usa & canada
on a shoestring

Robert Reid, Becca Blond, Loretta Chilcoat, Jeremy Chipman, Tom Downs,
Michael Grosberg, Jeff Hill, Graham Neale, Andrew Dean Nystrom, Michael Read,
Emily K Wolman

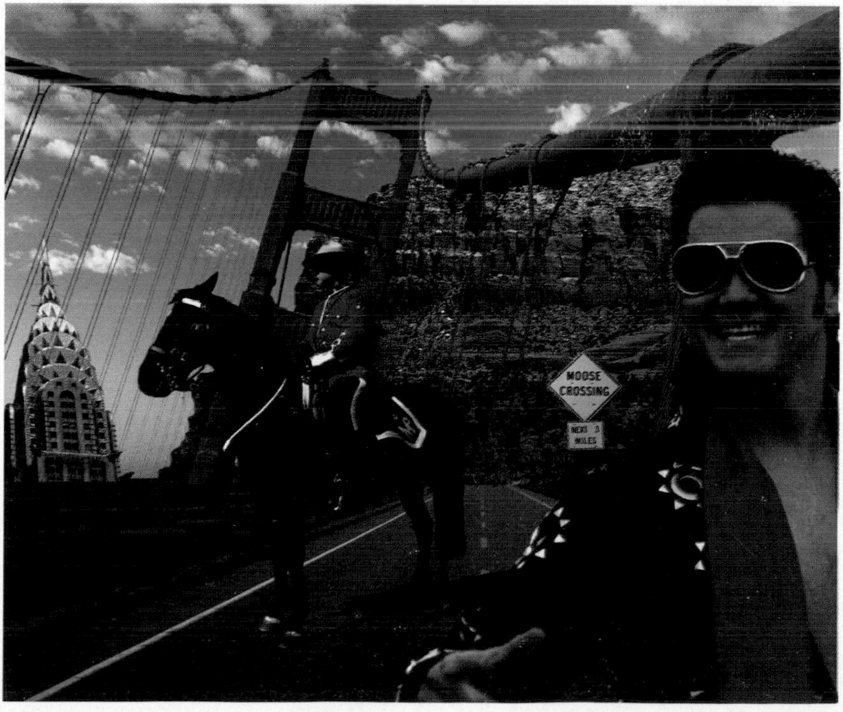

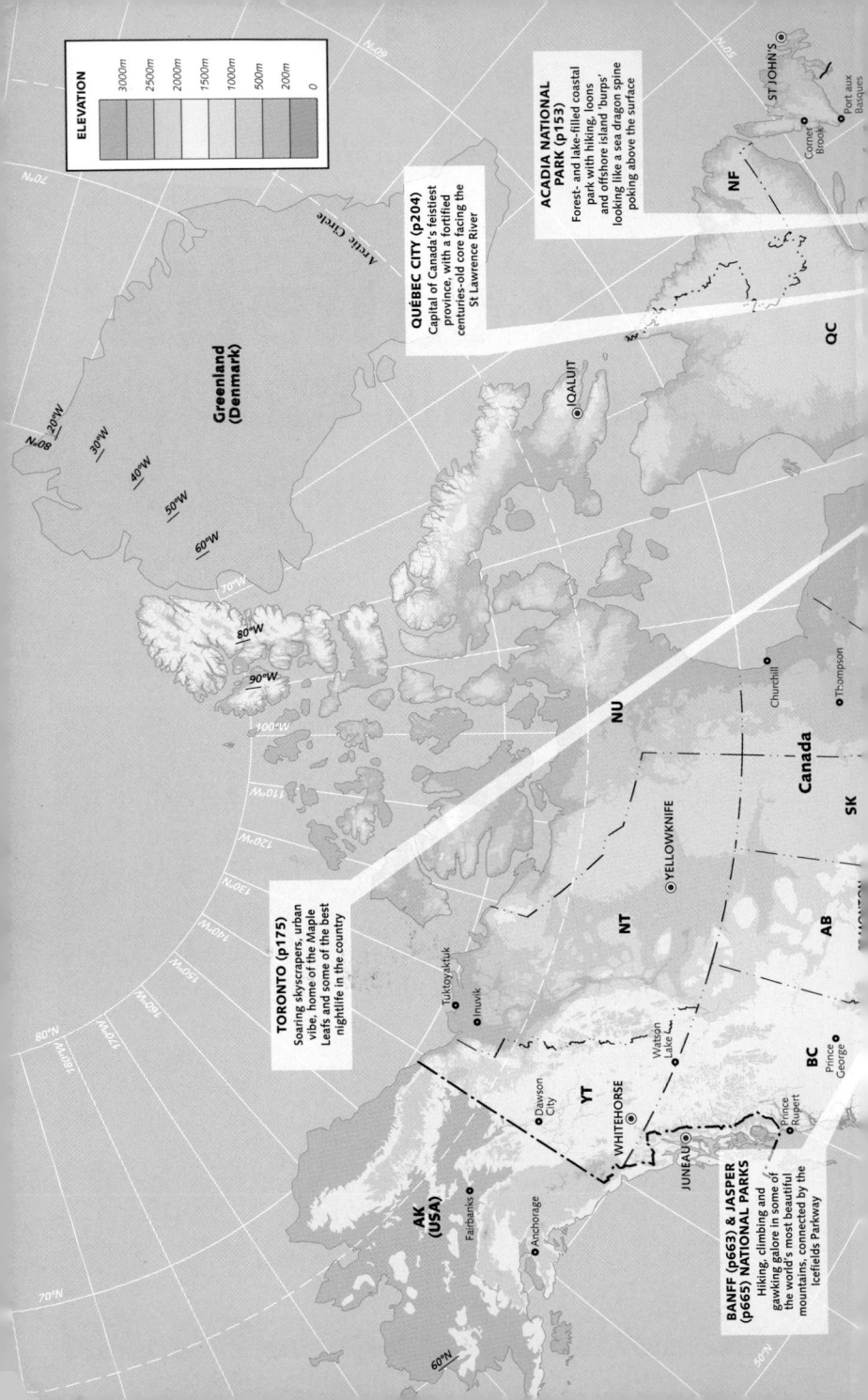

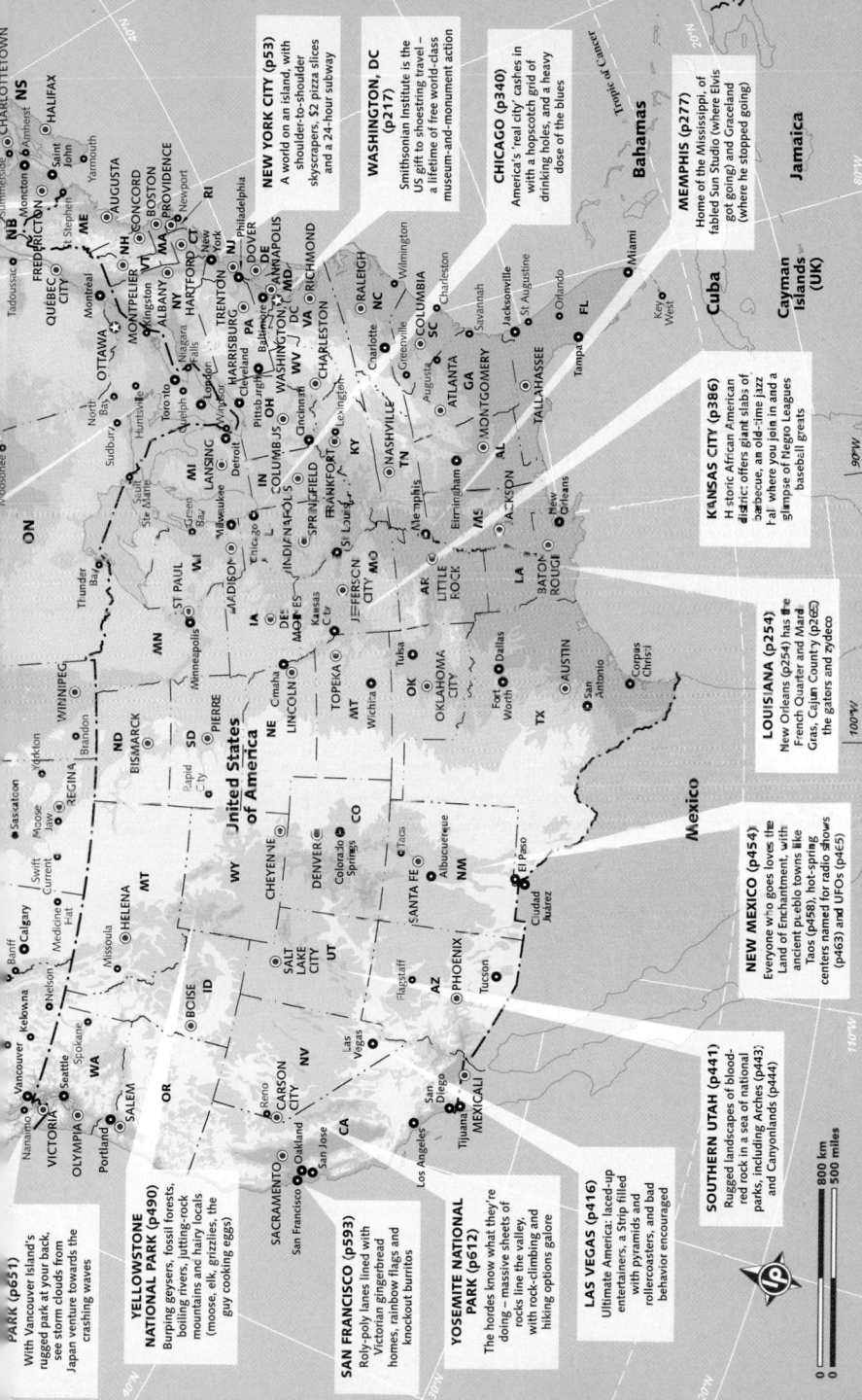

Responsible Travel

Think traveling responsibly is something for developing countries only? Not by a long shot. Some 42 million visitors come to the USA alone each year, and Americans make over a billion annual trips around its big self – which all accounts for nearly $600 billion of spending. That's big numbers – a lot of footfall, snapped photos, finger-points and wads of cash tossed about. Reckless tourists – some call them 'ugly' – can offend the cultures they witness and destroy the nature they gawk at.

Responsible travel is more than putting your candy bar wrappers in bins and recycling empty beer cans. It's knowing where your money goes, and rewarding the good guys who enact environmentally friendly parks and urban plans.

HOW YOU CAN HELP

- **Don't litter** Americans and Canadians have less tolerance for trashing up their cities, highways and parks than just about anybody on earth. Fines – big ones – add to the appeal of keeping it clean.
- **Volunteer** It's official: volunteering is the new travel. Spend a day chipping in on a community garden in a devastated urban district, or spend weeks building shelter or teaching kids on an Indian Reservation.
- **Go without wheels** It's car country for sure, but minimize your impact by taking public transport or lingering in cities with ped- and bike-friendly infrastructures; Toronto, for example, gives out a free 'green map' (see www.greentourism.ca).
- **First Americans** Much of Native America (or First Nations in Canada) is heartbreakingly poor. Take local guides for insight, pick up knickknacks made by the community, stay in tribe-run casino hotels – and don't intrude into local customs if it's frowned upon (some 'powwows' included, as well as hikes up some sacred mountains); if in doubt, ask.
- **Ask before you click** No matter whom you want to immortalize in print or digital film, ask first. It's rude not to.
- **Buy local** Get your produce from a farmers market and employ community-run tourist services.

INTERNET RESOURCES

- **www.sustainabletravel.org** BEST is an organization that strives to serve as as a leading source of knowledge on innovative travel industry practises that advance the communities' and all travelers' interests. Its website states that it aims to support the economic and cultural sustainability of destinations.
- **www.futureforests.com** Future Forests is a British-based organization that funds tree-planting to offset the impact of air travel.
- **www.handmadeinamerica** North Carolina–based community tourism organization.
- **www.lnt.org** Outlines how to camp and hike without making an impact.
- **www.planeta.com** Scores of links and info on worldwide ecotourism.
- **www.tourismconcern.org.uk** Tourism Concern is a British-based organization that strives to promote ethical tourism.

BOOKS

For more on how not to damage the lands we visit (and listings of ecotour groups), read *The Good Alternative Travel Guide* (Tourism Concern) or Mark Mann's outstanding *The Community Tourism Guide*.

Contents

The Authors

ROBERT REID
Coordinating Author, New York City, Great Plains

Growing up in Oklahoma, Robert frequently went on road trips in all directions – mountains, city smog, unfortunate camping trips and Rolling Stones concerts. After studying journalism, he left for NYC, where he worked at (don't laugh) *House Beautiful* magazine and spent his first months in a slummy basement pad in the East Village. After living in Vietnam, Robert joined Lonely Planet and worked in the Oakland, Melbourne and London offices. He's now a full-time writer and a proud new Brooklynite.

BECCA BLOND
Washington, DC & the Capital Region,
Rocky Mountains (Colorado)

A Washington, DC native who calls Boulder, CO home, Becca was addicted to travel at an early age, and has seen much of the USA, Asia, Western Europe and Africa. Even if she had money, she'd travel on a budget because she finds the people she meets along the way to be so interesting. When not on the road, which isn't often, she likes to relax at home, not think about airplanes and explore the outdoors.

LORETTA CHILCOAT
Florida

Loretta grew up in the cornfields of Maryland's Eastern Shore and her first trip to Florida was in sixth grade, which scarred her for life when her hot pink jelly shoes produced an abnormal sunburn pattern on her feet. Undaunted, she's returned to the Sunshine State many times. She's made Florida's coastline her beat, swimming with dolphins and surviving a hurricane in the Keys, ghostly encounters in St Augustine and Biker Week (with no money!) in Daytona.

JEREMY CHIPMAN
New England

Jeremy grew up near Boston and attended the University of Massachusetts around the same time that a Pixies song made the school semifamous. Having traveled the world extensively, he nonetheless appreciated the opportunity to explore the familiar territory of New England, to sample numerous clam shacks, and to try to use Red Sox tickets as a tax write-off. Jeremy has lived in the San Francisco Bay Area for more than a decade and is currently completing a Masters degree in product design.

TOM DOWNS
The South (New Orleans, Louisiana, Mississippi, Memphis,
Nashville, Eastern Tennessee, Kentucky), Great Lakes,
California (San Francisco, Around San Francisco, Sierra Nevada,
Northern Mountains)

Tom has traveled across the USA by every mode of transit with the exception of canoe. He has lived in San Francisco, Los Angeles, New Orleans and New York City, and he has been fortunate to write about these places for Lonely Planet.

MICHAEL GROSBERG
Mid-Atlantic

Michael was raised in the Washington, DC area and vacationed all over the Mid-Atlantic region due to his father's unanalyzed fear of flight. He studied philosophy in Michigan and Israel, worked in the Northern Marianas and took a long trip through Asia. Then he drove across the country, up to Alaska and back to the east coast through the northern states. He then left for journalism and nongovernment organization work in South Africa. He pursued graduate work in literature in NYC and now teaches at university.

JEFF HILL
Texas

Sadly, Jeff will never be allowed to sport one of the coveted 'Texas Native' license plates on his pickup. As the saying goes, he wasn't born in the Lone Star State but got there as soon as he could, after a misspent youth in Michigan and various temporary travel destinations. He has lived in Austin with his wife, Lori, since the mid 1990s, where he has worked as a travel editor and freelance writer. He spends his leisure time sampling the secondhand smoke in honky-tonks all across the state.

GRAHAM NEALE
Eastern Canada, Western Canada

Excerpt from conversations between Graham and random people after he moved from the north to the south side of the 49th parallel in 1999: 'I'm gonna write a book.' 'What about?' 'Canada.' Big words from an unproven jackass from Vancouver. A Canucks fan and unofficial spokesperson of all things Canadian (except Céline Dion and the Leafs), Graham's seen the country from both sides, knows where it's better and where his heart is, and wishes he'd coined the phrase, 'The world needs more Canada.'

ANDREW DEAN NYSTROM
Southwest, Rocky Mountains (Wyoming, Montana), California (Los Angeles, South Coast, The Deserts, Central Coast, North Coast), Alaska

Born in Denver and raised along the Pacific, Andrew retraced many of his favorite experiences for this book. He's conducted scientific studies in the Yellowstone National Park backcountry, contributed to a dozen LP titles, and is doing field research for a hiking book about Yellowstone and the Grand Tetons. He now lives in Alta, California.

MICHAEL READ
The South (North Carolina, South Carolina, Alabama, Georgia)

A longtime resident of North Carolina's Central Piedmont during his formative years, Michael can still switch on that honeyed Southern twang to get out of a jam. Formerly a senior designer for the award-winning lonelyplanet.com website, Michael jumped the fence in 2003 to hit the road as a full-time travel writer. He contributed to Lonely Planet's most recent edition of *Mexico* and is the co-author of *Great Smoky Mountains & Shenendoah National Parks*.

EMILY K WOLMAN
Rocky Mountains (Idaho), Pacific Northwest

Emily's first overseas trip was to Barcelona, where she was thrilled to discover that bartenders would serve her beer at age 15. Since then, her passion for wonder and wandering has led her to five continents and all over the USA. Despite countless Pacific Northwest trips over the years, Emily – an off-the-beaten-track traveler – didn't ascend the Space Needle until she was researching this book. Funny the things we do for work. When she's home in Oakland, California, Emily's mainstay is freelance editing.

CONTRIBUTING AUTHORS

Jeff Greenwald wrote the USA & Canada Outdoors chapter. He is author of five travel books, is a contributing editor for several magazines, and is executive director of Ethical Traveler, which is dedicated to human rights and environmental protection.

David Goldberg, MD wrote the Health chapter. He did his training in internal medicine and infectious diseases at Columbia-Presbyterian Medical Center in NYC, where he served as voluntary faculty. He is now an infectious diseases specialist in Scarsdale, New York.

Destination USA & Canada

The amazing rock formations of Bryce Canyon National Park (p447), Utah, USA

Whoa ho! The USA and Canada – the world's third- and second-largest countries – offer heartbeat-skipping moments on the countless miles (or kilometers) stretching from sea to sea. Highlights start in the cities – big-time 21st-century wonders where international communities zip around on well-oiled public transport – and continue in the sticks, where you'll find canyons the color of red fudge, moose sipping from your swimming hole, rocky-top mountains coated in snow and head-butting goats, banjo or blues or rural chitchat on the AM dial, big-buckled cowboys saying 'yup' at fillin' stations and surfers saying 'dude' by the beach, kitschy over-sized cows at stop-offs under big skies the size of worlds, and fresh buffalo hoof–creased blades in tallgrass. The people – a smiling bunch often – ain't bad either.

Save for getting around, it *can* be done on the cheap. Fifteen-buck hostels and free camp-sites abound, looks at landmarks from the Statue of Liberty to the Golden Gate Bridge are free, and specialty meals sell for prices that keep locals' eyebrows in place. It's car country, yessirree – and god it's good to see with a set of wheels – but so much can be seen by bus, train, cycle or boot too.

It's big, this USA and Canada stuff. Worth the hype? Yup.

NEIL SETCHFIELD

View from the Empire State Building (p63), New York City, USA

HIGHLIGHTS

BEST CITIES

New York City America's greatest city, the Big Apple runs all hours and brims with icons, monuments and museums (p53)

Chicago soaring skyscrapers on huge Lake Michigan, culture and ethnic districts, but most importantly Chi-town can outdrink your city, pal (p340)

New Orleans saints and drunkards alike march under cast-iron balconies along the Big Easy's French Quarter, seasoned in voodoo, boiled crawfish and the thick Southern-style humidity (p254)

San Francisco foggy in summer, glorious in the fall, the City by the Bay is implausibly gorgeous, with cable-car tracks, gingerbread Victorians, Dr Seuss–like roly-poly hills and a celebration of anything oddball (p593)

Vancouver Canada's best city: towering mountains meet sci fi–flavored downtown, rain forests and totem poles, ferries to islands, a booming Chinatown life and a serious 'Vansterdam' reputation (p630)

BEST COLLEGE TOWNS

Boulder on the Rockies' front range, hip(pie) Boulder begs its locals to get outside: in summer the town creek welcomes tubing (drunk) students, and nearby canyons draw rock climbers (p477)

Austin so unlike the rest of the state, with an entrenched music scene, a wing-flapping bat colony and artsy crowd all but drowning out more conservative folk like former resident George W Bush (p396)

Eugene Eugene scores for its punk Whiteaker district and the prototype for Moe's Tavern from *The Simpsons*; Eugene may well out-doobie any campus in the country (p546)

Chapel Hill once home to pre-pro Michael Jordan, Chapel Hill cultivates indie rock for its laid-back, left-leaning UNC (p296)

Boston OK it's a city, but Boston bubbles with dozens of schools, bookstores and bars on both sides of the James River; up in Cambridge, famed Harvard dates from the 17th century (p120)

The stunning scenery at Jasper National Park (p665), Alberta, Canada

BEST NATIONAL PARKS

Big Three ▪ atop an impressive list stand Yosemite (sheer cliffs, lush valleys; p613), Yellowstone (the world's first national park, brimming with wildlife; p490) and the Grand Canyon (277-mile-long gash in the earth; p428)

Glacier ▪ Montana's rugged Glacier has lakes filled with flotillas of ice still melting in summer and head-butting goats on snow-covered peaks (p505)

Olympic ▪ boots required – Olympic's glaciated mountains, remote waterfalls and mossy rain forests sit well away from the roads (p529)

Southern Utah ▪ earth in its most Mars like state: barren, rugged arches of blood-red stone mix with canyons of white, pink and red rock; see Canyonlands (p444), Arches (p443), Bryce Canyon (p447) and Zion (p447)

Jasper ▪ with fewer camera-toters than Banff, Jasper boasts head-butting goats (real bad mofos, these guys), underground rivers, limestone gorges, white-water rafting and more than a handful of marmots (p665)

BEST ACTIVITIES

Canoeing & kayaking ▪ lake-hop in Minnesota's Boundary Waters (p379) or take in the waterways at Ontario's Algonquin Provincial Park (p192)

Rock climbing ▪ go for short or long climbs at Wyoming's rugged Grand Teton National Park (p494) or scale the Half Dome at Yosemite (p613)

White-water rafting ▪ take a tumble down Idaho's pristine Class IV 3000ft Middle Fork of the Salmon River (p510); plunge over waterfalls between towers of sandstone rock on West Virginia's New and Gauley Rivers (p248)

Skiing ▪ head to Utah's Wasatch Mountains around Salt Lake City (p450) to spray powder at Park City (Olympics? check), Alta (cheap lifts? got it), Sundance (Robert Redford sightings? you betcha); up north the powder awaits 2010 at Whistler in BC's interior (p662)

Being a nut ▪ saner nuts can hang-glide where aviation was born in North Carolina (p297), or serious ones can jump out of a more modern air-jalopy at Gardiner, New York (p108)

Not as mysterious as Stonehenge, but worth checking out is Carhenge (p389), Nebraska, USA

BEST HOSTELS

HI Clay Hotel & International Hostel, Miami ■ century-old art-deco beaut – where Al Capone rolled the dice – now offers dorms within walking distance of South Beach nightclubs (p326)

ADK Adirondack Loj, New York State ■ sit-back lodge sits lakeside on the edge of Adirondack hiking and cross-country ski trails (p111)

Charleston's Historic Hostel ■ Southern charm casts its grip onto every chair-rocking guest; best is that it's a short stroll from the historic district bars and the water (p302)

Wilderness Hostels, Alberta ■ along the Icefields Parkway from Banff to Jasper are 10 hostels with hikes, rock climbing and ping-pong (p666)

HI Redwood National Park Hostel ■ northern California's superb hangout hostel is right across from the Pacific and near hiking trails that lead past half the state's towering redwoods (p629)

BEST OFF-THE-BEATEN-TRACK PLACES

Sequoia & Kings Canyon, California ■ when Yosemite is crawling with visitors, these national parks offer elbow space (and then some), the world's largest tree and views below and above an 8200ft divot of earth (p619)

Nebraska Panhandle ■ the Great Plains' prehistoric sea floors haven't made much of a dent on mainstream itineraries, but a car-made replica of Stonehenge (p389) and Crazy Horse's death site (p389) are worth a go

Wisconsin ■ Milwaukee (p369) is home to Harley and beer; try Madison (p371) for student life, and Green Bay (p372) on game day; two-laners take in the Mississippi or 19th-century villages in Door County (p373)

Cape Breton Highlands, Nova Scotia ■ Canada's great park is no secret, but way off most itineraries: cliff-hanging hikes to backcountry campsites and whale sightings off the rocky coast; take a kilt for Scottish lore (p209)

West Texas ■ the Lone Star State is underrated, particularly out west, where you can see unexplained lights at Marfa (p409), one of the most unlikely art centers in the USA, plus loose 'land-o-lost' boulders and hot springs on the Rio Grande at Big Bend National Park (p409)

ITINERARIES

The following itineraries are built to maximize the intake on the long haul. You're better off with a car, though some of these itineraries can be followed loosely by bus or train. If time is endless, loop along several over many months, or just see where the wind takes you.

COAST-TO-COAST TRIPS

Northern Crossing: New York City to Seattle

After several days soaking up **New York City** (p53) – without a car – head 'upstate' to see the granola-spiced town of **Woodstock** (p109) in the kicking-back Catskills. Cross New York and base yourself at the hostel in **Buffalo** (p113) to see the international **Niagara Falls** (p187) – eat north of the border for a wee bit less – then follow Lake Erie (Hwy 5 bypasses the toll) to rock and roll's birthplace (in nomenclature, not beats) to see the Hall of Fame and drink a cold beer in the Flats in way overlooked **Cleveland** (p358). If time allows, take toll-free US 20, stopping in **South Bend, Indiana** (p358) to pay respects to (or diss) the Notre Dame football team, or a hike at the great-all-year **Indiana Dunes** (p358) facing Lake Michigan.

You'll need several days to take in **Chicago** (p340) and sample the deep-dish pizza, bars and blues, taking a peek from one of the landmark sky-scrapers (insiders prefer the second-tallest John Hancock Center).

Head up I-94 to surprising **Milwaukee** (p369), home of Laverne, Shirley and Harley-Davidson. Just west, **Madison** (p371) is a fun college town

How long?
3-5 weeks
When to Go?
July and August is peak season, curb months may be best, while snow blocks some roads in winter
Budget?
US$30-60 per day, US$70 or more in the cities

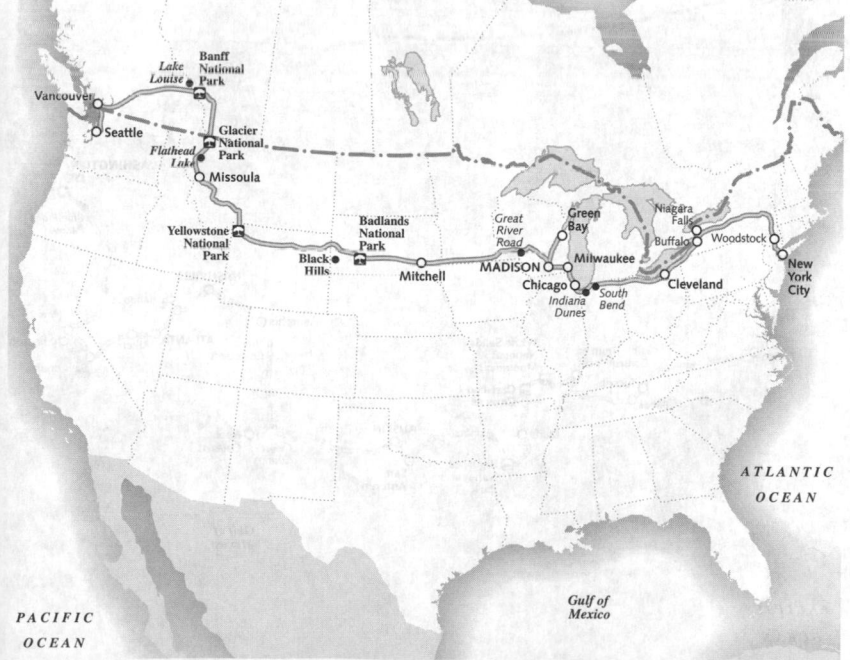

'Are we there yet?' was probably first uttered somewhere between the east and west coasts. This 4600-mile (7360km) route nags some of mid-America's most scenic areas – and drinking towns back east – while hitting top-tier national parks out west before pulling into Seattle.

perched betwixt two lakes and with a hostel downtown. In fall, consider detouring to **Green Bay** (p372) when 'cheeseheads' grill bratwursts before Packer football games – great even if you watch from a sports bar.

Travel via I-90, detour on the Mississippi's **Great River Rd** (p373) in La Crosse, before zipping across Minnesota where hills fade to fields. In South Dakota, break up the hours at the corn-covered civic center in **Mitchell** (p389) and take in the 41-mile ride (and an Indian taco) in the other-worldly **Badlands National Park** (p390). The huge **Black Hills area** (p390) warrants a few days for its mountains of men, Native American sights and lush wildlife; **Deadwood** (p391) has a hostel.

Way across Wyoming, **Yellowstone National Park** (p490) sports boiling rivers, geysers and abundant wildlife. Perhaps base yourself more cheaply in nearby **Cody** (p497). Head north to rejoin I-90 and stop for veggie food in the student town of **Missoula, Montana** (p503), then maybe pitch a tent at **Flathead Lake** (p505) before spending a few days in rugged **Glacier National Park** (p505) – watch out for grizzlies.

Hop the border to see Alberta's **Banff National Park** (p663) and **Lake Louise** (p665). Heading west, stop into **Vancouver** (p634) for super urban hikes and finish back stateside with a cup of coffee in **Seattle** (p516).

Southern Crossing: Washington, DC to San Diego

Once you've filled up on free museums in **Washington, DC** (p217), wander along the **Blue Ridge Parkway** (p235) through Virginia's Shenandoah Valley. Take I-77 through North Carolina to compare the South's two superb boozy coastal colonial masterpieces: South Carolina's **Charleston** (p300) and, just south, Georgia's **Savannah** (p309).

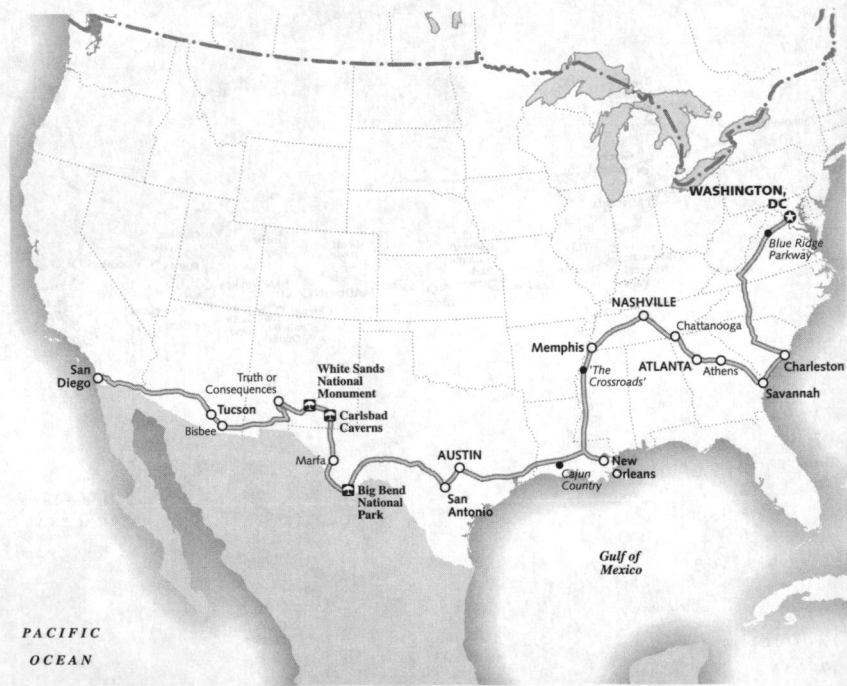

Say so long to the ocean, and see where REM got started at 40 Watt Club in **Athens** (p309), then take in African American sights in Sweet Auburn in **Atlanta** (p303), including Martin Luther King Jr's birthplace and grave. Both towns have hostels.

Over in Tennessee, oft-missed **Chattanooga** (p287) isn't just a funny name – the rushing Tennessee River has good rafting, downtown's pedestrian bridge is the world's longest and Civil War sites offer summit views over rocky-top mountains.

Take I-24 to **Nashville** (p282) and see the Grand Ole Opry Museum for free and proceed to **Memphis** (p277) where music fans get chills over Sun Studio and Graceland. Take Hwy 61 south into the **Mississippi Delta** (p274), where the legendary 'crossroads' tempts souls.

Plan on a couple of days minimum in **New Orleans** (p254), an irresistible blend of Dixieland jazz, voodoo, po-boys and all-hour drunkenness. Drop into French-speaking **Cajun Country** (p269) in the nearby bayou, perhaps splurging on a stay in a gator-surrounded houseboat (p270).

Skip Houston and go straight to **Austin** (p396), Texas' live music capital (booming loudest during March's South by Southwest festival). Get some Mexican food and a look at the Alamo in **San Antonio** (p401), then drive west – and it becomes serious West soon. Camp and hike where, it's said, 'God put all the rocks left over after making the world,' at **Big Bend National Park** (p409), then via scenic Hwy 170, then north speculate on the origins of the wacky **Marfa Lights** (p409).

Take lonely Hwy 54 north of I-10 into lesser-visited bits of New Mexico. Visit the 73-sq-mile (190-sq-km) **Carlsbad Caverns** (p466) and hike along a bat-dung trail. Dune-frolic for a day at the surreal **White Sands National Monument** (p464), then soothe sore muscles (or bum from driving) at spas in New Mexico's **Truth or Consequences** (p463).

Follow backroads through the Chihuahuan Desert (home to the curvy saguaro cacti) and spend a night in an old done-up trailer in **Bisbee** (p441) before taking in a day in surprisingly lively **Tucson** (p437) with a crazy lil' historic hostel and good in-town biking fun. Take I-8 across the Yuma Desert and into **San Diego** (p575).

Canadian Crossing: Vancouver to Québec City

Hike and eat your way through **Vancouver** (p634), where mountain trailheads brush shoulders with nude beaches and Chinatown. Pop over to Vancouver Island for whale-watching opportunities and a bout with the ass-kicking **West Coast Trail** (p651) – or perhaps ferry-hop around the **Southern Gulf Islands** (p654).

From Vancouver, don't rush to Banff. Head north along Hwy 99 from Vancouver to **Whistler** (p655), which is one of the great North American ski resorts (open all year). Stop for good pickings in the – What's this? Desert? Cor blimey! – **Okanagan Valley** (p659), with various fruit harvests from late June to October, and grab a bunk in **Kelowna** (p660) on the lip of a lake. If time allows, wind your way on Rte 6 southeast to **Nelson** (p661), an artist hangout with many a bong raised to dull the pain from biking/skiing/boarding wipeouts. Back north on the Trans Canada Hwy, stop to reflect on emerald **Lake Louise** (p665), canoe past critters and hike up does-that-sucker-end snow-capped mountains in **Banff National Park** (p663), then take the Icefields Parkway 144 miles (230km) north past a stream of 'wilderness hostels' to **Jasper National Park** (p665).

From Jasper, take Hwy 16 out of the mountains into Saskatchewan, where plains stretch into headaches left and right. **Saskatoon** (p670) is the prettiest city for miles and miles. Way east, massive-for-the-plains

How long?
2-5 weeks
When to Go?
Best is May or June, September or October; most roads OK in winter, but even the South gets chilly
Budget?
US$50-100 per day

Heading west, green turns all shades of beige as the Southwest begins and space gets stretched to lunar-like proportions. This 4400-mile (7040km) shadoobee Is the best cross-country trip for winter, while heat and humidity can be unbearable in summer.

How long?
4-6 weeks
When to Go?
June to October is best, although summer is busiest
Budget?
C$40-80 per day

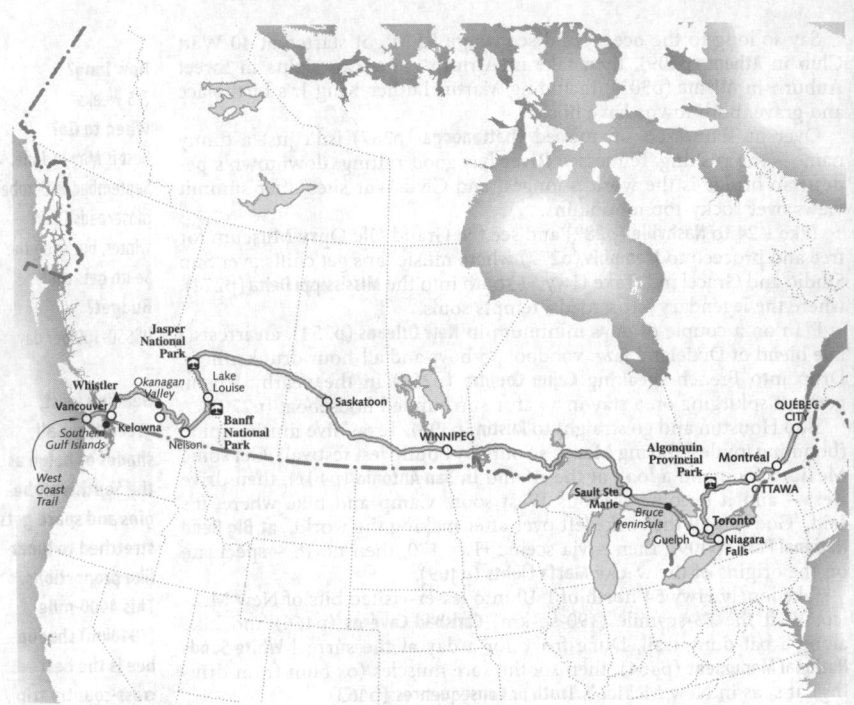

This 4200-mile (6720km) crossing snubs the USA. Buses and trains, or an internal flight, make it feasible if you don't have a car, but with time you can catch plenty of water, trees, mountains, moose, beer and 'beaver-tail' (a doughnut-type snack, not the real thing).

Winnipeg (p671) with plenty of history, a French quarter to poke around and some cheap and good ballet.

East of Thunder Bay in Ontario, the Trans Canada Hwy skirts cliffs along Lake Superior. Stay in the fun **Sault Ste Marie** (p194). Detour south via Rte 6 to the C$27 car ferry 'short cut' to lake-sandwiched **Bruce Peninsula** (p194) for unreal scuba and kayaking options. Rte 6 snakes south to **Guelph** (p192), worthy for its crew of jackasses and a mug of Sleeman's. Stick with the (better) Canadian side at **Niagara Falls** (p187), then plan on a couple of days in **Toronto** (p175), which earns its (self) horn-blowing rep with tower views, the Hockey Hall of Fame and full-moon canoe trips on the harbor.

Detour north to **Algonquin Provincial Park** (p192), a perfect slice of Canada with wolves howling from hilltops over clean, clear lakes – just get a canoe and go. Southeast in the capital **Ottawa** (p189), bunk in the jail hostel, snack on a famed 'beavertail,' see a re-creation of an aboriginal village, and – if in winter – skate with commuters on the frozen canal.

Get out your French phrasebook over in Québec. Plan a few days for **Montréal** (p195), with partying and bagels that hold their own with New York City's. Watch out for freshwater whales in the St Lawrence River, which leads northeast to the province's cobblestone capital, **Québec City** (p204). Retell your trip's tale to the city's goat, Batisse.

REGIONAL TRIPS

East Coast: Boston to Miami

A good introduction to old America, **Boston** (p120) is kept young (and tipsy) with its vast array of colleges and fervor at Red Sox baseball games.

Head to a hostel way out on **Cape Cod** (p140) and spring for a lobster, before taking a cheap bus (or driving) to **New York City** (p53), where the budget needs some wriggling room; you need at least five days. Stop where American independence began at **Philadelphia** (p91) for a Philly cheesesteak and a run up the *Rocky* steps. Scandal-ridden **Washington, DC** (p217) is the country's best budget deal with a lifetime's worth of free world-class monuments and museums.

The South begins across the Potomac River in Virginia, where a stack of Civil War battlefields can be visited, including **Bull Run** (p231), site of a southern rout that kicked off the four-year war. From south of Front Royal, take the **Skyline Drive** (p235) through Virginia's rolling Shenandoah Valley. Nearby, the university town of **Charlottesville** (p234) boasts Thomas Jefferson's Monticello (seen on the back of the nickel), while one-time Confederate capital **Richmond** (p232) has more free attractions, including a canal walk, an old estate and a former POW Civil War camp.

Via I-95, stop in North Carolina's lab-heavy 'Triangle' to catch a Durham Bulls baseball game in **Durham** (p296) or some indie rock where Michael Jordan learned hoop geometry in the college town of **Chapel Hill** (p296). Get back to the sea at way-out **Cape Hatteras National Seashore** (p298), rich with bird life and empty beaches; consider a US$65 hang-gliding splurge up in **Kitty Hawk** (p297), where the Wright Brothers made their first flight in 1903.

The Southern drawl thickens in South Carolina's must-see coastal colonial town of **Charleston** (p300), with snaking backstreets lined with weepy willows and antebellum mansions, plus a boozy scene reached on foot from the superb hangout, Charleston Historic Hostel. Its Georgian

How long?
3-5 weeks
When to Go?
July and August is busy season when the denser east fills with vacationing families; shoot for June or September (if swimming), or May or October (if not)
Budget?
US$40-60 per day, US$70-100 in the cities

A 2300-mile (3680km) ramble down the east coast pays nod to the country's colonial centers and beaches that become more beautiful as the locals' lingo starts to slur. Frequent bus and train connections make much of it possible without a car. The northeast's regional 'Chinatown buses' have the best deals.

cohort **Savannah** (p309) is another moss-covered oak antebellum paradise; one club has *free* drinks after midnight. Consider taking the ferry to **Cumberland Island** (p313) for sandy beaches, roaming horses and oak-shaded campsites.

In Florida, laze at the terrific Pirate Haus Hostel in **St Augustine** (p328), the USA's oldest colonial city. Mid-state, take in **Disney World** (p332) in Orlando – perhaps with comp tickets if you can schmooze them – then finish up in **Miami Beach** (p319), where you can club and sleep in style a walk away from pastel art-deco wonders and the beach, and cool off with a Cuban *batido* (milk shake) in Little Havana's Calle Ocho (p324).

West Coast: Los Angeles to Vancouver

From **Los Angeles** (p560), take fabled Hwy 1, built where roads shouldn't be: on landsliding fault lines and skirting rocky bluffs overlooking the Pacific. Stay a night in the college beach town **Santa Barbara** (p585), for nice beaches, bopping nightlife and a peek into a Spanish Moorish–styled courthouse.

If you're camping, reserve your tent spot beforehand in Hwy 1's cliff-clutching **Big Sur** (p588). North, hike around the rocky coast – or dive offshore – at the **Point Lobos State Reserve** (p589) in Carmel, then bunk in a hostel near Cannery Row in **Monterey** (p589) or up in less touristy, boho-with-boardwalk **Santa Cruz** (p591). Best, however, is the Pigeon Point Lighthouse hostel in **Pescadero** (p592), on Hwy 1 north of Santa Cruz. Leave Hwy 1, via Hwy 17, north to **San Francisco** (p593) for a few days in and around the bay, then rejoin Hwy 1 on the north side of the Golden Gate Bridge.

How long?
2-4 weeks

When to Go?
Summer's best for swimming, but coastal towns near big cities get busy, busy, busy on weekends

Budget?
US$40-80 per day

Those with cars mustn't miss the cliff-hugging two-laners that weave their way high above Pacific waves up and down the West Coast. This 1900-mile (3040km) route takes in whale and seal hangouts, towering redwoods, glacier-cut mountains, gentle and rough surf, and five of the countries' most inviting cities.

Technically part of another continental plate, **Point Reyes National Seashore** (p609) has a hostel and miles of often-empty beaches – incomparable if the sun's shining.

Hwy 1 ends at US 101, about 120 miles (192km) south of the **Redwood National Park** (p628), home to the famed big trees and a superb hostel overlooking the ocean. Backtrack inland on scenic **Hwy 299** (p622) and get a glimpse of **Mt Shasta** (p622) on the way to Oregon.

Take US 97 towards **Crater Lake National Park** (p553), with drives along the country's deepest lake – don't expect to retrieve dropped coins. Back on the Pacific, on the **Oregon Coast** (p549) stay in a Mongolian-style yurt or take your pick of amazing sea-facing camp spots. The hostel north of **Cannon Beach** (p550) rents kayaks for cheap. Save at least a day for **Portland** (p535), simmering with tasty beers and lively locals. Just east, drive along the **Columbia River Gorge** (p543) and take in huckleberry-picking hikes.

In Washington, the hostel in seaport town **Port Angeles** (p530) is near glaciated Mt Olympus and the crystal-clear lakes and rain forests and falls – enough already! – of **Olympic National Park** (p529). In **Seattle** (p516), take the local caffeine high up the Space Needle and then catch a show at the Crocodile Cafe where grunge got going. Ferry, hike and/or kayak around some of the 457 **San Juan Islands** (p532) before pulling into **Vancouver** (p634) and on into British Columbia.

California & Southwest Loop: from San Francisco

After you've had your fill of Mission burritos and drinks in **San Francisco** (p593), head south on the coastal winner Hwy 1. Stop to camp and hike in the thick of it at **Big Sur** (p588), then witness what media millionaires

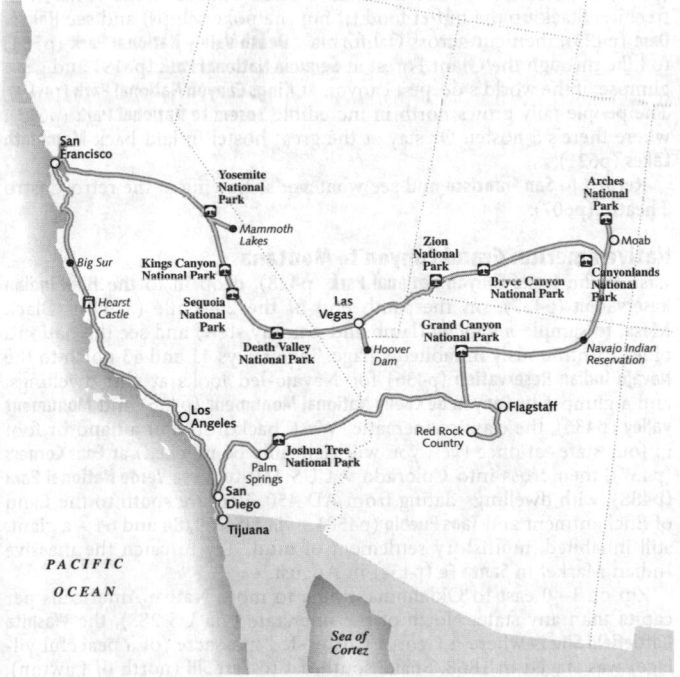

Got your national parks pass yet? This 2475-mile (3985km) trip, starting and ending in the City by the Bay, loops some of America's best parks offering forested rocky mountains with climbing and bears, wide-open deserts and red archways of stone. City life is good, too, from Vegas' neon, Hollywood's star scene and San Diego's surf.

build at the worth-the-US$18-ticket **Hearst Castle** (p588), inspiration for *Citizen Kane*. Next stop, **Los Angeles** (p560), baby, where you'll need at least a few days just to get around the lovely sprawling mess. Crash at a seaside hostel and don't miss the free billion-dollar Getty Center. Check the surf south in **San Diego** (p575) and trolley down to **Tijuana, Mexico** (p581) to pay respects to the birthplace of the margarita (upside down and right side up).

Go for a martini in '20s-era Hollywood playground **Palm Springs** (p582), with a big gay and lesbian scene, then get U2 on California at nearby **Joshua Tree National Park** (p583), 30 miles (48km) away. Buy a national parks annual pass from any entrance.

Cross into Arizona to cool, ponderosa-perforated **Flagstaff** (p434) for a peek through the telescope that found Pluto and looks at nearby **Red Rock Country** (p434). Then, the big mama **Grand Canyon National Park** (p428); you'll need to reserve way, way ahead for rafting trips (or try to bum a group's spare space by showing up with some cases of beer); the North Rim (just over there!) is some 250 miles (400km) by road – worth it to escape the crowds. Take a Navajo-led walk to cliff dwellings in the **Navajo Indian Reservation** (p436).

You'll want a week or more in Utah. If you're not camping, set up shop in laid-back **Moab** (p442) for hikes in area national parks: the Mars-like **Arches** (p443) and, with 4WD, the roads of rugged-to-the-point-of-decay **Canyonlands** (p444). Retrace your tire treads south and go via scenic Hwys 95 and 12 to the spires and pinnacles of **Bryce Canyon National Park** (p447) and colorful **Zion National Park** (p447).

As soon as you can say 'I'm sick of this wilderness crap,' **Las Vegas** (p416) beckons across the horizon. Pricier central sleeps come with freebies. Stack up the buffet food (if not the poker chips) and see **Hoover Dam** (p425), then cut across California's **Death Valley National Park** (p584) to hike through the Giant Forest at **Sequoia National Park** (p619) and get a glimpse of the world's deepest canyon at **Kings Canyon National Park** (p619). The people tally grows north in incredible **Yosemite National Park** (p613), where there's a hostel. Or stay at the great hostel in laid-back **Mammoth Lakes** (p621).

Return to **San Francisco** and see whatever's showing at the retro Castro Theatre (p607).

Native America: Grand Canyon to Montana

East of the **Grand Canyon National Park** (p428), drop in to the **Hopi Indian Reservation** (p437), on the south end of the 200-mile (320km) Black Mesa, to sample *noqkwivi* (lamb and hominy stew) and see the nation's oldest continuously inhabited village. Take Hwys 41 and 43 north to the **Navajo Indian Reservation** (p436) for Navajo-led looks at cliff dwellings, and a glimpse of **Canyon de Chelly National Monument** (p436) and **Monument Valley** (p436), the classic cinematic 'West' backdrop. Put a hand or foot in four states at once (yes, you will rightfully be mocked) at **Four Corners** (p437), then cross into Colorado via US 160 to **Mesa Verde National Park** (p488), with dwellings dating from AD 450. Venture south to the Land of Enchantment and **Taos Pueblo** (p458) – via US 160, 84 and 64 – a giant, still inhabited, multistory settlement of mud. Try to catch the massive Indian Market in **Santa Fe** (p454) in August.

Zip on I-40 east to Oklahoma, home to more Native Americans per capita than any state. North of the interstate (via US 283), the **Washita Battlefield Site** is where a George Custer–led massacre (of a peaceful village) was staged in 1868. Snake southeast to **Fort Sill** (north of Lawton),

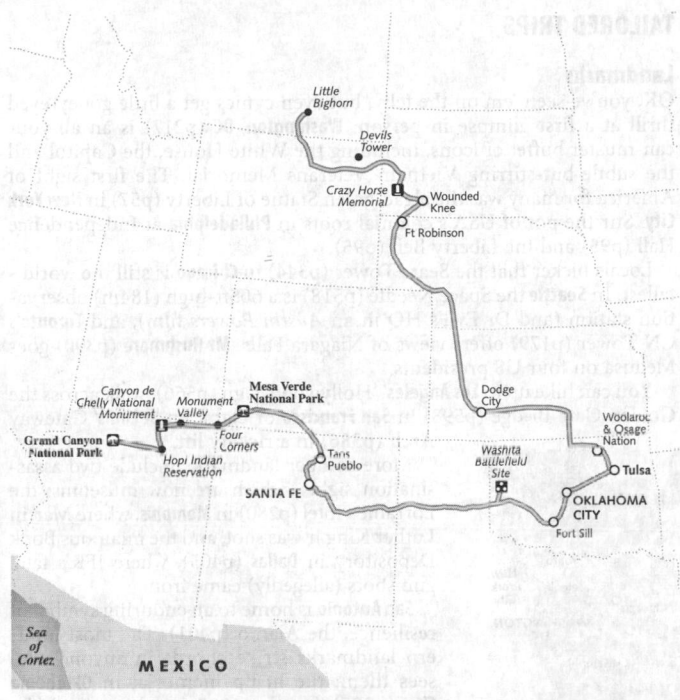

Before cowboys fastened their lassos (and bluecoat soldiers bullied their way west), the land was filled with diverse cultures settled in pueblos or roaming after buffalo herds. Things have changed, but Native America still lives. You'll need your own wheels for this 2900-mile (4640km) jaunt on lesser-known two-laners.

where Apache prisoner-for-life Geronimo is buried. Settled in a wild one-day land rush in 1889 (some left a day sooner than allowed – prompting Oklahoma's nickname 'Sooner State'), **Oklahoma City** (p384) stages the country's biggest Native American festival in June and is home to the National Cowboy & Western Heritage Museum. Two of the nation's best collections of Western art are northeast at Thomas Gilcrease Museum in **Tulsa** (p385), and at **Woolaroc** (p385), located on Osage Nation. Stop in small cemeteries to ponder the many deaths in the 1920s, when schemers murdered Osage for lucrative property rights in this once oil-rich area.

Bounce along country lanes north to Kansas' cow-town **Dodge City** (p386) and see real wagon ruts from the Santa Fe Trail and a hokey re-creation of its wild days. Take the country's loneliest road, US 83, north to Nebraska and west to the remarkable landmarks of the **Nebraska Panhandle** (p389); a good place to stay is in the 19th-century barracks at **Fort Robinson** (p389) where Crazy Horse was killed.

Crazy Horse was fighting for the still-contested **Black Hills** (p389), north in South Dakota. Outside the hills, **Pine Ridge Indian Reservation** (p391) is the current somber home of the Sioux and the once-bloodied fields of **Wounded Knee** (p391). The in-progress **Crazy Horse Memorial** (p390) will some day dwarf presidential Mt Rushmore, as intended. West in Wyoming, **Devils Tower** (p499), looking like a god's finger–scraped mound, was a sacred sight. Go north on Hwys 59 and US 212 to **Little Bighorn** (p502), where Custer and his men lost their scalps in the most famous moment of the Sioux Wars.

Turn the dial to the Native American radio stations when you are on reservations.

How long?
3-4 weeks
When to Go?
May, June, September or October are the best times; summer months get hot in the Southwest and see the most tourists
Budget?
US$40-70 per day

TAILORED TRIPS

Landmarks

OK, you've seen 'em on the telly, but even cynics get a little gooey-eyed thrill at a first glimpse in person. **Washington, DC** (p217) is an all-you-can-muster buffet of icons, including the White House, the Capitol and the subtle-but-stirring Vietnam Veterans Memorial. The first sight of America for many was the algae-green Statue of Liberty (p57) in **New York City**. Stir the pot of USA's colonial roots in **Philadelphia** at Independence Hall (p95) and the Liberty Bell (p95).

Locals bicker that the Sears Tower (p344) in **Chicago** is still the world's tallest. In **Seattle** the Space Needle (p518) is a 605ft-high (184m) observation station (and Dr Evil's HQ in an *Austin Powers* film), and **Toronto's** CN Tower (p179) offers views of Niagara Falls. **Mt Rushmore** (p390) goes Medusa on four US presidents.

You can hike up to **Los Angeles'** 'Hollywood' sign (p566), walk across the Golden Gate Bridge (p598) in **San Francisco** or clank up **St Louis'** Gateway Arch (p386) in a rickety lift.

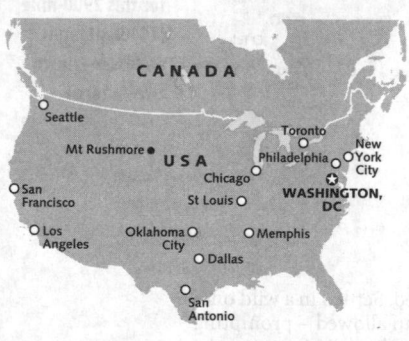

More-somber landmarks include two assassination sights, which are now museums: the Lorraine Hotel (p280) in **Memphis**, where Martin Luther King Jr was shot; and the infamous Book Depository in **Dallas** (p405), where JFK's fatal gun shots (allegedly) came from.

San Antonio is home to an enduring symbol of resilience, the Alamo (p401). The most modern landmarks strike chords in anyone who sees them: the lit-up memorial in **Oklahoma City** (p385) for the 1995 bombing, and the shocking clearing at the World Trade Center site (p58) in **New York City**.

Roadside Attractions

In the build-it-and-they-will-come column are bizarre human-built creations begging for a stop. The Dakotas are kings of the absurd. In South Dakota, Mitchell is home to a 275,000-ear **Corn Palace** (p389), and west is **Wall Drug** (p390), with signs all over the world advertising its 5¢ coffee and nut-ball games. Up north, North Dakota has the **world's largest Holstein cow** (p391).

Mountains made of men are the most grandiose pull-off-to-see. South Dakota's Black Hills have two – presidential **Mt Rushmore** (p390), a national landmark; and in-progress **Crazy Horse Memorial** (p390). Down South, **Stone Mountain** (p309) celebrates the Civil War's confederate heroes.

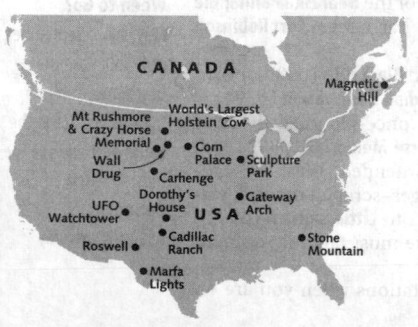

Some say if something don't work no more, then build something from it, son. Texas' **Cadillac Ranch** (p408) inspired a Boss song, and Nebraska's **Carhenge** (p389) parodies Stonehenge. Outside Madison, Wisconsin, **Sculpture Park** (p372) is a towering grab bag of scrap metal.

Wizard of Oz fans should watch out for munchkin droppings outside (the replica of) **Dorothy's House** (p386) in Liberal, Kansas.

The **Gateway Arch** (p386) looms over downtown St Louis like a UFO remnant. Hooper,

Colorado has a **UFO Watchtower** (p487), with campsites, and **Roswell, New Mexico** (p465) has devoted itself to a purported 1947 visit by green friends. In New Brunswick, Moncton's **Magnetic Hill** (p209) pulls a car 'uphill.' The nightly **Marfa Lights** (p409) in Texas defy explanation. Maybe transmitted laser belches from Pluto pranksters?

Without Wheels

Reality check: in car country, it's less smooth getting from A to B, *and* getting around B once you're there, without a car. Here's a list of places easily enjoyed with just your legs or a subway pass.

Some major cities have a proper well-oiled public transport system. **New York City** (p53), **Philadelphia** (p91) and **Chicago** (p340) have 24-hour subway or elevated train services. Others run on limited hours, including the color-coded 'T' in **Boston** (p120), plus **Washington, DC** (p217), **Montréal** (p195) and **Toronto** (p175). Sparing a little room for profanity at the occasional glitch, you'll be OK getting around on bus, tram, train, ferry or cable car in **San Francisco** (p593), **Portland, Oregon** (p535), **Seattle** (p516) and **Vancouver** (p634)

Best are towns with walkable cores you never have to leave. Sights, bars and hostels along the cobblestone lanes of historic **Charleston** (p300), **Savannah** (p309) and **Québec City** (p204) are (generally) within sneaker distance. As are sand, sun and clubbing in compact **Miami Beach** (p319). More people stumble around the French Quarter in **New Orleans** (p254) than walk. Student towns (p12) tend to be more pedestrian-friendly.

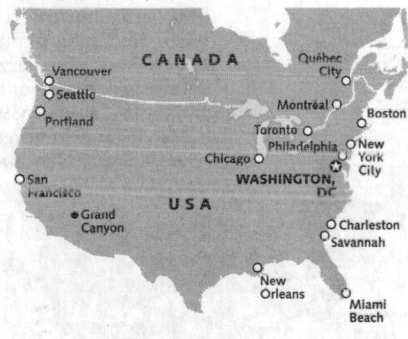

Some national parks encourage use of a shuttle service to get to and fro – thus minimizing the number of cars in the natural habitat. Many roads at the **Grand Canyon** (p428) are accessible only by its free shuttle anyway (but bus service *to* the canyon is limited). Hikers could take the 2167-mile (3467km) **Appalachian Trail** (p153) from Maine to Georgia (takes five to seven months).

If you prefer self-motorized wheels – aka bicycles – to cars, see p707 .

D.R.I.N.K.I.N.G.

Mentioning 'tasty American beer' is a sure laugh for Central Europe comedians, but American and Canadian drink can ruin livers with the best of them. For the 'bad' stuff, visit the Budweiser brewery in **St Louis** (p386) or Miller Brewing Company in **Milwaukee** (p369). Microbreweries make the better brew (eg Anchor Steam in San Francisco, Shiner Bock in Texas); some offer tours, including Sleeman's up in **Guelph** (p192), Brooklyn Brewery in **Brooklyn, New York** (p80), and Samuel Adams in **Boston** (p120). Boston also has a top-shelf Irish bar scene. There are also many beer-makers in the **Pacific Northwest** (p512) and **Colorado** (p478), which is home to the September **Denver** Great American Beer Festival (p474). **Portland** stages a brewers' fest in July (p539).

Many glasses clink, with varying accuracy, in the USA's northeast quarter. **Chicago** (p351), **Philadelphia** (p98) and even **Cleveland** (p360) take their drinking *very* seriously, and **New York City** (p78) is no stranger to intoxicants – the name 'Manhattan' is thought to come from a Native American term for 'inebriation.'

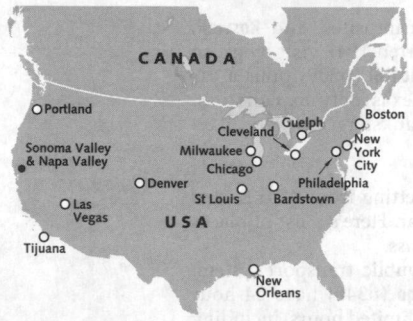

Yet the most advanced drinking bingers seem to gravitate elsewhere: **New Orleans** (p266), **Las Vegas** (p423) and **Tijuana, Mexico** (p581), where you can walk into the birthplace of margaritas (a lime-ified tequila cocktail made for the weak gringo, which quickly took off north of the border).

It's not all beer, though. Grape fermenting gets going all over, but wineries in California's **Sonoma and Napa Valleys** (p609) rightly reign amongst the world's finest. Or sample a sweet decanter of bourbon in its birthplace, **Bardstown, Kentucky** (p291).

Music Sights

With *Bringing It All Back Home* in 1965, Bob Dylan sassily reminded Beatlemania fans where much of modern music (blues, jazz, rock, country, western swing, big band) was rooted.

All music fans must stop in **Memphis** (p278) for goose-pimpled looks at Sun Studio and – seriously worth it – Elvis' Graceland. Down south, see the haunting source of the blues at the historic 'crossroads' outside **Clarksdale** (p274). Chess Studios in **Chicago** (p340) became another blues mecca. **Detroit** (p365) is home to Motown and the White Stripes. Hometown hero Chuck Berry still plays monthly at Blueberry Hill in **St Louis** (p386). Join in all-night jazz sessions in **Kansas City** (p387), or booze it up in the sweaty Dixie jazz halls of **New Orleans** (p266).

Indie rock fans should visit **Athens** (p309) – where REM and the B-52s got it going; **Austin** (p396) – home to the South-by-Southwest music fest in March (and hundreds of guitar-based bands year-round); or **Seattle** (p526) – where Nirvana kicked off grunge (not to mention heavy metal's

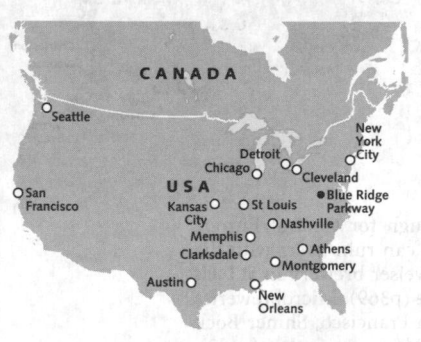

arse). Though Starship claimed to have built the city on rock and roll, Noise Pop in **San Francisco** (p602) attracts a stash of new talent. **Cleveland** (p359) is home to the Rock and Roll Hall of Fame, while the Country Music Hall of Fame in **Nashville** (p284) focuses on country twang. Relive Hank Williams' stripped-down country appeal in **Montgomery** (p314).

When on the **Blue Ridge Parkway** (p235) listen out for bluegrass on the radio, or stop for Friday night jamborees in Floyd, Virginia.

Musicians of all types dream most of taking a bite of the Big Apple; while in **New York City** (p62), check out the rowdy cheer-or-boo amateur night at the Apollo Theatre in Harlem.

Ethnic Enclaves

Though only one in five Americans and Canadians carry a passport, there's more than Disney World for those seeking so-called international flavor.

Impressive Chinatowns around both countries offer top-notch budget food and flopping-fish markets that you just don't find at Wal-Mart. Can't-miss examples include the ever-expanding one in **New York City** (p59), a dainty looker in **San Francisco** (p598) and – for food's sake, the best – **Toronto** (p180) and **Vancouver** (p639) up in Canada. Of all things,

'Little Saigon' in **Oklahoma City** (p385) serves some of the country's best Vietnamese *pho* noodle soup.

The USA's largest French-speaking area is in **Cajun Country, Louisiana** (p369), where zydeco rocks at bars and down-home crawfish *étouffée* fills bellies. **Québec City** (p204) and **Montréal** (p195) are sizable French-speaking cities with a super *Canadien*-spun version of French food.

Outside Philadelphia, **Lancaster County** (p100) is a famous Amish community where traditional-minded locals get about by horse buggy and cook up hearty meals to sample. Ohio's **Amish County** (p361) is similar. Iowa's **Amana Colonies** (p388) have embraced certain aspects of technology – they're famed for their refrigerators actually – while less traditional German towns are in Texas' **Hill Country** (p400).

The USA is home to many fun Mexican and Latin American neighborhoods, including Olvera St in **Los Angeles** (p567), the Mission in **San Francisco** (p598), Market Sq in **San Antonio** (p401) and Little Havana in **Miami** (p324).

Some cities have it all. **Chicago** (p345) boasts exciting districts devoted to its Latino, Chinese, Ukrainian, Chinese and Orthodox Jewish residents.

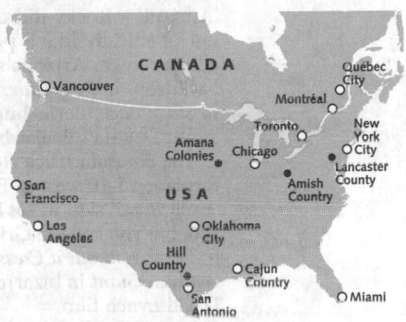

'I Like the Animals'

Wild animals tend to dine, stroll, defecate and love one another where there are fewest people to watch. All Rockies' parks offer prime viewing, including Wyoming's **Grand Teton National Park** (p494), which in spring and early summer bubbles with active moose, elk and bison.

Whales blow water off the shores of both coasts. In **Cape Breton, Nova Scotia** (p209), one boat outfitter 'guarantees' sightings from April to October for C$25, or you can head out from **Boston** (p129) for US$30. Ace spots to watch from land are Washington's **San Juan Islands** (p532) or BC's **Saturna Island** (p652). In summer killer whales feed on migrating salmon at **Johnstone Strait** near Telegraph Cove (p653).

Ontario's **Algonquin Provincial Park** (p192) is moose-a-rama. Hikes at Michigan's vehicle-free **Isle Royale National Park** (p368) go by swimming moose, and campers get a wolf serenade.

Alaska is serious bear country. Polar bears do the Manitoba Dance in remote **Churchill** (p671), while grizzlies often loiter trailside in Rocky Mountain parks like **Waterton Lakes National Park** (p667) in Alberta. Mountain goats butt heads in nearby **Glacier National Park** (p505), with no tip jars in sight.

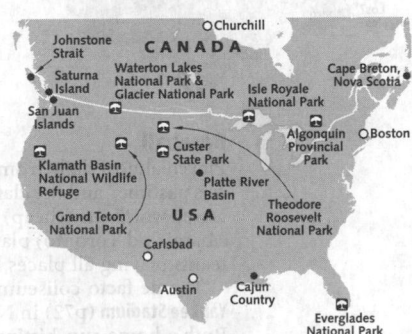

Venture into gator country down south, including Florida's **Everglades National Park** (p329), or via a US$15 swamp cruise in Louisiana's **Cajun Country** (p271).

The buffalo are returning to the plains. See loads at North Dakota's overlooked **Theodore Roosevelt National Park** (p391) or at South Dakota's **Custer State Park** (p390).

The eagle, the USA's symbol, fights to flourish. An important site for its regrowth is California's **Klamath Basin National Wildlife Refuge**. For nine million years, hundreds of thousands of sand hill cranes have roosted in February and March off I-80 in Nebraska's Platte River Basin (between Kearney and Grand Island). See a million-plus bats flap wings in **Austin** (p397) or **Carlsbad** (p466).

Film & TV Sights

American films flood world cinemas with images of the USA. Running up the **Rocky steps** at the Philadelphia Museum of Art (p96), as Sly did in the boxing movie, is the US equivalent of crossing Abbey Rd, but don't yell 'Adrian!' – Rocky did that in the ring. Alfred Hitchcock's *Vertigo* plays out practically like a postcard of 1960s **San Francisco** (p593) with sights all over town. Arizona's stark **Monument Valley** (p436) has provided stark backdrops in *Easy Rider* and *Forrest Gump,* but it made its celluloid debut in *Stagecoach.* Eerie 'bug world' scenes in *Starship Troopers* took place in South Dakota's **Badlands** (p390).

The dinosaur truck stop for *Pee-Wee's Big Adventure* is in **Cabazon**, California, on I-10 west of Palm Springs. Nothing says movies more than the 'Hollywood' sign in **Los Angeles** (p566). Studio tours here cost out the wazoo, but you can see Griffith Observatory, where cliff-diving cars zoomed in *Rebel Without a Cause,* for free. Speaking of James Dean, he filmed his last film *Giant* in bizarre **Marfa** (p409), which itself has the feel of a B-side David Lynch film.

Stop at the Geneva Steel complex in Vineyard, Utah (off I-15 between Salt Lake City and Provo) to see where Kevin Bacon did his little dance in *Footloose.* The Eisenstein 'baby carriage' tribute in *The Untouchables* was filmed in **Chicago's Union Station** (p354). While in **Minnesota** (p374), where *Fargo* was filmed, count the 'you betchas' uttered. The club scenes in *Purple Rain* – where Prince shows 'em all, yeah – were shot at still-strong First Ave in **Minneapolis** (p378).

Dare to swim off **Martha's Vineyard** (p143) in Massachusetts, where *Jaws* did his dining. You've seen more of **Vancouver** (p634) than you know, as filmsters spend more than US$1 billion annually for city-meets-nature backdrops in films like *Catwoman* and *Rumble in the Bronx.*

Of course **New York City** is a film set in itself. Woody Allen fans can stay at a death scene from *Manhattan Murder Mystery* at the Hotel 17 (p75) and watch sunrise on the bench overlooking the Queensboro Bridge as seen in *Manhattan* (p67).

You can get yourself on the small screen, be it Oprah or David Letterman. TV shows in **New York** (p81) and **Los Angeles** (p568) offer tickets for studio audiences; you'll need to plan way ahead.

CANADA

Vancouver · Badlands National Park · Minneapolis · Martha's Vineyard · San Francisco · Vineyard · Chicago · Philadelphia · New York City · USA · Monument Valley · Los Angeles · Cabazon · Marfa

Baseball

Played almost daily from April to October, baseball bills itself as 'America's pastime,' and the clank of a last-out ball sent bouncing on green grass is well worth the (cheap) ticket price. Most big cities (from Los Angeles to Miami and Toronto) play big-time ball, with little leaguers and semi-pro teams playing all places between.

The de facto coliseum of the sport is, despite Red Sox fans' protests, **Yankee Stadium** (p72) in New York City, where the field was built for Babe Ruth's home-run hitting style. Baseball began – most agree – upstate in Cooperstown, where you can visit the **National Baseball Hall of Fame** (p110). Kansas City's **Negro Leagues Baseball Museum** (p387) highlights African American teams that flourished when baseball was segregated. In Kentucky, stop to buy a famed **Louisville Slugger bat** (p290) from the eponymous museum.

Losers are loved just as much as winners: the **Milwaukee Brewers** (p369) have never won the World Series, the **Boston Red Sox** (p134) won three times in the 1910s and didn't win again until 2004, and the **Chicago Cubs** (p353), playing in ivy-lined Wrigley Stadium, haven't hoisted the banner since 1908. In Baltimore, the **Orioles** (p241) play at the urban-inspired Camden Yards, near Babe Ruth's birthplace.

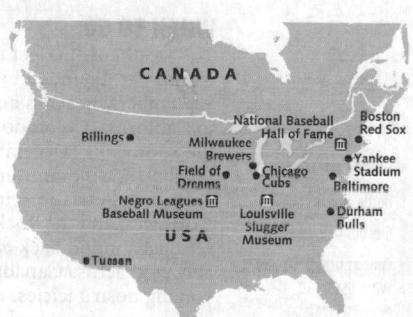

Seen in the film *Bull Durham* starring Kevin Costner, the **Durham Bulls** (p296) are the nation's most famous minor-league team. If Costner's your thing, run the bases from his film *Field of Dreams* (p388) outside Dyersville, Iowa, on US 20 west of Dubuque. More fun minor-league action gets going in **Billings** (p501), Montana and **Tucson** (p438), Arizona.

Great baseball movies include *Eight Men Out* (about the 1919 World Series fix), *The Natural* and *Bad News Bears* (with a drunk coaching foul-mouthed little leaguers).

Dream Sleeps

Bend your budget a bit here and there and you'll get some seriously memorable places to hang your hat. The ultimate is on a gator-guarded **Cajun Country houseboat** (p270), or on a **Mississippi River tugboat** up in St Paul (p377). Architecture fans should make it to Bartlesville, Oklahoma – no, hold on a sec – to stay in a **Frank Lloyd Wright skyscraper** (p385) with the rooms redone as Frank intended.

Test your fate with a night in Oregon's **Timberline Lodge** (p546), the outside of *The Shining* hotel, or where Nixon's own curse began at the infamous **Watergate** in Washington, DC (p226).

In the Mississippi Delta, pick away on old instruments in fixed-up **sharecropper cabins** (p274). In Kentucky's bourbon country, you can stay in the historic overnighter for the too-boozed-up – a refashioned **prison cell B&B** (p290).

Campy (not camping) fans in California should splurge for a room at San Luis Obispo's ultra-kitsch **Madonna Inn** (p587), or at the **Railroad Park Resort** (p623), with rooms made in old train cars in the shadow of Mt Shasta. Of course the king of camp are **Vegas' Strip resorts** (p422), fashioned like Egyptian ruins and Venetian canals.

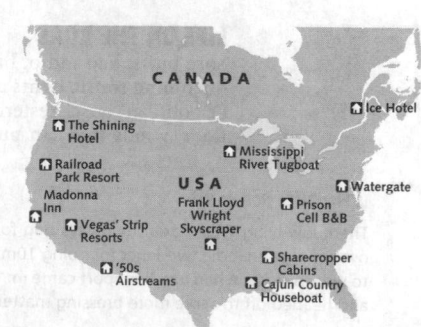

In Bisbee, Arizona, bunk down in pure-cool, decked-out **'50s Airstream** trailers (p441) from US$40 per night.

If you have, oh C$550 or so, stay in Québec City's famed **Ice Hotel** (p206) in winter, or tour it for C$14.

See Fast Facts on every chapter's title page for the best hostel by region, or p14 for the best five overall.

Getting Started

See Climate Charts (p687) for more information.

Traveling in these two huge countries is pretty much a breeze. Most people speak English, the infrastructure is solid and free travel info is everywhere. That said, go-and-see-what-happens traveling has its limits. This chapter addresses some pre-trip issues to consider before popping on the road; more information is in the alphabetized Directory chapter (p683).

WHEN TO GO

The weather is perfect *somewhere* any time of year. Main holiday season is summer, bounded by Memorial Day (late May) and Labor Day (early September). Beaches and parks fill up. Ski areas (from British Columbia to California, Colorado to Alberta, New England to Québec) boom when the snow falls (December to March or April). In peak tourist seasons, hotel rates will jump up and rooms can sell out.

Regional variations in weather should be considered. July in the Pacific Northwest and the Rockies is wonderful, but brutal in the Southwest (and seriously humid back east). February's fine for San Francisco, but miserably cold across Canada (and much of the USA), unless you're skiing or you dig nostril icicles. For regional breakdowns, see the Fast Facts boxes at the start of regional chapters.

If you visit in curb season – spring and fall – you'll miss the peak travel crunch and have greater access while not freezing (too much) in northerly cities like Toronto, Chicago or New York. Consider festivals (p691) before making plans too.

COSTS & MONEY

The further you go and the longer you stay, the more you'll spend. In recent years, the US and Canadian dollars have dipped in strength versus the British pound and the euro. (Exchange rates are listed on the inside front cover.) You're generally fine to get around with an ATM or cash card (p694) and most businesses accept travelers checks and credit cards. Daily costs range from around US$30 to more than US$100 per day; it differs for each region and the ranges are given in the Fast Facts box that starts each chapter.

While daily costs in Canada are a little less – museum tickets, hotels, doughnuts, hockey games – some transport (eg flights) tends to be a little more.

LIFE ON THE ROAD

Sore butts, bad radio, bad coffee – and pure freedom. A whirlwind of oncoming traffic lights and billboards advertising a resort, a truck stop or political cause. Yesterday's neon-colored french fries squashed on the floor, winds that can push the car window out of its socket. Sunshine

---

HOW MUCH?

Bottle of water: US$1

City bus fare: free–US$2

Concert tickets: Strokes or Wilco US$15-30, Prince US$75-100

Hostel bunk: US$10-35

Hotel double room: New York US$100, Dallas US$60, Thunder Bay C$46

Internet access: per hr US$3-5

Museum admission: Toronto's Hockey Hall of Fame C$12, Cleveland's Rock'n'Roll Hall of Fame US$20, LA's Getty Center free

Newspaper: US$0.50-3

Pint of beer: US$2.50-5

WHOOPS! *Robert Reid*

Them low-lying West Texan highways beg for speed, but highway patrols can lurk. I got pulled over on a panhandle two-laner for going 10mph too fast and a gap-toothed drawling cop started to write a ticket when a radio report came in: 'The Wilsons' hound is loose.' He gave me a warning and headed off to serve more pressing matters. Saved by a runaway hound.

10 TIPS TO STAY ON A BUDGET

First off, crash with friends. Or friends of friends. But that's not all:

- **Bidding for travel** With Internet sites like www.priceline.com and www.hotwire.com, you can score super-cheap three- and four-star hotel rooms for a song. Grand Hyatt Chicago for US$45? Yep. See p684 for more budget lodging tips.

- **Discounts** Take a student ID to save on museums, airfare, bus tickets etc.

- **Drive-away cars** If you're without wheels, consider driving private vehicles from X to Y for the cost of gas; see p707.

- **Free leap frog** From overseas, buy a ticket to the opposite coast (from London to California) with a free stopover in New York City; treat each as a hub and get a regional-based Rent-a-Wreck (p711) or bus around.

- **Make meals** This rocket-science report just in: making meals (peanut butter, ramen noodles) saves money; take a sandwich to a park or a bench.

- **National Parks pass** A US$50 annual pass gets you into all of the US parks, paying for itself quickly (particularly in the park-frenzied west). Most parks sell them or you can buy online (https://buy.nationalparks.org).

- **Plan reasonably** Don't set your budget up to lose. To properly gauge the money you'll need, use the regional budgetary breakdowns in this book, and then add some. Don't forget gas if you're driving, at roughly US$2 per 40 or 50 miles.

- **Read the fine print** The devil's in the detail for things such as phone cards (connection charges), car rentals (sky-high insurance) and hotel rooms (taxes). Buyer beware.

- **Slooow it down buddy** If you stay longer in a place, or see fewer places, you can cut travel costs and give yourself time to find the cheaper ways of seeing things and eating. Also slow it down on the road – stay under the speed limit to avoid tickets.

- **Work** Hostel exchange programs, bar work or (if you have the visa) as a temp; see p700.

filling big skies that stretch a world away. Donning a jacket on a blazingly humid day for the blasting air conditioner in a big-ass mall (see p375 for the biggest of the big). A nod from a skeptical cowboy, a hurried sigh from a city slicker walking past. Six hours of fields, then an isolated hill, sitting alone like an outcast kid in the lunch playground. A day of bouncing along invisibly on a big city's streets – museum, landmark, park, snack, department store – then sitting on the subway between two strangers' lively talk, inviting you, with a quick smiling glance, to join in. Suddenly the city includes you.

John Lennon said 'life is what happens when you're making other plans.' And many highs of a trip – particularly to such a vast region as the USA and Canada, where the concept of the modern 'road trip' was born – come somewhere between here and there.

CONDUCT

All in all, Americans and Canadians are a very friendly bunch. Even reported rudies in New York can be engaged in lively conversation on sidewalks. Most anywhere, if you show a peep of interest in local life, you'll open up a chatterbox.

Smiling is a way of life. Often strangers nod or give a slight smile – try to return it. Even jaded city hipsters are expected to return a 'How are you?' with a cheerful 'Great, you?', whether true or not. A sense of optimism pervades many aspects of life here – loads of North Americans

WHAT TO TAKE?

Everything you might need can be found in North America, and there's always secondhand Goodwill stores if you need an extra sweater.

- **ATM card** Check with your bank to make sure you can use yours here.
- **Digital camera** Save on film and avoid those scary new airport X-rays.
- **Driver's license** Your national one's OK (for a year in the US, three months in Canada), but get an International Driving Permit if yours doesn't have a photo ID or you plan to take a drive-away car (p707).
- **Laundry gear** Save money with quick-dry clothes, a clothesline and a sink plug.
- **Passport** Even US and Canadian travelers may need a passport to check into some hostels.
- **Photocopies** Make copies of your passport, air tickets and travel insurance forms.
- **Sneakers or hiking boots** Token motherly advice, but scores forget how much *more* they'll walk on vacation.
- **Student ID** Many museums offer discounts.
- **Visas** You won't get in without one; see p698.
- **Your tunes** Whether CDs, MP3s, an iPod or old-school cassettes, bring and share your music.

prefer not to sit back and make snide remarks over a failure or burp in life, but rather roll up their sleeves to fix it.

Many folks here are mystified by the British sense of humor, but not all. Canadians proudly claim a stronger grip on The Funny than Americans, having produced so many well-known comics: Mike Myers, Jim Carrey, Dan Aykroyd, John Candy, Martin Short, Eugene Levy, all the *Kids in the Hall* blokes and William Shatner.

Outside the cities, it can be considered bad taste to flaunt feelings – certainly for gay couples (p691) – or talk loudly in public. Cursing at family restaurants will grant you stares from neighboring diners. If you have 'ANARCHY & HATE' painted on a leather jacket and wear a blue Mohawk, good for you. But you will be stared at.

Don't be offended or surprised by a complete lack of awareness of your home country. Historically rather isolated from global exchange, Americans are usually intrigued by foreigners, but a certain standoffishness may exist (particularly in rural areas). When the talking gets going, you may have to remind them that Ireland is not part of England. Or stomach the ol' chestnut 'Yes, we sure bailed you out of

WELL-TRAVELED READS

- *On the Road* by Jack Kerouac – its heydays of thumbing are largely past, but here's America's best celebration of the roadways
- *Blue Highways* by William Least Heat-Moon – travelogue follows a 13,000-mile US circuit of two-laners and everyday America
- *Travels with Charley* by John Steinbeck – sharp, funny trip around the country in a trailer in 1962; Charley's a poodle if you didn't know
- *Great Plains* by Ian Frazier – zigzagging across that central stretch of prairies, bison trails, Native American sites and fenced-off missile silos in that part of the US *no one* visits

DOS & DON'TS

- Don't rush to criticize the USA or the president, unless the person you're with takes the lead.
- Do tip your waiter (15% to 20%), bartender ($1 per drink) and taxi driver (10% to 15%).
- Don't smoke anywhere without asking first, as most states have nonsmoking laws.
- Don't kiss good ol' boys on the cheek or wrap your arms around their beer-gut frame in a long embrace. Outside cities, most men shake hands, partner.
- Do call American football 'football' and European football 'soccer,' or skip the latter entirely.

dubya dubya two' – totally ridiculous, but meant fairly good-naturedly all the same.

Many of the people hold a totally unironic devotion to God. Mom'n'pop shops, motels and restaurants often have framed quotes from the Bible – though other religions too – up on the wall. If religion ain't your thing, it's probably not worth debating with the guy serving you eggs and turkey bacon.

People generally love their hometowns, states and regions. If you want to break the ice with anyone, hide any negative feelings you may have. As in life anywhere, if you respect folks, you'll get it back.

TOP 10 AMERICAN ALBUMS

If you're wanting the perfect soundtrack for the road trip, consider these standouts. Apologies to Bob Dylan, Snoop Dogg and the wonderful world of heavy metal.

- **Alt rock** *Doolittle* (1988) by the Pixies – Nirvana called their 1991 landmark 'Smells like Teen Spirit' a 'Pixies rip-off'
- **Blues** *King of the Delta Blues* (1997) by Robert Johnson – all modern music's roads eventually lead back to the Mississippi crossroads where, legend has it, Robert sold his soul to the devil in the 1920s; also Muddy Waters
- **Country (Folk)** *American Recordings* (1994) by Johnny Cash – the first of the Man in Black's stripped-down man-and-his-guitar comeback albums; also try Woody Guthrie
- **Country (Twang)** *20 Greatest Hits* (1990) by Hank Williams – barebones country, Hank put the tears in beer when country wasn't cool; also anything Loretta Lynn
- **Funk** *Funk Power: 1970* (1996) by James Brown – less heard than JB's early '60s stuff, his '70s brand bounces with Bootsy Collins on bass, sometimes lingering on as good funk should
- **Hip-hop** *Fear of a Black Planet* (1990) by Public Enemy – politically charged blitzkrieg from when rap was 'rap' and you could sample what you wanted
- **Jazz** *Money Jungle* (1962) by Duke Ellington, Charles Mingus and Max Roach – holy summit of jazz greats from swing and bop eras; hard to overlook Miles Davis too
- **Pop** *Pet Sounds* (1967) by the Beach Boys – Brian Wilson ups the ante on lite surf rock, causing McCartney's eyebrows to raise and lean into *Sergeant Pepper's*
- **Punk rock** *The Ramones* (1976) by the Ramones – New York City punk rock band that kept the leather on for their three-chord songs even for 100°F midday shows
- **Rock and roll** *The Velvet Underground* (1967) by the Velvet Underground – Lou Reed and company's debut takes in cross-dressing and heroin; also Replacements' *Let it Be* is a lost beer-soaked classic from the '80s, and the Pretenders are cool

ARRIVING SOMEWHERE NOT IN THIS BOOK

This book doesn't cover it all. Keep the following in mind when you pull into places like, oh, Harrisburg, Pennsylvania:

- Most towns have proud visitors centers – visit for free coffee, maps, coupons and advice.
- Many small towns have signs leading to chain-free 'Historic Downtown' or 'Main Street'.
- Interstates tend to bypass old downtowns; clusters of fast-food and motel chains are out by the interstate, while more interesting (sometimes cheaper) mom'n'pop shops are in town.
- At each stop, take the 'ask one question challenge.' Whether it's the gas pumper or a sandwich-maker at a grocery store, ask something about the town – eg why Pierre is pronounced 'peer' – for (often) an earful of insider commentary.
- Stop at a random small-town museum and ask the curator to show you around; often they collect the stuff themselves and will be delighted at the interest.

Also watch for 'If You've Got a Few More Days…' boxes in each chapter that highlight places – including many tucked away on back roads – to steer toward.

Snapshots

CURRENT EVENTS

On pace to out-weird the 1960s, the 2000s (someone needs to name this crazy decade already) started in a wave of anxiety with the potential computer meltdown of Y2K, which arrived without incident. In November 2000, George W Bush edged out Al Gore in electoral votes (certainly not the popular count) in the USA's most controversial presidential election. Then September 11. In its aftermath, the Bush administration tightened the borders and in 2002 created the Department of Homeland Security, which made (among other things) the USA Canada border crossing just that little bit more annoying. The Patriot Act, however, greatly expanded the government's surveillance and search powers that many likened as too close to Orwell's *1984* for comfort.

Most Americans are now somewhat used to the blipping 'yellow warnings' for terrorist threats that stream across TV sets, while 'September 11' has joined the daily lexicon.

Much has divided the USA. Bush's strategy to improve the declining economy was to lower taxes, increase defense budgets and allow huge annual deficits (Reaganomics anyone?). Alienating many world administrations (and peoples), the USA invaded Iraq in early 2003 and eventually captured Saddam Hussein when he was found hiding in a hole in the ground. The US military transferred power to a democratic Iraqi government in June 2004, though had no immediate plans for withdrawal. The first year's death count surpassed that of the first four years of the Vietnam War.

Harkening back to the '60s, many apolitical Americans became outspoken supporters or dissidents of Bush and the war, and movies themselves became banners for beliefs, including politicized films like Michael Moore's *Fahrenheit September 11* and Mel Gibson's *The Passion of the Christ*.

Meanwhile, Canada refused to support the Iraq war, but sent troops to Afghanistan and keeps more troops in the UN peacekeeping force than any other nation. At home, Canada legalized medical marijuana in 2001 and toyed with decriminalization completely (it remains a big no-no down south). A domestic source of contention are First Nations land rights based on old treaties; this stems from the 1973 land claims policy, which recognized First Nations lands based on treaties.

Gay marriage became another huge divisive factor for both countries (and distraction from life during wartime); some pointed to the Bible, others pointed to legal implications and the appeal of the heart. Vermont and Massachusetts legalized it, as have Ontario, British Columbia and Québec; when the San Francisco mayor deemed California's anti-marriage stance unconstitutional, same sex couples flocked to city hall to be wed. President Bush took a beating when his bill to amend the Constitution (to forbid it) triggered no reaction in Congress. He ended up by saying the states 'can do what they want to.'

For now, the states – in one of the more heated presidential elections in recent history – said they were happy enough with Bush's first term to re-elect him to another four years in the November 2004 election. Bush beat Democrat Senator from Massachusetts John Kerry by over four million popular votes.

So big we don't need to leave it. Under 20% of Americans have passports – that's 230 million people content to get their international fix at Disney World. Up north, about 23% of Canadians carry passports.

HISTORY
'I See Land, Sir'

The first humans in the region walked here some 20,000 to 30,000 years ago over a convenient land bridge once connecting present-day Siberia and Alaska. Between 40 and 75 million Native Americans lived in diverse tribal nations – some as nomads, some in wood-hut or pueblo settlements – by the time European jaws first dropped at the scene.

Following Italian Christopher Columbus' ventures in the Caribbean, swarms of eager, gold-seeking (sometimes throat-slitting) Spaniards, French, Dutch and Brits trickled in. Some British business types settled the colony of Jamestown, Virginia in 1607, while ultraconservative Protestant pilgrims from England founded Plymouth, Massachusetts in 1620. Despite leaky boats, hardships and malaria, both settlements survived, largely thanks to help from local Native American tribes who gave food and showed how to grow crops. Thankful Pilgrims staged a harvest festival, which has come to be known as Thanksgiving.

In 1664 the British kicked the Dutch out of New Amsterdam (now a humble town called – hold on a sec…oh yeah – New York City) and had established 13 colonies (from Maine to Georgia) by 1733.

> Dee Brown's *Bury My Heart at Wounded Knee* is a great overview of the tragedies of Native Americans in the last half of the 1800s.

Battling the French

Not big fans of each other, Britain and France duked it out for North American land rights in the French and Indian War. A young colonial general, George Washington, led a first strike against French troops in 1754, two years before war was officially declared. The French army, aided by First Nations tribes, fought unconventionally, easily picking off British troops marching in rows.

The tide turned in 1758, when the British wrestled control of the Bay of St Lawrence, then overpowering Québec City in 1759 (which saw both British leader James Wolfe and French leader Marquis de Montcalm fall in battle), and finally Montréal and Detroit in 1760. France conceded lands east of the Mississippi River to the British formally in 1763, western lands to Spain, and their grip of the Americas was lost to the ages. Various Native Americans kept up the fight, however, for over a century more.

Independence

> Of the eight soldiers involved in the Boston Massacre jailed and tried for murder, all but two were acquitted on the grounds of self defense. The two were found guilty of manslaughter and claimed the benefit of clergy (the chance to make penance instead of being executed).

The British government jacked up taxes in the colonies to pay for wars on the other side of the globe, and locals got fed up. In 1770 some drunken Bostonians attacked a group of British soldiers resulting in the Boston Massacre (former slave Crispus Attucks was the first killed), and three years later a group of the discontented dressed up like Indians dumped tea cargo into the Boston Harbor. Continental Congresses met in 1774 and 1775 in Philadelphia to discuss how to deal with this mess (eg 'taxation without representation') and assembled a ragtag army led by George Washington. The defiant Declaration of Independence was signed in Philadelphia on

TIMELINE

1012: Theorized American forays by Vikings, who may have made it as far as present-day Poteau, Oklahoma		**1620:** Mayflower lands in Cape Cod, and 204 legs hit Cape Cod with fervor

AD 500	1000	1500	1600	1700

1000: Construction starts of settlements by Taos people in present-day New Mexico

1492: Columbus and posse pop up at America's door

1759: The *merde* hits the painted hand fan as British take Québec, ending French rule in Canada

July 4, 1776, and the resulting Revolutionary War saw colonials hiding behind bushes to pick off the clearly visible red-coated British troops. French support (in supplies mostly) helped turn the tide, and led to the unlikely British surrender at Yorktown, Virginia, in 1781.

Some kiss-assy locals showed their allegiance to the crown by foregoing the conflict and relocating to Canada, helping balance the number of British and French in the tense peace up north.

In 1789 Washington became the first president of the USA, with the capital in New York City. Third president Thomas Jefferson doubled the USA's size with the Louisiana Purchase in 1803 ($15 million for most of everything between St Louis and Seattle – good deal). The little inconclusive War of 1812 broke out as the ever-testy relations between Britain and the states worsened, highlighted by the British army burning down the new capital of Washington, DC. Canada got into the action, too, exchanging a few border raids with the Americans, to little effect. The war ended in a draw in 1814.

Sherman Alexie is an outspoken author with many pull-no-punches books such as *Ten Little Indians* (2003) and *Custer Died For Your Sins* (1988)

Expansion, War & Lies

The US rushed into the rest of the 19th century with the gusto of a toddler on its first steps. Administrations after Jefferson's continued the westward gaze, as part of the 'gimme gimme' Manifest Destiny philosophy that all of North America simply was bound to become USA. Ask Mexico, goaded into a war that cost it half its northern territory.

As the US expanded, the issue of 'free state' versus 'slave state' hovered over every new state. (Following the Missouri Compromise of 1854, Texas even cut off part of its panhandle to maintain its 'slave state' status – the sliver is now the Oklahoma panhandle.) The South was solely based on cotton-producing plantations and slave labor. The so-called Underground Railroad assisted slaves escaping to the free north.

After anti-slavery advocate Abraham Lincoln was elected president in 1860, southern states broke off, forming the Confederate State of America, and declared war on the USA. The bloody Civil War followed (estimated deaths exceeded half a million) with reckless northern leaders mounting casualties against the far out-resourced, outnumbered Confederate army, led by Virginian General Robert E Lee. Following key Union (northern) victories in July 1863 at Gettysburg, Pennsylvania, and Vicksburg, Mississippi, the war slid into an inevitable, but messy, Union victory by April 1865. Lincoln didn't live to see it, though, as he was shot and killed April 14, 1865.

Following the Civil War, many Union vets kept their uniforms on to assist westward migration and settlement. That meant fighting Indians and defending a lot of false promises regarding land rights. A small sort of payback occurred in June 1876, when General George Custer lost his scalp at Little Big Horn in Montana to the hands of Sioux (he had it coming). In 2004 the US capital (finally!) acknowledged Native American

Based on Alexie's writing, *Smoke Signals* (1988) was the first Native American-made film. Kevin Costner's film *Dances With Wolves* (1990) is kept pretty authentic – half is told in Lakota tongue

1848: Victory in President Polk's controversial war with Mexico gives USA Texas and parts of present-day Southwest

1861: Predecessor to Royal Canadian Mounted Police forms; the outfits came later

1800	1850	1860	1880	1890

1776: American colonies sign Declaration of Independence on July 4

1861: First of USA's nine presidents with facial hair (Lincoln) takes office; Civil War erupts

1877: First game of hockey with rules – rules? *Sacre bleu!* – staged in Montréal

TOP CIVIL RIGHTS SIGHTS

- **Rosa Parks Museum**, Montgomery, Alabama (p314)
- **Martin Luther King Junior National Historic Site**, Atlanta, Georgia (p305)
- **National Civil Rights Museum**, Memphis, Tennessee (p280)
- **Brown versus the Board of Education National Historic Site**, Topeka, Kansas (p387)

history by opening a museum on the Mall, Washington, DC (p221). (Still waiting for a national museum dedicated to African American history and slavery…)

Canada spent most of the 19th century defining itself too. After rebellions in both Upper Canada (Ontario) and Lower Canada (Québec), the two united in 1840. Britain was keen not to lose another colony. In 1867 Britain formed the Dominion of Canada (Ontario to Nova Scotia) and John Macdonald became the first prime minister. He added Manitoba to the Dominion of Canada in 1870, but it took hanging an uppity French-Canadian leader Louis Riel to do it. Look for Chester Brown's comic-strip bio *Louis Riel* (2003; Drawn & Quarterly) that lovingly tells the tale.

Boom & Bust

The industrial age of the 19th century and early 20th saw millionaires get made – Andrew Carnegie via steel, John D Rockefeller via Standard Oil, Henry Ford via cars and the modern assembly line – and millions of new Americans (Italians, German, Irish, East European Jews) pour in, often through Ellis Island in New York City (p57). New factories needed new hands of course, but work conditions were far from ideal (as gruesomely described in Upton Sinclair's 1906 novel *The Jungle*). Labor unions would follow, helping guarantee the 40-hour work week, banning child exploitation and breaking up monopolies.

Expansionist American eyes turned abroad too. A greedy war movement (spurred on by publisher William Randolph Hearst, as parodied in the 1941 film *Citizen Kane*) led to the quick, one-sided Spanish-American War, where the US picked up the Philippines, Guam, Puerto Rico and rights to Cuba, later contested by Fidel Castro. In the early 1900s, the US wrestled rights for Panama from its Colombian rulers and built the Panama Canal by 1914.

The USA initially tried to keep out of the Great War (later known as WWI), but jumped in by 1917 to tip the balance toward the Allies (and get a share of the spoils afterward). Canada immediately jumped into WWI, despite Québec's bitter opposition to the draft.

Responding to the 'Roaring '20s' excesses (a time when money, jazz and flappers ruled the roost), religious conservatives ushered in Prohibition,

1931: Canada becomes a voluntary member of the Commonwealth

1964: Hockey great Tim Horton establishes Canada's famed doughnut chain

| 1900 | 1930 | 1940 | 1950 | 1960 |

1896: Ice-cream cone invented in New York City

1933: Franklin Roosevelt's New Deal plan counters Great Depression; prohibition ends, drinking binges begin

1955: First McDonald's and Disneyland open

which – gasp – constitutionally outlawed liquor and spawned a new industry of organized crime. In Chicago trigger-happy gangs were run by Al Capone who snuck in his booze from Canada past Royal Canadian Mounted Police. The Canadians' two-decade flirtation with Prohibition had ended (in most parts) by 1920; Capone was finally taken down for tax evasion (see the tale in the 1987 film *The Untouchables*). When Prohibition was repealed in 1933, gangs switched to prostitution and drugs.

A decade of indulgence crashed suddenly in October 1929 when the stock market collapsed and ripple effects were felt through the land and around the globe. Millions lost homes, farms and businesses, and the Great Depression set off. Amidst it the Dust Bowl added to the misery of the Great Plains, as many 'Okies' migrated west (as told in John Steinbeck's *The Grapes of Wrath*). Democrat Franklin Roosevelt was elected president in 1932 and quickly become one of the USA's most pivotal figures with his New Deal policies and the introduction of (rather radically) many social programs (eg social security).

What, More Wars?

Canada followed Britain's declaration of war against Germany in September 1939. The Japanese attack of Pearl Harbor, Hawaii, and Germany's declaration of war against the USA four days later, brought the USA full-fledged into WWII. With a little luck, the US defeated larger Japanese forces at Midway Islands in June 1942, igniting an island hop toward Tokyo.

The Allied forces' D-Day invasion of France on June 6, 1944 brought some relief to Soviet forces who had been savagely fighting Germans in Eastern Europe for three years. Following Germany's surrender in May 1945, attention turned fully to the Pacific, but an invasion of the Japanese mainland was avoided by dropping atomic bombs on Hiroshima and Nagasaki in August 1945.

Immediately following WWII, tension built between the USA and the Soviet Union as a four decade–long Cold War kicked off: capitalism versus communism, with only the threat of mutual nuclear destruction keeping the powers from direct war. In Korea, Soviet- and Chinese-supported North Korea invaded South Korea, with the US and its allies keeping it from being overrun.

DID YOU KNOW?

The attack on Pearl Harbor commenced at 7:55am on Sunday, December 7 1941

HAIR TODAY, GONE TOMORROW

Conspiracy! Al Gore made headlines for growing a beard after losing the 2000 presidential election. While noble, it came too late to affect the USA's **PO-PACS-HUF** (Period of Presidents and Candidates Sporting Hair upon Face), which lasted from 1861 to 1948. For more, see http://explorers .whyte.com/presbeards.htm – possibly the best website of all time. Canada's last prime minister with facial hair – Louis St Laurent, he had a 'stache – *lost* the 1957 election.

1981: MTV starts, and ultimately killed the radio star

2000: US 'gives back' Panama Canal to Panama, South Park's 'Blame Canada' song earns nomination

| 1970 | 1980 | 1990 | 2000 |

1974: Nixon lowers speed limit to 55mph, resigns (over Watergate)

1987: US speed limits raised to 65mph, following Sammy Hagar's lame single 'I Can't Drive 55'

After President John F Kennedy was assassinated in November 1963, President Lyndon Johnson pushed through major Civil Rights legislation that came years after violent struggles in the South and the emergence of leaders like Martin Luther King Jr and Malcolm X.

Escalation of the space program – a race to the moon against the USSR – was 'won' when Americans landed there in July 1969 (a month before Woodstock, man). But Johnson's committal of half a million US troops to Vietnam to fight communist North Vietnam divided the country. While Canada officially stayed out of the conflict, many Canadians did not; thousands crossed the border to legally join the US armed forces (while some 30,000 Americans crossed north to dodge the draft). Finally the USA left, heads down, in 1973, leaving the South for the communists, who took it in April 1975, half a year after President Richard Nixon resigned in scandal following a burglary at the Watergate office complex in the capital.

Parties & Payback

The world got a shock in 1973 when Arab nations decided not to trade with countries friendly to Israel (USA and Western Europe allies), thus

launching a competition for petroleum resources that continues to linger (punctuated by the 444-day Iran Hostage crisis in 1979, which helped Reagan take the presidency from a befuddled Carter administration). Amid this, disco provided the soundtrack, and cocaine and birth control pills the fuel, to an unrestrained spirit till AIDS and the '80s crept in.

Ever-cheerful former actor Reagan put taking care of the Commies atop the agenda. He built up defense and offered huge tax cuts that prompted economic growth (and record budget deficits), and Ronnie generally gets credit for winning the Cold War, as the USSR toppled back to Russia. His hapless successor George Bush I had to wrestle with the mess for four years, then was followed up by political moderate Democrat Bill Clinton who had the fortune to ride the technology boom of the '90s, sending unemployment below 2%. Despite unprecedented popularity, Clinton had his enemies. When he lied about an affair with intern Monica Lewinsky, he narrowly escaped being removed from office by a Republican-controlled Congress.

THE CULTURE

Built from the countries' first inhabitants and immigrants from all over the world, the USA and Canada drip with culture (ie it's not just TV).

The People

The US population is an estimated 288.4 million, making it the world's third most populous nation (after India and China). In the 1990s the USA grew by 10% due to immigration, and the influx has continued despite September 11 and an economic downturn. About 75% of the country are white. By some measures in 2003, the Hispanic population (12.5% from the 2000 census) has surpassed African Americans to become the 'largest minority.'

Canada adds another 31.7 million souls to the region. For the first time in a century, Canada's growth rate in the last half of the '90s was under the USA's (though still above most developed nations). Immigration has tipped from Western Europe and the UK in the 1990s, with a huge influx of Asians, Africans, Latin Americans and Eastern Europeans in more recent years.

See p26 for Ethnic Enclaves around the region.

Religion

Though there is no official religion in either country, freedom of religion is one of the founding rights of the USA. The US Constitution calls for separation between church and state, but many visitors are surprised at how closely that religion stuff can be tied to government (eg 'In God We Trust' on money). 'Under God' was added to the pledge of allegiance in 1954, though prayer in schools (currently a no-no) is a hot source of debate in more conservative circles. Religion is the backbone to ongoing debates on abortion and gay marriage.

Most of the US population is Christian (approximately 54% Protestant, 24% Roman Catholic). The sometimes mocked Bible Belt (from Kentucky and Tennessee westward to Oklahoma and Texas) is home to the most devoted folks and heart of the fundamentalist Southern Baptist church. Other religions, of course, are represented too. About 2.2% of the country is Jewish, and there are sizeable populations of Muslims, Buddhists, Hindus and traditional Native American religions.

In Canada, seven in 10 people are Roman Catholics and Protestants, though the percentage is waning slightly (dropping several percent in the past decade), due to the influx of 'imported religions' from immigrants.

Overheard at an Oklahoma rodeo: 'They may have taken prayers out of school, but they're not taking it out of rodeo.'

Architecture

The first colonials were more keen to worship, eat corn and reproduce than think about expanding the art of architecture, and unsurprisingly the first century or two of building largely reflected the European manors, cottages and palaces they knew from back in Europe.

After the Revolutionary War, the USA adopted neoclassicism as a style suited for a new republic. Thomas Jefferson designed the Virginia State Capital and his home Monticello after Roman designs. Charles Bulfinch put a Federal touch, paralleling English Georgian style, on the US Capitol in Washington, DC.

Beginning in the 1850s, iron-frame buildings (and the elevator) allowed more freedom and design. Skyscrapers started their shoulder-to-shoulder race upward, beginning with Louis Sullivan's 13-story Guaranty Building in Buffalo, followed by more famed buildings in Chicago and New York City.

Frank Lloyd Wright, architecture's golden child of the 20th century, worked on sculptural 'prairie houses' that took the (rich folks') home to new places (such as Fallingwater in Pennsylvania; p105) and his school Taliesin in Wisconsin (p372).

Art deco – an immediate hit after its 1925 Paris exposition – changed the 20th century, evident in the 1930 Chrysler Building and 1931 Empire State Building in New York. Nazi-fleeing Bauhaus architects brought the sculptural glass-walled hit-or-miss international style to the USA, inspiring Ludwig Mies van der Rohe.

A healthy dose of retro postmodern nods by architects like Michael Graves and Philip Johnson followed. One of the most famous architects today is Canadian Frank Gehry, influenced by installation art, with superb asymmetrical designs.

For an up close and personal look at some of the USA's great buildings, check out www.greatbuildings.com/places/usa.html

DID YOU KNOW?

There are approximately 10 million bricks in the Empire State Building.

Art

The first real American art trends began in the 1820s with romantic landscapes capturing the Hudson River Valley in the east (Thomas Cole), then later with Western images captured by German-born Albert Bierstadt, and Native American and 'cowboy art' by George Catlin, Frederic Remington and Charles Russell.

Romanticism turned to realism as the 19th century faded to the 20th, with more subdued works by artists such as Edward Hopper, Thomas Hart Benton and Grant Wood (who did the much parodied *American Gothic,* housed at the Chicago Art Institute). Norman Rockwell gave an idealized view of life on magazine covers from the 1920s to 1960s.

During this period, modern art evolved, with abstract painters like Joseph Stella and ever-popular Georgia O'Keefe. New York became the de facto avant-garde capital following WWII, with Jackson Pollock's 'action paintings' and Mark Rothko's bold squares of color. This evolved into Pop Art such as Roy Lichtenstein's comic book art and Andy Warhol's incorporation of cartoonesque advertising. Performance art and mixed media art (Bruce Nauman is a good example) has generally picked up the baton in more recent years. New York's Whitney Museum (p67) focuses on modern American art.

Music

It can't be denied: clefs bass and treble of the USA have changed the world. Blues developed out of slaves' work songs, or 'shouts,' and out of spiritual call-and-response themes, both adaptations from African music. It spread across the South after the Civil War, where folks like Robert Johnson plucked town to town in the 1920s on an old guitar; miraculously he was recorded. After WWII, blues migrated to Chicago, where the amped-up variety got going with artists like Muddy Waters, Robert Lee Hooker and Buddy Guy.

More instrumental, but of the same stock, jazz began, it's believed, at slave gatherings in New Orleans in the early 1800s. Early variations included ragtime and Dixieland jazz. The great jazz age of the 1920s and '30s, when big-band leaders like Duke Ellington and Count Basie expanded the sound, coincided with the Harlem Renaissance in New York. Singers like Ella Fitzgerald and Billie Holiday combined blues and jazz.

After the WWII, a reaction to big-band swing was bebop or bop jazz, lead by sax player Lester Young and a crop of legends to follow: Charlie Parker, Dizzy Gillespie and Thelonius Monk. As jazz broke and remade molds, new pioneers stepped in to travel the permutations of hard-bop, cool jazz, avant-garde and fusion, including Miles Davis, John Coltrane and Charles Mingus.

Possibly the polar opposite is the foot-stompin' country-and-western music that emerged in Applachian Mountains from the pickin' instruments brought over by Scottish, Irish and English immigrants. The Grand Ole Opry in Nashville (p284) opened its stage to the radio in 1925, helping nationalize the twang. In Kentucky, Bill Monroe combined country, jazz and blues to create bluegrass. Rock-influenced variety became rockabilly in the 1960s, and sales finally soared in the 1970s and '80s, with folks like Dolly Parton, George Strait and Garth Brooks selling millions. (And more recently Shania Twain from Ontario.)

Folk has never really hit the biggest stages. Depression-era songsters like Woody Guthrie and Pete Seeger seeped into the '60s, inspiring rock and roll straddlers like Bob Dylan and Canadian Neil Young. Celtic-based music lingers in pockets of Canada's Martitime Provinces.

Some say rock and roll was born in 1954 with Elvis' 'That's All Right,' but purists maintain the first rock record was Bill Haley and the Comets' 'Rock Around the Clock' the same year. Its complex sound – a mix of guitar-driven blues, country-and-western and black R & B – was backed up by counter-cultural, sexually charged lyrics aimed squarely at the youth. The USA scrambled initially to counter the British invasion in the early 1960s when the Beatles and Stones dominated, but upped the ante with Dylan's rock records, Jimi Hendrix's guitar, the Velvet Underground's experimentation, and (to a lesser degree) the Grateful Dead's drug-dealt psychedelia.

The Ramones gave rock a needed kick in the ass in the mid '70s with their two-minute punk bursts. With MTV starting in 1981, music became more visual. Some fogies withstood the superficial make-up (Bruce Springsteen, Tom Petty), some thrived off it (Van Halen, Aerosmith), while alternative rock longed to keep things legit (REM, Talking Heads, Pixies).

DID YOU KNOW? The Carpenters signature song 'We've Only Just Begun' was originally part of a TV commercial for a California bank.

In the early 1990s, grunge rock – led by Nirvana and Kurt Cobain's flannel shirt – rallied against hair metal bands like Poison. When the mainstream got a hold of this new 'alternative,' much of it died, but bands like Pavement and Sonic Youth kept things interesting way below the radar. The two-piece White Stripes' Zeppelin-ified blues gave a limping rock a needed jolt with their stripped-down sound, spurring a host of bass-free bands like the Yeah Yeah Yeahs.

No longer a new kid on the block, hip-hop arose out of black and Puerto Rican street culture in New York's South Bronx in the 1970s, where turntable DJs scratched over disco songs. Harlem's Sugar Hill Gang recorded the first rap hit, 'Rapper's Delight,' in 1979. As never heard before, rapid-fire lyrics dominated the repetitive structure, which included samples of well-known songs. Early groups gave urgent voice to political and social problems, such as Public Enemy, De La Soul and Run DMC. Out on the west coast, 'gangsta rap' took off with bands like NWA glorifying guns, drugs and prostitution. The murders of Tupac Shakur and Biggie Smalls in 1997 curbed its popularity. White rap has always been on the fringe. Detroit's Eminem helped expand hip-hop to the white teenage market. And 20 years old, the Beastie Boys remain the most enduring hip-hop band.

Electronica music in various forms – melodic trance (such as pop-electronica star Moby) and more rhythmic drums-and-bass or jungle – has added a synth scape to speakers in nightclubs, at home and in car commercials.

Memorize all US states and Canadian provinces. See p696 for a full alphabetical list. Name the capitals in case of a tie. Tip: no one remembers Lansing, Michigan.

Literature

Young Americans are forced to read early examples of national literature such as James Fenimore Cooper's fussy *The Last of the Mohicans* (1826), Herman Melville's get-to-the-point-already *Moby Dick* (1851) or Edgar Allan Poe's super gruesome tales such as *The Tell-Tale Heart* (1843) – nothing like a dead beating heart to pique interest. Literarily speaking, things really got going after the Civil War. Mark Twain's *Huckleberry Finn* (1884) – the tale of a runaway boy and a slave drifting down an antebellum Mississippi – is a masterpiece of 'anti-intellectual' story telling. Young Canadians don't get far without reading soldier John McCrae's 1915 poem *In Flanders Fields*. Canadian WP Kinsella writes of contemporary First Nations life, but is best known for *Shoeless Joe* (1982), which was made into the film *Field of Dreams*.

Following WWI, 'Lost Generation' writers took the 'anti' stance a step farther, with works reflecting a growing disillusionment with the modern world. Examples include F Scott Fitzgerald's *The Great Gatsby* (1925), Ernest Hemingway's *The Sun Also Rises* (1926), John Steinbeck's *The Grapes of Wrath* (1939) and, later on, JD Salinger's *The Catcher in the Rye* (1951).

Their successors, the Beat Generation, took off in the 1950s. Big names included Jack Kerouac (*On the Road,* 1957), poet Allen Ginsberg (*Howl,* 1956) and William S Burroughs (*Naked Lunch*, 1959). Current literary lights include Dave Eggers, David Foster Wallace, Johnathan Letham and Canadian Douglas Coupland.

The first major African-American works were powerful essays, including Frederick Douglass' powerful autobiography (1845), which fueled the anti-slavery movement, and WEB Du Bois' *The Souls of Black Folk* (1903). Post-WWII classic novels include Richard Wright's *Black Boy* (1945) and James Baldwin's *Go Tell It on the Mountain* (1953).

Sports

Many sports are an all-consuming pastime (and business) in the USA and Canada. Baseball gets the overseas hype – and seeing a minor- or major-league game is cheap, laid-back summer fun (p28; also see mlb .com; frequent games from April to October). But football (an evolved rugby played as leaves wither in fall) is number one during fall and winter. Its stop-and-start pacing frustrates some first-time watchers. NFL pro football (www.nfl.com; played Sunday and Monday, August to January) gets most headlines – particularly for the Super Bowl, a pseudo-holiday in late January – but NCAA college football's old traditions (eg a wagon led on the field by tiny ponies after a score), quaintly dated helmets and heated-to-hatred rivalries most resemble the rugby, European soccer or footie vibe from abroad. NFL and many college tickets are costly and tough to get; try sports bars in college towns or Texas' super high-school variety on Friday nights. Canada's pro league (www.cfl.ca; weekly games June to November) alters the rules slightly.

NBA basketball (www.nba.com; frequent games October to June) – with its helmet-less personalities in clear view – is fast approaching football for favorite sport. Its college alternative finishes off in March Madness, a thrilling single-elimination tournament that has mass appeal. Women's basketball is staying strong (www.wnba.com; frequent games May to October).

Up in Canada, ice hockey reigns, and the popular NHL major league (www.nhl.com; frequent games September to May) crosses international boundaries. At the time of going to print, the NHL was in a 'lockout' with its players over salary caps and the 2004 to 2005 season was likely to be missed. Some theorize that the league is hurting after expanding too much into less hockey-oriented places in southern USA.

Soccer struggles for life here – the women's league failed despite an enthusiastic start following the US win in the 1999 World Cup – though the men's league (www.mlsnet.com) still plays weekly April to October.

Hard to beat a can of Bud at a rodeo – big or large – found all over the countries' western states. The sport – Spanish for 'to surround' – started with Spanish horse tamers in the west in the late 1700s and was picked up in the 19th century by tobacco-chewing types like Buffalo Bill Cody. Several events are judged, including saddle bronc and bull riding, tie-down roping and barrel races. See schedules at www.prorodeo.com or ask at visitors centers. The biggest and baddest rodeo is the Calgary Stampede (p668; www.calgarystampede.com), held in July. Smaller ones include the superb African-American rodeo in Boley, Oklahoma (p381), and Saturday night rodeo in, of all places, New Jersey (p107).

ENVIRONMENT
The Land

The USA covers 3.79 million sq miles (6.06 million sq km). Canada is a wee bit portlier at 3.81 million sq miles (6.09 million sq km). (Only Russia

The easy-to-hate Manchester Uniteds of the USA include the Dallas Cowboys ('America's team'; NFL), Notre Dame Fighting Irish (NCAA football), Los Angeles Lakers (NBA), Duke Blue Devils (NCAA basketball) and New York Yankees (ML baseball)

is bigger.) The continental USA is made up of 48 states, with huge Alaska (northwest of Canada) and Hawaii rounding it out at 50. USA's external territories include Puerto Rico, Guam, American Samoa and the US Virgin Islands. Canada has 10 provinces and three territories.

Climate is all over the place. Most of the USA's 'lower 48' are temperate, particularly in the east. Hawaii and Florida are tropical, Alaska is arctic and the Great Plains are semiarid. Canada's warmest areas run along the US border, where most of the people are located.

Geologically, the lands were bent and shaped about 50 to 60 million years ago, when ice sheets covered much of the continent. In the past few million years, rain, rivers and wind have polished the results, most dramatically in the Southwest desert canyons.

DID YOU KNOW?

The deadliest hurricane in Canadian history was in September 1775, when 4000 people died along the south coast of Newfoundland.

Wildlife

The marching boots of civilization wreaked some serious havoc on the living things that once flourished coast to coast. As forest and prairies became cities, highways and farms, things changed. Notably gone are most of the USA's 100 million buffalo, which roamed between the Mississippi and the Rocky Mountains as recently as 150 years ago. Named from an Aztec word, coyotes – the roaming 'little wolf' – get nods in much Native American and cowboy lore – still having their way with North American deer, rodents and farm animals despite decades of barbed wire and shotguns. One angry farmer complained, 'They ain't fooling around with my sheep, they're eating them!' Respect.

In 1903 President Theodore Roosevelt founded the first bird sanctuary, giving birth to the National Wildlife Refuge System (NWRS), today managed by the US Fish & Wildlife Service (www.fws.gov), which oversees 95 million acres. One success story is the American alligator, once on the brink of extinction, but now found frightening birds and fish throughout the southeast. Bald eagles, grizzly bears and grey wolves have now recovered to sustainable populations.

Contrary to popular belief, only one alligator has been found in the New York City sewer system, a 125lb specimen found by four boys in 1935.

Only 1% of the vast tallgrass prairies of the Great Plains now remain, and only 4% of the original redwood forests, while a full quarter of Canada remains forested. Many native plant species are left to thrive in only isolated, federally protected refuges. The best examples of what the continent used to be like are the diverse Yellowstone (p490) and Great Smoky Mountain National Parks (p294). Not to mention Canada's national and provincial parks, including Jasper National Park (p665) and Ontario's Algonquin Provincial Park (p192). See p27 for best places to view wildlife.

National Parks

The USA's National Park Service (NPS; www.nps.gov) manages more than 380 federally protected sites covering an area the size of England and Scotland combined. Its 53 national parks are the crowning glory and cover the breadth of the USA's natural highlights (mountains, caves, deserts, swamps, volcanoes and rainforests). These are reasonably popular, particularly in

---

TOP RIDICULOUS RODENT: PRAIRIE DOG

Sitting plop on their butts from Texas to Manitoba, and west to the Rockies, these fat short-eared rodents (tailless squirrels essentially) create vast (sometimes farm-ruining) 'towns' of intricate tunnels that extend miles – one found in Texas ran 250 miles. Listen for hilarious squeaks from 'guards', who can alert friends as to the kind of predator approaching (hawk, badger, coyote, popsicle-toting brat from Cincinnati).

summer, and the NPS governs with varying degrees of strictness, eg Zion (p447) doesn't allow cars during summer. Most have camping and rather expensive lodges, with cheaper stays being offered in base towns nearby.

Canada's 39 national parks are managed by Canadian Heritage–Parks Canada (www.parkscanada.pch.gc.ca).

FOOD

Big meals make big folks. Order fries at a steakhouse and get the full fryer basket's worth lopped on a plate, an iced tea comes quart size, sweetened and with free refills. Meat – off the bone, in bloody slabs, ground into burgers, mashed into loaf – is the name of the game. And dessert, often hot cobbler with ice cream melting on the side, is expected.

Well, that's one way into American or Canadian dining. But that's far from the reality on the road. Waves of immigrants – from past centuries, from last week – add a diverse stamp onto the food landscape, with Indian, Thai and Vietnamese meals increasingly becoming a chosen option for families nationwide.

Breakfast follows the English school of thought – BIG with eggs, bacon, sausage, bread, jams – not just a roll. A super tradition is weekend brunch – a leisurely late breakfast, often with a cocktail, at bigger cities' cafés and restaurants.

Here's a regional breakdown of what you can expect, watch for, and avoid:

Canada Québec has real-deal French dining; Canada's Chinatowns (Vancouver, Toronto, Montréal) have more authentic ingredients than make it through US customs.

Great Plains Look for lamb fries (aka Rocky Mountain oysters, aka fried calf testicles), served whole or sliced; some Native American locations serve 'Indian tacos' in deep-fried flour shells; Kansas City's mammoth spicy barbecue portions give the bread slices an inferiority complex.

Mid-Atlantic Philadelphia gave the world the lovely grilled cheesesteak (a roll stuffed with beef, cheese and onions); Amish restaurants in Pennsylvania serve home-style German food; good crab eating in Chesapeake Bay.

New England Seafood specialties like Maine's prized lobster and the regional clam chowder; 'raw bars' serve oysters cold from the sea; the clambake (sung about by Elvis) is a ritual meal dating from Native American traditions; Vermont makes a mean maple syrup.

New York The City has it all, particularly famed for its bagels and pizza slices (p76); thriving Chinatown is best for Vietnamese actually.

TOP FIVE FAST FOODS

Some fast-food stops are better than others. Here are the tops of the multistate chains. But do look out for Tommy's in Southern California too.

- **A&W** (www.awrestaurants.com) National drive-in, started in the 1920s, still serves root beer in frosty mugs, though numbers are starting to wane to the mega-muscle of Sonic.

- **Dairy Queen** (www.dairyqueen.com) Royal head of small-town dipped cones; plenty of greasy meals too.

- **In-n-Out Burgers** (www.in-n-out.com) Old-school burger stand (featured in *The Big Lebowski*) in California, Arizona and Nevada; the best fast-food burger there is.

- **Taco Bueno** (www.tacobueno.com) Flashy taco sellers in Texas, Oklahoma and Kansas, superior to Taco Bell; the bean burrito makes a handy car-jousting weapon, if in need.

- **Waffle House** (www.wafflehouse.com) Breakfast means waffles and grits all day at the House throughout the South and Midwest.

Pacific Northwest Produces crispy apples and wonderful mushrooms and berries; Seattle toots its love for the coffee bean.

Southern Here you go, heavy countryfied cooking; for breakfast you *must try* grits and buttery biscuits coated in gravy; barbecue is big stuff here (Texas' beef brisket, Carolinas' pulled pork), as is peach cobbler a la mode in Georgia; iced tea is practically served in buckets; spicy Cajun food (rice-based jambalaya, shrimp gumbo stew, blackened catfish) is of the nation's best – all is often served with a 'here you go, sugar'.

Southwest & California Heavy Mexican influence in the former Spanish territory; let the hungover awake with a big plate of *huevos rancheros;* taco trucks serve superb tacos for $1 or so; San Francisco has arguably the country's finest dining.

See the D.R.I.N.K.I.N.G tailored trip (p25) for highlights of booze and beer around the region.

TIME TO EAT!

- **New Year's Day** Black-eyed peas supposedly bring in a happy new year
- **Superbowl Sunday** Bad snacks, burgers and beer around the TV set
- **July 4** Barbecue outdoors till the firework displays
- **Halloween** (October 31) Children dressed as demons go door to door for candy
- **Thanksgiving & Christmas** Roasted turkey, pecan and pumpkin pies

---

USA & Canada
Outdoors Jeff Greenwald

Log on to www
.recreationusa.com for
exhaustive coverage of
activities in the USA, while
www.travelcanada.ca will
satisfy those heading to
Canada.

COREY RICH

Rock climbing in Yosemite National Park (p613), California, USA

Imagine my surprise. After 20 years of cross-country hitchhiking, African vagabonding, Himalayan trekking, and Micronesian wreck diving, the most terrifying place I'd ever been was right at home – on a bicycle.

The Slickrock Bike Trail, in the heart of Utah's gorgeous redrock country, is where it all began. My friend James and I rented bikes in Moab and took them out to the so-called 'Practice Loop': a 4-mile circuit just east of Slickrock, designed to test your two-wheeler skills.

'Practice Loop, huh? Isn't that for little kids with training wheels?' I guffawed. 'Let's check it out anyway,' James suggested.

Half an hour later I found myself a mile into the Loop, paralyzed with fear. The trail had climbed to a hilltop, and now dropped away with the dizzying pitch of a roller coaster. The ground was hard as cement and ready to flay me alive. I recalled my joke – but even training wheels wouldn't help if I skidded over the nearby cliff.

Somehow, by blind luck, I survived. But the incident taught me a lesson: never underestimate how wild the wild places in the USA and Canada can be. Not all of them are dangerous – but most have a raw, rugged beauty unlike anything you've ever tasted before.

New York, San Francisco, Montréal and Vancouver are serious fun – but to find the soul of the USA or Canada, you've got to visit the national parks and monuments. The variety alone will blow you away. From the dunes of California's Death Valley to the soaring, pyramidal peaks of Canada's Banff National Park; from the grizzly bears of Yellowstone to the alligators of the Everglades – you'll find infinite opportunities to experience the eye-popping, jaw-dropping wilderness that met (and sometimes devoured) the first Western explorers to the New World.

So drink up the museums and nightlife, then get yourself into the wild. You'll soon understand why actor and outdoorsman Steve McQueen once said, 'I'd rather wake up in the middle of nowhere than in any city on earth.'

SKIING & SNOWBOARDING

In the mid-1970s, when the world was young, a guy named Jake Burton Carpenter set up a workshop and began to build 'snowboards' in his Vermont garage. Jake was a snurfer – a snow-surfer – but he dreamed of a day when his passion would break into the mainstream. It didn't take long. Vermont became the ground zero of snowboarding, and Burton Snowboards kick-started what's now a snowballing industry.

On powdered slopes across the USA and Canada, snowboarding has become as popular as downhill skiing. Riding the lifts of Sun Valley, Lake Placid or Telluride, you'll see airdogs gaping the ski tracks – or cratering into moguls. Though Vermont remains the heart of snowboard culture, you won't find the white stuff there in July. Don't despair: the Hortstman's Glacier in Canada's Mt Whistler region (which will host the 2010 Winter Olympics) is winter's summer home.

Skiing is one of the world's great rushes, but it isn't cheap. When you add up the rentals and lift tickets, it amounts to a major splurge. I learned to ski in Telluride, and it was worth every nickel – but for my next trip, I'll head up north. Canadian lift tickets are much more affordable, and the slopes of Québec's Mont Tremblant or Banff's Sunshine Village are as good as anything you'll find in Utah or the American Rockies.

One of the best websites for those planning a skiing holiday in the USA is www.goski.com /usa.htm. If you're headed north to Canada then www.skicanada.org will point you in the right direction.

And while you're out there, don't forget those tooth-and-claw snow sports: dog sledding and skijoring (being pulled along on skis by a horse). Who hasn't dreamed of crossing Canada's Monashee Mountains on skis, towed at top speed by a pair of huskies? (Okay, neither have I – but hey, let's try it!)

CYCLING & MOUNTAIN BIKING

Want to be able to say you saw the USA or Canada? I mean, *really* saw it, in a way few others can match? Grab yourself two months, a big chunk of change and a serious hydration system – and sign up for one of the 4200-mile (that's 6720km) cross-country rides offered by a few select outfitters. Oh yeah, you'll need one more thing: the most comfortable bike seat in the world.

If you're not that crazy, there are still plenty of terrific rides that will show you the backcountry with less chafing. South Dakota's Mickelson

Trail, for example, cuts across the Black Hills National Forest for 110 gritty miles (177km), following the old roads used by gold miners. Another sure bet is the 206-mile (332km), hut-to-hut ride between Telluride, Colorado, and Moab, Utah. Both towns are drop-dead gorgeous, and the scenery in between will make you feel like you've landed in a John Wayne film.

Across the Canadian border, the Icefield Parkway between Jasper and Banff is a six-day, inn-to-inn route that breezes past mountain lakes and cracking glaciers – some of which reach down to the roadsides.

Plenty of cities are bike-friendly, too: Montréal, Boulder, Austin and Portland, to name just four. But some of the best cycling in America is found around San Francisco – where you can fill your tires near Haight-Ashbury and ride over the Golden Gate Bridge toward the Marin Headlands. The toughest biking challenge in the States? Keeping your eyes on the road while cruising beneath those soaring golden towers.

DIVING & SURFING

Ninety feet below the surface of Monterey Bay, I felt like I'd entered an underwater cathedral. Diving in California's giant kelp forests, I could almost forget the frigid ocean water rushing in through the neck of my wet suit. In every direction, gigantic kelp stalks rose toward the glittering surface, swaying like very tall belly dancers. Sunlight filtered through the fronds, turning them into stained-glass windows.

> Surfing was originally developed by the Ngaru people of the Hawaiian islands before the 15th century, but didn't really catch on until the early 20th century.

Throughout the year, California's coastal waters host an amazing variety of life: colorful nudibranchs that look like miniature flying carpets, wild dolphins, and enormous gray whales on their annual migration between Mexico and Alaska. Across the USA, there's more terrific diving (and warmer water!) in the Florida Keys – once you get out of the mangrove swamps and onto the outer reefs. Canada boasts some good diving, too – notably in the lakes of Ontario's Bruce Peninsula, where the ill-tempered waters around Fathom Five Marine Park have turned 21 known sail and steam ships into popular wreck dives.

If waves are your passion, some of the best surf in the continental USA breaks off the beaches of Santa Cruz. The names of these sites are part of surfing legend: Steamer Lane, Pleasure Point, Sharks, Mavericks. Equally famous are the town's funky brew-pubs – great places to share travelers' tales. And if you can, take the high trail west to Hawaii, the winter home of big waves, where the famed Pipe Masters competition draws the world's best surfers to Oahu's north shore during November and December.

ROCK CLIMBING

Aside from hosting the world's oldest (and weirdest-looking) trees, the high desert of California's Joshua Tree National Park is covered with rock called 'pinkish monzogranite.' The only thing more fun than saying it is climbing it – and countless climbers have perfected their moves on these noble boulders. Driving through the park, you'll spot solo climbers, teams and classes (look for the tangled piles of rope) almost everywhere. With over 5000 climbs to choose from, you'll think you've landed in the Flintstones' answer to Disneyland.

Almost everyone with a thing for rocks has seen mind-boggling pictures of climbers bivouacking on El Capitan or Half Dome in Yosemite National Park; but it's not all about going up. Near Zion National Park in Utah, five-day canyoneering classes teach the fine art of going down: rappelling off of sheer sandstone cliffs into glorious redrock canyons.

If you're not planning to cross the Mississippi, upstate New York's Shawangunk Ridge is where many East Coast climbers – including myself – tied their first billets. There are lots of great climbs in the 'Gunks,' but Trapps Cliff is where you'll probably end up: more than two solid kilometers of 70m wall (1.24 miles of 230ft wall), with hundreds of possible routes. That's about enough for one summer, ya think?

Canada's west coast also offers superb climbing, just northwest of Vancouver. The Squamish Valley is famous for the nine-pitch, 2200ft (660m) Grand Wall of the Stawamus Chief – a monolithic face first climbed, incredibly, in the 1960s. So whether you're a bumblie, a betty or a bongle (Google 'rock-climbing slang'), British Columbia might just be the place where you find your personal pucker factor.

HIKING & BACKPACKING

Growing up in the East Coast suburbs, it was a total revelation when I moved west and discovered there was more to outdoor recreation than shopping malls. The first place I ever camped was the Point Reyes National Seashore, a spectacular wilderness just an hour's drive north of San Francisco. I'll never forget waking up that first morning in Coast Camp, watching a family of raccoons wrestling the cheese out of my backpack.

Point Reyes is still my favorite spot on earth. About 30 places vie for second place: from Death Valley's awesome Mosaic Canyon to the mind-blowing Joint Trail in Utah's Canyonlands; from the chlorophyll-drunk woods of Kentucky to the bubbling calderas of Hawaii Big Island. This is one of the most irresistible things about the USA and Canada: almost anywhere you go (except for a few of the flat, dusty parts where they mostly grow corn), you'll find great hiking and backpacking within striking distance. And the further you wander from the parking lots, the more solitude – and wildlife – you'll find.

Any of North America's hundreds of national parks, monuments and preserves offer terrific hikes, from wheelchair-accessible routes to screaming scrambles over snowbound passes. Looking for *real* commitment? The Appalachian Trail stretches from Maine to Georgia, while the Pacific Coast Trail leads from Canada to Mexico – we're talking 2650 miles or 4266km, passing through six of North America's seven ecological zones. It's hard to believe, but about 300 hikers go for it every year. Give it a shot – but watch out for your cheese.

Two National Park units bear the Rockefeller name: John D Rockefeller Parkway (connecting Grand Teton and Yellowstone) and Marsh-Billings–Rockefeller National Historical Park in Vermont.

WATERWAYS

The New River – don't ask me how it got its name – is the oldest river in the western hemisphere. Slicing from North Carolina into West Virginia, it cuts a gorge that ranges from 700ft to 1300ft deep (210m to 390m). Known as the 'Grand Canyon of the East,' the river drops 240ft in just 14 miles (72m in 22.5km), churning up white-water rapids to rival anything found in the American West.

The New is one of West Virginia's three most stompin' rafting and kayaking rivers – and there are six more, in the same neighborhood, for less experienced (or insane) water rats. In the western states, the astonishing Owyhee flows from Idaho into Oregon, passing towering hoodoos shaped like abstract sculptures. And if you're the organized type who can plan things a few years in advance, you might try for a spot on the Colorado itself: the mother of all rivers for kayakers, paddlers and rafters worldwide.

But don't be fooled by big-name hype. There are hundreds of places to enjoy surface tension all over the USA and Canada – even if your idea

DID YOU KNOW?

The Miramichi River in New Brunswick produces almost half of all rod-caught Atlantic salmon in North America.

TOP 10 USA & CANADA OUTDOOR ACTIVITIES

▪ **Schussing** the vertical in Whistler-Blackcomb, British Columbia (www.whistelerblackcomb
.com), 8171 acres of the best skiing in North America, from bunny slope to Crazy Canuck (the
local version of Black Diamond).

▪ **Paddling a sea kayak** through the rugged islands of Maine's Stonington Archipelago,
enjoying close encounters with seals, ospreys, puffins and whales; check out www.coast
guides.com/kayak/kayak.html.

▪ **Scuba Diving** amid the giant kelp forests of Bluefish or Whaler's Cove in the Point Lobos
State Reserve, Monterey, California (pt-lobos.parks.state.ca.us/scuba/scuba.shtml).

▪ **White-water rafting** on the boiling Nantahala River, outside of Cherokee, North Carolina.

▪ **Mountain biking** the Slickrock Trail in Moab, Utah (better start with the Practice Loop,
pardner).

▪ **Snowboarding** where it all began, in the Green Mountains of Vermont.

▪ **Snorkeling** among the yellow tangs, parrotfish and humuhumunukunukuapua'a (Hawaii's
state fish) of Hanauma Bay, on the southern shore of Oahu.

▪ **Hiking** the 17-mile trail to the dizzying summit of Ansel Adam's favorite peak – Half Dome
(8842ft or 2653m) – in California's breathtaking Yosemite National Park.

▪ **Canoeing** Ten Thousand Islands, Everglades National Park, South Florida.

▪ **Cross-Country skiing** across the rim of a great (and hopefully dormant) volcanic caldera,
1000ft (300m) above the sapphire waters of Oregon's Crater Lake National Park.

of a rough paddle is floating along in an inner tube with a beer in your
hand. Rentals and instruction are yours for the asking, from Georgia's
Chattooga rapids to Washington's Olympic Peninsula; from Alberta's
Oldman River to Hawaii Napali Coast. Hire kayaks in Monterey Bay for
a close encounter of the otter kind, or paddle through a cypress swamp
in Bayou Gravenburg, about 80 miles (129km) from New Orleans. As the
Louisiana alligator said (after using a chomped paddle as a toothpick):
'It's all good.'

New York City

HIGHLIGHTS

- **Central Park** Massive respite from Manhattan's urban sprawl (p66)
- **Brooklyn Bridge** Elevated pedestrian walkway on the city's greatest bridge (p58)
- **Chelsea's gallery ghetto** 200 free galleries (p63)
- **Chinatown** $1 noodles, cheap T-shirts and toys and floppy-fish markets (p59)
- **East Village** Rock and roll, Little India, booze and brunch (p59)
- **Off the beaten track** Ha! Nowhere in NYC is off the beaten track
- **Best journey** The Staten Island Ferry for a free close-up look at the Statue of Liberty (p57)

FAST FACTS

- **Area** 309 sq miles (half of London)

- **Budget** $70-120 per day

- **Costs** dorm bed $25-37, one-week Metro-Card for buses & subways $21, 'I ♥ NYC' T-shirt $3

- **Driving times** what, you're driving? Bwahahahahahaha!

- **Famous for** oh, you know already

- **Language** just about every known language is spoken here

- **Population** 8,008,000

- **Phrases** *fuhgeddaboutit* (kindly refrain from remembering this), *fuck you* (taxi to taxi lingo)

- **Seasons** year-round tourist season, best weather is September to November and May to June

- **Tasty treats** pizza slices, hot dogs, bagels

- **Time** GMT minus 5 hours

- **Top hostel** Jazz on the Park (p74)

TRAVEL HINTS

If you're renting a car, major companies do cheaper deals from Newark International Airport than from JFK or La Guardia. Save money by having a picnic in Central Park for lunch. And stay as long as you can afford to.

The world's greatest city – no doubt about it – welcomes and shuns slow-talkin' bumpkins and jaded jet-setters in the same breath. That everything imaginable is here (people, culture, stuff) means you're welcome to jump in, but just don't slow up the pace.

With a set of sneakers, New York's greatest glory is free to see – get lost along random sidewalks of remarkably differentiated neighborhoods (Wall St's money-grabbing bustle, the East Village's combat boots, Chelsea's art galleries, Harlem's African-American lore,

Brooklyn Heights' brownstones) and enjoy thrills of sudden glimpses of world-class icons (Empire State Building, Statue of Liberty, Central Park).

The legacy of the Big Apple's eternal 'my building is better and bigger than your building' mentality is seen below a shady canyon of art-deco and modern buildings. Equally exciting are little things, like seeing smoke pouring out of manhole covers, honking taxis weaving over street lanes, munching on a world-class bagel snack for a buck, witnessing deli owners on a smoke break yapping across the street from each other, and all sorts of no-bullshit commuters clicking heels past you as you stop to gawk. Then there's the night. There are great cities, and then there's New York. Those who don't love it just aren't into the city thing.

HISTORY

Inhabited by Native Americans for some 11,000 years before Europeans showed up, the island was known as 'Manahactanienk' (place of inebriation) by the 'Lenape' when pants-buckled Dutch bought it for $24 in 1625. Soon the subsequent New Amsterdam governor Peter Stuyvesant tried to fight the 'inebriation' by banning alcohol (and some religions). When the British bloodlessly took over in 1664, few complained.

After the American Revolution, New York City became the first federal capital in 1789. In the next hundred years, the population grew from 33,000 to well past a million. Economic and racial tensions rose too. During the Civil War, race riots broke out as poor whites blamed job loss to an increasing black population. In the 1880s and '90s, millionaires such as Andrew Carnegie, John D Rockefeller and John Jacob Astor built giant public works that still stand proudly.

The boroughs – Brooklyn, Bronx, Queens and Staten Island – joined the metropolis of Manhattan in 1898 to help house the growing number of New Yorkers. By 1905, four out of five New Yorkers were either immigrants or immigrants' children.

In the decades following WWII things declined, capping with rioters looting millions of dollars of goods during a 1977 power outage. The Reagan years, led locally by mayor Ed Koch, brought a yuppified cash-in (as typified in the film *Wall Street*).

During mayor Rudy Giuliani's reign, a severe crackdown on crime and 'quality of life' issues (including some gay bars, as well as the homeless and graffiti) helped the city become one of the USA's safest big cities, though many complain that the gap between rich and poor widened.

On September 11, 2001, the World Trade Center was struck by hijacked planes and was destroyed within two hours. Giuliani emerged as a hero, rallying a clean-up and keeping the calm. Mayor Michael Bloomberg now tries to carve out his own legacy.

THE CULTURE

When the world watches you, whether it be in movies, sports, news, music or art, confidence builds. Even many born-and-bred New Yorkers see no problem in their often shocking ignorance of US and world geography, or nothing vain about wearing an 'I ♥ NY' T-shirt.

Slow-talking time-takers (at the front of busy bagel lines or ticket kiosks) won't win friends. Still, the idea that New Yorkers are fast-talking a-holes who won't help a person in need is myth. Ask for directions and you'll get 'em. Many locals justify the grind-grime-bum-rush-roar of city life with the philosophy that 'I can do anything I want anytime I want because New York has it all,' but then do little but work. But, no doubt, in good weather, New Yorkers revel in joy in their 'back yards' like Central Park.

The New Yorkers of the movies ('doncha tink dat goil iz poidy?') are more commonly found in the boroughs – particularly Brooklyn, where so many film stars hail from.

THE BIG ISSUE: NEW BROOKLYN?

As the metropolis started jockeying heavy-duty to host the 2012 Olympics, Brooklyn was looking to up the ante as well. In January 2004, developer Bruce Ratner bought the New Jersey Nets NBA franchise and aimed to move them to Brooklyn by 2007. The move hinges on the opening of a 21-acre, $250 billion Atlantic Yards project that would overhaul Atlantic Ave between Flatbush and Vanderbilt Aves, ousting dozens from their homes. Most Brooklynites would love to see pro sports back in the borough (the baseball Dodgers left in 1958 for Los Angeles and it's still wept over), but many think it's too much to send residents packing in the name of big money.

ORIENTATION

When most travelers think of 'New York', it's usually the island of Manhattan on their minds. While it's true most attractions are centered here, don't snub the boroughs, particularly Brooklyn, which for hipsters, is the most happening place in town.

Where the Hudson River meets the Long Island Sound (near the Atlantic), New York City (NYC) is made up of five boroughs: Manhattan, Brooklyn, Queens, the Bronx and Staten Island.

North of its historic southern end, most of Manhattan is an easy-to-understand grid pattern, with numbered streets increasing by digit to the north, and (mostly) numbered avenues rising to the west. North–south Broadway cuts diagonally through the whole mess. Pick up the free subway and bus route maps from station kiosks.

Lonely Planet's *New York City* map is also useful.

INFORMATION
Bookstores

Barnes & Noble (Map pp64-5; ☎ 212-253-0810; 33 E 17th St; ☯ 10am-10pm) On Union Square, this branch carries loads of LP titles.

Bluestockings (Map pp60-1; ☎ 212-777-6028; 172 Allen St; ☯ 1-10pm) Indie bookshop/café owned by women and strong on dyke writings and rad readings.

Borders (Map pp64-5; ☎ 212-823-9775; 10 Columbus Circle; ☯ 8am-10pm Mon-Fri, 10am-10pm Sat, 11am-8pm) In new shops at Columbus Circle mall.

Oscar Wilde Bookshop (Map pp60-1; ☎ 212-255-8097; 15 Christopher St; ☯ 11am-7pm) World's oldest gay and lesbian bookstore.

Strand Book Store (Map pp60-1; ☎ 212-473-1452; 828 Broadway; ☯ 9:30am-10:30pm Mon-Sat, 11am-10:30pm Sun) New York's favorite used bookstore (open since 1927) has unruly tight aisles under towering racks of books. Some travel guides, lots of NYC maps.

Used Book Café (Map pp60-1; ☎ 212-334-3324; 126 Crosby St; ☯ 10am-9pm Mon-Fri, noon-9pm Sat, noon-7pm Sun) Proceeds go to AIDS charity.

Emergency

Crime victims services (☎ 212-577-7777)
Gay & Lesbian Anti-Violence Project (☎ 212-714-1141)
Legal Aid Society (☎ 212-577-3300)
New York Police Department (☎ 212-374-5000)

Internet Access

Apple Store SoHo (Map pp60-1; 13 Prince St) Free Internet for 'browsers.'

NYC FREEBIES

Aside from parks, bridge walks and churches, these sights are always free:

- **Astoria Pool** (p72)
- **Chelsea's gallery ghetto** (p63)
- **East Village community gardens** (p59)
- **Grant's Tomb** (p68)
- **National Museum of the American Indian** (p58)
- **New York Public Library** (p66)
- **New York Unearthed** (p58)
- **Schomburg Center for Research in Black Culture** (p68)
- **Staten Island Ferry** (p58)

The following offer freebie fun at designated times:

- **Brooklyn Brewery tours** (p80) All day Saturday
- **Brooklyn Botanic Garden** (p69) All day Tuesday and 10am to noon on Saturday
- **Bryant Park films** (p66) 8pm Monday in summer
- **Downtown Boathouse kayaking** (p72) Saturday and Sunday mid-May to mid-October
- **Jewish Museum** (p68) 5pm to 8pm Thursday
- **MoMA** (p67) 4pm to 7:45pm Friday
- **Whitney Museum of American Art** (p67) 6pm to 9pm Friday

GETTING INTO TOWN

Buses stop at **Port Authority Bus Terminal** (Map pp64-5) and some budget companies stop in Chinatown, and Amtrak trains pull in at **Penn Station** (Map pp64-5) – all are near the subway.

If arriving by air, the three airports (JFK and La Guardia in Queens, and Newark in New Jersey) have frequent shuttle services. **New York Airport Service Express Bus** (☎ 718-875-8200, $13 one way), leaves every 15 minutes to/from Port Authority, Penn Station and Grand Central Terminal. **Super Shuttle Manhattan** (☎ 800-258-3826, $17-19) goes direct to/from hotels.

The **Air Ride line** (☎ 800-247-7433) has information on transportation to and from all three airports.

■ **To/From JFK** Taxi vouchers and shuttle tickets are available from desks near baggage claim. The taxi from JFK to Midtown is a fixed $30 (not including bridge/tunnel tolls and tip); the other direction costs about $45. By subway, a new AirTrain ($5) connects the Howard Beach–JFK subway station en route to/from Manhattan. The AirTrain – a rip off actually, a bus used to make the trip for free – takes about 15 minutes to connect the subway station with the airport terminals.

■ **To/From La Guardia** Taxis are metered to/from La Guardia – it's about $40 to/from Midtown in light traffic, plus tolls and tip. A shuttle is about $15. From the terminal, take either Q60 bus to the N, W stop at Astoria Blvd in Queens, or Q33 to 7 subway stop at 74th St–Broadway in Queens. The trip will take at least an hour.

■ **To/From Newark** A taxi from Midtown to Newark International Airport costs about $55, plus tolls and tip. Allow 40 minutes to an hour. Shuttles cost about $18, or you can take a bus to/from the Port Authority Bus Terminal ($11).

Getting Around Town

Following is a list of Manhattan's key neighborhoods and their busiest subway access points.

■ **Financial District** (much of Lower Manhattan, centering at Wall St) Subway A, C, J, M, Z, 2, 3, 4, 5 to Fulton St–Broadway Nassau–Cortland St

■ **Chinatown & Little Italy** (around Canal St, east of Broadway) Subway J, M, N, Q, R, W, Z, 6 to Canal St

■ **Tribeca** (south of Canal St, west of Broadway) Subway 1, 9 to Canal St

■ **SoHo** (between Canal & Houston Sts, west of Broadway) Subway C, E to Spring St or N, R, W to Prince St

■ **Lower East Side** (between Houston St & Chinatown, east of Christie St) Subway F, V to Lower East Side–2 Ave

■ **East Village & Alphabet City** (between E 14th & Houston Sts, east of Broadway) Subway 6 to Astor Pl

■ **Greenwich Village** (between W 14th & Houston Sts, west of Broadway) Subway A, B, C, D, E, F, V to W 4th St

■ **Chelsea** (between W 14th & 28th Sts, west of Broadway) Subway 1, 9, C, E to 23rd St

■ **Midtown West** (expanding from Times Square, between W 59th & W 34th Sts, west of Sixth Ave) Subway A, C, E to 42nd St–Port Authority Bus Terminal or N, Q, R, S, W, 1, 2, 3, 7, 9 to Times Sq–42nd St

■ **Midtown East** (expanding from Grand Central Terminal, between E 59th & W 34th Sts, east of Sixth Ave) Subway S, 4, 5, 6, 7 to Grand Central–42nd St

■ **Upper West Side** (west of Central Park) Subway A, B, C, D, 1, 9 to 59th St–Columbus Circle or 1, 2, 3, 9 to 72nd St

■ **Upper East Side** (east of Central Park) Subway N, R, W, 4, 5, 6 to Lexington Ave–59th St or 4, 5, 6 to 86th St

■ **Harlem** (north of Central Park, centered on 125th St) 2, 3, A, B, C, D to 125th St

EasyEverything (Map pp64-5; ☎ 212-391-9611; 234 W 42 St; ☼ 24hr) Here you'll find around 800 PCs, for as little as $1.

Net Zone (Map pp64-5; ☎ 212-239-0770; 28 W 32nd St; ☼ 10-2am)

Media

National Public Radio airs on WNYC 820AM and 93.9 FM.

Publications worth checking out include:

New York Times (www.nytimes.com; Mon-Sat $1, Sun $3; daily)

Time Out New York (www.timeoutny.com; $3; every Tue) Best listings for theater and art.

Village Voice (www.villagevoice.com; free; every Wed) Best entertainment listings.

Medical Services

Columbia-Presbyterian Eastside (Map pp70-1; ☎ 212-326-8500; 16 E 60 St)

New York University Medical Center (Map pp64-5; ☎ 212-263-5550; 462 First Ave)

Money

ATMs are everywhere; all-hour delis (convenience stores) have some with $1.50 fees and a $100 limit.

Commerce Bank (☎ 888-751-9000), with many locations, is open daily, as is the Chinatown branch of **Chase Manhattan Bank** (Mott & Canal Sts).

Post

General post office (Map pp64-5;421 Eighth Ave at 33rd St; www.ny.com/general/postoffices.html; ☼ 24hr)

Telephone

You need to dial the area code for all local calls (☎ 212 and 646 for Manhattan, 718 and 357 for the boroughs).

Toilets

There are OK toilets in many parks, including Washington Square Park.

Tourist Information

NYC & Company Theater District (Map pp64-5; ☎ 212-484-1200; www.visitnyc.com; 810 Seventh Ave btwn 52nd & 53rd Sts); Lower Manhattan (Map pp60-1; City Hall Park at Broadway) Harlem (Map pp70-1; 163 W 125th St at Adam Clayton Powell Blvd) This is the city's official tourist arm.

Times Square Visitors Center (Map pp64-5; ☎ 212-768-1569; www.timessquarebid.org; Broadway btwn 46th & 47th St) Staff speak 10 languages.

STA Travel (Map pp60-1; ☎ 212-473-6100; www.statravel.com; 30 Third Ave, East Village; ☼ Mon-Sat) Six locations in NYC; see website for other locations.

DANGERS & ANNOYANCES

New York is kinda proud of its 'you're not in Kansas anymore' rep, but things have seriously gotten safer and cleaner in recent years. Crime has dropped 69% since the early '90s, and there was all but a parade to celebrate falling out of the murder rate top five list. According to a 2003 FBI report, New York City has the third-safest murder rate for a US city of over one million. If you're worried about getting on the subway, consider this: there are four reported robberies a day while 4.5 million use it daily.

Don't flare jewelry or unzipped bags, particularly in busy areas like Canal St. If you're out late, share a taxi back to the hostel to minimize risk.

Rats (really big ones) can be an annoyance. Treat each sighting (usually on subway tracks, beside dumpsters) as some kind of guessing game – whoever gets closest to the total count wins.

SIGHTS
New York Harbor

The long-time first glimpse of the USA for immigrants and foreigners, the harbor (snug between Brooklyn, Staten Island, Manhattan and New Jersey) needs to be got out and into to appreciate the city scope.

The USA's most enduring landmark, the **Statue of Liberty** (☎ 212-363-3200; www.nps.gov/stli; ☼ ferries leave every 30 min 9:30am-3:30pm; ferry ticket incl Ellis I $10), a gift from the French in 1865, stands on a rocky NYC island (though technically behind New Jersey state lines). After September 11, the climb to the crown has been closed off, but close-up views, the museum and observation deck more than make up for the trip.

The ferry (Map pp60-1) leaves from a terminal at Battery Park City. For ferry info call ☎ 212-269-5755, or check www.statue oflibertyferry.com.

After the statue, the ferry stops at **Ellis Island** (☎ 212-363-3200; www.nps.gov/elis; admission free), NYC's main immigration station from 1892 to 1954 when 12 million passed through the halls. Several galleries,

GOING TO GOVERNOR'S

The newest kid on New York Harbor's block of attractions, **Governor's Island** (☎ 212-514-8296; www.nps.goc/gois; admission incl ferry $5) reopened in 2003 after 200 years off-limits to civilians. A longstanding military base, Governor's Island's legacy traces the development of the nation. George Washington erected forts here in 1776 to ward off the British; later, the island held Confederate prisoners during the Civil War, and housed the headquarters for the US First Army during WWII. Declared a national monument in 2001, the park reopened in 2003 to great fanfare. Ranger-led hiking tours (1½ hours, 1.5 miles) loop the island, affording unreal vistas of Manhattan, Brooklyn and New York Harbor. Check the website or call for times and ferry location; presently ferries leave from South Street Seaport (Map pp60-1).

beginning with the Baggage Room, tell the fascinating story (eg anarchists were sent back). Recorded tales from Ellis immigrants can be heard on phones. Plan on half a day for Ellis Island and the Statue of Liberty.

An alternative (and free) way to travel into the harbor is aboard the **Staten Island Ferry** (Map pp60-1; ☎ 718-815-2628; www.siferry.com; admission free), which takes 70,000 passengers (mostly commuters) on the 25-minute, five-mile trip going nearby the Statue of Liberty 103 times a day. One departs every 15 or 20 minutes weekdays (or every 30 minutes on weekends) from 6am to 7pm, roughly hourly otherwise.

Lower Manhattan   Map pp60-1

Busy by day, deserted by night, much of Lower Manhattan's financial district follows the cute crooked Dutch plan from the New Amsterdam days in the mid-17th century including literal names (Beaver St is where pelts were traded etc).

On Manhattan's southern tip, **Battery Park** (near the ferries for Staten Island and the Statue of Liberty) is home to **Castle Clinton**, an early 19th-century fort. In the old Customs House just north, the **National Museum of the American Indian** (☎ 212-514-3700; 1 Bowling Green; admission free; 🕙 10am-5pm Fri-Wed, 10am-8pm Thu) has the nation's largest Native American art collection. Facing it, the broken-off

spears along the wrought-iron fence surrounding **Bowling Green** were broken off to use as bullets in the Revolutionary War. Many tourist photos are made of the **Charging Bull statue** nearby – often focusing on the bull's remarkable testicles.

Nearby, the interesting **New York Unearthed** (☎ 212-748-8628; 17 State St; admission free; 🕙 noon-5pm Mon-Fri) dusts off finds (from subway tunnels, construction sites etc) dating from 6000 years of local history.

Pier 17's touristy **South Street Seaport** has a ho-hum mall but the 11-block historic district boasts a hey-ho location on the East River next to the Brooklyn Bridge (it also has public toilets).

To the west, you can link up with the riverside **boardwalk** heading north toward **Hudson River Park**.

WALL ST

Several blocks north of Battery Park, look up along Wall St (named for a Dutch barrier) at historic buildings – **14 Wall St** has a Greek temple–top, **40 Wall St** once lost the battle for 'tallest building' to the Chrysler Building, and the **New York Stock Exchange** (☎ 212-656-5168; 8 Broad St), not open to the public.

Also here is **Federal Hall** (☎ 212-825-6888; 26 Wall St; admission free; 🕙 9am-5pm Mon-Fri), with a museum telling how George Washington took the presidential oath here in 1789.

BROOKLYN BRIDGE

High up in the do-this-now list is a 30-minute walk over the Brooklyn Bridge, the world's first steel suspension bridge. Its 1596ft span made it the world's longest when it opened in 1883.

The boardwalk **pedestrian/bicyclist path** was added in the early 1980s – stay out of the bike lane in lieu of furious biker comments. Walking it to or from Brooklyn allows knock-out looks at the waterfront and the bridge's glorious stone arches and cables. Continue on for a looksee of historic **Brooklyn Heights** (p69).

The bridge is just east of **City Hall** (Broadway, btwn Chinatown & WTC site) or accessed in Brooklyn from the High St stop on the A, C subway line.

WORLD TRADE CENTER SITE

Little can prepare you for the gaping hole or frenzied construction at the WTC site, at

Church St, a block west of Broadway at Fulton St. Walls with building history displays line the site, and an elevated **observation deck** (admission free) is on the south side. The surrounding buildings are slowly being repaired, though some still show damage. On July 4, 2004, Mayor Bloomberg laid the cornerstone for the 1776ft-tall Freedom Tower to occupy the sight by 2015. The tower, part of a *Reflecting Absence* memorial, would be the world's tallest building.

Chinatown & Little Italy

In Chinatown, on and off **Canal St**, some 150,000 residents (many speaking only Cantonese) work stands and shops selling wind-up toys, two-for-a-buck pork buns, NYC T-shirts, pirated CDs, cheap noodles and flopping or cut-up fish. Canal St marks the former site of a canal that once carried butchers' bloody discards from a (now filled-in) lake.

Columbus Park (Map pp60-1; btwn Worth & Bayard Sts) is a lively spot with shoulder-to-shoulder crowds looking over games of mah-jongg. Its southern point roughly marks Five Points, when this was an Irish neighborhood (as depicted in the film *Gangs of New York*).

What's left of the once thriving Little Italy is the first couple blocks north on Mulberry St. Food's so-so and pricey, but have a drink with Frank's spirit at **Mare Chiaro** (p78).

SoHo & Tribeca

A few dozen blocks of brick streets and Civil War–era cast-iron buildings line these trendy neighborhoods that are heavy with restaurants, retail outlets and well-to-do lofts. Translucent elevated walkways loom over the entry of **Apple Store SoHo** (Map pp60-1; ☎ 212-226-3126; 103 Prince St), plus there's free email access. Rem Koolhaus's elaborate **Prada Store** (☎ 212-334-8888; 575 Broadway; ☽ 11am-7pm Mon-Fri, noon-6pm Sat & Sun) is worth a peek too.

Lower East Side

Manhattan's designated entry-level cheap neighborhood, style oozes from the LES's brick tenement buildings and tight side streets that have been home to countless immigrants from Eastern Europe and Latin America. The latest resident-in-force is the hipster – particularly visible on and around the nightlife-mad nexus of **Orchard St** between Houston and Delancey, with bars aplenty.

The very best place to uncover old six-per-room tenement life is at the excellent **Lower East Side Tenement Museum** (Map pp60-1; ☎ 212-431-0233; www.tenement.org; 90 Orchard St; tours $10; ☽ 11am-5:30pm), with guided tours of reconstructed depression-era immigrant dwellings of the late 19th and early 20th centuries.

East Village   Map pp60-1

Work up your jaded, disinterested looks before hitting the E-Vill sidewalks. The main artery of New York's coolest neighborhood, **St Marks Place** (cleanly betwixt E 7th and 9th Sts) is punk enough to break the street-numbering grid. Along these streets, and east in the quainter-than-it-used-to-be **Alphabet City** of Aves A, B, C, D, are great vintage clothing shops, tattoo/piercing parlors, bars, used CD stores, and profane T-shirt shops (mom will love a 'New York Fucking City' one).

The 16-acre **Tompkins Square Park**, at St Marks Pl and Ave A, was a dirty, druggy (though lively) 'tent city' of squatters until they were pushed out in 1991, sparking the Tompkins Square Riot (mentioned in Lou Reed's *New York* album). The only squatting these days is from fashionistas' pets in the dog park.

Splurgers can consider a dip at the **Russian & Turkish Baths** (☎ 212-473-8806; www.russianturkishbaths.com; 268 E 10th St; admission $25; ☽ daily), open since 1892. Before AIDS, it was a notorious gay romping ground. Admission includes lockers, pool, sauna and sun deck. Most hours are for men and women, call.

Peek (or picnic) at Alphabet City's free **community gardens**, green havens made from abandoned lots: the **6 & B Garden** (www.6bgarden.org; E 6 St & Ave B) and the twin plots of **9th St Garden** and **La Plaza Cultural** (E 9 St & Ave C).

Greenwich Village   Map pp60-1

Home to radicals, beatniks, folk singers, freedom-seeking gays and lesbians, marijuana advocates and Jimi Hendrix, the crooked streets of 19th-century townhouses in Greenwich Village (aka West Village) has always been a hotbed for the alternative.

In addition to the following, be sure to walk down Bleecker St and on side nooks, such as **75½ Bedford St**, a skinny 9.5ft-wide

A | B | C | D | E | F

1

See Midtown & Chelsea Map (pp64–5)

Chelsea Market

18th St

W 17th St
W 16th St
W 15th St
14th St
8th Ave–14th St
6th Ave–14th St
W 14th St
W 13th St
E 13th St
E 12th St
W 12th St
W 11th St

Union Square

Stuyvesant Square
E 16th St
E 15th St
First Ave Loop
14th St Loop

Stuyvesant Town
3rd Ave
1st Ave
E 14th St

14th St–Union Sq

John Murphy Park

95
56
109
53
17
7
57
46
111
48
87
116
103
94
13

Little W 12th St
Meatpacking District
Gansevoort

Horatio St
Jane St
Bethune St
Abington Square
Bank St
Perry St
Charles St

West Side Hwy
Hudson St
Greenwich St
Washington St

Jefferson Market Library

W 10th St
W 9th St
W 8th St
E 8th St
8th St NYU
Astor Pl

Washington North Square

Washington Square Park

Washington Square South

New York University

W 3rd St
Bleecker St

Greenwich Village

Christopher Park
Christopher St–Sheridan Square
James J Walker Park
St Luke in the Fields

88
5
28
16
23
112
77
76
59
92
19
42
81
12
24

E 11th St
E 10th St
E 9th St
St Marks Pl
E 8th St
E 7th St
E 6th St
E 5th St
E 4th St
E 3rd St
E 2nd St

Tompkins Square Park
East Village
Alphabet City

6
73
78
14
67
39
37
55
115
62
11
101
70
60
86
45
21 30

St Luke's Pl
Morton St
Leroy St
Clarkson St
Houston St

W Houston St
Prince St
Spring St
Soho

Broadway
Broadway-Lafayette St
Bleecker St
2nd Ave

Nolita

E 1st St
E Houston St

Hamilton Fish Park

61
85
51
100
98
102
99
91
2
36
90
117
105
74

Lower East Side
Delancey St–Essex St

Bernard Downing Playground

Bowery
Kenmare St
Spring St

Sarah D Roosevelt Parkway

Delancey St

107
114
79
80
69
31
47
93
15
38
110
50
96
75
8
1

Little Italy

Grand St
Broome St
Watts St
Grand St
Canal St

Hudson River
Holland Tunnel
West Side Hwy

Hudson Square

Howard St
Canal St
Lispenard St
Walker St

W H Seward Park

East Broadway

119
72
84
58
82
120

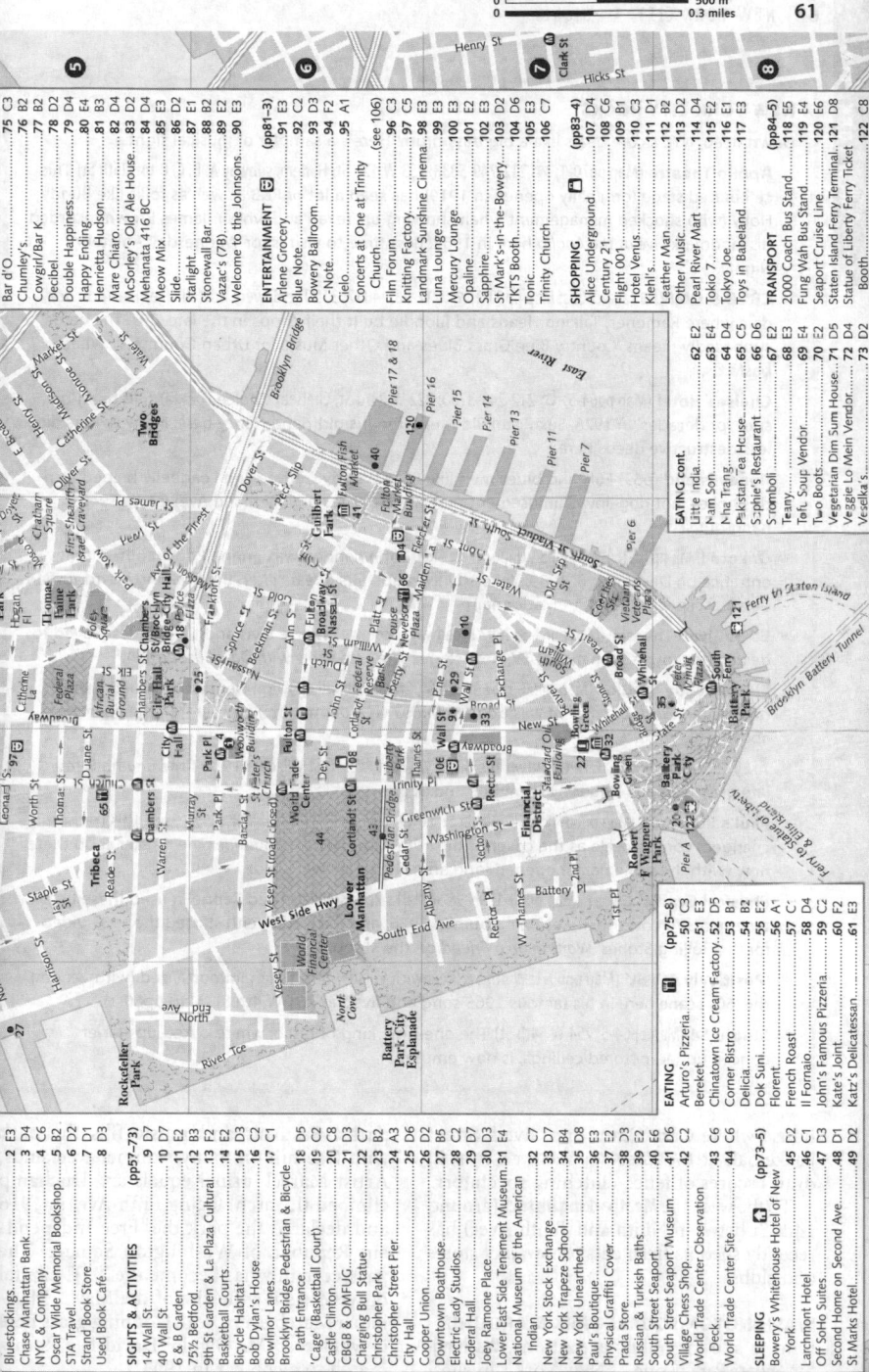

NEW YORK CITY ROCKS

Down deep, NYC's core beats like a big bass drum. Here's a sampler of musical sights:

- **Apollo Theatre** (Map pp70-1; ☎ 212-749-5838; 253 W 125 St, Harlem, subway A, B, C, D to 125th St) This celebrated stage (originally opened in 1919) has seen a lot of R&B as well as folks like Buddy Holly (who shocked management when showing up Texan and white). James Brown recorded his landmark *Live at the Apollo* here in 1962. Best time to visit is for Wednesday Amateur Night.

- **CBGB & OMFUG** (aka CBGBs; Map pp60-1; ☎ 212-982-4052; 315 The Bowery, East Village) Famed rock dive where Ramones, Talking Heads and Blondie built their chops in the late '70s. The name supposedly means 'Country Blue Grass Blues and Other Music for Urban Gourmets.' Whacky bastards.

- **Chelsea Hotel** (Map pp64-5; ☎ 212-243-3700; 222 W 23rd St, Chelsea) Choice rock and lit hang-out spot for decades. In 1978, Sex Pistol Sid murdered his girlfriend Nancy here. Many writers did less-destructive deeds here.

- **Coney Island** (p69) Folk and blues men like Okie Woody Guthrie and Leadbelly helped turn this hokey, hot dog–lovin' amusement park area (particularly Mermaid Ave) into a 1940s hang-out scene.

- **Dakota** (Map pp70-1; 1 W 72nd St, Upper West Side) John Lennon was gunned down outside the entrance on December 8, 1980; Yoko still lives upstairs. (Years later, the building board turned down prospective resident Madonna.)

- **Ed Sullivan Theater** (Map pp64-5; 1697 Broadway, Midtown) Where Elvis and the Beatles played to deafening crowds on national TV, now stages *The Late Show with David Letterman*.

- **Electric Lady Studios** (Map pp60-1; 52 W 8th St, Greenwich Village) Jimi Hendrix recorded here (though his *Electric Ladyland* was done in Midtown – damn, Jimi) and slept in the apartment above.

- **Joey Ramone Place** (E 2nd St, btwn The Bowery & First Aves, East Village) In 2003 the city honored late great Ramone singer by naming E 2nd St after him.

- **Paul's Boutique** (Map pp60-1; 99 Rivington St, Lower East Side) The Beastie Boys used this (rather changed) corner locale as the cover of the 1989 album *Paul's Boutique*. The hipster shop there now (with the same name) opened long after the beats were laid.

- **Physical Graffiti Cover** (Map pp60-1; 96-98 St Marks Pl, East Village) Led Zeppelin used these two tenements to cover their *Kashmir* album in 1976, and Mick and Keith started the 1981 video for the Rolling Stones' *Waiting on a Friend* on the stoop.

- **'Positively 4th St'** (Map pp60-1; W 4th St, Greenwich Village) Bob Dylan immortalized (with venom) the '60s scene here in his famous 1965 song and lived at 161 W 4th St (Map pp60-1).

- **Studio 54** (Map pp64-5; 254 W 54th St) The one-time king of disco, where coked-up starlets danced under mirrored ceilings, is now empty.

house where Cary Grant once lived. Street basketball at the **'Cage'** (cnr Sixth Ave & W 4th St) draws scores of fence-clutching spectators.

To the west, the **Meatpacking District** (around 14th St between Ninth and Tenth Aves) has recently shed its fresh cuts for swanky stores and clubs.

WASHINGTON SQUARE PARK & AROUND

Once a site for public executions, **Washington Square Park** is one of New York's liveliest parks. Festivals and music fills the park with free fun on many summer weekends. Artist Marcel 'urinal equals art' Duchamp climbed the arch, facing Fifth Ave, in 1916 and declared the park the 'Free Independent Republic of Washington Square.' The park certainly has become the NYC capital of weed, as it's the site of the May 1 Marijuana March every year. Copping grass here is what cost 'Mr Gigolo' David Lee Roth a march to a cop car in 1993.

Surrounding the park is **New York University** (☎ 212-998-4636; www.nyu.edu; info center 50 W 4th St), which has been slowly overtaking many buildings in the area.

The blocks south of the park (the former beatnik HQ) have become a de facto 'Greenwich trainer' for tourists. On Thompson St, are several chess shops, including **Village Chess Shop** (☎ 212-475-9580; 230 Thompson St; ☺ 11am-midnight), where you can stop to play a crusty crew of regulars for $1 per hour.

CHRISTOPHER STREET

Under plenty of rainbow flags, Christopher St is home to sex shops, bars and **Oscar Wilde Bookstore** (p55), the landmark gay bookstore. In 1969 a gay rebellion against meddling cops set off at the site of the **Stonewall Bar** (☎ 212-463-0950; 53 Christopher St). Outside, **Christopher Park** (Christopher St & Seventh Ave) has lifelike statues of two same-sex couples, watched over by the statue of bastard Philip Sheridan, a 19th-century general who uttered 'the only good Indian is a dead Indian.'

At the street's end, past the sweet **Leather Man** (p84), is **Christopher Street Pier**, a one-time domain of 'pier queens' (depicted in the 1990 film *Paris is Burning*), and now a magnet for Downtowners of all stripes.

Chelsea & Union Square

If it's not clear enough on the streets, 'Chelsea boys' aren't gangs of brutes looking for tourists' wallets, but handsome muscled gay men looking for…well.

In the past decade Chelsea has become Manhattan's chief **gallery district** (btwn W 20th & 29th Sts btwn Tenth & Eleventh Aves), with 200-plus galleries displaying recent modern art of tomorrow's masters (photographs and paintings, but also outrageous life-sized installations that bring some to say 'bull crap, my five-year-old could do better than that'). It's a shoestringer's dream. The galleries are open 10am to 6pm Tuesday to Sunday and are free. The main action is on W 22nd St.

Other sights include the famous **Chelsea Hotel** (p62) and (west in the Flatiron District) the wafer-thin 1902 **Flatiron Building** (Map pp64-5; Fifth Ave & 23 St), the world's first steel-frame skyscraper and (briefly) the globe's tallest.

Pick up fresh produce (vegetables, apple ciders etc) and organic breads from upstate at the **Greenmarket Farmers Market** (Map pp64-5; Union Sq; ☺ 8am-6pm Mon, Wed, Fri & Sat).

Midtown   Map pp64-5

Heart of business, commerce and tourism, this is where many New Yorkers come to work, and tourists stand to gape.

A few districts worth strolling around are the western part of Midtown West (west of Sixth Ave) including the **Garment District** (along Seventh Ave between Times Square and W 34th St), home to prime-time fashion; and **Herald Square** (at the convergence of Broadway, Sixth Ave and W 34th St), famed for Macy's department store. Another interesting area, **Hell's Kitchen** (on and off Eighth and Ninth Aves, between W 34th and 50th Sts), is a one-time miscreant hood romanticized in *West Side Story*, and now cleaning up with its new name of 'Clinton' – still plenty of greasy diners and dive bars a hop from the Times Square hordes.

East of Sixth Ave, the famed avenues and streets warrant your foot soles a time or two: **Park Ave** (classy apartment buildings), **Madison Ave** (publishing HQ for many), **42nd St** (leading from Grand Central Terminal to Bryant Park, then Times Square) and the **'diamond district'** along E 47th St (between Fifth and Sixth Aves).

Head up **Fifth Ave**, Midtown's swankest stretch – **Tiffany & Co** (p84), among others – from 42nd St and Central Park South.

EMPIRE STATE BUILDING

One triumphant sign of progress during the Great Depression, this limestone classic **skyscraper** (☎ 212-736-3100; www.esbnyc.com; 350 Fifth Ave at E 34th St; admission $11; ☺ 9:30am-midnight) was constructed (102 floors, 1472 ft) in just 410 days with seven million man-hours clocked. Two years after opening, a (fake) King Kong climbed its antennae, and in 1945 a (real) B25 accidentally crashed into the 79th floor, killing 14 people. Since September 11, it's again NYC's tallest building, standing like a comforting friend over the city. Views from the two observation decks have always been the city's best. Go early or late to bypass biggest lines (up to two or three hours).

TIMES SQUARE

The days of New York's theater district (at the convergence of Broadway and Seventh Ave, between W 42nd and W 47th Sts) brushing elbows with W 42nd St porn, prostitution and dope have joined the leagues of lore.

A

B

C

D

1

2

3

4

5

6

W 60th St

W 59th St

W 58th St

W 57th St

W 56th St

W 55th St

W 54th St

W 53rd St

W 52nd St

W 51st St

W 50th St

W 49th St

W 48th St

W 47th St

W 46th St

W 45th St

W 44th St

W 43rd St

W 42nd St

W 41st St

W 40th St

W 39th St

W 38th St

W 37th St

W 36th St

W 35th St

W 34th St

W 33rd St

W 32nd St

W 31st St

W 30th St

W 29th St

W 28th St

W 27th St

W 26th St

W 25th St

W 24th St

W 23rd St

W 22nd St

W 21st St

W 20th St

W 19th St

W 18th St

W 17th St

W 16th St

W 15th St

59th St-
Columbus
Circle

Central Park South

The Pond

Columbus Cir

2

57th St

57th St

53

55th St

79

56th St

77
64

7th Ave

27

14

86

73

5th

55

56

20

Dewitt
Clinton
Park

50th St

8

21

44

50

Worldwide
Plaza

65 75

49th St

47th-50th Sts-
Rockefeller Center

24 78

17

22

10

40

80

Theater
District

69

25

5

60

47th St

9

29

45

88

Hell's
Kitchen

58

Times
Square

Midtown

81

42nd St

42nd St

3 Times Sq
42nd St

42 St-
Bryant
Park

Bryant
Park

42

23

85

49

Broadway

54

Jacob Javits
Convention
Center

Koreatown

39

Garment
District

34th St Penn
Station

68

Herald
Square

48

34th St-
Herald Sq

83

62

15

33rd St

33

32nd St

4

90 84

W 32nd St

6

31st St

38

30

33

Chelsea
Park

28th St

London
Terrace
Gardens

Chelsea

52 41

23rd St

67

61

66

Flatiron
District

31

32

57

59

63

18th St

51

Chelsea
Piers

Chelsea
Market

Hudson River

Twelfth Ave (West Side Hwy)

Eleventh Ave

Tenth Ave

Ninth Ave

Eighth Ave

Seventh Ave

Broadway

Sixth Ave (Ave of the Americas)

Fifth Ave

West Side Hwy

8th Ave-
14th St

14th St

6th Ave-
14th St

W 14th St

11

13

Pier 83

Pier 81

Un
Sqi

70

M
S

65

0 — 500 m
0 — 0.3 miles

INFORMATION
Barnes & Noble...............................1 E6
Borders...2 C1
EasyEverything...............................3 C3
General Post Office.........................4 C4
Gray Line Visitors Center................5 C2
Net Zone..6 D4
New York University Medical
  Center...7 F4
NYC & Company.............................8 C2
Times Square Visitors Center..........9 C2

SIGHTS & ACTIVITIES (pp57–73)
Atlas Statue..................................10 D2
Chelsea Piers.................................11 B5
Chrysler Building...........................12 E3
Circle-Line Sightseeing..................13 A3
Ed Sullivan Theater.......................14 C1
Empire State Building.....................15 D4
Flatiron Building............................16 D5
GE Building...................................17 D2
Grand Central Terminal.................18 E3
Greenmarket Farmers' Market.......19 E6
Museum of Modern Art
  (MoMA)......................................20 D1
Museum of Television & Radio.....21 D2
NBC Studios..................................22 D2
New York Public Library.................23 D3
Radio City Music Hall....................24 D2
Rockefeller Center.........................25 D2
St Patrick's Cathedral....................26 D2
Studio 54......................................27 C1
United Nations..............................28 F2

SLEEPING (pp73–5)
Big Apple Hostel............................29 D2
Chelsea Center Hostel...................30 C4
Chelsea Hotel................................31 C5
Chelsea International Hostel...........32 C6
Chelsea Star Hotel.........................33 C4
Gershwin Hotel.............................34 D5
Hotel 17.......................................35 E6
Jazz on the Town...........................36 E1
Vanderbilt YMCA...........................37 E2
Wolcott Hotel................................38 D4

EATING (pp75–8)
Cho Dang Goi...............................39 D4
Daisy May's BBQ...........................40 D2
F&B...41 C5
Il Forno Toscano...........................42 D3
Indian Fast Food...........................43 E1
Island Burgers & Shakes................44 B2
Miriam's Falafel............................45 C4
Prime Burger.................................46 D2
Republic..47 E6
Soul Fixins....................................48 C4

DRINKING (pp78–81)
Bryant Park Café & Grill................49 D3
Campbell Apartment..................(see 18)
Druids...50 B2
SBNY...51 D6
Serena......................................(see 31)
Trailer Park Lounge & Grill............52 C5

ENTERTAINMENT (pp81–3)
Carnegie Hall................................53 C1
Club Shelter..................................54 D3
Exit2...55 A1
Jon Stewart Daily Show
  Studio..56 B1
Joyce Theater................................57 C6
MTV Studios..................................58 C3
Roxy..59 B6
TKTS Booth....................................60 C2

SHOPPING (pp83–4)
Annex Antique Fair & Flea
  Market..61 D5
B&H Photo-Video..........................62 C4
Barney's Co-Op.............................63 C6
Bergdorf Goodman.......................64 D1
Colony...65 C2
Flea Market...................................66 D5
Garage Antique Fair......................67 D5
Macy's...68 D4
Manny's Music..............................69 C2
New York Transit Museum
  Shop..(see 18)
Otto Tootsi Plohound....................70 D6
Paragon Athletic Goods.................71 E6
Saks Fifth Ave...............................72 D2
Takashimaya.................................73 D1
Tiffany & Co..................................74 D1
Tin Pan Alley.................................75 C2

TRANSPORT (pp84–5)
Aer Lingus....................................76 E1
Aeromexico...................................77 D1
Air Canada....................................78 D2
Air France......................................79 D1
American Airlines...........................80 D2
British Airways...............................81 D3
Continental Airlines.......................82 E3
Delta/Delta Song......................(see 82)
KLM Royal Dutch Airlines..........(see 82)
Lufthansa......................................83 D4
Penn Station.................................84 C4
Port Authority Bus Terminal..........85 C3
Qantas Airways.............................86 D1
United Airlines..........................(see 82)
US Airways....................................87 E3

OTHER
Intrepid Sea-Air-Space
  Museum......................................88 A2
Irving Plaza...................................89 E6
Madison Square Garden................90 C4

And though it's fashionable for New Yorkers to sigh disapprovingly over its new 'Disney-fied' self, the lit-up billboards and influx of TV networks like MTV, some of the world's biggest shops (Toys 'R' Us has an indoor Ferris wheel) and a buffed-up singing cowboy in his undies – has ensured its energy hasn't changed. On New Year's Eve, a million come to see the crystal ball drop. The square is named after the *New York Times*, a long-time resident.

ALONG 42ND ST

A couple of blocks east of Times Square is **Bryant Park** (☎ 212-768-4242; www.bryantpark.org; W 42nd St at Sixth Ave), a rare green spot with Parisian-style chairs set in the shade.

On the east side of the park (and accessed around the corner on Fifth Ave), the huge beaux arts **New York Public Library** (☎ 212-930-0830; www.nyplorg; E 42nd St & Fifth Ave; ⊗ 11am-7:30pm Tue-Wed, 10am-6pm Thu-Sat), dedicated in 1911, is a super Midtown retreat with lofty halls of marble and gilded ceilings. It has free exhibits downstairs (including stacks of famed manuscripts) and a vast 3rd-floor reading room seating 500 bottoms.

New York's most dramatic public space, **Grand Central Terminal** (www.grandcentralterminal.com; 42nd St & Park Ave), aka Grand Central Station, serves subway and commuter trains. Built in 1913, it boasts 75ft glass-encased catwalks, looming balconies, and constellations on the vaulted ceiling (accidentally done backwards). There's a small tourist info center here, and food in the basement.

Just east, the **Chrysler Building** (405 Lexington Ave) is an art-deco masterpiece from 1930 with jutted-out gargoyles way up. (It's closed to the public.)

ROCKEFELLER CENTER & AROUND

The art-deco **Rockefeller Center** (☎ 212-632-3975; www.rockefellercenter.com; Fifth Ave, btwn E 48th & 51st Sts) is decorated with **art pieces** from the 1930s. See Mexican artist Diego Riviera's entry mural for the center-piece 70-story

GE Building. The statue of **Prometheus** overlooks the ice rink and **Atlas** on Fifth Ave faces ornate **St Patrick's Cathedral** (Fifth Ave at E 50th St).

The GE Building is the HQ for **NBC Studios** (☎ 212-664-3700; www.shopnbc.com). The glass-enclosed *Today Show* is broadcast weekday mornings from the building across W 48th St.

West, on Sixth Ave, is the **Radio City Music Hall** (☎ 212-247-4777; www.radiocity.com; 51st St & Sixth Ave), the famed 6000 art-deco seater.

UNITED NATIONS

The headquarters of the **UN** (☎ 212-963-7539; First Ave & E 46th St; tours adult/student \$10.50/8; ⊗ 9:30am-4:45pm) is technically on a slice of international territory overlooking the East River. Tours (which visit the General Assembly) leave every 30 minutes in English (less frequently in other languages).

MUSEUM OF MODERN ART

Always a city favorite, the **MoMA** (☎ 212-708-9400; www.moma.org; 11 W 53rd St; adult/student \$12/8.50, pay what you wish after 4pm Fri; ⊗ 10am-5pm Mon, Thu, Sat & Sun, 10am-7:45pm Fri) doubled its space in 2004 to house its 135,000 art pieces (including Van Gogh's *The Starry Night*, among others). It's far easier to conquer in a few hours than the Met. Good films are shown too.

MUSEUM OF TELEVISION & RADIO

Couch potatoes mustn't miss the smorgasbord of 50,000 American TV and radio programs available to enjoy with the click of a mouse at this popular **museum** (☎ 212-621-6800; www.mtr.org; 25 W 52nd St; adult/student \$10/8; ⊗ noon-6pm Tue, Wed & Fri-Sun, noon-8pm Thu), off Fifth Ave. Old radio programs are great, but most visitors dive into TV's yesteryears (eg Arnold getting caught water ballooning on *Different Strokes*).

Central Park   Map pp70-1

This 843-acre **park** (☎ 212-360-3444; www.centralparknyc.org) sits smack-dab in Manhattan's belly, a break for urban insanity and a testament to thinking ahead. It was created in the 1860s and '70s by Frederick Law Olmstead and Calvert Vaux (who also made Brooklyn's Prospect Park) as a leisure space on NYC's (at the time) northern fringe. Don't venture into the park at night.

BUDGET TIP

Catch Bryant Park's free Monday-night summer outdoor film series. Arrive early with a bottle of wine before hordes pack the lawn. Films begin at 8pm (June to August).

The park starts from 59th St at its south border and runs to 110th St. East–west borders are Central Park West (just east of Columbus Ave) and Fifth Ave. For park information, visit the **Dairy** (☎ 212-794-6564; Central Park at 65th St; ☽ 11am-4pm Tue-Sat).

There's a lot of life here on nice days – joggers, skaters, cyclists, soccer, softball, tennis, picnics. One focal point is the **Great Lawn** (btwn 72nd & 86th Sts), where the New York Philharmonic Orchestra plays in summer. Nearby is the **Delacorte Theater**, home to the annual Shakespeare in the Park; the hill-top panoramic **Belvedere Castle**; the leafy **Ramble**, a birding and gay-male cruising ground; and **Loeb Boathouse** (☎ 212-517-2233; btwn 74th & 75th Sts; rowboats per hr $10, bikes per hr $9-15), on a lake (not as dirty as Woody Allen suggests in *Manhattan*).

Situated at the W 72nd St entrance, **Strawberry Fields** is dedicated to John Lennon, who lived nearby (p62).

Joggers love the 1.8 mile circle around the central **Jacqueline Kennedy Onassis Reservoir** (btwn 86th & 96th Sts), where Jackie O used to run.

Winter skating at **Wollman Rink** (☎ 212-439-6900; btwn 62nd & 63rd Sts; ice skating $8.50, skate rental $4.75) is best at night.

In spring and fall, hundreds of birds drop in; the **New York Audubon Society** (☎ 212-691-7483; www.nycas.org) holds birding tours for $6. Call for info.

Upper West Side

Map pp70-1

West of Central Park, this Yuppie residential hood is where Tom Hanks and Meg Ryan met up in *You've Got Mail* and it sees most action along Broadway, Columbus and Amsterdam Aves. **H&H Bagel** (p77) is a NYC institution.

Showing off fossils, mastodons and whatnot since 1869, the huge and wonderful **American Museum of Natural History** (☎ 212-769-5000; www.amnh.org; Central Park West & W 79th St; adult/student $12/9, free after 4:45pm; ☽ 10am-5:45pm) delights science dweebs and dummies. It's famed for three large dinosaur halls, a giant (fake) blue whale, a 3-D star show in the Hayden Planetarium (at extra cost), and roaming guides who get giddy over questions. There's live jazz and drinks from 6pm to 8pm Friday. Afterward stop by the nearby fossil shop **Maxila & Mandible** (☎ 212-724-6173; 451 Columbus Ave); fossilized dung is $18.

MUSEUM PASS

A terrific deal is the **CityPass** (www.citypass .com). Good for nine days, the pass covers admission to the Empire State Building observatory, American Museum of Natural History, Intrepid Sea-Air-Space Museum, the Circle Line, Modern Museum of Art and Guggenheim Museum. The pass costs $45, a saving of 30% to 50%. Buy it at participating sights.

Upper East Side

Map pp70-1

Dismissed by many as staid, uptight conservative turf, the Upper East Side still boasts some of the city's finest museums. Watch dawn arrive from the park bench at the end of E 59th St, as Woody Allen and Diane Keaton did in *Manhattan*.

METROPOLITAN MUSEUM OF ART

The city's number one attraction, with five million visits a year, the **Met** (☎ 212-535-7710; www.metmuseum.org; Fifth Ave & E 82nd St; suggested donation adult/student $12/7; ☽ 9:30am-5:30pm Tue-Thu & Sun, 9:30am-9pm Fri & Sat) positively drips in culture. Its staggering collection of two million objects – a 17th-century Stradivarius, the Egyptian Temple of Dendur from 15 BC, the iconic *Washington Crossing the Delaware*, European classics like Jean van Eyck's *Crucifixion*, even baseball cards – are thematically laid out. Free tours are worthwhile. On Friday evenings, you can top off the arting with a terrace cocktail (p79).

OTHER MUSEUMS

As famed for its building – a Frank Lloyd Wright's toilet-bowl spiral building – as its 20th-century art, the **Solomon R Guggenheim Museum** (☎ 212-423-3500; www.guggenheim.org; 1071 Fifth Ave; adult/student $15/10; ☽ 10am-5:45pm Sat-Wed, 10am-8pm Fri) features 5000 permanent works (Pollock, Kandinsky, Degas, Mapplethorpe) and changing exhibits seen on a (some say constricting-to-art) coiled inclined ramp.

A rebel in the hood is the brutal rock-like building housing the **Whitney Museum of American Art** (☎ 212-570-3600; www.whitney.org; 945 Madison Ave; adult/student $12/9.50, pay what you wish after 6pm Fri; ☽ 11am-4:30pm Tue, 11am-6pm Wed, 11am-9pm Fri, 11am-6pm Sat & Sun), which proudly fills its halls with cutting-edge art (and also fogies like Rothko, O'Keefe and Hopper).

The **Cooper-Hewitt National Design Museum** (Map pp70-1; ☎ 212-849-8400; www.si.edu/ndm; 2 E 91st St; adult/student $10/7; ☺ 10am-5pm Tue-Thu, 10am-9pm Fri, 10am-6pm Sat, noon-6pm Sun) is in a 64-room mansion built in 1901 with superb architectural and textile exhibits, plus a knock-out terrace.

The **Jewish Museum** (☎ 212-423-3200; www.jewishmuseum.org; 1109 Fifth Ave at E 92nd St; adult/student $10/7.50, pay what you wish after 5pm Thu; ☺ 11am-5:45pm Sun-Wed, 11am-8pm Thu, 11am-3pm Fri) packs in 30,000 Judaica items. Trace the city's past at the interesting **Museum of the City of New York** (☎ 212-534-1672; www.mcny.org; 1220 Fifth Ave btwn E 103rd & 104th Sts; suggested donation adult/student $7/4; ☺ 10am-5pm Wed-Sun).

ROOSEVELT ISLAND

The tram ride up from the bowels of the Upper East Side over the East River to Roosevelt Island is the city's most unusual ride. The place is weird: soccer-pitch thin, with (rather drab) housing blocks, a single street, and the one-time home to a prison and mental hospital, but city views from the riverside walk are tip-top.

Trams leave from 60th St at Second Ave every 15 minutes from 6am to 2am Sunday to Thursday and until 3:30am Friday and Saturday. The one-way fare is $1.50. The F train also stops at Roosevelt Island.

Harlem & Northern Manhattan   Map pp70-1

The USA's most famous African-American neighborhood has seen a renaissance in recent years, with camera-carrying tourists busing in for soul food and to attend a gospel-fueled church service. Along 125th St (between Fifth and Eighth Aves) is where the action is – home of the **Apollo Theater** (p62) and Bill Clinton's post-presidential offices.

South of 125th St on Fifth Ave is **Marcus Garvey Park**, with a clock tower atop a rocky bluff. **Harlem Market** (☎ 212-987-8131; 116th St, btwn Lenox & Fifth Aves; ☺ 10am-5pm) sells African bric-a-brac.

The **Schomburg Center for Research in Black Culture** (☎ 212-491-2200; www.nypl.org/research/sc/sc.html; 515 Lenox Ave at 135th St; admission free; ☺ noon-8pm Tue & Wed, noon-6pm Thu & Fri, 10am-6pm Sat) features the USA's biggest collection of African-American–related photos, recordings and rare books.

North of the Upper West Side, from W 110th to 125th Sts, **Morningside Heights** is an accessible neighborhood, that's home to the **Cathedral of St John the Divine** (☎ 212-316-7540; W 112th St & Amsterdam Ave), the world's third largest. It's been under construction since 1892 – that's right, still not done. Don't miss the pop-art Keith Haring–designed altar. A few blocks north is the **Columbia University** (☎ 212-854-1754; Broadway, btwn W 114th & 121st Sts). Overlooking the Hudson, **Grant's Tomb** (☎ 212-666-1640; www.nps.gov/gegr; Riverside Dr & W 122nd St; admission free; ☺ 9am-5pm) is a Greek-inspired marvel holding the remains of the Civil War hero (and less heroic president).

Far north, in the Washington Heights neighborhood at Manhattan's northern tip, the **Cloisters** (☎ 212-923-3700; www.metmuseum.org; suggested donation adult/student $12/7; ☺ 9:30am-4:45pm Tue-Sun) was built from imported fragments of French and Spanish monasteries. It houses the Met's medieval frescos and tapestries. Entry to the **Met** (p67) includes the Cloisters, which is an outside annexe of the Met way up here in northern Manhattan. Go via subway A to Dyckman St.

Outer Boroughs

NYC's four outer boroughs – Brooklyn, Queens, the Bronx and Staten Island – may see far fewer visitors to big bro Manhattan, but doncha tell them they're not New York. Together they comprise 92% of the NYC metropolis area.

BROOKLYN

No NYC trip is complete without seeing booming Brooklyn. Attractions include some

---

GLORY BE TO GOSPEL

An old saying goes, 'in Harlem there's a bar on every corner and a church on every block.' Witnessing rollicking, deeply moving gospel choruses (mostly Baptist) belt out to Jesus on Sunday mornings has long been a popular attraction for bus groups and indie venturers. If you go, be respectful.

The most popular service is at the historic **Abyssinian Baptist Church** (☎ 212-862-7474; 132 W 138th St; services 9am & 11am Sun; subway 2, 3 to 135th St), followed by **Mother African Methodist Episcopal Zion Church** (☎ 212-234-1545; 146 W 137th St; subway 2, 3 to 135th St), around the corner.

of New York's best, including Coney Island and the Brooklyn Museum of Art. **Brooklyn Tourism & Visitors Center** (☎ 718-802-3846; www .brooklyn-usa.org; 209 Joralemon St; ☑ 10am-6pm Mon-Fri; subway 2, 3, 4, 5 to Borough Hall) has info.

Across the Brooklyn Bridge, veer south to historic **Brooklyn Heights** ('what New York used to look like,' some claim), with 19th-century town houses and a promenade overlooking Lower Manhattan. Just north of the bridge is **Dumbo**, a warehouse-turned-artists-loft area; its riverside **Empire-Fulton Ferry State Park** (☎ 718-858-4708; admission free) has front-row spots of Brooklyn and Manhattan bridges.

Inland, bordering mammoth Prospect Park, **Park Slope's** Fifth and Seventh Aves are worth a stroll for boutiques, books, bars and restaurants. Hipster ex-Manhattanites have been transforming Brooklyn's humble-by-looks **Williamsburg** into the 'new East Village' for a decade.

The country's biggest art museum after the Met, the **Brooklyn Museum of Art** (☎ 718-638-5000; www.brooklynmuseum.org; 200 Eastern Parkway; adult/student $6/3, incl Botanic Garden $9.50/5; ☑ 10am-5pm Wed-Fri, 11am-6pm Sat & Sun; subway 2, 3 to Eastern Pkwy–Brooklyn Museum), affectionately called BAM, is a certifiable A-lister. Features include the Americas' biggest Egyptian collection, art deco period rooms, 58 pieces by Rodin (look for the broken-nose guy), and an 1899 film of Brooklyn Bridge.

Behind BAM, the lush **Brooklyn Botanic Garden** (☎ 718-623-7200; www.bbg.org; 1000 Washington Ave; adult/student $5/3, free on Tue & 10am-noon Sat; ☑ 8am-6pm Tue-Fri, 10am-6pm Sat & Sun; subway 2, 3 to Eastern Pkwy–Brooklyn Museum, B, Q, S to Prospect Park) has 15 gardens and some serious bonsai. Made by the Central Park architects, **Prospect Park** (☎ 718-965-8951; www.prospectpark .org; subway B, Q, S to Prospect Park, 2, 3 to Grand Army Plaza, F to 15 St–Prospect Park) is a huge 526 acres with broad meadows, bike paths and lakes filled with lots of action on sunny days.

The city's HQ for greasy trashy water fun, **Coney Island** (subway D, F to Coney I–Stillwell Av; a 50-min ride from Midtown) still packs 'em in for **Nathan's Famous** hot dogs (p78), the 'shoot the freak' games, boardwalk beers, a big-time July 4 celebration, and rickety rides dating from the 1920s, such as the **Cyclone roller coaster** ($5). Rides run from about noon to 10pm from mid-June to Labor Day. Some of the city's best pizza is found at **Totonno's** (p76).

A mile north is **Brighton Beach** (subway B, Q to Brighton Beach), an interesting, well-kept Russian community with lots of Cyrillic and canned caviar.

To strut Travolta style under the elevated train line (à la *Saturday Night Fever*), take the D or M subway to 20 Ave in Bensonhurst and walk along 86th St.

QUEENS

Best introduced by its city-searing elevated subway line that passes so many immigrant hoods (Irish, Indian, Latin American, Korean, Chinese etc) that it's been deemed a historical trail (the 7 line), Queens doesn't get the press, but visiting it makes you wonder why.

In Long Island City (just across the river), and under MoMA's wing, **PS1 Contemporary Art Center** (☎ 718-784-2084; www.ps1.org; 22-25 Jackson Ave at 46th Ave; suggested donation adult/student $5/2; ☑ noon-6pm Thu-Mon; subway E, V to 23 St–Ely Ave, 7 to 45 Rd–Court House Sq) hosts some of the city's edgiest modern art and is housed in a 19th-century school. Check out the **graffiti** show on nearby Pearson St, under the No 7 train line.

Built for the 1939 World's Fair with bizarre Cold War–era additions, the 1225-acre **Flushing Meadows Corona Park** (subway 7 to Willets Point–Shea Stadium) is home to the massive stainless steel **Unisphere**, the annual US Open tennis competition in August and September and plenty of soccer games. Shea Stadium (the Mets' home) is just north. The park's best attraction is a startling 895,000-piece, all-inclusive miniature panorama of NYC at the **Queens Museum of Art** (☎ 718-592-9700; adult/student $5/2.50; ☑ 10am-5pm Wed-Fri, noon-5pm Sat & Sun).

THE BRONX

Rougher at the edges, the Bronx is like the 'New York for New Yorkers,' confident to the point of all-out attitude.

The lush **Bronx Zoo** (☎ 718-367-1010; www.bronx zoo.com; admission $11/8 Apr-Oct/Nov-Mar; ☑ 10am-5pm; subway 2, 5 to Pelham Pkwy) is one of the country's best, with two million folks yearly coming to see polar bears, gorillas, penguins, zebras, giraffes, bison and bats to name just a few. From the station, head south on White Plains Rd, right on Lydig Ave, right on Bronx Park East, and left to Bronx River Parkway Gate.

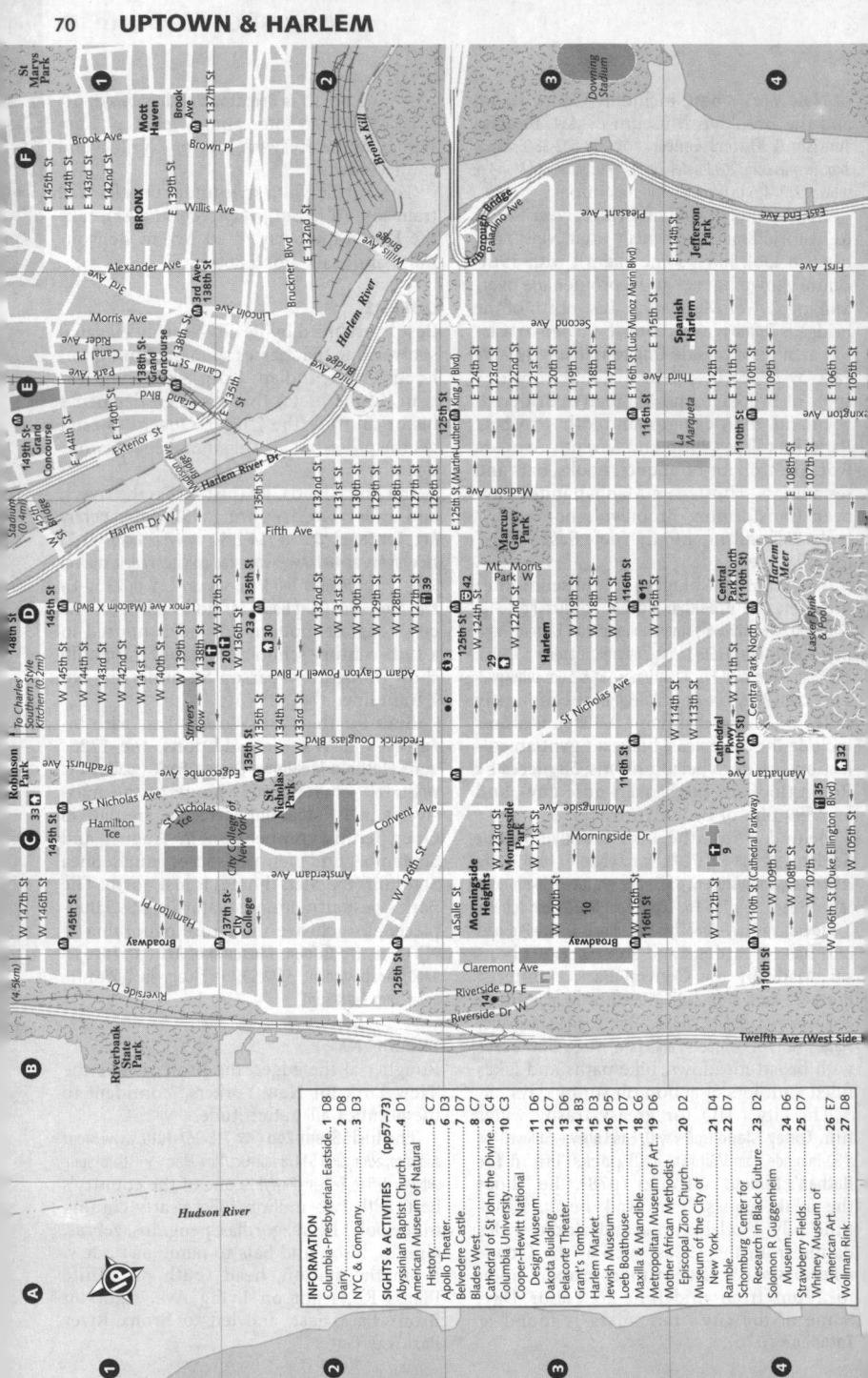

INFORMATION	
Columbia-Presbyterian Eastside...1	D8
Dairy...2	D8
NYC & Company...3	D3

SIGHTS & ACTIVITIES (pp57–73)	
Abyssinian Baptist Church...4	D1
American Museum of Natural History...5	C7
Apollo Theater...6	D3
Belvedere Castle...7	D7
Blades West...8	C7
Cathedral of St John the Divine...9	C4
Columbia University...10	C3
Cooper-Hewitt National Design Museum...11	D6
Dakota Building...12	C7
Delacorte Theater...13	D6
Grant's Tomb...14	B3
Harlem Market...15	D3
Jewish Museum...16	D5
Loeb Boathouse...17	D7
Maxilla & Mandible...18	C6
Metropolitan Museum of Art...19	D6
Mother African Methodist Episcopal Zion Church...20	D2
Museum of the City of New York...21	D4
Ramble...22	D7
Schomburg Center for Research in Black Culture...23	D2
Solomon R Guggenheim Museum...24	D6
Strawberry Fields...25	D7
Whitney Museum of American Art...26	E7
Wollman Rink...27	D8

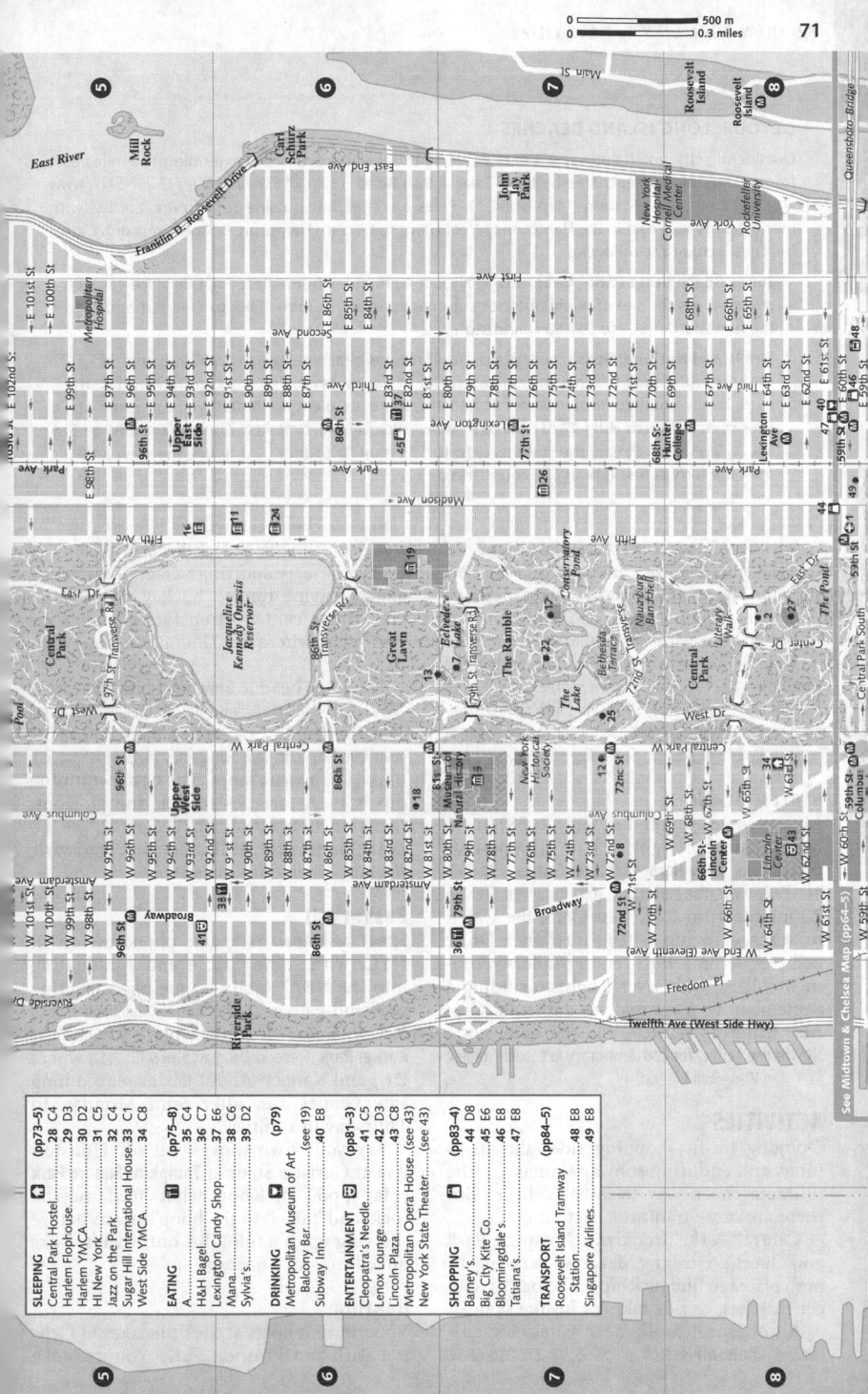

0 — 500 m
0 — 0.3 miles

SLEEPING (pp73–5)
Central Park Hostel......28 C4
Harlem FlopHouse......29 D3
Harlem YMCA......30 D2
HI New York......31 C5
Jazz on the Park......32 C4
Sugar Hill International House...33 C1
West Side YMCA......34 C8

EATING (pp75–8)
A......35 C4
H&H Bagel......36 C7
Lexington Candy Shop......37 E6
Mana......38 C6
Sylvia's......39 D2

DRINKING (p79)
Metropolitan Museum of Art......(see 19)
Balcony Bar......(see 19)
Subway Inn......40 E8

ENTERTAINMENT (pp81–3)
Cleopatra's Needle......41 C5
Lenox Lounge......42 D3
Lincoln Center......43 C8
Metropolitan Opera House......(see 43)
New York State Theater......(see 43)

SHOPPING (pp83–4)
Barney's......44 D8
Big City Kite Co......45 E6
Bloomingdale's......46 E8
Tatiana's......47 E8

TRANSPORT (pp84–5)
Roosevelt Island Tramway Station......48 E8
Singapore Airlines......49 E8

See Midtown & Chelsea Map (pp64–5)

DETOUR: LONG ISLAND BEACHES

Outside the city, you'll find super beaches along this well-named island extending 120 miles east from Manhattan, all reachable by **Long Island Rail Road** (LIRR; ☎ 631-231-5477, 718-217-5477; www .mta.info) from Penn Station (Map pp64-5). Fares are cheapest outside rush hours. Locals (with money) party way east in the Hamptons (West Hampton, South Hampton, Bridgehampton). Closer beaches include the following:

■ **Jones Beach State Park** (☎ 631-785-1600) Just 40 minutes from Midtown, this place can get crowded. It's the site of many outdoor summer concerts. Take the LIRR to Freeport and then the free shuttle ($12 to $17.50 roundtrip).

■ **Fire Island National Seashore** (☎ 631-289-4810) This beach fills a narrow 32-mile barrier offshore with sandy beaches, no cars and a lot of happy gay folks. On its western end is the more family-oriented Robert Moses State Park. There are plenty of hotels; you can camp at sites such as **Watch Hill** (☎ 631-289-9336; www.watchhillfi.com; campsites $28). Take the LIRR to Bay Shore, Sayville or Patchogue stations ($16 to $25 roundtrip; about 1½ hours one way) and then the ferry across (about $12 roundtrip).

Afterwards walk west via Fordham Rd to **Belmont/Arthur Ave** (Subway B, D to Fordham Rd), perhaps New York's most kept-real Italian-American neighborhood. You will see plenty of pasta shops with wine-splattered menus.

Take an hour-long tour of fabled **Yankee Stadium** (☎ 718-579-4531; www.yankees.com; E 161st St & River Ave; tours $12-25; ☼ 10am-4pm Mon-Fri, 10am-noon Sat when team is on road, 10am-noon Mon-Fri when at home; subway B, D, 4 to 161 St–Yankee Stadium).

STATEN ISLAND
Most people get off the ferry (p58) from Manhattan, then right back on. The best attraction is **Snug Harbor Cultural Center** (☎ 718-448-2500; www.snug-harbor.org; 1000 Richmond Tce), a 20-minute grim walk west along the water, or reached by bus S40. It's a rather Doric complex set in a 19th-century sailors retirement village, with several sights including a September 11 memorial, an authentic Chinese Scholar's Garden, and the quite good **Newhouse Center for Contemporary Art** (adult/student $2/1; ☼ 10am-5pm Tue-Sun).

ACTIVITIES
Dodging traffic, hopping sidewalk droppings and enduring subway saunas are the ultimate cheap way to sweat a little. But there are more traditional activities.

Central Park, Brooklyn's Prospect Park and Queens' Flushing Meadows Park are superb places to find pick-up basketball or soccer matches, or ride bikes or in-line skate.

Another catch-all, near Chelsea's galleries, **Chelsea Piers** (Map pp64-5; ☎ 212-336-6666; www.chelseapiers.com; West Side Hwy, btwn W 16th & 22nd Sts) is a 30-acre sporting village (of bowling alleys, driving ranges, hockey rinks, pools and fitness centers) transformed from the 1910 piers where the *Titanic* was bound for in 1912.

Kingpins head to **Bowlmor Lanes** (Map pp60-1; ☎ 212-255-8188; 110 University Pl, Greenwich Village; ☼ 11-4am Mon & Fri, 11-1am Tue & Wed, noon-2am Thu, noon-4am Sat, noon-1am Sun; games $6.45-$8, shoes $5), the city's favorite lanes. The best swimming dip is in Astoria Queens at the glorious, riverside **Astoria Pool** (☎ 718-626-8620; 19th St & 23rd Dr; admission free; ☼ 11am-7pm summer; subway N, W to Astoria Blvd), built in 1936.

Basketball
Street basketball is a cult phenomenon in NYC, with some city legends graduating into the NBA. A city league plays exciting weekend games at the **'Cage'** (Map pp60-1; Sixth Ave & W 4th St). A legendary place to watch is **Rucker Park** (Frederick Douglass Blvd & 155th St) where Dr J and Kareem Abdul Jabaar played long ago. Games run after 6pm Monday to Thursday in summer.

Try your own moves out off Houston Ave at Christie St, or at **Tompkins Square Park** (Map pp60-1). Know what 'feed me the rock' and 'take it to the hoop' means before showing up in a full NBA outfit with socks pulled to your kneecaps.

Boating
You can rent boats at the little lakes in Central Park and Prospect Park. You can take

cruises of the New York Harbor from **South Street Seaport** (Map pp60-1) and aboard the **Schooner Adirondack** (☎ 646-336-5270; Chelsea Piers).

The deal of the city, however, is at **Downtown Boathouse** (Map pp60-1; ☎ 646-613-0740; www.downtownboathouse.org; Pier 26, btwn Chambers & Canal Sts; ☺ 9am-6pm Sat & Sun mid-May–mid-Oct), which offers free 20-minute kayaking (with equipment and tips).

Cycling & In-line Skating

Central Park's roads are for bikers and bladers only on weekends. You can ride along the river around nearly all of Manhattan – it gets a bit dodgier up north. The traffic-halting-plea-for-more-bike-lanes – Critical Mass – is a city-wide rally starting at 7pm on the last Friday of the month from Union Square.

The best place for tips and bikes is at **Bicycle Habitat** (Map pp60-1; ☎ 212-431-3315; www.bicyclehabitat.com; 244 Lafayette St; ☺ 10am-7pm Mon-Thu, 10am-6pm Fri-Sun; bike hire per day $25-30). You can also rent bikes at **Loeb Boathouse** (p67) in Central Park.

Rent in-line skates in the Upper West at **Blades West** (Map pp70-1; ☎ 212-787-3911; 120 W 72nd St; incl pads $22) or in Brooklyn's Park Slope at **3rd Street Skate Co** (☎ 718-768-9500; 207 Seventh Ave; per day $20; subway F to 7th Ave).

TOURS

Big Onion Walking Tours (☎ 212-439-1090; www.bigonion.com; adult/student $12/10) These guys draw locals too for their lovingly led two-hour thematic tours (eg Gangs of New York, Historic Harlem) of NYC's past and present.

Gray Line (Map pp64-5; ☎ 800-669-0051; www.graylinenewyork.com; Eighth Ave, btwn W 47th & 48th Sts; all loops 2-day ticket $50, Downtown or Uptown loop $40) Runs those cute red double-decker tour buses, featuring hop-on/off loops around the city. Hell, save the cash (and look less silly) by plotting your own tour with the help of free bus maps and a $7 MetroCard (p85).

Circle-Line Sightseeing (Map pp64-5; ☎ 212-563-3200; www.circleline.com; cruise $26; ☺ Mar-Dec) A fun island circuit by water. It takes three hours, leaving from Pier 83 at W 42nd St on the Hudson River.

FESTIVALS & EVENTS

For additional information of special events in the city, visit www.nycvisit.com.

Restaurant Week January and June. High-profile restaurants offer three-course lunches/dinners for $20/30.

St Patrick's Day Parade March 17. Massive Fifth Ave parade slash party.

Tribeca Film Festival (www.tribecafilmfestival.com) May. Robert DeNiro's annual Downtown film fest.

Fleet Week Late-May to early June. Docked ships bring a city full of uniformed sailors to the streets.

Mermaid Parade June. Costumes of the sea hit Coney Island's Boardwalk.

Lesbian, Gay, Bisexual & Transgender Pride All of June. Gay Pride month is topped with a Fifth Ave parade (last Sunday of month).

Central Park Summerstage (www.summerstage.org) Bands galore, some for free

Shakespeare in the Park Everyone's favorite Bill gets his due with free summer shows at Central Park's Delacorte Theatre (www.publictheater.org).

Macy's Fourth of July Fireworks Independence Day. The tradition over the East River begins at 9pm.

Howl! Festival (www.howlfestival.com) August. Weeklong arts showcase celebrates the East Village.

San Genarro Festival (www.sangenarro.org) September. Little Italy's colorful carnival fest (as seen in *Godfather II*).

Dumbo Art Under the Bridge (www.dumboartscenter.org). Autumn art celebration in Brooklyn.

Halloween Parade October 31. Freaks and geeks prance around Greenwich Village.

New York City Marathon (www.nycmarathon.org) First week of November. Spaces for the 26-mile run are chosen by lottery.

Macy's Thanksgiving Day Parade Fourth Thursday of November. Giant floats drift down Broadway from W 72nd St to W 34th St.

New Year's Eve December. Raucous Times Square countdown draws a million.

SLEEPING

Many hotels keep the same rates even if you have another person or two crammed in. If you're from a cool place (London, Berlin, Tokyo, LA etc) try to arrange room swaps online (www.craigslist.com is a good bet).

Hostels

All hostels here are open 24 hours. Most are huge, but do fill. Try to reserve a week or two in advance. Prices include tax. Peak-season rates (summer and Christmas) are

---

RENT YOUR OWN

Check out www.craigslist.com for advertised rooms, www.roomiematch.com for a roommate, www.vrbo.com for rentals by owner, or the following agencies:

- **CitySonnet** (☎ 212-614-3034; www
  .westvillagebb.com; guest rooms from $80,
  private apartments from $135) Lots of hip
  Downtown private apartments.

- **Manhattan Lodgings** (☎ 212-677-7616;
  www.manhattanlodgings.com; apartments from
  $125-400 nightly, from $1550 monthly, hosted
  stays $105-140)

---

listed here; prices usually drop by $2 or $3 during the low season.

DOWNTOWN & MIDTOWN

Chelsea Center Hostel (Map pp64-5; ☎ 212-643-0214; www.chelseacenterhostel.com; 313 W 29th St; dm incl breakfast $33; ✄ ▢) This quiet, 18-bed hostel with mixed and female-only dorms, is more personal than most. Clean bathrooms and night lights. Better is the **East Village location**; call for info.

Chelsea International Hostel (Map pp64-5; ☎ 212-647-0010; www.chelseahostel.com; 251 W 20th St, Chelsea; dm/r $28/70; ▢) A festive, international scene and central location – with views of the Empire State Building from the outside deck – helps compensate for the slightly boxy rooms (it's big: 350 beds). Bunk rooms sleep four to six. Amenities include kitchens, lockers and laundry. Dorm beds with air-con cost $32. Everyone must show a passport to check in (even US citizens), and there's a two-week max stay.

Big Apple Hostel (Map pp64-5; ☎ 212-302-2603; www.bigapplehostel.com; 119 W 45th St, Midtown; dm/ d $36/100; ✄ ▢) Big Apple has dozens of four-bunk rooms right off Times Square. Staff are not there to make friends.

Bowery's Whitehouse Hotel of New York (Map pp60-1; ☎ 212-477-5623; www.whitehousehotelofny.com; 340 The Bowery; s/d $30/60; ▢) Now run by an enthusiastic lawyer, this fascinating East Village relic from the Bowery's crusty flophouse days still houses transient residents in one wing, and Euro backpackers in another. Hostel-like rooms are bare-bone cubicles, with lattice ceilings (sound carries), but are secure and clean.

UPTOWN

Jazz on the Park (Map pp70-1; ☎ 212-932-1600; www .jazzhostel.com; 36 W 106th St btwn Central Park West & Manhattan Ave, Upper West Side; dm incl breakfast $31-37, d $100; ✄ ▢) This recently refurbished flop is way cool for a hostel. Rooms are small, with standard wood-frame bunks (numbering four to 12 bunks per room), but there's a beautiful roof deck and brick lounge that hosts local jazz acts. There's a TV room, lockers and laundry. The deck at its new cousin **Jazz on the Town** (Map pp64-5; ☎ 212-651-3260; 130 E 57th St btwn Lexington & Park Aves; dm incl breakfast $27-44, r $90; ✄) overlooks Midtown.

HI New York (Map pp70-1; ☎ 212-932-2300; www .hinewyork.org; 891 Amsterdam Ave at 103rd St, Upper West Side; dm $29-35, nonmembers extra $3, r with/without bathroom $135/120; ✄ ▢) The USA's biggest hostel – try 600 dorm beds in a former hospital – has clean safe rooms with four to a dozen beds in each. It has lockers, TV lounges and kitchens. Breakfast is $3. Some partying gets done on the big-ass patio out back. Staff are nice for such a huge thing.

Sugar Hill International House (Map pp70-1; ☎ 212-283-1490; 722 St Nicholas Ave at 146th St; dm $25) Bare-bones and way north but clean, Sugar Hill offers standard bunk beds (six to 10 per room) in a renovated 19th-century limestone home. Kitchen facilities, locked storage space. The daily rate drops to $20 for longer stays.

Central Park Hostel (Map pp70-1; ☎ 212-678-0491; www.centralparkhostel.com; 19 W 103 St, Upper West Side; dm $26-30, r $75; ✄ ▢) A recently converted five-floor brownstone with four-, six- and eight-bunk rooms (about 200 beds in all). There's no kitchen.

Hotels

Prices don't include the 13.625% city and state tax and $2 hotel tax lopped on.

SPLURGE!

Chelsea Hotel (Map pp64-5; ☎ 212-243-3700; 222 W 23rd St, Chelsea; r from $135; ✄) New York's most (in)famous inn (and cultural landmark; though some guests – Sid's and Nancy's anyway – left in body bags) is aware of its lore and prices accordingly. Each of the irresistible high-ceilinged rooms nevertheless carry its own style. Cheapest rooms have shared bath.

IT'S FUN TO STAY AT THE Y

The **YMCA** (www.ymca.net) lets rooms to men and women travelers. Prices below include tax; all rooms have shared bath and no air-conditioning. Rooms are clean, secure and offer pool access, but – no offense to the Village People – most people tend to be happier at a hostel. Branches include:

- **Flushing** (☎ 718-961-6880; 138-46 Northern Blvd, Flushing, Queens; s/d $50/70; subway 7 to Flushing–Main St, 1 mile south on Main St)

- **Greenpoint** (☎ 718-389-3700; 99 Meserole Ave, Brooklyn; s/d $45/80, weekly $400; subway G to Nassau Ave, two blocks north via Manhattan Ave)

- **Harlem** (Map pp70-1; ☎ 212-281-4100; 180 W 135th St; s/d $70/75; subway 2, 3 to 135th St)

- **Vanderbilt** (Map pp64-5; ☎ 212-756-9600; 224 E 47th St, Midtown; s/d $70/75)

- **West Side** (Map pp70-1; ☎ 212-875-4100; 5 W 63rd St, Upper West Side; s/d $70/75)

DOWNTOWN & CHELSEA

Off SoHo Suites (Map pp60-1; ☎ 212-979-9815, 800-633-7646; www.offsoho.com; 11 Rivington St, Lower East Side; r $80) Cheap prices and a super location more than make up for tacky decoration. Some rockers sleep here. Week or longer stays get a 10% discount.

Larchmont Hotel (Map pp60-1; ☎ 212-989-9333; www.larchmonthotel.com; 27 W 11th St, Greenwich Village; s/d $80/109) This cozy European-like inn boasts 52 rooms, shared bathroom, communal kitchens and a plum spot on a leafy block. Be sure to reserve ahead.

Gershwin Hotel (Map pp64-5; ☎ 212-545-8000; www.gershwinhotel.com; 7 E 27th St, Flatiron District; dm/r $35/100; subway 6 to 28th St; 🕸) Four blocks north of the Flatiron Building, this popular and bohemian spot (half youth hostel, half hotel) is buzzing with original artwork, touring bands and a cool new lobby bar.

Chelsea Star Hotel (Map pp64-5; ☎ 212-244-7827; www.starhotelny.com; 300 W 30th St, Chelsea; dm $30, d with shared bathroom $80-90; 🕸) European-style hotel with private themed rooms (eg Star Trek, Madame Butterfly, Cher) – some more inviting than others. A lovely mixed crowd lingers on the patio and bikes and skates are for rent.

St Marks Hotel (Map pp70-1; ☎ 212-674-2192; 2 St Marks Pl, East Village; s/d $90/100) Ignore the dodgy steps up from St Marks' bustle. The rooms are clean and have character (though try to snag a room in back, away from piercing and tattooing cries). Rooms have teeny sinks, bathrooms, mounted TVs and full-length mirrors.

Second Home on Second Ave (Map pp70-1; ☎ 212-677-3161; www.secondhome.citysearch.com; 221 2nd Ave btwn 13th & 14th Sts, d incl breakfast $105-185) This tidy boutique B&B has seven themed rooms (Peruvian, Caribbean, modern) and soundproof windows; the cheaper ones have shared bathrooms.

MIDTOWN & UPTOWN

Harlem Flophouse (Map pp70-1; ☎ 212-662-0678; www.harlemflophouse.com; 242 W 123rd St; s/d $65/90) With nods to Harlem's jazz era, this four room beaut has large spaces, glossed wood floors, tin and plastered ceilings, wooden shutters and heaps of decorative moldings.

Hotel 17 (Map pp64-5; ☎ 212-475-2845; www.hotel17ny.com; 225 E 17th St, Midtown; s/d/tr $70/90/110; 🅿 🕸 🖳) This popular spot has serious character – seen in a dark light in Woody Allen's *Manhattan Murder Mystery*. There's an old-fashioned elevator, vintage wallpaper and worn but chic charm to the small, quiet rooms.

Wolcott Hotel (Map pp64-5; ☎ 212-268-2900; 4 W 31st St, Midtown; s/d $100/120; 🕸) John Duncan, the architect of Grant's Tomb, designed this 280-room beaux-arts hotel. Rooms are small, but are a great deal, and the gilded lobby is stunning.

EATING

High-class and cheap-ass eateries sit side by side all over town. Don't leave without sampling a lazy weekend brunch on side streets in Greenwich Village, East Village and the Lower East Side. All-hour delis (corner-store markets) are everywhere, but bigger grocery stores are cheaper.

Lower Manhattan   Map pp60-1
Sophie's Restaurant (☎ 212-269-0909; 205 Pearl St; mains $6-8; ☺ Mon-Fri) Downtown nine-to-fivers line up for steaming plates of rice and beans and *café con leche* (coffee with steamed milk) at lunch time.

Pakistan Tea House (☎ 212-240-9800; 176 Church St; mains $6-8) From lunch to way late night, this Tribeca shop heats up tasty curries and rotis for clubbers to sober up.

Chinatown   Map pp60-1
Street vendors churning out the goods for a buck include **veggie lo mein** (cnr Canal & Mulberry Sts) and **tofu soup** (cnr Grand & Christie Sts). Southeast Asian fruits (durian, longan etc) are a bit more pricey.

Weekend morning dim sum is big. **Vegetarian Dim Sum House** (☎ 212-577-7176; 24 Pell St; mains $8-12) is a (rare friendly) Chinese eatery, serving crowd-pleasing mock-meat meals.

Vietnamese food is generally a bit cheaper (and tastier) than Chinese food. **Nha Trang** (☎ 212-233-5948; 87 Baxter St; mains $5-8) is one of a couple of scenester restaurants on the block; things are a bit more low key at **Nam Son** (☎ 212-966-6507; 245 Reade St; mains $4-12). At both, *bún* (vermicelli noodles) dishes and *pho* (beef noodle soups) are $4 or $5.

Get a green tea ice-cream chaser at the **Chinatown Ice Cream Factory** (☎ 212-608-4170; 65 Bayard St; s scoop $2.75).

Lower East Side   Map pp60-1
Bereket (☎ 212-475-7700; 187 E Houston St; mains $4-7; ☺ 24hr) Keep it old-school and Istanbulesque here with excellent stuffed grape leaves and bean stews ready for late-nighters.

Teany (☎ 212-475-9190; 90 Rivington St; mains $6-12) Co-owned by techno-pop star Moby, Teany serves veggie and vegan meals, and close to 100 types of tea, in a small candle-lit setting.

Katz's Delicatessen (☎ 212-254-2246; 205 E Houston St; mains $5-12) OK, so Meg Ryan did her fake orgasm thing in *When Harry Met Sally* here at this old-world deli with corned beef sandwiches and scramby eggs.

East Village   Map pp60-1
For shoestring dining, don't miss the 20-some restaurants of **Little India** (aka Little Bangladesh) on and around E 6th St between First and Second Aves. Most serve $4 vegetable curries with all-you-want rice.

NEW YORK PIZZA

Walk-up pizzerias around town serve thin-crust $1.50 or $2 slices – the most reliable, quick, tasty meal this side of a bagel. But fresh brick-oven pizzerias' $12 to $20 pies put the 'New York' in 'New York pizza.' So who does it best? Here's the top three for each.

Take-away Slices

- **John's Famous Pizzeria** (Map pp60-1; ☎ 212-243-1680; 278 Bleecker St, Greenwich Village) West side's premier grab-a-slice stop.

- **Stromboli** (Map pp60-1; ☎ 212-673-3691; 85 St Marks Pl, East Village) Less lore than some, but a must for late-night sober-up snacking.

- **Two Boots** (Map pp60-1; ☎ 212-254-1919; 42 Ave A, East Village) The 'Boots' refers to Italy and Louisiana. Go Cajun with crawfish or BBQ shrimp. All have cornmeal-dusted crusts.

Sit-down Pies

- **Arturo's Pizzeria** (Map pp60-1; ☎ 212-677-3820; 106 W Houston St, Greenwich Village) Bustling dining room with piano music.

- **Grimaldi's** (Map pp60-1; ☎ 718-858-4300; 19 Old Fulton St, Brooklyn Heights) Under the Brooklyn Bridge, with checkered table tops and Frank on the walls and jukebox.

- **Totonno's** (☎ 718-372-8606; 1524 Neptune Ave, Coney Island; ☺ Wed-Sun) Two blocks from the boardwalk (between 15th and 16th Sts), Totonno's has served mouthwatering pies since 1924.

STREET EATS

Many of Midtown's carts-on-wheel vendors get higher marks for lunch spots, rather than actual sit-down restaurants. And most are near sitting areas and fountains – perfect for a recoup between museums. Street eats are available roughly from 11am to 3:30pm Monday to Friday.

■ **Daisy May's BBQ** (Map pp64-5; cnr W 50th St & Sixth Ave; chili $6) All-meat chili, with hunks of beef stewed in a rich red sauce.

■ **Indian Fast Food** (Map pp64-5; cnr Park Ave & E 53rd St; mains $4-5) This street vendor mixes up the veggie and meat curries daily (saag, chicken tikka, navrattan korma and so on).

■ **Miriam's Falafel** (Map pp64-5; cnr W 46th St & Sixth Ave; kosher falafel $4) Locals swear, with frightening passion, that Miriam makes the city's best veggie falafel. Comes with hummus-smeared pita and green hot sauce.

Restaurants packed with tables glow under a sea of Christmas lights and tacky designs, and offer ice cream, naan bread or papadums 'on the house' to beckon diners. At most, you can bring in your own beer or wine.

Veselka's (☎ 212-228-9682; 144 Second Ave; mains $5-10; ☺ 24hr) Joey Ramone went for farina at breakfast at this Ukrainian diner famed for all-hours cheese blintzes, buffalo burgers and bowls of borscht with challah bread.

Dok Suni (☎ 212-477-9506; 119 First Ave; mains $9-15) Superb Korean eatery with old-script wallpaper, a full bar and big bottles of Korean beer. The tofu soup bursts with flavor as does the beef *moochim* (grilled beef served atop a spicy salad).

Kate's Joint (☎ 212-777-7059; 58 Ave B; mains $6-10) For all-veggie, but refreshingly greasy, pickings.

Greenwich Village   Map pp60-1

French Roast (☎ 212-533-2233; 458 Sixth Ave at W 11th St; mains $10-18; ☺ 24hr) Filled with out-of-bed 20-somethings, the Roast serves up tasty steak frites and tofu stir fry in a big airy dining space.

Florent (☎ 212-989-5779; 69 Gansevoort St; mains $9-13; ☺ 24hr) This Meatpacking District hangout fills tummies of wee-hour clubbers with French dishes plus lots of breakfasts, burgers and blood sausages.

Corner Bistro (☎ 212-242-2002; 331 W 4th St; burgers $4-7) Unforgettable burgers and ice-cold beers.

Chelsea   Map pp64-5

F&B (☎ 646-486-4441; 269 W 23rd St; mains $3-6) A block from the galleries, F&B is a bright cube-like spot with stools. It serves beef and tofu dogs with 10 types of toppings.

Republic (☎ 212-627-7168; 37 Union Sq West; mains $4-9) Facing Union Square, the Republic is a delicious bargain serving pan-Asian meals (tofu udon soup, spinach noodles with soy lime sauce) in a huge space.

Midtown   Map pp64-5

Island Burgers & Shakes (☎ 212-307-7934; 766 Ninth Ave; burgers $6-8) Northwest of Times Square, the surf-themed Island serves up fajitas, Thai salads as well as classic BLTs. Most opt for the namesake burgers and shakes.

Soul Fixins (☎ 212-736-1345; 371 W 34th St at Ninth Ave; mains $8-14) Tiny storefront, heated by simmering pots of collards, candied yams and other down-South specialties. The $5 breakfast of fish or eggs (with grits of course) is a filling day-starter.

Cho Dang Goi (☎ 212-695-8222; 55 W 35th St; mains $10-15) Korean youngsters flock to this authentic eatery in Koreatown for meals studded with bits of homemade tofu. The *bibimbops* (a medley of veggies and grilled meat that you assemble into mini sandwiches) are mean. Plenty of super sticky-rice dishes too.

ESSENTIAL INFO: HOW TO ORDER A SLICE

When ordering New York pizza (a must), say 'gimme a slice, guy' and *not* 'a piece of cheese pizza please.' Or indicate by topping (only): 'one mushroom.' If you muster 'I'll take an oven-warmed piece of cheese pizza with pepperoni slices carefully spread equidistantly on top,' you can *fuhgeddaboutit*. Practice your skills at one of the city's choice pizza joints (opposite).

> **SPLURGE!**
>
> **Delicia** (Map pp60-1; ☎ 212-242-2002; 322 W 11th St; mains $12-15; ☺ dinner Tue-Sat) Duck into this cozy Brazilian eatery below street level and you'll feel like you're entering someone's home. The food can't be beat. Get a minty *caipirhnah* (rum drink) with knock-out meals, including veggie *feijoada* (black-bean stew with yucca and oranges), tender cod fish croquettes and butternut squash baked with shrimp and cilantro (coriander) in coconut milk.

Prime Burger (☎ 212-759-4729; 5 E 51st St; burgers $5; closed Sat & Sun in summer, Sun other times) This classic Midtown diner has been feeding quick lunches to area workers since its 1937 birthday. Inside it smacks of its history. Sit up front in the swivel-tray seats for your burger or crab cake sandwich.

Uptown

H&H (Map pp70-1; ☎ 212-595-8003; 2239 Broadway; bagels $1; ☺ 24hr) Join the lines out the door for New York's best bagels sold hot around the clock. Take a bag to the Bagel-Eating Grounds (aka Central Park).

A (Map pp70-1; ☎ 212-531-1643; 947 Columbus Ave; mains $8-13; ☺ Tue-Sat dinner) This closet-sized miracle cooks up delicious cheap Caribbean-fusion food. Staff are little-town friendly, and the BYOB policy is the gravy.

Mana (Map pp70-1; ☎ 212-787-1110; 646 Amsterdam Ave; mains $9-15) Greens, grains and beans change daily at this simple eatery serving pure veggie food (including great weekend brunches) for health-conscious locals.

Lexington Candy Shop (Map pp70-1; ☎ 212-288-0057; 1226 Lexington Ave at E 83rd St; mains $5-10) This picture-perfect Upper East Side lunch spot is complete with an old-fashioned soda fountain, serving egg creams, malts and cheap diner fare.

Sylvia's (☎ 212-996-0660; 328 Malcolm X Blvd; mains $10-15) The owner of this long-time famous Harlem eatery still sweats in the kitchen herself some days, and the Sunday gospel brunch – with singing and grits – is a real-deal affair.

Charles' Southern Style Kitchen (☎ 212-926-4313; 2839 Frederick Douglass Blvd Ave btwn 151st & 152nd Sts; mains $5-7; subway A, B, C, D to 145th St) A notch down on the down-home scale, Charles serves Harlem's best fried chicken with $10 all-you-can eat lunches, $12 at dinner.

Brooklyn

Tom's Restaurant (☎ 718-636-9738; 782 Washington Ave; mains $2.75-8; ☺ Mon-Sat) Three blocks from the Brooklyn Museum of Art, this happy greasy spoon (inspiration of Suzanne Vega's song) woos locals with its friendly service (staff bring by 'cold orange slices' and cookies) and cheap breakfast and lunch. Two eggs, toast, coffee, home fries or grits costs $2.75.

Nathan's Famous (☎ 718-946-2202; 1310 Surf Ave; hot dogs $2.75) Right outside the subway at Coney Island, Nathan's has been serving *the* all-beef dog with sauerkraut since 1916.

DRINKING

Bars in bottle-shaped Manhattan cover everything from high-gloss swank to seedy sleaze dives with sticky floors. There's no smoking except in 'cigar bars' or on open-air patios. All bars and lounges listed here – just a sip of a sip of a very large keg – are open early afternoon to 2am or 4am daily unless otherwise noted. It's assumed bars are open from early afternoon to 1am or 2am daily; exceptions are noted.

Also see Boozing in Billyburg (p80).

Chinatown & Little Italy   Map pp60-1

Double Happiness (☎ 212-941-1282; 173 Mott St) Too cool to be signed, this subterranean bar (reached by steep stone steps) has candle-lit nooks and pricey drinks (about $8).

Mare Chiaro (☎ 212-226-9345; 176 1/2 Mulberry St) This former Sinatra hangout, used as a backdrop in *The Godfather*, has cheap drinks ($4 or so)? C'mon.

Mehanata 416 BC (☎ 212-625-0981; 416 Broadway; ☺ 6pm-late Tue-Sun) Aka 'the Bulgarian bar,' this drunken dance hall feels Soviet bloc all the way. The unsigned door looks dodgy, the paneled walls a bit dicey, feet stick to the floors from last night's Zagorka beer spills and DJs pump the tunes for bliss- (and beer-) filled Slavs and those who know about it. Tip: *blagodariya* means thank you.

Lower East Side   Map pp60-1

There's much more to choose from here.

Adultworld (☎ 212-253-0035; 116 Suffolk St; ☺ Tue-Sun) Totally unsigned (who needs signs in the Side?) and reached by down-then-up staircases, this funhouse blares the rock and swirls the drinks for $7.

Happy Ending (☎ 212-334-9676; 302 Broome St; ☺ Tue-Sun) A former Asian massage parlor and bathhouse (note the old showerheads) with many sweet cocktails (around $7).

Welcome to the Johnsons (☎ 212-420-9911; 123 Rivington St) Brady Bunch–like bar with an almost off-the-set living-room environment. Beer's cheap ($4), as long as you don't play ball in the house.

East Village   Map pp60-1

Some bars date from back before punk went 'punque.'

Decibel (☎ 212-979-2733; 240 E 9th St; ☺ 8pm-3am Mon-Sat, 8pm-1am Sun) Entering easy-to-miss Decibel is like stepping into 19th-century Japan, with a tiny wooden bar up front, and a fully decked-out tavern out back where it's easy to lose yourself within the huge sake list for hours (beer and drinks are $4 to $10). Tasty snacks are on offer too. Oh, and you might see Uma.

McSorley's Old Ale House (☎ 212-473-9148; 15 E 7th St) Manhattan's oldest bar has deep dust-caked chandeliers and the sawdust floors look every bit its 1854 birthday. Women weren't allowed here till 1970 and it retains a masculine, but welcoming, edge. Lovingly gruff waiters slam two short beers (an order comes in pairs, $2 each) on your table.

Vazac's (☎ 212-473-8840; 108 Ave B; ☺ 5pm-4am) All the prowling Downtown youth call this landmark, with pinball and a horseshoe bar,

'7B' for its location. It'll be expected you know what band is on the jukebox.

Greenwich Village   Map pp60-1

Bar d'O (☎ 212-627-1580; 29 Bedford St; ☺ evenings) Plush lounge with frequent drag acts attracting chic straights and gays.

Chumley's (☎ 212-675-4449; 86 Bedford St) Oozing with its prohibition-era speakeasy history, Chumley's remains discreet – look for the air-con unit hanging out over an unsigned door.

Cowgirl/Bar K (☎ 212-633-1133; 519 Hudson St) Hipster urbanites meet for okra martinis and cheese-covered Fritos in this long-time popular yee-haw bar and lounge.

Chelsea   Map pp64-5

Serena (☎ 212-255-4646; 222 W 23rd St; ☺ Mon-Sat) This cool Chelsea Hotel underground lounge is a DJ-spinning, velvet-rope out front sort of place with $8 drinks.

Trailer Park Lounge & Grill (☎ 212-463-8000; 271 W 23rd St) Chelsea's white trash is gay and straight at this fun bar with greasy burgers, a collection of velvet Elvises (who can stop at a dozen?), fruit cocktails and loads of rum-based drinks served with paper umbrellas (about $6).

Midtown   Map pp64-5

Il Forno Toscano (Bryant Park) Screw dive bars when you can get afternoon $4 drafts in this sun-soaked setting.

Campbell Apartment (☎ 212-953-0409; Grand Central Terminal) Booze splurgers with credit cards should get a mixed cocktail or two ($12 each, ouch!) at this classy wrought-iron, glass-door trustee office in the station. There's live music on Saturday.

Druids (☎ 212-307-6410; 736 Tenth Ave) This Hell's Kitchen Irish pub has a popular garden out back, serving $4 beers to local theater workers.

Upper East Side   Map pp60-1
Metropolitan Museum of Art Balcony Bar (☎ 212-535-7710; 1000 Fifth Ave; ☽ 4-8pm Fri & Sat) NYC's most elegant boozing, with live string quar-

tet and a garden bar up on the roof over-looking Central Park. Drinks are about $7.

Subway Inn (☎ 212-223-8929; 143 E 60th St) Return to earth from Bloomingdale's across the street at this classic dive.

CLUBBING
The club scene changes constantly due to an unending battle with the city over drug activity and noise. Clubs – unlike bars and lounges – feature dance floors and DJs. Check *Time Out New York* or *Paper* (www.papermag.com) for the latest.

BOOZING IN BILLYBURG

When it comes to hipster crawls, Manhattan is *so* 1990s. These days, hip-a-fied 20-something drinkers pay a nod to the Williamsburg gods by eating and drinking their way around Brooklyn's coolest hood, just across from 14th St. Drinking holes are a bit spaced out and some serve meals – plan on eating over here. Following is a sampler.

From the Bedford Ave stop on the L subway line, exit to Williamsburg's café- and shop-line street and go a block south to the **Abbey** (1; ☎ 718-599-4400; 536 Driggs St; ☽ 3pm-4am), an old-time pub drawing gay and straight locals. A couple of blocks north, pre-boom **Brooklyn Ale House** (2; ☎ 718-302-9811; 103 Berry St; ☽ 3pm-4am) pours seriously strong cocktails – the TV plays on mute so the bartender can keep an eye on Oklahoma football games. If your timing's right, stop by **Brooklyn Brewery** (3; ☎ 718-486-7440; www.brooklynbrewery.com; 79 N 11th St; happy hr 6-10pm Fri & Sat, free tours noon-5pm Sat).

Head back to Berry St. If you're hungry, resto/bar **Planet Thai** (4; ☎ 718-559-5758; 133 N 7th St; ☽ 4pm-midnight) is cheap despite its ultra-hip L-shaped high-ceiling space – try elevated row-boat fountain and DJs! Nearby is another even swanker Thai-meets-aquatics legend, **SEA Thai** (5; ☎ 718-384-8850; 114 N 6th St; ☽ 11:30am-1 or 2am), with reflecting pool before Buddha, loads of cocktails and higher-priced curries. Both work as bars too.

Head back to Berry, past many options, and make your way to Metropolitan Ave, where a couple of blocks down is **Black Betty** (6; ☎ 718-599-0243; 366 Metropolitan Ave; ☽ 7pm-4am), an Arabian-

themed bar with live music and DJs playing to a tight dance floor. After the underpass, veer left to roomy **Union Pool Hall** (7; ☎ 718-609-0484; 484 Union Ave; ☽ 5pm-4am) with rockabilly DJs and outdoor smoke garden.

Back under the underpass, step into the homey classic **Pete's Candy Store** (8; ☎ 718-302-3770; www.petescandystore.com; 709 Lorimer St; ☽ 5pm-2am or 4am), with themed nights (jazz, country, Scrabble) and a lively backyard. A car service is back next to Union, or the Lorimer St stop on the L, a block away. Taxis roll down Bedford Ave.

If you're sober enough, another irreversibly hip place is **Diner** (9; ☎ 718-486-3077; 85 Broadway; ☽ 11-4am), housed in old Pullman, where cocktails are strongest when you sit at the bar. The food (particularly brunch or splurging daily specials) is superb. Go via Bedford St.

Cielo (Map pp60-1; ☎ 212-645-5700; 18 Little West 12th St, Meatpacking District; admission $10) Intimate spot with multi-culti crowd dancing to Latin-spiced house.

Club Shelter (Map pp64-5; ☎ 212-719-4479; 20 W 39th St btwn Fifth & Sixth Aves, Midtown; admission $10-20) Saturday is best, with DJ Timmy Regisford spinning house, while Lovergirl packs in cruising lesbians on other floors.

Exit2 (Map pp64-5; ☎ 212-582-8282; 610 W 56th St, Hell's Kitchen; subway A, B, C, D, 1, 9 to Columbus Circle; admission $25) DJ Junior Vasquez spins Saturday night from a private $8-million booth, easy to get lost in the maze of thematic rooms.

Opaline (Map pp60-1; ☎ 212 995-8684; 85 Ave A, Alphabet City; admission $10) Lush subterranean lounge becomes Area 10009 on Friday, a queer-friendly dance-fest.

Roxy (Map pp64-5; ☎ 212-677-0404; 515 W 18th St, Chelsea; admission $15-25) Legendary megaclub with Tuesday roller disco and shirtless gay-male Saturday night bash.

Sapphire (Map pp60-1; ☎ 212-777-5153; 249 El-dridge St, Lower East Side; admission $5) This tiny, hoppin' venue sees plenty of steamy dancing on a tight dance floor.

ENTERTAINMENT

Time Out New York and *Village Voice* are the best guides to nightlife. Higher culture – stuff like ballet – is well covered in the Friday and Sunday *New York Times* and *New Yorker*.

Washington Square Park usually has some sort of free spectacle going on.

Theater & Dance

Centered around Times Square, Broadway is home to the city's big-time musical and plays, like newcomer *Wicked* (a prequel to the *Wizard of Oz*) or stand-bys like *Beauty*

BE ON TV!

The following shows offer free seats to their broadcasts:

■ **Daily Show with John Stewart** Call ☎ 212-586-2477 three months ahead of time, or call 11:30am Friday for last-minute seats of the following week. The **studio** (Map pp64-5) is at 514 W 54th St.

■ **Late Show with David Letterman** Email www.cbs.com/lateshow, or call ☎ 212-247-6497 at 11am on day of taping. It's held at the **Ed Sullivan Theater** (Map pp64-5; 1697 Broadway, Midtown).

■ **Saturday Night Live** Email snltickets@nbc.com in August, or line up by 8:15am on day of show at **NBC Studios** (Map pp64-5; 50th St btwn Fifth & Sixth Aves) for lottery tickets (16 and older).

■ **Total Request Live** Line up at **MTV Studios** (Map pp64-5; 1515 Broadway) by noon weekdays, for the show, which begins at 3:30pm, or call ☎ 212-398-8549 in advance; audience is for ages 16 to 24 only.

---

and the Beast. 'Off Broadway' simply refers to smaller theaters (200 or fewer seats) and more experimental 'Off-off Broadway' even smaller (under 100 seats). Read up about what's showing in *Time Out New York* or you can check reviews online at www.broadwayworld.com or www.talkinbroadway.com/allthatchat.

American Ballet Theatre (www.abt.org) Stages spring and summer shows at the Metropolitan Opera House.

New York State Theater (Map pp70-1; ☎ 212-870-5570; www.nycballet.com; Lincoln Center, Broadway & 63rd St) Home to the New York City Ballet, which caps its season with *The Nutcracker* in December.

Student-rush tickets are $10 online or at the office on the day of performance.

For more experimental dance, see what's on at the **Joyce Theater** (Map pp64-5; ☎ 212-242-0800; www.joyce.org; 175 Eighth Ave, Chelsea) or **Danspace Project at St Mark's-in-the-Bowery** (Map pp60-1; ☎ 212-674-8194; Second Ave & E 10th St, East Village).

HALF-PRICED BROADWAY TICKETS

The cash-only **TKTS Booth** (Map pp64-5; ☎ 212-768-1818; www.tdf.org; Broadway & 47th St; ☺ 3-8pm Mon-Sat evening performances, 10am-2pm Wed & Sat matinees, 11am-3pm Sun matinees, 3-8pm Sun evenings) sells same-day tickets to Broadway and off-Broadway productions for 25 or 50% off, plus a $3 booking fee. Look for the bright orange sign, or the lines. There's a new stand at **South Street Seaport** (Map pp60-1; John & Front Sts; ☺ Mon-Sat).

Cinemas

Film Forum (Map pp60-1; ☎ 212-727-8110; www
.filmforum.com; 209 W Houston St, SoHo) This is the
city's No 1 indie film theater with double
features and oddball films that aren't shown
elsewhere. Seats aren't the comfiest.

Landmark Sunshine Cinema (Map pp60-1; ☎ 212-
777-3456 ext 687; 143 Houston St) A newish art-
house cinema in the Lower East Side.

Sports

New Yorkers loves their sports, particularly
the Yankees, Knicks, Giants and Rangers –
or whoever's winning.

Skip the *Times* for sports coverage and go
straight to the back pages of the *Daily News*
for fiery, no-punches-pulled accounts. Seeing football is way pricey ($200 or more from
scalpers) and Knicks seats are a challenge.

Best to watch is baseball, with day games,
loads of lore and frequent home games
from April to October. Check **Ticketmaster**
(☎ 800-462-2849, 212-307-7171; www.ticketmaster
.com) or **StubHub** (☎ 866-788-2482; www.stubhub
.com), a ticket-trade board. Bus service from
Port Authority Bus Terminal goes to Giants
Stadium for $3.25.

One of pro tennis's grand slam tourna-
ments, the popular **US Open** (www.us open.org) is
held in Queens in August and September.

Giants (☎ 201-935-811, tickets ☎ 201-935-8222;
www.giants.com; Giants Stadium, East Rutherford, NJ)
NFL football. Tickets are sold out years in advance and your
only hope is through a scalper.

Islanders (☎ 631-888-9000; www.nyislanders.com;
Nassau Veterans Memorial Coliseum, Uniondale, Long I;
tickets $31-160) NHL hockey, out on Long Island.

Jets (☎ 516-560-8200 ext 1; www.newyorkjets.com; Giants Stadium, East Rutherford, NJ) NFL football. As popular
as the Giants and the same story for tickets applies.

Knicks (☎ 212-465-5867; www.nyknicks.com; Madison
Square Garden, Seventh Ave & 33rd St; tickets $55-160)
NBA basketball.

Liberty (☎ 212-465-6293; www.nyliberty.com; Madison
Square Garden; tickets $10-65) WNBA women's basketball.

MetroStars (☎ 201-583-7000; www.metrostars.com;
Giants Stadium, East Rutherford, NJ; tickets $18-38) Soccer
from April to October.

Mets (☎ 718-507-8499; www.mets.com; Shea Stadium,
123-01 Roosevelt Ave, Flushing, Queens; tickets $5-48;
subway 7 to Willets Point–Shea Stadium) Major League
baseball.

New Jersey Devils (☎ 201-935-6050; www.new
jerseydevils.com; Continental Airlines Arena, East
Rutherford, NJ; tickets $20-90) NHL hockey.

New Jersey Nets (☎ 800-765-6387; www.njnets;
Continental Airlines Arena, East Rutherford, NJ; tickets
$40-500) NBA basketball, may be moving to Brooklyn.

Rangers (☎ 212-465-6741; www.nyrangers.com;
Madison Square Garden; tickets $30-160) NHL hockey.

Yankees (☎ 718-293-6000; www.yankees.com; Yankee
Stadium, 161st St & River Ave; tickets $10-70; subway B, D
or 4 to 161 St–Yankee Stadium) Major League baseball.

Live Music

CLASSICAL MUSIC & OPERA

Soaking in the more uppity pleasures can get
costly (starting at $50 a pop), but most have
cheap seats starting at $15 or so.

Carnegie Hall (Map pp64-5; ☎ 212-247-7800; www
.carnegiehall.org; 154 W 57th St) Open since 1891, this
historic hall hosts visiting philharmonics.

Metropolitan Opera House (☎ 212-362-6000;
www.metopera.org). Part of the 16-acre **Lincoln
Center** (Map pp70-1; W 64th St & Amsterdam Ave) the
opera season runs from September to April.
Tickets start at $55, but the standing-room
tickets are a bargain at $12 (sold at 10am
Saturday for the following week).

Trinity Church (Map pp60-1; ☎ 212-602-0747;
www.trinitywallstreet.org; Broadway & Wall St) Holds
'Concerts at One' (1pm) for $2.

Brooklyn Academy of Music (BAM; ☎ 718-636-
4100; www.bam.org; 30 Lafayette Ave; subway B, Q, 2, 3,
5 or 5 to Atlantic Ave). Some of the most cutting-
edge experimental work (big with dance
and theater too) is staged here.

ROCK & HIP-HOP   Map pp60-1

Big-name venues, like Roseland, Irving Plaza
and Madison Square Garden host often (immediately) sold-out shows of big-name acts.
Check the *Village Voice*. The following are
more low-key clubs in the Lower East Side:

Arlene Grocery (☎ 212-358-1633; www.arlene
-grocery.com; 95 Stanton St) A '90s vet, deli-turned-
club stages great free shows nightly, plus
has cheap beer.

Luna Lounge (☎ 212-260-2323; 171 Ludlow St)
Local acts and up-and-coming indie darlings
(the Strokes included) play the back stage.

Mercury Lounge (☎ 212-260-4700; www.mercury
loungenyc.com; 217 E Houston St) Beloved long-term
space with good sound, ample dance space
for indie rockers galore.

JAZZ & EXPERIMENTAL

Blue Note (Map pp60-1; ☎ 212-475-8592; www.blue
note.net; 131 W 3rd St, Greenwich Village) Famous club,
with high covers and *serious* jazz fans.

Cleopatra's Needle (Map pp70-1; ☎ 212-769-6969; www.cleopatrasneedleny.com; 2485 Broadway btwn W 92nd & 93rd Sts, Upper West Side) Late-night open-mic jams swag till 4am. There's a $10 drink/food minimum, but no cover.

C-Note (Map pp60-1; ☎ 212-677-8142; www.thecnote.com; 157 Ave C, East Village) Down-and-dirty space with free jazz and blues – open jams conquer Saturday.

Lenox Lounge (Map pp70-1; ☎ 212-427-0253; www.lenoxlounge.com; 288 Malcolm X Blvd btwn 124th & 125th Sts, Harlem) Jazz-cat haven hip with down-towners. Sunday is a soulful gay soiree.

Knitting Factory (Map pp60-1; ☎ 212-219-3055; www.knittingfactory.com; 74 Leonard St, Tribeca) Long influence in NY jazz, experimental music and spoken word.

Tonic (Map pp60-1; ☎ 212-358-7501; www.tonicnyc.com; 107 Norfolk St, Lower East Side) Elixir of the avant-garde, has kids like John Zorn and Kim Gordon.

SHOPPING

New York's department stores, vintage bou-tiques, CD shops, street vendors and entre-preneurial trolling clerks ('Rolex? You want a Rolex?') vie against museums and monu-ments for the city's premier attraction. Some say it's no contest: shopping takes gold.

SoHo
Map pp60-1

Find sportier versions of Uptown classy designers on these oft-trod brick streets. Start at Prince St or West Broadway. Along Broadway are discount shoe and jeans shops. Lafayette St is edgier, with DJ paraphernalia that'll look down on the subway.

Alice Underground (☎ 212-431-9067; 481 Broadway; ☼ 11am-7pm) Well-organized vintage stock.

Hotel Venus (☎ 212-966-4066; 382 W Broadway; ☼ 11am-8pm) Home to Patricia Field (who dressed up the characters in *Sex and the City*

TOP FIVE CHEAP NYC GIFTS

- **'I ♥ NYC' shirts** About $3 at Times Square and Chinatown
- **Knock-off Yankees cap** $10; everyone else's wearing 'em
- **Strand Book Store tote bag** (p55) $6; stuff your purchases in a canvas bag from the city's greatest bookstore
- **Subway-print gear** From the **New York Transit Museum Shop** (Map pp64-5; ☎ 212-878-0106; Grand Central Terminal, Shuttle Passage)
- **Metro map** Free from subway clerks, you cheapskate

---

fame), this shop puts a bang into the SoHo scene: colored wigs and loads of spandex.

Pearl River Mart (☎ 212-431-4770; 477 Broadway; ☼ 10am-7pm) One-stop 'Chinatown' sampler (actually north of Canal St) with two floors of teapots, dragon dresses, wind-up clocks and kites.

Lower East Side

Many small boutiques stocking local or Jap-anese designers' clothes are found around Ludlow and Orchard Sts. A famed sex-toy shop for women is **Toys in Babeland** (Map pp60-1; ☎ 212-375-1701; www.babeland.com; 94 Rivington St; ☼ noon-10pm Mon-Sat, noon-7pm Sun).

East Village
Map pp60-1

NYC's spirited rock-and-roll hood runs on and off St Marks Pl. Don't miss leafy bou-tique-lined E 7th and 9th Sts.

Kiehl's (☎ 212-677-3171, 800-543-4571; 109 Third Ave; ☼ 10am-7pm Mon-Sat, noon-6pm Sun) NYC's favorite skin-care maker since 1851.

CRAZY DISCOUNT COUTURE

Fashion's a big thing here, but you won't need to bust your budget for that Pucci scarf. NYC has a couple of key clearing houses for cut-rate, high-end couture and accessories. A New York City legend directly across from the WTC site, **Century 21** (Map pp60-1; ☎ 212-227-9092; 22 Cortland St; ☼ 7:45am-8pm Mon-Fri, 10am-8pm Sat, 11am-7pm Sun) sports four floors packed-to-the-neck with discounted top-tier designers' wares. Way further afield (1½ hours north of the city in fact), **Woodbury Common Premium Outlets** (☎ 845-928-4000; www.premiumoutlets.com; 498 Red Apple Court, Central Valley, NY) is home to over 200 stores selling (often) marked-down collections. Bus up with **Gray Line New York** (☎ 212-445-0848, 800-669-0051 ext 3; roundtrip $35); leaving daily 8:30am to 2:45pm, returning 3:30pm to 9:25pm.

SHOPPING SPLURGES

Many Manhattan department stores are worth a peek even if you can't afford a key chain.

- **Barneys** (Map pp70-1; ☎ 212-826-8900; 660 Madison Ave)
- **Bergdorf Goodman** (Map pp64-5; ☎ 212-753-7300; 754 Fifth Ave)
- **Bloomingdale's** (Map pp70-1; ☎ 212-705-2000; 1000 Third Ave at 59th St)
- **Saks Fifth Ave** (Map pp64-5; ☎ 212-753-4000; 611 Fifth Ave at 50th St)
- **Takashimaya** (Map pp64-5; ☎ 212-350-0100; 693 Fifth Ave)
- **Tiffany & Co** (Map pp64-5; ☎ 212-755-8000; 727 Fifth Ave)

Other Music (☎ 212-477-8150; 15 E 4th St; 🕙 noon-9pm Mon-Fri, noon-8pm Sat, noon-7pm Sun) Facing Tower Records, this everything-indie CD store offers anything 'other': offbeat lounge, psychedelic, electronica, indie-rock.

Two hole-in-the-wall consignment shops are **Tokio 7** (☎ 212-353-8443; 64 E 7th St; 🕙 noon-8:30pm Mon-Sat, noon-8pm Sun) and **Tokyo Joe** (☎ 212-473-0724; 334 E 11th St; 🕙 noon-9pm).

Greenwich Village   Map pp60-1
Hit Bleecker St for used CDs and vinyl, guitars and all sorts of condoms. There's some Goth and cheap leather shoes on W 8th St, east of Sixth Ave.

Flight 001 (☎ 212-691-1001; 96 Greenwich Ave; 🕙 11am-8:30pm Mon-Fri, 11am-8pm Sat, noon-6pm Sun) Cool travel gear and LP guides.

Leather Man (☎ 212-243-5339; 111 Christopher St; 🕙 noon-10pm, noon-8pm) This long-time sex shop has a lot of leather, clothes and toys.

Chelsea & Union Square   Map pp64-5
Barneys Co-Op (☎ 212-593-7800; 236 W 18th St; 🕙 11am-8pm Mon-Fri, 11am-7pm Sat, noon-6pm Sun)

Best during its wild warehouse sales (February and August).

Otto Tootsi Plohound (☎ 212-460-8650; 137 Fifth Ave; 🕙 11:30am-7:30pm Mon-Fri, 11am-8pm Sat, noon-7pm Sun) Great NYC mini-chain for designer shoes. Usually a sales rack. Clearance sales are in January and July.

Paragon Athletic Goods (☎ 212-255-8036; 867 Broadway; 🕙 10am-8pm Mon-Sat, 11:30am-7pm Sun) NYC's best sports and outdoor collection.

Midtown & Uptown
Fifth Ave is about chic wear for the fat-walleted swank set; classy boutiques line Madison Ave from 70th St through the 70s.

B&H Photo-Video (Map pp64-5; ☎ 212-502-6200; www.bhphotovideo.com; 420 Ninth Ave; 🕙 9am-7pm Mon-Thu, 9am-1pm Fri, 10am-5pm Sun) Classic crazed camera shop with some used gear.

Big City Kite Co (Map pp70-1; ☎ 212-472-2623; 1210 Lexington Ave; 🕙 11am-6:30pm Mon-Wed & Fri, 11am-7:30pm Thu, 10am-6pm Sat) Big funny kites for Central Park's airways.

Colony (Map pp64-5; ☎ 212-265-2050; 1619 Broadway; 🕙 9:30am-midnight) At site of Tin Pan Alley, historic Colony is the king of karaoke CDs, sheet music and memorabilia (Dylan's harmonica from 1961 costs $10,000).

Macy's (Map pp64-5; ☎ 212-695-4400; 151 W 34th St at Broadway; 🕙 10am-8:30pm Mon-Sat, 11am-7pm Sun) The world's largest department store.

Manny's Music (Map pp64-5; ☎ 212-819-0576; 156 W 48th St; 🕙 10am-7pm Mon-Sat, noon-6pm Sun) Pick up guitar strings where the Stones bought the 'Satisfaction' distortion pedal.

Tatiana's (Map pp70-1; ☎ 212-755-7744; 767 Lexington Ave; 🕙 11am-7pm Mon-Fri, 11am-6pm Sat) Super consignment shop, with women's designer labels – many are worn once, then cast away from affluent locals.

GETTING THERE & AWAY
Air
Most international flights land at **John F Kennedy International Airport** (JFK; information line ☎ 718-244-4444; Queens), 15 miles southeast of

---

CHELSEA MARKETS

Hitting Chelsea's flea markets on weekends is as 'New York' as bagels or the Yankees. At Sixth Ave, the **Annex Antique Fair & Flea Market** (Map pp64-5; ☎ 212-243-5343; 107-111 W 25th St; admission $1; 🕙 dawn-dusk Sat & Sun) features dozens of open-air stalls hawking watches, cameras, records and owners' dogs to pet. Just south, is a free **flea market** (Map pp64-5; Sixth Ave & W 24th St). Another freebie, the **Garage Antique Fair** (Map pp64-5; 112 W 25th St) is good for eyewear and old posters.

Midtown. **La Guardia Airport** (☎ 718-533-3400; Queens), closer to Manhattan, has mostly domestic flights.

About 10 miles west of Manhattan, New Jersey's **Newark International Airport** (☎ 973-961-6000) is just as accessible, with a large international terminal. You'll often pick up cheaper airfares flying into or out of Newark. It's a hub for Continental Airlines.

Most major airlines have offices in the city; for a complete list see (p702).

Bus

Most buses arrive and depart from the **Port Authority Bus Terminal** (Map pp64-5; ☎ 212-564-8484; 41st St & Eighth Ave), including **Greyhound** (☎ 212-971-6300) with links to Buffalo, Boston, Philadelphia and Washington, DC. Greyhound's international office here (p706) helps foreign travelers and sells bus passes. **Peter Pan Trailways** (☎ 800-343-9999) has a daily express bus to Boston ($42) and **Short Line** (☎ 212-736-4700), offers connections to upstate New York and New Jersey.

Cheaper deals are found at new 'sidewalk terminal' (possibly even legal) bus services in Chinatown: **Fung Wah** (Map pp60-1; ☎ 212-925-8889; www.fungwahbus.com; 139 Canal St) goes to Boston ($10) hourly 7am to 10pm; **2000 Coach** (Map pp60-1; www.2000coach.com; 88 E Broadway) goes to Philadelphia ($12) and DC ($20). On weekends it gets frantic with sidewalk waits. Other stands have buses to Cincinnati and Virginia Beach.

Train

Pennsylvania Station (Penn Station; Map pp64-5; 33rd St btwn Seventh & Eighth Aves) is the departure point for all **Amtrak trains** (☎ 800-872-7245). The **Long Island Rail Road** (LIRR; ☎ 718-217-5477) has its own platform at Penn Station for commuters to Brooklyn, Queens and the suburbs of Long Island. **New Jersey Transit trains** (☎ 973-762-5100) go from Penn Station to the Jersey suburbs and Jersey Shore. **Metro North Rail Road** (☎ 212-532-4900; Grand Central Terminal), which serves northern suburbs and Connecticut, is the only commuter train company using Grand Central Terminal.

PATH (☎ 800-234-7284) has a separate 24-hour subway system that runs up Sixth Ave to 33rd St and then on to Hoboken and Newark ($1.50).

GETTING AROUND

Gone are the days of the subway token: the **MetroCard** is used on buses and subways. It's $2 per ride, $7 for an unlimited one-day pass and $21 for a week. A ride includes free transfers from subway to city bus within two hours. Cyclists will find wide wheels are best for the city's pockmarked streets. Wear a helmet and watch for taxi doors.

Car & Motorcycle

A bad place to be driving, with the street-grid getting choked at rush hour. Parking in Manhattan is difficult or expensive. Be wary of clearly signed street-cleaning rules. Parking garages in Midtown charge at least $35 during the day. Cheaper lots are found on West St in Chelsea (around $18). Find a side-street spot for free in Williamsburg.

Airports have offices for major rental companies (it's cheapest in Newark). An excellent family-run car-rental company, **Autoteam USA** (☎ 866-438-8326, 732-727-7272; www .autoteamusa.com; South Amboy, NJ) rents cars from $30/175/600 daily/weekly/monthly (1000 miles per week free).

Public Transportation

White-and-blue city buses operate 24 hours a day. You need exact change of $2 (no pennies or bills) or a MetroCard to board. Ask for a transfer to another bus when boarding if you're not carrying a MetroCard. Bus maps are available at subway and train stations. Some 'limited stop' buses pull over only every 10 blocks or so. 'Express' buses are for outer-borough commuters.

Running 24 hours a day, and serving four million folks a day, the subway is run by the **New York City Transit Authority** (☎ 718-330-1234; www.mta.info), which celebrated its 100th birthday in 2004. Ask for a free map at stations. On maps, local stops are solid black dots, express stops are white dots.

Taxi

The average fare is nearly $9. Flagfall is $2.50, plus 30¢ for every fifth of a mile and 20¢ a minute while stuck in traffic; from 8pm to 6am, a 50¢ nighttime surcharge is tacked on to your fare. The passenger must pay any bridge or tunnel tolls and tip 10% to 15% (minimum 50¢).

Mid-Atlantic

HIGHLIGHTS

- **Philadelphia** Colonial American theme park with students and nightlife keeping the 21st century fun (p91)
- **Atlantic City** East coast version of Las Vegas, but with a beach (p107)
- **Whale watching** See the largest New Jersey natives – whales – swimming in the waters off Cape May (p107)
- **Bobsledding** Put your head down and pray like an Olympian careening downhill at Lake Placid (p111)
- **Off the beaten track** The mirage-like waters of the St Lawrence River on the Canadian border (p111)
- **Best journey** Rivers, mountains, forests roll by like a beautiful movie on the train from NYC to the Adirondacks and beyond (p110)

FAST FACTS

- **Area** 100,000 sq miles
- **Big Cities** Philadelphia (population 1,586,600), Pittsburgh (369,600), Buffalo (292,700)
- **Budget** $30-60 per day
- **Costs** hostel in Philadelphia $18, bus from NYC to Atlantic City $24, Amish boy & girl saltshakers $6
- **Driving times** NYC to Philadelphia 2 hours, Philadelphia to Pittsburg 6 hours, NYC to Niagara Falls 8 hours
- **Famous for** kitschy boardwalks, beautiful waterfalls, sports fanatics, real people
- **Population** 40 million (including NYC)
- **Phrases** *yo* (hello), *youse* (you all), *critters* (flies, skunks, any annoying animal)
- **Seasons** high (May-Aug & Nov 25–Jan 1), low (Sep-Oct & Jan-Apr)
- **States** Pennsylvania, New Jersey, New York
- **Tasty treats** cheesesteaks *(jeez-take)*, Buffalo wings, saltwater taffy
- **Time** East Coast, GMT minus 6 hours
- **Top hostel** HI-AYH Tibbett's Point Lighthouse (p112)

TRAVEL HINTS

Many museums, sights and camping grounds are closed during the winter. Take the nontoll roads to save some cash.

Full of places where jaded city-dwellers escape to seek simple lives, where artists retreat for inspiration, and where pretty houses line main streets, the Mid-Atlantic is a region of defining American locales. It's provincial in many ways, with rough-around-the-edges towns hoping to reinvent themselves as tourist destinations, promoting museums dedicated to obscure achievements or industries well past their glory days. Even though it's the most populated and industrialized part of the US, the Mid-Atlantic is also proof that America really is a nation of small places, many here set amidst stunning scenery but overlooked in a country so large.

City lovers can still get their fill, from river-rich Pittsburgh and bohemian Buffalo to the historic gem that is Philadelphia. But the character of the region and its true appeal lie outside the cities, in the tranquil rural hideaways and wilderness. This is where you'll find the spellbinding Niagara Falls, gorgeous Jersey Shore, and mountainous Adirondacks, reaching skyward just a few hours north of New York City.

HISTORY

Native American settlement was sparse when Europeans first arrived here. The area was probably home to fewer than 100,000 people, comprising only two major cultural groups: the Algonquians and the Iroquois.

French fur trappers and traders on the St Lawrence River reached the region by the mid-16th century, and in 1609, Henry Hudson found, named and sailed up the Hudson River, claiming the land for the Dutch, who started several settlements in 'New Netherlands.' The Iroquois soon controlled the booming fur trade, selling to Dutch, English and French agents.

The tiny Dutch settlement on Manhattan Island surrendered to a Royal Navy warship in 1664, in the midst of a series of Anglo-Dutch wars. The new colonial power created two territories, called 'New York' and 'New Jersey.' In the prolonged French and Indian War (1754–63) the British defeated the French to secure control of northeast America. The shift of Indian allegiances away from the French was a crucial factor in the British victory. The new British territory, extending to the Mississippi, was made a short-lived Indian reserve.

Pennsylvania played a leading role in the Revolutionary War (1775–83). New York and New Jersey loyalties were split, but important battles still occurred in all three states. Many Iroquois allied themselves with the British, and they suffered badly from military defeats, disease, European encroachment and bitter reprisals. Entire communities were wiped out, and much of their land was deeded to Revolutionary War veterans. Farmers then displaced the Algonquians from coastal areas and river valleys.

Railways linked the major cities as early as the 1840s. The population grew with waves of immigration, starting with the Irish in the 1840s and 1850s. Natural resources, abundant labor and unfettered capitalism transformed the region into a powerhouse of industry and commerce. During the Civil War (1861–65), the Mid-Atlantic states supplied men and material for Union forces.

After the Civil War, the American West was opened by steel railroad tracks made in Pittsburgh, the engines of growth used Pennsylvania coal and oil, and the profits went back to the 'robber barons' (the super-rich industrialists and financiers) in New York. All the region's cities were swollen with immigrants – blacks from the South, Chinese from California, and over 12 million Europeans who arrived at Ellis Island, in the middle of New York Harbor. The growth, industry, wealth, cultural diversity and constant flow of people continue in the Mid-Atlantic states to this day.

THE CULTURE

While it's almost impossible to define a Mid-Atlantic character and residents would never identify themselves regionally in the same way as, say, a Southerner would, the people in general do share a conflicted relationship between urban and rural ways of life. New York City looms like an alien mothership, and serves as a sort of Rorschach test: mention it in conversation and the respondent will opine whether said city is a cosmopolitan shangri-la for bored suburbanites, or a seething megalopolis full of jaded people to avoid. Even the most secluded up-stater will have a say on it.

There are other large cities in the region responsible for the constant movement of

MID-ATLANTIC STATES

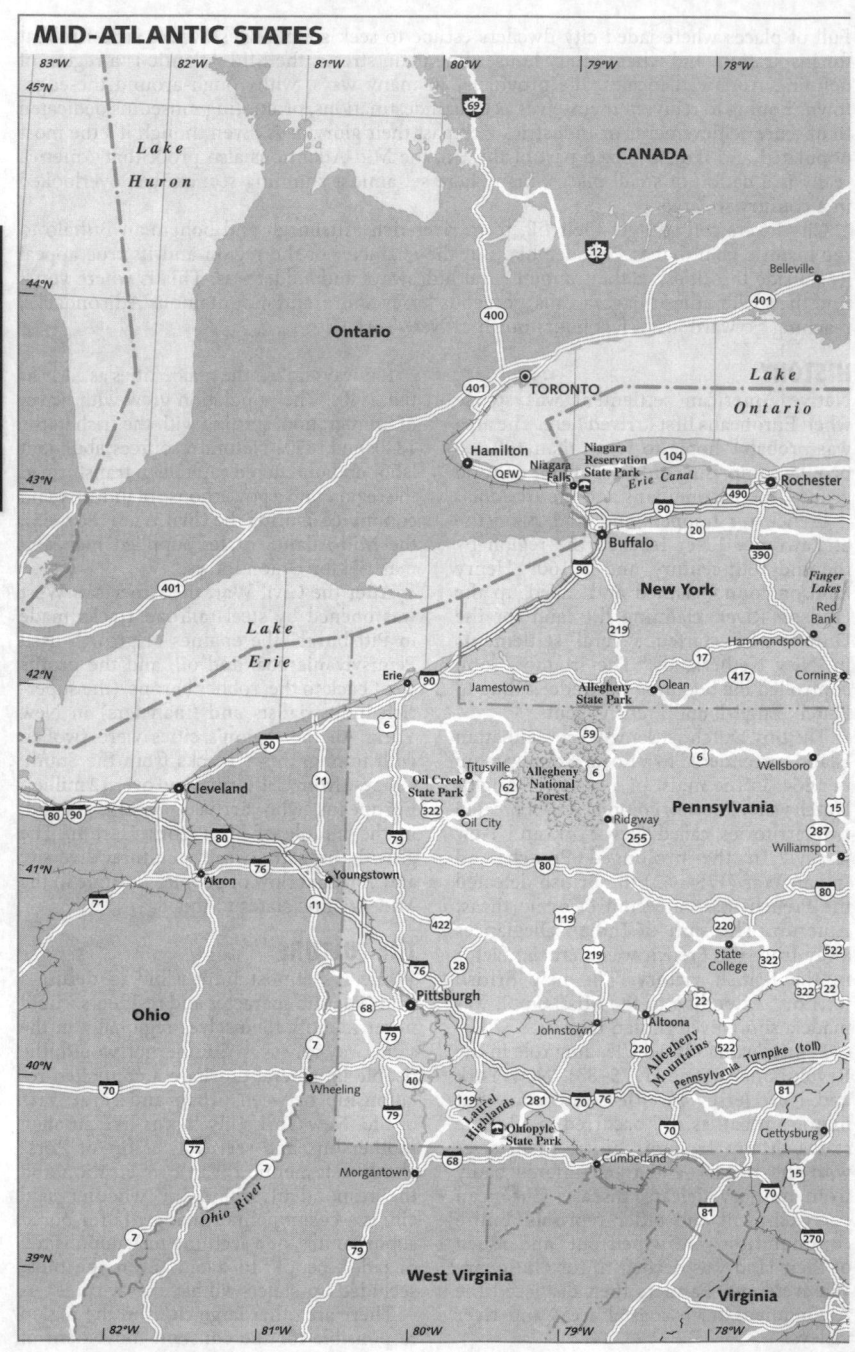

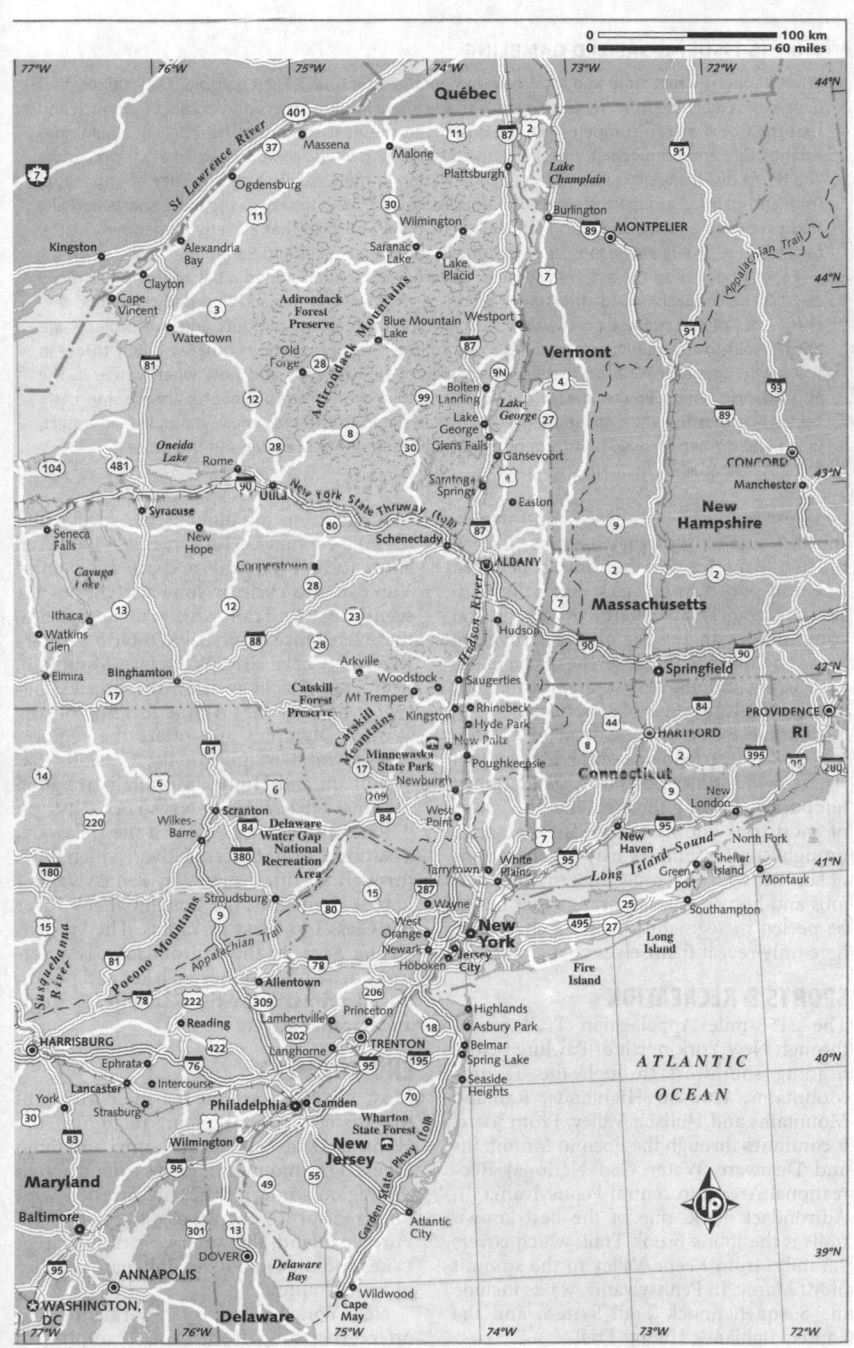

THE BIG ISSUE: LEGALIZED GAMBLING

What happens when state and local governments need money? They gamble. They call on that *deux ex* slot machine from Vegas to restock their coffers hoping voters don't object too much and that their casinos can compete with the casinos in the next state over. New Jersey already has Atlantic City and Connecticut has the Native American–owned Foxwoods, so what's a poor state like NY to do? It's finally allowed the Cayuga Nation in the Catskills, after decades of opposition from anti-gaming groups and local communities, to add video lottery to the more sportsman-like harness racing already on tap in Monticello, NY, giving birth to that cleverly named hybrid, the racino. Three others are already open in Buffalo, the Finger Lakes and Saratoga.

Eager to get in on the act, Pennsylvania Governor Ed Rendell signed a bill approving as many as 61,000 slot machines for the state hoping to rival Nevada in gambling-derived public revenue. Lots of the monies go towards cash-strapped education budgets and the projects are always sold to the public as a harmless way to cut taxes, property or otherwise. But throw in the newly opened casino on the New York side of Niagara Falls and now when you're in the Mid-Atlantic region you're always only a short drive away from a place to drop some cash. Critics fear that the state governments will get addicted to the easy money and, like an addict, won't know when to stop, transforming communities in unforeseen ways in the process.

peoples between wealthy, comfortable suburbs and gritty urban centers, like in much of America. But the contrast between rich and poor can be stark especially with skyrocketing real estate prices. Rural communities in the region are struggling more and more to integrate the urban exiles who bring money and sophistication but also a perceived sense of superiority.

In some locales if you dress or act too 'big city' your friendly greeting may be met with a cold shoulder or shrug. You are just temporary, passing through, like the waves of industrial booms and busts that once brought comfort and security to generations of families who now must fight to keep their jobs and homes. Like an orange that has to be peeled in segments, people's characters here only reveal themselves over time.

SPORTS & RECREATION

The 2158-mile Appalachian Trail passes through New York north of Pawling before heading southwest through the Taconic Mountains, Hudson Highlands, Ramapo Mountains and Hudson Valley. From there, it continues through the Pocono Mountains and Delaware Water Gap National Recreational Area into central Pennsylvania. In Adirondack Park, one of the best-known trails is the Johns Brook Trail, which covers 9.5 miles from Keene Valley to the summit of Mt Marcy. In Pennsylvania, walks include the Susquehannock Trail System and the Laurel Highlands Hiking Trail.

A bicycling highlight is the spectacular 35-mile Mohawk–Hudson Bike/Hike Trail along former railroads and canal towpaths. You can also cycle on long stretches of the scenic Seaway Trail, which runs parallel to the St Lawrence River, Lake Ontario, Niagara River and Lake Erie. Whiteface Mountain, near Lake Placid in the Adirondacks, has twice hosted the Alpine events of the Winter Olympics and offers the region's best downhill skiing. In the Catskills, Ski Windham and Hunter Mountain are good ski areas fairly close to New York City.

Rafts and canoes go down the Delaware, a National Wild & Scenic River, which flows through all three states. In Pennsylvania's Laurel Highlands, the Youghiogheny River has Class I to Class IV rapids. The St Regis Canoe Area, in the Adirondacks, is a network of 58 interconnected lakes and ponds, linked primarily by the Raquette, St Regis and Saranac Rivers.

ENVIRONMENT

Most big cities are on the main rivers of the eastern coastal plain, including the Hudson, Delaware, Susquehanna and Ohio Rivers. Low mountain ranges extend across the region's interior, heavily forested with pine, red spruce, maple, oak, ash and birch. Further inland, the waterways of the Great Lakes and the Ohio River link many smaller industrial cities.

New York has protected parklands that offer everything from beach camping to mountain climbing. For entrance to state-run parks, you can purchase the $60 Empire Passport, which gives you access to almost all of the 164 state parks and 50 Department of Environmental Conservation forest preserve areas for one year. In New Jersey, the Wharton State Forest, with more than 110,000 acres, is notable for being the largest single tract of land within the state's park system. Pennsylvania's Lake Erie region has the only surf beach in the state.

The following places all provide useful information about the area's national and state parks:

Natural Resources (www.dcnr.state.pa.us/)

New Jersey State Park Service (www.state.nj.us /dep/forestry)

New York State Parks (www.nysparks.state.ny.us/)

Pennsylvania Department of Conservation &

TRANSPORTATION

The big cities all have airports, but New York's John F Kennedy (JFK) is the region's major international gateway. Alternatives include Newark Liberty International Airport; La Guardia, in Queens, and Philadelphia International Airport where airlines offer good deals on domestic fares. Try **Southwest** (www.southwest.com) or **AirTran** (www.airtran.com).

New Jersey Transit trains from New York City's Penn Station service the Jersey Shore as far as Bay Head, and also make connections to the Trenton and Princeton areas. The 24-hour underground PATH train connects New York City with Hoboken, Newark and Jersey City ($2). Seastreak and NY Waterway ferries cross the Hudson from the west side of Manhattan to spots in New Jersey.

Greyhound buses serve main US towns, as well as Canada. **Peter Pan Trailways** (☎ 800-343-9999; www.peterpan.com) and **Adirondack Trailways** (☎ 800-225-6815) are both regional bus lines. Amtrak provides commuter rail services throughout the New York metropolitan area.

When it comes to getting around, it's all about having a car but rentals are expensive in New York State and especially New York City so check out rates in New Jersey. Hitchhiking is not only illegal on major highways, it's just not done these days for fear of being picked up by a lunatic.

In New Jersey the main roadways are the New Jersey Turnpike, which crosses the state diagonally from New York to Philadelphia, and the much more pleasant Garden State Parkway, which runs along the Jersey Shore all the way south to Cape May.

PHILADELPHIA

At once the heart of the British colonial experiment and the intellectual and spiritual motor of its demise, blue-collar, working class Philadelphia is also becoming part of history. Vibrant universities, world-class museums, performing-arts centers, and a thriving nightlife scene offset any notion that Philadelphia is only for school field trips. Although the style of architecture has become ubiquitous across the states – you'll see bland versions of it in schools in almost every neighborhood – the older, preserved buildings in Philadelphia provide a picture of what colonial American cities once looked like.

Though urban renewal has been going on for decades, some parts of the city formerly populated by industrial workers are blighted and worlds away from the carefully manicured lawns and park service glutted historic district around the Liberty Bell and Independence Hall. Although it may seem like a little sibling to NYC less than a two-hour drive away, Philadelphia is a more representative example of what east-coast city living is like.

HISTORY

There's probably no American city in which history seems so alive and visible. An estimated 2000 buildings from the 18th century still stand and countless 19th-century homes and commercial buildings survive.

Philadelphia was a planned city, born in 1682, the creation of idealistic English Quaker William Penn, who borrowed the name from antiquity; it's Greek and means 'brotherly love.' By the late 1760s Philadelphia was the largest city in North America, with about 25,000 residents, and it was the colonial center of the arts, science and medicine spearheaded by Benjamin Franklin, the city's most prominent citizen.

As tensions mounted with England over its taxation policies, Philadelphia leaders articulated American grievances and then

MID-ATLANTIC

PHILADELPHIA

INFORMATION
Drexel University...................1 A4
Giovanni's Room....................2 D6
Graduate Hospital.................3 C6
Independence Visitors Center.....4 E5
Ing Direct.............................5 C5
National Park Service
   Visitors Center...................6 F5
Pennsylvania Hospital............7 E6
Philadelphia Java Co..............8 E6
Philadelphia Main Post Office...9 A4
Post Office..........................10 F5
Robin's Bookstore.................11 D5
Thomas Cook......................12 C4

SIGHTS & ACTIVITIES (pp95-6)
African American Museum
   in Philadelphia..................13 E4
Arch St Meeting House..........14 F4

Boathouse Row....................15 A1
Carpenters' Hall...................16 F5
City Hall..............................17 D4
Congress Hall...................(see 22)
Eastern State Penitentiary......18 C2
Elfreth's Alley.......................19 F4
Franklin Institute Science Museum...20 C3
Free Library of Philadelphia....21 C3
Independence Hall...............22 F5
Liberty Bell Center...............23 E5
Library Hall.........................24 E5
Mantua Maker's Museum House...(see 19)
Mütter Museum....................25 B4
National Constitution Center...26 E4
National Museum of American
   Jewish History..................27 F5
Old City Hall.....................(see 22)
Pennsylvania Academy
   of the Fine Arts................28 D4

Philadelphia Museum of Art....29 B2
Philosophical Hall.............(see 22)
Rodin Museum.....................30 B3

SLEEPING (p97)
HI Bank St Hostel.................31 F5
Thomas Bond House B&B.......32 F5

EATING (pp97–8)
Bridget Foy's.......................33 F6
Famous 4th Street Deli..........34 E6
Jamaican Jerk Hut................35 C6
Patou.................................36 F5
Penang..............................37 E4
Pink Rose Pastry Shop..........38 E6
Reading Terminal Market........39 D4
Silk City Diner.....................40 F3
Smokey Joe's Tavern.............41 A5
Vietnam..............................42 D4

0   500 m
0   0.3 miles

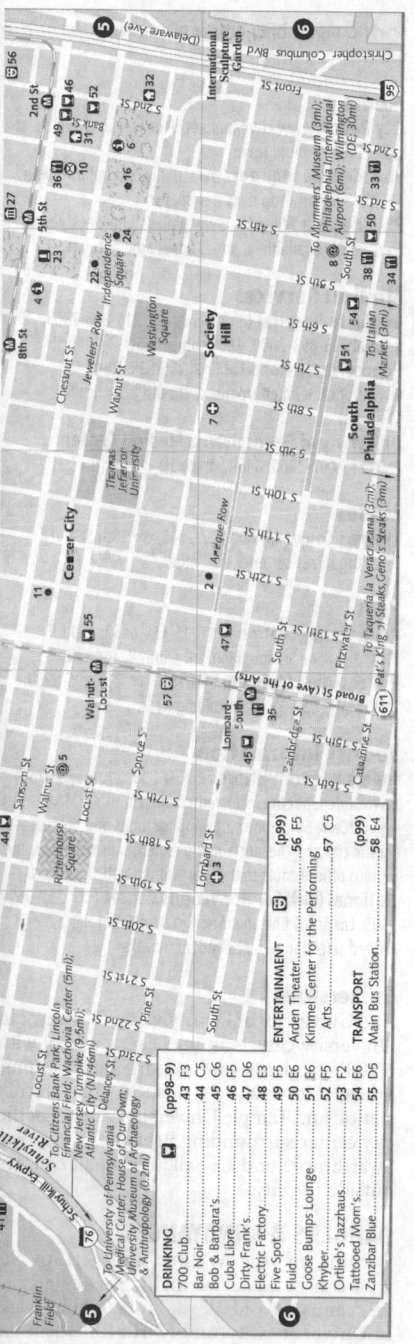

MID-ATLANTIC

when war broke, patriot leaders meeting in the Pennsylvania State House, later nicknamed 'Independence Hall,' would declare independence in 1776 and draw up a constitution for a new nation in 1787. And Philadelphia would become the capital of the new nation from 1790 to 1800 while Washington, DC, found itself under construction.

The years that followed the revolution were a glorious period for the city when it was both the American capital and state capital. Moving into the 19th century, Philadelphia quickly lost its pre-eminence in population, finance and shipping to New York City. Early in the 19th century Philadelphia became a national leader in the manufacture and use of steam engines, and the early textile industry. It emerged from the Civil War as America's leading industrial city and by the end of the century the city housed more than 7000 factories, mills and small workshops.

In the decades following WWII Philadelphia saw a mass exodus of industry. By the 1960s there were clear patterns of malaise. While Philadelphia's population continued to decline in the 1990s, the decade saw major development and renewed energy at the city's core. Many old neighborhoods were gentrified, residential neighborhoods close to downtown boomed and a new city skyline took shape as several gleaming skyscrapers sprouted.

ORIENTATION

Most sights are within walking distance of each other, or a short bus ride away. East-west streets are named; north–south streets are numbered, except for Broad and Front Sts and progress numerically starting from the Delaware River.

Historic Philadelphia includes Independence National Historic Park and Old City, which extends east to the waterfront. West of the historic district is Center City, home to Penn Sq and City Hall. The Delaware and Schuylkill (skoo-kill) Rivers border South Philadelphia, which features the colorful Italian Market, restaurants and bars. West of the Schuylkill, University City has two important campuses and a major museum. Northwest Philadelphia includes the genteel suburbs of Chestnut Hill and Germantown, plus the hip and growing Manayunk. The

---

GETTING INTO TOWN

The Septa R1 airport railway line ($5.50) and door-to-door shuttle-bus services ($8 to $10) run to the airport. A one-way cab fare from the airport to Center City costs about $20.

Buses stop at the **main bus station** (1001 Filbert St) in town while Amtrak and New Jersey Transit trains stop at 30th St Station, in University City from where it's a 15-minute walk into the city.

South St area, between S 2nd, 10th, Pine and Fitzwater Sts, has bohemian boutiques, bars, eateries and music venues.

INFORMATION
Bookstores

Giovanni's Room (☎ 215-923-2960; 345 S 12th St) Gay and lesbian books and periodicals.

House of Our Own (☎ 215-222-1576; 3920 Spruce St) Used books, small-press publications and frequent readings.

Robin's Bookstore (☎ 215-735-9600; 108 S 13th St) Philly's oldest independent bookstore.

Emergency

Philadelphia Suicide & Crisis Center (☎ 215-686-4420)

Rape crisis center (☎ 215-985-3333)

Traveler's Aid Society (☎ 215-523-7580; www.travelersaid.org; 1201 Chestnut St, 12th fl) A nonprofit agency that helps stranded travelers in distress.

Internet Access

Free Internet access can be sought at any branch of the Free Library of Philadelphia.

Free Library of Philadelphia (☎ 215-686-5322; 1901 Vine St; ☒ 9am-9pm Mon-Thu, 9am-6pm Fri, 9am-5pm Sat, 1-5pm Sun) The largest and grandest.

ING Direct (☎ 215-731-1410; 17th & Walnut Sts; ☒ 7am-7pm Mon-Fri) A bank and café with free access.

Philadelphia Java Co (☎ 215-928-1811; 518 S 4th St; per hr $2; ☒ 7am-10pm) In Society Hill. Bring your laptop and a few bucks for the Wi-Fi.

Internet Resources

www.centercityphila.org For information on all summer in the city events.

www.gophila.com For information about the Philadelphia area.

www.septa.org For information on the public transportation system.

www.campusphilly.org For student events and activities.

Media

City Paper (www.citypaper.net) Free weekly available at street boxes around town.

Philadelphia Inquirer (www.philly.com/mld/inquirer; 55¢) The region's top daily newspaper.

Philadelphia Weekly (www.philadelphiaweekly.com) Free weekly available at street boxes around town.

Medical Services

Graduate Hospital (emergency ☎ 215-893-2353, general 215-893-2000; 1800 Lombard St; ☒ 24hr)

Pennsylvania Hospital (☎ 215-829-3000; www.uphs.upenn.edu/pahosp; cnr 8th & Spruce Sts; ☒ 24hr)

University of Pennsylvania Medical Center (☎ 215-662-4000; 3400 Spruce St; ☒ 24hr)

Money

Thomas Cook (☎ 800-287-7362; cnr 18th St & JFK Blvd) Organizes currency exchange.

Post

Penn Center Station (☎ 215-568-6452; 1500 JFK Blvd; ☒ 8am-5:30pm Mon-Fri) Centrally located.

Philadelphia Main Post Office (☎ 215-895-8980; 2970 Market St; ☒ 6am-midnight)

Tourist Information

Independence Visitors Center (☎ 800-537-7676; www.independencevisitorcenter.com; cnr 6th & Market Sts; ☒ 8:30am-5pm) One stop shop for maps and brochures for the city and the surrounding region; sells tickets for the various official tours that depart from nearby locations.

National Park Service Visitors Center (☎ 215-965-2305; cnr 3rd & Chestnut Sts; ☒ 9am-5pm) Has a more limited selection of maps and information.

Universities

The University of Pennsylvania (U Penn), in University City, is an Ivy League school with 30,000 students and a gorgeous campus. Drexel University is close to the Amtrak station and Temple University is north of the city center surrounding Broad St. Villanova, Swarthmore and La Salle are small colleges outside the city.

DANGERS & ANNOYANCES

Downtown, the Walnut and S 13th Sts area can be sleazy at night, particularly at weekends. Avoid West Philadelphia, west of University City, and North Philadelphia

Also avoid the subway at night, unless you're with a few thousand fans attending a sports event in South Philly.

SIGHTS

While most of Philly's better-known historic sites – the Liberty Bell, Carpenters' Hall etc – are concentrated in the Independence National Historic Park, there's something to see in plenty of other neighborhoods, too. Old City is rich with history, Center City is bursting with arts and culture, South Philadelphia is home to the Italian Market, and University City feels like an entirely different town in itself.

Independence National Historic Park

Dubbed 'America's most historic square mile,' this L-shaped 45-acre park recently added the **National Constitution Center** (☎ 866 917-1787; www.constitutioncenter.org; admission $6; ☾ 9:30am-5pm). Who knew civil, legal and political rights could be so fun? History teachers take note: pressing and touching things makes learning more digestible. Determine whether you could have voted in 1860 or listen to debates concerning state's rights and monetary policy. Seriously, it's a good time.

Carpenters' Hall (☾ Tue-Sun), the USA's oldest trade guild (1724), was the site of the First Continental Congress in 1774. **Library Hall** is where you'll find a copy of the Declaration of Independence, handwritten in a letter by Thomas Jefferson.

To get inside **Independence Hall** (☾ 9am-5pm), the 'birthplace of American government,' where delegates from the 13 colonies met to approve the Declaration of Independence on July 4, 1776, you must join one of the frequent tours. Cool thing is, they're free. **Congress Hall** (cnr S 6th & Chestnut Sts; ☾ 9am-5pm),

meanwhile, was the meeting place for the US Congress when Philly was the nation's capital. **Old City Hall** (☾ 11am-5pm), finished in 1791, was home to the US Supreme Court until 1800. **Philosophical Hall** (☎ 215-440-3400; ☾ 10am-5pm Wed-Sun Mar–Labor Day, 10am-4pm Thu-Sun Labor Day–Mar), just south of Old City Hall, is HQ of the American Philosophical Society, founded in 1743 by Benjamin Franklin.

Made in London and tolled at the first public reading of the Declaration of Independence, the iconic Liberty Bell recently moved into its own museum at the **Liberty Bell Center** (cnr 6th & Chestnut; admission free; ☾ 9am-5pm). Film clips help explain how the bell, unusable since 1846, came into celebrity.

Old City & Society Hill

Along with Society Hill, Old City – the area bounded by Walnut, Vine, Front and 6th Sts – was early Philadelphia. The 1970s saw revitalization, with many warehouses converted into apartments, galleries and small businesses. **Elfreth's Alley** is believed to be the oldest continuously occupied street in the USA.

The **National Museum of American Jewish History** (☎ 215-923-3811; www.nmajh.org; 55 N 5th St; adult/student $4/3; ☾ 10am-5pm Mon-Thu, 10am-3pm Fri, noon-5pm Sun) features exhibits that examine the historical role of Jews in the USA. **Arch St Meeting House** (320 Arch St; admission by donation; ☾ Mon-Sat) is the country's largest Quaker meeting house, and the **African American Museum in Philadelphia** (☎ 215-574-0380; www.aampmuseum.org; 701 Arch St; adult/student $6/4; ☾ 10am-5pm Tue-Sat, noon-5pm Sun) contains some excellent collections about black history and culture.

Residential **Society Hill** to the south is a lovely place to aimlessly stroll and take in 18th and 19th century architecture.

FREAKY PHILLY

For a change from the regular museum runs, try the following two off-the-wall options.

Skip med school and visit the seriously twisted **Mütter Museum** (☎ 215-563-3737; www.collphyphil.org; 19 S 22nd St, btwn Market & Chestnut Sts; adult/student $9/6; ☾ 10am-5pm) to learn all about the history of medicine in the US. If the giant and dwarf skeletons and Grover Cleveland's jaw tumor don't turn you off you might be doctor material.

A visit to the old **Eastern State Penitentiary** (☎ 215-236-3300; www.easternstate.org; cnr 22nd St & Fairmount Ave; admission $9; ☾ 10am-5pm Wed-Sun), a few blocks from the Museum of Art, will scare the most wayward of people straight. The penitentiary opened in 1829 and features Al Capone's cell and death row. It turns into a top-notch haunted house all October for Halloween.

South Philadelphia

A Mardi Gras–like celebration of food, the **Italian Market** (🕑 Tue-Sat; 9th St below Christian St) is a highlight of South Philadelphia. It's the country's largest outdoor market, hawking fresh produce and cheeses and homemade pastas, fish and butchered meats.

In the midst of it all is the **Mummers Museum** (☎ 215-336-3050; 1100 S 2nd St; admission $3.50; 🕑 9:30am-4:30pm Tue-Sat, noon-4:30pm Sun), celebrating the tradition of disguise and masquerade. It has an integral role in the famed Mummers Parade, taking place here every New Year's Day. Catch live music on Tuesday nights in summer.

Center City & Around

Trees and statues decorate **Rittenhouse Sq**, a genteel and popular spot for an afternoon break. Ornate and impressive, **City Hall** (☎ 215-686-1776; cnr Broad & Market Sts; admission by donation; 🕑 12:30-2pm) stands tall in Penn Sq, topped by a bronze statue of William Penn. **Pennsylvania Academy of the Fine Arts** (☎ 215-972-7600; www.pafa.org; 118 N Broad St; admission $5) has a museum with works by American painters.

Benjamin Franklin Parkway

Modeled after the Champs Elysées in Paris, the parkway is a center of museums and other landmarks. It's easy to get lost in the **Philadelphia Museum of Art** (☎ 215-763-8100; www.philamuseum.org; 26th St; admission $10, pay what you wish Sun; 🕑 10am-5pm Tue, Thu, Sat & Sun, 10am-8:45pm Wed & Fri), one of the nation's largest and most important. Run up the grand stairway like Sylvester Stallone in the 1976 flick *Rocky*. **Franklin Institute Science Museum** (☎ 215-448-1200; 20th St; admission $13; 🕑 9:30am-5pm) is where hands-on science displays were pioneered. You'll find some of the French sculptor's works at the **Rodin Museum** (☎ 215-763-8100; www.rodinmuseum.org; 22nd St; suggested donation $3; 🕑 10am-5pm Tue-Sun).

University City

An Ivy League School, **University of Pennsylvania**, commonly called 'U Penn,' was founded in 1740. The campus makes a pleasant afternoon stroll. Drexel University is nearby. While you're here, don't miss the romantic, neoclassical **30th St Station**, beautifully lit at night. **University Museum of Archaeology & Anthropology** (☎ 215-898-4000; cnr 33rd & Spruce Sts; admission $5; 🕑 10am-4:30pm Tue-Sat, 1-5pm Sun) contains ancient archaeological treasures.

Fairmount Park

Divided into east and west by the **Schuylkill River**, huge Fairmount Park is the largest landscaped city park in the world, 10 times the size of Central Park in New York City. On the east bank, **Boathouse Row** has Victorian-era rowing clubs. **Philadelphia Zoo** (☎ 215-243-1100; www.phillyzoo.com; 3400 W Girard Ave; admission $11; 🕑 9:30am-5pm), the country's oldest zoo, has been modernized with naturalistic habitats.

Though the aesthetic and educational ideas of its founder have provoked controversy, the **Barnes Foundation Gallery** (☎ 610-667-0290; www.barnesfoundation.org; 300 N Latches Lane; admission $5; 🕑 9:30am-5pm Fri-Sun) has a world-class art collection. Reservations are required.

ACTIVITIES

The best spots for cycling and rollerblading include Fairmount Park and the towpaths that run alongside the neighborhood of Manayunk. For advice and group rides, contact the **Bicycle Club of Philadelphia** (☎ 215-843-1093; www.phillybikeclub.org). Runners should also head to the park, which has tree-lined trails that range from 2 to 10 miles in length.

TOURS

Philadelphia Trolley Works (☎ 215-925-8687; tours $20) Hop on and off at designated stops on this 1½-hour narrated trolley trip. Tours start by the Liberty Bell.

Phlash Bus (☎ 215-474-5274; www.phillyphlash.com; all-day pass $4) A one-hour, affordable do-it-yourself tour (no tour guide, although you do have a map) that takes you to about 25 sites in a bright purple van. It runs from 10am to 6pm May through November.

Ghost Tour (☎ 215-413-1997; www.ghosttour.com; tours $15) Who knew history could be so frightening? This is a candlelight walking tour through Independence Park and Society Hill every night from April to November. It starts at 5th and Chestnut Sts at 7:30pm.

FESTIVALS & EVENTS

Mummers Parade January 1. A very Philly parade, an elaborate celebration of costumes.

South St Mardi Gras for Fat Tuesday Mid-February. Music and booze in the streets.

Annual Jam on the River Memorial Day weekend. Excellent music lineup, from folkies to jam bands.

9th Street Italian Market Festival First weekend in June. Two-day food and music party.

SLEEPING

Downtown is expensive. There are a bunch of cheap motels near the airport at Exit 9A on I-95 but it's far from the center.

Bank Street Hostel (☎ 215-922-0222, 800-392-4678; www.bankstreethostel.com; 32 S Bank St; dm $18-21; ☒ ▣) The location can't be beat although accommodation is basic dormitory style. Just blocks from major sights and nightlife, however the 1am weekend curfew could cramp your style. It accepts cash only.

Chamounix Mansion International Youth Hostel (☎ 215-878-3676, 800-379-0017; www.philahostel.org; 3250 Chamounix Dr; dm $15; ☒) Further out but slightly nicer this converted mansion is in West Fairmount Park. Check in is from 8am to 11am and 4:30pm to midnight and there's a midnight curfew. There are free bikes for use.

Timberlane Campground (☎ 856-43-6677; www.timberlanecampground.com; 117 Timberlane Rd; campsites $24) A 15-minute drive across the Delaware River in Clarksboro, NJ, this is the closest campsite to Philadelphia. Reservations are recommended.

SPLURGE!

Thomas Bond House B&B (☎ 215-923-8523; www.winston-salem-inn.com/philadelphia; 129 S 2nd St; r $95-115, ste $145-175; Septa 2nd St Station, bus No 9, 12, 21, 42, 57) You'll feel like a Founding Father at this B&B owned by the National Park Service and part of Independence National Historical Park. The building dates from 1769, with later additions made in 1824, 1840 and a more recent renovation in our century. The rooms may be small, but they are laden with history as the framed documents mounted throughout the house attest to. Breakfast is light on weekdays and substantial on weekends.

EATING

Shiny trucks serve cheap eats like falafels and burgers to the city's office workers at several spots in town. Try near 20th and Market Sts, and especially around Penn Sq where they line up around 36th and Spruce Sts, 34th and Spruce Sts, and 36th and Walnut Sts.

Chinatown & South Street Area

Penang (☎ 215-413-2531; 117 N 10th St; mains $5-16) This place attracts the late-night throngs

---

PHILLY CHEESESTEAKS

Just like the legend of the North American yeti and the Marlboro man, the origin of the Philly cheesesteak is shrouded in mystery. Not. Eureka! Behold the cheesesteak, invented here at **Pat's King of Steaks** (☎ 215-468-1546; 9th & Passyunk Ave; cheesesteaks $5-6, cash only; ☒ 24hr). But more impressive than the giant crowds who show up after bars close are the smaller numbers having a steak for breakfast at 9am. Forever thumbing its nose at Pat's is **Geno's Steaks** (☎ 215-389-0659; 1219 S 9th St; cheesesteaks $5-6, cash only; ☒ 24hr) whose bright and colorful signage can be seen for miles but more importantly by its rival across the street.

---

lured by sizeable portions and cheap prices (most items cost less than $8). Try the mango shrimp or ginger duck.

Vietnam (☎ 215-592-1163; 221 N 11th St; mains $9-11) The low prices seem out of place in such a relatively elegant dining room. The crispy spring rolls and catfish stand out.

Pink Rose Pastry Shop (☎ 215-592-0565; 630 S 4th St; cakes $5-6, pies $5) A cute place to go with a cute name. Pink outside, flowers and doilys inside set the mood for elaborate cakes, tarts and other pastries. There's also a simple breakfast and lunch menu.

Famous 4th St Deli (☎ 215-922-3274; 700 S 4th St; mains $6-10) Family owned and run place usually referred to as 'the Famous'; the Reuben is special.

Taqueria la Veracruzana (☎ 215-465-1440; 908 Washington St; burritos $5, mains $8-10) With Taqueria's juicy burritos, South Philly's emerging Mexican population stakes a claim to the city's food landscape around the corner from the bustling Italian market.

Center City & Around

Reading Terminal Market (☎ 215-922-2317; www.readingterminalmarket.org; cnr 12th & Arch Sts; mains $2-8; ☒ 8am-6pm Mon-Sat) Even the most demanding of foodies on a budget can find happiness here. Choose from fresh Amish cheeses and Thai desserts, to falafel, cheesesteaks, salad bars, sushi, Peking duck and great Mexican.

Silk City Diner (☎ 215-592-8838; 425 Spring Garden St at N 5th St; mains $6-11) A 1940s classic, open 24 hours with entertainment some nights.

SPLURGE!

Patou (☎ 215-928-2987; 312 Market St; brunch $10, dinner mains $18-29) Colonial America couldn't feel further away at this newcomer on the dining scene. It's stylish and designed almost all in blue and white. Try the *pan grillé Francais*, banana-stuffed *brioche*, French toast with vanilla *créme fraiche* and chocolate.

Stephen Starr restaurants dominate the trendy Philly dining scene. You won't be disappointed at the following: **Buddakhan** (☎ 215-574-9440; 325 Chestnut St), **Tangerine** (☎ 215-627-5116; 232 Market St), **Morimoto** (☎ 215-413-9070; 723 Chestnut St), **Angelina** (☎ 215-925-6889; 706 Chestnut St) or **El Vez** (☎ 215-928-9800; 121 S 13th St).

Jamaican Jerk Hut (☎ 545-8644; 1436 South St; mains $7) Come for the delicious home-style Caribbean food, stay for the Bob Marley themed backyard veranda. Grab a plate of jerk chicken and plantain stew and listen to the live music on weekend nights.

Bridget Foy's (☎ 215-922-1813; 200 South St; lunch mains $7-12) Neighborhood standby dishing up unpretentious fare like meat loaf and crab cakes. The chichimanga is a good deal, still only $9 for dinner.

University City

White Dog Café (☎ 215-386-9224; 3420 Sansom St; lunch & brunch mains $8-12, dinner mains $16-25) Looking like a B&B minus the bedrooms, the White Dog's menu changes seasonally, but is always heavy on the organic. It's popular for Sunday brunch.

Smokey Joe's Tavern (☎ 215-222-0770; 208 S 40th St; burgers $6) Locals and UPenn students rub elbows here, between Locust and Walnut Sts. On offer is typical pub fare, heavy on the frying.

Lee's Hoagie House (☎ 215-387-0905; 4034 Walnut St; hoagies $5) A candidate in the competition everyone has an opinion about – best cheesesteak. Lee's does tasty shakes and chicken fingers too.

DRINKING
Bars

Most bars stay open until 2am. Check the free Thursday *City Paper* and the Wednesday *Philadelphia Weekly* for city events. A diverse crowd frequents the pubs around South St and those around 2nd St near Chestnut St, close to the Bank St Hostel, on weekends. Newly hot Columbus Blvd (Delaware Ave) has lots of nightclubs and restaurants popular with students. Gay and lesbian weekly *Au Courant* (free) lists events for Philadelphia and the surrounding area. Most clubs that attract gay clientele are around Camac, South 12th and South 13th St. Manyunk, a short train ride from the center is another spot for a pub crawl.

Bar Noir (☎ 215-569-9333; 112 S 18th St) Early evenings at this Philly institution since the punk '70s are tame but by the time midnight rolls around, elbow room is hard to come by.

Dirty Frank's (☎ 215-732-5010; 347 S 13th St) Forget your creative failures at this dive bar patronized by art students.

Bob & Barbara's (☎ 215-545-4511; 1509 South St) Sexual orientation is anyone's guess at the Thursday night drag shows. An old-school jazz band plays other nights and Tuesday is ping pong night. Pabst Blue Ribbon is the drink of choice.

Tattooed Mom's (☎ 215-238-9880; 530 South St) Guys with metal disks in their ears and white girls with dreadlocks and tattoos hang out upstairs. Graffiti covers the walls and the jukebox is loud.

700 Club (☎ 215-386-3408; 700 N 2nd St) A place that helped to establish Northern Liberties as a hip destination. Trendy music plays in the bar downstairs and DJs spin in the small upstairs lounge every night but Sunday.

Goose Bumps Lounge (☎ 215-923-4481; 611 S 7th St) This place serves $2 drinks everyday from 5pm to 8pm – enough said. DJs spin jazz to house to trip hop.

New Deck Tavern (☎ 215-386-4600; 3408 Sansom St) In University City, students enjoy a choice of 18 draft beers.

Live Music

Zanzibar Blue (☎ 215-732-4500; www.zanzibarblue.com; 200 S Broad St; admission $5-30) Big stars call classy and elegant Zanzibar Blue home. National acts usually play on weekends but there's jazz seven nights a week.

Ortlieb's Jazzhaus (☎ 215-922-1035; 847 N 3rd St; occasional admission $5; ☾ shows 8pm-midnight) Once a ramshackle brewery lunchroom, Ortlieb's has kept the stuffed buffalo head and added a stellar jazz line up.

Khyber (☎ 215-238-5888; www.thekhyber.com; 56 S 2nd St; admission $5-15) Trendy Old City stops at the door to this down-and-dirty old Rock bar. Live music nightly. The Strokes made it big while they were the Khyber's resident band.

Five Spot (☎ 215-574-0070; 5 S Bank St; admission $5-10) Across from the Bank St Hostel, the Five Spot has two floors and sometimes two simultaneous acts. Tuesday nights feature female DJs and hip-hop artists.

Fluid (☎ 215-629-0565; 613 S 4th St; admission $5-10) Young crowds like to bust it end up at this smallish hot spot, but not until after midnight. DJs play hip-hop, house and techno. The entrance is an unmarked blue door on Kater St.

Cuba Libre (☎ 215-627-0666; 10 S 2nd St) The only prop missing at Cuba Libre is Castro, but the commandante would probably find the scene too decadent. Have a few mojitos and salsa like you're in Havana.

Electric Factory (☎ 215-336-2000; 421 N 7th St; tickets $15-40; ☉ box office noon-6pm Mon-Sat) Big acts come to this Clear Channel venue.

ENTERTAINMENT

The premier cultural destination is Broad St south of City Hall, called the 'Ave of the Arts.' For most entertainment, buy tickets from **Ticketmaster** (☎ 215-336-2000) or **Upstages** (☎ 215-569-9700), which offers half-price, same-day tickets. Wander through the 40-plus art galleries, most between Front and Third and Market and Vine Sts, on the first Friday of every month. There's a great vibe. Doors open from 5pm to 9pm.

Arden Theater (☎ 215-922-1122; www.ardentheat er.org; 40 N 2nd St; tickets $24-40) One of the best theater experiences in all of Philadelphia. Revivals mix with ambitious contemporary productions.

Philadelphia is a hardcore sporting town, the kind where face painting is a common fashion response to playoff success. All the major sporting venues are in South Philadelphia – take the Septa train to Pattison Station and then bus No 17. The Major League baseball **Philadelphia Phillies** play at Citizen's Bank Park; the **Philadelphia Eagles** play at Lincoln Financial Field; the NBA's (basketball) **76ers** and NHL's (hockey) **Flyers** share the Wachovia Center at 3601 S Broad St. Call **Ticketmaster** (☎ 215-336-2000; www.ticketmaster.com; tickets $15-85).

Annenberg Center for the Performing Arts (☎ 215-898-3900; www.pennpresents.org; 3680 Walnut St; adult $10-50, discounts available for students) Depending on the schedule, you might catch a Senegalese percussion orchestra or 1970s rocker Patti Smith giving a lecture. You can catch most shows, which run from September through May.

Mann Center for the Performing Arts (☎ 215-893-1999; www.manncenter.org; 5201 Parkside Ave; tickets $10-130) In addition to being the summer home of the Philadelphia Orchestra, the Mann's summer season presents a little bit of everything, from flamenco to the Mormon Tabernacle Choir, from Weird Al Yankovic to Shakespeare.

Kimmel Center for the Performing Arts (☎ 215-893-1999; www.kimmelcenter.org; 260 S Broad St) Home of eight performing arts organizations including the Philadelphia orchestra. The roof garden has great views of the city skyline.

GETTING THERE & AWAY

Philadelphia International Airport (☎ 800-745-4283, 215-937 6937; www.phl.org), 8 miles southwest of Center City on I-76, has direct flights to/from Europe, the Caribbean, Canada and more than 100 US cities.

Bus travel to NYC is reasonable. **Today Travel** (☎ 212-964-6334; www.todaybus.com) and **New Century Travel** (☎ 215-627-2666; www.2000coach .com) offer $20 roundtrip tickets between Philadelphia and NYC's Chinatown. More expensive **Greyhound** (☎ 800-231-2222, 215-931-4014; 1001 Filbert St), **New Jersey Transit** (☎ 800-772-3606, 215-569-3752) and **Capitol Trailways** (☎ 800-444-2877) buses stop at the **main bus station** (1001 Filbert St). Daily buses run to New York ($21, two hours); Atlantic City ($6.60, 1½ hours); and Washington, DC ($19, 3½ hours). Buses also make less-frequent trips to Lancaster and several stops along the Jersey Shore.

Amtrak (☎ 800-872-7245) trains stop at 30th St Station, in University City. Philadelphia is on Amtrak's Northeast Corridor route between Richmond, Virginia and Boston, Massachusetts. There are also trains west to Lancaster, Pittsburgh and Chicago, and south to Florida. One-way fares include New York (from $50, 1½ hours); Washington, DC ($50, two hours); and Pittsburgh ($40, eight hours). **New Jersey Transit** (☎ 800-228-8246) has a frequent rail service to Atlantic City ($6.60, 1½ hours). To get to and from NYC it's much cheaper to take a Septa train from 30th St station to Trenton, where you can transfer to a New Jersey Transit commuter train to NYC's Penn Station ($17, 2¼ hours).

GETTING AROUND

Septa (☎ 215-580-7800; www.septa.org) operates the subways and buses. Its three subway routes are the Market–Frankford, Broad St and Subway–Surface along Market St (one way $3 to $6; 50¢ to 75¢ less off-peak). Most Septa bus trips cost $2 (plus 60¢ for a transfer); a DayPass ($5.50) and weekly pass ($19) allow unlimited rides on city transit vehicles. Shuttle buses that stop at most major stops take up the slack around midnight when the subway shuts down.

For taxis call **Quaker City Cab** (☎ 215-728-8000) or **Olde City Taxi** (☎ 215-338-0838).

EASTERN PENNSYLVANIA

PENNSYLVANIA DUTCH COUNTRY

Between Blue Ball and Intercourse lies Amish (ah-mish) country. Anabaptist sects, persecuted in their native Switzerland, settled here in the southeast region of Pennsylvania, in an area about 20 by 15 miles, east of Lancaster starting in the early 1700s. Speaking German dialects, they became known as 'Dutch' (from 'Deutsch'). Most Pennsylvania Dutch live on farms, and their beliefs vary from sect to sect. Many do not use electricity, and most opt for horse-drawn buggies – which may seem less than charming when trying to pass in your car.

However, don't be disappointed if you see teenagers shopping for stereos at Best Buy. Even with a set of written and unwritten laws called the Ordnung that governs everyday life, it's impossible to keep modernity and consumerism at bay and luring youths away. Don't expect lots of interaction with the people who, while obviously not museum exhibits, have opened windows into their culture with tourism revenue in mind.

To escape the crowds and learn about the region, rent a bike, pack some food and explore the numerous back roads. You may also consider hiring a guide for a private tour, or simply visiting in winter, when tourism is down. Craft shops sell quilts, wooden furniture and faceless dolls. Farmers' markets are very popular for pies, preserves, fresh fruit and vegetables.

Lancaster & Around

The pleasant town of Lancaster 70 miles from Philadelphia was briefly the US capital in September 1777, when Congress stopped here overnight.

INFORMATION

Chamber of Commerce (☎ 717-397-3531; 100 Queen St; 🕙 8am-5pm Mon-Fri) In downtown Lancaster, provides information.
Visitors center (☎ 717-299-8901; www.padutch country.com; 🕙 9am-5pm) Off Rte 30 in Lancaster.

SIGHTS & ACTIVITIES

The touristy **Central Market** (Penn Sq; 🕙 6am-4:30pm Tue & Fri, 6am-2pm Sat) offers good food and crafts.

The very friendly **People's Place** (☎ 800-390-8436; Rte 340; admission $5; 🕙 10am-5pm Mon-Sat) in Intercourse gives a sensitive overview of Amish and Mennonite life with a *Who Are the Amish?* documentary.

Bird-in-Hand has craft stores, restaurants and a farmers market. **Abe's Buggy Rides** (☎ 717-392-1794; admission $10) does a 2-mile tour. **Amish Farm & House** (☎ 717-394-6185; www .amishfarmandhouse.com; admission $7) is an original farmhouse with a tour describing Amish culture.

In Lititz, visitors come for the **Sturgis Pretzel House** (☎ 717-626-4354; www.sturgispretzel .com; Rte 772; admission $2; 🕙 9am-5pm Mon-Sat), the USA's first pretzel factory. The nearby **Ephrata Cloister** (☎ 717-733-6600; 632 W Main St; admission $7; 🕙 9am-5pm Mon-Sat, 9am-noon Sun), a collection of medieval-style buildings, is where the Pietists lived and worked under rigorous conditions.

TOURS

Amish Country Tours (☎ 717-768-3600) Runs 2½-hour bus tours that take back roads and visit farms (from $20).
Lancaster County Bicycle Tours (☎ 717-768-8366) Rents bikes and leads intimate tours that visit an Amish home and grocery store ($50 per half day).

SLEEPING

There are a slew of inns in Amish country, and you will find cheap motels along the southeast portion of Rte 462/Rte 30.

Red Caboose Motel (☎ 717-687-5000; www.red caboosemotel.com; r $79; 🕸) Take a well-earned sleep in a restored caboose at this aptly named place in Strasbourg.

Beacon Hill Camping (☎ 717-768-8875; www .beaconhillcamping.com; Rte 772; campsites/cabins $24/50) In Intercourse, this place has a range of family-friendly sites.

EATING & DRINKING

To sample one of the famous family-style restaurants and lots and lots of bland food, be prepared to rub elbows with packs of fellow tourists. The experience is part of coming to Amish country though.

Miller's Smorgasbord (☎ 717-687-6621; 2811 Lincoln Hwy E; mains $23) Between Intercourse and Bird-In-Hand, this is definitely a stand-out option.

Bird in Hand Family Restaurant (☎ 717-768-8266; breakfast/lunch/dinner buffet $6/8.50/11) Gorge on all-you-can eat buffets at Bird in Hand.

Chimney Corner Restaurant (☎ 717-626-4/07; Rte 772; mains $10) Locals get their Pennsylvania Dutch grub at this family-owned restaurant in Lititz.

Bube's Brewery (☎ 717-653-2056; 102 N Market St) There's a *biergarten* at this Mount Joy drinking place.

GETTING THERE & AROUND

The **Capitol Trailways & Greyhound terminal**, at the train station, has buses to Philadelphia ($15, two hours) and Pittsburgh ($38, five hours). **Amtrak** has trains to and from Philadelphia ($13, 1¼ hours) and Pittsburgh ($85, six hours).

RRTA (☎ 717-397-4246) local buses link the main towns.

GETTYSBURG

At the site of one of the bloodiest battles of the Civil War, and where Lincoln delivered the Gettysburg Address, tranquility now reigns at this small, history-laden town, 145 miles west of Philadelphia. The **Gettysburg Convention & Visitors Bureau** (☎ 717-334-6274; www.gettysburg.com; 35 Carlisle St; 🕙 8:30am-5:30pm) has a comprehensive list of attractions.

The 8-sq-mile National Military Park encompasses most of the area of the three-day battle. South of the visitors center, **Cemetery Ridge** is the site of Pickett's Charge, where the Confederates suffered 80% casualties. In the evening, you can mingle with the battle spirits on the eerie **Ghosts of Gettysburg Candlelight Walking Tours** (☎ 717-337-0445; admission $6.50).

The annual **Civil War Heritage Days** (☎ 717-334-6274) festival, taking place from the last weekend of June through the first weekend of July, features living history encampments, battle re-enactments, a lecture series and book fair.

WESTERN PENNSYLVANIA

In a state so large it's to be expected that geography in part determines identity. The further west you go the closer you are to the rest of America. While Philadelphia and its environs are firmly ensconced culturally in the east coast, residents of Pittsburgh and western PA are proud to identity themselves as part of the city or immediate region, relishing their proximity to the 'heartland.' As the terrain becomes more rugged, the people more blue collar, and the towns less familiar, you begin to appreciate the sheer size and diversity of this one state.

PITTSBURGH

To most Americans, Pittsburgh conjures stark images of steel and coal factories. But today's city, still somewhat of a secret even to East Coasters, is absolutely teeming with culture and beauty. University of Pittsburgh, Carnegie Mellon University and Duquesne University are all large presences in town, with sprawling campuses and bustling academic crowds.

The city's location at a major river junction made it a colonial-era trading center; iron

---

PITTSBURGH-ISMS

Here are a few to help you understand the locals:

- *up'ere* (up there).
- *Stillers* (Steelers football team).
- *youns* (you all).
- *and'nat* (and that, meaningless gibberish that Pittsburghers tend to add to the end of every sentence).

and steel industries boomed until the 1960s and 1970s, when competition from newer, more efficient steelworks overseas devastated heavy industries and closed factories. These days, a scrappy, blue-collar element remains, as do distinct, closely knit neighborhoods, a growing white-collar workforce and marked ethnic diversity. Air quality and civic amenity have improved greatly from the closure of many old industrial plants, with much of the city now clean and green.

Orientation

The city, spread among a series of rivers and connected by seven bridges (all with footpaths), is not easily traversed on foot unless you're exploring one neighborhood at a time. The mystical-sounding Golden Triangle, between the converging Monongahela and Allegheny Rivers, is Pittsburgh's downtown, now comprehensively (if a bit soullessly) renovated. Just northeast of here, the Strip offers warehouses, ethnic food stores, cheap restaurants and clubs on Penn and Smallman Aves. Across the Allegheny, the North Side has the big new sports stadiums, several museums and appealing neighborhoods around Allegheny Sq.

Across the Monongahela River, the South Side slopes up to Mt Washington; incline railways allow access to the views from the top. E Carson St has numerous clubs, galleries and restaurants and is one of the most happening areas. East of downtown is Oakland, the university area. Squirrel Hill, a Jewish neighborhood with upscale boutiques, some great restaurants and a small-town feel, is further east.

Information

Carnegie Library of Pittsburgh (☎ 412-622-3114; 4400 Forbes Ave) Access the Internet for free.

Pittsburgh Convention & Visitors Bureau (☎ 412-281-7711, 800-366-0093; www.visitpittsburgh .com; Liberty Ave; ☺ 9am-5pm Mon-Fri, 9am-3pm Sat & Sun) Publishes the *Official Visitors Guide* and provides maps and tourist advice.

Pittsburgh Council for International Visitors (☎ 412-624-7800; www.pciv.org; 315 S Bellefield Ave)

University of Pittsburgh Book Center (4000 Fifth Ave) Good bookstore.

Sights

Points of interest in Pittsburgh are scattered everywhere, and its spread-out nature makes it a difficult place to cover thoroughly on foot. Stick to public buses, which are quite reliable, and you'll get to see it all, from the historic buildings of the Golden Triangle and the intellectual pockets of Oakland to the kosher delis of Squirrel Hill and the quirky mix of museums and sports on Pittsburgh's North Side.

GOLDEN TRIANGLE

Although it's been renovated into a modern, generic landscape, downtown – parts of which feel quite abandoned after weekday business hours – still has a few fine older buildings, such as Kaufmann's department store. At the triangle's tip is **Point State Park**, which is popular during summer with strollers, runners and loungers. The nicely remodeled brick warehouse that is the **Senator John Heinz Pittsburgh Regional History Center** (☎ 412-454-6000; www.pghhistory.org; 1212 Smallman Ave; admission $6; ☺ 10am-5pm) offers a good take on the region's past.

NORTH SIDE

Development of the area is in high gear. There are lots of new office buildings and restaurants – all part of the renaissance the city and state are banking on. While it feels most populated when its **PNC Park** is filled with sports fans, the area is also a big draw for museum buffs. **Andy Warhol Museum** (☎ 412-237-8300; www.warhol.org; 117 Sandusky St; admission $8; ☺ 10am-5pm Tue-Thu, Sat & Sun, 10am-10pm Fri), just over the 7th St Bridge, exhibits the work of the Pittsburgh native famous for his pop art and avant-garde movies.

Modern-art enthusiasts should also check out the **Mattress Factory** (☎ 412-231-3169; www.mattress.org; 500 Sampsonia Way; admission $8, free Thu; ☺ 10am-5pm Tue-Fri, 10am-7pm Sat, 1-5pm Sun), featuring edgy installations.

Carnegie Science Center (☎ 412-237-3400; www .carnegiesciencecenter.org; 1 Allegheny Ave; admission $14; ☺ 10am-5pm Sun-Thu, 10am-7pm Fri & Sat) is a cut above the average hands-on science museum. Across the street is **Sportsworks** (☎ 412-237-3400; 333 Allegheny Ave; admission $14; ☺ 10am-5pm) an amusement park for sports junkies. Race against a life-sized video screen image of Olympic sprinter Jackie Joyner-Kersee or pilot a motion-simulated bobsled.

You can see more than 500 exotic and endangered bird species at the **National Aviary**

(☎ 412-321-4364; www.aviary.org; W Commons, Allegheny Sq; admission $5; ☺ 9am-5pm), many flying freely in high-ceilinged aviaries that you can walk through.

SOUTH SIDE & MT WASHINGTON

Monongahela Incline (☎ 412-442-2000; roundtrip $3.50; ☺ 5:30-12:45am) and **Duquesne Incline** (☎ 412-381-1665; roundtrip $3.50; ☺ 5:30-12:45am) are the funicular railroads that run up and down Mt Washington's steep slopes. (Duquesne is pronounced doo-*kane*.) They're what remains of last century's 15 incline railroads, which served to open the South Side – featuring the bustling nighttime strip of E Carson St – to suburban development.

OAKLAND AREA

The University of Pittsburgh and Carnegie Mellon University are here, surrounded by streets that are packed with cheap eateries, cafés, shops and student-packed multifamily homes.

Carnegie Museum of Art (☎ 412-622-3131; www .cmoa.org; 4400 Forbes Ave; admission $8; ☺ 10am-5pm Tue-Sat, noon-5pm Sun) has a terrific collection of impressionist, post-impressionist and modern American paintings, plus a very fine architecture exhibit.

A useful landmark is the **Cathedral of Learning** (☎ 412 624 6000; 157 Cathedral of Learning; admission free, tours $3; ☺ 9am-2:30pm Mon-Sat, 11:30am-2:30pm Sun), a rather grand 42-story Gothic tower at the University of Pittsburgh campus.

Frick Art & Historical Center (☎ 412-371-0600; www.frickart.org; 7227 Reynolds St; admission $10; ☺ 10am-5pm Tue-Sat, noon-6pm Sun), located in Point Breeze, east of Oakland, displays some of Frick's Flemish, French and Italian paintings. The **Car & Carriage Museum** includes assorted Frickmobiles such as a 1914 Rolls Royce, but the highlight is **Clayton**, the restored 1872 mansion of industrialist Henry Clay Frick.

SQUIRREL HILL & SHADYSIDE

These upscale neighborhoods feature wide streets and huge, beautiful homes, truly excellent restaurants and eclectic shops. Squirrel Hill, home to Pittsburgh's large Jewish population, contains the city's best kosher eateries, butchers and Judaica shops.

Festivals & Events

Greek Food Festival Early May. Souvlakia and spanakopita draw thousands.

Pittsburgh Blues Festival July 16–18. On the grounds of Pittsburgh Brewing Company.

Pittsburgh Three Rivers Regatta Early August. Sails soar on the three rivers.

Pittsburgh Vintage Grand Prix July. Car races galore.

Sleeping

Budget accommodation is a problem since the only hostel closed. For pure bargains look 10 miles west of town at Moon Run, off the I-79 at exit 16, Steubenville Pike, where there's a predictable choice of chains with rooms averaging $45 per night. **Pittsburgh Bed & Breakfast Association** (☎ 724-352-4899; www.pittsburghbnb.com) can put you in touch with the local inn that best fits your taste.

Eating

Head to the Strip, where you'll find it all.

Primanti Brothers (☎ 412-263-2142; 46 18th St; sandwiches $4.75; ☺ 24hr) A Pittsburgh must. Sandwiches with the deli meat of your choice served over french fries (yes french fries) and coleslaw, packed into two big pieces of fresh Italian bread. Heartburn extreme.

Pennsylvania Macaroni Co (☎ 412-471-8330; 2010-12 Penn Ave) Sells quality Italian foods.

Downtown is not the culinary headquarters of Pittsburgh by any means. If you're too hungry to wait until you reach the South Side or Squirrel Hill, here are a few to try.

DeLuca's (☎ 412-566-2195; 2015 Penn Ave; mains $4-7) Self-described as home of the 'best breakfast in town.' The behemoth omelettes, strong coffee and greasy-spoon charm have crowds waiting patiently on the sidewalk each weekend.

My Ngoc (☎ 412-765-1150; 1120 Penn Ave; mains $7-11) Cheap Vietnamese and Chinese dishes.

On and around Forbes Ave in Oakland, cheap places cater to local students.

Original Hot Dog Shoppe (☎ 412-621-7388; 3901 Forbes Ave; hot dogs $2) Known simply as the 'O' this local institution is great at 3am when you don't care what goes in your body. Dogs and fries are what make this place famous but it also does cheap pizza ($4) and all kinds of subs, sandwiches and ribs.

LuLu's Noodle Shop & YumWok Pan Asian Diner (☎ 412-687-7777; 400 S Craig St; mains $5-8) A cute

MID-ATLANTIC

spot serving noodle bowls, great stir-fries and Thai-style salads.

Tom's Diner (☎ 412-488-0900; 1715 E Carson St; mains $7-12; ☽ 24hr) Brightly lit Tom's Diner serves up the all-American favorites, such as baked fish and tuna casserole, in a nifty 1950s setting.

Pittsburgh's sizeable Jewish population means there's lots of kosher food on offer. Squirrel Hill has plenty of veggie options (all are closed on Saturday for the Jewish Sabbath).

Eat'n Park (☎ 412-422-7203; 1816 Murray Ave; breakfast $4; ☽ 24hr) A great spot for late night 'breakfast', this chain is a local institution.

Milky Way Dairy & Vegetarian Restaurant (☎ 412-421-3121; 2120 Murray Ave; mains $5-7) Serving pizzas, falafel, vegetarian meatball hoagies and the Middle Eastern specialty, *melawach* (fried dough).

Drinking

Most nightlife is centered around the South Side, along the E Carson St strip. Try Iron City Beer, brewed locally since 1861.

BARS

Church Brew Works (☎ 412-688-8200; 3525 Liberty Ave) Secular or religious, this microbrewery in a former Catholic church makes blasphemy fun. Since parishioners stopped coming, the confessionals and the pulpit now store beer vats. Four house beers are on tap and the *pierogies* and pizza are divine.

Del's (☎ 412-683-1448; 4428 Liberty Ave) Another joint in Bloomfield, the bar at Del's is a good place for a drink. There's karaoke on Friday nights and the restaurant does tasty Italian food.

Zythos (☎ 412-481-2234; 2108 E Carson St) A mellow, trendy pub with specialty martinis. Upstairs **Memphis Lounge** is a darker, sultrier lounge featuring DJs who spin hip-hop, house and deep grooves.

Forbes Field Tavern (☎ 412-431-9500; 2901 Sarah St) A true locals' hang out where you will find endless Pittsburgh Pirates memorabilia, a down-to-earth crowd and cheap plates of good 'n' greasy *pierogi* (a pocket in dough, filled with vegetables, fruit or cheese).

Hemingway's Café (☎ 412-621-4100; 3911 Forbes Ave) In Oakland, Hemingway's is a college pub that packs 'em in for cheap drinks, friendly crowds and occasional poetry and fiction readings.

LIVE MUSIC

South Side's E Carson St is the place for rock, R & B and all-round funk.

Nick's Fat City (☎ 412-481-6880; 1601 E Carson St) A local favorite for rock and alternative bands.

Club Café (☎ 412-431-4950; 56 S 12th St) Inside a retro-cool building that's all tile and neon, Club Café is a formal bar with plush booths and a live jazz and blues show.

Lava Lounge (☎ 412-431-5282; 2204 E Carson St) Doles out rock and blues.

Metropol (☎ 412-261-2232; 1600 Smallman Ave) At the Strip. For clubbers.

World (☎ 412-261-2221; 1650 Smallman) Adjacent to Metropol, the World, formerly Rosebud, spins hip-hop, house, trance and acid jazz.

To hear good jazz, head to **Dowe's on 9th** (☎ 412-281-9225; 121 Ninth St) and **Club Café** (☎ 412-431-4950; 56-58 S 12th St).

Entertainment

Grab the *Pittsburgh City Paper*, a free alternative weekly with extensive arts listings.

Pittsburgh Cultural Trust (☎ 412-471-6070; www.pgharts.org; 803 Liberty Ave) Promotes all downtown arts, from dance and theater to visual art and opera; the website has links to all main arts venues.

Benedum Center for the Performing Arts (☎ 412-456-6666; 719 Liberty Ave; tickets from $15) Benedum hosts dance, ballet, opera and Broadway shows.

Byham Theater (☎ 412-456-6666; 101 6th St) This midsized venue hosts theater and dance performances.

Harris Theater (☎ 412-682-4111; 800 Liberty Ave) A wide variety of art-house films, often part of film festivals, play at this restored theater.

Andy Warhol Museum (☎ 412-237-8300; www.warhol.org; 117 Sandusky St) An eclectic venue, also used by comedy troupes, music groups and lecturers. Art-house films play here too.

Pittsburgh's sports teams relish their gritty and blue-collar reputations. Pittsburgh University football and basketball games can get out of hand in a good way. On the North Side, just by the Allegheny River, is **PNC Park** (☎ 412-321-2827; www.pirateball.com), where the Major League baseball Pittsburgh Pirates play. The NFL Pittsburgh Steelers play at **Heinz Field** (☎ 412-323-1200; www.pittsburghsteelers.com) and the NHL

Pittsburgh Penguins suit up in the **Civic Arena** (☎ 412-642-1800; www.pittsburghpenguins.com).

Getting There & Away

Pittsburgh International Airport, about 18 miles from downtown, has direct connections to Europe, Canada and major US cities.

Greyhound has frequent buses to Philadelphia ($40, seven hours), New York ($55, 11 hours) and Chicago ($60, eight to 12 hours). Amtrak trains head to Philadelphia ($40, eight hours), New York ($65, 10 hours) and Chicago ($60, 10 hours).

Getting Around

Port Authority Transit (PAT; ☎ 412-442-2000; 345 Sixth Ave) operates buses and a light rail system called the 'T' Bus and T fares range from free to $2.75. For taxis, try **Yellow Cab** (☎ 412-665-8100). Unmarked cabs may be uninsured or unsafe.

AROUND PITTSBURGH

The rolling, wooded hills of the Laurel Highlands and **Ohiopyle State Park**, just 40 miles southeast of Pittsburgh, hide the whitewater mecca of the Youghiogheny River ('Yough,' pronounced yock) and the little riverfront village of Ohiopyle (oh-*hi*-oh-pile) on Rte 381. The **park office** (☎ 724-329-8591; ☻ 8am-4pm Apr-Oct, 8am-4pm Mon-Fri Nov-Mar) and visitors center is at the end of the old steel railway bridge.

Tired of hostels? Imagine living at **Fallingwater** (☎ 724-329-8501; www.wpconline.org/falling waterhome.htm; Rte 381; admission Mon-Fri $12, Sat & Sun $15; ☻ 10am-4pm Tue-Sun Mar-Nov), arguably the most famous private residence in the US. Completed in 1939 as a weekend retreat for the Kaufmanns, owners of the Pittsburgh department store, a waterfall drops through several levels of the home. Reservations are recommended.

NEW JERSEY

Anyone who's seen the HBO hit drama *The Sopranos* knows that behind the veneer of dull New Jersey suburbia there's a lot of mob stuff going on. Hey, it helps to spice things up. Of course neither the newly popular image of Mafia-heavy Sopranoland nor the more enduring one of billowing smokestacks is really accurate. There are McMansions and

guys who speak with thick Jersey accents. There are strange smells emanating from industries congregated around the turnpike and harbors near NYC. However, there's also plenty of high-tech headquarters and sophisticated, progressive people living well in towns off the highways.

Some New Yorkers see the state as a refuge, a safety valve for when they're ready to flee the city for a comfortable place to live and raise a family. But you'll feel instantly nostalgic after spending time on one of its 127 miles of beaches, longing for one more carefree, warm sun-drenched day. Get off at an exit, flee the malls and you are privy to a beautiful side of New Jersey: a surprising 40% of the state is forest, and 25% is farmland.

NORTHERN & CENTRAL NEW JERSEY

Across the river from lower Manhattan, **Hoboken** has become an attractive choice for young professionals fleeing the skyrocketing rental market in Manhattan. From the Path Station to Steven's Institute of Technology, the university that occupies the northern part of the city, the bars and restaurants that line Washington St generally exude a post-collegiate fraternity atmosphere, but several are good live-music venues. **Maxwell's** (☎ 201-653-1703; 1039 Washington St) is a famous club for emerging and established acts. At **Goldhawk** (☎ 201-420-7989; 936 Park Ave), Tuesdays is Latin night.

Although it's only a 10-minute trip from NYC's Penn Station on the Path train, most worldly New Yorkers never see anything but the airport in **Newark**. Get off at Newark's Penn Station and walk the streets of the Ironbound District, a vibrant Portuguese community. Ferry St is lined with excellent restaurants, pastry shops and music stores. Always bustling **Seabra's Marisqueira** (☎ 973-465-1250; 87 Madison St; mains around $8) does delicious barbecued shrimp and bowls of mussels.

The Delaware River meanders through 40 miles of the **Delaware Water Gap National Recreation Area** in West Jersey, carving the 1400ft-deep Kittatinny Ridge chasm at the southern end. Activities include canoeing, swimming, rock climbing, horseback riding and hiking – the Appalachian Trail passes through the area. The park straddles the New Jersey–Pennsylvania border. From

MID-ATLANTIC

BELIEVE IT OR NOT, THESE ARE MUSEUMS

For some reason, the Mid-Atlantic has cornered the oddball-museum market:

- **Museum of Early American Farm Machinery & Very Old Horse Saddles With A History** (☎ 724-438-5180; Chalk Hill, PA) Pretty self-explanatory don't you think?

- **National Shrine of North American Martyrs** (☎ 518-853-3033; Auriesville, NY) To the memory of the Martyred Jesuits and Blessed Indian maiden.

- **Easton Museum of Pez Dispensers** (☎ 610-253-9794; Philadelphia, PA) Everyone needs a Pez dispenser, right?

- **Original American Kazoo Museum** (☎ 716-992-3960; Eden, NY) The kazoo capital of the world.

- **Jell-O Gallery Museum** (☎ 888-442-1932; Le Roy, NY) Dedicated to 'America's most famous dessert'.

- **Lucy-Desi Museum** (☎ 716-484-0800; Jamestown, NY) Dedicated to the life and times of the great Lucille Ball.

- **National Toy Hall of Fame** (☎ 585-263-2700; Rochester, NY) Kid heaven.

- **Shoe Museum** (☎ 215-625-5243; Philadelphia, PA) Tonic for your soles.

New Jersey, exit I-80 at the **Kittatinny Point Visitors Center** (☎ 908-496-4458; ☹ 9am-5pm).

Nothing conjures up the Ivy League like the tony town of **Princeton** and its university. The effects of privilege and learning, the manicured lawns, the lovely architecture and noteworthy historic sites all combine to produce the feeling of being in a rather comfy cocoon. Nassau and Witherspoon Sts are the main streets. Grab some breakfast or affordable lunchtime sandwiches at **PJ's Pancake House** (☎ 609-924-1353; 154 Nassau St; mains $6-10).

JERSEY SHORE

When people do think of New Jersey, they probably think of the shore. This stretch of beach from Sandy Hook in the north to Cape May in the south, boasts a coastline that rivals the beauty of more well-known resorts in the southern United States. Depending on your tastes, you'll find the kitschy beach towns either an obnoxious intrusion or fun examples of quintessentially American vacation spots. Whatever your perspective, no amount of drunken carousers – and you may be one of them – and Ripley's Believe or Not museums can detract from the pleasure of a dip in the Atlantic or contemplating the sun dropping behind the horizon.

Northern Beaches

At the northern tip of the Jersey Shore, **Sandy Hook National Recreation Area** (☎ 732-872-

5970; per car $10; ☹ dawn-dusk) is a sandy, 6-mile-long peninsula at the entrance to New York Harbor. Most of the area is undeveloped, and the ocean side of the peninsula has massive **beaches** (including a nude beach at parking lot G) lined on the inland side by an extensive system of bike trails.

With the demolition of the once iconic Palace Amusements, an enduring symbol of American kitsch as much synonymous with the community of **Asbury Park** as Bruce Springsteen, an era came to an end. What comes next is not entirely clear but developers promise that the town won't suffer a major decline like the one it went through after 'the Boss' (Bruce Springsteen) arrived at the **Stone Pony** (☎ 732-502-0600; 913 Ocean Ave) nightclub (still offering live music at weekends) in the 1970s. While it still has areas that should be avoided after dark, a visit to Asbury Park is rewarding to see the town before gentrification surely sets in. **Sonny's** (☎ 732-774-6262; 574 Cookman Ave; mains $9-13) serves authentic Southern cuisine.

Not-so-straitlaced **Belmar** seems to attract a younger crowd, and can get pretty rowdy when the bars close at 2am. **Carol's Guest House** (☎ 732-681-4422; www.carolsguesthouse.com; 201 11th Ave; r from $45; ☒) has a wraparound front porch and is only a block from the ocean.

Barnegat Peninsula, a narrow barrier island/ sand spit, extends some 22 miles south from Point Pleasant. In its center, **Seaside Heights** sucks in the wild 20-something summer crowds with beaches, boardwalks, bars and two amusement piers. Occupying the southern third of Barnegat Peninsula is **Island Beach State Park** (☎ 732-793-0506; per car $7), a flat 3000-acre stretch of dunes and wetlands.

Atlantic City

If you pause and look past the blinging lights and white noise of clanking quarters you'll see busloads of retirees making a beeline for the slots. Inside the casinos that never see the light of day, it's easy to forget there's a wide white-sand beach just outside and boarded-up shop windows a few blocks in the other direction. But that's just the point in Atlantic City. The massive structures blocking the seafront pale in ostentation compared to Vegas, but billionaire developer and outsized personality Donald Trump has put his stamp on the city, especially in the form of the Trump Taj Mahal – a perfect metaphor for the city's identity. Seen from afar, the grand pastel colored minarets appear like a fantastic mirage but viewed up close from the boardwalk they reveal themselves as the shoddy knock-offs they are.

Despite, or because of, this Atlantic City is still a fascinating place to visit at least once. If gambling isn't your thing, the Boardwalk offers up an all-star roster of summer indulgence, from funnel cakes to go-carts to cheesy gift shops. And even on a perfect sunny day the odds are you'll find room to spread out on the free beach while most take their chances on a riskier form of pleasure inside.

Next to the Atlantic City Convention Center on the boardwalk there is a **visitors center** (☎ 609-449-7130, 1-888-22-84748; www.atlanticcity.nj.com; ☻ 9:30am-5:30pm), which has maps and other information. Check out the *Atlantic City Weekly* (www.acweekly.com) for entertainment and events listings.

Built in 1870, the **Boardwalk** was the first in the world. Enjoy a walk or a hand-pushed rolling chair ride ($5 and up depending on how far you go). The **Miss America Pageant**, held every September in the Convention Hall is the city's signature event. There are numerous arcades, but the best entertainment is at the **Central Pier & Speedway** (☎ 345-5219; cnr Boardwalk & Tennessee) and **Steel Pier amusement park** (☎ 898-7645; www.steelpier.com; cnr Boardwalk & Virginia). The nearby residential towns of Margate and Ventnor have very nice beaches that charge a nominal fee.

Staying in the towering hotels can be cheap or extravagant, depending on the season, with rooms ranging from $50 in winter to $300 in summer. Otherwise, your best bet is the string of motels lining Pacific and Atlantic Avens. **Irish Pub Inn** (☎ 609-344-9063; www.theirishpub; 164 St James Pl; d $45; ☒) is a good place and has a lively pub with $6 dinner specials. **Shady Pines Campground** (☎ 652-1516; 443 S 6th Ave; campsites $33; ☒) is 6 miles away.

All casinos have several restaurants and usually at least one all-you-can-eat buffet. The prices aren't cheap ($15 for lunch, $19 for dinner) and the quality and service is spotty. Some casinos offer food coupons with your bus ticket. While the Boardwalk serves up hamburgers, and every imaginable fast-food, heartier food can be found away from the casino strip. A few blocks inland, **Mexico Lindo** (☎ 609-345-1880; 2435 Atlantic Ave; mains $7-11) is a favorite offering among the Mexican locals.

Greyhound ($28), Academy ($24), and New Jersey Transit ($25) buses run from New York (six hours roundtrip) and from Philadelphia (about $14 roundtrip, 1½ hours one way). Remember that casinos refund most of the fare in coins.

Southern Beaches

From Ocean City, the northernmost barrier island, south to Sea Isle, Avalon, Stone Harbor, the Wildwoods and Cape May on the state's southern tip, the full spectrum of the beach idyll is on display, from elegant and quaint family resorts to frathouse-style party scenes.

Cape May is the country's oldest seashore resort and the only place in the state where

---

EAST COAST COWBOYS

Cowtown Rodeo (☎ 856-769-3200; www.cowtownrodeo.com; Rte 40, Pilesgrove, NJ; admission $12; ☻ 7:30pm Sat May-Sep) America's longest running Saturday night rodeo is held from May through September. It's 8 miles east of the Delaware Memorial Bridge, about 50 miles west of Atlantic City.

the sun rises and sets over the water. In addition to 600 gingerbread-style houses, the city boasts a 157ft lighthouse, whale watching and bird-watching, attracting everyone from suburban families to a substantial gay crowd.

The white, sandy **beach** (1-/3-day/weekly pass $4/8/11) is the attraction in summer months. The **Cape May Whale Watcher** (☎ 609-884-5445; www.capemaywhalewatcher.com; 2nd Ave & Wilson Dr) 'guarantees' sighting a marine mammal – whale or dolphin – on its ocean tour (three hours, $30).

The best budget option is the **Hotel Clinton** (☎ 609-884-3993, off-season 516-799-8889; 202 Perry St; r $40-50; 🞰). The town is overflowing with smaller B&Bs and there are almost two dozen well-equipped campgrounds nearby. See www.newjerseycampgrounds.com.

North of Cape May, the three towns of **North Wildwood**, **Wildwood** and **Wildwood Crest** are an archaeological find of whitewashed motels with flashing neon signs, turquoise curtains and pink doors. Wildwood Crest really is an especially kitschy slice of 1950s Americana. Wildwood is the main focus, a party town popular with teens and young overseas visitors. The Wildwood **tourist office** (☎ 609-729-4000; www.gwcoc.com) hands out information on self-guided tours. The beach is free, and there are rides on the pier. About 250 motels offer rooms for $50 to $200.

UPSTATE NEW YORK

When a certain breed of New Yorker says they're going 'upstate,' they're usually referring to sweet retreats along the Hudson or in the Catskills. But New York State stretches way up to Canada and has some magnificent wilderness and surprisingly rural areas. You can reach many of the pretty main towns by bus or train, but to explore the countryside, you need a car. Take a train to a town like Albany and rent one there – you'll avoid driving in NYC. Most campgrounds are closed in the winter.

HUDSON VALLEY

You don't have to be part of the New York elite to enjoy the winding roads, picturesque farms, Victorian cottages, apple orchards and old-money mansions along the Hudson

> **SPLURGE!**
>
> **Blue Sky Ranch** (☎ 845-255-9538; www.ranch skydive.com; per jump $185) One of the busiest skydiving drop zones in the US is in nearby Gardiner. Blue Sky Ranch will you let you off at 13,000ft to fall and float down to the valley floor.

River. **Hudson Valley Tourism** (☎ 800-232-4782; www.hvnet.com) has regional information about sites and events.

On the west side, 40 miles north of New York City, **Harriman State Park** (☎ 845-786-5003; Palisades Parkway) and adjacent **Bear Mountain State Park** (☎ 845-786-2701; Rte 9W) offer hiking in summer, wildflowers in spring, gold foliage in fall and cross-country skiing in winter.

Two showcases of contemporary and avant garde art worth a visit are the **Dia: Beacon** (☎ 845-440-0100; www.diabeacon.org; 3 Beekman St; adult/student $10/7; ☉ 11am-6pm Thu-Mon) and the **Storm King Art Center** (☎ 845-534-3115; www .stormkingartcenter.org; Old Pleasant Hill Rd, Mountainville; admission $9; ☉ 11am-5pm Wed-Sun Apr-Nov) among 400 acres of rolling hills.

Looking to enlist or just learn about the history of war? Stop at **West Point**, the strategic fort that became the US Military Academy in 1802. The **visitors center** (☎ 845-938-2638; ☉ 9am-4:45pm) in Highland Falls has exhibits and maps and can tell you when cadets will parade in their finery.

The largest town on the Hudson's east bank, **Poughkeepsie** (puh-*kip*-see) is famous for **Vassar**, a private liberal-arts college that admitted only women until 1969.

Despite the natural foodstores, meditation, yoga, and aromatherapy centers, **New Paltz**, caters just as equally to fun-seeking students at the State University of New York and eco-friendly visitors. Be thankful that this wilderness with panoramic views of the Shawangunk Mountains (pronounced *shon*-gum, and known as Shon-gum or just 'the Gunks'), is not as popular as the Adirondacks or Catskills.

Lake Minnewaska is actually only pleasantly cool during the summer months. While some sources say the lake's name means 'frozen waters', others say it means 'white rock', although both claim that the word is derived from a nonlocal Indian dialect, while others insist that the name was simply pulled out of a hat by Alfred Smiley, who purchased the lake in 1875. The name of the lake was Coxing Pond until it was renamed by Smiley.

A small corner of the lake, replete with an equally small rocky beach and pier, is a great place to cool off after a long hike in the **Minnewaska State Park Preserve** (☎ 255-0752; per car $6), 12,000 acres of wild, beautiful landscape.

For **rock climbing** either at Minnewaska or Mohonk, get information and gear at **Rock & Snow** (☎ 845-255-1311; www.rocksnow.com; 44 Main St) or the **Inner Wall** (☎ 845-255 7625; www .theInnerwall.com; 234 Main St) in New Paltz.

New Paltz Hostel (☎ 845-255-6676; www.new paltzhostel.com; dm/d $24/61) is really a converted private home conveniently located on Main St, next door to the Trailways Bus Station. Reservations are recommended in summer.

CATSKILLS

The cultural battle lines have already been drawn only a few years after NYC publishing types and other urbanites seeking a hideaway more 'authentic' than the Hamptons began snapping up property in this scenic region of quaint small towns, farms, and gorgeous countryside. Even though it's quite easy to identify the 'new-money interlopers' from long term year-round residents, the rural feel of the area has not yet been compromised.

The focus of the Catskills has moved north in recent years. Most of the 'Borscht Belt' resorts in the southern Catskills, once enormous holiday spots for New York's Jewish families, have closed. Part of a grand scheme to rejuvenate the region, long contested and controversial plans to open a Native American–run casino in Monticello have recently taken a small step forward. If you're short of time stick to Rte 28, which crosses the Catskills west of Woodstock, then winds past the Ashokan Reservoir and through the 'French Catskills'. Along this route are great restaurants, campgrounds, inexpensive lodgings and plenty of character.

In Arkville, **Belleayre Hostel** (☎ 845-245-4200; www.belleayre-hostel.com; Pine Hill; dm $20), off Main St, is very rustic with cheap bunks.

Even to those who were born long after the now legendary concert, **Woodstock** 10 miles northwest of Kingston, symbolizes the tumultuous 1960s, when US youth questioned authority, experimented with freedom and redefined popular culture. Today it's a combination of quaint and hip. The famous 1969 Woodstock music festival actually occurred in Bethel, a town over 40 miles southwest, where a simple plaque marks the famous spot. Two not-so-peaceful spin-offs, also named 'Woodstock,' took place in nearby Saugerties (1994) and Rome (1999).

You'll find plenty of fine inns in the area, but backpackers should head to the nearby **Rip Van Winkle Campground** (☎ 845-246-8334; 149 Blue Mountain Rd, Saugerties; campsites $24-28) for cheap, well-maintained sites.

MID-ATLANTIC

TOP FIVE NEW YORK PARKS

- **Adirondack Forest Preserve** (☎ 518-846-8016; www.adk.com) The High Peaks region by Lake Placid gets all the glory, but the lakes around Blue Mountain are heaven on earth.

- **Catskill Forest Preserve** (☎ 845-586-2611; www.catskillcenter.org) Waterfalls, winding mountain roads and wacky Woodstock will bring out the inner tree-hugger in everyone.

- **Harriman & Bear Mountain State Parks** (☎ 845-786-2701; www.nysparks.state.nu/us/parks) Just outside of New York City, these adjacent parks in the scenic Hudson Highlands give cooped-up city folk a chance to ramble in the woods.

- **Minnewaska State Park** (☎ 845-256-0579; www.nysparks.state.ny.us/parks) Dark, cool lakes, winding streams and a dramatic mountain range are enough to make the most jaded city dweller love the outdoors.

- **Niagara Reservation State Park** (☎ 716-278-1796; www.nysparks.state.ny.us/parks) If you think the topography of the East Coast is too subdued, get to this impressive gorge and world-famous waterfalls.

Cooperstown

You don't need to be a little leaguer or hardcore baseball fan to make the pilgrimage to Cooperstown but it sure does help. You won't see a *Field of Dreams* style tableau of fathers and sons playing catch under the moonlight, although thanks to the main street's brick buildings and the national baseball institution, Cooperstown, 50 miles west of Albany is pure Americana.

The scenery around Ostego Lake is stunning. **Chamber of commerce** (☎ 607-547-9983; www.cooperstownchamber.org; 31 Chestnut St; 9am-7pm) provides visitors information.

Cooperstown is defined by the **National Baseball Hall of Fame & Museum** (☎ 607-547-7200; 25 Main St; www.baseballhalloffame.org; admission $9.50; 9am-5pm Sep-May, 9am-9pm Memorial Day–Labor Day), a shrine to the national sport.

Accommodations range from homey B&Bs to more basic campgrounds, most north of Cooperstown perched along Rte 80 on the western shore of Ostego Lake. Local residents rent out rooms at affordable prices especially for longer stays. **Ringwood Farms Campground** (☎ 800-231-9114; www.ringwoodfarms.com; 7489 Rte 80; campsites & dm $15;) has some secluded spots for camping and a pool. The hostel caters primarily to large groups.

Saratoga Springs

Not to be confused with warm, soothing swimming holes, the waters in **Saratoga Springs**, are in fact cold and heated to serve the tastes of individual customers at a handful of day spas in town. Despite the continued encroachment of large retail chains found everywhere, the main commercial street retains something of the artsy, laidback feel of a college town and it's rightly known for its performing arts, horse racing and Victorian-era residential streets. The **visitors center** (☎ 518-587-3241; www.saratoga.com; 9am-4pm daily Apr-Nov, closed Sun Dec-Mar) is in a former trolley station across from Congress Park where you can drink from differently flavored spring-fed fountains.

Saratoga Spa State Park (☎ 518-584-2535; 19 Roosevelt Dr; per car $4; dawn-dusk) offers the full-service Lincoln and Roosevelt mineral baths for $18 each, along with golf courses, an Olympic-sized pool complex, multiuse trails and ice rinks. It's also where you'll find the **Saratoga Performing Arts Center** (☎ 518-587-3330; www.spac.org; Hall of Springs), the summer home of the New York City Ballet and Philadelphia Orchestra (tickets around $15 to $55). From late July through September, fans of horse racing flock to the **Saratoga Race Course** (☎ 518-584-6200), the country's oldest active thoroughbred racetrack.

Camp amidst a spring-fed lake and pine trees at **Adirondack Adventure Resorts** (☎ 800-340-2267; www.adirondackadventureresorts.com; 265 Brigham Rd; campsites $30) around 5 miles away in Greenfield Center. Independent motels along Rte 9/S Broadway (exit 13N) are the most affordable. **Top Hill Motel** (☎ 800-852-9759; 3290 S Broadway, Rte 9; r $55;) is one of the cheapest.

Plenty of cafés and restaurants line Broadway and the side streets. **Esperanto** (☎ 518-587-4236; 6½ Caroline St; mains $6) is casual and cheap. Choose from Mexican, Thai, and Middle Eastern specialties. The burritos are especially good.

THE ADIRONDACKS

Adirondack Park's six million acres include towns, mountains, lakes, rivers and more than 2000 miles of superb hiking trails. The Adirondack Forest Preserve covers 40% of the park; the state constitution designates it as 'forever wild' – a good thing, because the peaks and valleys and lakes rival the best in the state. There's good trout, salmon and pike fishing, along with excellent camping spots (despite the biting black flies, a summer nuisance). July and August are glorious in the Adirondacks.

You can set up camp anywhere on state land as long as it isn't above 4000ft, within 150ft of water or within 100ft of a trail. About 60% of the Adirondacks is privately owned and only a few owners allow public access, so don't ignore the 'No Trespassing' signs.

Greyhound and Adirondack Trailways have a few routes within the region.

Amtrak trains stop at stations in Westport, 37 miles east of Lake Placid, and Fort Edward/Glens Falls, 16 miles from Lake George. Both are on the Adirondack line that travels from New York City to Montréal. The journey is quite scenic; the train goes along the Hudson River on and off until Albany, and then through dense forests.

It seems almost every road through the Adirondack Park could be called a scenic route and most are only two lanes wide. Rte

---

BUNK DOWN AMID HIGH PEAKS

ADK Adirondak Loj (☺ 518-523-3441; www.adk.org; Heart Lake Rd/Adirondak Loj Rd; campsites $23-32, dm $34-45, d $110) Sitting on Heart Lake at the feet of the High Peaks, this large lodge serves as a base for exploring the nearby hiking and skiing trails. Inside, are rocking chairs in front of a large fireplace and a good library of books and magazines on the Adirondacks. Accommodations include private rooms, four- to six-person dorms and 18-person dorms all with wooden bunks, thick and firm mattresses and, if you're lucky enough to get a bunk facing the lake, great views.

There is also an adjacent campground with tent, lean-tos and canvas cabin sites in pretty woods. This is your best choice in the bottom-end accommodations bracket – if not in any bracket.

All Loj room rates include breakfast; if you want dinner ($14), arrange it in advance. The food is served family-style at long tables. Breakfast is $5 for those in cabins, lean-tos and tents. Trail lunches can be ordered in advance for $5.50.

---

30 is an especially beautiful road that runs for 160 miles from the Great Sacandaga Lake in the south to Malone outside the northern boundary of the park.

Lake George

It's always a surprise to come upon a place so beautiful and yet so little known outside the immediate region. The forested peaks of the Adirondacks frame the clear blue water of 32-mile-long Lake George at the park's southeastern entrance. Civilization seems far away along the more wild northern shoreline while it's on full display at its tacky and touristy best in the village of Lake George, the gateway to the Adirondacks. The House of Frankenstein Wax Museum in the village says it all. You can get away from the boardwalk-style shops at the small sandy public beach just to the east. For a quiet and an even more spectacular view of the lake, head to the village of **Bolten Landing**, 10 miles north. Several companies run rafting and tubing trips down the nearby stretch of the Hudson and Sacandaga Rivers including **Adirondack River Outfitters** (☎ 800-525-7238; www.aroadventure.com; Rte 9 N, Lake Luzerne) and **Tubby Tubes Company** (☎ 518-696-5454; www.tubbytubestubing.com; 1372 Lake Ave, Lake Luzerne).

The state maintains some really remote **campgrounds** (reservations ☎ 800-456-2267) on Lake George's islands. The **Lake George Battleground Public Campground** (☎ 518-668-3348; campsites $10-16), at the southern end of town, has 50 shaded sites. Canada St/Rte 9 is lined with motels.

Lake Placid

Synonymous with the US Hockey team's improbable victory over the heavily favored Russians in the 1980 Olympics, and still a training center for aspiring Olympians, you don't have to be an elite athlete to appreciate the area's beauty. The **visitors center** (☎ 518-523-2445; www.lakeplacid.com; 216 Main St; ☺ 8am-4pm) disperses maps and information about skiing, fishing, cycling and hiking.

On Main St, the **Olympic Center Ice Arenas** (☎ 518-523-3325; www.orda.org/olymmpcenter.html; Main St; admission $5; ☺ 8am-9:30pm) has four ice rinks that are now used for training, hockey and ice shows (tours available). Ski jumpers train year-round at the **Olympic Ski Jump Complex** (☎ 518-523-2202; www.orda.org/skijump.html; Rte 73; ☺ 9am-4pm), which is southeast of town. Take the elevator to the top ($8) for Olympic-sized fear. Rollercoasters have nothing on the adrenaline rush you get shooting through the bobsled or luge runs at **Mt Van Hoevenberg Olympic Sports Complex** (☎ 518-523-4436; www.orda.org/mtvan.html; bobsled summer/winter $30/40, luge winter $25; ☺ 10am-12:30pm & 1:30-4pm Wed-Sun). A professional driver is supplied, weather permitting.

There are other options other than **ADK Adirondack Loj** (p111). **High Peaks Hostel** (☎ 518-523-4951; www.highpeakshostel.com; 59 Sentinel Rd; dm/d $20/48), a private hostel in a home 0.5 miles from the Adirondack Trailways bus stop and the **Jack Rabitt Inn** (☎ 800-584-7006; www.jackrabittinn.com; Rte 73; dm/d $20/60; ☐ ☒).

ST LAWRENCE RIVER

It's difficult to believe this is in the same state as the behemoth New York City. Formerly a swank playground for the rich, the **Thousand Islands** region draws boaters, campers and even scuba divers looking to explore the watery paradise surrounding the 1890 tiny islands dotting the wide St

MID-ATLANTIC

SCENIC DRIVE – SEAWAY TRAIL

Leisurely making its way through small towns and villages, the New York State Seaway Trail is a 450-mile scenic driving and bicycling route on a series of highways following the seaway through New York (and northern Pennsylvania) along the St Lawrence River, Lake Ontario and Lake Erie. The well-marked trail includes Rtes 104, 3, 12E, 12 and 37 (from Oswego to Massena) and provides an interesting alternative to superhighways. Green and white 'Seaway Trail' signs help guide you along the historic route. There are also 42 brown and white interpretive signs along the trail, marking events that took place here during the War of 1812. Much of the trail makes for magnificent driving – you'll hug the deep, deep blue waters of Lake Ontario sprinkled with colorful fishing boats or meander through fields, across streams and past dilapidated red barns.

Lawrence River east of Lake Ontario, some no larger than rocky outcroppings. Check out the **1000 Islands International Tourism Council** (☎ 800-847-5263; www.visit1000islands.com; ⏱ 9am-5pm).

The relaxing village of **Cape Vincent** is at the western end of the St Lawrence River, where it meets Lake Ontario. Its **Burnham Point State Park** (☎ 315-654-2324; Rte 12E; campsites \$20) has small, wooded, lakeside campsites. Further east, **Alexandria Bay** (Alex Bay), an early-20th-century resort town, has lost some of its charm but remains the departure point for ferries to Heart Island and lovely **Boldt Castle** (☎ 800-847-5263; www.boldtcastle.com; admission \$4.75; ⏱ 10am-6:30pm mid-May–Sep).

If you've made it this far don't pass up the chance to stay at this still functioning 1854 lakeside lighthouse 3 miles west of town. **HI-AYH Tibbetts Point Lighthouse Hostel** (☎ 315-654-3450; 33439 County Rte 6; ⏱ May 15–Oct 24; dm \$14) has dorms in two white houses, formerly the lighthouse-keepers' quarters and the entire place is on the National Historic Register. The drive alone is worth the trip. Sit in the garden and listen to the crashing waves. There is a 9:30am to 5pm lockout.

During summer **Thousand Islands Bus Line** (☎ 315-788-8146; 540 State St, Watertown) runs from Watertown to several Thousand Islands towns, including Alexandria Bay and Clayton.

FINGER LAKES REGION

Eleven long, narrow lakes stretch north to south and form the fingers of this western New York region. It's an ideal place for boating, fishing, cycling, hiking and cross-country skiing, and the rolling hills are the state's best wine-growing region. The **New York Wine & Grape Foundation** (☎ 315-536-7442; www.newyorkwines.org), in Penn Yan, distributes free brochures about wine trails. The Genesee River cuts through several gorges in **Letchworth State Park**, an hour southwest of Rochester near Castile. **Watkins Glen State Park** on the southern shore of Seneca Lake also has lots of waterfalls, hiking and swimming.

Ithaca

It's a little corny, but the T-shirt tagline 'Ithaca is Gorge-ous' is entirely true. Add the arty and laid-back university town vibe and you'll want to enroll. For tourist information, head straight to the **visitors center** (☎ 800-284-8422; www.visitithaca.com; 904 E Shore Dr; ⏱ 9am-5pm Mon-Fri, 10am-5pm Sat). Ithaca Falls is visible from Cayuga St.

Ithaca's suburbs and its surrounding countryside are interspersed with waterfalls, gorges and gorgeous parks, popular with hikers and rock climbers. Eight miles north on Rte 89, the spectacular **Taughannock Falls** spill 215ft into the steep gorge below; **Taughannock Falls State Park** (☎ 607-387-6739; Rte 89) has two major hiking trails, craggy gorges, tent-trailer sites and cabins. **Buttermilk Falls State Park** (Rte 13S) creek descends more than 500ft in series of cascades; **Treman State Park** has a spectacular swimming pool below the falls; there's nude sunbathing at **Six Mile Creek** above the dam and at **Potter's Falls**.

Founded in 1865, **Cornell University** boasts a lovely campus, that sits high on a hill, overlooking the picturesque town below. The striking, modern **Johnson Museum of Fine Art** (☎ 607-255-6464; www.museum.cornell.edu; University Ave; admission free; ⏱ 10am-5pm Tue-Sun) has some major exhibits and a nice view from its top floor.

For sleeping, a real gem of a find is the **Elmshade Guest House** (☎ 607-273-1707; 402 South Albany St; r \$35-125; ✿ ▯), a private home on a quiet street offering eight spotless, tasteful rooms. A hearty breakfast is included.

Moosewood Restaurant (Café DeWitt; ☎ 607-273-9610; 215 N Cayuga St; soup $2, mains $7-12), an acclaimed natural foods eatery has a changing menu. Try the Texas two-bean chili soup, mushroom pecan burgers, and Navajo peach crumble. Locals set up tents at the **Ithaca Farmers Market** (www.ithacamarket.com; Third St off Rte 13n; ⊗ 9am-2pm Sat Apr-Dec, Sun & Tue Jun-Oct) on a Cayuaga Lake inlet, selling agricultural produce, from flowers to honey, ready-to-eat-meals and fresh baked goods. Popular **Glenwood Pines** (☎ 607-273-3709; 1213 Taughannock Blvd; pinesburger $3.75), 4 miles north of Ithaca, does burgers and onion rings.

Pick up a free copy of the weekly *Ithaca Times* to check out live music around town. **Chapter House** (☎ 607-277-9782; 400 Stewart Ave) is no-frills, grungy, and fun. There are 50-plus brews on tap. **Micawber's** (☎ 607-273-9243; 118 N Aurora St) has live music and dancing

WESTERN NEW YORK

The Erie Canal spawned a number of early industrial centers along its route between Albany and Buffalo. Tracing the canal is an alternative to the I-90 toll route, and a more interesting way to get to Niagara Falls (see p187), 430 miles northwest of New York City. Plus, the canal's towpaths are ideal for easy-going cycling trips. Unfortunately, two of the region's biggest cities, Syracuse and Rochester, don't really warrant visits.

Buffalo

Known for its spicy hot chicken wings and painfully cold and snowy winters, Buffalo has quite a bit more going for it, from impressive art museums and architecture to bustling shopping areas and sprawling university campuses. There's an inspiring presence of young, hip and stylish college students.

A post-WWII decline in the city's traditional industries hit hard, the population fell, and much of the inner city became badly run-down. Recent urban renewal has improved the downtown area, and the huge student population adds another dimension to a city still known for its working-class roots and football fanatics.

Despite harsh winters, the city is dubbed 'the Miami of the North' because of its pleasant, sunny weather during May to September.

INFORMATION

Visitors center (☎ 716-852-0511; www.gobuffalo niagara.com; 617 Main St) Has good walking-tour pamphlets.

SIGHTS

Architecture aficionados will love the city. **Prudential Building** (28 Church St), designed by Louis Sullivan in 1895 as the Guaranty Building, was the first modern skyscraper. The stunning art deco **city hall** (65 Niagara Sq) was constructed in 1931 and boasts a roof observatory with excellent views of the city. Six **Frank Lloyd Wright houses** are a highlight, however most are privately occupied.

North of downtown, beautiful Delaware Park was designed by Frederick Law Olmsted. Its jewel is the not to-be-missed **Albright-Knox Art Gallery** (☎ 716-882-8700; www .albrightknox.org; 1285 Elmwood Ave; admission $6, free Wed; ⊗ 11am-5pm Tue-Sat, noon-5pm Sun), a big museum with outstanding French impressionists and contemporary American works. The birth of the present-day Buffalo art scene can be credited to an institution called **Hallwalls** (☎ 716-854-1694; www.hallwalls.org; 341 Delaware). Relocated to a former church building downtown, it hosts literary and music events and contemporary art exhibitions.

Allentown is a traditionally very 'funky' neighborhood. It's quite vibrant, if at times

---

IF YOU'VE GOT A FEW MORE DAYS IN THE MID-ATLANTIC

- **Albany, Rochester & Syracuse** For what students do best, visit these New York college towns.

- **Lake Champlain** Separating the Adirondacks in New York from the Green Mountains in Vermont, this long sliver of water extends all the way to Canada.

- **Grand Canyon of Pennsylvania** North-central Pennsylvania's smaller, forested version, great for hikes and rafting.

sleazy. The Elmwood strip, which stretches along Elmwood Ave, between Allen St and Delaware Park, is somewhat newer, dotted with hip cafés, restaurants, and bookstores. Another cool stretch is Main St, between Hertel and Kenmore, which is quickly becoming gentrified.

Woodlawn Beach State Park (S-3585 Lake Shore Rd; www.nysparks.com) is a mile-long stretch of sandy beach on Lake Erie.

FESTIVALS & EVENTS

The following festivals are big, noisy and cheap:

Allentown Arts Festival June 12 and 13.
Taste of Buffalo July 10 and 11.

SLEEPING

Hostel Buffalo (☎ 716-852-5222; www.hostelbuffalo .com; 667 Main St; dm/d $20/55) In the heart of the Theater District, this big, airy hostel has 52 beds in immaculate dorms. There is no lockout during summer and the staff know what's up in the city. The roundtrip bus service to Niagara Falls costs $4.50.

Most of the cheap chain motels are located near Buffalo's I-90 and I-290 exits.

EATING

Kuni's Sushi (☎ 716-881-6819; 752 Elmwood Ave; sushi $2.75-4.50) Easily the best place for sushi, this small place is always busy.

Duff's Sheridan Patio (☎ 716-834-6234; 3651 Sheridan Dr; wings 10/20 $7.50/13) Some say Duff's has the best wings in the city.

Charlie the Butcher's Kitchen (☎ 716-633-8330; 1065 Wherle Dr; sandwiches $3-6) Another Buffalo

---

ANCHOR BAR

You need only four words at Buffalo's most famous restaurant – mild, medium, hot or suicidal. Okay, maybe five – beer appears to also be essential. The **Anchor Bar** (☎ 716-886-8920; 1047 Main St; mains $6-15) invented Buffalo chicken wings in 1964. Located in a marginal neighborhood, the bar still packs in crowds most days of the week. Wings come in single and double orders ($8 and $12 respectively). The sauce is mouthwatering and the chicken itself is perfect (not too fatty). Not convinced? The Anchor Bar also has a full menu of seafood, pasta, pizza, chicken and sandwiches.

---

specialty. Order the 'beef on weck', roast beef on kimmelweck roll (like a kaiser roll) at this casual diner.

Ted's (☎ 716-691-7883; 2351 Niagara Falls Blvd; footlong hot dog $2) Ted's has been around since 1927. There are several around town serving up red-hot hot dogs and onion rings.

Gabriel's Gate (☎ 716-886-0602; 145 Allen St; mains from $9) For ribs and steaks and crisp chicken wings in a historic Allentown home.

ENTERTAINMENT

The Chippewa St pub strip is mobbed with trashed frat boys and sorority girls. The best sources for information on nightlife and theater productions are the Friday edition of the *Buffalo News* and *ArtVoice*.

Lance Diamond Show (☎ 716-856-3550; www .lancediamond.net; Elmwood Lounge, 14 Lafayette Sq) Still going strong after open heart surgery, known as the 'best dressed and hardest working showman in Buffalo,' Lance Diamond stages an old-school lounge act on Friday nights.

Nietzsche's (☎ 716-886-8539; 248 Allen St) Ani DiFranco got her start here. Up and coming folk and bluegrass artists perform almost nightly hoping for similar success. You'll pay $1.50 for Labatt beer from 4pm to 8pm.

Two-Two-Three Allen (Old Pink, the Pink Flamingo; ☎ 716-884-4338; 223 Allen St) A dark dive bar full of bikers, students and artists.

Several gay bars are clustered around the south end of Elmwood, including **Fugazi** (☎ 716-881-3588; 503 Franklin St) and **Friends** (☎ 716-883-7855; 16 Allen St).

Minor League AAA **Buffalo Bisons** (☎ 716-846-2000; www.bisons.com; 275 Washington St; Apr 10–Sep 5) games beat the big boys for fun. Tickets, food and beer are also cheaper.

Locals worship the NFL **Buffalo Bills** (☎ 716-648-1800) football team and the **Buffalo Sabres** (☎ 716-855-4100; HSBC Arena) ice-hockey team.

GETTING THERE & AROUND

Bus No 40 ($4.50 roundtrip) and No 60 run regularly between the downtown Buffalo transit center and the Niagara Falls transit center, a short walk from the falls.

New York Trailways, Greyhound and NFTA operate from the Metro Transportation Center (cnr Ellicott & Eagle Sts).

From the downtown Amtrak train station, you can catch trains to New York City ($60, 7½ hours).

New England

HIGHLIGHTS

- **Boston** A historic, eminently walkable city teeming with a youthful energy (p120)
- **Acadia National Park** Some of the most dramatic scenery on the entire Atlantic Coast, and the perfect place to watch the sunrise (p153)
- **Martha's Vineyard** Quintessential New England island with a funky history (p143)
- **Providence** Reborn as a Boston alternative for great food, shopping and culture (p163)
- **Off the beaten track** The islands of Lake Champlain, wedged between mainland Vermont and New York State, are undervisited gems (p158)
- **Best journey** A road trip from quirky Brattleboro to lively Burlington, via Vermont's ultra-scenic Rte 100

FAST FACTS

- **Area** 71,997 sq miles (about half the size of California)
- **Big cities** Boston (population 3 million), Providence (175,000), Portland (65,000)
- **Budget** $50-80 per day
- **Costs** bed in Boston youth hostel $25, New Haven to Brattleboro train ticket $37, cup of clam chowder in Portland $4
- **Driving times** Boston to New York 4½ hours, Portland to Bar Harbor 4 hours, Burlington to Montréal, Canada 2 hours
- **Famous for** Cape Cod beaches, Maine fishing villages, Vermont landscapes, Boston historical sights, taciturn locals, snowy winters, humid summers
- **Languages** English, of a sort, where the 'r' becomes 'h' ('cah' and 'pahk' for 'car' and 'park')
- **Population** 14,205,480
- **Phrases** *wicked* (very, as in 'that test was wicked hard'), *Yankees suck* (the predictable chant of Red Sox fans)
- **Seasons** unpredictable year-round, but usually cold and snowy in winter, hot and

humid in summer and blissful for six weeks of spring and fall each

- **States** Massachusetts, Maine, New Hampshire, Vermont, Rhode Island, Connecticut
- **Tasty treats** Saltwater taffy, maple candy, New Haven pizza, Maine lobster and Dunkin' Donuts coffee (regular = lots of milk and *lots* of sugar)
- **Time** GMT minus 5 hours
- **Top hostel** HI Truro, Cape Cod (p143)

TRAVEL HINTS

Check the Internet for discounts on Amtrak and commuter rail rides across the region. They're often competitively priced compared to a bus ride, and make for a much more pleasant and scenic journey, especially through Vermont and along the Connecticut coastline.

The six states that comprise New England – Massachusetts, Maine, New Hampshire, Vermont, Rhode Island and Connecticut – share an identity that is both quintessentially American and steadfastly separate from the rest of the country. While the region's rich history and culture ooze from almost every city and town, everything else about New England will come across as rather modest in scale and unassuming in nature – at least by bold, brash American standards. Still, it adds up to a collection of picturesque villages, secluded beaches, pristine lakes, panoramic mountains and dramatic coastline.

New Englanders may be somewhat taciturn by nature, but the weight of tradition is counterbalanced by a new energy as the region becomes more ethnically diverse. You'll experience it in Boston, where the old-world streets are now home to more diverse cultures, trendy shops and stylish restaurants. There's postcard-perfect Provincetown, a seaside village that has morphed into the East Coast's most gay-friendly vacation spot. And formerly sleepy industrial cities such as Providence, Portland and Burlington are being reborn as edgy centers of urbanity.

HISTORY

New England's history begins with the Algonquin peoples, native inhabitants who lived by raising foodstuffs, hunting, and fishing the abundant coastal waters. In the early 1600s European explorers such as Englishman John Smith (who christened the region 'New England' in 1614) set the stage for a wave of colonization, inaugurated by the Pilgrims, whose ship the *Mayflower* landed at Plymouth Rock in 1620.

The colonies expanded and thrived (mostly at the expense of the shrinking native population) for the next 130 years. However, there was increasing resentment towards the British crown, focused on the colonists' lack of representation in parliament and the excessive taxes being imposed. Things came to a head with the battles of Lexington and Concord on April 18, 1775, the unofficial start of the Revolutionary War (1775–83) that birthed a nation.

Following the Revolutionary War, New England's natural economic strengths – fishing, whaling and commerce – took hold. The region's rushing rivers became engines that powered its industrial mills. Post–Civil War, as the country grew, agriculture moved to the Great Plains, industry moved south to take advantage of cheaper labor and electricity eliminated the need for lamps illuminated by whale oil.

The Great Depression of the 1930s hit New England hard, but the region's shipyards boomed during WWII. The rest of the 20th century saw the region become an undisputed center of education, medicine and finance. Today biotechnology and tourism are two of the linchpins of the regional economy.

THE CULTURE

Ask any American to describe the stereotypical New Englander and they'll probably conjure up a taciturn, hardscrabble farmer or fisherman who talks about the weather, if he talks at all. No one would ever characterize the people who live here as the world's friendliest or most outgoing. Truth be told, in many ways New Englanders are different from the rest of their compatriots: fiercely independent, somewhat sarcastic and fatalistic, fiscally conservative and socially liberal (or at least libertarian). It takes a certain personality to survive the brutal winters and steamy summers without throwing up one's hands and running off to California. People live here because they always have, and the region's sense of history and generational bonds are matched only by those in the South.

That said, the region is going through unmistakable changes, many of them positive.

THE BIG ISSUE

Who would have guessed that low-key New England would end up at the center of the national row over gay marriage? And yet Vermont and Massachusetts have both played the role of protagonist in interpreting pre-existing state laws. Vermont currently allows civil unions, while in 2004 Massachusetts became the first state in the USA to legalize gay marriage – much to the chagrin of its Mormon and Republican governor, Mitt Romney. At the time of writing, thousands of gay and lesbian couples have tied the knot in the Bay State and the sky has yet to fall.

The insular, parochial 'townie' of yore is giving way to a more diverse population, as waves of immigrants, especially from Central America and Southeast Asia, build communities in cities and towns all over the region. With the old industries dying out, cities like Portland, Providence and Burlington have seen the future and chosen to remake themselves as centers of arts and culture. (The old mill town of North Adams, Massachusetts, has attracted a whole colony of artists.) Best of all, the famous New England reserve is inexorably falling by the wayside; whether by design or evolution, folks here are opening up and engaging with visitors.

SPORTS & RECREATION

Living in a region with weather that's rarely conducive to outdoor sports doesn't stop New Englanders from being top-flight spectators, which they are with a passion. The New England Patriots, winners of the NFL's Super Bowl in 2002 and 2004, have reached historic heights of popularity, while the six states' baseball fans continue to relive the 2004 World Series, which the Boston Red Sox won for the first time since 1918. Men's and women's college basketball is king in Connecticut, while college hockey is a big winter draw in Maine, New Hampshire and Vermont.

For activity-oriented folks, New England's mountains, lakes, forests and coastline provide options year-round: hiking, biking, sailing, canoeing, rafting, skiing, snowboarding and ice-skating. You can also go indoors and try your luck at candlepin bowling, a variation on tenpin bowling with a cruel, regionally appropriate twist: no one has ever bowled a perfect game of candlepins.

ARTS & ENTERTAINMENT

New Englanders take pride in their contributions to American (and human) culture, which may explain why Boston has historically described itself as the 'Athens of America.' Many great names in American literature were either born or lived part of their lives here: Nathaniel Hawthorne, Henry Thoreau, Henry Wadsworth-Longfellow, Emily Dickinson, WEB DuBois and Jack Kerouac, to name a few. New England artists as different as John Singer Sargent and Norman Rockwell are famous for capturing the essence of their portrait subjects.

The photogenic villages of the region have served as the setting for countless films, including *Dolores Claiborne* (coastal Maine), *Jaws* (Martha's Vineyard), and *Mystic Pizza* (Mystic, Connecticut).

Most of New England's contributions to the world of recorded music have come from Boston, where bands like Aerosmith, the Pixies and (ahem) New Kids on the Block first rose to prominence. Out in Western Massachusetts, Pioneer Valley's college scene spawned alt-rock guitar god J Mascis, aka Dinosaur Junior. Burlington, Vermont, birthed Phish, the most popular jam band of its day.

ENVIRONMENT

The indelible impact of human activity on the environment is evident in New England. In recent years the coastal states, especially Massachusetts, have seen a horrifying collapse of their once-mighty fishing industry. How much of this is due to global warming and how much to overfishing by the fleets is subject to debate, but it's undeniable that both have played a role. A nascent movement afoot to try to reverse the damage is running into predictable opposition from those whose livelihood depends on the daily catch.

Even though New England has a much smaller percentage of government-owned land than other parts of the country, its cities and towns tend to have zoning laws that discourage sprawl. On the coastline, there are plenty of unspoilt bogs, marshes and rocky cliffs. Further inland, the region is covered with forests – dense groves of oak, maple, beech and other deciduous trees whose vibrant autumn foliage attracts tourists from around the world for a few precious weeks in late September and early October. Despite the short growing season and often rocky, unforgiving soil, the climate is just fine for maple syrup, apples, blueberries, cranberries, corn and more.

National & State Parks

Acadia National Park (p153), on the coast of Maine, is New England's only national park, but there are significant tracts of land across the northern states (especially New

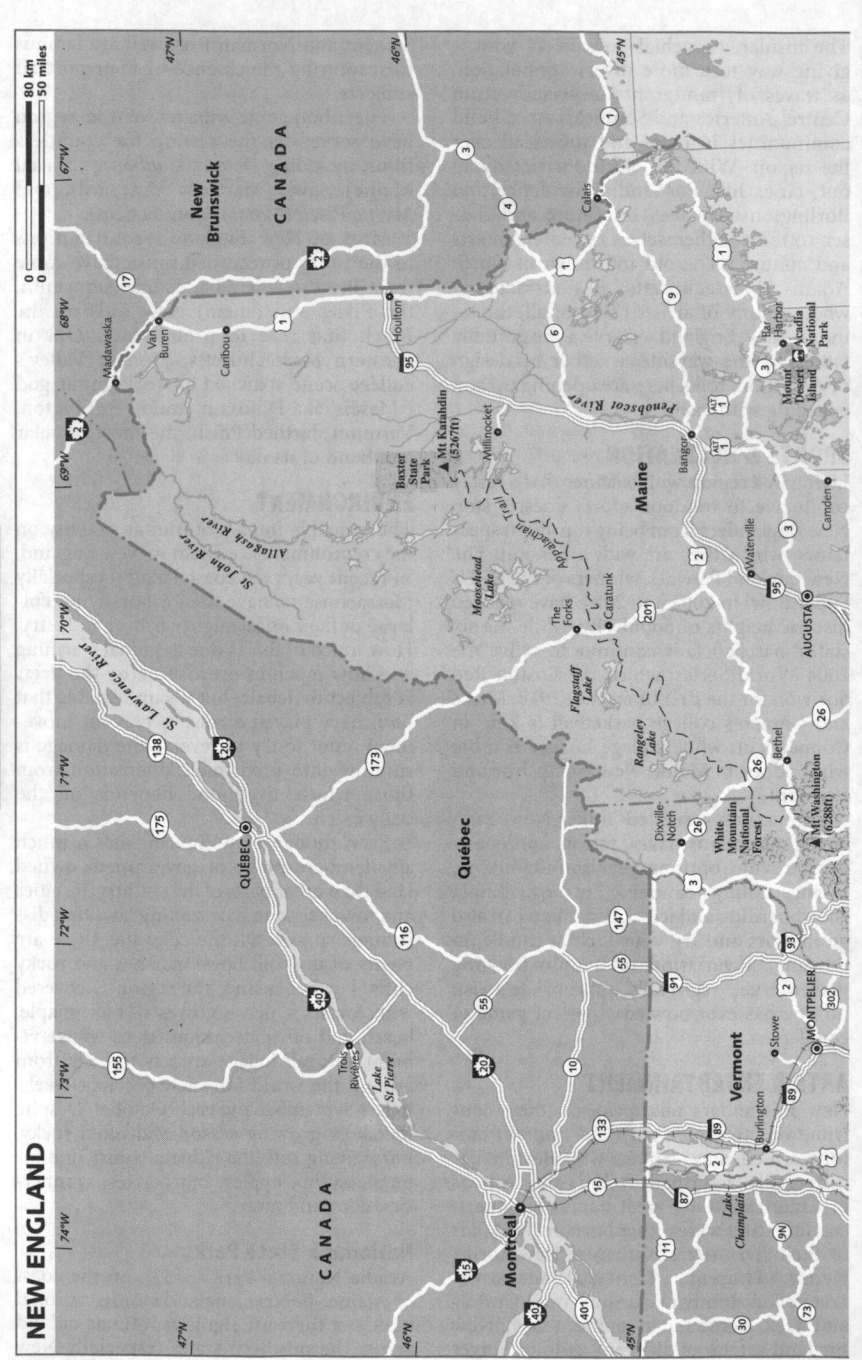

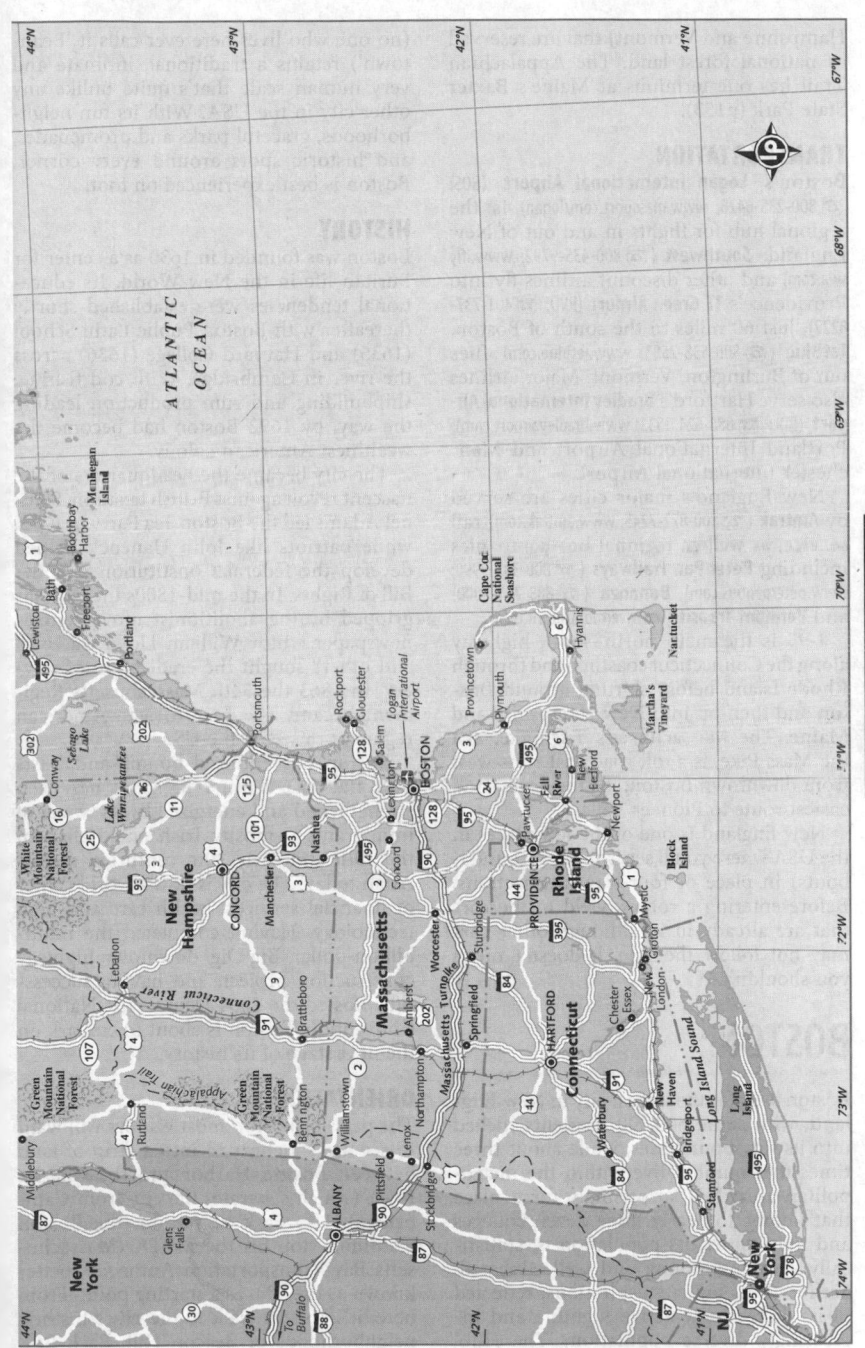

Hampshire and Vermont) that are reserved as national forest land. The Appalachian Trail has one terminus at Maine's Baxter State Park (p153).

TRANSPORTATION

Boston's **Logan International Airport** (BOS; ☎ 800-235-6426; www.massport.com/logan) is the regional hub for flights in and out of New England. **Southwest** (☎ 800-435-9792; www.ifly swa.com) and other discount airlines fly into Providence's **TF Green Airport** (PVD; ☎ 401-737-8222), just 60 miles to the south of Boston. **JetBlue** (☎ 800-538-2583; www.jetblue.com) flies out of Burlington, Vermont. Major airlines also serve Hartford's **Bradley International Airport** (BDL; ☎ 888-624-1533; www.bradleyairport.com), Portland International Airport and Manchester International Airport.

New England's major cities are served by **Amtrak** (☎ 800-872-7245; www.amtrak.com) rail service, as well as regional bus companies including **Peter Pan Trailways** (☎ 800-343-9999; www.peterpanbus.com), **Bonanza** (☎ 888-751-8800) and **Vermont Transit** (www.vermonttransit.com).

I-95 is the main north–south highway along the Connecticut coastline and through Rhode Island before skirting around Boston and then up into New Hampshire and Maine. The Massachusetts Turnpike, aka the Mass Pike, is a toll road that runs west from downtown Boston; it's the fastest and easiest route to Pioneer Valley.

New England is one of the few places in the USA where you'll see 'rotaries' (roundabouts) in place of four-way intersections. Before entering a rotary, yield to the cars that are already in it: although other cars may not follow the rule, it doesn't mean you shouldn't.

BOSTON

Boston is by far the largest city in New England, with some 600,000 residents tucked into its tidy boundaries, while about three times that number live within the metropolitan area. Not surprisingly for a place that's home to nearly three dozen colleges and universities, its population is, statistically speaking, young and well educated. Yet for all its big-city aspirations, reflected in its increasingly active nightlife and increasingly diverse population, 'The Hub'

(no one who lives here ever calls it 'Beantown') retains a traditional, intimate and very human scale that's quite unlike any other city in the USA. With its fun neighborhoods, graceful parks and promenades, and historic spots around every corner, Boston is best experienced on foot.

HISTORY

Boston was founded in 1630 as a center for Puritan life in the New World. Its educational tendencies were established shortly thereafter with Boston Public Latin School (1635) and Harvard College (1636) across the river in Cambridge. With cod fishing, shipbuilding and rum production leading the way, by 1692 Boston had become the wealthiest American colony.

The city became the headquarters of the nascent revolt against British taxation. Samuel Adams led the Boston Tea Party in 1773, while patriots like John Hancock helped develop the federal Constitution and the Bill of Rights. In the mid-1800s the city was gripped by the abolitionist movement as newspaper editor William Lloyd Garrison and others sought the eradication of slavery. In 1863 the 54th Massachusetts Regiment became the first African-American regiment raised in the USA.

Boston has endured booms and busts over the past century or so. It has been strengthened and energized by its waves of immigrants – mostly Irish and Italian in the 19th and early 20th centuries, mostly Asian today. The city is now a world center of financial services, health care and high technology. Having completed the multi-billion-dollar 'Big Dig' downtown highway construction project, and having successfully hosted the 2004 Democratic National Convention, Boston is about to embark on the next stage of its history.

ORIENTATION

The parts of Boston most visitors will want to see are shoehorned into a strip of land between Boston Harbor and the Charles River (which separates the city from Cambridge). Use Park St station, the Boston Common stop on the MBTA (Massachusetts Bay Transportation Authority, better known as the 'T'), as a starting point. From here, it's a short walk to the city's historic neighborhoods of Beacon Hill, Back Bay,

---

GETTING INTO TOWN

From Logan International Airport, downtown Boston is accessible via the MBTA ($1.25). Take a free shuttle bus (Nos 22, 33 and 55) from any of the airport terminals to the new, modern Airport station. Hop on any inbound Blue Line train. Get off at State St or Government Center station.

Amtrak trains and most of the major bus lines roll into South Station, a few blocks from the Financial District and the Downtown Crossing shopping area. There's an MBTA Red Line station here for subway trains to Cambridge.

North End and South End. From Boston Common, a series of parallel boulevards (Boylston, Newbury and Beacon Sts) radiate westward towards Kenmore Sq and the western suburbs. From Park St station, you can catch trains to Harvard Sq and Cambridge.

INFORMATION
Bookstores
Borders (☎ 617-557-7188; 10-24 School St) This Downtown Crossing branch of the chain has a huge selection of books and a café.
Trident Booksellers & Cafe (☎ 617-267-8688; 338 Newbury St) New Age and academic books.
We Think the World of You (☎ 617-574-5000; 540 Tremont St) Specializes in gay and lesbian titles.

Internet Access
Boston Public Library (☎ 617-536-5400; 700 Boylston St; free 15-min access) Free for 15 minutes on certain 'express' computers; sign up for visitor courtesy card at circulation desk to get a whole hour of free terminal usage.
NewburyOpen.net (☎ 617-267-9716; 3rd fl, 252 Newbury St; www.newburyopen.net; per 15 min/hr $3/5) Promotes cheap and easy wi-fi access. Its main Internet café provides computers for email, web, online gaming and burning CDs.

Media
Boston Globe (www.boston.com/globe/) New England's largest daily paper; serious broadsheet with solid coverage of politics and an excellent sports section.
Boston Herald (www.bostonherald.com) Daily tabloid with more conservative politics than the *Globe* and strong local reporting.
Boston Phoenix (www.bostonphoenix.com) Free alternative weekly, available Thursday, with comprehensive arts and entertainment listings.
WBUR (90.9FM) News and talk shows from National Public Radio and BBC World Service.

Medical Services
Beth Israel Deaconess Medical Center (☎ 617-754-2400; cnr Deaconess Rd & Brookline Ave)

Brigham & Women's Hospital (☎ 617-732-5500; 75 Francis St)
Massachusetts General Hospital (☎ 617-726-2000; 55 Fruit St, off Cambridge St)

Money
There are ATMs most everywhere downtown, especially along Boylston St and near Government Center.
Fleet Foreign Currency Exchange(☎ 877-353-3839; 100 Federal St)

Post
Main US post office (☎ 617-654-5326; 25 Dorchester Ave; ☒ 24hr) One block southeast of South Station.

Toilets
Boston's public toilet situation is somewhat improved with the addition of forest-green pay toilet pods scattered throughout downtown. They cost 50¢. If you don't have coin change, try a restaurant.

Tourist Information
Boston Common Visitors Information Center (☎ 617-426-3115; www.bostonusa.com; cnr Tremont & West Sts; ☒ 8:30am-5pm Mon-Sat, 9am-5pm Sun) Friendly, knowledgeable staff as well as a great selection of maps, brochures and discount coupons.
Boston National Historical Park Visitor Center (☎ 617-242-5642; www.nps.gov/bost; 15 State St, opposite the Old State House; ☒ 9am-5pm) A good source of Freedom Trail information.
Greater Boston Convention & Visitors Bureau Booth (Prudential Center, 800 Boylston St; ☒ 9am-5pm)

Universities
Boston and neighboring Cambridge are higher-education meccas. There are some 35 institutions in the area, but these are the most prominent ones in Boston proper:
Boston College (☎ 617-552-8000; www.bc.edu; Commonwealth Ave, Chestnut Hill)

Boston University (☎ 617-353-2000; www.bu.edu; Commonwealth Ave)
Massachusetts College of Art (☎ 617-232-1555; www.massart.edu; 621 Huntington Ave)
Northeastern University (☎ 617-373-2000; www .neu.edu; Huntington Ave)
University of Massachusetts, Boston (☎ 617-287-5000; www.umb.edu; Morrisey Blvd)

SIGHTS

Sightseeing Boston is like taking American History 101. Before checking out the attractions, check the tourist info offices for discount coupons to major museums and tours. You can also save money (and avoid ticket lines) by purchasing a **Boston CityPass** ($36.75), which covers admission at the New England Aquarium, Museum of Science, Museum of Fine Arts, JFK Library, Skywalk Observatory and Harvard Museum of Natural History. A combo ticket for the Paul Revere House, Old State House and Old South Meeting House ($10) is available at Boston National Historical Park Visitor Center.

Beacon Hill

Old money rules along Beacon Hill's narrow streets, where gas lamps burn 24 hours a day in front of the Federalist townhouses where 'Boston Brahmins' reside. The Boston Brahmins originally came from Europe (England, mostly) and settled the city in the 1600s. Don't miss tiny Acorn St, often called 'the most photographed street in America.'

Begin at **Massachusetts State House** (☎ 617-727-3676; cnr Beacon & Park Sts; admission free; ☯ 10am-4pm Mon-Fri), the majestic capitol building built in 1798 and fittingly topped by a golden dome. Call about tours.

Directly across the street from the State House is the **Robert Gould Shaw Memorial**, dedicated to the leader and troops of the 54th Massachusetts Regiment, the first African-American troop to fight for the Union in the Civil War.

To the left is the entrance to **Boston Common**. Established in 1634, it's the oldest public park in the USA and is a great place to kick back on the cheap. True to its name, the common hosts concerts, political rallies, plays and numerous other public events during the year. The Frog Pond is great for wading on a hot summer day, or ice-skating during winter. Get your free culture fix at Shakespeare on the Common performances (www.wangcenter.org) held during July and August.

Right near Boston Common's Park St station entrance is the starting point for the **Freedom Trail** (☎ 617-357-8300), a Boston highlight. This 2.5-mile path, marked on the sidewalk by an unbroken line of red (paint or brick), passes some of Boston's most historic sights, including the Park St Church, Old Corner Bookstore and Bunker Hill Monument, before ending at the Charlestown Navy Yard. Free maps are available from the **visitor center** (15 State St).

The smaller **Public Garden**, across Charles St from Boston Common, is the oldest botanical garden in the country. Most tourists make a beeline for the **Swan Boats** (☎ 617-522-1966; admission $2.50; ☯ 10am-5pm late Jun–early Sep), established in 1877 and still going strong. The tranquil ride on the garden's central Lagoon is one of Boston's enduring traditions. Also be sure to catch the **'Make Way for Ducklings' statue**, which gets high marks for cuteness.

The **Museum of Afro-American History** (☎ 617-725-0022; 46 Joy St; admission free; ☯ 10am-4pm Mon-Sat) celebrates the accomplishments of African-Americans during America's colonial period. The museum has created a 1.6-mile Black Heritage Trail that passes historic sites in and around Beacon Hill; ask for a free map at the museum. Nearby, the **African Meeting House** (☎ 617-725-0022; 8 Smith Ct) dates back to 1806 and is the oldest African-American church in the USA still standing.

Charles St, the commercial heart of Beacon Hill, has fine shops and restaurants. Just off Charles St is the old **firehouse** (127 Mt Vernon St) where MTV's *The Real World: Boston* was filmed.

Government Center, North End & Charlestown

Across Congress St from Boston's modern City Hall is historic **Fanueil** (fan-yul) **Hall** (☎ 617-242-5675; ☯ 9am-5pm), a very handsome 18th-century brick building capped by a weathervane. Used in the 1700s for local meetings to oppose British rule, today it's the gateway to Fanueil Hall Marketplace and centerpiece for the city's tourist trade. Three long granite buildings – North Market,

South Market and the central Quincy Market – house shops, bars, restaurants and nightclubs, street performers keep the camera clickers busy.

The **Old State House** (☎ 617-720-3290; 206 Washington St; adult/student $5/4; ☺ 9am-6pm) served as the seat for the colonial and original state governments when it was built in 1713. It was also the site of the Boston Massacre. Today it's a museum of Boston history.

On a December night in 1773, 5000 pissed-off colonists gathered at the **Old South Meeting House** (☎ 617-482-6439; 310 Washington St; adult/student $5/4; ☺ 9:30am-5pm summer, 10am-4pm winter), the largest colonial building in the city, to protest the British taxation on tea, leading to the infamous Boston Tea Party and subsequent American Revolution.

The centerpiece of Boston's waterfront, the **New England Aquarium** (☎ 617-973-5200; Central Wharf; admission $16; ☺ 9am-5pm Mon-Fri, 9am-6pm Sat, Sun & holidays) is notable for its circular, Guggenheim-esque ramp surrounding the 200,000-gallon Giant Ocean Tank, full of sharks, manta rays, sea turtles and lots of other aquatic life. The sea lion presentation in the adjacent *Discovery* ship is quite entertaining. The aquarium also operates daily, four-hour whale-watching cruises from April to October.

Museum of Science (☎ 617-723-2500; Science Park; admission $14 exhibit halls, $8.50 planetarium, laser shows & Omni Theater; ☺ 9am-5pm Sat Thu, 9am-9pm Fri), between Boston and Cambridge on a strip of land above the Charles River, has enthralled kids of all ages for decades with more than 500 hands-on exhibits that are both educational and entertaining. Check out the Theater of Electricity, containing the world's largest Van de Graaf generator, or one of the planetarium's trippy laser-light shows set to rock music.

Steeped in history, North End is Boston's compact and tight-knit Italian neighborhood, with charming streets and delicious eateries. **Paul Revere House** (☎ 617-523-2338; 19 North Sq; adult/student $3/2.50; ☺ 9:30am-5:15pm Apr 15–Oct 31, 9:30am-4:15pm Nov 1–Apr 14, closed Mon Jan-Mar), a wooden building built in 1680, is the oldest in Boston and the only surviving building from the original city. It features period furnishings and examples of the famous patriot's work. Nearby is the beautiful Georgian-style **Old North Church** (☎ 617-523-6676; 193 Salem St; ☺ 9am-6pm Jun-Oct, 9am-5pm Nov-May), formerly Christ Church, where two lanterns hung out on April 18, 1775, warned Revere and other messengers of British soldiers' water-based approach ('One if by land, two if by sea'). Just down Hull St from Old North Church lies **Copp's Hill Burying Ground**, an ancient cemetery from the late 1600s.

Across the Charles River from North End is Charlestown, a quaint neighborhood that has undergone significant gentrification in the past decade. Its historic centerpiece is **Charlestown Navy Yard** (☎ 617-242-5601; admission free; ☺ daily Apr-Oct, Thu-Sat Nov-Mar, tours on the half-hr 10:30am-3:30pm), which serviced the US Navy for nearly 200 years until 1974. It's where the USS *Constitution*, known as 'Old Ironsides,' built in 1797 and the world's oldest commissioned warship still afloat, is docked. Within walking distance of the navy yard is **Bunker Hill Monument** (☎ 617-242-5641; Monument Sq; admission free; ☺ 9am-4:30pm), a 221ft obelisk commemorating the first major battle in the Revolutionary War. Visitors can hike the 294 steps to the top for a great view of downtown Boston.

Back Bay

Back Bay, west of Boston Common, is lined with fancy brownstone residences. Its majestic boulevards, including Newbury St, the city's toniest shopping address, are perfect for strolling.

The **Esplanade**, a swath of greenery that runs between Storrow Dr and the Charles River, is a pedestrian paradise, with miles of paths for walking, running and cycling. If you're an experienced boater, small sailboats can be rented at **Community Boating** (☎ 617-523-1038; The Esplanade, Back Bay; ☺ Apr-Oct) for a sail on the Charles. During summer, the art deco **Hatch Memorial Shell**, accessible by a pedestrian bridge on the corner of Arlington and Beacon Sts, is the site of free concerts and, every Friday night, free movies at sunset.

Copley Sq, bounded by Boylston, Clarendon and Dartmouth Sts and St James Ave, is anchored by the gorgeous **Trinity Church** (☎ 617-536-0944; 206 Clarendon St; admission free). This national landmark, designed by architect HH Richardson, features a cozy, brightly colored interior. On the other side of Dartmouth St sits the venerable **Boston Public Library** (☎ 617-536-5400; 700 Boylston St; ☺ 9am-9pm

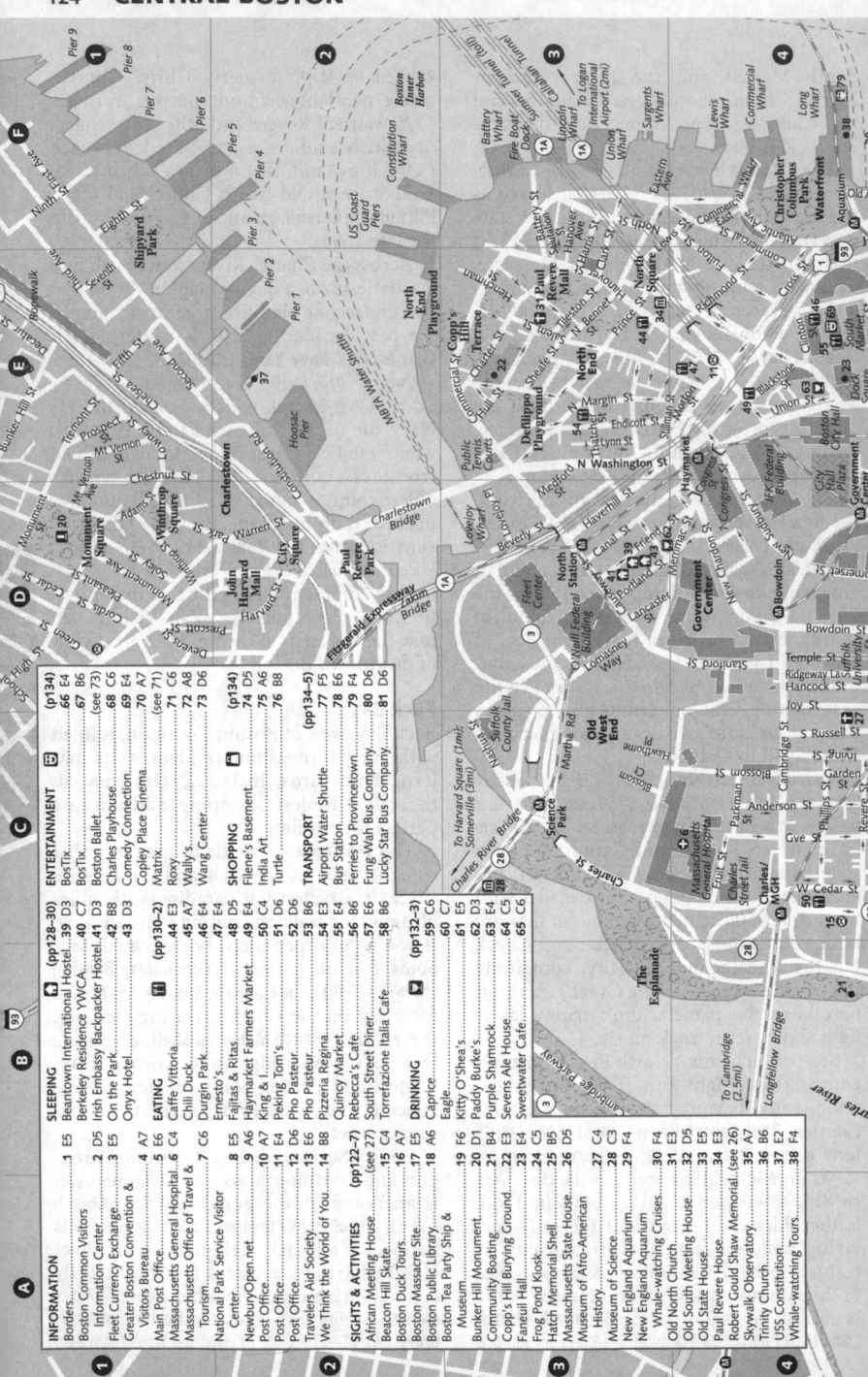

INFORMATION

Borders.................................1	E5
Boston Common Visitors	
Information Center.................2	D5
Fleet Currency Exchange.........3	E5
Greater Boston Convention &	
Visitors Bureau....................4	A7
Main Post Office....................5	E6
Massachusetts General Hospital..6	C4
Massachusetts Office of Travel &	
Tourism............................7	C6
National Park Service Visitor	
Center............................8	E5
NewburyOpen.net.................9	A6
Post Office..........................10	A7
Post Office..........................11	E4
Post Office..........................12	D6
Travelers Aid Society.............13	E6
We Think the World of You....14	B8

SIGHTS & ACTIVITIES (pp122–7)

African Meeting House.......(see 27)	
Beacon Hill Skate..................15	C4
Boston Duck Tours................16	A7
Boston Massacre Site.............17	E5
Boston Tea Party Ship &	
Museum...........................18	A6
Bunker Hill Monument...........19	F6
Community Boating................20	D1
Copp's Hill Burying Ground.....21	B4
Faneuil Hall.........................22	E3
Frog Pond Kiosk...................23	E4
Hatch Memorial Shell.............24	C5
Massachusetts State House......25	B5
Museum of Afro-American	
History.............................26	D5
New England Aquarium..........27	C4
Old North Church..................28	C3
Old South Meeting House........29	F4
Old State House....................30	F4
Paul Revere House.................31	E3
Robert Gould Shaw Memorial..(see 26)	
Science Museum...................32	D5
Skywalk Observatory.............35	A7
Trinity Church.......................36	B6
USS Constitution....................37	E2
Whale-watching Tours............38	F4

SLEEPING 🛌 (pp128–30)

Beantown International Hostel..39	D3
Berkeley Residence YWCA........40	C7
Irish Embassy Backpacker Hostel..41	D3
On the Park.........................42	B8
Onyx Hotel..........................43	D3

EATING 🍴 (pp130–2)

Caffe Vittoria.......................44	E3
Chili Duck...........................45	A7
Durgin Park.........................46	E4
Ernesto's............................47	E4
Fajitas & Ritas......................48	D5
Haymarket Farmers Market......49	E4
King & I..............................50	C4
Peking Tom's.......................51	D6
Pho Pasteur.........................52	D6
Pho Pasteur.........................53	B6
Pizzeria Regina.....................54	E3
Quincy Market......................55	E4
Rebecca's Cafe.....................56	B6
South Street Diner.................57	E6
Torrefazione Italia Cafe...........58	B6

DRINKING 🍷 (pp132–3)

Caprice...............................59	C6
Eagle.................................60	C7
Kitty O'Shea's......................61	E5
Paddy Burke's......................62	D3
Purple Shamrock...................63	E4
Sevens Ale House..................64	C5
Sweetwater Cafe...................65	C6

ENTERTAINMENT 🎭 (p134)

BosTix................................66	E4
BosTix................................67	B6
Boston Ballet...................(see 73)	
Charles Playhouse.................68	C6
Comedy Connection..............69	E4
Copley Place Cinema..............70	A7
Matrix...........................(see 71)	
Roxy.................................71	D6
Wally's..............................72	A8
Wang Center.......................73	D6

SHOPPING 🛍 (p134)

Filene's Basement..................74	D5
India Art............................75	A6
Turtle...............................76	B8

TRANSPORT (pp134–5)

Airport Water Shuttle.............77	F5
Bus Station.........................78	E6
Ferries to Provincetown..........79	F4
Fung Wah Bus Company.........80	D6
Lucky Star Bus Company.........81	D6

Mon-Thu, 9am-5pm Fri & Sat, 1-5pm Sun); be sure to visit its awe-inspiring Bates Hall Reading Room and peaceful inner courtyard.

Eight-block-long Newbury St is Boston's most glamorous, and the best place in the city to do some serious people watching. At its eastern end, near the Ritz Carlton at Arlington St, Georgio Armani, Ann Taylor and assorted art galleries (ie 'old money') predominate. If you have to ask how much something costs, you probably can't afford it. In the middle blocks are outdoor cafés and famous chains stores such as Niketown and the Gap. Toward the western end at Massachusetts Ave, the crowd leans toward punks, fashionistas and international students. The McCormick Gallery at the **Boston Architectural Center** (☎ 617-262-5000; 320 Newbury St; admission free; 🕙 8:30am-10:30pm Mon-Thu, 8:30am-9pm Fri, 9am-5pm Sat, noon-5pm Sun) has interesting exhibits about the city's buildings.

For a panoramic view of Boston, head up to the **Skywalk Observatory** (☎ 617-859-0648; 50th fl, Prudential Center, 800 Boylston St; admission $9.50; 🕙 10am-10pm), which includes exhibits on city history. Further down Boylston St, the **Institute of Contemporary Art** (ICA; ☎ 617-266-5152; 955 Boylston St; adult/student $7/5; 🕙 noon-5pm Tue, Wed & Fri, noon-9pm Thu, 11am-5pm Sat & Sun) showcases cutting-edge works by current artists. The ICA is scheduled to move into a new location along the waterfront in 2006.

The **Christian Science Church** (☎ 617-450-3790; 175 Huntington Ave; admission free; 🕙 10am-4pm Mon-Sat, 11:30am-4pm Sun) complex may be one of Boston's most underrated sights. The church itself accommodates 4000 worshippers and features a 13,000-pipe organ. Inside the adjacent Mary Baker Eddy Library for the Betterment of Humanity is the **Mapparium** (☎ 617-450-7000; 200 Massachusetts Ave; adult/student $5/3; 🕙 10am-5pm Tue-Sun), an enormous stained-glass globe (political boundaries c 1935) through which visitors can walk. The stone benches facing the Christian Science Plaza's 200yd-long reflecting pool are ideal places to relax.

Kenmore Sq & Fenway

Kenmore Sq isn't really a square – it's a converging point for Beacon St, Commonwealth Ave and Brookline Ave, as well as a hang-out for students at nearby Boston University. To get here, look for the giant Citgo sign (flashing neon at night) perched above the Buckminster Hotel. The adjacent Fenway neighborhood is home to Fenway Park and a couple of world-class museums.

The **Museum of Fine Arts** (☎ 617-267-9300; 465 Huntington Ave; adult/student $15/13; 🕙 10am-4:45pm Sat-Tue, 10am-9:45pm Wed-Fri) has Boston's largest collection of artworks from around the world, with more than 350,000 prints, paintings, photographs, textiles and fashion arts. Hold onto your ticket; if you can't see (or handle) it all in one visit, you can come back for another visit on the same ticket within 30 days.

One of the most remarkable museums in the USA, the **Isabella Stuart Gardner Museum**

A PLACE TO BELIEVE

No visit to Boston would be complete without a guided tour of **Fenway Park** (☎ 617-226-6666; 4 Yawkey Way; admission $10; tours hourly 9am-4pm), the home of major-league baseball's Red Sox. One of America's longest-running dramas, the Sox are the subject of year-round obsession by fans both local and far-flung: ('Red Sox Nation'). Though many celebrated baseball stars – including Ted Williams, Jim Rice, and Pedro Martinez – have played for the club, the Sox suffered through 86 years of futility and heartbreaking defeats after winning the 1918 World Series. Then came their stunning 2004 championship season – including a back-from-the-dead playoff victory over the despised archrival New York Yankees – which enthralled the entire country and put to rest all talk of a 'curse.' It isn't possible to overstate how much New Englanders care about this team: just tune in to the post-game call-in shows on WEEI (850AM) radio or read any of the half-dozen books about the Sox that come out every year.

New ownership has spruced up historic, quirky Fenway, which dates back to 1912 (it opened days before the *Titanic* sank), but it remains the smallest ballpark in the major leagues, with only about 35,000 seats to meet a much larger demand. **Tickets** (☎ 877-733-7699; admission $12-75) for a regular season game are extremely hard to come by. Your best bet is to wait in line outside Gate C on Lansdowne St, where unused tickets go on sale two hours before each home game.

(☎ 617-566-1401; 280 Fenway; adult/student $10/5; ☺ 11am-5pm Tue-Sun), a beautiful 1903 Venetian-style palazzo, houses the eclectic art collection of Mrs Gardner. Her personal vision is clearly on display, with works by Rembrandt, Raphael, Botticelli and Sargent, although the building and meticulously landscaped garden courtyard may be bigger stars than the collection. Superb classical and jazz concerts are held in the museum on many weekend days during the year.

Near the Boston University campus, the **Photographic Resource Center** (☎ 617-975-0600; 832 Commonwealth Ave; admission $3, free Thu & last weekend each month; ☺ 10am-6pm Tue-Fri, 10am-8pm Thu, noon-5pm Sat & Sun) presents vital and acclaimed work by modern photographers in its storefront gallery.

Columbia Point

John F Kennedy Library & Museum (☎ 617-514-1600; Columbia Point; adult/student $10/8; ☺ 9am-5pm) celebrates the life of the USA's 35th president with multimedia, pictures, documents and other ephemera of American politics. Take the T's Red Line to JFK/UMass and get on the free shuttle bus to the museum.

Across the road, the **Commonwealth Museum** (☎ 617-727-9268; 220 Morrisey Blvd; admission free; ☺ 9am-5pm Mon-Fri, 9am-3pm Sat) has rotating exhibits on Massachusetts history in two modest-sized galleries. They cover such subjects as the state's Civil War soldiers and the artifacts uncovered during the 'Big Dig' construction project.

Jamaica Plain

Part of the 'Emerald Necklace,' designed by Frederick Law Olmsted, the **Arnold Arboretum** (☎ 617-524-1718; 125 Arborway; admission free; ☺ sunrise-sunset) is a 265-acre botanical wonderland. Visitors can walk or cycle among thousands of different trees, flowers and shrubs.

Take the MBTA Orange Line to Forest Hills and walk on for a quarter-mile northwest.

Brookline

A suburb that's surrounded on three sides by Boston, Brookline is home to a modest house that was John F Kennedy's birthplace and childhood residence.

The **John Fitzgerald Kennedy National Historic Site** (☎ 617-566-7937; 83 Beals St; admission $3; ☺ 10am-4:30pm Wed-Sun May-Oct) can be reached by taking the MBTA Green Line to Coolidge Corner and walking down Harvard St.

ACTIVITIES

Community Boating (☎ 617-523-1038; The Esplanade; ☺ Apr-Oct) rents sailboats, windsurfers and kayaks from its boathouse on the Charles River by the Charles St footbridge.

Beacon Hill Skate (☎ 617-482-7400; 135 Charles St, Beacon Hill) rents in-line skates by the hour or by the day.

Frog Pond, on Boston Common, becomes an ice-skating rink from mid-November to mid-March. Rent skates and lockers at the adjacent **klosk** (☎ 617-635-2120; Beacon Hill; admission $3, skates $7, lockers $1).

WALKING TOUR

In pedestrian-friendly Boston, just about any neighborhood is worth exploring by foot for a few hours. For the visitor, though, no other walking tour offers the rewards, both visual and gastronomic, of North End's tight-knit, old-world ambience.

Begin at the foot of Salem St, filled with classic neighborhood shops run by Italian immigrants. At 57 Salem St you can pick up domestic and imported nuts, raisins, fudge and other snacks at **Dairy Fresh Candies (1)**, established by the Matara family in 1957.

Continue up Salem and hang a right at Parmenter St – you might well pass neighborhood old-timers sitting on the sidewalk in folding beach chairs and carrying on animated conversations in Italian. Walk into No 25, the unassuming **North End Public Library (2)**, and wander to the back of the main room. There you'll find a huge-scale model of Venice's Doge's Palace.

Keep walking down Parmenter until you reach Hanover St, North End's major commercial street, and chock-full of great pastry shops and cafés. Taking a left onto Hanover, you'll reach **Caffe Vittoria (3)** at No 290. Stop here for Boston's best cappuccino and the retro, mid-20th-century vibe. Resume walking, cross Prince St and on your left you'll see the Peace Garden fronting the 1873 **St Leonard's Roman Catholic Church (4)**, the first church in New England built by Italian immigrants.

A few blocks away on the left is **Paul Revere Mall**, an inviting brick plaza highlighted by an

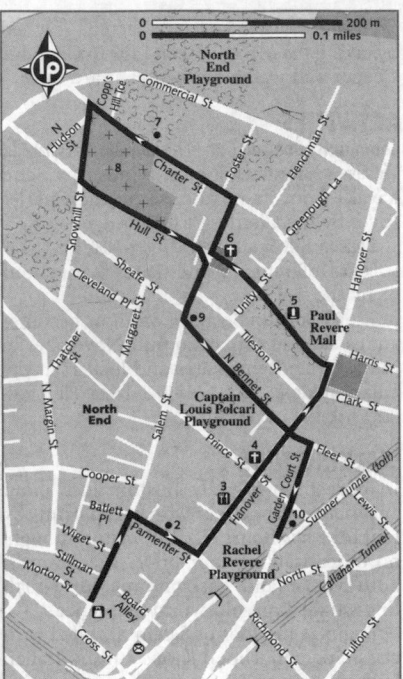

you can explore the Paul Revere House at No 19; the 1710 Pierce/Hichborn House, former residence of Revere's cousin, at No 29; and the Mariner's House, an 1838 home for visiting seamen, at No 11. Finish your tour, and your bag of Dairy Fresh snacks, down the street at Rachel Revere Playground.

TOURS

Samuel Adams Brewery (☎ 617-368-5080; 30 Germania St, Jamaica Plain; admission $2; tours 2pm Thu, 2pm & 5:30pm Fri, noon, 1pm & 2pm Sat; also 2pm Wed May-Aug) offers tours of its factory, aka the Boston Beer Museum, including a taste of its popular ales. Take the MBTA Orange Line to Stony Brook. **Harpoon Brewery** (☎ 888-427-7666; 306 Northern Ave; admission free; 11:30am-5:30pm Tue-Sat, tours 3pm Tue-Thu, 1pm & 3pm Fri & Sat) offers a similar tour at its South Boston plant.

Boston Duck Tours (☎ 617-723-3825; www.bostonducktours.com) runs cheesy but entertaining tours around the city on board renovated WWII amphibious landing vehicles (half truck, half boat), first on the city streets and then on the Charles River. You might have to quack, but it's all just goofy fun.

FESTIVALS & EVENTS

Boston Marathon (Patriots Day, third Monday in April) A century-old road race that's still going strong. Upward of one million fans line the 26.2-mile route between the village of Hopkinton and Copley Sq in Back Bay.

Boston Harborfest (late June) Eat clam chowder, visit ships, listen to free concerts on City Hall Plaza. Repeat.

Head of the Charles Regatta (October) This weekend-long event, pitting some of the world's top rowing teams against one another, draws more than 300,000 spectators to the banks of the Charles River.

First Night (December 31) Many cities have copied Boston's highly successful festival that ends the old year and starts off the new with an evening of cultural performances, colorful ice sculptures and a midnight fireworks display.

SLEEPING

Boston can be mighty expensive for bedding down, but it also has a number of centrally located hostels and affordable guesthouses (especially if two or more share a room). Make reservations well in advance during high season (June to August) and book way, way, way ahead if you're coming in late May; that's when all of the colleges and universities in the area hold graduation ceremonies.

equestrian **statue (5)** of the great patriot himself. Revere was actually born on Hanover St, lived on nearby North Sq and died on Charter St. Have a seat and watch people come and go, or read the many historical markers against the wall. At the end of the mall is the famed **Old North Church (6)**, the former Christ Church. Wander around the corner, back to Salem St, and enter this important site of American Revolutionary history.

Where Salem dead ends at Charter St, make a left until you reach **Copp's Hill Terrace (7)**, a multilevel public park that affords great views of the USS *Constitution* and Charlestown across the Charles River. Take a left onto Snowhill St and then left again onto Hull St, to **Copp's Hill Burying Ground (8)**. After perusing the ancient grave markers, continue on Hull, turn right back onto Salem and then left onto North Bennet St. At this corner is the **North Bennet School (9)**, currently used as a school for woodworkers, jewelers and other artisans.

Follow North Bennet St to Garden Court St, turn right and you'll end up at **North Sq (10)**, a triangular patch of cobblestone. Here

---

SPLURGE!

Between April and October, whale-watching tours are one of the most popular activities for visitors to Boston. Most of the trips involve a 30-mile boat trip east of the city, out to the 800-sq-mile Stellwagen Bank, a prime ocean feeding area for humpback, finback and minke whales. You'll probably also see dolphins (who love to swim alongside the boats), birds and other sea life. Most watches are narrated by an on-board naturalist, and most of the tour operators 'guarantee' a whale sighting; you'll get a free ticket for another trip if you don't see one. Be sure to bring a jacket or sweater; even on a warm day offshore conditions can be windy at best and inclement at worst. Don't forget rubber-soled shoes, sunscreen and sunglasses, and (of course) camera and film. Trips leave from Central or Rowes Wharf. Take the MBTA Blue Line to Aquarium station. Reservations are recommended on weekends and holidays. Discount coupons are often available at visitors centers.

The following companies offer tours:

- **New England Aquarium** (☎ 617-973-5281; adult/student $29/26)
- **Massachusetts Bay Lines** (☎ 617-542-8000; admission $29)
- **Boston Harbor Cruises** (☎ 617-227-4321; admission $30)

For more information on bed and breakfasts in Boston, call the **Bed & Breakfast Associates Bay Colony** (☎ 781-449-5302; info@bnbboston.com).

Hostels

HI Boston (☎ 617-536-9455; www.bostonhostel.org; 12 Hemenway St, Fenway; dm $27-35; ⊗ 24hr; ✕ ✕ ☐) Close to the popular Landsdowne St nightspots, this 205-bed hostel offers some plum amenities such as a locker and lamp per bed, common rooms, a laundry room, and bathrooms stocked with hairdryers, shampoo and shower gel. What really makes it, though, are nightly social events like free movies and Irish pub crawls. Word's out though; reservations essential year-round.

HI Fenway Summer Hostel (☎ 617-267-8599; fenway@bostonhostel.org; 575 Commonwealth Ave, Kenmore Sq; dm $33-39, r $99-120; ⊗ 24hr May 31–mid-Aug; ✕ ✕ ☐) This former Howard Johnsons in Kenmore Sq serves as an overflow hostel during summer months, with 465 beds spread among 100 rooms on eight floors. Private rooms (each with bathroom) work well for large groups, families and couples. Breakfast is served, but there's no kitchen.

Beantown International Hostel (☎ 617-723-0800; 222 Friend St, Government Center; dm $25; ⊗ curfew 2.15am, checkout 10am; ✕ ☐) and **Irish Embassy Backpacker Hostel** (☎ 617-973-4841; 232-34 Friend St, Government Center; dm $25; ✕ ☐) These two private hostels on the fringes of North Station offer bare-bones yet clean accommodations. The 52-bed Beantown and 50-bed Irish Embassy feature wheelchair-accessible dorm rooms with free lockers, laundry and a free buffet on Thursday and Friday at nearby McGunn's Pub. The choice location, mere blocks from Quincy Market and North End, draws a large European contingent. Be sure to reserve at least a week in advance and get your breakfast elsewhere – it's not offered here.

YMCA of Greater Boston (☎ 617-536-7800; 316 Huntington Ave, South End; s/d/t $46/66/81, key deposit $5) Sparse, institutional and impersonal are the best words to describe many of the 39 rooms here. Still, it's hard to beat the price for private, secure accommodations near the Museum of Fine Arts and Symphony Hall. Rooms are available for men and women June through August; the rest of the year, it's men only. Prices include breakfast and use of the Y's fine exercise facilities. Be sure to make reservations at least two weeks in advance.

Berkeley Residence YWCA (☎ 617-375-2524; rooms_berkeley@ywcaboston.org; 40 Berkeley St, South End; r $56-99) Located in the heart of charming South End, this 200-room women-only dormitory provides guests with phones, a central TV, dining room, living room, laundry room and 24-hour security. A $2 membership fee is required.

Guesthouses & Hotels

Midtown Hotel (☎ 617-262-1000; www.midtownhotel.com; 220 Huntington Ave, South End; r $89-239; P ✕ ☐ ✕) If you're traveling with others, and for some reason you've chosen to drive in Boston, this is probably the place for you.

There's free parking at this two-story hotel near the Prudential Center, as well as a private pool and clean, comfortable rooms.

On the Park (☎ 888-486-6018; 166 West Canton St, South End; r with shared bathroom $95-110; ☒ ☒) This charming South End B&B, run by a colorful couple, is a 4th-floor walk-up in a Victorian townhouse. Although there are only two guest rooms, they're both cozy and comfortable, and there is a main sitting room with TV. A generous continental breakfast is included.

463 Beacon St Guest House (☎ 617-536-1302; www.463beacon.com; 463 Beacon St, Back Bay; r $69-139; ☒) This renovated 19th-century brownstone is located on a quiet Back Bay street. There are 20 rooms on six floors, and each one includes a mini-fridge and microwave oven. The rooms with bay windows that face Beacon St, such as Room 40, are especially bright and cheery. Breakfast is not included and there's no elevator – be prepared to climb stairs – but there's no room tax either. If you're staying longer, the innkeeper rents other apartments in the neighborhood starting at $500 per week.

Farrington Inn (☎ 800-767-5337; www.farrington inn.com; 23 Farrington Ave, Kenmore Sq; s/d/t with shared bathroom $55/75/95; ℗) This budget B&B near Boston University has a variety of lodging including studios and rooms with a kitchenette. Rates include parking and free local phone service.

Anthony's Town House (☎ 617-566-3972; 1085 Beacon St, Brookline; s/d with semi-private bathroom

---

$50/90; ☒ ☒) Near Kenmore Sq, just across the Brookline town line, this immaculate family-run guesthouse has been open since 1944. All 10 rooms have large walk-in closets, cable TV and plush furnishings. The staff goes to great lengths for guests. Reservations are recommended; be sure to ask for seasonal rates and weekly discounts.

EATING

Boston's diversity of cultures means that there is now a great variety of relatively inexpensive ethnic restaurants to go along with the old reliable brewpubs and pizza places that have long served the city's large and budget-conscious student population.

Beacon Hill, Government Center & North End

King & I (☎ 617-227-3320; 145 Charles St; mains $8-11) This cozy Thai restaurant on Beacon Hill features a large menu of curries and noodle dishes.

Quincy Market (☎ 617-523-1300) Choose from more than 40 eateries in three buildings, including the main colonnade, which is one of the most visited food halls in the world. Bordered by Clinton, Chatham and Commercial Sts.

Durgin Park (☎ 617-227-2038; 340 Faneuil Hall Marketplace; mains $8-25) A Boston institution, Durgin Park's family-style seating and somewhat curt service are part of the place's charm. Dig into hearty New England specialties such as Yankee Pot Roast and Baked Scallops.

Haymarket Farmers Market (Blackstone St) Boston's historic open-air market is held every Friday and Saturday. Be prepared to buy your fruits and vegetables by the pound, not by the item, and check for freshness.

Pizzeria Regina (☎ 617-227-0765; 11 Thatcher St; pizzas $8-17) Boston's oldest brick-oven pizzeria and still its most famous. Join the line of tourists waiting for a taste of authentic thin-crust pies.

Ernesto's (☎ 617-523-1373; 69 Salem St; pizza slices $2.75-4.50) Want some pizza without Regina's crowds? This tiny storefront spot in the heart of North End is a really great place for monster-sized slices.

Downtown Crossing & Chinatown

Fajitas & Ritas (☎ 617-426-1222; 23 West St; mains $6-12) The Downtown Crossing branch of this

---

SPLURGE!

Onyx Hotel (☎ 617-557-9955; www.onyxhotel .com; 155 Portland St, Government Center; r from $229; ℗ ☒ ☒ ☐ ☒) If you really want to go all out and experience Boston like a movie star or captain of industry, check into this luxurious, ultra-hip hotel – anointed 'The Official Hotel of the Britney Spears Tour' – located a couple of blocks away from the Fleet Center. The 112 stylish guest rooms are designed with a subtle palette of solid earth tones, and feature a CD player, WebTV, nightly turn-down service and more. There's also free access to the hotel's health club, morning weekday town-car service to the Financial District (if you need it), and an evening wine reception.

popular, budget-friendly Tex-Mex eatery offers extremely generous portions. Its tasty margaritas nicely complement the food.

Peking Tom's (☎ 617-482-6282; 25 Kingston St; mains $6-20; ☽ to 1am) Unlike most Chinatown restaurants, Peking Tom's features stylish décor and subdued lighting. Reasonably priced Cantonese dishes are both familiar (crab Rangoon) and unique (orange and tamarind glazed spare ribs). Along with the exotic tropical drinks, it's a winning combination that draws a crowd.

South Street Diner (☎ 617-350-0028; 178 Kneeland St; mains $5-10; ☽ 24hr) This traditional 1950s diner is open 24-7 and serves up home-style servings of burgers, steak and fish, not to mention 22 different beers.

Back Bay & South End

Newbury Pizza & Subs (☎ 617-536-9451; 225 Newbury St; pizza slices $2.25-2.75) Somewhat out of place on its upscale street, this basement-level eatery nevertheless dishes out solid pizzas and sub sandwiches.

Torrefazzione Italia (☎ 617-424-0951; 85 Newbury St) This upscale café chain has a prime Newbury St locale that comes complete with an outdoor patio – perfect for downing an espresso, munching on a biscotti and watching the world go by.

Pho Pasteur (☎ 617-262-8200; 119 Newbury St; mains $7-15) The smallish Newbury St branch of what is considered Boston's top Vietnamese restaurant has outstanding noodle soups. There's another branch at Chinatown.

Rebecca's Café (☎ 617-267-1122; 112 Newbury St; mains $5-8) The best bet for low-carb, vegetarian and other healthy menu items, Rebecca's offers a daily Blue Plate special ($6.75) main dish served with salad and bread.

Men-Tei (☎ 617-425-0066; 66 Hereford St; mains $7-11) This hole-in-the-wall Japanese restaurant offers a dizzying array of noodle and rice dishes.

Chilli Duck (☎ 617-236-5208; 829 Boylston St; mains $6-14) Colorful décor serves as the setting for this basement restaurant that serves signature Thai curries and vegetarian specialties.

Bob the Chef's (☎ 617-536-6204; 604 Columbus Ave; mains $7-15) A cozy South End joint that provides jazz as the background to filling Southern comfort food – fried chicken, jambalaya, collard greens and candied yams. Don't miss the all-you-can-eat Sunday brunch ($19) accompanied by live music.

Kenmore Sq & Fenway

Ankara Cafe (☎ 617-437-0404; 472 Commonwealth Ave; mains $5-14) A tiny, friendly eatery that makes pizzas, wraps, paninis and triple-decker sandwiches named after area colleges.

Boston Billiard Club (☎ 617-536-7665; 126 Brookline Ave; mains $6-8) A Fenway bar that doubles as a budget traveler's best friend: it pours $1 draft beers and serves $1 hot dogs on Red Sox game days.

Fresh City (☎ 617-424-7907; Landmark Center, 201 Brookline Ave; mains $5-8) Wraps, salads and Asian noodle dishes and smoothies in a clean, caféteria-style setting.

T Anthony (☎ 617-734-7708; 1016 Commonwealth Ave; pizzas $6-14) This longtime Boston University hang-out dishes out pizza slices, subs and other cheap eats all day long.

Brown Sugar Café (☎ 617-266-2928; 129 Jersey St; mains $7-15) A highly regarded Thai restaurant serving specialties with names like 'avocado dancing' and 'three stooges'.

El Pelon Taqueria (☎ 617-262-9090; 92 Peterborough St; burritos $4-6) From burritos to *tamales* to *quesadillas*, this no-frills storefront eatery has some very good, very filling, very authentic Mexican dishes.

Buteco (☎ 617-247-9508; 130 Jersey St; mains $8-13) Specializing in Brazilian cooking, this Fenway neighborhood restaurant is a meat lover's paradise, although there are some vegetarian and fish dishes as well. Try the *bife a mineira* (steak).

Jamaica Plain

'JP' may not be well known to most tourists, but it's one of the city's hippest neighborhoods, with a number of stylish eateries and budget restaurants. Take the MBTA Orange Line to Green St.

Bella Luna (☎ 617-524-6060; 405 Centre St; mains $5-18) This art-filled dining room, located upstairs from the Milky Way bar (p133), offers especially delicious pasta dishes and flavorful gourmet pizzas.

La Pupusa Guanaca (☎ 617-524-4900; 378 Centre St; mains $4-7) This tiny restaurant (three tables) in Hyde Sq produces delicious Salvadoran *pupusas* – cornmeal pancakes filled with some combination of beans, cheese and meat. If there isn't room to sit down, take them to go and head next door to the Brendan Behan Pub.

Jake's Boss BBQ (☎ 617-983-3701; 3492 Washington St; mains $8-16) The affable Kenton Jacobs (aka

'Jake') cooks up mesquite- and hickory-smoked pork ribs for a grateful clientele. There's also beef brisket, chicken and the usual Southern fixins. And the legendary Doyle's Pub is just across the street.

June Bug Cafe (☎ 617-522-2393; 403a Centre St; sandwiches $5.75-7) A casual café with a menu of custom-made veggie and meat sandwiches as well as a create-your-own-omelet brunch.

Brookline

Chef Choy's House (☎ 617-566-2275; 354 Chestnut Hill Ave; mains $6-11) This restaurant serves up cheap, filling, high-quality Chinese food in the Boston College neighborhood of Cleveland Circle. The Mongolian sliced lamb is highly recommended.

Rubin's (☎ 617-731-8787; 500 Harvard St; mains $6-16) A true New York–style delicatessen, Rubin's hot pastrami sandwiches and potato pancakes make it one of the most popular gathering places for Brookline's sizable Jewish population.

DRINKING

Boston holds its own with the great drinking cities of the world, despite the Mayberry-esque 1am closing time for bars that compares unfavorably with New York City. (Nightclubs stay open until 2am.) If you're headed out for an evening of imbibing, bring some legitimate photo ID; without it – and without being 21 – you won't get in anywhere.

Bars

Boston Beer Works (☎ 617-536-2337; 61 Brookline Ave, Fenway) The place to go before and after Red Sox games, this enormous bar, conveniently situated across the street from Fenway Park, has more than a dozen microbrews, produced in-house, on tap. It's also a full-service restaurant.

Jillian's (☎ 617-437-0300; 145 Ipswich St, Fenway) This über-hip alcohol-entertainment complex has three floors of drinking-related activity. Jillian's itself, located on the 2nd floor, has loads of comfortable seating, more than 50 pool and billiards tables, foosball, darts and table tennis. The 3rd-floor **Lucky Strike Lanes** (per game $4.50-5.95, shoe rentals $3.50) features 16 bowling lanes, lots of couches and a 50ft-long bar. **Tequila Rain** (☎ 617-859-0030; 3 Lansdowne St), on the ground

floor, promises 'Spring Break 52 Weeks a Year.' DJs spin Top 40 and hip-hop Friday and Saturday.

Tiki Room (☎ 617-351-2580; 1 Lansdowne St, Fenway; ⊗ Tue-Sat) A tropical-themed club pouring Scorpion Bowls and other sweet drinks to wash down Polynesian snacks.

Cask 'n' Flagon (☎ 617-536-4840; 62 Brookline Ave, Kenmore Sq) This longtime Fenway bar offers shoestring specials like $5 pitchers of beer and half-priced appetizers.

Audobon Circle (☎ 617-421-1910; 838 Beacon St, Kenmore Sq) Aiming toward a slightly more sophisticated crowd, this spacious bar, a good place for larger groups, serves draft beers and a full menu of tequilas.

Sonsie (☎ 617-351-2500; 327 Newbury St, Back Bay) A popular see-and-be-seen spot that draws more than its fair share of beautiful people and European students with bulging wallets. Skip the expensive meal and have a pretty drink at the 50ft-long mahogany bar. Red Room Lounge downstairs serves cocktails Wednesday to Saturday nights.

Top of the Hub (☎ 617-536-1175; 800 Boylston St, Back Bay) Head to the 52nd floor of the Prudential Center, bypass the ultra-expensive restaurant of the same name and discover this casual bar-lounge where the view is fantastic, the drinks don't cost much more than at an average bar and there's live jazz nightly – with no cover charge.

Eagle (☎ 617-542-4494; 520 Tremont St, South End) DJs spin seven nights a week at this popular gay hang-out in South End.

Sevens Ale House (☎ 617-523-9074; 77 Charles St, Beacon Hill) A cloistered, rustic pub on Beacon Hill, which has the beers to match the atmosphere – bottled British and Irish brews like Sam Smith and Newcastle Brown are among the offerings.

Sweetwater Cafe (☎ 617-351-2515; 3 Boylston Pl, Theater District) This casual alleyway bar in the Theater District serves $2.50 Pabst Blue Ribbon draft beer during happy hour. Later in the evening, there's live acoustic music and no cover charge.

Caprice (☎ 617-292-0080; 275 Tremont St, Theater District) Part of the Roxy entertainment complex, this fashionable downtown bar and lounge features comfortable sofas and red pool tables.

Purple Shamrock (☎ 617-227-2060; 1 Union St, Government Center) The young, just-legal-to-drink crowd hits Faneuil Hall and this nightspot

TOP FIVE BOSTON IRISH BARS

With such a large population of Irish descent, Boston is an Irish-pub crawler's heaven. While there are dozens to choose from, here are five worth stopping by for a tipple:

■ **Brendan Behan** (☎ 617-522-5386; 378 Centre St, Jamaica Plain) This classic, dark, intimate pub in Jamaica Plain draws in a diverse neighborhood crowd.

■ **Doyle's** (☎ 617-524-2345; 3484 Washington St, Jamaica Plain) Beloved local landmark saloon that dates back to 1882. A perfect place to spend St Patrick's Day.

■ **Paddy Burke's** (☎ 617-367-8370; 132 Portland St, Government Center) Located on Boston's smallest block, the bar and the old brick building that houses it are shoehorned between two side streets. Guinness on draft, and there's a burger-and-beer special ($7.75).

■ **Crossroads Irish Pub** (☎ 617-262-7371; 495 Beacon St, Back Bay) Friendly staff, a great selection of beers, free appetizers daily from 5pm to 7pm, and nightly activities – including Irish music with no cover charge on Monday night – are part of this pub's drawing power.

■ **Kitty O'Shea's** (☎ 617-725-0100; 131 State St, Financial District) Traditional Irish bar in the heart of the Financial District. Has live music Thursday to Saturday and a DJ on Saturday night.

for live bands on Friday and Saturday and for DJs the rest of the week.

Silhouette (☎ 617-254-9306; 200 Brighton Ave, Allston) Out in the college ghetto hinterland of Allston, this no-frills bar with the neon sign out front draws artsy 20-somethings from the 'hood.

Sunset Grill & Tap (☎ 617-254-1331; 130 Brighton Ave, Allston) With 112 beers on tap, 380 beers in bottles and any brew you'd like in the famous 'yard glass' of ale, it's safe to say that this place is Boston's beer central. Burgers, fries and other pub grub are available to help soak up the alcohol.

Kells (☎ 617-623-9910; 161 Brighton Ave, Allston) A popular college bar and dance club that gets extremely crowded on Friday and Saturday nights.

Live Music

Paradise Rock Club (☎ 617-562-8800; 969 Commonwealth Ave, Kenmore Sq) A landmark nightspot that hosts nationally known rock artists. The front room, Paradise, presents more alternative, edgier acts.

Bill's Bar & Lounge (☎ 617-421-9678; 5 Lansdowne St, Fenway) A UN of live music – punk, metal, funk, ska and reggae – all presented in a modest, un-Lansdowne-like environment.

Wally's (☎ 617-424-1408; 427 Massachusetts Ave, South End) This venerable South End dive bar near Symphony Hall is entering its seventh decade of showcasing live jazz acts.

Milky Way (☎ 617-524-3740; 403 Centre St, Jamaica Plain) Jamaica Plain locals come to this basement club all week long for the live music, pool tables, bowling alley and hip bar. On Saturday night it attracts a really big crowd for Mango's Latin Dance Club – complete with salsa lessons.

Midway Cafe (☎ 617-524-9038; 3496 Washington St, Jamaica Plain) An unpretentious, mellow joint smack in the heart of Jamaica Plain that hosts local rock, folk and blues acts six nights a week.

CLUBBING

Roxy (☎ 617-338-7699; 279 Tremont St, Theater District) and **Matrix** (☎ 617-542-4077; 275 Tremont St, Theater District) Self-proclaimed as Boston's hottest nightspots, the upstairs Roxy and smaller, downstairs Matrix host events as diverse as fashion shows and live music, but their bread and butter is dancing, including 18- and-over nights on Friday.

Avalon (☎ 617-262-2424; 15 Lansdowne St, Fenway) A big dance club best known for its 'Avaland' Friday night lineup of multiple DJs. Sunday's gay night is the biggest in Boston.

Axis (☎ 617-262-2437; 13 Lansdowne St, Fenway) The undisputed king of Lansdowne St college nightlife. Open to the 19-year-old-and-up crowd from Monday to Friday, Axis is the place to go for dancing six nights a week, including gay night on Monday.

Embassy (☎ 617-536-2100; 30 Lansdowne St, Fenway) Lansdowne St's upscale club, popular with the European student crowd and heavy on the international disco.

NEW ENGLAND

ENTERTAINMENT
Cinemas
Copley Place (☎ 617-369-5000; 100 Huntington Ave, South End) This 11-screen cinema shows a variety of first-run films.

Coolidge Corner Theater (☎ 617-734-2500; 290 Harvard St, Brookline) Recently refurbished 1933 art deco movie house in Brookline shows first-run independent films and classic movies.

Performing Arts
BosTix (www.artsboston.org) has kiosks in both Copley Sq and Fanueil Hall Marketplace selling half-price, day-of-show tickets for major theater productions.

Symphony Hall (☎ 617-266-1492; 301 Massachusetts Ave, South End) The center of classical music in the city, this is where the highly regarded Boston Symphony Orchestra and the beloved Boston Pops both perform.

New England Conservatory of Music (☎ 617-585-1122; Jordan Hall, 30 Gainsborough St, South End) Free performances of classical and jazz music are held here.

Comedy Connection (☎ 617-248-9700; Quincy Market, Government Center) Hosts national and local comedy acts.

Wang Center (☎ 617-482-9393; 270 Tremont St, Theater District) This landmark theater presents the Boston Ballet, opera and musicals.

Charles Playhouse (☎ 617-426-5225, 74 Warrenton St, Theater District; adult/student $34/20; 1 show nightly Tue-Fri, 2 shows Sat & Sun) The long-running 'Shear Madness,' a comedy-mystery that takes place in a hair salon, varies according to the (welcome) audience participation and whatever current events the script references that night.

Boston Center for the Arts (☎ 617-426-5000; 539 Tremont St, South End) The historic Cyclorama building in South End houses this urban cultural village with three theaters, the Mills Gallery and 50 artists studios.

There are many free concerts held at the **Hatch Memorial Shell** (☎ 617-727-9547; Charles River Esplanade, Back Bay), including the Boston Pops' July 4th concert, complete with huge crowds and huge fireworks. The City of Boston shows free movies here on Friday night during summer.

Sports
The **Boston Red Sox** play baseball at **Fenway Park** (☎ 617-226-6000; 4 Yawkey Way, Fenway; tickets $12-110) between April and October.

Between late October and April, the NBA **Boston Celtics** (☎ 617-523-3030; tickets $10-170) play basketball and the NHL **Boston Bruins** (☎ 617-624-1900; tickets $19-99) strut their stuff on the hockey rink at the **Fleet Center** (150 Causeway St, Government Center).

At sparkling new **Gillette Stadium** in Foxboro, 25 miles south of Boston and accessible via MBTA commuter rail from South Station, the NFL **New England Patriots** (☎ 508-543-8200; tickets $49-99) play football from September to December and the MLS **New England Revolution** (☎ 877-438-7387; tickets $16-32) play pro soccer from April to October.

SHOPPING
There are hundreds of stores in and around Boston. The following is just a sample of what's out there:

Filene's Basement (☎ 617-542-2011; 426 Washington St) Legendary Boston bargain outlet in the basement of Filene's flagship Downtown Crossing store. Unless you're a masochist, avoid the unruly mobs during the annual wedding gown sale.

Newbury Comics (☎ 617-236-4930; 332 Newbury St, Back Bay) Venerable regional chain store stocking independent music, CDs, DVDs, Red Sox paraphernalia and comics.

Condom World (☎ 617-267-7233; 332 Newbury St, Back Bay) 'Protect and serve,' the store's slogan, needs no further explanation.

India Art (☎ 617-266-6539; 223 Newbury St, Back Bay) Henna tattoos, incense and more.

Turtle (☎ 617-266-2610; 619a Tremont St, South End) South End boutique selling stylish clothing and pieces by new designers.

Brookline Booksmith (☎ 617-566-6660; 279 Harvard St, Brookline) Superb independent bookstore in Brookline's Coolidge Corner.

GETTING THERE & AWAY
Logan International Airport (BOS; ☎ 800-235-6426) is conveniently located across the water in East Boston, just a couple of miles from downtown via the Callahan Tunnel, the Ted Williams Tunnel or the MBTA Blue Line's Airport station. It handles many domestic and international flights.

Amtrak (☎ 800-872-7245) trains arrive and depart from both Back Bay and South Stations. **Bonanza** (☎ 888-751-8800), **Greyhound** (☎ 800-231-2222) and **Peter Pan** (☎ 800-237-8747) bus lines also stop at South Station. All have regular service to Portland, Providence, New Haven and New York.

CHINATOWN BUS

Much as low-cost, discount airlines have changed the way Europeans travel on the continent, so too have the Chinatown buses changed the way people travel between Boston and New York City. Started in the mid-1990s, these incredibly inexpensive bus rides (one way $10) have become the transportation of choice for students, backpackers and low-income families shuttling between the two cities. The buses themselves are generally clean, generally timely (between four and five hours each way, depending on traffic), but generally not for those seeking peace and quiet – besides being packed full with passengers, the bus operators seem to believe that showing on-board videos of old Jackie Chan and Arnold Schwarzenegger action movies, with the volume turned to 11, is a great way to keep folks entertained during the trip. Still, you can't beat the price, and there are two major competitors to choose from, with buses departing daily, every hour on the hour, from early morning to late evening.

■ **Fung Wah** (☎ 617-338-1163; www.fungwahbus.com; 68 Beach St)

■ **Lucky Star** (☎ 617-426-8801; www.luckystarbus.com; 42b Harrison Ave)

Bay State Cruises (☎ 617-748-1428) operates ferries from the Commonwealth Pier in South Boston to Provincetown on Cape Cod.

GETTING AROUND

The **Massachusetts Bay Transportation Authority** (MBTA; ☎ 617-222-3200; www.mbta.com), better known as the 'T', operates the USA's oldest underground railway. Four color-coded subway lines (Green, Red, Orange and Blue) serve Boston, Cambridge, Brookline and the outlying suburbs, with hub stations at Park St, Downtown Crossing, State St and Government Center. (Hint: don't waste time and money traveling on the T for just one or two stops within Boston's compact downtown.) 'Inbound' trains are those headed toward downtown, whereas 'Outbound' trains are headed away from downtown. Check the destinations before boarding.

It ain't New York, but Boston generally has enough taxis to serve the needs of late-night tipplers who have missed the last train. Try **Metro Cab** (☎ 617-782-5500) and **Town Taxi** (☎ 617-536-5000).

Cars and motorcycles are *not* recommended. Traffic, parking and the fact that all you'll want to see is easily reachable by foot or the T make having a car here crazy. You should only rent cars – at the airport or at many downtown locations – if you need one for traveling to another destination.

There are many places where you can rent bikes in Boston, including **Back Bay Bicycles** (☎ 617-247-2336; 366 Commonwealth Ave).

AROUND BOSTON

CAMBRIDGE

Cambridge, directly across the Charles River from Boston, is the home of Ivy League flagship Harvard University, the first institute of higher education in the USA, and the high-tech-oriented Massachusetts Institute of Technology (MIT). It's not for nothing that Cambridge is know for its 'Left Bank' culture – as well as having the world's largest concentration of bookstores, this is a mecca of progressive politics. For the visitor, Harvard Sq offers great shopping and eating, while nearby Central Sq and Porter Sq have their share of nightlife.

Take the MBTA Red Line to Harvard Sq station.

Sights

As you exit the Harvard T station, you'll step right into **Harvard Sq**. This triangular expanse of brick is in essence the heart of Cambridge: a hang-out spot for students, break-dancers, young punks and petition-carrying activists. A few yards away are **Out Of Town News**, a kiosk that sells magazines and newspapers from around the world, and **Au Bon Pain** (☎ 617-497-9797; 1316 Mass Ave), a café whose outdoor patio is a popular rendezvous spot and the site of many an impromptu chess tournament. Across the street lies the **Harvard Coop** (☎ 617-499-2000; 1400 Mass Ave), the country's oldest college cooperative, with student necessities and much more spread across two adjacent buildings.

NEW ENGLAND

Founded in 1636, **Harvard University** (☎ 617-495-1000; www.harvard.edu) remains the jewel of American universities. Its illustrious history, handsome, ivy-covered buildings and numerous points of interest make it a popular destination – even for visitors not applying for admission. Campus tours leave from the **Holyoke Center** (☎ 617-495-1573; 1350 Massachusetts Ave; admission free; tours 10am & 2pm Mon-Fri, 2pm Sat Sep-May; 10am, 11:15am, 2pm & 3:15pm Mon-Sat mid-Jun–mid-Aug).

The campus has an amazing collection of museums. The **Harvard Museums of Natural History** (☎ 617-495-3045; 26 Oxford St; adult/student $7.50/6, admission free 9am-noon Sun, 3-5pm Wed Sep-May; 9am-5pm) combines the school's collections from its botanical, mineralogical and comparative zoology museums. The adjacent **Peabody Museum of Archeology & Ethnology** (☎ 617-496-1027; 11 Divinity Ave) is devoted to the anthropological history of human culture. The **Fogg Art Museum** (☎ 617-495-9400; 32 Quincy St; adult/student $6.50/5, admission free 10am-noon Sat; 10am-5pm Mon-Sat, 1-5pm Sun) surveys Western art since medieval times. Admission to the Fogg also gets you into the Northern European–centric **Busch-Reisinger Museum**, housed in the same building; and the Asian art–oriented **Arthur Sackler Museum** (485 Broadway). To save money, pick up a **Harvard Hot Ticket** (adult/student $10/8), available at any of the above locations; it's good for single admission to every Harvard museum.

Much further down Massachusetts Ave is the **Massachusetts Institute of Technology** (MIT; ☎ 617-253-1000; www.mit.edu). Easy jokes about plastic-rimmed glasses and pocket protectors aside, MIT has been a hot spot for scientific research since its founding in 1861. The campus is a riot of interesting architecture, from the modernist **List Visual Art Center** (20 Ames St) to the controversial Frank Gehry–designed **Stata Center** (32 Vassar St). There are also free **campus tours** (departing from lobby of Bldg 7, 77 Massachusetts Ave; tours 10am & 2pm Mon-Fri). East Campus is a short walk from the MBTA Red Line's Kendall Sq station.

MIT Museum (☎ 617-253-4444; 265 Massachusetts Ave; adult/student $5/2, free 3rd Sun each month; 10am-5pm Tue-Fri, noon-5pm Sat & Sun), dedicated to the work of the school's famous scientists and engineers, shows the layperson just how geeks have inherited the earth. Exhibits focus on robots and artificial intelligence as well as architecture, kinetic sculpture and more.

Eating

Mr Bartley's Burger Cottage (☎ 617-354-6559; 1246 Massachusetts Ave; burgers $5-10) While Harvard Sq rapidly gentrifies, Bartley's is that old college standby: the greasy spoon. This compact restaurant packs in the crowds for its juicy grilled hamburgers with a wide variety of toppings and pretty clever names. Viagra burger, anyone?

Grendel's Den (☎ 617-491-1160; 89 Winthrop St; mains $6-9) This longtime eatery (established 1271) serves up pub food and a $4 express lunch. For those on a budget, all menu items are half-price daily from 5pm to 7pm and from 9pm to 11:30pm Sunday to Thursday.

Enormous Room (☎ 617-491-5550; 567 Massachusetts Ave; mains $14) As much a chill-out spot as a restaurant, this Central Sq space serves up terrific North African–inspired dishes to patrons seated, communal style, on plush sofas and chairs. Sit back and relax: the only menu choice here is meat or vegetarian.

Cambridge Common (☎ 617-547-1228; 1667 Massachusetts Ave; mains $5-13) As well as its popular Sunday brunch, this large restaurant serves reasonably priced American dishes. The full bar has 24 brews on draft.

Anna's Taqueria (☎ 617-661-8500; 822 Somerville Ave; mains $3-7) The Porter Sq outpost of the wildly popular local Mexican restaurant chain. The burritos here are consistently voted best in greater Boston.

Bluefin (☎ 617-497-8022; Ste 1, 1815 Massachusetts Ave; mains $4-12) One of numerous Japanese restaurants inside the Porter Exchange building, Bluefin offers inexpensive sushi, sashimi and other specialties in a casual setting.

Indian Club (☎ 617-491-7750; 1755 Massachusetts Ave; mains $9-15) This charming restaurant serves a full menu of tandooris, biryanis and masalas. The friendly staff serves a 12-course lunch buffet on weekends for $7.95.

Sugar & Spice (☎ 617-868-4200; 1933 Massachusetts Ave; mains $8-14) Cheap and filling Thai food on the outskirts of Porter Sq. Try the drunken noodles or the intriguingly named 'lovely couple'.

Ice-cream aficionados are well served by Cambridge. Two especially good spots for the cool dessert are **Christina's Ice Cream** (☎ 617-492-7021; 1255 Cambridge St) located in Inman Sq, and **Toscanini's** (☎ 617-491-5877; 899 Main St), voted as having 'the world's best ice cream' by no less an authority than the *New York Times*.

Drinking

BARS

Shay's (☎ 617-864-9161; 58 JFK St) The patio of this pub and wine bar facing JFK Park is populated by a great mix of students, foreign visitors, bohemians and whoever else wants to join the party. Happy hour (5pm to 8pm) often sees a line forming for a chance at some alfresco drinking.

Border Cafe (☎ 617-864-6100; 32 Church St) This Tex-Mex joint in the heart of Harvard Sq has excellent margaritas and a college-age crowd ready to drink them.

Redline (☎ 617-491-9851; 59 JFK St) A Harvard hot spot that features DJs spinning music Wednesday through Saturday.

Algiers (☎ 617-492-1557; 40 Brattle St) Right above the Brattle St Theater, this restaurant-café serves hot drinks, Italian sodas and snack foods, and is the perfect place for post-movie discussions. Look for seating on the 2nd-floor outdoor deck overlooking Brattle St.

Café Pamplona (12 Bow St) This tiny remnant of Cambridge's beatnik culture from the 1950s and '60s is one of the last remaining coffeehouses from that era.

River Gods (☎ 617-576-1881; 125 River St) A Central Sq Irish bar with hip décor, low-priced drinks and guest DJs spinning a variety of tunes every night of the week from 9pm. The low-budget college crowd comes here in droves to listen to free music.

Phoenix Landing (☎ 617-576-6260; 512 Massachusetts Ave) An 'alternative Irish bar' that features dancing and DJs nightly, and also shows live English Premier League soccer and international rugby matches.

Miracle of Science (☎ 617-868-2866; 321 Massachusetts Ave) This triangular, upscale bar near the MIT campus is the watering hole of choice for local engineering students and their cool, humanities-major friends.

LIVE MUSIC

Middle East Café (☎ 617-864-3278; 472 Massachusetts Ave) If a big-name band is playing in Cambridge, it's probably playing here. There are four different rooms for music, from the headlining rockers downstairs to the acoustic singer-songwriters upstairs.

TT The Bear's (☎ 617-492-2327; 10 Brookline St) A tiny dive showcasing up-and-coming indie rock acts.

Manray (☎ 617-864-0400; 21 Brookline St) This place was Goth before Goth was popular,

and it keeps marching to its own beat today. Campus Thursday attracts a gay crowd.

Western Front (☎ 617-492-7772; 343 Western Ave) This long-running reggae-tinged nightclub has expanded into dance hall and hip-hop.

Club Passim (☎ 617-492-5300; 47 Palmer St) The best folk music club in greater Boston is well known for its open-mike nights.

Lizard Lounge (☎ 617-547-0759; 1667 Massachusetts Ave) This dark, basement alternative nightspot has great live jazz, poetry slams, rock and roll, open-mike night comedy and more. There's no cover charge for the 'Soul-Low' acoustic set before 9pm every night except Sunday.

Toad (☎ 617-497-4950; 1912 Massachusetts Ave) A cozy Porter Sq club that serves up free, rootsy country and blues music seven nights a week, and usually two sets every evening.

Entertainment

Cinema buffs won't want to miss classic movies at the venerable **Brattle Theater** (☎ 617-876-6837; 40 Brattle St), challenging documentaries at the **Harvard Film Archive** (☎ 617-495-4700; 24 Quincy St) or first-run independent flicks at the **Kendall Square Cinema** (☎ 617-499-1996; 1 Kendall Sq).

The renowned **American Repertory Theater** (☎ 617-547-8300; 64 Brattle St), best known as the A-R-T, stages classic and new plays at Harvard's Loeb Drama Center. Student rush tickets are available 30 minutes before curtain.

The performance art space **Zeitgeist Gallery** (☎ 617-876-6060; 1353 Cambridge St), located in out-of-the-way Inman Sq, has something edgy and new going on every night of the week.

Shopping

Planet Aid (☎ 617-354-6413; 30 JFK St) Vintage clothing for men and women.

Twisted Village Records (12b Eliot St) Improv and beat and rock from the self-described 'purveyors of obscure music.'

Million Year Picnic (☎ 617-492-6763; 99 Mt Auburn St) Sells comics, graphic novels and other items for the bookish.

Museum of Useful Things (49b Brattle St) Design fetish central. Mostly functional household items, many of them stainless steel.

Black Ink (☎ 617-497-1221; 5 Brattle St) This small store mixes kitsch items and artsy stationery.

Cardullo's (☎ 617-491-8888; 6 Brattle St) Longtime gourmet food shop. Stocks cheeses from around the world, sells wine gums and Yorkie Bars for homesick Brits.

NEW ENGLAND

BOOK 'EM

Cambridge has the world's highest concentration of bookstores. Browse to your heart's content at these bastions of bibliophiles:

- **Globe Corner Bookstore** (☎ 617-497-6277; 28 Church St) Excellent selection of travel books and maps.

- **Harvard Bookstore** (☎ 617-661-1515; 1256 Massachusetts Ave) Established in 1932, this sprawling independent store is well stocked with literary and scholarly works.

- **Schoenhof's Foreign Books** (☎ 617-547-8855; 76a Mt Auburn St) Sells dictionaries and textbooks for more than 700 languages and dialects, as well as fiction and nonfiction in many European languages.

- **HL Mendelsohn Fine European Books** (☎ 617-576-3634; 1640 Massachusetts Ave) This tiny garden shop, set back from the street, specializes in architectural monographs and international design books.

- **McIntyre & Moore Booksellers** (☎ 617-629-4840; 255 Elm St) Used books about almost every subject imaginable. Located in Somerville's Davis Sq.

SOMERVILLE

With new restaurants, cafés and nightspots, Somerville's Davis Sq is quickly turning into the new outpost of hip on the 'other' side of the Charles River. Take the MBTA Red Line to Davis Sq.

Redbones (☎ 617-628-2200; 55 Chester St; mains $8-16), the neighborhood's purveyor of moist, rich St Louis–style barbecued pork ribs, offers a cheap lunch buffet. It also serves a gaggle of rare beers in the basement bar, **Under Bones**. You can grab a coffee and grab some sofa seat at the **Someday Café** (☎ 617-623-3323; 51 Davis Sq), or play some pool and hang out with the funky crowd at **Diesel Café** (☎ 617-629-8717; 257 Elm St).

Burren (☎ 617-776-6896; 247 Elm St) is a great, friendly pub that features traditional Irish music performed nightly in the front room. A few doors down, the **Sligo Pub** (☎ 617-623-9651; 237 Elm St), a classic dive bar, draws a mix of grizzled barflies and hipsters.

Open for nearly four decades, **Johnny D's** (☎ 617-776-2004; 17 Holland St) continues to bring an incredibly eclectic collection of live musical acts to its stage seven nights a week. The equally historic **Somerville Theater** (☎ 617-625-5700; 55 Davis Sq) programs second-run films, comedians, fund-raisers and musicians such as Jonathan Richman.

LEXINGTON & CONCORD

Lexington, 15 miles west of Boston on Rte 2, is where the Revolutionary War began in 1775. The British redcoats then marched west toward Concord, where they battled (and were defeated by) the American minutemen at the town's North Bridge. You can revisit this momentous bit of history at the **Minute Man National Historic Park** (☎ 978-369-6993; 174 Liberty St, Concord; admission free; 🕙 9am-5pm Apr-Oct, 11am-3pm Nov-Mar) and along the 5.5-mile Battle Rd Trail, suitable for walking or biking. The **National Heritage Museum** (☎ 781-861-6559; 33 Marrett Rd; admission free; 🕙 10am-5pm Mon-Sat, noon-5pm Sun) has a number of interesting rotating exhibits.

Concord is also home to many historic sites related to American literature, including the **Wayside** (☎ 978-369-6993; 455 Lexington Rd), the former home of author Nathaniel Hawthorne; the **Ralph Waldo Emerson House** (☎ 978-369-2236; 28 Cambridge Turnpike); and Louisa May Alcott's **Orchard House** (☎ 978-369-4118; 399 Lexington Rd). Three miles south of Concord's Monument Sq is **Walden Pond**, where Henry David Thoreau was inspired to write *Walden*. Historical significance notwithstanding, it's a great place to swim.

SALEM

This North Shore city, located 18 miles north of Boston, is famous for its role in the growth of America's maritime trade – and for its infamous witch trials. It makes a great day trip. Take the MBTA Rockport/Newburyport commuter rail line from Boston's North Station and get off at Salem.

Sights

Begin your visit at the **National Park Regional Visitors Center** (☎ 978-740-1650; 2 New Liberty St; admission free), housed in a refurbished armory. There are lots of good exhibits on maritime history, a 30-minute film about Salem's textile industries and a model of the vessel *Friendship*.

DUNKIN' DONUTS

It won't take very long for observant travelers to notice that in New England the pink-and-orange logo of the Dunkin' Donuts chain is even more prevalent than that of Starbucks Coffee. Although it's a global company, with thousands of stores in far-flung locales such as New Zealand and Qatar, Dunkin' Donuts started in Quincy, Massachusetts, in 1950, and remains headquartered here. Millions of New Englanders have grown up on its doughy, sugary pastries and old-style coffee, heavy on the cream and sugar. Even today, in a world of Atkins dieters and countless breakfast choices, there's a perverse fondness for the familiar, comfortable consistency of Dunkin' Donuts doughnuts. Watch for the appearance of its products in any Farrelly Brothers movie (especially *There's Something About Mary*) and you'll see what we mean. For a true taste of New England, a honey-glazed doughnut and a coffee should do the trick for just a couple of dollars.

Appropriately housed in a sinister-looking Gothic Revival building, the **Salem Witch Museum** (☎ 978-744-1692; Washington Sq, Salem Common; admission $6.50; ☯ 10am-5pm Sep-Jun, 10am-7pm Jul Aug) examines the Salem witch trials of 1692 and the hysteria they brought about (19 innocent people were hanged). The presentation features 13 stage sets and is based on actual trial documents.

At the corner of Essex and New Liberty Sts is the **Peabody Essex Museum** (☎ 978-745-9500; East India Sq; adult/student $13/9; ☯ 10am-5pm). The oldest continually operating museum in the country, this so-called 'mini-Smithsonian' features a superb collection of art from around New England and the corners of the world. The beautiful new wing, which was designed by famed architect Moshe Safdie, features an expansive glass atrium seamlessly integrated into the old building. As well as rotating exhibits, highlights include the Yin Yu Tang House (an authentic Chinese home that was meticulously dismantled in its original location and then rebuilt on museum grounds) and monumental model of the 15ft-long RMS *Queen Elizabeth*.

The **House of the Seven Gables** (☎ 978-744-0991; 54 Turner St; admission $11; ☯ 10am-5pm Nov-Jun, 10am-7pm Jul-Oct), constructed in 1688, is the oldest surviving mansion in New England and is one of the United State's rare post-medieval homes. This is where Salem native and famed 19th-century romance novelist Nathaniel Hawthorne was born. The house tour also includes a visit to the Colonial Revival gardens and educates visitors about the maritime trade that landed Salem on the map.

The **Salem Witch House** (☎ 978-744-8815; 310 Essex St; admission $7; ☯ 10am-5pm Jul, Aug & Oct; call for hr other months), home of witch trials judge Jonathan Corwin, conveys the Puritan colonists' lifestyle and is also an excellent example of 17th-century post-and-beam construction.

Just past Pickering Wharf, you'll pass **Derby Wharf**, home of the USS *Friendship*. The nearby Derby Wharf Light Station was installed in 1871 and still serves as a navigation aide to ships.

Tree-lined, broad **Chestnut St** features landmark Federalist mansions and is well worth a walk.

Sleeping
Winter Island Park (☎ 978-745-9430; 50 Winter Island Rd; campsites $25; Ⓟ), operated by the city of Salem, offers overnight camping less than a mile from the center of town on Salem Harbor. Showers and bathrooms are open 24 hours. You can hang out at the park's 'Waikiki Beach' and explore the bunkers of Fort Pickering, which dates back to 1643. **Days Inn Boston/Salem** (☎ 978-777-1030; www.daysinndanvers.com; 152 Endicott St; r $69-119; Ⓟ ⊠ ⊠ ⊠) has 130 rooms, an outdoor pool and free continental breakfast, just 3 miles from Salem in Danvers.

Eating
In a Pig's Eye (☎ 978-741-4436; 148 Derby St; mains $4-8) is a reasonably priced sit-down lunch spot serving sandwiches, salads and Mexican specialties. The **Boston Hot Dog Company** (☎ 978-744-2320; 60 Washington St; hot dogs $1.85-3.25) serves gourmet weiners along with homemade baked beans, coleslaw and draft root beer. **Captain Dusty's** (☎ 978-744-0777; 143 Derby St) is a purveyor of fine and tasty homemade ice cream, with a large variety of flavors and toppings.

NEW ENGLAND

CAPE COD & THE ISLANDS

The narrow strip of land that forms a crescent between Massachusetts Bay and the Atlantic Ocean is *the* vacation spot for New Englanders during summer. That's when throngs of visitors flood Provincetown's bustling streets, tan themselves on miles of white-sand beaches, explore the dunes of Cape Cod National Seashore and bike the island roads of Martha's Vineyard and Nantucket. High season (mid-June through September) here can be frightfully expensive, but the abundance of hostels in the region make it manageable for budget travelers, while the scenery makes it completely worth it.

CAPE COD
Provincetown

Everyone thinks the *Mayflower* first dropped anchor in Plymouth, but the Pilgrims' first stop in the New World was actually Provincetown, at the very tip of Cape Cod. Provincetown was incorporated in 1727, and in the mid-20th century became popular with artists and bohemians. Today Provincetown has morphed into a gay-friendly vacation mecca; a quick walk down Commercial St, the 3-mile long, Carnaval-esque center of town activity, will confirm this.

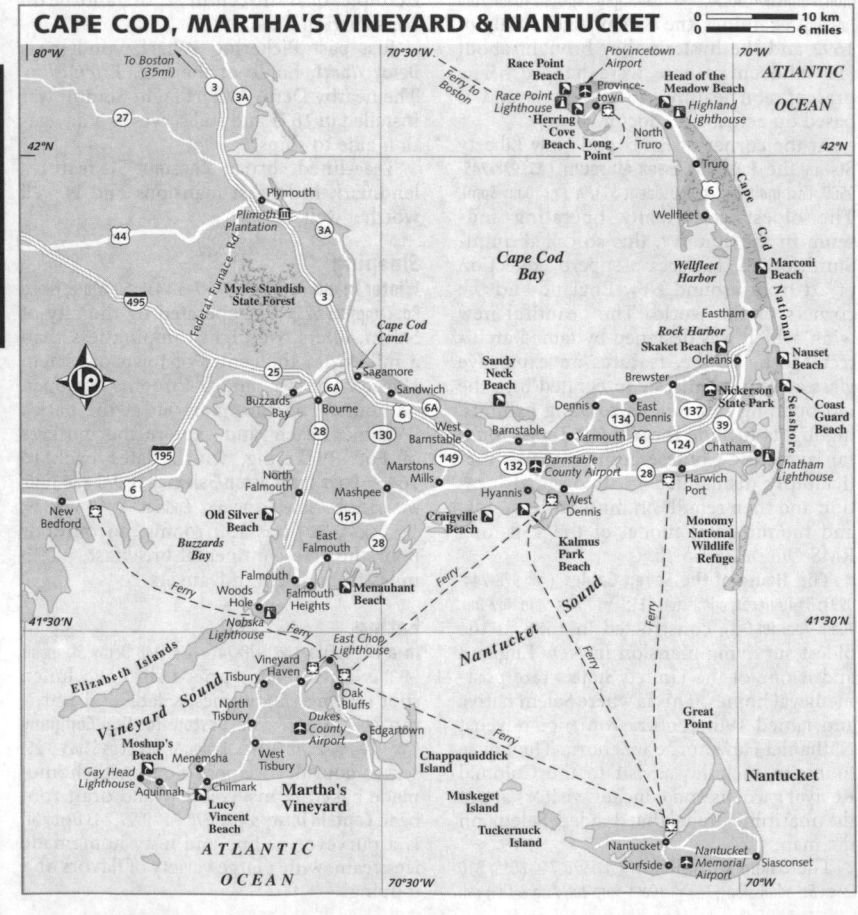

CAPE COD, MARTHA'S VINEYARD & NANTUCKET

INFORMATION
Outer Cape Health Services (☎ 508-487-9395; 49 Harry Kemp Way)

Provincetown Bookshop (246 Commercial St) Small but well-stocked bookstore.

Provincetown Chamber of Commerce (☎ 508-487-3424; 307 Commercial St at MacMillan Wharf)

Provincetown Public Library (☎ 508-487-7094; 330 Commercial St) Free Internet access; sign up at the front desk.

Seamen's Saving Bank (☎ 508-487-0035; 221 Commercial St)

US Post office (☎ 508-487-3580; 219 Commercial St)

WOMR (92.1FM) Community radio station.

SIGHTS & ACTIVITIES
Commercial St is the main street in town. The far western and eastern ends are narrow (barely 15ft wide) and quiet, with charming, immaculate cottages and homes on either side. The middle section around MacMillan Wharf is a cacophony of bars, restaurants, high-end shops and drag queens promoting the evening's entertainment. Most visitors heading out to the nearby seashore get around by bike.

The 253ft-high **Pilgrim Monument** (☎ 508-487-1310; High Pole Hill; adult/student $7/5, free 9am-noon Sun; ☒ 9am-5pm April 1–Nov 30, to 7pm Jul & Aug), the tallest all-granite structure in the world, is Provincetown's most prominent landmark. It commemorates the 'first landing' of the *Mayflower* Pilgrims in Provincetown on November 21, 1620, and offers views of the town and Cape Cod National Seashore.

Provincetown Art Association & Museum (☎ 508-487-1750; 460 Commercial St; admission $2) celebrates and collects nearly a century's worth of work by local artists. A renovated and expanded exhibit space is scheduled to open in 2005.

Interactive periscopes provide visitors with a virtual tour of underwater sea life at **Stellwagen Bank National Marine Sanctuary** (☎ 508-487-3622; 115 Bradford St; admission free; ☒ 11am-6pm Thu-Sun early–mid-May, Sep & Oct; 10am-7pm daily late May–Sep 1).

The walk across a dyke to the square-shaped **Wood End Light** is almost as interesting as the lighthouse itself. At the western end of Commercial St, the dike passes a salt marsh that's full of crabs, fish, snails and birds. The tide here rises and falls 8ft every six hours, so make sure you time your visit correctly.

On the outskirts of town, west-facing **Herring Cove Beach** is one of the few spots on the East Coast that you can watch the sun set over the ocean. Nearby, just off Race Point Rd, **Province Lands Visitors Center** (☎ 508-487-1256; ☒ 9am-5pm May-Oct) has interactive exhibits, films about the sand dunes and an observation deck with a 360-degree view of Cape Cod's tip.

Gale Force Bikes (☎ 508-487-4849; 144 Bradford St; beach cruisers per day $12-19) rents mountain bikes and beach cruisers, while **Venture Athletics** (☎ 508-487-9442; 237 Commercial St; kayaks per half-day $25-35) has kayaks for paddling in Provincetown Harbor and runs guided kayaking tours ($45 to $65). For a splurge, try a whale-watching trip with **Dolphin Fleet** (☎ 800-826-9300) or **Portuguese Princess** (☎ 508-487-2651).

SLEEPING
Be warned, Provincetown's lodgings can be incredibly pricey during summer.

Outermost Hostel (☎ 508-487-4378; outermost@ mindspring.com; 28 Winslow St; dm $25; Ⓟ) The jury is still out on this conveniently located, but bare-bones, non-HI hostel. Twenty-five bunk beds are spread between a number of Spartan cottages, and there's a miniscule kitchen for cooking. Only recommended for hardy travelers who don't need peace and quiet.

White Horse Inn (☎ 508-487-1790; 500 Commercial St; s $50-70, d $70-100) Affable innkeeper Frank Schaefer is a ravenous art collector who counts locals John Waters and Norman Mailer as buddies. There are 11 clean, cozy rooms of varying size, all nicely decorated.

EATING
Tofu A Go-Go (☎ 508-487-6237; 336 Commercial St; mains $5-12; ☒ lunch) This somewhat quirky vegetarian restaurant makes sandwiches, burritos and hot plates with names like 'Giant Rodan' and 'El Melto.'

Karoo Kafe (☎ 508-487-6630; 338 Commercial St; mains $4-11) The South African owner here serves some unusual dishes from his native land – like *bobotie*, a curried meatloaf – as well as burgers and salads.

Provincetown House of Pizza (☎ 508-487-6655; 50 Bradford St; pizzas $6-14) offers slices, subs and other pizza specialties to dine in, take out or for delivery.

Bubula's by the Bay (☎ 508-487-0773; 183 Commercial St; mains $8-26) This somewhat pricey restaurant has a nice outdoor patio facing Commercial St and seating with harbor views. After hours, there's live entertainment and a bar that's open until 1am.

Provincetown Portuguese Bakery (☎ 508-487-1803; 299 Commercial St; bifana sandwich $4) caters to the area's large Portuguese population with sandwiches and sweet specialties like *malasada*, a fried dough.

To eat in Provincetown on the cheap, try one of these grab-and-go places offering sandwiches and the like:

Big Daddy's Burritos (☎ 508-487-4432; 205 Commercial St)

Blue Light (☎ 508-487-3466; 225 Commercial St)

Mojo's (☎ 508-487-3140; Ryder St at MacMillan Wharf)

Coffee Pot (☎ 508-487-9715; 315 Commercial St, Lopes Sq)

Provincetown General Store (☎ 508-487-0300; 147 Commercial St)

DRINKING
Old Colony Tap (☎ 508-487-2361; 323 Commercial St) is a grizzled old seafaring pub that has buoys decorating the walls and serves longneck bottles of Pabst beer.

CLUBBING
Provincetown is awash with gay nightclubs and one-man/woman shows by drag queens. Some of the big spots include the multi-room **Crown & Anchor** (☎ 508-487-1430; 247 Commercial St), the biggest nightclub in town; the **Governor Bradford** (☎ 508-487-9618; 312 Commercial St), site of 'Drag Karaoke' every weekend night at 9:30pm; the **Boatslip Resort** (☎ 508-487-1669; 161 Commercial St), home of the world's largest T-Dance from 4pm to 7pm; and the **Post Office Cabaret** (☎ 508-487-9793; 209 Commercial St), which hosts comedians and other outrageous performers.

ENTERTAINMENT
New Art Cinema (☎ 508-487-4269; 214 & 237 Commercial St) shows first-run films at two locations along Commercial St.

Provincetown Theater (☎ 508-487-9793; 238 Bradford St) is the beautiful new home of the town's two resident theater companies, **Provincetown Repertory Theater** (☎ 508-487-0600) and **Provincetown Theater Company** (☎ 508-487-8673).

GETTING THERE & AWAY
Boston Harbor Cruises (☎ 617-227-4321) runs a high-speed ferry that covers the trip from Boston's Long Wharf to Provincetown's MacMillan Wharf in 1½ hours (one way/round trip $37/58). **Bay State Cruise Company** (☎ 617-748-1428) runs a similar express ferry as well as a less expensive, more leisurely Boston–Provincetown boat (one way/round trip $18/29) that departs from Boston's World Trade Center Seaport and takes about three hours.

Plymouth & Brockton Bus Lines (☎ 508-746-0378) runs between Boston's South Station and Provincetown ($25, 3½ hours), with stops all along the Outer Cape.

GETTING AROUND
From late spring to early fall, the **Breeze** (☎ 800-352-7155) runs a daily Provincetown–North Truro shuttle ($1) with stops that include Herring Cove and Race Point Beaches.

Cape Cod National Seashore
Henry Thoreau once referred to Cape Cod as the 'bared and bended arm of Massachusetts.' The outer part of that arm is a natural work in progress, with dramatic sand dunes and an ever-shifting shoreline whose natural beauty is unequaled. Thanks to Cape Cod resident and US President John F Kennedy, 43,000 acres of Outer Cape land and 40 miles of ocean beach received official protection status in the 1960s, giving birth to **Cape Cod National Seashore** (☎ 508-349-3785; www.nps.gov/caco). This park boasts historic lighthouses, three cycling trails and – judging by the packed parking lots and overflowing summertime crowds – six of the best beaches in the USA: Coast Guard, Marconi, Nauset Light, Head of the Meadow, Race Point and Herring Cove. Each beach is equipped with bathrooms and outdoor showers. Daily beach parking is $10 (free after 5pm); arriving by bike or on foot, entry is $3. Check with the two visitor centers, Salt Pond (p143) in Eastham and Province Lands (p141) in Provincetown, for more information.

Truro
Highland (Cape Cod) Light (☎ 508-487-1121; off S Highland Rd; tours $3; ☉ 10am-5:30pm) is the Cape's oldest lighthouse, established in 1798. Due to beach erosion, it was moved back 250ft in 1996 to stop it falling into the sea. The adjacent **Highland House Museum** (☎ 508-487-3397;

admission $3; (⊙ 10am-4:30pm) displays a collection of artifacts from the Truro Historical Society.

Truro Vineyards of Cape Cod (☎ 508-487-6200; Rte 6A; ⊙ noon-5pm daily summer, noon-4pm Fri-Sun winter) offers tours, tastings and a wine-making display. It's $5 for all the wine you can sample – and you get to keep the glass.

Truro Transfer Station (Rte 6, 0.5mi south of Pamet Rd; ⊙ 8am-3:30pm) – that is, the town's garbage dump – features a Swap Shop, a medium-sized room filled with clothing, books, records and tools. It's free of charge to take or leave anything (hopefully you'll do both). You could conceivably pick up some smart-looking wardrobe for the rest of your travels, or discard an old outfit that someone else could use.

HI Truro (☎ 508-349 3880; trurohostel@yahoo.com; North Pamet Rd; dm $22-27; ⊙ late Jun–Sep; P ✕) is one of the gems in the American hostel system. This beautiful old Coast Guard building with a shaded front porch and original wainscoting is just two minutes' walk from a gorgeous beach. The 42 beds are spread among male, female and co-ed dorms, with large common areas and a huge kitchen. If they're not busy, the gregarious staff will drive over to the South Truro Post Office and pick up guests arriving on the Bonanza bus. As the hostel is only open between late June and the first week in September, reservations are highly recommended, and essential on weekends.

Wellfleet

On January 19, 1903, a 48-word message addressed to Edward VII, King of England, from US President Theodore Roosevelt, became the first wireless transmission across the Atlantic. **Marconi Station**, located on a beach bluff off Rte 6, commemorates the site where that message was sent and features a model of the original telegraph station.

The **Cape Cod Rail Trail**, a former railroad right of way, has been brilliantly converted into 25 miles of biking trails past cranberry bogs, salt marshes and freshwater ponds. It runs all the way from Wellfleet to the town of Dennis on the mid-Cape.

On cloudy and rainy days, the **Wellfleet Flea Market** (☎ 508-349-2520; ⊙ 7am-4pm Wed, Thu, Sat & Sun summer, Sat & Sun only spring & fall), held at the Wellfleet Drive-In, is a nice diversion and a bargain-hunter's bonanza.

Paine's Campground (☎ 508-349-3007; 180 Old Country Rd; campsites per night $30; P) is located minutes from area beaches and has wooded sites, including a couples-only quiet area. If you ask, the staff might point you in the direction of a secret swimming pond nearby.

Mac's Seafood (☎ 508-349-9611; 265 Commercial St; clam roll with fries $11), beautifully situated on Wellfleet Harbor, is a family-style restaurant that serves clam rolls, fried oysters and other sinful delights. Guests can eat at picnic tables as the sun sets.

WHAT (☎ 866-282-9428; 1 Kendrick Ave; tickets $23), the Wellfleet Harbor Actors Theater, is renowned for its adventurous theater.

Beachcomber (☎ 508-349-6055; Cahoon Hollow Rd), a burger-and-beer hang-out, features the unmissable Incredible Casuals playing every Sunday in summer.

Eastham

Salt Pond Visitors Center (☎ 508-255-3421; Rte 6; ⊙ 9am-4:30pm) is the southern entry point for Cape Cod National Seashore. The recently renovated center has educational exhibits and is staffed to assist with trip planning.

HI Mid-Cape Eastham (☎ 508 255-2785; midcape hostel@yahoo.com; 75 Goody Hallet Dr; dm $20-27, $10 key deposit; ⊙ late May-mid-Sep; P ✕ 🖳) In a quiet, wooded setting near the path of the Cape Cod Rail Trail and the public Skaket Beach on Cape Cod Bay. There are 48 beds spread across seven cabins aligned in a horseshoe, as well as a main building with kitchen, dining room and living room (equipped with TV, VCR and Internet access). This hostel attracts lots of cycling and youth groups, so reservations are recommended. Guests can rent kayaks for four hours ($35 to $49) and paddle around the bay.

MARTHA'S VINEYARD

Located just a few miles off the coast of Cape Cod, Martha's Vineyard is a world unto itself. Make that many worlds: a (highly recommended) bike ride around this island's 100 sq miles takes in the colorful Victorian cottages and nightlife of Oak Bluffs, the elegant colonial seaport of Edgartown and the breathtaking beauty of Aquinnah's cliffs.

Get visitor information from the **Martha's Vineyard Chamber of Commerce** (☎ 508-693-0085; www.mvy.com; Beach Rd, Vineyard Haven; ⊙ 9am-5pm Mon-Fri year-round, also 10am-4pm Sat & noon-4pm Sun late May–early Sep).

NEW ENGLAND

> **BUDGET TIP**
>
> All taxis on the island are vans. If you're going out for a night on the town, it'll save money to find a group of fellow travelers headed in the same direction who are amenable to leaving and returning at around the same time.

Vineyard Haven

Most ferries arrive in this handsome harbor that's part of the larger town called Tisbury. Most tourists head off the boat onto the town's Main St, which is full of restaurants and shops. **Bunch of Grapes Bookstore** (☎ 508-693-2291; 44 Main St) has a good selection of Martha's Vineyard history, literature and nonfiction for your beach reading.

Sandwich Haven Pizza (☎ 508-696-8383; Beach St; pizzas $6.50-15), across from Cumberland Farms, serves inexpensive slices. Pick up grocery supplies at **Stop & Shop** (☎ 508-693-8339; 50 S Water St).

Martha's Bike Rentals (☎ 508-693-6593; Five Corners) is a good place to rent bikes (per day $20) for tooling around the island. Guests staying at the hostel in West Tisbury receive a special rate on rentals and get their bikes delivered directly.

The only camping on the island, **Martha's Vineyard Family Camping** (☎ 508-693-3772; 569 Edgartown Rd; campsites $40, cabins $105-125) offers campsites and a few no-frills cabins.

Oak Bluffs

Undoubtedly the most interesting town on Martha's Vineyard, Oak Bluffs began as a site for Methodist revival meetings in the mid-1800s. The enormous, open-air **Trinity Park Tabernacle**, from 1879, is only the biggest legacy of the MV Camp Meeting Association – the others are the charming, brightly colored gingerbread cottages surrounding the tabernacle (and scattered throughout town), and the tight-knit African-American community that has developed here.

Oak Bluffs is also home to the 1876 **Flying Horse Carousel** (Circuit Ave at Lake Ave; rides $1), the oldest in America, and the **East Chop Lighthouse** (Vineyard Haven–Oak Bluffs Rd), with fine ocean views.

Biscuits (☎ 508-693-2033; 26 Lake Ave; mains $5-8; ☺ breakfast & lunch) serves breakfast and lunch dishes.

Season's Eatery & Pub (☎ 508-693-7129; 19 Circuit Ave; mains $7-15) serves the cheapest draft beer in Oak Bluffs and $4 pints of Offshore Ale microbrew, along with a standard menu of seafood, pasta and burgers. The adjacent **Atlantic Connection** (☎ 508-693-7129) is a raucous nightclub with dancing and live bands.

Edgartown

The most staid of the Vineyard communities, Edgartown's large Greek Revival and colonial homes speak to the wealth of its founding whaling captains and merchants. Among numerous historic properties is the 1843 **Old Whaling Church** on Main St, now used as a performing arts center. Wander over to **Memorial Wharf**, the island's largest harbor, filled with stately yachts and the tiny car ferry that chugs back and forth to neighboring, wooded Chappaquiddick Island. **South Beach**, a few miles south of town, is the 18-to-25 crowd's beach of choice.

West Tisbury & Chilmark

Tiny West Tisbury and Chilmark are part of the Vineyard's more rural 'up-island' area. Their roads are dotted with rolling fields and brief peeks of ocean vistas. Chilmark's coast includes the clothing-optional **Lucy Vincent Beach**.

Just inside the entrance to the **Abel Hill Cemetery**, on West Tisbury–Chilmark South Rd, is the grave of legendary comedian John Belushi. The star of *Animal House* and *The Blues Brothers* spent his summers in Chilmark before his untimely death. Look for fans' beer-bottle caps and foreign coins and the gravestone that proclaims Belushi's epitaph: 'I May Be Gone, But Rock 'n' Roll Lives On.'

The centrally located **HI Martha's Vineyard** (☎ 508-693-2665; mvhostel@yahoo.com; Edgartown–West Tisbury Rd; dm $20-27; ☺ Apr-Oct; ℗ ☒ ▣) is next to a bike path and a state forest in West Tisbury. The first purpose-built hostel in the USA, this 1955 saltbox homestead has 74 beds, a common room with fireplace, and a large kitchen with pedal-operated sinks. The outside grounds have a bike shelter, ping-pong table, beach volleyball, outdoor showers and barbecue grill. The hostel is usually full during July and August, so advance reservations are highly recommended. (You can book a specific dorm online.) Ask about off-season weekly rates.

Back Alley's (☎ 508-693-8401; 1045 State Rd), a bakery and deli in West Tisbury, sells bagels, sandwiches and other supplies for a day at the beach. **Chilmark Chocolates** (☎ 508-645-3013; State Rd), just down the road from the Chilmark General Store, produces mouthwatering chocolates in varieties such as mint, almond, toffee and raisin. Learning disabled students help run the shop, which was also an 'early adopter' of the solar paneling that powers the store.

Menemsha & Aquinnah

The fishing village immortalized in the movie *Jaws*, Menemsha features a nice beach – a very popular place to watch the sunset – and a harbor filled with local draggers and recreational boats. You can pick up whatever the catch of the day might be at **Larsen's Fish Market** (☎ 508-645-2680; 56 Basin Rd) or fried clams at **Bite** (☎ 508-645-9239; 29 Basin Rd).

Formerly known as Gay Head, Aquinnah contains the Vineyard's most dramatic view, a sweeping panorama of the Atlantic Ocean from atop the 150ft-high **Aquinnah Cliffs**. These distinctly colored bluffs, land owned by the Wampanog Indians, overlook a 400ft-long beach. The 1844 **Gay Head Light** (☎ 508-627 4441) is constructed from red bricks made from the cliffs. Popular **Moshup's Beach** is another clothing-optional swimming spot.

Getting There & Away

Bonanza Bus Lines (☎ 888-751-8800) operates a service from Boston and New York to Woods Hole, the transfer point for the ferry. If you're leaving a car on the mainland, a free shuttle bus travels between the Palmer St parking lot ($8 per calendar day) and the ferry terminal.

The **Steamship Authority** (☎ 508-477-8600) runs ferries between Woods Hole and Martha's Vineyard (one way per adult/adult and bicycle $6/9, 45 minutes, 25 daily). Most dock at Vineyard Haven, although a few head to Oak Bluffs. Don't waste money bringing a car on the ferry – it costs $57 to do so in summer and is impossible without advanced reservations.

If you're already on the mid-Cape, **Hy-Line Cruises** (☎ 508-778-2600) operates ferries from Hyannis to Oak Bluffs (one way per adult/student and bicycle $14.50/19.50, 90 minutes).

Getting Around

Biking is the best way to get around the island, but even in low season roads are narrow and can be crowed. If there isn't a dedicated bike path, be sure to hold your ground and let cars pass you on the left.

Martha's Vineyard Transit Authority (VTA; ☎ 508-693-9440) runs 10 different bus routes around the island. One-way fares are $1 per town, including the one from which you depart. If you're planning on riding the bus a lot, pick up a $6 pass, good for one day of unlimited travel.

NANTUCKET

Nantucket may be smaller and less developed than Martha's Vineyard – nearly 40% of the island is conservation land – but it's just as popular with vacationers. The former whaling port is beloved for its fine beaches, quaint houses and cycling-friendly roads. Get more information from the **Nantucket Chamber of Commerce** (☎ 508-228-1700; www.nantucketchamber.org; 48 Main St).

HI – Nantucket (☎ 508-228-0433; nantuckethostel@yahoo.com; 31 Western Ave; dm $20-27), better known as the Star of the Sea Hostel, is 3.5 miles from the ferry in Surfside and is accessible by bike, bus or taxi. The former Lifesaving Station, listed on the National Register of Historic Places, has 49 beds and is across the street from the beach. Reservations are essential.

The **Steamship Authority** (☎ 508-477-8600) runs ferries from the Ocean St dock on Hyannis on Cape Cod for the trip to Nantucket (one way per adult/student and bicycle $14/20, 2¼ hours).

WESTERN MASSACHUSETTS

Western Massachusetts is two hours by car from Boston but feels like it's worlds away. Connecticut River Valley, better known as Pioneer Valley, is home to a number of rural farming communities where tobacco leaves are still grown, and vibrant college towns like Amherst and Northampton. There are five colleges in the valley – Amherst College, Hampshire College, Smith College, Mount Holyoke College and the University of Massachusetts. The very high concentration of students and academics means that there's always some interesting art or cultural event going on.

Peter Pan (☎ 800-343-9999) and **Greyhound** (☎ 800-231-2222) bus lines provide frequent service to Boston and New York while the **Amtrak** (☎ 800-872-7245) service to New York and Montréal stops in both towns once daily. **Pioneer Valley Transportation Authority** (PVTA; ☎ 413-586-5806; www.pvta.com) offers bus services to the entire area, with the Northampton to Amherst route having the most frequent service.

Cyclists can enjoy a leisurely ride between Northampton and Amherst on the **Norwottuck Rail Trail**, a 10-mile-long right of way that's been converted to a bike path. It crosses the Connecticut River on a historic 1500ft-long iron bridge. You can rent bikes at the Amherst end of the trail from **Valley Bicycles** (☎ 413-256-0880; 319 Main St) for $15/25 per half/full day.

NORTHAMPTON

Northampton (some call it 'Noho' but most locals refer to it as 'Hamp') is said to have more creative folks per square foot than any other burg between Montréal and New York City. It's also a hotbed of progressive politics and boasts a large lesbian population. Easily walkable, with a collection of shops, restaurants, nightclubs and cafés that would be impressive for a city many times its size, this might well be the best college town in the country.

Maps and brochures are available at the **Greater Northampton Chamber of Commerce** (☎ 413-584-1900; www.northamptonuncommon.com; 99 Pleasant St).

Sights

The campus of **Smith College** (☎ 413-584-2700; www.smith.edu), an all-women college founded in 1875, is spread over 125 beautiful, verdant acres. The **Smith College Museum of Art** (☎ 413-585-2770; admission free; Elm St at Bedford Tce; ☉ 10am-4pm Tue-Sat, noon-4pm Sun) possesses a 25,000-object collection, primarily of 19th- and 20th-century masterworks, making this one of the best art museums at any liberal arts college in the country. The campus residence halls and academic buildings are a collection of beautiful old brick and stone buildings from colonial to Gothic gingerbread.

Historic Northampton (☎ 413-584-6011; 46 Bridge St; admission free; ☉ 10am-4pm Tue-Fri, noon-4pm Sat & Sun) houses 50,000 objects in its three colonial-era buildings, a repository of Connecticut Valley history – everything from photographs to furniture to toys.

Look Memorial Park (☎ 413-584-5457), on Rte 9 in Florence, has more than 150 acres of public space in which to spread out a picnic basket, as well as mini-golf, pedal boats and bumper boats.

Skinner State Park offers stupendous views of the Connecticut River and Pioneer Valley from atop Holyoke Range. Take Rte 47 off Rte 9 in Hadley to get here. The auto road is accessible April through November, and it can be hiked year-round. At the top of Mount Holyoke, the **Summit House** (admission free; ☉ Sat & Sun May-Oct) features historical displays and hosts special concerts during the year. There are picnic tables and hiking trails near the summit.

Sleeping

Best Western (☎ 413-586-1500; 117 Consz St; r from $74; P ☒ ☒ ☒) Standard rooms and complimentary deluxe breakfast. Located a short walk from downtown Northampton.

10 Lupine House (☎ 413-586-9766; www.lupine house.com; 185 North Main St, Florence; r $70-90; ☒) This three-bedroom guesthouse in Florence, 2 miles from downtown Northampton on Rte 9, has rooms with private bathrooms and serves up a good homemade continental breakfast.

Eating & Drinking

For being such a college town, Northampton's food offerings are decidedly upscale. There are, however, a number of cheap places to eat and drink.

Sylvester's (☎ 413-586-5343; 111 Pleasant St; mains $5-9) This extremely popular downtown restaurant is named after a 19th-century diet guru and serves delicious sandwiches on homemade breads; especially recommended is its BLTA (bacon, lettuce, tomato and avocado).

Teapot (☎ 413-585-0880; 116 Main St; mains $7-16) Popular, award-winning Chinese and Japanese cuisine with an airy interior and upscale décor. Chinese lunch specialties start at $5.

Bela (☎ 413-586-8011; 68 Masonic St; daily specials lunch $7, dinner $10) A very intimate storefront restaurant serving vegetarian dishes made with tofu, tempeh and pastas.

Haymarket Cafe (☎ 413-586-9969; 185 Main St; mains $4.50-7.25) Northampton's coolest hangout spots for bohemians and caffeine addicts. Two sprawling floors of seating and a sign behind the counter that boasts 'Coffee: I'll Sleep When I'm Dead.'

Tunnel Bar (☎ 413-586-5366; cnr Strong Ave & Pearl St) This bar, housed below Northampton's elegant old railroad station, really *is* a tunnel. Sit in plush chairs and enjoy the fine woodwork at this long, narrow nightspot while you drink somewhat pricey but tasty cocktails and wines.

Ye Ol' Watering Hole (☎ 413-584-9748; 287 Pleasant St) Hundreds (and we mean *hundreds*) of vintage beer cans line the walls at this old timers' dive where the valley's blue-collar crowd crosses path with students and scenesters. Cheap drinks, two pool tables and a Golden Tee video game.

Entertainment

Academy of Music (☎ 413-584-8435; 274 Main St) One of the oldest movie houses in the USA, and one of the most beautiful, too. Shows first-run independent films.

Calvin Theater (☎ 413-584-1444; 19 King St) Historic movie house converted to concert hall. Hosts a number of folk-rock acts.

Iron Horse Cafe (☎ 413-584-0610; 20 Center St) This cozy storefront café offers a great opportunity to see musicians perform in an intimate environment.

Pearl Street Nightclub (☎ 413-584-7771; 10 Pearl St) Big dance nights upstairs, live concerts by college rock bands downstairs.

New Century Theater (☎ 413-587-3933; tickets $10-22) One of the best regional theater companies in the US, the troupe stages works by the likes of Wendy Wasserstein and Kenneth Lonergan. Performances are at the Mendenhall Center at Smith College campus.

AMHERST

Amherst is 10 miles east of Northampton on Rte 9. Pick up visitor information at the kiosk on Amherst Common, or from the **Amherst Area Chamber of Commerce** (☎ 413-253-0700; www.amherstcommon.com; 409 Main St).

Sights

Famed 19th-century poet Emily Dickinson was known as the 'Belle of Amherst,' and the history of her life here is put on display at the **Dickinson Homestead** (☎ 413-542-8161; 280 Main St; adult/student $8/7; tours on the hr 10am-5pm Wed-Sat, 1-5pm Sun Jun-Aug; call for spring & fall hr), where she grew up and wrote much of her famous work. Her grave is nearby at the West Cemetery on Triangle St.

Amherst College (☎ 413-542-2000; www.amherst.edu; 100 Boltwood Ave) is right in the center of town and is home to the **Mead Art Museum** (☎ 413-542-2335; admission free; ☻ 10am-4:30pm Tue-Sun, closed summer).

The sprawling **University of Massachusetts** (UMass; ☎ 413-545-0111; www.umass.edu) campus houses the **Fine Arts Center** (☎ 413-545-2511; Haigis Mall; tickets $5-12), a monstrous concrete building that hosts nearly 100 performing arts events per year in its main hall and presents cutting-edge dramatic plays in its New World Theater.

Puffers Pond, 2 miles north of town, has a wooded, secluded beach area that fills with students and locals on a warm day. Take East Pleasant St to Sand Hill Rd and then turn right onto State St.

Hampshire College (☎ 413-549-4600; 893 West St), approximately 5 miles south of Amherst on Rte 116, has two new museums on its campus. The **Eric Carle Museum of Picture Book Art** (☎ 413-658-1100; 125 West Bay Rd; adult/student $4/2; ☻ 10am-4pm Tue-Sat, noon-4pm Sun) celebrates book illustrations from around the world and has an art studio where aspiring artists can give it a try. Next door, the **National Yiddish Book Center** (☎ 413-256-4900; 1021 West St; admission free; ☻ 10am-3:30pm Mon-Fri, 11am-4pm Sun) is devoted to Yiddish culture and literature.

Just outside the Hampshire campus, the **Atkins Farms Country Market** (☎ 413-253-9528; cnr Rte 116 & Bay Rd) has a great selection of fresh produce, syrups and a scratch bakery with tasty treats.

Sleeping

Campus Center Hotel (☎ 413-549-6000; Campus Center, UMass; r $72-109; P ☐) Operated by UMass students majoring in hospitality, this hotel has 116 guest rooms, many with views overlooking the Campus Pond. Free continental breakfast.

Amherst B&B (☎ 413-256-6151; 132 Farmington Rd; r $70; P ☒) This private home in a quiet neighborhood has two guest rooms, an in-ground pool, and includes a full breakfast.

Amherst Motel (☎ 413-256-8122; 408 Northampton Rd; d $60-80; [P] [X] [🐾] [🍴]) Simple and inexpensive lodging (30 furnished apartments and 14 hotel rooms) on Rte 9 near the UMass campus.

Eating & Drinking

Pub (☎ 413-549-1200; 15 East Pleasant St; mains $6-16) This casual dining spot is popular with both students and local families. The menu includes burgers, wraps, barbecued ribs and salads, not to mention 40 microbrews.

Antonio's by the Slice (☎ 413-253-0808; 31 North Pleasant St; pizza slices $1.50-2.75) Rolls out pizza slices with unique toppings that include steak and seafood (shrimp, crabmeat etc). The staff efficiently handle the takeout needs of the students who crowd the counter area.

Bub's BBQ (☎ 413-548-9630; Rte 116; mains $10-14; ☽ Tue-Sun) A taste of the South in Pioneer Valley. Barbecued chicken, ribs and sausages are all served on glorified picnic tables while country music plays soothingly over the speakers.

Black Sheep Cafe (☎ 413-256-1706; 79 Main St) An Amherst mainstay whose bakery stocks fresh breads, cakes and cookies. Expect a long line for coffee in the morning.

Spoke (33 E Pleasant St) This longtime hangout for UMass students has weekly drink specials, and free pool Monday evenings.

Moan & Dove (☎ 413-256-1710; 460 West St) European-style pub near Hampshire College campus, with 150 bottled beers and 20 draft beers.

SOUTH HADLEY

South Hadley is the smallest of the Pioneer Valley's college towns and is the site of **Mount Holyoke College** (☎ 413-538-2000; www .mtholyoke.edu; 50 College St), an attractive campus that features an exceptional **art museum** (☎ 413-538-2245; Lower Lake Rd; admission free; ☽ 11am-5pm Tue-Fri, 1-5pm Sat & Sun).

Main Moon (☎ 413-533-8839; 11 College St; mains $4-13) has Chinese food on a student budget. The Village Commons houses stores and eateries, including **Tailgate Picnic Deli & Market** (☎ 413-532-7597; 7 College St) for food supplies, the **Thirsty Mind** (☎ 413-538-9303; 19 College St) for café drinks, and the **Tower Theater** (☎ 413-533-3456; 19 College St) for first-run films.

SPRINGFIELD

A 30-minute drive south of Northampton on I-91, the city of Springfield is best known as the birthplace of basketball. This is where in 1891 Dr James Naismith first taught his students to throw a medicine ball into peach baskets, blissfully unaware that his invented sport would one day turn baggy shorts and $150 sneakers into full-blown fashion statements. The history of the game is on full display at the **Basketball Hall of Fame** (☎ 413-781-6500; 1000 West Columbus Ave; admission $16; ☽ 10am-6pm), a sprawling riverside complex that features exhibits, interactive kiosks and memorabilia worn by the great Michael Jordan and other legends.

While you're in the city, head on over to the Quadrangle at the corner of State and Chestnut Sts to see the **Dr Seuss National Memorial Sculpture Garden**, honoring Springfield's native son and children's book author Theodor Seuss Geisel. There are bronze statues of the Lorax, Horton the Elephant and the Cat in the Hat.

SCENIC DRIVE: RTE 2

Rte 2 runs from Boston all the way to the New York border along the northern edge of Massachusetts. Known as the Mohawk Trail, this scenic road is a great way to explore the rural parts of western Massachusetts. Start just west of where Rte 2 and I-91 meet, in **Shelburne Falls**, home to the Bridge of Flowers – a cornucopia of flowers that crosses the Deerfield River – and nearby potholes ground out of granite during the glacial ages. Stop in Florida – the town, that is – and **Whitcomb Summit** (2240ft), the trail's highest point. Follow Rte 2 downward, past the scenic overlook at Hairpin Turn, into North Adams, a former mill town that is now home to the celebrated Massachusetts Museum of Contemporary Art, better known as the **MASS MoCA** (☎ 413-664-4481; 87 Marshall St; admission $9; ☽ 11am-5pm Mon & Wed-Sun Sep-Jun, 10am-6pm daily Jul & Aug). In **Williamstown**, near the intersection of Rtes 2 and 7, is the **Williams College Museum of Art** (☎ 413-597-2429; 15 Lawrence Hall Dr; admission free; ☽ 10am-5pm Tue-Sat, 1-5pm Sun) and the **Clark Art Institute** (☎ 413-458-2303; 225 South St; ☽ 10am-5pm Tue-Sun Sep-Jun, daily Jul & Aug).

MAINE

Most people's knowledge of Maine comes from the novels and films of horror fiction guru (and native son) Stephen King. Visitors to New England's largest state probably won't meet any of King's creepy characters, but they will get to experience the dramatic natural rocky coastline and charming rural villages, as well as take part in the multitude of activities in bustling Portland.

PORTLAND

Like many of New England's formerly somnolent burgs, Portland, Maine's largest city, has experienced a renaissance in recent years. Artists, designers and other creative professionals have moved in and fixed up old Victorians in the West End and brick rowhouses along the waterfront. Portland's manageable size makes it perfect for browsing in galleries and exploring the city's maritime history.

Central Portland nestles on Casco Bay, wedged between Back Cove to the west and Portland Harbor to the east. The two main streets run parallel to one another: Commercial St runs by the water's edge along the length of the Old Port, the refurbished waterfront district, while up the hill, Congress St traverses downtown sights such as Monument Sq and the Portland Museum of Art. Between the two, and west of State St, the West End is a charming neighborhood of tree-lined streets and refurbished Edwardian and Victorian rowhouses.

Information

Portland Phoenix is the free weekly arts guide. The **Convention & Visitors Bureau of Greater Portland** (☎ 207-772-5800; www.visitport land.com; 245 Commercial St) has free maps and brochures of the area.

Sights & Activities

The **Old Port**, Portland's gentrified waterfront district, centers on the restored historic buildings of Commercial St, whose focus has shifted from shipping to shopping. The port's maze of cobblestone side streets houses art galleries, creative firms and some cozy pubs. At the eastern end of the port, the **Maine Narrow Gauge Railroad Co & Museum** (☎ 207-828-0814; 58 Fore St; admission $6; 10am-4pm) lovingly preserves the state's existing narrow-gauge (2ft) railroad equipment – everything from boxcars to flatcars to cabooses. Trains depart the museum on the hour between 11am and 4pm for the brief journey along Casco Bay. In this area you'll also find the **Shipyard Brewing Company** (☎ 800-273-9253; 86 Newbury St; 3-5pm Mon-Fri, noon-5pm Sat & Sun), which offers free tours from May to December.

Anchoring the city's arts District on the western edge of downtown, the **Portland Museum of Art** (☎ 207-775-6148; 7 Congress Sq; adult/student $8/6, free 5-9pm Fri; 10am-5pm Tue-Sun, 10am-9pm Fri) holds three centuries' worth of artwork in a modern brick edifice designed by IM Pei. It includes pieces by Andrew Wyeth, Winslow Homer and Robert Indiana. Just down the street, the **Institute of Contemporary Art** (☎ 207-879-5742; 522 Congress St; admission free; 11am-5pm Wed-Sun, 11am-7pm Thu, 11am-8pm 1st Fri each month) showcases cutting-edge, contemporary work in the Maine College of Art's historic Porteous building. Equally interesting, the **Museum of African Culture** (☎ 207-871-7188; 122 Spring St; admission $5; 10:30am-4pm Tue-Fri, 12:30-4pm Sat) collects masks and other artifacts from sub-Saharan Africa and features rotating exhibits.

Maine Historical Society (☎ 207-774-1822; 489 Congress St; admission $7; 10am-4pm Mon-Sat, noon-4pm Sun May-Oct) operates a one-acre campus downtown. The admission includes access to the main edifice, a large museum that spotlights Maine's rich history, and the **Wadsworth-Longfellow House** (☎ 207-879-0427; 485 Congress St), a restored 1850s colonial residence that was the home of poet Henry Wadsworth-Longfellow. There's also a research library on the grounds.

At the eastern end of Congress St is the only remaining maritime signal tower in the US, **Portland Observatory** (☎ 207-774-5561; 138 Congress St; admission $5; 10am-5pm late May–early Oct). If you're willing to ascend its 103 steps, the reward is good views of Casco Bay and downtown.

Fort Williams State Park, a 15-minute drive south of downtown on Rte 77, is a sprawling green space whose history as a military fortification dates back to the 19th century. **Portland Head Light** (☎ 207-799-2661; 1000 Shore Rd, Cape Elizabeth; admission $2; 10am-4pm Jun-Oct), the world's most photographed lighthouse, sits on its grounds.

GLOBAL WARNING

Don't miss Eartha, the world's largest rotating globe (5600lb, and 130ft in circumference) at the **Map Store** (☎ 207-846-7100; 2 DeLorme Dr) in Yarmouth, between Portland and Freeport. Take I-95 exit 52 to I-295 exit 17.

Portland's connection with the sea makes it a great place to splurge and take a ride on a sailing ship. The **Portland Schooner Company** (☎ 207-766-2500; tickets $25-35) operates daily, two-hour sails on Casco Bay aboard the elegant 72ft-long *Bagheera*. The **Old Port Mariner Fleet** (☎ 207-775-0727) operates daytime and sunset seafaring tours that travel past the bay's seven lighthouses, as well as whale-watching and deep-sea fishing cruises.

Sleeping

Portland is not the most friendly city for budget travelers – there's no youth hostel or comparable dormitory-style accommodations. However, the city's West End has some B&Bs that are a reasonable option for two to four people traveling together. Lodging for October foliage-watching season fills up well in advance.

Inn at St John's (☎ 207-773-6481; www.innatstjohn.com; 939 Congress St; r with breakfast $55-175; P ⊠ 💻) One block from Union station, and across the street from the bus station, this is the oldest continuing operating inn in Portland, dating back to 1897. It has 39 charming European rooms with flowery wallprints and vintage wooden furniture. Ask for a room facing away from noisy Congress St.

Percy Inn (☎ 207-871-7638; www.percyinn.com; 15 Pine St; r with breakfast $89-199; P ⊠ 🐾) An 1830 Federal-style brick rowhouse, this renovated boarding house has spacious, well-appointed rooms named after literary giants like Henry Longfellow and Dorothy Parker. There's also a player grand piano and a 400-title movie library. A large continental breakfast is included. Call innkeeper (and former travel writer) Dale Northrup if you're a late arrival; unsold rooms have a special last-minute rate.

Travelodge (☎ 207-774-6101; www.travelodgeportland.com; 1200 Brighton Ave; r $59-89; P 🐾 💻 🐕) For those with cars, this chain motel with

131 standard rooms is the cheapest option close to downtown (5 miles southwest of here). Take I-95 to exit 48.

Wassamki Springs (☎ 207-839-4276; www.wassamkisprings.com; 56 Saco St; campsites $34; P), in nearby Scarborough, is the closest campground to Portland. Take I-95 to Rte 22.

Eating

Portland has an ever-increasing variety of restaurants that will satisfy most any palate. The place to begin isn't a restaurant at all, but **Portland Public Market** (☎ 207-228-2000; 25 Preble St; ⏰ 9am-7pm Mon-Sat, 10am-5pm Sun). This downtown food hall houses 25 locally owned businesses serving fresh and prepared chow. It's ideal for picking up fresh fruit, wines, pizza, sushi and more. Take it to go or eat it beneath the market's distinctive 70ft-high ceiling.

Gilbert's Chowderhouse (☎ 207-871-5636; 92 Commercial St; mains $7-21) In a long, narrow waterfront dining room that looks like it's been there forever, Gilbert's dishes out good, cheap, filling seafood – not just clam chowder but lobster rolls, clam rolls and more. It also pours $4 glasses of Shipyard Ale, a regional microbrew.

Saigon Thinh Thanh (☎ 207-773-2932; 608 Congress St; mains $6-14; ⏰ Mon-Sat) Consistently voted one of Portland's best restaurants, this downtown eatery serves reasonably priced Vietnamese food and a large number of vegetarian dishes.

Norm's East End Grill (☎ 207-253-1700; 47 Middle St; mains $8-17) The down-home atmosphere of this barbecue joint spills over into the huge portions like Mom used to make – one serving is almost enough for two people. The baby back ribs are exceptional.

Dogfish Café (☎ 207-253-5400; 953 Congress St; mains $7-10) Salads, wraps and grilled meats are on the menu at this casual spot across from the bus station.

Bangkok Thai (☎ 207-879-4089; 671 Congress St; mains $5-9; ⏰ Mon-Sat) The former site of a greasy spoon diner is now a place for affordable, high-quality Thai dishes.

Ezo African Restaurant (☎ 207-772-1796; 51 Oak St; mains $6-15) This tiny family-run eatery, located on an easy-to-miss downtown side street, serves filling African stews for both vegetarians and meat eaters alike.

Granny's Burrito (☎ 207-761-0751; 420 Fore St; mains $5-10) Locals love this purveyor of cheap Mexican food, where the burritos include things like mango and Jamaican jerk chicken.

On the waterfront, **Standard Baking Company** (☎ 207-773-2112; 75 Commercial St; ⊙ breakfast & lunch) serves up tasty homemade breads and pastries, while **Portland Coffee Roasting Company** (☎ 207-772-9044; 111 Commercial St) is a great place to soak up the atmosphere of the Old Port district.

Drinking

Gritty McDuff's (☎ 207-772-2739; 396 Fore St) A combination casual bar and brewing company that serves award-winning bitters, browns and stouts. Because it's in the Old Port district, it only feels like it's been here forever – it actually opened in 1988.

Ri Ra (☎ 207-761-4446; 72 Commercial St) This authentic Irish pub right on the waterfront offers $2.75 draft-night specials, live music, a trivia quiz every Tuesday night and dancing every Friday night.

Bull Feeney's (☎ 207-773-7210; 375 Fore St) One of Portland's most popular bars and nightspots serves up free appetizers at happy hour (4pm to 7pm), free live music Thursday to Saturday nights and special $2 draft beers nightly.

Downtown Lounge (☎ 207-828-9944; 606 Congress St) A small, hip bar that specializes in martinis but also has happy hour tap specials and a small food menu. Its dark, cozy décor attracts lots of local artists.

Entertainment

Space (☎ 207-828-5600; 538 Congress St) is a self-described 'alternative arts venue' that presents exhibits, screens documentary films and hosts indie rock bands.

Center for Cultural Exchange (☎ 207-761-0591; 1 Longfellow Sq) This local arts organization caters to Southern Maine's growing ethnic community. Its downtown space contains a café and tiny, 220-seat performance space.

Comedy Connection (☎ 207-774-5554; 16 Custom House Wharf; tickets $6-10) Local and national stand-up comedians perform here Thursday through Sunday.

Merrill Auditorium (☎ 207-842-0800; 477 Congress St) showcases opera, theater and ballet.

The historic **State Theater** (207-780-8265; 609 Congress St) hosts live concerts by nationally touring bands.

You can watch prospective Boston Red Sox baseball players at charming **Hadlock Field** (☎ 800 936 3647; 271 Park Ave; tickets $6-8), home of the minor-league Portland Sea Dogs.

Getting There & Around

Portland is served by **Amtrak** (☎ 800-872-7245) at Union station and by both **Vermont Transit** (☎ 800-552-8737; www.vermonttransit.com) and **Concord Trailways** (☎ 800-639-3317; www.concordtrailways.com) at the **Greyhound Transit** (☎ 207-772-6587; 950 Congress St). Major airlines fly into the **Portland International Jetport** (☎ 207-774-7301; www.portlandjetport.org).

The free **Portland Explorer** (☎ 207-772-4457; www.portlandexplorer.org) connects visitors traveling between the airport, outlying hotels and downtown Portland. It runs a single route six times daily Sunday to Friday and 10 times on Saturday. **Metro Bus** (☎ 207-774-0351) offers seven routes and more frequent service for the $1 fare.

FREEPORT

A 30-minute drive north of Portland, Rte 1 passes through Freeport, the 'birthplace of Maine,' a quintessential New England village that has been reborn as a shoppers' mecca. The beautiful colonial houses that line Main St are now facades for outlet

NEW ENGLAND

stores, including the flagship store of **LL Bean** (☎ 800-559-0747; 95 Main St), which is open 24 hours a day, 365 days a year. Other famous names offering up bargains are **Banana Republic** (☎ 207-865-0559; 39 Main St), **Gap** (☎ 207-865-4452; 35 Main St) and **Abercrombie & Fitch** (☎ 207-865-4641; 55 Main St), which is housed in a 1905 Carnegie building.

To get here without a car, take the **Freeport Explorer** (☎ 207-772-4457), a bus that runs to and from Portland on Saturday and Sunday May to December ($10, three daily).

Super 8 Motel (☎ 207-865-1408; 506 US Rte 1; r $45-90; P ⊠ ⊠) has charmless but functional rooms on the outskirts of town.

Right in the center of town are numerous food stalls along Main St that sell hot dogs, lobster rolls, crab rolls and lemonade. **Isabella's Sticky Buns Café & Bakery** (☎ 207-865-6635; 2 School St; sticky buns $1.85) is a good place for breakfast or a snack.

BAR HARBOR

More than just a staging area for visitors to Acadia National Park or ferry passengers headed for Nova Scotia, the attractive resort town of Bar Harbor offers a number of interesting sights and activities. Check in with the **Bar Harbor Chamber of Commerce** (☎ 888-540-9990; www.barharbormaine.com; 93 Cottage St).

Sights & Activities

The **Abbe Museum** (Bar Harbor ☎ 207-288-3519; 26 Mt Desert St; admission $6; ☼ 9am-5pm; Sieur de Monts Spring admission $2; ☼ 9am-4pm late May–mid-Oct) presents 10,000 years worth of Maine's rich Native American history in the form of objects and artifacts. There are two locations – one in downtown Bar Harbor and one at Sieur de Monts Spring in the heart of Acadia National Park.

The **Whale Museum** (West St; admission free; ☼ noon-8pm) is a gift shop–cum–educational center that displays a 22ft-long minke whale vertebrae inside its front doors. It also offers a good primer on the biology of whales and other sea mammals.

Being adjacent to a national park, Bar Harbor is naturally bustling with outdoor companies offering everything from whale-watching tours to hang gliding, rock climbing, mountain biking and more. **Bar Harbor Whale Watch Company** (☎ 207-288-2386; 1 West St) offers 1½-hour jaunts ($19) around Frenchman Bay hauling lobster traps and viewing

harbor seals in their natural habitat, as well as half-day fishing trips ($40) where you can try your hand at catching cod, mackerel and pollack. **National Park Sea Kayak Tours** (☎ 207-288-0342; 39 Cottage St) offers half-day, one-way and round-trip tours of Acadia by kayak ($45). **Bar Harbor Bicycle Shop** (☎ 207-288-3886; 141 Cottage St) rents tandems and high-performance bikes ($15 to $20 per day) to explore Mount Desert Island. **Acadia Mountain Guides Climbing School** (☎ 207-288-8186; 198 Main St; per half/full day $50/75) provides instruction for beginning rock climbers on the island's pink granite sea cliffs. If you'd like to splurge, try **Island Soaring Glider Rides** (☎ 207-667-7627; 1/2 passengers $89/119), which has thrilling 'Acadia Special' glider-plane flights.

Sleeping

HI Bar Harbor (☎ 207-288-5587; www.barharborhostel .com; 321 Main St; dm $21-24; P ⊠ ⊠) The Bar Harbor hostel reopened in 2004 at this renovated farmhouse a short walk from the Greyhound bus station. It has 30 beds in two single-sex dormitories, one private room ($75), a kitchen, dining room and an outdoor deck. The staff organizes various nightly activities, and continental breakfast is included. Open from April 1 to November; call for reservations. Check-in is 5pm.

Mt Desert Island YWCA (☎ 207-288-5008; 36 Mt Desert St; dm/s/d $27/37/64) provides lodging for women only; by late April it's usually booked for the entire summer. **Robbins Motel** (☎ 207-288-4659; Rte 3; d $56; P ⊠ ⊠), a few miles out of town, has spare, nonsmoking rooms and an outdoor heated pool.

Eating

Morning Glory Bakery (☎ 207-288-3041; 39 Rodick St; sandwiches $5) serves up delicious, fresh sandwiches on fresh rolls. **Eden** (☎ 288-4422; 78 West St; mains $11-16) offers vegetarian food in a simple environment. **Skelly's Pure Fries & More** (37 Cottage St; mains $2.50-5.50) fries fish and potatoes in 100% soybean oil with no cholesterol. If you're hankering for some fresh seafood, **West St Café** (☎ 207-288-5242; 76 West St) offers an 'Early Bird Special' before 6:30pm ($18.95) that includes Maine lobster, a cup of clam chowder and hot blueberry pie.

Entertainment

Reel Pizza Cinerama (☎ 207-288-3811; 33 Kennebec Pl) shows first-run independent films and also serves pizzas. Seven nights a week during summer, **Improv Acadia** (☎ 207-288-2503; 15 Cottage St; tickets $12) invites audience participation for its comedic stylings. The art deco **Criterion Theater** (☎ 207-288-3441; 35 Cottage St) is on the National Registry of Historic Places and shows first-run films.

Getting There & Away

Vermont Transit (☎ 800-451-3292) has bus service to Bar Harbor from both Boston and Portland.

Bay Ferries (☎ 888-249-7245; 65 Main St) operates *The Cat*, a high-speed, 900-passenger boat that whisks travelers between Bar Harbor and Great Yarmouth in Nova Scotia, Canada, in under three hours (adult $45 to $55, car $85 to $155). Catch the ferry at the **Bar Harbor Terminal** (121 Eden St) on the waterfront. Special one-day, round-trip fares are available from $49. Sailings are at 8am daily, with another 4pm sailing between late June and early September.

ACADIA NATIONAL PARK

Occupying most of Mount Desert Island, the Schoodic Peninsula and Isle au Haut, **Acadia National Park** rewards budget travelers who have journeyed this far up the Maine coast. The only national park in the northeastern USA, Acadia features an undulating landscape sculpted by glaciation with a stunning variety of mountains and lakes, ocean beaches and tide pools, plants and mammals – all within a relatively tidy 62 sq miles. Visitors can enjoy a chilly dip in the ocean at gorgeous Sand Beach, watch the crashing Atlantic surf from Otter Cliffs, follow a nature trail around Jordan Pond and join the hardy group of early birds atop 1530ft-high Cadillac Mountain (they're among the first people in America who get to watch the sun rise). There are some 120 miles of hiking trails, as well as 57 miles of historic carriage (broken stone) roads, car-free and ideal for cyclists. The carriage roads cross above and below 17 stone bridges around the park, gifts from John D Rockefeller Junior.

The park has two campgrounds. **Blackwoods** (☎ 800-365-2267; ME 3; campsites $14-20), 5 miles south of Bar Harbor, has 310 sites that are open year-round but available during summer by reservation only. **Seawall** (Rte 102A; campsites $14-20), 4 miles south of Southwest Harbor, is open between late May and late September and is first-come, first-served.

Drivers can access views, trails and campgrounds via the 27-mile **Park Loop Rd** that connects Sieur de Monts, Spring Area, Sand Beach, Thunder Hole, Cadillac Mountain and Jordan Pond. For those without their own vehicle, the **Island Explorer** (☎ 207-288-4573) shuttle bus is a convenient way to get around the park. There are seven routes originating in Bar Harbor that run to various corners of Acadia National Park, with some running as frequently as every 30 minutes.

The park maintains a **Hulls Cove Visitor Center** (☎ 207-288-3338; www.nps.gov/acad; ME 3) that dispenses maps and useful tourist information. This is also where you can pay the park's entrance fee (low/high season $10/20), which is good for a seven-day visit.

BAXTER STATE PARK

In the vast inland expanse of northern Maine, **Baxter State Park** (☎ 207-723-5140; www.baxterstateparkauthority.com) is notable for having within its boundaries **Mt Katahdin** (5267ft), the state's highest mountain, and the north end of the **Appalachian Trail** (AT; ☎ 304-535-6278; www.nps.gov/appa). The 'AT' covers more than 2100 miles of federal- and state-protected land between here and Georgia, including 281 very isolated miles in the state of Maine itself. Most of the amazing backpackers who hike the entire AT finish up here in late summer or early fall. For those just interested in day hikes or overnight camping, the state park offers 180 miles of hiking trails and 1200 campsites. Advance reservations are recommended as the park tends to fill up early in summer. To get here by car, take I-95 to exit 244 in Medway and follow Rte 11 to Rte 157.

There's great white-water rafting in the area. The **New England Outdoor Center** (☎ 800-766-7238), in nearby Millinocket, organizes guided trips on the Penobscot River.

NEW HAMPSHIRE

Known as the Granite State, New Hampshire has earned a reputation as a haven for rock-hard, fiercely independent-minded

NEW ENGLAND

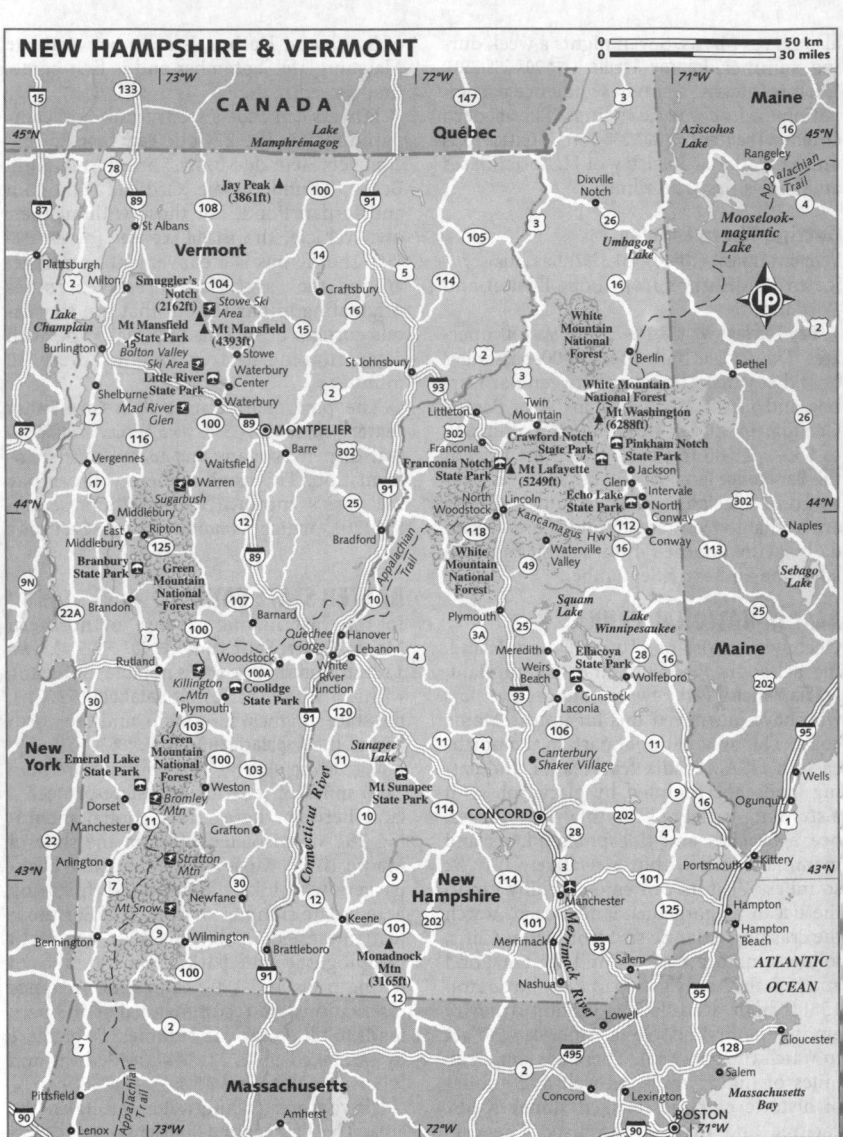

NEW HAMPSHIRE & VERMONT

NEW ENGLAND

people. The 'Live Free or Die' slogan on their car license plates is more of a proud mantra than a suggestion. There's a wide variety of scenery, from the historic seaport town of Portsmouth in the south to the peaks of the White Mountains in the north. Bonus for budget travelers: the state has no sales tax.

PORTSMOUTH

A classic New England seaport, Portsmouth's historic, preserved downtown is a maze of winding streets and narrow brick rowhouses. It lies along the mouth of the Piscataqua River, across the water from Kittery, Maine. The area is easily walkable, with most of the activity converging on the corner of Market and Congress Sts. Pick up information, maps and a Portsmouth Harbor Trail Guide at the **Greater Portsmouth Chamber of Commerce** (☎ 603-436-3988; www.port city.org; 500 Market St).

Sights

Strawbery Banke Museum (☎ 603-433-1100; 64 Marcy St; admission $15; ☉ 10am-5pm Mon-Sat, noon-5pm Sun May-Oct) In a neighborhood that was once known as Puddle Dock, this waterfront collection of historic homes and period gardens harkens back to the days of Strawbery Banke, the original name of Portsmouth. During winter the museum is open only for guided walking tours ($10). Tickets are good for a two-day period.

USS Albacore (☎ 603-436-3680; 600 Market St; admission $5; ☉ 9:30am-5pm late May–early Oct, 9:30am-3:30pm early Oct–late May) Explore this decommissioned US Navy submarine, whose teardrop hull design became a model for other nations' subs. Marvel at how, somehow, 55 men once worked in very cramped quarters. Take I-95 to exit 7.

Portsmouth has a number of lovingly preserved historic homes, including the **John Paul Jones House** (☎ 603-436-8420; 43 Middle St; admission $6; ☉ 11am-5pm late May–mid-Oct), the **Wentworth Gardner & Tobias Lear Houses** (☎ 603-436-4406; Mechanic St; admission $5; ☉ Wentworth–Gardner House 1-4pm Tue-Sun, Tobias Lear House 1-4pm Wed, both open mid-Jun–mid-Oct), and the **Warner House** (☎ 603-436-5909; 150 Daniel St; admission $5; ☉ 11am-4pm Mon-Sat, noon-4pm Sun early Jun–Oct). All are within the downtown area.

Portsmouth Harbor Cruises (☎ 603-436-8084; Ceres St Dock; adult $11-18; ☉ mid-May–end Oct) provides a good overview of the area's rich nautical history from the Piscataqua to the Isle of Shoals.

Sleeping

Motel 6 (☎ 603-334-6606; 3 Gosling Rd; r $65-85; P ⊠ ⊠ ⊠) A 108-room chain hotel 3 miles northwest of downtown Portsmouth. If you're driving, go west on Rte 4, follow the exit to Gosling Rd and turn right.

Great Bay Camping (☎ 603-778-0226; 56 Rte 108; campsites $22-32; P ⊠) Wooded campground on the banks of the Squamscott River with 95 sites, boat access to the Atlantic Ocean and canoe rentals. By car, take I-95 North to Rte 101 West. Follow signs to Rte 108 and drive north for 4.5 miles.

Eating & Drinking

Portsmouth Gas Light Company (☎ 603-430-9122; 64 Market St) This brick-oven pizzeria features a $6.50 all-you-can-eat buffet during weekday lunches that includes pizza, garlic bread, pasta and a 16oz soft drink with free refills.

Portsmouth Brewery (☎ 603-431-1115; 56 Market St; mains $6-23) This expansive brewpub with an impressive and extensive menu features everything from burgers to thin-crust pizzas to *cioppino* (an Italian stew) made with fresh seafood – not to mention a massive selection of beers.

Friendly Toast (☎ 603-430-2154; 121 Congress St; mains $3-8) Spacious, funky restaurant with tattooed servers, pop art décor and 1950s Formica booths. It's not just style over substance, though; the food is uniformly terrific, especially the filling breakfasts.

O'Naturals (☎ 603-319-0101; 100 Market St; mains $5-8) This environmentally responsible restaurant, located on the 2nd floor of an office building, offers healthy dishes such as Asian noodles, tossed salads and flatbread sandwiches.

Molly Malone's (☎ 603-433-7233; 177 State St) Irish pub located upstairs in an historic, elegant rowhouse. Serves a variety of lagers and ales, including the tasty Shipyard Old Thumper. A full-service, moderately priced steakhouse is downstairs.

Entertainment

The acclaimed **Seacoast Repertory Theater** (☎ 603-433-4472; 125 Bow St; tickets $22-32) performs various dramatic works in the historic 1892 Bow St Theater. The historic **Music Hall** (☎ 603-436-2400; 28 Chestnut St) presents theater, music and dance, as well as an excellent summer movie series.

Getting There & Around

C & J Trailways (☎ 603-430-1100) makes daily runs between Boston and Portsmouth; the trip takes approximately 90 minutes. You'll be dropped off at the **Trailway Transportation Center** (185 Grafton Dr, Pease Tradeport)

The **COAST** bus (☎ 603-743-5777; www.coastbus .org; tickets $1) provides transportation from downtown Portsmouth to the New Hampshire seacoast towns of Dover, Newington and Rochester. The **Downtown Loop Trolley** (tickets 50¢; ☉ 10:30am-5:30pm late Jun–early Sep) covers most major central attractions.

NEW ENGLAND

LAKE WINNIPESAUKEE AREA

Holding some 625 billion gallons of water, Lake Winnipesaukee, the largest in New Hampshire, is a popular outdoor destination for New Englanders. It's dotted with towns geared toward mindless summer diversions such as mini-golf and waterslides. Although the miles of tacky commercial strips can be a bit much, the scenic views make up for it.

By car, take I-93 to Rte 11 into Laconia then follow Rte 3 north to Weirs Beach and Meredith. **Concord Trailways** (☎ 800-639-3317; www.concordtrailways.com) offers twice-daily service from Boston's South Station to the Mountain Mart on Rte 25 in Meredith.

In Laconia, the **Greater Laconia/Weirs Beach Chamber of Commerce** (☎ 603-524-5531; 11 Veterans Sq), in an old train station, has maps and good advice. In the same building, the **Black Cat Café** (☎ 603-524-3233; 17 Veterans Sq; mains $3-7) serves coffee, sandwiches and big cookies in a funky space with cozy sofas. **Greater Laconia Transit Agency** (GLTA; ☎ 603-528-2496; www.gltabus.org) operates limited bus service between Laconia and other towns along the lake.

Nearby in Guilford, **Ellacoya State Beach** (☎ 603-293-7821; NH 11; admission $3) has a 600ft lakeside beach, picnic area and campground. During summer, Gunstock, the local ski resort, also operates a **campground** (☎ 800-486-7862; NH 11A; campsites $25; P 🐾). **Patrick's Pub & Eatery** (☎ 603-293-0841) serves meat, seafood and pasta meals, with live entertainment on weekends.

When it comes to riding go-karts and stuffing your face with fried dough, Weirs Beach is unequaled. While you're here, don't miss the chance to explore all corners of the lake aboard the **M/S Mount Washington** (☎ 603-366-5531; Lakeside Ave; adult $16-19), which offers two-hour scenic daytime cruises as well as Wednesday night singles dance cruises. A smaller **US Mail boat** ($16, 11am and 2pm Monday to Saturday) takes passengers on its delivery route to less traveled corners of the lake. **Lakeview Hotel Motel & Cottages** (☎ 603-366-4621; r $38-95; 🍴 P 🐾) is just 100yd from Weirs Beach Boardwalk. **Kellerhaus** (☎ 603-366-4466; Rte 3), New Hampshire's oldest maker of candy and ice cream, has a make-your-own-ice-cream-sundae buffet. **Weirs Beach Drive-In** (☎ 603-366-4723) is one of the last outdoor cinemas of its kind.

In the town of Moultonborough, **Castle in the Clouds** (☎ 603-476-2352; Rte 171; admission $10; ⏲ 10am-4:30pm Sat & Sun May, daily Jun-Oct) is an architectural hodgepodge of a mansion built in 1913. Tours of this unique estate feature great views of the lake and the Ossippee mountain range.

WHITE MOUNTAINS

Active types love the White Mountains, and with good reason. This area is blessed with terrific hiking, camping and skiing. There are dramatic vistas around every curve in the road, and the most dramatic vista of all from atop Mt Washington (6288ft), New England's highest peak.

Take Rte 16 to Conway, then head north on Rte 16 to Mt Washington or west on Rte 302 or Rte 112 (the Kancamagus Hwy) to Franconia Notch. **Concord Trailways** (☎ 603-228-3300) stops in Conway and North Conway.

Information

Mt Washington Valley Chamber of Commerce (☎ 800-367-3364; www.mtwashingtonvalley.org; 2617 Main St, North Conway)

White Mountains Visitors Center (☎ 800-346-3687; www.visitwhitemountains.com; 200 Kangamagus Hwy, North Woodstock; ⏲ 8:30am-5pm)

Sights & Activities

At 6288ft, **Mt Washington** is the tallest mountain in New England. It also proudly boasts the 'world's worst weather': a wind speed of 234mph was recorded at the peak observatory in 1931. Most days it's just overcast and windy at the summit, but if you're lucky enough to be here on a clear day, the views are superb. To reach the top, take the historic 8-mile **Auto Rd** (☎ 603-466-3988; car & driver $18, each additional adult passenger $7) from Rte 16, or splurge and hop aboard the **Cog Railway** (☎ 800-922-8825; tickets $49), the oldest mountain-climbing railway in the world.

Wildcat Mountain (☎ 888-754-9453), on Rte 16 in Pinkham Notch, features a gondola skyride, the 70ft Glen Ellis falls (a 2-mile hike from the parking lot) and great skiing terrain in winter.

Conway Scenic Railroad (☎ 603-356-5251; round trip $11-56; ⏲ late Jun–late Oct) runs a variety of excursions from North Conway Depot station across Mt Washington Valley and through dramatic Crawford Notch. It's one of the most scenic train rides in the country, especially during peak foliage season in late September and early October.

A 34.5-mile-long stretch of NH 112, the **Kangamacus Highway** (named after a 17th-century Native American chief) is a unique road. As it runs through the heart of the White Mountain National Forest, there are no honky-tonk cafés, gas stations or billboards. The only turnouts are for dramatic overlooks of the Presidential Mountain Range, quiet picnic sites and miles of hiking trails. First-come, first-served camping is permitted at six highway campgrounds including Blackberry Crossing and Passaconaway. Pick up maps and information at the **Saco Ranger District Office** (☎ 603-447-5448; 33 Kancamagus Hwy) near Conway at the eastern end.

An equally dramatic drive is the one through the deep, rocky gorge of **Franconia Notch State Park**. Get maps and info at the park **visitors center** (☎ 603 745 8391; I-93 exit 34A). Nearby, **Cannon Mountain** (☎ 603-823-8800; I-93 exit 34B) has rides to the top on its aerial tramway (round trip $10; ☯ 9am-5pm mid-May mid Oct) and walking tours of the **Flume Gorge** (☎ 603-745-8391; Rte 3; admission $8; ☯ 9am-5pm May & Jun, Sep & Oct; 9am-5:30pm Jul & Aug).

Saco Canoe Rental Company (☎ 603-447-2737; 328 Rte 16, Conway; kayaks per day $15) rents 'fun-yaks' – inflatable rubber kayaks – for trips along the nearby Saco River.

Sleeping

HI Albert P Lester Memorial Hostel (☎ 603-447-1001; conwayhostel@yahoo.com; 36 Washington St, Conway; dm $19-22; ☒ ☐) This clean, colonial Conway farmhouse has 45 beds, four private rooms and Internet access. On the doorstep to White Mountains National Forest, it attracts hikers and outdoor adventurers, as well as European students staying here while visiting the country on work visas.

Eating

Chinook Café (☎ 603-447-6300; 80 Main St, Conway; sandwiches $2.75-7.25; ☯ lunch) Puts just about anything you want on bread, from peanut butter and jelly to white bean and Portabello in a bruschette.

Cafe Noche (☎ 603-447-5050; 147 Main St, Conway; mains $5-10) A popular family restaurant that serves a Tex-Mex menu of enchiladas, fajitas and chimichangas.

Michael's Roadside Diner (☎ 603-374-2280; Rte 302, Bartlett; ☯ 24hr Fri & Sat) In nearby Bartlett, offers burgers, hot dogs and the famed Friday night fish fry.

VERMONT

The majestic Green Mountain State, Vermont arguably has the prettiest landscapes in America east of the Mississippi River. Inarguably, it's the least populated state in New England. For visitors this means that outside of Burlington, the major city, you won't see many people as you travel on quiet two-lane roads, admire panoramic vistas, stop in picturesque villages and take advantage of the state's many outdoor offerings: hiking and swimming in summer, skiing in winter.

For travel info, dial ☎ 511 within Vermont, ☎ 1-800-837668 out of state, or check www.511VT.com.

BURLINGTON

Burlington, 'The Queen City,' has always enjoyed its regal location on the eastern shore of Lake Champlain. This liberal college town – home to five institutions of higher education, including the University of Vermont – also lays claim to political and musical icons. Bernie Sanders, the only Socialist in the US Congress, was once mayor of the city, and the jam band Phish started by playing local Burlington nightclubs. Residents and visitors alike can take advantage of year-round outdoor activities from sailing to skiing.

Downtown Burlington can be reached by car on I-89. Take exit 14 West and follow Main St into town. The downtown area is laid out in a grid and is easy to navigate on foot. Main St runs all the way down to the shores of Lake Champlain and intersects with Church St Marketplace, the city's main pedestrian mall. The weekly *Seven Days* covers Burlington's arts and entertainment scene. **Lake Champlain Regional Chamber of Commerce** (☎ 802-863-3489; www.vermont.org; 60 Main St) serves the info.

Sights

Burlington's downtown is easily navigable by foot, and there's no better place to start than at the foot of Main St on the banks of **Lake Champlain**. At 120 miles long, 12 miles wide at its widest point, 400ft deep at its deepest point, with a mean depth of 40ft, it's the sixth-largest freshwater lake in the US. There are great views across to New York State and the Adirondacks from

Waterfront Park, one block over on College St, or from the band shell at Battery Park on Lakeview Tce. The 9-mile-long **Burlington Bike Path** runs north to the Winooski River Trail Bridge.

ECHO Lake Aquarium & Science Center (☎ 802-864-1848; 1 College St; adult/student $9/8; ⏰ 10am-5pm Fri-Wed, 10am-8pm Thu), a new educational science museum, opened on the Burlington waterfront in 2003. It displays aquatic habitats, live species, interactive exhibits and has a multimedia theater.

Away from the lake, Main St rises up a hill to the heart of Burlington's downtown area. The architecturally significant **Church St Marketplace** (☎ 802-863-1648), a four-block pedestrian mall, is lined with more than 100 great shops, restaurants and bars. There are also galleries like the **Firehouse Center for Visual Arts** (135 Church St). When the weather is nice, the mall is filled with street vendors, entertainers and the crush of human activity day and night, and the outdoor patios have a European feel to them.

At the top of Main St is the attractive **University of Vermont** (☎ 802-656-3131; www.uvm.edu) campus, home of the **Robert Hull Fleming Museum** (☎ 802-656-0750; 61 Colchester Ave; adult/student $5/3; ⏰ 9am-4pm Tue-Fri, 1-5pm Sat & Sun Labor Day–Apr 30; noon-4pm Tue-Fri, 1-5pm Sat & Sun May 1–Labor Day). This beautiful beaux arts–style building houses over 20,000 objects from around Vermont and every corner of the world. It also boasts funky traveling exhibits such as Lou Reed's Andy Warhol collection.

On the outskirts of town, **Shelburne Museum** (☎ 802-985-3346; US Rte 7; adult/student $18/13; ⏰ 10am-5pm May 1–Oct 31) contains a superb, diverse collection of folk and decorative art on a 45-acre estate comprising historic buildings, peaceful gardens and the 220ft steamboat *Ticonderoga*. Take exit 13 off I-89.

Vermont Teddy Bear Company (☎ 802-985-3001; US Rte 7, Shelburne; admission $2; ⏰ 9am-6pm Mon-Sat, 10am-5pm Sun) has been manufacturing its hyper-popular stuffed bears for more than two decades, and it's reached the point where it's willing to pull back the curtain and show you how it's done. You can even make your very own bear on the premises. Located approximately 1 mile south of the village of Shelburne.

Burton World Headquarters (☎ 802-660-3200; 80 Industrial Parkway) is the main factory of the popular manufacturer of snowboarding gear and apparel. Don't miss the lobby display tracing the development of the snowboard from 1977 to the present day. The factory also houses a prototype shop and a hip flagship store.

Activities

Burlington is less than a two-hour drive from five major ski resorts: Stowe, Smuggler's Notch, Sugarbush, Bolton Valley and Killington. The **Ski Rack** (☎ 800-882-4530; 85 Main St; skis per day $30, bikes per hr/day $10/22) rents skis in winter and bikes in summer.

If you're headed out to Lake Champlain, **Waterfont Boat Rentals** (☎ 802-864-4858; Perkins

---

BACKROADS VERMONT

If you've gotten as far north in Vermont as Burlington, it's worth a bit of extra driving to explore the dazzling and relatively undiscovered **Lake Champlain Islands**. Between Vermont mainland and New York State are five different slivers of land surrounded by water: the rural communities of South Hero, Grand Isle, North Hero, Isle La Motte and Alburg – the last of which is technically a peninsula whose only land connection is to Canada. Part of the charm of these islands is their geographic separateness; they're literally their own little worlds. There are historic attractions like St Anne's Shrine on Isle La Motte, and the Hyde Log Cabin, one of the oldest in the country, on Grand Isle. There are also offbeat finds like the miniature stone castles that surround South Hero, built throughout the mid-20th century by a local gardener named Harry Barber. You can explore the wildlife and wetlands of Alburg Dunes State Park, then stop by Sunburger's in Grand Isle to choose from among 83 flavors of soft-serve ice cream. There are good fishing spots throughout, many beaches for swimming and even a few places to camp.

To explore the islands, drive north from Burlington on I-89 and take exit 17 to Rte 2 headed west. You'll soon pass over a causeway that leads to South Hero, 'the garden spot of Vermont' and the start of 27 miles of gently rolling terrain – a quiet corner of a state that's quite peaceful to begin with.

Pier at Maple St; kayaks per hr/day $10/35, motorboats per hr/day $40/140) rents kayaks and motorboats.

Petra Cliffs (☎ 866-657-3872; 105 Briggs St), Vermont's largest indoor climbing gym, offers rock-climbing programs for beginners.

Tours

Lake Champlain Chocolates (☎ 802-864-1807; 750 Pine St; 9am-2pm Mon-Fri) This Pine St factory offers a free, hourly tour of this olfactory and gustatory heaven. Free confectionery samples are available. The popular chocolates are also sold at a downtown **store** (☎ 802-862-5185; 63 Church St).

Magic Hat Brewery (☎ 802-658-2739; 5 Bartlett Bay Rd, South Burlington) offers free tours Wednesday through Saturday, including a free sample of its beers produced using 'ancient alchemy and modern-day science.'

Green Mountain Railroad Corp (☎ 802-463-3069; College St station; round trip $10; 10am, noon, 2pm, 4pm Sat & Sun late Jun–late Aug) operates the *Champlain Valley Flyer* between Burlington and Shelburne. The scenic train ride takes one hour.

Lake Champlain Shoreline Cruises (☎ 802-862-8300) offers lake cruises aboard the *Spirit of Ethan Allen II*.

Sleeping

Burlington's beds get snapped up in autumn during leaf-peeping season, and in May, when the five area colleges hold graduation ceremonies.

Mrs Farrell's Home Hostel (☎ 802-865-3730; dm member/nonmember $19.70/23.20; ☽ Apr 1–Oct 31; ⓟ ⊠ ▣) This tiny but cozy six-bed hostel is, as advertised, a home in a residential neighborhood about 5 miles north of (and a 20-minute bus ride from) downtown. You'll need to call for directions. Telephone between 4pm and 6pm local time to make advance reservations, which are required. There's a two-night minimum stay.

North Beach Campground (☎ 802-862-0942; 60 Institute Rd; campsites $25; ⓟ) Located 3 miles north of downtown, this campground has 68 campsites along the wooded shores of Lake Champlain, as well as picnic grounds, bathroom and shower facilities, and a beach with lifeguards. Canoes and kayaks are available for rent.

Hartwell House Bed & Breakfast (☎ 802-658-0242; hartwell@together.net; 170 Ferguson Ave; r $55-70; ⓟ ⓡ) A quiet neighborhood B&B where guests can warm up in front of the living

room fireplace or go for a swim in the pool. With only two rooms available, you'll need to make reservations here in advance.

Eating & Drinking

Being a college town, Burlington has plenty of cheap eats and lots of bars with drink specials.

Handy's Lunch (☎ 802-864-5963; 74 Maple St; mains $2-6; ☽ breakfast & lunch) A tried-and-true local spot near the waterfront, Handy's offers horseshoe-counter seating and a bargain breakfast special of eggs, toast and coffee for about $3.

Mr Mike's Pizza (☎ 802-864-0072; 206 Main St; pizza slices $2-3) Cranks out cheap pizza slices and calzones for hungry and alcohol-fueled UVM students. The adjacent Clubhouse Bar gives alliterative monikers to its nightly drink specials, like 'whiskey weekend' and 'tequila Tuesdays.'

Manhattan Pizza & Pub (☎ 802-658-6776; 167 Main St) All-you-can-eat pizza specials for less than $7, and karaoke at 10pm on Thursday, Friday and Saturday.

Vermont Pub & Brewery (☎ 802-865-0500; 144 College St; mains $5-14) Burgers, salads and a great selection of microbrews,

Five Spice Café (☎ 802-864-4045; 175 Church St; mains $9-18.) Pan Asian restaurant serving traditional dishes from Thailand, Indonesia, Vietnam, Burma and China.

Ri Ra's (☎ 802-860-9401; 123 Church St) An Irish pub housed in a former bank, with live DJs on Friday night.

Other Place (☎ 802-863-5803; 4 N Winooski Ave) A mellow dive bar with open-air seating, pool tables and cheap drinks.

Breakwater Cafe & Grill (☎ 802-658-6276; King St at Battery St) This top waterfront spot serves food, pours drinks, hosts live entertainment and has an outdoor patio from which you can watch the sun setting over the Adirondack mountains across Lake Champlain.

Entertainment

Nectar's (☎ 802-658-4771; 188 Main St) Dating back to 1975 – the wise elder of Burlington nightlife – this is where the jam band Phish got its start. Nectar's still packs in the students on weekend nights. Upstairs, **Club Metronome** (☎ 802-865-4563) offers DJs and nationally touring rock bands.

Red Square (☎ 802-859-8909; 136 Church St) This is a hip, tiny scenester bar year-round and overflows its crowds into the adjacent alleyway for live bands on summer nights.

Millennium (☎ 802-660-2088; 165 Church St) Presents live music and visiting, nationally known DJs. Cheap draft beer and shots from Wednesday to Saturday.

Flynn Center/FlynnSpace (☎ 802-863-5966; 147-153 Main St) These two neighboring venues – one a 1500-seat art deco theater, the other a tiny 150-seat performance space – host concerts, classes and festivals.

Vermont Expos (☎ 802-655-4200; tickets $5-6), a short-season minor-league baseball team, plays at the oldest minor-league ballpark, Centennial Field. Take East Ave to Colchester Ave.

Sunset Drive-In (☎ 802-862-1800; Porter's Point Rd off Rte 127) is one of the last old-time bits of Americana, a summer drive-in theater with four screens showing first-run movies from April to October.

Getting There & Away

An increasing number of low-fare airlines, most notably **Jet Blue** (☎ 800-538-2583;

THANK YOU, CHERRY

The most popular tourist attraction in Vermont isn't a museum or a mall – it's the **Ben & Jerry's Ice Cream Factory Tour** (☎ 866-258-6877; Rte 100, Waterbury; admission $3; ☺ 9am-5pm), drawing more than 300,000 visitors a year to its plant 2 miles north of Waterbury center. The half-hour tours begin with a short film that explains the company's history and long-standing progressive business practices. Then it's on to a room overlooking the production floor, where 24,000 gallons a day of popular flavors like 'cherry Garcia' and 'chocolate chip cookie dough' are produced. Visitors pass by the Quality Assurance lab, whose taste-testing staff have perhaps the best job in America, and then finally there's a room at the end where generous samples are provided. You're also welcome to simply hang out, free of charge, at the colorful picnic tables and Adirondack chairs dotting the factory grounds, or visit the 'Flavor Graveyard', where tombstones commemorate such 'Greatest Misses' as 'peanut butter and jelly', and 'Miz Jelena's sweet potato pie'. To get to the factory, take exit 10 off I-89.

www.jetblue.com) and **Independence Air** (☎ 800-359-3594; www.flyi.com), fly into **Burlington International Airport** (☎ 802-863-1889).

Vermont Transit (☎ 800-552-8737) provides bus service between Burlington's terminal (345 Pine St) and major East Coast cities including Boston, New York and Montréal.

Lake Champlain Ferries (☎ 802-864-9804; www .ferries.com) operates auto ferry service across the lake between Vermont and New York State at three different points. Depart from the Burlington ferry terminal, at the foot of King St, for the crossing to Port Kent, New York (round trip per adult $6.75, car and driver $25, one hour). There's also a 20-minute crossing at the lake's southern end between Charlotte and Essex, New York, and year-round 24-hour service from Grand Isle to Plattsburgh, New York, a 12-minute journey. Both trips are $4.50 for an adult round trip and $14 round trip for a car and driver.

Getting Around

Chittenden County Transportation Authority (CCTA ☎ 802-864-2282; www.cctaride.org) provides $1 bus service throughout greater Burlington. It also operates an express bus (one way $3) to Montpelier along I-89.

MONTPELIER

Vermont's pretty and progressive state capital, Montpelier is a small town of around 10,000 people, some 40 miles east of Burlington on I-89. It can easily be explored in about half a day. The **Amtrak** (☎ 800-872-7245) *Vermonter* stops here. There's travel information at the **Capitol Region Visitors Center** (134 State St; ☺ 8am-5pm).

Befitting its sparse population, the Vermont **State House** (State St) is quite modest in size. If not for its gold-leaf dome and handsome, locally quarried granite, it could be mistaken for a county courthouse. **Guided tours** (☎ 802-828-2228; admission free; tours 10am, 3:30pm Mon-Fri, 11am-2:30pm Sat Jul–mid-Oct) are available by appointment. Next door is the **Vermont Historical Society Museum & Store** (10 State St; adult/student $5/3; ☺ Tue-Sat 10am-4pm year round, also noon-4pm Sun May-Oct), housed inside the graceful Pavilion building.

In nearby **Barre** is the **Rock of Ages Visitor Center** (☎ 802-476-3119; 558 Graniteville Rd, Graniteville admission free; ☺ 8:30am-5pm Mon-Sat, noon-5pm Sun May-Oct), with exhibits and displays of the granite produced in local quarries and used around the world. Artisans here transform granite into memorials and statues. For a closer look, take the narrated shuttle tour ($4) of the EL Smith Quarry, the world's largest-dimension granite quarry. Take I-89 exit 6 to Rte 63.

Set back from the street, **Thrush Tavern** (☎ 802-223-2030; 107 State St; mains $4-11) is frequented by employees from the State House next door. Hearty burgers, soups, salads and daily specials are on the menu, and there is beer on tap. **Julio's** (☎ 802-229-9348; 54 State St; mains $6-11) serves moderately priced Mexican food and has outdoor seating. **Capitol Grounds** (☎ 802-223-7800; 45 State St) is a breakfast spot for coffee and freshly baked pastries.

MIDDLEBURY

This classic New England college town has a handsome village green and a narrow, picturesque main street full of shops and cafés. It's located on Rte 7 near the border with New York State, about 35 miles south of Burlington.

Sights & Activities

Middlebury College (☎ 802-443-3000; www.middlebury.edu; 131 S Main St; tours 10am & 2pm Mon-Fri, also 10am Sat Aug & Sep, Oct & Nov) offers free tours of its verdant campus throughout the academic year. The **Middlebury College Museum of Art** (☎ 802-443-5007; S Main St; admission is free;

⊙ 10am-5pm Tue-Fri, noon-5pm Sat & Sun) has a strong collection of European and American paintings as well as contemporary photographs.

The **Henry Sheldon Museum of Vermont History** (☎ 802-388-2117; 1 Park St; adult/student $5/3.50; ⊙ 10am-5pm Mon-Sat), housed in an 1829 Federal-style brick house, features a variety of furniture, clothing and tools from the state's past.

Equine lovers will not want to miss the University of Vermont's **Morgan Horse Farm** (☎ 802-388-2011; Horse Farm Rd; adult $4; ⊙ 9am-4pm May-Oct), whose rolling pastures are home to dozens of registered stallions. Go west on VT125 and then north on VT23.

Silver Lake, a lovely, boat-free mountain swimming hole just outside of town, is a popular escape for Middlebury College students. Take VT53 south and then hike 1 mile up from the parking lot.

Sleeping

Blue Spruce Motel (☎ 802-388-4091; Rte 7; cottages $65-75; P ⊠) This clean, comfortable motel on the outskirts of Middlebury has 22 rooms, some with kitchenettes.

Branbury State Park (☎ 802-247-5925; 3570 Lake Dunmore Rd, Salisbury; campsites $16; P) This place has 45 campsites on either side of the road, including some right along Lake Dunmore. The price includes access to a swimming beach, fishing, boating and hiking. Take VT7 south to VT53 south.

NEW ENGLAND

SCENIC DRIVE: RTE 100

It's safe to say that Rte 100 is the backbone of Vermont. For one thing, it literally runs through the center of the state. For another, a drive on this rural road contains everything the state is known for: mountains, ski resorts, charming villages with town commons and church steeples – and cows. Lots and lots of cows.

Begin near the road's southern terminus in Wilmington. You'll drive just a few miles before reaching **Mt Snow** (☎ 800-451-4211), the self-proclaimed mountain bike capital of the east, with miles of steep, technical terrain that hosts national competitions during the summer months. Continuing north, you'll reach **Weston**, a beautiful albeit touristy town. Pick up a jug of Grade A maple syrup at its distinctive **Vermont General Store**. When you reach **Plymouth**, take a brief detour onto Rte 100A to see the birthplace of US President Calvin Coolidge. Back on the road, you'll soon reach **Killington** (☎ 802-422-6200), a year-round resort that offers hiking, rock climbing and an alpine slide in summer and 200 ski runs across seven mountains in winter. You'll soon hit a stretch of dairy farms, farmers and those aforementioned cows. Pass through scenic Waterbury, stop off at the **Ben & Jerry's Factory** (see the boxed text p160) for ice cream, then soldier on to luxurious **Stowe**. Wander around this scenic village, then top off the day by driving to the top of Vermont's highest mountain on the nearby **Mt Mansfield Auto Toll Rd** (☎ 800-253-4754; cars $17). The entire drive should take four to six hours.

Eating

A&W Drive-In (☎ 802-388-2876; Rte 7; mains $3-5; ☺ summer only) The only drive-in restaurant in the state, with curbside service provided by servers on roller skates. The fast-food menu even includes falafel.

American Flatbread (☎ 802-388-3300; at the Marble Works; pizzas $12-16; ☺ dinner Fri & Sat) Specializes in all-natural pizzas, large enough for two to three people and topped with locally raised meats and organic vegetables.

Entertainment

At the **Middlebury College Language Schools** (☎ 802-443-5510) there are free screenings of obscure international films every Saturday night from early June to early August at the Dana Auditorium on campus. All films are subtitled in English. One small catch: visitors are asked to refrain from using English during the screenings so as not to distract from the students' study of the language in question.

BRATTLEBORO

With a very vibrant arts community, quirky shops and a scenic location on the banks of the Connecticut River across from New Hampshire, it's no surprise that Brattleboro has been voted one of the top five small towns in America. Take exit 5 off I-91. **Amtrak** (☎ 800-872-7245) and **Vermont Transit** (☎ 802-254-6066) both make stops here.

Check in at the **Brattleboro Area Chamber of Commerce** (☎ 802-254-4565; www.brattleboro.com; 180 Main St).

Sights & Activities

Brattleboro's **Main St** includes the gorgeous art deco Latchis building, which houses three movie theaters and a hotel; and the River Garden, a semi-enclosed public space with terrace views of the Connecticut River. Climb Mt Wantastiquet, on the New Hampshire side of the river, for a great view of town.

Brattleboro Museum & Art Center (☎ 802-257-0124; 10 Vernon St; adult/student $4/2; ☺ 11am-5pm Wed-Mon), housed in the 1915 Union train station, showcases contemporary works by regional artists in a variety of mediums – photography, painting and video installations.

At 984ft long, rising 35ft over a series of 51 pools, the **Connecticut River Fish Ladder** (Governor Hunt Rd; admission free; ☺ 8am-5pm May-Jul) helps out the spawning habits of American shad and Atlantic salmon. A viewing gallery lets visitors watch the drama unfold. Take VT142 south towards Vernon.

Brattleboro is a Nordic skiing mecca, with miles of trails boasting views of the Connecticut River and the West River Valley. The **Harris Hill Ski Jump** (☎ 877-254-4565; Cedar St), one of the few Olympic-sized, 70m ski jumps in the USA, hosts international competitions every February.

Sleeping

Latchis Hotel (☎ 802-254-6300; 50 Main St; r $60-110; ☐ ☒) One of only two art deco–style buildings in the entire state, this historic hotel (upstairs from the equally dazzling Latchis Theater) has been carefully restored to its past grandeur.

Fort Dummer State Park (☎ 802-254-2610; 434 Old Guilford Rd; campsites/lean-tos $14/21; ☐) A heavily forested campground with 51 campsites and 10 lean-to shelters. Take I-91 to exit 1, go north a few hundred yards on US 5, 0.5 miles east on Fairground Rd, then a mile south on Main St and Old Guilford Rd.

Eating & Drinking

Amy's Bakery Arts Café (☎ 802-251-1071; 113 Main St; mains $3-8) One of the town's free trade-certified coffee shops, Amy's also serves up soups, salads, sandwiches and a view overlooking the river.

Riverview Café (☎ 802-254-9841; 36 Bridge St; mains $9-20) An acclaimed restaurant with a contemporary menu emphasizing ingredients made from fresh local produce and local products. The patio views of the Connecticut River are a nice bonus. Good for a splurge meal or for just enjoying any of 10 microbrews from the rooftop bar.

Brattleboro Food Co-op (☎ 802-257-0236; 2 Main St) This Brookside Plaza grocer sells a variety of organic foods in its market and deli.

McNeill's Brewery (☎ 802-254-2553; 90 Elliot St) This casual, spacious hang-out features an excellent selection of microbrewed beers.

Entertainment

Hooker-Dunham Theater & Gallery (☎ 802-254-9276; 139 Main St) hosts musicians, comedians and playwrights, while the adjacent 1100-sq-ft gallery has exhibits by local and visiting artists. Memorial Park has outdoors **Shakespeare in the Park** (☎ 802-254-4636; tickets $5) in June.

RHODE ISLAND

The USA's smallest state was founded by Roger Williams, who sought to create a haven from religious persecution. These days, Rhode Island offers a different kind of escape: its main attractions are culinary, cultural and historical, from the revitalized state capital of Providence to the spectacular mansions and relaxing beaches of Newport.

PROVIDENCE

The rebirth of Providence, the capital of Rhode Island, may be New England's biggest success story of the past few years. What was once a depressed, corrupt, crime-ridden burg has turned into a stylish, artsy, happening city that's a destination in its own right. From the revitalized downtown area along the spruced-up Providence River to the historic homes that line the streets of East Side (home of Brown University), this is one place that's worth a visit.

Downtown Providence lies along two rivers, the eponymous Providence and the Woonasquatucket. East Side, the city's most scenic area – where the Brown and Rhode Island School of Design (RISD) campuses are located – is just east of downtown. Federal Hill, a heavily Italian neighborhood, runs along Atwells Ave and Broadway on the other side of I-95.

The *Providence Phoenix* is the city's alternative weekly. **Providence-Warwick Convention & Visitors Bureau** (☎ 401-274-1636; www.go providence.com; One W Exchange St; ❂ 8:30am-5pm Mon-Fri) dispenses street maps, brochures and discount coupons.

Sights & Activities

East Side has a number of great streets to wander along. Benefit St is a lovely promenade of historic colonial and Victorian homes with back patios overlooking downtown and the river. Thayer St is the lively college strip. It adjoins Brown University's verdant campus, a collection of grassy courtyards filled with ivy-covered brick buildings. Wickenden St has a number of shops and cafés, and there's a farmers market every Tuesday from 2pm to 6pm from mid-June to late October.

Federal Hill, the Italian neighborhood, is centered around the restaurants and food shops on Atwells Ave.

Rhode Island's historic center of government, the **State House** (☎ 401-222-2357; 82 Smith St; admission free; ❂ 9am-3:30pm Mon-Fri) is an elegant building with a large marble dome built between 1895 and 1904. It houses artifacts such as the Royal Charter of 1663 from England's King Charles II.

With a dazzling collection of 65,000 pieces, **RISD Museum of Art** (☎ 401-454-6500; 224 Benefit St; adult/student $8/3, free 10am-1pm Sun, 5-9pm 3rd Thu each month & all day last Sat each month; ❂ 10am-5pm Tue-Sun, to 9pm 3rd Thu each month) is the place in Providence to see Egyptian metals, Japanese prints, textiles, 18th-century porcelain figures and lots more. Visitors can view 300 years of American and British silverworks inside Pendleton House, a two-story historic residence that forms part of the museum. The beautifully arranged galleries are filled with gems and yet are not at all overwhelming.

The **David Winton Bell Gallery** (☎ 401-863-2932; 64 College St; admission free; ❂ 11am-4pm Mon-Fri, 1-4pm Sat & Sun) inside the List Art Center features the latest in contemporary art.

Roger Williams State Park & Zoo (☎ 401-785-3510; www.rogerwilliamsparkzoo.org; 1000 Elmwood Ave; park/zoo free/$10; ❂ 9am-5pm Mon-Fri, 9am-6pm Sat & Sun spring & summer; 9am-4pm daily fall & winter) The 'Jewel of Providence' attracts 3.5 million visitors per year. This sprawling park contains botanical gardens, a Museum of Natural History and a planetarium. The zoo has polar bears, a tropical rainforest and 160 species. Take I-95 to exit 17.

Russian Sub Museum (☎ 401-521-3600; www .saratogamuseum.org; Collier Point Park, Allens Ave; admission $8; ❂ 10am-6pm) Hop aboard *Juliett 484*, a former Soviet nuclear cruise missile submarine now docked on the river. This sub was used in the movie *K19: The Widowmaker*.

Culinary Archives & Museum (☎ 401-598-2805; www.culinary.org; 315 Harborside Blvd; adult/student $7/3; ❂ 9am-5pm Mon-Sat) Known as the 'Smithsonian Institution of the Food Industry,' this quirky museum contains a half-million-item collection devoted to the history of dining out.

Fleet Skating Center (☎ 401-331-5544; 2 Kennedy Plaza) Located right downtown, this large outdoor rink is available to the public for ice-skating in winter and rollerblading in summer. Rentals available.

East Bay Bike Path (☎ 800-233-1637) is a paved route that runs along the edges of

---

ARTISTIC LICENSE

On the third Thursday of every month, **Gallery Night** (www.gallerynight.info) offers visitors a taste of Providence's burgeoning art scene. On Gallery Night, the **RISD Museum of Art** (☎ 401-454-6500; 224 Benefit St; adult/student $8/3, admission free 10am-1pm Sun, 5-9pm 3rd Thu each month & all day last Sat each month; ☻ 10am-5pm Tue-Sun, 10am-9pm 3rd Thu each month) provides free admission from 5pm to 9pm, and includes free, one-on-one instruction from a professional artist or educator (materials are provided). There's also a free Art Bus that loops continuously around a dozen of Providence's museums and galleries.

Naragansett Bay for 15 miles between East Providence's Washington Bridge and the town of Bristol.

Sleeping

Providence is sadly lacking in cheap hotels. Your best bet for (relatively) affordable lodging is to stay at a roadside chain a few miles out of town.

Six miles from Providence in Seekonk, Massachusetts, the **Johnson & Wales Inn** (☎ 508-336-8700; www.jwinn.com; 213 Taunton Ave; r $89-145; P ✕ ☷) has 86 well-appointed guest rooms. The hotel doubles as a training facility for culinary and hospitality students attending Johnson and Wales University.

In neighboring Pawtucket, **Comfort Inn** (☎ 401-723-6700; 2 George St; r from $79; P ✕ ☷) offers rooms with standard amenities and continental breakfast. Take I-95 to exit 27.

If you'd like to stay in Providence and are willing to splurge, the beautiful Italianate **Old Court Bed & Breakfast** (☎ 401-752-2002; 144 Benefit St; r $95-175; ✕ ☷) features a variety of 19th-century-styled rooms with high ceilings and antique furnishings. A large homemade breakfast is served daily.

Eating & Drinking

Arcade (☎ 401-598-1199; 65 Weybosset St) The nation's oldest indoor marketplace, a National Historic Landmark, houses a number of inexpensive lunchtime spots.

Bob & Timmy's (☎ 401-453-2221; 32 Spruce St; pizzas $9-13) Delicious wood-grilled, square-shaped pizzas with fresh toppings of produce, wild mushrooms and a legendary pink vodka sauce. Very good and quite cheap.

Cuban Revolution (☎ 401-331-8829; 149 Washington St; mains $4-8) Funky, pro-Castro downtown restaurant wears its politics on its metaphorical sleeve and serves Cuban sandwiches, platters and salads. Good combination specials are under $10. Try the Goya ginger beer.

East Side Pockets (☎ 401-453-1100; 278 Thayer St; mains $4-7) Immensely popular Thayer St Middle Eastern joint serves falafels, wraps and gyros to Brown University students on a tight budget.

Spike's Junkyard Dogs (☎ 85 Richmond St; 401-421-0830; junkyard dogs $3.25) A brightly lit place right near a gaggle of bars, the better to serve the gastronomic needs of late-night drinkers. Chicken, subs, buffalo wings and lots of fried foods.

Trinity Brewhouse (☎ 401-453-2337; 186 Fountain St; mains $6-22; ☻ to 1am Sun-Thu, to 2am Fri & Sat) Rhode Island's largest brewery is also a fully functioning restaurant, specializing in pub food that complements the beer: Black Angus burgers, fish and chips, shepherd's pie and more.

Red Fez (☎ 401-272-1212; 49 Peck St) This cozy 2nd-floor bar on the edge of downtown is popular with RISD students, whose esoteric artistic tastes are reflected in the Russian Constructivist wall posters and indie rock blasting on the speakers. Serves a number of microbrews on tap.

Liquid Lounge (☎ 401-454-3434; 165 Angell St) Near the Brown University campus, this basement bar runs numerous beer promotions (including $1.50 Rolling Rock bottles at all times) and provides free use of its pool table from 7pm to 10pm.

Haven Brothers Diner (Kennedy Plaza) A Providence tradition, this greasy food truck magically appears in front of City Hall every evening and stays open until the early morning hours.

Entertainment

WaterFire Providence (☎ 401-273-1155; www .waterfire.org) This fire sculpture installation created by artist Barnaby Evans, features dozens of floating bonfires set along the downtown rivers as music plays over speakers. The free event takes place on certain evenings between May and October.

Providence Performing Arts Center (☎ 401-421-2787; 220 Weybosset St) Historic, 3000-seat theater that hosts Broadway shows, live concerts and nationally known musical acts.

AS220 (☎ 401-831-9327; www.as220.org; 115 Empire St) An open forum for the arts, this collective mounts exhibits and presents live music, often in its downtown performance space.

Lupo's at the Strand (☎ 401-331-5876; 79 Washington St) Downtown performance venue hosts reggae, rock and hip-hop acts.

Living Room (☎ 401-521-5200; 23 Rathbone St) Tiny, longtime dive that gives rock bands their start.

Avon Cinema (☎ 401-421-3315; 260 Thayer St) Shows first-run independent films.

Sports

The **Providence Bruins** (☎ 401-273-5000), a minor-league ice hockey team, plays at the **Dunkin' Donuts Center** (☎ 401-331-0700), known affectionately as 'The Dunk.'

North of Providence in the neighboring city of Pawtucket the **Pawtucket Red Sox** (☎ 401-724-7300) play minor-league baseball at McCoy Stadium.

Shopping

Risdworks (☎ 401-277-4949; 10 Westminster St) Sells art and designer products produced by RISD graduates and faculty.

Armageddon Shop (☎ 401-521-6667; 436 Broadway) Federal Hill shop with a superb collection of used and obscure vinyl (mostly punk and metal) and alternative magazines.

Tom's Tracks (☎ 401-274-0820; 281 Thayer St) New and used CDs and records.

Getting There & Away

Providence is 50 miles (about a one-hour drive) from Boston on I-95 South, which continues through Rhode Island and on into Connecticut.

Bonanza (☎ 888-751-8800) and **Greyhound** (☎ 800-231-2222) bus lines both serve Providence from all major East Coast cities. Kennedy Plaza, between City Hall and Federal Court House, is the downtown intermodal transportation site.

Amtrak (☎ 800-872-7245) trains stop right in the center of town, but if you have the extra time, the slower **MBTA Commuter Rail** (☎ 800-392-6100) runs from here to Boston for just $6 one way.

TF Green Airport (PVD; ☎ 401-737-8222), located 10 minutes south of downtown in the city of Warwick, is often less expensive than flying into Boston's Logan. It is served by Southwest Airlines, US Airways, Delta and other major carriers.

Getting Around

The **Rhode Island Public Transit Authority** (RIPTA; ☎ 800-244-0444) operates a bus service throughout Providence and to Newport as well. Its Providence Link Green Line trolley ($1) runs every 10 to 20 minutes from East Side traveling through downtown and onto Federal Hill.

NEWPORT

The beautiful seaside resort town of Newport, situated on the southern end of Naragansett Bay, has historically been a playground for the super-rich. It's the US home of the America's Cup sailing races, and boasts superbly maintained colonial houses and enormous mansions. Budget travelers may experience a bit of sticker shock at the prices of accommodations and Thames (pronounced thaymz, not temz) St eateries, but Newport's sights and activities warrant a visit.

Upon arriving, check in at the **Newport Visitor Info & Transportation Center** (☎ 401-845-9123; www.gonewport.com; 23America's Cup Ave; ⊙ 9am-5pm) for more information.

Sights & Activities

What happens when some of the richest people in early-20th-century America decide to build their summer homes on the Rhode Island coast? You get the **Newport Mansions** (☎ 401-847-1000; www.newportmansions.org; tours $23-32; call for times), which have to be seen to be believed. These enormous architectural and landscaping jewels range in style from Gothic Revival to classic Victorian, and there are dozens of them spread on either side of Bellevue Ave. For a more affordable sampling of these grand houses, **Belcourt Castle** (☎ 401-846-0669; 657 Bellevue Ave; adult/student $10/8; ⊙ noon-5pm Wed-Sun) offers hourly guided tours of the opulent 60-room estate.

You can get great exterior views of the mansions without spending a penny. The 3.5-mile **Cliff Walk** is a free public path that winds past the sprawling lawns and mansions of Newport's Gilded Age on one side and the Atlantic Ocean on the other. It begins at Memorial Blvd and ends at Ledge

Rd. Parts of the Cliff Walk are steep, so be sure to wear good walking shoes.

International Tennis Hall of Fame (☎ 401-849-3990; 194 Bellevue Ave; adult/student $8/6; ⊙ 9:30am-5pm) houses the largest tennis museum in the world amid six acres of Victorian-era social ambience. Learn about the game and its great players, and swing a racket on the grass courts of the Casino.

Touro Synagogue (☎ 401-847-4794; 85 Touro St; admission free; ⊙ 10am-5pm), dedicated in 1763, is the oldest synagogue in the US. It's worth checking out for its interesting combination of classical Italian architecture and Sephardic Jewish ritualism. A Jewish cemetery and park honoring colonial Jewish leaders are on the grounds.

Fort Adams State Park (☎ 401-847-2400; Harrison Ave; admission free; ⊙ sunrise-sunset) is America's largest coastal fort and was used to defend Naragansett Bay from 1799 to 1945. You can explore the gun tiers and enjoy a great view of Newport Harbor.

Easton's Beach (☎ 401-848-6491; 175 Memorial Blvd), known to locals as 'First Beach,' gets packed with sunbathers on weekends, but it's still a great place to catch a tan and splash around in the bay, and even surf if the waves are just right.

Newport Sailing (☎ 401-848-2266) offers half-day sailing lessons as well as a one-hour sailing tour around Newport Harbor for $18 per person.

Scooters (☎ 401-619-0573; 411 Thames St) hires bicycles.

Sleeping

Newport is frightfully expensive when it comes to hotels and B&Bs. Your best options

---

IF YOU HAVE A FEW MORE DAYS ON RHODE ISLAND

Tiny, 11-sq-mile **Block Island**, 12 miles off the Rhode Island coast, makes for a relaxing escape. It has 17 miles of beaches, two lighthouses and miles of nature trails (a quarter of the island is preserved open space). Regular, daily **ferry service** (☎ 401-783-4613) departs from Point Judith on the mainland (one way $8.30). For accommodation information, contact the **Block Island Tourism Council** (☎ 800-383-2474, ext 63; www.blockislandinfo.com).

---

are **Motel 6** (☎ 401-848-0600; 249 JT Connell Hwy; r $69-95; P 🞩) and the **Seaview Inn** (☎ 401-846-5000; 240 Aquidneck Ave; r $69-229; P 🞩 🞩). **Admiral Weaver Inn** (☎ 401-849-0051; www.admiral weaverinn.com; 28 Weaver Ave; r $65-169; 🞩) often has special packages that include gourmet breakfast and free parking.

Eating & Drinking

Sapo Freaky Burrito (☎ 401-847-7276; 16 Broadway; burritos $5.50-6.25; ⊙ Mon-Sat) Offers cheap Mexican food.

Istanbul Coffee House (☎ 401-841-5828; 2 Broadway; veg plate $11; ⊙ Tue-Sun) Serves up dolma, baklava and a Turkish coffee that's sure to get you wired.

Aidan's (☎ 401-845-9311; 1 Broadway; mains $4-15) A traditional Irish pub with an extensive selection of draft beers. The 'Irish brunch' on weekends comes with pot of Irish tea.

Pop (☎ 401-846-8456; 162 Broadway) This ultra-stylish bar, whose restrooms are labeled 'Us' and 'Them,' attracts lots of young people after 9pm. It serves drinks until 1am and munchies until midnight. There's dancing and karaoke on Friday and Saturday.

Jack & Josie's (☎ 401-851-6900; 111 Broadway; mains $7-12) Serves coffee, juices and snacks amid a hip diner with modern furnishings, wireless Internet access and a plasma-screen TV.

White Horse Tavern (☎ 401-849-3600; 26 Marlborough St) Be sure to get at least one drink here. The 1673 building is the oldest operating tavern in the US.

Entertainment

One Pelham East (☎ 401-847-9460; 270 Thames St) A large bar with a small stage that hosts local rock groups and alternative cover bands. It's popular with tourists and locals alike.

Jane Pickens Theater (☎ 401-846-5252; 49 Touro St) Independent and first-run movies in a historic brick building on charming Washington Sq.

Getting There & Away

Rhode Island Public Transit Authority (RIPTA; ☎ 800-244-0444) runs buses to and from Providence ($13.50, 1½ hours). **Bonanza** (888-751-8800) stops here as well.

RIPTA also offers ferry service (one way $7, six daily) between Newport's Gateway Center and Providence's **Point St Ferry Landing** (40 Point St).

Getting Around

RIPTA has a number of bus routes around town. Pick up an all-day pass ($5); it also provides discounted admission at many Newport sights.

CONNECTICUT

Connecticut is one part quintessential New England – best reflected in the seafaring towns along the southeastern coast – and one part New York–centric, especially urban (and urbane) New Haven on the southwestern coast.

Most major airlines, including United, American, Continental and Southwest, fly into Connecticut's **Bradley International Airport** (BDL; ☎ 888-624-1533; www.bradleyairport.com), just outside of Hartford.

SOUTHEASTERN COAST

Mystic & Around

The pretty seaside village of Mystic is probably best known as the setting for the Julia Roberts film *Mystic Pizza*, but it has a rich maritime tradition that long precedes this. The **Mystic Chamber of Commerce** (☎ 860-572-9578; www.mysticchamber.org; 14 Holmes St; 9am-5pm Mon-Fri) provides information for visitors.

Mystic Seaport (☎ 888-973-2767; adult/student $17/15; 9am-5pm Apr-Oct, 10am-4pm Nov-Mar), also known as the Museum of America & the Sea, covers much of America's maritime history throughout its sprawling 19th-century village. Highlights include the largest collection of nautical photographs in the world and the National Historic Landmark vessel *Sabino*, a 1908 passenger ship. On-site artisans still practice and will demonstrate traditional shipbuilding methods. The seaport is 1 mile south of I-95 on Rte 27.

The **Mystic Aquarium** (☎ 860-572-5955; 55 Coogan Blvd; admission $15; 9am-6pm Mar-Dec, 10am-5pm Mon-Fri & 9am-6pm Sat & Sun Dec-Mar) has more than 6000 creatures on view, including baby alligators and beluga whales.

Seven miles north of Mystic off I-95 exit 92, the **Mashantucket Pequot Museum & Research Center** (☎ 800-411-9671; 110 Pequot Trail, off CT 24; admission $15; 9am-5pm) is the world's largest Native American museum, using high-tech interactive exhibits, videos and dioramas to convey local tribal culture.

A nonprofit environmental sanctuary, the **Denison Pequotsepos Nature Center** (☎ 860-536-1216; 109 Pequotsepos Rd; admission $6; 9am-5pm Mon-Sat, 10am-4pm Sun) educates visitors about the woodland, wetland and meadow habitats along the Connecticut shore. There's excellent wildlife viewing along 8 miles of trails.

Voodoo Grill (☎ 860-572-4422; 12 Water St; mains $5-12) serves up burgers, po-boys and barbecued Creole dishes. **Mystic Pizza** (☎ 860-536-3700; 56 West Main St; pizza slices $2.50), the restaurant that inspired the movie that launched Julia Roberts' career, serves filling pizza slices to go and also offers a sit-down service. Grab a pint in the colonial-style pub at the **Captain Daniel Packer Inne** (☎ 860 536-3555; 32 Water St), housed within a 250-year-old historic landmark.

Seaport Campground (☎ 860-536-4044; 45 Campground Rd, CT 184; campsites $33) has 130 campsites, a swimming pool and a modem hookup at the main office.

Groton & New London

Groton and New London are both coastal towns that have played a prominent role in manufacturing submarines and other military elements for the USA's nautical defenses. Groton's **US Navy Submarine Force Museum** (☎ 800-343-0079; 1 Crystal Lake Rd; admission free; 9am-5pm Wed-Mon, 1-5pm Tue May 15–Oct 31; 9am-4pm Wed-Mon, closed Tue Nov 1–May 14) and New London's **US Coast Guard Academy Museum** (☎ 860-444-8511; 15 Mohegan Ave, CT 32; admission free; 9am-5pm Mon-Fri, 10am-5pm Sat, noon-5pm Sun) reflect the area's naval history. The **Lyman Allyn Art Museum** (☎ 860-443-2545; 625 Williams St, New London) exhibits a variety of international classical and ethnic art.

IF YOU HAVE A FEW MORE DAYS IN CONNECTICUT

Hartford, Connecticut's capital, offers up the **State Capitol**, the **Mark Twain House** and the **Wadsworth Atheneum**, the oldest public art museum in the US. **Gillette Castle**, in East Haddam, is a 24-room mansion that's part of a large state park. **Dudleyville** is reputed to be 'the most haunted town in America.'

NEW HAVEN

The first planned city in the US, not to mention the birthplace of the Frisbee and the lollipop, New Haven is the largest city on the Connecticut coastline. Founded in 1638 by Puritans escaping persecution in Anglican England, it's dominated today by the presence of Yale University, a school that wouldn't look out of place in the Old Country. Yale and the finest pizza in the world make New Haven well worth a visit.

INFO New Haven (☎ 203-773-9494; www.infonewhaven.com; 1000 Chapel St), the visitors center on New Haven Green, stays open seven days a week to dispense maps, brochures and calendars.

Sights

Like Harvard University to the north, **Yale University** (www.yale.edu) is one of the most elite educational institutions in the US – after all, the last three presidents (George HW Bush, Bill Clinton and George W Bush) all studied here. The campus is a riot of Gothic and Tudor-style buildings, as well as modern edifices such as Eero Saarinen's David S Ingalls Hockey Rink (aka 'The Whale') and Gordon Bunshaft's **Beinecke Rare Book & Manuscript Library** (☎ 203-432-2977; 121 Wall St; admission free; 🕑 8:30am-8pm Mon-Thu, 8:30am-5pm Fri), behind whose translucent marble windows is housed one of the world's few remaining Gutenberg bibles. Free campus tours leave from the **Yale Visitor Center** (☎ 203-432-2300; 149 Elm St; 🕑 10:30am & 2pm Mon-Fri,1:30pm Sat & Sun).

Generally acknowledged as having the best collection of British artwork outside the UK, the **Yale Center for British Art** (☎ 203-432-2800; 1080 Chapel St; admission free; 🕑 10am-5pm Tue-Sat, noon-5pm Sun) – the last commissioned work of architect Louis Kahn – features rotating exhibits and films, as well as concerts and lectures throughout the year.

Across the street stands the 1928 Italian Gothic–style Swartwout building housing the oldest college art museum in the country, the **Yale University Art Gallery** (☎ 203-432-0600; 1111 Chapel St; admission free; 🕑 10am-5pm Tue-Sat, noon-5pm Sun). It displays pieces from ancient Greece to the present day. There are classic works by Edward Hopper and Winslow Homer, as well as a great collection of decorative furnishings. The 1953 Louis Kahn–designed wing is being renovated and is scheduled to reopen in 2005.

At the **Peabody Museum of Natural History** (☎ 203-432-5050; 170 Whitney Ave; adult/student $7/5, admission free 2-5pm Thu; 🕑 10am-5pm Mon-Sat, noon-5pm Sun), the collection comprises 11 million specimens and artifacts. Highlights include the internationally renowned festival of fossils in the Great Hall of Dinosaurs, housed against a backdrop of Rudolph Zallinger's award-winning mural *The Age of Reptiles*, which covers 300 million years of earth history in 110ft.

If museum going tires you out, take a load off on **New Haven Green**, a beautiful open park, National Historic Landmark and the center of the city's nine squares. It's bordered by College, Chapel, Church and Elm Sts.

Sleeping

Hotel Duncan (1151 Chapel St; r $44-112) Just a few blocks from New Haven Green, this old hotel in an 1894 high-rise features a creaky elevator, worn but clean rooms and spacious suites. You'll be in good company – hundreds of famous actors including Gene Hackman and James Earl Jones have called this place home while performing at local theaters.

Eating

New Haven is justifiably famous among gourmets and gourmands for its pizza. Popular legend has it that in 1900 the first pizza ever made in America was produced here by Italian immigrant Frank Pepe, based on his family's tomato pie recipe. History is still made today, one mouthwatering brick-oven pizza at a time, at **Frank Pepe Pizzeria** (☎ 203-865-5762; 157 Wooster St; pizzas $6-21; 🕑 Wed-Mon) and its adjacent annex, the **Spot** (☎ 203-865-7602; 163 Wooster St; 🕑 Tue-Sun). Expect a long wait almost any time of day to eat here, and it gets especially crowded at dinnertime.

Lots of locals believe that **Modern's Apizza** (☎ 203-776-5306; 874 State St; pizzas $5.75-18) serves up pies as good as, if not better than, Pepe's, and without the throng of tourists.

Louis' Lunch (☎ 203-562-5507; 261 Crown St; burgers $4.50) This tiny, cramped eatery with arched doors and Gothic windows served America's first hamburger at this site in 1895, and to this day it's still cooking a goof, no-frills burger (cheese, tomato and onion are the only available toppings) on toasted bread.

Yankee Doodle (☎ 203-865-1074; 258 Elm St; ☒ breakfast & lunch) This 1950s hole-in-the-wall greasy spoon offers counter service and atmosphere to spare.

Ivy Noodle (☎ 203-562-8800; 316 Elm St; mains $3-8) This popular student spot serves very cheap and filling Asian noodle dishes along with traditional Chinese mainstays.

Entertainment

New Haven has a strong theatrical tradition, thanks to its geographic proximity to the Great White Way (Broadway) in New York. The three professional troupes in town have launched the careers of Meryl Streep and the like. Performances are held at these venues:

Yale University Theater (☎ 203-432-1310; 254 York St)

Yale Cabaret (☎ 203-432-1566; 217 Park St)

Yale Repertory Theater (☎ 203-432-1234; 1120 Chapel St)

Long Wharf Theater (☎ 203-787-4282; 222 Sargent Dr)

Palace Theater (☎ 203-789-2122; 246 College St)

New Theater (☎ 203-432-1234; 1156 Chapel St)

Schubert Theater (☎ 800-228-6622; 247 College St) This venerable hall has presented more than 600 Broadway tryouts in its illustrious history, including the premier performances of such beloved musicals as *Oklahoma* and *Damn Yankees*.

Toad's Place (☎ 203-562-5589; 300 York St) This intimate nightclub plays host to rock acts of various sizes. The Rolling Stones once kicked off a stadium tour here, so you never know who might be appearing.

Getting There & Away

New Haven is two hours' drive northeast of New York City on I-95. **Amtrak** (☎ 800-872-7245) trains and the **Metro-North Railroad** (☎ 800-638-7646) both stop at Union station, as do **Peter Pan** (☎ 800-237-8747) and **Greyhound** (☎ 203-772-2470) bus lines. All offer connections to New York City, Hartford, Springfield and Boston.

Eastern Canada

HIGHLIGHTS

- **Toronto** Explore the tightly knit patchwork of neighborhoods (p175)
- **Montréal** Historic by day, wild by night (p195)
- **Biggest surprise** Photos and postcards don't do justice to the charm of Québec City (p204)
- **Off the beaten track** Bruce Peninsula's scenic shorelines and stunning sunsets (p194)
- **Best journey** Go mainstream; start in Detroit and race up Hwy 401, stopping in Toronto and Kingston before detouring to Ottawa and continuing to Montréal and Québec City

FAST FACTS

- **Area** 907,655 sq km

- **Big cities** Toronto (population 4.7 million), Montréal (3.4 million), Ottawa (785,000), Halifax (335,000), Québec City (167,000)

- **Budget** $40-80 per day

- **Costs** campsite $15-30, hostel $18-30, 1L can of maple syrup $6-10

- **Driving times** Toronto to Montréal 6 hours, Montréal to Halifax 10 hours, Toronto to Winnipeg 28 hours

- **Famous for** CN Tower, ice hockey, moose and beavers, maple trees, Maritime affability, Hwy 401, rocks and trees, snow

- **Languages** English in Ontario, predominantly French with some English in Québec, English with a thick Irish-like accent in the Maritimes

- **Population** 20,933,254

- **Phrases** *Put on a toque* (pronounced took) *and let's go get a two-four* (connotes desire to put on a wooly cap and go out to pick up a case of beer); *Take off, hoser* (made famous by Bob and Doug McKenzie, but rarely used today, connotes semi-friendly and ubiquitous comeback)

- **Seasons** hot, muggy summers; cold and wet winters, with frequent snow and ice storms; beautiful spring and fall don't last long.

- **Provinces** Ontario, Québec, Nova Scotia, New Brunswick, Prince Edward Island, Newfoundland & Labrador

- **Tasty treats** Montréal bagels, smoked-meat sandwiches and poutine, Ottawa beavertails, St John's fish & chips

- **Time** Eastern, Atlantic and Newfoundland Time Zones

- **Top hostel** city – Canadiana Guesthouse & Backpackers, Toronto (p182); country – Chalet Beaumont, Val David (p204)

TRAVEL HINTS

Don't make fun of Mounties; it's never been funny. Bringing your own wine to Québec restaurants is cheaper and encouraged. Get a railpass if you plan on using the train more than a few times. Knowledgeably talking about hockey will earn new friends and possibly free drinks.

Nobody spends any amount of time between the northern shores of Lake Superior and the eastern shores of the Atlantic Ocean without drinking Canadian beer (the good and bad), hearing about hockey and noticing just how simple life can be. There are no steadfast rules, no unwritten codes, no secret plans, just a bunch of people appreciating what they have and, more importantly, being proud of their home.

Visitors to Eastern Canada are awestruck by the vast wilderness, the thunderous spray of Niagara Falls, the craggy yet stunning beauty of the Maritimes and the endless energy of Québec. Even CN Tower draws cries of 'I can see it!' when visitors approach Toronto for the first time. But what really helps people settle in and get around are the sociability and sense of community seen and felt everywhere, despite it being the biggest 'half' of the world's second-biggest country.

HISTORY

Don't believe everything the history books say. European discovery of North America happened on the northeast shores of Labrador when Scandinavian Vikings settled 500 years before Columbus.

John Cabot was the first documented European explorer to walk on the shores of east coast Canada in 1497. He was unimpressed with the rocky, barren landscape, but his reports of waters so thick with codfish one could walk on the surface spawned a fishing industry that built and supported the Maritimes for almost half a millennia. In the past decade, the fishing industry has been hit hard: stocks are low and federal restrictions are tight.

From the very start of those fishing days, France and Britain bantered and squabbled for control. As settlement made its way inland, British-built forts and communities would be taken by the French, retaken by the British, set on fire by the British, rebuilt by the French or any variation on that theme. Britain finally won in 1759 with a battle victory on the Plains of Abraham at Québec City. However, when thousands of British Loyalists fled the American Revolution in the 1770s, the area divided into the British Upper (today Ontario) and French Lower (Québec) Canada. Though France's New World influence had been waning, political positions, voices and beliefs let the world know they were still around and have been ever since.

Throughout it all, dozens of aboriginal groups have had to watch their land of 10,000 years get settled and exploited through fishing, the 18th-century fur trade and centuries of modernization since. Be it the Algonquin in southern Ontario, Iroquois and Ojibway north of there, Mohawk along the St Lawrence River, Innu in northern Québec, or Mi'kmaw in Nova Scotia, European visitors were almost always welcomed with excited hesitation and cautious optimism and almost always later regarded with resentment.

THE CULTURE

There was a beer commercial on Canadian TV a few years ago. It involved a mid-20s male with semi-short, dark hair in blue jeans and a plaid shirt walking sheepishly across a stage to a microphone under a spotlight. He timidly starts off with 'Hey,' before recounting things that he is not (lumberjack), people he doesn't know (Jimmy from Canada) and things he doesn't say ('aboot'). His voice grows stronger as he starts to list things he does believe and things he does say before confidently proclaiming, 'I am Canadian!'

That commercial still lives strong today on the Internet, T-shirts, posters and other commercial goods.

THE BIG ISSUE: SEPARATISM FADING

Once the most hotly contested issue in the region, Canadians occasionally still debate the proposal that Québec secede from the Canadian federation and form an independent nation. During the 1960s, the Front de libération du Québec (FLQ) launched a decade of violent advocacy involving kidnapping, murder and martial law. Québecers have twice voted down formal sovereignty referenda; the second in 1995 by a margin of less than 1%. Bloc Québecois (prosovereignty party) support began to decline in federal elections but won two-thirds of Québec's seats in the House of Commons (a return to its highest levels of representation) in the 2004 election. Nevertheless, by and large most Canadians are way over it.

EASTERN CANADA

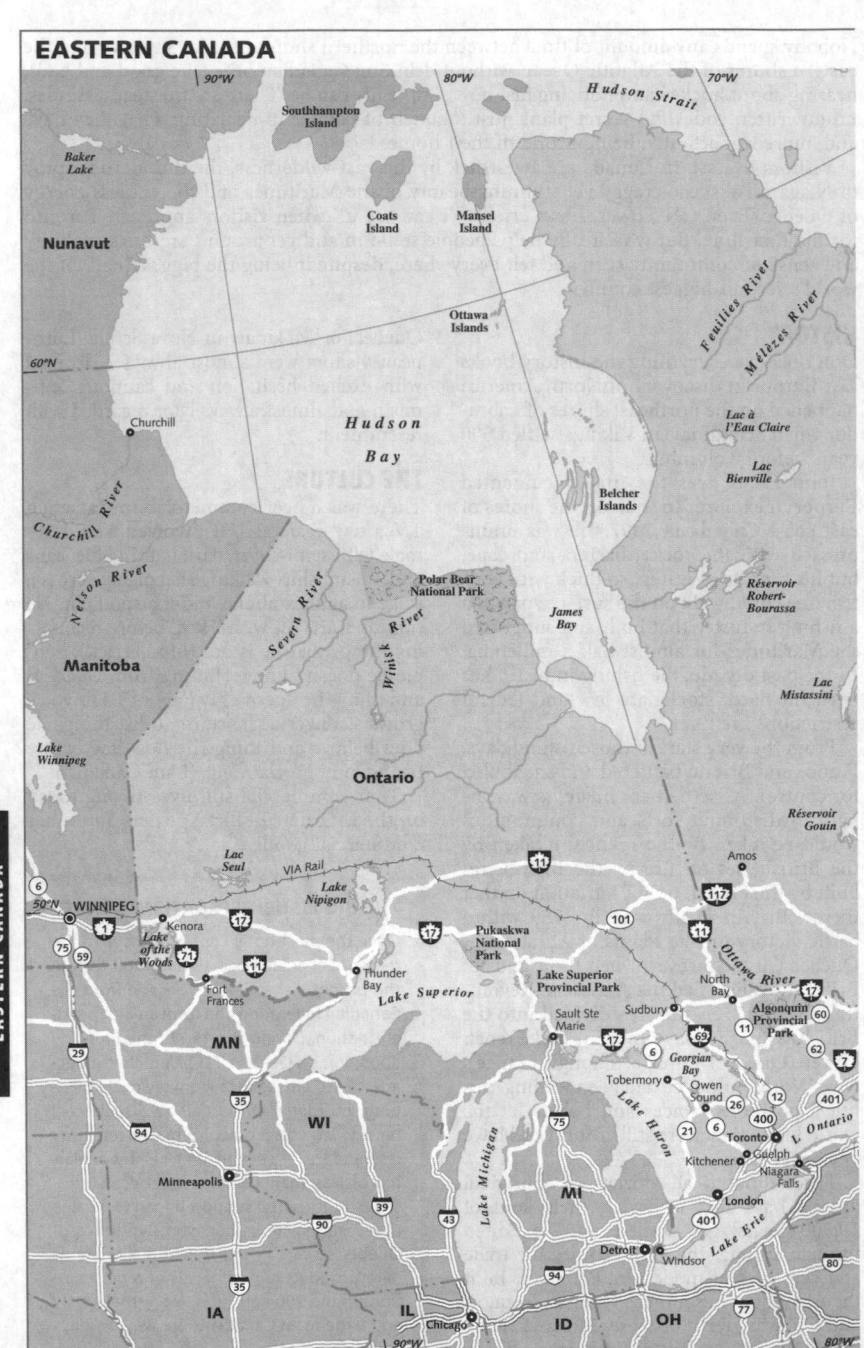

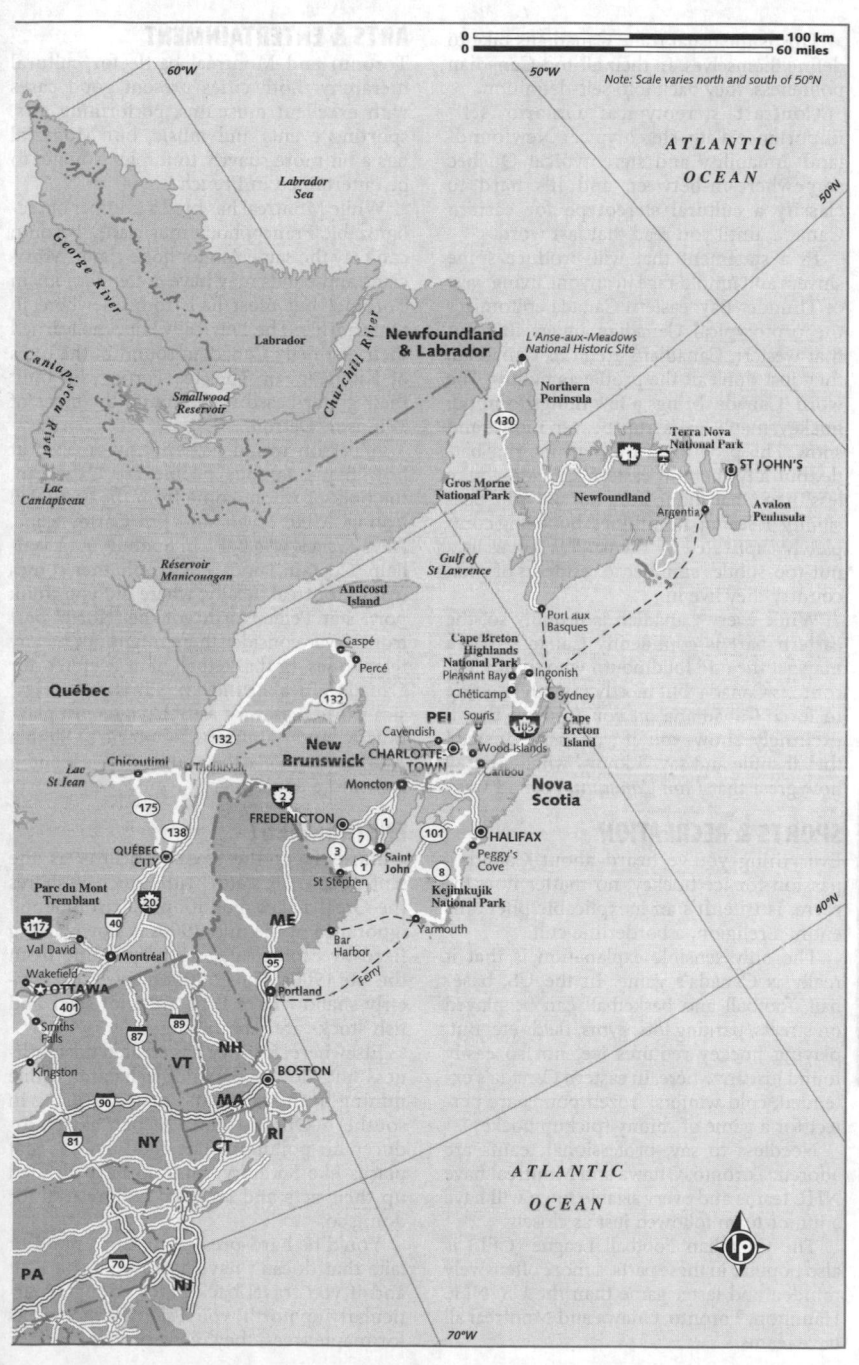

This is the usual route Canadians take to define themselves. In their all-too-Canadian politeness, they back into self-definition.

Contrast stereotypical Ontario self-importance with stereotypical Newfoundland amiability and stereotypical Québec somewhere-in-between and it's hard to classify a cultural stereotype for eastern Canada, until you read that last word.

In a statement that will produce spine shivers and untold rage in anyone living west of Thunder Bay: eastern Canada epitomizes the prototypical Canadian image. It's not that western Canadians aren't *as* Canadian, they just don't fit the profile as tightly. The word 'Canada' brings a few things to mind: hockey, maple leaf/syrup, beaver, moose and snow. This produces a love/hate internal battle, but anywhere in eastern Canada you're less than a half-hour from not only the possibility of seeing these things, but being completely captivated by them. This serves as a not-too-subtle reminder to residents of what country they live in.

While every Canadian is proudly so, the eastern part is confidently Canadian. You may get the odd loudmouth who thinks Toronto *is* Canada, but mostly nobody is going to force Canadiana on you (though they'll excitingly show you if you ask). Instead they'll smile and say, 'I know' when you say how great that *I am Canadian* beer ad was.

SPORTS & RECREATION

Everything you've heard about Canada's passion for ice hockey, no matter how bizarre, is true. It's an inexplicable phenomenon, a religion, a borderline cult.

The only sensible explanation is that it really is Canada's game. In the US, baseball, football and basketball can be played on streets, parking lots, gyms, fields etc. But, playing hockey requires ice, not so easily found just anywhere. In eastern Canada's extended, cold winters, frozen ponds are perfect for a game of shinny (pickup hockey).

Needless to say, professional teams are adored. Toronto, Ottawa and Montréal have NHL teams and every sizable town will have a junior team followed just as closely.

The Canadian Football League (CFL) is also popular in these parts, a more offensively minded and faster game than the US' NFL. Hamilton, Toronto, Ottawa and Montréal all have teams.

ARTS & ENTERTAINMENT

Toronto and Montréal battle for cultural hierarchy. Both cities present good cases with excellent museums, performing arts, sporting events and music, but Montréal has a bit more suavity to it, plus you get to be entertained in French.

While Montréal has bred a number of recognizable Francophone musicians, Toronto can't lay the same Anglophone claim. Musicians and bands may have gotten famous in Toronto, but most hail from elsewhere in Ontario, like The Tragically Hip who learned their distinctly Canadian sound in the pubs of Kingston, or The Tea Party, who built their guitar-based rock around the blues of Windsor–Detroit.

A person would be seriously amazed at how many famous people are Canadian, the bulk of whom come from the east. Neil Young, Mike Myers and Jim Carrey aside, Alex Trebek was born in Sudbury and William 'Captain James T Kirk' Shatner comes from Montréal. Really, where did you think porn star Peter North got the 'North' part from? Ever consider there might not be any telephones or basketball if it weren't for Canada? In a Britney vs Christina vs Jessica world, Ottawa's Avril Lavigne just plays music, and Timmins, Ontario's Shania Twain, has made the country-rock blend a little more appealing.

ENVIRONMENT

Ontario faces the same concerns as the half-dozen US states with which it shares the Great Lakes: pollution. Environmental ignorance of the mid-1900s is slowly being fixed by ecological sensitivity dating from the late 1900s. The pollution levels, particularly shallow Lake Erie, are a lot safer and fish stocks are rebounding.

Elsewhere, forestry has created unsightliness and destroyed wildlife habitat, while mining in the north and manufacturing in southern Ontario and Québec have produced air pollution. The good news is that places like Sudbury, Ontario have cleaned up their acts and received UN awards for doing so.

You'd be hard-pressed to find a pond or lake that doesn't have a beaver lodge in it and if you travel back roads enough (particularly up north) you'll see that moose. As for maple trees, they're everywhere.

If you have a chance to visit anything protected by **Parks Canada** (☎ 888-773-8888; www.pc.gc.ca; camping reservations ☎ 877-737-3783; www.pccamping.ca) do it. You'll be treated to ecologies that epitomize the region. Provincial parks are only slightly less stunning where a moose may poke a nose (or just a nostril – some are big) in your tent. Some provincial and national campgrounds are reservable (for a fee) and it's recommended you do so.

TRANSPORTATION
Toronto's Pearson International Airport is the main air hub but flights to Montréal or St John's might be cheaper from Europe.

Greyhound runs all over Ontario, to/ from the US and to/from some Québec cities. Further east, bus lines and shuttles compete for business. **Ontario Northland** (☎ 705-472-4500, 800-363-7512; www.ontc.on.ca) has been running buses and trains in northern and eastern Ontario for about a century. **Moose Travel** (☎ 905-853-4762, 888-816-6673, www .moosenetwork.com) is a fun and practical bus company/tour operator offering affordable jump-on/jump-off trips in Ontario and Québec.

VIA Rail runs frequently along the Windsor–Québec City corridor and connects Toronto with western Canada, Montréal with Halifax. Five days' advance purchase will save you some bucks. The biggest savings is a Corridor Pass for southern Ontario and Québec, a Canrail Pass (cheaper October to June) for traveling the country or a North American Rail Pass for North America travelers.

I AM TRANS-CANADIAN

For the 'true' Trans Canada Hwy in the confusing east just follow the numbered maple leaves.

- **Ontario** Hwy 17 (don't be fooled by Hwy 11, it's a clever ruse)
- **Québec** Hwy 20
- **New Brunswick** Hwy 2
- **PEI** Hwy 1
- **Nova Scotia** Hwy 104, then 105 in Cape Breton
- **Newfoundland** Hwy 1

The Trans Canada Hwy does some funny things at the Manitoba/Ontario border. It ceases to be Hwy 1 for parts and it splits in two in northern Ontario (see also the boxed text on this page).

Those accustomed to four-lane divided highways in the US are in for a bit of a shock. While Hwy 401 (Canada's busiest) from Windsor to Québec City will satiate your interstate-culture withdrawal, two-lane back roads are the norm and they can get a bit tedious. Bring CDs, enjoy the scenery and watch for deer or moose – they will *seriously* wreck your vehicle on impact.

TORONTO

Toronto has a vibrancy and vitality that often goes overlooked. Being the biggest Canadian city, it's also open to the biggest criticisms and elsewhere in the country you'll hear references to 'Center of the Universe' or 'New York wannabe' and silly, 'T-dot' attempts at defining its own hip-hop. But the city is a fascinating mix of personalities and cultures where the buttoned-down world is dissolving into one of colorful and funky urban-toed looseness.

Toronto is, in every essence of the word, a city. There are parks and tree-lined streets, but there's no getting away from the sky-reaching buildings and urban vibe. Toronto is also, in every sense of the word, dynamic. List any metropolitan activity and you can do it here. Hit a world-class theater or sports-bar? Done. Go clubbing all night? Done. Walk a shoreline path among upscale condos? Done. Eat a bowl of noodles in a park with stockbrokers, college students, lesbians, travelers from Cuba and Leaf fans? Done.

Toronto? Do it.

HISTORY
In the 17th century, present-day Toronto was Seneca Aboriginal land. Étienne Brûlé, on a trip with Samuel de Champlain in 1615, was the first European to see the site. The Aboriginals did not particularly relish the visit. The chilly reception, ongoing suspicion and ill will temporarily impeded further French development. It wasn't until around 1720 that the French established a fur-trading post and mission in what's now the city's west end.

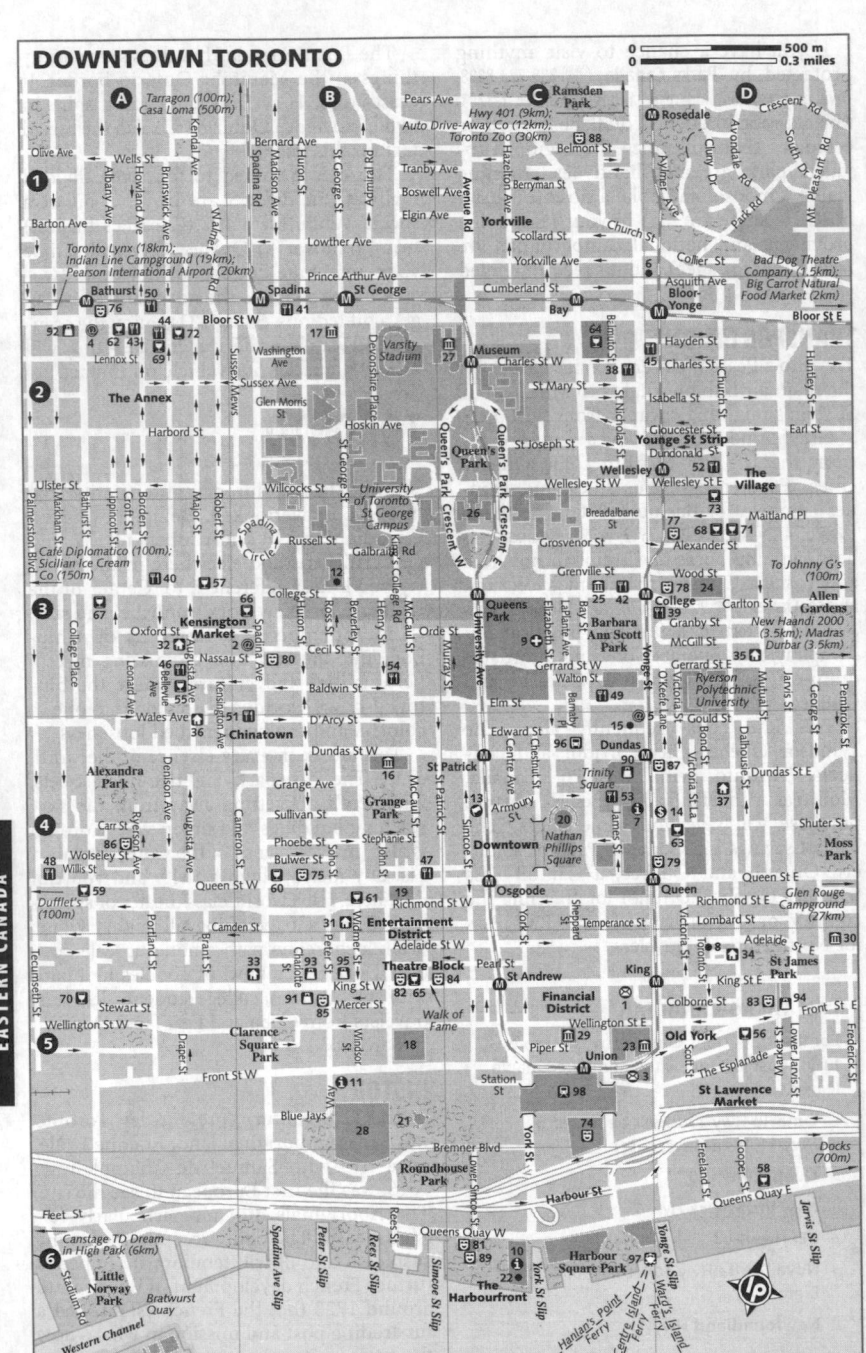

DOWNTOWN TORONTO

In 1793 the British took over and John Simcoe, lieutenant governor of the new Upper Canada, chose the site as the capital (formerly at Niagara-on-the-Lake) and founded a town that became known as York. During the War of 1812, the American forces reached Fort York on April 27, 1813, and after a short struggle overcame British and Ojibwe troops. The Americans looted and razed York, but held it for only six days before Canadian troops kicked them out and chased them all the way back to the US political headquarters in Washington.

In 1834, with William Lyon Mackenzie as the first mayor, York was renamed Toronto, an Aboriginal name meaning 'meeting place.' The Victorian city, controlled by conservative politicians, became 'Toronto the Good,' a tag that only began to fade in the 1970s. Religious restraints (it was illegal to hire a horse on Sunday) and strong anti-vice laws were responsible. Not long ago, curtains were drawn in department-store windows on Sunday, because window-shopping was sinful, and movies couldn't be screened.

Like many big cities, Toronto had a great fire; in 1904 about five hectares of the inner city burned, leveling 122 buildings. Amazingly, no one was killed. By the 1920s Bay St was booming, in part because gold, silver and uranium mines had been discovered in northern Ontario.

In 1941, 80% of the population was Anglo-Celtic. But the city began to change after WWII. Close to one million immigrants have arrived since then. Italians make up the largest non-British ethnic group. But since the 1970s Portuguese, Chilean, Greek, Southeast Asian, Chinese and West Indian immigrants have rolled into the city in waves. This influx of new tongues, customs and food has livened up a place once thought to be a hopeless case of one-dimensional Anglo reserve.

In 1998 when five cities were incorporated into the Megacity, Toronto became the largest city in Canada and the fifth largest in North America.

That's certainly a long way from its beginnings as the second-choice capital after pastoral Niagara.

EASTERN CANADA

ORIENTATION

Greater Toronto spreads from the northwest shore of Lake Ontario with downtown situated in the center. It's quite easy to stay oriented in downtown's north–south/east–west grid, which contains most of the city's major points of interest. Use the CN Tower to gather your bearings, it's near the shoreline in the east–west center of downtown. If you can't see it, try three things: turn around; move a little bit to see if it's hiding behind a building; or check if you're still in Ontario.

The main north–south artery, Yonge (yung) St, separates the 'east' and 'west' street designations. Lined with stores, bars, restaurants, cinemas and the like, Queen St is Yonge's east–west counterpart cutting through the particularly lively Entertainment District.

INFORMATION

Bookstores

Open Air (☎ 416-363-0719; 25 Toronto St) Travel and outdoor activity books, guides, maps.
World's Biggest Bookstore (☎ 416-977-7009; 20 Edward St) Chapters warehouse-style outpost with discounts.

Emergency

Toronto Rape Crisis Centre (☎ 416-597-8808)

Internet Access

Yonge St has places to check email, usually $3 per hour.

Cyber Share (☎ 416-593-4229; 404 Spadina Ave; per hr $3)
Insomnia Internet Bar Café (☎ 416-588-3907; 563 Bloor St W; per hr $5) Fully licensed café/lounge serves and surfs until late.
Internet Centre (☎ 416-408-0400; 324 Yonge St; per hr $3)

Libraries

Metropolitan Toronto Reference Library
(☎ 416-395-5577; 789 Yonge St) Internet terminals on the main floor and huge multi-lingual section on 5th.

Media

PRINT

eye Free weekly entertainment rag.
Metro Popular free daily paper.
Now Free weekly newspaper.
Toronto Star Daily newspaper.
Toronto Sun Daily tabloid.

RADIO

CBC (94.1FM; 99.1FM) National and local news and programming.
CFNY (102.1 FM) Alternative; good entertainment source.
CHIN (100.7 FM) Multilingual/multicultural.
CILQ (107.7 FM) Classic rock.

Medical Services

Medical clinics around town have walk-in service and some are open until 9pm.
Toronto General Hospital (☎ 416-340-4611; 200 Elizabeth St) For 24-hour emergencies. Near Queen's Park.

GETTING INTO TOWN

You'll fly into Pearson International Airport 24km northwest of downtown. Catch the 20-minute express 192 Airport Rocket ($2.25) from any of three terminals to Kipling Station on the Bloor–Danforth subway, which heads into the north part of downtown. If your flight comes in at an ungodly hour (2am to 5am), sleep on the floor or take the 300 Bloor–Danforth from Terminal 2 or 3.

Convenient **Pacific Western Airport Express** (☎ 905-564-6333; www.torontoairportexpress.com; $15.50) runs every 20 minutes from all terminals to major hotels, City Hall and the bus and train stations. The trip takes about 80 minutes.

A 45-minute taxi ride is limited to $43 by tariff laws, but there's a $10 charge (per drop) for multiple drop offs.

The bus station and Union Station are right downtown and a 15- to 45-minute walk from the hostels. If you're dog-tired there's a subway on the lower level of Union Station or two blocks from the bus station. Those with energy can head straight out the Union Station front doors (away from CN Tower) and left up University Ave for the Entertainment District, which is halfway between the bus station and CN Tower.

Yonge St exit off Hwy 401 and York St off Gardiner Expressway (from the Queen Elizabeth Way) lead downtown.

Money

Banks and ATMs are all over the city.
World Currency Exchange (☎ 416-214-4761; 277 Yonge St) Currency-exchange houses generally have better hours and rates.

Post

Toronto's first post office (☎ 416-865-1833, 260 Adelaide St E; ☒ 9am-4pm) Worth a few minutes for photos and models from Toronto's baby-years. Letters can be written in pen and inkwell and sealed with wax.
GPO (☎ 416-365-0656; 25 The Esplanade; ☒ 8am-5:45pm) Pick up general delivery (poste restante) here. Mail should be addressed: [Recipient's Name]; General Delivery; Postal Station A, Toronto, ON; M5W 1A1.

Canada Post offices are closed weekends; some drugstores have postal outlets with extended hours.
Commerce Court Station (25 King St W)
University of Toronto Bookstore (214 College St) Open Saturdays.

Toilets

The best options for relief are shopping malls. Hotel lobbies often have toilets; restaurants will send you away unless you're eating there.

Tourist Information

Ontario Travel Information Centre (☎ 800-668-2746; 220 Yonge St, Level 1; ☒ 10am-9pm Mon-Fri, 9:30am-7pm Sat, noon-5pm Sun) Ontario and Toronto information desk in Eaton Centre.
Tourism Toronto (☎ 416-203-2500, 800-363-1990; www.torontotourism.com); Main Office (207 Queens Way W, 5th fl; ☒ 9am-5pm Mon-Fri); Metro Convention Centre (225 Front St W; ☒ 8am-8pm)

SIGHTS

Save money and hassles with **Citypass** (www .citypass.com; $46) available online or at its six attractions: CN Tower, Art Gallery of Ontario, Royal Ontario Museum, Casa Loma, Ontario Science Centre and Toronto Zoo. A lot of places give HI discounts.

Entertainment District

At 553m, **CN Tower** (☎ 416-868-6937; www.cntower .ca; 301 Front St; glass fl/top deck $19/23; ☒ 9am-10pm Sun-Thu, 9am-10:30pm Fri & Sat), the world's largest freestanding structure will immediately draw you like a homing-beacon. The better thing to do is visit after you've got a feel for the city and reflect on where you've been.

DID YOU SAY FREE?

That four-letter F word is music to the budget traveler's ear. Free viewing times:

- ■ **Art Gallery of Ontario** (p180; ☒ 6-8:30pm Wed)

- ■ **Bata Shoe Museum** (p180; ☒ 5-8pm Thu)

- ■ **Royal Ontario Museum** (p180; ☒ 4:30-8pm Fri)

Make sure it's a clear day so you can see Niagara Falls; if it's cloudy don't bother.

At the base of the tower – and drawing affectionate references as 'Toronto's cock & balls' – **SkyDome** (☎ 416-341-3663, tours 416-341-2770; 1 Blue Jays Way; tour $12.50; tours 11am-4pm) isn't quite up there with Fenway and Wrigley, but the retractable roof evokes minor heart-stutters from baseball fans. Tours sometimes go onto the field, but a bleacher (tiered, uncovered) seat is cheaper with better ambience.

Whether or not you've heard of 'icing' or 'one-timer,' after perusing international hockey's trophy case (the Stanley Cup) and garage-sale of memorabilia (your country's jersey) and visited the Montréal Canadiens locker room at the **Hockey Hall of Fame** (☎ 416-360-7765; 30 Yonge St; adult $12; ☒ 9:30am-6pm Mon-Sat), hockey will become your life.

The Hollywoodesque **Walk of Fame** (King St W btwn John & Simcoe Sts) is sure to elicit more than one 'I didn't know he/she is Canadian.' See Canada's contemporary history through the eyes of those who lived and documented it at the **Canadian Broadcasting Corporation** (CBC; ☎ 416-205-5574; 250 Front St W; free, tours adult/student $7/5; ☒ 9am-5pm Mon-Fri, noon-4pm Sat). It has an eclectic museum with a collection of broadcasting items and proud-Canadian stories. **ChumCity/City-TV** (☎ 416-591-5757, tours 416-591-7400 ext 2770; 299 Queent St W; tours free), home to most of Canada's alternative programming, is in the heart of the action. Go press your face against the ground-level studio windows of **Much Music** (Canada's MTV) or call for a tour.

Harbourfront

South of everything, shoreline paths and green spaces (and skyrocketing glass condos) look onto Toronto Harbour. It's a very

EASTERN CANADA

INSTEAD OF CN TOWER

Enjoy a $5 beer in the **Panorama Lounge** (☎ 416-967-0000; 55 Bloor St W; ☺ 5pm-2am) on the 51st floor of Manulife Centre – try to dress semi-nice. The views aren't *as* good, but they're still outstanding, and there's a patio open in summer.

---

relaxing place to eat lunch, take a walk or catch some entertainment: practicing guitarists, torch jugglers and sometimes free shows are at **York Quay Centre's** outdoor stage.

On sunny, muggy days, breezy relief happens on a **ferry** (☎ 416-392-8193; Harbour Sq Park; adult/student return $6/3.50; ☺ 8am-11:30pm summer, varies seasonally) – as good as the harbor tour – to **Toronto Islands**, where the south shore looks onto Lake Ontario's horizon. Take the ferry to **Centre Island**, follow the paths to the south shore, then west to **Gibraltar Point Lighthouse**, Toronto's oldest landmark and best vantage for sunsets. Head north (past **Hanlon Point Beach**, Toronto's only nudie) to ferry back from **Hanlon's Point**.

Financial District

The right angles of modern, glass-and-concrete skyscrapers distinctly define the serious part of Toronto. Underneath it all the **PATH** (www.city.toronto.on.ca) network – signs point to entrances – connects downtown to itself in the world's longest continually running shopping complex.

Under the Freedom Arches, the concrete plaza **Nathan Phillips Square** (cnr Queen & Bay Sts) is full of street-performers, concerts, demonstrators, businesspeople, skateboarders and rollerbladers (ice skating in the winter). It's all in front of **City Hall** (☎ 416-338-0338; ☺ 9am-5pm Mon-Fri), looking like a spaceship engulfed by a giant clam. Take the self-guided tour for the outrageous engineering of the massive upper-floor column and the **Mural of Nails** (all 100,000 of them).

The **Toronto Dominion Galley of Inuit Art** (☎ 416-982-8473; 79 Wellington St W; free; ☺ 8am-6pm Mon-Fri, 10am-4pm Sat & Sun) houses a glass-cube maze in an impressive collection of stone and bone Inuit carvings in the lobby.

Not just another gallery, the **Art Gallery of Ontario** (☎ 416-979-6648; www.ago.net; 317 Dundas St W; adult/student $12/9; ☺ 11am-6pm Tue-Fri, to 8:30pm Wed, 10am-5:30pm Sat & Sun) combines fine-art

sterility and art-for-you real-worldliness. It focuses mainly on paintings from the 14th-century to the present, with behind-the-scenes displays and free galleries of in-storage works.

Queen's Park

North of downtown this huge park's grounds are full of Frisbee games, picnickers, students and backpackers. Looking south from the intersection of Ave Rd and Bloor St is arguably the best Toronto-skyline view from up close. The buildings of the University of Toronto campus range from spiky, limestone structures like the 1859-built **University College Building** to buildings of the present. The stately and strong **Provincial Parliament Buildings** (☎ 416-325-7500; University Ave; free; ☺ 9am-5pm, closed weekends Sep-May) are in outstanding condition considering they were built in 1892. Take a tour of the marble and oak interior.

At the north end of the park, the 'high-heeled-ly' regarded **Bata Shoe Museum** (☎ 416-979-7799; www.batashoemuseum.ca; 327 Bloor St W; adult/student $6/4; ☺ 10am-5pm Tue-Sat, to 8pm Thu, noon-5pm Sun) looks at the 4000-year history of footwear, from Inuit sealskin shoes of necessity to unnecessarily luxurious celebrity foot-fashion. Two blocks east, the five-story **Royal Ontario Museum** (☎ 416-586-5551; www.rom.on.ca; 100 Queen's Park; adult/student $10/7; ☺ 10am-6pm, to 9:30pm Fri) is Canada's largest covering the natural sciences, art and archeology.

East of the park, the **police museum** (☎ 416-808-7020; www.torontopolice.on.ca; 40 College St; free; ☺ 10am-4:30pm Mon-Fri, also noon-5pm Sat & Sun summer) celebrates 170 years of Toronto's finest through stories, displays and everyone's favorite: confiscated weapons. Further east, lay your hands on history and touch the now-vacant **Maple Leaf Gardens** (cnr Church & College Sts).

Other Neighborhoods

Spadina Ave from Dundas St to College St has all the sights and smells associated with **Chinatown**: cheap eats, street vendors and grocers with Asian remedies. West of there, **Kensington Market's** multicultural strip contrasts with downtown. Fishmongers, delis, textile vendors and open-air markets spill out onto the street, fighting for room among the shoppers, buskers and speech-makers. To the north, along Bloor St west of

Spandina Ave, the **Annex** is an energetic and animated blend of immigrants, students, professors and other professionals making for an unforgettable stroll.

Outside Downtown

The 98-room, 'medieval' castle-cum-mansion **Casa Loma** (☎ 416-923-1171; www.casaloma .org; 1 Austin Tce; adult/child $10/6; ♥ 10am-4pm) illustrates why it sometimes sucks to be rich. With secret passageways and completed in 1914, it's a thing of boyhood dreams, but it was lived in only a few years before Sir Henry Pellat went broke. Take the subway to Dupont, walk two blocks north and climb the 110 steps.

The huge **Toronto Zoo** (☎ 416-392-5900; www .torontozoo.com; Meadowvale Rd; admission $18; ♥ 9am-7:30pm summer, varies seasonally) has 5000 animals and if you're not heading into the wilderness, Canadian Domain is the next best thing. Take the Bloor–Danforth subway east to Kennedy for Scarborough, subway to Scarborough Centre, then the No 194 Zoo Rocket bus.

ACTIVITIES

The **Toronto Bicycling Network** (☎ 416-766-1985; www.tbn.on.ca) is an excellent resource and Toronto has plenty of bike shops. The **Martin Goodman Trail** is the busiest and best-maintained path along the waterfront, eventually connecting with the **Lake Ontario Waterfront Trail**. Toronto Islands are more about scenic pedals than fitness rides.

Harbourfront Canoe & Kayak Centre (☎ 416-203-2277; www.paddletoronto.com; 283a Queens Quay W; kayak per hr/day $20/50, canoe $20/40, tours from $50) rents out equipment, but also has kick-ass tours – sunrise or full-moon paddles through Toronto Islands.

In winter ice-skate for free at **City Hall** and **Harbourfront**; both have rentals.

Windsurfing rentals are available at Kew Beach (east of downtown). You'll find a bit more privacy at Sunnyside Beach (west of downtown).

TOURS

Following the Discovery Walks **Downtown Walk** (6km; 2hr) plaques through the city is an excellent way to orient yourself.

JoJo Tours (☎ 416-201-6465, 888-202-3513; www .interlog.com/~jojotour; May-Oct/Nov-Apr; $50/40) JoJo (Davia) herself picks up at hostels and drives the 11-person

bus to Niagara Falls, stopping at wineries and Niagara-on-the-Lake, making for a personal trip.

Magic Bus (☎ 416-516-7433, 877-856-6610; www.furtherstill.com; from $37) Anything goes on Niagara or cottage-country tours and pub-crawls in the colorful buses.

Muddy York Walking Tours (☎ 416-487-9017; www .muddyyorktours.com; adult/student $10/8) Excitingly animated historical recounts of Toronto's seldom-told stories, from the macabre to the royal.

ROMwalks (☎ 416-586-5513; depart 6pm Wed & 2pm Sun summer) Free, rain-or-shine historical jaunts by Royal Ontario Museum.

University of Toronto (☎ 416-978-5000; depart visitors center, 25 King's College Cir; 11am, also 2pm Mon-Fri) Free campus tours illustrating buildings' histories.

FESTIVALS & EVENTS

Taste of Little Italy (☎ 416-240-9338; www.tasteof littleitaly.com; mid-Jun) Free music-and-food street party each June.

Canada Day (Jul 1) Everywhere in the city celebrates Canada's birthday.

CHIN Picnic (www.chinradio.com; early Jul) Free four-day multicultural party with music, food and sports and beer.

Festival Of Fire (early Jul) Three-night firework Harbourfront display.

Caribana (www.caribana.com; mid-Jul–early Aug) Caribbean festival featuring steel-drum, calypso music, Carnival-costumed parade (Jul 31).

Caravan (☎ 416-977-0466; www.caravan-org.com; $25; early Sep) Nine days of cultural exchange.

International Festival of Authors (www.readings .org; late Oct) Dozens of well-known writers read and discuss.

SLEEPING

Most hostels are an easy walk from the train or bus stations and right where you want to be, in (or close enough to) the bar-peppered **Entertainment District** and the multicultural **Kensington Market**. Most also have HI, ISIC and student discounts, reduced weekly rates and lower prices in the off-season. Prices given are for nonmembers.

BUDGET TIP

Beware 'budget' places that list $20 to $30 rooms with only one at that price, then try to hard-sell a $75 'suite.' Trust your gut, there *are* some shady places. Other places are budget in every sense of the word.

EASTERN CANADA

Canadiana Guesthouse & Backpackers (☎ 416-598-9090, 877-215-1225; www.canadianalodging.com; 42 Widmer St; dm $25-28, s/d $50/60; 😵) In five side-by-side Entertainment District Victorians you'll find Toronto's best-run and ever-growing hostel. There are no more than six hand-made bunks per comforting white-and-yellow, country-colored room. Outside patios, 'Chili Night,' pub crawls and a communal feel make it hard to get homesick.

Global Village Backpackers (☎ 416-703-8540, 888-844-7875; www.globalbackpackers.com; 460 King St W; dm/q/d $25/28/60) Toronto's party-hostel. Random color schemes decorate the walls, the downstairs pub is honestly fun and the brick patio entertains on summer nights. Has a travel desk with discount connections.

Planet Traveler's Hostel (☎ 416-599-6789; www.theplanettraveler.com; 175 Augusta Ave; dm/d/tr with breakfast $25/65/80; 💻) Like housesitting with a couple of dozen strangers, this Victorian in Kensington Market has just 20 dorm beds and nine private rooms, so it doesn't get over crowded.

Neill-Wycik College Hotel (☎ 416-977-2320, 800-268-4358; www.neill-wycik.com; 96 Gerrard St E; dm/s/d/tr/q with breakfast $27/44/66/88/105; 😎 mid-May–mid-Aug) Institutional linoleum floors and concrete walls in this 22-story college residence are offset by knockout views and splashes of color. Awesome rooftop patios.

HI-Toronto (☎ 416-971-4440, 877-848-8737; www.hihostels.ca/toronto; 76 Church St; dm/q/s/d $26/27/70/74) The 5th-floor patio is a great city escape and the above rooms are slightly larger. Everything is clean and usable in what may once have been a sewage system downstairs, but don't expect lots of sunlight while playing pool or using the kitchen.

College Hostel (☎ 416-929-4777; www.collegehostel.com; 280 Augusta Ave; dm/s/d from $25/55/70; 💻) Smack in the middle of Kensington's verve

---

SPLURGE!

Valhalla Inn (☎ 416-239-2391; www.valhalla-inn.com; 1 Valhalla Inn Rd; r from $100; 🍴) Among the chains, Valhalla's unsterile environment stands out. Dark colors and soft lighting make the standard rooms not seem so standard and the outdoor patios offer your last (or first) glimpse of CN Tower. A good gateway sleep as it's only a five-minute shuttle from the airport.

---

is this former apartment complex with exceptionally clean rooms. Private rooms have TV and phones; all rooms have balconies.

Toronto Budget Hostel (☎ 416-703-3939 ext 132; www.torontohostel.com; 223 Church St; dm/r $25/60) A little sterile and characterless, but downtown and clean.

Indian Line Campground (☎ 416-661-6600; iline @trca.on.ca; Indian Line Rd; campsite $22) With 240 sites on the airport's east side, it's noisy as hell but there are lots of gardens and it's a cheap cab-ride in the morning.

Glen Rouge Campground (☎ 416-392-2541; Kingston Rd; campsite $22) Its 120 campsites of the RV/wooded variety are east of the city close to trails and beach. Reached via GO Trains on a long trip.

EATING

Toronto is a city where dirty hovels rub shoulders with chic bistros, where you can get a smoked-meat sandwich next door to a fine-dining jazz café. For the most part you can slum with locals on **Yonge** or **Bloor Sts** west of Spadina St and find an endless string of pizza and sandwich take-out counters between coffeehouses and cafés.

Two major health-food stores are the **Big Carrot Natural Food Market** (☎ 416-466-2129; 348 Danforth Ave) and the more central **Baldwin Natural Foods** (☎ 416-979-1777; 201/2 Baldwin St).

St Lawrence Market (☎ 416-392-7219; 92 Front St E; 😎 7am-5pm Tue-Sun) is a more upscale farmers' market, but it's possible to find bargains. Just to the north, local farmers sell produce from the backs of their trucks at St Lawrence Hall on weekends.

Street food in Toronto isn't bad, and you'll find the best-tasting dogs in the Financial or Entertainment Districts. The chip wagons in Harbourfront lack British authenticity, but are a valiant North American effort.

Toronto doesn't have its 'own' dish, but you'll find an unexpected number of Montréal smoked-meat delis, and **Mel's Montreal Delicatessen** (☎ 416-966-8881; 440 Bloor St W; sandwiches $5-9; 😎 24hr), which hand cuts the meat, is always busy and one of the favorites.

You're never far from an **Amato Pizza** (College St ☎ 416-972-6286; 380 College St; slice $2-3; Queen St ☎ 416-703-8116; 534 Queen St E; Yonge St ☎ 416-977-8989; 429 Yonge St), which has a good reputation among students and an even better crust. Eaton Centre or the underground PATH network have good food courts.

College caféterias like **Ryerson Polytechnic University Cafeteria** (☎ 416-979-5000; Jorgenson Hall, cnr Gerrard E & Victoria Sts; mains $4-10) or the hidden gem **Catering Masters Tartu Buffeteria** (☎ 416-924-7651; 310 Bloor St W; mains $4-7) have soups and sandwiches and excellent daily specials for next to nothing prepared by chefs-in-training.

Downtown

Trinity Square Café (☎ 416-598-2010; Trinity Sq; soup & sandwiches $3-7) In Holy Trinity Church, this tiny café's limited menu of a couple of daily specials and soups attracts the local suits and hardhats.

Fran's Diner (☎ 416-923-9867; 20 College St; mains $6 10; ☼ 24hr) Fran's isn't a throwback – she's an original with the same red vinyl seats and checkerboard floor. She's good for late night grub after clubbing and music, food and fun all the time.

Slack Alice (☎ 416-969-8742; 562 Church St; mains $6-10) This primarily lesbian spot has wide-open doors and a widely-varied-but-focused menu, keeping it a Church St favorite for years. Mondays are half-price. Pad Thai and other weekly specials energizes the diners who rowdy it up in the late-night bar-and-DJ scene.

Kensington Market

In **Kensington Market** (Augusta St btwn Dundas & College Sts) the cheese shops are exhaustive, the fruit and vegetable stands colorful and bartering expected.

King's Café (☎ 416-591-1340; 192 Augusta Ave; mains $6-10) Dishes from simple green beans to complex sushi. The focus is Asian (the soups are delicious) and Indian plates (vegetable curry) with a few combo platters.

Café Diplomatico (☎ 416-534-4637; 594 College St; mains $4-12) 'The Dip,' a longtime casual favorite, relies on the pizza, calzone and pasta menu that made it locally famous, especially for patio fun.

Sicilian Ice Cream Co (☎ 416-531-7716; 712 College St; ice-cream $3-6) For delicious tartufo, sherbets, gelato and just plain ol' ice cream, this old-fashioned parlor serves it up with nostalgia.

Chinatown

Yung Sing Pastry Shop (☎ 416-979-2832; 22 Baldwin St; snacks $2-5) A no-frills, takeaway Chinese bakery.

ALL YOU CAN EAT

When you pay for a meal, you want five. Welcome to Indulgenceville.

- **Korean Grill House** (☎ 416-263-9850; 214 Queen St W; lunch/dinner $9/13) Before reaching over the table for your significant other's hand or getting upset at the raw meat you've been served, relax. The metal plate in front of you is searingly hot and it's cook-your-own at this busy, colorfully plain eatery of fun.

- **Le Commensal** (☎ 416-596-9364; 655 Bay St; per 100g $1.69) Vegetarian buffet with fresher than fresh ingredients. Stick to lighter ingredients.

- **New Haandi 2000** (☎ 416-469-9696; 1401 Gerrard St E; lunch/dinner buffet $8/10) Kitschy furniture and sedate servers are irrelevant when Indian food is this outstanding.

Phô' Hu'ng (☎ 416-593-4274; 350 Spadina Ave; pho $5-7, vermicelli $6-9) If noisy and messy defines good eating then the constant clatter from chaotic tables puts this place on top. It has an awesome selection of pho and vermicelli dishes, including plenty for the veggies.

The Annex

Fresh (☎ 416-531-2635; 521 Bloor St W; mains $5-10) This is a city fave for vegan fare and absence of earnestness. Sandwiches, meatless burgers and pasta complement smoothies and shakes.

Future Bakery & Café (☎ 416-922-5875; 483 Bloor St W) This down-to-earth hangout is well used and well appreciated. The walk-up counter lends to just-a-coffeehouse/bakeshop mentality, but it's just as good a place for a full meal. Three-egg, all-day breakfasts cost $4.

The Village

Green Mango (☎ 416-920-5448; 707 Yonge St; mains $8-10) This headquarters of four local locations defies logic. Indiscreet lighting and intimate settings do not show up on the menu and they don't cheap out on excellent rice and noodle dishes.

Johnny G's (☎ 416-928-1358; 474 Parliament St; mains $5-8) This tiny diner with a confidently simple menu of all-day breakfasts and

EASTERN CANADA

burgers is the epitome of cheap comfort food. Cooks in white aprons and paper hats add to the atmosphere of small tables and unhurriedness.

7 West Café (☎ 416-928-9041; 7 Charles St W; sandwiches $6-10; ⏲ 24hr) The whole of this old house is greater than the sum of its parts: café, restaurant and bar. The salads and sandwiches are goodly simple, and the hangout is good for shooting pool and having fun.

Outside Downtown

Madras Durbar (☎ 416-465-4116, 1435 Gerrard St E; mains $5-10) Ambience and décor are an afterthought but this place is a steal. Flavor explosions served on silver platters include *masala dosai* (crepe) – so big it hangs off your plate.

La hacienda (☎ 416-703-3377; 640 Queen St W; mains $6-11) It's dark, the tables and chairs are beat up and don't match and the menu is limited with only a few daily specials, but it's a perfect place for all-day egg breakfasts and burritos.

Dufflet's (☎ 416-504-2870; 787 Queen St W; desserts $3-6) Solidly pastel and minimalist in design, this Toronto institution still makes damn good cakes, tarts and brownies.

DRINKING

The wonderfully unappealing orange-and-white signs lead to The Beer Store. For liquor and wine, find a green-and-white Liquor Control Board of Ontario (LCBO) sign. There's no shortage of drinking venues but FYI: Toronto recently imposed a bylaw banning smoking in *all* establishments.

Clubs stay open, *sans* alcohol, until 3am or 4am and ridiculously priced after-hours places can be found, but it's a word-of-mouth thing.

Bars

Peel Pub (☎ 416-977-0003; 276 King St W) You're about to find several hundred drinking buddies in this cavernous cellar with rows of caféteria tables and sports on TV. Plan on spending at least one night here drinking cheap, being loud and swearing lots.

Wheat Sheaf Tavern (☎ 416-504-9912; 667 King St W) When you're this old and draw the honest crowd, character just happens. The Sheaf is Toronto's oldest pub and serves some of the stiffest drinks at cheap prices ($3 highballs).

Ye Olde Brunswick House (☎ 416-964-2242; 481 Bloor St W) A student hangout that's part pub, part frat house and always crazy. The kind of place where you'll be drinking with the staff until 6am and where it's not uncommon to lose your friends, your shoes, or both.

Red Room (☎ 416-929-9964; 444 Spadina Ave) Exquisitely dank and a bit musty, as if your friend from high school with the rad basement moved to Toronto and opened a café-bar. Down pints or sip from 200 teas.

Sneaky Dee's (☎ 416-603-3090; 431 College St) Another hangout bar with the smoky aroma of decades of cigarettes and beer-stained floors. It's cheap, it's lively; it's colorful in all aspects.

Amadeus (☎ 416-591-1245; 184 Augusta Ave) Amadeus is a place that doesn't care about upkeep – just about opening the Kensington Market patio, spreading out the plastic chairs and making sure the taps are clean.

C'est What? (☎ 416-867-9499; 67 Front St E) Board games, Coffee Porter, well used, Rye Beer, good fun, woodsy appeal, 20 whiskies, go drink, have fun.

Live Music

Grossman's (☎ 416-977-7000; 379 Spadina Ave; no cover) Blissfully grotty and one of the cheapest spots in town, set lists are tossed and bands just jam. There's live music every night, mainly blues but some big-names of all genres have graced Grossman's stage. It's hit or miss, between enjoyable and magic.

Horseshoe Tavern (☎ 416-598-4753; 370 Queen St W; cover $3-10) Toronto's most loved bar, the 'shoe presents music played with real instruments and launches careers of future stars.

Massey Hall (☎ 416-872-4255; 178 Victoria St) Toronto's oldest concert hall has excellent acoustics and intimacy great for concerts.

Free Times Café (☎ 416-967-1078; 320 College St) Homey and cozy mainstay for folk music.

Healy's (☎ 416-703-5882; 178 Bathurst St) Excellent rock and blues in Jeff Healy's house.

Lee's Palace (☎ 416-532-1598; 529 Bloor St W) Guitar-string-busting, finger-bleeding, foot-stomping rock bar.

Tranzac (☎ 416-923-8137; 292 Brunswick Ave; no cover) Down Under theme, open to all with good folk music every night.

Gay & Lesbian Venues

Toronto's huge gay culture is centered on Church St in downtown's northeast corner, which is also known as the **Village** or the 'gay ghetto.' It's a lively residential/commercial mix with businesses, bars and patios catering to the queer community but you don't have to be gay to have a gay time.

Zelda's (☎ 416-922-2526; 542 Church St) Oh the fun that's had on Saturday nights' Martini Madness. Use your imagination and bring it to the show. Drag shows and other theme nights dot Zelda's calendar.

Woody's (☎ 416-972-0887; 467 Church St) is a long-time favorite, very wild and popular gay bar and **Tango** (☎ 416-972-1662; 510 Church St) is for the ladies.

CLUBBING

The **Entertainment District** is jammed on weekends. Wander around and check out the people in line for 'your' place. Cover ranges from zero to $20. Check with your hostel or www.clubvibes.com for 'skip the line' deals.

Guvernment (☎ 416-869-0045; www.theguvernment.com; 132 Queens Quay E; cover $10) This Toronto standard with no-attitude is about let-it-all-hang out good times. At least one of the six dance floors will have something for you, and the outdoor patios are a welcome, hot summer night's relief.

Docks (☎ 416-461-3625; www.thedocks.com, 11 Polson St; cover $10) If you can't have fun at Docks, go back to bed. More of a complex than a nightclub, the driving range, outdoor pool, batting cages and more are open all day. The activities aren't free, but just watching is fun. At night, the fun doesn't stop: inside dance floors, outside bars and a fantastic view across the water.

Joker Club (☎ 416-598-1313; 318 Richmond St W; cover $10) Three stories of pool tables, hip-hop, house or Top 40, crowned by a huge rooftop patio. Chill in the white leather couches or pop'n'lock to a million dollars of sound and light.

ENTERTAINMENT

Now magazine has complete entertainment listings. Thursday's *Star*, Friday's *Sun* and Saturday's *Globe & Mail* also list events.

Most tickets go through **Tickemaster** (☎ 416-870-8000; www.tickemaster.ca) or venue box offices, which may have same-day discounts. **TO Tix** (☎ 416-536-6468 ext 40; cnr Dundas & Yonge Sts; noon-6pm Tue-Sun) sells half-price leftover tickets, in person only, for same-day shows.

Harbourfront Centre (☎ 416-973-3000; www.harbourfront.on.ca; 235 Queens Quay) runs York Quay Centre, which is a covered outdoor concert venue with performances (some free) nearly every night.

Cinemas

Repertory film houses are cheaper than first-run theaters and an inexpensive membership saves even more. Weekday matinees will be cheaper everywhere.

Bloor Cinema (☎ 416-516-2330; 506 Bloor St W) Excellent little movie-house popular with students showing new and old alternative movies.

Carlton Cinemas (☎ 416-598-2309; 20 Carlton St) Nonmainstream new releases and a licensed café.

Rainbow Cinemas (☎ 416-214-7006; 80 Front Street E) First run movies at cheaper prices.

Comedy Clubs

Second City (☎ 416-343-0011; 56 Blue Jays Way; adult/student Mon-Thu $20/12) Sketch comedy institution for 40 years and fostered Dan Aykroyd, John Candy and Mike Myers.

ALTdot (☎ 416-596-1908; 332 Queen St W; cover $5-15; 9pm Mon) Has free 'Coming Soon' shows after 11pm some nights at the Rivoli.

Bad Dog Theatre Company (☎ 416-491-3115; 138 Danforth Ave; cover $7-10) Hilarious improv with local talent.

Sports

Tickets are always available from scalpers prior to games, but wait until after start time for better deals. The **Air Canada Centre** (ACC; ☎ 416-977-1641; www.theaircanadacentre.com; 40 Bay St) is Toronto's entertainment complex on the Harbourfront.

Toronto Maple Leafs (☎ 416-815-5700; www.mapleleafs.com; ACC; ticket $25-375) The grammatically incorrect Maple Leafs are the New York Yankees, Manchester United or Collingwood of the hockey world – loved by their fans, hated by everyone else. If you get a chance, it's a truly passionate experience. Constantly sold out, but some are tickets released game day.

Toronto Rock (☎ 416-596-3075; www.torontorock.com; ticket $19-48; Jan-Apr) The national game, lacrosse, is inexpensive, rough, fast and fun.

Toronto Raptors (☎ 416-366-3865; www.raptors.com; ACC; ticket $25-175; Skydome; Oct-Apr) NBA's only Canadian team.

EASTERN CANADA

Toronto Blue Jays (☎ 416-341-1000, 888-654-6529; www.bluejays.com; ticket $9-56) Sitting in the cheap seats at the Skydome, then moving down to the good seats, at a ball game is a perfect summer evening or afternoon.

Toronto Argonauts (☎ 416-341-2700; www.argonauts.ca; adult $15-50, student $12-45; Skydome) The Argos play an exciting and fast brand of Canadian League Football.

Toronto Roadrunners (☎ 416-263-3267, 868-631-3925; www.torontoroadrunners.ca; ticket $25-35) For a cheaper hockey alternative featuring future superstars, catch the minor-league team to the Edmonton Oilers.

Theater

The engaging alternative theater of **Theatre Passe Muraille** (☎ 416-504-7529; www.passemuraille.on.ca; 16 Ryerson St; ☽ Sep-May) and **Tarragon** (☎ 416-536-5018; www.tarragontheatre.com; 30 Bridgman Ave; ☽ Oct-May) are pay-what-you-can for debuts and Sunday matinees.

Canstage TD Dream in High Park (☎ 416-392-1111; High Park, Parkside Dr; suggested donation $15; ☽ 8pm Tue-Sun Jun-Aug) Inexpensive Shakespeare outdoor performances. Bring blankets and snacks, and show up early.

Toronto Truck Theatre (☎ 416-922-0084; 94 Belmont St; ticket $26) Been playing Agatha Christie's *The Mousetrap* since 1976 so they've gotten pretty good at it.

Toronto's lavish and elegant theaters:

Royal Alexandra Theatre (☎ 416-872-1212; 260 King St W)

Princess of Wales Theatre (☎ 416-872-1212; 300 King St W)

Elgin & Winter Garden Theatre Centre (☎ 416-314-2901; 189 Yonge St) Double-decker style.

Buddies in Bad Times Theatre (☎ 416-975-8555; www.buddiesinbadtimestheatre.com; 12 Alexander St) Showcases alternative queer theater.

SHOPPING

Toronto's biggest mall is the **Eaton Centre** (220 Yonge St). You can snag funky bargains among used- and vintage-clothing shops in **Kensington Market** (p180) or the Sunday antique and flea market in **St Lawrence Market** (p182).

Before heading into the bush you'll find cheap gear at **Trailhead** (☎ 416-977-7031; 370 King St W), **Mountain Equipment Co-op** (☎ 416-340-2667; 400 King St W) and **Europe Bound Outfitters** (☎ 416-205-9992; 383 King St W); the latter two do rentals.

Honest Ed's Discount Store (☎ 416-537-1574; 581 Bloor St W) An area landmark, the gaudy signs draw people from around the globe for cheap kitsch, clothes and knickknacks. 'Come in and get lost' is the invitation to the organized chaos of Ed Mirvish's subtlety.

GETTING THERE & AWAY
Air

Pearson International Airport (code YYZ; ☎ 416-776-3000; www.gtaa.com) is a mini-city so make sure the bus/taxi/shuttle drops you at the right terminal.

Bus

Save money and hassles and get your bus ticket at **Metro Toronto Coach Terminal** (☎ 419-393-7911; 610 Bay St) a few days ahead of time, especially for weekend travel.

Discounted quasi-legal van services between Toronto and Montréal or Ottawa advertise in *Now* or *Metro*. It's 'meet here, pay cash, go.' Beware, most won't have insurance coverage.

Car

Check hostel ride boards for drive-sharing. You may get lucky and find an **Auto Drive-Away Co** (☎ 416-225-7754, 800-561-2658; www.torontodriveaway.com; 5803 Yonge St) vehicle going your way. Check classifieds in weekend newspapers or travel ads in *Now* and *Metro*.

Train

Grand old **Union Station** (65 Front St W) is the hub of VIA Rail's regional service, and terminus for its three-times-a-week train to the west coast. There's frequent service along the Québec City–Windsor Corridor and branches to southwestern Ontario, including Niagara Falls. Trains transfer at Montréal (p204) to the Maritimes.

GETTING AROUND
Public Transportation

Toronto Transit Commission (TTC; ☎ 416-393-4636; 1-ride/5-ride/day pass $2.25/9.50/7.75) oversees an extensive network of buses, subways and streetcars. Single fares (exact change on buses) or tokens are good for an hour so ask for a transfer. Get a daypass if you'll be using transit all day after 9:30am. They're available, along with five-ticket booklets, from subway stations and convenience stores. Toronto is one of the few North American cities still using streetcars; they roll east–west St Clair Ave, College, Dundas, Queen and King Sts, and north–south Spadina Ave.

GO trains (☎ 416-869-3200; www.gotransit.com) runs daily trains from Union Station to a few stops in town on their way to the suburbs. Though they rely on the honor system, there are random ticket inspections.

Taxi

Flagging a cab is quite easy downtown. If you want a sure thing:

416-TAXICAB (☎ 416-829-4222)
Beck Taxi (☎ 416-751-5555)
Co-op Cabs (☎ 416-504-2667)
Royal Taxi (☎ 416-777-9222)

LAKE ONTARIO

The most eastern Great Lake has a special affinity with Ontarians. Not counting the urban tangle on the western shores, northern Lake Ontario is the most accessible Cottage Country, full of leafy forests and blue lakes. If you've only got a few days to spend in Ontario, try a daytrip to Niagara Falls and a few stops along the north shore.

From Toronto, busy Hwy 401 follows Lake Ontario's north shore into Québec and Queen's Elizabeth Way (QEW) curves south to Niagara Falls. Busy border crossings into New York happen at Niagara Falls and Thousand Islands and Cornwall off Hwy 401. **Coach Canada** (☎ 800-461-7661; www.coachcanada.com) has competitive rates (often cheaper than Greyhound) on a half-dozen scheduled routes around Ontario and into New York.

NIAGARA FALLS

Armed with zeal and the ridiculous the US and Canada are engaged in an ongoing war of who's better, which started decades ago, and the battleground is a loud neon mess with the natural wonder Niagara Falls caught in the middle.

Renowned as the honeymoon capital of the continent, this international hotspot has the ability to dazzle. The sheer power of the freefalling water will amaze, and the glitz of Canada's Clifton Hill or the USA's casinos will stimulate.

Orientation & Information

Niagara Falls, NY and Niagara Falls, ON engage in an international staredown across the Niagara River. **Rainbow Bridge** (car/pedestrian US$2.50/0.50) spans the international creek and connects downtowns, accessed via Robert Moses Parkway (US) or Rte 420 (Canada).

Canadian Clifton Hill leads west of the falls, with stimuli-confusing, Las Vegasian attractions that actually have nothing to do with water. For more serenity, Niagara Parkway leads downstream to 'normal' town, with the train and bus stations and hostels.

In Canada, get city and park information, maps and coupons adjacent to the falls at **Table Rock Complex** (☎ 905 371 0254, 877-642-7275; www.niagaraparks.com; ☾ 9am-11pm, 9am-4pm Sep-May). USA side, **Orin Lehman State Park Visitors Center** (☎ 716-278-1796; Prospect Park; ☾ 9am-5pm) shows a good film about the falls ($3). The **visitors bureau** (☎ 800-338-7890; 4th & Niagara Sts; ☾ 8:30am-5pm) is beside the US bus terminal.

INSTEAD OF ACTING LIKE A JACKASS

Before hopping in a barrel for a fall of bravado, bring your leg down off the railing, put your pants back on and listen. The first recorded 'fall' was 1901 and five of the 14 since couldn't try a second time.

Favor those odds? Consider, a jet-ski rider with parachute and an experienced kayaker didn't make it. Successful Kirk Jones, the Fall of Shame 2003 entry, was the first to go without a device, so being That Guy isn't possible.

Also consider, if successful, you'll appear in front of a judge for illegally performing a stunt (it's a real law, one with a $10,000 fine) or given a psych profile for attempted suicide.

Not as thrilling, but cheaper and lawfully safer, try a larger-than-life trip at **IMAX Niagara Falls** (☎ 905-358-3611; 6170 Fallsview Blvd; admission $12) and its free exhibit of original barrels or the USA's **Daredevil Museum** (☎ 716-282-4046; www.niagarafallslive.com; 303 Rainbow Blvd).

If you still want to go, barrels have had the most success – really.

Sights & Activities

Really, it's better in Canada. **Bridal Veil Falls** are best seen from Canada, but the USA's **Prospect Point Observation Tower** ($0.50) elevates visitors to a vista.

The more famous **Horseshoe Falls** produce a spray felt from afar but seen up-close from the Canadian side of the border. Come early with coffee to the observation deck at Table Rock for unobstructed photos and no crowds. The USA has a viewpoint after crossing the bridge to **Goat Island** to Terrapin Point. Colored spotlights light up the falls every night.

To really experience the thundering falls (without actually bailing over them) **Maid of the Mist** (☎ 905-358-5781; www.maidofthemist.com; 5920 Niagara Parkway; adult C$13, US$11.50; ☝ 9am-7:15pm Jun-Aug, to 5:45pm early Jun, varies seasonally, closed Nov-Feb) has been leaving both sides to bob and bounce in the pool since 1846.

Save a few dollars with **Niagara Falls & Great Gorge Adventure Pass** ($32): good for the main sites and People Mover (p188).

Journey Behind the Falls (☎ 905-354-1551; 6650 Niagara Parkway; adult/child $10/6; ☝ 9am-5:30pm Mon-Fri, 9am-7:30pm Sat & Sun) leads through rock-cut tunnels halfway down the cliff (raincoats provided). The steel barge *Old Scow*, 1km

---

> **DETOUR: NIAGARA'S USA SIDE**
>
> The elevator on the north corner of the USA's Goat Island descends to **Cave of the Winds** (☎ 716-278-1730; admission $8), where walkways go within 25ft of the cataracts (raincoats provided). **Devil's Hole State Park** (Robert Moses Pkwy) walkway leads 300ft into the gorge for a spectacular view.
>
> **HI-AYH Niagara Falls** (☎ 716-282-3700; 1101 Ferry Ave; dm $18) has seven dormitory rooms with four, six or eight bunks to a room, a living room, laundry and kitchen facilities.
>
> **Niagara Falls Campground** (☎ 716-731-3434, 800-525-8505; 2405 Niagara Falls Blvd/Rte 62; campsite $21) is 7 miles east of Niagara Falls.
>
> **Top of the Falls Restaurant** (☎ 716-278-0337; Goat Island; lunch $6-9, dinner $13-25) has views of the falls through large windows – especially brilliant at sunset. It's cheaper at lunch, or you can belly-up to the bar. **Flying Saucer Drive Inn** (☎ 716-356-4553; 6768 Lundy Ln; mains $4-6) serves carhop-delivered burgers and $0.99 two-egg breakfasts.

to the south, is waiting to fall since its 1918 rock-lodging.

North of Niagara, quaint and historic Queenston has **Laura Secord Homestead** (☎ 905-262-4851; 29 Queenston St; adult $2.50; ☝ 10am-4pm May–mid-Oct). Famous as a chocolate goddess (yes, there's a shop), Lo also played a significant part in the War of 1812.

Sleeping

The hostels are close to the train and bus stations and just a 30-minute walk to the falls.

HI-Niagara Falls (☎ 905-357-0770, 888-749-0058; www.hihostels.ca/niagrafalls; 4549 Cataract Ave; dm/r/s $23/30/56) This industrial-looking but quite comfortable-feeling hostel offers 90 solid, iron bunks. Veg potlucks happen every Sunday evening.

Backpacker's International Inn (☎ 905-357-4266, 800-891-7022; niagarafallshostel@hotmail.com; 4219 Huron St; dm/d $29/50) This 19th-century home is reminiscent of Niagara's early days and charm.

Lyons House Hostel (☎ 905-354-6425; lyonshouse hostel@cogeco.ca; 5741 McGrail Ave; dm/d $20/50) The closest hostel to the falls sits quietly among the touristic chaos.

Eating & Drinking

Under Clifton Hill's neon lights food is cheap, buffets are plentiful and it's quantity over quality. Local growers host a **Farmers Market** (cnr Park & Chrysler Sts; ☝ 7am-2pm Sat).

Daily Planet (☎ 905-371-1722; 4573 Queen St; mains $5-10) Escape the mobs for beer and a pub-grub meal or Mexican dish.

Niagara Falls Brewing Co (☎ 905-356-2739; 6863 Lundy's Lane; mains $6-12) Fall into a good brew while enjoying a burger or one-handed snack. Tours (free, make reservations) include samples.

Getting There & Around

Greyhound, Coach Canada, and Amtrak stop on both sides of the Falls. VIA Rail stops in Canada. From the USA's **NFTA bus terminal** (4th & Niagara Sts), bus No 40 goes to Buffalo ($1.85, one hour) for air connections.

Check for daytrips departing from Toronto (p181).

People Mover (☎ 905-357-9340; daypass adult/child $6/3; ☝ May–mid-Oct) loops around Canada's side from Rapids View to Queenston. **Niagara Transit** (☎ 905-356-1179; www.niagaratransit.com;

SCENIC DRIVE: THOUSAND ISLANDS PARKWAY

Hwy 401 follows the Canadian shore of the St Lawrence, and **Thousand Islands Bridge** (C$3, US$2) rises high above it all while crossing to Alexandria Bay, NY and I-81. Follow the yellow signs for **Thousand Islands Parkway** from Hwy 401 between Gananoque (gan-an-*awk*-way) and Mallory-town Landing. You'll take a trip parallel to the unbelievably blue St Lawrence, dotted with vividly green mounds that make up Thousand Islands' Cottage Country. There is also a **bikeway** along the parkway for 35km, with frequent picnic areas, before rejoining the highway. In tiny Morrisburg, re-created **Upper Canada Village** (☎ 613-543-4328, 800-437-2233; www.uppercanadavillage.com; adult/ student $17/11; ⊙ 9:30am-5pm mid-May–mid-Oct) has a functional working blacksmith's shop, sawmill, and farm brought to life by costumed characters. Busy and bold **Three Nations Bridge** crosses the St Lawrence from Cornwall (birthplace of factory lighting) to Massena, NY.

---

1 ride/daypass $3/6; ⊙ mid-May–Nov) shuttles to Canadian attractions. **Viewmobile trolley** (☎ 716-282-0028; daypass $5) does a USA loop.

KINGSTON

With a legitimate claim as Canada's Hockey Town, five prisons, a military college, a student-mecca and the eastern point of the Great Lakes, Kingston can't help but be fun. As Canada's first capital, it's got history too.

Take Division St off Hwy 401 to one-way Princess St, the main drag. Get the self-guided walking tour map at **Kingston Tourism** (☎ 613-548-4415, 888-855-4555; www.kingstoncanada .com; ⊙ 9am-8pm daily Jul & Aug, 9am-5pm Mon-Fri, 10am-4pm Sat & Sun Sep–Jun).

About 2km west of downtown along the lakeshore, **Correctional Service of Canada Museum** (☎ 613-530-3122; 555 King St W; free; ⊙ 9am-4pm Mon-Fri, 10am-4pm Sat & Sun May-Sep) has cool exhibits and teaches you how to bust out of jail...you know, just in case. Across the harbor, **Fort Henry** (☎ 613-542-7388; www.forthenry .com; Fort Henry Dr; adult/student $11/8.75; ⊙ 10am-5pm late-May–Oct) was built on its hilltop perch in 1832 to protect the country. It's still a military college with impeccable grounds.

The crew's quarters on retired 64m ice-breaker **Alexander Henry** (☎ 613-542-2261; www .marmus.ca; 55 Ontario St; dm $32; ⊙ May-Oct) are cramped and viewless, but authentic. Inviting **Louise House** (☎ 613-531-8237; www.hihostels .ca/kingston; 329 Johnson St; dm $23.50, s/d incl breakfast $35/50; ⊙ May-Aug) is an 1847 landmark home and HI summer-only hostel.

Downtown has almost a dozen pubs and you'll talk (listen) hockey at all of them. **Toucan** (☎ 613-544-1966; 76 Princess St) is most welcoming and cheap. Rock concerts at **AJ's Hangar** (☎ 613-547-3657; 393 Princess St) are truly phenomenal.

Cheap fun and Canadian-passion happen during **Kingston Frontenacs** (☎ 613-542-4042; www.kingstonfrontenacs.com; adult/student $13/11; ⊙ Sep-Mar) games at **Kingston Memorial Centre** (303 York St).

Greyhound, Coach Canada and VIA Rail all stop here.

EASTERN ONTARIO

It's amazing how natural and relaxed things start to feel almost immediately north of Hwy 401, close to the Québec border. Algonquin Provincial Park is the ecological highlight and Ottawa is worth more than an afternoon.

OTTAWA

Welcome to Canada's capital. Ottawa's appeal is that the main residents are students and politicians – both infamous for lengthy summer vacations – so visitors define the summertime fun. Long considered a ho-hum town, 'Silicon Valley of the North' has earned a lively and cultural reputation with established museums and emerging nightlife.

Orientation

Parliament Hill ('the Hill') is perched on the south shore of the Ottawa River; Byward Market ('the Market') is situated east across the Rideau Canal ('the Canal'). Québec province and the City Formerly Known as Hull, Gatineau, are located north across the river.

Information

Major banks and currency-exchange offices have branches on Sparks St.

EASTERN CANADA

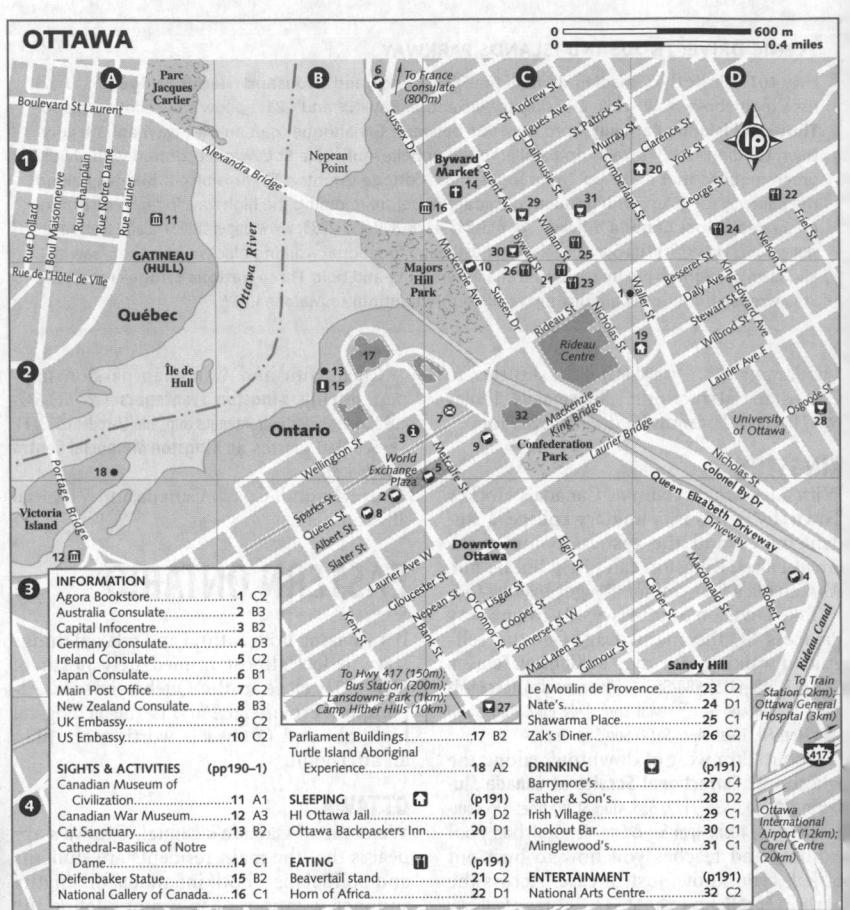

OTTAWA

INFORMATION
Agora Bookstore........................1 C2
Australia Consulate....................2 B3
Capital Infocentre....................3 B2
Germany Consulate....................4 D3
Ireland Consulate....................5 C2
Japan Consulate....................6 B1
Main Post Office....................7 C2
New Zealand Consulate............8 B3
UK Embassy....................9 C2
US Embassy....................10 C2

SIGHTS & ACTIVITIES (pp190–1)
Canadian Museum of
Civilization....................11 A1
Canadian War Museum............12 A3
Cat Sanctuary....................13 B2
Cathedral-Basilica of Notre
Dame....................14 C1
Deifenbaker Statue....................15 B2
National Gallery of Canada......16 C1

Parliament Buildings....................17 B2
Turtle Island Aboriginal
Experience....................18 A2

SLEEPING 🛏 (p191)
HI Ottawa Jail....................19 D2
Ottawa Backpackers Inn............20 D1

EATING 🍴 (p191)
Beavertail stand....................21 C2
Horn of Africa....................22 D1

Le Moulin de Provence............23 C2
Nate's....................24 D1
Shawarma Place....................25 C1
Zak's Diner....................26 C1

DRINKING 🍷 (p191)
Barrymore's....................27 C4
Father & Son's....................28 D2
Irish Village....................29 C1
Lookout Bar....................30 C1
Minglewood's....................31 C1

ENTERTAINMENT (p191)
National Arts Centre....................32 C2

Agora Bookstore (☎ 613-562-4672; 145 Besserer St;
per hr $5; 🕑 Mon-Sat) Internet café like your buddy's
apartment with HI discounts.

Capital Infocentre (☎ 613-239-5000, 800-465-1867;
www.ottawatourism.ca; 90 Wellington St;
🕑 8:30am-9pm daily, 9am-5pm Mon-Fri only Labor Day–
Victoria Day) Near the Hill, with 24-hour touch-screen
display outside.

Main Post Office (☎ 613-844-1545; 59 Sparks St)

Ottawa General Hospital (☎ 613-737-7777;
501 Smyth Rd) Southeast of downtown.

Sights & Activities

On the **Hill**, Canada's federal **Parliament
Buildings** display government importance
(with a view) above the Ottawa River; grab
a self-guided map. Show up early for the

Changing of the Guard (🕑 10am late Jun-Aug) and
sign up for a **tour** (☎ 613-992-4793, 866-599-
4999; free; 🕑 9am-7:30pm Mon-Fri, 9am-4:30pm Sat &
Sun summer) for current-day **Centre Block** and
Confederation-era **Eastern Block**. Don't miss
striking **Peace Tower** views and come back at
night for the **Sound & Light Show**.

Make sure to rub **Deifenbaker**'s left foot
for luck and visit the doll-housed **cat sanctuary** of strays cared for by 'Catman of the
Hill' René Chartrand.

The **Market** is an always-busy, mainly-
pedestrian attraction in itself. The popular
glass-and-granite **National Gallery of Canada**
(☎ 613-990-1985; www.national.gallery.ca; 380 Sussex Dr; permanent collection free; 🕑 10am-5pm, to 8pm
Thu, closed Mon & Tue Oct-Apr) seems to have one

SPLURGE!

Bungee (☎ 613-459-3714, 877-828-8170; www
.bungee.ca; 1st jump $100; ☒ 11am-6pm week-
ends May-Oct, 3-6pm Mon-Fri Jul & Aug) Go big,
and jump 200ft into a limestone quarry with
Bungee (call for Ottawa shuttle). Shoppers
Drug Marts have discount coupons ($77).

hundred galleries emphasizing Canadian
artists, most of them excellent.

Go inside **Cathedral-Basilica of Notre Dame**
(Guigues Ave; free; ☒ 7am-6pm) in late afternoon
when light streams through the stained-
glass windows. With a new home from
2005, the **Canadian War Museum** (☎ 613-776-
8600; www.warmuseum.ca; 330 Sussex Dr; adult/student
$4/3, free 4-8pm Thu, half-price Sun; ☒ 9:30am-5pm, to
8pm Thu, closed Mon Oct-May) exhibits Canada's
military history from 1812 to Korea.

Turtle Island Aboriginal Experience (☎ 613-
564-9494; www.aboriginalexperiences.com; Victoria Island; packages from $7; ☒ 11am-6pm May-Sep) is a
replicated village of aboriginal culture and
traditions.

Ottawa is famous for **ice-skating** the Canal,
of which 7.8km are maintained and lined
with rental shacks and huts serving beavertails (hot, flat, yummy doughnuts) and
hot cocoa.

Festivals & Events

Winterlude (☎ 613-239-5000, 800-465-1867; www
.canadascapital.gc.ca/winterlude; early Feb) Huge fest
along the frozen canal.

Canada Day (Jul 1) Canada's birthday, Canada's capital.
Party!

Sleeping

Ottawa Backpackers Inn (☎ 613-241-3402, 888-
394-0334; www.ottawahostel.com; 203 York St; dm/d/r
$19/38/55) Beat-up couches on the porch sug-
gest ghetto house, but this is a comfortable
19th-century home near the market.

HI Ottawa Jail (☎ 613-235-2595; www.hihostels
.ca/ottawa; 75 Nicholas St; dm/r $25/59) This is the

spot of Canada's last public hanging and an
18th-century (haunted) jail. Sleep tight.

Camp Hither Hills (☎ 613-822-0509; fax 613-822-
6413; 5227 Bank St; Hwy 31; campsites $20; ☒ mid-May-Oct)
Park-like setting 10km south of downtown
(500m from transit).

Eating

Line up at the **Beavertail stand** (cnr William &
George; beavertails $3-4) for Ottawa's signature
indulgence. **Le Moulin de Provence** (☎ 613-241-
9152; 55 Byward Market; items $2-6) has good coffees
and excellent pastries.

Zak's Diner (☎ 613-241-2401; 16 Byward St; mains $5-
10; ☒ 24hr Fri & Sat) For after-drinking munchies
and/or hangovers, Zak's 1950s-ness has the
cure. Colossal sundaes.

Shawarma Place (☎ 613 562 3662; 284 Dalhousie
St; shawarmas $5-7) Delicious tangy-spicy Leba-
nese food at excellent prices, it's open late
just outside the Market.

Nate's (☎ 613-789-9191; 316 Rideau St; mains $4-
7) The $5 breakfast will fill you up; for $7
you'll be stuffed.

Horn of Africa (☎ 613-789-0025; 364 Rideau St;
mains $6-11) As much a hangout and experi-
ence as a restaurant, the Ethiopian food is
spicy and unbeatably priced.

It's a good hump to Chinatown, don't
blink or you might miss it. Go south from
the river on Bronson Ave to Somerset St for
noodles. A few blocks west is Little Italy.

Drinking

Express is the city's free entertainment
weekly; *Capital Xtra* is aimed towards gays
and lesbians.

Father & Son's (☎ 613-234-1173; 112½ Osgoode St)
'F&S' is a pseudo-college bar. It's loud, open
and has – $10 pitchers.

Irish Village (☎ 613-562-0674; 67 Clarence St)
Emerald-Isle design has four pubs (Heart
& Crown, Snug, Mother McGintey's and
Black Rose) meeting in the middle so peo-
ple meet and mingle.

Minglewood's (☎ 613-562-2611; 101 York St) The
Market's all-time fun bar with a loud pub

EASTERN CANADA

GETTING INTO TOWN

Bus No 97 Kanata–Stittsville ($2.60) heads east from the airport on the Transitway (express bus
route through downtown), which is also used by bus No 95 Nepean, south from the train station.
The bus station is 1.5km (30 minutes' walk) from the Hill; catch bus No 4 Ottawa–Rockcliffe north
on Kent St.

BACK-ROADS ONTARIO

West of Toronto, get off Hwy 401 (and escape the 140km/h herds). Since you've probably been drinking their beer, you should tour **Sleeman's Brewery** (☎ 519-822-1834, 800-268-8537; www .sleeman.com; 551 Clair Rd; tour $4; 7-9pm Mon-Fri) in Guelph. If you haven't had a Sleeman's, for shame; drink one and take a tour. Also visit the pastoral refuge for abused, heartwarming jackasses at **Donkey Sanctuary of Canada** (☎ 519-836-1697; www.donkeysanctuary.ca; 6981 Puslinch Concession Rd; donation; ⊙ 9am-4pm Wed & Sun May-Nov). Make sure to hit **Bluesfest** (☎ 519-851-6202; www.theblues fest.com; ⊙ mid-Jul) in London and North America's largest **Oktoberfest** (☎ 519-570-4267, 888-294-4267; www.oktoberfest.ca; ⊙ early-mid-Oct) in Kitchener.

The **Bruce Trail** is a well-loved footpath stretching 780km over private and public lands from Queenston (north of Niagara Falls) up the Bruce Peninsula. It's a worthwhile hike for a day or week – contact **Bruce Trail Association** (☎ 800-665-4453; www.brucetrail.org).

---

downstairs, 2nd-floor sportsbar and pool tables and tiny dance floor up top.

Barrymore's (☎ 613-233-0307; 323 Bank St) The best of the upstairs patios.

Lookout Bar (☎ 613-789-1624; 41 York St) Multi-tiered, gay-and-lesbian fave, in the Market.

Entertainment
PERFORMING ARTS
National Arts Centre (NAC; ☎ 613-755-1111; 53 Elgin St) Ottawa's performance complex. Make friends with students who are able to buy $9.50 tickets through Live Rush (www.liverush.ca).

SPORTS
OC Transpo runs special buses to venues on game day.

Corel Centre (☎ 613-599-0300; Hwy 17) Don't be confused by all the Leaf fans, Ottawa has its own NHL team: the **Ottawa Senators** (☎ 613-599-0250; www.ottawasenators.com; ticket $21-190).

Lansdowne Park (☎ 613-580-2429; 1015 Bank St) CFL games are played by the **Ottawa Renegades** (www.ottawarenegades.net; ticket $34-70).

Getting There & Around
All Canadian, and some US, airlines fly to **Ottawa International Airport** (code: YOW; ☎ 613-248-2000; www.ottawa-airport.ca). Greyhound and VIA Rail stop here on Toronto–Montréal routes. Almost every **OC Transpo** (☎ 613-741-4390; www .octranspo.com; fare/daypass $2.60/6) route connects with the Transitway. Offices, including at Rideau Centre, answer questions and sell tickets (cheaper than regular fares).

AROUND OTTAWA
Cold-War fans will appreciate **Diefenbunker** (☎ 613-839-0007; www.diefenbunker.ca; 3911 Carp Rd; Carp; adult/student $14/12.50; ⊙ 11am-3pm summer,

varies seasonally), Canada's underground bomb shelter located 35km east in Carp.

In Gatineau, the **Canadian Museum of Civil ization** (☎ 819-776-7000, 800-555-5621; 100 Rue Lau rier; adult/student $10/6, half-price Sun; ⊙ 9am-6pm daily May-Aug, 9am-5pm Tue-Sun Oct-Apr, to 9pm Thu year-round) contrasts Canada's aboriginal and European history as a fantastic collection of totems watches Parliament.

Wakefield, 15km north of Ottawa, acts as gateway to Gatineau Parc. Wild daytrips travel the deceptively fast and turbulent Ot tawa River. **Ottawa Adventures** (☎ 800-690-7238 www.ottawaadventure.com; daytrip with camping from $78) is cheaper and has a shuttle operator from Ot tawa ($26). Other outfitters include **Owl Raft ing** (☎ 800-461-7238; www.owl-mkc.ca/owl; daytrip/2-day midweek $90/180, campsite with breakfast $15) and **Rive Run** (☎ 800-267-8504; www.riverrunners.com; daytrip 2-day midweek $95/199, campsite per person $10).

With 80 acres linked to Gatineau Parc there are heaps of outdoor possibilities a **Gatineau Parc International Hostel** (☎ 819-459-3180; carman@magma.ca; Carman Rd; dm $18-20). The sauna is a plus. Ask about bush treks.

Greyhound stops here; ask the bus-driver for hostel drop off.

ALGONQUIN PROVINCIAL PARK
Inspiration for Group of Seven painting and Tragically Hip songs, **Algonquin** (☎ 705-633-5572; www.algonquinpark.on.ca; admission $12, camp site/backcountry $25/9) epitomizes stereotypica Canada: clear lakes, green hills and howlin wolves; a must for canoeists and hikers.

The main road, Hwy 60, runs acros the southern edge. **Algonquin Visitor Cente** (☎ 613-637-2828; Hwy 6; ⊙ 10am-5pm, to 9pm mid Jun–Sep, to 4pm Sat & Sun Nov–mid-Apr), inside th west gate has awesome dioramas.

You should see **wildlife** from Hwy 6 and it's guaranteed if you head into the bush. Park staff comically conduct '**howling sessions**' on Thursday nights in August to converse with wolves, stop and listen.

Rental outfitters are in and around the park, but check Ottawa or Toronto for deals. **Algonquin Outfitters** (☎ 705-635-2243, 800-469-4948; www.algonquinoutfitters.com; rentals per day from $26) has four locations around the park: Oxtongue, Huntsville, Opeongo and Brent. The **Portage Store** (☎ 705-633-5622; www.portagestore.com; Canoe Lake; packages per day from $40) has several packages. Both have guided tours.

Campground reservations are essential and there's plenty of backcountry. West of the park, hostel-log-cabins at **Wolf Den** (☎ 705-635-9336; www.wolfdenbunkhouse.com; 3429 Hwy 60, Oxtongue Lake; dm/s/d $18/50/54) are rustic and fun. Hammond Transport stops here. A three-story block with windows, **Hi-South Algonquin** (☎ 613 338 2080, 800-595-8064; www.hihos tels.ca/maynooth; Hwy 62; dm/s/d $21/25/$35) in Maynooth, 25km from the east gate, is a nicely converted Arlington hotel.

Getting There & Away

Hammond Transportation (☎ 705-645-5431; www .hammondtransportation.com; ☿ Jul-early Sep) connects with Ontario Northland Monday, Wednesday and Friday in Huntsville for $28. **Moose Travel** (p175; ☿ May-Sep) goes from Toronto for $95. Both have 'drop us here' service. Greyhound stops at Hunstville and Maynooth.

If you've got wheels and/or gear, beat the crowds and access the park off northern Hwy 17.

SMITHS FALLS

If you're thinking, 'man, I could really go for five pounds of chocolate' then luckily **Hershey** – yes that Hershey – **Chocolate Factory** (☎ 613-283-3300; 1 Hershey Dr; free; ☿ 9am-5pm), off Hwy 43, gives Willie Wonka–style tours. Cheap bags of chocolate scraps, as well as discounted bars and stuff.

GREAT LAKES ONTARIO

Ontario is essentially separated from the US by water. North of Lake Erie, Hwy 401 speeds towards Windsor, connecting with Detroit, MI. Lakes Superior and Huron border Northern Ontario and some of the most untramped wilderness on the entire continent. A trip to the north is essentially a trip in itself, as you cannot simply go 'for a day' and return – but the wilderness experience is so rewarding it's worth the extra days or weeks that you'll miss out on elsewhere.

Hwy 401 leads from Toronto to Detroit in a continual reminder of the interstate culture. Hwy 17 is the road most-traveled through the north, Hwy 11 takes longer but passes closer to untouched lands.

VIA Rail's Toronto–Vancouver *The Canadian* passes nowhere near any roads in the north and allows hop-off service for hardcore paddlers and hikers wherever they like. **Algoma Central Railway** (ACR; ☎ 705-946-7300, 800-242-9287; www.algomacentral railway.com; one-way $14-109) offers similar service from Sault Ste Marie.

SCENIC DRIVE: LAKE SUPERIOR SHORELINE

Sheer cliffs rising from sandy beaches interrupt misty forests and rocky hills as Hwy 17 flirts with Lake Superior's shore between Sault Ste Marie and Thunder Bay. As one of only two throughways to western Canada, it's a forced bit of scenery and, like a male being offered the chance to be an underwear-model photographer, don't look a gift-horse in the mouth.

Though 690km may not sound bad, this is a long haul through rock cuttings and inlets. Often peaceful, sometimes brutal and occasionally furious, ever-present Lake Superior is a canoeing haven and big ship graveyard. Refresh with a swim if you dare.

Break-up the journey by playing the Wildlife Checklist Game, learning Gordon Lightfoot lyrics or stopping for a picnic or a seven-day hike at **Lake Superior Provincial Park** (☎ 705-856-2284; Hwy 17; vehicle $9.50; backcountry/front country site $7.50/18-30) or **Pukaskwa** (*puk*-ah-sah; ☎ 807-229-0801; Hwy 627; adult $4.50; backcountry/front country campsite $5-8/21-23). Don't repeat 'rocks and trees' more than a dozen times consecutively and remind yourself that it could be a lifetime before you're in untouched wilderness again. Pack lots of CDs (no Bryan Adams), expect diner food along the way and always have your camera ready.

SPLURGE!

Fathom Five National Marine Park (☎ 519-596-2233; admission $4.50, backcountry $8, diver $15) The Bruce Peninsula is an 80km-long limestone outcrop flanked by rocky shores and sandy beaches of Lake Huron on the west and Georgian Bay on the east. Spectacular waters and shores at the north end around Tobermory, especially those protected by the marine park, are renowned diving and kayaking spots.

Diving

Cold, cold, cold but the waters are incredibly clear and lake floors are littered with shipwrecks of century-old maritime mistakes. If you've got skills and gear, register at **Diver Registration & Visitor Center** (☎ 519-596-2503; Cyprus Lake Rd; ☒ 8am-4:30pm). If you're in need, **G&S Watersports** (☎ 519-596-2200; www.gswatersports.com; 8 Bay St S; day/weekend rental $70/100, open-water single/multiple $675/475, courses from $150) takes care of that.

Kayaking

With the rocky shores of Georgian Bay at your back, a Lake Huron sunset is unforgettable. **Paddling Gourmet** (☎ 519-596-8343; www.paddlinggourmet.com; 129 Bay St; sunset/half day/full day $45/60/125-160) takes small group on relaxed paddles with flexible itineraries. 'Jungle Jane' enthusiastically lives up to her name and she's in love with Bruce. For calmer waters on inland lakes, **Thorncrest Outfitters** (☎ 519-596-8908, 888-345-2925; www.thorncrestoutfitters.com; Hwy 6; full day $45) aims trips at beginners in addition to Georgian Bay trips.

Getting There & Away

Greyhound stops in Owen Sound. **Laidlaw Transit** (☎ 519-376-5712, 519-376-5375; ☒ Fri-Sun Jun-Sep) runs between there and Tobermory for $20. Thorncrest Outfitters also runs shuttles ($25). For a shortcut to Northern Ontario via pretty Manitoulin Island, **Ontario Ferries** (☎ 800-265-3163; www .ontarioferries.com; adult/car $12.50/27; ☒ May-Oct) runs daily; reserve ahead.

WINDSOR

Laying claim to being the only Canadian city *south* of mainland USA, Windsor is a busy border crossing to Detroit: MI via the **Ambassador Bridge** (C$4, US$2.75), or the **Detroit–Windsor Tunnel** (C$3.50, US$2.50).

It's not uncommon for insanely busy line ups. Kill some time at the posh **Casino Windsor** (☎ 519-258-7878; www.casinowindsor.com; 445 Riverside Dr W), overlooking the river. Or enjoy a picnic, Detroit's skyline and 3-D art under the Ambassador Bridge.

Greyhound stops downtown, some buses continue to Detroit. VIA Rail also stops but you'll need to cross to Detroit for Amtrak; take **Transit Windsor** (☎ 519-944-4141; $2.35) bus No 2 from the station and transfer to the Tunnel Bus ($2.75).

SAULT STE MARIE

Pretty and fun, at the meeting of Lakes Huron and Superior, 'The Soo' will immediately be in your top-five favorite stopovers.

You can count up to 80 freighters each summer day passing through the last set of locks on the St Lawrence Seaway. **Art Gallery of Algoma** (☎ 705-949-9067; www.artgalleryofalgoma .on.ca; 10 East St; admission by donation; ☒ 10am-5pm Mon-Sat) has local and aboriginal art.

The frontier **Algonquin Hotel** (☎ 705-253-2311, 888-269-7728; www.hihostels.ca/saultstemarie; 864 Queen St E; dm $23) has clean and quiet rooms. Thick slabs of Canadian bacon are served at **Muio's** (☎ 705-254-7105; 685 Queen St E; mains $5-12), a 1950s diner. Drinking is half-price in Michigan but try the ambience at locally constructed **Loplops Lounge** (☎ 705-945-0754; 651 Queen St E), with its awesome polished-steel bar.

The **International Bridge** crosses to Sault Ste Marie, MI. Greyhound stops here.

THUNDER BAY

Thunder Bay is an unlikely urban mess plunked among the woods at the western edge of the Great Lakes. Its charm emerges slowly once the culture-shock wears off and melts into comfort and surprising cosmopolitanism.

Pagoda information centre (☎ 807-684-3670; cnr Red River Rd & Water St; ☒ 9am-5pm May-Sep) is central and **Tourism Thunder Bay** (☎ 807-983-2041,

800-667-8386; Hwy 17; 8:30am-8:30pm mid-Jun–Aug, 9am-5pm Sep–mid-Jun) is 6km east of town.

In July, **Thunder Bay Blues Festival** (807-684-3509, 800-463-8817; www.tbayblues.ca) and **Thunder Bay Fringe Theatre Festival** (807-344-1343; www.tbfringe.com) are fun and cheap.

Happily messy **Thunder Bay Backpackers Inn** (807-683-3995, 866-424-5687; tbaybackpackers inn@shaw.ca; 139 Machar Ave; dm/s/d $20/23/46) has *Leave it to Beaver* charisma and a basement sauna ($8). On eight acres of wooded lakeside bliss 18km east of town, **Thunder Bay International Hostel** (807-983-2042; www.thunder bayhostel.com; 1594 Lakeshore Dr; dm/campsite $19/12) has campsites, a house, a cabin and an old bus. Greyhound will pick up/drop off here.

Westjet also stops here.

WEST TO MANITOBA

Heading west from Thunder Bay the highway splits at Shabaqua Corners; Hwy 17 is quicker, Hwy 11 is better-looking.

Big ol' Kenora has excellent little **Lake-of-the-Woods Museum** (807-467-2105; 300 Main St; admission $2; 9am-5pm) following the timeline of aboriginal origins to industrial degradation of the present.

Well northwest of Kenora, **Serenity on the River** (807-543-3107, dellalitkowski@hotmail.com; Olson Rd; dm $20) has water frontage reached via Rte 596.

Fort Frances is a busy border crossing to International Falls, MN.

QUÉBEC

Canada's least-understood province is a cultural and natural experience. Party all night in Montréal, enjoy visible history in Québec City or travel north through boreal forests and small communities. English-speakers will be fine in the cities and experience a bit of a language barrier elsewhere; French-speakers will learn new dialects and ways to swear. Separatist desire and '*nous sommes Québec, you are Canada*' views aren't as prevalent as they were decades ago.

The province is served by bus lines including **Voyageur** (800-661-8747; www.grey hound.ca), **Orléans Express** (888-999-3977; www .orleansexpress.com) and **Limocar** (866-700-8899; www.limocar.com). **Allô Stop** (514-985-3032; www .allostop.com; membership $6) hooks drivers up with passengers who are traveling between

a few Québec destinations. A one-year membership is required, and you may meet at random locations (never dangerous). **Autotaxi** (www.autotaxi.com) is a Web-based bulletin board for ride sharing.

Overall, it's a fun province and proud of its French heritage. Big smiles and lots of laughter are seen and heard everywhere, making truth of the axiom, joie de vivre!

MONTRÉAL

Québec's largest city has an intangible verve that won't let you get bored. Glitzy-glam downtown, fun residential neighborhoods and stoic Old Town come together in European-North Americanism. The smoking section of Canada' label, tangy smoked-meat sandwiches and unhealthy poutine serve as metaphors for Montréalers love of life and indulgence. Bilingual presence and packed streets mix with vibrancy of nightlife, museums, sports and history all watched over by the city's namesake, Mont Royal.

Orientation

Montréal is a southwest–northeast oriented island with the St Lawrence River on its southwestern shore. Plateau Mont Royal rises northeast of downtown; Vieux Montréal (Old Town, 17th- to 19th century downtown) is sandwiched between there and the river. Chinatown lies north of Old Town and the residentially fun Quartier Latin, the Plateau and the Village are all to the east. Blvd René-Levesque and Rue Ste Catherine are the main east–west roads through downtown; northwest–southeast is Rue University.

Getting around on foot in downtown is lively and fun; getting lost in Old Town is not impossible and also fun. The Métro system easily takes you elsewhere.

To minimize confusion and maximize fun, street and place-names in the text are in French, just like real life.

Information
INTERNET ACCESS
Cyber Ground (514-842-1726; 3672 Blvd St Laurent; per hr $3)

MEDIA
English-language weeklies are the *Montréal Mirror* and *Hour*; French counterparts are *Voir* and *Ici*.

INFORMATION
Centre Infotouriste..........................1 C4
Cyber Ground....................................2 F2
Main Post Office...............................3 D4
Post Office (Poste Restante)..........4 E5
Royal Victoria Hospital.....................5 D2
Tourist information booth................6 F6
Tourist Information Bureau of
   Montréal.......................................7 F5
Uniglobe..8 B4
US Consulate.....................................9 D4

SIGHTS & ACTIVITIES   (pp198–200)
Basilique Notre Dame.....................10 E5
Cathédrale Marie Reine du
   Monde..11 C4
Centre Canadien d'Architecture...12 A4
Chalet du Mont Royal....................13 C2
Cross of Montréal...........................14 D1
Hôtel de Ville...................................15 F5
Musée d'Art Contemporain..........16 E4
Musée des Beaux Arts....................17 B3
Musée McCord.................................18 D3
Patinoire du Bassin Bonsecours...19 F6
Pointe à Callière Museum of
   Archaeology & History.............20 E6
Sailors' Memorial Clock Tower.....21 G6
Sculpture Garden............................22 A4
Terrasses Bonsecours......................23 G6
Vélo Aventure.................................24 E6
Vélo Québec's La Maison des
   Cyclistes......................................25 H1

SLEEPING   🏠   (pp200–1)
Auberge Alternative........................26 E6
HI Auberge de Jeunesse de
   Montréal.......................................27 B4
Le Gîte du Parc Lafontaine............28 H2
Le Gîte du Plateau Mont Royal.....29 F3
McGill University Residences.........30 D1
UQAM Residences...........................31 F4
YWCA...32 B4

EATING   🍽   (pp201–2)
Amelio's..33 E3
Amine..34 G3
Bato Thai..35 H4
Ben's...36 C4
Café St Paul......................................37 E6

Chez José..38 F1
Govinda Jaya Jaya...........................39 F1
Jardin de Jade..................................40 F4
La Paryse..41 F3
Mazurka..42 F2
Peel Pub..43 C4
Pho Viet..44 G3
Reuben's...45 D4

DRINKING   🍸   (pp202–3)
Café Campus....................................46 F2
Cathédral...47 F2
Comedy Nest...................................48 B4
Funky Town......................................49 C4
Gerts...50 C3
Hurley's Irish Pub............................51 B4
JinXi..52 G1
Jupiter Room....................................53 F1
L'Air du Temps.................................54 E6
Les Deux Pierrots.............................55 F5
McLean's Pub...................................56 C4
Pub St Paul.......................................57 F5
Pub Ste Elisabeth............................58 F4
Stereo...59 G4

ENTERTAINMENT   🎭   (p203)
Bell Centre.......................................60 C5
Foufounes Electriques.....................61 D2
Molson Stadium...............................62 D1
Montréal Alouettes....................(see 62)
Montreal Canadiens...................(see 60)
Monument National Theatre.........63 F4

National Film Board........................64 F3
Orchestre Symphonique de
   Montréal.................................(see 65)
Place des Arts..................................65 E4
Théâtre de Quat' Sous....................66 F2

TRANSPORT   (p204)
Gare Centrale..................................67 D4
Station Centrale de l'Autobus........68 G3

0 _____ 600 m
0 _____ 0.4 miles

E **F** **G** **H**

Plateau Mont Royal

To Fairmount Bagel (1.2km)

Rue Rachel Est
52
Rue Rivard

Ave Bureau
Rue Rachel Est
25

Ave Calixa Lavallée

1

Rue du Parc
38 39

Ave Duluth Ouest
Ave Duluth Est

Parc Lafontaine

Rue St Urbain
Boul St Laurent
Rue Bagg
Ave Henri Julien
Rue Drolet

Rue Napoléon
Rue Napoléon

53
Rue St Cuthbert

Plateau du Montréal

Ave Calixa Lavallée

Hôpital Hôtel Dieu de Montréal

47
Rue Roy Est
Rue Roy Est
Rue Berri
Rue St André

Université du Québec à Montréal

335

Ave du Parc Lafontaine

138

Olympic Village (4km); Mirabel International Airport (50km)

2

Ave des Pins Ouest
Ave des Pins Est

Rue Guilbault
2
66
Rue St Denis
Rue St Hubert

Sherbrooke

Hôpital Notre-Dame

Rue Clark
46
Rue de l'Hôtel de Ville

Carré St Louis
Rue de Malines
Rue Cherrier

Parc Persillier Lachapelle

28

Rue Prince Arthur Ouest
42
Ave Laval
Rue de Rigaud

Rue Sherbrooke Est
Rue Montcalm

Ave du Parc
Rue Jeanne Mance
Rue St François
Rue St Urbain
Rue Clark
33
Rue Milton

Ave Duluth Est

Rue de la Visitation
Rue Alexcque
Rue St Christophe
Rue St André
Rue St Hubert

Rue LaFontaine

3

The Village

Rue Sherbrooke Ouest

29
Rue St Norbert
Rue St Denis

Quartier Latin

41
Rue Ontario Est
Ave Savoie

Rue Ontario Ouest
34
Rue Robin
Rue Logan

Rue Emery

Ave Amherst
Rue St Timothée

64
68

Boul de Maisonneuve Est

M Place des Arts
05

St Laurent
M
Berri-UQAM
M
Beaudry
M

44

16
Complexe Desjardins

Rue de Bullion
61
58
Rue Ste Catherine Est

Place Émilie-Gamelin

59
Rue Ste Catherine Est
55
Rue Plessis

4

63
Place de la Paix

Université du Québec à Montréal

Ave de l'Esplanade Émile Gamelin

Rue St André
Rue St Christophe

Boul René Lévesque Est

40
Boul René Lévesque Est
Boul René Lévesque Est
31
Rue de La Gauchetière
Rue St Denis
Rue Berri
Rue Labelle

Rue Montcalm
Rue Beaudy
Rue St Timothée
Rue St André
Rue Wolfe
Rue Panet

Chinatown

Place d'Armes
M

Ave Viger Est

Champ de Mars

Ave Viger Est

720

Viger Ouest
4

Autoroute Ville Marie
720

Rue St Antoine Est
Rue St Louis

Rue Berri

5

Rlle des Fortifications

Champ de Mars
15

Rue du Champ de Mars

Place d'Armes
Rue Notre Dame Est
10

Vieux Montréal

7
Place Jacques Cartier

Rue St Paul Est

Rue Bonsecours
Rue St Gabriel
Rue St Claude
Rue Cosford

37
55
57
Rue de la Commune Est

19
21

20
54
Place Royale

Parc du Bassin Bonsecours

Bassin de l'Horloge

Quai de l'Horloge

Pl d'Youville

24
6
Bassin Jacques Cartier
Ferry Terminal
23

St Lawrence River

6

Rue de la Commune Ouest
Rue St Pierre

Bassin King Edward

Quai King Edward

Quai Jacques Cartier

Ferry to Parc Jean-Drapeau

Bassin Alexandra

Quai Alexandra

GETTING INTO TOWN

Outside Pierre-Elliot-Trudeau International arrivals hall, bus No 204 Cardinal Est goes to Dorval Bus Transfer Station and you'll switch to No 211 Bord-du-Lac Est, going to Lionel Groulx Métro station. The whole deal takes about an hour to get downtown, easily done on one ticket ($2.50). **Aérobus** (☎ 514-931-9002; one way/roundtrip $12/21.75) shuttles between the airports and Place Bonaventure downtown, you'll then take the free shuttle to your hostel.

The underground train station is also at Place Bonaventure; Station Centrale de l'Autobus is the bus station two blocks from the Berri–UQAM Métro station in Quatier Latin.

Coming from the west, branch off Hwy 20 to Hwy 720 and take Rue University exit for downtown.

MEDICAL SERVICES

For nonemergencies, walk-in clinics live all over the city.

Queen Elizabeth Health Complex (☎ 514-485-5013; 2100 Rue Marlowe) Community-owned and friendly.
Royal Victoria Hospital (☎ 514-934-1934; 687 Ave des Pins Ouest) Best hospital option for English-speaking patients. Non-Canadians must pay deposit and accept responsibility for all costs; check your insurance.

MONEY

You'll find banks downtown and ATMs everywhere.

Uniglobe (☎ 514-845-5849; 1385a Rue Ste Catherine Ouest) Offers HI discounts on exchange rates.

POST

Post offices are closed weekends. Blue-and-red signs in drugstores indicate postal outlets with extended hours.

Main post office (☎ 514-846-5401; 1250 Rue University)

Direct poste restante (general delivery) mail to: [Recipient's Name]; Poste Restante; Station Place d'Armes; 435 Rue St Antoine; Montréal, QC; H2Z 1H0 and **pick up** (🕓 8:30am-5:30pm Mon-Fri) within two weeks.

TOURIST INFORMATION

Centre Infotouriste (www.bonjourquebec.com; 1001 Rue Square Dorchester; 🕓 7am-8pm, 9am-6pm Sep-May) City's main information office offers city and provincial help. Extremely well organized and contains a bookstore, currency exchange counter and Internet terminals.
Central Switchboard (☎ 514-873-2015, 877-266-5687) Handles tourist information.
Tourist Information Booth (Quai King Edward; 🕓 10am-7pm summer) Seasonal kiosk.
Tourist Information Bureau of Montréal (www.tourisme-montreal.org; 174 Rue Notre Dame Est; 🕓 9am-7pm Jun-Aug, 9am-5pm Sep-May)

Sights

Most of Montréal's best things are close to the city center, others are easily accessed by Métro. Museum freaks will love the **Montréal Museum Pass** (☎ 514-873-2015, 877-266-5687; $20), good for access to 20 museums for two-of-three consecutive days. It's available from tourist info centers or museums.

VIEUX MONTRÉAL

Old Town, the oldest section of the city (17th-century), has random-directional cobblestone streets lined with stone buildings. With the waterfront never far away, it's a must for romantics and architecture lovers.

Place Jacques Cartier (btwn St-Paul & Notre Dame) is a cobblestone strip filling and spilling with visitors, vendors, horse-drawn carriages and musicians in summer. A fiberglass replica of Nelson's Column, **Colonne Nelson** (Nelson was the British admiral who defeated the French and Spanish fleet at Trafalgar), and the statue of obscure French admiral **Jean Vauquelin** erected in response, epitomize French–British tensions.

Hôtel de Ville (City Hall; ☎ 514-872-1111; 275 Rue Notre Dame Est; free; 🕓 8:30am-4:30pm Mon-Fri) towers over Place Jacques Cartier to the east and marks where Charles de Gaulle cried 'Vive le Québec libre!' to the masses from the balcony, fueling the fires of the Québec separatist movement.

A few blocks west, the **Basilique Notre Dame** (☎ 514-842-2925; 110 Rue Notre Dame Ouest; adult/student $4/2; 🕓 8:30am-4:30pm) exhibits architectural splendor. Completed in 1823, it holds 5000 people among magnificently detailed woodcarvings, gold plating and colorful backlighting. A religious multimedia sound-and-light show, **Et la Lumiére fut** (admission $10; 🕓 6:30pm & 8:30pm Tue-Sat) re-creates its history.

In the west end near **Place Royale** (cnr Rue de la Commune & Pl d'Youville), Montréal's first small fort, **Musée d'Archéologie et d'Histoire Pointe à Callière** (☎ 514-872-9150; www.pacmuseum.qc.ca; 350 Place Royale; adult/student $10/6; ☼ 10am-5pm Tue-Fri, 11am-5pm Sat & Sun) details in underground ruins Montréal's beginnings.

Attractive green space and recreational trails front the piers of **Vieux Port** (www.vieux portdemontreal.com), a busy spot in the summer full of picnickers, buskers, vendors, concerts, joggers, bikers and fiddlers. **Quai de l'Horloge** has the observation **Sailors' Memorial Clock Tower** (☎ 514-496-7678). Between there and **Quai Jacques Cartier** are food stands, stages, the huge flea market and **Parc du Bassin Bonsecours**, a grassy islanded expanse crisscrossed with footbridges.

Across the water, unsystematic concrete blocks thrown together make **Habitat 67**, a complex designed for the World's Fair as residential experimentalism.

DOWNTOWN

Downtown mixes modern skyscrapers with classic architecture.

Musée des Beaux Arts (☎ 514-285-2000; www .mmfa.qc.ca; 1379 Rue Sherbrooke Ouest; free, adult/ student temporary exhibits $12/6, half-price 5:30-9pm Wed; ☼ 11am-5pm, to 9pm Wed, closed Mon Sep-Jun) is Montréal's fine art gallery with Canadian, contemporary, worldwide and classic pieces displayed in two buildings. Temporary and permanent exhibits mingle nicely so you'll find Rembrandt beside Random Artist.

With a heavy focus on Québecois artists (think winterscapes), **Musée d'Art Contemporain** (☎ 514-847-6226; www.macm.org; 185 Rue Ste Catherine Ouest; adult/student $6/4, free 6-9pm Wed; ☼ 11am-6pm Tue-Sun, to 9pm Wed) boasts more than 6000 works.

In one of Montréal's most boxy-yet-subtly-attractive buildings, the **Centre Canadien d'Architecture** (☎ 514-939-7026; www.cca .qc.ca; 1920 Rue Baile; adult/student $8/5, students free Thu, everyone free 5:30-8pm Thu; ☼ 10am-5pm Wed-Sun, to 9pm Thu) will teach you a thing or two. Fanatics will love the place; others will find at least some interest in buttresses or in the history of lawn care. The **sculpture garden** across Blvd René Lévesque is impressively lit up at night.

Cathédrale Marie Reine du Monde (☎ 514-866-1661; 1085 Rue de la Cathédrale; free; ☼ 8am-7:30pm) is a magnificent, scaled-down version of St Peter's Basilica in Rome. Duck in for a look at the copper-and-gold leaf altar.

Near the McGill campus, **Musée McCord** (☎ 514-398-7100; www.mccord-museum.qc.ca; 690 Rue Sherbrooke Ouest; adult/student $10/5.50; ☼ 10am-6pm Tue-Fri, 10am-5pm Sat-Mon, closed Mon Sep-May) has over a million artifacts illustrating Canada's early European settlement from 1700.

The picturesque campus of **McGill University** (☎ 514-398-4455; 845 Rue Sherbrooke Ouest) is good for the legs (lots of hills) and eyes (lots of Victorian architecture and views).

Draped around the extinct volcano and staring over the island of Montréal is **Parc du Mont Royal** (☎ 514-872-6559; www.lemontroyal .qc.ca), known as 'the Mountain' and covered with paths, ponds and maple trees. **Chalet du Mont Royal** (excellent southward view) and **Observatoire de l'Est** (popular make-out spot) are lookouts connected by the half-hour park trail. The famous **Cross of Montréal** (a 1924 version of Paul de Chomedey, sieur de Maisonneuve's 1643 one), 1km northeast of Chalet du Mont Royal, is lit up at night and visible all over the city.

OLYMPIC VILLAGE

The leftovers from the 1976 Olympics are east of downtown, accessible from the Viau Métro stop. **Tourist Hall** (☎ 514-252-8687; 4141 Ave Pierre de Coubertin) is a three-story information center and ticket office. An Olympic Park combination ticket (adult/student $15.25/8.50) or ticket including Biodôme and Jardin Botanique (p200; $27/13.50) is the best value.

Walking around **Olympic Park** (tour adult/ student $7/5.25) is historically hysterical, if not hysterically historical. Montréalers claim to smoke so much because cigarette-sales taxes go towards grounds repair and paying for scandal and corruption involved with its buildings. Take **Stade Olympique** (Olympic Stadium). In addition to a 55-ton beam collapsing and the roof caving in due to snow, the cables of the **Montréal Tower** don't work, but that matters little as the roof it's meant to lift has too many holes. Yet the stadium still manages to host games, concerts and trade shows.

Biodôme (☎ 514-868-3000; www.biodome.qc.ca; 4777 Ave Pierre de Coubertin; adult/student $11.75/9; ☼ 9am-6pm) is an indoor zoo with four ecosystems, 4000 animals and 5000 plants. Recent renovations are improving the exhibits and the ever-popular penguins are always good for a laugh. Across the street (free shuttle) **Jardin Botanique & Insectarium** (☎ 514-872-1400; 4101 Rue Sherbrooke Est; adult/student $11.75/9; ⏲ 9am-9pm summer) is a massive floral collection of themed gardens like greenhoused cactii or the Zen-like Japanese Garden. The Insectarium is full of live and dead creepy crawlies, bugs as big as your fist and the dazzling outdoor **Butterfly House**.

PARC JEAN DRAPEAU

South of downtown in the St Lawrence River, **Parc Jean Drapeau** (☎ 514-872-4537; www.parcjeandrapeau.com) is made up of grassy islands. Take the **water shuttle** (☎ 514-281-8000; ticket $3.50; ⏲ 7:10am-10:30pm) from Quai Jacques Cartier (p198) or bike over Pont de la Concorde. You'll find an information kiosk near the Jean-Drapeau Métro stop.

Find sensational views of the city from **Île Ste Hélène** and pathways that stroll among pavilions of the **1967 World's Fair**. Fifteen million tons of earth excavated from construction of the Métro made **Île Notre Dame**. It's criss-crossed with canals and pretty garden walkways.

OTHER NEIGHBORHOODS

Quartier Latin, between Rue St Denis Blvd de Maisonneuve and Rue Sherbrooke, has lots of young people, open-air places and music spots. It's a good place to go slumming, and the side alleyways can uncover hidden bars and adventures. To the north, the **Plateau du Montréal** is much of the same with more multiethnicity and inexpensive Victorians with wrought-iron fences. Known by many as 'the Main,' Rue St Denis and Blvd St-Laurent are the major strips.

The area of Rue Ste Catherine Est between Rue St Hubert and Ave Papineau is where Montréal's gay community revitalizes itself in the **Village**. This once neglected part of town is quickly becoming a comfortable confluence of people from all walks of life and sexualities.

Activities

CYCLING & INLINE SKATING

With about 350km of bike paths, several magazines have voted Montréal the best city in North America for cyclists. Tourist offices have good free maps and **Vélo Québec's La Maison des Cyclistes** (☎ 514-521-8356;

www.velo.qc.ca; 1251 Rue Rachel Est; day $25) is an excellent resource for all things bike.

Vélo Aventure (☎ 514-847-0666; Vieux Port; per hr/day $7/22, weekends $7.50/25) rents bikes, skates and other gear by Old Port and major bike paths.

Circuit Gilles Villeneuve, the Formula 1 Grand Prix track in Parc Jean Drapeau, is popular with skaters.

ICE SKATING

The **Patinoire du Bassin Bonsecours** (☎ 514-496-7678; admission $3, rental $6), inside the Parc du Bassin Bonsecours at the Vieux Port, and **Lac aux Castors** (☎ 514-872-6559; Parc du Mont Royal; admission free; rental $6) are Montréal's popular outdoor skating rinks in winter.

Invite yourself to play in an outdoor hockey game for a memorable event. Players will be happier to share thermoses of mulled wine and cries of 'But!' (goal) than be concerned about your skill level. Informal matches take place wherever there's ice.

Tours

Guidatour (☎ 514-844-4021; www.guidatour.qc.ca; adult/student $14/12; 11am-12:30pm & 1:30-3pm Jun-Oct) Historical tours by historical people.
Old Montréal Ghost Trail (☎ 514-868-0303; www.phvm.qc.ca; adult/student $15/12; 8:30pm Jun-Aug) Somewhat campy tours hunt ghosts, follow ghosts or visit historical crime scenes.

Festivals & Events

Le Mondial Fireworks Festival (www.lemondialsaq.com; Jul-Aug) International fireworks competition on Île Ste Hélène seen from Jacques Cartier bridge.
International Jazz Festival (☎ 514-871-1881, 888-515-0515; www.montrealjazzfest.com; late Jun-early Jul) Loads of free shows in small clubs.
Just for Laughs Comedy Festival (☎ 514-845-3155, 888-244-3155; www.hahaha.com; ⏲ mid-Jul) Montréal's best-known fest brings in no-names and big names to keep audiences rolling in the aisles.
Les FrancoFolies de Montréal (☎ 514-876-8989; www.francofolies.com; late Jul-early Aug) Fun-filled shows featuring excellent bands and singers doing tributes to French-language artists.

Sleeping

Auberge Alternative (☎ 514-282-8069; www.auberge-alternative.qc.ca; 358 Rue St-Pierre; dm/s/d $19/55/55) Formerly a three-story brick warehouse, there's an instant reassurance found at this hostel on a quiet street in Old Montréal.

The colorful quarters inspire friendliness and the 19th-century construction brings settled comfort.

HI Auberge de Jeunesse Montréal (☎ 514-843-3317, 866-843-3317; www.hostellingmontreal.com; 1030 Rue Mackay; dm/s/d $28/58/58) The huge white building with red awnings west of Old Montréal has a hotel layout but a hostel vibe. The café/pub in the basement serves cheap beer and tasty sandwiches. Non-Canadians need to have/buy a membership. It also runs a shuttle to **HI-Mont Tremblant** (p204; ☎ 866-425-6008; return with Mt Tremblant stay $25).

Hostel Montréal (☎ 877-350-4483; www.hostelmontreal.com; dm/s/d $23/50/60; Le Gîte du Plateau Mont-Royal ☎ 514-284-1276; 185 Rue Sherbrooke Est; Le Gîte du Parc Lafontaine ☎ 514-522-3910; 1250 Rue Sherbrooke Est) These two old houses aren't far from each other and both have a B&B feel and are close to the action of the Plateau.

YWCA (☎ 514-866-9941; www.ydesfemmesmtl.org; 1355 Blvd René-Lévesque Ouest; s/d with shared bathroom $60/75) A complete revamp gave this Y an almost-hotel luxury. Everyone is welcome to stay, women get to use the gym and nobody will complain about cleanliness or downtown location.

UQAM Residences (☎ 514-987-6669; www.residences-uqam.qc.ca; 303 Blvd René-Lévesque; s in 8-/3-/2 bed room $39.50/49/55, ste $80; ☺ mid-May–mid-Aug) Splashes of color and modern furniture bring the bright, sunny rooms to life and make the city views that much better.

McGill University Residences (☎ 514-398-8299; reserve.residences@mcgill.ca; 3935 Rue University; s $35-45; ☺ mid-May–mid-Aug; ☐) The college-dorm rooms in two residences have tranquility and convenience. The rooms will be cleaner than the dorm you left back home.

Eating

Due to the French culture, Montréalers rarely eat at home. You'll find the densest concentration of restaurants ('restos,' or with a bar attached: 'restosbars') in Quartier Latin or the Plateau, but anywhere in town you won't be far from a cheap diner, café or wagon.

Most have a 'bring your own wine' (BYOW) policy; they'll gladly pour you a glass of whatever you've brought.

Head to the clock tower from the Lionel-Grouix Métro to the two-story **Atwater Market** (☎ 514-935-5716; 138 Ave Atwater) with plenty of vendors outside and delis, bakeries and specialty shops inside in the vaulted hall. It's a bit fashionable, but you'll get by.

DOWNTOWN, CHINATOWN & VIEUX MONTRÉAL

Café St Paul (☎ 514-844-7225; 143 Rue St Paul Ouest; breakfast $4-10, lunch $6-13) The chrome-and-black diner seating totally contrasts with the century-old, wood-beam construction in this popular little café. An excellent spot for breakfast, it's super busy early morning and lunchtime, but all yours in between.

Peel Pub (☎ 514-844-6769; 1107 Rue Ste Catherine Ouest; mains $3-10) Not only does this loud, fun, underground college hangout have a dirt-cheap menu of burgers, chicken, pizzas and greasy fries, drinks are equally cheap and you could end up staying all night.

Amelio's (☎ 514-845-8396; 201 Rue Milton; pizzas $8-12, lunch specials $5) Follow the students in the 'McGill ghetto.' Indiscreet lighting and brickwork create a warm atmosphere; generously topped pizzas warm the bellies.

Jardin de Jade (☎ 514-866-3127; 67 Lagauchetiére Ouest; lunch/2-5pm/dinner buffet $7.75/6.75/9.95) The seemingly chaotic and random exhibit of dishes makes a little more sense once you make your way around the half-dozen buffet displays.

QUARTIER LATIN & THE VILLAGE

Amine (☎ 514-287-9043; 1655 Rue St Denis; items $3-5) Underground and under $5, this little grab-and-go spot is clean, with good soups and sandwiches.

La Paryse (☎ 514-842-2040; 302 Rue Ontario Est; burgers, sandwiches $5-7, soups $2.50-4) This small café makes a case for the thickest, juiciest burgers in town. The massive amounts of toppings are about as overboard as the neo-retro rooms and it all comes together with hip and fun attitude.

Pho Viet (☎ 514-522-4116; 1663 Rue Amherst; pho $4-7; ☺ Mon-Sat) Bright orange walls and excellent Vietnamese food at affordable prices have made this a Village favorite.

Bato Thai (☎ 514-524-6705; 1310 Rue Ste Catherine Est; mains $7-17, bargain daily specials $8) Fresh and tasty ingredients in generous portions of Thai food at the boat-shaped bar.

THE PLATEAU

Chez José (☎ 514-845-0693; 173 Ave Duluth Est; mains $4-7) This cramped little place is known for brunch time crêpes and omelettes, but the

MONTRÉAL TRIATHLON

To truly experience Montréal cuisine, bypass the chic cafés and head into the trenches for a trio of only-in-Montréal eating events.

Start the day sharing a dozen bagels rivaling those in Manhattan from **Fairmount Bagel** (☎ 514-272-0667; 74 Fairmount Ave Ouest; dozen bagels $3.50-5; ☿ 24hr) and the decades-old Jewish family recipe. Away from everything, but a good warm-up. It's chaotically loud behind the counter, but the bagels are warm and delicious. Go to the Laurier Métro, walk west on Blvd St Joseph, then right on Rue St Urban.

For lunch, it's Québec's famous coronary –on-a-plate topped with cheese: poutine. Fries layered with gravy layered with cheese curds (leftovers from cheese-making process – much tastier than it sounds) is a 'dish' you'll find in almost every restaurant in town. The seedier-looking the place, the better the taste. Warning: it's not a delicacy, not at all good for you and highly addictive.

The dinner leg involves Montréal's famous smoked-meat sandwiches.

Ben's (☎ 514-844-1000; 990 Blvd de Maisonneuve Ouest; sandwiches $5-9) This caféteria/diner institution with the synthetically-infatuated décor of the 1950s and menu plastered on the back wall has men in white shirts and black bow ties serving stacked-high sandwiches.

Rueben's (☎ 514-866-1029; 888 Rue St Catherine Ouest; sandwiches $5-9) Walk down the steps into the dark green-and-wood interior and the cling-clang of dishes of this classic. Thin pieces of rye barely hold the greasy sandwich together and you'll have trouble getting your mouth around it, but man is it good.

Well done, triathlon complete. For a cool-down routine find a place to nap.

---

daily soups ($3) and fresh empanadas ($3) are a real treat. The ambience is the real draw here, with marine-theme walls, friendly service and an eccentric, bilingual clientele.

Mazurka (☎ 514-844-3539; 64 Rue Prince Arthur Est; mains $5-13) Four levels of din and clatter serving Polish dishes, the ultimate comfort food. Everything is good and hearty (including possibly the best borscht of your life) and the daily special ($5) makes a great lunch or smallish dinner.

Govinda Jaya Jaya (☎ 514-284-5255; 263 Rue Duluth Est; lunch/dinner $7/9) The gold-and-wood, East-meets-West décor sets up eating comfort from a selection of about a dozen vegetarian and vegan Indian buffet dishes.

Drinking

BARS

Montréal is as close to a city that never sleeps as Canada will get. Downtown (Rues Peel and Stanley) and Quartier Latin (Blvd St Laurent) are crawling with people – last call is at 3am. Places start picking up at 11pm. Expect long lines and to be checked to make sure you're cool enough.

Mirror and *Hour* free weeklies have complete listings. Check monthly *Nightlife* for hot clubs and music trends. *Fugues* is a free, partially bilingual, monthly for gays and lesbians.

McLean's Pub (☎ 514-393-3132; 1210 Rue Peel) Two-dozen taps and a healthy Scotch selection means it's drinkin' time in this typical pub with a lot of wood, a mostly Anglophone crowd and good times.

Café Campus (☎ 514-844-1010; 57 Rue Prince Arthur Est) One of the most popular student clubs is a great place mid-week with '80s hits, French rock and live bands.

Pub St Paul (☎ 514-874-0485; 124 Rue St Paul Est) This wooden pub goes against the grain and doesn't gouge you on prices. Not the cheapest place, but Old Town is fun, a $6 pint ain't bad and it's got pool tables.

Pub Ste-Élisabeth (☎ 514-286-4302; 1412 Rue Ste Élisabeth) Among the seedy strip-clubs, this little spot with a brick terrace is becoming one of the better places to chill.

LIVE MUSIC

Les Deux Pierrots (☎ 514-861-1686; 104 Rue St Paul Est; cover $5; ☿ Thu-Sat) This two-story, three-decades-old club is like being in a washing machine on spin cycle. Several thousand people go nuts for French, solo acoustic sets or '80s cover bands.

Hurley's Irish Pub (☎ 514-861-4111; 1125 Rue Crescent) Tourists are accepted as locals at the big bar or stone fireplace. Acoustic guitar and/or fiddlers play most nights and football or soccer matches are shown every night.

L'Air du Temps (☎ 514-842-2003; 191 Rue St Paul Ouest; cover after 9:30pm $5) This smoky dark place with the small wooden stage is perfect for legendary, intimate shows. Don't expect a large beer or drink menu; do expect to be blown away by great jazz.

Clubbing

Stereo (☎ 514-282-3307; 858 Rue Ste Catherine Est; ☺ Thu-Sat) Owing its popularity to wicked in-house and imported DJs, this club stays open after-hours.

Foufounes Électriques (☎ 514-844-5538; 87 Rue Ste Catherine Est) Students, alternafreaks and trendies come here to shake their 'electric buttocks.' New lights and sounds and a video screen punch the punk and hardcore into your senses while the décor is weird.

Gerts (☎ 514-398-3319; 3840 Rue McTavish) McGill's college bar pipes down in summertime, but the dance floor is still active and loud with girls/boys to meet.

Jupiter Room (☎ 514-844-9696; 3872 Rue St Laurent) With no attempt to conceal exposed plumbing or decaying walls, Jupiter brings in suits and students to drink cheap high-balls, dance to Top 40, relax and have a good time.

JinXi (☎ 514-985 5464; 410 Rue Rachel Est; ☺ Wed-Sat) This landmark of Montréal's house music scene attracts 20-somethings, with reputed DJs and overstuffed couches.

Funky Town (☎ 514-282-8387; 1454a Rue Peel) Almost a living museum, this flashing-dance-floor disco isn't cheap, but it's worth a drink or two just to see, strut and get your mojo on.

Cathédral (☎ 514-842-4721; 3781 Rue St Laurent) Weekends are a can't miss at this Gothic-looking club with a predominantly franco-phone crowd.

Entertainment

For major concerts, shows, festivals and sporting events, purchase tickets from the box office or **Admission** (☎ 514-790-1245, 800-361-4595; www.admission.com). **Ticketmaster** (☎ 514-790-1111; www.ticketmaster.ca) sells concert and theater tickets.

SPORTS

Scalpers charge more than face value, but you can snag a deal after the game starts. Try to be discreet and check the tickets before you buy.

Bell Centre (☎ 514-932-2582; www.centre-molson .com; 1260 de la Gauchetière Ouest) The most successful professional team in North America, the **Montréal Canadiens** (☎ 514-790-1245; www .canadiens.com; $22-160), have won the Stanley Cup 24 times. Watching Les Habitants ('The Habs') is an exciting event not to be missed (F the Leafs).

Molson Stadium (1255 Rue University) The **Montréal Alouettes** (☎ 514-254-2400; www.alouettes.net; $20-110; ☺ Jun-Oct) almost always bring fun times and good Canadian football games to McGill University.

The **Montréal Expos** Major League baseball team couldn't fight the inevitable and has been sold and officially moved to Washington, DC.

CLASSICAL MUSIC

The main performing arts center, **Place des Arts** (☎ 514-842-2112; www.pda.qc.ca; 175 Rue Ste Catherine Ouest), is home to **Orchestre Symphonique de Montréal** (☎ 514-842-9951) and publishes monthly *Calendrier des Spectacles*. McGill University also has impressive classical music concerts.

THEATER

Monument National Theatre (☎ 514-871-2224; 1182 Blvd St Laurent) This classic holds regular student rehearsals of mostly French dramas.

Théâtre de Quat' Sous (☎ 514-845-7277; 100 Ave des Pins Est) Intellectual and experimental drama.

Terrasses Bonsecours (www.terrassesbonsecours .com; Quai Jacques Cartier; free) Open-air films, concerts and performances *en français* (in French) from Tuesday to Saturday on summer evenings.

COMEDY CLUBS

Comedy Nest (☎ 514-932-6378; www.comedynest .com; 1740 Blvd René Lévesque; admission $3-12, student discounts; ☺ Wed-Sat) Unknown talent and always funny storytellers offer side-splitting entertainment with a dash of cabaret.

CINEMAS

National Film Board (☎ 514-496-6895; 1564 Rue St Denis; admission free-$3) Shows regular screenings for cheap, but the coolest part is **Cinérobothèque** (adult/student hr $3/2), a robot who gets your movie from one of 6000 videodiscs to use in an individual, stereo-equipped chair with personal monitor.

Getting There & Around

Of Montréal's two airports **Pierre-Elliot-Trudeau International Airport** (code: YUL), formerly Dorval, serves domestic, US and overseas flights while charters use **Mirabel International Airport** (code: YMX).

Buses use **Station Centrale de l'Autobus** (☎ 514-842-2281; 505 Rue de Maisonneuve Est) and trains use **Gare Centrale** (☎ 514-989-2626; 895 Rue de la Gauchetière Ouest). Part of the VIA Rail Québec–Windsor *Corridor*, it's also a busy hub for trains to the Maritimes and Amtrak trains to the US. Montréal is one of Allô Stop's destinations.

Around town, drivers do *Deathrace 2000* impressions so be careful when crossing the street. Montréal's public transit, **STCUM** (☎ 514-786-4636; www.stcum.qc.ca; 1-trip/6-trip/daypass/3-day $2.50/11/8/16), has an excellent and convenient bus and Métro (subway) system. Single fares require exact change on buses Ask for a transfer, which is good for 90 minutes and will get you anywhere. Save a few bucks with multi-ticket strips or daypasses.

QUÉBEC CITY

What Montréal is to hooking up, Québec City is to falling in love. Montréal's cheeky rhythm is replaced here by the pulse of deep history and the sweep of romantic vistas. The provincial capital is old, but certainly not geriatric. It has a quiet energy all seasons and there's no escaping the fact you're only a very small part of its timeline.

Orientation

Though the city is small, you're going to get lost at least eight times – the streets are 300 years old and run in all directions. Most places of interest are in the area surrounded by the can't-miss walls, perched on the cliffs of Cap Diamant above and west of the St Lawrence River. Vieux Québec (Old Town) is divided into Haute Ville (Upper Town) and Basse Ville (Lower Town). Unless you're on a cliff in front of either, La Citadelle will be south of you and the castle-style Château Frontenac will be to the east. Free maps from the tourist centers are essential.

Keep the bus station or train station to your back as you walk up steep Rue St Nicolas and even-steeper Côte du Palais to Old Town. Alternatively, bus No 800 goes to Place d'Youville; a short walk goes to the other side of the walls.

Information

Centre Infotouriste (☎ 418-649-2608; 800-363-7777; www.bonjourquebec.com; 12 Rue Ste Anne; ☺ 8:30am-7:30pm Jul & Aug, 9am-5pm Sep-Jun) Extremely busy provincial and city office.
Discovery Pavilion (☎ 418-648-4071; 835 Ave Wilfred Laurier; ☺ 9am-5:30pm) Information on historic sites.
e-club (1045 Rue St-Jean; per hr $6) Internet access.
Kiosk Frontenac (Terrasse Dufferin) Seasonal booth near Château Frontenac.
L'Hôtel Dieu de Québec (☎ 525-4444; 11 Côte de Palais) Central Hospital.

BACK-ROADS QUÉBEC

Charlevoix & Sangeunay

A drive up the north coast of the St Lawrence River and onto Lac St Jean takes you through real Francophone communities and all their idiosyncrasies, hospitalities and Maple Sugar Shacks. You might see whales, you will see stunning scenery. Return via Rte 175 through the wilderness of **Parc de la Jacques Cartier** (☎ 418-848-3169; 800-665-6527; admission $3.50) and enormous **Réserve Faunique des Laurentides** (☎ 418-848-2422; Rte 175; admission $3.50).

The Laurentians

Rte 15 from Montréal leads to **Mont Tremblant** (☎ 514-876-1445, 866-836-3030; www.tremblant.com), *the* place to ski in eastern Canada. **HI-Mont Tremblant** (☎ 819-425-3760; www.hihostels.ca/mont tremblant; 2213 Chemin du Village Mont-Tremblant; dm $22) has a shuttle from HI-Auberge de Jeunesse Montréal. The same folks who run Whistler-Blackcomb (p655) have given Tremblant more commercial appeal (bigger crowds, more expensive). On the way there, Val Morin and Val David have over a dozen local ski hills and endless kilometers of cross-country skiing. In Val David, the hardly-a-hostel, chalet-esque **Chalet Beaumont** (☎ 819-322-1972; 1451 Beaumont St; dm $20, r $43-69) has a mountain setting, a sauna and a fun pub downstairs.

Spring, summer and fall bring your mountain bike or hiking shoes.

Transchange International (☎ 418-694-6906; 43 Rue de Buade; ☻ 8am-10pm) Currency exchange.
Upper Town Postal Station (☎ 418-694-6102; 5 Rue du Fort)
Vieux-Québec Tourist Office (☎ 418-649-2608; www.quebecregion.com; 835 Ave Wilfrid Laurier; ☻ 8:30am-7:30pm summer, varies seasonally) Less-busy city office above Discovery Pavilion.

Sights

Québec City is its own attraction and museum. Those cobblestone streets and buildings all have historic and/or architectural interest. Get the *Official Tourist Guide* from the tourist office or an information center for in-depth descriptions and directions.

VIEUX QUÉBEC

The jagged and restored wall, technically the **'Fortifications of Québec,'** surrounding Old Town is a national historic site and great vantage point on the city and its history. The 4.5km circuit can be walked; feel free to play commander and make exploding noises every time you pass a cannon.

La Citadelle (☎ 418-694-2815; www.lacitadelle.qc .ca; Côte de la Citadelle; adult/student $8/7; ☻ 9am-6pm summer, varies seasonally, closed Nov-Apr) is a military stronghold inside the half-star-shaped moat/wall on a cliff above the St Lawrence. Started by the French, completed by the British and used to defend against the Americans, today it's home to Canada's Royal 22s. It's also a military-history museum with tours and the stoically impressive **Changing-of-the-Guard** (☻ 10am summer) with uniformed officers and Batisse, the goat mascot.

Château Frontenac (1 Rue des Carrières) overlooks the entire city and is said to be the world's most photographed hotel. Quebec City is full of churches, but the towering **Notre-Dame de Québec Basilica-Cathedral** (☎ 418-694-0665; 20 Rue De Buade; free; ☻ 8am-4pm) makes the rest seem lame.

Musée d'Art Inuit (☎ 418-694-1828; 39 Rue St Louis; adult/student $6/4; ☻ 9:30am-5:30pm) has one of the best collections of Inuit carvings and sculptures in the country.

Get to Lower Town using the **Escalier Casse-Cou** (Break-Neck Stairs) off steep Rue Côte de la Montagne or take the **funicular** (angled elevator; ticket $1.50) from Terrasse Dufferin. At the bottom, **Rue du Petit Champlain** is possibly the narrowest and oldest street in North America and one of the busiest. Lined with expensive shops and cafés in 17th-century buildings, it's a fun place to see a slice of tourist life and amazingly detailed murals. On the waterfront by the ferry, **Place Royale** was where Champlain first settled Québec. Four hundred years later, it's still possible to look up at the cliffs and be awestruck.

Musée de la Civilisation (☎ 418-643-2158; 85 Rue Dalhousie; adult/student $8/5; Tue free Nov–May; ☻ 9:30am-6:30pm late-Jun-Aug, 10am-5pm Tue-Sun Sep–late-Jun) traces the interlocking histories of Québec in its three fascinating permanent galleries.

OUTSIDE THE WALLS

Formerly a blood-soaked area of carnage, the appropriately named and ironically beautiful **Battlefields Park** runs southwest from the Citadelle. Green hills, colorful gardens and dramatic cliffs make it perfect for biking, strolling or picnicking. A standout fine-art gallery at the west end of the park, **Musée Nationale des Beaux-Arts du Québec** (☎ 418-643-2150, 866-220-2150; www.mnba .qc.ca; permanent collection free; ☻ 10am-6pm, to 5pm Tue-Sun Sep May, to 9pm Wed) contains excellent Québecois and international art.

West of Old Town, step into the tiny-but-decadent **Choco-Musée** (☎ 418-524-2122; 634 Rue St-Jean) to learn everything you did, and didn't, want to know about chocolate. The cemetery at **St Matthew Church** (755 Rue St-Jean), now a library, has some thought-provoking 200-year-old epitaphs.

A walk north (down Côte de Palais) from Old Town is impressive and scenic, and the **Gare du Palais** and **Palais de Justice** are worth a look. West of there is the neighborhood of **St Roch**, where you can slum with locals.

Tours

Guided walking tours offer specialized knowledge and point out things like cannonballs wedged into trees.
Ferrry to Lévis (☎ 418-644-3704; Place Royale; one-way $2.50) As good as more expensive boat tours.
La Compagnie des Six Associés (☎ 418-692-3033; www.sixassocies.com; Centre Infotouriste; tours from $12) Costumed guides walk and talk about murders, ghosts, alcohol and hookers.
Paul Gaston l'Anglais (☎ 418-529-3422; 2hr tour $15) Affable archeologist Paul gives excellent, thematically diverse walking tours.

EASTERN CANADA

Festivals & Events

Winter Carnival (www.carnaval.qc.ca; early Feb) The icy football game is only part of the fun at Québec City's most famous event. Parades, ice sculptures, music and lots of drinking all over Old Town makes up some of the rest. Don't miss the ice-slide behind Château Frontenac.

Fête Nationale du Québec (www.snqc.qc.ca; Jun 24)

Summer Festival (☎ 888-992-5200; www.infofestival .com; early–mid-Jul) Free shows, concerts, drama and dance in Old Town squares and parks.

Sleeping

Auberge Internationale de Québec (☎ 418-694-0775; www.cisq.org; 19 Rue Ste Ursule; dm $24, s/d with bathroom $60/65) Huge (over 280 beds) and friendly, the almost-too-clean dorms let you sleep well. The location is central to everything and the downstairs lounge is fun-loud.

Auberge de la Paix (☎ 418-694-0735; www.auberge delapaix.com; 31 Rue Couillard; dm with breakfast $19.50) Handmade bunks, hardwood floors and a welcoming feel make this 19th-century home an excellent hostel.

SPLURGE!

Ice Hotel (☎ 418-875-4522; 877-505-0423; www.icehotel-canada.com; 143 Rte Duchesnay, Ste Catherine de la Jacques Cartier; d from $550, tour $14) A half-hour drive west of Québec City, Canada's famously perishable Ice Hotel is available for touring or sleeping on ice. **Sherpa Plein Air** (☎ 418-640-7437, 877-640-7437; www.sherpapleinair.com; with/without tour $40/30) provides transportation.

Eating

Eating inside the walls is rarely cheap, but there are a few hidden gems. Outside, your best bets are fun **Rue St Jean** west of Old Town, or **Rue St Paul** east of the train station, which is where the huge **Old Port Market** is full of local vendors and an endless supply of maple syrup.

Most places will have a BYOW policy and sometimes 'table d'hôte' (complete meal) can be a better bargain.

Marché Richelieu (☎ 418-692-3647; 1097 Rue St Jean) For self-catering, this place is a well-stocked grocer/deli full of produce, cheeses, wine and breads from the in-house bakery.

Casse-Crêpe Breton (☎ 418-692-0438; 1136 Rue St Jean; crêpes $4-7) Sweet or savory, it's hard to beat this tiny, unassuming and lively spot for overstuffed crêpes. Expect a wait.

Kookening Kafé (☎ 418-521-2800; 565 Rue St-Jean; mains $7-12) Colorful, small, and fun, don't come here if you're in a hurry. A casual 'we'll open when we open and you'll eat when it's done' attitude only heightens the charm of personally prepared Mexican dishes.

Buffet de l'Antiquaire (☎ 418-692-2661; 95 Rue St Paul; mains $4-7) In Lower Old Town it's as real as it gets. Québec home-cooking (lots of meat) ridiculously underpriced and chaotic.

Chez Temporel (☎ 418-694-1813; 25 Rue Couillard; items $3-6) It would be easy to miss this local, favorite hole-in-the-wall if it weren't for the commotion. The coffees and pastries are damn good and it serves light lunches.

Restaurant Liban (☎ 418-694-1888; 23 Rue d'Auteuil; mains under $5) A little dingy, but a good takeout option, this hidden spot serves tasty Lebanese food.

Drinking

Rue St Jean is the happening street and Grand Allée is trendy and expensive. Check Thursday's French *Voir* for listings.

BARS

Pub St Alexandre (☎ 418-694-7075; 1087 Rue St Jean) Always packed and comfortably noisy, be prepared to make decisions like which 10 of the 200 kinds of beer or dozen scotches you're going to have.

L'Inox (☎ 418-692-2877; 38 Rue St André) A younger crowd comes here for some river-view patio-time and 4pm to 8pm happy hour ($4 pints). Learn the beer-making craft at the small museum.

LIVE MUSIC

Fou-Bar (☎ 418-522-1987; 525 Rue St Jean) This dark, sultry and small spot is perfect for almost-in-your-lap jazz or acoustic sets.

Chez son Père (☎ 418-692-5308; 24 Rue St Stanislas) This *boîtes à chanson* (house of songs) has been bringing energetic, folksy chanson-niers and hand-clapping, foot-stomping crowds together for years.

Clubbing

Chez Dagobert (☎ 418-522-0393; 600 Grand-Allée Est) The formulaic good-sound-with-excellent-light-show principle at 'Dag' works like a charm. Mostly pop-rock, some R & B and live bands.

IF YOU'VE GOT A FEW MORE DAYS IN QUÉBEC

- **Île d'Orléans** Québec City is visible from its shores, but pastoral serenity in the middle of the St Lawrence is miles from everywhere. Stay at the stone manor **Auberge le P'tit Bonheur** (☎ 418-829-2588; 183-186 Côte Lafleur; dm $19).

- **Gaspé Peninsula** Known locally as 'La Gaspésie,' the surprisingly undeveloped north coast is full of stunning scenery (chance to see whales) and dotted with small French communities. VIA Rail's *Le Chaleur* travels inland, but all routes go to touristy Gaspé and slightly less-touristy Percé on the east coast. Visit **Rocher Percé** and stay at converted red barn **La Maison Rouge** (☎ 418-782-2227; rmasse@globetrotter.net; 125 Rte 132 at Rue Biard, Percé; dm/s/d $20/40/60).

- **Îles de la Madeleine** Eastern Canada's Caribbean replaces sandy beaches with red cliffs, palms with maple trees and warm weather with…well, Eastern Canada weather but this collection is island paradise full of free-minded travelers. Get there through Souris, PEI via **CTMA** (☎ 418-986-3278, 888-9863278; www.ctma.ca; adult/bike/car $40/10/75). Stay at spacious, yet intimate and quiet **Auberge Internationale des Îles** (☎ 418-986-4505; www.hihostels.ca/ilesde lamadeleine; 74 Chemin du Camping; campsite/dm/d $15-20/28/50) on Île du Cap aux Meules.

Aviatic Club (☎ 418-522-3555; 450 Rue de la Gare du Palais) In the train station and misleadingly pretentious looking, it's uber-casual and cheaper than you'd expect.

Le Drague (☎ 418-649-7212; 815 Rue St Augustin; ◷ noon-late) Québec's small gay scene's star is a multi-faceted bar with three different rooms and vibes. Drag shows Sunday.

Shopping

The **Old Port Market** is the best spot to pick up Canadian specialties like ciders, honeys and, duh, maple syrup. **Rue de Trésor**, by Château Frontenac has some surprisingly affordable local art.

The oldest grocery store in North America (1871), **JA Moisan Épicier** (☎ 418-522-0685; 699 Rue St Jean) has nothing past its expiration date, but does have timeless appeal.

Getting There & Around

Air Canada, Jetsgo and a few others use **Jean Lesage International Airport** (code: YQB; ☎ 418-640-2700; www.aeroportdequebec.com) to connect with select Canadian and US cities.

Orléans Express and VIA Rail use the **Gare du Palais** (450 Rue de la Gare-du-Palais) or the next-door **bus station** (☎ 418-525-3000; 320 Rue Abraham Martin). It's the end of the line for Via Rail's Windsor–Québec *Corridor*; shuttles connect with **Charny** (2326 Rue de la Gare) across the river for trains to the Gaspé Peninsula and the Maritimes. Allô Stop charges $15 from Montréal.

The only transport between town and the airport is a taxi ($27).

Many **bike paths** run through and around the city; the tourist office sells a detailed map, *Greater Québec Cycling Trails*. **Cyclo Services** (☎ 418-692-4052; 160 Rue du Quai St André; hr/day $10/25) rents and leads tours.

Motorcycles are not permitted within the walls and **Réseau du Transport de la Capitale** (RTC; ☎ 418-621-1000; www.stcuq.qc.ca; 1-ride/daypass $2.50/5.45) buses you around town if you're too lame to walk.

THE MARITIMES

Welcome to the Maritimes: come for a beer, sing for the night. Well known for colorful fishing towns and craggy shoreline cliffs greeting relentless waves, the Maritimes – New Brunswick, Nova Scotia, Prince Edward Island, Newfoundland and Labrador – is also one of the friendliest and most fun parts of the continent. No matter where you are, locals will be happy to help with an empty tank or broken shoulder strap; and they'll always be more than happy to knock back a few pints with you. Throughout the Maritimes, pubs host traditional **cei-lidhs** (*kay*-lees; aka kitchen parties): gleeful Celtic music and dance not to be missed.

Acadian Coach Lines (☎ 800-567-5151; www.smt bus.com) acts as a Greyhound replacement in the Maritimes. Private shuttle buses compete with the bus companies all over the Maritimes. Check with visitors centers for those operating in your area. **Salty Bear Adventure Tours** (☎ 902-446-3866, 866-458-2327; www.saltybear.ca;

2-/4-/6-day tour $109/249/319) runs some budget-oriented tours around Nova Scotia with HI discounts. **Marine Atlantic** (☎ 800-341-7981; www.marine-atlantic.ca; adult/vehicle $27/77) runs ferries between Port aux Basques, Newfoundland and North Sydney, Nova Scotia. **Northumberland Ferries Ltd** (☎ 888-249-7245; www.nfl-bay.com) ferries between Nova Scotia and PEI, New Brunswick and Bar Harbor, ME. **Scotia Prince** (☎ 866-412-5270; www.scotiaprince.com; adult/vehicle US$85/105; mid-Apr–early Nov) travels from Portland, ME and Yarmouth, Nova Scotia.

Halifax, Moncton and St John's are busy airports.

HALIFAX

Spend a day or two in Halifax, Nova Scotia, and you can understand why some stay for a lifetime. It's more than the sea air, ever-changing weather and stunning scenery; it's the slow pace and new friends. With a long history, Halifax has a confident, strong self-image and enough good-naturedness to make you want to stay…maybe a lifetime.

Halifax Harbour makes downtown's east shore. Eight blocks west is the hill with the Citadel. Rte 102 leads right downtown. Check the helpful **visitor information center** (www.halifaxinfo.com; Downtown ☎ 902-490-5946; 1595 Barrington St; ⏱ 8:30am-8pm, to 4:30pm Mon-Fri Sep-May; Airport ☎ 902-873-1223; ⏱ 9am-9pm; Waterfront ☎ 902-424-4248; 1655 Lower Water St; ⏱ 8:30am-8pm, to 4:30 Wed-Sun Oct-May).

Sights

Among the **Historic Properties** (1869 Upper Water St) built between 1800 and 1905 is **Privateer's Warehouse** which was used to store pirate booty.

Dominant and defensive **Citadel National Historic Site** (☎ 902-426-5080; off Sackville St; adult $9, off-season discounts; ⏱ 9am-6pm) sits in its odd-angled fortress atop Halifax's central hill. The **Old Town Clock** has been keeping time for 200 years.

If you see one maritime museum on the Atlantic, see the **Maritime Museum of the Atlantic** (☎ 902-424-7490; www.museum.gov.ns.ca/mma; 1675 Lower Water St; admission $8, $4 Nov-Apr; ⏱ 9:30am-5:30pm, to 8pm Tue-Thu summer). Formerly a chandlery (ship-gear shop), you can still smell charred ropes and pump a hand-operated foghorn.

Canada's Ellis Island, **Pier 21** saw over a million immigrants between 1928 and 1971. Visit the **museum** (☎ 902-425-7770; www.pier21.ns.ca; 1055 Marginal Rd; adult/student $7.75/5.50; ⏱ 9:30am-5:30pm May-Nov).

Acadian entertainers come from as far as Louisiana for the **Grou Tyme Acadian Festival** (www.groutyme.com; late Jul).

Sleeping

Halifax Heritage House Hostel (☎ 902-422-3863; www.hihostels.ca/halifax; 1253 Barrington St; dm/r $24/57) This place has weekly pub-crawls, steep staircases and big common rooms; fun just happens.

Halifax Backpackers Hostel (☎ 902-431-3170; www.halifaxbackpackers.com; 2193 Gottingen St; dm/s/d $20/35/50) Don't be daunted by this hostel's storefront look (cool possible-Mafia reference), inside it's bright and solid.

> **SPLURGE!**
>
> **Halliburton House Inn** (☎ 902-420-0658; www.halliburton.ns.ca; 5184 Morris St; r incl breakfast $140-180) Three downtown homes have inexpensive rooms with balconies overlooking the garden patio. Indiscreet lighting and a definite gold hue put you in the lap of luxury.

Eating & Drinking

North America's oldest, **Halifax Farmers Market** (☎ 902-490-4043; 1496 Lower Water St; ⏱ 7am-1pm) is a labyrinth of maple syrup, berries, wine and cheese in Keith's Brewery Building. **Harbourside Market** (mains $9-12) in Historic Properties has open-beam woodiness and a brewpub.

Making a case for the most atmospheric pub is **Henry House** (☎ 902-423-5660; 1222 Barrington St). With enough character and grime, **Split Crow** (☎ 902-422-4366; 1855 Granville St) could be Halifax's first drinking hole. Hipsters and 'actors & writers' jam up **Economy Shoe Shop** (☎ 902-423-8845; 1663 Argyle St) on weekends.

Entertainment

When Nirvana's label signed local-band Sloan in the mid-1990s, Halifax became 'New Seattle' and everyone wore flannel, yet maritime-folk lives on. **Marquee** (☎ 902-429-3020; 2037 Gottingen St; cover $6-25) is raucously used by touring bands and big-name locals; lesser-knowns start downstairs in **Hell's Kitchen**. 'Liquordome,' err, the **Dome** (☎ 902-422-5453;

IF YOU'VE GOT A FEW EXTRA DAYS IN THE MARITIMES

New Brunswick

■ **Moncton** A name that's fun to say and a couple of natural oddities. **Magnetic Hill** (☎ 506-858-8841; Mountain Rd; vehicle $5, free after-hr; ☼ 8am-8pm mid-May–mid-Sep) defies the laws of everything as vehicles line up to be 'pulled' uphill, seriously. It's hit-or-miss between anti-climactic and spectacular when **Tidal Bore Park** (east end of Main St) looks onto tidal waves ranging from a few centimeters to 1m.

■ **Saint John** Stunning when sunny, atmospheric when foggy, always spell out in full and *never* call it St John's ('that city in Newfoundland'). Spawning international ignorance as the country's only beer **Moosehead Brewery** (☎ 506-635-7020; 49 Main St W; ☼ 9am-5pm Mon-Wed, 9am-9pm Thu & Fri, 10am-5pm Sat) sometimes has tours. Tides cause 'upstream' rapids at **Reversing Falls**.

Nova Scotia

■ **Kejimkujik National Park** Inland park contains pristine backcountry ideal for multi-day trips, particularly by canoe.

■ **Peggy's Cove** The little fishing town 30km west of Halifax is so Maritime. Come before 10am (sunrise is even better), take a roll's-worth of pictures and leave before the masses.

Prince Edward Island

■ **Prince Edward Island National Park** Heaving dunes and dramatic red-sandstone bluffs provide startling backdrops for some of the island's finest stretches of sand.

■ **Cavendish** Home of Canada's most famously fictional sweetheart, Anne Shirley, who blew apart the boys-are-better-than-girls myth in Lucy Maud Montgomery's *Anne of Green Gables*.

■ **Souris** Named after furious French screaming at crop-ravaging mice, they come all the way from Nashville for **PEI Bluegrass & Oldtime Music Festival** (☎ 902 569 3153; www.bluegrasspei .com; early Jul).

Newfoundland & Labrador

■ **L'Anse aux Meadows National Historic Site** 1000-year-old remains of Scandinavia and Greenland **Viking settlement** (☎ 709-623-2608; Rte 436; adult/child under 17/family $7/5.50/17.50; ☼ 9am-5pm Jun–mid-Oct, to 8pm mid-Jun–early Sep).

1740 Argyle St) has a live-music venue (the Attic) and three nightclubs. Shake it.

Excited crowds love the **Halifax Mooseheads** (www.halifaxmooseheads.ca; adult/student $13.50/9) junior hockey games at **Halifax Metro Centre** (☎ 902-451-1221; 5284 Duke St).

Getting There & Around

Halifax International Airport (code: YHZ; ☎ 902-873-4422; www.hiaa.ca) is 39km northeast of town. **Airbus** (☎ 902-873-2091; one-way/return $12/20) travels to/from the airport and major hotels. **Scotia Shuttle** (☎ 902-435-9686, 800-898-5883), **Reliable Shuttle** (☎ 902-435-3434, 800-435-3434) and **Inverness Shuttle Service** (☎ 902-945-2000, 888-826-2477) travel to Cape Breton. Acadian Lines and VIA Rail stop downtown.

Metro Transit (☎ 902-490-6600; 1-ride/20 tickets $1.75/$30) runs the city bus system.

CAPE BRETON HIGHLANDS NATIONAL PARK

Technically an island, but tell folks you're going to Cape Breton Island and you'll sound like a tourist. This is quintessential Atlantic Canada: waves pounding on rugged coasts; colorful fishing villages; pint-clinking, beer-spilling, folk-playing pubs. Come for a couple of days walking back roads or come for an evening, just come.

Despite all the coastal scenery around the Maritimes, nothing can quite prepare you for Canada's dramatic **Cape Breton Highlands National Park** (adult/group $5/12.50). Granite pillars and cliffs stubbornly brave the sea, and mountains rise to a boreal plateau before dropping back on the opposite coast. The **information centers** (☺ 9am-5pm mid-May–mid-Oct, 8am-8pm summer; Chéticamp ☎ 902-224-2306; 16646 Cabot Trail; Ingonish ☎ 902-285-2535; 37677 Cabot Trail) at the park's southern boundary have maps and advice.

Activities

A one-stop shop, **Sea Spray Outdoor Adventures** (☎ 902-383-2732; www.cabot-trail-outdoors.com; 1141 White Point Rd, Dingwall; bike half-/full-day $25/35; ☺ 9am-5pm Jun–mid-Oct) rents bikes (and replaces break-downs), plans hikes, teaches kayaking, and leads cross-country and backcountry downhill ski-trips.

HIKING

Two-dozen gorgeous trails concentrated along the coasts range from wheelchair-accessible paths to do-I-*look*-like-Spiderman climbs.

Skyline (8.7km roundtrip; 100m gain; 2-3hr) Awesome views of west coast atop French Mountain.

Coastal (11km roundtrip; 30m gain; 3-4hr) Feel sea-mist and hear sea-sounds along beaches and cliffs.

Fishing Cove (16km roundtrip; 330m descent; 10-12hr; backcountry campsite $18) Mind-blowing hike to back-country campsite at mouth of rugged Fishing Cove. Can be done in a very long day or take steeper and shorter hike (6km roundtrip) from a second trailhead about 5km north.

CYCLING

The park is a popular cycling destination, but not for rookies: dicey roads shared with large RVs and lots of hills. Of the four inland mountain biking trails, only **Branch Pond Lookoff Trail** offers ocean views.

SKIING

Groomed **ski trails** (adult daypass $5) take you on the same summertime hikes and lead to off-trail downhill. There are campsites

($10) along the trail and shelters at **Black Brook** ($20) and **Mary Ann Falls** ($30).

WHALE-WATCHING

Captain Mark's Whale & Seal Cruise (☎ 902-224-1316, 888-754-5112; www.whaleandsealcruise.com; Pleasant Bay; adult $25; ☺ mid-May–Sep) guarantees whale-sightings.

Sleeping

Six drive-in, first-come-first-served **campgrounds** (serviced/unserviced $21/27) have services in summer, but can still be used off-season ($17). **Chéticamp** (162 campsites; east coast) and **Broad Cove** (256 campsites; west coast) are the busiest; **Corney Brook** (20 campsites; east coast) is the most stunning.

In nearby Pleasant Bay, **Cabot Trail Hostel** (☎ 902-224-1976; www.cabottrail.com/hostel; 23349 Cabot Trail; dm $24) provides a perfect base for exploring.

ST JOHN'S

As honestly good-natured as they come St John's (Britain's first overseas colony and North America's oldest city) has never tried to be anything but a fishing village.

The streets in St John's can be confusing, but most lead to water. The end of the Trans Canada is 'Mile 0'. **City Tourist Office** (☎ 709-576-8106; www.stjohns.ca; 348 Water St; ☺ 9am-4:30pm, Mon-Fri Sep–mid-Jun) is downtown. Parks Canada has multi-site passes for St John's (daypass adult/group $5.50/14) and Newfoundland (7-days, adult/group $26/65) sites.

You can't miss it, so head east to **Signal Hill National Historic Site**, site of the last North American Seven Years' War battle. The glorious view (maybe see icebergs) is worth the trip alone, playing with cannons at **Queen's Battery & Barracks** is a bonus. There's a 1.7km trail to **Cabot Tower**, where Guglielmo Marconi received the first wireless transatlantic message in 1901. The interior of the **Anglican**

SCREECH

Immediately upon entering a bar, you'll be asked: 'Is You a Screecher?' Nod confidently and order a pint. Do otherwise, show even the slightest bit of inquiry, and a full shot glass, or worse, rocks glass will be forced into your hand. It's too late for you now, you must drink, or rather: you must swallow. Loosely described as homemade rum, 'drinking' Screech is similar to 'accepting' a live grenade. What you're about to down makes moonshine taste like 30-year-old scotch.

A good-humored initiation to visitors, that 20-grit-sandpaper-feeling in your throat can be shared with folks back home: Screech is sold in liquor stores.

Cathedral of St John the Baptist (☎ 709-726-5677; 22 Church St) burnt in the Great Fire of 1892 and was rebuilt around the stone skeleton in 1905.

About 15km southeast, **Cape Spear National Historical Site** (☎ 709-772-5367; Blackhead Rd; adult/group $3.50/8.75, free mid-Oct–mid-May) has WWII stuff and spectacular cliffs of 'The Most Easterly Point in North America.'

Sagging **Downtown Hostel** (☎ 709-754-7658; downtownhostel@yahoo.com; 25 Young St; dm $23) is so charismatic and fun you won't notice the crooked homemade furniture and steeply plunging floors.

It's a fish and chips town, but culinary diversions have blasphemously been creeping into St John's. If you're a purist, **Ches's** (☎ 709-726-2373; 5-9 Freshwater Rd; fish & chips $5-8) or **Chucky's Fish N'Ships** (☎ 709-579-7888; 10 King's Rd; mains $5-11) are the spots.

Pluck out any watering hole along George St: energetic **O' Reilly's** (☎ 709-722-4853; 15 George St) and screeching **Christian's Pub** (☎ 709-753-9100; 23 George St) are excellent starting points. Past Signal Hill, **Quidi Vidi Brewing** (☎ 709-738-4040; 15 Barrows Rd; tour & tasting $6; ☽ noon-4pm Mon-Fri) offers tours and lovely iceberg-water beer.

Mile One Stadium (☎ 709-576-7657; 50 New Gower St) Despite Toronto affiliation, St John's fills the stands to see their **Maple Leafs** (www.sj mapleleafs.ca; tickets $18.50-20.50), minor-league team to the NHL franchise.

Flights might be cheaper than Toronto or Montréal between Europe and **St John's International Airport** (code: YYT; www.stjohnsairport .com). It's 6km north and **Dave Gulliver Cabs** (☎ 709-722-0003; $17.50-20) goes to town. DRL stops here and various shore taxis radiate to parts of Newfoundland.

Washington, DC & the Capital Region

HIGHLIGHTS

- **Adams-Morgan, Shaw & U Street** Enjoy flavor-packed food from Africa or Latin America at outdoor cafés, then head to the myriad bars and clubs (p220)
- **Museum hopping around the National Mall** Whatever your fancy, DC has a museum for it, and, best off all, most are free. Don't miss the International Spy Museum (p222)
- **Southern West Virginia** Raft the wild and wonderful New and Gauley Rivers (p248)
- **Atlantic Coast beaches** From the beaches of Ocean City, MD (p242), Virginia Beach, VA (p233), and Dewey Beach, DE (p246), to the gay scene at Rehoboth Beach, DE (p245)
- **Off the beaten track** Get lost in remote southwestern Virginia. In the Shenandoah Valley Region life moves slower and bluegrass music fills the air (p234)
- **Best journey** Drive the Blue Ridge Parkway though the southern Appalachian mountains in fall, when the trees put on an out-of-this-world beautiful display (p235)

FAST FACTS

- **Area** 121,242 sq miles
- **Big cities** Washington, DC (population 565,000), Baltimore (651,154), Richmond (207,000)
- **Budget** $40-60 per day
- **Costs** hostel bed $16, DC–Baltimore train ticket $5.75, most DC museums free!
- **Driving times** DC to New York City 5 hours, Richmond to DC 2 hours, DC to Ocean City 3 hours
- **Famous for** politics, the White House, Smithsonian Institute, beach towns
- **Languages** English
- **Population** 16,291,900
- **Phrases** Who'd you vote for in the last election? Do you work on the Hill?
- **Seasons** high Memorial Day (mid-May) to Labor Day (mid-Aug)
- **States** Washington, DC, Virginia, Maryland, Delaware, West Virginia

- **Tasty treats** crab cakes, Ethiopian food, international fare from all over the globe
- **Time** GMT minus 5 hours
- **Top hostel** Washington International Student Center (p224)

TRAVEL HINTS

Beware of post–September 11 security changes in DC. Walking into many national buildings is a no-no. Museums may periodically shut if the nation's terrorist threat level increases.

If you picture the Capital Region as a giant artichoke, Washington, DC would surely be the heart. But even though the nation's capital yields the greatest chunk of meat, the rest of the region still packs in plenty of flavor.

A world-class cosmopolitan city, DC is home to national symbols like the White House and the Capitol. It's filled with vibrant neighborhoods where the air is thick with exotic smells and thumping with reggae music. But like the political parties that shape it, DC is a city with two faces. Dig beneath the shiny marble surface and you'll find a grittier side – boarded-up buildings, graffiti-filled walls, poor people. Experiencing this face, however, is imperative to understanding the dynamics shaping the city and the country as a whole.

Beyond DC, limitless adventures await. Blue collar Baltimore offers boundless partying, the Chesapeake Bay cherished maritime heritage explorations. Swim the warm Atlantic, watch wild ponies frolic on sandy white dunes, eat fistfuls of famous Maryland blue crabs. Virginia's Blue Ridge Mountains offer hikes through lush, green forests and over rolling, blue hills, while West Virginia's Appalachia just might yield that little bit of heaven John Denver sings about.

HISTORY

Early European settlements in the Capital Region were variously assisted and resisted by Native Americans. While the tale of how a chieftain's daughter named Pocahontas saved the life of English captain John Smith is now a treasured American legend, the bulk of the region's Native American history is far less romantic. Inhabitants of many European and Native American settlements engaged in 'Indian Wars,' though European-borne diseases proved far more devastating than warfare, wiping out whole tribes. Today, only a handful of Native American communities remain on isolated reservations in Virginia.

In 1624 the British founded the royal colony of Virginia, in honor of the 'Virgin Queen' Elizabeth, liberally claiming all territory in a strip from the Atlantic Coast to the west. The English soon absorbed Dutch and Swedish settlements on the Delaware coast, established in 1631 and 1638, respectively. In 1634 a royal grant enabled Lord Baltimore to establish an independent Catholic colony, which he named 'Maryland.' To resolve early territorial disputes among Maryland, Delaware and Pennsylvania, a pair of English astronomers mapped out their namesake 'Mason-Dixon line,' which later represented the boundary between the industrial North and the slaveholding South.

During the Revolutionary War, the region saw both the initial defeat of the Continental Army at the Battle of Brandywine Creek (1777) and the final surrender of the British at Yorktown (1781). Virginians were influential in the 1787 Constitutional Convention, and four of the new republic's first five presidents came from that state.

The site of Washington was selected as a convenient point between Northern and Southern states after a post–Revolutionary War compromise. The new capital's position proved strategic during the Civil War. While Maryland and Delaware were technically 'slave states,' they chose to remain in the Union. Virginia seceded and established the capital of the Confederacy in Richmond. The mountainous western part of Virginia was admitted to the Union as a separate state, West Virginia, in 1863 to grant Lincoln the votes needed to advance Emancipation.

After the Civil War, the coastal urban corridor became increasingly developed. The mountain regions, particularly West Virginia, remain much less developed; boom-to-bust coal production peaked here in the early 20th century.

THE BIG ISSUE: DC STATEHOOD

Washingtonians will talk your ear off about taxation without representation and the unfairness of it all. Basically, the city is within the federal enclave of the District of Columbia, and, as a federal protectorate, DC has a political life more closely resembling a colony than a state. The municipal government must operate under the imposing oversight of the federal government. In fact, District residents only won the right to vote in presidential elections in 1961. And DC's hard-fought struggle for congressional representation has so far earned it only nonvoting representatives.

WASHINGTON, DC & THE CAPITAL REGION

Today the area is still growing professionally and economically, despite the slumping economy (particularly tourism) and the impact that September 11, 2001, had on the DC area.

THE CULTURE

A patriotic renaissance in this region followed the September 11, 2001 terrorist attacks. American flags flew in suburban yards and showed up on bumper stickers and car windows. Although the region has always been patriotic – DC is the birthplace of democracy, Maryland is the home of the Star-Spangled Banner, Virginia has churned out many US presidents – the events of September 11, 2001 saw a rekindling of an 'I'm proud to be an American' mentality that was deeper than party lines.

Washington is a company town, the company being the federal government. About a third of DC workers are employed by the government, in either federal or city bureaucracies. African-Americans represent about 60% of the city's population, one of the highest percentages of blacks in the country.' Other ethnic groups include growing numbers of Asians (2.7%) and Hispanics (7.9%). Despite this diverse population, DC is one of the most segregated cities in the county, the 31% of the population that is white lives almost exclusively in Northwest DC. Violent crime between ethnic groups in DC has always been a problem in fact until 2002 DC claimed the dubious distinction of 'murder capital,' with more murders per capita than any other city in the nation. Many of these deaths are attributed to ethnic gang warfare.

The city's economic boundaries are as sharp as its racial ones. About 20% of the population falls below the poverty line, and most of this segment is black. This percentage is eight points above the national average, which – in a city with the second-highest per capita income in the country – demonstrates a disturbing economic disparity.

Beyond DC, life moves at a slower pace. The rural mountainous areas of Virginia and West Virginia are quite poor and often shunned by city folks – some going as far as to call inhabitants of Appalachia 'hicks' and 'inbreeds.' Travel to these areas, however, and despite pockets of abject poverty you'll find friendly, intelligent folks trying to get by as best they can. The southern portion of Virginia still identifies itself with the 'Old South,' and here you may be confronted with Confederate flags on trucks and derogatory racial slurs sliding easily off white tongues.

SPORTS & RECREATION

Washington, DC and Baltimore, MD are the regions sports' cities. In DC fall means football season and the celebrated Washington Redskins. The 'Skins of late have been trying to recapture their glory days of the 1980s, when they won two Super Bowls. But they still inspire face-painting, beer-guzzling fans and sell out every game.

Baltimore's had a little better luck. In 2000 its football team, the Baltimore Ravens, won the Super Bowl. The city is also home to the Baltimore Orioles, a major-league baseball team.

Back in DC, the city's National Basketball Association (NBA) team, the Washington Wizards, generated a lot of publicity when Michael Jordan bought into the team's ownership and came out of retirement to play. He could not reverse the Wizard's fortunes, however, and left DC under bad circumstances in 2003.

The Washington Capitals – dubbed the 'Caps' – are the National Hockey League (NHL) team.

ARTS & ENTERTAINMENT

Washington is the showcase of American arts, home to such prestigious venues as the National Gallery and the Kennedy Center. The National Symphony Orchestra and the National Theatre embody everything their titles imply: top-notch music and theater. Likewise, Washington's architecture and city design is the product of founding fathers and city planners who intended to construct a capital city befitting a powerful nation. The result is that Washington's arts scene – where it is most visible and most acclaimed – is national rather than local in scope.

Often overlooked, however, is another arts scene – a scene representative of DC but not necessarily of the USA. It is edgier, blacker, more organic and more experimental. It is colored by the experiences of the city's African-American and immigrant populations, lending diversity and ethnicity. It dances around the edges of the more conservative national scene and discreetly tests its boundaries. Loads of smaller art galleries and community theaters around the city are the backbone of this vibrant scene.

Outside the metropolitan region, art and music play an important role in local lifestyles. Southern Virginia produces acclaimed bluegrass music, while strumming a dulcimer (a skinny wooden string instrument plucked in a similar manner to a guitar) is popular in the rural areas of Virginia and West Virginia. Both Maryland and Delaware host numerous museums filled with work by local and nationally recognized artists.

ENVIRONMENT

The region's coastal areas include a low, flat, 100-mile-wide coastal plain as well as the 'Delmarva' (Delaware–Maryland–Virginia) Peninsula between Chesapeake and Delaware Bays. Chesapeake Bay is an estuary, where some 48 navigable rivers join the sea in a geographically and culturally distinct region called the 'Tidewater.'

Further inland, the undulating Piedmont Plateau holds the region's farmlands and many of its cities and towns. The Appalachian range, which forms a barrier to the northwest, has a number of subsidiary ranges, including the Allegheny Mountains and Blue Ridge Mountains. The fabled Shenandoah Valley lies between them. On the west side of the Alleghenies, the principal rivers of heavily forested West Virginia drain inland to the Ohio River system.

Many large mammals have disappeared, but black bears and white-tailed deer are still common. The coastal and tidewater areas are great for bird-watching. Migratory and wintering waterfowl include snow geese, tundra swans, mallards, killdeers, sandpipers and ospreys. Raptors include golden eagles and American bald eagles. Environmental concerns in the region focus on the Chesapeake Bay watershed, and many Maryland residents sport special Chesapeake Bay license plates, where a proportion of the fee paid for the plate goes to preserving the bay. As North America's largest estuary, the bay is home to more than 3600 species of plant and animal, and more than 16 million people. Pollution, chemical contamination and overfishing led to

the death of many native species. Today the Chesapeake Bay is still trying to replenish once-abundant seafood and other marine life and clean up its waters, but the future is looking brighter. The US government and voluntary organizations are working together to preserve this fragile ecosystem.

The region has numerous state parks and recreation areas, as well as two national parks: Great Falls National Park/ C&O Canal National Park, just outside of Washington, DC in Virginia and Maryland; and Shenandoah National Park, about 70 miles west of DC in Virginia. Portions of the Appalachian Trail run through Maryland, Virginia and West Virginia.

TRANSPORTATION

Washington, DC is the main entry point into the region by air. Three major airports service the metropolitan area:

Baltimore-Washington International Airport (BWI; ☎ 410-859-7111) Thirty-five miles north of Washington, DC and 10 miles south of Baltimore.

Ronald Reagan National Airport (DCA; ☎ 703-417-8000) Washington, DC.

Washington Dulles International Airport (IAD; ☎ 703-572-2700) Twenty-six miles west of Washington.

Buses are the budget alternative for reaching many smaller cities not served by air or rail (though travelers should check car rental rates and packages to compare costs). Nearly every city has a **Greyhound** (www.greyhound.com) bus station or stop. **Trailways** (www.trailways.com) is another bus line that often uses the same terminals. See individual city sections for more on local and regional bus transit.

Amtrak (www.amtrak.com for fares & schedules) and the regional **MARC** (www.mtamaryland.com) system provide rail transit to Washington, DC and other regional destinations.

You'll need a car for extensive exploring outside major cities. For more information on Transportation in the USA, see p707.

Washington, DC is ringed by I-495, also known as the Beltway. I-95 is the north-south vein throughout the region and branches off from the Beltway. To travel to the beaches you'll take US 50 east. Other major highways heading west from DC into Virginia and West Virginia are Hwys 66, 81 and 64.

WASHINGTON, DC

In the nation's capital, it's all about the party. And we're not just talking along partisan lines – DC is a city that knows how to play. Young, vibrant and cosmopolitan, there's an exotic sauciness in the air here, especially in summer when temperatures soar and college interns filter in for a taste of power. Work hard, play hard seems to be the motto of the young and restless. And when the sun sinks low over the Potomac, seemingly straight-laced Congressional aids, lobbyists and lawyers trade Capitol Hill deal brokering for dingy bars and happy-hour martinis (although the talk at the table can stay political well into the night), then shift into overdrive at one of DC's many nightclubs.

Whether you're into watching a history-making session of Congress, reliving the past at a world-famous museum or drowning the present in a foaming pitcher of beer, America's capital is sure to serve an interactive lesson in American history for dinner, with a hearty slice of American life for dessert.

HISTORY

Various capitals were considered for the fledgling US republic before Congress decided upon the site across the river from George Washington's home at Mt Vernon. People started calling it 'the city of Washington,' and the name stuck.

The brand-new Capitol was torched in the War of 1812. Washington was eventually rebuilt and its ailing infrastructure was overhauled in the 1870s. A late-19th-century beautification plan contributed landscaping, parks and monuments, but as late as the 1960s John F Kennedy derided it as 'a city of Southern efficiency and Northern charm.' However, DC gained hope in the '60s when reporters started calling John and Jackie Kennedy's home Camelot.

New corporate commitment to the downtown area has created a spectacular sports arena, the MCI Center and a giant conference center, which is engendering urban renewal. Crime is at a 25-year low. New restaurants, clubs and boutique hotels are bursting forth all over the city. Meanwhile, a number of once-segregated neighborhoods such as Capitol Hill, Shaw, Adams-Morgan and U St are becoming more racially diverse, making the optimism surrounding such renewal very palpable.

ORIENTATION

Originally carved as a diamond from neighboring Virginia and Maryland, Washington, DC is bounded by the Potomac River on one side and by Maryland on all others. It lost its original shape by retroceding land to Virginia in 1837, and today's city measures 69 sq miles. It's ringed by a freeway (I-495/95) called the Beltway, which separates urban insiders from suburbanites.

From the Capitol, the city is divided into four quadrants – northwest, northeast, southeast and southwest – along axes that follow N Capitol St, E Capitol St, S Capitol St and the National Mall. Identical addresses appear in each quadrant. Most visitor attractions are in the northwest quadrant.

North–south streets are referred to by numbers, while east–west streets are ordered alphabetically (with no B, J, X, Y or

---

GETTING INTO TOWN

Three major airports, Reagan National, Washington Dulles and Baltimore-Washington International (BWI) Airport, serve DC. Metrobus No 5A ($2, hourly) leaves from the Washington Dulles car-hire area to central DC (L'Enfant Plaza). There's not much space for luggage, however.

From Reagan National, you can hop onto the Metro, which will take you into the city. From BWI, take an Amtrak or regional MARC commuter train ($9) to Union Station. There's a free shuttle between the airport and the rail station.

If you arrive by bus you'll be dropped at 1005 1st St NE. The neighborhood is rather rough, so it may be worth taking a cab eight blocks to Union Station, where you can catch the Metro.

For door-to-door van service between all three airports and downtown DC, try **SuperShuttle** (☎ 800-258-3826). Fares are $10 to Reagan National, $22 to Washington Dulles and $28 to BWI (return fares vary according to destination).

INFORMATION

American Express	1 C3
Chamber of Commerce Visitors Center	2 D4
CyberStop Café	3 C2
George Washington University Hospital	4 B4
Kramerbooks	5 B2
Lambda Rising	6 B2
Main Post Office	7 G2
Thomas Cook	8 C3
Washington Hospital Center	9 E1
White House Visitors Center	10 C4

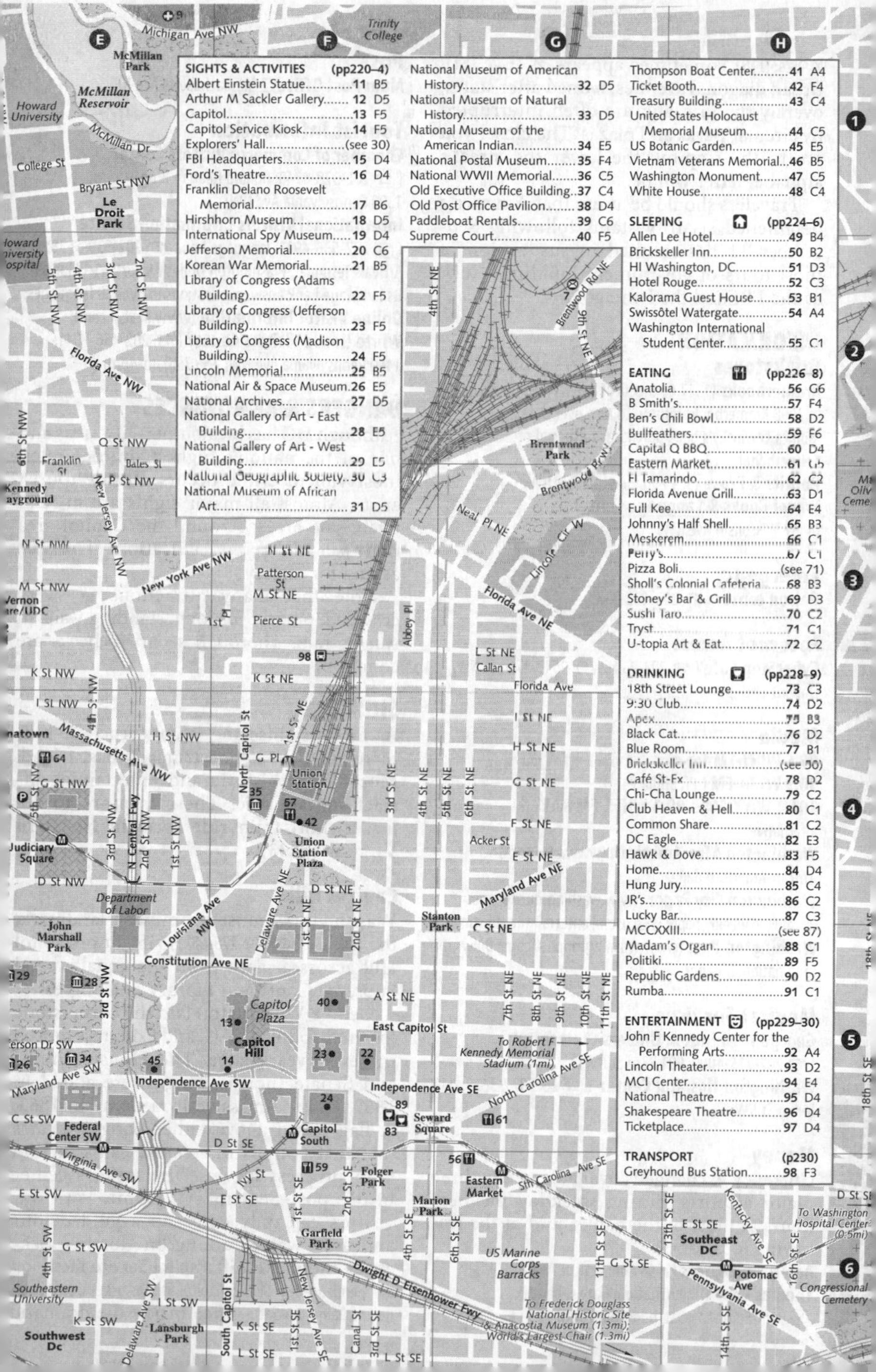

0 ——— 500 m
0 ——— 0.3 miles

SIGHTS & ACTIVITIES (pp220–4)

Albert Einstein Statue	**11** B5
Arthur M Sackler Gallery	**12** D5
Capitol	**13** F5
Capitol Service Kiosk	**14** F5
Explorers' Hall	(see 30)
FBI Headquarters	**15** D4
Ford's Theatre	**16** D4
Franklin Delano Roosevelt Memorial	**17** B6
Hirshhorn Museum	**18** D5
International Spy Museum	**19** D4
Jefferson Memorial	**20** C6
Korean War Memorial	**21** B5
Library of Congress (Adams Building)	**22** F5
Library of Congress (Jefferson Building)	**23** F5
Library of Congress (Madison Building)	**24** F5
Lincoln Memorial	**25** B5
National Air & Space Museum	**26** E5
National Archives	**27** D5
National Gallery of Art - East Building	**28** E5
National Gallery of Art - West Building	**29** E5
National Geographic Society	**30** C3
National Museum of African Art	**31** D5
National Museum of American History	**32** D5
National Museum of Natural History	**33** D5
National Museum of the American Indian	**34** E5
National Postal Museum	**35** F4
National WWII Memorial	**36** C5
Old Executive Office Building	**37** C4
Old Post Office Pavilion	**38** D4
Paddleboat Rentals	**39** C6
Supreme Court	**40** F5
Thompson Boat Center	**41** A4
Ticket Booth	**42** F4
Treasury Building	**43** C4
United States Holocaust Memorial Museum	**44** C5
US Botanic Garden	**45** E5
Vietnam Veterans Memorial	**46** B5
Washington Monument	**47** C5
White House	**48** C4

SLEEPING 🏠 (pp224–6)

Allen Lee Hotel	**49** B4
Brickskeller Inn	**50** B2
HI Washington, DC	**51** D3
Hotel Rouge	**52** C2
Kalorama Guest House	**53** B1
Swissôtel Watergate	**54** A4
Washington International Student Center	**55** C1

EATING 🍴 (pp226–8)

Anatolia	**56** G6
B Smith's	**57** F4
Ben's Chili Bowl	**58** D2
Bullfeathers	**59** F6
Capital Q BBQ	**60** D4
Eastern Market	**61** G6
H Tamarindo	**62** C2
Florida Avenue Grill	**63** D1
Full Kee	**64** E4
Johnny's Half Shell	**65** B3
Meskerem	**66** C1
Perry's	**67** C1
Pizza Boli	(see 71)
Sholl's Colonial Cafeteria	**68** B3
Stoney's Bar & Grill	**69** D3
Sushi Taro	**70** C2
Tryst	**71** C1
U-topia Art & Eat	**72** C2

DRINKING 🍸 (pp228–9)

18th Street Lounge	**73** C3
9:30 Club	**74** D2
Apex	**75** B3
Black Cat	**76** D2
Blue Room	**77** B1
Brickskeller Inn	(see 50)
Café St-Ex	**78** D2
Chi-Cha Lounge	**79** C2
Club Heaven & Hell	**80** C1
Common Share	**81** C2
DC Eagle	**82** E3
Hawk & Dove	**83** F5
Home	**84** D4
Hung Jury	**85** C4
JR's	**86** C2
Lucky Bar	**87** C3
MCCXXIII	(see 87)
Madam's Organ	**88** C1
Politiki	**89** F5
Republic Gardens	**90** D2
Rumba	**91** C1

ENTERTAINMENT 🎭 (pp229–30)

John F Kennedy Center for the Performing Arts	**92** A4
Lincoln Theater	**93** D2
MCI Center	**94** E4
National Theatre	**95** D4
Shakespeare Theatre	**96** D4
Ticketplace	**97** D4

TRANSPORT (p230)

Greyhound Bus Station	**98** F3

Z Sts; I St sometimes appears as 'Eye' St). Broad diagonal avenues, named after states, overlay the grid and are often interrupted by circular parks and plazas. The closer you are to the Capitol, the lower the street's alphabet letter will be.

Travelers should be aware that America's heightened security status following September 11 has resulted in suspension of most tours of government buildings, such as the FBI and the Pentagon.

INFORMATION
Bookstores
Kramerbooks (1517 Connecticut Ave NW, Dupont Circle) In 1998 Kramerbooks refused to turn over details of Monica Lewinsky's book purchases to special prosecutor Kenneth Starr.
Politics & Prose (5015 Connecticut Ave NW)
Travel Books & Language Center (4437 Wisconsin Ave NW)

Emergency
Poison center (☎ 202-625-3333)

Internet Access
CyberStop Cafe (☎ 202-234-2470; 1513 17th St NW, Dupont Circle)

Media
99.5 WIHT-FM Top 40.
90.9 WETA-FM NPR affiliate.
101.1 WIYY-FM & 99.1 WHFS-FM Rock and alternative.
Washington Afro-American (www.afro.com) African-American daily.
Washington City Paper (www.washingtoncitypaper .com) Free weekly paper with useful entertainment listings.
Washington Post (www.washingtonpost.com) Daily city (and national) paper.

Medical Services
George Washington University Hospital (☎ 202-715-4000; 901 23rd St NW)
Washington Hospital Center (☎ 202-877-3627; 110 Irving St NW)

Money
Currency exchange is available at the three major airports, during weekday business hours at most of the banks, and at the following locations:
American Express (1150 Connecticut Ave NW)
Thomas Cook (Union Station, Gate G booth; ☾ 9am-5pm Mon-Sat, noon-6pm Sun)

Post
Main Post Office (2 Massachusetts Ave NE)

Tourist Information
Chamber of Commerce Visitors Center (☎ 202-328-4748; Ronald Reagan Bldg, 1300 Pennsylvania Ave NW)
International Visitors Information Service (☎ 202-536-4911, language bank ☎ 202-939-5538; Arrivals Terminal, Washington Dulles Airport; ☾ Mon-Fri) Its language bank answers questions in over 50 languages.
Online Visitor Information (www.dcvisit.com)
White House Visitors Center (☎ 202-456-7041; 1450 Pennsylvania Ave NW; ☾ 7:30am-4pm)

DANGERS & ANNOYANCES
Although DC has bleak inner-city areas and one of the nation's highest murder rates, most violent crime occurs outside tourist areas. Almost all major sights are in relatively safe areas. Around the Capitol area there's a higher concentration of people asking for money.

Note that many attractions get very crowded; prepare for long, standing waits in sun or rain. Thorough security checks are common.

SIGHTS
As far as sightseeing is concerned, Washington, DC is a shoestringer's best friend. Most of the historic and entertaining attractions are free. There is more to see just a short train ride away in Northern Virginia (p233).

Capitol Hill
Washington's most prominent landmark, the **Capitol** (☎ 202-225-6827) sits atop Capitol Hill across a plaza from the equally regal Supreme Court and Library of Congress.

George Washington laid the cornerstone for the Capitol in 1793, and Congress moved in seven years later. The House (south) and Senate (north) wings were added in 1857, and the massive iron dome in 1863. A flag raised above either wing indicates that that body is in session. Construction is in progress on a secure visitors center in this post–September 11 time. For now, visitors can only enter on a guided tour and must wait in a long line for free tickets at the makeshift **Capitol Service Kiosk** (cnr Independence Ave SE & S Capitol St SW; ticket distribution begins 9am Mon-Sat). Once inside the dramatic central **Rotunda**, note the Constantino Brumidi fresco inside the dome and the hallway murals and ceilings.

Housed in an imposing 1935 marble building is the **Supreme Court**, the highest court in the land. Visitors can watch oral arguments (Monday to Wednesday from October to April) and bench sittings (Monday, mid-May to June). Arrive early to get in line.

Just north of the Capitol is Washington's most impressive gateway, **Union Station** (☎ 202-371-9441; cnr Massachusetts Ave & 1st St NE). A massive, beautifully restored 1908 beaux arts building, its great hall was modeled on the Roman baths of Diocletian. It hosts Amtrak, Metro and commuter rail stations, as well as shops, restaurants and cinemas.

The revamped **US Botanic Garden** (☎ 202-225-8333; 245 First St; admission free; ☉ 10am-5pm), filled with more than 26,000 plants, is also worth a wander.

National Mall

This 400ft-wide green expanse stretching from the Potomac River to Capitol Hill is home to DC's most famous monuments and museums. It's also renowned for mass gatherings designed to influence public policy, such as anti-Vietnam War protests in the 1960s and Martin Luther King Junior's 'I Have a Dream' speech.

SMITHSONIAN INSTITUTION

In 1826 Englishman James Smithsonian, without ever visiting the United States, willed $4,100,000 to the country to found an 'establishment for the increase and diffusion of knowledge.' Today's Smithsonian Institution has a collection so large that only 1% is on display at any given point. Admission to museums is free; all are open from 10:30am to 5pm and closed on December 25. Dial ☎ 202-633-1000 for information about the museums listed below (just a sampling, there are many more).

The **National Museum of American History's** (The Mall, cnr 14th & Constitution Ave SW) eclectic collection includes the original American flag, first ladies' inauguration ball gowns, Archie Bunker's armchair (from TV's All in the Family), a whites-only Woolworth's lunch counter, and touching memorabilia left at the Vietnam Memorial. The best part is the factitiously perfect turn-of-the-20th-century ice-cream parlor in the basement. Rest your legs while savoring a hot fudge sundae.

The **National Museum of Natural History** (The Mall, cnr 10th St & Constitution Ave SW) has such highlights as a towering 13ft elephant, the 45-carat Hope diamond and a life-size model of a blue whale.

The cavernous halls of the **National Air & Space Museum** (cnr 6th St & Independence Ave SW), one of the world's most popular museums, holds full-size air and spacecraft, from the Wright brothers' flyer and Charles Lindbergh's Spirit of St Louis to the Apollo 11 command module. Make sure to touch the sliver of the moon for good luck.

A huge collection of 20th-century sculptures can been seen at the **Hirshhorn Museum** (cnr 7th St & Independence Ave SW), while the **National Museum of African Art** (950 Independence Ave SW) and **Arthur M Sackler Gallery** (1050 Independence Ave SW) showcase African and Asian art.

The brand new **National Museum of the American Indian** (cnr 4th St & Independence Ave SW), located in a splendid building, features permanent and temporary exhibitions on Native American culture and history. Exhibitions seek to educate the public about the many different tribes and how they live today. Although some of the exhibits are a little heavy on reading and light on artifacts, the museum just opened and has lots of potential.

NATIONAL GALLERY OF ART

This famous **gallery** (☎ 202-737-4215; www.nga.gov; Constitution Ave btwn 3rd & 4th Sts NW; admission free; ☉ 10am-5.30pm) exhibits primarily European art from the Middle Ages to the early 20th century, including a lone da Vinci in its neoclassical west wing. In the east wing there's a four-story atrium with a Calder mobile, plus various abstract and modern works.

WASHINGTON MONUMENT

A 555ft-tall white obelisk, the **Washington Monument** (☎ 202-426-6841; admission free; ☉ 9am-4:45pm) rises above the Mall, offering wonderful views, especially at night. There's free admission, but tickets, available from the **kiosk** (cnr 15th St & Madison Dr), are required.

LINCOLN MEMORIAL

Visit this imposing **monument** (☎ 202-426-6895; cnr 23rd St & West Potomac Park NW; ☉ 24hr) after the sun has set for a solemn and stunning sight. Dedicated to the 16th US president, it resembles a Greek temple and the statue's hands read 'A' and 'L' in American sign language.

US HOLOCAUST MEMORIAL MUSEUM

The events of Nazi Germany are laid bare in stark and grim detail at this haunting **memorial** (☎ 202-488-0400; www.ushmm.org; 100 Raoul Wallenberg Plaza SW, formerly 15th St; admission free; ☒ 10am-5.30pm) to WWII Holocaust victims. You'll be sure to leave in a somber mood, but the experience is one of those gruesome, yet necessary, moments. Crowds necessitate tickets (limit of four per person), distributed from 10am.

NATIONAL WWII MEMORIAL

Opened in 2004 to great fanfare, the **National WWII Memorial** (☎ 202-426-6841; cnr 17th St & Constitution Ave NW; ☒ 24hr), DC's newest, honors the 16 million Americans who served in the armed forces during the war, and the 400,000 that died. It offers classic district views – the Washington Monument to the east, the Lincoln Memorial to the west – on a massive paved plaza. Look out for the wall with 4000 gold stars, each signifying 100 military deaths centered between two low waterfalls.

VIETNAM VETERANS MEMORIAL

More than 58,000 names are etched into two black marble walls at the **Vietnam Veterans Memorial** (☎ 202-634-1568; cnr Constitution Ave & Henry Bacon Drive NW; ☒ 24hr), one name for every American killed or who disappeared during the Vietnam War. Designed by Maya Lin, a 21-year-old student, in a national competition, it's now DC's most visited memorial.

SPY TIME

The highlight of downtown DC is a visit to the **International Spy Museum** (☎ 202-393-7798; 800 F St NW; admission $11; ☒ 10am-8pm Apr-Oct, 10am-6pm Nov-Mar). If you've ever wanted to step into James Bond's shoes and live a glamorous spy life, this is the place to learn the secrets. DC's hottest attraction illustrates high-tech gadgetry, notorious spy cases, secret methods and the not-so-pleasant consequences of being an international person of mystery. Lines form early.

Names are inscribed chronologically from date of death.

Across the Mall, the **Korean War Memorial** (☎ 202-619-7222; south of Lincoln Memorial reflecting pool; ☒ 24hr) consists of an eerie troop of 19 stone soldiers.

TIDAL BASIN

The scenic Tidal Basin, southwest of the National Mall, is lined with cherry trees, a gift from Japan, which blossom in spring. **Paddleboat rentals** (per hr $7) are available at the boathouse.

Designed to mimic the Monticello home of the third president, the domed **Jefferson Memorial** (☎ 202-426-6822; 900 Ohio St SW; ☒ 24hr), has Jefferson's writings etched on the inside walls.

Although Franklin Delano Roosevelt entreated no memorial 'larger than his desk' be built in his honor, the 1997 **Franklin Delano Roosevelt Memorial** (☎ 202-426-6841; Ohio St NW; ☒ 24hr) includes a water sculpture with stone-etched quotes and a seated statue of the 32nd president (the only president elected for four terms).

White House & Around

Since 1800 every US president has lived at 1600 Pennsylvania Ave. Additions to the **White House** include Franklin Roosevelt's pool, Truman's 2nd-story porch, George Bush Senior's horseshoe-throwing lane, Clinton's jogging track and George W Bush's T-ball field. Unfortunately, following the September 11 attacks tours of the building are no longer offered to the general public. Still, it's worth snapping a picture of the outside.

The 1883 Greek Revival **Treasury Building** (☎ 202-622-0896), next to the White House, is decorated with golden eagles, ornate balustrades and a two-story marble Cash Room. On the White House's other side is the **Old Executive Office Building** (☎ 202-395-5895), which contains the offices of White House staff.

Within downtown's **National Archives** (☎ 202-501-5000; www.archives.gov/index.html; 700 Pennsylvania Ave NW; admission free; ☒ 8:45am-5pm Mon & Wed, 8:45am-9pm Tue, Thu & Fri, 8:45am-4:45pm Sat) are gallery displays of blockbuster originals: the Declaration of Independence, the Constitution, the Bill of Rights and one of four remaining versions of the 1297 Magna Carta.

TOP FIVE QUIRKY DC SIGHTS

When you're tired of looking at stoic monuments or relic-stuffed museums, check out the other side of DC. You'll find the city to be a gold mine for artifacts from the slightly offbeat to the downright bizarre.

- **Squished Penny Museum** (☎ 202-986-5644; www.squishedpenny.com; Northwest Washington; admission by appointment only, phone for directions) has an unusual collection of – you heard it – squished pennies, coins and other ephemera from around the world. Exhibited in the owners' living room, it gives new meaning to the term *common cents*.

- See the famous exterior of the **Exorcist House** (3600 Prospect St NW, Georgetown) and its steep staircase from the movie *Exorcist,* which gave many people nightmares in the '70s. The steps in the film are at the end of M Street in Georgetown, across from the Key Bridge.

- The stuffed body of Owney, the unofficial postal mascot, rests behind glass at the **National Postal Museum** (☎ 202-633-9849; cnr 1st & Massachusetts Ave NE). Adopted by the postal service in 1888, he 'worked' as a mail carrier until 1897 when he died from a mysterious gunshot wound.

- Ever wonder what the world's largest hairball looks like? Wishes do come true at the **National Museum of Health & Medicine** (☎ 202-782-2200; cnr 6900 Georgia Ave & Elder St NW; admission free; ☺ 10am-5:30pm). There's a fascinating display that shares the oddball category with pieces of Abraham Lincoln's skull and a touchable human stomach.

- In Anacostia on V St, the **world's largest chair** towers over Martin Luther King Dr; at 19ft of pure mahogany, no one is sure how it got there.

Dupont Circle

Once a marshland, the Dupont Circle area, north of the White House, is the heart of gay and lesbian DC (see p229) and home to Washington's diplomatic community. Scenic Dupont Circle itself is at Connecticut and Massachusetts Aves, though the term generally refers to the entire neighborhood, which offers restaurants, cafés, clubs and boutiques. It's a fabulous area for a stroll or a people-watching picnic in the park. Rotating exhibits on worldwide expeditions, and some spectacular photography, are found at the **National Geographic Society's Explorers Hall** (☎ 202-857-7588; 1145 17 St NW; admission free; ☺ 9am-5pm Mon-Sat, 10am-5pm Sun).

Adams-Morgan, Shaw & U Street

Ethnic and bohemian, eclectic and electric, and sometimes downright gritty, this area should not be missed. At night, reggae music pumps from dark and dingy clubs and mixes with house and hip-hop in places with throbbing neon lights. Ultra fashionably dressed trendsetters dance with dread-locked Rasta and the air is thick with aromas of exotic ethnic cuisine. In the daytime wander past offbeat boutiques, then stop at an outdoor café for a latte.

The heart of Adams-Morgan is 18th St between Florida Ave and Columbia Rd, and along Columbia Rd itself. To the east, Shaw & U Street is a largely African-American neighborhood stretching from around Thomas Circle to Meridian Hill Park and from N Capitol St to 15th St NW.

Back in the 1930s, **Lincoln Theater** (☎ 202-328-6000; 1215 U St NW) was a high point on the 'chitlin' circuit' of African-American entertainment, hosting such celebrities as DC native Duke Ellington. Today, it showcases a little bit of everything. Riots following the 1968 assassination of Martin Luther King Junior devastated the commercial district, but recently Shaw & U St enjoyed a modern-day renaissance with the reopening of the historic theater, and new cafés, shops and clubs. Once a downtrodden and sometimes dangerous area, today it's one of DC's top nightlife destinations.

Georgetown

Lined with major chain retailers, bars and restaurants, this elegant and refined neighborhood features cobbled, tree-lined streets, 18th-century brick row houses and **Georgetown University**, Bill Clinton's alma mater. Fashionable and full of yuppies and

---

DETOUR – GREAT FALLS NATIONAL PARK

Fourteen miles upriver from Georgetown, the normally placid Potomac cascades 77ft down a series of beautiful, treacherous rapids known as Great Falls. The C&O Canal was built to allow barges to bypass the falls. Today there are parks on both sides of the river providing glorious views of the falls as well as hiking, cycling and picnicking spots. From the towpath out of Georgetown you can hook up with the park in Maryland, where its called **C&O Canal National Historical Park**; on the Virginia side it's **Great Falls National Park**. The entrance to both parks is per car/walker $5/3.

---

college kids, day or night it's an exciting place to explore.

The **Chesapeake & Ohio (C&O) Canal towpath** is great for walking or biking. Head north along the towpath from Georgetown and you'll quickly leave the city behind. With the canal on one side and the Potomac River on the other, it's a serene experience. **Big Wheel Bikes** (☎ 202-337-0254; 1034 33rd St; per hr/day from $5/25) is a good bike rental if you'd rather cruise the towpath. You can also rent boats to paddle the mighty Potomac; try **Thompson Boat Center** (☎ 202-333-9543; 2900 Virginia Ave; kayaks & canoes per hr $8).

Upper Northwest

The massive high-Gothic **Washington National Cathedral** (☎ 202-537-6200) is an Episcopal venue for state funerals, including Ronald Reagan's, and other high-profile events. It's open to the public during the day. **Rock Creek Park** starts at the Potomac River, extends north through DC and boasts terrific biking and hiking. The **National Zoological Park** (☎ 202-357-2700; 3000 Connecticut Ave NW; admission free; ⏰ 6am-8pm Apr 6–Oct 25, 6am-6pm Oct 26–Apr 5) follows the contour of its woodland canyon setting and boasts some 2000 species in natural habitats. Don't miss the famous pandas.

Waterfront & Anacostia

At the southwestern waterfront, a really nice promenade along the Washington Channel has great sunsets and overrated seafood restaurants. Across the Anacostia River in hard-luck Anacostia, the **Frederick Douglass National Historic Site** (☎ 202-426-5960; 1411 West St SE; admission free; ⏰ 9am-4pm) is the hilltop home of the abolitionist and former slave; the visitors center screens a biographical film. The Smithsonian's **Anacostia Museum** (☎ 202-287-3307; 1901 Fort PI SE; admission free; ⏰ 10am-5pm) is a national resource for African-American culture and operates

rotating exhibits. Anacostia has a well-earned reputation for violent crime; take a cab from Anacostia Metro.

TOURS

Tourmobile Sightseeing (☎ 202-554-5100, 888-868-7707; www.tourmobile.com; tours $20) is an open-air trolley, which adapts to both cold and wet weather and runs its convenient trams daily between all the major sights. Ticket booths are at the Washington Monument and Union Station. The spectacular 'Washington by night' tour is a must for viewing the monuments by illumination and moonlight.

Scandal Tours (☎ 202-783-7212; Old Post Office Pavilion; tours $27; 1pm Sat Apr-Sep) gives you all the gossip about DC's infamous spots (expanding daily), covering George Washington to George W Bush.

FESTIVALS & EVENTS

National Cherry Blossom Festival (☎ 202-547-1500; www.nationalcherryblossomfestival.org) DC's chance to bloom, this internationally known event is held late March to early April when the trees blossom.

Smithsonian's Folklife Festival (☎ 202-357-2700; www.folklife.si.edu) This fun family event, held over two weekends in June and July, features distinctive regional folk art, crafts, food and music.

Independence Day Also big here, celebrated on July 4 with parades, concerts and fireworks.

SLEEPING

DC has a variety of budget accommodation. It's also a business town, so hotel rates can drop as much as 50% on weekends.

Washington International Student Center (☎ 202-667-7681; dcstudentcentr@aol.com; 2451 18th St NW; dm $20; ⏰ 24hr; ✕ 🖵) Located in lively Adams-Morgan, this small hostel has a great, friendly atmosphere and major pluses: within walking distance of major sites, convenient to the bus and Metro, free breakfast, and free pickup from the train or bus station. You'll also find cable TV and Internet access.

HI Washington, DC (☎ 202-737-2333; www.hi washingtondc.org; 1009 11th St NW at K St; dm members/ nonmembers $20/29; ☽ 24hr; ⌨) Remodeled in 2002, this 270-bed hostel is a hot spot for budget travelers, with good amenities such as a theater-style TV room, Internet access, coin laundry and luggage storage. It also organizes events and free VIP club passes. Reservations and photo ID are required.

Kalorama Guest House (☎ 202-667-6369; fax 202-319-1262; 1854 Mintwood Pl NW; s/d with shared bathroom from $45/50; ☷) What a find! This charming place is an oasis in an ocean of overpriced lodging. Extremely friendly innkeepers greet visitors with hot or cold beverages, depending on the season, and escort you to simple rooms with period furniture. Close

to Adams-Morgan and many major sites, you'll find a community fridge, sunroom, free local calls and best of all – an afternoon sherry.

Brickskeller Inn (☎ 202-293-1885; 1523 22nd St NW; s/d with shared bathroom $55/75; ☷) Centrally located in Dupont Circle, this inn is above the famous saloon of the same name (see p228). Rooms are basic but clean and come with TVs and telephones. There are coin-operated laundry facilities on the 2nd floor.

Allen Lee Hotel (☎ 202-296-3518; www.allenlee hotel.com; 2224 F St NW; s/d/4-person r with shared bathroom $45/62/85; ☷) More than a little shabby, with peeling paint and stained carpets, don't expect a classy hotel stay here. The location, however is perfect (and in a very safe neighborhood) and the rooms themselves

---

TOP FIVE SCANDALS

Washington media loves nothing more than a good scandal (and, some argue, devotes too many hours to trying to sniff one out). We offer here only a brief primer.

■ **Smoking Gun: Vista Hotel** It was in room No 727 that former DC Mayor Marion Barry uttered his timeless sobriquet 'Bitch set me up!' when the FBI caught him taking a friendly puff of crack in the company of ex model (and police informant) Rasheeda Moore. The widely broadcast FBI video of his toke horrified a city lacerated by crack violence, but didn't stop it from re-electing Barry in 1994. The Vista has since changed its name to the Wyndham Washington Hotel.

■ **Scandal Central: Watergate** This chi-chi apartment-hotel complex has lent its name to generations of political crime. It all started when Committee to Re-Elect the President (CREEP) operatives were found here, hiding under a desk after trying to bug Democratic National Committee headquarters. Thus was launched Woodward and Bernstein's investigation, which would eventually topple Nixon. Later, Monica Lewinsky hid out here during the Clinton sex scandal.

■ **Swimming for it: Tidal Basin** In 1974 Arkansas Representative Wilbur Mills was stopped for speeding, whereupon his companion – the stripper Fanne Foxe, known as the 'Argentine Firecracker' – leapt into the Basin to escape. The 65-year-old chairman of the House Ways & Means Committee and his 38-year-old friend were both several sheets to the wind. Unfortunately for Mills' political career, a TV cameraman was there to film the fun.

■ **What's Your Position, Congressman?: Capitol Steps** John Jenrette was a little-known South Carolina Representative until he embroiled himself in the bribery scandal dubbed Abscam (after Abdul Enterprises Ltd, the faux company set up by the FBI to offer money to congressmen in return for political favors). Jenrette's troubles were compounded when his ex-wife Rita revealed to *Playboy* magazine that she and her erstwhile husband used to slip out during dull late-night congressional sessions for an alfresco quickie on the Capitol's hallowed marble steps.

■ **Stool Pigeon Sushi: Pentagon City Food Court** It was by the sushi bar that Monica Lewinsky awaited Linda Tripp, her lunch date (and betrayer), who led Ken Starr's agents down the mall escalators to snap her up for questioning. Who knew a food court could provide such a media fiesta?

SPLURGE!

Hotel Rouge (☎ 202-667-9827; www.rouge hotel.com; 1315 16th St NW; r from $120; ✖ ▢) Pure fun. Stylish and luxurious with wild red décor, the rooms offer flat-screen TVs, in-room computers with high-speed Internet access and stainless steel kitchenettes. There's even a complimentary Bloody Mary bar and cold pizzas.

Swissôtel Watergate (☎ 202-965-2300; 2650 Virginia Ave NW; r from $175; ✖ ✖) One of the world's most infamous hotels due to its famous 'plumbing' convention (see p225), it's nonetheless luxurious and fully serviced. Elegant marble bathrooms and a fitness center with spa and sauna compete with panoramic balconies on which to plot your own scheme to uncover DC's secrets.

---

are clean. If appearances aren't important, and especially if you're traveling in a group of four, it's not a bad option.

EATING

Dining is a great adventure in DC, where around every corner a different slice of the world is waiting to be discovered. Among numerous ethnic enclaves, **Adams-Morgan** is known for its amazing Ethiopian restaurants and vibrant **Chinatown** for authentic homeland dishes.

Capitol Hill

Eastern Market (225 7th St SE; food from $2) This is a must for market eats, with an international smorgasbord of food stalls.

Bullfeathers (☎ 202-543-5005; 410 1st St SE; mains $5) Feel like an extra from the *West Wing* TV show at this popular Capitol Hill hangout, named after Teddy Roosevelt's favorite expression, and decorated much like the time he was president.

Anatolia (☎ 202-544-4753; 633 Pennsylvania Ave SE; mains $5) Duck into this mysteriously lit restaurant for authentic and inexpensive Turkish dishes, and make sure you don't forget to finish with a hit of strong, sublime coffee.

B Smith's (☎ 202-289-6188; 50 Massachusetts Ave NE; mains $10) A taste of New Orleans (with hot Cajun food and soulful southern soups) in a wild, spacious room adjacent to Union Station.

White House Area & Downtown

Full Kee (☎ 202-371-2233; 509 H St NW; mains $5) Despite the dingy exterior you'd be crazy to pass up this excellent Chinese restaurant, a well-guarded local secret. Expect a lengthy, cheap menu that includes savory roast pork, inventive soups and delectable dumplings. Food is served until 2am daily.

Capital Q BBQ (☎ 202-347-8396; 707 H St NW; mains $4.50) A must for Texas-style barbecue lovers, with piled-high portions of smoked meat and plenty o' slaw on the side; try the brisket sandwich.

Sholl's Colonial Cafeteria (☎ 202-296-3065; 1990 K St NW; mains $5) This cultural icon sells regional rock-bottom cafeteria fare such as baked chicken and mashed potatoes.

Stoney's Bar & Grill (☎ 202-347-9163; 1307 L St NW; mains $5) Near the youth hostel, this homey dive is a dirt cheap choice for American fare, burger-and-beer deals and half-price specials.

Dupont Circle & Around

Nam Viet (☎ 202-237-1015; 3419 Connecticut Ave NW; mains from $5) Eat here for delicious Vietnamese cuisine, some of the city's best, not the lackluster décor. The rich *pho* soup is cold-day comfort food, while the more substantial dishes come with delicate palate-pleasing sauces. The restaurant is north of Dupont Circle; use the Cleveland Park metro stop.

Johnny's Half Shell (☎ 202-296-2021; 2002 P St NW; mains from $12) A popular, casual oyster bar and café, it's a must to sample Maryland crab cakes, fried-oyster po-boys and sautéed soft-shell crabs. The friendly bar boasts strong drinks.

Sushi Taro (☎ 202-462-8999; 1503 17th St NW; mains $13) The drab exterior is an unfortunate entrance to a superb sushi bar with traditional rolls, steaming soups and more authentic cuisine as evidenced by its dedicated Japanese clientele.

Adams-Morgan

Meskerem (☎ 202-462-4100; 2434 18th St NW; mains from $10) A favorite for Ethiopian fare, Meskerem features three floors of African-themed rooms and great open spaces. Try the upper level with colorful walls and either low, cushioned seats or window perches – perfect for people watching.

El Tamarindo (☎ 202-328-3660; 1785 Florida Ave NW; mains $5-10) The waitress arrives with

LATE NIGHT GRUB

If you're trying to sop up the alcohol running through your blood with a little 3am grease after a wild night at the Adams-Morgan clubs, then do as the locals do and head to **Pizza Boli** (☎ 202-462-3100; 2455 18th St NW; slices $3) for a positively gigantic slice of oily pizza. You'll eat standing up on the street (or in some cases slumped over the curb). For a more sedate eating experience, head to **Georgetown Café** (☎ 202-333-0215; 1623 Wisconsin Ave; mains from $5). The place claims to stay open 24 hours, although it's been known to shut early on slow nights. Greasy-spoon American fare, steaming mugs of coffee and bleary-eyed partygoers greet you late at night.

water and chips and spicy homemade salsa as soon as you sit down at this friendly neighborhood Mexican restaurant. It's a good place to fill up before heading out on the town. The menu is large and inexpensive, the margaritas or pitchers of Sangria strong and tasty.

Tryst (☎ 202-232-5500; 2459 18th St NW; sandwiches from $6) Sink into the comfortable shabby-chic couch, order an overstuffed sandwich and chai latte in the afternoon (or try a cocktail after dark) and make eye contact with the beautiful stranger across the room. Low-key coffee house by day, meat-market bar by night, Tryst is a funky favorite hangout at any hour.

Perry's (☎ 202-234-6218; 1811 Columbia Rd NW; mains from $10) The sprawling rooftop deck is sublime for alfresco summer dining with steaks, seafood and even a sushi bar. The views of the city are quite incredible, and outrageous Sunday brunches accompanied by singing drag queens are really a sight to behold. If you're looking for attitude, you'll find it at Perry's.

Shaw & U Street

Utopia Art & Eat (☎ 202-483-7669; 1418 U St NW; mains $10) An artistic feast for the senses, with creative North African–Cajun fusion cuisine set among local artwork and live daily jazz; don't miss the funky bar.

Ben's Chili Bowl (☎ 202-667-0909; 1213 U St NW; mains $7) A DC cultural institution, this famous dive is actually better known for its 'greasy diner' atmosphere than the quality of its food. That said, the half-smokes and chili bowls are some of the best around – not too spicy, not too pricey.

Florida Avenue Grill (☎ 202-265-1586; 1100 Florida Ave NW; mains $5) Another cultural institution, this place serves fried catfish and collard greens along a well-worn counter; check out the celebrity wall behind it.

Georgetown

Pizza Paradiso (☎ 202-337-1245; 3282 M Street NW; pizzas from $8) Locals rave about this casual restaurant serving wood-oven pizza with scrumptious toppings to crowds of starving patrons. The pizza crust is perfect – light, crisp and a little flaky.

SPLURGE!

Sequoia (☎ 202-944-4200; 3000 K St; mains $8-21) With views to die for and mouthwatering seafood, this classic Georgetown restaurant pleases all your senses. Overlooking the Potomac River, try the more casual outdoor patio where the menu is a little cheaper and the sunsets spectacular. Inside it's all white linen and china and suits. Inside or out the food is creative and elegant and the service excellent. At night Sequoia is a popular drinking spot with Washington's preppy pretty people. You'll pay royally to drink your Corona at the packed outside bar, but it's quite a social experience.

Bethesda

Just over the line in Maryland, Bethesda has enough restaurants to keep you eating (and eating well) for months to come. Easily accessible by the Metro, it's a fun place to wander and has a less chaotic air than much of the city. Check out the area around Woodmont and Bethesda Aves.

Rio Grande Cafe (☎ 301-656-2981; 4780 Bethesda Ave; mains from $8) With consistent lines out the door, this is one of the city's most popular stops for Tex-Mex. The fajitas are some of the best in the business. Make sure to order a margarita or a 'swirl'; these drinks are packed with enough booze to get you at least a little tipsy. Portions are large and appetizers double as meals, especially if you fill up on the free chips and salsa first.

Penang (☎ 301-657-2878; 4933 Bethesda Ave; mains from $7) You can eat like a king at this authentic Malaysian restaurant between 11:30am and 3pm Monday to Friday. For $8 you get soup, salad, appetizer, drink and a noodle dish. Otherwise portions are large, delicious and almost all can be made vegetarian. Try the *kari mee* noodle soup ($7). Don't let the outside discourage you; inside the place is intimate Asian chic.

Raku (☎ 301-718-8680; 7420 Woodmont Ave; mains from $7) We just love the yellow curry udon noodles with chicken. They come bursting with flavor in a fantastically large soupy bowl. The Asian diner, with sparse yet edgy sophisticated décor, also does yummy sushi and has a big sake menu and sidewalk seating for warm days.

DRINKING

There's no shortage of fantastic watering holes in the nation's capital. The greatest concentration is in **Adams-Morgan**, **U Street** and **Georgetown**. Bars are generally open day and night and last call is between 2am and 3am. And you can still light up a cigarette in DC bars.

Capitol Hill

Politiki (☎ 202-546-1001; 319 Pennsylvania Ave SE) A fun, three-story bar with three very different themes offering concoctions ranging from coconut rumrunners to long-neck bottles to dirty martinis. Hint: the higher you go, the more 'refined' the crowd.

Hawk & Dove (☎ 202-546-1001; 329 Pennsylvania Ave SE) A hot spot for everybody from political junkies to House pages, with free-food happy hours and intimate corner booths perfect for chilling over boutique martinis and creating the next District scandal.

White House Area, Dupont Circle & Downtown

Eighteenth Street Lounge (☎ 202-466-3922; 1212 18th St NW) Dress to impress or you won't get in to this swanky place known for hosting acclaimed international DJs. The décor ranges from gold upholstered couches and candelabras to blue wills, gilded mirrors, marble tables and flickering candles.

Brickskeller Inn (☎ 202-293-1885; 1523 22nd St NW) With a drink menu as thick as a bible, this is heaven for beer worshippers, and probably the best place to grab a brew

in DC – if you can choose from the 110C around-the-world varieties.

Lucky Bar (☎ 202-331-3733; 1221 Connecticut Ave NW) Catering to the city's young and poor, this dive-like place offers $7 domestic pitchers on Friday and $2 Budweisers on Thursday. There's a dance floor, a poo table and free salsa and meringue lessons on Monday.

MCCXXIII (☎ 202-822-1800; 808 1223 Connecticut Ave NW) Above and beyond swank, you'll need to be dressed to the nines to enter this trendy club. Past the velvet ropes, Roman temple meets industrial in a spatial illusion feat Dance the night away with Washington' exclusive set.

Home (☎ 202-638-4663; 911 F St NW) Smaller more intimate, and as cliché as it sounds more like home than other velvet-rop nightclubs, this relative newcomer on th DC circuit features armless couches fo lounging and multiple dance floors.

Adams-Morgan, Shaw & U Street

Blue Room (☎ 202-332-0800; 2321 18th St NW) Blue i the word at this two-level bar and nightclu (blue velvet curtains in the bathrooms? with the 2nd floor mixing trippy candle and chill attitude. This place is one of th hottest venues on this crowded street.

Common Share (☎ 202-518-6847; 2003 18th St NW Think you can't drink in DC on a budget You've hit the mother lode here, where a drinks are $2, that's right, only $2. The onl drawbacks are large and loud crowds, an standing room only.

Café Saint-Ex (☎ 202-265-7839; 1847 14th St NW Modeled after a Parisian brasserie, Sain Ex features pressed-tin ceilings, tobacco stained walls and French Art Deco déco upstairs. French flair defines the baseme lounge with old movie-theater seats line against a wall underneath a TV screenir films from a time past. DJs spin all types music down here.

Madam's Organ (☎ 202-667-5370; 2461 18th NW) An area staple with nightly blues, blu grass or jazz sessions. Red-headed women natural or dyed – get half-price rolling rock

Rumba Café (☎ 202-588-5501; 2443 18th St N The *mojitos* (Cuban cocktails) are poss bly the best in town at this tiny eclect Brazilian restaurant-club. It hosts live Lat bands in its shabby-chic interior and has delicious tapas menu (from $4).

GAY & LESBIAN DC

Home to more than 30 national gay and lesbian organizations and more than 300 social, athletic, religious and political support groups, DC is one of the most gay-friendly cities in the USA. Often the scene of huge gay rights marches, gay pride is an integral part of DC's character.

Dupont Circle is by far the city's most gay-friendly neighborhood, with numerous gay-owned businesses and the bulk of the city's nightlife options clustered on 17th St NW between P and R Sts NW and along P St west of the circle. Another hot spot is the club and bar scene on Pennsylvania Ave and around Capitol Hill. You'll find popular male strip clubs – one of the few places in the US where full nudity is legal – in Southeast DC near the Navy Yard Metro station. Take a cab here after dark.

Lambda Rising (☎ 202-462-6969; 1625 Connecticut Ave NW) is the landmark bi-gay bookstore in Dupont Circle, and has free flyers on local entertainment. It serves as a popular community gathering place. **La Cage** (☎ 202-554-3615; 18 O St SE) attracts a male go-go dancing crowd, while **DC Eagle** (☎ 202-347-6025; 639 New York Ave NW) is 'leather and Levi's,' with shirtless men the norm. **Apex** (☎ 202-296-0505; 1415 22nd St NW; admission $8), at P St, is a popular steamy club, **Hung Jury** (☎ 202-785-8181; 1819 H St NW) is the most well-known lesbian bar and **JR's** (☎ 202-328-0090; 1519 17th St NW) is a friendly Dupont Circle hangout. And there's always the casual, mixed crowd at Georgetown's **Mr Henry's** (4321 Wisconsin Ave NW).

Club Heaven & Hell (☎ 202-667-4355; 2327 18th St NW) A perennial favorite with the college crowd, this hot spot hosts Heaven (upstairs) with thematic dance parties to flashing disco lights, and Hell (downstairs), which is grittier and attracts hard drinkers. The large outdoor patio in Heaven overlooks the 18th St strip and is popular on steamy nights.

Republic Gardens (☎ 202-232-2710; 1355 U St) History is thick at Republic Gardens, which draws a mostly African-American crowd. It was once one of the city's hottest jazz clubs. Duke Ellington and Pearl Baily were frequent performers, but today the music is mostly dominated by hip-hop. Full of understated elegance, it draws a professional crowd.

Chi-Cha Lounge (☎ 202-234-8400; 1624 U St NW) Located in Shaw, Chi-Cha Lounge is where the Middle East comes to DC with Latin American fare and flair. Soak up the jazz along with the low, cushioned seats and hookahs.

9:30 Club (☎ 202-393-0930; 815 V St NW) This spacious dive, featuring two floors and a mid-size stage, is the best place to see well-known rock acts.

Black Cat (☎ 202-667-7960; 1811 14th St) Dave Grohl is part owner of this amazing club – and if you don't know who he is, you probably won't like the bands that have gigs here. More intimate than the 9:30 Club, it boasts an equally impressive roster of bands.

Georgetown

Mr Smith's (☎ 202-333-3104; 1218 Wisconsin Ave NW) This is a casual well-worn hangout with some great happy-hour specials and a lush back patio that hops all year long. From 4pm to 7pm there are half-price rail drinks and appetizers.

Tombs (☎ 202-337-6668; cnr 36th & Sts) If it looks familiar, think back to the '80s; this was the setting for *St Elmo's Fire*. Today it's a local feel-good fave with university students and those looking to escape the yuppie-filled urban bars.

Georgetown Station (☎ 202-333-6122; 3125 M St NW) Restaurant by day, South Beach–style nightclub at night, this place has affordable happy hours and a VIP lounge upstairs.

ENTERTAINMENT

The *Washington Post*'s 'Weekend' section and the free weekly *Washington City Paper* are useful for planning your time out. Conveniently located at the Old Post Office Pavilion, **Ticketplace** (☎ 202-842-5387; 1100 Pennsylvania Ave NW; ☙ Tue-Sat) sells same-day concert and show tickets at half-price.

Theater

DC's theater district (such as it is) is east of Dupont Circle around 14th St, P and Q Sts NW.

John F Kennedy Center for the Performing Arts (☎ 202-467-4600; www.kennedy-center.org; 2700 F St NW; ☙ daily) The National Symphony and

Washington Chamber Symphony perform here; this is also home to the **Washington Opera** (www.dc-opera.org), of which Placido Domingo is artistic director.

National Theater (☎ 202-628-6161; 1321 Pennsylvania Ave NW) Opened in 1835, this is Washington's oldest continuously operating theater and hosts everything from plays to musicals.

Shakespeare Theater (☎ 202-547-1122; 450 7th St NW) An evocative venue, it produces, what else, Shakespeare's works.

Sports

Washington Redskins (☎ 301-276-6060) Three-time NFL champions play at FedEx Field, east of DC in Maryland.

Robert F Kennedy Memorial Stadium (RFK; ☎ 202-547-9077; 2400 E Capitol St SE btwn 7th & 8th Sts) This stadium is home to DC United, winners of the inaugural US soccer championship (1996), and the women's soccer team **Washington Freedom** (☎ 202-547-3137), featuring Mia Hamm.

MCI Center (tickets & information ☎ 202-628-3200, 202-432-7328) The NBA Washington Wizards, the WNBA Washington Mystics, the NHL Washington Capitals ice hockey team and the Washington Power lacrosse team all play at this downtown stadium.

GETTING THERE & AWAY

For air connections, see p702.

Bus

Greyhound (☎ 800-231-2222l; 1005 1st St NE) and **Peter Pan Trailways** (☎ 800-343-9999; 1005 1st St NE) have offices in a very seedy part of Washington, DC. Take a cab through this rough neighborhood to the nearest Metro station, Union Station, eight blocks away. There is at least one bus a day to the following cities: Baltimore, MD ($11, one hour), Charlestown, WVA ($60, 10 hours), New York City ($42, 4½ hours), Philadelphia, PA ($22, four hours) and Richmond, VA ($18, 2¼ hours).

In addition, **New Century Travel** (☎ 202-789-8222; 513 H St NW) runs a bus to New York City for $35.

Train

Union Station (☎ 202-371-9441; 50 Massachusetts Ave NE), DC's major transport hub, connects directly to the Metro and Amtrak.

MARC (☎ 800-325-7245) commuter trains run Monday to Friday to many regional cities, including Baltimore and Harpers Ferry, West Virginia. **Amtrak** (☎ 800-872-7245) has services to and around the region and further afield destinations including New York City, Chicago, and New Orleans.

GETTING AROUND
Car & Taxi

Drivers beware: middle lanes of some streets change direction during rush hour. Street parking is often scarce, especially around Georgetown and the Mall. Taxis, which operate on a zone system, charge a base rate of $5 per zone and are plentiful in the central city. Try the following:

Capitol (☎ 202-546-2400)
Diamond (☎ 202-387-6200)
Yellow Cab (☎ 202-544-1212)

Metro

Metrorail (☎ 202-637-7000) runs to most sights, hotel and business districts, and to the Maryland and Virginia suburbs. Trains operate 5:30pm to midnight weekdays, 8am to 1am weekends. Machines inside stations sell computerized fare cards. Fares (from $1.20) depend on distance traveled and time of day. All-day excursion passes cost $5.

Metrobus (☎ 202-637-7000) operates buses throughout the city and suburbs (from $1.20). The L2, along 18th St through Adams-Morgan (connecting with Woodley Park and Foggy Bottom Metro stations), and the D5, from Union Station to Georgetown's central M St strip, are handy routes.

Train

Amtrak and regional MARC commuter trains operate between DC's Union Station and a rail terminal near BWI ($9 one way; a 10-minute free shuttle is provided to BWI proper).

VIRGINIA

A large scoop of American history (the Revolutionary and Civil War periods especially) is served alongside a generous portion of rolling blue-green hills in this pretty state. Virginia is divided into distinct regions. Cosmopolitan Northern Virginia is so closely connected to DC it's really considered an extension of the city – many folks commute into the district for work

Southern Virginia is far removed from DC. Accents grow thicker, tobacco plants blanket fields and genteel, sometimes slightly faded towns dot the countryside.

NORTHERN VIRGINIA
Arlington National Cemetery
Veterans from every US war since the Revolution are buried at this 612-acre national cemetery (☎ 703-692-0931; ☺ 8am-7pm Apr 1–Sep 30, 8am-5pm rest of year). In fact this is the final resting place for over 225,000 military personnel and their dependents. The **Tomb of the Unknowns** represents unknown soldiers killed in action. Military guards retain a round-the-clock vigil, and an impressive sight is the ritual changing of the guard (every hour or half-hour). An eternal flame marks the **grave of John F Kennedy**, next to those of Jacqueline Kennedy Onassis and two of her infant children. The grave of Robert Kennedy is nearby, marked with a cross.

Alexandria
Walkable blocks of attractive brick row houses in the historic district find modern uses as restaurants, taverns and shops in quaint Alexandria. The **visitors center** (☎ 800-388-9119; www.funside.com; 221 King St; ☺ 9am-5pm) issues discount tickets to historic sights and free parking permits (know your license plate number).

The **Torpedo Factory Art Center** (☎ 703-838-4565; 105 N Union St; admission free; ☺ 10am-5pm), in a funky modern building, displays the work of local artists. Northwest of town, **Fort Ward Museum & Historic Site** (☎ 703-838-4848; 4301 W Braddock Rd; admission free; ☺ 9am-4pm Tue-Sat, noon-5pm Sun, park open 9am-dusk) preserves one of the largest of the 162 Civil War fortifications known as the Defenses of Washington.

At **Five Guys** (☎ 703-671-1606; 4626 King St; mains $5) the hamburgers are served big, sloppy and dripping with grease and toppings. If all you're looking for is a meal on a bun, you can't beat this dive burger joint for value and taste. You'll often have to fight for a seat.

DC's Metro and Amtrak service the King St station; local buses cover the mile to the visitors center.

Mt Vernon
A meticulous restoration that affords a glimpse of 18th-century farm life makes George Washington's country estate of

Mt Vernon (☎ 703-780-2000; www.mountvernon.org; admission $9; ☺ 9am-5pm) one of the nation's most visited historic sites. Beautifully situated on the banks of the Potomac in Virginia, the estate holds a 19-room country house, immaculate gardens, slaves' quarters, a working farm and Washington's tomb. Mt Vernon is only 16 miles south of DC by road; you can take the Metro to Huntington, then bus No 11P to the estate.

Manassas Battlefield
South of where Washington Dulles Airport now stands, major Civil War battles known collectively as the Battles of Bull Run (by the North) or Battles of Manassas (by the South) were fought in July 1861 and August 1862. Most thought the war would be decided on the day of the first battle, and DC's elite traveled to the field to watch the 'cute skirmish.' Instead of a day at the races, however, they witnessed a bloody and embarrassing rout by the Confederates. The **Manassas National Battlefield Park Visitors Center** (☎ 703-361-1339; ☺ daylight) is the start of a good self-guided tour ($2).

Fredericksburg
History is palatable in Fredericksburg. Captain John Smith visited the site as early as 1608, George Washington grew up here and James Monroe practised law here. On the Rappahannock River, the city features an attractive, 40-block historic district packed with museums, shops and restaurants.

The biggest attraction is the **Fredericksburg & Spotsylvania National Military Park** (☎ 540-373-6122; 1013 Lafayette Blvd; admission $4; ☺ 9am-5pm Mon-Sat, 11am-5pm Sun, 11am-4pm Dec-Feb), which preserves four crucial Civil War battlefields. Among them is Chancellorsville, where General Stonewall Jackson received his fatal wound.

Fredericksburg Colonial Inn (☎ 540-371-5666; 1707 Princess Anne St; r from $65; P ☒) is a scaled-down version of Tara, with 30 rooms exuding antebellum atmosphere.

Goolrick's (☎ 540-373-3411; 901 Caroline St; mains $8), the oldest continually operating soda fountain in the US, serves great, inexpensive lunches and thick milk shakes.

Weekday **commuter trains** (☎ 800-742-3873; www.vre.org) are the cheapest way (per person $7) to reach Fredericksburg from DC. They depart from Union Station and drop you at the train station on Caroline St. Buses come into the **Greyhound/Trailways depot** (☎ 540-373-2103; 1400 Jefferson Davis Hwy).

RICHMOND

Exuding a certain air of the antebellum old South with wide, tree-lined boulevards, gracious houses and restaurants serving home-style southern cooking, Richmond was the linchpin of the Confederacy during the Civil War.

Orientation & Information

Richmond is about 100 miles south of DC on I-95. The James River bisects the city, with most attractions to the north. The most happening neighborhoods are Shockoe Slip, a restored warehouse district on E Cary St between 12th & 15th Sts downtown; the Fan district, south of Monument Ave; and Carytown, in the west end.

For information try the **Richmond Region Visitor Center** (☎ 804-783-7450; www.richmond.com/visitors; 405 N 3rd St; ☽ 9am-5pm).

Sights

A must-see for fans of the writer, the **Edgar Allan Poe Museum** (☎ 804-648-5523; 1914 E Main St; admission $6; ☽ 10am-5pm Tue-Sat, 11am-5pm Sun) is an enchanting shrine containing the world's largest collection of Poe memorabilia. In fact, Poe wrote some of his darkest stories about a block over from the museum.

A former grand estate, **Maymont** (☎ 804-358-7166; 1700 Hampton St; admission free; ☽ 10am-5pm) is now the most visited attraction in Richmond – and so it should be. With an exotic mix of Japanese and Italian gardens, an arboretum and nature center, grassy hills and plenty of open areas for afternoon pick-up games of Frisbee, it's a great place to spend a warm afternoon.

Jackson Ward, an African-American community known as Little Africa in the late 19th century, is now a national historic landmark district. The **Black History Museum & Cultural Center of Virginia** (☎ 804-780-9093; Clay St; admission $4; ☽ Tue-Sat 10am-5pm, 11am-5pm Sun), in a fine Greek Revival building, highlights the achievements of black Virginians.

The **Virginia Museum of Fine Arts** (☎ 804-340-1400; 2800 Grove Ave; admission free; ☽ 11am-5pm Wed-Sun) has a remarkable repertoire of European works (Monet, Goya, Picasso), sacred Himalayan art and the largest Fabergé egg collection on display outside Russia. It's well worth exploring.

Activities

The 1.5-mile **Canal Walk** along the James River is an ambitious waterfront redevelopment. There are 12 stops, and the city's history is carefully highlighted. One of the stops, Belle Isle, was a former POW camp for Union soldiers and today is a lovely outdoor excursion, with a climbing wall, hiking and biking trails, and access to the white-water rapids (up to class V) that run through downtown Richmond. The island is accessible by a wavy footbridge at the Tredegar Iron Works.

Sleeping

Budget options are rare. You may find cheaper rates at the chain motels spread across town. These are the city's most interesting budget-ish options.

Massad House Motel (☎ 804-648-2893; 11 N 4th St; r from $55; ☒) Not only the cheapest option, but also centrally located for exploring downtown. Small rooms are equipped with cable TV in a boarding house–style building. The friendly, 24-hour desk clerk has plenty of entertainment suggestions.

Linden Row Inn (☎ 804-783-7000; www.lindenrowinn.com; 100 E Franklin St; r from $100; ☒) Rumored to be the place where Poe played as a child, this intimate inn occupies antebellum row houses that are set around a balcony-lined courtyard.

Mr Patrick Henry's Inn (☎ 804-644-1322; 2300 E Broad St; r from $95; ☒) Named for the fiery American patriot, this place suffers from a slight identity problem, also housing a gourmet restaurant and an English-themed pub in the basement, but remains a perfect cozy respite from the city.

Eating

The happenin' eats are found in the **Fan**, **Carytown** and E Cary St in **Shockoe Slip**.

3rd St Diner (☎ 804-788-4750; 218 Main St; mains $8; ☽ 24hr) Guns 'n' Roses at 8am? You bet. This hole-in-the-wall diner attracts an eclectic crowd from truck drivers to drag queens. Bring an appetite and lose the attitude, because this dive serves it up quick, no frills, 24-7.

Star-lite (☎ 804-254-2667; 2600 W Main St; mains under $20) Traditionally known as a great

---

IF YOU'VE GOT A COUPLE MORE DAYS IN THE CAPITAL REGION

Jam packed with historical sights and natural attractions, this region could keep you entertained for months. If you've got a little extra time on your hands, consider the following:

- **Colonial Williamsburg** At one time the capital of England's largest, richest and most popular colony, it's now a restored historic district in Virginia containing dozens of authentic 17th- and 18th-century buildings, including shops and taverns. Don't miss the nighttime Original Ghosts of Williamsburg tour – it's a chilling experience and may even frighten those who swear they don't get scared. Williamsburg is 150 miles southeast of DC off I-64.

- **Appomattox** Robert E Lee surrendered the Army of Northern Virginia to Ulysses S Grant at Appomattox in Virginia. Today the compact village, 90 miles southwest of Richmond off US 460, is preserved within a 1300-acre park, which houses a museum and an evocative pedestrian-only village.

- **Shepherdstown** An unexpected little West Virginian jewel, this is the oldest town in the state (dating back to 1762). It's a sophisticated college town with several restaurants, cafés and arty shops. Shepherdstown is in the northeastern portion of the state, close to Harpers Ferry.

---

corner bar, Star-lite's food is simply too outstanding not to highlight as well – they make meatloaf a must try! The menu ranges from simple Reubens to scallops Rockefeller, and the brunches are even better. The outdoor patio is great in summer.

Double T's Barbeque (☎ 804-353-9861; 2907 W Cary St; mains $7-13) Just follow the smokehouse scent to this wooden shack and some of the best barbecue you'll ever have. Choose from six kinds of barbecue sauce and rib-stickin' sides like homemade cornbread, Southern-style potato salad and fried apples.

Village Café (☎ 804-353-8204; 1001 W Grace St; mains from $3) Near Star-lite, Village Café is a funky little eatery serving cheese boards, among other things. It's been referred to as 'a counter with a culture behind it.'

Drinking & Entertainment

You can't throw a bottle cap in the Fan, Carytown or Shockoe Slip without hitting a bar or club; E and W Cary Sts and W Main St have the most action.

Richbrau Brewing Co (☎ 804-644-3018; 1214 E Cary St) Despite the Wal Mart–size megaclub and bar here, lines still wrap around the block. It's worth the wait for sheer madness on the thumping two-story dance floor, the billiards rooms and many, many bars, known for their boutique ales.

Swingers (☎ 804-648-1003; 12 N 18th St) Here the blood-red walls and mahogany bar melt into one of the hottest watering holes downtown. Downstairs it's live rock bands and billiards, an *über* hip lounge above.

The gay and lesbian scene plays out in Carytown. **Babes** (☎ 804-359-9338; 3166 W Cary St) and **Cosmopolitan** (☎ 804-355-5527; 3156 W Cary St) are well-known gay clubs. **Godfrey's** (☎ 804-648-3957; 308 E Grace St) is part of a circle of gay bars along Grace St, affectionately known as the fruit loop.

Byrd Theater (☎ 804-353-9911; 2908 W Cary St; tickets $2) At this fabulous old theater, Wurlitzer organ concerts precede recent movies.

Getting There & Around

The **Greyhound/Trailways** bus terminal (☎ 804-254-5938; 2910 N Blvd) offers the usual services. **Greater Richmond Transit Company** (GRTC; ☎ 804-358-4782; base fare $1.25, exact change only) runs local buses. The local GRTC bus No 27 runs to/from downtown. **Amtrak** (☎ 800-872-7245) stops off way north of town at 7519 Staples Mill Rd.

VIRGINIA BEACH

In the summer, burgeoning Virginia Beach attracts young revelers to its crowded 6-mile beach. Neon lights, rowdy boardwalk bars, golden sand and blue surf draw sun worshippers from around the region, all looking for a party. I-264 takes you straight to the beach and the **visitors center** (☎ 800-822-3224; www.vbfun.com; 2100 Parks Ave).

Surfing is permitted at the beach's southern end, near Rudee Inlet, and alongside the 14th St pier.

You couldn't ask for a prettier campground than the bayfront **First Landing State Park** (☎ 757-412-2300; Cape Henry; campsites/cabins

$21/80). **Angie's Guest Cottage & Hostel** (☎ 757-428-4690; www.angiescottage.com; 302 24th St; dm/s/d $15/40/60; 🐾) is one block from the beach, has a kitchen and sundeck, and boogie boards and beach mats for guests. The staff are friendly.

All are welcomed with blintzes, 'penicillin soup,' packed deli sandwiches and monster pies and cakes at the **Jewish Mother** (☎ 757-422-5430; 3108 Pacific Ave; sandwiches from $5). A crude stage hosts live music nightly. Get a psychic reading with your organic sandwich at **Heritage Cafe & Deli** (☎ 757-428-0500; 314 Laskin Rd; sandwiches from $5).

Among the myriad of tacky clubs and bars between 17th and 23rd Sts around Pacific and Atlantic Aves, **Ocean Eddie's** (☎ 757-425-7742; 14th St Pier) has wild Friday-night bashes to the strains of a country/R & B band.

Greyhound (☎ 757-422-2998) services Virginia Beach.

CHARLOTTESVILLE

Impressive architecture and magnolia-lined streets set against a Blue Ridge Mountain backdrop help make this smart university town Virginia's Cambridge. As the home of Thomas Jefferson and the University of Virginia, Charlottesville is a pleasant place to get lost for an afternoon or two.

The helpful **Charlottesville/Albemarle Convention & Visitors Bureau** (☎ 877-386-1102; Rte 20s; www.charlottesvilletourism.org) is near the I-64 exit 121A.

East of town, Thomas Jefferson's magnificent home, **Monticello** (☎ 804-984-9822; admission $13; 🕑 8am-5pm Mar-Oct, 9am-4:30pm Nov-Feb), is full of Jefferson's quirky inventions and French-inspired innovations. Jefferson's tomb is downhill. Its inscription, noting the author of the Declaration of Independence and Virginia's religious freedom statute, was chosen by Jefferson himself. Daily tours include a plantation-community tour that exposes the rather complicated past of the slave owner who declared all men to be equal.

The cheapest sleeping option is at the **Charlottesville KOA** (☎ 434-296-9881; 3825 Red Hill Rd; campsites/cabins $20/36; 🐾 🈂), which has rustic cabins, grassy camping spots, a small lake and plenty of trees. A slightly costlier option, but still good value for money, is the **English Inn** (☎ 434-971-9900; 2000 Morton Dr; r from $75; 🐾 🈂), a tidy motel with a great pool, near the Rtes 29 and 250 bypass.

Inexpensive student eateries crowd the **Corner**, the busy commercial district adjacent to UVA grounds. Try **Miller's** (☎ 434-971-8511; 109 W Main St; mains $5), an unpretentious jazz dive with smoke, junk food and character. It's also a wildly popular college band venue that's grown a little weary of its famous ties to the Dave Matthews Band.

Excellent French bistro cuisine is served at the **C&O Restaurant** (☎ 434-971-7044; 515 E Water St; mains $12). It's a funky dive that was once a train workers' boardinghouse.

Charlottesville is easily accessible by **Amtrak** (☎ 434-296-4559; 810 W Main St) and the **Greyhound/Trailways terminal** (☎ 434-295-5131; 310 W Main St). A free trolley runs through the historic district.

SHENANDOAH VALLEY REGION

Far from the bustle of Washington, DC, life moves slower in the southwestern corner of the state. Here you'll find the beautiful Shenandoah Valley, a land of rolling, blue-green mountains and lush forests studded with Civil War historic sites.

DETOUR – CHINCOTEAGUE ISLAND

This legendary island, tucked behind Maryland's windswept Assateague Island (see p244), is famous for its July roundup, when the wild ponies that inhabit the Assateague Island refuge are auctioned off after their ceremonious swim across the channel. One particular pony, Misty, caught the fancy of author Marguerite Henry, who came to see her swim in 1946 as part of her book research. She made friends with a Chincoteague family who purchased the pony, and later acquired Misty for herself. The pony and family were immortalized in the Misty of Chincoteague novel, and many American school children grow up reading about Misty and her equally famous foal, Stormy.

The island's **chamber of commerce** (☎ 757-336-6161) has great maps for the scenic hiking and biking trails up to and into the **Chincoteague National Wildlife Refuge** (☎ 757-336-6122; admission $5), which protects migratory waterfowl. Chincoteague is across the 17-mile Chesapeake Bay bridge-tunnel ($10) from Virginia Beach.

SCENIC DRIVE – BLUE RIDGE PARKWAY

Without a doubt one of the prettiest drives in the nation, the Blue Ridge Parkway (www.blue ridgeparkway.org) traverses the southern Appalachian ridge from Shenandoah National Park at Mile 0 to North Carolina's Great Smoky Mountains National Park at Mile 469. Wildflowers bloom in spring, and fall colors are spectacular on the winding country road. In winter, snow can cause the parkway to close at times. High-quality National Park Service (NPS) campgrounds and visitors centers are open May to October. To drive the entire parkway would take days, but if you just want to explore a portion of it, allocate at least three hours. To break up the scenery, detour often.

A stop well worth making for gritty, Friday-night bluegrass jamborees is the tiny town of **Floyd** (Mile 154) and the famous **Floyd's Country Store** (206 S Locust St; adult $2). Further south, **Mabry Mill** (☎ 540-952-2947), at Meadows of Dan, is one of the most photogenic objects in the state.

The parkway has nine **campgrounds** (☎ 800-933-7275; campsites $9), four in Virginia:

- **Otter Creek** (Mile 61) Year-round.
- **Peaks of Otter** (Mile 86) Seasonal.
- **Roanoke Mountain** (Mile 120) Seasonal.
- **Rocky Knob** (Mile 167) Seasonal, plus full facility cabins.

The **HI Blue Ridge Country** (☎ 540-236-4962; Mile 214.5; dm $15) offers dorm lodging with views.

Travel further west and the land becomes more remote. Often the brunt of city-dweller jokes, the people of Appalachia have seen hard times since the coal-mining industry collapsed almost a century ago. Poor towns feature peeling paint and sagging porches, but plenty of character. Don't judge a place on a first drive through. Instead, get out and wander around. In quintessential small-town America, you'll discover kind-hearted folks, hear strains of bluegrass in the air and find run-down bars that will quench your thirst with a beer and burger. Public transportation is limited, so it's best to have your own wheels. I-81 and the Blue Ridge Parkway are the main veins through the region.

Shenandoah National Park

Easy on the eyes, this beautiful **park** (☎ 540-999-2243; www.nps.gov/shen; admission per vehicle/cyclist $10/5) features gentle bluish mountains and deep-green forests to explore. The park's jewel is **Skyline Drive**, which crosses the spine of the Blue Ridge Mountains in 105 miles from Front Royal in the north to Rockfish Gap in the south. It's spectacular in spring and fall.

Two visitors centers, **Dickey Ridge** (☎ 540-635-3566; Mile 4.6 in the north) and **Byrd** (☎ 540-999-3500; Mile 51 in the south), have maps, backcountry permits, and information on hiking (the Appalachian Trail frequently crosses Skyline), horseback riding, hang gliding, biking (only on public roads) and other activities.

Camping (☎ 800-365-CAMP reservations; campsites $14) is available at four National Parks Service (NPS) campgrounds: Mathews Arm (Mile 22.1), Big Meadows (Mile 51.3), Lewis Mountain (Mile 57.5) and Loft Mountain (Mile 79.5). Reservations are required only at Big Meadows from May to November. For not-so-rough lodging, try **Lewis Mountain** (☎ 800-999-4714; Mile 57.5; cabins weekdays/weekends from $60/85).

Natural Bridge

A young George Washington uncovered this awesome 215ft-high natural **arch** (☎ 540-291-2121; admission $10), off I-81, on a scouting mission (look close to see his initials carved into the side). Skip the tacky resort and museums surrounding this natural wonder. Instead, head to rushing waterfalls beyond the arch for a picnic lunch with a view. The nearby **Yogi Bear Jellystone Park** (☎ 540-291-2727; www .campnbr.com; Natural Bridge Station; campsites/cabins $22/45; 2-night minimum in summer; ⚘) is a great camping resort for single travelers. It boasts waterfront and wooded accommodation options, a swimming lake with beach, stocked trout pond and canoe and tube rentals.

A **National Forest Service (NFS) ranger station** (☎ 540-291-2189), across from the resort, provides information about recreation and camping in nearby forest service areas, including $10 campsites at Cave Mountain Lake, 8 miles south.

MARYLAND

There's something for everyone in Maryland – party hard on her beaches or eat a crab cake sandwich in working-class Baltimore. Explore the watery playground of the Chesapeake Bay, swim blissfully in a mountain lake, or relive the colonial days in Annapolis.

BALTIMORE

A great, hard-working, ball-playing, no-nonsense US city where the blood largely runs blue, Baltimore is a friendly place in a state of constant change. Dramatic and continuing redevelopment has transformed the gritty city into an exciting modern destination. Neighborhoods are full of little idiosyncrasies and bursting with personality, while the Inner Harbor's waterfront promenade is urban redevelopment exemplified. The city's undeniable importance in shaping American history is highlighted in numerous attractions, and there's a plethora of nightlife if you're looking to stay up late.

Orientation

The Inner Harbor is the heart of tourist activity. Downtown's business district is immediately north and west of the Inner Harbor, climbing uphill to the swank Mt Vernon district. East of the Inner Harbor (accessible by water taxi) are Little Italy, Fells Point and Canton. The Camden Yards Sports Complex borders the Inner Harbor to the West. Federal Hill is south of the Inner Harbor.

GETTING INTO TOWN

Light Rail runs from Baltimore-Washington International (BWI) Airport to downtown's Lexington Market and costs $1.35. If you want to go directly to the Inner Harbor, the SuperShuttle airport-van will take you there for $12. Buy tickets at the ground transportation desk at C Pier.

The Greyhound bus station is about 1.5 miles from the Inner Harbor. Catch the local bus No 27 or, if it's nice, walk northwest up Haines St, turn right on Russell St and right again on Pratt St.

Information

BOOKSTORES

Barnes & Noble (☎ 410-385-1709; Power Plant, Inner Harbor) Massive bookstore chain.
Book Thing (☎ 410-662-5631; 2645 N Charles St) Free books.

EMERGENCY

Poison Center (☎ 800-222-1212)

INTERNET ACCESS

Enoch Pratt Free Library (☎ 410-396-5430; 400 Cathedral St) Only venue in town with free Internet access.

MEDICAL SERVICES

Johns Hopkins Hospital (☎ 410-955-5000; 600 N Wolfe St)
Maryland General Hospital (☎ 800-492-5538; 22 S Greene St)

MONEY

American Express (☎ 410-837-3100; 100 E Pratt St)

POST

Main Post Office (☎ 410-347-4425; 900 E Fayette St; ⏱ 8:30am-5pm Mon-Fri, 8:30am-4pm Sat)

TOURIST INFORMATION

Baltimore Area Visitors Center (☎ 410-837-4636, 877-225-8466; www.baltimore.org; 451 Light St)

Dangers & Annoyances

Baltimore is an urban city with urban problems. That said, the city is fine to explore with the usual precautions. Areas west of Howard St hold little attraction for visitors and are best avoided, especially at night. On the northern edge of the city, North Ave is an absolute no go. If you're visiting Little Italy, stay to the well-lit streets and don't go west of Eastern Ave – there are only empty lots and project housing beyond.

Sights

The majority of attractions are compactly located around the Inner Harbor and east and north throughout Baltimore's quaint neighborhoods. Water taxis are the best way to see the downtown attractions.

INNER HARBOR

Thanks to major revitalization projects, the Inner Harbor is packed with attractions and is a great place to spend the afternoon. The epicenter of tourist activity is **Harborplace,**

BALTIMORE

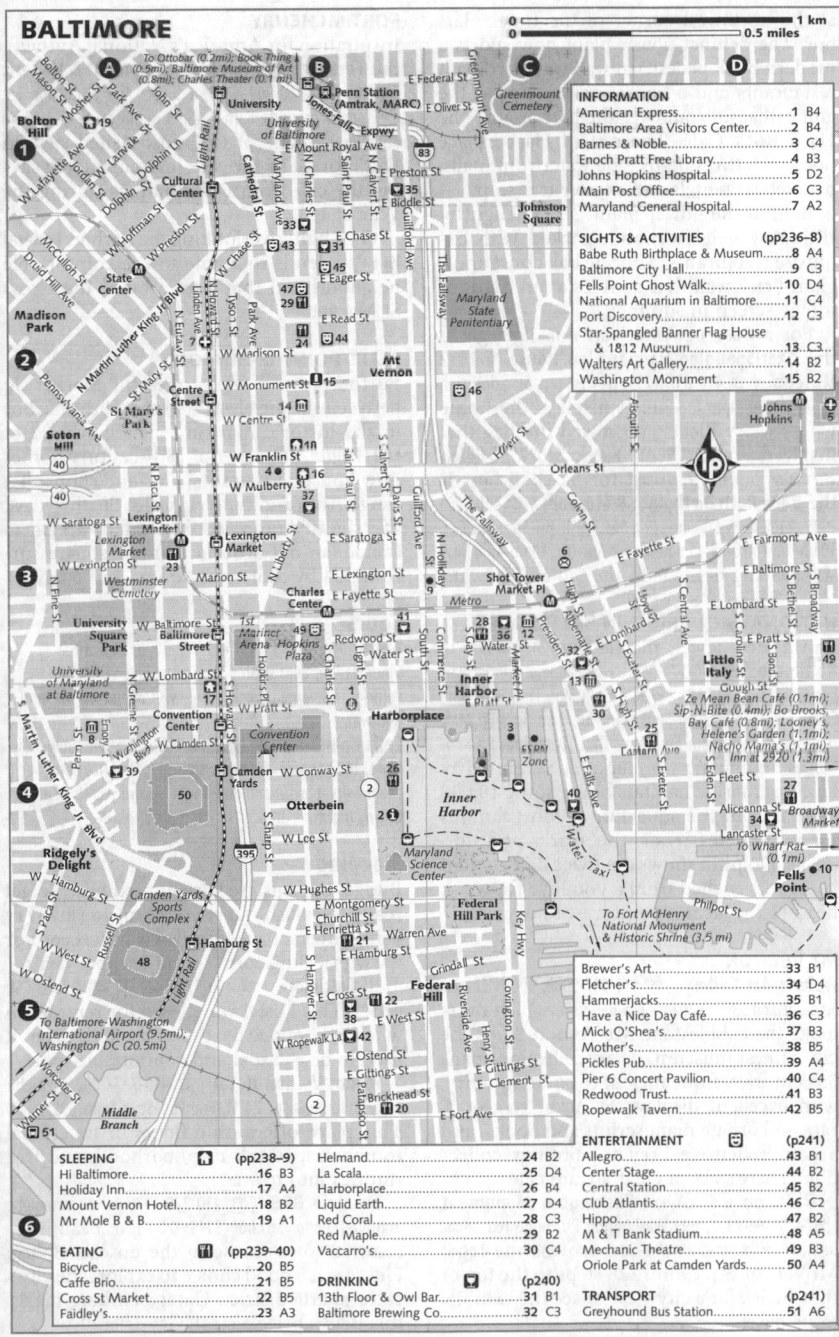

INFORMATION
American Express	1 B4
Baltimore Area Visitors Center	2 C4
Barnes & Noble	3 C4
Enoch Pratt Free Library	4 B3
Johns Hopkins Hospital	5 D2
Main Post Office	6 C3
Maryland General Hospital	7 A2

SIGHTS & ACTIVITIES (pp236–8)
Babe Ruth Birthplace & Museum	8 A4
Baltimore City Hall	9 C3
Fells Point Ghost Walk	10 D4
National Aquarium in Baltimore	11 C4
Port Discovery	12 C3
Star-Spangled Banner Flag House & 1812 Museum	13 C3
Walters Art Gallery	14 B2
Washington Monument	15 B2

SLEEPING (pp238–9)
Hi Baltimore	16 B3
Holiday Inn	17 A4
Mount Vernon Hotel	18 B2
Mr Mole B & B	19 A1

EATING (pp239–40)
Bicycle	20 B5
Caffe Brio	21 B5
Cross St Market	22 B5
Faidley's	23 A3
Helmand	24 B2
La Scala	25 D4
Harborplace	26 B4
Liquid Earth	27 D4
Red Coral	28 C3
Red Maple	29 B2
Vaccaro's	30 C4

DRINKING (p240)
13th Floor & Owl Bar	31 B1
Baltimore Brewing Co	32 C3
Brewer's Art	33 B1
Fletcher's	34 D4
Hammerjacks	35 B1
Have a Nice Day Café	36 C3
Mick O'Shea's	37 B3
Mother's	38 B5
Pickles Pub	39 A4
Pier 6 Concert Pavilion	40 C4
Redwood Trust	41 B3
Ropewalk Tavern	42 B5

ENTERTAINMENT (p241)
Allegro	43 B1
Center Stage	44 B2
Central Station	45 B2
Club Atlantis	46 C2
Hippo	47 B2
M & T Bank Stadium	48 A5
Mechanic Theatre	49 B3
Oriole Park at Camden Yards	50 A4

TRANSPORT (p241)
Greyhound Bus Station	51 A6

at the northwest corner of the Inner Harbor. The defunct power plant now sports a modern brick pedestrian walkway lined with restaurants and a bookstore as giant as the guitar that juts out over the harbor atop the Hard Rock Café. The rest of Harborplace hops with two side-by-side waterfront malls, paddleboat rentals and a water-taxi stop.

Behind the power plant is the delightful **Little Italy** neighborhood, packed with exquisite restaurants, a boccie ball court and a giant brick wall that doubles as an outdoor movie screen in summer.

For a dose of American nostalgia go to the **Star-Spangled Banner Flag House & 1812 Museum** (☎ 410-837-1793; 844 E Pratt St; admission $5; ☽ 10am-4pm Tue-Sat). It displays the home where Mary Pickersgill sewed the flag that inspired Francis Scott Key's *Star-Spangled Banner* poem. A must for baseball fans is the **Babe Ruth Birthplace & Museum** (☎ 410-727-1539; 216 Emory St; admission $6; ☽ 10am-5pm Apr-Oct, 10am-7pm on Orioles home games Apr-Oct, 10am-4pm Nov-Mar), paying homage to the Sultan of Swat.

NATIONAL AQUARIUM IN BALTIMORE

Baltimore's jewel, the **National Aquarium in Baltimore** (☎ 410-576-3800; www.aqua.org; Inner Harbor; admission $17.50; ☽ 9am-6pm Mon-Thu, 9am-8pm Fri-Sun Jul & Aug; 9am-5pm Mon-Thu, 9am-8pm Fri Mar-Jun, Sep & Oct; 10am-5pm Mon-Thu, 10am-8pm Fri Nov-Feb) is an aquatic wonderland. Seven twisty levels of marine habitats house some 10,000 animals, but the aquarium is most famous for its finned friends: the sharks and dolphins. Dolphin shows are twice daily, and if you get drenched from a goodbye fin wave, head to the steamy rainforest to dry out.

MT VERNON

Walters Art Gallery (☎ 410-547-9000; 600 N Charles St; admission $8; ☽ 10am-5pm Tue-Sun), which overlooks the cobblestone Mt Vernon Sq, is the city's finest museum. Its art collection spans 55 centuries, from ancient to contemporary, with excellent displays of Asian treasures, rare and ornate manuscripts and books, and a comprehensive French-paintings collection. There's also a great atrium café.

Baltimore's own **Washington Monument** (☎ 410-396-7837; 699 Washington Pl; suggested donation $1; ☽ dawn-dusk Wed-Sun) crowns the regal Mt Vernon Sq. Climb 228 steps to the top of the obelisk for a city view or see the exhibits in its base.

FORT MCHENRY

Inspiration for America's National Anthem, the **Fort McHenry National Monument & Historic Shrine** (☎ 410-962-4290; 1 E Fort Ave; admission $5; ☽ fort & grounds 8am-7:45pm summer, 8am-4:45pm otherwise) is one of the most-visited sites in Baltimore. The fort was instrumental in saving the city from British attack during the War of 1812.

On a bluff overlooking the harbor, **Federal Hill Park** lends its name to the comfortable neighborhood that's set around the Cross St Market.

FELLS POINT & CANTON

Further east, cobblestones fill Market Sq between the **Broadway Market** and the harbor in the historic maritime neighborhood of **Fells Point**. A number of 18th-century homes now house restaurants, bars and shops that range from funky to upscale. Further east, the slightly more sophisticated streets of **Canton** fan out around a grassy square surrounded by more restaurants and bars.

Tours

Baltimore Ducks (☎ 410-727-3825; 25 Light St, Inner Harbor; admission $22) Amphibious WWII military vehicles nicknamed 'Ducks' show visitors the city via land and water.

Fells Point Ghost Walk (☎ 410-342-5000; Amuse toy store, 1623 Thames St; admission $12; Mar-Nov) Uncover the tawdry, playful and downright bizarre secrets of a bawdy maritime area.

Sleeping

Budget options are very limited here, so get ready to splash out if you want to stay. Try using Internet sites like www.hotels.com or www.priceline.com to find cheaper deals.

HI Baltimore (☎ 410-576-8880; 17 W Mulberry St; dm $25) This hostel was closed for renovation when we stopped by; call to see if it's open. It used to be a casual and comfortable spot.

Mount Vernon Hotel (☎ 410-727-2000; www.bic .edu/mtvernon.asp; 24 W Franklin St; r from $95; 🏿) This place offers nine floors of functional rooms in a swank neighborhood, and free shuttles into town.

Mr Mole B&B (☎ 410-728-1179; www.mrmolebb .com; 1601 Bolton St; r from $119; 🏿) This beautifully restored town house in the upscale Bolton Hill area is a good choice to explore the city's cultural arts district. Garage parking makes this B&B's price a steal. Gay-friendly.

> **SPLURGE!**
>
> **Inn at 2920** (☎ 410-342-4450; www.theinn at 2920.com; 2920 Elliott St; r from $155; 🔀 🖵) Most everywhere to stay in Baltimore is a bit of a splurge, but this modern B&B a few steps from Canton Sq is a great splash-out. There is gourmet breakfast, high-speed Internet access, Jacuzzi tubs and, best of all, beds to die for.

Holiday Inn (☎ 410-685-3500; www.holidayinn .com; 301 W Lombard St; r from $130; 🅿 🔀 🖳) A mere block from the Camden Yards Sports Complex, Holiday Inn is central to downtown, and has a huge indoor pool and guest laundry facilities.

Eating

Known for its outstanding steamed crabs, Baltimore's culinary options are ever expanding with Italian, Asian, Middle Eastern and comfort foods. The Power Plant Live complex, in the Inner Harbor, has numerous open-air options from sushi to Cuban to steakhouses.

INNER HARBOR & LITTLE ITALY

Harborplace (☎ 410-332-4191; cnr Pratt & Light Sts; mains from $2) Two pavilions contain a giant food court, as well as many popular national and chain restaurants. You can get anything here – from fast food to elegant sit-down dinners. Try one of the seafood stands for inexpensive crab cake sandwiches (priced from $7).

Vaccarro's (☎ 410-685-4905; 222 Albemarle St; desserts from $3) Truly sinful cannoli, rum cakes and homemade gelati from this Italian institution are absolute heaven. Attempt all-you-can-eat Mondays if you dare (6pm to 9pm, $11).

Red Coral (☎ 410-528-1925; 614 Water St; mains $12) Silent loops of kung fu movies are shown on flat-screen TVs mounted on rich red walls at this urban sushi joint. At dinnertime it is an intimate place, but afterwards, get ready to get rowdy when the tables are cleared away and a high-energy dance club moves in.

Bo Brooks (☎ 410-558-0202; 2701 Boston St; mains $10) There are only two things you need to order here for a true taste of Maryland: platters of steamed crabs by the dozen ($35), thrown ceremoniously down on newspaper-covered tables, and a cold pitcher of beer.

Faidley's (☎ 410-727-4898; Lexington Market; mains from $5) This seatless favorite has a popular raw bar known for $1 oysters plus enormous lump crab cakes.

MT VERNON

Helmand (☎ 410-752-0311; 806 N Charles St; mains from $12) Deservedly the best of Baltimore's handful of Afghan restaurants, Helmand's daring menu of leek-filled ravioli and pan-fried pumpkin are incredible.

Red Maple (☎ 410-547-0149; 930 N Charles St; mains $4-10) Here you'll find a groovy mix of exotic cocktails and Asian-inspired tapas in a gorgeous setting with red satin walls. Themed evenings. No jeans.

FEDERAL HILL

Caffe Brio (☎ 410-234-0235; 902 S Charles St; mains $4-11) This trendy vegetarian eatery is a neighborhood favorite and displays the work of local artists. It's within walking distance of Camden Yards.

Bicycle (☎ 410-234-1900; 1444 Light St; mains from $12) Striking colored walls and a hip, art gallery feel accent the French, South American and Asian tastes. Large parties can grab the 14-person table in the garden.

FELLS POINT & CANTON

Broadway Market (btwn Fleet & Lancaster Sts; food from $3) In two buildings, this market has a health food and herb shop, and several places to sit and eat; the water taxi stops nearby.

Liquid Earth (☎ 410-276-6606; 1626 Aliceanna St; mains $6-11) The totally veggie menu at this funky place has everything from vegan soups to organic sandwiches.

Sip-N-Bite (☎ 410-675-7077; 2200 Boston St; mains $6-11) Not very much has changed at this bare-bones diner since it opened in 1940 – including prices – serving up 24-hour breakfasts and an expansive menu. Cash only.

> **SPLURGE!**
>
> **La Scala** (☎ 410-783-9209; 1012 Eastern Ave; mains $14-30) Oh so worth the price for Little Italy's best. Here you'll find creamy risotto, penne and gnocchi dishes that melt on the tongue, and a wine list that'd make even the Godfather cry.

Helene's Garden (☎ 410-276-2233; 2908 O'Donnell St; mains $18-24, half-price Wed) Visit on Wednesday night when the expensive main dishes are half-price. Helene's is an artsy and intimate place serving innovative dishes, from seafood to free-range chicken.

Ze Mean Bean Café (☎ 410-675-5999; 1759 Fleet St; mains from $12) A cross between a mountain lodge and a European café, Ze Mean Bean Café serves up hearty Eastern European plates of pierogi, Ukrainian borscht and chicken Kiev, all dished out home style.

Bay Café (☎ 410-522-3377; 2809 Boston St; mains $12-24) This is a great place to grab jerk chicken, shrimp salad or a burger in the summer glow of an outdoor tiki torch. The sandy beach opens onto a view of the Patapsco River.

Nacho Mama's (☎ 410-675-0898; 2907 O'Donnell St; mains from $12) This shrine to Elvis and Natty Bo beer, once locally brewed, serves a jumble of meals from mom's meatloaf to loaded quesadillas.

Drinking

The V-shaped Water St area teems with people in summer attending open-air block parties. The new Power Plant Live complex across from the National Aquarium has a cluster of bars and dance clubs, including a frenetic open-air patio that comes alive in summer. And a lively, lovely bunch of bars spill people into Canton Sq throughout the year.

BARS

Mick O'Shea's (☎ 410-539-7504; 328 N Charles St) Baltimore's Irish mayor makes frequent stops here, playing traditional Irish music with his band.

13th Floor & Owl Bar (☎ 410-347-0888; 1 E Chase St) Atop the gothic Belvedere Hotel, 13th Floor's soothing neon lights beckon long drinking sessions to the tune of nightly live music from 9:30pm. A nostalgic throwback to '50s Baltimore, 1st-floor Owl Bar, also in the Belvedere Hotel, has a long wooden bar – just like in the *Shining* – that attracts a big martini-sippin' university crowd.

Brewer's Art (☎ 410-547-9310; 1106 N Charles St) This is a subterranean cave that mesmerizes the senses with an overwhelming selection of beers.

Mother's (☎ 410-244-8686; 1113 S Charles St) Here is a classic Baltimore neighborhood bar where the drinks flow freely. You'll be called

'Hon' more than once, and the Purple Patio is the meeting spot for wing specials and post–football game discussions.

Hammerjacks (☎ 410-234-0044; 316 Guilford Ave; ✇ Thu-Sat) This two-level nightclub and bar leans toward the big-hair band music of the '80s and books live bands accordingly. You'll find great happy-hour buffets and drink specials, plus plenty of parking (a rarity in Baltimore).

Baltimore Brewing Co (☎ 410-837-5000; 104 Albemarle St) This is a popular watering hole with a range of local brews.

Ropewalk Tavern (☎ 410-727-1298; 1209 S Charles St) A historical and quite roomy bar, Ropewalk Tavern has exposed brick and a wood-beam ceiling. It's the kind of place where America's founding fathers would have polished off a few. Fortunately, so can you, with more than 150 tempting ales to choose from.

Wharf Rat (☎ 410-276-9034; 801 S Ann St) The authentic maritime decorations, brass bars and dark lighting take drinkers back to a turn-of-the-20th-century pub; try the 'three for $3' local brew samples. Spirits of a non-alcoholic nature are rumored to frequent the fireplace area.

Pickles Pub (☎ 410-752-1784; 520 Washington Blvd) Directly across the street from the Camden Yards Sports Complex, fans meet here for pre-game bevies and burgers.

LIVE MUSIC

Redwood Trust (☎ 410-659-9500; 202 E Redwood St; admission $10) This two-level dance club is a former bank and it mimics South Beach clubs, with VIP lounges along with couch-sitting fees.

Have a Nice Day Café (☎ 410-385-8669; 34 Market Pl, Power Plant Live; admission $3-8) This café plays a groovy mix of '70s, '80s and electronica on a Billie Jean–style light-up dance floor.

Fletcher's (☎ 410-558-1889; 701 S Bond St; admission $5) For live music, this is downtown Baltimore's best venue for alternative rock bands, where you can get a pint for less than $5.

Ottobar (☎ 410-243-3535; 2549 N Howard St; admission $3-8) The roomy Ottobar rocks with punk, indie and new wave bands from around the country.

Pier 6 Concert Pavilion (☎ 410-625-3100; Inner Harbor) This amphitheater draws big country and rock names in the summer.

GAY & LESBIAN BALTIMORE

Though it does not have a huge population of gays and lesbians (most flock to DC's hot spots), Mt Vernon is the predominantly gay enclave. Check out www.bgp.org or www.outinbaltimore .com for more comprehensive listings.

Hippo (☎ 410-547-0069; 1 W Eager St) This is the city's largest gay club, with ladies' and men's tea, cabaret and outrageously themed dance nights.

Allegro (☎ 410-837-3906; 1101 Cathedral St; admission $3) Also a popular dance club, Allegro is where boywatch and lava lounge themes play out on the dance floor.

Central Station (☎ 410-752-7133; 1001 N Charles St) This energetic bar is where house diva Ms Tia gets the mixed crowd going with karaoke, drag shows and *Will & Grace* TV nights.

Club Atlantis (☎ 410-717-9099; 615 The Fallsway) John Waters' fans will recognize Club Atlantis as the Fudge Palace from the movie *Pecker*.

Entertainment

Baltimoreans' love for their sports teams and historic theaters is contagious.

THEATER

Theater options include the following:

Center Stage (☎ 410-332-0033; 700 N Calvert St) Alternative plays.

Mechanic Theatre (☎ 410-625-4269; 25 Hopkins Plaza) Touring Broadway productions.

CINEMAS

Charles Theatre (☎ 410-727-3456; 1711 N Charles St) The best art-house cinema in the city, Charles Theatre screens new releases, revivals and art films.

SPORTS

Tailgating parties in parking lots and bars that keep their taps open late on game nights are the norm in Baltimore.

The Baltimore Orioles play at **Oriole Park at Camden Yards** (☎ 888-484-2473; http://baltimore. orioles.mlb.com; 333 W Camden St; ☙ Apr–Oct), while the 2000 Super Bowl champion Baltimore Ravens play football at the **M&T Bank Stadium** (☎ 800-551-7328; www.baltimoreravens.com) next door.

Horse racing is big in this area, especially at **Pimlico** (www.marylandracing.com), where the second jewel of the Triple Crown, the Preakness, is held to great fanfare.

Getting There & Away
BUS

From the **Greyhound Bus Station** (☎ 410-752-1393; 2110 Haines St) daily buses run to Philadelphia, Pennsylvania ($18, 2½ hours), New York ($37, four hours) and Washington, DC ($10, one hour).

TRAIN

Trains stop at Baltimore's **Penn Station** (1515 N Charles St). Amtrak runs multiple times daily to Philadelphia ($43, 1½ hours), New York ($70, 2¼ hours) and Washington, DC ($14, 40 minutes). MARC operates weekday commuter trains to and from Washington, DC (one way/return $5.75/11.50). This is the cheapest, most convenient way to travel between these cities.

Getting Around

Baltimore-Washington International Airport (BWI) is 10 miles south of downtown via Rte 295.

Downtown sights are relatively compact and taxis are plentiful and inexpensive. If you are driving, many Inner Harbor garages charge cheaper 'In before' prices if you park there before or after rush hours.

Seaport Taxi (☎ 410-675-2900; Inner Harbor; admission $5) and **Ed Kane's Water Taxi** (☎ 410-563-3901; Inner Harbor; admission $5) land at many of the harborside attractions and neighborhoods.

Single bus fares within the city cost $1.35 and an all-day pass is $3 (correct change required).

ANNAPOLIS

Narrow lanes lined with brick row houses and original 18th-century architecture give Maryland's capital its charm. Deeply rooted in its colonial past, Annapolis is a lively and picturesque place. Home to the US Naval Academy (established in 1845), it's also well known as America's Sailing Capital – there are 17 miles of waterfront, and more than 2500 vessels are docked here. Annapolis is about 30 miles east of Washington, DC off Hwy 50.

There's a **visitors center** (☎ 410-280-0445; www .visit-annapolis.org; 26 West St; ☺ 9am-5pm) and a seasonal information booth at City Dock.

Sights & Activities

Think of the State House as a wheel hub from which most attractions fan out, leading straight down to the **City Dock** and the **historic waterfront**. Most water-based activities originate from the dock area, while tours are handled straight from the visitors center.

The prestigious **US Naval Academy** is the undergraduate college of the US Navy. The **Armel-Leftwich Visitor Center** (☎ 410-263-6933; Gate 1 at the City Dock entrance; fee for tours; photo ID required) has a film, tours and interactive exhibits about the 338-acre yard (never 'campus'). Most visitors come to see the formation daily at 12:05pm sharp. This is when the 4000 midshipmen and midshipwomen conduct a 20-minute military marching display in the plaza around their massive dormitory – a memorable spectacle.

The country's oldest state capitol in continuous legislative use, the stately 1772 **Maryland State House** (☎ 410-974-3400; ☺ 9am-5pm Mon-Fri, 10am-4pm Sat & Sun; photo ID required) also served as the fledgling national capitol for a short time from 1733 to 1734, when it housed the Continental Congress. The Senate is in action here from January to April.

Annapolis has many sailing schools, cruises and bareboat (sail-it-yourself) charters. **Watermark Cruises** (☎ 410-268-7600; City Dock; sailing cruises from $25) is the best, with daily cruises, sunset sails and excursions around Annapolis. The 74ft schooner **Woodwind** (☎ 410-263-7837; 80 Compromise St; day sailing/sunset cruises $25/27; ☺ May-Oct) offers two-hour cruises. The 19-mile **Baltimore & Annapolis Trail** (☎ 410-222-6244) is a popular recreational route that follows the old B&A Short Line Railroad.

Sleeping & Eating

The capital has many cozy B&Bs but few budget options, except for chain hotels outside the historic district. You're in better luck in the eating department. Annapolis brims with an eclectic assortment of eateries. The majority of restaurants line City Dock and Main St. As the T-shirts proclaim, 'Annapolis is a drinking town with a sailing problem' – so there's no shortage of nightlife.

ScotLaur Inn (☎ 410-268-5665; www.scotlaurinn .com; 165 Main St; r from $75) There are 10 simple, newly furnished B&B rooms in the heart of the historic district at this good-value inn.

Gibson's Lodgings of Annapolis (☎ 410-268-5555; www.aumcyber.com/gibson; 110 Prince George St; r with shared bathroom from $70) Rooms are in three separate buildings, two of which are old Annapolis homes, and feature antique furnishings. There's a pretty garden courtyard. Rates include a full continental breakfast.

Country Inn & Suites (☎ 800-456-4000, 410-571-6700; www.countryinnsdestinationguide.com; 2600 Housley Rd; r from $110; 🐾) A surprisingly charming chain hotel that offers free shuttles to the historic district and both an indoor and outdoor pool.

49 West Cafe (☎ 410-626-9796; 49 West St; mains $2-12) Grab one of the books or newspapers scattered around this casual café that encourages lingering. Food is light gourmet and there is live classical and jazz music Tuesday to Saturday nights. The giant appetizers make a meal, or you can try the slippery $1 oyster shooters and platefuls of other catches of the day in this historic waterfront tavern.

Buddy's Crabs & Ribs (☎ 410-626-1100; 100 Main St; mains $12) This boisterous eatery draws a young crowd. The emphasis is on seafood and ribs.

Chick & Ruth's Deli (☎ 410-269-6737; 165 Main St; mains under $10; ☺ 24hr) This deli doubles as a 24-hour diner, where reciting the Pledge of Allegiance is mandatory every morning at 8:30am (9:30am weekends).

Rams Head Tavern (☎ 410-268-4545; 33 West St; mains from $6) One of the town's top nightlife destinations, this place also features sophisticated pub grub – try one of the burgers. There are 170 beers to choose from, including local brews. The small stage inexplicably attracts national bands and performers (concert tickets from $10).

Getting There & Around

Greyhound runs buses to Washington, DC ($11.50, one hour, at least daily). **Annapolis Transit** (☎ 410-263-7964) buses and trolleys provide local transport.

OCEAN CITY

Known as OC, Maryland's mammoth Atlantic coast resort swells in summer when Coppertone-slicked beachgoers crowd the boardwalk corn-dog stands and Skee-Ball arcades, and cruise the Coastal Hwy lined with budget motels. Slightly sleazy, very American, OC is a party destination and young Washingtonians flock here by the hundreds on the weekends. It's about 140 miles east of DC on Hwy 50.

The **visitors center** (☎ 410-289-8181; cnr Coastal Hwy & 40th St; ☼ 9am-5pm) in the swank convention center can help you find lodging and more.

Extending 2.5 miles from the inlet to 27th St, the **boardwalk** is the center of the action. Try the **Jolly Roger Amusement Park** (☎ 410-289-3477; cnr Thirtieth St & Coastal Hwy; admission $30; ☼ 2pm-midnight) for roller-coaster action or the **Splash Mountain Water Park** (☎ 410-289-6962; 7401 Philadelphia Ave; admission $30; ☼ 10am-9pm) for crazy water rides. An early morning bike ride down the boardwalk is a pleasant diversion from all the sand. Check out **Continental Cycle** (☎ 410-524-1313; cnr 73rd St & Coastal Hwy; per hr from $4) for rentals. Or you could take the free option and just hang out on the long golden sand beach.

Sleeping

Of the 9500 guest rooms in town, the cheapest can be found around the inlet at the south end and throughout town on the bay side. Rates drop dramatically in the off season (March to April and November to December). The rates below are for the summer season.

Surf Villa (☎ 410-289-9434, 888-333-7873; www .surfvilla.com; 705 N Baltimore Ave; r weekdays/weekends from $79/99; ☒) This is a comfy hotel boasting rocking chairs, ocean-view rooms, as well as shower and changing facilities on checkout days.

King Charles Hotel (☎ 410-289-6141; www.king charleshotel.com; 1209 Baltimore Ave; r weekdays/ weekends from $83/101; ☒) This place feels like a summer cottage and is an outstanding deal for high season. It's centrally located half a block from the beach in the heart of the boardwalk action.

Ocean City Campground (☎ 410-524-7601; www .occamping.com; 70th St on Coastal Hwy; campsites $32) Situated just one block from the beach, this friendly park is surrounded by plenty of amusements, as well as a convenient local bus stop out the front (for more camping options see Detour – Assateague Island, p244).

Eating & Drinking

Plenty of cheap eats line the **boardwalk** and **Coastal Hwy** (watch for many all-you-can-eat and early-bird deals, particularly on seafood). Make sure to buy a big bucket of Thrashers french fries from one of the stands on the boardwalk. Douse them with vinegar and salt. It's an OC tradition. An influx of dance clubs cluster around the boardwalk's southern tip.

Paul Revere Smorgasbord (☎ 410-524-1776; 2nd & Boardwalk; buffet $9) To really fill up, do as the starving college students do and head here on Friday or Saturday nights for the all-you-can-eat colonial feast – heavy on meat, fish and, of course, crabs. The food isn't the best out there, but you can't beat the price. If you arrive between 4pm and 4:30pm it's even cheaper!

Phillip's Restaurant at 21st Street (☎ 410-289-6821; 2004 Philadelphia Ave; mains from $10) Though now synonymous with crabs in the DC region (Phillip's operates restaurants throughout the capital region), it all started in Ocean City. The restaurant is a casual place, with white paper on the tables and a huge menu emphasizing crabs, which is what you should order.

Buxy's Salty Dog Saloon (☎ 410-289-0973; cnr 28th St & Bayside; mains from $6) The casual (and often boisterous) Salty Dog delivers inexpensive burgers. There's a daily happy hour and lunch specials.

Dumser's (☎ 410-250-5543; 12305 Coastal Hwy; lunch from $3, dinner from $7) A long-time local favorite, this country kitchen–style place serves comfort food – think fried chicken and tasty crab cakes. It started as an ice-cream parlor, and the creamy concoction is still a mainstay. There are more than 20 varieties of sundaes to choose from.

Seacrets (☎ 410-524-4900; 117 W 49th St) A Jamaican-themed bar and club straight out of MTV's *Spring Break*, Seacrets has beach parties, spring-loaded indoor dance floors, and watery areas where you can drift in an inner tube while sipping your drinks.

Scandals Night Club & Sports Bar (☎ 410-723-0500; 44th St Shopping Center) Catering to 20-somethings looking to drink, Scandals has fish bowl draft beers, a packed dance floor and a sports bar.

Party Block (☎ 410-289-6331; 17th St & Coastal Hwy; entry before/after 10pm free/$5) Combining four wild nightclubs, it offers a slightly

DETOUR – ASSATEAGUE ISLAND

This beautiful 37-mile-long barrier island preserves a rare stretch of undeveloped seashore. Legendary herds of wild horses roam free on the island. Its lower third is in Virginia (see p234). Get maps and information at the **Barrier Island Visitors Center** (☎ 410-641-1441; Rte 611).

Two **campgrounds** (☎ 800-365-2267; campsites $10-14) maintained by the NPS are near the access road. **Backcountry camping** (permit $5, plus NPS entry fee $5) is a great alternative if you're searching for serenity. **Assateague State Park** (☎ 410-641-2120; campsites $20) offers 350 campsites with bathrooms and hot showers.

raunchy yet fun clubbing experience and plenty of bikini contests.

Getting There & Around

Carolina Trailways (☎ 410-289-9307; cnr 2nd St & Philadelphia Ave) has regular buses to major regional cities. The **Ocean City Municipal Bus Service** (☎ 410-723-1607; day pass $1; ☽ daily) runs the length of the beach.

WESTERN MARYLAND

This obscure region offers mountain recreation set against scenic Appalachian landscapes and significant Civil War sites, most notably Antietam.

Frederick

A popular stop along the Civil War trail (it's halfway between the blockbuster battlefields of Gettysburg and Antietam), Frederick is a quiet place with a 50-square-block historic district retaining many 18th- and 19th-century buildings.

The **visitors center** (☎ 301-663-8687; 19 E Church St at Market St) conducts weekend walking tours ($4.50).

The **National Museum of Civil War Medicine** (☎ 301-695-1864; 48 E Patrick St; admission $6.50; ☽ 10am-5pm Mon-Sat, 11am-5pm Sun), Frederick's premier attraction, guides visitors through a personal look at the health conditions soldiers faced on the battlefields and beyond.

You can camp at **Gambrill State Park** (☎ 301-271-7574; Rte 40; campsites from $10), 5 miles northwest of town. Chain-motel rooms at around $65 are south of town off I-270.

Taverns, a deli and an Irish pub can be found along Market St. **Mudd Puddle** (☎ 301-620-4323; 124 S Carroll St; sandwiches from $4) prepares tasty, inexpensive Italian sandwiches.

Frederick is 50 miles northwest of DC and accessible via **Greyhound** (☎ 301-663-3311; E All Saints St) and weekday-only **MARC** (☎ 301-228-2888; 141 B&O Ave at East Ave) trains.

Deep Creek Lake

In the extreme west, Maryland's largest lake is a great place to play – in any season. In the summer, water sports dominate, in the winter, it's the ski slopes. Our favorite time to visit is in the fall, when the Allegany Mountains turn a vibrant red and orange. Stop by the **visitors center** (☎ 301-387-4386; www .garrettchamber.com; 15 Visitors Center Dr) for information on all outdoor activities.

Boating is the most popular summer activity and there are numerous places to pick one up along US Rte 219. Canoes cost about $6 per hour, fishing boats about $15 and ski boats start at about $20 an hour. Try **Aquatic Center** (☎ 301-387-8233; 634 Deep Creek Dr).

Deep Creek Lake State Park (☎ 301-387-5563; State Park Rd; admission $2; ☽ 8am-sunset summer, 8am-4pm winter) has a number of hiking trails, ranging from easy to difficult. Try the Indian Turnip Trail. At 2.5 miles, it's the park's most scenic. The park also features an 800ft sandy beach, great for swimming on a hot summer day.

In winter, Deep Creek Lake is home to Maryland's only ski area, **Wisp Resort** (☎ 301-387-4911; www.gcnet.net/wisp; 290 Marsh Hill Rd; lift tickets from $35; ☽ Dec-Mar). There are 23 ski runs for all levels, including long scenic trails, fast runs through the forest and a straight-down-the-face run with lots of moguls for those wanting more adventure.

Stay on the shores of the lake at the **Point View Inn** (☎ 301-387-5555; 609 Deep Creek Dr; r from $50). The motel-style rooms have porches overlooking the lake and most feature some type of antique furnishings. The state park has 112 campsites ($25).

The **Deep Creek Brewing Company & Restaurant** (☎ 301-387-2182; 75 Visitor Center Dr; mains from $7) serves hearty pub grub and handcrafted beers, created on the premises. It's a casual spot in a gorgeous location. Picture windows offer lake views, and there are high ceilings and a fireplace. It's behind the visitors center.

DETOUR – ANTIETAM NATIONAL BATTLEFIELD

Called 'Sharpsburg' by Southerners, the Battle of Antietam (ann-tee-tum) was the bloodiest day of the Civil War and in US history. On September 17, 1862, General Lee's first invasion of the North was stalled in a tactical stalemate that left 23,000 dead, wounded or missing. As a comparison, that's nine times the number of US soldiers killed in the D-Day invasion in WWII. The battlefield and surrounding area are solemn and haunting, uncluttered save for plaques and statues. Living-history demonstrations are conducted monthly from June to December.

The **visitors center** (☎ 301-432-5124; State Rd 65; 3-day pass $3; ☼ 8:30am-6pm) offers driving-tour pamphlets and audiotapes ($5) to guide you past 8 miles of evocative landmarks; free summer talks and walks are also available.

Enjoy a gourmet sandwich on the deck at **Canoe on the Run** (☎ 301-387-5933; 2622 Deep Creek Dr; sandwiches from $3). It also serves beer, wine, coffee and pastries.

Deep Creek Lake is best reached by car. From the east or the west take I-68 to US Rte 219.

DELAWARE

Most people fly through Delaware so fast, on their way to somewhere else, they hardly notice they've entered a new state. But the Delaware seashore has some classic East Coast beaches that are always hopping with young partygoers in the summer. Beyond these destinations, however, the region holds few attractions for the budget traveler.

WILMINGTON

Located in the wooded and green Brandywine Valley, Delaware's largest city makes a decent stop-off if you're tired of driving on I-95. In the process of reinventing itself, the new Riverfront, south of the downtown, is turning old warehouses and other industrial sites into shops, restaurants and museums. The city's central commercial district is along Market St, and here you'll find more museums, boutiques and restaurants.

The **visitors center** (☎ 302-652-4088; www.visitwilmingtonde.com; 100 W 10th St) offers the usual information. A mile from downtown, the **Delaware Art Museum** (☎ 302-571-9590; 800 S Madison St; adult/student $7/2.50; ☼ 10am-6pm Tue, Thu & Fri, 10am-9pm Wed, 10am-5pm Sat, 1-5pm Sun) is known for its holdings of American art (from 1840 to the present).

The **Fairfield Inn** (☎ 302-292-1500; 65 Geoffrey Dr; r from $60; ☒ ☒) offers good-value accommodation in nicely furnished rooms. There's a

complimentary continental breakfast in the morning.

Brandywine Brewing Company Restaurant & Brewery (☎ 302-984-2800; cnr 9th & Orange Sts; mains from $7) offers a constantly rotating selection of beers, as well as American cuisine in a relaxed setting.

The **Backstage Cafe** (☎ 302-778-2000; 100 S West St; mains from $8), on the Riverfront, offers happy-hour specials, DJ dancing and occasionally live bands. The menu features everything from pasta and pizza to sandwiches, and music memorabilia graces the walls.

DELAWARE SEASHORE

The 28 miles of pristine, sandy Atlantic Ocean beaches are the best reason to linger (and party) in the tiny state. Many businesses, campgrounds and services are open only for an extended summer season when prices are highest; off-season bargains abound.

Rehoboth Beach

Long known as a fashionable gay resort, downtown Rehoboth is a vibrant old seaside town tucked behind a very tacky stretch of Hwy 1 (follow signs to the resort area). Poodle Beach, at the southern tip of the boardwalk, is primarily gay, while lesbians congregate at North Shores Beach at the south end of Cape Henlopen State Park. Straight folks shouldn't feel excluded – the beach attracts all types.

The main drag, Rehoboth Ave, is lined with restaurants, food stalls and souvenir shops, from the easy-to-miss **visitors center** (☎ 302-227-2233; 501 Rehoboth Ave) to the mile-long beach boardwalk.

SLEEPING
Rehoboth Guest House (☎ 302-227-4117; www.guesthse.com/reho; 40 Maryland Ave; r with shared

bathroom from $70; 💢 💽) Gay owned and operated, this cool guesthouse is wildly popular for its afternoon wine-and-cheese parties, private sunbathing decks and immaculate rooms, not to mention its five-minute walk to the boardwalk. Reservations are highly recommended.

Summer Place Hotel (☎ 302-226-0766; www.reho bothsummerplace.com; 30 Olive Ave; r weekdays/weekends $80/120; 💢) You'll find the best budget option here, with a choice between spacious condos and comfy hotel-style rooms with refrigerators, microwaves and TV.

Royal Rose Inn B&B (☎ 302-226-2535; www.royal roseinn.com; 41 Baltimore Ave; r from $115; 💢) This place is a great bang for your buck, with a rooftop hot tub, screened porch and sundeck; it's just a block from the boardwalk.

Big Oaks Campground (☎ 302-645-6838; www .bigoakscamping.com; Rte 1 & Rd 270; campsites $32; 💽) Family-friendly and just 3 miles from the boardwalk, Big Oaks has a pool and playground. Beach shuttles are available.

EATING & ENTERTAINMENT

The beach boardwalk and Rehoboth Ave are a smorgasbord of quick food and bars.

Corner Cupboard (☎ 302-227-8553; 50 Park Ave; mains $10) This is a standout for its tucked-away location and Eastern Shore cookin'.

Sydney's Blues & Jazz (☎ 302-227-1339; 25 Christian St; mains from $13) Black-and-white photos of Hollywood royalty grace the walls, and gold and silver mobiles are suspended from the ceiling at this eclectic place that serves tasty Creole dishes and nightly jazz and blues.

Dogfish Head (☎ 302-226-2739; 320 Rehoboth Ave) The vast wine and beer selections here will keep you moving to the high-energy live music.

Blue Moon (☎ 302-227-6515; 35 Baltimore Ave) Popular at happy hour with gay men, it's an old favorite.

GETTING THERE & AROUND

Greyhound/Carolina Trailways (☎ 919-833-3601) buses stop on Rehoboth Ave.

Dewey Beach

Rehoboth's wild little sister, further south along Hwy 1, is best known for its frantic nightlife. When the sun goes down, throngs of under-30s swarm the streets and quickly forget their sunburns after downing a couple at the numerous watering holes.

If you're searching for seafood, head to **Crabbers' Cove** (☎ 302-227-4888; Dickenson St; mains from $10). This open-air seafood restaurant features all-you-can-eat specials and various other seafood dishes.

Obie's by the Sea (☎ 302-227-6261; cnr Virginia & Olive Aves; mains from $5) offers open-air dining right on the beach (as well as an indoor dining room upstairs) and a menu of sandwiches, burgers, ribs and salads. On weekends a DJ spins and revelers dance.

The town's two most popular nightspots are the **Rusty Rudder** (☎ 302-227-3888; 113 Dickenson St), which holds nightly deck parties overlooking the bay, and the **Bottle & Cork** (☎ 302-227-8545; Dagsworthy St), known for bringing in excellent live bands, with the Dave Matthews Band and Joan Jett among its past repertoire. The Bottle & Cork is a large place that can get really, really rowdy.

Reach Dewey Beach from Rehoboth on the **Jolly Trolley** (☎ 302-227-1197; ⌚ late May-late Aug). It departs from the boardwalk and Rehoboth Ave on Rehoboth Beach ($1.50).

WEST VIRGINIA

West Virginia comes complete with the unflattering stereotypes of hillbillies and front-yard appliances. The reality is completely different. Though it remains one of the more economically depressed states, there are jewels tucked within the hills of Appalachia in the form of ruggedly beautiful terrain, churning white-water rivers and charming towns that glitter far brighter than the way in which they are perceived.

HARPERS FERRY

Rich history and tremendous recreational opportunities collide on a scenic spit of land where the Shenandoah and Potomac Rivers meet to form the boundaries of three states. Abolitionist John Brown's famous raid of the federal armory in 1859 put Harpers Ferry on the map. Brown wanted to arm slaves and spark a national rebellion against slavery. His ambition died once he was caught and hanged, but the incident helped precipitate the Civil War. Today little has altered the town's antebellum appearance (the town was declared a National Historic Park in 1986), and visitors and residents alike wander down the steep cobblestone lanes.

Activities

The most fun in Harpers Ferry takes place on the hiking and biking trails or on the river. Passing through town, the 2160-mile Appalachian Trail (AT) is headquartered at the **Appalachian Trail Conference** (☎ 304-535-6331; www.atconf.org; cnr Washington & Jackson Sts; ☒ Apr-Oct), a tremendous resource for local hikers as well as backpackers. Day hikers can also scale the Maryland Heights Trail past Civil War fortifications or the Loudoun Heights Trail for scenic river views.

River Riders (☎ 800-326-7238; www.riverriders .com; 408 Alstadts Hill Rd; per half-day $27) is a one-stop shop for adventure sports. Rent bikes to explore the **C&O Canal** towpath. The scenic path follows the Potomac River. It's not exactly technical mountain biking stuff, but it's a beautiful ride. Or take raft and kayak trips down the Shenandoah River (Class I-III). The rafting costs $49, the kayaking $59. Try the kayaking if you're looking for more of an adrenalin rush. A cheaper (and equally fun) option is tubing. For $24 the company will give you a tube, life jacket and shuttle transport to and from the Potomac River. You're then on your own to negotiate the Class I-III rapids.

Sleeping & Eating

HI Harpers Ferry Lodge (☎ 301-834-7652; www .harpersferryhostel.org; 19123 Sandy Hook Rd; dm members/ nonmembers $15/17; closed Nov–mid-Mar) You'll find this lodge 2.5 miles from the train station in Knoxville, MD. It has the usual hostel amenities, as well as an outdoor campfire, and a bike and inner tube, which hostel guests can borrow.

Harpers Ferry KOA (☎ 304-535-6895; campsites/ cabins $26/42; ☒ year-round; ☒) Two miles southwest on Hwy 340, Harpers Ferry KOA is a good camping option that also offers rustic cabins. The heated Olympic-sized pool is an added bonus.

Last Resort Inn (☎ 304-535-2812; 280 Clay St; weekdays/weekends r $80/90; ☒) For a bit of a splash-out, this place boasts a magnificent view of three states and two rivers from its sweeping porch.

Anvil (☎ 304-535-2582; 1270 Washington St; mains 11-23) Here you'll find seafood and steak mains and fun happy hours.

Mountain House Cafe (☎ 304-525-2339; 179 High St; mains $5) This café serves up fresh salads and sandwiches in the backyard rose garden.

Getting There & Around

Daily **Amtrak** (☎ 800-872-7245) and **MARC** (☎ 800-325-7245) trains run between the historic-district station and Washington's Union Station (bikes are permitted if disassembled and boxed).

BERKELEY SPRINGS

Once the haunt of George Washington and co, today Berkeley Springs is a charming microcosm of spiritualism, artistic expression and soul-pampering spa centers; it boasts more masseuses in town than lawyers.

Don't let the clinical appearance deter you from a soak in the Roman-style baths at **Berkeley Springs State Park** (☎ 304-258-2711; bath with/without massage $38/20; ☒ 10am-4:30pm); it's a fantastic deal!

It's rare to find a classy place that still offers inexpensive rooms with shared bath rooms, but the **Berkeley Inn & Spa** (☎ 800-822-6630; www.theinnandspa.com; 1 Market St; r with shared bathroom from $49; ☒), across from the park, does just that. Another recommended option is the holistic **Coolfont Resort** (☎ 304-258-4500; 3621 Cold Run Valley Rd; campsites/r $20/95; ☒) for a *Dirty Dancing* camp-like setting spread over 1300 acres. The resort offers a variety of activities and lodging options.

Get a bite to eat, buy a local piece of artwork and listen to live entertainment at the casual **Tari's** (☎ 304-258-1196; 123 N Washington St; mains $10-25), or try one of the innovative sandwiches at **Inspirations Café & Bakery** (☎ 304-258-2292; 174 N Washington St; sandwiches $6.50).

MONONGAHELA NATIONAL FOREST

With 1400 sq miles of wild rivers, caves and dense forests, this vast expanse of rugged terrain in the Allegheny Mountains is what earned West Virginia the nickname 'Colorado of the East.' More than 850 miles of trails include the 124-mile **Allegheny Trail**, for hiking and backpacking, and the scenic 75-mile rails-to-trails **Greenbrier River Trail**, popular with cyclists.

Elkins, at the forest's western boundary, is a good base of operations. Here the **NFS Office** (☎ 304-636-1800; 200 Sycamore St; campsites/ primitive sites $5/free) distributes recreation directories for hiking, biking and camping. And **Fat Tire Cycle** (☎ 304-636-0969; 101 Randolph Ave) rents gear and sponsors excursions.

Snowshoe Mountain (☎ 877-441-4386; www .snowshoemtn.com; lift tickets $36, summer bike passes

> **SPLURGE!**
>
> Want to fly through a remote canyon on a rubber raft? Travel past towering sandstone cliffs, and fiery red and brilliant yellow trees in the fall? Want to plunge over waterfalls, get jostled on roller-coaster waves? Start your heart racing a little? Then you've come to the right spot. It's here you will find the New and Gauley Rivers, which offer some of the best Class V rafting in the country. On the Lower New (the best stretch of the New for adventure junkies), you'll encounter the first rapid just after you've put in, and they'll keep coming for the next three hours. At one point the river drops 32ft in less than a quarter of a mile.
>
> The best of the Gauley is rafted on select dates in September and October, when an immense amount of water is released from Summersville Dam to create stomach-churning world-class white water (the river is ranked among the top 10 in the world). Trips fill up fast, so booking ahead is advised. It's cheaper to raft the New during the week when trips cost $50. The Gauley starts at $70.
>
> Among the many state-licensed rafting outfitters in the area, **USA Raft** (☎ 800-872-7232; www .usaraft.com; Appalachian Dr; trips from $50) stands out.

from $15) is the state's largest downhill resort and serves as a mountain-biking center from spring to fall (rentals and excursions available).

Other highlights include the surreal landscapes at **Seneca Rocks**, 35 miles southeast of Elkins, which attract rock climbers to demanding challenges up 900ft-tall sandstone strata. **Seneca Shadows Campground** (☎ 877-444-6777; campsites from $13), 1 mile east, is handy to the rocks.

SOUTHERN WEST VIRGINIA

A mecca for white-water rafting (not to mention hiking, mountain biking and cross-country skiing), this is a must-not-miss region for anyone addicted to adrenalin. Fayetteville is the starting point for rafting. Once a sleepy blue-collar town, it's now an anchor for numerous river-running operations, and with the transformation comes good food, good drink and good shops.

Mountain Laurel RV Park/Campground (☎ 304-574-0188; Laurel Creek Rd at Rte 19; per person $6) is a cheap camping option in town. If you want to stay in style, nearby **Hawk's Nest State Park**

(☎ 304-658-5212; Hwy 60; r from $70), northwest of Fayetteville, offers views from its rim-top lodge. In summer it operates an aerial tram down to the river, where you can catch a cruising boat ride (tram closed Monday). Just south of Fayetteville is **Babcock State Park** (☎ 304-438-3004; State Rte 41 S; campsites/cabins $15/68), which offers accommodation, boat rentals and 15 miles of trails. **Elliot's Whitewater Grill** (☎ 304-574-3443; Laurel Cres & Rte 19; mains $9) is a good place to relax after rafting.

Between Hinton and Fayetteville you'll find 63,000 acres of stunning landscape protected at the **New River Gorge National River**. The 1000ft-deep gorge is the dramatic setting for rafting on the New River. At one point the river falls 750ft in 50 miles, creating the New's best sets of rapids. The crowning man-made attraction is the **gorge bridge**. It's the second-highest bridge in the US and the longest single-arch steel bridge in the world. The **Canyon Rim Visitor Center** (☎ 304-574-2115; US Rte 19 at Fayetteville) is the best place from which to view the bridge. Rim and gorge trails offer beautiful views. There are four free basic **camping areas**.

The South

HIGHLIGHTS

- **New Orleans** The cradle of jazz throws a huge party in its exotic setting (p254)
- **Charleston** Rocking nightlife, antebellum grandeur and two great hostels (p300)
- **Nashville** Dig down to the roots of country music at age-old honkytonks and the Country Music Hall of Fame (p282)
- **Cajun Country** Boogie to zydeco grooves and paddle the bayous alongside alligators (p269)
- **Off the beaten track** Hippy-dippy Asheville, NC, rocks with jam bands and is an idyllic base for venturing into the Blue Ridge and Smoky Mountains (p293)
- **Best Journey** A broad circuit could take in New Orleans (p254), Memphis (p277), Nashville (p282) and the Great Smoky Mountains National Park (p294), seguing into Savannah (p309), Charleston (p300) and the North Carolina Coast (p297)

FAST FACTS

- **Area** 426,100 sq miles

- **Big cities** Atlanta (population 3.6 million), Charlotte (1.3 million), Memphis (650,000), Nashville (570,000), New Orleans (485,000), Louisville (256,000)

- **Budget** $50-100 per day

- **Costs** campsites $16-30, bed in hostel $18-22, pulled-pork sandwich $4

- **Driving times** New Orleans to Memphis 6 hours, Raleigh to Atlanta 7 hours, Charlotte to Louisville 9 hours

- **Famous for** Civil War, Southern hospitality, belles and dandies, hillbillies, Bible Belt, jazz, blues and country music

- **Language** English, Cajun French is spoken throughout southern Louisiana

- **Population** 44,412,964

- **Phrases** *y'all* (you all, or you), *Dixie* (nickname for the South), *cotton-pickin'* (an infrequent substitute for 'mother-fuckin')

- **Seasons** summer (Jun-Aug) is humid, with the threat of hurricanes, spring (Mar-May) and fall (Sep-Nov) are warm, in winter (Dec-Feb) it snows infrequently along the Gulf, but the north gets dustings and the odd blizzard

- **States** Louisiana, Arkansas, Mississippi, Alabama, Tennessee, Kentucky, North Carolina, South Carolina, Georgia

- **Tasty treats** gumbo, boiled crawfish, pecan pie, fried chicken, chitterlings (fried pork intestines)

- **Time** Eastern Time Zone

- **Top hostel** Charleston Historic Hostel in Charleston, South Carolina (p302)

TRAVEL HINTS

Stop at state welcome centers for hotel discount coupons. Alligators can move with surprising speed, so don't get too close. Bring a hollow leg if going to New Orleans.

Much like the country girl of a country boy's dreams, the South is beautiful and a little bit trashy. And, not unlike Dolly Parton's smile, it's warm, crazy and shrewd. Southern hospitality is at once welcoming and kind of scary.

This is a land where alligators lurk beneath exotic Spanish mosses and kudzu vines threaten to reclaim old barns. Placid cotton plantations silently evoke their turbulent, not-so-distant past. Blue-grassy knolls nourish magnificent thoroughbreds for the urgent thrust of horse races. Bible-thumpers keep guns in their living rooms. Lacy iron balconies and antebellum columns conceal the Tennessee Williams dramas unfolding within. Being nosey visitors, we are interested. Very interested.

The South really isn't always so cotton-pickin' complicated, though. The people are friendly and generous and know how to have fun. After all, this is America's sweatbox, the well-spring of the nation's jazz, blues, country-and-western, rockabilly, gospel and blue-grass traditions. Soulful kitchens fuel rising spirits with fried catfish, truckstop biscuits, Virginia ham, barbecued pork shoulder, boiled crawfish and Creole gumbo. It's bad for the arteries, wondrous for the heart.

For the shoestringer, good news: you'll get more for your dollars in this part of the US.

HISTORY

As early as the 16th century, European explorers started arriving along the East Coast. They came from several directions and, as elsewhere in the country, their presence wreaked havoc on the Native Indians. Immigration increased sharply in the early 18th century. The 1803 Louisiana Purchase brought the land west of the Mississippi under US control and even more settlers.

President Andrew Jackson signed the Indian Removal Act in 1830, requiring the South's 'Five Civilized Tribes' – Cherokee, Choctaw, Chickasaw, Creek and Seminole – to relocate to 'Indian Territory' west of the Mississippi. A few isolated groups stayed, but most of the South was 'cleared' for settlement.

When the invention of the cotton gin mechanized the process of removing seeds from raw cotton, large-scale cotton growing became profitable. Cotton *was* the

Southern economy, but it was heavily dependent on Northern financiers who took much of the wealth back North.

Politically strong plantation owners depended on slave labor. When Lincoln was elected US president on an antislavery platform, all nine states except Kentucky seceded and most were devastated by the Civil War (1860–64) that followed. The Confederate states were readmitted to the Union only after they had abolished slavery and provided for black suffrage. Once readmitted, however, white elites imposed 'Jim Crow' laws designed to restrict black voting. White supremacist organizations like the Ku Klux Klan (KKK) were born and racial segregation became the norm.

In 1954, the US Supreme Court ruled that segregation of public schools was unconstitutional. Southern states did not accept this and the next 10 years saw demonstrations, protests and civil action aimed at desegregation and black political representation. Mississippi closed its public schools rather than let blacks enroll. Black students sat for days at North Carolina lunch counters waiting to be served. Segregated buses were boycotted for 13 months in Alabama. Under the leadership of Martin Luther King Jr, the protests were nonviolent, but often met with violent reaction.

The past few decades have been much more peaceful, but the South continues to grapple with its turbulent past. Phrases like the 'New South' suggest the region taking strides to move on. But while some in the South see the future in former president Bill Clinton's moderately progressive terms, the

---

THE BIG ISSUE: REBEL FLAGS

Those durned Confederate flags just don't seem to go away. You see them mostly on trucks driven by good ole boys, some of whom proclaim *not* to be racist. You can also see remnants of the old 'stars and bars' motif on many state flags throughout the region. This reluctance to let go of the rebellious symbol is by and large a sign of regional pride. But to many Southern blacks, whites' fondness for the old Rebel symbol suggests a powerful, haunting nostalgia for slavery times.

rise in neo-conservativism and Christian fundamentalism throughout the region suggest the old wounds haven't healed yet.

THE CULTURE

The South has pretty much gotten over the Civil War (1860–64). The decaying images of a defeated South, which lingered for more than a century, are all but gone now. The old mansions have been spiffed up, the KKK is much diminished in stature, and racial integration has become the law of the land.

For the most part, whites and blacks seem to maintain a cordial noncoexistence. Interaction is common, but rarely intimate. Blacks hold public office in many cities across the South, and blacks and whites mix in schools, stores and public places. Yet racism and racial inequality are still a reality. Educated Southerners, black and white, are quite open about these issues. They often see the rest of the country as somewhat hypocritical in its belief that racial problems are something particular to the South.

The South is known as the 'Bible Belt' because of the predominance of Southern Baptists in the region, and spiritual conviction is commonplace among whites and blacks. The region's mainstream is politically conservative, largely due to religious beliefs, as well as a strong appreciation for traditional ways of life and the right to bear arms.

Conservative standards of dress prevail, even in informal situations: for those wearing a T-shirt and jeans, the T-shirt usually tucked in. White and black men in southern Louisiana share a predilection for white Stetson hats, worn at a jaunty angle. On dance floors of Cajun or zydeco music clubs, the hats tipping one way and then t'other are dashing indeed. Southerners generally value a good time. Great music and rib-sticking food are the foundations for public festivals, church functions and family gatherings. Generational divides so common elsewhere in the country are less prevalent in the South, where social events typically draw young and old alike.

There are isolated pockets where people are deeply suspicious of strangers, but on the whole Southerners are a friendly, easygoing people. Even in large cities like New Orleans, perfect strangers strolling an uncrowded sidewalk are likely to wish each other a good morning. Making conversation is not hard to do, as people generally take an interest in travelers and often are eager to be helpful in some small way.

SPORTS & RECREATION

With its diverse topography, the South offers outdoor enthusiasts plenty of options. Along the coastal regions of North Carolina, South Carolina and Georgia, there is simply nothing better than getting a wave's-eye view from a kayak. Abundant outfitters offer guided trips through coastal rivers and marshes, and abundant hire companies make renting boats a breeze.

In Louisiana, just slipping through the swamps in a canoe or on a gator tour will transport you into another world. Truly excellent mountain biking, camping and hiking abounds in the Blue Ridge and Great Smoky Mountains in Tennessee, North Carolina and Kentucky.

Horseback riding is a fun way to explore trails and green pastures, especially in Tennessee and Kentucky, where farms offer horseback riding to guests.

ARTS & ENTERTAINMENT

Music is the South's great gift, so little wonder many a traveler goes hunting for some blues in the Mississippi Delta, jazz in New Orleans, soul music in Memphis, country-and-western in Nashville, Cajun and zydeco in southern Louisiana, bluegrass in Kentucky and traditional folk ballads in the hills of Tennessee. One can certainly be satisfied sticking to such a plan, but the music of the South tends to bleed and blend in all directions, so these musical forms can be heard throughout the region. And the South rocks and raps, too. You might encounter surf-tinged instrumentals and jam bands in the Carolinas, trombone-wielding hip-hoppers in New Orleans, alt-rockers in Athens, Georgia, or metal-heads in the land of Elvis.

The Southern gift of the gab has translated brilliantly to the written page, and many of the USA's great writers are or were Southerners. Prose dense as kudzu vines has flowed from the pens of William Faulkner, Eudora Welty, Walker Percy, Flannery O'Connor, James Agee, Harry Crews, Zora Neale Hurston, Robert Penn Warren and Larry Brown. The South's great playwright, Tennessee Williams, didn't produce light entertainment either.

THE SOUTH

THE SOUTH

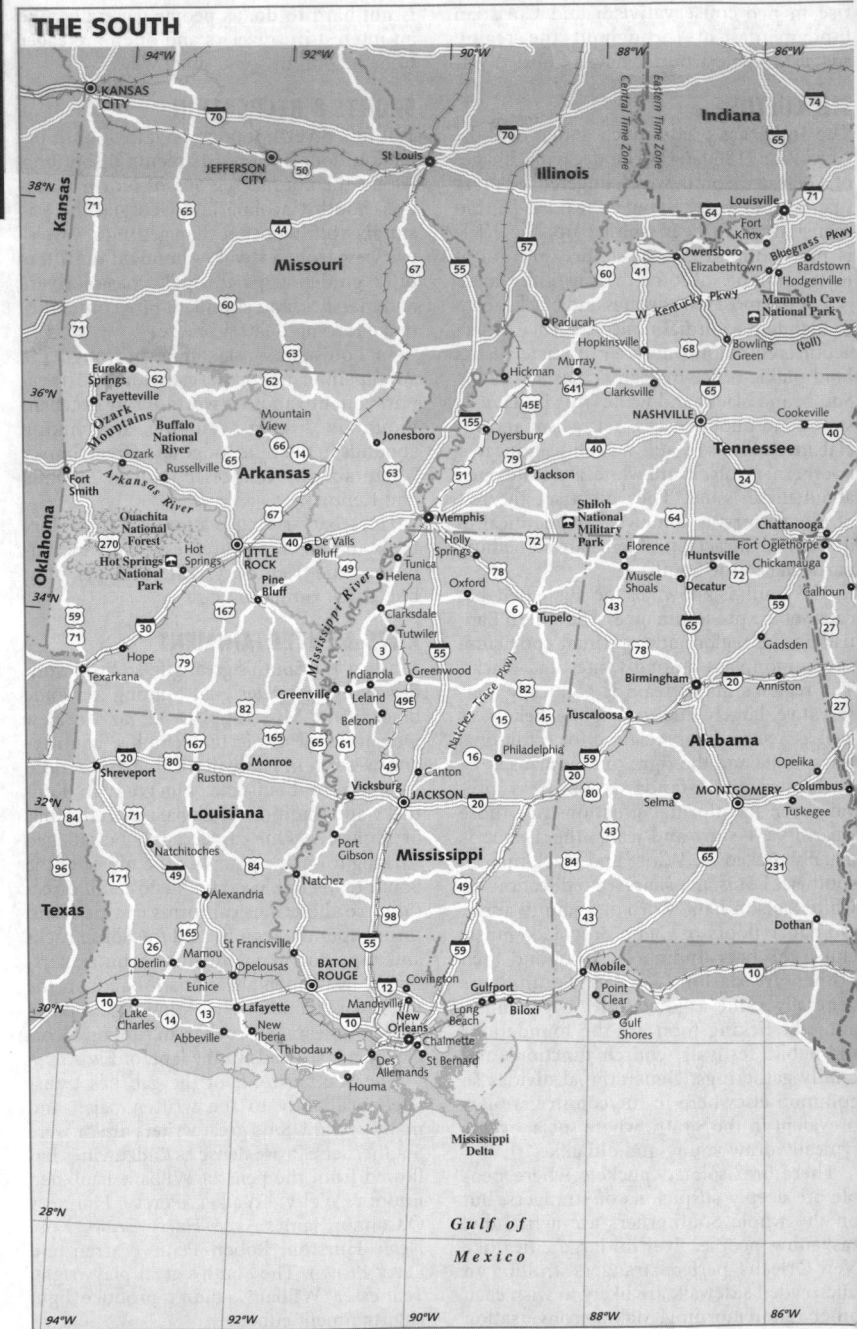

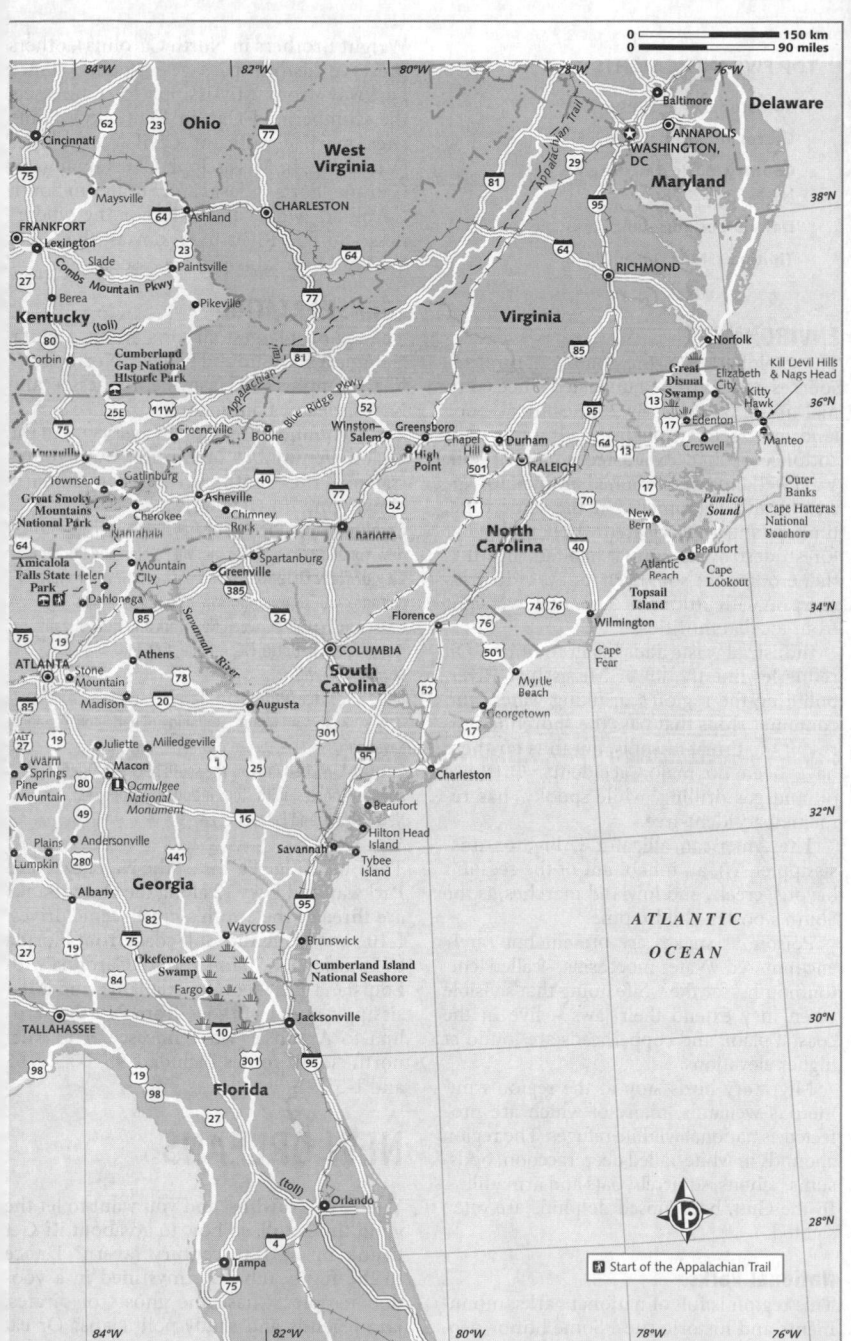

Start of the Appalachian Trail

TOP FIVE MUSIC SIGHTS

- **Sun Studio**, Memphis (p279)
- **Graceland**, Memphis (p278)
- **Country Music Hall of Fame**, Nashville (p284)
- **Delta Blues Museum**, Clarksdale (p274)
- **Tipitina's**, New Orleans (p267)

ENVIRONMENT

The exploitation of the South's natural resources has continued unabated since colonial times. By the early 20th century, poor land management of the singly important cotton crop had exhausted southern soil. Vital wetlands were drained or filled for agricultural development. At the same time, timber companies cleared whole regions of forest, destroying animal habitats and further eroding the soil. Even today, industries carry on with little environmental oversight from local authorities.

Industrial waste adds insult to injury. Oil refineries line the lower Mississippi River, polluting the region's drinking water, and container ships that pass the shoreline represent the threat of spills, but thus far there have been no major accidents. Offshore oil and gas drilling, while spooky, has remained accident-free.

The American alligator (Alligator mississippiensis), an inhabitant of the region's bayous, creeks and lowland marches, is the South's poster-child reptile.

Poisonous snakes are present but rarely encountered. Water moccasins – called 'cottonmouths' for the white lining that's visible when they extend their jaws – live in the coastal plain, and copperheads are found at higher elevations.

Migratory birds stop at the region's numerous wetlands, many of which are protected as national wildlife refuges. The region abounds in white-tailed deer, raccoon, opossums, rabbits, squirrels, bats and armadillos. In the Gulf, bottlenosed dolphins are often sighted.

National Parks

This region is full of national parks, monuments and historic sites. Some honor people (Martin Luther King Jr in Georgia, the Wright Brothers in North Carolina), others preserve historic passages (Natchez Trace Parkway from Mississippi to Tennessee, the Cumberland Gap in Kentucky). Some sites mark significant Civil War battles (Vicksburg in Mississippi, Chickamauga in Georgia, Forts Pulaski and Sumter in South Carolina), while others honor the wilderness (Buffalo River in Arkansas, the Great Smoky Mountains in Tennessee).

TRANSPORTATION

The region's largest airports are in Atlanta, Georgia; Charlotte and Raleigh, North Carolina; Memphis and Nashville, Tennessee; and New Orleans, Louisiana.

Greyhound buses stop in every city in the region. A number of Amtrak train routes traverse the South, several conveniently converging on New Orleans.

Carolinian and Piedmont Travels inland from New York City to Charlotte, NC, via Raleigh and Durham.

City of New Orleans Travels between New Orleans and Chicago, with stops at Jackson, MS, and Memphis.

Crescent Travels between New York and New Orleans, stopping at Charlotte, NC; Atlanta, GA; and Birmingham, AL.

Silver Service/Palmetto Travels between New York City and Miami, stopping at Charleston, SC, and Savannah, GA.

Sunset Limited Crosses the south between Orlando, FL and Los Angeles, with stops including Mobile, AL; New Orleans and Lafayette, LA.

The Blue Ridge Parkway, the Natchez Trace Parkway and Hwy 12 along the Outer Banks are three of the South's most scenic drives. I-10 runs along the Gulf coast from Florida to Louisiana; I-20 links South Carolina with Louisiana via Georgia, Alabama and Mississippi; and I-40 goes from North Carolina to Arkansas via Tennessee. The chief north–south routes include I-95, I-75, I-65 and I-55.

NEW ORLEANS

You're in 'Nawlins' and you want to let the good times roll, so how to go about it? Get drunk in an 18th-century tavern? Dance to the funky tuba? Be mystified in a voodoo temple? Chase the ghosts of pirates, jazz legends and shady politicians? Or eat to your heart's content, slurping gumbo, scarfing down oyster po-boy sandwiches and boiled crawfish until you're fit to burst? In the tradition of the best entertainment capitals, New Orleans disregards the old credo to 'leave 'em wanting more.' The Big Easy aims to satiate, no doubt about it.

New Orleans has a vibrant, old-school panache that lends a certain dignity to otherwise debauched activities. Amid the French Quarter's Creole cottages and cast-iron balconies, the sonorous echoes of trad jazz, modern jazz, funky brass, R & B and soul music put bounce in the bar-hopper's stride. Succulent restaurant aromas recall a history infused with African, Spanish, French, Italian and Caribbean cultural influences.

Though its famous month-long Mardi Gras celebration and Jazz Festival up the ante for craziness and fun, New Orleans is a blast anytime. When things are quiet in early morning or late afternoon, New Orleans reveals its many sober charms.

HISTORY

The town of Nouvelle Orléans was founded as a French outpost in 1718 by Jean Baptiste Le Moyne de Bienville. Early settlers arrived from France, Canada and Germany, and the French imported thousands of African slaves and ex-convicts from the jails of the mother country. Many slaves earned their freedom and assumed an established place in the Creole community as *les gens de couleur libres* (free people of color). Unsuccessful in conventional commerce, the city developed a reputation for smuggling.

In 1762, the vast Louisiana territory, including New Orleans, was transferred to the Spanish, who were responsible for building the French Quarter as it still looks today. The French resumed control in 1800, but three years later Napoleon negotiated the Louisiana Purchase with the US. The resulting influx of Anglo Americans led to an expansion of the city into the Central Business District (CBD), Garden District and Uptown. By 1840 New Orleans was the US's fourth-largest city, with over 100,000 people.

New Orleans survived the Civil War intact after an early surrender to Union forces. However, the end of the plantation economy and the declining importance of river traffic hit New Orleans hard, and its economy languished until oil and petrochemical industries developed in the 1950s.

GETTING INTO TOWN

From the airport, the **Jefferson Transit Airport Express** (☎ 504-737-7433; fare $1.50) runs bus E2 to Tulane Ave opposite New Orleans Public Library. From there it's a few blocks walk to the French Quarter. From the airport you can also take the **Airport Shuttle** (☎ 504-522-3500; one way per person $10) to downtown hotels. Taxis to downtown cost $28 for one or two people, $12 more for each additional passenger.

Greyhound and Amtrak both stop at Union Passenger Terminal, on the corner of Loyola and Howard Aves in the CBD. It's a 15-minute walk to the Quarter from there. City buses stop across Loyola Ave, corner of Howard Ave (look for the sheltered stop). Get bus No 17 to the edge of the Quarter, at the corner of Rampart and Canal Sts. Taxis from the station to the Quarter cost $5.

It is in New Orleans, some say, that jazz music was born at the end of the 19th century. If that claim is somewhat exaggerated, clearly New Orleans, more than any other place, contributed to the early development of the music.

ORIENTATION

New Orleans is wedged between the Mississippi River to the south and Lake Pontchartrain to the north. The historic French Quarter *(Vieux Carré)* consists of 80 blocks around Jackson Sq. Canal St separates the Quarter from the CBD, which extends to the freeway overpass at Lee Circle. Beyond that, following St Charles Ave, are the Lower Garden District, a ramshackle neighborhood with a bohemian enclave, and the lovely Garden District, known for its historic homes. St Charles Ave follows the river into Uptown and the Riverbend area (populated by many students of Tulane and Loyola universities).

The Tremé district, across Rampart St from the French Quarter, is a predominantly black residential district. Faubourg Marigny, a creative enclave, is centered on Frenchmen St, downriver from the French Quarter. The rugged Bywater district of the city is even further downriver.

Workable maps of the city are available at the New Orleans Welcome Center in Jackson Sq (p258). Lonely Planet's *New*

500 m
0.3 miles

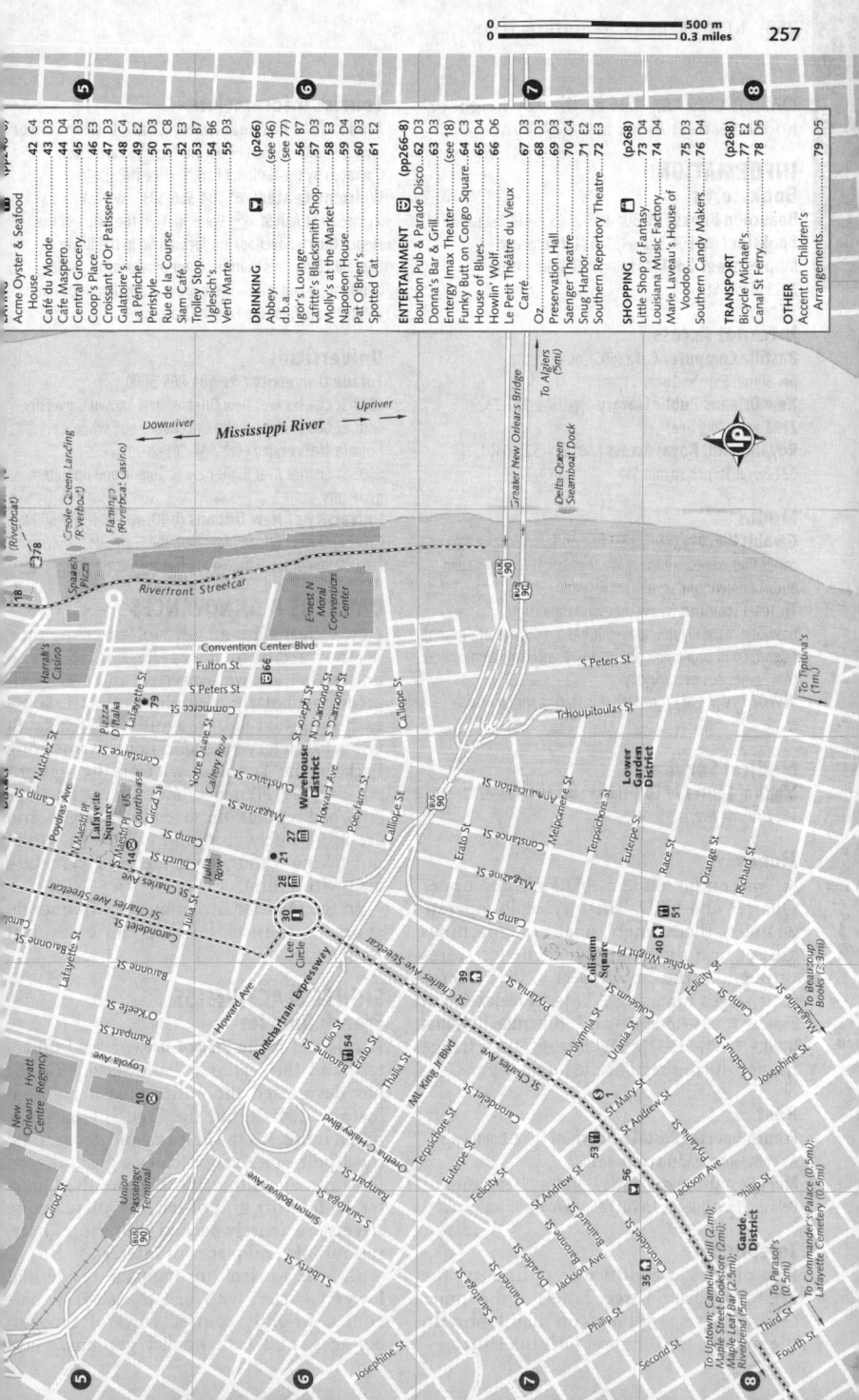

Orleans City Map has all the key neighborhoods, a street index and key sights.

INFORMATION
Bookstores
Beaucoup Books (☎ 504-895-2663; 5414 Magazine St)
Bookstar (☎ 504-523-6411; 414 N Peters St)
Maple Street Bookstore (☎ 504-866-4916; 7529 Maple St)

Internet Access
Bastille Computer Café (605 Toulouse St; per 30min $5; ☼ 10am-11pm)
New Orleans Public Library (☎ 504-529-7323; 219 Loyola Ave; free)
Royal Blend, Royal Access (☎ 504-525-0401; 621 Royal St; per 30 min $5)

Media
Gambit Weekly (www.bestofneworleans.com) A free paper that comes out every Wednesday. It features solid entertainment and restaurant listings.
Times-Picayune (www.timespicayune.com) New Orleans' daily newspaper. It has a daily entertainment calendar and *Lagniappe*, an extensive entertainment guide that comes out every Friday.
WWOZ (90.7 FM) Tune into this station for Louisiana music.

Medical Services
Medical Center of Louisiana (☎ 504-903-2311; 1532 Tulane Ave)

Money
ATMs can be found at banks in the upper Quarter and CBD. These typically operate 24 hours. Increasingly, small cash machines are set up in bars and convenience stores throughout the city. Expect $2 to $3 service charges for using ATMs. **Travelex** (airport branch ☎ 504-465-9647) and **Hibernia National Bank** (☎ 504-533-5712; 313 Carondelet St) exchange money during regular business hours.

Post
French Quarter Postal Emporium (1000 Bourbon St) A central independent postal shop.
Main Post Office (701 Loyola Ave) All mail sent to General Delivery, New Orleans, LA 70112, goes to this branch.

Telephone
Pay phones are difficult to find in the French Quarter. Larger hotels in the upper Quarter have pay phones off their lobby. In the middle, try Bourbon Orleans Hotel.

Tourist Information
Jean Lafitte National Historic Park Visitor Center (☎ 504-589-2636; 419 Decatur St; ☼ 9am-5pm) Operated by the National Park Service (NPS).
Welcome Center (☎ 504-566-3031; www.bigeasy.com; 529 St Ann St; ☼ 9am-5pm) In the heart of the French Quarter overlooking Jackson Sq in the lower Pontalba Bldg, this visitors center provides lots of free information and maps. There are also smaller information kiosks throughout the French Quarter.

Universities
Tulane University (☎ 504-865-5000; 6823 St Charles Ave) New Orleans' best known university, with 22,000 students in its 11 colleges and schools.
Loyola University (☎ 504-865-2011; 6363 St Charles Ave) Right next to Tulane and operated by Jesuits.
University of New Orleans (UNO; ☎ 504-280-6000; Lakefront) New Orleans' largest public campus (16,000 students), with a good history department.

DANGERS & ANNOYANCES
New Orleans has a high violent-crime rate; it's not a city to be careless in. Stick to places that are well traveled and well peopled, particularly at night, and save some cash for a taxi fare to avoid dark walks. St Louis Cemetery No 1 and Louis Armstrong Park, in the Tremé district on the western edge of the French Quarter have particularly bad reputations, even by daylight, and are more safely visited in groups (if you're not taking a tour, coincide your cemetery visit with tours).

In the Quarter, street hustlers frequently approach tourists, but you can easily just walk away.

SIGHTS & ACTIVITIES
French Quarter
Locals call it the **Vieux Carré**, or 'Old Quarter,' and the National Park Service (NPS) has designated the entire area a national historic district, but the French Quarter is much more. It's the cultural and geographic focal point of New Orleans – ground zero for any visit to the city. Explore the Quarter on foot. Its grid of narrow, picturesque streets are densely packed with shops, bars, restaurants and places of interest.

Be sure to stroll through the residential lower Quarter, with ornate cast-iron balconies, brightly colored rows of shotgun cottages, and lush pocket gardens. Gays

NEW ORLEANS CEMETERIES

New Orleans' high-water table makes it difficult to bury bodies in the ground. Long ago, repeatedly resurfacing cadavers during heavy storms necessitated above-ground burials, with bodies placed in the stately family tombs and long rows of 'oven' vaults you'll see here.

Just outside the Tremé District is **St Louis Cemetery No 1** (Rampart St; admission free; ⊙ 8am-3pm), New Orleans' oldest cemetery. You don't need to be especially morose or Gothic to appreciate this crumbling beauty. Wandering at leisure, you'll appreciate the decayed statuary and ornate ironwork and stumble, literally, upon many historic tombs.

Naturally, St Louis Cemetery has many intriguing skeletons in its closets. Voodoo Queen Marie Laveau purportedly rests here, in a family crypt with the names Glapion, Laveau and Paris (branches of her family) etched on its marble front. Demented scenes from the 1969 film *Easy Rider* were filmed in the cemetery, and local lore maintains that a headless statue, on the Italian Society tomb, was decapitated by actor Dennis Hopper.

At the corner of Prytania St and Washington Ave you'll see the walls of **Lafayette Cemetery No 1** (admission free; ⊙ 9am-2:30pm), established in 1833. As in all of New Orleans' cemeteries, crypts here are above ground, with the magnificent marble monuments of the wealthy touching the overcrowded, oven-like tombs of the poor. You'll notice many German and Irish names on the tombs, almost all from 19th-century yellow fever epidemics. In 1995, author Anne Rice staged a faux funeral here – for herself, of course.

A caveat: don't enter the cemeteries alone; if the ghosts don't get you, the muggers might.

and party-happy itinerants populate this onetime Sicilian sector. Then hit the upper Quarter, with lascivious signs and boisterous tourist bars along Bourbon St, and the tony antique shops and galleries on Royal and Chartres Sts.

Beautiful **Jackson Square**, in the heart of Vieux Carré, is the best starting point for visitors. The traditional symmetry of French and Spanish colonial architecture contrasts with the square's modern cultural milieu. An assortment of street musicians (ranging from the genuinely talented to the genuinely bizarre) perform for a few bits tossed in the hat, while artists, jewelry vendors and tarot-card readers flashily offer their wares and services. That magnificent triple spired wedding-cake presiding over the square is **St Louis Cathedral**, a 1794 gem designed by Gilberto Guillemard.

On the north side of the cathedral, the 1813 **Presbytère** (☎ 504-568-6968; 751 Chartres St; admission $5; ⊙ 9am-5pm Tue-Sun) was designed by Guillemard as a rectory. It's now home to a Mardi Gras museum, with comprehensive displays of over-the-top masks and costumes, hand-painted parade floats, historic photos and documentary videos. This museum offers as good an insight into the city's mindset as you'll find anywhere.

Don't miss the fascinating, somewhat chaotic **Historic Voodoo Museum** (☎ 504-523-7685;

724 Dumaine St; admission $7; ⊙ 10am-8pm), which explores the exotic form of spiritual expression known here as voodoo, first brought to New Orleans by West African slaves who came on ships via Haiti. In New Orleans, voodoo fused with Catholicism, and saints and deities became interchangeable for followers of both religions. Much of the city's intriguing lore involves supernatural voodoo activities.

A trading site since pre-Columbian times, the **French Market** (⊙ 24hr) has three different markets. The open-air **Farmers Market** has a good stock of fresh fruit, vegetables, kitchen supplies, hot sauces, garlic strings and cookbooks. Cafés, such as the enjoyable **Café du Monde**, have occupied the French Market's upper end since 1860. Café du Monde's shaded patio tables are a great place to stop and passively watch Jackson Square entertainers and characters do their thing. For tacky souvenirs, peruse the **Flea Market's** aisles of inexpensive Mardi Gras masks and dolls, preserved alligator heads (which, of course, you really need to have) and CDs of dubious origin.

To get out on the Mississippi River, hop aboard the **Steamboat Natchez** (p262) for a boat ride up and down the Big Muddy. The boat dock is near Jackson Square – just listen for the sweet and very loud calliope (playing groovy renditions of old Barry

Manilow hits and the like), which is played on board prior to departure.

CBD & Warehouse District

On the upriver side of Canal St, the CBD and Warehouse District comprise the American commercial section that was established after the Louisiana Purchase in 1803. The Warehouse District is a fashionably gentrified area with restaurants and art galleries.

The **Canal St Ferry** (admission free; ☽ 6am-midnight) from the foot of Canal St is the best way to admire the city from the traditional river approach. The ferry crosses to the sleepy town of Algiers, which is worth a brief stroll.

Aquarium of the Americas (☎ 504-581-4629; Canal St; admission $15; ☽ 9:30am-6pm) simulates an eclectic selection of watery habitats including the Mississippi River and Delta wetlands. You can buy combination tickets to the Imax theater next door and to the excellent Audubon Zoo in Uptown (p260) – boats from Woldenberg Park will take you there.

To get an idea about what was on the minds of Confederate soldiers and their girlfriends, stop by the surprisingly engaging **Confederate Civil War Museum** (☎ 504-523-4522; 929 Camp St; admission $5; ☽ 10am-4pm Mon-Sat). There's no underlying political statement, and the topic of slavery is conspicuously absent, but this museum's generous array of personal effects – playing cards, undergarments, love letters and guns – are fascinating and oddly touching. A block away, General Robert E Lee, standing atop his monument at **Lee Circle**, continues to fix his gaze northward.

For contrast, get an idea of what goes on inside the heads of modern artists at the **Contemporary Arts Center** (CAC; ☎ 504-523-1216; 900 Camp St; adult/student $5/3; ☽ 11am-5pm Tue-Sun). In a renovated warehouse, this is a cool place to hang out, even if just to grab a coffee and check your email. The galleries, in converted warehouses, exhibit brilliant sculpture and multimedia performances, and the center has two performance spaces for plays, dance and concerts.

Ogden Museum of Southern Art (☎ 504-539-9600; 925 Camp St; admission $10; ☽ 10am-5pm Tue-Sun) began with the stellar collection of entrepreneur Roger Houston Ogden. The museum is affiliated with the Smithsonian Institute

in Washington DC, giving it access to that bottomless collection.

Half a world away from Normandy, the **National D-Day Museum** (☎ 504-527-6012; 923 Magazine St; admission $10; ☽ 9am-5pm) is a worthwhile stop for its eyewitness accounts of the Allied invasion, planes, weaponry and landing craft.

Garden District & Uptown

This is where you'll find the upper crust of New Orleans, as well as lovely Audubon Park. In this part of town, sightseeing is primarily about admiring beautiful buildings and graceful gardens, but at night there are good restaurants and clubs that draw out funseekers from New Orleans' highly regarded Uptown universities.

Heading Uptown is always a good excuse to hop aboard the **St Charles Ave streetcar** (fare $1.25; ☽ 24hr). The electric cars date to the 1920s. Slide into a window seat on one of the mahogany benches and enjoy the relentless panorama of 19th-century mansions, stately old churches and age-old live oak trees. The streetcar runs the entire length of St Charles Ave – some 5 miles – then hooks onto Carrollton Ave, in the Riverbend neighborhood, for just a few blocks.

It's worth disembarking in the **Garden District** for a walk around. Get off at Jackson Ave, head a block towards the river to Prytania St, a shaded residential thoroughfare lined with landmark homes, and wander around from there.

Further Uptown, near the more socially diverse Riverbend area, **Tulane** and **Loyola** universities occupy adjacent campuses. It doesn't take long to explore the small campuses. Be sure to drop by Tulane's University Center, which has a bulletin board for information on apartment rentals, sublets, ride shares and jobs. Also get information here about free open-air concerts on Friday afternoons in the spring.

Among the USA's best zoos, the **Audubon Zoological Gardens** (☎ 504-861-2537; 6500 Magazine St; admission $11; ☽ 9am-5pm) is the headquarters of the Audubon Institute, which also maintains the Aquarium of the Americas. Its Louisiana Swamp exhibit displays flora and fauna in a Cajun cultural setting, with alligators, bobcats, red foxes, black bears and snapping turtles. The nicest way to get there is by a zoo cruise from Woldenberg

Park, downtown. Combined tickets ($20) for the aquarium and zoo are available.

Esplanade Ridge & City Park

Esplanade Ave, a quiet and genteel thoroughfare with an oak-shaded median and many gorgeous 19th-century houses, runs from the lower edge of the French Quarter all the way out to City Park. Besides hosting the regular horseracing season, the **Fair Grounds**, a block off Esplanade near City Park, is also the site of the huge springtime New Orleans Jazz and Heritage Festival. Just before the entrance to City Park, **Bayou St John** snakes through the neighborhood. Follow it a couple of blocks down, away from the park, into a placid enclave with a variety of residential architectural styles. From a pedestrian bridge you'll sometimes see old-timers working crab traps in the bayou.

Acquired in 1850, the 1500 acre City Park is famous for its huge moss-draped live oaks and scenic bayou lagoons, especially along the narrow strip fronting City Park Ave. A stand of oak trees known as the **Dueling Oaks**, near the Museum of Art, were long ago the site of many pistol duels between hot-headed Creoles.

The **New Orleans Museum of Art** (☎ 504-488-2631; 1 Collins Diboll Circle; admission $6; ☒ 10am-5pm Tue-Sun, noon-8pm Thu) was founded in 1910. On Thursday night it's free to see the museum's extensive collection. A **Botanical Garden** (☎ 504-482-4888; admission $3; ☒ 10am-4:30pm Tue-Sun) features a stunning art-deco pool and fountain amid its native and exotic plants.

Lakeshore Park

This park stretches nearly 10 miles along a narrow shoreline strip fronting Lake Pontchartrain. It's where locals come to jog, bike, skate or check each other out – but not to swim in the polluted water.

FRENCH QUARTER WALKING TOUR

The French Quarter's narrow streets and passageways feature elegant architectural vestiges of the 18th-century Spanish colony. But the Quarter also has its mysterious charms, seen best at a slow, leisurely pace.

Begin your walk at the **Presbytère (1)**, on Jackson Sq, and head down Chartres St to the corner of Ursulines Ave and the **Ursuline Convent (2)**. Built in 1745–50, it's the oldest structure in the Quarter and the only

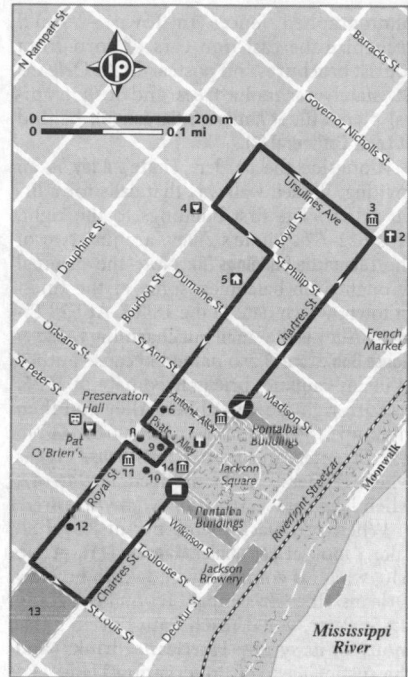

French-colonial building still standing in New Orleans.

Directly across Chartres St, at No 1113, the 1826 **Beauregard-Keyes House (3)** combines Creole- and American-style design. Civil War General PGT Beauregard rented rooms here, and author Francis Parkinson Keyes lived here from 1942 to 1970.

Continue up Ursulines Ave and then left onto Bourbon St. The ramshackle one-story structure, on the corner of St Philip St, is a great little tavern and National Historic Landmark called **Lafitte's Blacksmith Shop (4)**. Legend has it that the pirate Jean Lafitte ran a blacksmith shop here with his brother. True or not, it's always nice to drink in a bar that has its own stories. Head down St Philip St and back to Royal St, then take a right.

When it comes to classic New Orleans postcard images, Royal St takes the prize. Many of the structures along the following stretch are graced by cast-iron galleries and potted plants hanging from the balconies. Take it slow and appreciate the details.

At No 915 the **Cornstalk Hotel (5)** stands right behind one of the most frequently photographed fences in town – you'll recognize the cast-iron ears of corn from tourist brochures and postcards. At Orleans St, stately magnolia trees and lush tropical plants fill **St Anthony's Garden (6)**, behind **St Louis Cathedral (7)**.

Alongside the garden, **Pirate's Alley** is an inviting, shaded walkway that calls for a little detour. The first buildings to the right, Nos 622–624 Pirate's Alley, are just two of the **Labranche Buildings (8)**. Note the original wrought-iron balconies, some of the finest in town, which date to the 1840s. At 624 Pirate's Alley is the small but charming **Faulkner House Bookstore (9)**, so named because author William Faulkner briefly lived here in 1925.

Turn right down Cabildo Alley and then right up St Peter St, toward Royal St. At No 632 St Peter, the **Avart-Peretti House (10)** is where Tennessee Williams lived in 1946–47, when he wrote *A Streetcar Named Desire.*

When you reach the corner of Royal St, take a look at **LeMonnier Mansion (11)**, at No 640, which is commonly known to be New Orleans' first 'skyscraper.' If you kept going up St Peter, you'd reach Pat O'Brien's (famous for its syrupy 'Hurricane' drinks) and the rustic facade of Preservation Hall.

Turn left on Royal St. At No 520, a carriageway leads to the picturesque **Brulatour Courtyard (12)**, made famous by the countless artists who have drawn and painted it. On the next block, the massive 1909 **State Supreme Court Building (13)** was the setting for many scenes from the movie *JFK.* The white-marble and terracotta facade stands in attractive contrast to the rest of the Quarter.

Head down St Louis St to Chartres St and turn left. As Jackson Sq comes into view, you'll reach the Presbytère's near-identical twin, the **Cabildo (14)**. Have a seat on the benches in front. Relax and enjoy the lively street musicians.

TOURS

The Jean Lafitte National Historic Park Visitor Center (p258) offers free walking tours of the French Quarter at 9:30am (show up at 9am).

Royal Carriages (☎ 504-943-8820; fare per half hour $12.50; 9am-midnight) It's a touristy cliché, but a carriage ride through the French Quarter is still a great way to see the narrow streets at a gentle pace. The drivers are entertaining, if not always historically precise. Tours depart from Jackson Sq.

Historic New Orleans Walking Tours (☎ 504-947-2120; www.tourneworleans.com; admission $12-15) Great and informative walks through the Quarter, the Garden District, and St Louis Cemetery No 1. Call or check the website for times.

Steamboat Natchez (☎ 504-586-8777; www.steamboatnatchez.com; admission $19-26; departs 11:30am & 2:30pm) New Orleans' only steamboat, which was the traditional mode to travel the river. Cruises take two hours; skip the on-board buffet lunch. Buy tickets at the boat dock behind JAX Brewery at the foot of Toulouse St.

NEW ORLEANS JAZZ & HERITAGE FESTIVAL

New Orleans' second-biggest reason to party, 'Jazz Fest,' began as a celebration of the city's 250th birthday in 1968, attracting famous jazz players like Louis Armstrong and Duke Ellington. It moved to the Fair Grounds in 1972, expanded to two weekends in late April and early May and began showcasing different musical forms in addition to jazz. Today, it's a musical feast serving up rock, blues, R & B, gospel, zydeco, bluegrass, reggae, and, yep, jazz, on a dozen stages, give or take. Whatever your tunes of choice, you'll hear them at the festival.

What's great for the shoestringer is that Jazz Fest is genuinely cheap. Daily passes good for the hundreds of acts each day cost $20 in advance, or $25 at the gate. Bargains extend to food and drink, and, come hunger, vendors' food booths overflow with in-season boiled crawfish, oyster and catfish po-boys, jambalaya and barbecue galore. Bring your dancing shoes, sunscreen, a hat, some water and a blanket for chilling between shows.

The Jazz Fest schedule comes out in January and it's a good idea to make reservations as soon as possible. Hotels fill up, so if you've got friends in town, give 'em a ring. The Fair Grounds are open 11am to 7pm, but Jazz Fest festivities continue well into the wee hours in bars and clubs throughout New Orleans.

For more information, contact or write to the **New Orleans Jazz & Heritage Festival** (☎ 504-522-4786; www.nojazzfest.com; 1205 N Rampart St, New Orleans, LA 70116). Tickets are available through **TicketMaster** (☎ 504-522-5555).

FESTIVALS & EVENTS

Just after New Year's Eve (no slouch celebration here), New Orleans residents break out the king cakes and spirits to begin celebrating Carnival, which culminates in the Mardi Gras madness. Arthur Hardy's *Mardi Gras Guide* contains a good history along with detailed descriptions and maps of all parades.

Mardi Gras January or February.

St Patrick's Day March 17th. Debauched fun at Molly's on the Market in the Quarter and Parasol's in the Irish Channel spills out of the bars into the street.

French Quarter Festival Mid-April. Touted as a 'warm-up' to the Jazz Fest, but with key differences: it's in the Quarter and it's free. Great music, delicious food.

New Orleans Jazz & Heritage Festival Late April and early May.

Halloween October. A natural fit for New Orleans, where the entire French Quarter becomes a huge costume party.

Celebration of the Oaks December. All New Orleans seems to light up for the holidays, but City Park easily tops the rest of town with this drive-thru Santa-in-Vegas experience.

SLEEPING

The best values tend to be a ways out from the French Quarter, but, fortunately, public transit makes getting to and from them fast and easy. The prices below are high-season non-festival rates. Room rates peak during Mardi Gras and Jazz Fest, but in the hot summer months prices fall by as much as 50%. Hotel sales-tax amounts to 13%, plus $1 per person per night.

HI Marquette House Hostel (☎ 504 523 3014; www.hiayh.org; 2253 Carondelet St; dm $18-21, r from $50; ❌ ▣) Quiet and impressively clean, this 176-bed facility on the edge of the Garden District comprises four renovated buildings. Picnic tables in the backyard are an ideal place to meet fellow travelers. Igor's bar, around the block, doubles as a 24-hour laundry. The French Quarter is just a 10-minute ride from here on the St Charles Streetcar. Parking is available on the street.

India House Backpackers Hostel (☎ 504-821-1904; www.indiahousehostel.com; 124 S Lopez St; dm 15; r from $40; ▣ ▣ ❌) It's a free-spirited, disheveled sort of hostel, but India House is the fun place to be, especially in warmer months when backyard pool parties are in session. Three old houses have dorms, and there are private 'Cajun shacks' out back. Canal St streetcars link this mid-city hostel with the French Quarter, about 15 minutes away.

Lamothe House (☎ 504-947-1161; www.new-orleans .org; 621 Esplanade Ave; r $60-100; ▣ ❌ ❌ ▣) Just outside the Quarter on a beautiful tree-lined block, Lamothe House offers Creole elegance at an affordable price. Rooms open up to courtyard gardens, and continental breakfast is served in a stately old parlor. This is very convenient to exploring the Quarter and Marigny.

Mazant Guesthouse (☎ 504 944-2662; Info@mazant guesthouse.com; 906 Mazant St; r $40-50; ▣ ❌ ❌) In the Bywater, about a mile below the French Quarter, the Mazant offers comfortable lodging in a former plantation house. Its rooms, some with private bath, are furnished with slightly worn antiques, and the kitchen is great for getting to know fellow travelers while you're peeling vegetables. Vaughan's, an eccentric local tavern, is just a few blocks away.

French Quarter Guest House (☎ 800-529-5489; www.frenchquartergh.com; 623 Ursulines St; d $50-90; ▣ $12 ❌) If central French Quarter digs are your gig, this former Creole house, replete with old slave quarters, often has very reasonable rates. Rooms are clean and modern and a light breakfast is served in the pleasant courtyard.

St Vincent's Guest House (☎ 504-523-3411; www .stvincentsguesthouse.com; 1507 Magazine St; r $60-90; ▣ ❌ ❌ ▣) Originally an orphanage, the house's modernized rooms don't feel haunted by its former young tenants. At times, St Vincent's seems poorly managed, but guests seem mostly satisfied with what they get at this price.

Prytania Park Hotel (☎ 504-524-0427, 888-498-7594; www.prytaniaparkhotel.com; 1525 Prytania St; r from $60; ▣ ❌ ❌) One block from the streetcar line in the Garden District, this modern motel is adjoined to a restored 1850s guesthouse. It has 49 small but nicely appointed rooms, with refrigerators and microwaves, and it offers a free shuttle to the French Quarter.

Empress Hotel (☎ 888-524-9200; www.empress hotel.com; 1317 Ursulines St; r $25-50; ⓟ ⊠) It's in the dodgy Tremé District, but the Empress' rates are unbeatable. Rooms are basic and clean and the French Quarter is just four blocks away. Drive or take a cab at night.

SPLURGE!

Columns Hotel (☎ 504-899-9308; www.the columns.com; 3811 St Charles Ave; r $110-180; ⊠) Uptown, this stately 1883 mansion exudes old South luxury. Rooms are not particularly fancy, but the hotel is famous for its lively bar. A full Southern breakfast is thrown into the deal.

Other reasonable places include **Olde Town Inn** (☎ 504-949-5815; 1001 Marigny St; r $40-90; ⓟ), in the Faubourg Marigny, and **Ursuline Guest House** (☎ 504-525-8509; 708 Ursulines Ave; r $50-125; ⓟ ⊠) in the French Quarter.

The best camping near New Orleans is in **St Bernard Parish State Park** (☎ 504-682-2101; campsites $12), about 13 miles south near the Mississippi. The park has lagoons, nature trails and a swimming pool. Take Hwy 46 along the east bank to Bayou Rd and turn right on Hwy 39.

EATING

With its strong Creole, Cajun, French and African-American influences, this is a city that enjoys its food. The best news is that you can eat well in New Orleans without spending a lot of money.

French Quarter

Café du Monde (☎ 504-581-2914; 800 Decatur St; beignets $2.50; ⏱ 24hr) This New Orleans institution keeps its prices low despite its proximity to the French Market and Jackson Sq. It's a great place to kick off a morning with a café au lait and those irresistible piping-hot *beignets* (deep-fried pastries dusted with powdered sugar).

Central Grocery (☎ 504-523-1620; 923 Decatur St; sandwiches $6-8; ⏱ 8am-5:30pm Mon-Sat, 9am-5:30pm Sun) The *muffaletta* sandwich was invented by a Sicilian immigrant here way back in 1906. Today, it's still the best place in town to get the sandwich: a round, seeded loaf of bread filled with ham, salami and provolone, drizzled with olive relish. Buy one to share, then chase it with a Barq's root beer.

Verti Marte (☎ 504-525-4767; 1201 Royal St; mains $4-7; ⏱ 24hr) Those in the know drop by this busy little neighborhood market anytime day or night for quick take-out fare (it also delivers in the Quarter and the Marigny) The menu seems endless, but stick with basics like po-boys, seafood sandwiches and hot daily chef specials.

Croissant d'Or Patisserie (☎ 504-524-4663; 617 Ursulines Ave; mains $3-5) At this little bakery in the upper Quarter start your day with a fine pastry and coffee. Or come by for lunch

---

SPLURGE!

New Orleans has long been touted as one of America's great culinary capitals. The local cuisine is truly unique, and most visitors are flat-out astounded. You want to find out for yourself what the hype's all about, but most of the city's celebrated menus begin at around $20 a plate. So, where to break the budget?

Here are just a few of New Orleans' very best high-end eateries.

Peristyle (☎ 504-593-9535; 1041 Dumaine St; starters $8-16, mains $24-30; ⏱ dinner Tue-Sat) Chef Anne Kearney's intimate Provençal restaurant is one of New Orleans' more romantic spots for dinner. Delectable, traditional fare is prepared and served in a contemporary and most attractive fashion. Reservations essential.

Commander's Palace (☎ 504-899-8221; 1403 Washington Ave; lunch $14-25, dinner $22-35) The training ground for such fine New Orleans chefs as Emeril Lagasse and Paul Prodhomme, Commander's Palace offers outstanding old-style Creole cuisine with fresh, local ingredients. Reservations and a jacket (for men) required.

Galatoire's (☎ 504-525-2021; 209 Bourbon St; mains $17-35; ⏱ Tue-Sun) Local devotees so love this revered Creole establishment that to die here over a plate of, say, grilled *pompano* is considered a *belle mort*, or good death. Try the daily special for the freshest taste. Expect to wait outside for a table. A fine spot for lunch or dinner.

PO-BOYS & WHERE TO GET 'EM

They're not unlike heroes or submarine sandwiches, but what a treat po-boys are. So named because they've always been considered sustenance for the local hoi polloi, po-boys come in fried oyster, shredded roast beef, fried shrimp, fried catfish, and numerous other varieties. Order them 'dressed' with lettuce, tomatoes and mayonnaise for a perfectly satisfying and affordable meal. (They can also be 'undressed,' if that thrills you.) Po-boys turn up on lunchtime menus all over town, but here are a couple of specialist shops to mull over while working up your appetite.

Parasol's (☎ 504-899-2054; 2533 Constance St; po-boys $6) Locals will almost always direct you to this Irish Channel bar for the finest shredded roast beef po-boys.

Domilise's Po-Boys (☎ 504-899-9126; 5240 Annunciation St; po-boys $7) If you're looking for a humble little shack with a great big fryer, look no further. An immense Domilise fried shrimp po-boy qualifies as essential Uptown eating.

and fluffy quiches, croissant sandwiches and tasty gumbo.

Cafe Maspero (☎ 504-523-6250; 601 Decatur St; mains $5-9) Hungry travelers instinctively end up here, and for good reason: cheap, filling grub. This is a good spot for that steaming plate of red beans and rice you know you must have in New Orleans, or an immense catfish sandwich. Wash it down with cold draught Abita ale.

Acme Oyster & Seafood House (☎ 504-522-5973; 724 Iberville St; mains $6-10) Out-of-towners and locals flock to this old-school oyster bar – its reputation for shucking the city's best oysters, along with seafood gumbo and po-boys, has lasted since its inception in 1910.

Coop's Place (☎ 504-525-9053; 1109 Decatur St; mains $6-15) Local characters think of this as a friendly tavern that's good for cold beer and a game of pool, but we like to drop by for inexpensive Louisiana cuisine. It does a great sausage and red beans plate, and the rabbit jambalaya's equally tasty.

Faubourg Marigny

Siam Café (☎ 504-949-1750; 435 Esplanade Ave; mains $7-12; ♥ 5pm-2am) Dimly lit, small restaurant serving Thai standards, with spicy curries and vegetarian dishes.

La Péniche (☎ 504-943-1460; 1940 Dauphine St; burgers $6-10; ♥ 24hr Tue-Thu) This popular, late-night dinner spot serves greasy diner fare, but it gets interesting late at night when partiers from the Quarter start trickling in.

Garden District & Uptown

Uglesich's (☎ 504-523-8751; 1238 Baronne St; lunch $8-15; ♥ 11am-2pm Mon-Fri) It's a trek to get to this little family-run joint, but no one's ever left saying it wasn't worth the trouble.

Uglesich's dishes up authentic Louisiana cuisine in suitable down-home environs. Sample from the top notch oyster bar before feasting on fresh seafood specials. The 'trout muddy waters' qualifies as a local classic. Or you can settle for a drop-dead-delicious po-boy sandwich.

Rue de la Course (☎ 504-899-0242; 3128 Magazine St; baked goods $2-4; ♥ 7:30am-11pm) In Uptown, get strong coffee here and observe an always interesting crowd.

Camellia Grill (☎ 504-866-9573; 626 S Carrollton Ave; mains $2-8) At this Riverbend institution, snappy, gregarious waiters have been serving well-made short-order fare since the late 1940s. Fluffy omelettes and pecan waffles fly off the grill at all hours. If breakfast

LATE-NIGHT GRUB

New Orleans is an all-night sort of town, but even here most chefs eventually get tired and go to bed. Kitchens start to close at around 10pm or 11pm. Here's a quick cheat-sheet of restaurants that can be counted on past the midnight hour, all reviewed in these pages:

- **Café du Monde**, French Quarter, 24hr (p264)
- **Verti Marte**, French Quarter, 24hr (p264)
- **Siam Café**, Marigny, until 2am (left)
- **La Péniche**, Marigny, 24hr Tue-Thu (opposite)
- **Camellia Grill**, Riverbend, until 3am on weekends (above)
- **Trolley Stop**, Garden District, 24hr (p266)

anytime isn't your thing, burgers and fries ought to do you.

Trolley Stop (☎ 504-523-0090; 1923 St Charles Ave; burgers $6-10; ✹ 24hr) This former filling station serves a crazily diverse mix of customers with greasy burgers, eggs and potatoes. A convenient pit stop for guests of the nearby hostel.

DRINKING

New Orleans keeps its carnival atmosphere stoked around the clock year-round. Nonstop music spills out of clubs and bars, luring passersby in for one more drink. Most bars serve a 'hurricane,' with dark rum, white rum, orange juice, pineapple juice and grenadine in a hurricane-lantern shaped glass. Also common are the gin fizz and mint julep. You can get plastic 'go cups' at any bar; it's legal to drink in the streets but illegal to have open glass containers. A good many bars feature live music – jazz combos or acoustic soloists – and there's often no cover. Fun bars can be found throughout the French Quarter, along Frenchmen St in the Marigny and near the universities in the Riverbend area.

d.b.a. (☎ 504-942-3731; 618 Frenchmen St) A local hipster haunt, d.b.a. has the city's broadest beer selection and is a good stop if you're doing a Frenchmen St bar crawl. It often has live music and there's rarely a cover charge.

Spotted Cat (☎ 504-943-3887; 623 Frenchmen St) The friendly patrons don't seem to mind sharing a good thing in this little local. What's the good thing, you ask? Smart jazz and swing combos and stylishly casual

ambience. Well worth dropping by. Admission's free, but the beer's marked up.

Molly's at the Market (☎ 504-525-5169; 110? Decatur St) Irish cultural center of the French Quarter serves Guinness and grill fare to a diverse mix of local characters.

Abbey (☎ 504-523-7150; 1123 Decatur St) This dark little tavern, decorated with stained glass cathedral windows, draws a punky crowd. Cool place, top jukebox.

Napoleon House (☎ 504-524-9752; 500 Chartres St) Having opened its doors way back in 1797, this ancient haunt has seen it all, including years of decay. Its well-worn stuccoed walls haven't seen a dab of paint in what must be decades, lending the place an above-it-all sort of dignity. Grab a *muffaletta* and a beer here.

Pat O'Brien's (☎ 504-525-4823; 718 Peter St) New Orleans' most famous tourist bar claims to have introduced the sugary sweet hurricane to the world. A raucous party always seems to be happening in the labyrinthine series of alcoves and courtyards.

Lafitte's Blacksmith Shop (☎ 504-523-0066; 94 Bourbon St) A well-worn corner bar lit strictly from candles with a singalong piano situated in the rear.

Igor's Lounge (☎ 504-522-2145; 2133 St Charles Ave) Loose and entertaining, this dive never closes, and has a greasy grill, pool tables and washing machines.

ENTERTAINMENT

To order tickets for events in New Orleans call **TicketMaster** (☎ 504-522-5555). There are several outlets in town.

Live Music

Generations of New Orleans club owners have thrived by promoting a combination of music and booze. Look out for shows by local performers like jazz trumpeter Kermit Ruffins, piano virtuoso Henry Butler, Latin jazz combo Los Hombres Calientes and the Dirty Dozen Brass Band. The free monthly *Offbeat* and weekly *Gambit* are your best sources if you want to read reviews and catch performances.

Mid-City Rock & Bowl (☎ 504-482-3133; 4133 Carrollton Ave; cover $5-10) Get thee to the Rock & Bowl, where you can shake and shimmy to some of New Orleans' best R & B and zydeco music, bowl a few frames between sets, and swill beer with a dynamic, electric

---

INSTEAD OF...

Instead of heading to Bourbon St, where the nightlife caters strictly for tourists and conventioneers, mix with a younger, more local crowd on lower Decatur St, where the bars exude a slightly seamy, raucous atmosphere. Check out **Molly's at the Market** (right) or the **Abbey** (right) along this strip. Or repair to atmospheric Frenchmen St, in the Faubourg Marigny, where you can barhop slick hipster hangs and sultry cool caverns with tight live bands. Try **d.b.a.** (above) the **Spotted Cat** (above) or **Snug Harbor** (opposite).

GAY & LESBIAN NEW ORLEANS

New Orleans has a large and spirited gay and lesbian community, based primarily in the lower Quarter and the Faubourg Marigny. A number of shops, bars, restaurants and guesthouses in these areas have a special appeal for locals and visitors.

Lesbian & Gay Community Center (☎ 504-945-1103; 2114 Decatur St; ⏲ 2-6pm), in the Marigny, is a great place to pick up free information. You can also use the bulletin board, library and cultural services. Nearby, **Faubourg Marigny Book Store** (☎ 504-943-9875; 600 Frenchmen St) is the South's oldest gay bookstore and is a good place to find out about the local gay and lesbian scene.

A quick way to get up on gay culture in New Orleans is to take the **Gay Heritage Tour** (☎ 504-945-6789; admission $20), led by colorful guide Robert Batson. These tours don't happen every day, so call to find out when and where to meet.

Same-sex couples will feel welcome at most hotels, but a few cater specifically to gays, including **Lion's Inn B&B** (☎ 504-945-2339; www.lionsinn.com; 2517 Chartres St; r $50-110), in a renovated Creole house. **Bywater Bed & Breakfast** (☎ 504-944-8438; www.bywaterbnb.com; 1026 Clouet St; r $65-75) is an artsy lesbian house with three guestrooms.

Gay-friendly restaurants are ubiquitous, but **La Peniche** (☎ 504-943-1460; 1940 Dauphine St; mains $7-15; ⏲ 24hr Thu-Tue) and **Clover Grill** (☎ 504-598-1010; 900 Bourbon St; mains $3-8; ⏲ 24hr) are especially known for their surly, flirtatious waiters and late-night intrigue.

Oz (☎ 504-593-9491; 800 Bourbon St) and **Bourbon Pub & Parade Disco** (☎ 504-529-2107; 801 Bourbon St) are throbbing bars/dance clubs with daily happy hours. Parade Disco has a Sunday 'Tea Dance' from 5pm to 10pm with free draft beer. Bars abound along Burgundy and Dauphine Sts in the Quarter.

crowd. It's located at the corner of Tulane and Carrollton Aves, about 15 minutes' drive from the Quarter.

House of Blues (☎ 504-529-2583; 255 Decatur St; cover $7-25) Certainly this is one of the best live-music venues in town. The calendar fills with fine rock, country and alternative acts. The Sunday Gospel Brunch will fortify your soul.

Tipitina's (☎ 504-895-8477; 501 Napoleon Ave; cover $10-20) This legendary music club is where the Neville Brothers and the Meters regularly rocked the city until dawn in the 1970s. The bar is marked by a bust of Henry Roland Byrd (1918–80), or 'Professor Longhair,' whose 1953 hit 'Tipitina' inspired the club's name.

Preservation Hall (☎ 504-522-2841; 726 St Peter St; cover $5) A historically significant place, this worn music hall attracts veteran jazz musicians. Get there early to get a seat, or stand outside and listen through the open shutters.

Donna's Bar & Grill (☎ 504-596-6914; 800 N Rampart St; cover $5-15) This little sweatbox touts itself as New Orleans' 'Brass Band Headquarters'. Local jazz talent gets booked, and those who aren't booked often stop by to jam. Monday night the club dishes out free red beans and barbecue.

Funky Butt on Congo Square (☎ 504-558-0872; 714 N Rampart St; cover $5-15) With a swanky, sexy atmosphere, the Funky Butt usually turns up the heat, with modern jazz, Latin rhythms and a lively crowd.

Snug Harbor (☎ 504-949-0696; 626 Frenchmen St; cover $10-25) This club, in Faubourg Marigny, is the city's premier contemporary jazz venue. Expect regular performances by Ellis Marsalis (Wynton and Branford's dad) and a revolving door of touring artists.

Howlin' Wolf (☎ 504-523-2551; 828 S Peters St; cover $5-15) One of the best live-music venues in town, this Warehouse District club attracts local talent as well as touring rock and alt-rock bands.

Maple Leaf Bar (☎ 504-866-9359; 8316 Oak St; cover $5-10) The best of the Riverbend clubs, Maple Leaf packs a wild crowd into it's pressed-tin music hall. Look for bluesman Walter 'Wolfman' Washington, zydeco star Rockin' Dopsie Jr and the Rebirth Jazz Band. Always a good show.

Vaughan's (☎ 504-947-5562; 800 Lesseps St; cover $10) Swing down to the lower Bywater on Thursday night for Kermit Ruffins' weekly jazz jam at Vaughan's. Consummate showman, Kermit makes the deal more enticing by serving up barbecue from the back of his pick-up truck. Show starts around 11pm.

Theater

Contemporary Arts Center (☎ 504-528-3800; 900 Camp St; adult/student $5/3; ☺ 11am-5pm Tue-Sun) This is the premier venue for New Orleans' cutting-edge performances.

Saenger Theatre (☎ 504-524-2490; 143 N Rampart St) Major touring troupes perform at this ornate and finely restored 1927 theater.

Le Petit Théâtre du Vieux Carré (☎ 504-522-2081; 616 St Peter St) One of the oldest theater groups in the US. Classic and contemporary Southern plays.

Southern Repertory Theatre (☎ 504-861-8163; 333 Canal Place) On the 3rd floor of the Canal Place Shopping Center, it presents classic and contemporary Southern plays.

Cinemas

Canal Place Cinemas (☎ 504-581-5400; 333 Canal St, 3rd floor) Head to this conveniently located multiplex for the latest mainstream and art releases.

Prytania Theatre (☎ 504-891-2787; 5339 Prytania St) This old Uptown movie house was built in the 1920s and screens independent and art films.

Sports

Louisiana Superdome (☎ 504-587-3810; 1500 Poydras Ave; tickets $22-50) The 60,000-seat superdome is home to the NFL New Orleans Saints and every few years it hosts the Super Bowl. The NBA's New Orleans Hornets play in the Superdome. In January, the dome hosts the NCAA (college) Sugar Bowl.

Fair Grounds Race Track (☎ 504-944-5515; 1751 Gentilly Blvd) Horseracing is a New Orleans tradition at the Fair Grounds Race Track. The racing season lasts from November to March.

SHOPPING

You've already perused the flea market at the Farmers Market, but do you want to take home something distinctly New Orleanian that won't end up laying on the closet floor? Here are some interesting stores to check out:

Louisiana Music Factory (☎ 504-586-1094; 210 Decatur St) Here's where you'll find the best selection of local and regional CDs.

Little Shop of Fantasy (☎ 504-529-4243; 515 St Louis St) If you've got the Mardi Gras spirit, go to this emporium of hand-crafted masks and party attire.

Marie Laveau's House of Voodoo (☎ 504-581-3751; 739 Bourbon St) There are some great souvenirs here: voodoo love potions and intriguing masks and statuary, many of them handmade and painted, with some old specimens. Very nice for the shrine back home.

Southern Candy Makers (☎ 504-523-5544; 334 Decatur St) Pralines, those sugary Southern confections, make a nice gift for friends. A box of these'll easily fit in your carry-on bag.

GETTING THERE & AWAY

Louis Armstrong New Orleans International Airport (☎ 504-464-0831; www.flymsy.com; 900 Airline Hwy), 11 miles west of the city, handles mostly domestic flights.

Greyhound (☎ 800-231-2222, in Spanish ☎ 800-531-5332) buses run from the **Union Passenger Terminal** (☎ 504-524-7571; 1001 Loyola Ave), west of the Warehouse District. Regular services go to Baton Rouge, Memphis, Nashville and Atlanta.

Amtrak (☎ 504-528-1610, 800-872-7245) trains also operate from the Union Passenger Terminal.

GETTING AROUND
Car & Motorcycle

Bringing a car to downtown New Orleans is often a costly proposition. During daytime, street parking has a two-hour limit. Parking garages in the upper (southern) part of the Quarter charge about $5 for the first hour, or $20 for 24 hours.

Public Transportation

The **Regional Transit Authority** (RTA; ☎ 504-248-3900) runs the local bus service. Fares are $1.50, plus 25¢ for transfers; express buses will set you back $1.50. Exact change is required. RTA Visitor Passes for one/three days cost $5/12.

The RTA also operates three streetcar lines: on St Charles Ave, Canal Blvd and along the River levee in the French Quarter and CBD. Fares are $1.50.

Bicycle

You can rent bicycles at **Bicycle Michael's** (☎ 504-945-9505; 622 Frenchmen St; bicycle per hour/day $7.50/20), in Faubourg Marigny. Reservations are needed during festivals, but no otherwise.

AROUND LOUISIANA

New Orleans is surrounded by alligator swamps, bayous, antebellum plantation homes and Cajun communities where the music parties start early and end late on Saturdays. You'll have more than enough incentive to get out into Louisiana's vital countryside.

BARATARIA PRESERVE

A great way to learn about swamplands is to visit this unit of the Jean Lafitte National Historic Park. Set in an area originally settled by Isleños (Canary Islanders) in 1779, it offers hiking and canoe trips into the swamp and a good introduction to the wetlands environment. Even a brief walk on the boardwalks that wend their way through the swamp will yield sightings of gators and egrets.

Start at the **NPS Visitors Center** (☎ 504-589-2330; Hwy 3134; ⊙ 9am-5pm), 1 mile west of Hwy 45, where you can pick up a map or join a ranger-led walk.

Bayou Barn (☎ 504-689-2663; canoes per 2hr $15; ⊙ Tue-Sun) rents canoes. It's on the Bayou de Familles just outside the park, and is a pleasantly funky restaurant compound of tin-topped weatherbeaten buildings on the opposite side of the intersection. Cajun or zydeco bands play to lively local crowds at **dances** (admission $5; ⊙ noon-6pm) held most Sundays.

RIVER ROAD

Antebellum plantation homes line the east and west banks of the Mississippi River between New Orleans and Baton Rouge. First indigo, then cotton, rice and sugarcane brought great wealth to these plantations, many of which are open to the public as historic sites, usually with costumed guides leading 45- to 60-minute tours. Many present a romantic picture of plantation life, focusing on the lovely architecture, ornate gardens and genteel lifestyle of antebellum Louisiana. Most gloss over the story of plantation slaves, who lived in relative squalor.

Laura Plantation (☎ 225-265-7690; 2247 Hwy 18; admission $10; ⊙ 9:30am-5pm) In Vacherie, this is an unassuming French Creole plantation constructed in 1905. Unlike other tours, this ever-evolving and popular plantation thoughtfully addresses the role of slavery. You get a good picture of what life was like for both master and slave via accounts from the lives of the Creole women who ran the place for generations.

Oak Alley Plantation (☎ 225-265-2151; 3645 Hwy 18; admission $10; ⊙ 9am-5pm) A dramatic approach, with a 0.25-mile canopy of 28 live oaks lining the entry, leads to this grand Greek Revival–style house. It's one of the most beautiful remnants of the 'old South.'

River Road African-American Museum & Gallery (☎ 225-474-5553; www.africanamericanmuseum .org; 406 Charles St, Donaldsonville; museum/walking tour $4/15; ⊙ 9am-5pm) The important history of African-Americans in Louisiana is told in this excellent museum, in the historic town of Donaldsonville. In addition to exhibits about plantation slavery and the slaves' journey to freedom via the underground railroad, Hambrick gives 45-minute walking tours of Donaldsonville, which was a prosperous city for blacks after the Civil War.

CAJUN COUNTRY

This part of southern Louisiana, stretching from the Mississippi River to the Texas border, is home to the largest French-speaking minority in the US. French settlers who were exiled by the British in 1755 from L'Acadie (now Nova Scotia, Canada) sought refuge in Louisiana but were shunted to the western swamplands. Houma and Chitimacha Indians taught their new neighbors to trap, fish, hunt and eat crawfish. These Indians corrupted 'Acadian' to 'Cagian' – hence 'Cajun.' Cajun culture has remained distinct from mainstream culture in many ways.

The logical starting point is Lafayette, 130 miles west of New Orleans, but the real Cajun experience is found in small towns, bayous and rural back roads. Cajun and zydeco music rocks out at bars and restaurants, *fais-do-do* (Cajun dances) are mostly held on weekends, and Cajun food (jambalaya, crawfish *étouffée*, shrimp bisque) is available everywhere.

Lafayette

This small city isn't exceptionally attractive, but the University of Louisiana at Lafayette (ULL), with 17,000 'Ragin' Cajuns,' gives Lafayette some college-town vitality. It's a convenient base, with hotels and a hostel, if you're exploring the region.

SPLURGE!

What better way to get to know Louisiana's wetlands than to sleep in them on a houseboat? **Houseboat Adventures** (☎ 337-228-7484, 800-491-4662; www.houseboat-adventures.com; 1399 Henderson Levee Rd, Breaux Bridge; 2 nights small/big boat $390/460; 🕱) makes it possible, with a fleet of six smartly accoutered houseboats (sleeping up to four or six people) that are towed into secluded corners of the vast Atchafalaya swamp. The boats have kitchens, so bring your vittles and an accordion and sing the night away with a chorus of frogs and cicadas. The gators swim right by, so don't sleep walk. Rowboats are included for exploring the swamp. As the price stays the same regardless the size of your party, this is a splurge that's more affordable if you are traveling in a pack. Advance reservations required.

From I-10, exit 103A, the Evangeline Thruway (Hwy 167) goes to the center of town via the **visitors center** (☎ 337-232-3737, 800-346-1958; 1400 NW Evangeline Thruway; 🕒 8:30am-5pm Mon-Fri, 9am-5pm Sat & Sun).

SIGHTS & ACTIVITIES

Vermilionville (☎ 337-233-4077; 300 Fisher Rd; adult/student $8/5; 🕒 10am-4pm Tue-Sun) Docents in period costumes guide you through a 19th-century Cajun village at this living history and folklife museum. Bands perform shows daily in the barn, and there are daily cooking demonstrations and tastings.

Acadian Village (☎ 337-981-2364; 200 Greenleaf Dr; admission $6.50; 🕒 10am-5pm) is less glitzy than Vermilionville and is favored by locals. Follow a brick path around a rippling bayou to some restored houses, craft shops and a church.

The best NPS museum in Cajun Country is the **Acadian Cultural Center** (☎ 337-232-0789; 501 Fisher Rd; admission free; 🕒 8am-5pm). Interactive displays – like a Cajun joke-telling booth – give life to local folkways.

SLEEPING

Lafayette offers nearly 4000 hotel and B&B rooms. All the usual chains are present at or near exits 101 and 103, off I-10. Budget rates will cost around $40 to $50 for double rooms.

Blue Moon Saloon & Guesthouse (☎ 337-234-2422, 877-766-2583; www.bluemoonhostel.com; 215 E Convent St; dm $15, r $30-55; 🕱) This tidy old home, with dormitories and private rooms, is a fun place to stay. The 'saloon,' set up on the back porch, features live music Wednesday to Sunday nights. The friendly owners are fountains of local information. It's south of I-10 exit 101, within walking distance of downtown.

EATING

Many places offer one-stop entertainment, dancing and regional cuisine. Markets, convenience stores and even gas stations keep a pot of hot *boudin* (pork-and-rice-filled sausage) by the cash register, a sure sign you're in Cajun country.

T-Coons (☎ 337-232-3803; 740 Jefferson Blvd; mains $5-7) The local favorite for crawfish omelettes in the morning and plates of smothered rabbit or jambalaya for lunch.

Old Tyme Grocery (☎ 337-235-8165; 218 W St Mary St; po-boys $5) Excellent shrimp or roast beef po-boys at lunch or dinner.

Cedar Deli (☎ 337-233-5460; 1115 Jefferson Blvd; mains $4-6) This Syrian-owned deli serves falafels, as well as veggie and meat *muffalettas*.

ENTERTAINMENT

To find out who's playing in the clubs, look for the free weekly *Times*.

El Sid O's (☎ 337-237-1959; 1523 Martin Luther King Dr) For zydeco, try El Sid O's at St Antoine St, a big and welcoming cinderblock joint.

Hamilton's Club (☎ 337-991-0783; 1808 Verot School Rd) For zydeco.

Grant St Dance Hall (☎ 337-237-2255; 113 W Grant St; cover $10-20) For a more eclectic menu of musical offerings, head to this cavernous warehouse on Grant St.

GETTING THERE & AWAY

Greyhound (☎ 337-235-1541) operates from a hub beside the central commercial district, making 11 runs daily to New Orleans. Amtrak also stops here.

Cajun Wetlands

In 1755, *le Grand Dérangement*, the British expulsion of the rural French settlers from Acadia, created a homeless population of Acadians who searched for decades for a place to settle. In 1785, seven boatloads of exiles arrived in New Orleans. By the early 19th century, some 3000 to 4000 Acadians arrived to occupy the swamplands southwest of New Orleans. Here, they eked out a living based upon fishing and trapping and developed a culture substantially different from the Cajuns who settled further inland in the prairie region, where animal husbandry and farming were the primary vocations. Southeast of Lafayette, along US 90 beside the **Atchafalaya Basin**, the heart of the Cajun wetlands is a lowland area of dense vegetation, swamps, lakes and bayous.

New Iberia was settled by the Spanish in 1779 and makes a good base for exploring the area. The town prospered on the sugarcane of surrounding plantations. Today, the town's best-known native son is mystery writer James Lee Burke, whose novels often take place in and around New Iberia and feature Detective Dave Robicheaux.

A cheap place to stay with basic but clean rooms is the **Teche Motel** (☎ 337-369-3756; 1830 Main St; r $40; P ⊠). On Hwy 14, chain hotels vie for traveler business. A favorite weekday breakfast and lunch spot is the **LagniappeToo Café** (☎ 337-365-9419; 204 E Main St; mains $5-9). It also serves dinner on Friday and Saturday. For delicious boiled seafood, locals head a few miles north of town along I-49/Hwy 90 to the simple **Guiding Star** (☎ 337-365 9113; mains $8-12; ☺ 3-10pm). If you need crawfish-cracking lessons, this is the place to come.

Just 60 miles southwest of New Orleans, **Thibodaux** (*ti*-ba-doh) sits at the confluence of two bayous. The big attraction here is the **Wetlands Cajun Cultural Center** (☎ 985-448-1375; 314 St Mary St; ☺ 9am-8pm Mon, 8am-5pm Tue-Fri, 9am-5pm Sat & Sun), a spacious museum and gallery operated by the NPS. Exhibits cover virtually every aspect of Cajun life in the wetlands, from music to the environmental impacts of trapping and oil exploration. Local musicians jam here Monday evenings from 6pm to 8pm.

Cajun Prairie

As the elevation rises north of Lafayette, the land dries out and the roads become more predictable than in the southern wetlands. The simple geometry of grain silos echoes those of the Midwest, and it's no surprise Midwestern farmers were some of the earliest rice growers in the region. This entire area is fertile ground for Cajun and zydeco music, fishing camps and crawfish boils.

Opelousas has a historic city center and a museum covering Indian, Acadian and Creole cultures. On the main square, **Palace Cafe** (☎ 337-942-2142; mains $6-10) does great crawfish *étoufée* and bisque.

Top zydeco venues include **Slim's Y-Ki-Ki** (☎ 337-942-9980), a few miles up Washington St, and **Richard's** (☎ 337-543-8223), 8 miles west in Lawtell. **Plaisance**, northwest of Opelousas, hosts the **Southwest Louisiana Zydeco Festival** (☎ 337-942-2392; www.zydeco.org) at the end of August.

In **Eunice**, the **Prairie Acadian Cultural Center** (☎ 337-457-8490; cnr Third St & Park Ave) is part of Jean Lafitte National Historic Park. Displays introduce visitors to Acadian heritage and map the immigration of French men

---

SWAMP TOURS

You haven't experienced Louisiana unless you've been out in a swamp, and the easiest way to get to one is to join a swamp tour. Many tours can be arranged from New Orleans, with shuttle rides to and from the swamps. You can also choose among the many companies established on landings along the levee road in Henderson. To get there, take I-10, exit 115 (between Baton Rouge and Lafayette), head south and turn left onto Hwy 352.

Here are a couple other suggestions elsewhere in the Cajun Wetlands:

■ **Cajun Man's Swamp Cruise** (☎ 985-868-4625; www.cajunman.com; Hwy 90; admission $15)
Ten miles west of Houma, this is run by Black Guidry, who serenades his passengers with a bit of accordion music, while piloting them through a scenic slice of swamp, his trusty dog Gator Bait at his side.

■ **Annie Miller's Son's Swamp & Marsh Tours** (☎ 985-868-4758; www.annie-miller.com; 3718 Southdown Mandalay Rd, Houma; admission $15) Eight miles west of Houma, the son of the legendary swamp guide Annie Miller (who died in 2004) has taken up his mom's tracks.

and women to Louisiana. The **Liberty Theater** (☎ 337-457-7389; cnr S Second St & Park Ave) is best known for its **Rendez-vous des Cajuns** (admission $5), a Saturday-night *fais-do-do* broadcast on local radio stations. Surrounded by woods, **Cajun Campground** (☎ 318-457-5753; 552 Hwy 190; campsites $10, cabins $55) has a pool, small store, playground and small lake. The seven cabins have kitchenettes.

Mamou, the self-proclaimed 'Cajun Music Capital,' backs its claim with a crazy little 8am booze fest, a live traditional Cajun band and charming country waltzes every Saturday morning at **Fred's Lounge** (☎ 337-468-5411; 420 6th St).

ARKANSAS

Once a jumping-off point for frontier expeditions to the west and south, Arkansas later attracted visitors with its natural hot springs. Today it promotes itself as 'the Natural State,' with camping, fishing and hunting in the Ozark and Ouachita Mountains. Some unnatural attractions include sites associated with former US president Bill Clinton, civil-rights history and quirky hillbilly culture.

The **Department of Parks & Tourism** (☎ 501-682-7777, 800-628-8725; www.arkansastravel.com; 1 Capitol Mall, Little Rock, AR 72201) sends out a vacation plan kit on request.

LITTLE ROCK

Downtown Little Rock is like a sleepy small town with some great big-city characteristics. Recent redevelopment of the downtown and riverfront areas has really spruced things up, bringing a level of sophistication to the staid 19th- and 20th-century

> **SPLURGE!**
>
> **Peabody Little Rock** (☎ 501-906-4000, 800-723-2639; www.peabodylittlerock.com; 3 Statehouse Plaza; from $120; P ⊠ ✕) This gorgeous hotel, sister to the famous Peabody Hotel in Memphis, TN, recently underwent a $40 million reconstruction. Its 418 rooms offer the height of luxury and run the gamut from standard rooms to deluxe suites. Amenities include in-room babysitters, a five-star restaurant and bar overlooking the river.

architecture. Across the river, North Little Rock is a growing enclave of shops and restaurants stretching alongside the long riverfront park, whose trails are great for walking or jogging. The **visitors center** (☎ 877-220-2568; www.littlerock.com; 615 E Capitol; 🕙 8am-6pm) is housed in the 1842 Curran Hall.

The best place in the city to stroll around is the **River Market District**, an area of shops and restaurants anchored on W Markham St and President Clinton Ave and along the banks of the Arkansas River. **Riverfront Park** provides a pleasant, walkable area along the riverbank. At the park's eastern end you might discern the little rock for which the city is named. Nearby, the **River Market** has a good food court and outdoor spaces overlooking the water.

Completed in fall 2004, the **William J Clinton Presidential Center** (☎ 501-370-5050; www.clintonpresidentialcenter.com; 1200 E President Clinton Ave) houses the largest archival collection in presidential history, along with a museum, replica of the oval office and plenty of parkland.

Perhaps the most compelling attraction in Little Rock is the NPS's **Central High Museum & Visitor Center** (☎ 501-374-1957; 2125 W Daisy L Gatson Bates Dr; admission free; 🕙 10am-4pm Mon-Sat, 1-4pm Sun), housed in a restored 1950s-era Mobil gas station opposite the school where, in 1957, nine black teenagers defied the state's policy of racially segregated schooling and enrolled. While the center shows what happened to the 'Little Rock Nine' after they enrolled, the school itself, now thoroughly integrated, is closed to visitors.

Because of government and convention center traffic, it's difficult to find inexpensive hotels right in the downtown area, though rates can downright plummet midweek when there's no convention in town. All of the usual budget-oriented motels can be found off the interstates. **Super 8** (☎ 800-359-4827; 8115 Frenchman's Lane; r from $40) is a logical choice

The food court at **River Market** (🕙 7am-6pm Mon-Sat) is an economical place for breakfast or lunch. You'll find everything from fresh fruit and pastries, to Greek, Lebanese, burgers and barbecue.

Sim's Bar-B-Que (☎ 501-372-1148; 109 Main St; $4-8; 🕙 Mon-Sat) One of the oldest restaurants in town, where locals flock for ribs and pork sandwiches.

ARKANSAS RIVER VALLEY

Upstream from Little Rock, I-40 is the fast route, but **US 64** is studded with small-town Americana: **Atkins**, the 'Pickle Capital of Arkansas' (try fried dill pickle); **Russellville**, home of Jimmy Lile Custom Knives, as used in the Rambo movies; **Clarksville**, a college town and capital of 'Arkansas Peach Country'; **Ozark**, where the bridge across the river is rated by the Institute of Steel Construction as 'one of the 16 most beautiful long spans in the US'; **Altus**, the center of Arkansas' Germanic wine-growing region; and **Alma**, 'Spinach Capital of the World,' with a massive can of spinach and a statue of Popeye.

HOT SPRINGS

Hot Springs National Park, 55 miles southwest of Little Rock, is almost surrounded by the city of Hot Springs. The thermal waters spout a million gallons of 143°F water daily from 47 natural springs. People come for the waters, but also the Victorian architecture scenes from Bill Clinton's boyhood. Elaborate old bathhouses line up on Bathhouse Row, behind shady magnolias on the east side of Central Ave.

For city information and a useful map of Clinton-related sites, go to the **Convention & Visitors Bureau** (☎ 501-321-2277, 800-543-2284; www.hotsprings.org; 134 Convention Blvd; ⊗ 8am-5pm Mon-Fri).

Spa-resort hotels have private bathhouses, or you can visit the **Buckstaff Bathhouse** (☎ 501-623-2308; www.buckstaffbaths.com; just south of the Fordyce; thermal bath/Swedish massage $18/20; ⊗ Mon-Sat). A promenade runs around the hillside behind Bathhouse Row, where some springs survive in a more-or-less natural state. A network of trails covers **Hot Springs Mountain**, and a scenic drive goes all the way to the top, where the 216ft **Hot Springs Mountain Tower** (☎ 501-623-6025; admission $6; ⊗ 9am-6pm) affords magnificent views of the surrounding mountains, which are covered with dogwood, hickory, oak and pine – especially lovely in the spring and fall. **National Park Duck Tours** (☎ 501-321-2911; 418 Central Ave) offers boat tours and the **Belle of Hot Springs** (☎ 501-525-4438; www.belleriverboat .com; 5200 Central Ave; cruises $12-30) does cruises on Lake Hamilton.

The NPS's attractive **Gulpha Gorge Campground** (☎ 501-624-3383; campsites $12), 2 miles northeast of downtown off Hwy 70B, has 43 campsites (no showers, hookups or reservations). The cheap motels are on the highways around town. Ask at the visitors bureau for a list of lakeside rental properties and area B&Bs.

Friendly **Alpine Inn** (☎ 501-624-9164; 741 Park Ave/Hwy 7 N; r from $35; ⓟ ⊠ ⊗) is a great value and less than a mile to Bathhouse Row. The 15 tidy rooms have coffeemakers and hairdryers, and some have kitchenettes.

NOT A DAM IN SIGHT

Although it mightn't look like the Colorado or the Columbia, the Buffalo National River sure is purty. Administered by the NPS, the river flows beneath dramatic bluffs through unspoiled Ozark forest.

Evidence of human occupation dates back some 10,000 years to the Archaic Indians, but this wild and naturally bountiful area kept even modern Ozarks settlers self-sufficient and isolated. They developed a distinct dialect, along with unique craft skills and musical traits that continue today. Thanks to its National River designation in 1972, the Buffalo is one of the few remaining unpolluted, free-flowing rivers in the country. Starting as a trickle in the Boston Mountains, the river travels 150 miles along an ancient riverbed until pouring into the White River. Brilliant limestone bluffs, waterfalls and pristine wilderness make this a great spot for camping, hiking and canoeing.

The best way to see the park is by canoe or raft. Outfitters such as **Wild Bill's** (☎ 800-554-8657; www.ozark-float.com) and **Buffalo Outdoor Center** (☎ 800-221-5514; www.buffaloriver.com) can arrange canoes or rafting trips for around $40 per person. They can also arrange hiking tours, fishing trips and horseback riding.

The **Buffalo National River** (☎ 870-741-5443; www.nps.gov/buff) has three designated wilderness areas, the most accessible is through the **Tyler Bend Visitors Center** (☎ 870-439-2502, 11 miles north of Marshall on I-65; ⊗ 8am-5pm Sep-Jun). Other access points are at **Pruitt** (☎ 870-446-5373), 5 miles north of Jasper on Hwy 7, and **Buffalo Point** (☎ 870-449-4311), 17 miles south of Yellville Hwy 14.

There are lots of places to grab a bite along the Central Ave tourist strip. Two of the best include: **Granny's Kitchen** (☎ 501-624-6183; 362 Central Ave; mains $5-10), where you'll find good down-home breakfast, lunch or dinner; and **Faded Rose** (☎ 501-624-3200; 210 Central Ave; mains $8-12), which serves up inexpensive New Orleans cuisine.

Bill Clinton's favorite boyhood barbecue was **McClard's** (☎ 501-624-9586, 505 Albert Pike; mains $6-9), southwest of the center, where you can fill up on sweet, succulent ribs, pork, beef and slaw.

MISSISSIPPI

If y'all are looking for the Deep South, this is it. Dirt poor, rural, backwards, neglected, left for the kudzu – that pretty well describes much of the state of Mississippi. It's a strangely appealing scramble of natural greenery and agricultural refuse, particularly in the ever slumping Delta, where time seems to stand still as cypress stumps in stagnant water. It is Mississippi's refined side that jars the mind. Decades ago the state was a grisly civil rights battlefield, and yet the towering antebellum homes of Natchez, having weathered the storm, appear unperturbed as ever. Long after novelist William Faulkner dragged his retinue of ghosts through Mississippi's parlors, Oxford, where Faulkner lived, seems a pleasant college town.

Their state is as intense as it sounds, but Mississippians don't dwell on it too much. They're a friendly people who more often than not welcome a stranger with cold beer, iced tea, tender barbecue and blues grooves in shambling juke joints. Through the heart of the state lovely Natchez Trace Parkway runs its long, winding course over a peaceful countryside, from Natchez to Tupelo (humble origins of Elvis Presley) and beyond.

MISSISSIPPI DELTA

The Mississippi Delta is haunted by the ghosts of those who, many decades ago, sang the distinctive Delta blues. Charlie Patton, Robert Johnson, Muddy Waters, BB King and dozens of others lived, worked and performed in the Delta. Their blues, usually a simple combination of vocals and complex guitar finger-picking, were by turns tragic, disquieting, weary, spiritual, belligerent, uplifting. Most visitors come looking for remnants of this past, and, with a willingness to venture from the main highways, they find it. However, the best bluesmen died or moved on long ago, and the Delta still has the feel of a place that has been left behind.

Mostly what you'll encounter here is a third-world montage of cotton fields and small, impoverished towns. Economic stagnation is evident in the rows of abandoned shops and run-down houses and groups of people hanging around street corners and on front porches. Long-abandoned commissaries and rusted farm equipment pop up along the road, and painted signs fade away on the sides of buildings.

The Delta stretches for 250 miles from Memphis to Vicksburg. Technically it's an alluvial plain rather than a river delta. Regular blues festivals occur in towns throughout the Delta, and local performers play small 'juke joints' most weekends (p274).

Clarksdale

More than any other Delta town, Clarksdale celebrates its blues heritage, making this a good base for blues travelers. The Delta's northernmost town of any significant size, it was a jumping-off point for African Americans catching trains to Memphis or Chicago. Muddy Waters lived near hear, and Bessie Smith died in a hospital in Clarksdale.

Downtown is the few blocks where the railroad tracks meet the Sunflower River. Across the tracks, in a rough-looking part of town along Martin Luther King Jr Blvd, are several eateries and juke joints, with lots of people hanging out in front of boarded-up stores. At the town's south side, Hwys 61 and 49 meet at what locals refer to as the **crossroads**. You can't miss the tin guitars that mark the spot. Does this busy intersection look like a good place to sell your soul to the devil? Some locals will have you believe Robert Johnson did just that, right here.

Delta Blues Museum (☎ 601-627-6820; www.delta bluesmuseum.org; 1 Blues Alley; admission $6; ⊙ 9am-5pm Mon-Sat). In the old train station, this museum is a must-see for blues pilgrims. You can get maps and charts that plot musical milestones, see an effigy of Muddy Waters and peruse a modest collection of artifacts.

The **Sunflower River Blues & Gospel Festival** (☎ 662-627-6805; www.sunflowerfest.org) is staged on the first weekend in August.

Shack Up Inn (☎ 662-624-8329; www.shackupinn.com; r $50-75; P ✕) At Hopson Plantation, 2 miles south on the west side of Hwy 49, it provides much more than a place to lay your head. A night or two in one of the Shack Up's refurbished sharecropper cabins offers a totally unique experience that'll immerse you in Delta life. The cabins are filled with old furniture and musical instruments, and the more expensive ones sleep up to four people. The old commissary is an atmospheric sight for frequent live-music performances, and the owners are great sources for information.

Uptown Motor Inn (☎ 662 627 3251; 305 E 2nd St; d $30; P ✕) Recently updated rooms, with refrigerators and microwave ovens, make this central motel great value. Most Clarksdale sights are within blocks from here.

Abe's (☎ 662-624-9947; 616 State St; mains $3-6) At the crossroads, look for the tall sign with the black pig in bow-tie. Abe's has been providing Clarksdale with pork sandwiches since 1924.

Musical events are often publicized by word-of-mouth and on last-minute posters around town. Usually only one juke joint features live entertainment on any given night. A good starting point is **Ground Zero** (☎ 662-621-0990; 387 Delta St), by the Blues Museum. It's owned by actor Morgan Freeman, who lives near Clarksdale. On the other side of the tracks, try **Red's** (☎ 662-627-3166; 395 Sunflower Ave), with the huge barbecue pit out front, or **Smitty's** (377 Yazoo Ave).

Greyhound (☎ 662-627-7893; 1604 State St) buses run to several cities including Memphis, TN ($20, 1½ hours), and New Orleans, LA ($74, 10 hours).

Around Clarksdale

About 17 miles south, **Stovall Farms** is a former plantation where Muddy Waters lived and worked. In **Tutwiler**, an outdoor mural illustrates WC Handy's first exposure to the blues in 1903. Further south on Hwy 49, **Parchman Penitentiary** has been a temporary home for many bluesmen and the subject of several songs – the 'Midnight Special' was the weekend train bringing prison visitors.

Tiny **Merigold** has two draws: **Crawdad's** (☎ 662-748-2254; mains $6-10), a barn-sized res-

> ### THE EMPRESS' DEATHBED
>
> On September 26, 1937, jazz singer Bessie Smith (b 1894) was in a car accident near Clarksdale. She was brought to the Riverside Hotel, which then was a black medical clinic, and there she died. Legend has it she was sent here after being refused at the whites-only hospital, but this is now considered untrue. You can visit the **Riverside Hotel** (☎ 662-624-9163; 615 Sunflower Ave; r $30-40), or stay a night in one of the basic rooms. If the proprietor is in a talkative mood, he'll share stories from the old days, when musicians lived in the hotel, and show you the room in which Bessie is believed to have died.

taurant with walls of animal heads and generous portions; and **Poor Monkey's Lounge** (☎ 662-748-2254), a tumble-down juke joint along a dirt road that's welcoming to strangers. Call for odd opening hours and slightly confusing directions.

VICKSBURG

The high bluffs overlooking the Mississippi made Vicksburg a strategic location in the Civil War. General Ulysses S Grant besieged the city for 47 days, until its surrender on July 4, 1863. The major sights are readily accessible from I-20 exit 4B (Clay St). Get information at the **visitors center** (☎ 601-636-9421, 800-221-3536; cnr Clay & Washington Sts). The cobblestone blocks of Washington St, near the river, are lined with restaurants and shops. Riverboat casinos glitter down on the banks.

The **National Military Park** (☎ 601-636-0583; www.nps.gov/vick; per car $5; ☉ 8am-5pm), north of I-20 on Clay St, is the city's huge attraction. An 18-mile driving tour passes historic markers explaining Civil War key events that occurred here. The museum relates some fascinating, oft-overlooked history.

Hillcrest Motel (☎ 601-638-1491; 40 Hwy 80; s/d $26/32; P ✕) This is a slightly run down, but perfectly serviceable motel.

Walnut Hills (☎ 601-638-4910; 1214 Adams St; mains $7-12; ☉ Sun-Fri) For traditional Southern favorites, drop by this charming old house near downtown. Meals are served family style at big round tables (you can also just order your own 'blue plate special').

OXFORD

Cultivated, bustling and prosperous Oxford is home to the University of Mississippi ('Ole Miss'). William Faulkner mythologized the area in his disturbing tales of (mythical) Yoknapatawpha County. In 1962 ugly riots accompanied the enrollment of James Meredith, the first black student at Ole Miss. The university and town are now quietly integrated, with galleries, bookstores and cafés grouped around Courthouse Sq. It's a vibrant, artsy town and well worth a stop.

The university, a mile or so west of the town square, has a very attractive campus shaded by magnolias and dogwoods. Its **Center for the Study of Southern Culture** (☎ 662-915-5993; admission free) covers everything from Southern folklore to Elvis cults.

From 1930 until his death in 1962, William Faulkner lived and worked at **Rowan Oak** (☎ 662-234-3284; Old Taylor Rd; admission free; ✆ 10am-noon & 2-4pm Tue-Sat, 2-4pm Sun). The sparsely furnished house, built in 1840, attracts literary pilgrims and aspiring writers.

Ole Miss Motel (☎ 662-234-2424; 1517 University Ave; d $45; P ❉) Budgeters will find a good option here at this family-run establishment just a few blocks away from the square.

Coffee Bistro (☎ 662-281-8188; 107 N 13th St; mains $3-7) In an artsy interior just off the square and serving pastries, sandwiches and espresso drinks, this is a great spot for people-watching. There's live entertainment most nights.

TUPELO

Charming Tupelo is the birthplace of Elvis Presley – it's the King's manger, you might say. There's an Elvis Presley Festival in June.

The Natchez Trace Parkway and Hwy 78 intersect northeast of downtown. Get information at the Tupelo **visitors center** (☎ 662-841-6521, 800-533-0611; 399 E Main St; ✆ Mon-Fri).

Elvis Presley's Birthplace (☎ 662-841-1245; 306 Elvis Presley Blvd; admission all sights $7/3.50; ✆ 9am-5:30pm Mon-Sat, 1-4pm Sun) is east of downtown off Hwy 78. The 15-acre park complex contains the two-room shotgun built by Elvis' dad, a museum displaying personal items and a gift shop that has plastic 1970s Elvis sunglasses.

All American Inn (☎ 662-844-5610; 767 East Main St; r from $30; P ❉) Between downtown and Elvis' house, this place has a suitable leftover '50s look and large, comfortable rooms.

Johnnie's Drive In (☎ 662-842-6748; 908 E Main St; mains $3-6; ✆ Mon-Sat) Stop by this classic little barbecue joint for cheap meat – eat in a wooden booth or in the car.

Two state parks on either side of town, **Tombigbee** (☎ 662-842-7669; campsites $13) southeast of town, and **Trace** (☎ 662-489-2958; campsites $13) to the west, have fishing, swimming and camping.

Greyhound (☎ 662-842-4557; 201 Commerce St), operates daily buses to Memphis ($30, 2½ hours).

NATCHEZ

This is the opulent side of the old South. The wedding-cake antebellum architecture of Natchez, perched on a bluff overlooking the Mississippi, attracts tourists, especially during spring and fall when local mansions open for visitors. First drop by the **visitors center** (☎ 601-446-6345, 800-647-6724; www.natchez.ms.us; 640 S Canal St; ✆ 8:30am-5pm Mon-Sat, 9am-4pm Sun) to see which houses are open for tours.

SCENIC DRIVE: NATCHEZ TRACE PARKWAY

Early European explorers followed this Indian route, and French explorers set up trading posts at its northern and southern ends. In the late 18th century, traders coming downriver would sell their cargo, boats and timber rafts, and return north on foot. The route became a US post road and was later widened to serve as a military road. When steamboats arrived the road was supplanted by river traffic, and the trace fell into disuse until it was revived as a national historic route in the 1930s.

Today the Natchez Trace Parkway is a scenic two-lane road through woodlands and pasture from Natchez to Nashville, TN. The **parkway headquarters** (☎ 662-680-4025, 800-305-7417; Milepost 266; ✆ 8am-5pm) and visitors center are in Tupelo, and several other centers also distribute maps and information. Commercial vehicles are banned, and there are no businesses or advertising on the roadside. The parkway is popular for bicycle touring, and driving along it is pleasant but slow. Doing the entire Trace is best done in two days.

The following **historic houses** are open for tours year-round:

House on Ellicott's Hill (☎ 601-442-2011; 211 N Canal St; admission $6; 🕙 9am-4pm)

Longwood (☎ 601-442-5193; 140 Lower Woodville Rd; admission $6; 🕙 9am-4:30pm)

Melrose (☎ 601-446-5790; 1 Melrose-Montebello Parkway; admission $6; 🕙 9am-4pm)

Rosalie (☎ 601-445-4555; 100 Orleans St; admission $6; 🕙 9am-4pm)

Stanton Hall (☎ 601-442-6282; 401 High St; admission $6; 🕙 9am-4:30pm)

Sleeping & Eating

The shady, 50-site **Natchez State Park** (☎ 601-442-2658; campsites $9, cabins $62) is 10 miles north at the start of the Natchez Trace. The prefab, air-con cabins sleep up to six people.

Natchez Inn (☎ 601-442-0221; 218 John R Junkin Dr; r $35; **P** 🐾) This no-frills budget choice offers basic but clean rooms.

Carriage House (☎ 601-445-5151; 401 High St; mains $8-12; 🕙 lunch daily) A plate of expertly fried chicken on the grounds of Stanton Hall will surely enhance your Natchez day.

Magnolia Grill (☎ 601-446-7670; 49 Silver St; mains $8-15) The oldest restaurant on the bluff specializes in good surf-and-turf fare.

Getting There & Around

Greyhound stops here. Downtown attractions are walkable, or you can catch a trolley bus at the depot downtown. Rent bikes at the **Natchez Bicycle Center** (☎ 601-446-7794; www.natchezbicyclecenter.com; 334 Main St; bicycle per day $20; 🕙 10am-5:30pm Mon-Fri, 10am-3pm Sat).

MEMPHIS

This is where rock got rolling. It's where soul music dug its grooves into the American consciousness. The great Martin Luther King Jr, was murdered here at the height of the Civil Rights movement. Elvis made this city the seat of his power. Little wonder so many travelers are intrigued by Memphis.

The town fills with music fans during the burgeoning Memphis in May.

HISTORY

Memphis was incorporated in 1826 and prospered on the expanding cotton trade of the Mississippi Delta. Early in the Civil War Union troops occupied the city, but postwar collapse of the cotton trade was far more devastating. A yellow-fever epidemic in 1878 claimed more than 5000 lives and many white residents abandoned the city. The black community revived the town. A former slave named Robert Church became a prominent landowner, civic leader and millionaire, and by the 1920s Beale St was the hub of social, civic and business activity, but it was equally well known as a place of gambling, drinking and prostitution.

WC Handy's 'Beale Street Blues' established Memphis as a center of blues music, and in the 1950s local recording company Sun Records cut tracks for blues, soul, R & B and rockabilly artists, both white and black.

The old downtown was largely abandoned by the 1970s, and Beale St was nearly demolished to make way for 'redevelopment.' Instead, a restoration program revived the entertainment district.

ORIENTATION

Downtown Memphis runs along the east bank of the Mississippi, with Riverside Dr and a promenade parallel to the river. The main tourist district is the area bounded by Union Ave and Beale St, and 2nd and 4th Sts. Further east, Union Ave and Overton Sq have shops, bars and restaurants. Graceland is 3 miles south of town on Elvis Presley Blvd.

INFORMATION
Internet Access

Café Francisco (🕙 901-578-8002; 400 N Main St; per min 25¢; 🕙 7am-10pm Mon-Fri, 8am-10pm Sat, 8am-6pm Sun) In the Pinch district, this café has wireless Internet and terminals for customer use.

Public Library (3030 Poplar Ave; 🕙 9am-9pm Mon-Thu, 9am-6pm Fri & Sat, 1-5pm Sun)

Media

Commercial Appeal (www.gomemphis.com) Daily newspaper.

Memphis Flyer (www.memphisflyer.com) Pick up the free weekly, which comes out on Thursday and is chock-full of entertainment listings.

Medical Services

St Jude's Research Hospital (☎ 901-495-3306; 332 N Lauderdale)

Money

ATMs are widely available around town. If you need to go into a bank, try the **First**

THE SOUTH

MEMPHIS

Tennessee Bank (☎ 888-382-6654; 165 Madison Ave; ☺ 8am-4pm Mon-Fri, 10am-2pm Sat).

Post
Main Post Office (555 South 3rd St) There's another outlet at 1 N Front St.

Tourist Information
Tennessee State Visitor Center (☎ 901-543-5333, 888-633-9099; 119 Riverside Dr; ☺ 9am-5pm) Well stocked with brochures for the whole state. The helpful staff can assist you to find hotel deals in Memphis.

DANGERS & ANNOYANCES
Memphis is a friendly city but has its share of crime. Stick to populated areas, or take cabs if you stray far at night.

SIGHTS & ACTIVITIES
Graceland
For an utterly fascinating insight into a great American success story, do not miss the chance to see **Graceland** (☎ 901-332-3322, 800-238-2000; www.elvis.com; 3734 Elvis Presley Blvd; admission mansion $18, all attractions $27; ☺ 9am-5pm Mon-Sat & 10am-4pm Sun Mar-Oct, 10am-4pm Mon, Wed-Sun Nov-Mar, closed Tue Nov-Mar).

Elvis bought the house and 500-acre farm surrounding it in 1957 after recording a string of number-one hits for RCA Records. He was 22 years old at the time, and some of the alterations made during his two-decade residence in the house suggest he never lost his playful, boyish sense of grandeur. There's a jungle room with green

THE SOUTH

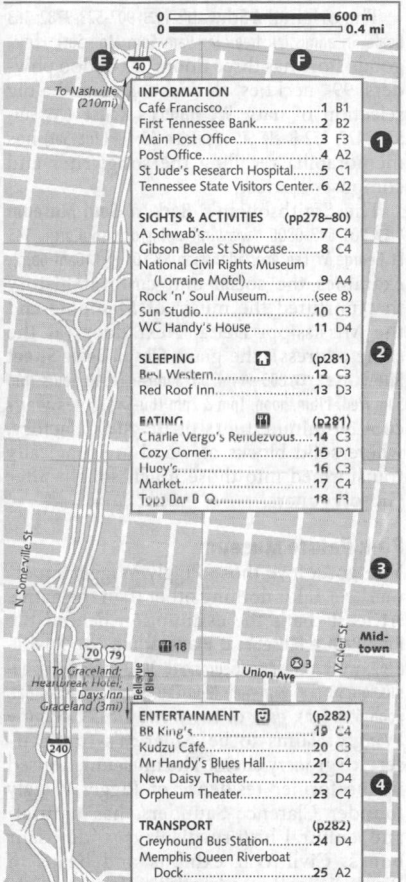

shag carpeting on the ceiling, a swank TV room with three monitors (which Elvis is rumored to have enjoyed shooting at) and an immense, unsightly racquetball gym in the back yard, where hundreds of gold and platinum discs now hang above mannequins sporting the King's sequined threads from his flamboyant cape-donning days.

The upstairs rooms are off-limits, so we are denied a look at the famous toilet where the King reputedly met his maker. But since Elvis is buried on the grounds, in a prayer garden next to the swimming pool, we are able to pay respects in perhaps a more appropriate setting.

The Graceland experience can only be described as a confusion of admiration and bemusement. It's an odd privilege to freely scrutinize the man's personal effects, in his own home. The tours inevitably draw a mix of diehard worshippers, casual fans, earnest sociology professors and the perversely curious. All are fully rewarded.

The 1½-hour mansion tour is a recording narrated by ex-wife Priscilla, with sound bites from Elvis and his daughter, Lisa Marie. You can pay for the package and see the entire estate, or you can pay to see the individual sights, which include the **mansion** (admission $18), the 'Sincerely Elvis' **memorabilia collection** (admission $6), the **car museum** (admission $8) and an **aircraft collection** (admission $7).

Sun Studio

For some fans, Memphis' No 1 musical shrine is **Sun Studio** (☎ 901-521-0664, 800-441-6249; www.sunstudio.com; 706 Union Ave; admission $9.50; ☼ 10am-6pm) It offers a simple, one-room, 30-minute tour that packs a punch because so many important events took place here during the 1950s. Some say rock and roll took its first flight in this tiny studio when Elvis Presley recorded his legendary 'Sun Sessions' here in 1954. Others argue that rock began in 1951, when Jackie Brenston's 'Rocket 88' was recorded at Sun.

Sam Phillips opened Sun in the early 1950s, initially concentrating on blues artists like Howlin' Wolf, BB King and Ike Turner. After Elvis passed through, Sun churned out greats such as Jerry Lee Lewis, Carl Perkins, Johnny Cash and Roy Orbison. The studio is still operating at night, favored by artists seeking that unique Sun sound. During the day guests can stand amid vintage instruments and recording gear and soak it all in.

HITS RECORDED AT SUN

- **Jackie Brenston** *Rocket 88*
- **Little Junior Parker** *Mystery Train*
- **Elvis Presley** *That's All Right*
- **Jerry Lee Lewis** *Great Balls of Fire, Whole Lotta Shakin' Goin On*
- **Johnny Cash** *I Walk the Line, Folsom Prison Blues*
- **Carl Perkins** *Blue Suede Shoes*
- **Roy Orbison** *Ooby Dooby*

HITS RECORDED AT STAX

- **Wilson Pickett** *In the Midnight Hour*
- **Otis Redding** *Dock of the Bay*
- **Booker T & the MGs** *Green Onions*
- **Sam & Dave** *Soul Man*
- **Isaac Hayes** *By the Time I Get to Phoenix*

Stax Museum of American Soul Music

If the **Stax Museum** (☎ 901-942-7685; www.stax museum.com; 926 E McLemore Ave; admission $9) fails to give visitors goose pimples it's because the original building was demolished long ago. The museum stands at the original address, however, and looks the same, with a theater marquee emblazoned with the words 'Soulsville USA.' Indeed, this was soul music's epicenter in the 1960s, when Otis Redding, Carla Thomas, Booker T & the MGs and Wilson Pickett recorded here. It's worth visiting for the photos, displays of '60s and '70s peacock clothing and, above all, Isaac Hayes' 1972 Superfly Cadillac outfitted with shag fur carpeting and 24-karat gold exterior trim.

National Civil Rights Museum

From the street, the **Lorraine Motel**, where Martin Luther King Jr was fatally shot on April 4, 1968, appears eerily frozen in time. Cadillacs from the 1960s are parked out the front and a memorial wreath hangs on the balcony in front of Room 6, where Dr King spent his last night. Inside, the hotel has been disemboweled and is now part of the monumental **National Civil Rights Museum** (☎ 901-521-9699; www.civilrightsmuseum.org; 450 Mulberry St; admission $10; ☉ 9am-5pm Wed-Sat, 1-5pm Sun). Five blocks south of Beale St, this museum brings to light one of the most significant moments in modern American history. Documentary photos and audio displays chronicle key events in civil rights history.

Beale Street

The strip from 2nd to 4th Sts is filled with clubs, restaurants, souvenir shops and neon signs – a veritable theme park of the blues. Only one of the stores is an original from Beale St's heyday in the early 1900s. It's easy and safe to walk around.

The original **A Schwab's** (☎ 907-523-9782; 163 Beale St; admission free; ☉ 9am-5pm Mon-Sat) dry-goods store has three floors of voodoo powders, 99¢ neckties, clerical collars and a big selection of hats. **WC Handy's House** (☎ 901-527-3427; 352 Beale St; admission $3; ☉ Tue-Sat) has memorabilia recalling the songwriter and composer's career.

The Smithsonian's **Rock 'n' Soul Museum** (☎ 901-543-0800; www.memphisrocknsoul.org; 145 Lt George W Lee Ave; admission $8.50; ☉ 10am-6pm), examines the social and cultural history that nurtured the music of Memphis and the Mississippi Delta. Next door (at the same address), the giant **Gibson Beale Street Showcase** (☎ 800-444-4766; admission $10; tours 1pm Sun-Wed, 11am, noon, 1pm & 2pm Thu-Sat) gives way-cool 30-minute tours of its guitar factory, where solid blocks of wood are magically transformed into those much sought after Gibson guitars.

Pink Palace Museum

You gotta love those Piggly Wiggly super-markets, if for nothing other than the name. At least that's the assumption behind the **Pink Palace Museum & Planetarium** (☎ 901-320-6362; www.memphismuseums.org; 3050 Central Ave; admission $8; ☉ 9am-4pm Mon-Thu, 9am-9pm Fri & Sat, noon-6pm Sun), east of town off US 72. Piggly Wiggly claims to be America's first self-service grocery chain. The museum, housed in the former residence of Piggly Wiggly founder Clarence Saunders, has natural- and cultural-history displays – dinosaur bones, Civil War exhibits and heaps of Piggly Wiggly memorabilia. It's certainly a very interesting premise. There is also a planetarium and Imax theater; tickets are sold separately.

TOURS

Memphis Queen (☎ 901-527-5694, 800-221-6197; www.memphisqueen.com; Riverside Dr at Monroe Ave; sightseeing cruise $15, music cruise with buffet $40) Riverboat rides aboard the *Memphis Queen* depart from the foot of Monroe Ave at Riverside Dr. Tour times fluctuate monthly so call ahead.

Memphis Rock'n'Roll Tours (☎ 901-359-3102; www.memphisrocktour.com; admission from $20) Offers a wide variety of music-related tours that take in studios, churches, juke joints, cemeteries and barbecue joints; call ahead for times.

Horse-drawn carriage (30min rides for 2 people $35) Departs from Beale St or outside the Peabody Hotel.

ELVIS WEEK

Each year in mid-August Memphis is flooded – not by the Mississippi River, but by Elvis impersonators of all ages. They are joined by devoted pilgrims, retro '50s swingers, average Joes and photographers. They come to mark the latest anniversary of the King's death on August 16, 1977. They congregate around Graceland, where they add to the graffiti on the brick wall out front. They strut, they weep, they laugh, they make spectacles of themselves. In other words, the fans steal the show. To become a part of this extraordinary event, plan ahead – reserve accommodations, get those sideburns started, have a sequined cape tailored. Check the Elvis website (www.elvis .com) for dates.

SLEEPING

If you want to save on accommodations, you'll find cheap highway-side motels across the river in West Memphis, Arkansas, where chain places cluster at I-40, exit 279. Tax on accommodations in Memphis is a stiff 15%.

Memphis-Graceland Campground (☎ 901-396-7125; 3691 Elvis Presley Blvd, campsites $22-27, cabins $33; ☑) You can play horseshoes with fellow Elvis fans at this RV park. The cabins are a good deal, but you'll need a sleeping bag. It's across the street from Graceland, behind the Heartbreak Hotel.

Red Roof Inn (☎ 901-526-1050; www.accor.na.com; 42 S Camilla St; d $50-70; P ☒ ☑) This is a clean option just 0.5 miles east of downtown Memphis. A complimentary continental breakfast is included.

Super 8 Motel Downtown Memphis (☎ 901-948-9005; 340 W Illinois Ave; r $33-43; P ☒) It's a bit run down and in an isolated pocket next to the Memphis–Arkansas Bridge, but downtown's just a mile away and the rooms are certainly adequate. Get coupons at the visitor center for the lowest price. Follow Crump Blvd until it becomes I-55 and take exit 12C.

Days Inn Graceland (☎ 901-346-5500; 3839 Elvis Presley Blvd; d $50-60; P ☒ ☑) With its guitar-shaped pool and free Elvis movies, this chain bends over backwards to make Elvis fans at home. Just a few blocks from Graceland.

Heartbreak Hotel (☎ 901-332-1000, 877-777-0606; www.heartbreakhotel.net; 3677 Elvis Presley Blvd; r $90-120; P ☒ ☑) OK, so it's not at the end of Lonely St, but the Heartbreak Hotel, behind Graceland's parking lot, is all about Elvis. The King's movies play in every room and the pool is shaped like a heart. Free shuttle to Beale St at night.

Best Western (☎ 901-527-4100, 800-380-3236; 164 Union Ave; r $70-100; P $5 ☒) Though slightly dated, this is a great choice for its location,

three blocks from Beale St. Rooms have hair dryers and coffeemakers. The hotel has a great lobby and fitness center.

EATING

Memphis is a carnivore's paradise, with some of the USA's best barbecue joints. The focus is on pork – in particular, chopped pork shoulder served in a sandwich (or 'pulled pork') and dry-rubbed ribs. Vegetarians will find their choices sadly limited.

Cozy Corner (☎ 901-527-9158; 745 N Parkway; mains $5-10) A nondescript and very friendly neighborhood barbecue joint, Cozy Corner is well worth the five-minute drive from downtown. In the opinion of many, this is as good as it gets.

Payne's (☎ 901-272-1523; 1762 Lamar Ave; barbecue $4-8) Another highly lauded barbecue joint is Payne's, in an old filling station along Hwy 78. Pork-shoulder sandwiches, topped with coleslaw, are the way to go here.

Market (☎ 900-543-8400; 119 S Main St; mains $2-7) This grocery store and deli is a healthy stop for delicious salads, sandwiches and fresh juices. There are tables in the adjacent mall, and the river is nearby for a picnic.

Charlie Vergo's Rendezvous (☎ 901-523-2746; 53 S 2nd St; mains $8-20; ☯ dinner Tue-Sat, lunch Fri & Sat) This jumping joint, on an alley off Union Ave, specializes in dry ribs, which are charcoal broiled rather than smoked. The service is friendly and the family atmosphere very upbeat.

Tops Bar-B-Q (☎ 901-725-7527; 1286 Union Ave; mains $6-10) With many locations, including this one in Midtown, Tops has been a favorite for cheap barbecue since 1952.

Huey's (☎ 901-527-2700; 77 S 2nd St; mains $5-9; ☯ to 3am) Long favored for creating the best burgers in town, Huey's is a good bet for casual pub food, right on the edge of the Beale St action.

ENTERTAINMENT
Live Music
The clubs that made Beale St famous were long gone when the city decided to revive the historic entertainment strip. What exists now has a theme-park atmosphere. But why complain about a blues-infused block party? There's little going on elsewhere in town.

BB King's (☎ 901-524-5464; 143 Beale St) BB's anchors the Beale St scene. It always has great live music, and there's usually no cover, but the beer's expensive.

Mr Handy's Blues Hall (☎ 901-528-0150; 182 Beale St) The most atmospheric club on Beale St has live blues every night.

Kudzu Café (☎ 901-525-4924; 603 Monroe Ave) Near downtown, Kudzu has comedy and regular guitar-pickin' contests.

New Daisy Theater (☎ 901-525-8979; www.newdaisy.com; 330 Beale St; shows at 7pm) This hip, all-ages venue hosts a variety of live-music shows. Call to see what's playing.

Sports
Memphis Redbirds (☎ 901-721-6000; tickets $5-17) The hometown AAA minor league baseball team plays frequent games before an enthusiastic crowd in its classic-style downtown yard, Autozone Park.

Memphis Grizzlies (☎ 901-678-2331) The NBA Memphis Grizzlies currently play basketball at FedEx Forum.

Theater
Orpheum Theater (☎ 901-743-2787; 203 S Main St) This is a 1928-era vaudeville palace, that has been restored as a venue for Broadway shows and major concerts.

GETTING THERE & AROUND
Memphis International Airport (☎ 901-922-8000; 2491 Winchester Rd) is 20 miles southeast of downtown via I-55; a taxi to or from downtown runs at about $30. The cheapest ride from the airport is aboard public bus No 32, which goes to midtown Memphis. Catch the bus outside the baggage claim, and ask the driver for a transfer. Also ask which transfer to make to get to your hotel. The fare is $1.25, plus 10¢ for the transfer. The **Downtown Airport Shuttle** (DASH; ☎ 901-522-1677; one way per person $15) serves most downtown hotels. If you factor in these costs, it might make sense to stay in a more expensive hotel that provides free airport shuttle.

Greyhound (☎ 901-523-1184; 203 Union Ave) operates frequent buses to Nashville and New Orleans.

Amtrak (☎ 901-526-0052; 545 S Main St) goes to Chicago and New Orleans.

The Sun Studio Shuttle runs a free hourly circuit to the city's music sites, including Graceland, the Stax Museum, Beale St and Sun Studio.

Local buses are run by the **Memphis Area Transit Authority** (MATA; ☎ 901-722-7100; www.matatransit.com). The **Main St Trolley** (☎ 901-274-6282; fare 60¢) runs vintage trolley cars on a loop from the Amtrak station to the Pyramid via Main St and Riverside Dr.

NASHVILLE

You could be forgiven for arriving in the country music capital expecting to meet honky-tonk women and lovesick troubadours. Well, it ain't exactly like that, folks. Nashville's about the *business* of country music – the recording and publishing and star-making that turns little-known talents into household names. Nashville characters these days are singer-songwriters and cowboy-booted publishing execs on cell phones. But Nashville shows visitors a good time. Almost every bar and many restaurants in town feature live music, from traditional country-and-western revivalists to slick Shania wannabes. Nashville has many attractions, from the fantastic Country Music Hall of Fame and the Grand Ole Opry House, to major league sports teams. It also has friendly people, cheap food and an unrivaled assortment of tacky souvenirs.

HISTORY
Central Tennessee was a land of migratory Shawnee until Europeans established Fort Nashborough in 1779. The legendary Daniel Boone brought emigrants over the Appalachians from the East.

Renamed 'Nashville,' the town became an important railroad junction with a riverboat connection to the Mississippi, and it was a strategic point during the Civil War. It surrendered to federal troops in 1862, and Andrew Johnson (then a US senator) was appointed military governor, imposing martial law until 1865. Confederate troops were destroyed in the 1864 Battle of Nashville.

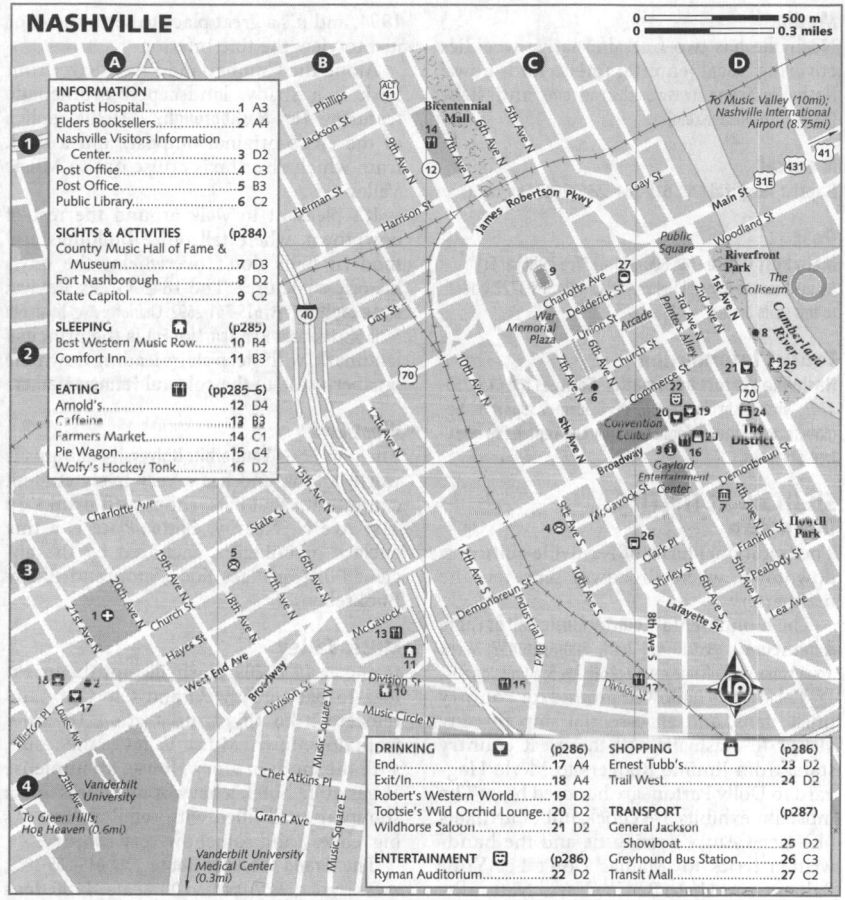

NASHVILLE

0 — 500 m
0 — 0.3 miles

INFORMATION
Baptist Hospital..........................1 A3
Elders Booksellers.....................2 A4
Nashville Visitors Information
Center..................................3 D2
Post Office..............................4 C3
Post Office..............................5 B3
Public Library..........................6 C2

SIGHTS & ACTIVITIES (p284)
Country Music Hall of Fame &
Museum................................7 D3
Fort Nashborough.....................8 D2
State Capitol...........................9 C2

SLEEPING (p285)
Best Western Music Row...........10 B4
Comfort Inn............................11 B3

EATING (pp285–6)
Arnold's.................................12 D4
Caffeine.................................13 B3
Farmers Market.......................14 C1
Pie Wagon.............................15 C4
Wolfy's Hockey Tonk...............16 D2

DRINKING (p286)
End.......................................17 A4
Exit/In...................................18 A4
Robert's Western World...........19 D2
Tootsie's Wild Orchid Lounge...20 D2
Wildhorse Saloon....................21 D2

ENTERTAINMENT (p286)
Ryman Auditorium...................22 D2

SHOPPING (p286)
Ernest Tubb's..........................23 D2
Trail West..............................24 D2

TRANSPORT (p287)
General Jackson
Showboat..............................25 D2
Greyhound Bus Station............26 C3
Transit Mall............................27 C2

From 1925, Nashville became known for its live-broadcast Barn Dance, later renamed the 'Grand Ole Opry.' Its popularity soared, the city proclaimed itself the 'country-music capital of the world,' and recording studios sprang up.

Today, Nashville draws a wide mix of friendly locals and talented transients who play small stages and hope their dreams will come true. The resulting glut of musicians and songwriters has created an exciting, ever-evolving music scene.

ORIENTATION

Nashville sits on a rise beside the Cumberland River, with the capitol at the highest point. The compact downtown slopes south to Broadway, the city's central artery and main entertainment strip. Across the river is the Coliseum where the Titans play. On the West Side are Vanderbilt University and a slew of restaurants and rock clubs. Northeast of town, the Briley Parkway leads to Music Valley and the Grand Ole Opry.

INFORMATION
Bookstores
Elders Booksellers (☎ 615-327-1867;
2115 Elliston Pl; ◷ Mon-Sat) An excellent used bookstore on the West Side.

Internet Access
Public Library (Church St, btwn 6th & 7th Sts;
free access)

Media

Nashville has two free alternative weeklies covering local entertainment and news: **Nashville Scene** (www.nashscene.com) and **Rage** (www.nashvillerage.com).

Medical

Baptist Hospital (☎ 615-284-5555; 2000 Church St)

Post

Main Post Office (☎ 800-275-8777; 525 Royal St) All mail sent to General Delivery, Nashville, TN 3722 goes to this main branch.

Tourist Information

Nashville Visitors Information Center (☎ 615-259-4747; www.nashvillecvb.com; ☽ 8:30am-5:30pm) In the glass tower of the Gaylord Entertainment Center. Provides free city maps.

SIGHTS & ACTIVITIES
Downtown

The traditional heart of Nashville culture is downtown, where Broadway serves as the main artery.

The monumental **Country Music Hall of Fame & Museum** (☎ 615-416-2001, 800-852-6437; www .countrymusichalloffame.com; 222 5th Ave S; admission $16; ☽ 10am-6pm) is hallowed ground for country music fans, and an essential stop for any visitor to Nashville. All the great country stars, from Jimmie Rodgers to Merle Haggard to Dolly Parton, are honored here. The museum exhibits are chock-full of artifacts like Gene Autry's string tie and the handwritten lyrics to 'Mamas Don't Let Your Babies Grow Up to Be Cowboys.' Naturally, Elvis' solid-gold Cadillac convertible upstages everything else. The state-of-the-art displays include touch screens that allow access to recordings and photos from the Country Music Foundation's enormous archives. There's country karaoke and live performances as well.

The **Ryman Auditorium** (☎ 615-254-1445; 116 5th Ave N; tours $6; ☽ 8:30am-4pm) is where the Grand Ole Opry began. It was built in 1890 by Thomas Ryman, a former riverboat captain who 'got the call' late in life and dedicated this huge, gabled, brick tabernacle to spiritual music. The Ryman's Saturday-night Barn Dance became the Grand Ole Opry in the 1930s, and stayed here for 31 years, until it moved out to the Opryland complex in 1974. The Ryman reopened in

1994, and it's a great place to see a show, or just to view the fine interior.

Along the Cumberland River, Riverfront Park is a shady, landscaped promenade featuring **Fort Nashborough**, a 1930s replica of the city's original outpost, and a dock from which river taxis cruise out to Music Valley.

It's pleasant to walk around the rest of downtown, where tall office buildings and modern halls don't overwhelm the city's historic structures. The 1845 Greek Revival **state capitol** (☎ 615-741-2692; Charlotte Ave, btwn 6th & 7th Sts; free tours 9am-4pm Mon-Fri) is the principal landmark, with steep stairs leading down the northern side to the colorful **Farmers Market**.

West End

The gorgeous **Vanderbilt University** campus is worth a look and has a very lively student community that eats, shops and drinks on 21st Ave N. Nearby, **Elliston Place** is a tiny enclave of bohemia anchored by the ancient Elliston Place Soda Shop and Elders Booksellers.

Music Valley

In the early 1970s, Nashville got the bright idea to pack up the Grand Ole Opry and relocate it to this tourist zone 10 miles from downtown. Music Valley is the result, with the modern Opry House, an immense Vegas-style hotel, a bevy of museums and a shopping mall filled with retail chains. It's big, cheesy and somehow very *country*.

The **Grand Ole Opry House** (☎ 615-889-3060; www.opry.com; 2802 Opryland Dr) seats 4400 fans for its year-round Friday and Saturday night shows. Guided backstage tours are offered daily by reservation ($9). The **Grand Ole Opry Museum** (☎ 615-889-3060; 2802 Opryland Dr; admission free; ☽ 10:30am-6pm, closed Jan & Feb) across the plaza tells the story of the Opry with wax characters, colorful costumes and artifacts. Don't miss the Patsy Cline classic – a 1950s rec-room diorama.

Next door, the Opry Mills Mall houses an Imax cinema, theme restaurants and the **Gibson Bluegrass Showcase** (☎ 615-514-2200; admission free; ☽ 10am-6pm), a working factory and concert venue where you can see banjos, mandolins and resonator guitars made.

Worth a quick stop, the **Willie Nelson Museum** (☎ 615-885-1515; 2613 McGavock Pike; admission $3.50; ☽ 9am-5pm, until 9pm May-Sep), displays the troubadour's guitars and gold records. The nearby **Music City Wax Museum** (☎ 615-883-3612; admission $3.50; ☯ 9am-5pm, until 9pm May-Sep), features wax statues of costumed country stars that look as lifelike as some of the real ones gracing the Opry stage.

To drive to Music Valley take Hwy 155 (Briley Parkway) exits 11 and 12B. It's also reachable by riverboat.

TOURS

General Jackson Showboat (☎ 615-871-5043; www .generaljackson.com; 2812 Opryland Dr; admission cruise only $10, buffet & show $38) has trips on the Cumberland River from downtown Nashville to the Opry Land Hotel.

SLEEPING

There's nothing very cheap downtown, and nothing especially worth a splurge. Freeways and fast-moving parkways slice through Nashville in all directions, so staying a few miles from the center is not a major inconvenience if you have a car. There are clusters of budget motels on all sides of downtown, on I-40 and I-65. They charge around $30 to $60 for rooms. The chains around Music Row, a few blocks from downtown music clubs, are slightly more expensive. Reasonable options are available in Music Valley great if Opryland is the primary focus of your visit. Be aware hotel tax in Nashville adds 14.25%.

Opryland KOA Kampground (☎ 615-889-0286, 800-562-7789; www.koa.com; 2626 Music Valley Dr; campsites $32; P ☂) At the north end of Music Valley, and with 460 tent and RV sites and every convenience you can think of, this is the best place for tenting near Nashville.

Drake Motel (☎ 615-256-7770; 420 Murfreesboro Rd; d $30-45; P ☒ ☂) Just a few minutes drive from downtown, the Drake is a cheap and convenient option, with loads of nostalgia. The vintage neon sign says 'Stay Where the Stars Stay,' which surely refers to stars of 40 years ago, but the Drake retains some of its former motel glory.

Best Western Music Row (☎ 615-242-1631, 800-528-1234; 1407 Division St; r from $50; P ☂) Not far from the action on Broadway (though it's a long walk), this standard hotel near Music Row is a good option. Comparable amenities can be found nearby at **Comfort Inn** (☎ 615-255-9977; 1501 Demonbreun St; r $60-80; P ☒ ☒ ☂).

Motel 6 (☎ 615-227-969 6; 311 W Trinity Ln; r $33-48; P ☒ ☒ ☂) This chain is a cheap, clean and easy option midway between Opryland and downtown. It's off I-65, exit 87. Close by, an adequate alternative is **Best Value Inn** (☎ 615-226-9805; 2403 Brick Church Pike; r $30-45; P ☒ ☒).

Guesthouse Inn & Suites (☎ 615-329-1000; 800-777-4904; 1909 Hayes St; r $60-90; P ☒) This nondescript hotel, near Vanderbuilt University, is neat and well run and a quick drive from downtown.

Fiddlers Inn (☎ 615-885-1440; 2410 Music Valley Dr; r $50 80; P ☂) This family-oriented hotel is a reasonable choice if you want to see shows at the Grand Ole Opry. Comparable offerings can be found at **Red Roof Inns** (☎ 615-889-0090, 2460 Music Valley Dr; r $50 80; P ☒ ☂)

EATING

The true taste of Nashville can best be found in cinderblock cabins in the industrial zone south of Broadway, where Southern slop comes in heaping portions. We're talking meat-and-threes. What's the 'three,' you ask? Greens, beans or potatoes, typically cooked in pork fat. These joints serve you cafeteria style.

Arnold's (☎ 615-256-4455; 605 8th Ave S; mains $5-8; ☯ 10:30am-2:30pm Mon-Fri) You can't beat the meat at Arnold's, a long-time local favorite for the ubiquitous meat-and-three. Happy folks line up to get into this roadhouse cafeteria for savory carved meats, catfish, fried green tomatoes, turnip greens and lemon ice-box pie.

Pie Wagon (☎ 615-256-5893; 1302 Division St; mains $4-8; ☯ 10:30am-3pm Mon-Fri) A Nashville institution since 1922, the Pie Wagon is another great place for meat-and-threes. The current location, with a clean, utilitarian atmosphere, has a loyal following for its homey Southern cuisine and hot chicken.

Wolfy's Hockey Tonk (☎ 615-251-1621; 425 Broadway; mains $5-10) We're not sure, but this may be the only hockey-mad tavern south of the Mason-Dixon line. Wolfy's kitchen serves up solid burger fare and sandwiches, including a fine veg Reuben. It's right on the strip, and has free live music when there's not an important game on.

Hog Heaven (☎ 329-1234; 115 27th Ave N; barbecue $3-7; ☯ Mon-Sat) Nashville's best barbecue comes from this tumbledown cinderblock box, opposite Centennial Park. Once you've ordered a pork plate or sandwich from the small window you can either settle at a picnic table on the premises, or mosey over to the park with it.

Pancake Pantry (☎ 615-383-9333; 1796 21st Ave S; mains $6-9) Nashvillians come in droves to eat fluffy hotcakes at this bustling West Side family restaurant. If the house specialty doesn't tempt you, order ham and eggs or a sandwich.

Farmers Market (8th Ave N at Jackson St) Near the state capitol, this daily market has food stalls that sell a variety of cheap food, including gyros, empanadas, *muffalettas*, Reubens and more.

Caffeine (☎ 615-259-4993; 1516 Demonbreun St; mains $6-7) If you're tired of the weak Joe served elsewhere in town, head to this West Side hangout. It's also good for light sandwiches and wraps. There's live music at night.

DRINKING & ENTERTAINMENT

Broadway's where live musicians set the woods on fire. Talented country, folk, bluegrass, Southern-rock and blues performers play the smoky honky-tonks and bars that line the strip. Clubs and brewpubs along 2nd St cater to crowds less hell-bent on hearing country music. Many places are free Monday to Friday or if you arrive early enough. In the bars musicians typically play for tips.

Live Music

Grand Ole Opry (☎ 615-871-6779; www.opry.com; 2802 Opryland Dr; admission $24-28; ⏱ 7:30pm Fri, 6:30pm & 9:30pm Sat) Though the Opry has a variety of shows, the production Friday and Saturday evenings is a lavish tribute to classic Nashville Country music.

Ryman Auditorium (tickets ☎ 615-458-8700, info 615-889-3060; 116 5th Ave; ticket prices vary) Often called the 'mother church of country music,' the Ryman was the home of the Grand Ole Opry from 1943 to 1974. The Ryman's excellent acoustics, historic charm and large seating capacity have kept it the premier venue in town. If you see a show here, it'll no doubt be a memorable experience.

Robert's Western World (☎ 615-244-9552; 416 Broadway) Fans of traditional country-and-western gather in this cool spot on the strip – a genuine, honky-tonk style tavern, well used over the years. It's a friendly, good-time kind of a place that attracts chain-

smoking old-timers, sparkly retro-cowboys and tourists named Sven. Cover bands take the stage in the afternoon and keep going through the night.

Tootsie's Wild Orchid Lounge (☎ 615-726-7937; 422 Broadway) Truly a must-visit for anyone, Tootsies is a venerated dive where up-and-coming country musicians play. It's not unusual for big stars, whose photos cover the walls, to stop by for a jam.

Wildhorse Saloon (☎ 615-902-8200; 120 2nd Ave N; cover $4-10) Young locals crowd into this large club for new country music. The saloon offers free dance lessons, so you'll be doing the Rebel Slide and Cowboy Stomp before you know it.

Bluebird Cafe (☎ 615-383-1461; 4104 Hillsboro Rd; cover free-$10) In an unassuming strip mall in suburban Green Hills area (5 miles west of the District), the Bluebird attracts some of the city's most talented singer-songwriters.

Exit/In (☎ 615-321-3340; 2208 Elliston Pl; cover varies) Hard rocker and western beats are the name of the game here. Touring bands draw the college crowd.

End (☎ 615-321-4457; 2219 Elliston Pl; cover varies) This tiny shack behind a parking lot is Nashville's premier grunge spot, doling out a steady bill of rock and alternative bands.

Sports

Tennessee Titans (☎ 615-565-4000) The local NFL team plays in the Coliseum, across the river from downtown.

Nashville Sounds (☎ 615-242-4371) A minor-league AAA baseball team, the Sounds play at homey Greer Stadium, with its smart-looking guitar-shaped scoreboard.

Nashville Predators (☎ 615-770-2300) Who'd have imagined? NHL hockey in the land of twang guitars? The Preds play at the Gaylord Entertainment Center.

SHOPPING

Ernest Tubb's (☎ 615-255-7503; 417 Broadway) The legendary Ernest Tubb's has a great selection of country and bluegrass.

Trail West (☎ 615-255-7030; 219 Broadway) Walk in looking like a German backpacker, re-emerge looking like Roy Rogers. At least get a smart embroidered shirt!

GETTING THERE & AROUND

Nashville International Airport (☎ 615-275-1662), 8 miles east of town, is not a major air hub.

GET SOUR MASHED

Off Hwy 55 in Lynchburg (population 361), you'll come to the only place in the world that distills Tennessee's famous sour mash whiskey. **Jack Daniel's Distillery** (☎ 931-759-6180; www.jackdaniels.com; tours free; ☽ 9am-4:30pm) offers interesting and colorful hour-long tours of the historic site.

MTA bus No 18 links the airport and downtown; the **Gray Line Airport Express** (☎ 615-883-5555; one-way/return $11/17; ☽ 6am-11pm) serves downtown and West End hotels.

Greyhound (☎ 615-255-3556; 200 8th Ave S) stops here.

The **Metropolitan Transit Authority** (MTA, ☎ 615-862-5950; fare $1.45) operates city buses. Bus No 18 connects the airport and downtown. There are express buses to Music Valley.

EASTERN TENNESSEE

Largely a rural region with unhurried towns dotting the hills and river valleys, Eastern Tennessee boasts spectacular scenery and a wide range of outdoor activities. The region's two main urban areas, Knoxville and Chattanooga, are pleasant riverside cities with lively college populations, good restaurants and an easygoing energy.

CHATTANOOGA

Once a polluted industrial burg, today Chattanooga is one of the most appealing small cities in the South. During the day, many visitors take in the world-class aquarium or one of the nearby Civil War battlefield parks. Others test their skill or courage with the region's celebrated climbing, rafting, hang-gliding or skydiving opportunities. At dusk, the broad Tennessee River becomes the center of attention as it gently meanders through the heart of town. The once-condemned Walnut St pedestrian bridge, claimed to be the longest in the world at nearly half a mile, spans the river to connect downtown with the Frazier St corridor. Along the river, in Coolidge Park, both children and adults frolic in the fountain, making Chattanooga as nice a place to spend a warm evening as one could hope for.

Chattanooga was born of one of the great injustices of the early USA: it served as the embarkation point for the forced removal of the Cherokee along the 'Trail of Tears.' The town and its environs was a key strategic point during the Civil War, and several important battles were fought nearby at Lookout Mountain and Chickamauga.

Chattanooga sits on the Tennessee–Georgia border at the junction of I-75 and I-24. Most of the city's main sights are within a few blocks of the **visitors center** (☎ 423-856-8687, 800-322-3344; www.chattanoogafun.com; 2 Broad St; ☽ daily) at the corner of 2nd and Broad Sts.

Sights & Activities

Absolutely a must-see, **Tennessee Aquarium** (☎ 800 262 0695; www.tnaqua.org; 1 Broad St; admission $14; ☽ daily) is the world's largest freshwater aquarium. Part of the aquarium, an **Imax theater** (☎ 800-762-0695; 201 Chestnut St; admission $7.75) shows the latest offerings of gargantuan cinema. Nearby, **Ross's Landing** is a good place to start a riverfront stroll.

Chattanooga Regional History Museum (☎ 423-265-3247; 400 Chestnut St; adult $4; ☽ daily) does a good job depicting the area's history with extra attention paid to the Cherokee Indians and Chattanooga's role in the Civil War.

Some of Chattanooga's oldest and best-known attractions are outside the city at nearby **Lookout Mountain** (☎ 706-820-4030; www.lookoutmtnattractions.com; 827 East Brow Rd; admission $35; ☽ vary by season). These include the Incline Railway, underground caverns called Ruby Falls, and Rock City – a garden with a dramatic cliff top overlook and waterfall. The admission gets you into all three attractions. **Point Park**, at the mountain's summit, is part of the NPS's **Chickamauga & Chattanooga National Military Park** (admission $2) complex. Admission to the **visitors center** (☎ 423-866-9241; ☽ daily), which tells gripping stories of the bloody 1863 Civil War battles that were fought here, is free. To walk on the battlefields is a powerful experience that brings home the magnitude of the struggle.

From March to mid-November, dozens of companies offer rafting adventures on the beautiful but vengeful **Ocoee River**, an hour east of Chattanooga and the site of the 1996 Olympic Whitewater Competition. Two of the best are **Sunburst Adventures** (Benton, TN; ☎ 800-247-8388) and **Outdoor Adventure Rafting** (Ocoee, TN; ☎ 800-627-7636).

Lookout Mountain Flight Park (☎ 706-398-3541, 800-688-5637; www.hanglide.com; Rising Fawn, GA) offers hang gliding instruction and exhilarating tandem flights. **Rock Creek Outfitters** (☎ 423-265-5969; 100 Tremont St) rents climbing equipment. Climbing guides and information are available at the **Adventure Guild** (☎ 423-266-5709; 149 River St). Bring your own wheels and shred a rail at **Sanctuary Skate Park** (☎ 423-267-4005; 1801 Carter St nr Finley Stadium; 3hr session $10).

Sleeping

Sadly, Chattanooga has no youth hostel, and all of the lodging options downtown are pricey. Budget motels can be found along I-24 at exits 178 and 181A.

The independently run **King's Lodge** (☎ 423-698-8944, 800-251-7702; I-24 exit 181A, 2400 West Side Dr; s/d $45/50; P ⚥) has great views of the city and clean, no-nonsense rooms with fridges. The **Cascades Motel** (☎ 423-698-1571; I-24 exit 181A, turn right, go 1 mile to 3625 Ringgold Rd; s/d $35/39; P ⚥) is similarly appointed but less scenic.

There are many campgrounds around Chattanooga. On the western edge of Lookout Mountain in northwestern Georgia, 29 miles from Chattanooga, **Cloudland Canyon State Park** (☎ 800-864-7275; Rising Fawn, GA, Rte 136, 8 miles east of Trenton & I-59; car/walk-in/backcountry campsites $19/10/4; P ⚥) has spectacular scenery and many walk-in and backcountry campsites. Less lovely, but closer to Chattanooga, is **Raccoon Mountain RV Park & Campground** (☎ 423-821-9403; primitive campsites $13-15), to the west at I-24 exit 174.

Eating

There are plenty of good, inexpensive spots to eat.

Sticky Fingers (☎ 423-265-7427; 420 Broad St; lunch $6-8, mains $10-15) Serving it wet, dry, sweet or hot, this place has the best ribs, chicken and barbecue in town.

Lupis Pizza Pies (☎ 423-266-5874; 406a Broad St; slices from $1.50, pizzas $9.25) Dark and funky, this excellent pizzeria sells great pies.

Mudpie (423-267-9043; 12 Frazier Ave; mains $6-9) On the other side of the river, this pleasant restaurant has an extensive menu of classic American food and several filling vegetarian options.

Greyfriar's (☎ 423-267-0376; 406b Broad St; 💻) This coffeehouse, with Internet access, is a good stop for a light breakfast.

For really cheap grub, try **Memo Grill** (☎ 423-267-7283; 430 E ML King Blvd; meals $3-6) and their signature dish, Memo's Chopped Wieners. Some people find the aforementioned chopped hot dogs, swimming in a sea of watery chili, to be irresistible. Others don't.

Drinking & Entertainment

Chattanoogans love music, and you can expect to hear rootsy American sounds in this town, be it old-time, bluegrass or just the blues. Turn to the free weekly alternative paper *The Pulse* for entertainment and restaurant listings.

Local (☎ 423-265-2171; 231 ML King Jr Blvd) Regional bands turn up the volume Wednesday to Saturday nights.

Lamar's (☎ 423-266-0988; 1018 ML King Jr Blvd) Velvet wallpaper, soul food, a classic jukebox and the stiffest drink in town.

Pickle Barrel (☎ 423-266-1103; 1012 Market St) Cruddy but beloved, Chattanooga's oldest bar has a pleasing patio and balconies.

Getting There & Around

Chattanooga's modest airport is just east of the city, as is the **Greyhound station** (☎ 423-892-1277; 960 Airport Rd).

Free electric shuttle buses ply the center. The visitors center has a route map.

KNOXVILLE

With its energetic student culture and a veneer of hipster new South slackerdom, Knoxville is a pleasant place to kick it for an evening or two while you regroup in preparation for attacking the Great Smoky Mountains National Park (p294), a two-hour drive away. While the town lacks dynamic attractions, it does offer its great Old City historic district, where you'll find plenty of old bars, restaurants and music halls.

Knoxville resides in the southwestern corner of Tennessee. The brand new **visitors center** (☎ 865-971-4440, 800-727-8045; www.knoxtsc .com; 301 S Gay St, Old City; 🕘 9am-5pm Mon-Sat, 1-5pm Sun) dispenses the usual brochures and historical information.

On the edge of downtown are two noteworthy historical sights. The 1792 **Blount Mansion** (☎ 865-525-2375; 200 W Hill Ave; admission $5; 🕘 9:30-5pm Mon-Sat) was the residence of a distinguished early governor. A few blocks up Hill St is a replica of **James White's**

Fort (☎ 865-525-6514; 205 E Hill Ave; admission $4; ☺ 9:30am-4:30pm Mon-Sat); the original, built in 1786, was the town's first house.

Sleeping

For budget accommodations, check out the offerings north of downtown on I-40 at exits 394 and 398, and south of the center at exits 378A and 378B. Closer to the action is one of the region's blessed few youth hostels.

Knoxville Hostel (☎ 865-546-8090; FourZeroFour East@aol.com; 404 E Fourth Ave; member/nonmember incl breakfast $15/18; ☺ office 8-11:30am, 1-6pm Mon-Fri),within walking distance of Greyhound and the Old City, occupies an old house with two bunkrooms, a cozy living area and communal kitchens and bathrooms. The neighborhood strikes some as slightly eerie at night, but others find this appealing. If you arrive by bus after dark, call the hostel for a pickup. Reservations recommended.

Days Inn (☎ 865-521-5000; 1719 Lake Ave; r from $70; P ❀) This impeccable service-oriented hotel off Cumberland Ave has pricey rooms but a great location near the university.

KOA Kampground (☎ 865-933-6393; at I-40/I-75, exit 117; campsites $19-22) Your best bet for camping close to the city.

Eating

Tomato Head (☎ 865-933-4067; 12 Market Sq; sandwiches $5, mains $8-10) With stamped-tin ceilings and an ever-changing art gallery, this downtown favorite serves inventive Italian and Southwestern fare, and delicious brunches.

Sun Spot (☎ 865-637-4663; 1909 Cumberland Ave, mains $6-10) Vegetarians and carnivores dine amiably together at this collegiate favorite, but only the latter can enjoy the blackened salmon quesadillas.

Barley's Taproom & Pizzeria (☎ 865-521-0092; 200 E Jackson Ave, Old City; slices from $2, whole pies $6-18) This place has good pizza, great live bluegrass music, and $2 pints until 6pm every day.

Entertainment

Pilot Light (☎ 865-524-8188; 106 E Jackson Ave, Old City) This hole-in-the-wall rock club books alternative bands.

Blue Cats (☎ 865-544-4300; 125 E Jackson Ave, Old City) A party atmosphere pervades this large music hall booking national acts.

Getting There & Away

Knoxville is at the crossroads of I-75 and I-40, about 180 miles east of Nashville. **Greyhound** (☎ 865-522-5144; 100 E Magnolia Ave) stops here.

KENTUCKY

Kentucky has its place in the American imagination as the birthplace of Abraham Lincoln, Colonel Saunders and bluegrass music. It's the wellspring of Bourbon whiskey, a pastoral land where, in the sunburst of late spring, thoroughbreds kick up the turf at Churchill Downs and blades of grass shine like gunmetal on rolling pastures. We know that much and, it seems, not much else. The state begs to be examined more closely.

The boundary between Eastern and Central time goes through the middle of Kentucky. If you go from Mammoth Cave to Lincoln's birthplace, you'll arrive an hour later than you thought.

LOUISVILLE

Not counting Derby Week, Louisville is a quiet, workaday burg. It's a fairly industrial city on the banks of the Ohio River, with a traditional American downtown, charming neighborhoods and pretty parks. Most locals refer to their city as 'Luahvul.' Louisville has its attractions but is noticeably short on restaurants and cheap lodging.

The I-64 freeway runs directly to the heart of the city and an inner (I-264) and outer (I-265) ring road circle it. The **visitors center** (☎ 502-582-3732, 888-568-4784; 221 S 4th St; ☺ 9am-5pm Mon-Fri) runs an outlet in the convention center. Surf the Web free at the **public library** (301 York St) downtown.

Sights
CHURCHILL DOWNS

Home to the Kentucky Derby, **Churchill Downs** (☎ 502-636-4400, 800-283-3729; www.churchill downs.com; 700 Central Ave), 3 miles south of downtown, is the mother church of American racetracks. If you'll miss the Derby, you can still see the ponies run here. During the racing season, from April through to November, $2 gets you into the Downs.

The **Kentucky Derby Museum** (☎ 502-637-7097; www.derbymuseum.org; Gate 1, Central Ave; admission $9; ☺ 8am-5pm Mon-Sat, noon-5pm Sun), on the grounds

THE KENTUCKY DERBY

A two-minute horse race on the first Saturday of May is the highlight of Louisville's calendar. Short as the actual event may be, the town's hotels are jam-packed during the weeklong build-up, and rates are double or triple the norm. If you're hoping to get in on the action, you might need a friend with an available couch to crash on.

It's near impossible for an out-of-towner without ties to the local aristocracy to get tickets for the grandstand at **Churchill Downs**. Never fear: on Derby Day, $40 gets you into the crowded Paddock party scene (no seat) if you arrive by 6am. It's so crowded you won't see much of the race, but you'll be with the hoi polloi who really know how to have fun.

Races at the Downs during the week leading up to the Derby are inexpensive (admission $2) and charged with Derby Week energy.

of the Downs, is a rewarding stop for race fans. It has displays on horses, jockeys and mint juleps, an awesome 360-degree audio-visual about the race, and visitors can take a tour of the track (reserve a spot for that).

LOUISVILLE SLUGGER MUSEUM
It's easy to spot the **Louisville Slugger Museum** (☎ 502-588-7228; www.sluggermuseum.org; 800 W Main St; admission $8; ❨ 9am-5pm Mon-Sat year-round, noon-5pm Sun Apr-Oct). Just look for the 120ft baseball bat leaning against the building on Main St. Since 1884, Hillerich & Bradsby Co have been making the famous Louisville Slugger baseball bat, favored by Big Leaguers from Honus Wagner to Derek Jeter. During a visit here you can watch the wooden bats being crafted in the factory. The admission fee includes a video, baseball exhibits, a plant tour, enthusiastic guides and a collection of baseball memorabilia. The prized souvenir is a personalized bat, with your own name grilled into the pine. Note: bat production halts on Sunday.

Tours
The **Belle of Louisville** (☎ 502-574-2355, 800-832-0011; www.belleoflouisville.org; admission $12), a 1914-era stern-wheeler, does scenic two-hour sightseeing cruises on the Ohio River, departing from the 4th St Wharf.

Sleeping
The cheapest motels are on the outskirts, especially around I-65 near the airport.

Emily Boone Home Hostel (☎ 502-585-3430; 102 Pope St; dm $10) Provides three futon beds with kitchen facilities in a private home. Space is limited, so call first.

Ramada (☎ 502-637-6336; 2912 Crittenden Dr; r from $50; ▣ ❇ ▣) A few miles from downtown,

this bland but tidy chain offers easy access to Churchill Downs. Take I-264 exit 11.

Eating
Lynn's Paradise Cafe (☎ 502-583-3447; 984 Barret Ave; breakfast & lunch $5-12, dinner $8-16; ❨ closed Mon night) Arty and kitschy Lynn's, south of downtown off Baxter Ave, is the place to go for delectable omelettes, breakfast burritos and homemade granola. For lunch or dinner, tuck into a splendid meatloaf and mashed potatoes platter. It's fun and satisfying.

Heine Bros Coffee (☎ 502-456-5108; 1295 Bardstown Rd; light mains $2-7) A young, intelligent crowd gathers at this local coffee shop. Good strong coffee and panini sandwiches are on offer.

Entertainment
The free weekly *Leo* lists gigs and entertainment options.

Jillians (☎ 502-589-9090; www.jillians.com; 630 Barret Ave) The fun and popular Jillians is a bar, restaurant and live-music venue all rolled into one.

Palace Theater (☎ 502-583-4555; 625 4th Ave) The 1928 Palace Theater is a wonderfully ornate venue for theater and concerts.

Getting There & Around
Louisville International Airport (☎ 502-367-4636) is 5 miles south of town on I-65. Get there by cab ($15) or local bus No 2. Greyhound stops here. Local buses are run by **TARC** (☎ 502-585-1234; 1000 W Broadway), based at the Union Station depot.

CENTRAL KENTUCKY
This is beautiful, rural country, with small towns and whiskey distilleries. Take a leisurely drive down scenic Hwy 31 south of

Louisville to enjoy the rolling green hills and painted barns.

About 40 miles south of Louisville is sleepy **Bardstown**, proud 'Bourbon Capital of the World.' Among the local distilleries, **Maker's Mark** (☎ 270-865-2099; admission free; � Mon-Sat 10:30am-3:30pm), in nearby Loretto, is clearly the best, with its historic still house and affordable top-shelf spirits. **Jim Beam** (☎ 502-543-9877; admission free; ☎ 9am-4:30pm Mon-Sat, 1pm-4pm Sun), in nearby Clermont, is best loved for its fine 'small batch' subsidiaries Knob Creek, Booker's and Baker's. Top off your Bourbon jag with a visit to Bardstown's very cool **Oscar Getz Museum of Whiskey History** (☎ 502-348-2999; 114 N 5th St; ☎ 10am-4pm Mon-Sat, noon-4pm Sun), with its nostalgic collection of naturally aged barrels, bottles and copper stills.

The town really comes alive during mid-September for the **Kentucky Bourbon Festival** (☎ 270-638-4877; www.kybourbonfestival.com). The **visitors center** (☎ 502-348-4877, 800-638-4877), just east of the square, has a walking-tour map of historic sights.

Motels include pleasant **Old Bardstown Inn** (☎ 502-349-0776; 510 E Stephen Foster Ave; d $60; ℗ ☒ ☒) and the family-run **Wilson Motel** (☎ 502-348-3364; 530 N 3rd St; d $50; ℗ ☒), north of Court Sq in the historic district. The **Jailer's Inn** (☎ 502-348-5551; 111 W Stephen Foster Ave; jail cells $70, r $105-125) is a renovated jailhouse with fancy B&B rooms and utilitarian jail cells with bunks (for a more 'captivating experience').

Hodgenville, further south on Hwy 31E, is home to the **Abraham Lincoln Birthplace National Historic Site** (☎ 270-358-3137; admission free; ☎ 8am-5pm). The story of the Babe Lincoln and his log cabin origins are as well known to Americans as the tale of Jesus in the

stable. However, the log-cabin here is not the actual one Lincoln was born in. It's promoted as his 'symbolic birthplace.' Lincoln was born somewhere near this spot. Adding interest to the site, certainly, is the Greek temple constructed around the cabin.

MAMMOTH CAVE NATIONAL PARK

Between Bowling Green and Elizabethtown, **Mammoth Cave National Park** (☎ 270-758-2328; www.nps.gov/maca; exit 53 from I-65) has the most extensive cave system on earth. With some 350 miles of surveyed passageways, Mammoth is at least three times bigger than any other known cave. Tourists started visiting around 1810 and guided tours have been offered since the 1830s. The area became a national park in 1926.

To see the caves, take a **ranger-guided tour** (☎ 800-967-2283; tours $8-20). It's wise to book ahead, especially in summer. Tours range from easy to strenuous, from about one hour to four hours. An easy, 30-minute unguided tour costs only $4.

Aboveground attractions of the Green River, the hiking trails and the natural forest are also alluring. The visitors center issues permits for backcountry camping (free) and has excellent publications. The caves are in the central time zone, an hour earlier than Louisville.

Mammoth Cave Hotel (☎ 270-758-2225; s/d $65/70, cabins $45), near the visitors center, has an inexpensive coffee shop and restaurant. The hotel and cottages have power, but the cabins do not. Three developed campgrounds have campsites ($16) with water and toilets. Call for reservations.

There are more tourist amenities along Hwy 70, between the park and Cave City. This is a great little run of corny attractions

---

IF YOU'VE GOT A FEW MORE DAYS IN KENTUCKY

Apart from horses grazing on the bluegrass fields around Lexington, the image most people have of Kentucky is **hillbilly country**. To get there, head to the far eastern part of the state, where the Cumberland and Appalachian Mountains straddle the jagged Kentucky-Virginia border. It's a remote, rural region of hollers, rivers and scenic two-lane blacktops connecting tiny towns that once were home to coalminers.

The **Daniel Boone Parkway** (Hwy 421) connects Manchester to Hyden, via the vast **Daniel Boone National Forest** (☎ 859-745-3100; www.southernregion.fs.fed.us/boone; campsites $8-22), with its rich variety of plants and wildlife and an extensive trail system. Hwy 421 continues south to Harlan County, heart of Kentucky mining country. From here, follow Hwy 119 to **Pikesville**, where the annual **Hatfield-McCoy Reunion Festival** (☎ 800-844-7453; www.real-mccoys.com) is held in mid-June.

that bend over backwards to tickle your funnybone: concrete dinosaurs, waterslides, miniature golf courses, teepees, and cute motels and cabins. Greyhound buses go to nearby Cave City, I-65 exit 53, which has touristy attractions and facilities.

LEXINGTON

In the heart of Bluegrass Country, Lexington is the shared turf of University of Kentucky students and jet-setters of the thoroughbred-racehorse industry. Most of Lexington's best attractions are outside the city, in the sublimely beautiful horse country. On a fine day, the area seems like the loveliest place on earth, with gently rolling hills, brilliant green grass, handsome houses, shady trees and picturesque plank fences receding into the distance. The barns are often more imposing than the houses, and the aristocratic thoroughbreds prance around like they own the place (which, given racing purses, they probably do). A loop around Paris Pike, Iron Works Pike, Yarnallton Rd and Old Frankfort Pike will take you past many horse farms, but scenic detours are recommended. Pick up good maps and area information from the **visitors center** (☎ 859-233-7299, 800-845-3959; 301 E Vine St; ☺ 8:30am-5pm Mon-Fri, 10am-4pm Sat).

Sights & Activities
KENTUCKY HORSE PARK
A working horse farm, educational theme park and equestrian sports center the **Kentucky Horse Park** (☎ 859-233-4303, 800-678-8813; www.kyhorsepark.com; 4089 Iron Works Parkway; admission $14; ☺ 9am-5pm mid-Mar–Nov, 9am-5pm Wed-Sun Dec–mid-Mar) sits on 1200 acres just north of Lexington. A visit to the horse farm will delight horse lovers and could convert anyone who isn't. Demonstrations of riding, horse breeds and equipment are included. Also included, the **International Museum of the Horse** follows the horse through human history, describing its role in hunting, transport, warfare and sport. Seasonal horseback riding costs $14. You can camp here, too (p292).

THOROUGHBRED CENTER
Most farms are closed to the public, but you can visit the **Thoroughbred Center** (☎ 859-293-1853; www.thethoroughbredcenter.com; 3380 Paris Pike; admission $10; tours 9am, 10:30am & 1pm Mon-Fri, 9am & 10:30am Sat Apr-Nov, by appointment Nov-Mar).

Tours of this working thoroughbred training facility take in stables, practice tracks and paddocks.

KEENELAND RACE COURSE
Horses earn their living 32 days a year at this exciting **race course** (☎ 859-254-3412, 800-456-3412; www.keeneland.com; 4201 Versailles Rd; admission $3-13), west of town on US 60, Versailles Rd (that's ver-*sales*). The spring and fall racing seasons are in April and October. From March to November, you can watch the champions train from sunrise to 10am. Afterward, you can enjoy breakfast in the track kitchen.

HORSEBACK RIDING
So you're itching to get in the saddle? Several working ranches around Lexington offer **horseback riding** to both newbie and experienced riders.

Whispering Woods (☎ 859-570-9663; 265 Wright Land; 1hr/full-day trail rides $20/60; ☺ May-Oct), in Georgetown, offers guided trail rides.

Deer Run Stables (☎ 859-527-6339), in Combs Ferry off Hwy 627, also offers guided trips. Call ahead for directions and reservations.

Tours
Blue Grass Tours (☎ 859-252-5744; www.bluegrasstours.com; from $25) Takes visitors to Keeneland or private horse farms and will pick up downtown.

Horse Farm Tours (☎ 859-268-2906; www.horsefarmtours.com; admission $25; tours 9am & 1pm Mon-Sun) Picks up at Lexington hotels and offers two tours daily to working horse farms. Reservations required.

Sleeping
The visitors center has a listing of highway motels, most of which charge about $45.

Super 8 (☎ 859-231-6300; 925 Newtown Pike; r $38-53; P) Just a few minutes' drive from the center of town, this chain is also close to Keeneland.

Kentucky Horse Park (☎ 859-259-4257, 800-370-6416; 4089 Iron Works Parkway; paved/primitive campsites $23/13) The convenient campground with 260 paved campsites on the Horse Park farm is open year-round. There's a pool, showers, laundry and more. Some 'primitive' campsites are also available.

Eating
Alfalfa's (☎ 859-253-0014; 557 S Limestone St; mains $6-12) Near the university, this vegetarian

place serves up good breakfasts and sand-wiches. Dig right into the hearty buckwheat pancakes.

Billy's Hickory Pit Bar-B-Q (☎ 859-269-9593; 101 Cochran Rd; mains $6-15) A longtime institution for inexpensive Kentucky-style smoked meats. This is a place to try 'burgoo,' Kentucky's own satisfying beef stew.

Drinking & Entertainment

For beer, bourbon and bar food, try friendly watering holes like **Cheapside** (☎ 859-254-0046; 131 Cheapside St), with a tropical patio. Cheapside, **Two Keys Tavern** (☎ 859-254 5000; 333 S Limestone St) and **A1A** (☎ 859-231-7263; 367 E Main St) all have live music.

Getting There & Around

Greyhound stops here. **Lex-Tran** (☎ 859-253-4636) runs local buses (No 6 goes to the Greyhound stop).

NORTH CAROLINA

If you have a predilection for gorgeous sce-nic byways, protected sandy beaches and verdant green forests that seem to go on forever, this is the state for you. Conversely, if you love mountain music, chili dogs, stock car racing or chainsaw sculpture – or think you might if properly exposed – North Carolina has no lack of attractions to satisfy your quirky soul.

Most travelers tend to skirt through the business-oriented urban centers of the cen-tral Piedmont, sticking instead to coastal routes (via the islands of the Outer Banks) and through the Appalachian Mountains, especially along the unforgettable Blue Ridge Parkway and in the Great Smoky Mountains National Park.

ASHEVILLE

Asheville's boosters exhort you to refer to their exceedingly pleasant western North Carolina city as the 'Paris of the South.' Perhaps they've never seen the bright lights of Paris. Notwithstanding, their enthusiasm for Asheville's bohemian pleasures is not misplaced. By day the streets are filled with hipsters perusing the used clothing shops or comparing tattoos. At night the sweet-smelling mountain air is graced with the sounds of musicians tuning their instruments

as the many clubs and cafés open their doors to showcase the local music scene.

The **visitors center** (☎ 828-258-6101, 800-257-1300; 151 Haywood St; ☒ 8:30am-5:30pm Mon-Fri, 9am-5pm Sat & Sun) is at I-240 exit 4C.

The **public library** (☎ 828-251-4991; 67 Haywood Ave; ☒ 10am-8pm Mon-Thu, until 6pm Fri, until 5pm Sat) has free Internet access.

Biltmore Estate (☎ 800-295-4730; www.biltmore.com; adult $40; ☒ 8:30am-5pm), with 250 rooms, is a gorgeous, sprawling estate billed as America's largest private house. Built for the filthy-rich Vanderbilt family as a holiday home, the 1895 mansion and gardens are styled after a French château and is over-whelmingly sumptuous in scale and decora-tion. Plan to spend hours viewing the estate to justify the hefty admission charges.

Thomas Wolfe Memorial (☎ 828-253-8304; 52 N Market St; adult $1; ☒ 9am-5pm Tue-Sat & 1-5pm Sun Apr-Oct, 10am-4pm Tue-Sat & 1-4pm Sun Nov-Mar) is the recently restored, local literary landmark, an early 1900s boardinghouse that was the model for 'Dixieland' in Wolfe's novel *Look Homeward Angel*.

Asheville is heaven on earth for outdoor activity enthusiasts. Recommended provid-ers include:

Bio-Wheels (☎ 828-232-0300; 76 Biltmore Ave; day rentals/tours from $35/150) Cycle the Blue Ridge.

Fordbrook Stables (☎ 828-667-1021; 120 Fordbrook Rd; 1hr/2hr/half-day guided rides $25/50/85) Ride wooded trails with beautiful views.

Climbmax Mountain Guides (☎ 828-252-9996; 43 Wall St; full-day rock climbing tours from $165) Also operates an indoor climbing center.

Sleeping

Chain motels cluster north of downtown at Merrimon Ave, with rates averaging $50 to $60. East on Tunnel Rd at I-240 Exit 6 are some independent places such as the nondescript **Blue Ridge Motor Lodge** (☎ 828-254-0805; 60 Tunnel Rd; r $40-60; P ☒). For local color try the **Mountaineer Inn** (☎ 828-254-5331, 800-255-4080; 155 Tunnel Rd; r from $45; P ☒ ☒) with its towering neon hillbilly sign and cedar-walled rooms.

Camping best bets:

French Broad River Campground (☎ 828-658-0772; 1030 Old Marshall Hwy; campsites off/on the river $17/19) Riverside campground 15 minutes north of downtown.

Bear Creek Campground (☎ 828-253-0798; I-40 exit 47, 81 S Bear Creek Rd; campsites without/with electricity $20/22) Primarily an RV park, it has full facilities.

Eating

Downtown has many interesting eateries.

Blue Moon Bakery & Café (☎ 828-252-6063; 60 Biltmore Ave; mains $6-10) A good stop for breakfast and sandwiches.

Laughing Seed Café (☎ 828-252-3445; 40 Wall St; lunch $6-10, dinner specialties $13-15; ☺ Wed-Mon) This veggie haunt offers great vegetarian dishes and organic Green Man beer.

Over Easy Breakfast Café (☎ 828-236-3533; 32 Broadway; breakfast $4-8) For stick-to-your-ribs breakfasts, hit this old-style diner with healthy fare and vegetarian options.

Noodle Shop (☎ 828-250-9898; 3 Pack Sq; mains $6-13) Excellent Chinese food and sidewalk tables with a privileged view of the square.

Drinking & Entertainment

Asheville has a rich music scene and plenty of good bars. To see what's on, pick up a copy of the free alternative weekly *Mountain Xpress or the Smoky Mountain News*.

Vincent's Ear (☎ 828-259-9119; 68-B N Lexington Ave) This amiable darkened hovel serves coffee and light meals by day, beer in the afternoon, and ear-splitting live music at night.

Orange Peel Social Aid & Pleasure Club (☎ 828-225-5851; www.theorangepeel.net; 101 N Biltmore Ave) Quality funk, punk and alt-country acts do their thing at this excellent music hall.

Smokey After Dark (☎ 828-253-2155; 18 Broadway) This gay bar still retains the ambience of its roadhouse origins. Pool tables and people in-the-know.

Hannah Flanagan's Irish Pub (☎ 828-252-1922; 27 Biltmore Ave) If beer comprises your agenda, this pub has dozens to choose from.

Fine Arts Theatre (☎ 828-232-1536; 36 Vanderbilt) The latest art-house films screened here.

Getting There & Around

Greyhound (☎ 828-253-8451; 2 Tunnel Rd) stops here. **Asheville Transit** (☎ 828-253-5691; www.ashevilletransit.com; bus fare $0.75) provides a limited local bus service.

GREAT SMOKY MOUNTAINS NATIONAL PARK

Straddling the border with Tennessee, this much-visited national park is loved for its gorgeous scarps of blue, hazy mountains, its phenomenal biodiversity and rustic vernacular architecture. Hikers – particularly those who venture into the backcountry – are rewarded with lush, old-growth forests, magical waterfalls, and the occasional glimpse of bear or fox. Autumnal visitors delight in the gorgeous fall colors, while those who come in May or June are treated to an astonishing variety of wildflowers.

Most visitors – and there are more than 10 million each year – enter the park via the gateway towns of **Gatlinburg, TN** or **Cherokee, NC**. Both towns are crowded and touristy, but have plenty of lodging and campgrounds – head to Cherokee for the cheapest options (although the town's services largely close November to February).

In the park, exhaustive information about camping and outdoor activities including hiking, biking, horseback riding can be obtained at one of the **visitors centers** (Occonaluftee ☎ 828-497-1900; Hwy 441, near Cherokee, NC; Sugarlands ☎ 865-436-1291; Hwy 441, near Gatlinburg, TN; ☺ daily Mar-Nov, off-season hours vary).

Ten **campgrounds** (☎ 800-365-CAMP; campsites $12-20) can accommodate thousands, although during the high season it can sometimes be difficult to procure a site. Some of the

---

IF YOU'VE GOT A FEW MORE DAYS IN NORTH CAROLINA

Chimney Rock Park (☎ 828-625-9611; admission $14; ☺ 8:30am-6:30pm) The photogenic, 26-story 'chimney' in the heart of this private park affords stunning views, but the real draw is the exciting hike around the cliffs to a 404ft waterfall.

Hot Springs Spa & Campground (☎ 828-622-7676; 315 Bridge St, Hot Springs, NC; regular/riverside/deluxe campsites $10/20/25, cabins from $40; ☺ 9am-11pm) Pamper your weary traveler's bones at this backwoods spa 35 miles northwest of Asheville. Curative mineral baths in secluded outdoor settings start at $10 per hour; well-priced massage also is available.

Nantahala Outdoor Center (☎ 888-662-2199; www.noc.com) With white-water adventure centers on the Nantahala, French Broad, Nolichucky and Chattooga rivers – all within easy driving distance of Asheville – this trusted outfitter leads rafting trips starting at $70 per person, and offers kayaking workshops. To reach the main campus on the Nantahala River, Take I-40 West to US 74 West; the center is 50 miles down this road.

more popular campgrounds take reservations. Only Cades Cove and Smokemont are open year-round; others are open March through October. Backcountry camping requires a permit. These can be obtained free at visitors centers or ranger stations.

THE TRIANGLE

Smack in the middle of the state is the Research Triangle, comprised of Chapel Hill, Durham and Raleigh. Together, these small cities form the high tech and scientific research capital of the 'New South.' Each town is home to a major university with its attendant student culture and bitter basketball rivalries. Durham and Raleigh have their share of interesting attractions, but if you've got a hankering to make a night of it head to Chapel Hill for its famous music scene and ever-growing array of bars and restaurants.

Sadly, the Triangle has few budget lodging options, but if you're traveling with a tent there is a terrific lakeside campground between Chapel Hill and Raleigh (p296).

For area entertainment listings, pick up the free *Spectator* or the *Independent* weekly papers.

VISITORS CENTERS

Pick up information and walking tour brochures at area **visitors centers** (Raleigh Capital Area Visitors Center; ☎ 919-733-3456; 5 E Edenton St at the North Carolina Museum of History; ☉ 8am-5pm Mon-Fri, 10am-5pm Sat, 1-4pm Sun; Durham Durham Visitors Center; ☎ 919-687-0288, 800-446-8604; www.durham-nc.com; 101 E Morgan St; ☉ 8:30am-5pm Mon-Fri, 10am-2pm Sat; Chapel Hill Chapel Hill–Orange County Visitors Bureau; ☎ 919-968-2060, 888-968-2060; www.chocvb.org; 501 W Franklin St; ☉ 8:30am-5pm Mon-Fri, 10am-2pm Sat).

GETTING THERE & AROUND

Raleigh–Durham International Airport (☎ 919-840-2123; www.rdu.com), a significant hub, is a 25-minute drive northwest of downtown Raleigh. **Carolina Trailways/Greyhound** (Raleigh ☎ 919-834-8275; 314 W Jones Rd; Durham ☎ 919-687-4800; 820 Morgan St; Chapel Hill ☎ 919-942-3356; 310 Columbia St) serve Raleigh and Durham with limited trips to Chapel Hill. **Amtrak** (☎ 919-471-3399; 302 W Cabarrus St) serves Raleigh. The **Triangle Transit Authority** (☎ 919-549-9999; www.ridetta.org; adult $1.50) operates buses linking Raleigh, Durham and Chapel Hill, and all three to the airport.

> **BUDGET TIP: INTERNET ACCESS**
>
> With a surprising lack of internet cafés in the Triangle, your best bets for logging on are at the public libraries at **Raleigh** (State Library; ☎ 919-733-3683; 109 E Jones St, 1 block south of the Visitors Center; ☉ Mon-Fri), **Durham** (Durham County Public Library; ☎ 919-560-0100; 300 N Roxboro St, near the visitors center; ☉ Mon-Sat) and **Chapel Hill** (Chapel Hill Public Library; ☎ 919-968-2777; 100 Library Rd; ☉ daily).

Raleigh

Some people might call Raleigh, well, dull. This would be impolite. While its low-key cultural scene is not going to be the primary subject of your letters home, this capital city in the Triangle's southeastern corner does offer a few good diversions, including three excellent museums.

The **North Carolina Museum of History** (☎ 919-715-0200; ncmuseumofhistory.org; 5 E Edenton St; admission free; ☉ 9am-5pm Tue-Sat, noon-5pm Sun), downtown near the Capitol, has a good chronological exhibit and a Wright brothers' airplane model.

The world's only dinosaur specimen with a heart is kept at the modern, airy **North Carolina Museum of Natural Sciences** (☎ 919-733-7450; www.naturalsciences.org; 11 W Jones St; admission free; ☉ 9am-5pm Mon-Sat, noon-5pm Sun).

On the western fringe of town, **North Carolina Museum of Art** (☎ 919-839-6262; www.ncartmuseum.org; 2110 Blue Ridge Rd; admission free; ☉ 9am-5pm Wed-Sat, 10am-5pm Sun) has a fine collection and an excellent outdoor Summer concert and film series.

The cheapest lodging can be found 2.5 miles northeast of downtown on Capital Blvd, about 1 mile inside the I-440 perimeter road. Downtown, **Days Inn** (☎ 919-828-9081; 300 N Dawson St; r $55; Ⓟ ⊠) has 55 basic but clean rooms.

Big Ed's (☎ 919-836-9909; 220 Wolfe St; mains $7-10; ☉ 7am-2pm Mon-Fri, 7am-noon Sat) This barn-looking place is *the* spot for a delicious country breakfast, like cured ham and eggs, grits and gravy.

Sadlack's (☎ 919-828-9190; 2116 Hillsborough St; sandwiches $3-6) This time-honored slacker hangout has inexpensive foot-long sandwiches, but the real reason to come is to get the lowdown from the hipsters that hang out here.

CAMPING IN THE TRIANGLE

Sadly, the Triangle area has a dearth of pension-class lodging, or even inexpensive motels. One way around this is to set up a tent at the **Jordan Lake State Recreation Area Crosswinds Campground** (☎ 919-362-0586; campsites with/without electricity $20/15, primitive $9). Huge Jordan Lake is lovely to behold, and even lovelier to swim in. The campground has showers, and is situated off the beaten track equidistant from Chapel Hill and Raleigh. From Raleigh, travel west 16 miles from the I-40 split on Hwy 64, turn right on Farrington Rd, and immediately look for the signs. From Chapel Hill, travel 11.5 miles on Mt Carmel Church Road from US 15/501 S.

Durham

The town where Lucky Strikes cigarettes were born has over the years diminished in importance as a tobacco center. These days it's a renowned medical research center and lively student town, in the 'pinnacle' of the Research Triangle. There are two hubs of activity. **Brightleaf Sq** on the east side of downtown is a recycled tobacco warehouse with restaurants and upscale shops, and 0.5 miles northeast, adjacent to the Duke University campus, is the student-filled **Ninth St District**.

See the humble origins of the Duke family and have an uncritical look at a historic mid-19th century tobacco farm at **Duke Homestead** (☎ 919-477-5498; 2828 Duke Homestead Rd; admission free; ☽ 10am-4pm Tue-Sat), on the north side of town.

One enjoyable way to spend an afternoon or evening is at the **Durham Bulls Athletic Park** (☎ 919-956-2855; www.durhambulls.com; 409 Blackwell St; tickets $4.50-8.50). The wildly popular Bulls, a minor-league baseball team that shot to fame after the 1988 flick *Bull Durham*, plays home games April through September.

Best Value Carolina Duke Inn (☎ 919-286-0771, 800-438-1158; 2517 Guess Rd; d $55; P ✷) This well-run motor inn provides the best value in the entire Triangle area. Located off I-85 at exit 175, it has 182 spacious rooms, most with cable TVs, microwaves, fridges and coffeemakers.

For dining, seek out the Brightleaf complex downtown and at Ninth St alongside the university campus.

Blue Corn Cafe (☎ 919-286-9600; 716B Ninth St; lunch $4-7, dinner $6-10) This worldly little place with sidewalk tables serves very toothsome dishes influenced by Cuban, Puerto Rican and Mexican cuisine.

Fishmongers (☎ 919-682-0128; 806 W Main St; lunch $6-9) A great seafood and crab joint.

Joe & Jo's (☎ 919-688-3222; 427 W Main St) This amiable downtown watering hole has great burgers and in-the-know barkeeps.

Chapel Hill

Providing a delightful impetus for potential visitors, arch-conservative senator Jesse Helms famously called this left-leaning university town a 'zoo' and proposed building a wall around it. As one veteran bartender reports, some of the folks from Chapel Hill weren't necessarily against the proposal, as it would have conversely served to keep the right-wingers *out*.

Chapel Hill, in the western corner of the Triangle, is the quintessential college town. The University of North Carolina (UNC), founded in 1789, was one of the nation's first state universities and has many fine old buildings. The music scene – particularly for roots American and alternative rock – is smokin', as is the basketball: Michael Jordan first took flight here.

Downtown is situated about 2 miles northwest of the Hwy 15/501 bypass. The main drag is Franklin St, with some funky clothing shops, bars and eateries on its northern side and the UNC campus towards the south; the same street enters Carrboro to the west.

Morehead Planetarium (schedule ☎ 919-549-6863, tickets 919-843-7997; www.moreheadplanetarium.org; 250 E Franklin St; admission $4.75; ☽ 12:30-5pm Sun-Wed, 10am-5pm & 6:30-9:30pm Thu-Sat) features science exhibits and celestial shows under its big dome.

Days Inn (☎ 919-929-3090, fax 919-929-8170; 1312 N Fordham Blvd; d from $80) This predictably comfortable chain has rooms with microwave, mini-fridge and free continental breakfast. It is the closest affordable option to downtown Chapel Hill.

Red Roof Inn (☎ 919-489-9421; 5623 Chapel Hill Blvd, I-40 exit 270; s/d $65/70; P ✷) About 4 miles north at Hwy 15/501, this comfortable chain motel seems steep for what you get, but quite reasonable when compared to other area hotels.

EATING & DRINKING

When university is not in session, you will feel like you have the whole town to yourself – not necessarily a good thing if you've come to wallow in revelry. Most restaurants and nightspots are along Franklin St.

Mama Dip's Country Kitchen (☎ 919-942-5837; 408 W Rosemary St; lunch or dinner $6-14) Get your daily servings of 'down home' yams, okra, chitlins or ribs at this time-honored country cooking institution.

Hector's (☎ 919-942-9420; 201 E Franklin; meals $2-6) This place is a late-night favorite among inebriated students for its cheap eats, perfect french fries, gyros and vegetarian, Greek-grilled cheese sandwiches.

Time Out (☎ 919-927 2425; 133 W Franklin; meals $3-5) Also open late, it serves filling biscuits, fried chicken and country vegetables.

Cave (☎ 919-968-9308; 452 W Franklin St) Cheap beer in a dank faux cave with live music and pool. Isn't this why you came?

West End Wine Bar (☎ 919-967-6790; 450 W Franklin) Wine with legs, DJs with mellow grooves, and a moon-drenched roof deck.

Chapel Hill's music scene has produced the likes of Ben Folds, Squirrel Nut Zippers, Chicken Wire Gang and Superchunk. See the next big thing at the following venues.

Cat's Cradle (☎ 919-968-4345; 300 E Main St) This is one of the seminal music halls that defined college indie rock; over the years everyone's played here.

Local 506 (☎ 919-942-5506; 506 W Franklin St) Bands like Zen Frisbee and Snatches of Pink got their start here.

Another good option is **Go! Room 4** (☎ 919-969-1400; 100-F Brewer Lane).

NORTH CAROLINA COAST

Traveling eastward, the landscape of North Carolina gradually recedes from the lofty peaks of the Blue Ridge to the gentle sandy plains that characterize the state's coastal region. At the terminus of land exists the **Outer Banks**, a fragile necklace of barrier islands that encircle the entire length of North Carolina's coast. In between are a series of estuaries, sounds and enclosed tidal lagoons.

It's a seascape awash in history. On Roanoke Island, the first permanent colony in the 'new world' was founded with the building of Fort Raleigh in 1585; it mysteriously vanished only a few years later. In the ensuing centuries, pirates roamed the tempestuous waters of the Outer Banks. Here more than a thousand vessels were shipwrecked, earning these waters the grim epithet 'The Graveyard of the Atlantic.' Faring better than their maritime counterparts, the Wright brothers taught us to fly in 1903 with a 12-second hop across a stretch of sand near Kitty Hawk in the first heavier-than-air powered aircraft.

Hwy 12 runs along this chain of barrier islands, curving east of Albermarle and Pamlico Sounds in a 100-mile arc. From north to south, **Bodle Island**, **Roanoke Island**, **Hatteras Island** and **Ocracoke Island** are linked by bridges and ferries. Out of season, things are very quiet and many businesses and campgrounds close. Much of the central islands is protected national seashore, with a few small towns and a wild, windswept beauty.

Most of the tourist attractions and facilities are along a 16-mile strip of Bodie Island, in the contiguous towns of **Kitty Hawk**, **Kill Devil Hills** and **Nags Head**. The best sources of information are at the **visitors centers** (Kitty Hawk ☎ 252-261-4644; Milepost 1½; ☼ 9am-5:30pm year-round; Manteo ☎ 252-473-2138, 800-446-6262; US 64/264; ☼ 9am-5:30pm Mon-Fri, noon-4pm Sat & Sun year-round).

BACKROADS NC: BYNUM

For a satisfying day trip, head 9.5 miles south of Chapel Hill on US 15/501 to the tiny town of Bynum, population 220. Take a left turn on Bynum Rd and the next left on Bynum Church Rd. Your reward will be a privileged viewing of the **homestead of noted folk artist Clyde Jones**, whose property is a virtual zoo of whimsical, hand-painted creatures pieced together from logs and detritus. Nearly all of Jones' neighbors keep at least one of his creations as a pet. After a walk across the one-lane bridge spanning the pretty Haw River, head back to the highway for lunch at **Allen & Son Bar-B-Que** (☎ 919-542-2294; 5650 US15/501; sandwiches $1.50-4, plates $4.75-7). Or, if you're fortunate enough to be there on a Friday evening in the spring or summer, take in an open-air string-band performance at the **Bynum General Store** (☎ 919-542-1858; performances 7pm).

No public transport exists to or on the Outer Banks. Free car ferries between Hatteras and Ocracoke Islands run at least hourly from 5am to midnight; bookings aren't necessary. **Ferries** (☎ 800-345-1665; per car $15) run between Ocracoke and Cedar Island (2½ hours) every two hours or so and should be reserved, especially in summer. **Ferries** (☎ 800-773-1094) also link Ocracoke and Swan Quarter on the mainland.

Sights

The **Wright Brothers National Monument**, near Milepost 8, honors Wilbur and Orville's achievement with a striking 80-ton granite monument embellished with art-deco wings atop a sand dune. Exhibits at the **visitors center** (☎ 252-441-7430; admission $3; ☽ 9am-5pm) trace the Wrights' painstaking development work in Dayton, Ohio, and the experiments conducted at summer camps here over several years. See replicas of their 1902 glider and 1903 powered Flyer, with informative hourly talks.

Fort Raleigh National Historic Site, on Roanoke Island, saw the first English colonies in North America meet with total failure. The **visitors center** (☎ 252-473-5772; ☽ 9am-6pm) has exhibits, artifacts and a free film about Native Americans and English settlers that will spark your imagination.

The **Lost Colony Outdoor Drama** is an immensely popular and long-running show that dramatizes the debacle. It plays from mid-June through to August at 8:30pm in the **Waterside Theater** (☎ 252-473-3414, 866-468-7630; www.thelostcolony.org; admission $16-20).

With graceful grounds and gardens, **Elizabethan Gardens** (☎ 252-473-3234; adult/student $6/4; ☽ daily in summer 9am-6pm) make a picturesque association with the England from 400 years ago.

CAPE HATTERAS NATIONAL SEASHORE

Saving much of the Outer Banks area from overdevelopment, a 70-mile long protected strand of barrier islands arcs out into the Atlantic and back again. Natural attractions include local and migratory water birds, marshes, woodlands, dunes and miles of empty beaches. Three **visitors centers** (Bodie ☎ 252-441-5711; Hatteras ☎ 252-995-4474; Ocracoke ☎ 252-928-4531; ☽ 9am-6pm in summer, hours vary in winter) serve the park on the main islands.

The **park headquarters** (☎ 252-473-2111; www.nps .gov/caha; 1401 National Park Dr) is in Manteo.

Pea Island National Wildlife Refuge (☎ 252-473-1131; admission free; ☽ 9am-4pm Mar-Nov, 9am-4pm Thu-Sun rest of the year), at the northern end of Hatteras Island, is a great place for watching wildlife along the nature trails and observation points.

Lighthouses are spaced all along the Outer Banks. The spirally striped Cape Hatteras Lighthouse is the tallest brick lighthouse in the US. You can climb the **257 steps** (admission $6; ☽ Apr-Oct), and check out the **visitors center** (☎ 252-995-4474; ☽ year-round).

The village of **Ocracoke** revels in its pirate past: Edward Teach, also known as Blackbeard, used to hide out in the area.

Tours

Popular outdoor activities and tours include swimming, surfing, kayaking, fishing, sailing, windsurfing, diving, hang-gliding and cycling – all well catered for in the northern resort areas. The following outfitters are recommended.

Kitty Hawk Kites Outdoors (☎ 252-441-4124, 800-334-4777; skate/bicycle/kayak/sailboat hire $10/15/60/80) At Jockey's Ridge State Park in Nags Head. Hang-gliding lessons ($65 and up), equipment rentals, and a variety of tours and courses.

Ocean Atlantic Rentals (☎ 252-441-7823, 800-635-9559; www.oar-nc.com; Milepost 10; bicycle/surfboard/kayak hire per day $10/15/30, per week $35/45/90)

Nags Head Diving (☎ 252-473-1356; 406 Uppowoc St, Manteo) Dive instruction and gear rentals.

Whalebone Surf Shop (☎ 252-261-8737; 4900A N Croatan Hwy) Equipment and information.

Sleeping & Eating

The area has hundreds of motels, efficiencies and B&Bs, but many close up shop in winter and most of them are booked solid in summer. The visitors centers can offer referrals.

Outer Banks International Hostel (☎ 252-261-2294, 877-453-2545; www.outerbankshostel.com; 1004 W Kitty Hawk Rd; dm member/nonmember $19/23, r $55/65, campsites $17) In a pleasant but out-of-the-way location, this friendly hostel has a communal kitchen, outdoor grill and camping. Internet access is available, as are rental tents and coin laundry.

High-season rates are listed for the following hotels and campgrounds. Expect to pay considerably less during low season.

Lightkeeper's Guest House (☎ 252-928-1821; Ocracoke; d $80, cuppola room $90; ☾ Mar-Dec; Ⓟ) This peaceful house in Ocracoke, built by a former lighthouse keeper near his beloved beacon, has real charm and a sunny cuppola room with 360-degree views.

Frisco Woods (☎ 252-995-5208; Hwy 12, Frisco; campsites $35, cabins for up to 4/6 $65/75; Ⓟ ⓧ Ⓡ) This campground caters mainly for RVs, but it does have good rustic cabins and a few secluded natural campsites. Open March to December.

The NPS runs a few summer-only **campgrounds** (☎ 800-365-2267; http://reservations.nps.gov; campsites $20), with cold-water showers and easy beach access. These are **Oregon Inlet**, near the Bodie Island lighthouse, **Cape Point** and **Frisco** near the Cape Hatteras lighthouse and **Ocracoke** on Ocracoke Island. Only sites at Ocracoke can be reserved; others are first come, first-served.

The main tourist strip on Bodie Island has the most restaurants and nightlife, but only in season. The following are all non-chain places open for lunch and dinner year-round on Beach Rd.

Black Pelican (☎ 252-261-3171; Milepost 4; mains $10-20) This restaurant in an old lifesaving station and telegraph office serves terrific seafood and wood-fired pizzas.

Awful Arthur's Oyster Bar (☎ 252-441-5955; Milepost 6; lunch $6-10, dinner $10-15) Another surefire bet for seafood.

Jolly Roger (☎ 252-441-6530; Milepost 6.75; meals $6-10) This small family place is good for breakfast, lunch or an inexpensive dinner.

WILMINGTON

This beautiful coastal city on the Cape Fear River has one of the largest historic districts in the USA and is only a short distance from the beaches of the Atlantic. Sometimes called 'Wilmywood' due to the presence of the largest film production facilities east of Los Angeles, Wilmington and environs have been the backdrop of hundreds of movies and TV shows – but don't expect to encounter A-list stars sauntering down the boulevards!

The **visitors center** (☎ 910-341-4030, 800-222-4757; 24 N 3rd St; ☾ 9am-5pm Mon-Fri, 10am-5pm Sat & Sun), in the 1892 courthouse building, has a walking-tour map and details of several historic houses.

Cape Fear Museum (☎ 910-341-4350; 814 Market St; admission $5; ☾ 9am-5pm Tue-Sat, 1-5pm Sun)

includes a model of Wilmington in the blockade-running 1860s, and a small display about local legend Michael Jordan.

Take a **river taxi** (round-trip $4) or cross the Cape Fear Bridge to reach the **Battleship North Carolina** (☎ 910-251-5797; admission $9; ☾ year-round). This 44,000-ton monster – the epitome of sea power when launched – now aims its cannons squarely at downtown.

If your big toe aches to be dipped into the Atlantic, head down US421 to the salty resort town of **Carolina Beach** or the less-crowded **Kure Beach**. Accessible via US74, **Wrightsville Beach** is one of the two barrier islands on the Cape Fear Coast, and boasts an uncluttered 5-mile stretch of white sand.

Whitey's El-Berta Motor Inn (☎ 800-866-9448; 910 799 1214; 4505 Market St, Hwy 17; s/d $45/52; Ⓟ ⓧ ⓧ Ⓡ) This worn but clean motor lodge on the road into town is adjacent to Whitey's Restaurant, still serving good country cooking after 50 years.

Fat Tony's Pub (☎ 910-343-8881; 131 N Front St; slices/pizzas from $1.50/9, mains $6-9) This Italian place brags about the quality of its sausage and meat balls. And frankly, they *are* delicious. Extensive beer and late night menu.

Barbary Coast (☎ 910 762-8996; 116 S Front St) This bar, the oldest in Wilmington, is decrepit and lovable.

Soap Box Laundro-Lounge (☎ 828-251-8500; 255 N Front St) The hipsters flock to this two-level club for bizarre karaoke, heavy metal bingo and the best local bands. They also come to do their laundry.

Getting There & Away
Greyhound (☎ 910-762-6073; 201 Hartnett St) stops here.

SOUTH CAROLINA

South Carolina's pride and joy is the elegant colonial port of Charleston, with its opulent mansions and effervescent nightlife. But to limit your time in the Palmetto State to its most famous city would be like drinking a Charleston Cocktail without the cherry brandy. This is to say that on South Carolina's roads less traveled you'll discover sweet beaches, many fascinating old towns and miles of country roads that wind past farmlands, white clapboard churches and crumbling sharecropper shacks. Keep

THE SOUTH

your eyes open and take it slow: in South Carolina, the South reveals many of its best-kept secrets.

CHARLESTON

A few days spent lazing around on Charleston's charming streets may well turn out to be the high point of your excursion into the American South.

Right from the time of its founding around 300 years ago, Charleston has rapidly grown into a prosperous lady gussied up for her genteel callers. The celebratory nightlife and sophisticated cultural scene, along with a couple of good hostels, make Charleston a must-visit for the shoestring traveler.

Orientation

The metro area sprawls over a broad stretch of coastal plains and islands, but the historic heart is compact, about 4 sq miles at the southern tip of a peninsula between the Cooper and Ashley Rivers. I-26 goes to North Charleston and the airport. Hwy 17, the main coastal road, cuts across the Charleston peninsula as the Crosstown Expressway.

Information

BOOKSTORES

Waldenbooks (☎ 843-853-1736; 120 Market St)

INTERNET ACCESS

Charleston Public Library (☎ 843-805-6930; 68 Calhoun St; free access)

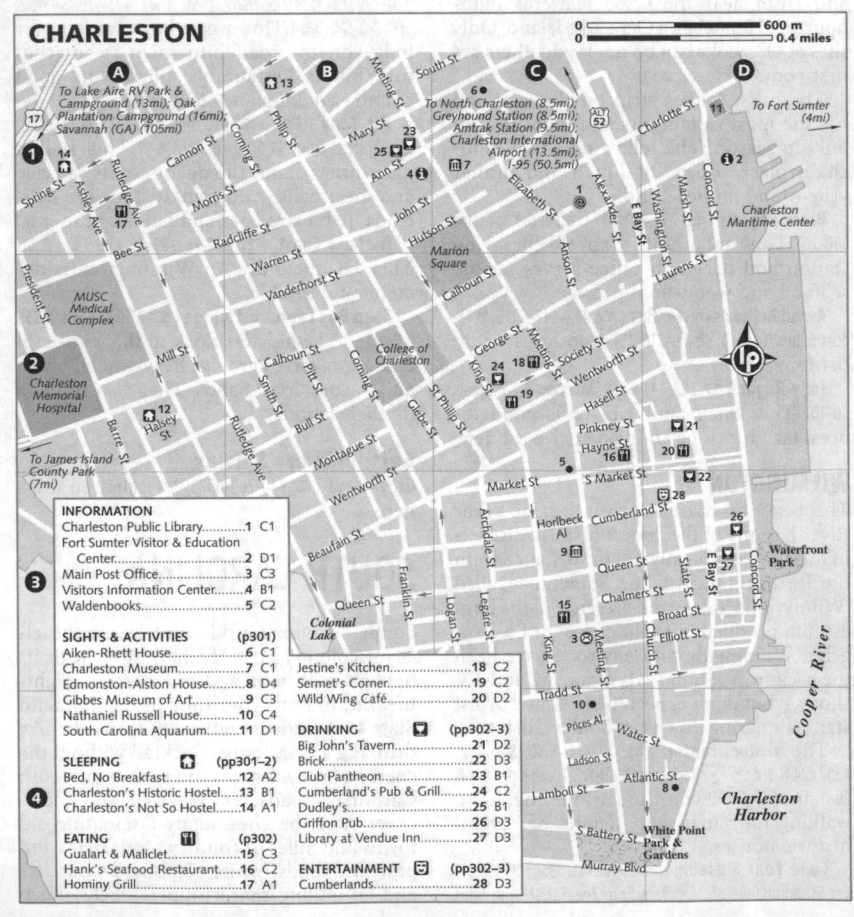

CHARLESTON

0 ——— 600 m
0 ——— 0.4 miles

INFORMATION
Charleston Public Library............**1** C1
Fort Sumter Visitor & Education
  Center..**2** D1
Main Post Office..........................**3** C3
Visitors Information Center.........**4** B1
Waldenbooks...............................**5** C2

SIGHTS & ACTIVITIES (p301)
Aiken-Rhett House........................**6** C1
Charleston Museum......................**7** C1
Edmonston-Alston House.............**8** D4
Gibbes Museum of Art.................**9** C3
Nathaniel Russell House.............**10** C4
South Carolina Aquarium...........**11** D1

SLEEPING (pp301–2)
Bed, No Breakfast........................**12** A2
Charleston's Historic Hostel......**13** B1
Charleston's Not So Hostel.......**14** A1

EATING (p302)
Gualart & Maliclet.......................**15** C3
Hank's Seafood Restaurant.......**16** C2
Hominy Grill...............................**17** A1

Jestine's Kitchen.........................**18** C2
Sermet's Corner...........................**19** C2
Wild Wing Café............................**20** D2

DRINKING (pp302–3)
Big John's Tavern........................**21** D2
Brick..**22** D3
Club Pantheon............................**23** B1
Cumberland's Pub & Grill..........**24** C2
Dudley's......................................**25** B1
Griffon Pub..................................**26** D3
Library at Vendue Inn.................**27** D3

ENTERTAINMENT (pp302–3)
Cumberlands...............................**28** D3

Cooper River

Charleston Harbor

MEDIA
Post & Courier Charleston's daily newspaper publishes *Preview*, a weekly what's-on guide each Friday.
Charleston City Paper An alternative weekly, published on Wednesday.

MEDICAL SERVICES
Charleston Memorial Hospital (☎ 843-577-0690; 326 Calhoun St)

POST
Main Post Office (☎ 843-577-0690; 83 Broad St)

TOURIST INFORMATION
Visitors Information Center (☎ 843-853-8000; 375 Meeting St; ☽ 8:30am-5pm) The well-stocked and helpful center can give advice on accommodations and tours.

Sights & Activities
Charleston's main attraction is the city itself, especially the quarter south of Beaufain St and east of King St, where you can wander along elegant thoroughfares and quaint, bending backstreets. There are maps with walking tours, but an aimless stroll is just as good.

HISTORIC HOUSES
Quite a few fine historic houses are open to visitors. Discounted combination tickets may tempt you to see more, but one or two will be enough for most. Most houses are open 10am to 5pm Monday to Saturday and 1pm to 5pm Sunday, and run guided tours every half hour. Admission is $7 to $9. Following are a few of the most interesting.

Nathaniel Russell House (☎ 843-724-8481; 51 Meeting St) is an 1808 gem noted for its spiral staircase. **Aiken-Rhett House** (☎ 843-723-1159; 48 Elizabeth St) is the only surviving urban plantation; the 1818 house includes well-preserved slave quarters. The 1828 harbor-front **Edmonston-Alston House** (☎ 843-722-7171; 21 E Bay St) has lots of portraits, porcelain and artifacts from a well-to-do family.

MUSEUMS
Charleston Museum (☎ 843-722-2996; www.charlestonmuseum.com; 360 Meeting St; admission $9; ☽ 9am-5pm Mon-Sat, 1-5pm Sun) Founded in 1773, this institution features a fascinating collection of artifacts pertaining to the cultural and natural history of the South Carolina low country.

GETTING INTO TOWN
If arriving by bus or train, take the Carta 'Dorchester/Waylyn' bus to the historic district; return on the 'Navy Yard: 5 Mile Dorchester Rd' bus. Shuttle buses operate between the airport and downtown for $10 per person (one way).

Gibbes Museum of Art (☎ 843-722-2706; www.gibbes.com; 135 Meeting St; admission $7; ☽ 10am-5pm Tue-Sat, 1-5pm Sun) With a collection of over 15,000 objects, the Gibbes showcases an exceptional range of art forms.

AQUARIUM WHARF
The fabulous **South Carolina Aquarium** (☎ 843-720-1990; www.scaquarium.com; 100 Aquarium Wharf; admission $14; ☽ 9am-6pm, until 5pm Aug-Jun) has more than 60 incredible exhibits on fish, reptiles and other wildlife indigenous to the Carolina coast. Definitely a must-see.

FORT SUMTER
Confederates fired the first shots of the Civil War at Fort Sumter, an artificial island at the entrance to Charleston Harbor, where the Union army had retreated. A few original guns and fortifications, and the obvious strategic location give a feel for the momentous history here, and there's a good little museum as well. To get here, take a boat with **Fort Sumter Tours** (☎ 843-881-7337; admission $12) from Liberty Sq next to the aquarium. The tour takes about 2¼ hours.

Festivals & Events
Spoleto Festival USA (☎ 843-579-3100; www.spoletousa.org) Charleston's premier cultural event – held annually the first two weeks of June – features opera, music, drama, dance, film and more, all free or moderately priced. Concurrent is the **Piccolo Spoleto** festival focusing on experimental theatre, music and media. Advance planning for accommodations is essential.

Sleeping
Staying in the historic downtown is the most attractive option, but it's expensive, especially at weekends and during special events. Fortunately, the city is blessed with not one but two good hostels: an embarrassment of riches!

Charleston Historic Hostel (☎ 843-478-1446; www.charlestonhostel.com; 194 St Philip St; dm/d $19/40; Ⓟ ☒ 🖳) This highly regarded hostel is a laid-back, friendly place with very simple but clean accommodations, free laundry and a shared living room, kitchen and piazza. Spacious porches, a well-stocked kitchen, and proximity to King St and the historic district makes this traveler's haven a fantastic value.

Charleston's Not So Hostel (☎ 843-722-8383; www.notsohostel.com; dm $19, d $35-50; Ⓟ ☒ 🖳) In a sort of sketchy but up-and-coming area in the Canonborough neighborhood, this eco-friendly hostel is housed in two old, rambling houses; request a spot in the main house.

Motel 6 (☎ 843-556-5144; 2058 Savannah Hwy; s/d $70/75; Ⓟ ☒ 🐾) and **EconoLodge** (☎ 843-571-1880; 2237 Savannah Hwy; s/d $70/80; Ⓟ ☒) are two predictably efficient options on Highway 17, about 5 miles south of town. Prices listed are weekend rates (Friday to Sunday); at other times you'll pay at least 15% less.

Bed, No Breakfast (☎ 843-723-4450; 16 Halsey St; r $80-100) This small, friendly pension-style place has two rooms and a shared bath. It's a great option if it has rooms available. Be sure to call ahead. Cash or checks only.

Three campgrounds southwest of Charleston offer shuttle services downtown:

Oak Plantation Campground (☎ 843-766-5936; 3540 Savannah Hwy; campsites & RV sites $14-18)

Lake Aire RV Park & Campground (☎ 843-571-1271; at Hwy 17 & Hwy 162; campsites $11-18)

James Island County Park (☎ 843-795-9884, 800-743-7275; 871 Riverland Dr; campsites/RV sites $18/24, cabins $100) The nicest campground of the three.

Eating

Pity the carb-counters; they will never know the bliss of a buttery biscuit. Everyone else, get ready for some sumptuous low-country chow! While the cuisine scene is heavy on the country cooking, Charleston's world-class chefs and hash-slingers alike are serving up something for everybody.

Jestine's Kitchen (☎ 843-722-7224; 251 Meeting St; meals 5-12; ☾ Tue-Sun) The soul food here is lovingly prepared and delicious. The menu was handed down by local darling Jestine Matthews who lived for 112 years and whose beguiling portrait gazes down on folks chowing on scrumptious dishes like shrimp-and-grits with Coca-Cola cake for desert.

Gaulart & Maliclet (☎ 843-577-9797; 98 Broad St; lunch $6-8, dinner $7-14; ☾ Mon-Sat) This small, cheerful café bills itself as 'Fast and French' (referring to the food, not the waitress). Smoking is discouraged, so save your pack of Gauloises for the sidewalk.

Hominy Grill (☎ 843-937-0930; 207 Rutledge Ave; meals $6-14) You can't beat the breakfasts at this Southern cooking paradise. Don't deny yourself the shrimp sautéed with scallions, mushrooms and bacon over cheese grits with a high-rise biscuit on the side.

Sermet's Corner (☎ 843-853-7775; 276 King St; meals $7-11) Sermet, the owner, cooks excellent panini sandwiches and delicious grub, like crab burgers served with sweet potato fries. Upstairs, the Mezzanine has couches and a lounge-like atmosphere; it's a great place to go for drinks.

Wild Wing Café (36 N Market St; meals $5-10) Its Chernobyl wings threaten meltdown. With 25 different wing flavors and burgers, quesadillas and other big portions, you get bang for your buck here.

Hank's Seafood Restaurant (☎ 843-723-3474; 10 Hayne St; meals $15-24; ☾ dinner) Locals go here for crab soup and other low-country dishes.

Drinking & Entertainment

Let's face it, there are some strange laws in South Carolina. For instance, tattooing is illegal, but body piercing is not. And then there's the law that requires bars to serve liquor from tiny bottles (thankfully, beer is exempted). We really shouldn't quibble: Charleston has arguably the best bar scene in the Southeast. The highest concentration of watering holes are around Market and E Bay Sts.

Griffon Pub (☎ 843-723-1700; 18 Vendue Range) A popular Celtic-style place with excellent bar food.

Big John's Tavern (☎ 843-723-3483; 251 E Bay) This gritty dive is beloved for its friendly bar staff and unusual decor (look up).

Brick (☎ 843-720-7788; 213B E Bay) Pleasing booths, weathered brick, loud rock and roll and generous drink specials make this a good spot for tying one on.

Cumberland's Pub & Grill (☎ 843-577-9469; 301 King St) This popular pub has live music nearly every night.

Dudley's (☎ 843-577-6779; 42 Ann St) If the cast of *Cheers* were gay, then they would drink at Dudley's.

Club Pantheon (☎ 843-577-2582; 28 Ann St) This high-energy gay dance club serves a mixed crowd composed of voyeurs, wallflowers and dance-floor divas.

Library at Vendue Inn (☎ 843-723-0486; 23 Vendue Range) A nice place to catch the sunset from the rooftop bar.

Cumberlands (☎ 843-577-9469; 26 Cumberland St) Live blues and regional acts.

Getting There & Around

To reach Charleston by car from the north coast or south coast, make use of Hwy 17. From I-95, take I-26 west for an hour to Charleston.

Charleston International Airport (☎ 843-767-7009), is 12 miles outside of town in North Charleston.

Greyhound (☎ 843-744-5341, 3610 Dorchester Rd), **Amtrak** (☎ 843-744-8264; 4565 Gaynor Ave) and **Charleston Area Regional Transportation Authority** (CARTA; ☎ 843-747-0922; www.ridecarta.com) runs city buses, as well as the Downtown Area Shuttle (DASH). The fare is $1.25, or $4 for an all-day pass (for the DASH and all CARTA buses).

AROUND CHARLESTON

There's plenty for you to see in the surrounding area, ranging from fine old plantations and historic forts to retired superpower technology.

Patriot's Point Naval & Maritime Museum (☎ 843-884-2727; admission $13; 🕒 9am-5pm), on the east side of the Cooper River, features the aircraft carrier USS *Yorktown*, a WWII veteran. You can also tour a submarine, destroyer, Coast Guard cutter and re-created 'fire base' from Vietnam.

Popular **beaches** are: Folly Island, only a 15-minute drive from downtown via Hwy 17 south to Hwy 171; and Isle of Palms, 12 miles from Charleston via Hwy 17 north to Hwy 517.

Edisto Island is only 45 minutes from Charleston but remains largely uncommercialized. **Edisto Beach State Park** (☎ 843-869-2756; campsites/cabin $25/80) rents two-bedroom marsh-front cabins (sleeping up to six people) that are furnished with air-con, and contain kitchens, running water and screened-in porches. The campground has oceanfront or marsh-front campsites with water and power. The walk-in, marsh-front campsites are peaceful and lovely.

The truly magnificent **Magnolia Plantation** (☎ 843-571-1266; admission $16; 🕒 8am-5:50pm Mar-Oct), 10 miles northwest of Charleston off Hwy 61, has a 50-acre garden with azaleas and camellias, and the Audubon Swamp Garden, with alligators and cypresses ($5). You can also pay extra to take boat tours, train tours and view the well-furnished Reconstruction-era house.

Beaufort began as a British colony in 1711 and became wealthy with the boom in sea-island cotton. Today the town is a tidy grid on a small peninsula, with fine 18th-century houses facing the estuary.

ATLANTA

When William T Sherman's army laid siege to Atlanta in 1864, burning it to the ground, none could have imagined the vanquished town would rise from the ashes to become one of the United States' most cosmopolitan cities. A bustling, left-leaning nexus of business, culture and nightlife, Atlanta's sprawling geography can be daunting for first-time visitors. The payoff comes in the form of great restaurants, diverse shopping, distinct neighborhoods that seem like friendly small towns, and hopping nightlife that makes for the biggest party in the Southeast.

HISTORY

Atlanta was created as a railroad junction in 1837. Because of its rail links and safe location, it became a major Confederate transportation and munitions center, like honey for General William T Sherman whose Union forces invaded Georgia in 1864.

Most of Atlanta was destroyed during the siege, and it worsened when retreating Confederates purposely destroyed their own ammunition. Sherman's army stayed in Atlanta for about 10 weeks. When they left they burned everything; leaving more than 90% of Atlanta's buildings in ruins.

After the war, Atlanta became the epitome of the 'new South,' a concept that entailed reconciliation with the north, the promotion of industrialized agriculture, and a progressive business outlook.

However, in the decades following Reconstruction, separate black and white societies developed and segregation deepened. Public sit-ins and demonstrations in the early

THE SOUTH

1960s led by Atlanta native Reverend Martin Luther King Jr, prompted city business leaders to sign a joint agreement to desegregate.

Atlanta's century of boosterism culminated when it hosted the 1996 Summer Olympic Games. Atlanta put on her prettiest dress and CNN beamed her picture worldwide. People took notice.

ORIENTATION

The sprawling Atlanta metro area sits inside a wide circle of freeway, which is called I-285 or, locally, 'the Perimeter.' Inside the circle, I-20 travels east–west, while I-75 and I-85 run north–south. I-75 and I-85 become a single road – 'the downtown connector' – as the roads pass through the city center.

DOWNTOWN ATLANTA

INFORMATION	
Atlanta Convention and Visitors Bureau	1 A4
Atlanta Medical Center	2 B4
Borders Books Music & Cafe	3 C2
Maasty Computers Internet Cafe	4 C2
Main Post Office	5 A5
Outwrite Bookstore & Coffeehouse	6 B2
Post Office	7 A1
Post Office	8 D1
Public Library	9 A4

SIGHTS & ACTIVITIES	(pp305–6)
Ebenezer Baptist Church (new)	10 B4
Ebenezer Baptist Church (original)	11 B5
King Center for Non-Violent Social Change	12 B5
Martin Luther King Jr Gravesite	13 B5
MLK Jr Birthplace	14 C5
MLK Jr National Historic Site Visitors Center	15 B4
Skate Escape	16 B1
World of Coca-Cola	17 A5

SLEEPING	(p307)
Atlanta Youth Hostel	18 B3
Highland Inn	19 D3

EATING	(p307)
Aprés Diem	20 C1
Flying Biscuit Café	21 B1
Red Chair	22 C1
Soul Vegetarian South	23 D3
Surin of Thailand	24 D2
Varsity	25 A3

DRINKING	(pp307–8)
Backstreet	26 A2
Eleven50	27 A1
Fontaine's	28 D1
Righteous Room	29 D2
Vortex Bar & Grill	30 A2

ENTERTAINMENT	(p308)
Blind Willie's	31 D2
Fox Theatre	32 A3

Peachtree and Piedmont Sts are the main north–south arteries, but be forewarned: you'll find that a hundred other streets, roads and avenues are also called Peachtree. Many streets also change names suddenly, so if you're driving, it's a good idea to plot your route on a map beforehand.

INFORMATION
Bookstores
Borders Books Music & Cafe (☎ 404-607-7903; 650 Ponce De Leon Ave NE)

Internet Access
Maasty Computers Internet Café (☎ 404-294-8095; www.maastyinternetcafe.com; 736 Ponce de Leon Ave NE; per hour $10; ☺ daily) Across from City Hall East, Maasty has laptop rentals and Internet connectivity.
Public Library (☎ 404-730-1700; 1 Margaret Mitchell Sq; ☺ 9am-9pm Mon-Thu, 9am-6pm Fri & Sat, 2-6pm Sun) Free Internet access at this main branch.

Media
Creative Loafing (www.atlanta.creativeloafing.com) This free weekly lists essential arts, music and theatre events. Released each Wednesday.
Southern Voice (www.sovo.com) This free gay weekly is released on Friday.

Medical Services
Atlanta Medical Center (☎ 404-265-4000; 303 Parkway Dr NE)
Piedmont Hospital (☎ 404-605-5000; 1968 Peachtree Rd NW)

Post
Main Post Office (☎ 404-521-9843; Federal Center, 41 Marietta St NW) Runs a poste-restante service. Mail addressed to General Delivery, Atlanta, GA 30301 can be picked up here.

Tourist Information
Atlanta Convention & Visitors Bureau (☎ 404-222-6688; www.atlanta.net; 233 Peachtree St; ☺ 8:30am-5:30pm Mon-Fri)

DANGERS & ANNOYANCES
Atlanta has a big-city, high-crime rate. Downtown is safe enough during the day, but at night the streets get eerily deserted. Stick to the well-populated areas.

Atlanta is a car town and doesn't cater well to pedestrians. Because of its the car-centricity, you'll find a lot of aggressive and

---

GETTING INTO TOWN

A **Metropolitan Atlanta Rapid Transit Authority rail line** (Marta; ticket $1.75; 20 minutes) travels to/from the airport to downtown. This is a great choice for getting to and from the airport. The **Atlanta Airport Shuttle** (☎ 404-524-3400, 800-842-2770; tickets $15-20) also transports passengers to hotels all over the city in a minibus. All the major car rental agencies have desks at the baggage-claim level.

---

speedy drivers. Be kind to your blood pressure and stay off the highways at rush hour.

SIGHTS & ACTIVITIES
Downtown
On weekdays, downtown Atlanta bustles with conventioneers and business folk, but on most evenings and weekends the bustle turns to a shuffle. Despite this complaint, there are a few worthwhile attractions.

Centennial Olympic Park (☎ 404-872-5338), on the west side of downtown, is a 21-acre legacy of green space from the 1996 Olympic Games.

World of Coca-Cola (☎ 404-676-5151; www.wocc atlanta.com; 55 Martin Luther King Jr Dr; admission $7; ☺ 9am-5pm Mon-Sat, 11am-5pm Sun, until 6pm Mon-Sat Jun-Aug) strives mightily to convince you that Coca-Cola is not just a soft drink, but rather one of the world's major cultural icons. It features memorabilia and a living, breathing soda jerk (but don't call him that to his face).

Next to Centennial Olympic Park is **CNN Center** (☎ 404-827-2300, 877-266-8687; admission $8; ☺ 9am-5pm), headquarters of the cable-TV news service. The popular 50-minute CNN tour (every 20 minutes), a behind-the-scenes glance at the world's busiest news organization, includes the CNN Headline News desk and a mock control room.

Sweet Auburn
Auburn Ave was the thumping commercial and cultural heart of African-American culture in the 1900s. Today, a collection of sights are associated with Sweet Auburn's most famous son: Martin Luther King Jr, who was born on Auburn and preached on Auburn and whose grave now looks onto the street.

The **Martin Luther King Jr National Historic Site Visitors Center** (☎ 404-331-5190; www.nps.gov /malu; 450 Auburn Ave NE; ☯ 9am-5pm, in summer until 6pm) has informative and moving exhibits and dispenses a map and brochure of area sights and exhibits. From here, guided tours leave for the **Martin Luther King Jr Birthplace** (501 Auburn Ave), a simple house where the future civil rights leader once cavorted with his siblings.

On Auburn Ave across from the visitors center, the **King Center for Non-Violent Social Change** (☎ 404-893-9882; 449 Auburn Ave NE) has more information on King's life and work. His **gravesite**, between the church and center, is surrounded by a long reflecting pool and can be viewed anytime.

Ebenezer Baptist Church (☎ 404-688-7263; 407 Auburn Ave NE; admission free; tours 9am-5pm Mon-Sat, 1-5pm Sun; ☯ to 6pm in summer) was the preaching ground for King, his father and grandfather, who were all pastors here. You can take a free tour of the original church, but Sunday services are now held at a new Ebenezer across the street.

All of the King sites are a few blocks' walk from Marta's King Memorial station.

Midtown

The streets of Midtown are filled with great bars, restaurants and cultural venues.

In the Woodruff Arts Center, the highlight is the **High Museum of Art** (☎ 404-733-4400; www.high.org; 1280 Peachtree St NE; adult/student $10/8; ☯ 10am-5pm Tue-Sat, noon-5pm Sun). Its collection includes European and American contemporary art and first-class African exhibits. The museum has special jazz nights (5pm to 10pm) on the third Friday of every month.

Piedmont Park

In the middle of Midtown, the Olmsted-designed **Piedmont Park** is a giant urban park and the setting of many cultural and music festivals. With its playgrounds, tennis courts, dog park, bike paths and in-line skating paths, it's a great place to spend a day without spending a dollar. On Thursday evenings in June, the free **Screen on the Green** features classic movies projected onto a big screen.

Rent bicycles or skates at **Skate Escape** (☎ 404-892-1292; 1086 Piedmont Ave NE at 12th St; per hr $6).

Grant Park & Oakland Cemetery

Grant Park is a large oasis of green on the edge of the city center. The park is home to the **Atlanta Cyclorama** (☎ 404-658-7625; adult $6; ☯ 9:30am-4:30pm), a circular painting 358ft around and 42ft high, depicting the 1864 Battle of Atlanta. Painted in 1886, this low-tech wonder is the largest painting in the world and is certainly worth a visit.

Next door, **Zoo Atlanta** (☎ 404-624-5600; www .zooatlanta.org; adult $16.50; ☯ 9:30am-4:30pm, 9:30am-5:30pm Sat & Sun during summer) provides natural environments, including an impressive large gorilla exhibit. The zoo's pride and joy are Lun Lun and Yang Yang, two of only a small population of giant panda bears in captivity.

Gone With the Wind author Margaret Mitchell and golf great Bobby Jones are buried in the **Oakland Cemetery** (☎ 404-688-2107; 248 Oakland Ave SE; admission free; ☯ 9am-5pm Mon-Fri), at Martin Luther King Jr Dr. Many very interesting Victorian and neoclassical monuments and mausoleums are scattered throughout the site. Stop at the visitors center for a **walking tour** brochure.

Points East

On a hilltop overlooking downtown, the **Jimmy Carter Library & Museum** (☎ 404-331-3942; www.cartercenter.org; 441 Freedom Parkway; admission $7; ☯ 9am-4:45pm Mon-Sat, noon-4:45pm Sun, library closed Sun) has exhibits highlighting Carter's 1977–81 presidency including a replica of the Oval Office.

Fernbank Museum of Natural History (☎ 404-929-6400; www.fernbank.edu/museum; 767 Clifton Rd NE; adult/student $12/11; ☯ 10am-5pm Mon-Sat, noon-5pm Sun) makes other museums seem hopelessly dull. With extensive exhibits on everything from reptiles to Egypt to seashells, and an Imax theater ($10), Fernbank is a great bet even if giant lizards don't rock your world. On **Martinis & Imax Fridays** (adult $5; ☯ 6:30-10pm Fri Jan-Nov), the lobby turns into a cocktail lounge and live jazz echoes through the bones of the world's largest dinosaur.

TOURS

More intriguing and economical than the usual bus tours are walking tours of the city's older neighborhoods. These are offered by the **Atlanta Preservation Center** (☎ 404-688-3353; www .preserveatlanta.com; 327 St Paul Ave; adult/student $10/5; ☯ Mar-Nov).

SLEEPING

Rates at downtown hotels tend to fluctuate wildly depending on whether there is a large convention in town. Weekdays are often cheaper, as are hotels away from downtown. Beware the cheap residential hotels in Atlanta. Many of them are dodgy places were you are liable to be solicited by prostitutes on the way to your room (and to boot they are considerably more expensive than the youth hostel!).

Atlanta Youth Hostel (☎ 404-875-9449, 800-473-9449; www.hostel-atlanta.com; 223 Ponce de Leon Ave at Myrtle St; dm $17-19; ☐) In a Victorian house in Midtown, this lively hostel has 80 dorm beds, and wins accolades for its cleanliness and good location. A kitchen, laundry, lockers, free morning coffee and doughnuts are available. The hostel's office is closed from noon to 5pm. It is four blocks east of the Marta North Ave station.

Highland Inn (☎ 404-874-5756; 888-256-7221; www .thehighlandinn.com; 644 N Highland Ave; r $70-106; P ☒) This European-style inn has a great location in the middle of Virginia Highland. With 100 clean and comfortable rooms, the inn hosted the entire Japanese media crew during the 1996 Olympics.

University Inn (☎ 800-654-8591; www.univinn.com; 1767 North Decatur Rd; r $65-134; P ☒ ☒ ☐ ☒) On the cusp of the Emory University campus, this low-key friendly inn offers rooms in four buildings. Most have kitchenettes and simple but pleasant furnishings. Breakfast and afternoon tea are included.

A cheap option is to stay somewhere along the Marta line, further outside the city, and take the train into the city for sightseeing. The trip by train to downtown should take 30 to 40 minutes.

Atlanta Inn (☎ 770-452-8500; 5114 Buford Hwy; r $50-60; P ☒) A mile south of the Marta Doraville station, this inn has worn, moderately clean rooms. Bus No 39 runs in front of the hotel to the station.

For camping around Atlanta see p309.

EATING

Chicken and waffles? Ox tails and cow feet? How about a tofu steak and banana cream pie? As to be expected, Atlanta does not disappoint with its big-town roster of excellent eateries.

Flying Biscuit Café Piedmont Ave (☎ 404-874-8887; 1101 Piedmont Ave at 10th St; breakfasts $6-10) McLendon Ave (1655 McLendon Ave nr L5P) Yum! A diverse, happy crowd enjoys a vegetarian-friendly menu featuring all-day breakfasts of omelettes, organic oatmeal pancakes, fried green tomatoes and tasty grits, all accompanied by the justifiably famous fluffy biscuits.

Soul Vegetarian South (☎ 404-875-1106; 652 N Highland Ave NE; dinners $6-12) If you think that soul food means chitterlings and hog jowls, head to this vegan paradise near L5P and order a barbecued tofu steak. Okay, it's not *really* soul food, but it is good for the soul.

Aprés Diem (☎ 404 872-3333; 931 Monroe Dr at 8th St; dinners $8-12; P) This urbane restaurant and cocktail bar really gets the groove going after sunset. Hipsters dine on delicious French and Italian fare on a capacious patio and in a swank, art-filled dining room as DJs spin loungecore from the corner.

Varsity (☎ 404-881-1706; 61 North Ave at Spring St; meals $1.50 5; P) The world's largest drive-in restaurant and an Atlanta institution since 1928. A glorified fast-food joint, the place is always packed with folks ordering walk-a-dogs (hot dogs), glorified steaks (burgers) and bags of rags (fries).

Fat Matt's Rib Shack (☎ 404-607-1622; 1811 Piedmont Rd NF; meals $7-11; P) Less than a mile north of Piedmont Park, this is a great place for quintessential southern barbecue. At night, up-and-coming jazz groups crank onstage from 8:30pm.

Surin of Thailand (☎ 404-892-7789; 810 N Highland Ave; meals $9 15) Among the string of bars and pubs in the Virginia Highland area, it has large tables that can handle the crowds who come for the reasonable prices and large portions of tasty Thai favorites.

DRINKING

There's a lot of heavy partying going on in Atlanta, especially in Virginia Highland, L5P, Midtown and Buckhead.

Fontaine's (☎ 404-872-0869; 1026 N Highland Ave) A great stop for evening cocktails.

Righteous Room (☎ 404-874-0939; 1051 Ponce de Leon Ave) This dark but cheerful local haunt has just the right ambience for knocking back copious amounts of beer.

Vortex Bar & Grill (☎ 404-688-1828; 438 Moreland Ave; burgers $6-10; P) This is the place for fantastic burgers and potent drinks with funny names (care for a 'Bitch on Wheels,' anyone?). Look for the giant skull and you'll find the front door.

> ### GAY & LESBIAN ATLANTA
>
> Find out why some folks call this town 'Hotlanta' by heading to Midtown or Ansley Sq (near Piedmont and Monroe) on a balmy summer evening, or anytime for that matter. By any measure, Atlanta is the gay capital of the South. The free weekly newspaper *Southern Voice* (www.sovo .com) will help get you oriented; or, you could just drop by one of the following spots.
>
> **Red Chair** (☎ 404-870-0532; 550-C Amsterdam Ave) One of Atlanta's most popular gay and lesbian bars, Red Chair has a full restaurant, cutting edge décor and huge screens showing the latest videos and movies.
>
> **Outwrite Bookstore & Coffeehouse** (☎ 404-607-0082; 991 Piedmont Ave) At 10th St in Midtown, this cheerful gay bookstore with a full coffee bar is a great place to hang out and survey the scene.
>
> **Charis Books & More** (☎ 404-524-0304; 1189 Euclid Ave NE) In Little Five Points, this is a crowded, well-stocked feminist and lesbian bookstore. From downtown, take North Ave; turn right on Moreland to Euclid Ave.
>
> **Backstreet** (☎ 404-873-1986; 845 Peachtree St NE; ☺ 24hr) This gigantic, storied dance club is the nexus of Hotlanta's late night party scene. There's a $5 cover and a $10 membership fee.

ENTERTAINMENT
Live Music
Eleven50 (☎ 404-874-0428; 1150 Peachtree Rd) In Midtown, this is a huge, multilevel dance club housed in an old theater.

Star Community Bar (☎ 404-681-9018; 437 Moreland Ave) In L5P, this spot draws a hip crowd to its live acts four nights a week. From downtown, take North Ave to Moreland Ave.

Blind Willie's (☎ 404-873-2583; 828 N Highland Ave) For serious blues, head to Blind Willie's, a well-established blues bar with local and occasional big-name acts.

Theater
Fox Theatre (☎ 404-881-2100; 660 Peachtree St NE) A spectacular 1929 movie palace with fanciful Moorish and Egyptian designs and 'Mighty Mo,' the second largest theatre organ in the world. It hosts Broadway shows, film festivals and concerts in a 5000-seat auditorium. If you can't make it to a performance, consider a **tour** (adult/student $10/5; 10am Mon, Wed & Thu, 10am & 11am Sat).

Center for Puppetry Arts (☎ 404-873-3391; www .puppet.org; 1404 Spring St NW at 18th; adults/students $8/7; ☺ 9am-5pm Mon-Sat, 11am-5pm Sun) The collection consists of over 1000 puppets from around the world. Try to see one of the full-stage puppet shows ($12). Take Peachtree St NE to 18th St; turn left to Spring St.

GETTING THERE & AROUND
Atlanta's huge **Hartsfield International Airport** (☎ 800-897-1910), 12 miles south of downtown, is a major regional hub and an international gateway.

The **Greyhound station** (☎ 404-584-1728; 232 Forsyth St) is next to the Marta Garnett station. The **Amtrak station** (☎ 404-881-3062, 800-872-7245; 1688 Peachtree St NW at Deering Rd) is 3 miles north of downtown. Take bus No 23 for about three-quarters of a mile from the Marta Arts Center station. The station is near the intersection of Peachtree St NE and Beverly Rd.

Driving in Atlanta can be infuriating and confusing. You'll often find yourself sitting in traffic jams, and it's easy to get disoriented – a good map really is an invaluable asset.

Because Atlanta is such a car-centric city, two-hour metered street parking is usually plentiful. Many parking garages offer reasonable rates (usually around $10 per day) for day-long parking.

Marta (☎ 404-848-4711; www.itsmarta.com; fares $1.75) operates a small but quite efficient rail system and an extensive bus network in Atlanta.

AROUND GEORGIA

It's not hard to see why the late, great Ray Charles kept singing that old sweet song with Georgia on his mind. The state is possessed of great natural beauty, and boasts two of the South's most exciting – albeit fundamentally different – cities: Atlanta and Savannah, a gorgeous relic of the antebellum south, visitors swoon to the lovely historic homes and public squares that are graced with ancient oaks draped with Spanish moss.

STONE MOUNTAIN PARK

This 3200-acre **park** (☎ 770-498-5690; per car $7, all attractions $17), 16 miles east of downtown Atlanta, is home to 825ft-high Stone Mountain, the world's largest outcrop of exposed granite. It's best known for the huge bas-relief carving of Confederate heroes Davis, Jackson and Lee – one of the largest such sculptures in the world. There's also a sky lift, hiking trails, an antebellum plantation, a railroad, laser show, camping and other attractions. The park is open daily and makes an excellent day trip.

Stone Mountain Family Campground (☎ 770-498-5710, 800-385-9807; www.stonemountainpark.com; campsites $23-45; P ⟨₽⟩) Georgia's largest campground has 441 campsites, laundry facilities, a volleyball court and is the best camping option near Atlanta.

The park is off Hwy 78 (I-285 exit 39). Bus No 120 can take you from the MARTA Avondale station to the village of Stone Mountain, where some buses continue into the park.

ATHENS

This attractive college town, 61 miles east of Atlanta, is a draw for its vibrant nightlife and world-famous music scene that served as proving grounds for the B-52s, REM and Widespread Panic. The downtown area is well supplied with music shops, bookstores, cafés, bars and clubs, which led *Rolling Stone* to call Athens the 'No. 1 College Music Scene in America.'

Housed in the town's oldest house, the **Athens Welcome Center** (☎ 706-353-1820; www.visitathensga.com; 280 E Dougherty St; ☉ Mon-Sat 10am-6pm, Sun noon-6pm) provides good information and offers bus tours ($15) of historic houses and sights. Ask for the brochure *A Walking Tour of Athens Music History*.

Internet access is free at the **public library** (☎ 706-613-3650; 2025 Baxter St; ☉ daily). If you've got a laptop and/or insomnia, a great alternative is **Hot Corner Cafe** (☎ 705-995-0622; 269 Hull St; ☉ 24hr), a hotspot with perfect coffee.

Seek out the free weekly publication **Flagpole** (www.flagpole.com) for comment and cultural-scene listings.

Sleeping

Hawkes-Nest Hostel (☎ 706-769-0563; bonmaya@bellsouth.net; 1760 McRee Mill Rd; house/cottage $10/18; P ⟨₽⟩) On seven acres near Watkinsville,

about 11 miles south of downtown Athens, this hostel is an extension of the owner's family house. The hostel has only two rooms, one inside the main house and one in a detached, rustic cottage. Guests use the kitchen and bathrooms inside the main house. Friendly owners Bonnie and Robert Murphy are helpful in planning activities around the area. Reservations are required.

Bulldog Inn (☎ 706-543-3611; 1225 Commerce Rd; s/d $45/55; P ⟨₽⟩) A very no-frills budget option just north of the city.

Sandy Creek Park (706-613-3631; 400 Bob Holman Rd; campsites $10, park entrance $2; ⟨₽⟩) At cool Lake Chapman, 5 miles north of town on US441, this county-run park has pleasant primitive campsites and opportunities for swimming, fishing and day-hiking.

Eating

Five Star Day Café (☎ 706-543-8552; 229 E Broad St; meals $5-7) An unpretentious little café with very reasonable prices, serving hot buttered soul chicken with Jamaican seasoning, pot roast, pesto pasta, Carolina barbecue and chicken-and-dumplings.

Grit (☎ 706-543-6592; 199 Prince Ave; meals $5-7) At lunch or dinner, this popular vegetarian place serves yummy things such as hummus and falafel, Indian curried vegetables, Italian pasta dishes and Mexican quesadillas.

Entertainment

Pick up the free weekly *Flagpole*.

LIVE MUSIC

Athens has more music clubs than you can shake a drum stick at. You might as well start your crawl at the famous **40 Watt Club** (☎ 706-549-7871; 285 W Washington St), where REM got its first exposure. It's still one of the best places in the South to catch up-and-coming bands. Another of the South's premiere live music halls is the **Georgia Theatre** (☎ 706-549-9918; 215 N Lumpkin St).

Getting There & Away

Southeastern Stages (☎ 706-549-2255; 220 W Broad St), a Greyhound connection service, serves Athens.

SAVANNAH

It's said that Savannah's beauty inspired Yankee general William T Sherman to spare it from the torch at the terminus of his devastating 'March to the Sea' in 1864.

Perhaps feeling a twinge of wistfulness for the destruction he had wrought, he instead offered the city and its 25,000 bales of cotton to President Abraham Lincoln as a Christmas present.

In the end, Sherman's restraint was a gift to posterity, for Savannah, with its mammoth live oak trees dripping with Spanish moss and its gorgeous streets lined with historic mansions and stately urban squares, is truly one of the USA's most hauntingly beautiful cities. Savannah preserves its own antebellum history in a way that only its low-country sister city, Charleston, can hope to rival.

Orientation

Savannah graces the Georgia coast, 105 miles south of Charleston. The city's Historic District is a rectangle bounded by Savannah River, Forsyth Park, E Broad St and Martin Luther King Jr Blvd. River St, the commercial strip of bars, restaurants and shops in converted cotton warehouses along the Savannah River, is the heart of the tourist district. City Market is an equally important area of shops and restaurants along the western edge of the Historic District at W St Julian St near Franklin Sq.

Twenty-one of Savannah's original 24 squares are the pillars of the historic districts. Each marks an exquisite place to relax among flower gardens, shade trees

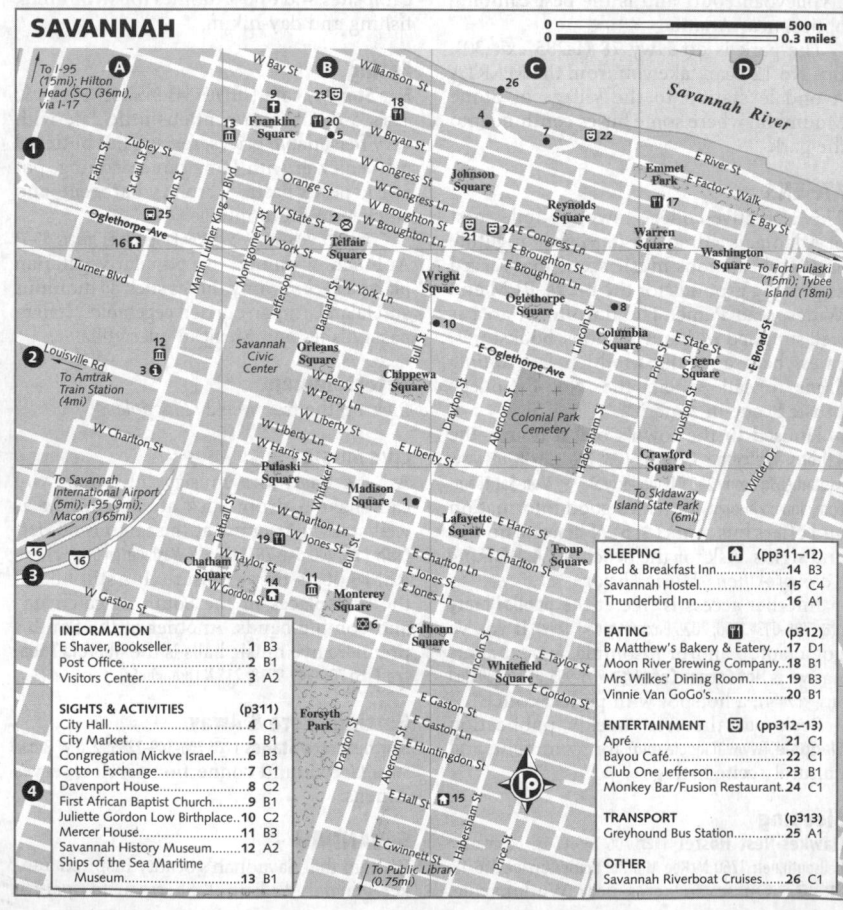

SAVANNAH

0 — 500 m
0 — 0.3 miles

and – usually – a monument to some notable person buried (such as Georgia's first settler James Oglethorpe) in the square. Bull St, running north–south, divides the east and west branches of streets.

Information
BOOKSTORES
E Shaver, Bookseller (☎ 912-234-7257; 326 Bull St) Excellent selection of region-specific titles.

INTERNET ACCESS
Public Library (☎ 912-652-3600; 2002 Bull St; 🕑 daily) Here, free internet access is yours for the asking.

POST
Post Office (☎ 912-235-4653; intersection of W State & Barnard Sts; 🕑 Mon-Sat)

TOURIST INFORMATION
Visitors Center (☎ 877 728 2662, 912-944-0455; www.savannahvisit.com; 301 Martin Luther King Jr Blvd; 🕑 8:30am-5pm Mon-Fri, 9am-5pm Sat & Sun)

Dangers & Annoyances
The Historic District is safe during the day but at night, use common-sense precautions and stay in well-lit, populated areas. Night crime is common in the neighborhoods that surround the Historic District.

Sights & Activities
Along the wharves of the Savannah River, on the northern edge of the Historic District, the **Riverfront** is Savannah's most popular tourist attraction. The main pedestrian artery is **River St**, a brick-and-cobblestone waterside promenade along a gallery of restored cotton warehouses. **Factor's Walk** promenade is essentially the upper level of buildings between River and Bay Sts and was the city's business center in the 19th century. Nearby are the gold-domed **City Hall** and **Cotton Exchange** buildings, guarded by lion statues and once one of the world's busiest exchanges.

Just behind the visitors center, the **Savannah History Museum** (☎ 912-238-1779; 303 Martin Luther King Jr Blvd; admission $4; 🕑 8:30am-5pm Mon-Fri, 9am-5pm Sat & Sun) is a good place to start a visit to Savannah's Historic District. The film and displays give a feel for the city's past.

Ships of the Sea Maritime Museum (☎ 912-232-1511; 41 Martin Luther King Jr Blvd; admission $7; 🕑 10am-5pm Tue-Sun) has attractive exhibits that focus on models of ships, particularly ones associated with the city, and nautical memorabilia.

Savannah has a number of elegant historic homes and houses of worship.

Davenport House (☎ 912-236-8097; Columbia Sq; admission $7; 🕑 10am-4pm Mon-Sat, 1-4pm Sun) was the first of Savannah's historic homes to be restored, and its 30-minute tour is exceptional for both its antique collection and the knowledge of the guides. If you have time for touring only one house, make it this one.

Other historic houses include the private **Mercer House** (429 Bull St on Monterey Sq), an immense red-brick Italianate mansion, and **Juliette Gordon Low Birthplace** (☎ 912-233-4501; 10 E Oglethorpe Ave; adult/student $7/5; 🕑 Thu-Tue), an upper-middle-class Victorian home dating from 1821.

Built in 1859 by slaves, **First African Baptist Church** (☎ 912-233-6597; 23 Montgomery St at Franklin Sq; admission free; 🕑 10am-3pm Mon-Fri) is the oldest African-American church in North America. Services are held on Sunday.

Congregation Mickve Israel (☎ 912-233-1547; 20 E Gordon St at Monterey Sq; admission by donation $2; 🕑 10am-noon, 2-4pm Mon-Fri) is the oldest Reform Judaism temple in the USA.

Tours
The visitors center is the best place to book tours, whether on foot, trolley, minibus or horse-drawn carriage ($19 for 50 minutes). Most of the city's tour operators begin and end their excursions from the center's parking lot. The classic paddleboats of **Savannah Riverboat Cruises** (☎ 912-232-6404; 9 E River St; admission $14; 🕑 2pm & 4pm) leave from east side of the Hyatt hotel for tours of the lowcountry marshes (one hour).

Sleeping
Savannah is well known for its dizzying array of B&Bs and romantic hotels. If you have the cash – most start above $100 – there's no better way to go. Unfortunately, lodging options for shoestringers are limited to a single hostel and a few chain places. If you've been holding out for a well-chosen splurge, Savannah will give you a lot of bang for the buck.

Savannah Hostel (☎ 912-236-7744; 304 E Hall St; dm $21, r $40-55) In a restored mansion in the Historic District two blocks from Forsyth

Park, this hostel has one dorm-style and several private rooms. The manager institutes a 10am to 5pm lock-out, and overall the place lacks a sense of atmosphere and community spirit, but the rooms are clean and secure and the location good. Closed December through February.

Thunderbird Inn (☎ 912-232-2661; 611 W Oglethorpe; s/d $56/70; P ⊠) This well-priced motor lodge across the street from the Greyhound terminal is recommended for its clean – if nondescript – rooms and superb location. However, if it's antebellum charm you're after, this is not the place.

Skidaway Island State Park (☎ 912-598-2300; Diamond Causeway; campsites with/without hook-up $24/22) Six miles southeast of the historic district, this shady park has pull-through campsites with water, elevated tent pads, barbecues and picnic tables. Take Liberty St east from downtown, turn right on Waters Ave and follow it to Diamond Causeway.

SPLURGE!

Bed & Breakfast Inn (☎ 912-238-0518; http://savannahbnb.com; 117 W Gordon St; r $80-150; P ⊠) Among Savannah's historic inns, the B&B Inn stands out for its value. Adjacent to Chatham Sq, the inn is an 1853 Federal row house. Its 16 rooms aren't as posh as those in some other inns, but then B&B Inn is less expensive. It's decorated in antiques, period reproduction pieces and oriental carpets, and it has a relaxing private garden and deck. You get hearty breakfasts with eggs and fresh fruits.

Eating

Get ready to feast! Savannah offers a legion of dining experiences, from gourmet Southern food to wild fusion combos with fresh seafood. Many restaurants are concentrated along the waterfront and in City Market, on W Congress St. Restaurants are also scattered throughout the Historic District.

B Matthew's Bakery & Eatery (☎ 912-233-1319; 325 E Bay St; pastries $2-4, sandwiches $4-6) There is simply no better place to spend a lazy morning in Savannah than this sensuous café at the east end of the Historic District. The owners have converted a run-down bar (dating from 1791!) into an attractive mix of tables and window seats. Try the house

specialty: the delicious Blackeyed Peacake Sandwich.

Vinnie Van GoGo's (☎ 912-233-6394; 317 W Bryan St; pizzas $12-16) You can get a killer 14-inch New York–style pizza with two toppings for $15. It also sells pizza by the slice, calzones and domestic and imported beers. This hangout isn't much to look at, but the tables outside are great for people-watching. Cash only.

Mrs Wilkes' Dining Room (☎ 912-232-5997; 107 W Jones St; meals $12-20) A longtime favorite for sociable Southern-style breakfasts and lunches, this family-style eatery packs its guests around long tables, three meals a day. No credit cards.

Moon River Brewing Company (☎ 912-447-0943; 21 W Bay St; sandwiches $5-8) You'll find this aromatic brewpub in an 1821 building a block from the Riverfront. Heavy with the scent of hops from the vats, it attracts a young crowd with its homemade beers and a menu ranging from buffalo wings to burgers and sandwiches.

Drinking

For an up-to-date list of events at clubs and bars, check out Thursday's *Savannah Morning News* and the weeklies *Connect Savannah* and *Creative Loafing*.

Monkey Bar/Fusion Restaurant (☎ 912-232-0755; 8 E Broughton St) It rocks! Owner Wendy Snowden and her clientele ooze an authentic, artsy glam, giving the place the feel of an indie film party. The American-Asian fusion cuisine is just as far out there.

Bayou Café (☎ 912-233-6411; 14 N Abercorn St) Between Bay and River Sts, across from the Hampton Inn, the Bayou is a gritty place, popular with partying students. It also has music every night, mostly alternative and country-rock.

Apré (☎ 912-238-8888; 2 E Broughton St; cover $10) Set above Il Pasticcio restaurant, Apré is the hippest club in town. The music is hard house and dance. At weekends the crowd gets fancier and older (25 to 35). The club gets packed, particularly between midnight and 1:30am when the booze is FREE.

Club One Jefferson (☎ 912-232-0200; www.club one-online.com; 1 Jefferson St) Savannah's premier gay venue, Club One features drag shows, pool tables and a large dance floor. Although its clientele is mostly gay, straight party animals also come here to dance and see the most excellent drag queens.

Getting There & Away

Savannah International Airport (☎ 912-964-0514) is located about 5 miles west of downtown off I-16.

Greyhound (☎ 912-232-2135; 610 W Oglethorpe Ave) buses stop here.

The **Amtrak station** (☎ 800-872-7245, 912-234-2611) is 4 miles from City Hall and served only by taxis.

Getting Around

Coastal Transportation (☎ 912-964-5999; adult $21) provides a shuttle from the airport to downtown. **Chatham Area Transit** (CAT; ☎ 912-233-5767) operates local buses, including a free shuttle that makes its way around the Historic District.

THE GEORGIA COAST

The Georgia coast is a place of startling beauty – the scurrying for hiding places and great egrets looking for their next meal; and mile after mile of cordgrass swaying with the wind.

The tiny community of **Tybee Island** (☎ 912-786-5444, 800-868-2322; www.tybeevisit.com; 1st St/US Hwy 80; ☯ 9:30am-5pm), 18 miles east of Savannah at the end of US 80, offers 3 miles of wide, sandy beach, good for swimming and castle building. The beautiful 154ft-tall Tybee Island Lighthouse is the oldest in Georgia and still in use. The neighboring Tybee Island Museum is in the basement of Fort Screvens, which operated from 1897 to 1947.

Cumberland Island National Seashore (☎ 912-882-4335; www.nps.gov/cuis/; admission $4), 115 miles south of Savannah, provides an isolated, maritime wilderness with 16 miles of wide, sandy beach that you might have all to yourself. The island's interior is characterized by a maritime forest. Feral horses roam the island and are a common sight around the mansion ruins, in the interdune meadows and occasionally on the beach.

The only public access to the island is via the ferry **Cumberland Queen** (☎ 912-882-4335; admission $12; ☯ 10am-4pm Mon-Fri), which leaves from the dock in the nearby town of St Marys. Reservations are recommended. October through February, the ferry does not operate on Tuesday or Wednesday.

Camping is available at **Sea Camp Beach** (☎ 912-882-4335; per person $4), a pristine, developed campground set among magnificent live oaks. Each of the campsites is surrounded by palmetto stands and comes with a raccoon box (to store your food, not your raccoons). Facilities include flush toilets, cold showers and drinking water.

ALABAMA

Alabama has no flashy destinations or world-famous parties, but to know its sleepy towns and charged history is to know something about the South. Perceived as a bastion of rednecks and rebels, the true nature of this place is considerably more complex and rewarding than the stereotype.

Alabama has long acted as an incendiary for radical change in America. Home to the first capital of the Confederacy and the birthplace of its flag, the state played a critical role in instigating the Civil War. A century later in the mid-1950s, the state became the locus for many of the Civil Rights movement's triumphs and bloody tragedies.

Whether you've come to celebrate the country's oldest Mardi Gras in Mobile or to learn about the struggle for black civil rights, you'll see why some folks say that in the Deep South, Alabama is the 'deep' part.

MOBILE

Like its bratty sister New Orleans, 120 miles to the southwest, Mobile (mo-*beel*) finds good reason to break out the bourbon each February for Mardi Gras. Here, however, the local code of decorum keeps the bacchanalian debauchery to a minimum, in keeping with Mobile's mellow charms and lack of ostentation. We'll just say that in Mobile the bourbon is *sipped,* and leave it at that.

Founded by the French in the early 18th century and one of the United States' oldest cities, Mobile today remains steeped in antebellum charm. Its shady boulevards and four historic districts are exceedingly pleasant for ambling.

Pick up walking and driving tours of the historic districts at the **visitors center** (☎ 251-208-7658, 800-566-2453; 150 S Royal St; ☯ Mon-Fri), part of the reconstructed **Fort Condé** (☎ 251-208-7304; admission free).

Across the street is the **Museum of Mobile** (☎ 251-208-7569; 111 S Royal St; admission $5; ☯ 9am-5pm Mon-Sat, 1-5pm Sun) with a pretty good collection of Mardi Gras costumes and maritime antiques.

Of course, Mobile's preeminent maritime antique is the **USS Alabama** (☎ 251-433-2703; 2703 Battleship Parkway; admission $10; ☺ 8am-6pm, until 4pm Oct-Mar), famous for escaping nine major WWII battles unscathed.

Mobile is famous for its antebellum architecture and several beautiful restored houses can be toured. These include **Oakleigh** (☎ 251-432-1281; 350 Oakleigh Pl; admission $6; ☺ Mon-Fri), an 1833 Greek Revival mansion. Find out about other old antebellum gems at the visitors center.

Sleeping

Mobile has no budget lodging downtown. Seven miles west of downtown several affordable motels line I-65 on the beltline between Exit 5A (Spring Hill Rd) and Exit 1 (Government Blvd). The best of these is the spacious, friendly and cheap **Olsson Motel** (☎ 251-661-5331, 800-332-1004; 4137 Government Blvd/ Hwy 90 W; s/d $35/40; Ⓟ ⊠). Of similar quality is the generic **Family Inn** (☎ 251-344-5500; 980 S Beltline Rd; d $40, Fri-Sat $50; Ⓟ ⊠), where the price includes continental breakfast.

Chickasabogue Park (☎ 251-574-2267; campsites with/without hookups $11/6) Pitch a tent in this lush and shady Alabama bottomland with moss-draped oaks and opportunities for a dip in the creek. Take I-65 to Exit 13 and look for the signs to Chickasabogue Park.

Eating & Drinking

The Dauphin St historic district is good for a night out on the town year-round with its ever-growing range of restaurants and watering holes.

Spot of Tea (☎ 251-433-9009; 310 Dauphin St; mains $6-10; ☺ breakfast & lunch) Oozing down-home Southern hospitality, this place has big breakfasts, thick sandwiches and an unbelievably rich crab bisque.

Wintzell's Oyster House (☎ 251-432-4605; 605 Dauphin St; mains $7-12) This lively joint serves 'em up fried, baked, in a sandwich or on the shell.

A&M Peanut Shop (☎ 251-438-9373; 209 Dauphin) Placate your sweet tooth here with the toothsome selection of handmade candies and delicious nuts, roasted before your eyes in a century-old contraption.

Charlene's (☎ 694-7070; 101 Dauphin St) This classy joint, good for a top-shelf cocktail, is on the ground floor of the South's first skyscraper, built in 1906.

Getting There & Away

Greyhound (2545 Government Blvd, west of downtown) and **Amtrak** (☎ 251-432-4052; 11 Government St) stop here.

MONTGOMERY

Montgomery has a long history of fomenting change in the American cultural landscape. Once a quiet cotton port, the town briefly became the capital of the Confederacy in 1861 after Alabama seceded from the United States. Nearly a century later in 1955 anger at segregation and Jim Crow laws came to a boil when a black woman named Rosa Parks refused to give up her seat to a white man on a Montgomery city bus. For 381 days, blacks boycotted city buses until the US Supreme Court finally ordered their desegregation.

Montgomery is in central Alabama, 160 miles north of Mobile. Today, it is mostly a sleepy government town with several moving civil rights sights. Many attractions are downtown and can be reached on foot. The **visitors center** (☎ 334-262-0013, 800-240-9452; www.visitingmontgomery.com; 300 Water St; ☺ 9am-5pm Mon-Sat, noon-4pm Sun) is in the historic Union Station, a gorgeous old railroad hub overlooking the river.

Outside the impressive headquarters of the Southern Poverty Law Center, the **Civil Rights Memorial** (400 Washington Ave; ☺ 24hr), a transcendent monument designed by Maya Lin, honors 40 martyrs of the Civil Rights movement. **Rosa Parks Museum** (☎ 334-241-8615; 252 Montgomery St; admission $5.50; ☺ Mon-Sat) tells the story of the woman who refused to move to the back of the bus, and screens a sophisticated video re-creation of the historic protest.

Tour the **Alabama State Capitol** (☎ 334-242-3935; 600 Dexter Ave; admission free; ☺ Mon-Sat) to see where Jefferson Davis took the oath of office. Only a block away is the **Dexter Avenue King Memorial Baptist Church** (☎ 334-263-3970; 454 Dexter Ave; guided tours 10am & 2pm Mon-Fri), where Rev Martin Luther King served as pastor and organized the Montgomery Bus Boycott.

Country music geeks will just not want to miss the **Hank Williams Museum** (☎ 334-262-3600; 118 Commerce St; admission $7; ☺ 9am-6pm Mon-Sat, noon-4pm Sun). On display is the country music legend's boots and suits, and even the baby-blue 1952 Cadillac he took his last breath in.

Sleeping

There is but one decent budget motel downtown. **Motel Town Plaza** (☎ 334-269-1561; 743 Madison Ave; s/d $33/40; P 🔀 🖵), within walking distance of the historic district, has basic, well-priced rooms with no personality whatsoever.

The same cannot be said for the ramshackle **Travel Inn** (☎ 334-288-2600; 970 West South Blvd, I-65 exit 168; s/d $26/31; P 🔀), the cheapest place in town. Its proximity to a truck stop means that you might hear voices whispering to you from behind the chain link fence. Less dicey but more expensive is the **Quality Inn** (☎ 334-277-1919, 800-228-5151; 5175 Carmichael Rd; d $60; P 🔀 🖭), a good value on the eastern bypass off Hwy 85, with a sauna, outdoor pool and comfortable rooms with coffeemakers.

Eating

Cheap, down-home Southern grub abounds in Montgomery.

Farmer's Market Cafeteria (☎ 334-262-1970; 315 N McDonough St; mains $4-6; ⏱ 5:30am-2pm Mon-Fri) The homey Southern breakfast keeps the crowd coming back to this local meeting place; at lunch there's more good country cooking and incredibly reasonable prices.

Montgomery Brewing Co (MBC; ☎ 334-834-2739; 12 W Jefferson St; mains $10-16) This lively hub of activity is a great place for a microbrew and salad, burger or savory steak.

Getting There & Away

Greyhound (☎ 334-286-0658; 950 W South Blvd) stops here.

BIRMINGHAM

This industrial revolution boomtown in north–central Alabama's Black Belt was built on once-rich veins of iron ore. The largest and most cosmopolitan city in Alabama, Birmingham has borne the brunt of many of the South's most daunting challenges. It was here where the Civil Rights movement faced its most anguished episodes. Today, Birmingham is finding its legs as a center for medical research, and a younger generation is bringing new vigor to its streets. Hipsters throng to Southside and Five Points South – off 20th St S (the main north–south thoroughfare) – where art-deco buildings house worthwhile shops, restaurants and nightclubs.

The **Birmingham Visitors Center** (☎ 205-458-8000, 800-458-8085; www.birminghamal.org; 2200 9th Ave N; ⏱ Mon-Fri) dispenses some informative brochures.

Perhaps the most worthwhile sight in town is the **Birmingham Civil Rights Institute** (☎ 205-328-9696, 866-328-9696; www.bcri.org; 520 16th St N; admission $8; ⏱ Mon-Sat). Here multimedia and artifacts tell the compelling story of racial segregation from WWI to the Civil Rights movement. The **16th St Baptist Church** (☎ 205-251-9402; at 6th Ave N; ⏱ Tue-Fri) stands as a memorial to the infamous 1963 Ku Klux Klan bombing that took the lives of four school-aged girls.

In the historic Carver Theatre, the **Alabama Jazz Hall of Fame** (☎ 205-254-2731; 1631 4th Ave N; admission free; ⏱ Tue-Sun) celebrates jazz musicians like Ella Fitzgerald, Nat King Cole and Duke Ellington. Nearby, at 4th Ave N and 18th St N, is the good-natured **Eddie Kendricks Memorial**, where beguiling statues of soul music sensations the Temptations hold court over a small park with piped-in music.

Birmingham's skyline is an extended rusty monument to the industrial revolution. Downtown, several ornate, early-20th-century, steel-framed skyscrapers still stand, some of them long empty. To the northeast are the imposing smokestacks of **Sloss Furnaces National Historic Landmark** (☎ 205-324-1911; 1st Ave nr 32nd St N; admission free; ⏱ Tue-Sun), a 32-acre blast furnace where pick iron was produced for over 100 years; it's now a museum and center for metal art.

Overlooking the Southside neighborhood is **Vulcan Park** (20th St S & Valley Ave), lorded over by a 56-ft-tall iron statue of the exceedingly buff Roman god of the forge.

Sleeping

There are a couple of budget places downtown. In Southside, the **Hospitality Inn** (☎ 205-322-0691; 2127 7th Ave S; s/d $45/50; P 🔀) has clean and comfortable wood-paneled rooms, but the neighborhood can be the wrong kind of lively at night. There is slightly less action at the no-frills **Royal Inn** (☎ 205-252-8041; 821 20th St S; s/d $45/50; P 🔀), but the dingy rooms are a little grim.

Microtel (☎ 205-945-5550, 800-275-8047; 251 Summit Parkway; s/d $38/42; P 🔀 🖭) South of Southside and halfway between downtown and Oak Mountain State Park, this place is clean and comfortable.

Oak Mountain State Park (☎ 205-620-2524; 15 miles south on 1-65, exit 246; tents $10-13, cabins $70-100) This wooded park is a good place to pitch a tent for a night, and has opportunities for swimming, fishing, hiking and tennis. The pleasant cabins sleep up to six and come with linens and simple kitchen.

Eating & Drinking

Birmingham has a good variety of authentic, cheap chow. Nowhere are these qualities more evident than at **Pete's Famous Hot Dogs** (☎ 205-252-2905; 1925 2nd Ave N; hot dogs $1.50), a tiny hole-in-the-wall that has been serving up chilidogs since 1920. Equally of the people is the old-timer **La Vase** (☎ 205-328-9327; 328 16th St N; mains $6-8; Tue-Sun) in the historic district, which serves cheap home-style soul food.

Fish Market Restaurant (☎ 205-332-3330; 611 21st St S; seafood mains $9-$10) On the south side of the tracks, this market-style joint serves seafood spiced the Cajun way, with a lengthy menu of southern side dishes and icebox pies.

Jim 'n Nicks BarBQ (☎ 205-323-7082; 744 29th St S; mains $9-13) In Southside, this place has true-blue barbecue done right. With a full bar and laid-back collegiate atmosphere, Jim 'n Nicks has everything you need for a night out.

Golden Temple Natural Grocery & Cafe (☎ 205-933-8933; 1901 11th Ave S; mains $4-7) A well-stocked, health-food store and café that serves meatless standards, Mexican fare and hearty soups.

Birmingham has plenty of good bars to keep night owls happy. Check the monthly *Black & White* for listings. The most popular nightclubs are in Southside.

Nick (☎ 205-252-3831; 2514 10th Ave S) The local proving ground for live bands.

22nd St Jazz Cafe (☎ 205-252-0407; 710 22nd St S) A cozy place for live jazz and blues.

Dave's (☎ 205-933-4030; 1128 20th St S) A quintessential saloon with talented bartenders, darts, and a particular ambience

Blue Monkey Lounge (☎ 205-933-9222; 1318 Cobb Lane, parallel 20th St S) Intimate nooks and crannies and lights turned down low.

Quest (☎ 205-251-4313; 416 24th St S) Gay club rocks all night, every night.

Getting There & Around

The **Birmingham International Airport** (☎ 205-595-0533) is about 5 miles northeast of downtown. **Greyhound** (☎ 205-251-3210; 618 19th St N) and **Amtrak** (☎ 205-324-3033; 1819 Morris Ave) stop here. **Metropolitan Area Express** (MAX; ☎ 205-521-0101; $1.25) runs local buses.

Florida

HIGHLIGHTS

- **South Beach** White coral beaches, legendary neon-clad art-deco hotels, and thumping nightlife that never ceases (p324)
- **Everglades National Park** Kayak through 10,000 lakes, and get within snout-range of the local residents (p329)
- **Daytona International Speedway** Experience the thrill of taking the curves at Daytona in an official NASCAR speed demon (p328)
- **Off the beaten track** Bar Bamboo, a shoestringer's best kept secret for great drinks and potential free passes to Walt Disney World (p333)
- **Best journey** See a side of Key West you never knew, on a bicycle with a passionate, machete-wielding tour guide (p330)

FLORIDA

FAST FACTS

- **Area** 58,560 sq miles (4,308 sq miles in water)
- **Big cities** Miami (population 3.9 million), Tampa (304,000), Orlando (188,000)
- **Budget** $30-70 per day
- **Costs** hostel in Miami $18, bus ride Miami–Orlando $40, bus ride Miami–Fort Lauderdale $10, *bocadillo* $4
- **Driving times** Miami to Orlando 4 hours, Miami to Key West 3½ hours, Miami to Daytona 5½ hours
- **Famous for** hot weather, picturesque beaches, oranges, alligators, year-round playground for rich and famous
- **Languages** Spanish, English
- **Population** 16 million
- **Phrases** *Hola, como estás?* (Hi, how are you?), *Un café Cubano por favor* (A Cuban coffee please), *Donde está la playa?* (Where is the beach?)
- **Seasons** high (Nov-Mar), low (Apr-Jun), hurricane (Jun-Oct)

- **Tasty treats** citrus (oranges and grapefruits), key lime pie, anything Cuban, especially café Cubano, *mojitos*, *ropa vieja*
- **Time** Eastern Time Zone
- **Top hostel** Gram's Place, Tampa (p333)

TRAVEL HINT

Snorkeling much? Buy a cheap mask, snorkel and fins to avoid rental charges – it's worth it to be able to wade out from any beach and swim up to the coral. Afterwards, donate your gear to a hostel if you don't want to take it with you.

FLORIDA

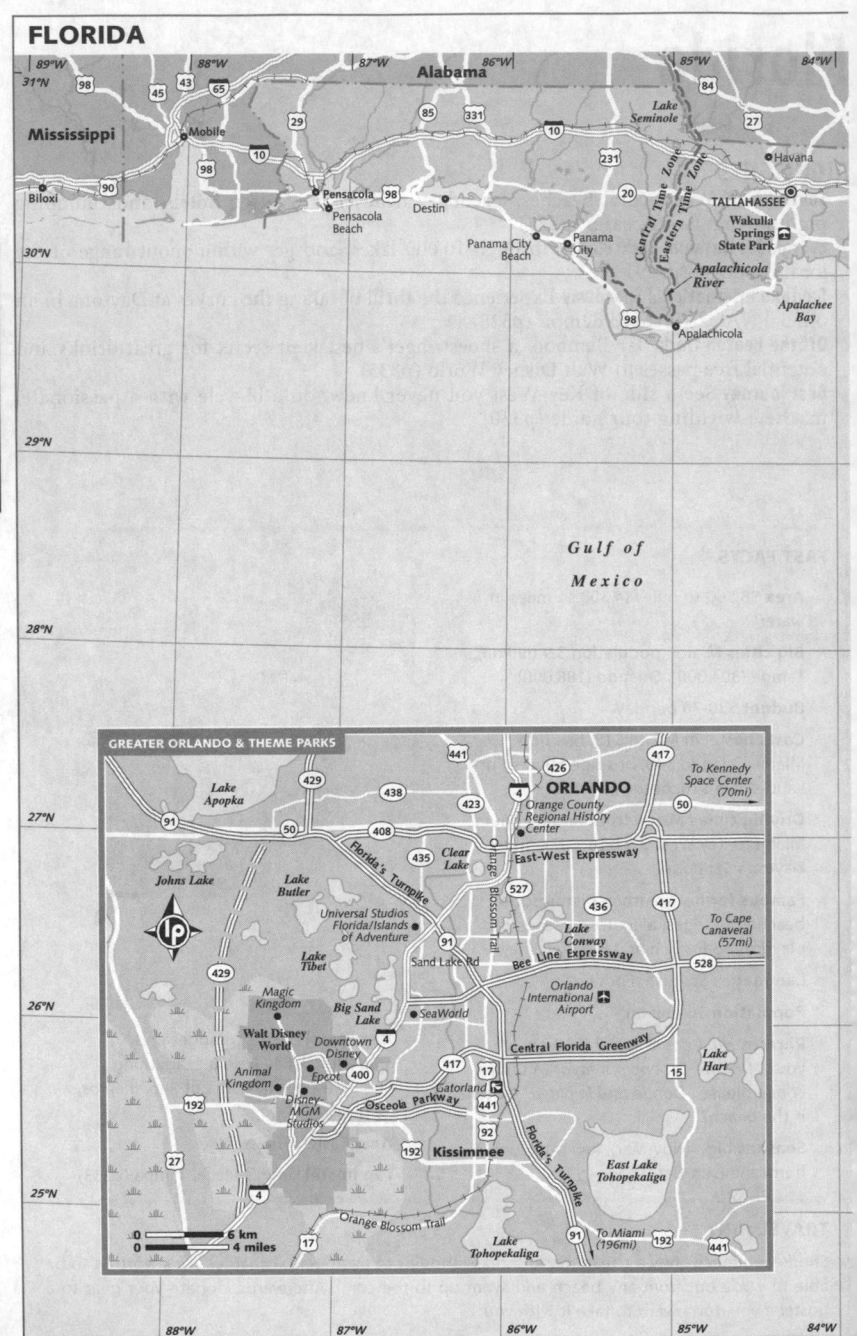

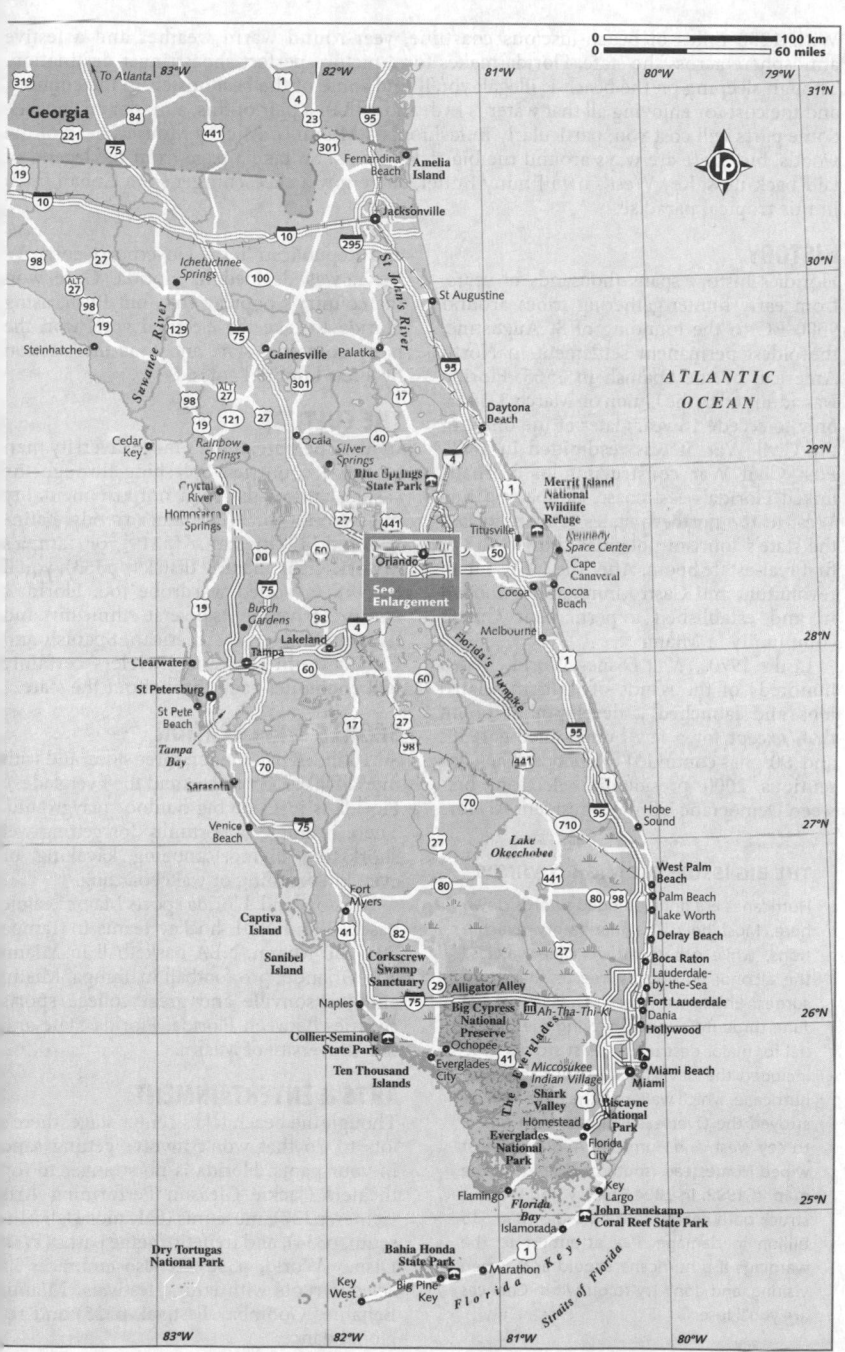

FLORIDA

With 1250 miles of beach-luscious coastline, year-round warm weather and a festive atmosphere across the state, Florida makes for a picture-perfect shoestringer destination. Though sleeping on the beach is illegal, you'll find some of the best hostels in the country, and the cost for enjoying all that water is little more than a pair of fins, a mask and snorkel. Some parts will cost you, particularly in fashionista Miami or Mickey Mouse's neck of the woods, but there are ways around the big-ticket items. So take a page from the legend of laid-back-ness, Key West's own Jimmy Buffet, and enjoy a cheeseburger (or a Cuban *frita*) in this tropical paradise.

FLORIDA

HISTORY

Florida's history spans thousands of years, from early hunter-gathering tribes around 9000 BC to the founding of St Augustine, the oldest permanent settlement in North America, by the Spanish in 1565. Florida was admitted to the Union on March 3, 1845, only to secede 16 years later at the onset of the Civil War. It was readmitted in 1868. Post–Civil War construction of railroads linked Florida's east coast, Tampa and Key West to the northern states. This unlocked the state's tourism potential and led to the first real-estate boom. After the 1959 Cuban revolution, anti-Castro immigrants flooded in and established a permanent Cuban community in Miami.

In the 1970s, Walt Disney World created hundreds of thousands of tourism-related jobs and launched a development boom that, except for a few bumps in the 1980s and '90s, has continued ever since. The contentious 2000 presidential election, between Democratic US Vice President Al Gore and Republican Texas Governor George W Bush, was decided in Florida. Gore won the country's popular vote, but Bush, using Florida to take the electoral vote, won the hotly contested state and thus the election by a few hundred votes.

THE CULTURE

In just one state, there's more diversity than in entire countries. Splashing through the casual, end-of-the-road outpost mentality of Key West (p330), Miami's trendy, Latin-flavored 'it' city status (p319), or Tampa's historic cigar-making district (p333), you'll do with a varied wardrobe too. Florida's culture thrives on its diverse ethnic mix and its roots in Native American, Spanish and Cuban traditions, and travelers certainly will encounter each throughout the state.

SPORTS & RECREATION

Surrounded by water on three sides, and with myriad lakes and rivers (and the Everglades), Florida is just one big outdoor playground. There is ample opportunity for getting wet snorkeling, diving, canoeing, kayaking, or even kiteboarding or wakeboarding.

Back on land, Florida sports Major League baseball and NHL hockey teams in Tampa Bay and Miami, NBA basketball in Miami and Orlando, pro football in Tampa, Miami and Jacksonville and great college sports rivalries between Florida, Florida State and the University of Miami.

ARTS & ENTERTAINMENT

Though the beach takes center stage, there's lots to do that won't involve getting sand in your pants. Florida is no stranger to top theaters (Jackie Gleason Performing Arts Center, p327), museums (Salvador Dalí Museum, p334), and frenetic theme parks (Walt Disney World, p332). It also embraces its eclectic roots with ethnic festivals (Miami Bahamas Goombay Festival, p325) and regional dance.

THE BIG ISSUE: THE MIGHTY WINDS

Hurricanes are double-edged swords down here. Most heed the mandatory evacuations, while others throw 'cane parties,' the alcohol flowing as free as the storm surges. Either way, they're a way of life June through October, packing the potential for major destruction. Past storms have included the devastating 1939 Labor Day hurricane, which walloped the Keys and destroyed the Overseas Railroad from Miami to Key West, and Hurricane Andrew almost wiped Homestead (south of Miami) off the map in 1992. In 2004 Charley and Frances struck both coasts, causing more than $15 billion in damage. Pay attention to the warnings if a hurricane should arise when visiting, and don't try to outwit it. Chances are you'll lose.

ENVIRONMENT

Florida's terrain is mainly flat, with coastal lowlands and low hills in the north and central regions. The south-central portion of the state is wetlands and reclaimed swampland. The coasts are protected by natural barrier islands and, in the south, coral reefs. The stretch of water between the barrier islands and mainland form the Intracoastal Waterway. In Miami and south Florida, the peak season is December through March, with warm, dry weather, big crowds and high prices. The dreaded hurricane season stretches from June to October – also the hottest and wettest time to be in Florida. Considering the extremely active 2004 hurricane activity, Florida residents (and businesses) are hoping for calmer seasons in the future.

National & State Parks

Florida has three national parks – Biscayne National Park (p329), Dry Tortugas National Park (p332), and Everglades National Park (p329). The **Florida Division of Recreation & Parks** (☎ 850-245-2157; www.floridastateparks.org; 3900 Commonwealth Blvd, Tallahassee 32399) manages the state's park system, of which there are 51 parks. Daily entrance fees are $4 to $5 for cars carrying up to eight people. Camping fees are $10 to $50 to enter the camping ground and then another $4 for the actual campsite itself, and reservations must be made through **ReserveAmerica** (☎ 800-326-3521; www.reserveamerica.com) and not through the individual parks.

TRANSPORTATION

Miami, Fort Lauderdale/Hollywood, Orlando and Tampa have major hub city airports. Fort Lauderdale and Miami airports are about 30 minutes apart, and it's almost always cheaper to fly into or out of Fort Lauderdale. Popular low-cost airlines that fly here are AirTran, Southwest Airlines, JetBlue, and Song. See p702 for further details.

Greyhound (☎ 800-229-9424; www.greyhound.com) has widespread bus services throughout the state, but bus travel can be extremely slow and not a good option if you're pressed for time.

The *Silver Meteor, Silver Star* and *Silver Palm* trains, run by **Amtrak** (☎ 800-872-7245; www.amtrak.com), travel daily between New York and Miami. The *Sunset Limited*

BUDGET TIP

Car rental rates in Florida tend to be relatively low: a small car might cost $29 per day or $135 per week. Drive-aways to Florida are common; for details see p707.

crosses the south between Los Angeles and Orlando three times weekly; see p711 for more information about Amtrak.

The **Tri-Rail** (☎ 800-874-7245; www.tri-rail.com) commuter system is certainly the cheapest mode of transportation between Fort Lauderdale and Miami, with stops at the three airports and bus connections to beaches, downtowns and neighboring cities. A transfer to the Metrorail at the end of the line will get you to Coconut Grove (p327). One-way fares are $2 to $5.50, and weekend and holiday fares are $4. It's slow but cheap.

MIAMI

Beautiful people in a glamorous atmosphere, glorious sunshine by day and killer all-night clubbing. Oh, did we mention the beautiful people? Miami is indeed many things to many people. It won't be the cheapest place to hang out (though lodging deals abound), but Miami is definitely something to write home about. Where else can you knock elbows with A-list celebs in sweaty nightclubs, watch cruise ships from your beach towel, or sip a high-octane Cuban coffee that would make your local coffee shop wince? Plus, its status as a major gay and lesbian playground ensures this city will always be en vogue.

Visitors will probably find that the city and the beach are a bit of a Jekyll and Hyde combination. The city is a little more conservative, with government offices, traditional neighborhoods and a wealth of fascinating historical sites. Yet when you hit the causeway to the beach, shed that three-piece suit for a two-piece bikini and crank the music and attitude. Lured by the low hum of neon-fronted art-deco hotels and the area's essence of pure fabulousness, most visitors bunk down in Miami Beach's 'South Beach' or 'SoBe' district, roughly 19 blocks packed with restaurants and clubs.

FLORIDA

GETTING INTO TOWN

From **Miami International Airport** (MIA; ☎ 305-876-7000, flight info ☎ 305-876-7770), public buses ($1.25) are accessible on Level 1 of Concourse E across from Customs. To get to the beaches, take the J bus to 41st St and Indian Creek Dr, then transfer to the C bus to 15th St and Washington Ave. Transfers are free. If arriving between 11:20pm and 7am, take the Airport Owl bus. For other destinations: downtown Miami (Bus 7); and Coral Gables (Bus 42). The **SuperShuttle** (☎ 305-871-2000) costs $10/12 to downtown/Miami Beach.

Greyhound has two major bus stops in the Miami area: **downtown** (36 NE 10th St) and **Omni** (Biscayne Blvd & NE 14th Tce). The C bus runs from either of these stations to the beaches. The **Airport Owl bus** (www.miamdade.gov/transit) runs to/from at the Omni bus station only.

Amtrak (☎ 305-835-1222; 8303 NW 37th Ave) is in North Miami's Hialeah neighborhood. For the beaches, take the L bus to Lincoln Rd.

So whether you choose sand or mainland, between the eclectic cultural mix of cuisines, the gorgeous weather, and totally nonstop partying, Miami's exciting youthfulness and it-city status has brought it a long way from the 'God's Waiting Room' moniker it had.

ORIENTATION

Greater Miami is a sprawling metropolis that includes suburbs such as Coral Gables and Coconut Grove (p325), and neighborhoods like Little Havana (p324). Miami is on the mainland, while the City of Miami Beach (including South Beach) is 4 miles east on a stretch of sand crowded with buildings.

Public transportation can get you anywhere, but chances are you'll spend most of your time in foot-friendly South Beach – roughly the stretch of beach from 1st to 21st Sts. A triumvirate of parallel streets (Ocean Dr, Collins Ave and Washington Ave) contains most of the action, as well as the pedestrian-only area of Lincoln Rd. The beachfront Ocean Dr is the most panoramic, while the club scene hops on Collins and Washington.

INFORMATION
Bookstores

Books & Books Coral Gables (☎ 305-442-4408; 265 Aragon Ave; ☺ 9am-11pm) Miami Beach (☎ 305-532-3222; 933 Lincoln Rd; ☺ 10am-11pm Mon-Thu & Sun, to midnight Fri & Sat) One of the finest independent bookstores in the US.
Downtown Book Center (☎ 305-377-9939; 247 SE 1st St, downtown Miami) Spanish-language books available here as well.
Lambda Passages Bookstore (☎ 305-754-6900; www.lambdapassages.com; 7545 Biscayne Blvd NE, downtown Miami; ☺ 11am-9pm Mon-Sat, noon-6pm Sun) For gay and lesbian travelers.

Emergency
Beach Patrol (☎ 305-673-7711; ☺ 24hr)
Rape Hotline (☎ 305-585-7273; ☺ 24hr)

Internet Access
Cybr Caffe (☎ 305-534-0057; www.cybrcaffe.com; 1574 Washington Ave, Miami Beach; ☺ 9am-1am Mon-Wed, 24hr Thu-Sun)
Kafka's Kafe (☎ 305-673-9669; http://kafkaskafe.com; 1464 Washington Ave, Miami Beach; ☺ 8am-midnight) Has a $3 per hour 'happy hour' from 8am to noon and 8pm to midnight.

Libraries
Miami Beach Library (☎ 305-535-4219; 2100 Collins Ave, Miami Beach; ☺ 9am-9pm Mon-Thu, to 6pm Fri & Sat) Free access on a screen-available basis.
Miami-Dade Public Library Downtown downtown Miami (☎ 305-375-2665; 101 W Flagler St; ☺ 9am-6pm Mon-Sat, to 9pm Thu, 1-5pm Sun Oct-Jun only); Miami Beach (☎ 305-535-4219; 2100 Collins Ave; ☺ 9:30am-9pm Mon-Thu, to 6pm Fri & Sat) Free access on a screen-available basis.

Media
El Nuevo Herald Spanish daily published by the *Miami Herald*.
Miami Herald The city's only major English-language daily. Entertainment section on Friday.
New Times Free alternative weekly with good listings of restaurants, clubs, bars and theater.
Wire Free gay weekly. All about partying on Miami Beach.

Medical Services
Miami Beach Community Health Center (☎ 305-538-8835; 710 Alton Rd, Miami Beach) Charges fees based on income.
Mount Sinai Medical Center (☎ 305-674-2121; 4300 Alton Rd, Miami Beach) The area's best emergency room. It also has a medical line on ☎ 305-674-2222.

MIAMI BEACH

500 m
0.3 miles

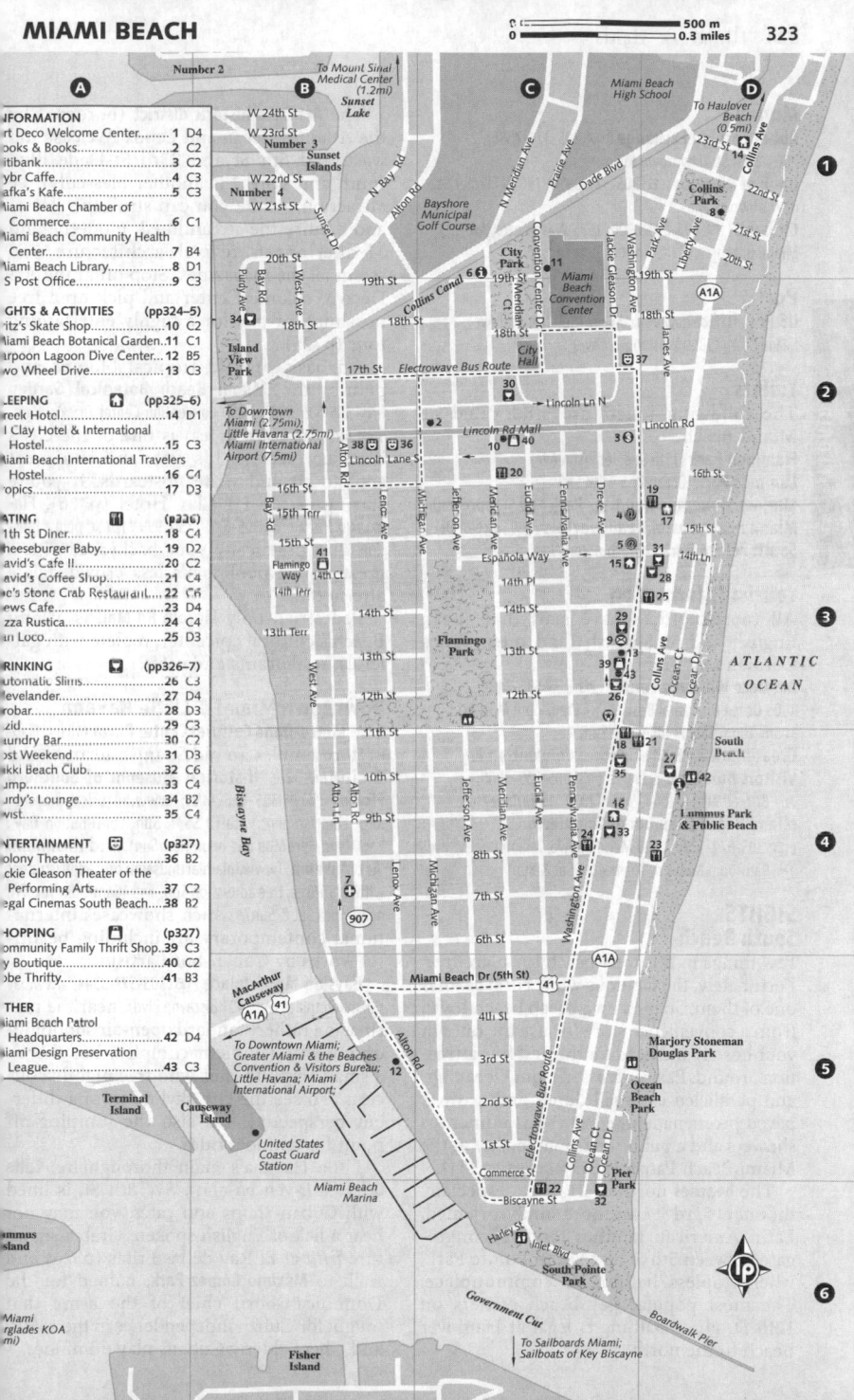

Money
Abbot Foreign Exchange (☎ 305-374-7885;
230 NE 1st St, downtown Miami)
Bank of America (☎ 305-373-0970; 150 W Flagler St,
downtown Miami)
Citibank (☎ 305-673-6900; 1685 Washington Ave,
Miami Beach)

Post
US Post Office downtown Miami (500 NW 2nd Ave);
Miami Beach (1300 Washington Ave)

Toilets
The following toilets are all located at
Miami Beach.
Flamingo Park (11th St & Jefferson Ave)
Lummus Park (Ocean Dr 5-15th Sts)
Marjory Stoneman Douglass Park (3rd St & Ocean Dr)
Miami Beach Patrol Headquarters (1001 Ocean Dr)
South Pointe Park (1 Washington Ave)

Tourist Information
All tourist offices have staff that speak
English and/or Spanish (and often times
German and French).
Art Deco Welcome Center (☎ 305-531-3484;
1000 Ocean Dr, Miami Beach; 11am-6pm Mon-Fri,
10am-10pm Sat, 11am-10pm Sun)
**Greater Miami & the Beaches Convention &
Visitors Bureau** main branch (☎ 305-539-3000;
701 Brickell Ave) Coconut Grove (2820 MacFarlane Rd)
Miami Beach Chamber of Commerce
(☎ 305-672-1270; 1920 Meridian Ave, Miami Beach;
9am-6pm Mon-Fri, 10am-4pm Sat & Sun)

SIGHTS
South Beach
Few things in this tony beach town are free.
Fortunately, the fabulous white coral **beach** is
one of them. So pick up a cheap beach towel
from a convenience store (or use the ones in
your hostel) and head for the best free attraction around. Easily accessed from Ocean Dr,
and paralleled by small dunes and a wavy,
paved promenade, the beach has numerous
showers and a public restroom facility at the
Miami Beach Patrol Headquarters (p324).

The **beaches** north of 21st St – especially
the one at 53rd St – are more family-oriented.
Latin American families tend to congregate between 5th St and South Pointe Park,
where topless bathing is commonplace.
The most popular gay beach centers on
12th St. Nude bathing is legal at Haulover
Beach to the north.

The **Art Deco historic district** (bordered by
the Atlantic Ocean and Lenox Ave east and
west, and 6th St and 23rd St-Dade Blvd
south and north) is another blessedly free
attraction, where you can stroll the streets
and admire the streamlined, moderne and
Mediterranean revival architecture you
see in all the magazines. Stop off at the Art
Deco Welcome Center and pick up a free
brochure, or pay for a highly entertaining
tour (p325).

An oasis of wild tropical blooms and
plants, the **Miami Beach Botanical Garden**
(☎ 305-535-8083; 2000 Convention Center Dr; 9am-
5pm Mon-Sat, from noon Sun) is one of the city's
best-kept secrets. It's free, and is a great
spot to sit and write postcards. If you're
staying at the HI Clay Hotel (p326), **Flamingo Park** (☎ 305-673-7730; 999 11th St; pool admission $3) is practically your backyard, with a
great public pool that's less crowded late
afternoon.

Pedestrian-only **Lincoln Rd Mall** is Miami
Beach's cultural epicenter, replete with galleries, restaurants and cafés.

Downtown Miami & Little Havana
The **Metro-Dade Cultural Center Plaza** (101 W Flagler St) resembles an old Spanish fortress and
includes the **Historical Museum of Southern
Florida** (☎ 305-375-1492; www.historical-museum
.org; adult/student with ID $5/4, Sun 'Contribution Day';
10am-5pm Mon-Sat, noon-5pm Sun), and the **Miami
Art Museum** (www.miamiartmuseum.org; adult/student
with ID $5/free, free admission Sun; 10am-5pm Tue-Fri,
noon-5pm Sat & Sun), which showcases international contemporary art including beautiful works by Cuban-born artists.

Bayside Marketplace (☎ 305-577-3344; www.bay
sidemarketplace.com; 401 Biscayne Blvd), near the marina, is a rather standard open-air shopping/
dining/entertainment complex, but there's
a small amphitheater with free nightly concerts. To see the city skyline from a different perspective, it's also the jumping-off
point for gondola rides.

Little Havana's main thoroughfare, **Calle
Ocho** (kah-yeh oh-cho), SW 8th St, is lined
with Cuban shops and cafés; you may not
hear a lick of English spoken. Grab a signature frita at El Ray de las Fritas (p326) and
walk to **Máximo Gómez Park**, named for the
Dominican-born chief of the army that
fought for Cuban independence in the 1890s,
and where elderly Cubans play dominoes.

Watch Cuban *tubaqueros* (tobacconists) hand roll cigars at **El Crédito Cigars** (☎ 305-858-4162; 1106 SW 8th St; admission free; ☉ 7am-6pm Mon-Fri, 7am-4pm Sat).

From the beaches, take bus K or C to the downtown Miami station, then transfer to the Little Havana Circulator bus, which covers downtown and Little Havana sites.

Coral Gables & Coconut Grove

A lovely, upscale city with a Mediterranean influence, Coral Gables has a handful of attractions, most enjoyably the superb **Venetian Pool** (☎ 305-460-5306; www.venetianpool.com; 2701 De Soto Blvd; admission $9; ☉ 10am-4:30pm Tue-Sun). Carved from a limestone quarry in 1923 and fed by springs, this is one of the oldest public swimming pools in the US – a playground of waterfalls and coves in an Italianate theme. Credit or debit cards are not accepted.

The site of the area's first major settlement, Coconut Grove is a former bohemian hangout that has evolved into a ritzy commercial hub, with the trendy **CocoWalk** shopping area a hub of hip nightclubs and bars. The 10-acre **Vizcaya Museum and Gardens** (☎ 305-250-9133; 3251 S Miami Ave; admission $12; ☉ 9:30am-4:30pm) is a glamorous Italian Renaissance–style villa built in 1916 by industrialist James Deering, with lush gardens overlooking Biscayne Bay. The moonlight garden tours ($5) give an awe-inspiring perspective of the grounds.

From the beaches, take bus K or C to the downtown Miami station, then transfer to bus 48 for Coconut Grove or bus 24 for Coral Gables and Vizcaya.

ACTIVITIES

No admission fare is required for the famous white-coral beach and its swimming, snorkeling and lounging possibilities.

Cycling & In-line Skating

Cruising by bike or blades is the most popular mode of transport, with the best venue along the promenade in South Beach. For rentals, try **Fritz's Skate Shop** (☎ 305-532-1954; 730 Lincoln Rd, Miami Beach; per hr/half-day/full-day $7/15/23; ☉ 10am-10pm) and **Two Wheel Drive** (☎ 305-534-2177; 1260 Washington Ave, Miami Beach; per hr/day $5/15; ☉ varies).

Water Sports

If your hostel doesn't have gear rentals, try **Tarpoon Lagoon Dive Center** (☎ 305-532-1445; 300 Alton Rd, Miami Beach Marina) for snorkel equipment. Otherwise, jump into the water with these outfits:

Miami Wakeboard (☎ 786-299-4285; www .miamiwakeboard.com; Wakeskate Slider Park) A thrilling combination of waterskiing and skateboarding.

Sailboards Miami (☎ 305-361-7245; 1 Rickenbacker Causeway; per hr $20-25; ☉ 9am-6pm)

Sailboats of Key Biscayne (☎ 305-361-0328; 4000 Crandon Park Blvd; per hr/day $27/130; ☉ 10am-6pm)

TOURS

Everything you always wanted to know about art deco in Miami Beach (including why the hotels are so small) is revealed by the **Miami Design Preservation League** (☎ 305-672-2014; www.mdpl.org; Ste 207, 1234 Washington Ave, Miami Beach) and its excellent **Deco District walking tours** (adult/student $20/15; tours 10:30am Sat, Sun & Wed, 6:30pm Thu); tours depart from the Art Deco Welcome Center, 1001 Ocean Dr. Self-guided audio tours cost $15/10. Its best tour, Deco Underworld, recaptures the city's sneaky Prohibition-era vibe and even uncovers Al Capone's secret office. It's only run a few times a year, so call ahead.

FESTIVALS & EVENTS

In March, the city lets loose for **Carnaval** (www .carnavalmiami.com) and the country's largest street party, the **Calle Ocho Festival** in Little Havana, which floods streets with craft vendors and samples of Cuban cuisine. Not only is the **Miami/Bahamas Goombay Festival** (www .goombayfestival.com) in June the largest black heritage festival in the nation, it's just downright awesome, with infectious rake 'n' scrape and junkanoo music, and soul food that'll stick to your ribs through winter.

SLEEPING

Miami Beach is blessed with good-value accommodations, some of which include a pool. Most hostels have reduced rates during summer, except for July, 4 and Labor Day, and they all run activities and city tours.

Creek Hotel (☎ 305-538-1951; 2360 Collins Ave; www.thecreeksouthbeach.com; dm/d $20/70; ✖ ☐ ☎) Creek Hotel has a pillow-filled theater, on-site café/Tiki Bar with the cheapest happy hour at the beach, game room, parking, and an excellent pool where the party-hearty international crowd take it into the dawn. The former Banana Bungalow just got a little hipper, with a state-of-the-art sound system and designer redecorated rooms. The so-called creek is really just a canal. No matter. The hotel close to the beach on the northern end of the Art Deco district.

HI Clay Hotel & International Hostel (☎ 305-534-2988; www.clayhotel.com; 1438 Washington Ave; dm/s $15/42; ✷ ▣) A classic, well-traveled hostel in the heart of all the beach action. This muted pink, 100-year-old Spanish-style complex offers everything from single-sex dorms to spacious suites with balconies, and the pretty Española Way pedestrian mall is right outside the front door.

Miami Beach International Travelers Hostel (☎ 305-534-0268; www.sobehostel.com; 236 9th St; dm members/nonmembers $14/16, d from $36; ✷ ▣) Don't let the rather rundown exterior fool you – inside is a totally cool world with 28 rooms (only four people per room), high-speed Internet, a movie lounge and no curfew. It's loud and busy, but also smack in the middle of the club and Art Deco district.

Tropics (☎ 305-531-0361; www.tropicshotel.com; 1550 Collins Ave; dm $16-19, d $50-75, tr $65-75, qd $75-90; ✷ ▣ ▨) The staff is just so darn friendly, and the Olympic-sized pool is a great place for picking up travelers tips. You'll need a passport to stay here, even if you're American.

For camping, try **Miami Everglades KOA Kampground** (☎ 800-562-7732, 305-233-5300; www.miamicamp.com; 20675 SW 162 Ave; tents/kabins $26/45, 1-/2-room lodge $80).

EATING

Cuban cuisine is king here. For cheap eats, a quick *bocadillo* (sandwich) and a *guarapo* (a drink of fresh sugar-cane juice) hit the spot, particularly in Little Havana. You can grab great meals in South Beach too, including the superfresh **Lincoln Rd farmers' market** (Lincoln Rd, Miami Beach; ☯ Sun), and grocery stores for quick picnic food and munchies.

11th St Diner (☎ 305-534-6373; 1065 Washington Ave, Miami Beach; mains $5-15) Excellent greasy-spoon (with a splash of Cuban on the side) for early noshers and night owls.

David's Cafe II (☎ 305-672-8707; 1654 Meridian Ave, Miami Beach; breakfast $4-7, buffet lunch $7.50) Traditional Cuban dishes of fried plantains and black beans and rice at this long-standing favorite, plus the take-out window at its second location, **David's Coffee Shop** (☎ 305-534-8736; 1058 Collins Ave, Miami Beach; ☯ 24hr).

Pizza Rustica (☎ 305-674-8244; 863 Washington Ave, Miami Beach; mains $5-9) An excellent assortment of fanciful pizza toppings and prime people-watching real estate is worth a $10 meal.

El Ray de las Fritas (1177 SW 8th St, Little Havana; mains $5-9) A trip to Calle Ocho is nothing until you grab one of El Ray's famous *fritas* (burger with shoestring fries on top) and thick *batidos* (milkshake).

News Cafe (☎ 305-538-6397; 800 Ocean Dr, Miami Beach; mains $9-12) Stick to the gigantic salads and sweet fruit plates to cut costs at this oceanfront, 24-hour landmark.

Joe's Stone Crab Restaurant (☎ 305-673-0365; 227 Biscayne St, Miami Beach; mains $12-45; ☯ closed mid-May–mid-Oct) Famous for its monstrous stone crab claws, you can beat the high price and endless line by ordering carry-out next door!

Satisfy late-night munchies at **Cheeseburger Baby** (☎ 305-531-7300; 1505 Washington Ave, Miami Beach; mains under $10) and **San Loco** (☎ 305-538-3009; 235 14th St, Miami Beach; tacos $5.50), with its deliciously sloppy 'Guaco Loco' tacos.

SPLURGE

'Miami Spice' month (www.miamirestaurant month.com) Eat like a king/queen/drag queen for an un-South Beach price in August when the oh-so-fabulous restaurants set prix-fix menus for dinner ($30 per person) and lunch ($20).

DRINKING

South Beach's ample café culture is evident by the colorful umbrella stands that dominate the Ocean Dr and Lincoln Rd promenades. Smoothies, martinis and high-octane Cuban coffee are the preferred drinks, best sipped outside. Following are a few of our favorite happy hours (most with free hors d'oeuvres) and rock joints.

Automatic Slims (☎ 305-695-0895; 1216 Washington Ave, Miami Beach) With a motto 'No cover, no VIP, no bullshit,' Slims is the anti-velvet rope authority in SoBe and rocks with live music amid the neon and stripper poles. Ladies drink free on Bike Night Thursday.

Laundry Bar (☎ 305-531-7700; 721 N Lincoln Lne, Miami Beach; basic wash $1.75) This hoppin' place is Miami's best place to be stuck doing your wash, with discount drinks some nights and a thumpin' backbeat that'll take you through the spin cycle.

Lost Weekend (☎ 305-672-1707; 218 Española Way, Miami Beach) is a comfy, relaxed dive, popular with the Clay Hotel crowd, with foosball, darts, pool, and nightly happy hours from 5pm, including $2 shots.

Purdy's Lounge (☎ 305-531-4622; 1811 Purdy Ave, Miami Beach) Retro meets your grandma's living room. Hip cocktails are slung back to live music Tuesday nights, and ladies can drink free Cosmos and martinis Thursday night.

Also recommended are the **Clevelander** (☎ 305-531-3485; 1020 Ocean Dr, Miami Beach), a cosmic oceanfront pickup joint with nightly two-for-one drinks; and **Jazid** (☎ 305-673-9372; 1342 Washington Ave, Miami Beach; cover Fri & Sat $10) for sophisticated jazz, soul and funk in a candlelit lounge.

CLUBBING
Cheap ain't the word here, as most velvet-rope clubs require a minimum $20 cover. Check hostels for reduced admissions, dress your best and sport your 'I belong here' attitude. The *New Times* reviews current clubs, but two must-dos are **Crobar** (☎ 305-531-5027; 1445 Washington Ave, Miami Beach; cover $25) in the renovated art deco Cameo Theatre; and the open-air **Nikki Beach Club** (☎ 305-538-1111; 1 Ocean Dr, Miami Beach; cover $20) where lounging is encouraged in hammocks and teepees.

ENTERTAINMENT
While nightlife gets the bulk of tourist attention, Miami enjoys stellar theater, sports and live music venues.

Cinemas & Theater
Matinees are only $4.25 at the opulent **Regal Cinemas South Beach** (☎ 305-674-6766; Lincoln Rd). See acts ranging from the Tibetan Monks to the Strokes at the **Jackie Gleason Theater of the Performing Arts** (☎ 305-673-7300; www.gleason theater.com; 1700 Washington Ave), or ballet and off-Broadway productions at art-deco **Colony Theater** (☎ 305-674-1026; 1040 Lincoln Rd).

Sports
The NFL's **Miami Dolphins** (☎ 305-620-2578; tickets $20-54; ☾ Sep-Dec) and the baseball's National League **Florida Marlins** (☎ 305-626-7400; tickets $4-55; ☾ Apr-Sep) play at **ProPlayer Stadium** (2269 Dan Marino Blvd, Miami). The NBA's **Miami Heat**

(☎ 305-577-4328; tickets $18-100; ☾ Nov-Apr) play hoops at **American Airlines Arena** (601 Biscayne Blvd, Miami), while hockey's **Florida Panthers** (☎ 954-835-8000; Office Depot Center Panther Pkwy, 136th St at Sunrise Blvd) skate at nearby Sunrise.

Watch and bet on the lightning-fast local court game at **Miami Jai Alai** (☎ 305-633-6400; 3500 NW 37th Ave, Miami; tickets $1-5).

SHOPPING
Designer boutiques reign supreme in South Beach. Dig through consignment shops like the **Community Family Thrift Shop** (1261 Washington Ave), **Fly Boutique** (650 Lincoln Rd) and **Sobe Thrifty** (1435 Alton Rd) for that perfect drag-queen evening gown or vintage Cuban shirt. Along **Calle Ocho** (SW 8th St, Little Havana) are cigar stores with hand-rolled stogies, and dozens of botanicas, the spiritual shops of the Santeria religion, which carry everything from lotions and potions to candles and soap that will aid a prayer or ward off a hex.

GETTING AROUND
See the boxed text p322 for details on transport into town.

The Electrowave is an electric bus operating on a loop around the South Beach area (fares $0.25). The **Tri-Rail** (☎ 800-874-7245) commuter system serves Miami (with a free transfer to Miami's transit system) and MIA, Fort Lauderdale and its airport ($3). The Metrorail line runs through downtown Miami ($1.25), and the 'Metromover' monorail ($0.25) loops over the downtown region.

ATLANTIC COAST

Attractions beckon up and down the coast, with the oldest US city and a pair of revered party towns to the north.

FORT LAUDERDALE

Once synonymous with 'Spring Break,' this city makes a great day-trip north from Miami. Most of the action is along Las Olas Blvd and the beach, but the Riverwalk is also an enjoyable entertainment area, less than a mile from the beach. The fun **Water Bus** (☎ 954-467-6677; www.watertaxi.com; 651 Seabreeze Blvd; day pass $5) taxis the waters around Las Olas Blvd. Fort Lauderdale is also a main place to search for crewing work on a variety of outbound vessels.

The king-daddy of backpacker institutions in these parts is **Floyd's International Youth Hostel & Crew House** (☎ 954-462-0631; www.floydshostel.com; 445 SE 16th St; dm $17, d $39-59; P ⊠ 🖳), with free pickup anywhere in Fort Lauderdale and its location close to crew placement agencies.

Lester's Diner (☎ 954-525-5641; 250 Hwy 84; mains $6-8; 🕑 24hr) is proud to be a greasy-spoon kind of joint and that's what people love about it. The **Bierbrunner German Bar** (☎ 954-462-1008; 425 Fort Lauderdale Beach Rd; mains $7-15) offers authentic schnitzel, sauerbraten and bratwurst with a belly-busting array of beers.

The **Suntrust Sunday Jazz Brunch** (☎ 954-828-5985; SW 2nd St; 🕑 11am-2pm Sun) is a free outdoor jazz concert on the first Sunday of the month. There's live blues and jazz nightly at **O'Hara's Pub & Jazz Cafe** (☎ 954-524-1764; 722 E Las Olas Blvd). **Beach Place** (17 S Atlantic Blvd) offers an all-in-one experience, with clubs, restaurants and shops, and **Club Cathode Ray** (☎ 954-462-8611; 1307 E Las Olas Blvd) remains a hip gay and lesbian dance spot.

Fort Lauderdale–Hollywood International Airport (FLL; ☎ 954-359-1200) is 20 minutes from Las Olas Blvd. BCT Bus No 1 goes from the airport to the Broward Central Terminal ($1). **Airport Express** (☎ 954-561-8888) runs shuttles (shared/private $8/30). Greyhound and Amtrak stop here too.

DAYTONA BEACH

The wild hedonism of Spring Break keeps Daytona Beach firmly in backpacker guides, and frat boys' itineraries, so if you're into nonstop partying, welcome home. **Spring Break** is usually in March, as is the Harley-packed Bike Week, so good luck finding cheap accommodation during this period. Your best bet is to get a group together and find a motel room along US 1 (rates drop under $35 in summer).

Daytona Beach is home to the **Daytona International Speedway** (☎ 386-254-2700, box office 386-253-7223; 1801 W International Speedway Blvd; admission $21.50), where you can fulfill your own Nascar dreams and splurge on the **Richard Petty Driving Experience** (☎ 800-737-3889; adult $135), which straps you in the passenger seat for three heart-pounding 150mph laps around the track.

Get a waterfront glimpse of gators with your sandwich at the ramshackle **Lighthouse Landing** (☎ 386-761-9271; 4940 S Peninsula Dr; mains $5-15), and put on your best racing leather for the high-energy dance club, **Razzles** (☎ 386-257-6236; 611 Seabreeze Blvd; cover $5-10).

ST AUGUSTINE

The nation's oldest city has its fair share of cheesy attractions (like a well marking Ponce de Leon's legendary 'Fountain of Youth'), but the imposing **Castillo de San Marcos National Monument** (☎ 904-829-6506; btwn San Marcos Ave & Matanzas River; admission $5; 🕑 8:45am-4:45pm) is a great old fort, reputed to be haunted. Look closely inside the cells for the eerie handwriting of past prisoners.

Across the **Bridge of Lions** is **Anastasia State Recreation Area** (☎ 904-461-2033; 1340A Hwy A1A S; per pedestrian/car $1/3.25, campsites $18-20; 🕑 8am-dusk). Lingering is encouraged here; there's a terrific beach, campsites, easy trails, and bird-watching activities. Rentals are available for windsurfing, kayaking, canoeing and sailing.

One of the coolest hostels on the East Coast, and frankly the best reason to come to St Augustine, is the **Pirate Haus Inn & Hostel** (☎ 904-808-1999; www.piratehaus.com; 32 Treasury St; dm/d $17/50; P ⊠ 🖳), which has everything going for it – terrific downtown location, comfy lodgings, a herb garden on the rooftop terrace, and all-you-can-eat pancake breakfasts included. The 'Guess Who's Coming to Dinner' program connects guests with local families for dinner, and if you're a historical re-enactor or cross-country cyclist, there's a discount on lodging.

IF YOU'VE GOT A FEW MORE DAYS IN FLORIDA...

■ **Panama City** A 27-mile-long barrier island flanked by tourist shlock.
■ **Kennedy Space Center** Indulge your inner space geek.

Visit the **Spanish Bakery** (☎ 904-471-3046; 42½ St George St; dishes $1-4; ❤ closes 3pm) for its heavenly sweet-potato turnover. Gamblers try your luck during 'Flip Night' at **Christophers** (across the Bridge of Lions) – if you call the flipped coin, your drink is free!

EVERGLADES NATIONAL PARK

The largest subtropical wilderness in the continental US is an amazing natural resource, with excellent outdoor activities, and a highly recommended youth hostel. It's 85 miles southwest of Miami. Take either I-395 (Florida Turnpike) or US 1 south to Florida City, then SR9336 for the main entrance.

The main entrance leads to the **Ernest F Coe Visitors Center** (☎ 305-242-7700; 40001 State Rd 9336; ❤ 24hr), a 45-minute drive from downtown Miami. It has interesting interactive exhibits, films, a bookstore and fun ranger-led activities such as slough slogs, hikes, talks and canoe trips. A few miles beyond is the **Royal Palm Visitors Center** (☎ 305-242-7700), the entryway to the short Gumbo-Limbo and Anhinga trails – favorites for wildlife viewing, especially in winter.

For information, contact **Everglades National Park** (☎ 305-242-7700; www.nps.gov/ever; 40001 State Rd 9336, Homestead). The park's five visitors centers are open daily 8am to 5pm.

It's a no-brainer – bring strong repellent for fierce mosquitoes in the summer. Never provoke or feed alligators, which are common. There's also the chance of spotting the highly endangered American crocodile, especially around the vicinity of Flamingo. Poisonous snakes, which you're not likely to see, include rattlesnakes, water moccasins and coral snakes. Wear long, thick socks and lace-up boots on hikes.

Shark Valley (☎ 305-221-8776; US 41), 25 miles west of Florida Turnpike, allows you to walk or cycle ($4.50 per hour) the alligator-strewn, 15-mile paved loop road. Those with less energy or interest in getting that close to nature can take a narrated two-hour tram tour ($11). The **Ten Thousand Islands** region is terrific for canoeing and kayaking past sandy beaches and shallow, brackish lagoons.

The excellent **Everglades Hostel & Tours** (☎ 800-372-3874, 305-248-1122; www.everglades hostel.com; 20 SW 2nd Ave; campsites/dm/d $10/14/35, semi-private d $26) is accessible by public transportation from Miami Beach and the airport, and it will even pick you up from the bus station. The hostel rents canoes and bikes to explore the park at your leisure, but the 'Alabama Jack' canoe tour ($20) is fantastic.

Pitch a tent at two locations in the park: **Long Pine Key Campground** (campsites $14), 7 miles from the main entrance, which has no showers; and **Flamingo Campground** (campsites $14), at the end of the main park road, which has a small grocery. There are hiking trails nearby. Reserve campsites through the **National Park Service** (NPS; ☎ 800-365-2267); if you're willing to brave the harsh summer heat, camping is free July to August.

Restaurants are scarce here, so bring food in (just make sure to take your trash out).

DETOUR: BISCAYNE NATIONAL PARK

One of the prettiest waterfront national parks, here you can spot endangered manatee and raceful sea turtles in the four diverse ecosystems (keys, coral reef, mangrove forest and bay). Anything beyond the **Dante Fascell Visitor Center** (☎ 305-230-7275; 9700 SW 328th Street, Homestead; ❤ 9am-5pm year-round) requires a boat as the park is 95% water. Fortunately, the center runs glass-bottom boats, dive and snorkel trips, and canoe and kayak rentals. **Camping** (per 2 tents or up to 6 people $10) is nothing short of perfect solitude, with just you, the echoes of a Black-crowned Night Heron, and a blessedly pollution-free night sky for stargazing.

FLORIDA

In Homestead, hit the **Farmers' Market Restaurant** (☎ 305-242-0008; 300 N Krome Ave; mains $6-14) for big breakfasts, and seafood and veggies for lunch and dinner, and in Everglades City try **Seafood Depot** (☎ 239-695-0075; 102 Collier Ave; mains $7-17) for fried fish and shrimp.

FLORIDA KEYS

Aiming southwest from Miami, the Florida Keys are sprinkled in a line out into the Atlantic Ocean. The Overseas Highway (US 1) links the islands like a loose chain of conch shells, and the populace hangs loose too, from the fish-happy folk at **Islamorada** to the spirited descendents of Hemingway (in spirit) and his cats (at his house) in **Key West**. It ain't known for bargains (though you can cut corners with picnics and a tent), but the Keys are unique American terrain, a right-of-passage pilgrimage for South Florida travel, and are literally the end of the road.

Hostels from the Everglades and Miami areas operate frequent day and overnight journeys to Key West, and there are a couple of well-rated beachfront camping options: **John Pennekamp Coral Reef State Park** (☎ 305-451-1202; www.pennekamppark.com; MM 102.5, US 1, Key Largo; vehicle with 1 person $2.50, with 2 or more $4 plus $0.50 per person, pedestrian $1.50, campsites $19), the first underwater park in the US, is the user-friendliest way to get out onto the Florida reef, and offers reasonably priced rentals on canoes, kayaks, powerboats and private glass-bottom boats. Glass-bottom boat tours ($18) depart regularly to **Molasses Reef**. The Keys' best beach is at **Bahia Honda State Park** (☎ 305-872-2353; www.floridastateparks.org; MM 37, US 1, Big Pine Key; admission $4; tents/waterfront cabins $19/110), a 524-acre park with nature trails, ranger-led programs, bike and kayak rentals, and snorkeling tours.

Advance booking is essential for camping at either of these places.

KEY WEST

Wasted away again here? You won't be the first one crooning that you are.

Sights & Activities

A mandatory, albeit crowded, rite of passage is the nightly **Sunset Celebration** (Mallory Sq); the blowing of the conch shell kicks off a night of revelry.

Beaches here are not what you think, with most made up of a stony bottom and sulfuric smell from the drying coral. **Smathers Beach** (S Roosevelt Blvd) and **Fort Zachary Taylor State Historic Site** (☎ 305-292-6713; Southard St; admission $2.50) are decent ones. Alternatively, take advantage of the myriad snorkeling trips offered by companies such as **Sebago Key West** (www.keywestsebago.com) or visit the community **swimming pool** (cnr Catherine & Thomas Sts; admission free).

Literary aficionados make the pilgrimage to the **Hemingway House** (☎ 305-294-1136; www.hemingwayhome.com; 907 Whitehead St; admission $10; ☯ 9am-5pm), home to the author from 1931 to 1940, and now overrun with friendly six-toed cats. Key West is also loaded with small attractions from its notorious 'wrecking' history, though many aren't worth the time and fee. Save your coin and just savor the town on foot.

For spooky fun, the **Key West Ghost Tour** (☎ 305-294-9255; www.hauntedtours.com; tours $15; 8pm & 9pm) has drained more than one traveler's digital camera batteries in front of the purported haunted houses.

More down to earth, the nutty **Lloyd Mager Bike Tour** (☎ 305-294-1882; tours $18, bicycles per day $6) is run by a transplanted New Jerseyite whose dislike for cars on the island comes out during his two-hour excursions of 'hidden' Key West. Don't be alarmed at the machete in his bike basket – it comes in handy later on the tour. Tours depart from Moped Hospital and reservations are required.

Must-haves in Key West: a pair of $6 local **Kino Sandals** (107 Fitzpatrick St); a slice of heavenly Oreo-crusted Key Lime Pie from **Kelly's Caribbean Bar & Grill** (301 Whitehead St; $5); and conch fritters at the legendary **Half Shell Raw Bar** (231 Margaret St; $6).

Sleeping

Key West Youth Hostel & SeaShell Motel (☎ 305-296-5719; www.keywesthostel.com; 718 South St; dm members/nonmembers $21/24, d $110; Ⓟ 🅧 🖳) Key West's hostel won't win any awards, but its prime location near Duval St can't be questioned. It's also the cheapest place in town, with bike rentals and free pickup from the bus station.

Boyd's Key West Campground (☎ 305-294-1465; boydscampground@aol.com; 6401 Maloney Ave; campsites nonwaterfront/waterfront $45/55; 🅡) On Stock Island, 12 miles from Old Town, Boyd's

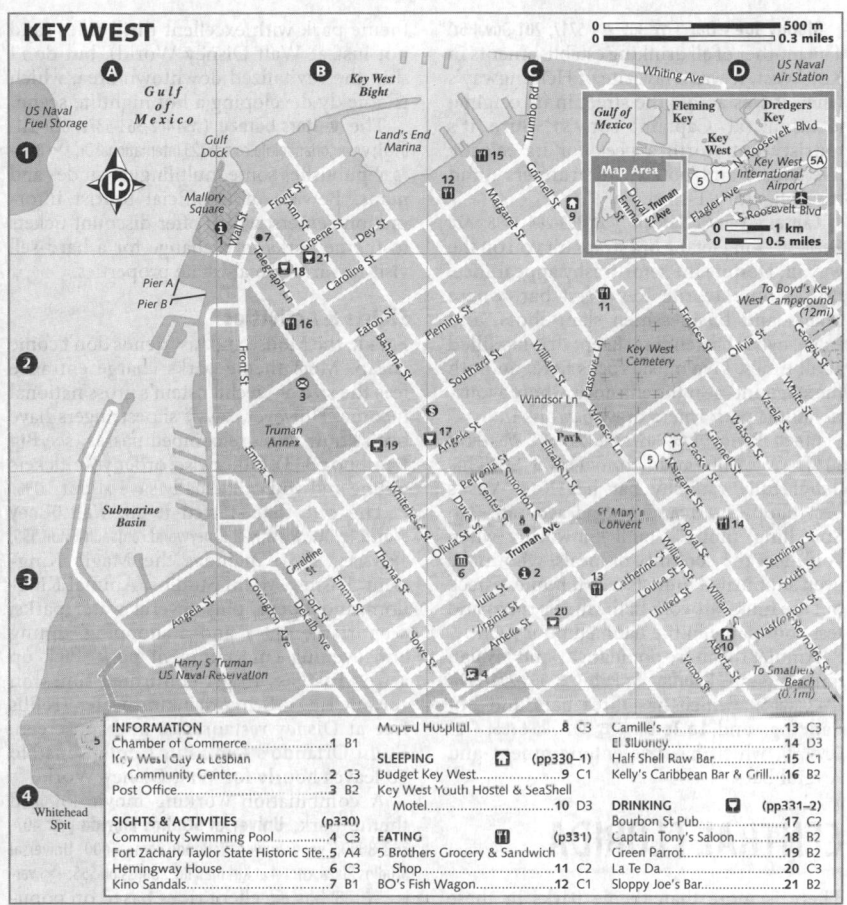

KEY WEST

INFORMATION
Chamber of Commerce....................1 B1
Key West Gay & Lesbian
 Community Center.......................2 C3
Post Office...3 B2

SIGHTS & ACTIVITIES (p330)
Community Swimming Pool..............4 C3
Fort Zachary Taylor State Historic Site..5 A4
Hemingway House.............................6 C3
Kino Sandals.....................................7 B1

Moped Hospital................................8 C3

SLEEPING 🏠 (pp330–1)
Budget Key West...............................9 C1
Key West Youth Hostel & SeaShell
 Motel...10 D3

EATING 🍴 (p331)
5 Brothers Grocery & Sandwich
 Shop..11 C2
BO's Fish Wagon..............................12 C1

Camille's..13 C3
El Siboney.......................................14 D3
Half Shell Raw Bar..........................15 C1
Kelly's Caribbean Bar & Grill.....16 B2

DRINKING 🍷 (pp331–2)
Bourbon St Pub................................17 C2
Captain Tony's Saloon....................18 B2
Green Parrot....................................19 B2
La Te Da..20 C3
Sloppy Joe's Bar..............................21 B2

doesn't offer much shade, but the grounds are immaculate and the big swimming pool provides blessed relief from the heat. In a pinch, chain hotels may bail you out.

Budget Key West (☎ 800-403-2866, 305-294-3333; www.budgetkeywest.com; 1031 Eaton St; d $90; 🛏) Upgrade your digs here in this spiffy, motel-like joint, steps from the activity at the Lands End Marina. All rooms come with microwaves, fridges, cable and a fantastically large bathroom you could do jumping jacks in. Free local calls are included.

Eating

El Siboney (☎ 305-296-4184; 900 Catherine St; mains $3-12; 🕙 11am-9:30pm Mon-Sat) Hands-down, this no-frills corner house, which might not even catch your eye, has the best Cuban food in Key West. Note that credit cards are not accepted.

Camille's (☎ 305-296-4811; 1202 Simonton St; mains $3-25) Serves swimsuit-busting breakfasts that will keep you fuelled all throughout the day.

Grab a quintessential Cuban mix sandwich at **5 Brothers Grocery & Sandwich Shop** (☎ 305-296-5205; 930 Southard St; mains $1-6; 🕙 closed Sun), or a fresh order of 'fish balls' at the shack-like **BO's Fish Wagon** (☎ 305-294-9272; 801 Caroline St).

Drinking

The 'Duval Crawl' is the famous bar-hopping activity.

Sloppy Joe's Bar (☎ 305-294-5717; 201 Duval St) The mother of all drinking establishments in Key West, it was a favorite of Hemingway's when it was across the street in its original location (at Captain Tony's). Sure it's touristy but worth a peek for its eclectic live music and potent Rumrunners…and the obligatory T-shirt.

Captain Tony's Saloon (☎ 305-294-1838; 428 Greene St) Don't let the bra straps hit you on the way in. Despite the semi-trashy appearance, this is our favorite Key West bar, where bikers and businessmen slam shots, and eagle-eyed bartenders keep drinks filled at all times. Live music rocks here, on both the stage and near the entrance, where acoustic guitar performers draw patrons in.

Green Parrot (☎ 305-294-6133; 601 Whitehead St) There is life away from Duval St! This delightfully raunchy bar has Key West's best happy hour and a dead-accurate 'No Snivelling' motto. You'll know why when you meet the cool mix of locals, who make even sunburned tourists feel at home. Check out the funky artwork in the men's room and test your game in the haunted pool room.

Among the more popular gay and lesbian hangouts are **Bourbon St Pub** (☎ 305-296-1992; 724 Duval St), which has three bars and hot dancing, and **La Te Da** (☎ 305-296-6706; 1125 Duval St), which has live entertainment and several bars.

CENTRAL FLORIDA

There is more than theme parks in these parts; happening nightlife, home-spun Cuban cigars, expansive beaches and Spanish surrealists all share billing with Uncle Walt.

ORLANDO

Utter 'Orlando,' and most think of the mouse. True, greater Orlando is an über theme park with excellent thrill rides (and not just at Walt Disney World), but don't skip the revitalized downtown area, which is quickly developing a hot nightlife scene.

The **visitors bureau** (☎ 407-363-5872, 800-551-0181; www.orlandoinfo.com; 8723 International Dr; ☯ 8am-7pm) publishes some multilingual guides and maps. Beware of unofficial tourist information centers, which offer discount tickets to theme parks in exchange for a hard-sell visit to various real-estate properties.

Sights & Activities

Face it, the Mouse and his friends don't come cheap. Most theme parks charge entrance fees the size of Liechtenstein's gross national income. However, savvy shoestringers have been know to score comped passes (see Big Bamboo p333). Otherwise, order your tickets online and you can usually save about 10%.

The one that started it all, **Walt Disney World** (WDW; www.waltdisneyworld.com; admission $55; ☯ varies; Ⓟ $7) includes the Magic Kingdom, Disney-MGM Studios, Animal Kingdom and Epcot, plus several water parks, a sports complex and a shopping, dining and evening entertainment park. Pick up a free FastPass to get confirmed times on certain rides. Bring drinking water (refills free at Disney restaurants) and sunscreen. From Orlando's Lynx Bus Center, bus No 50 leaves hourly for Walt Disney World.

A combination working movie lot and theme park, **Universal Studios Florida** (☎ 407-363-8000; www.universalorlando.com; 1000 Universal Studios Plaza, cnr I-4 at Kirkman Rd; admission $55; ☯ varies; Ⓟ $8) has excellent rides based on popular films. Its sister park, **Islands of Adventure** (admission $55) features slightly scarier roller coasters, thrilling rides and shows.

Aquatic acts are the deal at **SeaWorld** (☎ 407-351-3600; www.seaworld.com; 7007 SeaWorld Dr; admission $55, 10% off 7-day advance tickets online; Ⓟ $7), with a water-coaster ride and odd

---

SPLURGE

Dry Tortugas National Park A very long and pricey boat ride (three-hour roundtrip) from Key West, this never-completed military fort is now a prime snorkeling stop and bird-watching oasis. It's got a cool history, including its most famous prisoner, Dr Samuel A Mudd who unwittingly set John Wilkes Booth's leg after he assassinated President Lincoln. You want remote camping? You got it here, with only eight primitive campsites ($3) and, strangely enough, a lock down on toilets between 10am and 3pm. The **Yankee Freedom II** (☎ 305-294-7009; www.yankee freedom.com; adult/student with ID $130/120) leaves daily from Key West's Land's End Marina.

chances to swim with dolphins, while the classically tacky **Gatorland** (☎ 407-855-5496, 800-393-5297; www.gatorland.com; 14501 S Orange Blossom Trail; admission $20; ☺ 9am-dusk) features female wrestlers grappling the toothy critters.

Orlando before Disney is the bill at **Orange County Regional History Center** (☎ 407-836-8500; 65 E Central Blvd; adult/student with ID $7/6.50; ☺ 10am-5pm Mon-Sat, noon-5pm Sun), in a renovated 1927 courthouse that has a table into which infamous serial killer Ted Bundy scratched his name.

Orlando International Airport (☎ 407-825-2001) has easy connections to the major tourist areas via the local **Lynx Bus System** (☎ 407-841-8240; single/day/week pass $1.25/3/10). Taxis to International Dr and the theme-park corridor cost about $25 to $30, shuttle vans $15 to $20. Greyhound and Amtrak stop here.

Sleeping & Eating

Though there are hundreds of accommodations options (with the bulk of motel chains along International Dr, US 192 in Kissimmee and off I-4), travelers won't find much hostel-type lodging.

Palm Lakefront Resort & Hostel (☎ 407-396-1759; www.orlandohostels.com; 4840 W Irlo Bronson Hwy 192; dm/d/q $15/34/52) This converted motel is an exception to the motel chains. Though it looks like a dive at first glance, behind it is a coveted pool, pristine fountain, and sprawling waterfront where you can hang out on the pier. Catch Lynx buses out front to the theme parks. The owner was a former HI employee, so he knows what shoestringers need.

Big Bamboo (4849 W Irlo Bronson Hwy 192) Across the street from the hostel is this funky, crusty hotspot for theme park employees who can be generous with their comped passes. Don't miss the eye-popping assortment of cheap rum shooters.

Cafe Tu Tu Tango (☎ 407-248-2222; 8625 International Dr; mains $5-9) This multiethnic café feels like a crowded artists' loft, and the creative tapas are outstanding.

Downtown Orlando boasts a number of good, reasonably priced Vietnamese restaurants such as **Little Saigon** (☎ 407-423-8539; 1106 E Colonial Dr; mains $7-8.50) and **Pho 88** (☎ 407-897-3488; 730 N Mill Av; mains $4-8), both of which offer great spring rolls and soups of every description.

Drinking

Universal Studio CityWalk and Disney's Downtown Disney are mega entertainment, dining and shopping complexes with high covers. Save your pennies and head downtown for great, 'cover-less' happy hours. Go underground at **Lee's Tavern** (☎ 407-841-1565; 431 E Central Ave) for $1.50 drafts and free jukebox tunes, or enjoy plush couches and $4 namesake drinks at **Ybor's Martini Bar** (☎ 407-316-8006; 41 W Church St). **Room 3 Nine** (☎ 407-841-0390; 39 N Orange Ave) has an extensive lists of brews, which makes its two-for-one drafts all the better. Very close to the hostel, **Amigo's** (☎ 407-774-4334; 120 S Monterey Isle) makes fast friends with its half-price appetizers, $1 margaritas and it's raucous atmosphere.

TAMPA & AROUND

On the grittier side of the bay, Tampa is a bustling port city with a couple of notable attractions, mainly the revitalized 'Cigar Capital of the World' neighborhood of **Ybor City**, and the sweeping beaches of **St Petersburg**. There's another wonderful hostel here that's quickly topped our list of favorites too.

Learn about the previously bustling cigar industry at the **Ybor City Museum State Park** (☎ 813-247-6323; 1818 E 9th Ave, Tampa; admission $2; ☺ 9am-5pm) and watch free cigar-rolling demonstrations at **Gonzalez y Martinez Cigar Company** (☎ 813-248-8210; www.gonzalezymartinez .com; 2103 E 7th Ave, Tampa).

Gram's Place (☎ 813-221-0596; www.grams-inn -tampa.com; 3109 N Ola Ave, Tampa; dm $19-23, d $60-70; **P** ⌘) is a travel experience itself. Themed from musician Gram Parsons, this Key Westy outpost features the most unusual 'train car' dormitory; a treehouse-like roof deck; outdoor Jacuzzi; music room with pianos and musical instruments; and delightfully rare blues music piped throughout the complex. Yes, this *is* a hostel! If you don't mind a little walking and buses, it's well situated for downtown and Ybor City. Ask about discounts for longer stays.

Hyde Park historic district has two excellent, surprisingly inexpensive choices: **Cactus Club** (☎ 813-251-4089; www.cactusclub.com; 1601 Snow Ave; dishes from $7 ☺ varies) for fine Southwestern fare; and **Mise En Place Bistro** (☎ 813-839-3939; 2616 MacDill Ave; dishes from $7; ☺ closed Sun), one of Tampa's very best restaurants, which serves Floribbean cuisine.

Tampa International Airport (☎ 813-870-8700; 5503 W Spruce St) is close to downtown. Local HART bus No 30 runs from the airport to downtown Tampa (25 minutes, $1.30) and St Petersburg and the beaches (40 minutes, $1.30).

Greyhound and Amtrak stop in Tampa. **HARTline** (☎ 813-254-4278; single/day pass $1.25/3) local buses stop at the major sites and have bike racks. Electric streetcars run between downtown Tampa and Ybor City ($1).

St Petersburg

St Petersburg has the beaches that its sister city of Tampa lacks, plus the not-to-be-missed **Salvador Dalí Museum** (☎ 727-823-3767; www.salvadordalimuseum.org; 1000 3rd St S; adult/student with ID $13/7, after 5pm Thu $5; ⏱ 9:30am-5:30pm Mon-Sat, to 8pm Thu, noon-5:30pm Sun), which houses the largest collection of works by the artist outside Spain.

The **Looper trolley** links St Petersburg's museums and pier on a 30-minute narrated loop running from 11am to 5pm, starting at the St Petersburg Pier (fare $1).

Catch a baseball game in 'the Beach' section of **Tropicana Field** (☎ 888-326-7297; http://tampabay.devilrays.mlb.com; One Tropicana Field, St Petersburg), and watch Major League baseball's Tampa Bay Devil Rays play for only $6. **Pinellas Trail** (☎ 727-464-4751) is an awesome 34-mile urban biking, skating and walking trail that's oh-so-popular. It starts north of downtown at 34th St and Fairfield Ave and ends at US 19 in Tarpon Springs; pick up a free guidebook at visitors centers.

Great Lakes

HIGHLIGHTS

- **Chicago** Get a three-day CTA pass and explore the metropolis' dispersed neighborhoods (p344)
- **Milwaukee** The USA's crappy beer capital parties with gusto (p369)
- **Biggest surprise** Once denigrated as America's 'armpit', Cleveland has turned its riverfront warehouse district into a cool nightlife zone (p358)
- **Off the beaten track** The scraggly woods of Michigan's Upper Peninsula are not pristine, but the remote UP's strangeness makes it well worth a northward schlep (p367)
- **Best journey** Starting from Cleveland, do a loop-de-loop around Lake Michigan via Chicago, Milwaukee and the Upper Peninsula, with a short stop to see if Detroit is really as dismal as everyone says

FAST FACTS

- **Area:** 332,351 sq miles
- **Big cities** Chicago (population 2.9 million), Minneapolis–St Paul (2.4 million), Cleveland (1.8 million), Cincinnati (1.5 million), Detroit (955,000), Indianapolis (792,000), Milwaukee (600,000)
- **Budget** $40–80 per day
- **Costs:** campsite $10–20, hostel $18–34, burger and fries $3–8
- **Driving times** Chicago to Detroit 4 hours, Chicago to Minneapolis 7 hours, Minneapolis to Cleveland 10 hours
- **Famous for** Wrigley Field, Sears Tower, Milwaukee breweries, Abraham Lincoln sights in Springfield, 'cheesehead' Packer fans
- **Language** English with a Midwest nasal twang; various ethnic languages
- **Population** 50,074,516
- **Phrases** *Ya, you betcha* (connotes agreement or assurance in Minnesota)
- **Seasons** summer is hot and muggy; winter is brutally cold, with frequent snow storms; spring and fall are far too short
- **States** Illinois, Indiana, Ohio, Michigan, Wisconsin, Minnesota
- **Tasty treats** Cincinnati chili, Milwaukee bratwurst, Door County cherry pie, Michigan apples, Chicago deep-dish pizza
- **Time** Central and Eastern Time Zones
- **Top hostel** Mississippi Headwaters Hostel, Northern Minnesota (p379)

TRAVEL HINTS

A three-star hotel room in Chicago's Near North purchased through Priceline (www.priceline.com) can cost the same as a couple of bunks at the downtown hostel. Watch your speed on small highways, where nondescript county sheriff cars can sneak up on out-of-state vehicles. Tune into the radio for info during summer storms, when tornado 'watches' are frequent.

The Great Lakes states – Illinois, Wisconsin, Minnesota, Michigan, Ohio and Indiana – form the bulk of the Midwest. This is 'middle America,' where the beer is bad, the food is bland and the people are no-nonsense practitioners of the American way. Or so the script would have it. This part of the country springs frequent surprises on its visitors, and its oddities and eccentricities are refreshingly uncontrived.

Though predominantly a rural region, it is also known for its cities, most of which were written off as post-industrial scrap heaps only a decade or two ago. But urban comebacks are quite evident. Rust Belt jungles like Cleveland have converted warehouses into entertainment venues. Minneapolis is a hipster magnet, Milwaukee is reworking its quirky beer-and-brat image, and Detroit, still looking the neutron bomb victim, regularly spawns exciting rock, rap and electronica artists. Meanwhile Chicago thrives and hums as El trains lasso the Loop's skyscrapers.

The lakes themselves are huge inland seas, offering beaches, islands, dunes and lighthouses. Dairy cows and fruit orchards aplenty mean fresh pie and ice cream for the road-tripper seeking a quick slice of America's heartland. Most visitors come in summer, when the weather is fine for hiking, biking, canoeing and kayaking around the region's lakes and forests.

HISTORY

This fertile region has long been inhabited by advanced cultures like the Hopewell, which emerged around 200 BC, and the Mississippi River mound builders, who flourished from around AD 600. They began to decline around AD 1000, and when the first Europeans arrived in the early 17th century, the area was home to groups like the Miami, Shawnee and Winnebago.

The first Europeans were French voyageurs, who explored, traded for furs with the indigenous people and established missions and forts. But the French soon had rivals: the Ohio Company, a group of British entrepreneurs from England and Virginia, formed in 1748 to develop trade and control the Ohio Valley. Its explorations helped precipitate the French and Indian Wars (1754–61), after which Britain gained all the lands east of the Mississippi. Following the Revolutionary War, the area south of the Great Lakes became the new USA's Northwest Territory, which soon was divided into states.

The canals linking the Great Lakes to the area's river systems, built in the 1820s and '30s, along with railroad development in the next decades, stimulated settlement. But many conflicts erupted between the newcomers and the Native Americans in the region, including the bloody 1832 Black Hawk War that forced the removal of the indigenous people to areas west of the Mississippi.

Industries sprang up and grew quickly, fueled by resources of coal and iron, and urged on by Civil War demands. The work available brought huge influxes of European immigrants from Ireland (in the early and mid-19th century), Germany (in the mid- to late 19th century), Scandinavia (in the late 19th century), Italy and Russia (around the turn of the 20th century) and southern and eastern Europe (in the early 20th century). In addition, for decades after the Civil War a great number of African Americans migrated to the region's urban centers from the South.

The region prospered during WWII and through the 1950s. Then came 20 years of social turmoil and economic stagnation. The decline of manufacturing in the 1970s, particularly in the car industry, resulted in unemployment in many Rust Belt cities; Detroit and Cleveland were especially hard hit. The 1980s brought urban revitalization and a shift away from economic reliance on industry. In the past decade, growth in the light manufacturing,

---

THE BIG ISSUE: GOOD SPORTS

The Great Lakes are a sports-loving region, so it was big news when the Chicago Cubs almost made it to the World Series in 2003 (the lowly Cubs haven't been champions since before the US entered WWI). It was even bigger news when the Detroit Pistons took the NBA title away from the Los Angeles Lakers in 2004. Inter–Great Lakes football rivalries are legendary, with the Green Bay Packers historically on top.

service and high-tech sectors has meant better economic balance for the region. This process is continuing and the area's population has increased again, notably with newcomers from Asia and Mexico.

THE CULTURE

The Midwest is known as a bellwether of American sensibilities. It is the emotional median between the East Coast and California, and its inhabitants are far more rooted. They're typically perceived as deliberate and practical-minded, like to make up their own minds about things, are not easily flattered, and prefer a well reasoned argument over a hasty agreement. The American language, while not as colorful here as in the South, is used richly and with subtlety. It's no coincidence that novelist Ernest Hemingway hailed from this part of the country, where words are seldom wasted.

Midwestern cities do indulge in certain excesses, most notably Chicago's drive to outdistance the world (and specifically New York) in the skyscraper game. Chicagoans like to point out that the world's tallest structures, the Petronas Towers in Kuala Lumpur, are highest due to their crowning spires, which are merely decorative. The Sears Tower, by contrast, is a plain glass-curtain structure that reaches almost as high without the unnecessary flash. So, while discussing something so ostentatious as a 110-story skyscraper, Midwesterners are likely to emphasize function over fashion.

Underlying all Midwestern characteristics is a stolid regional pride that contrasts with the brashness of New Yorkers, the gumption of Texans, the flaky rootlessness of Californians. This level-headed pride is manifest in Wisconsin's freshly painted barns, in the tidiness of family-owned motel rooms in Michigan's Upper Peninsula, even in the way a Minneapolis housewife readily toots her horn if she catches you daydreaming at a traffic light. In Chicago, someone might say to you, 'This is the best city in the world. Anyone who tells you otherwise isn't from Chicago.' Certainly the second half of that statement is true. Chicagoans are completely infatuated with their city, and that's part of the charm of the place.

The region is more diverse than outsiders might expect. Immigrants from Mexico, Africa, the Middle East and Asia have established communities throughout the Midwest, mostly in the cities, where they are making welcomed contributions to local dining scenes. Recent generations are inevitably becoming more cosmopolitan, more adventurous. You'll notice that this part of the world is beginning to look outward for inspiration, in ways that nicely complement the region's solid sense of itself.

SPORTS & RECREATION

Baseball, football, basketball and ice hockey are all extremely popular in this part of the country. Cleveland, Detroit, Cincinnati, Chicago, Milwaukee and Minneapolis all have Major League baseball teams. All of the same cities have NFL teams (with the exception of Milwaukee, but Green Bay is nearby) and most have NBA basketball teams. Indianapolis has a football team and a basketball team. The WNBA is represented in cities throughout the region. NHL hockey teams also abound. The region offers ample hiking and biking opportunities in summer, but locals are particularly fond of canoeing on the many smaller lakes in northern Minnesota, Wisconsin and Michigan. The region's lakes and streams will also reward the angler. Popular winter sports include skiing and snowmobiling.

ARTS & ENTERTAINMENT

Chicago is one of the USA's cultural capitals, with excellent museums and consistently strong music and theater scenes. In fact, the Great Lakes region as a whole has long been fertile ground for writers and musicians. Theater is strong in Minneapolis.

During the Jazz Age Al Capone's gin joints promised ample work opportunities for musicians. Post-war black migration from Mississippi brought blues performers to Chicago, where electric blues was born and can be heard in clubs throughout the city to this day.

Detroit established itself as a soul music center in the 1960s, when the Motown label put local artists in the national limelight. Of late, the Motor City has devoted its energies in alt rock, with high-concept duo the White Stripes paving the way. Rap is also thriving in Detroit, with white rapper Eminem a most noted success.

Minneapolis produced prolific R & B artist Prince, along with a bevy of alt rockers

GREAT LAKES

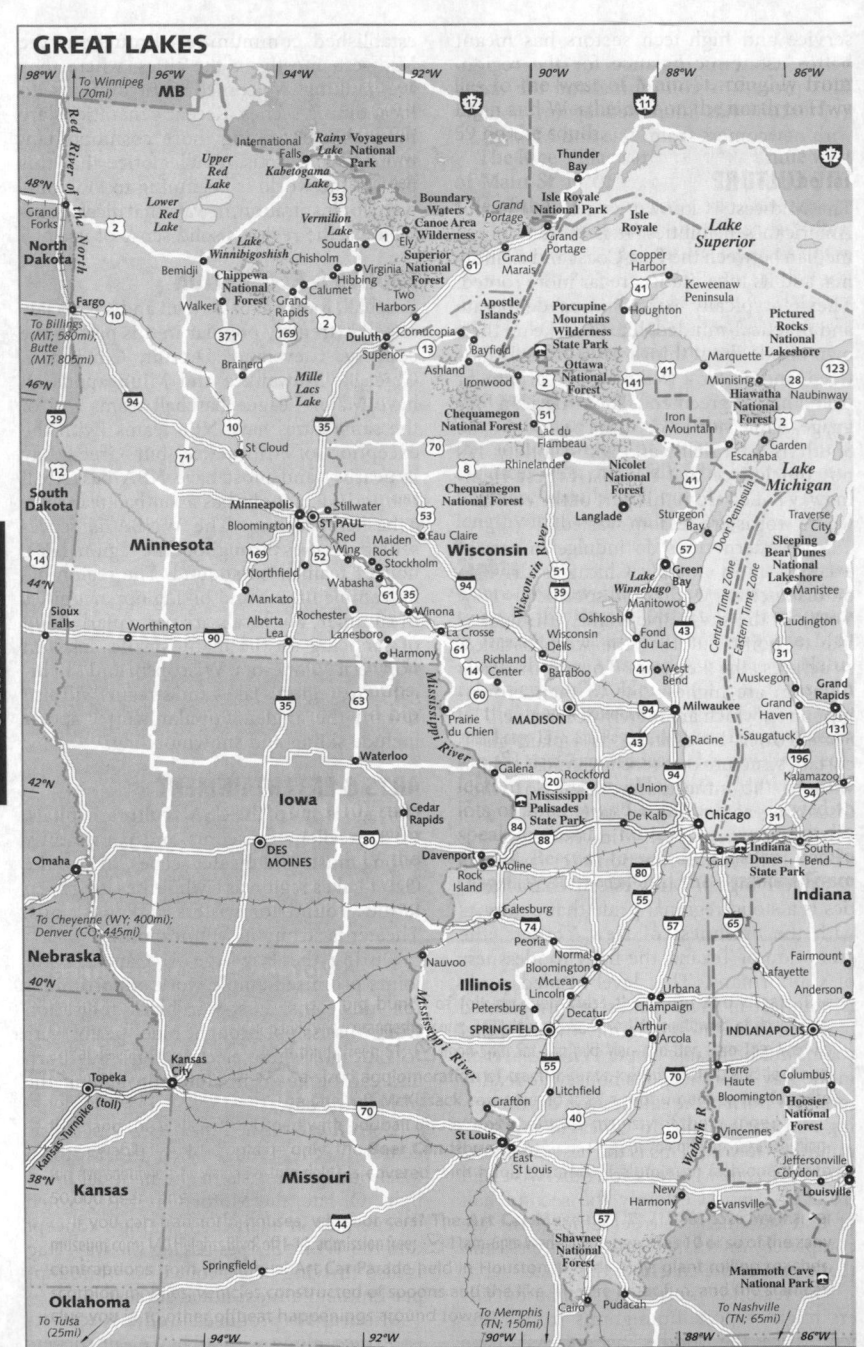

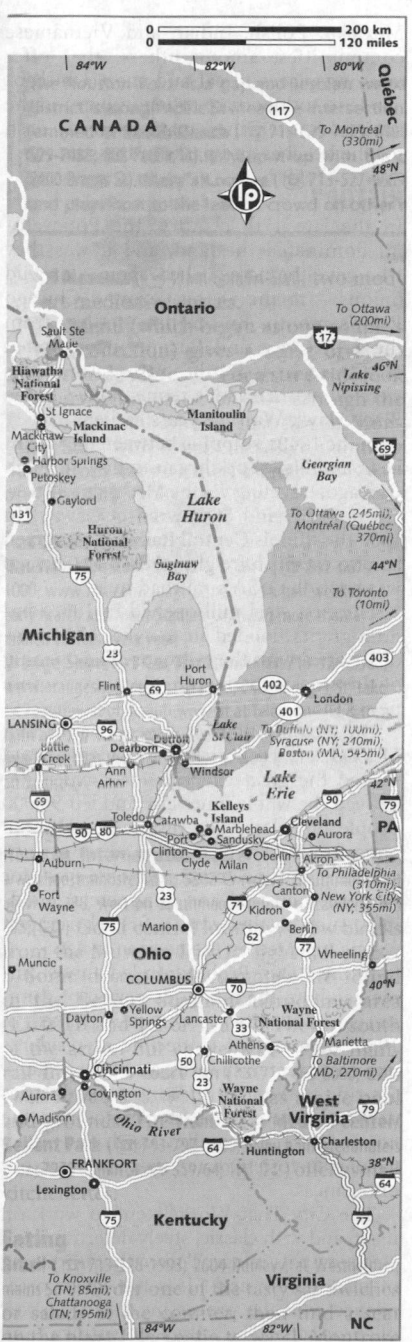

during the 1980s. Ohio bands include Guided By Voices, the Breeders and Devo. Defunct Smashing Pumpkins were a Chicago band. Jeffy Tweedy's Wilco still is.

Ernest Hemingway was born in Oak Park, Illinois. F Scott Fitzgerald came from St Paul, Minnesota. Carl Sandberg, Theodore Dreiser, Nelson Algren, Richard Wright and Saul Bellow all made Chicago their stomping grounds. Sherwood Anderson immortalized small town Ohio life, and Laura Ingalls Wilder chronicled life on the prairies of Wisconsin and Minnesota. Garrison Keillor's *Lake Wobegon Days*, Jim Harrison's *Farmer* and Elmore Leonard's *The Switch* are all contemporary tomes set around the Great Lakes.

ENVIRONMENT

Pollution is the chief environmental issue in the Midwest. The Great Lakes contain 15% of the world's fresh water, which makes them an invaluable natural resource, yet they were abused with reckless abandon during the industrialized periods through the 1960s. The shallowest of the Great Lakes, Erie, proved particularly vulnerable to pollution, which killed most of its fish by the 1970s. Images of a 'dead' Erie and a burning Cuyahoga River in Cleveland, in both cases the result of industrial pollution, helped radicalize America's environmental movement. With clean water laws and water treatment and pollution controls, fish stocks in some of the region's waterways are now rebounding. Industry has also been responsible for air pollution, particularly in the infamous Ohio Valley, where acid rain has been a problem.

Wildlife is abundant throughout the Lakes region. White-tailed deer populations are exploding in all six states, and small critters such as squirrel, opossum, raccoon and rabbit are as ubiquitous as ever. Larger mammals such as black bear, moose, beaver, elk and wolf have retreated to the dense forests of the far north. Bald eagles have made a remarkable recovery from the brink of extinction thanks to bans on certain pesticides and can be seen in huge numbers in Minnesota and along the Mississippi River.

National Parks

Several national parks and lakeshores are brushed across the Great Lakes region, including Voyageurs National Park in

Minnesota; Isle Royale and Pictured Rocks in Michigan; the Apostle Islands in Wisconsin; and Indiana Dunes. The Midwest office of the **National Park Service** (NPS; ☎ 402-221-3471; www.nps.gov) can provide general information; better is the park service's website, which has direct links and phone numbers for individual parks. Make camping reservations on the website or call ☎ 800-365-2267.

TRANSPORTATION

Chicago's O'Hare International Airport is the main air hub for the region. Heavy competition to Chicago means cheap airfares are frequently available for North American flights. Detroit, Cleveland and Minneapolis also have busy airports.

Greyhound (☎ 800-231-2222) connects major US and Canadian cities and towns.

Southeast Michigan (including Detroit) is the least expensive place in the region to rent cars. If you are traveling on major interstate highways (such as I-80 in Ohio), piles of change are useful for the tolls.

In winter, road closures due to heavy snow are not unusual. Keep a wool blanket in the car in case you get stuck in the snow or suffer a breakdown; don't rely on your car heater, which in an idling vehicle can cause carbon monoxide poisoning.

Keep an eye out for deer bounding across the road – they can make driving at night treacherous.

The national railroad network centers on Chicago, from where **Amtrak** (☎ 800-872-7245) runs trains regularly to major cities throughout the region and the rest of the USA.

CHICAGO

Chicago has a reputation to keep up as the 'most American of cities.' Along with its soaring skyscrapers and businesslike energy comes the roiling grittiness, the violence and aesthetic inconsistencies that epitomize American urban life. The Windy City also toddles as well as ever, through rain, sleet or snow. The city ranks among the USA's cultural meccas, with great theater, music, museums, architecture, sports teams and comedy clubs. Its 77 neighborhoods are bursting at the seams with vibrant Mexican, Polish, Indian and Vietnamese communities, among others, that offer amazing places to eat and shop. Chicagoans tend to hibernate (often in bars) in the blustery winter, then make a greedy dash for the beaches and parks in the summer.

HISTORY

In the late 17th century, the Potawatomi dominated the land, and it was they who gave the name 'Checaugou' – or wild onions – to the vicinity around Chicago River's mouth. By the time settlers from the East Coast and Europe incorporated as a town in 1837, the Native Americans were gone, their lands requisitioned in the Black Hawk War five years earlier.

In the 1840s, shipping between the Caribbean and New York began to flow through Chicago, traveling via the Mississippi River, Great Lakes and St Lawrence Seaway. In 1851 the Illinois Central Railroad was given land to establish freight yards, and Chicago was soon the USA's railroad hub.

The first steel mill opened in 1857, and immigrants flooded in to take jobs in industry and with the railroads. The opening of the stockyards in 1865 drew even more newcomers.

On October 8, 1871, legend has it that Mrs O'Leary's cow kicked over a lantern and started the great Chicago Fire, which destroyed the whole inner city and left 90,000 people homeless. The disaster became an opportunity to replace wide areas of substandard housing and create some space for modern industrial and commercial buildings, such as the world's first skyscraper, which appeared on the horizon in 1885.

In the 1920s, Prohibition led almost immediately to the infamous period of gangsterism. The city's population peaked in 1950, then started to decline as residents moved to outer suburbs and other states. Starting in the 1970s, traditional industries declined severely: the stockyards and the South Shore steel mills closed, and many smaller factories moved away or went out of business.

The City That Works went to work on itself, and with classic, steely determination cleaned up its image. Today, the processing of information and ideas has taken precedence over the processing and transport of products. The city's downtown and

---

GETTING INTO TOWN

Getting to the Loop from transit stations and airports is generally easy. From O'Hare Airport, the best way into town is on the CTA blue line train ($1.50), which runs 24 hours and can be caught under the Airport Hilton. From the luggage carousels, just follow the signs. If you're staying elsewhere in town, you'll need to transfer to another line, or a bus, in the Loop.

The far smaller Midway Airport is 11 miles southwest of the Loop. The CTA Orange Line runs between the two airports ($1.50). Other options to and from downtown are shuttles ($15 per person), taxis ($20 to $25) and Share-a-Ride ($14 per person).

Union Station, where Amtrak trains stop, is just a few blocks west of the Loop, within easy walking distance. CTA blue line trains stop two blocks away, at Clinton St.The main Greyhound station is not far from Union Station, also within walking distance of the Loop and close to the blue line station at Clinton St.

---

many of its neighborhoods are thriving, though areas of great poverty remain, particularly on the south side. Mayor Richard M Daley is Chicago's popular Democratic leader, continuing the tradition started by his father, who was mayor for 21 years.

ORIENTATION

The central downtown area is the Loop, a hub of skyscrapers and CTA trains. Beyond this, Chicago is a city of neighborhoods. Chicago's streets are laid out on a grid and numbered; Madison and State Sts are the grid's center. As you go north, south, east or west from here, each increase of 800 in street numbers corresponds to 1 mile. At every increase of 400, there is a major arterial street. For instance, Division St (1200 N) is followed by North Ave (1600 N) and Armitage Ave (2000 N), at which point you're 2.5 miles north of downtown. Pick up a copy of Lonely Planet's *Chicago City Map* for details.

INFORMATION
Bookstores
Savvy Traveler (☎ 312-913-9800; 310 S Michigan Ave)

Internet Access
Harold Washington Library Center (☎ 312-747-4300; 400 S State St) Free access in a grand building.
Hostelling International-Chicago (☎ 312-360-0300; 24 E Congress Parkway; per hr $6) Access your email here.

Media
The *Chicago Tribune* and *Chicago Sun-Times* are the competing dailies. Both publish excellent Friday entertainment sections. Look for the free *Reader*, a huge weekly paper out on Thursday with comprehensive event listings. *New City* is a smaller weekly freebie published on Wednesday.

Medical Services
Northwestern Memorial Hospital
(☎ 312-926-5188; 251 E Erie St)

Money
ATMs are plentiful downtown, with many concentrated near Chicago and Michigan Aves. To change money, try the currency exchange at Terminal 5 at O'Hare Airport or the following services in the Loop.
Travelex (☎ 312-807-4941; 19 S LaSalle St)
World's Money Exchange (☎ 312-641-2151; Suite M-11, 203 N LaSalle St, Loop)

Post
Fort Dearborn office (☎ 312-644-0485; 540 N Dearborn St)
Main post office (☎ 312-983-8182; 433 W Harrison St) Open 24 hours.

Telephone
For a public payphone a hotel lobby is your best bet. Even if you have a phone in your hotel room, use the lobby phone, which will charge 35¢ or 50¢ for a local call. By contrast, the same call may cost as much as $2 if you use the phone in your room.

Toilets
In the Loop and along the Miracle Mile (Michigan Ave) you will find toilets in large retail stores like Marshall Field or Borders. Sometimes, larger hotels also have rest rooms. Bars and restaurants have toilets, usually reserved for paying customers, but you can often slip in unnoticed – especially in fast-food chains.

GREAT LAKES

Water Filtration Plant
Navy Pier
Breakwater
Olive Park
Ohio St Beach
Lake Shore Park
Oak St Beach
N Lake Shore Dve
E Lake Shore Dve
Gold Coast
Seneca Park
Northwestern University Chicago Campus
Streeterville
Chicago River
E Wacker Dve
Family Golf Center
E Randolph St
Lake Path
Wildflower Works
Tennis Courts
Outdoor Music Pavilion
Millennium Park
Bank One Promenade
SBC Plaza
Wrigley Square
Illinois Center
N Columbus Dve
N Stetson Ave
River Esplanade
E North Water St
E Illinois St
E Ontario St
E Erie St
E Pearson St
E Chicago Ave
E Superior St
N Michigan Ave
E Division St
E Elm St
E Cedar St
E Bellevue Pl
E Oak St
E Walton St
E Chestnut St
N Rush St
Astor St
Mercury Chicago Skyline Cruises
E Wacker Pl
E Lake St
E Ohio St
E Grand Ave
N Wabash Ave
N State St
N Dearborn St
Clark/Division
Washington Square
Near North
Police Station
N Clark St
W Chestnut St
W Huron St
W Ohio St
W Grand Ave
W Illinois St
W Hubbard St
W Kinzie St
W Carroll Ave
W Wacker Dve
Chicago
Grand
State
Lake
Randolph
Washington
Madison
Clark
The Loop
W Madison St
W Monroe St
W Randolph St
N La Salle St
N Wells St
Merchandise Mart
N Franklin St
To Old Town; Lincoln Park; Wrigleyville; Andersonville; Far North
W Maple St
W Oak St
W Locust St
W Institute Pl
N Orleans St
W Ontario St
To Twin Anchors (0.5mi)
To Goose Island Brewery (0.3mi)
W Elm St
Cabrini-Green
N Sedgwick St
River North Gallery District
W Superior St
E Erie St
Kennedy Expressway
N Riverside Plaza
S Riverside Plaza
N West Water St
Canal St
Clinton
S Clinton
S Jefferson
S Desplaines
Richard B Ogilvie Transportation Center (Metra)
N Cleveland Ave
N Cambridge Ave
N Larrabee St
N Kingsbury St
N Howe St
Hobbie St
N Crosby St
W Division St
To DePaul University (2.2mi)
Chicago River
North Branch
Goose Island
N Hooker St
N Hickory Ave
To Ukranian Village (1.6mi)
W Chicago Ave
W Huron St
To Wicker Park; Bucktown
Grand
W Grand Ave
W Erie St
N Milwaukee Ave
W Fulton St
94
W Lake St
N Green St
W Randolph St
To Museum of Holography (50yd)
W Washington St
N Halsted
To United Center (1mi)
W Madison St
S Sangamon St
A
B
C
D
E
F
1
2
3
4

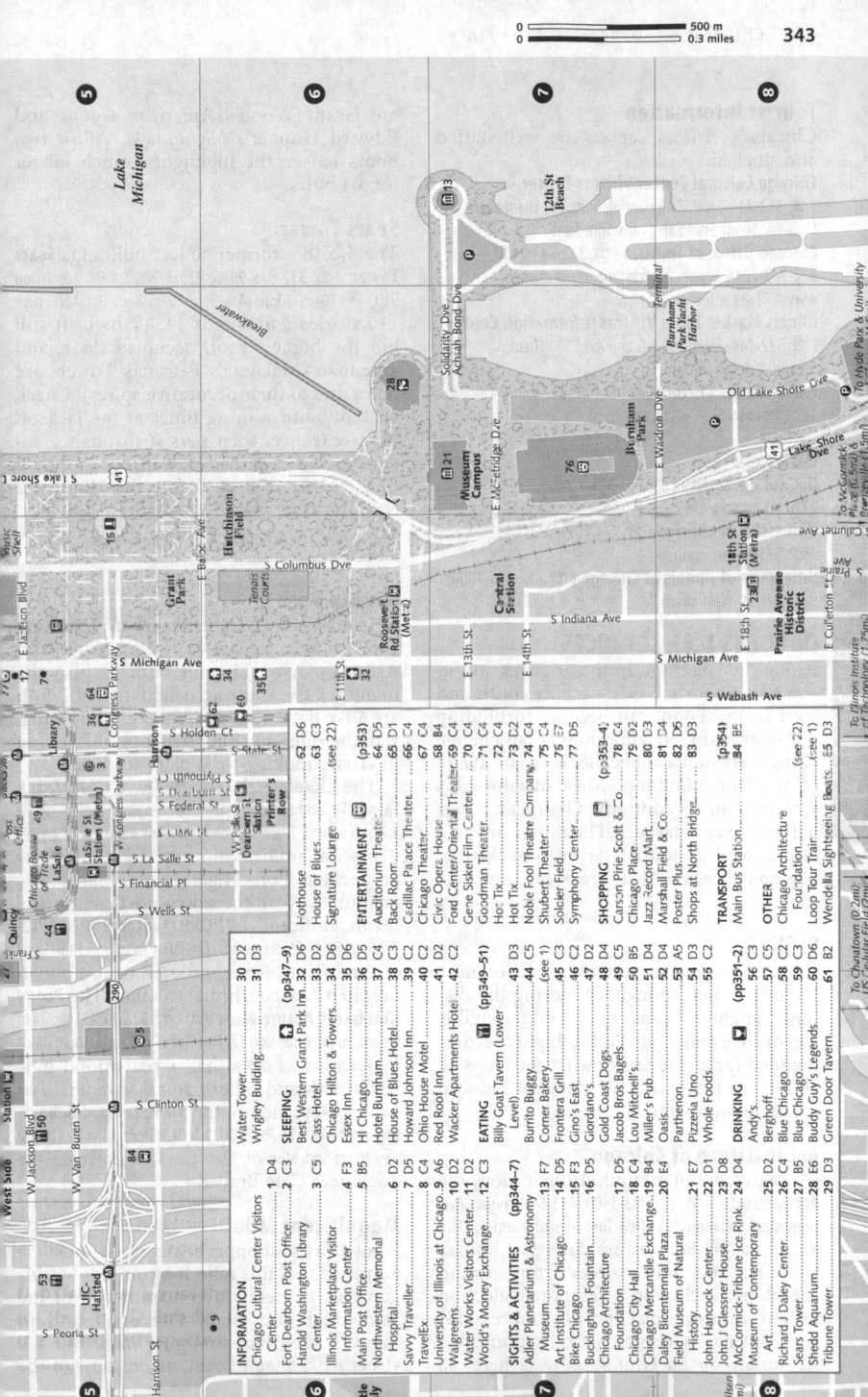

343

INFORMATION

Chicago Cultural Center Visitors Center	1 D4
Fort Dearborn Post Office	2 C3
Harold Washington Library Center	3 C5
Illinois Marketplace Visitor Information Center	4 F3
Main Post Office	5 B5
Northwestern Memorial Hospital	6 D2
Savvy Traveller	7 D5
TravelEx	8 C3
University of Illinois at Chicago	9 A6
Walgreens	10 D2
Water Works Visitors Center	11 D2
World's Money Exchange	12 C3

SIGHTS & ACTIVITIES (pp344–7)

Adler Planetarium & Astronomy Museum	13 F7
Art Institute of Chicago	14 D5
Bike Chicago	15 F3
Buckingham Fountain	16 D5
Chicago Architecture Foundation	17 D5
Chicago City Hall	18 C4
Chicago Mercantile Exchange	19 B4
Daley Bicentennial Plaza	20 E4
Field Museum of Natural History	21 E7
John Hancock Center	22 D1
John J Glessner House	23 D8
McCormick–Tribune Ice Rink	24 D4
Museum of Contemporary Art	25 D2
Richard J Daley Center	26 C4
Sears Tower	27 B5
Shedd Aquarium	28 E6
Tribune Tower	29 D3
Water Tower	30 D2
Wrigley Building	31 D3

SLEEPING (pp347–9)

Best Western Grant Park Inn	32 D6
Cass Hotel	33 D2
Chicago Hilton & Towers	34 D6
Essex Inn	35 D6
HI Chicago	36 C4
Hotel Burnham	37 C4
House of Blues Hotel	38 D3
Howard Johnson Inn	39 C2
Ohio House Motel	40 C2
Red Roof Inn	41 D2
Wacker Apartments Hotel	42 C2

EATING (pp349–51)

Billy Goat Tavern (Lower Level)	43 D3
Burrito Buggy	44 C5
Corner Bakery	(see 1)
Frontera Grill	45 C3
Gino's East	46 C2
Gold Coast Dogs	47 D2
Gordano's	48 D4
Jacob Bros Bagels	49 C5
Lou Mitchell's	50 B5
Miller's Pub	51 D4
Oasis	52 C4
Parthenon	53 A5
Pizzeria Uno	54 D3
Whole Foods	55 C2

DRINKING (pp351–2)

Andy's	56 C3
Berghoff	57 C5
Blue Chicago	58 C2
Blue Chicago	59 C3
Buddy Guy's Legends	60 D6
Green Door Tavern	61 B2

I-othouse	62 D6
House of Blues	63 C3
Signature Lounge	(see 22)

ENTERTAINMENT (p353)

Auditorium Theatre	64 D5
Back Room	65 D1
Cadillac Palace Theater	66 C4
Chicago Theater	67 C4
Civic Opera House	68 B4
Ford Center/Oriental Theater	69 C4
Gene Siskel Film Center	70 C4
Goodman Theater	71 C4
Hot Tix	72 C4
Hot Tix	73 D2
Noble Fool Theatre Company	74 C4
Solcier Field	75 E7
Symphony Center	77 D5

SHOPPING (pp353–4)

Carson Pirie Scott & Co	78 C4
Chicago Place	79 D2
Jazz Record Mart	80 D3
Marshall Field & Co	81 C4
Poster Plus	82 D5
Shops at North Bridge	83 D3

TRANSPORT (p354)

Main Bus Station	84 BE

OTHER

Chicago Architecture Foundation	(see 22)
Loop Tour Train	(see 1)
Wendella Sightseeing Boats	85 D3

Tourist Information

Chicago's visitors centers are well-staffed and stocked.

Chicago Cultural Center Visitors Center (☎ 312-744-2400; 77 E Randolph St; ⊙ 10am-6pm Mon-Fri, 10am-5pm Sat, 11am-5pm Sun)

Chicago Office of Tourism (☎ 312-744-2400, 877-244-2246; www.cityofchicago.org/tourism or www.877chicago.org)

Illinois Market Place Visitors Information Center (☎ 312-744-2400; 600 E Grand Ave; ⊙ 10am, closing varies 7-10pm)

Water Works Visitors Center (☎ 312-744-2400; 163 E Pearson St; ⊙ 7:30am-7pm)

Universities

DePaul University (☎ 773-325-7000; 2320 N Kenmore Ave)

University of Chicago (☎ 773-702-1234; 5801 S Ellis Ave, South Side)

University of Illinois at Chicago (☎ 312-996-7000; S Halsted St, West Loop)

DANGERS & ANNOYANCES

Along the lakefront, in major parks and in some neighborhoods, especially south and west of the Loop, can become forbidding places at night. Neighborhoods can change completely in just a few blocks, so be aware of your surroundings. Most of Chicago's violent crime is committed by street gangs battling over drug turf. The most common crimes against tourists are pickpocketing, bag snatching, vehicle break-ins and bike theft.

SIGHTS

Chicago's main attractions are in or near the city center, though sauntering the distant neighborhoods like Andersonville, Devon Ave and Hyde Park is highly recommended for a true feel of what the city's all about. Students with ID often get reduced museum admission.

Art Institute of Chicago

Chicago's premier cultural institution, the **Art Institute** (☎ 312-443-3600; 111 S Michigan Ave; suggested donation $10, free Tue; ⊙ 10:30am-4:30pm Mon-Fri, to 8pm Tue, 10am-5pm Sat & Sun) houses treasures and masterpieces from around the globe, including a fabulous selection of both impressionist and Postimpressionist paintings. Georges Seurat's pointillist *A Sunday on La Grande Jatte* is here; so

are Grant Wood's *American Gothic* and Edward Hopper's *Nighthawks*. Allow two hours to see the highlights, much longer for art buffs.

Sears Tower

The world's former tallest building, **Sears Tower** (☎ 312-875-9696; 233 S Wacker Dr; admission $10; ⊙ 10am-10pm May-Sep, 10am-8pm Oct-Apr) has 110 stories and stands 1454ft high. It still has the highest roof, occupied floor, and antennae (Malaysia's Petronas Towers are taller due to their decorative spires). Check visibility and waiting times at the Jackson Blvd entrance, then persist through a security check, series of waiting rooms, a film and more lines before the 70-second elevator ride to the 103rd-floor Skydeck. The John Hancock Center (p345) may be a better choice.

Lincoln Park

Lincoln Park is an urban oasis spanning 1200 leafy acres between North Ave and Ardmore Ave. 'Lincoln Park' is also the name for the abutting neighborhood. Both are alive day and night with people skating, walking dogs, pushing strollers and driving in circles looking for a place to park.

The **Lincoln Park Zoo** (☎ 312-742-2000; 2200 N Cannon Dr; admission free; ⊙ 10am-5pm summer, 10am-4:30pm winter, 10am-6:30pm Sat & Sun summer) is popular with families who stroll by the habitats of gorillas, lions, tigers and other exotic creatures. Near the zoo's north entrance, the magnificent 1891 **Conservatory** (☎ 312-742-7736; 2391 N Stockton Dr; admission free; ⊙ 9am-5pm) coaxes palms, ferns and orchids to flourish despite Chicago's brutal weather. The **Peggy Notebaert Nature Museum** (☎ 773-755-5100; 2430 N Cannon Dr; admission $7, free Thu; ⊙ 9am-4:30pm Mon-Fri, 10am-5pm Sat & Sun) has a year-round butterfly park and other natural wonders. For a duck's-eye view of the park, try **paddleboating** (☎ 312-742-2038; 2021 N Stockton; 30 min $10-15; ⊙ 10am-5pm Mon-Fri, 10am-6pm Sat & Sun) from the dock near Cafe Brauer.

Magnificent Mile

Known as a shopper's mecca, it must be admitted that this mile-long strip of Michigan Ave is merely a concentration of the same high-end chain retailers found in many a suburban shopping mall. But the street *looks* magnificent, as do most of the people strolling its sidewalks, and there's always a hum of excitement here.

Take a close look when passing by the gothic **Tribune Tower** (435 N Michigan Ave) to see chunks of the Taj Mahal, Parthenon and other famous structures embedded in the lower walls. The white terracotta exterior of the **Wrigley Building** (400 N Michigan Ave) glows day and night.

Gold Coast

Starting in 1882, Chicago's wealthy flocked to this neighborhood flanking the lake between Chicago and North Aves. Within 40 years, most of the Gold Coast was covered with mansions. Today the neighborhood giant is the 1127ft-tall **John Hancock Center** (☎ 312-751-3681; 875 N Michigan Ave; admission $9.50; ⟨⟩ 9am-11pm), which has a great 94th-floor observatory that's often less crowded than the one at Sears Tower and the view of the Loop and Lake Michigan is superior. Better yet, skip the observatory and head to the 96th-floor Signature Lounge, where the view is free if you buy a drink ($6 to $11).

The 154ft-tall, turreted **Water Tower** (cnr Chicago & Michigan Aves) is a defining city landmark;

it was the sole downtown survivor of the 1871 Great Fire.

The **Museum of Contemporary Art** (☎ 312-280-2660; 220 E Chicago Ave; adult/student $10/6, free Tue; ⟨⟩ 10am-8pm Tue, 10am-5pm Wed-Sun) displays head-scratching works by Franz Kline, René Magritte, Cindy Sherman and Andy Warhol.

To sample the Gold Coast's former grandeur, saunter down **N Astor St**, where gems include the 1887 mansions at 1308–1312 N Astor St, by architect John Wellborn Root; the Georgian Revival house at 1355 N Astor St; Frank Lloyd Wright's Charnley-Persky House at 1365 N Astor, which he proclaimed the 'first modern building'; and the 1929 art deco Russell House at 1444 N Astor St.

Grant Park

A plan by the Olmsted Brothers architectural firm turned a marshy lakefront wasteland into a park that has the formal lines of Versailles.

Its centerpiece, **Buckingham Fountain** (cnr Congress Parkway & Columbus Dr), is one of the world's largest, with a 1.5 million gallon capacity.

GREAT LAKES

A CITY OF NEIGHBORHOODS

Chicago is a kaleidoscope of neighborhoods encompassing every ethnic, racial and religious background. You really haven't made much of an effort to know the Windy City unless you've ventured beyond the Loop and Near North areas. Here are some neighborhoods worth exploring:

- **Pilsen** (Blue Line to 18th St) – Long a first stop for immigrants, this neighborhood is now predominantly Latino. 18th St has scores of taquerías, bakeries and small shops selling everything from devotional candles to Mariachi CDs.
- **Andersonville** (Red Line to Argyle St) – New Chinatown, around Argyle St, bustles with Vietnamese, Thai and Chinese eateries, while great bars along N Clark St host creative types, gays and yuppies who live in the neighborhood.
- **Wicker Park, Bucktown & Ukranian Village** (Blue Line to Damen Ave) – These three 'hoods are all in various stages of early gentrification, where young creative types are making a difference. Milwaukee Ave in Bucktown is lined with interesting shops, bars and restaurants.
- **Chinatown** (Red Line to Cermak–Chinatown) – This old neighborhood remains vibrant as ever. Head out early in the day for dim sum before perusing small shops selling herbs, tea and almond cookies.
- **Wrigleyville** (Red Line to Addison) – The streets around Wrigley Field are a Cubs fan's fantasyland, with sports bars and wonderful restaurants. A few blocks over, along Halsted St, Chicago's largest gay community has set up shop.
- **Far North** (Western Ave 49B bus) – Chicago's northernmost neighborhood is home to Indian women in jewel-toned saris, Muslim men in white skull-caps, Nigerian women in bright print robes, and Orthodox Jews in black yarmulkes. Good eating and interesting shopping can be done along Devon Ave.

The fountain squirts from 10am to 11pm April to October, accompanied at night by multicolored lights and music every hour on the hour.

Just north, the new **Millennium Park** (Michigan Ave, btwn Monroe & Randolph Sts) is slowly being completed. Visitors can ice skate at the outdoor rink during winter. Frank Gehry designed the band shell.

Museum Campus

This lakefront area south of Grant Park has three significant attractions side by side. Note that a City Pass costs $49 and will get you into all of these museums, plus the Art Institute and the Hancock Observatory.

SHEDD AQUARIUM

Top draws at the famous **Shedd Aquarium** (☎ 312-939-2438; 1200 S Lake Shore Dr; admission $23; ☾ 9am-5pm Mon-Fri Sep-May, 9am-6pm Mon-Fri Jun-Aug, 9am-6pm Sat & Sun year-round) include the Oceanarium, with its beluga whales and frolicking white-sided dolphins, and the new shark exhibit, where there's just five inches of Plexiglas between you and 30 or so fierce-looking swimmers.

FIELD MUSEUM OF NATURAL HISTORY

The mammoth **Field Museum** (☎ 312-922-9410; 1400 S Lake Shore Dr; admission $10; ☾ 9am-5pm) houses everything but the kitchen sink. Highlights include 'Africa,' a walk-through exhibit that moves from city streets to Saharan sand dunes, culminating in the hold of a slave ship; and Sue, the largest *Tyrannosaurus rex* skeleton yet discovered.

ADLER PLANETARIUM & ASTRONOMY MUSEUM

Touch a 1000lb meteorite in the interactive galleries at the **Adler Planetarium** (☎ 312-922-7827; 1300 S Lake Shore Dr; admission $13; ☾ 9:30am-4:30pm Mon-Fri, 9am-4:30pm Sat & Sun), then view the cosmos in a digital sky show controlled from your chair's armrest.

Mexican Fine Arts Center Museum

This vibrant **museum** (☎ 312-738-1503; 1852 W 19th St; admission free; ☾ 10am-5pm Tue-Sun), in Pilsen, is the largest Latino arts institution in the US. The art ranges from classical themed portraits to piles of carved minibus tires, and Mexico's turbulent, revolutionary history is well represented.

Willie Dixon's Blues Heaven

In a humble building in the Near South Side, the Chess brothers started a recording studio in 1957 and set out to record a great number of blues musicians who had migrated north from Mississippi and elsewhere. Muddy Waters, Howlin' Wolf, Bo Diddley, Chuck Berry and many other blues legends cut tracks here. Now incarnated as **Willie Dixon's Blues Heaven** (☎ 312-808-1286; 2120 S Michigan Ave; admission $10; ☾ 10am-4pm Mon-Fri, 11am-3pm Sat), it holds a collection of blues memorabilia.

Museum of Holography

This **museum** (☎ 312-226-1007; 1134 W Washington Blvd; admission $4; ☾ 12:30-4:30pm Wed-Sun) contains the world's largest collection of holograms (three-dimensional imaging), as well as an on-site school and laboratory dedicated to the science.

Hyde Park

At the prestigious **University of Chicago**, the heart of the Hyde Park enclave, graduate students outnumber undergrads, and some 73 Nobel prizes have been won. The bookish residents give the place an insulated, pleasant, small-town air. The area is easily reached via Metra Electric trains from the Randolph St station to 55th–56th–57th St station.

Of the numerous buildings that Frank Lloyd Wright designed in the Chicago area, none is more famous or influential than the **Robie House** (☎ 773-834-1847; 5757 S Woodlawn Ave; admission $9; tours 11am, 1pm & 3pm Mon-Fri, continuous 11am-3:30pm Sat & Sun). The resemblance of its horizontal lines to the flat landscape of the Midwestern prairie became known as the Prairie style. Inside are 174 art glass windows and doors.

The **DuSable Museum of African American History** (☎ 773-947-0600; 740 E 56th Pl; admission $3, free Sun; ☾ 10am-5pm Mon-Sat, noon-5pm Sun) has good artworks and exhibits on African Americans from slavery to the civil-rights era.

Cemeteries

Graceland Cemetery (☎ 773-525-1105; 4001 N Clark St, Andersonville; admission free; ☾ 8:30am-4:30pm Mon-Sat) is the resting place of local millionaires (George Pullman), architects (Daniel Burnham, Louis Sullivan) and retail magnates (including Marshall Field). Get a free map at the office to navigate the swirling paths.

Rosehill Cemetery (☎ 773-989-2170; 5800 N Ravenswood Ave, Andersonville; admission free; 🕒 8am-5pm) is Chicago's oldest and largest. WW Boyington designed the entrance gate in 1864 using the same gothic style as he used for the Water Tower. Free tours are offered at 10am on the first and third Saturday of the month, May to November.

ACTIVITIES

Tucked away in Chicago's 552 parks are public golf courses, ice rinks, swimming pools and more. Activities are free or low-cost, and the needed equipment is available for rent in the parks. Contact the **Chicago Park District** (☎ 312-742-7529; www.chicagoparkdistrict.com) for park information.

Bicycling

Chicago's flatness and 18.5-mile lakefront path make it a great city for cyclists. For rentals, try **Bike Chicago** (☎ 312-595-9600; www.bikechicago.com; 600 E Grand Ave, Navy Pier & North Ave Beach; bikes per day $34; 🕒 9am-7pm Apr-Oct, extended hours in summer). The company provides free tour maps and also rents in-line skates.

Boating

The **Chicago Sailing Club** (☎ 773-871-7245; www.chicagosailingclub.com; 2712 N Campbell Ave) offers all levels of instruction, including five-day beginner's classes for $395, or sailboats to rent from $35/55 per hour on weekdays/weekends. Departure from Belmont Harbor, where Belmont Ave meets Lake Michigan.

Kayaking

For a unique perspective, kayak down the Chicago River with **Wateriders Adventure Agents** (☎ 312-953-9287; www.wateriders.com) for $45 per person. Various tours take in architectural sights and ghost and gangster spots. Beginners are welcome.

Ice Skating

The Chicago Park District operates a first-class winter rink at **Daley Bicentennial Plaza** (☎ 312-742-7650; on the south side of E Randolph St in the park) and at the **McCormick-Tribune Ice Rink** (55 N Michigan Ave) in Millennium Park. Skate rental is just a few bucks.

TOURS

For a choice of excellent architectural tours by foot, bus or boat, contact the **Chicago Architecture Foundation** (☎ 312-922-3432; www.architecture.org; 875 N Michigan Ave, John Hancock Center, or 224 S Michigan Ave; tours year-round) The tours are highly recommended, especially those by boat; costs and times vary.

The 40-minute **Loop Tour Train** (1st fl, Chicago Cultural Center Visitors Center, 77 E Randolph St; tours 11:35am-1:35pm Sat May-Sep), guided by an Architecture Foundation docent, is a great way to see Chicago's buildings and learn the history of the elevated train (aka 'El'). Tickets for the free tours are first-come, first-served and must be obtained in person.

Chicago Greeter (☎ 312-744-8000; www.chicagogreeter.com; tours year-round) is a service in which a local Chicagoan takes you on a free personal tour customized by theme (architecture, history, gay and lesbian and more) or neighborhood. It lasts two to four hours, either by foot or complimentary public transportation, and must be reserved seven business days in advance.

Wendella Sightseeing Boats (☎ 312-337-1446; 400 N Michigan Ave; admission $18; Apr-Nov) offers 1½-hour tours of the river and lake. Various other lake cruises leave seasonally from Navy Pier.

FESTIVALS & EVENTS

Chicago has a full events calendar year-round, but the biggies are held in the summer. For exact dates and other details, call the **Mayor's Office of Special Events** (☎ 312-744-3315; www.cityofchicago.org/specialevents). Each of the following listed events is free and held downtown on a weekend, unless noted otherwise.

Blues Festival Chicago gets down for four days each June with the biggest free blues fest in the world.

Gospel Festival You'll be floored by gut-wrenching performances by singers straining to please Him, with a capital H. It's held in Grant Park in June.

Jazz Festival Big names on the national jazz scene converge on Chicago in September for this four-day fest.

Latin Music Festival The merengue, salsa and other Latin rhythms are as sultry as the late August weather.

Taste of Chicago Bridging June and July, this 10-day gastro-fest puts dozens of ethnic cuisines and celebrated chefs into tents and food stalls in Grant Park.

SLEEPING

Chicago is not known to be a cheap place to sleep, but there are ways around the exorbitant costs if you are flexible and creative. The best way is to reserve a room through an

Internet clearinghouse like Priceline (www .priceline.com). At the time of writing, we were seeing three-star rooms in the Near North and South Loop areas going for $50 (double occupancy) during the week. This is a tremendous deal when you consider a bunk at the downtown hostel costs almost as much. On weekends, and when big conventions trample through town, your options become much slimmer, so plan ahead to avoid unpleasant surprises. Taxes add 14.9% to the rates. The closest decent campgrounds are at least an hour away in any direction.

Hotels in **The Loop** are convenient to Grant Park, the museums and business district, but not near the best nightlife. Popular with visitors, the **Near North/Gold Coast** neighborhood has a plethora of places for eating, drinking, shopping and entertainment. Hotels in **Lincoln Park** are often cheaper than the big ones downtown and are near hip nightlife, with the Loop a short El ride away.

Hostels

HI Chicago (☎ 312-360-0300; www.hichicago.org; 24 E Congress Parkway; dm from $33; P $18 ⊠ 🖳) The prices are outrageous for a hostel, but this is far and away Chicago's best. It is immaculate, very central, and offers all kinds of bonuses, such as a staffed information desk, free volunteer-led tours, discount passes to museums and shows, an attached café and luggage storage ($1 per bag). The simple dorm rooms have six to 12 beds and attached bathrooms.

Chicago International Hostel (☎ 773-262-1011; www.chicagointernationalhostel.com; 6318 N Winthrop Ave; dm $17) Near Loyola University, this major year-round hostel housed in a 1960s building lies three blocks south of the Loyola El stop on Sheridan, then two blocks east. Though the location is safe enough, you're far from the action. On the El it's 35 minutes to Chicago Ave.

Arlington House (☎ 773-929-5380; www.arlington house.com; 616 W Arlington Pl; dm $24, d $54-68) This hostel, in an old brick building, has a great location in the heart of Lincoln Park. The cheaper private rooms have shared bathroom. The rooms have been renovated, but parking can be ugly.

International House of Chicago (☎ 773-753-2270; ihouse.uchicago.edu; 1414 E 59th St; s/d $50/82) At the University of Chicago, this beautiful

student dormitory lets out single and double rooms when available – typically in summer. Guests will enjoy the posh lounge, library and courtyard. There's a café and a kitchen, linen is included and downtown is 20-minutes away on the Metra train.

Hotels

Ohio House Motel (☎ 312-943-6000; 600 N LaSalle St; r $85-95; P ⊠) Smack in the heart of the city this vintage 1960s motor lodge certainly stands out. The rooms are just fine, if faded, and the attached coffee shop is a classic. The free parking is a considerable perk.

Howard Johnson Inn (☎ 312-664-8100; 720 N La-Salle St; r $79-139; P ⊠) The HoJo is another '60s-era motor lodge, complete with free parking. Again, we're talking timeless, not state-of-the-art, motel rooms.

House of Two Urns (☎ 773-235-1408, 877-896-8767; www.twourns.com; 1239 N Greenview Ave, Wicker Park; r $69-139; P ⊠) This excellent B&B is distinctive on several fronts: it's owned by artists and filled with antiques and original art, and it's located in Wicker Park near the hipster restaurant/bar scene. Take the CTA Blue Line to Division.

Cass Hotel (☎ 312-787-4030, 800-227-7850; www .casshotel.com; 640 N Wabash Ave; s $69-89, d $89-114; P $19 ⊠) The Cass isn't as flashy as many of its high-end neighbors, but its small, clean rooms win the day for their reasonable prices, as does the prime location in the Near North. It also has an offbeat bar that's good for a nightcap.

Red Roof Inn (☎ 312-787-3580; 162 E Ontario St; s/d $100/120; P $22 ⊠) Red Roof Inn has a great location just east of Michigan Ave, occupies a handsome 1930s building, and has the chain's dependable, utilitarian rooms.

Essex Inn (☎ 312-939-2800, 800-621-6909; www .essexinn.com; 800 S Michigan Ave; r $59-199; P $21 ⊠ 🖳 🖲) The Essex, opposite Grant Park just south of the Loop, has nice amenities – indoor pool, Internet access and free shuttle to the Miracle. Even nicer, the rooms and lobby have a dated feel, like maybe off the set of the *Bob Newhart Show*, which helps keep rates low. A pretty good deal.

Willows Hotel (☎ 773-528-8400, 800-787-3108; www.cityinns.com; 555 W Surf St; r $79-139; P $18 ⊠) In Lincoln Park, the Willows is a stylish little place with antique furnishings, and is within walking distance of the beach. The owners have two similar properties in

SPLURGE!

Chicago's worth a splurge, so why not go all the way and treat yourself to a night in one of the city's legendary posh hostelries. The following are fully outfitted with lavish furnishings, spit-spot service and cruise ship amenities.

House of Blues Hotel (☎ 312-245-0333, 800-235-6397; www.loewshotels.com; 333 N Dearborn St; r from $150; P $30 ⚄) You won't be wallowing in self-pity in this hipster haven, with its goofy and colorful decor.

Hotel Burnham (☎ 312-782-1111, 877-294-9712; www.burnhamhotel.com; 1 W Washington St; r $139-250; P $29 ⚄) The Burnham is housed in the landmark 1890s Reliance Building, precedent for the modern skyscraper. Discounts can drop rates as low as $99 during off-peak times.

Chicago Hilton & Towers (☎ 312-922-4400; 720 S Michigan Ave; s/d from $179/204; P $28 ⚄ 🍸) The Hilton was the largest hotel in the world when it opened in 1927. You can often get big discounts on weekends.

the neighborhood: **City Suites Hotel** (☎ 773-404-3400, 800-248-9108; 933 W Belmont Ave; r $79-139; P $18 ⚄), near the CTA Red Line Belmont station, and the **Majestic Hotel** (☎ 773-404-3499, 800-727-5108; 528 W Brompton Ave; r $79-139; P $19 ⚄), close to Wrigley Field and the Halsted St gay scene.

Wacker Apartments Hotel (☎ 312-787-1386; 111 W Huron Ave; s/d $55/60) If the name hasn't already scared you off, you might consider this slightly dicey cost-saving option. Yes, the Wacker is a residential hotel, and, yes, some of the residents are likely to be recent divorces or otherwise 'between lives.' Maybe you can live with it for a few nights.

EATING

Chicago is a great food town, and if you can you really ought to stretch the budget a bit to experience what the city can offer. The cultural hodgepodge that gives Chicago's neighborhoods their character translates into a mind-reeling, diverse restaurant scene. The city also has its own vaunted traditions, like deep-dish pizza, baby-back ribs and hot dogs buried in half a dozen toppings.

The Loop

Burrito Buggy (☎ 312-362-0199; 206 W Van Buren St; mains $4-7; ☽ lunch only) This quick and cheap lunch option serves big burritos, some of them containing unexpected ingredients. The barbecue chicken burrito includes mashed potatoes. The veggie burritos kick ass.

Oasis (☎ 312-558-1058; 21 N Wabash Ave; mains $3-6; ☽ until 5pm Mon-Sat) Hidden inside the Wabash Jewelers Mall is this dark little counter.

The falafel is crisped to perfection and the hummus is the best this side of Amman. Eat in or carry out to the nearby parks.

Miller's Pub (☎ 312-645-5377; 134 S Wabash Ave; mains $7-24; ☽ 11-4am) This bar/restaurant, with its entry shaded by the El tracks, just feels like Chicago. Celebrity photos, sports on TV, a friendly crowd and sweet ribs and bar food on the menu. Remember Miller's, as its late-late hours are sure to come in handy.

Jacob's Bros Bagels (☎ 312-922-2245; 53 W Jackson Blvd; bagels $1-4; ☽ lunch only) Chicago's not known for its bagels, but bagels are known to be cheap and filling. This place will fortify you for those long walks around town.

Corner Bakery (☎ 312-201-0805; 78 E Washington St; sandwiches $4-6) This chain of gourmet sandwich stores seems to occupy every corner in the Loop and is good for a fine sandwich or bowl of chili. At this outlet, in the Cultural Center, you can take your eats to the adjacent Atrium and listen to free lunchtime music.

Near North & Gold Coast

Billy Goat Tavern (☎ 312-222-1525; lower level, 430 N Michigan Ave; burgers $2-4) This bar and burger joint is the legendary haunt of *Tribune* and *Sun-Times* reporters. Only the dimmest of bulbs orders fries with their 'cheezborger' (recall John Belushi's famous *Saturday Night Live* skit: 'No fries – chips!').

Gold Coast Dogs (☎ 312-917-1677; 159 N Wabash Ave; mains $3-6) If you eat meat, you'll have to try a Chicago-style hot dog here. Your typical Chicago dog is piled high with onions, relish, mustard, hot peppers, celery salt and a warm pickle spear. The hotdog stand shares tables with a fried chicken chain, so

GREAT LAKES

CHICAGO DEEP-DISH PIZZA

Chicago-style pizza is absolutely nothing like any pizza that was ever tossed in Italy; lofting one of these deep-dish leviathans could actually hurt someone. To prepare their mammoth pies, pizza chefs line a special pan – not unlike a frying pan without a handle – with dough and then pile on the toppings. These include a red sauce, chopped plum tomatoes and a mountain of shredded, yellow mozzarella cheese. Of course, all the usual pizza toppings can be crammed into a Chicago pizza. Pizzeria Uno founder Ike Sewell claims to have invented Chicago-style pizza in 1943, but the competition won't admit having got the idea from Ike.

Here's where to go for the good stuff (the following are chains, found all over town):

Giordano's (☎ 312-951-0747l; 730 N Rush St; mains $8-26) Order the 'special,' stuffed with sausage, mushrooms, green peppers and onions.

Pizzeria Uno (☎ 312-321-1000; 29 E Ohio St; mains $8-26) Light, flaky crusts wrapped around piles of cheese and a herb-laced tomato sauce.

Gino's East (☎ 312-943-1124; 633 N Wells St; mains $7-25) The pizza's great, with a crispy cornmeal crust, and scribbling on the restaurant's walls is not only fun, it's condoned.

---

order take-out and take yer dog for a walk. You can also grab a burger here.

Frontera Grill (☎ 312-661-1434; 445 N Clark St; mains $12-22; ☺ Tue-Sun) Celebrity chef Rick Bayless's restaurant is a worthy splurge. The kitchen prepares innovative, high-end Mexican fare.

Whole Foods (☎ 312-932-9600; 50 W Huron St) This large supermarket has lots of organic and deli items.

Old Town

Twin Anchors (☎ 312-266-1616; 1655 N Sedgwick St; slab of ribs $20) This hugely popular, neighborhood tavern draws hordes of people on weekends to get at the baby back ribs. The huge slab is a splurge unless you're willing to share with a partner.

Lincoln Park

For those seeking out a raucous late-night munchie, two places do it well.

Wiener's Circle (☎ 773-477-7444; 2622 N Clark St; items $2-4; ☺ 11-4am Sun-Thu, 11-6am Fri & Sat) Famous for its unruly ambience (you have to shout out your order to be heard), its char-dogs and its heart-stopping cheddar fries.

Taco & Burrito Palace 2 (☎ 773-248-0740; 2441 N Halsted St; items $2-4; ☺ until 5am Fri & Sat) Does huge spicy pork burritos, chimichangas and soft tacos. It's a convenient stop after a night of heavy drinking at B.L.U.E.S. or Kingston Mines.

Bourgeois Pig (☎ 773-883-5282; 738 W Fullerton Pl; mains $6-7) An old-school lefty coffee shop, the Pig serves up strong java and good panini sandwiches.

Wrigleyville

You'll want to grab a bite before or after a game at Wrigley at one of the neighborhood's many diverse eateries. The neighborhood hums with activity most nights.

River Kwai (☎ 773-472-1013; 1650 W Belmont Ave; mains $5-8; ☺ 11pm-6am) It's somewhat scruffy, keeps exclusive late-late hours, and there's usually a long wait for one of the few tables, but Chicago night owls swear by the delicious seafood soup and pad Thai.

Leona's (☎ 773-327-8861; 3215 N Sheffield Ave; mains $8-17) Part of a legendary local chain, Leona's serves heaping portions of excellent pizza, sandwiches, lasagna and other Italian dishes.

Chicago Diner (☎ 773-935-6696; 3411 N Halsted; mains $8-11) This diner serves large portions of tofu omelets, tofu stroganoff, tofu loaf and tofu everything else.

Andersonville/Devon Avenue

These northern neighborhoods are bursting with inexpensive, unassuming Southeast Asian eateries.

Thai Binh (☎ 773-728-0283; 1113 W Argyle St; mains $6-13) This personable, family-owned Vietnamese restaurant has a huge selection of soups, rice plates and noodle dishes.

Kopi Traveler's Cafe (☎ 773-989-5674; 5317 N Clark St; mains $5-8) Kopi's has an Indonesian trekker vibe, from the pile of cushions to sit upon, to the bulletin board where travelers post flyers. The health-conscious menu features soups, salads and sandwiches.

Thai Pastry (☎ 773-784-5399; 4925 N Broadway; mains $5-9) The yummy pad Thai and clay-pot

GREAT LAKES

curries are excellent at this unpretentious Thai restaurant.

Wicker Park & Bucktown

Artists and hipsters hang out here these days. Take the CTA Blue Line to Damen or Western.

Irazu (☎ 773-252-5687; 1865 N Milwaukee Ave; mains $4-11; ☽ Mon-Sat) This jam-packed little Costa Rican joint dishes up wonderful toasted sandwiches (pressed, Cuban-style), huge burritos and pureed mango shakes.

Flo (☎ 312-243-0477; 1434 W Chicago Ave; mains $5-14; ☽ Tue-Sun) In nearby Ukranian Village, Flo is popular with 20-somethings who crave delicious, Southwestern breakfasts.

Cafe Laguardia (☎ 773-862-5996; 2111 W Armitage Ave; mains $5-15) This hip, family-run Cuban café has a jazzy atmosphere and serves great roasted pork sandwiches among other Caribbean specialties. Rev up with a round of mojitos.

Margies (☎ 773-384-1035; 1960 N Western Ave; mains $3-5; ☽ until midnight) You can eat here, but most locals come to this classic ice cream parlor to sink a spoon into an unbelievably rich sundae or attempt a foot-tall milkshake.

West Side & Pilsen

The West Side's ethnic enclaves offer good eats. Greek Town extends along S Halsted St, Little Italy is along Taylor St and the Mexican Pilsen enclave centers around W 18th St (the CTA Blue Line stops here, but you'll need wheels to reach the other areas easily).

Lou Mitchell's (☎ 312-939-3111; 565 W Jackson Blvd; mains $4-9; ☽ 7am-3pm) Near the train station, just west of the Loop, this old-style urban eatery is famed for chatty waitresses and breakfast standards done well and piled high on heavy crockery.

Nuevo Leon (☎ 312-421-1517; 1515 W 18th St; mains $3-5) One of Chicago's best-loved Mexican restaurants, Nuevo Leon is clearly on the tourist map but it hasn't resorted to tourist trap shortcuts or inflated prices. Delicious tacos, tamales and enchiladas are served at peso-size prices.

Parthenon (☎ 312-726-2407; 314 S Halsted St; mains $9-16) The waiters are busy, the colonnades are fake, some of the dishes are on fire and the customers at this Greektown favorite are uniformly happy.

Chinatown

From the CTA Red Line Cermak–Chinatown stop you can see the colorful shopfronts of Chinatown. It's mostly restaurants, and this is a good spot to grab a cheap plate of noodles or a rice plate.

Three Happiness (☎ 312-791-1228; 2130 S Wentworth Ave; mains $4-11) Not just one or two happinesses, but *three*. Chicagoans head here for generous portions of chop suey, egg foo young, and a retinue of meat and poultry dishes. Dim sum carts cruise the isles from 10am to 3pm.

DRINKING

Chicago is a toddling town, as Frank Sinatra famously noted many decades ago. The long cold winters and long hot summers are conducive to spending lots of time on stools and around tables with bottle, stein or glass in hand. Usual closing time is 2am, but many places stay open until 4am on weekdays and 5am on Saturday. In summer many boast beer gardens and outdoor seating.

Bars

Signature Lounge (☎ 312-787-7230; John Hancock Center, 875 N Michigan Ave) Have the Hancock Observatory view without the Hancock Observatory admission price. Shoot straight up to the 96th floor and order your beverage ($8 and up) while looking out over the glittering city.

Berghoff (☎ 312-427-3170; 17 W Adams St) Berghoff, in the Loop, was the first place in town to legally serve liquor when Prohibition was repealed. It has a great German bar and food is served in an adjacent dining room.

Olde Town Ale House (☎ 312-944-7020; 219 W North Ave) A longtime local favorite just around the corner from Second City, the Olde Towne is a good place to drop by with a few old pals. It warms up after 11pm. After a couple of rounds, the bar itself will feel like an old pal, too.

Hopleaf (☎ 773-334-9851; 5148 N Clark St) There are 200 beers available (30 on tap) at this wildly popular bar in Andersonville. With classic jazz and country music booming from the juke box, Belgian frites and mussels on a limited menu and an upbeat crowd, the Hopleaf generates good times.

Green Door Tavern (☎ 312-664-5496; 678 N Orleans St) Old Chicago atmosphere, excellent pub

GREAT LAKES

food and a congenial crowd make this a stellar spot in the River North area. It's a good place to watch the Cubbies play on TV and enjoy colorful commentary from vocal fans.

Simon's (☎ 773-878-0894; 5210 N Clark St) With good indie-rock tunes on the juke box, this long and narrow watering hole draws a smart 20-something crowd. It's in Andersonville. Great bar.

Goose Island Brewery (☎ 312-915-0071; 1800 N Clybourn Ave) Goose brews its excellent beers on site and serves tasty sandwiches.

Rainbo Club (☎ 773-489-5999; 1150 N Damen Ave) The Rainbo, in Wicker Park, has been a fertile brooding ground for generations of under-employed artists. On weekends, they're joined by suburbanites.

Ginger Man (☎ 773-549-2050; 3740 N Clark) This is a good-looking spot. With arty patrons, pool tables and a good beer selection it stands apart from the surrounding Wrigley sports bars.

Big Chicks (☎ 773-728-5511; 5024 N Sheridan Rd) Dancing gay boys pack the room until the wee hours on weekends, but Andersonville's Big Chicks is relatively sedate during the week, when it draws a mixed crowd.

Also recommended for relaxed drinking are the **Charleston** (☎ 773-489-4757; 2076 N Hoyne St Ave) and **Map Room** (☎ 773-252-7636; 1949 N Hoyne St Ave), both in Bucktown.

Live Music

Metro (☎ 773-549-3604; 3730 N Clark St, Wrigleyville) Local indie-rockers and big names play at Metro; its basement **Smart Bar** hosts dancing until dawn.

Hideout (☎ 773-227-4433; 1354 W Wabansia Ave) Tucked behind a factory in Wicker Park, Hideout is as hard to find as the name implies, but worth it for the laid-back atmosphere and excellent live folk, country and rock performances.

At **Double Door** (☎ 773-489-3160; 1572 N Milwaukee Ave) and **Empty Bottle** (☎ 773-276-3600; 1035 N Western Ave), the hard-edge Chicago alt-rock scene is epitomized in Wicker Park and Bucktown.

Noisy, hot and sweaty – as all blues bars should be – are **B.L.U.E.S.** (☎ 773-528-1012; 2519 N Halsted St) and **Kingston Mines** (☎ 773-477-4646; 2548 N Halsted St), which is conveniently located and draws the 4am crowd. They are both in Lincoln Park.

Green Mill (☎ 773-878-5552; 4802 N Broadway, Andersonville) The sultry 1930s atmosphere and top-notch jazz combos will conjure images of Capone-era Chicago. Indeed, this was one of Al's favorite spots, and it has aged gracefully.

Buddy Guy's Legends (☎ 312-427-0333; 754 S Wabash Ave) This place, a few blocks south of the Loop, gets the top blues acts in town, including the venerable Mr Guy himself.

Rosa's Lounge (☎ 773-342-0452; 3420 W Armitage Ave, West Side) This is a hardcore blues club that draws top local talent and dedicated fans to a somewhat dodgy West Side block. Take a cab.

House of Blues (☎ 312-923-2000; 329 N Dearborn St, Near North) In part owned by Blues Brother Dan Aykroyd, House of Blues is a large venue for all musical forms. Big name acts passing through weekly.

Blue Chicago (☎ 312-642-6261; 536 & 736 N Clark St) A pair of friendly clubs on easily accessed downtown blocks.

Back Room (☎ 312-751-2433; 1007 N Rush St, Near North) This jazz joint is so tiny it's like having a band in your bedroom.

Hothouse (☎ 312-362-9707; 31 E Balbo Ave) Hothouse is a beautiful room offering esoteric jazz and world music to a stylish crowd.

Andy's (☎ 312-642-6805; 11 E Hubbard St) This renowned club features both jazz and blues.

CLUBBING

The club scene ranges from hip snooty places to casual joints where all you do is dance. Covers range from nix to $20.

Berlin (☎ 773-348-4975; www.berlinchicago.com; 954 W Belmont Ave) No-attitude crowd is as mixed as the music.

Big Wig (☎ 773-235-9100; www.bigwignightclub.net; 1551 W Division St) One of Chi-town's best underground clubs is home to some of the freshest sounds around.

Red Dog (☎ 773-278-1009; 1958 W North Ave) Great DJ's, funk, hip-hop and house grooves and a mixed crowd liven up this kitschy warehouse club.

Sinibar (☎ 773-278-7797; 1540 N Milwaukee Ave) Funk and soul stir the exotic Moroccan decor.

Vision (☎ 312-266-1944; www.visionnightclub.com; 640 N Dearborn St) Some of the city's best techno parties make this a destination for dancers rather than poseurs.

ENTERTAINMENT

Check the *Reader* and other local media. **Hot Tix** (78 W Randolph St, 163 E Pearson St or 2301 N Clark St) sells same-day tickets at half the price.

Theater

Chicago's excellent reputation for stage drama is very well deserved. Following are the main companies.

Steppenwolf Theatre (☎ 312-335-1650; 1650 N Halsted St, Old Town) Hollywood-friendly.

Noble Fool Theatre Company (☎ 312-726-1156; 16 W Randolph St) A first-rate smaller house of farce.

Goodman Theater (☎ 312-443-3800; 170 N Dearborn St) Known for both new and classic works.

Victory Gardens (☎ 773-871-3000; 2257 N Lincoln Ave, Lincoln Park) Specializing in plays by Chicago authors.

Major performance venues include the following:

Auditorium Theater (☎ 312-922-2110; 50 E Congress Parkway)

Cadillac Palace Theater (☎ 312-977-1700; 151 W Randolph St)

Chicago Theater (☎ 312-443-1130; 175 N State St)

Ford Center/Oriental Theater (☎ 312-977-1700; 24 W Randolph St)

Shubert Theater (☎ 312-977-1700; 22 W Monroe St)

Sports

Chicago Cubs (☎ 773-404-2827; 1060 W Addison St) The Cubbies last won the World Series in 1908, but their fans still pack Wrigley Field, baseball's most charming and intimate stadium. It was built in 1916 and is known for its ivy-covered outfield wall. Take the CTA Red Line to Addison. Wrigley is 4.5 miles north of the Loop.

Chicago White Sox (☎ 312-674-1000; 333 W 35th St) The Chi-Sox play in antiseptic US Cellular Field. It's 4 miles south of the Loop and near the CTA Red Line Sox–35th station.

Chicago Bulls (☎ 312-455-4000; 1901 W Madison St) The Bulls play basketball in huge United Center, also used by the **Blackhawks** (☎ 312-455-7000) for hockey. It's about 2 miles west of the Loop. CTA runs special buses on game days; it's not safe to walk here.

Chicago Bears (☎ 847-615-2327; 425 E McFetridge Dr) 'Da Bears,' Chicago's NFL team, tackles at renovated Soldier Field. The **Chicago Fire** (☎ 312-705-7200) soccer team competes here as well.

Live Music

Symphony Center (☎ 312-294-3000; 220 S Michigan Ave) The Chicago Symphony Orchestra is headquartered in this superb center.

Civic Opera House (☎ 312-332-2244; 20 N Wacker Dr) The Lyric Opera of Chicago, one of the country's best, performs in the grand old opera house.

Grant Park Orchestra (☎ 312-742-7638) In summertime, watch for free classical concerts performed by the Grant Park Orchestra in Millennium Park.

Cinemas

Music Box Theatre (☎ 773-871-6604; 3733 N Southport Ave, Wrigleyville) Patrons are treated to live organ music and clouds rolling across the ceiling prior to their art films at this theater.

Gene Siskel Film Center (☎ 312-846-2800; 164 N State St) Offbeat films are screened here.

Comedy

Improvisational theater began in Chicago, and the city still nurtures the best in the business.

Second City (☎ 312-337-3992; 1616 N Wells St, Old Town) The place where John Belushi, Bill Murray and many others honed their wit.

Zanies (☎ 312-337-4027; 1548 N Wells St, Old Town) Chicago's best stand-up club.

Dance

Joffrey Ballet of Chicago (☎ 312-739-0120) A local dance company of great renown, Joffrey performs in various venues.

SHOPPING

The ultimate Chicago souvenir is a Cubs or White Sox cap, which can be bought anywhere tourists shop. If stumped, try the ballparks or the **Chicago Tribune Store** (☎ 312-222-3080; 435 N Michigan Ave).

Poster Plus (☎ 312-461-9277; 200 S Michigan Ave) Historical prints from Chicago World's Fairs and works of art from the 19th and 20th centuries. The Art Institute is right across the street, and also has a gift shop selling posters.

Jazz Record Mart (☎ 312-222-1467; 444 N Wabash Ave) Thoroughly stocked on Chicago blues and jazz CDs, as well as other artists in those genres.

Reckless Records (☎ 773-235-3727; 1532 N Milwaukee Ave) In Bucktown, this is Chicago's best indie-rock record and CD emporium.

GREAT LAKES

Chicago Comics (☎ 773-528-1983; 3244 N Clark St) The place to go for books by renowned local graphic artists such as Chris Ware, Ivan Brunetti or even Dan Clowes (who lived here during his early *Eightball* days). Superman and Simpsons products are also sold here.

Disgraceland (☎ 773-281-5875; 3338 N Clark St, Wrigleyville) Head here for contemporary second-hand clothing.

Large malls can be found along the Magnificent Mile, and include **Shops at North Bridge**, **Chicago Place**, **Water Tower Place** and **900 N Michigan**. In the Loop, the flagship **Marshall Field's** (☎ 312-781-1000; 111 N State St) and **Carson Pirie Scott & Co** (☎ 312-641-7000; 1 S State St) are Chicago's premier department stores from the turn of the 20th century.

GETTING THERE & AWAY
Air
O'Hare International Airport (ORD; ☎ 800-832-6352) is the world's busiest. It's huge but user-friendly, with good signs and maps. The smaller **Midway Airport** (MDW; ☎ 773-838-0600) has a new terminal and is used by domestic carriers like Southwest, and is which often have cheaper flights than airlines serving O'Hare.

Bus
The **main bus station** (☎ 312-408-5800; 630 W Harrison St) is just a few blocks west of the Loop. Greyhound has frequent buses to Cleveland ($46, eight hours), Detroit ($29, seven hours), Indianapolis ($34, four hours), Milwaukee ($15, two hours) and Minneapolis ($66, 10 hours).

Car
Car rental is subject to 18% tax. Many rental agencies have 24-hour desks at both airports (cheapest) and keep regular business hours around town (more expensive).

Train
Chicago's classic **Union Station** (225 S Canal St) is the hub for Amtrak's national and regional service. Daily trains go to Detroit ($41, six hours), Milwaukee ($20, 1½ hours), Cleveland ($78, seven hours) and St Paul ($97, eight hours).

GETTING AROUND
Public Transportation
The **Chicago Transit Authority** (CTA; ☎ 312-836-7000; www.transitchicago.com) operates the city bus network and train system that includes both elevated (El) and subway trains. CTA buses go everywhere from early morning to late evening. Two of the seven color-coded train lines – the Red Line, and the Blue Line to O'Hare International Airport – operate 24 hours. The other lines run from about 5am to 11pm daily. During the day, you should not have to wait more than 15 minutes for a train. Get free maps at any train station.

The standard fare on a bus or train is $1.50; transfers cost 30¢. On buses, you can use a fare card (called a Transit Card) or pay with exact change. On the train, you must use a Transit Card, sold from vending machines at train stations. Passes are available for one day ($5), two days ($9), three days ($12) and five days ($18), but not all stations sell them. You can buy them at the O'Hare station and other hubs, as well as through CTA's website.

Metra commuter trains (☎ 312-836-7000; www.metrarail.com) have 12 routes serving far corners of Chicago and the suburbs from four terminals ringing the Loop (LaSalle St Station, Randolph St Station, Richard B Ogilvie Transportation Center and Union Station). Some lines run daily, while others operate only during weekday rush hours. Metra fares cost $1.75 to $5 or more. An all-weekend ticket costs $5.

PACE (☎ 312-836-7000; www.pacebus.com) runs the suburban bus system that connects with city transport.

Much of the city train system is inaccessible to people with reduced mobility, but most buses are accessible.

Taxi
Cabs are plentiful in the Loop, north to Andersonville and west to Bucktown. In other areas, call **Yellow Cab** (☎ 312-829-4222) or **Flash Cab** (☎ 773-561-1444). Flagfall is $1.90, plus $1.60 per mile; a 15% tip is expected. If you venture outside city limits, you'll pay 1½ times the fare.

AROUND ILLINOIS

OAK PARK
Ernest Hemingway described his hometown, just 8 miles west of Chicago's Loop, as 'a village of wide lawns and narrow minds,' but it is more than that, no thanks to Papa.

From 1898 to 1908, architect Frank Lloyd Wright worked and lived in Oak Park and he left a legacy that's well worth seeing. The Oak Park **visitors center** (☎ 708-848-1500; 158 Forest Ave; 🕑 10am-4pm winter, 9am-5pm summer) sells an architectural walking-tour map ($3.25).

The **Frank Lloyd Wright Home & Studio** (☎ 708-848-1976; 951 Chicago Ave; admission $9; tours 11am, 1pm & 3pm Mon-Fri, every 20 min 11am-3:30pm Sat & Sun) provides tours of the home and other Wright-designed dwellings.

The **Ernest Hemingway Museum** (☎ 708-848-2222; 200 N Oak Park Ave; admission $7; 🕑 1-5pm Sun-Fri, 10am-5pm Sat) will thrill hardcore fans of the novelist. Admission includes access to **Hemingway's Birthplace** (339 N Oak Park Ave). The town is easily reached on the CTA Green Line.

SPRINGFIELD

Illinois' small state capital is the heart of the Land of Lincoln. Prior to being elected 16th president of the US, Abraham Lincoln practiced law here from 1837 to 1861. Springfield today offers a profusion of sights that pay homage to the stovepipe-hatted statesman, and many of the attractions are walkable downtown and cost little to nothing.

Information

Visitors center (☎ 217-789-2360; www.visit-springfieldillinois.com; 109 N 7th St; 🕑 8am-5pm Mon-Fri) Get your bearings with maps from this central visitors center.

Sights

Springfield's top draw is the **Lincoln Home** (☎ 217-492-4150; 426 S 7th St; admission free; 🕑 8:30am-5pm), where Abe and Mary Lincoln lived from 1844 until they moved to the White House in 1861. You'll see considerably more than just the home: the whole block has been preserved, and several structures are open to visitors.

The impressive **Lincoln's Tomb** sits in **Oak Ridge Cemetery** (☎ 217-782-2717; admission free; 🕑 9am-5pm), north of downtown. The gleam on the nose of Lincoln's bust, created by visitors' light touches, indicates that many feel oddly compelled to pay their respects by touching Abe's nose.

The **Lincoln Presidential Library & Museum** (☎ 217-524-7216; 1 Old State Capitol Plaza) contains the most complete Lincoln collection in the world, with many never-before-seen items.

Standing a block apart are the noteworthy **Lincoln-Herndon Law Offices** (☎ 217-785-7289; cnr 6th & Adams Sts; suggested donation $2; 🕑 9am-5pm Tue-Sat) and **Old State Capitol** (☎ 217-785-7961; cnr 5th & Adams Sts; suggested donation $2; 🕑 9am-5pm Tue-Sat). Both offer detailed tours covering Lincoln's early political life; the latter takes in his dramatic pre–Civil War debates with Stephen Douglas.

Lincoln-free attractions include the pristine 1904 **Dana-Thomas House** (☎ 217-782-6776; 301 E Lawrence St; admission $3; 🕑 9am-4pm Wed-Sun), one of Frank Lloyd Wright's Prairie-style masterworks, with an insightful tour; **Shea's Gas Station Museum** (☎ 217-522-0475; 2075 Peoria Rd; admission free; 🕑 7am-4pm Tue-Fri, 7am-noon Sat) with Rte 66 pumps and signs; and the sumptuous **State Capitol** (☎ 217-782-2099; cnr 2nd & Capitol Sts; admission free; 🕑 8am-4pm Mon-Fri, 9am-3pm Sat & Sun) with free tours.

SCENIC DRIVE: RTE 66

You can still get your kicks on parts of Rte 66, which was once the fastest path from Chicago to Los Angeles. Though the Illinois stretch of 66 is now almost totally superseded by I-55, the old route – affectionately called Main St, USA – still exists in scattered sections, and its associated Americana survives in towns bypassed by the interstate.

Burgers and fries are natural staples along the 'Mother Rd,' but seldom are they proffered by a grinning, 28ft fiberglass spaceman, as they are at the **Launching Pad Drive-In** (☎ 815-476-6535; mains $3-4) in Wilmington, 20 miles south of Joliet. The restaurant itself suspiciously resembles an old Sizzler, but this little family-owned greasy spoon delivers the goods.

Further south, a good section of old Rte 66 parallels I-55 through Litchfield. Grab a meal and piece of pie at **Ariston Cafe** (☎ 217-324-2023; mains $4-15), which has changed little since it opened in 1924, or see a $2 movie at the **Sky View Drive-In Theater** (☎ 217-324-4451) amidst the corn and soybean fields. Hotels are nearby on Rte 16.

Mount Olive has the classic 1926 **Soulsby Shell Station**, the route's oldest gas station; you can't fuel up here, but the owner plans to reopen with a Rte 66 museum.

GREAT LAKES

At the irresistibly macabre **Museum of Funeral Customs** (☎ 217-544-3480; 1440 Monument Ave; admission $3; 🕙 10am-4pm Tue-Sat, 1-4pm Sun), the roots of modern sterile death rituals are represented with a 1920s embalming room, horse-drawn hearses and implements used in the process.

Sleeping

Motel 6 (☎ 217-529-1633; 6010 S 6th St; r $35-45; P 🞤 🞤) This is just one of the many chain hotels lining I-55 east of town where you'll find budget prices.

The bland but clean **Carpenter Street Hotel** (☎ 217-789-9100, 888-779-9100; www.carpenterstreet hotel.com; 525 N 6th St; r $75; P 🞤) and the **Mansion View Inn** (☎ 217-544-7411, 800-252-1083; www .mansionview.com; 529 S 4th St; r from $80; P 🞤) are serviceable options near the center.

Eating

Cozy Dog Drive In (☎ 217-525-1992; 2935 S 6th St; corn dogs $1.50-3; 🕙 Mon-Sat) This is the corn dog's birthplace, and a Rte 66 legend to boot. Check out the memorabilia on the walls.

For an array of tasty meal options, cruise S 6th St between Monroe and Adams Sts. A local specialty is the 'horseshoe,' an artery-clogging fried meat sandwich covered with melted cheese; you can find these at **Brewhaus** (☎ 217-525-6399; 617 E Washington; horse-shoes $3-6; 🕙 Mon-Sat), a popular pub.

Getting There & Around

Greyhound and Amtrak stop here, with frequent service from Chicago.

INDIANA

The 'Hoosier State' is not on everybody's must-see list, but with many of the Midwest's main byways passing through, travelers to this part of the country are bound to see some of Indiana anyway. Much of the state is refreshingly free of mass commercialism, making Indiana's towns and cities pleasant and relaxing for a pit stop. Indiana also has a few surprises up its sleeve. For instance, it's little known that Columbus is one of the USA's premier architectural meccas, with schools, banks and fire stations designed by IM Pei, Eero Saarinen and other noted designers. Bloomington is a lively university town filled with ethnic restaurants and Tibetan

temples. The flourishing capital, Indianapolis, home to that famous 500-mile car race, has the nifty Indy 500 museum where you can take a spin around the race track.

INDIANAPOLIS

Car racing put Indianapolis on the map, and it's still the city's number one point of interest. Indy, as locals call it, had many early carmakers but they were eclipsed by the Detroit giants. Their legacy was a 2.5-mile rectangular test track that was used in 1911 for the first Indianapolis 500 race (won at an average speed of 75mph). Downtown is a vibrant mix of museums, nightlife and sporting venues, all watched over by the silent dome of the state capitol.

Orientation

Indianapolis is geometrically laid out, much like Washington DC, with diagonal avenues superimposed on a grid layout. Everything radiates from the massively impressive Monument Circle. Meridian St divides streets east from west; Washington St divides them north from south.

Information

Nuvo, distributed free on Wednesday, outlines Indy's arts, music and nightclub scene.

Visitors center (☎ 800-323-4639; cnr Washington & Illinois Sts in the Artsgarden Bldg; 🕙 10am-9pm Mon-Sat, noon-6pm Sun) Covers everything that *Nuvo* doesn't.

Sights & Activities

INDIANAPOLIS MOTOR SPEEDWAY

The Speedway, home of the **Indianapolis 500** motor race, is Indy's super-sight and an absolute must-see. The **Hall of Fame Museum** (☎ 317-484-6747; 4790 W 16th St; admission $3; 🕙 9am-5pm) features 75 sleek racing cars (including former Indy winners), a 500lb Tiffany trophy and a track tour ($3 extra). OK, so you're on a bus for the latter and not even beginning to burn rubber at 37mph; it's still fun to pretend when you pass the grandstand. **Tickets** (☎ 317-484-6700, 800-822-4639; www.imstix.com) are hard to come by for the big event, held each year on Memorial Day weekend in May and attended by 450,000 crazed fans. They cost anywhere from $20 to $140. Tickets for pre-race trials and practices are more likely (and cheaper).

Other races at the Speedway are the Nascar **Brickyard 400** in August and Formula One **US Grand Prix** in September.

WHITE RIVER STATE PARK

Sprawling White River State Park, at the edge of downtown, contains several worthwhile sights. The adobe **Eiteljorg Museum of American Indians and Western Art** (☎ 317-636-9378; 500 W Washington St; admission $7; ☺ 10am-5pm Mon-Sat, noon-5pm Sun) features Native American artifacts, such as basketry, pots and masks, as well as a fabulous US painting collection with works by Frederic Remington and Georgia O'Keeffe.

The **NCAA Hall of Champions** (☎ 800-735-6222; 700 W Washington St; admission $7; ☺ 10am-5pm Mon-Sat, noon-5pm Sun) is surprisingly popular, until you remember that most Hoosiers are renowned fanatics for hoops.

Sleeping

Hotels cost more and are usually full during race weeks in May, August and September. Look for low-cost motels off I-465, the freeway that circles Indianapolis.

Motel 6 (☎ 317-248-1231; 5241 W Bradbury St, off I-465 at Airport Expressway; r $36-56; P ⊠ ⊠) This is an inexpensive option 6 miles west of town.

Days Inn (☎ 317-637-6464; 401 E Washington St; r $64-89; P ⊠) This is good value for the downtown location. The lobby is stately with a fireplace; the rooms are clean. Breakfast is included.

Eating

Central Massachusetts Ave ('Mass Ave' to locals) is bounteous when the stomach growls. At lunch it's hard to beat the incredible range of cheap eats at the old **City Market** (on Market St, two blocks east of Monument Circle), filled with ethnic food stalls and produce vendors.

Mug 'N' Bun (☎ 317-244-5669; 5211 W 10th St; mains $3-4) The mugs are frosted and filled with a wonderful home-brewed root beer. The buns contain burgers, chilidogs and juicy tenderloins. At this vintage drive-in, located near the Speedway, you are served in your car.

Abbey Coffeehouse (☎ 317-269-8426; 771 Massachusetts Ave; mains $6-7) The Abbey is everything a good coffee shop should be: serene and arty, with comfy chairs. The sandwiches, wraps and vegetarian items are delicious.

Drinking

Downtown and Mass Ave have a few good watering holes; Broad Ripple has several.

Rathskeller (☎ 317-636-0396; 401 E Michigan St) This is a long-established German haunt, in the Athenaeum building, with traditional and modern fare and a busy biergarten pouring imported brews.

Slippery Noodle Inn (☎ 317-631-6974; 372 S Meridian St) The Noodle is the oldest bar in the state and has seen action as a whorehouse, slaughterhouse, gangster hangout and Underground Railroad station. Now it's an excellent blues club, with live music nightly, and it's cheap.

Entertainment

Indiana Pacers (☎ 317-917-2500; 125 S Pennsylvania St) This beloved NBA team plays basketball at Conseco Fieldhouse.

Indianapolis Colts (☎ 317-262-3389; 100 S Capitol Ave) Under the RCA Dome's vast fiberglass roof, 63,000 fans watch NFL football games.

GREAT LAKES

DETOUR: COLUMBUS, IN ARCHITECTURE

When you think of the USA's great architectural cities, Columbus, Indiana, doesn't quite leap to mind. But it should. Located 40 miles south of Indianapolis on I-65, Columbus is a remarkable gallery of physical design. Since the 1940s, the city and its leading corporations have commissioned some of the world's best architects, including Eero Saarinen, Richard Meier and IM Pei, to create both public and private buildings. Stop at the **visitors center** (☎ 812-378-2622; 506 5th St; ☺ 9am-5pm Mon-Sat Dec-Feb, 9am-5pm Mon-Sat, 10am-4pm Sun Mar-Nov) to pick up a self-guided tour map ($2) or join a **bus tour** (admission $9.50; ☺ 10am Mon-Fri, 10am & 2pm Sat, 11am Sun). Over 60 notable buildings are spread over a wide area (car required), but about 15 diverse works can be seen on foot downtown.

Motels are found on the city's outskirts on I-65. For a huge pork tenderloin sandwich, an Indiana specialty, drop by the **Columbus Bar** (☎ 812-372-5252; 322 4th St; mains $4-7), a classic bar and grill.

Getting There & Around

Indianapolis International Airport (☎ 317-487-7243; www.indianapolisairport.com) is 7 miles southwest of town. The No 8 Washington bus runs between the airport and downtown ($1, 30 minutes). Greyhound and Amtrak stop here.

IndyGo (☎ 317-635-3344; www.indygo.net) runs the local buses; the fare is $1.25.

BLOOMINGTON

One of the Midwest's great college towns, Bloomington is the lively, compact and colorful home of the 35,000 students of Indiana University. It's an essential stop in Indiana.

The town centers on Courthouse Sq, surrounded by restaurants, bars, bookshops and the historic facade of Fountain Sq Mall. The super-stocked **visitors center** (☎ 812-334-8900; www.visitbloomington.com; 2855 N Walnut St; ✆ 8am-5pm Mon-Fri, 9am-4pm Sat) is a few miles north of the center. Nearly everything else is walkable.

The colorful, prayer-flag-covered **Tibetan Cultural Center** (☎ 812-331-0014; 3655 Snoddy Rd; admission free; ✆ 10am-4pm, meditation session 1pm Sun) and stupa, as well as the **Dagom Gaden Tensung Ling Monastery** (☎ 812-339-0857; 102 Clubhouse Dr; ✆ call for hr), indicate Bloomington's significant Tibetan presence.

Look for cheap lodgings along N Walnut St near Rte 46. The limestone **Motel 6** (☎ 812-332-0820; 1800 N Walnut St; r $30-50; ✆ ✆) may be the chain's most attractive. Ten miles south of town, Lake Monroe makes a fine warm-weather outing, and there's camping at quiet **Paynetown Recreation Center** (☎ 812-837-9546; www.camp.in.gov; campsites $16-23).

For a town its size, Bloomington offers a mind-blowing array of ethnic restaurants – everything from Burmese to Eritrean to Mexican. Browse Kirkwood Ave and E 4th St. Charming **Little Tibet** (☎ 812-331-0122; 415 E 4th St; mains $6-8; ✆ Wed-Mon) offers specialties from the Himalayan homeland, as well as Thai-influenced dishes and curries. The **Scholar's Inn Bakehouse** (☎ 812-331-6029; 125 N College Ave; mains $3-9) is excellent for coffee and sandwiches. Pubs on Kirkwood Ave close to the university cater to the student crowd.

INDIANA DUNES

Hugely popular on summer days with sunbathers from Chicago and South Bend, **Indiana Dunes National Lakeshore** stretches along 20 miles of Lake Michigan shoreline. Windy winter weather make the dunes more desolate and moody, an equally unforgettable experience. Sandy beaches, dunes and woodlands are crisscrossed with hiking trails, which often afford glimpses of nearby steel mills and stark, industrial structures. The lakeshore is noted for its incredible variety of plant life – everything from cactus to grasslands to hardwood forests and pine trees. Beaches are usually open 8am to sunset daily. You can get here from Chicago (1½ hours) via the South Shore Metra train, which stops at Beverly Shores among other park locations.

Adjacent **Indiana Dunes State Park** (☎ 219-926-1952; www.duneland.com; end of Rte 49 near Chesterton; campsites $8-23) has year-round camping and takes reservations. **Al & Sally's Motel** (☎ 219-872-9131; 3221 Rte 12; s/d $65/75; ✆ ✆) is a good option between the park and Michigan City.

SOUTH BEND

The city of South Bend is known as the home of the University of Notre Dame, famous for its 'Fighting Irish' football team. To tour the pretty campus with its gold-domed administration building, *Lourdes Grotto* replica and *Touchdown Jesus* painting, start at the **visitors center** (☎ 574-631-5726, 111 Eck Center; ✆ 8am-5pm Mon-Sat, 10am-5pm Sun).

OHIO

The Buckeye State is mostly farmland, but is equally known for its large industrial cities, which flopped in the post-WWII era, only to come back magnificently in recent decades. Bisecting the state from the northeast to the southwest, you'll encounter Cleveland's post-industrial warehouse culture, the slow 18th-century pace of Amish life in central Ohio, and Cincinnati's intriguing old neighborhoods.

CLEVELAND

The Cuyahoga River, which snakes through the heart of Cleveland, no longer spontaneously combusts (as it did in 1969), but Cleveland still shows its visitors a good time. Once derided as the 'Mistake by the Lake,' this burgh, at the bottom-end of Lake

Erie, is a model of late-20th century urban renewal. It's well worth stopping here for a day or two to drive around and admire this Rust Belt beauty. The Flats area, along either side of the once notorious river, is particularly astonishing to behold. It's a unique agglomeration of narrow river, gentle bluffs, a panoply of 19th-century warehouses and, best of all, a maze of high bridges arching over smaller iron draw-bridges. A perfect day in Cleveland would include a visit to the Rock and Roll Hall of Fame or, in summer, to the downtown ballpark for a game, followed by a night of bar- and club-hopping in the Flats.

Orientation
Cleveland's center is Public Sq, dominated by the conspicuous Terminal Tower. Ontario St is the east–west dividing line. Ohio City, Tremont and Coventry are good areas nearby for eating and drinking.

Information
Star Plaza (☎ 216-771-9118; 1302 Euclid Ave; ☻ 11am-6pm Tue-Sat, 11am-3pm Sun) Has travel info.
Terminal Tower (☎ 216-621-7981; 1st fl, 50 Public Sq; ☻ 9am-4:30pm Mon-Fri) Also provides tourist information.

Sights
A tribute to rock music and the always fascinating culture that goes with it (from the genuinely wild to the smarmily con-trived), the **Rock & Roll Hall of Fame & Museum** (☎ 216-781-7625, 888-764-7625; www.rockhall.com; 1 Key Plaza; admission $20; ☻ 10am-5:30pm Thu-Tue, 10am-9pm Wed) is Cleveland's top attraction. The museum contains delightful esoterica such as Janis Joplin's psychedelic Porsche and Ray Charles' sunglasses, but this is much more than a Hard Rock Café–style collection of rock-star memorabilia. In-teractive multimedia exhibits trace the history and social context of rock music and the many performers who created it

and influenced it. Why is the museum in Cleveland? Because this is the hometown of Alan Freed, the disk jockey who popu-larized the term 'rock 'n' roll' in the early 1950s, and because the city lobbied hard and paid big. Be prepared for crowds.

Sleeping
Central Cleveland has a quite unexpected dearth of cheap lodging. For budget options head out on I-71, 9 miles west of town, and along Hwy 57 off I-80/90 (exit 145), 24 miles from downtown. Prices listed here do not include the 14.5% tax.

HI Stanford House (☎ 330-467-8711; hi-stanford hostel@juno.com; 6093 Stanford Rd; dm $16, linen $3; ☻ daily Apr-Dec, Thu-Mon Jan-Mar) This hostel sits peacefully in the leafy Cuyahoga Valley National Recreation Area, 22 miles south of Cleveland in Peninsula. The fine old farmhouse is surrounded by trails, and deer often bound by. The office is open 7am to 9am and 5pm to 10pm. It's not accessible by public transportation; call for directions.

Motel 6 (☎ 216-234-0990; 7219 Engle Rd; r $38-53) Near the airport, this outlet is typical for the cheapie chain.

Brownstone Inn (☎ 216-426-1753; 3649 Prospect Ave; r $65-125; P ☻) In an 1874 townhouse near downtown, this B&B has a big per-sonality. All five rooms in the Victorian townhouse have a private bathroom. Break-fast is served in the morning, aperitifs in the evening.

Comfort Inn (☎ 216-861-0001; 1800 Euclid Ave; r $63-149; P $6.50 ☻) Not far from the bus station, the rooms are of standard, decent quality.

GREAT LAKES

THE CLEVELAND COMEBACK
Cleveland reached its nadir in the 1960s and '70s, when the demise of the city's traditional industries led to urban blight and severe social problems. Ongoing renewal started in the 1980s, as derelict waterfronts became bustling restaurant, bar and entertainment precincts. Three 1990s developments had major impacts – new baseball and football stadiums became the focus of local civic pride, and the Rock & Roll Hall of Fame brought international attention.

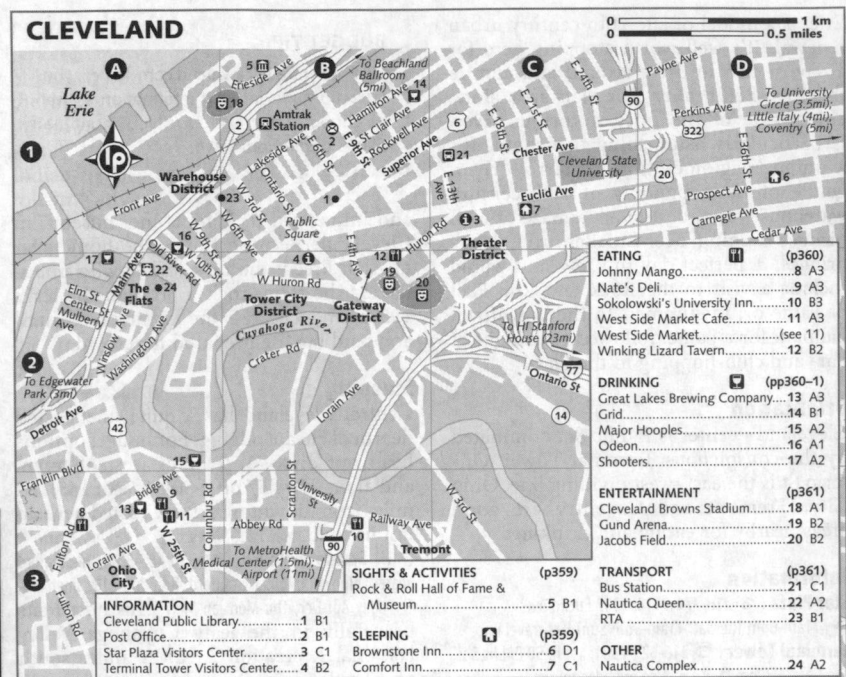

CLEVELAND

EATING	🍴	(p360)
Johnny Mango		8 A3
Nate's Deli		9 A3
Sokolowski's University Inn		10 B3
West Side Market Cafe		11 A3
West Side Market		(see 11)
Winking Lizard Tavern		12 A3

DRINKING	🍺	(pp360–1)
Great Lakes Brewing Company		13 A3
Grid		14 B1
Major Hooples		15 A2
Odeon		16 A1
Shooters		17 A2

ENTERTAINMENT		(p361)
Cleveland Browns Stadium		18 A1
Gund Arena		19 B2
Jacobs Field		20 B2

TRANSPORT		(p361)
Bus Station		21 C1
Nautica Queen		22 A2
RTA		23 B1

OTHER		
Nautica Complex		24 A2

SIGHTS & ACTIVITIES		(p359)
Rock & Roll Hall of Fame & Museum		5 B1

SLEEPING	🏠	(p359)
Brownstone Inn		6 D1
Comfort Inn		7 C1

INFORMATION		
Cleveland Public Library		1 B1
Post Office		2 B1
Star Plaza Visitors Center		3 C1
Terminal Tower Visitors Center		4 B2

Eating

West Side Market Cafe (☎ 216-579-6800; 1979 W 25th St; mains $4-7; ☯ Wed-Sat & Mon) This is a smart stop if you're craving well made breakfast and lunch fare and cheap fish and chicken mains.

West Side Market (cnr W 25th St & Lorain Ave; ☯ Mon, Wed, Fri & Sat) Adjacent the West Side Market Cafe in a local landmark building, this market overflows with fresh produce and prepared foods, especially on crowded Saturday mornings.

Nate's Deli (☎ 216-696-7529; 1923 W 25th St; mains $4-9; ☯ until 6pm Mon-Sat) Unassuming Nate's offers an uncommon mix of Middle Eastern dishes and deli sandwiches, with choices from reubens (corned beef, Swiss cheese and sauerkraut on rye) to stuffed grape-leaf platters.

Johnny Mango (☎ 216-575-1919; 3120 Bridge Ave; mains $5-15) The Caribbean-influenced food and drinks are as flavorful as the interior is colorful at this trendy joint. The menu includes a hearty vegetarian selection ~long with meat dishes, sangrias and Cuban *moj~* (rum cocktails).

Sokolowski's University Inn (☎ 216-771-9236; 1201 University Rd; mains $8-15; ☯ Mon-Sat) The portions are huge, enough to fuel the hungriest steelworker. It's cafeteria style, so grab a tray and fill it with plump pierogi, cabbage rolls and other rib-sticking Polish fare.

Winking Lizard Tavern (☎ 216-589-0313; 811 Huron Rd; mains $6-15) This hugely popular pub-grub outlet, thankfully named for its caged iguana, is a logical downtown stop before or after a sporting event.

Drinking

BARS

The Flats is a prime area for lively bars and clubs and easy eats.

Major Hooples (☎ 216-575-0483; 1930 Columbus Rd) Up a ways from the nightlife district, this is a welcoming watering hole that has Cleveland's best skyline view.

Great Lakes Brewing Company (2516 Market Ave; ☯ Mon-Sat) Elliott Ness had a shootout with criminals in this old building. Now it's a civilized place in which to order a house brew and a plate of satisfying pub grub. Ask the bartender to show you the bullet holes.

Shooters (☎ 216-861-6900; 1148 Main Ave) Shooters is worth seeking out for its great waterfront location, perfect for sunset gazing. Nearby, the restored Powerhouse building in the Nautica complex contains more bars and restaurants along the Cuyahoga.

LIVE MUSIC
Odeon (☎ 216-574-2525; 1295 Old River Rd) A rock club in the Flats.

Beachland Ballroom (☎ 216-383-1124; 15711 Waterloo Rd) Hip young bands play at this venue in East Cleveland about 5 miles east of downtown.

Clubbing
Grid (☎ 216-623-0113; 1437 St Clair Ave) A downtown gay dance venue.

Entertainment
The *Plain Dealer* is the city's daily newspaper, with a good Friday entertainment section. *Scene* is a free weekly entertainment paper, out on Wednesday.

Cleveland Indians (☎ 866-488-7423; 2401 Ontario St) Major League Baseball is played at downtown Jacobs Field.

Cleveland Cavaliers (☎ 216-241-2121; 1 Center Ct) The NBA Cavaliers and women's-league **Rockers** play basketball at the Gund Arena.

Cleveland Browns (☎ 440-891-5000; 1085 W 3rd St) The NFL's Browns play football at lakefront Browns Stadium.

Getting There & Around
Cleveland Hopkins International Airport (☎ 216-265-6030; www.clevelandairport.com) is 11 miles southwest of downtown and linked by the Regional Transit Authority Red Line train ($1.50).

Greyhound and Amtrak stop here. The **Regional Transit Authority** (RTA; ☎ 216-621-9500; 1240 W Sixth St) operates a decent bus and train system. The useful Waterfront Line train ($1.50) connects the Flats and other attractions to Tower City Center. Day passes ($3) are valid on buses and train.

AROUND CLEVELAND
In **Canton**, birthplace of the NFL, the popular **Pro Football Hall of Fame** (☎ 330-456-8207; 2121 George Halas Dr; admission $12; ☉ 9am-5pm) is a shrine for the gridiron-obsessed. Look for the football-shaped tower off I-77.

West of Cleveland, attractive **Oberlin** is an old-fashioned college town with noteworthy architecture by Cass Gilbert, Frank Lloyd Wright and Robert Venturi.

AMISH COUNTRY
Hmm. Shumptin's *amish* here. A visit to Amish Country is a trip back in time, as the Amish have famously resisted modernity for centuries now. Wayne and Holmes Counties, between Cleveland and Columbus (immediately east of I-71), have the USA's densest Amish concentration (followed by areas in Pennsylvania and Indiana).

Descendants of conservative Dutch-Swiss religious factions who migrated to the USA during the 18th century, the Amish continue to follow the *ordnung*, or way of life, in varying degrees. Many adhere to rules prohibiting the use of electricity, telephones and motorized vehicles. They wear traditional clothing, farm the land with plow and mule, and go to church in horse-drawn buggies. Others are not so strict, willingly accepting rides in cars from non-Amish, or even driving vehicles themselves.

Unfortunately, what would surely be a peaceful country scene is often disturbed by behemoth tour buses. Many Amish are happy to profit from this influx of outside dollars, but don't equate this to free photographic access – the Amish typically view photographs as taboo. Drive carefully, and slowly, as roads are narrow and curvaceous and there's always the chance of pulling up on a slow-moving buggy just round the bend. Many places are closed Sunday.

Near Berlin, east of Millersburg, is the **Amish & Mennonite Heritage Center** (☎ 330-893-3192; 5798 County Rd 77; admission $6; ☉ 9am-5pm Mon-Sat year-round, 9am-8pm Fri & Sat Jun-Oct), which offers concise explanations of the history and life of Amish. East of Berlin on Hwy 38, the **Amish Farm** (admission $4; ☉ 10am-5pm Mon-Fri, 10am-6pm Sat) offers tours and buggy rides.

Kidron, on Hwy 52 just north of Hwy 250, is worth a stop on Thursday, when the **Kidron Auction** takes place at the livestock barn. It's a view of 18th century commerce, as hundreds of buggies will be lined up along the roadside, and an interesting flea market rings the barn. Across the street, **Lehman's Store** is an absolute must-see. It's the Amish community's main purvey̲ of modern-looking products that ̲ electricity, as well as the sorts of daily items your great-grandparents probably used.

In quiet Walnut Creek, between Sugarcreek and Berlin just north of Hwy 39, check out the amazing **Amish Flea Market** (9am-5pm Fri & Sat), where you can find new or used (sometimes ancient) knickknacks, crafts, quilts, produce, antiques and delicious baked goods. Just north of Walnut Creek, along Hwy 515, **Yoder's** (330-893-2541; tours $2; 10am-5pm Mon-Sat mid-Apr–Oct) is another Amish farm that's open to visitors.

Tent campers can share grounds with RVs at **Amish Country Campsite** (330-359-5226; Hwy 62; campsite $14). This basic campground is 6 miles northeast of Berlin, just past Winesburg.

In the town of Millersburg, west of Berlin on Hwy 62, the historic **Hotel Millersburg** (330-674-1457; www.hotelmillersburg.com; 35 W Jackson St; r $40-99) has very basic, reasonably priced rooms (ask for an economy or twin room for the lowest rates). There's a modern, brightly lit tavern and dining room on the ground floor.

Boyd & Wurthman Restaurant (330-893-3287; Main St; mains from $5; Mon-Sat) is Berlin's most atmospheric eatery and serves homestyle cooking and attracts locals and tourists alike. Amish specialties like ham loaf and wedding steak (ground meat in mushroom sauce) join familiar American fare on the menu.

CINCINNATI

Cincy's a very Midwestern business center just across the Ohio River from the South. Its maze of freeway ramps appear designed to confound and deter visitors, but with a little wading you'll find the city's sweet spots. On a warm evening, take in a Reds game and admire the old river flowing past the outfield wall. Then walk the bridge into charming Covington, Kentucky, for drinks and dinner. Or hike up to Mt Adams, a gorgeous hilltop enclave with an active bar and dining scene.

Orientation

Downtown streets are laid out on a grid radiating from Fountain Sq. Mt Adams is east of downtown, beyond the snarl of freeway ramps, and the up-and-coming Over-the-Rhine neighborhood is immediately north of downtown. The snaking

Ohio River forms the city's southern boundary; charming Covington, Kentucky, lies across the water.

Information

Visitors Center (513-621-6994; 511 Walnut St; 10am-5pm Mon-Sat, noon-5pm Sun) Can help with tourist info.

Dangers & Annoyances

The area between the train station and downtown is best avoided on foot, and caution should be used at night in the Over-the-Rhine neighborhood, north of downtown.

Sights & Activities

DOWNTOWN

The elegant 1876 **Roebling Suspension Bridge** was a forerunner of John Roebling's famous Brooklyn Bridge in New York. At its foot is the **National Underground Railroad Freedom Center** (513-412-6100; www.freedomcenter.org; north bank of the Ohio River; admission $12; 10am-4pm Tue-Sat, 11am-4pm Sun), with exhibits on how slaves escaped to the north; Cincinnati was a prominent stop on the railroad and a center for abolitionist activities led by residents such as Harriet Beecher Stowe.

Fountain Sq (cnr 5th & Vine Sts), the city centerpiece, hosts the fancy old Spirit of the Waters fountain. **Carew Tower** (513-579-9735; 441 Vine St; admission $2; 10am-3pm Mon-Fri, 10am-4:45pm Sat & Sun) has a great view from its 49th-floor observation deck and a fine art deco interior. East of the square is the postmodern **Procter & Gamble world headquarters** (cnr 6th St & Broadway), often called the 'Dolly Parton Towers' due to its resemblance to the country singer's most prominent features.

A stroll along the riverfront will take you through several parks; one of them, **Bicentennial Commons** at Sawyer Point, features whimsical monuments and flying pigs. The pedestrian-only **Purple People Bridge** provides a unique crossing from Sawyer Point to Newport, Kentucky. You can also cross the **Taylor–Southgate Bridge** on foot.

MT ADAMS

It might be a bit of a stretch to compare Mt Adams, immediately east of downtown, to Paris' Montmarte, but this hilly 19th-century enclave of narrow, twisting streets, Victorian townhouses, galleries, bars and restaurants is certainly a pleasurable surprise. Two big attractions here are the **Cincinnati Art Museum** (☎ 513-721-5204; 953 Eden Park Dr; admission free; ☺ 11am-5pm Tue, Thu & Fri, 11am-9pm Wed, 10am-5pm Sat, noon-6pm Sun), with an emphasis on Middle Eastern and European arts as well as local works, and the **Krohn Conservatory** (☎ 513-421-4086; 1501 Eden Park Dr; admission free; ☺ 10am-5pm), which is a vast greenhouse with a rain forest, desert flora and superb seasonal flower shows. Most visitors just ascend the hill for a look around, a drink and a pause to enjoy the magnificent view from the hilltop Catholic church.

To drive here, follow 7th St east of downtown to Van Meter St, turn right and head up Elsinore Ave. For a strenuous 30-minute hike up the hill, take E 6th St, cross the bridge and then climb a long stairway.

COVINGTON & NEWPORT
Directly across the river is **Covington**, Kentucky, a historic and charming town that serves as a sort of bedroom community of Cincinnati. Covington's bustling **MainStrasse** was once a 19th-century German neighborhood; it is now full of shops, pubs and places to eat. A pleasant riverfront walk lies east of the Roebling Bridge.

Covington Landing, an area of floating bars and tour boats, is right by the south end of the Roebling Suspension Bridge. **BB Riverboats** (☎ 859-261-8500, 800-261-8586; 1 Madison Ave; tickets $13-40; call for schedules) takes off from here and plies the river in a nifty sightseeing paddle wheeler.

Festivals & Events
Riverfest (☎ 513-352-4000; www.webn.com/riverfest) Concerts and fireworks; Sunday of Labor Day weekend (early September).

Oktoberfest (www.oktoberfest-zinzinnati.com) German beer, brats and mania; mid-September.

Sleeping
Hotel tax is a tad cheaper on the Kentucky side at 10.24%, rather than the 16.5% charged in Cincinnati. Tax is not included in the following prices.

Cincinnati Riverfront Travelodge (☎ 859-291-4434; 222 York St; r $50-65; P ☒ ☒) Your best affordable option, at the Newport, Kentucky, end of the Taylor–Southgate Bridge, is this slightly dated Travelodge. Rooms are large and clean and north-facing rooms have

views of the river. Getting downtown and to the Red's ballpark entails a pleasant walk over the bridge.

Budget Host (☎ 513-559-1600; 3356 Central Parkway; r $45-85; P ☒) Trying hard to be bright and cheery, it's definitely the top cheapie in the uptown area along Central Parkway; exit at Hopple St, about 3 miles north of downtown on I-75, or take the No 20 bus.

Comfort Suites (☎ 859-291-6700; 420 Riverboat Row; r $80-130; P ☒) This is an OK, if pricey option near the Newport attractions.

Eating
In addition to downtown, good dining options are concentrated in Mt Adams, along the riverfront and in Clifton by the University of Cincinnati (try Calhoun, McMillan and Ludlow Sts).

Skyline Chili (☎ 513-721-4715; 1007 Vine St; mains $2-5) The 'five-way chili' served here is a Cincinnati classic. It consists of meat sauce (spiced with chocolate and cinnamon) with beans, cheese and onions served on a bed of spaghetti. Dare yourself – it's actually quite tasty. The chili dogs ($1.30) are the cheapest eats in town.

Kaldi's (☎ 513-241-3070; 1204 Main St; mains $5-9) In the transitional Over-the-Rhine neighborhood, north of downtown, Kaldi's coffee shop-bar-restaurant-bookstore is a bohemian respite. An eclectic crowd convenes in the hip, library-like atmosphere, and people often linger long after they've polished off their delicious food (particularly the vegetarian 'un-burger'). There's live music some evenings.

Rookwood Pottery Bistro (☎ 513-721-5456; 1077 Celestial St; mains $7-17) In a former pottery factory atop Mt Adams, the Rookwood warms the heart with delectable sandwiches and inventive mains, like mahi mahi served with pineapple salsa.

Findlay Market (cnr Findlay & Elm Sts; ☺ morning Mon & Tue, to 6pm Wed-Sat) This is a collection of vendors in little stores and stalls offering everything from fresh fish to organic jellies to Mediterranean spices. Saturday is the biggest day.

Chez Nora (☎ 606-491-8027; 530 Main St; mains $6-20) In Covington, this congenial dining spot has a rooftop terrace where jazz bands play. Light sandwich and salad fare and more elaborate meals are on the menu.

GREAT LAKES

Graeter's Ice Cream (☎ 513-381-0653; 41 E 4th St) Another local delicacy, this is the place to come for dessert. There are other locations around town.

Drinking

The city's German influence meant Cincinnati was once an oasis of beer – in the 1890s there were 1800 saloons for 297,000 people, guzzling two times more than the rest of the country. Mt Adams and Over-the-Rhine are still busy nightspots. Covington Landing has places on the river (in moored boats) that are refreshing on hot nights when there's a breeze.

Blind Lemon (☎ 513-241-3885; 936 Hatch St) Here's a sweet spot in Mt Adams, with an atmospheric courtyard. Live bands play outdoors on warm evenings. Inside, trains and other bric-a-brac hang from the ceiling.

Arnold's (☎ 513-421-6234; 210 E 8th St) Arnold's is a downtown oldie but goodie dating from 1861. There's live music nightly – often blue grass (a Kentucky influence, no doubt).

Jefferson Hall Saloon (☎ 513-723-9008; 1150 Main St) The cornerstone of the happening Over-the-Rhine district, Jefferson Hall regularly features obscure or well-known rock and blues acts.

Barrel House (☎ 513-421-2337; 22 E 12th St) A brew pub in Over-the-Rhine, Barrel House has a nice copper bar, good pizza and live music most nights.

Entertainment

CityBeat is a free weekly entertainment paper, out on Wednesday.

Cincinnati Reds (☎ 513-765-7000; 100 Main St) Cincy, home of the Reds, is a great baseball town, with the modern riverside Great American Ballpark and an undying love for the home team.

Cincinnati Bengals (☎ 513-621-3550; 1 Paul Brown Stadium) The local NFL team scrimmages a few blocks west, at Paul Brown Stadium.

Getting There & Around

Cincinnati's airport is actually in Kentucky, 13 miles south. To get downtown, take the **TANK bus** ($1.25) from Terminal 1 or 3.

Greyhound and Amtrak stop here. **Metro** (☎ 513-621-4455; 120 E 4th St) runs the local commuter buses. Fares are 80¢ during rush hour.

MICHIGAN

As Michigan's mitt-shaped Lower Peninsula reaches to touch the remote Upper Peninsula, the state plunges into the heart of the Great Lakes. In fact, the waters of four of the Great Lakes lap Michigan shores, which stretch some 3200 miles. It's a refreshing image, and for serious lovers of the great outdoors (particularly bowhunters and fishing enthusiasts) Michigan fulfils its promise. Of primary interest to the shoestring traveler is the chance to motor through the UP's peculiar towns and hike off into the wilderness for a day or two. You'll also want to have a look at the desolated cityscape that is Detroit. Ann Arbor, one of the Midwest's great college towns, also beckons.

Prior to the mid-1970s, the car industry dominated Michigan, but the state has since worked hard to diversify its economy. Still, manufacture of passenger cars and transportation equipment accounts for about one quarter of the annual gross state product. General Motors (GM), Ford and the Chrysler Group of Daimler Chrysler all maintain their headquarters in or near Detroit.

State Parks
Michigan state park information
(☎ 800-447-2757; www.midnrreservations.com)
Campground reservations accepted. Park entry requires a vehicle permit ($4/20 per day/year).

DETROIT

To be perfectly honest, Detroit is a pit, forever mired in a 'recovery' that never seems to coalesce. It's depressing, sure, but that's what's interesting about the place. Wide swathes of downtown are filled with empty lots and the boarded-up buildings that rose and fell with the fortunes of the auto industry. Such overt destitution represents a cold sore on the lip of the American Way, and perhaps it has also inspired the city's hard-edged musicians – Eminem and the White Stripes hail from the Motor City, and the local club scene is alive with creative energy.

Detroit's top sights, Motown and the Henry Ford Museum, are both truly one-of-a-kind attractions.

GREAT LAKES

THE MOTOR CITY STORY

At the turn of the 20th century, Detroit was a medium-size city of 285,000, known as a manufacturing center for horse-drawn carriages and bicycles. Thanks in part to the massive iron and copper mines in the Upper Peninsula, cheap transport on the Great Lakes and enterprising s ouls such as Henry Ford, the Dodge brothers and the Fisher brothers, Detroit quickly became the motor capital of the world. Ford in particular changed the fabric of US society. He didn't invent the automobile, as so many mistakenly believe, but he did perfect the assembly line manufacturing method and became one of the first industrialists to use mass production. The result was the Model T, the first car that the USA's middle class could afford to own.

Since its 1950s heyday, when Detroit's population exceeded two million, the city's fortunes have spiraled downwards. Racial tensions spurred violent riots, which peaked in 1967 and left blocks of the city smoldering. The oil shocks and inroads by the Japanese carmakers in the 1970s rocked the auto industry, and many residents packed up and fled to the suburbs. The city entered an era of deep decline, with its population eventually dropping below one million.

Today 80% of the city's residents are black, and the Motor City remains a culturally rich region, and a national center for African American culture.

Orientation

The glossy Renaissance Center, GM's headquarters, dominates the skyline, but the heart of Detroit is Hart Plaza, nestled alongside the Detroit River at the foot of Woodward Ave. Woodward is the city's main boulevard and heads north from the plaza all the way to Pontiac. The Mile Roads are major arteries east-west; 8 Mile (which entered the national consciousness thanks to local boy Eminem) forms the boundary between Detroit and the suburbs. Across the river lies Windsor, Canada. Detroit is a bit of a geographical oddity: it is the only US city that looks south to Canada.

Information

The *Metro Times*, distributed free on Wednesday, is the best guide to Detroit's arts, music and nightclub scene.

Detroit Convention & Visitors Bureau (☎ 313-202-1800; www.visitdetroit.com; 10th fl, 211 W Fort St; ☻ 9am-5pm Mon-Fri) Fill up on info here.

Dangers & Annoyances

The main streets (Woodward Ave, Jefferson Ave, Lafayette Blvd) with office buildings, restaurants, nightclubs and attractions are as safe as any other large USA city. Travelers should avoid the areas around 12th St where the 1967 riots began.

Sights & Activities

The **Motown Museum** (☎ 313-875-2264; 2648 W Grand Blvd; admission $8; ☻ 10am-6pm Tue-Sat), in Berry Gordy's old house, is where the small record label churned out a stunning string of stars and hits that ruled the pop and soul charts throughout the 1960s. Justifiably known as 'Hitsville USA,' Motown began in 1959. Stars that rose from the Motown label include Diana Ross, Marvin Gaye, the Four Tops, Smoky Robinson, Stevie Wonder, Gladys Knight and Michael Jackson. Gordy and Motown split for the glitz of Los Angeles in 1972, but you can still step into humble Studio A and see where the magic happened.

Detroit's melting pot is best experienced at the **Eastern Market**; on Tuesday and Saturday, the large halls at Gratiot Ave and Russell St are filled with bartering shoppers and vendors. Surrounding the open market are specialty shops, delis and restaurants.

Hamtramck, northeast of downtown, is a traditional Polish enclave with a 1940s-era shopping strip that's alive with restaurants and bars. The area is still largely Polish, with recent arrivals from Albania.

Greektown is the liveliest part of downtown, with restaurants, bakeries and casinos centered on Monroe St.

The **People Mover** (☎ 313-962-7245), Detroit's 3-mile elevated rail system, appears forlornly unpractical but it's cheap (50¢) and provides great views of the city and riverfront.

If the day is nice, head to **Belle Isle**, 2.5 miles northeast of downtown at E Jefferson Ave and E Grand Blvd. It's a good spot for a picnic and a view of the downtown skyline.

GREAT LAKES

Festivals & Events

Movement Festival (☎ 313-567-0080; www.movementfestival.com) The world's largest electronic music festival congregates in Hart Plaza over the Memorial Day weekend; admission is free.

Woodward Dream Cruise (☎ 888-493-2196; www.woodwarddreamcruise.com) More than 1.5 million people line Woodward Ave between Ferndale and Pontiac to watch thousands of classic cars cruise by on the third Saturday in August.

Sleeping

Room rates listed here do not include the 9% hotel tax.

HI Country Grandma's Home Hostel (☎ 734-753-4901; 22330 Bell Rd; dm $15; ☿ Apr-Sep) In New Boston, midway between Detroit and Ann Arbor (about a 20-minute drive either way), Grandma's is homey, with seven beds in two rooms. Reservations are required. It's not accessible by public transportation.

Shorecrest Motor Inn (☎ 313-568-3000, 800-992-9616; 1316 E Jefferson Ave; r $75-100; P ⊠) Shorecrest is the pick of the litter with clean, comfortable rooms just six blocks northeast of Hart Plaza. It has friendly, helpful staff.

Hotel Pontchartrain (☎ 313-965-0200; 2 Washington Blvd; r $89-169; P $17 ⊠ ⊠) This is a historic, full-amenity hotel downtown by Cobo Hall; rates are low when business is slow.

Affordable motels abound in the Detroit suburbs. From I-94, follow the signs for Merriman Rd when leaving the airport and take your pick.

Motel 6 (☎ 248-583-0500; 32700 Barrington Rd; r $36-46; P ⊠ ⊠) In the northern suburb of Madison Heights, this is about the cheapest around.

Pontiac Lake Recreation Area (☎ 248-666-1020; 7800 Gale Rd; campsites $20; ☿ May–mid-Oct) West of Pontiac on M-59 in Waterford, it's the closest state park with modern campsites.

Eating

Detroit restaurants reward their ethnically diverse patrons with large portions of authentic dishes at reasonable prices.

Lafayette Coney Island (☎ 313-964-8198; 118 Lafayette Blvd; mains $2-3; ☿ 24hr) Lafayette's minimalist menu consists of hot dogs smothered with chili and onions (ie a 'Coney'), burgers, fries, pies, doughnuts and beer. It's downtown. Cast-iron stomach required.

New Hellas Cafe (☎ 313-961-5544; 583 Monroe St; mains $7-12) Flaming cheese and the cry of 'Opa!' are a Detroit tradition at this bustling Greektown restaurant.

Cass Cafe (☎ 313-831-1400; 4620 Cass Ave; mains $5-9; ☿ noon-2am) An artsy kind of eatery serving soups, sandwiches and veggie beauties like the lentil walnut burger.

Jacoby's (☎ 313-962-7067; 624 Brush St; mains $7-12) Since 1904, this old tavern has been satisfying German cravings with sauerbraten, Wiener schnitzel and German beer.

Traffic Jam & Snug (☎ 313-831-9470; 511 W Canfield St; mains $8-20; ☿ Mon-Sat) Detroit's best brew-pub food.

Drinking

BARS

Motor City Brewing Works (☎ 313-832-2700; 470 W Canfield St; ☿ Wed-Sat) A small, intimate bar that makes its own brew.

Union Street Saloon (☎ 313-831-3965; 4145 Woodward Ave) This place has been around since the early 1900s and still attracts a mod crowd.

LIVE MUSIC

In recent years rock, rap and techno have pushed the city to the forefront of the music scene.

St Andrew's Hall (☎ 313-961-6358; 431 E Congress St) A legendary alternative band venue; downstairs is the **Shelter** (☎ 313-961-6358), a smaller music/dance club.

Magic Stick (☎ 313-833-9700; 4120 Woodward Ave) and larger **Majestic Theater** (☎ 313-833-9700; 4140 Woodward Ave) are side-by-side concert halls where indie rockers and rap djs perform. The complex also has bowling, billiards and a pizza joint.

X/S (☎ 313-963-9797; 1500 Woodward Ave) This techno hothouse is Detroit's top downtown spot for dancing, in an old piano store.

Entertainment

Detroit Pistons (☎ 248-377-0100; 2 Championship Dr) The Palace hosts the NBA Pistons and **Detroit Shock** women's team.

Detroit Redwings (☎ 313-396-7444; 600 Civic Center Dr) Detroit's much-loved pro hockey team plays at Joe Louis arena.

Detroit Lions (☎ 800-616-7627; cnr Brush & Adams Sts) This NFL team plays at downtown Ford Field.

Detroit Tigers (☎ 313-471-2255; 2100 Woodward Ave) The Tigers play Major League baseball at Comerica Park, downtown.

Getting There & Around

It is best to have your own wheels to get around the Motor City; public transportation is lacking, much to the big automakers' delight.

Metro Airport (☎ 734-247-7678; www.metroairport .com) is 15 miles southwest of Detroit. The Smart bus ($1.50) gets downtown in 1½ hours; catch it on the lower level of LC Smith Terminal.

The **Greyhound terminal** (☎ 313-961-8562; 1001 Howard St) is near Lodge Freeway. Amtrak also stops here.

The **Detroit Department of Transportation** (DDOT; ☎ 888-336-8287) handles the local bus service. The fare is $1.25, transfers 25¢.

AROUND DETROIT
Dearborn

If Detroit's auto industry rocks your boat, the **Henry Ford Museum** (☎ 313-271-1620; 20900 Oakwood Blvd; admission $14; ☒ 9:30am-5pm Mon-Sat, noon-5pm Sun), in this suburb 10 miles from Detroit, will tip it over. The huge showroom displays classic cars from the industry's origins right up to contemporary times. Some of the highlights are one-of-a-kind vehicles that were clearly designer indulgences. Equally interesting is the adjacent, outdoor **Greenfield Village** (☎ 313-271-1620; admission $20; ☒ 9am-5pm Mon-Sat, noon-5pm Sun Apr-Dec), which features historic old buildings shipped in from over the country, reconstructed and restored. Together the museums contain a wealth of Americana, such as the chair Lincoln was sitting in when he was assassinated, Edgar Allan Poe's writing desk and Thomas Edison's laboratory from Menlo Park. The museum and village are separate attractions, but you can get a combination ticket for one day ($26) or two ($48). The two-day pack includes admission to the **Ford Rouge Factory Tour** (☎ 313-982-6001), taking you behind the scenes of a Ford plant that has been assembling cars since the 1920s.

Ann Arbor

Leafy, liberal and bookish, Ann Arbor is home of the University of Michigan. The walkable downtown is loaded with coffee shops, bookstores, brewpubs and informal places in which to grab a cheap bite.

Ann Arbor's biggest events are the University of Michigan football games, a fall tradition attracting 115,000 fans per game.

Tickets are nearly impossible to purchase, especially when nemesis Ohio State is in town. You can try, or obtain tickets to other sporting events, by calling the **U of M Ticket Office** (☎ 734-764-0247).

Grab tasty Middle Eastern dishes at **Jerusalem Garden** (☎ 734-995-5060; 307 S Fifth Ave; mains $3-9). **Zingerman's Delicatessen** (☎ 734-663-3354; 422 Detroit St; mains $7-12) is regarded by many as one of the Midwest's finest. **Fleetwood Diner** (☎ 734-995-5502; 304 S Ashley St; mains $5-7; ☒ 24hr) is an atmospheric round-the-clock greasy spoon that attracts the studious and down at heel.

When darkness falls, head to the **Blind Pig** (☎ 734-996-8555; 208 S First St) or the **Ark** (☎ 734-761-1800; 316 S Main St), both nationally acclaimed venues for rock, blues and more. Live music and handcrafted beer are found at **Arbor Brewing Co** (☎ 734-213-1393; 114 E Washington St; mains $7-12).

UPPER PENINSULA

The UP is likely to be out of your way regardless where you're going, but that's part of the reason it's worth heading up this way. The area's isolation gives it its own identity, far from the chain-store driven mainstream. You can drive from the Mackinac Bridge to the Wisconsin state line in about six hours, or take your time cruising two-lane blacktops along an undeveloped shoreline and through rustic campgrounds and rural towns that time seems to have overlooked.

Many come here to get away from it all, which is what happens when you visit Isle Royale National Park, a 210-sq-mile island in Lake Superior. Pictured Rocks National Lakeshore and Tahquamenon Falls are also justifiably popular with visitors.

THE 'TOLEDO WAR'

The Upper Peninsula became part of Michigan state thanks to the 'Toledo War' of 1835–36, when the new state's militia faced off against the Ohio militia over rights to the city of Toledo. (Toledo hasn't enjoyed such popularity since.) Ohio won the dispute, with nary a drop of blood spilt, and Michigan was given the Upper Peninsula as consolation. Easy-going Wisconsin still hasn't gotten its back up over this turn of events.

GREAT LAKES

Sault Ste Marie & Around

Founded in 1668, Sault Ste Marie (Sault is pronounced 'soo') is the third-oldest city in the USA. The town is best known for its locks that raise and lower the 1000ft-long freighters between the different lake levels. **Soo Lock Park** is at the end of Water St in the heart of downtown. It features an interpretive center and observation decks from which you can watch the action. To get closer to the boats, go down to the adjacent walkway.

Most of Sault Ste Marie's motels are along the I-75 Business Loop and Ashmun St. Try the pleasant **Plaza Motor Motel** (☎ 906-635-1881, 888-809-1881; www.plazamotormotel.com; 3901 I-75 Business; r $33-81; ⊠), or the spiffy **Lockview Motel** (☎ 906-632-2491, 800-854-0745; www.lockview.com; 327 W Portage Ave; r $53-69; ⊙ May–mid-Oct; ⊠), across from Soo Locks.

Head straight to the ever popular **Antlers** (☎ 906-632-3571; 804 E Portage Ave; mains $8-20) if you want to enjoy a carnivorous feast amid a gallery of stuffed animal heads (animal rights enthusiasts beware). Huge steaks, burgers and ribs anchor the menu.

An hour's drive west of Sault Ste Marie, via M-28 and M-123, is the eastern UP's top attraction: lovely **Tahquamenon Falls**, with tea-colored waters tinted so by upstream hemlock leaves. The Upper Falls in **Tahquamenon Falls State Park** (☎ 906-492-3415; campsite $15-17; day-tripper $8 per vehicle) are 200ft across with a 50ft drop, making them the third-largest falls east of the Mississippi River. The Lower Falls are a series of smaller cascades best viewed by renting a **boat** (☎ 906-492-3457) and rowing across the river to an island. The large state park also has camping and excellent hiking, and there's a brew pub near the park entrance. North of the park, beyond the little town of Paradise, is the fascinating **Great Lakes Shipwreck Museum** (☎ 906-635-1742; 18335 N Whitefish Point Rd; admission $8.50; ⊙ 10am-6pm May-Oct), where the intriguing displays include items trawled up from sunken ships. More than 300 ships have sunk nearby in the congested sea lanes and unpredictable weather of the 'Graveyard of the Great Lakes.'

The M-123 leads to Paradise. **Curly's Paradise Motel** (☎ 906-492-3445; M-123; r from $50; ⊠) is a family-owned motel on the lake. There are numerous other well-kept mom-and-pop motels along this stretch of highway.

Pictured Rocks National Lakeshore

Along an isolated stretch of spectacular shoreline, these 200ft high cliffs are a lovely sight to behold, particularly in the late afternoon light. Head first to the gateway town of Munising, where you can book a 2½-hour boat tour with **Pictured Rock Boat Cruises** (☎ 906-387-2379; fare $27; ⊙ 9am-5pm late May–mid-Oct); boats depart from downtown on the hour in summer. You can also drive to **Miners Castle Overlook**, 12 miles east of Munising off M-58, for a good view.

Just offshore is **Grand Island**, part of the Hiawatha National Forest. Hop aboard the **Grand Island Ferry** (☎ 906-387-3503; round-trip $14; late May–mid-Oct) to get there, and rent a mountain bike ($15) from the ferry company to zip around.

Munising has lots of motels, including **Alger Falls Motel** (☎ 906-387-3536; www.algerfallsmotel.com; M-28 E; r $45-68).

IF YOU HAVE A FEW MORE DAYS IN MICHIGAN

Totally free of vehicles and roads, **Isle Royale National Park** (☎ 906-482-0984; www.nps.gov/isro; 800 E Lakeshore Dr; admission per person per night $4; ⊙ 8am-4:30pm Mon-Fri year-round, 8am-6pm Mon-Sat in summer), an island far off the coast of Michigan's Upper Peninsula, is certainly a place to go for peace and quiet – and to commune with moose and wolves (very cautiously). It is laced with 165 miles of hiking trails that connect dozens of campgrounds along Lake Superior and inland lakes. You must be totally prepared for this wilderness adventure, with a tent, camping stove, sleeping bags, food and water filter. The Isle Royale National Park Service headquarters is in Houghton.

From the dock outside the headquarters, the **Ranger III** (☎ 906-482-0984; round-trip $100; ⊙ 9am Tue & Fri) departs twice a week on the six-hour trip to Rock Harbor, at the east end of the island. Alternately, you can head 50 miles up the Keweenaw Peninsula to Copper Harbor (a beautiful drive), from where it's a 4½-hour trip aboard the **Isle Royale Queen** (☎ 906-289-4437; www.isleroyale.com; round-trip $100). You also can access Isle Royale from Grand Portage, MN. Bringing a kayak or canoe on the ferry costs about $40 more.

WISCONSIN

Wisconsin is a state of mind, a leisurely ride through crisp imagery of a bucolic Middle America that elsewhere has long faded away. Much of the state is a dairy wonderland of yawning pastures, laconic farmers and beautiful barns. Peaceful, peninsular Door County, with its subtle coastal light, bears an unexpected likeness to coastal New England. Wisconsin cities have their own peculiar charms: Milwaukee's a fun place to swill cheap beer and eat unhealthy food, while Green Bay is endearing for its football madness. Madison, a prototypical college town in a lovely, insular setting, captivates visitors with its sophisticated, worldly tastes.

State Parks

Wisconsin state park information (☎ 888-947-2757; www.dnr.state.wi.us) Park entry requires a vehicle permit ($10 per day). Campground reservations accepted.

MILWAUKEE

The beer's bad but the company's unbeatable in this fun-loving, mid-size city. Milwaukee's charming because it's comfortably unfashionable, as if the local citizenry figure there's no point putting on airs when worldly Chicago is a mere 1½ hours away. Downtown Milwaukee is attractive, with a narrow river wending through early 20th century buildings, and Harley riders regularly rumble through the city that birthed their hog of choice. Local sports fans only ask that their Brewers make a valiant effort to achieve a .500 record, and bowling remains a popular pastime. Surely, *Laverne and Shirley* are enjoying their golden years somewhere in town, chain-smoking filtered cigarettes in a local bar. Be sure to venture out to the workaday neighborhoods for a true taste of what this old burgh has to offer.

Orientation

Lake Michigan sits to the east of the city, and is rimmed by parkland. The inspired **Riverwalk** is a great system of redeveloped walking paths along both sides of the Milwaukee River downtown. Wisconsin Ave divides streets east from west. North and uth streets usually are numbered and in- ase as they head west from the lake.

Information

Visitors center (☎ 414-908-6205; 400 W Wisconsin Ave; 🕒 8am-5pm Mon-Fri, daily in summer) This makes a helpful stop.

Sights & Activities

Sights are spread out, but usually accessible by public buses.

HARLEY-DAVIDSON PLANT

In 1903 William Harley and Arthur Davidson, local schoolmates, built and sold their first Harley-Davidson motorcycle. A century later, the big bikes are a symbol of American manufacturing pride, and this **Harley-Davidson plant** (☎ 414-535-3666; 11700 W Capitol Dr; admission free; 🕒 usually 9:30am-1pm Mon, Wed & Fri), in the suburb of Wauwatosa (20 minutes from downtown Milwaukee) is where engines are built. (Body assembly goes on in York, Pennsylvania and Kansas City, Missouri.) The one-hour tours are kind of technical, but ultimate payoff comes when you get to sit in the saddle of a vintage bike. No open-shoes are permitted in the plant.

BREWERIES

Pabst and Schlitz have moved on, but Milwaukee is still known for its watery, working-class beer. Of course, that's not everyone's cup of tea, but it would be a shame not to join the legions of beer drinkers that line up for tours of the **Miller Brewing Company** (☎ 414-931-2337; 4251 W State St; admission free; 🕒 10:30am-3:30pm Mon-Sat). A most fascinating walk through the bottling and distribution areas will give you an idea of just how much brew the public consumes. Bring ID to participate in the generous tasting session.

For more swell times (and better beer), head out to the small-scale **Sprecher Brewing Company** (☎ 414-964-2739; 701 W Glendale Ave; admission $3; 🕒 4pm Fri, 1-3pm Sat), a microbrewery with a museum featuring memorabilia from long-gone Milwaukee breweries and a beer garden replete with oom-pah music. It's 5 miles north of downtown.

Festivals & Events

Milwaukee knows how to put on a party, so don't pass the opportunity to join in the fun. Call the **visitors center** (☎ 414-908-6205) for details.

German Fest (www.germanfest.com) July ends with this brew-ha-ha.

Irish Fest (www.irishfest.com) The shamrock crowd jigs in mid-August.

Polish Fest (www.polishfest.org) Polka's, Chopin recitals and the crowning of Miss Polish in late June.

PrideFest (www.pridefest.com) Milwaulkee's large gay and lesbian festival is in June.

Summerfest (☎ 800-273-3378; www.summer fest.com) The granddaddy of local festivals, with 11 days of music and merriment in late June and early July.

Sleeping

Rates listed here are for summertime; rooms can be 15% to 30% less in winter. The 14.6% tax is not included in the listed rates. Book ahead in summer.

HI Milwaukee Summer Hostel (☎ 414-288-3232, 414-961-2525; www.hostellingwisconsin.org; 525 N 17th St; dm from $17; Ⓟ $3.50 ⊠ ▣) Marquette University's South Residence Hall serves as a hostel during June and July. It's well-located, near public transportation and has the usual amenities (kitchen, laundry) plus room phones.

Try Howell Ave, which is located south near the airport, for cheap chain lodging, including **Motel 6** (☎ 414-482-4414; 5037 S Howell Ave; r $33-48; Ⓟ ⊠).

Ambassador Hotel (☎ 414-342-8400; www.ambass hotel.com; 2308 W Wisconsin Ave; r $69-99; Ⓟ ⊠) Near the Marquette University and not far from downtown, this old hotel has been modestly maintained over the years.

Astor Hotel (☎ 800-558-0200; www.theastorhotel .com; 924 E Juneau Ave; r $79-109; Ⓟ $3 ⊠ ▣) The Astor, which dates from 1918, has bright, spacious rooms, some with cool old furnishings, plus perks like a continental breakfast, free Internet and a convenient shuttle to nearby sights.

Best Western Inn Towne Hotel (☎ 414-224-8400; www.inntownehotel.com; 710 N Old World 3rd St; r $89-129; Ⓟ $10 ⊠) It's operated by a chain, but this old hotel offers good-quality rooms and vintage ambience right in the heart of downtown.

Eating

If all's going according to plan, you're in Milwaukee in time for the weekend, and you'll be partaking in a **Friday night fish fry**. This highly social tradition is observed throughout Wisconsin and all over Milwaukee. It costs around $10.

American Serb Memorial Hall (☎ 414-545-6030; 5101 W Oklahoma Ave; ☽ noon-9pm Fri) Southwest of downtown, this place has one of the best fish fries. A large crowd of regulars come for its all-you-can-eat baked cod, and visitors will feel welcome.

Safehouse (☎ 414-271-2007; 779 N Front St; mains $6-20) This most intriguing downtown spot is hidden away behind a door marked 'International Exports Ltd.' Once you've been buzzed in you'll step into a spy's world filled with sliding panels and secret passageways. It's a fun and original way to enjoy sandwiches and burgers and the like.

Nite-Owl Drive-In (☎ 414-483-2524; 83 E Layton Ave; mains $3-7; ☽ Tue-Sat) Head down towards the airport if you're a fan of unadulterated diners from the mid-20th century. This one's well-used and well-loved.

African Hut (☎ 414-765-1110; N 1107 N Old World 3rd St; mains $9-12; ☽ Mon-Sat) A wonderful place to go for exotic meat and vegetarian dishes with fabulous ingredients such as pounded yam, cassava and cooked-down peanuts blended with herbs, served amid some wild leopard-print walls.

A Milwaukee specialty is frozen custard, like ice cream only smoother and richer. **Leon's** (☎ 414-383-1784; 3131 S 27th St) and **Kopp's** (☎ 414-961-2006; 5373 N Port Washington Rd, Glendale) are popular purveyors.

Drinking

The beer legacy guarantees that a thirst-quenching array of golden nectar is available. Over a dozen bars and restaurants lie around N Water and E State Sts. More bars can be found in Walker's Point on 1st and 2nd Sts, and along Brady St between Astor and Farwell Sts.

THE BEV THAT MADE MILWAUKEE FAMOUS

German settlers started small breweries here in the mid-19th century, but the introduction of bulk brewing technology in the 1890s turned beer into a major Milwaukee industry. Schlitz ('the beer that made Milwaukee famous'), Pabst and Miller were all based here at one time, but among the majors, only Miller remains.

Gene & Mary's Holler House (☎ 414-647-9284; 2242 Lincoln Ave) A unique Milwaukee experience, this living-room/bar has antique, regulation-sized bowling lanes in the basement. Phone to see if the pin-setter will be on duty.

Von Trier (☎ 414-272-1775; 2235 N Farwell Ave) The German Von Trier is a long-standing, real-deal favorite, with plenty of good stuff on tap and a biergarten.

Water Street Brewery (☎ 414-272-1195; 1101 N Water St) The emphasis here is definitely on beer: Water Street brews several fine ones.

Entertainment

Shepherd Express is the free weekly entertainment paper available at bookstores and coffee shops.

Milwaukee Brewers (☎ 414-902-4000; 1 Brewers Way) The local National League team plays baseball in Miller Park, which has a retractable roof and real grass.

Milwaukee Bucks (☎ 414-227-0400; 1001 N 4th St) The NBA Bucks do their dribbling at the Bradley Center.

Getting There & Around

General Mitchell International Airport (☎ 414-747-5300; 5300 S Howell Ave) is 8 miles south of downtown. Take public bus No 80 ($1.50) downtown. Greyhound and Amtrak frequently pass through on the way to/from Chicago and onwards. **Badger Bus** (☎ 414-276-7490; 635 N James Lovell St) goes to Madison. The **Milwaukee County Transit System** (☎ 414-344-6711; www.ridemcts.com; 1942 N 17th Ave) provides efficient local bus service as well as a trolley-like bus – the 'Milwaukee Loop' – that runs downtown. Tickets cost $1.50.

MADISON

Wisconsin's small state capital surely rates among the country's best college towns. Ensconced on a narrow isthmus between Mendota and Monona lakes, the town feels wonderfully secluded and yet, as a stroll down lively State St makes obvious, its liberal-minded denizens have an abiding love for world cuisines and cultures. Come in spring, when locals and students take pleasure in biking and hiking around the lakes.

Information

Isthmus is the local entertainment paper.

Visitors center (☎ 608-255-2537; www.visitmadison .com; 615 E Washington Ave; ⊗ 8am-5pm Mon-Fri) Six blocks from Capitol Sq.

Sights & Activities

Head straight to State St, the shaded strip of student stores, bars, cafés and inexpensive international restaurants. It forms the axis between the capitol and the University of Wisconsin. This is where it's all happening.

The heart of town is boldly marked by the x-shaped **State Capitol** (☎ 608-266-0382; admission free; ⊗ 8am-6pm Mon-Fri, 8am-4pm Sat & Sun). It's a beaut, as pompous government structures go, and also the USA's largest capitol building outside Washington, DC. Tours are available on the hour most days.

The impeccable **Monona Terrace Community & Convention Center** (☎ 608-261-4000; 1 John Nolen Dr; admission free; ⊗ 8am-5pm; P $3), two blocks from the square, has a fabulous rooftop garden overlooking Lake Monona. It finally opened in 1997, 59 years after Frank Lloyd Wright designed it. Tours (adult/student $3/2) are offered at 1pm daily.

By all means, take advantage of the city's lakes and trails. For rentals, try **Yellow Jersey** (☎ 608-257-4737; 419 State St; bikes per day $10; ⊗ 10am-6pm Tue, Wed & Fri, 10am-8pm Mon & Thu, 9am-5pm Sat, noon-5pm Sun) for two-wheelers and **Carl's Paddlin' Canoe & Kayak** (☎ 608-284-0300; 110 N Thornton St; per day $30; ⊗ 10am-6pm Mon-Wed, 10am-8pm Thu & Fri, 10am-5pm Sat, noon-5pm Sun) for lake-faring craft.

Sleeping

HI Madison Hostel (☎ 608-441-0144; www.madison hostel.org; 141 S Butler St; dm/r $16/38) The hostel is right downtown. Linens and towels are free and there's a kitchen and laundry.

University Inn (☎ 608-285-8040; 441 N Frances St; r $69-149; P 🟦) This handy hotel is right by the State St action downtown.

Select Inn (☎ 608-249-1815; 4845 Hayes Rd; r $51-56; P 🟦) This Tyrolean knock-off with free high-speed Internet access stands out among the moderately priced motels off I-90/I-94. It's 6 miles from the center. Other motels can be found off Hwy 12/18 and along Washington Ave.

Eating & Drinking

Himal Chuli (☎ 608-251-9225; 318 State St; mains $7-11) This aromatic and cozy place serves up homemade Nepali fare, including vegetarian dishes.

Kabul (☎ 608-256-6322; 541 State St; mains $6-11) Head to Kabul for beautifully prepared Afghani food.

Michelangelo's (☎ 608-251-5299; 114 State St; mains $2-5) Michelangelo's is a pleasant hangout with an impressive array of fair trade coffees, sweets and sandwiches.

Cruising Williamson ('Willy') St turns up good Lao, Jamaican, Caribbean and other eateries.

Memorial Union (☎ 608-265-3000; 800 Langdon St) For a convivial beer, join the fun atmosphere at this bar located at the university. The lakeside patio is especially nice on warm afternoons.

Getting There & Away

The central **Greyhound station** (☎ 608-257-3050; 2 S Bedford St) is also used by the **Badger Bus** to Milwaukee.

AROUND MADISON

Taliesin, 40 miles west of Madison and 3 miles south of Spring Green, was the home of Frank Lloyd Wright for most of his life and is the site of his architectural school. It's now a major pilgrimage destination for fans and followers. The house was built in 1903, the Hillside Home School in 1932, and the **visitors center** (☎ 608-588-7900; www .taliesinpreservation.org; Rte 23; tours $15-75; 🕙 9-5pm May-Oct) was built in 1953. A wide range of guided tours covers various parts of the complex; reservations are required for the more lengthy ones. The two-hour walking tour ($15, no reservation needed) is a good introduction; the website details the more expensive tours.

Half a dozen motels are strung along Rte 14, north of Spring Green. **Usonian Inn** (☎ 877-876-6426; www.usonianinn.com; E 5116 Hwy 14; r $45-75; 🅿 🔀 ⊠) and the **Prairie House Motel** (☎ 800-588-2088; E4884 Hwy 14; r $32-65; 🅿 🔀 ⊠) were both inspired by Wright. South on Rte 23, **Tower Hill State Park** (☎ 608-588-2116; campsite $11) offers good, basic camping and walking trails.

Wright was born 27 miles northwest of Spring Green in **Richland Center**. He designed the **AD German Warehouse** (☎ 608-647-2808; 300 S Church St; admission $10; 🕙 May-Nov by appointment only) in 1915, and it's the only remaining example of his work from that decade, notable for its geometric concrete decorations. (Be aware that the building is privately owned, and it can be difficult reaching the proprietor to schedule a visit.)

Wisconsin is kind of famous for its oddballs and esoterica, and there's a concentration of quirky sights near Madison.

Scrap metal has been obsessively converted into art at the jaw-dropping **Sculpture Park** (admission free; 🕙 roughly 9am-5pm), 9 miles south of Baraboo on Hwy 12. It's the work of one Dr Evermor (aka Tom Every), who has single-mindedly and with exceptional skill welded old pipes, carburetors and other salvaged metal into a hallucinatory world of futuristic creatures and structures. The crowning glory is the giant, eggdomed Forevertron, cited by Guinness as the world's largest scrap metal sculpture. A visit here is highly recommended; look for sculptures along the highway marking the entrance.

The **Wisconsin Dells** is a mega-center of kitschy diversions, including family theme parks, water-skiing thrill shows and superminigolf courses, a jolting contrast to the natural appeal of the area with its scenic limestone formations carved by the Wisconsin River. To appreciate the original attraction, take a boat tour or walk the trails at Mirror Lake or Devil's Lake state parks; both have camping. For lodging, the area is chock-full of sterling relics from the early 1960s, including **Bridge View Motel** (☎ 608-254-6114; 1020 River Rd; r $35-65; 🔀 🔀 ⊠). Look for modest restaurants on Broadway Ave.

Baraboo, 20 miles northwest of Madison, was once the winter home of the Ringling Brothers Circus. **Circus World Museum** (☎ 608-356-0800; 550 Water St; admission summer/winter $15/7; 🕙 10am-4pm Mon-Sat, 11am-4pm Sun) preserves a nostalgic collection of wagons, posters and equipment from the touring big-top heydays. In summer, admission includes clowns, animals and acrobats doing the three-ring thing. In early July the little town holds its **Great Circus Festival** (☎ 866-693-1500) with a parade and big-top shows. Among numerous motels, sprawling **Spinning Wheel** (☎ 608-356-3933; www.spinningwheelmotel.com; 809 8th St; r in summer $59-77; 🔀 ⊠) is decent.

GREEN BAY

All the action here can be found during the fall at Lambeau Field, home of Green Bay's beloved NFL team, the Packers (winner of the first two Super Bowls and, mo

---

SCENIC DRIVE: GREAT RIVER ROAD

The Mississippi River forms most of Wisconsin's western border, and alongside it run some of the most scenic sections of the Great River Rd (Hwy 35) – the designated route that follows Old Man River from Minnesota to the Gulf of Mexico.

From Madison, head west on Hwy 18. You'll hit the River Rd at **Prairie du Chien**. Founded in 1673 as a French fur-trading post, the town's name quaintly honors the prairie dogs that once populated the area.

North of Prairie du Chien, the hilly riverside wends through the scene of the final battle in the bloody Black Hawk War. Historic markers tell part of the story of the war, which finished at the Battle of Bad Ax when Native American men, women and children were massacred trying to flee across the Mississippi.

Upstream, **La Crosse** is a fine riverside town with a historic center nestling restaurants and pubs. **Grandad Bluff** offers grand views of the river. It's east of town along Main St (which becomes Bliss Rd); follow Bliss Rd up the hill and then turn right on Grandad Bluff Rd. For area information, stop by the **visitors center** (☎ 608-782-2366; Riverside Park; ⏱ 8am-5pm Mon-Fri year-round, plus 10am-5pm Sat, noon-5pm Sun in summer). To bed down, try the friendly **Guest House Motel** (☎ 608-784-8840, 800-274-6873; 2622 Rose St; r $45-70; 🐾), with full English breakfast.

---

recently, the 1996 Super Bowl). The city was founded in the 1650s as a fur-trading post, but when shipping and the railroads converged on Green Bay, the town's bread and butter became packing agricultural products (which explains the team's name). The **visitors center** (☎ 920-494-9507, 888-867-3342; www .greenbay.org; 1901 S Oneida St; ⏱ 8am-4:30pm Mon-Fri) is by the football stadium, just off Lombardi Ave, south of downtown. The town core is on the east side of the Fox River around Walnut St. Green Bay is a gateway to scenic Door County.

Packer fans are unique not only for being such fanatical, die-hard supporters of their team: city residents actually *own* the team. They also wear huge foam cheese wedges on their heads. The **Green Bay Packer Hall of Fame** (☎ 920-499-4281; Lambeau Field; admission $10; ⏱ 9am-6pm, closed during home games) is indeed packed with memorabilia and has football movies and interactive exhibits, plus tours of the newly expanded stadium.

Bay Motel (☎ 920-494-3441; www.baymotelgreen bay.com; 1301 S Military Ave; r 39-70; 🐾 ✕ 🅿) A mile from Lambeau Field, this independent motel is tidy.

The usual chain cheapies can also be found around town.

DOOR COUNTY

With its rocky coastline, picturesque lighthouses, cherry orchards and sedate, picture-perfect 19th-century villages, you have to admit Door County is pretty fuckin' lovely.

The county is on a narrow peninsula jutting 60 miles into Lake Michigan. When traffic is light, looping around the peninsula on Hwy 57 and Hwy 42 is unbeatable. No public buses serve the peninsula, and not much stays open from November to April.

The most attractive part of the loop begins at **Sturgeon Bay**, the peninsula's main town. As you enter it stop at the knowledgeable **Chamber of Commerce** (☎ 920-743-4456; www.door county.com; 1015 Green Bay Rd; ⏱ 8:30am-5pm Mon-Thu, 8:30am-8pm Fri, 10am-4pm Sat & Sun mid-May–mid-Oct, 8:30am-4:30pm rest of year); on the porch a kiosk is accessible 24 hours a day with lodging information.

Sturgeon Bay also has the cheapest lodging. **Holiday Motel** (☎ 920-743-5571; www.holiday motelpm@charter.net; 29 N 2nd Ave; r $29-81; 🅿 ✕) is simple, presentable and has aged gracefully. At the kitschy **Chal-A-Motel** (☎ 920-743-6788; 3910 Hwy 42/57; r $59; 🐾) you'll share the premises with 1000 Barbie dolls, some mechanical elves, a DeLorean car and more. To the north, in Sister Bay, **Edge of Town Motel** (☎ 920-854-2012; 11092 Hwy 42; r $40-80; 🅿 ✕) is your basic vintage hideaway. All of the above are open year round. Excellent camping and sunset watching are available at **Peninsula State Park** (☎ 920-868-3258; campsites $12) by Fish Creek. Secluded **Newport State Park** (☎ 920-854-2500; campsites $12) offers camping, trails and solitude.

Many restaurants have a 'fish boil,' a regional specialty started by Scandinavian lumberjacks, in which whitefish, potatoes

GREAT LAKES

TOP FIVE GREAT LAKES DINERS

The Great Lakes states are rife with 1950s diners. Here are our top picks, all genuine articles (two of 'em in the Twin Cities):

■ **Nite-Owl Drive-In**, Milwaukee, WI (p370)

■ **Mug 'N' Bun**, Indianapolis, IN (p357)

■ **Cozy Dog Drive In**, Springfield, IL (p356)

■ **Band Box Diner**, Minneapolis, MN (p377)

■ **Mickey's Dining Car**, St Paul, MN (p377)

---

and onions are cooked in a cauldron. It's sedate, until the chef douses the flames with kerosene, and then whoosh! A fireball creates the requisite 'boil over' (which gets rid of the fish oil), signaling dinner is ready. Finish with Door's famous cherry pie.

At **Al Johnson's Swedish Kitchen** (☎ 920-854-2626; 704 Bay Shore Dr; mains $6-20), goats feed on the sod roof of this curiously atmospheric joint, while you will surely enjoy Swedish meatballs or a sandwich and a slice of cherry pie. Attractive **Summer Kitchen** (☎ 920-854-2131; Hwy 42, Ephraim; mains $6-17; ⏰ May-Oct) serves tasty breakfast, lunch and dinner. Also, sample the smoked fish available around Gills Rock.

MINNESOTA

Beyond Minneapolis and the huge number of lakes, few non-Minnesotans have much to say about this state, and most visitors skirt the southern end without bothering to find out what those vast hinterlands are all about. It's a shame, but understandable. Getting to know Minnesota requires an investment of time that few people are willing to make.

It's OK, though, because Minneapolis' culture and nightlife are a bonafide draw. More intrepid visitors will want to wet their paddles in the spectacular wilderness of the Boundary Waters Canoe Area or take in the raw beauty of the Iron Range or the gritty, freighter-filled port of Duluth.

Note that in 'Minne-snow-ta' (as residents sometimes call it), the white stuff can fall into May.

History

The Eastern Sioux were the primary inhabitants when the first French trappers arrived in the 17th century. Starting in the early 18th century, Ojibwa bands (also called Chippewa) moved into northeast Minnesota and, armed with guns traded by the French, pushed the Sioux southwest onto the prairie.

The area east of the Mississippi River became part of the US Northwest Territory in 1787, and the area west of the Mississippi was acquired from France in the 1803 Louisiana Purchase. Timber was the territory's first boom industry, and soon water-powered sawmills arose along the river. Wheat from the prairies also needed to be processed, and the state's first flour mills were built in the 1820s.

The population boomed in the 1880s, with mass immigration (especially from Scandinavia), development of the iron mines and expansion of the railroads. Since the 1920s, depleted forests and larger farms have meant a declining rural population, while industry and urban areas have grown.

State Parks

Minnesota state park information (☎ 866-857-2757; www.dnr.state.mn.us/state_parks) Campground reservations accepted. Park entry requires a vehicle permit ($7 per day).

MINNEAPOLIS

The hometown of the artist formerly known as 'Glyph' (Prince) is not really so weird a place, but there is a definite creative vibe here. Don't be put off by Minneapolis' impersonal downtown high-rises, which mostly were added in the 1960s and '70s. The cultural life of the city hums along Hennepin Ave and in pockets around town. Rock and roll, and theater are Mini-Apple's primary strengths, and the city abounds with venerable clubs and venues. Minneapolis is also endowed with a surprising number of good ethnic eateries – it's not just Swedish meatballs anymore.

Though fewer visitors will be drawn to older, quieter **St Paul**, the fact that these 'Twin Cities' are essentially joined at th hip (forming a metropolitan area of 2.3 million residents) naturally has a huge influence on the local culture.

As you walk the streets here, don't be embarrassed if you find yourself singing the theme song to *The Mary Tyler Moore Show*. You're gonna make it, kid.

Orientation

The Twin Cities form a metropolis on both sides of the generally hidden Mississippi River. On the west side, downtown Minneapolis – the beating heart of the two cities – is a modern grid of high-rise buildings, many linked by a series of enclosed overhead walkways called 'Skyways' (extremely welcome in winter). Uptown is actually southwest of downtown, with Hennepin Ave the main axis. Central St Paul is 10 miles to the east on I-94.

Information

Hip and really easy-to-navigate www.minneapolis.org has maps, coupons and other goodies.

Minneapolis visitors center (☎ 612-335-5827; cnr Nicollet Mall & 7th St S; ☺ 10am-7pm Mon-Fri, 10am-6pm Sat, noon-5pm Sun) Located in the city center.

Sights & Activities

The first-rate **Walker Art Center** (☎ 612-375-7622; 725 Vineland Pl; admission $6; ☺ 10am-5pm Tue, Wed, Fri & Sat, 10am-9pm Thu, 11am-5pm Sun) has a strong permanent collection of 20th-century art and photography, including big-name US painters and great US pop art.

Beside the Walker is the seven-acre **Minneapolis Sculpture Garden** (admission free; ☺ 6am-noon), studded with imaginative contemporary works like the oft-photographed spoon and cherry. The garden is connected to attractive Loring Park by a sculptural pedestrian bridge over I-94.

The **St Anthony Falls Heritage Trail**, on the north edge of downtown at the foot of Portland Ave, is a recommended 2-mile path that provides both interesting history (markers dot the route) and the city's best access to the banks of the Mississippi. View the cascading falls from the car-free Stone Arch Bridge. On the north side of the river, Main St SE has a stretch of redeveloped buildings housing restaurants and bars.

Within a mile or two of downtown, a ~ng of lakes circles the inner-city area.

THE MALL TO END ALL MALLS

Yes, it's a shopping mall, filled with the usual stores, movie theaters and food courts. But the **Mall of America** (☎ 952-883-8800; off I-494 at 24th Ave; ☺ 10am-9:30pm Mon-Sat, 11am-7pm Sun), in the southern suburb of Bloomington, is the USA's largest shopping center, and much more. Within its confines there is a hotel, a roller coaster, a full-scale aquarium, a bowling alley and many other features that go above and beyond the call of duty for a mall. The choice is yours: shop until you drop, or just stare on in amazement as others do it. The mall is well-served by local buses; No 180 is express.

Cedar Lake, Lake of the Isles, Lake Calhoun and Lake Harriet are surrounded by parks and comfortable suburbs. Cycling paths (cross-country ski trails in winter) meander around the lakes, where you can go boating in summer or ice-skating in winter. **Wirth Park**, just west of downtown, has the full gamut. **Thomas Beach**, on Lake Calhoun, is popular for swimming, biking and canoeing. Also visit **Minnehaha Park**, 6 miles south of downtown, to view the falls made famous by Longfellow's epic poem *Hiawatha*, though Longfellow never actually visited. Call the **Parks Board** (☎ 612-661-4875) for recreation information.

The **University of Minnesota**, by the river southeast of the center, is one of the USA's largest campuses, with over 50,000 students. Most of the campus is in the East Bank neighborhood. **Dinkytown**, based at 14th Ave SE and 4th St SE, is dense with student cafés and bookshops.

Calhoun Rental (☎ 612-373-3333; www.calhounrental.com; 1622 W Lake St; bike rentals per day $25; ☺ 10am-7pm) is an Uptown shop that rents bikes and tandems.

The **Minneapolis Park & Recreation Board** (☎ 612-370-4883; 3000 E Calhoun Parkway; ☺ 11am-7pm daily late May–early Sep, 11am-6pm Sat & Sun early Sep-Oct) rents a slew of vessels for getting out on Lake Calhoun. Canoe or kayak rental costs $10 per hour.

Festivals & Events

Minneapolis Aquatennial (☎ 612-376-7669; www.aquatennial.org) Ten days celebrating the ubiquitous lakes in mid-July.

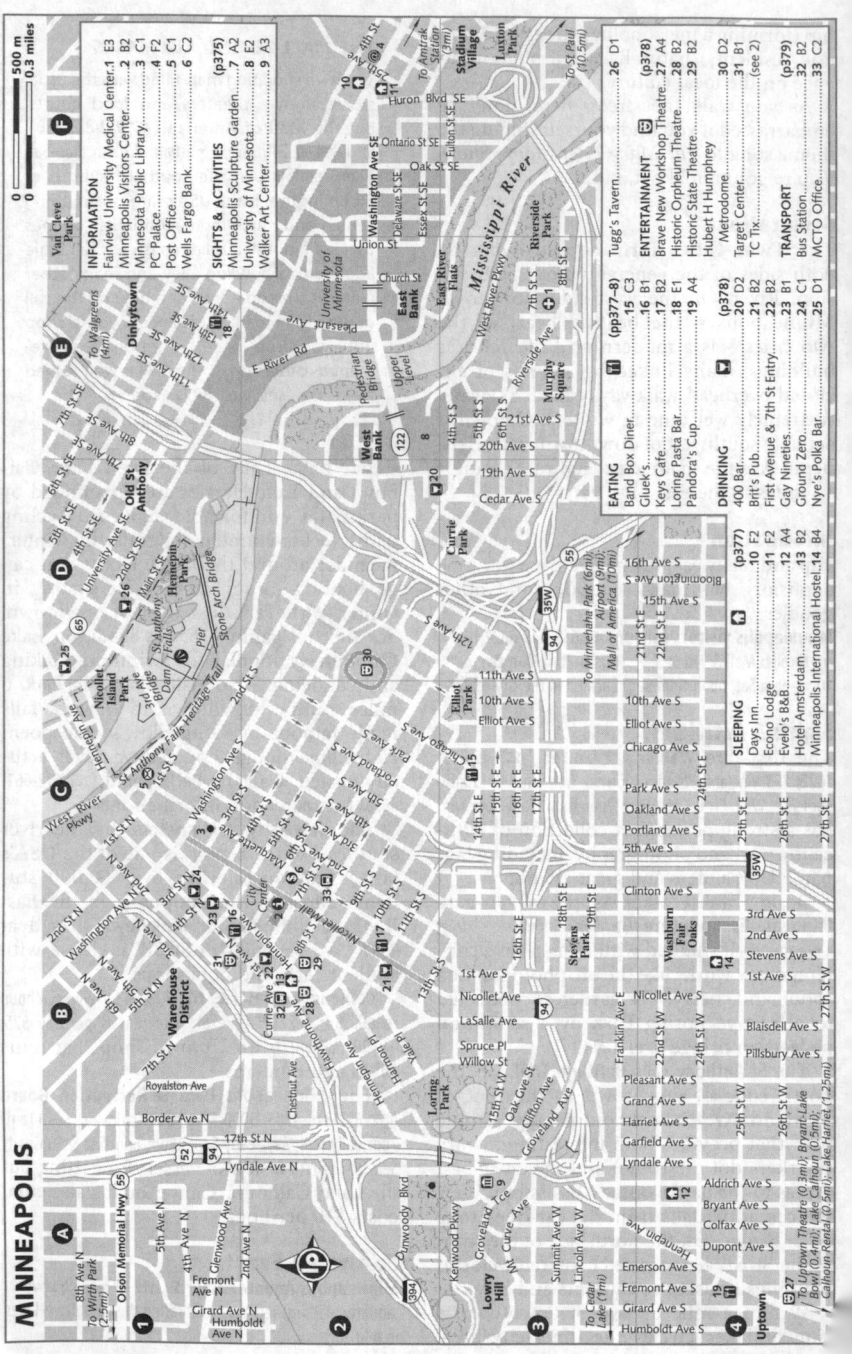

St Paul Winter Carnival (☎ 651-223-4700; www
.winter-carnival.com) Ten days of ice sculptures, ice skating
and ice fishing in January.

Sleeping

Room costs range toward the high end in
summer. The 13% tax is not included in the
following prices.

Minneapolis International Hostel (☎ 612-871-
3210; www.minneapolishostel.com; 2400 Stevens Ave S; dm
$20-24, r $29-49; P $5 ⊠ ⬜) This homey hos-
tel beside the Institute of Arts has antique
furniture, wood floors and fluffy quilts on
the beds. The building recently came under
new management, so some things may
change. Reservations are recommended;
$10 key deposit.

Hotel Amsterdam (☎ 612-288-0459; www.gaympls
.com; 828 Hennepin Ave; r $44-65; ⬜) The Amster-
dam is a busy, European-style, gay-friendly
hotel located above a bar downtown. The
rooms are utilitarian but clean, and all share
a bathroom.

Motel 6 (☎ 612-861-4491; 7640 Cedar Ave S; r $40-46;
P ⊠) Near the airport, a 10-minute drive
from downtown, this is a standard cheapie.
Others are nearby.

Econo Lodge (☎ 612-331-6000; 2500 University Ave
SE; r $60-80; P ⊠) The rooms here are more
than decent, and the price includes continental breakfast, making it the best value in
the bland university area. It's a 10-minute
bus ride from downtown.

Evelo's B&B (☎ 612-374-9656; sevelo@mpls.k12
.mn.us; 2301 Bryant Ave; s/d $60/77; ⊠) Evelo's is

> ### SPLURGE!
>
> **Covington Inn** (☎ 651-292-1411; www.coving
> toninn.com; Pier 1, Harriet I; r $140-235; P ⊠)
> Usually, blowing your budget on an expen-
> sive hotel room only means getting the
> conventional four walls dressed up with tas-
> seled curtains and newer towels and people
> expecting to be tipped at every turn. What
> you should get for the extra dough, though,
> is something really unique, such as a night
> onboard a tugboat on the Mississippi River.
> Turns out that's what you get at Coving-
> ton, in downtown St Paul. At night you can
> admire the way city lights sparkle on the
> river and over your morning coffee you
> can watch boat traffic gliding by. Breakfast
> is included.

in a quiet, tree-shaded neighborhood between the Walker Art Center and uptown.
The Victorian home has beautiful woodwork, lots of windows and light and comfy
rooms.

Days Inn (☎ 612-623-3999; 2407 University Ave SE;
r $59-109; P ⊠) This chain often caters to
people in town for events (when prices
move to the upper end of the spectrum).

Eating

Interesting dining options can be found
all over town. Nicollet Ave S between 14th
and 29th Sts is known as 'Eat Street' because it's particularly dense with Vietnamese, Mexican and other ethnic eateries.

Bryant-Lake Bowl (☎ 612-825-8949; 810 W lake
St; mains $5-14) Bowling alleys are not generally
known for great food, but this one defies
the odds with tasty home-style standards
and some inventive, multicultural zingers.
You can bowl, drink or just eat. The Monday night 'cheap date' special (pre-fix $25
for two) includes all the above.

Band Box Diner (☎ 612-332-0850; 729 S 10th St;
mains $2-6) You'll be impressed by the ex-
cellent breakfasts and lunches so carefully
prepared in this former railcar. French fries
made from scratch are almost unheard of
these days, but you can still get 'em in this
downtown joint.

Pandora's Cup (☎ 612-381-0700; 2516 Hennepin
Ave S; sandwiches $4-6) Pandora's is Uptown,
in a big, rambling house run by friendly
punks who make damn good coffee and
sandwiches.

Gluek's (☎ 612-338-6621; 16 6th St N; mains $7-16;
�), food until 11pm) For that old-school Minneapolis beerhall experience, Gluek's happy
hour (4pm to 6pm Monday to Friday) is
not to be missed: two-for-one pints and $2
brats and other filling fare. This landmark
has been dishing out German–American
classics since 1902.

Loring Pasta Bar (☎ 612-987-3444; 327 14th Ave
SE; mains $7-20) In a former drugstore in Dinky
Town, this is where you'll find the liveliest
college crowd noshing on pizzas, pastas and
meat dishes.

Keys Cafe (☎ 612-339-6399; 1007 Nicollet Mall;
mains $4-10) Bustling Keys, on the downtown
pedestrian mall, dishes up solid breakfasts
and sandwiches; try the caramel rolls.

Mickey's Dining Car (☎ 651-222-5633; 36 W 7th St;
mains $3-7) Over in downtown St Paul, Mickey's

is a truly timeless beauty, the kind of place where the waitress calls you 'honey' and regulars line the counter with their coffee cups and newspapers. The food is timeless, too: burgers, malts and apple pie, available 24 hours a day.

Drinking

BARS

The Warehouse district just north of downtown is where you'll find the highest concentration of bars and clubs.

Brit's Pub (☎ 612-332-3908; 1110 Nicollet Mall) It's not every day you go to a drinking establishment with a lawn-bowling green on its roof: there's a large selection of Scotch, port and beer to boot.

Tugg's Tavern (☎ 612-379-4404; 219 Main St SE) Tugg's draw is cheap happy hour specials (4pm to 6pm Monday to Friday) on its swell outdoor patio on the Mississippi River's revitalized north-side strip.

LIVE MUSIC

First Avenue & 7th St Entry (☎ 612-338-8388; 701 1st Ave N) Minneapolis' legendary club is smartly laid out, has solid bookings and usually draws a fun crowd.

Nye's Polka Bar (☎ 612-379-2021; 112 E Hennepin Ave) Nye's, just over the river from the Warehouse district, is a Polish–American supper club with this polka bar attached. From Thursday through Saturday, when the World's Most Dangerous Polka Band takes the stage, the old joint trembles. The best time you'll have.

400 Bar (☎ 612-332-2903; 400 Cedar Ave S) Lots of students convene at this place where live rock, funk and alternative bands play.

Clubbing

Gay Nineties (☎ 612-333-7755; 408 Hennepin Ave) You'll find dancing, dining, drag shows and both a gay and straight clientele at Gay Nineties.

Ground Zero (☎ 612-378-5115; 15 4th St NE; cover free–$5) This long-standing spot gets a mixed gay and straight dance crowd for recorded music.

Entertainment

City Pages and *Pulse* are weekly entertainment freebies. Minneapolis is lauded for its range of cinemas and fine theater troupes. **TC Tix** (☎ 612-288-2060; in the Minneapolis visitors center) provides same-day discounts.

CINEMAS

Uptown Theatre (☎ 612-825-6006; 2906 Hennepin Ave S) Catch art-house flicks here.

THEATER

In particular, look for plays and concerts at the following venues (all in Mini-Apple unless otherwise noted):

Brave New Workshop Theatre (☎ 612-332-6620; 2605 Hennepin Ave) An established venue for musical comedy and satire.

Fitzgerald Theater (☎ 651-290-1221; 10 E Exchange St, St Paul) Where Garrison Keillor tapes his *Prairie Home Companion* radio show.

Historic Orpheum Theatre (☎ 612-339-7007; 910 Hennepin Ave) The usual venue for Broadway shows and touring acts.

Historic State Theatre (☎ 612-339-7007; 805 Hennepin Ave) Also hosts Broadway shows and touring acts.

SPORTS

The **Minnesota Vikings** (☎ 612-338-4537) pro football team plays at **Hubert H Humphrey Metrodome** (900 5th St S), as do the **Twins** (☎ 612-338-9467) baseball team.

The **Timberwolves** (☎ 612-337-3865; 600 1st Ave N) play NBA games at Target Center, downtown. The Lynx women's team also plays here.

The **Wild** (☎ 651-222-9453; Kellogg Blvd) NHL team take the ice in St Paul's downtown Xcel Energy Center.

A REALLY COOL SPORT

For those uninitiated in northern ways, curling is a winter sport that involves sliding a heavy, hubcab-sized 'puck' down the ice toward a bulls-eye. It's actually played competitively in the Winter Olympics, but never seems to air on prime time TV. Nevertheless, it's popular in these parts, and if you're curious about it you should bop on down to St Paul during the curling season (November to March) and catch the action at the **St Paul Curling Club** (☎ 651-224-7408; www.stpaulcurlingclub.org; 470 Selby Ave).

Getting There & Around
Minneapolis–St Paul International Airport (☎ 612-726-5555; www.mspairport.com) is a major regional hub and home of Northwest Airlines, which operates several direct flights to Europe and throughout North America. The No 7 bus goes to downtown Minneapolis (45 minutes); the fare is $1.25 to $2.50. A light-rail line runs between the airport and downtown with the same low fares.

Greyhound has stations in **Minneapolis** (☎ 612-371-3323; 950 Hawthorne Ave) and **St Paul** (☎ 651-222-0509; 166 W University Ave).

The **Amtrak station** (☎ 651-644-1127; 730 Transfer Rd), off University Ave SE, is between the Twin Cities.

Metropolitan Council Transit Operations (MCTO; ☎ 612-373-3333) runs clean, frequent and well-used buses throughout the area (fare $1.25, plus 50¢ for express or rush hour buses).

NORTHERN MINNESOTA
Boundary Waters
This pristine region has more than a thousand lakes and streams in which to dip a paddle. It's possible to go just for the day, but most people opt for at least one night of camping, a wonderfully remote experience where it most likely will be you, the moose who's nuzzling the tent and a sky full of stars. **Permits** (☎ 877-550-6777; www.bwcaw.org), costing $10, are required for overnight stays; day permits, though free, are also required.

The gateway town of **Ely** has accommodations, restaurants and scores of outfitters.

> **IF YOU'VE GOT A FEW MORE DAYS IN MINNESOTA**
>
> **Voyageurs National Park** – *Way* up there, this watery park on the USA–Canada border is old French Canadian fur-trapping land, and best explored by canoe, kayak or motorboat.

Kawishiwi Wilderness Station (☎ 218-365-7561; ☺ 6am-6pm May-Sep) offers expert camping and canoeing details, trip suggestions and required permits.

Mississippi Headwaters
At **Itasca State Park** (☎ 218-266-2100; off Hwy 71 N; campsites $15-18) you can walk across the official headwaters of the mighty Mississippi, rent canoes or bikes, hike the trails and camp. The log **HI Mississippi Headwaters Hostel** (☎ 218-266-3415; www.himinnesota.org/headwaters; dm $15-22, r $30-64; ☺ daily in summer, Sat & Sun rest of year) is in the park.

On the western edge of the forest, neat and tidy **Bemidji** is an old lumber town with a well-preserved downtown and a giant statue of legendary logger Paul Bunyan and his faithful blue ox, Babe. Among the modest motels south of town is **Midway Motel** (☎ 218-751-1180; midway_motel@hotmail.com; 1000 Paul Bunyan Dr NE; r $40-55; ☒ Ⓟ). The **Greyhound** (☎ 218-751-7600) bus stops behind here. **Cyber Bugs Paradise Cafe** (☎ 218-444-2927; 311 3rd St NW; mains $2-5) has fine light lunches, espresso drinks and Internet access.

GREAT LAKES

Great Plains

HIGHLIGHTS

- **Black Hills & Badlands** South Dakota's huge natural wonders, with stone presidents and Native American history (p390)
- **St Louis & Kansas City** Missouri's two cities jockey for state rights; former has Arch and a French quarter, latter great jazz and barbecue (p386)
- **Theodore Roosevelt National Park** North Dakota's prime attraction provides the critters and scenery without the tourists (p391)
- **Rte 66** Oklahoma's stretch of the fabled two-lane road has more remaining miles than anywhere in the USA (p384)
- **Off the beaten track** Traipse around prehistoric sea floors in the Nebraska panhandle, with surreal Carhenge and giant cliffs overlooking the sparse scene (p389)

FAST FACTS

- **Area** 503,305 sq miles (bigger than France & Britain combined)
- **Big cities** Oklahoma City (population 506,132), Kansas City (443,500), Omaha (399,400), St Louis (338,400)
- **Budget** $40-60 per day
- **Costs** Deadwood, South Dakota hostel $13; Kansas City–St Louis bus fare $33; Oklahoma 'Sooner schooner' hat $25
- **Driving times** St Louis to Denver 14 hours, Minneapolis to Black Hills 11 hours, St Louis to Oklahoma City 8 hours
- **Famous for** tornadoes, Plains Indians, football, Lewis & Clark meeting Sacajawea, lovin' da Bible
- **Population** 17,940,377
- **Phrases** *I'm fixin' to…* (I'm going to…), *that's for neat* (that's neat), *Texas sucks* (no definition needed)
- **Seasons** High season is Memorial Day (mid-May) to Labor Day (mid-Aug)
- **States** Oklahoma, Missouri, Kansas, Iowa, Nebraska, South Dakota, North Dakota

- **Tasty treats** lamb fries (calf testicles; at many steakhouses; often debated whether 'tasty'), buffalo burgers, Indian tacos
- **Time** GMT minus 6 hours, GMT minus 7 hours (daylight savings observed)
- **Top hostel** St Louis' HI Huckleberry Finn, Missouri (p386)

TRAVEL HINTS

Bitching about flatlands? Drive toward a short horizon and see the plains drop dramatically to unveil a mountain-type view without the queasy ride up.

All real road trips cut through this mostly flat, much-scorned stretch of rolling fields of wheat where Native Americans heroically fought overpowering forces and bison roamed in the millions. These days, on the Plains' sweeping prehistoric sea floors, you're more likely to spot cowboy-hatted locals lassoing steer, cowgirls cursing over football and pickup trucks poking along two-lane pink highways and old Rte 66. Tornadoes outnumber tourists, some days. Give yourself a day off the interstate – there's some serious shine in the spur if you look (and some cheaper prices generally). Few people do, and you'll look cool at the Venice Beach hostel bragging about the 'rewarding gems of Nebraska.'

HISTORY

Spear-toting nomads hunted mammoths here 10,000 years before shiny-hatted Spaniards introduced the horse around 1630 and (dull-hatted) French explorers probed the prairies for furs. The US snagged much of it in the 1803 Louisiana Purchase.

The infamous forced resettlement of the Five Civilized Tribes along the 1838–39 'Trail of Tears' led to Oklahoma from back east (p250). Pioneers blazed west on trails such as the Santa Fe across Kansas, and cowboys made their myth on the cattle-drivin' Chisholm Trail from Texas to wild towns like Dodge City (p386).

Original occupants, including the Osage and Sioux, had different, but often tragic, fates. Many resettled in pockets of Oklahoma (the Osage luckily found their plots to be above the world's richest oil wells), others fought for lands once promised.

Railroad, barbed-wire and oil all brought change as the 20th century hovered. The 1930s dust bowl ruined farms and spurred many residents to say: 'enough of this crap – I'm heading west.'

THE CULTURE

Outside the big cities, farmers may tell you they prefer wide, open lands so they can 'see if anyone's coming.' With so few people around, locals can be slightly defensive at first – one 'perpendicular Viking' in South Dakota, a Swedish-American, talks to you at a 90-degree angle. If you show genuine interest in local issues, however, you're likely to get an earful. You'll find a lot of devotion to family, God and Republicans.

Listen to AM radio as often as you can. Commercial-free Native American stations play stuff like 'Stairway to Heaven' when pals drop by the studio and ask to hear it.

Ian Frazier's *Great Plains* is a super read about the area's people and sights, and the *Plains Folk* series by Jim Hoy and Tom ▪ern tackles old-time country living.

SPORTS & RECREATION

Football is *not* just a game here. Past gridiron heroes (such as Nebraska's Tom Osbourne and Oklahoma's JC Watts) often end up playing ball (successfully) in politics.

Small rodeo arenas perforate prairies outside many cow towns. A remarkable one is the African-American rodeo in Boley, Oklahoma (on Memorial Day weekend in late May), southwest of Tulsa. For info call ☎ 918-667-331.

A few states have made (or are making) bike trails, such as Missouri's Katy Trail State Park and Nebraska's Cowboy Trail east of Valentine (p388). You can spot wildlife on walks, particularly in South Dakota's Black Hills (p390) or North Dakota's Theodore Roosevelt National Park (p391).

ARTS & ENTERTAINMENT

Music has some strong roots in the Plains. Count Basie dominated the lush jazz scene in Kansas City, Chuck Berry still plays his

---

THE BIG ISSUE: WAL-MARTIZATION

Established over in Arkansas in 1962, Wal-Mart hasn't been subtle in its ploy: pumping cheap goods for low-income folks in one-horse towns – and then some. Its 3300 stores around the USA sell, on average, over $700 to every American annually and employ more workers than any other company. Often, Wal-Mart brings availability of gasoline, groceries, eyeglasses, blue jeans, electronics, guns, diapers etc to remote areas. But they take away the action from old-age moms'n'pops and brickstone downtowns. Another catch is censorship (eg anti-union Wal-Mart pulled a *Sports Illustrated* swimsuit issue from its shelves in 2003). Around the Great Plains, comparing quiet, sometimes boarded-up downtowns with booming Wal-Mart parking lots shows how effective these stores have been.

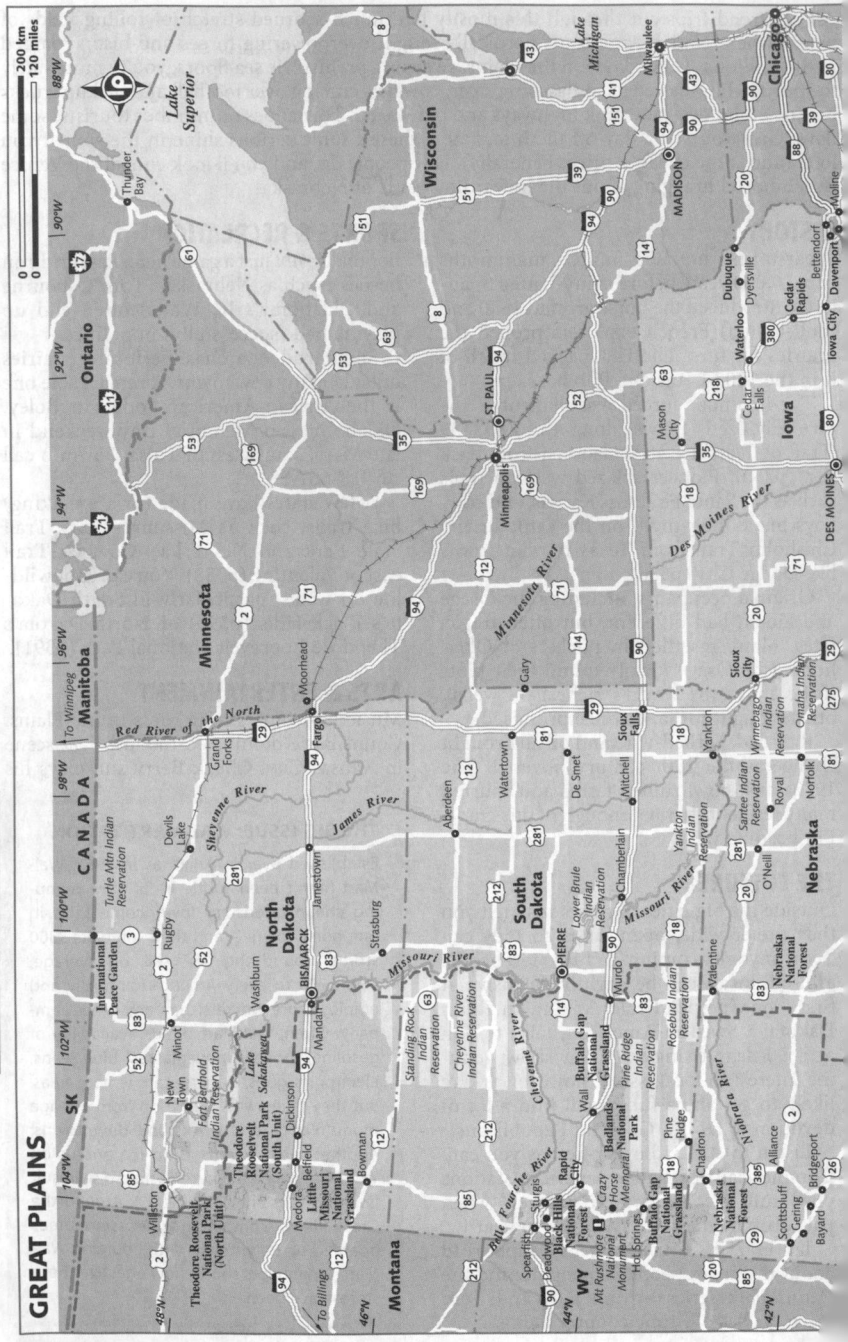

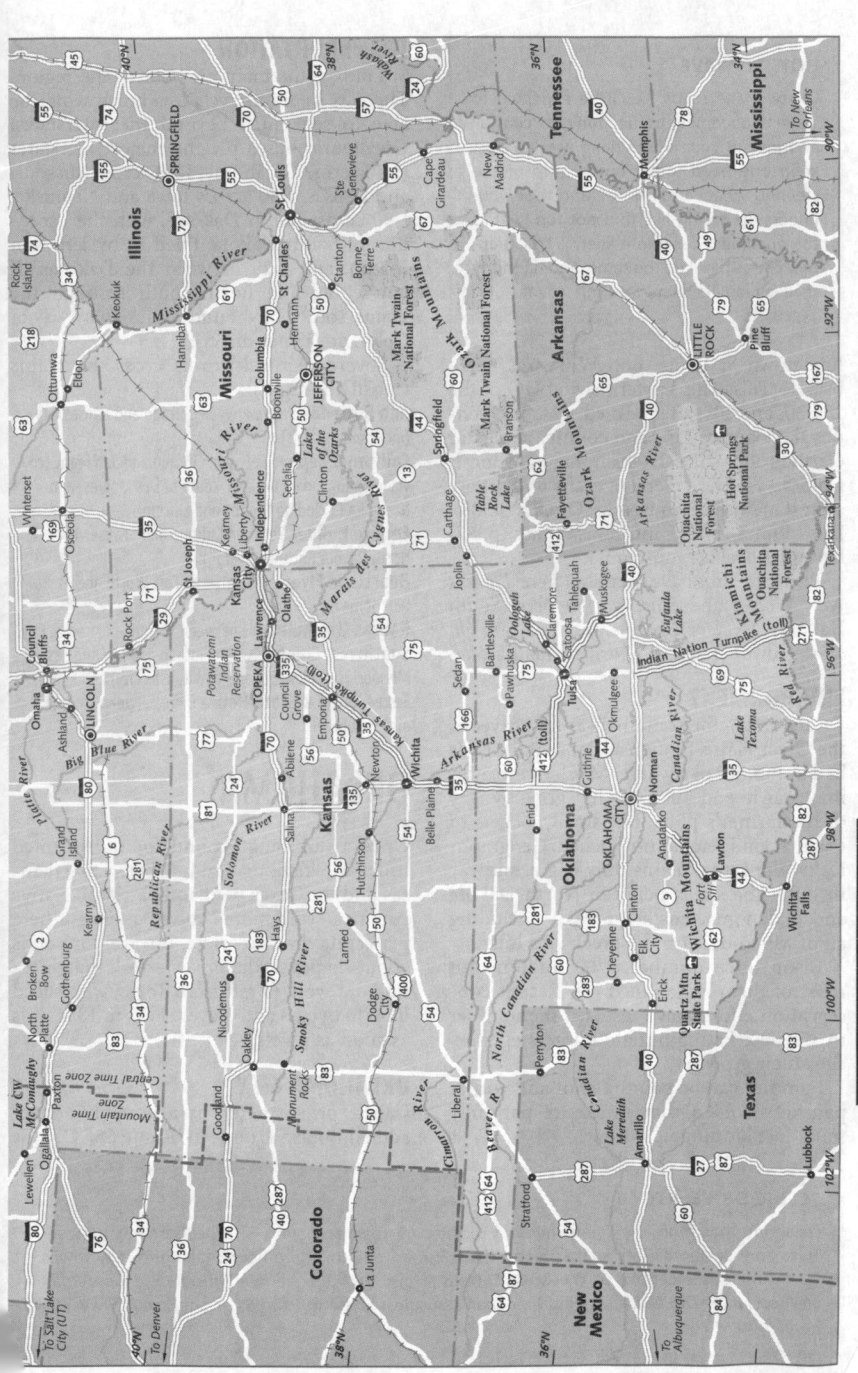

HOW TO WAVE

On two-lane roads, you'll be expected to wave to oncoming traffic. Don't go 'coastal' and extend your whole dang arm up. Just keep one hand (only) on the top of the steering wheel at all times, and raise your fingers up, spring-like (but not too fast) as the oncoming car (more likely a truck) approaches. They'll do the same. And harmony shall spread like wind through wheat.

hometown St Louis, Bob Wills was taken back to Tulsa (his western swing HQ of the 20s, 30s and 40s) after he died. Alt-rock weirdos the Flaming Lips and country superstar Garth Brooks still call Oklahoma state home. Colorful Native American crafts and art are seen at many local museums; Omaha (p388), Des Moines (p388) and Kansas City (p387) have real-deal art museums.

Plenty of films have been shot here: *Dances with Wolves* and *Starship Troopers* (South Dakota); *Field of Dreams* and *The Straight Story* (Iowa); and *The Outsiders* (Tulsa).

ENVIRONMENT

Under water for some half a billion years, the Great Plains is often as flat as if the gods had a slumber party here. Much of the original prairie and tall grass has gone by way of the farmer's plow, but small pockets of original land remain untouched. Geographically, the actual plains only begin midway through the states between North Dakota and Oklahoma. Eastern areas – including all of Missouri – can be green and hilly.

Bison once numbered 60 million, but most of them were killed off. Recent conservation efforts have restored the number to 150,000. Eating buffalo burgers encourages their growth.

Summer can be painfully hot and winter painfully cold. Other times are painfully mild; just kidding, it's fine.

TRANSPORTATION

St Louis is the main air hub for the region. The car- or motorcycle-less brave won't be able to see much beyond the interstates. Greyhound buses ply the major interstates (I-40 across Oklahoma, I-70 across Missouri and Kansas, I-80 across Iowa and Nebraska, I-90 across South Dakota), with the exception of South Dakota, filled in by Jefferson (p391), and I-29 between the Dakotas. If you're heading north–south through the Plains, some Greyhound routes go by way of Colorado (ie not direct).

Several Amtrak trains cross the plains (mostly at night):

Ann Rutledge Daily between Chicago and Kansas City (including St Louis).

California Zephyr Between Chicago and San Francisco via Iowa (including Osceola, south of Des Moines) and Nebraska (including Omaha and Lincoln).

Empire Builder Between Chicago and Seattle via North Dakota (including Fargo).

Heartland Flyer Daily between Fort Worth and Oklahoma City.

Kansas City Mule Daily between St Louis and Kansas City.

Southwest Chief Between Chicago and Los Angeles via Missouri (including St Louis and Kansas City) and Kansas.

Texas Eagle & State House Daily between Chicago and St Louis.

OKLAHOMA

Once a dumping ground for transplanted Indians, Oklahoma (on I-40 between Arkansas and the Texas panhandle) is still 'Native America,' with more Native Americans here per capita than any state. If travel for you is about shapes, Oklahoma's – with that 'erection out west' (a gift from Texas, who sliced it off to bypass anti-slavery laws in 1854) – is as good as it gets.

OKLAHOMA CITY

Called 'oh so pretty' by a possibly booze-addled Bobby Troupe in 'Route 66,' OKC is

---

SCENIC DRIVE: RTE 66

Oklahoma has more surviving miles of old Rte 66 than any state. The best stretch between Tulsa and Oklahoma City snakes along the toll road I-44 for three hours, taking in hilly towns. Go for the apple cobbler at the **Rock Café** in Stroud. Pick up the free *Official Oklahoma Route 66 Association Trip Guide*, available at many businesses along Rte 66, or check out www.okla homaroute66.com.

IF YOU'VE GOT A FEW MORE DAYS IN OKLAHOMA...

Oil town **Bartlesville** (42 miles north of Tulsa) neighbors the rolling Osage Hills, which were sung about in Bob Wills songs. In town, Frank Lloyd Wright's only skyscraper, the **Price Tower** (☎ 918-336-1000; www.pricetower.org; d from $145) can be toured ($8, from Tuesday to Sunday) or slept in. Just west, the super fun **Woolaroc Museum** (☎ 918-336-0307; admission $5; ⏰ 10am-5pm Wed-Sun) has enormous Native American art and relic collections, and a grouchy talking buffalo.

---

flat, mostly treeless and sprawled out like a Los Angeles without the sea or stars. That's cow town glory for you, and it oozes with the best of it.

Oklahoma's main interstates (I-44, I-35, I-40) pass through OKC. The Centennial Expressway (exit 126) heads north from I-40 at downtown past 23rd St (Little Saigon) to I-44 and Rte 66.

Get your lap steel from King Country 93.3 FM.

Sights

If cowboy lore tugs your lasso, the huge and super **National Cowboy & Western Heritage Museum** (☎ 405-478-2250; 1700 NE 63rd St; admission $8.50; ⏰ 9am-5pm) has plenty, including a rodeo room. Take Centennial Expressway north, then east on I-44. The chilling **Oklahoma City National Memorial** (5th St & Harvey Ave; admission free), downtown, marks the former site of the Alfred P Murrah Federal Building (destroyed on April 19, 1995 by American extremists, killing 168).

On Monday and Tuesday, drop by the doggie auction at **Oklahoma National Stockyards** (☎ 405-235-8675; 2500 Exchange Ave; admission free), south of I-40 west of downtown; bidding starts at 8am.

Festivals & Events

The **Red Earth Native American Cultural Festival** (☎ 405-427-5228), which is North America's largest Native American gathering, is held in June.

Sleeping & Eating

Many budget motels (including some rough ones) are on I-35 a few miles south of I-40. **Green Carpet Inn** (☎ 405-677-0551; 1629 S Prospect Ave; d $36) is good; use the first exit south of I-40. Get good Mexican chow on the Bricktown canal at **Chelinos** (☎ 405-235-3533; 15 E California Ave; mains from $7; ⏰ 11am-10pm or 11pm). The humble little Saigon neighborhood, around 23rd and Classen Blvd, serves very authentic

Vietnamese. Try **Pho Hoa** (☎ 405-521-8987; 901 NW 23rd St; beef noodle soup $5).

Junior's (☎ 405-848-5597; 2601 NW Expressway; ⏰ 11am-midnight Sun-Thu, 11-2am Fri & Sat) is a ruby-red bar/restaurant where many an oil man's illicit dealings got sprung.

Getting There & Away

Greyhound buses depart from the **Union Bus Station** (☎ 405-235-6425; 427 W Sheridan Ave). Daily **Amtrak** (100 S EK Gaylord Blvd) trains go to Fort Worth.

TULSA

One-time Oil Capital of the World, Tulsa is the state's prettiest city, but a bit quiet. KVOO 1170AM still gives Tulsa its oldtime twang. Climb up the TV evangelist's glass Prayer Tower at the Jetsons-meet-Jesus campus of **Oral Roberts University** (ORU; ☎ 918-495-7910; 7777 S Lewis Ave; ⏰ Tue-Sun), south of I-44 exit 227.

Northwest of downtown (off US 64, near Pine St), the **Thomas Gilcrease Museum** (☎ 918-596-2700; 1400 Gilcrease Museum Rd; admission $3; ⏰ 10am-4pm Tue-Sun) plays up its western art, with super 19th-century Remingtons in the house.

Cheapest sleeps are at old-timer motels west of the Arkansas River, off I-44. Also try the **Victorian Inn** (☎ 918-743-2009; 114 E Skelly Dr; s/d US$38/45; Ⓟ 🐾), off I-44 exit 226. Drinking happens at Brookside district, around 21st St and Peoria Ave.

Greyhound buses stop at Tulsa.

MISSOURI & KANSAS

Following I-70 across mid-America, Missouri offers the metropolises of St Louis and Kansas City, and some greenery (best is the hill-hugging web of small highways running through the southern Ozarks, south of I-44; best not josh locals about little Hwy PP though), while further west

Kansas opens way up, with grain elevator farm towns and worn ruts of 200-year-old pioneers' wagons.

ST LOUIS

East meets west in this giant Mississippi River town with a long French history, and (more recently) a century of mostly hard times – evident in Chevy Chase's humbling experience here in *Vacation*. Downtown, and the Arch, is not far from the strolling and drinking grounds in the gorgeous red-brick French Quarter of Soulard. It's home to a hostel and a big July 14 Bastille Day party.

Orientation & Information

North of downtown is ho-hum Laclede's Landing historic district, south is Soulard. A mile west is Market South, which meets dripping-with-boho-vibe Grand South Grand another mile south.

Downtown, **Explore St Louis** (☎ 314-342-5160; www.explorestlouis.com; 7th St & Washington Ave; ☺ Mon-Sat) has travel information. Tune into diverse community-run KDHX FM 88.1.

Sights

Decked in white, and towering over downtown, the **Gateway Arch** (☎ 314-982-1410; www .stlouisarch.com; 707 N 1st St; tram $8, with NP pass $5; ☺ 8am-10pm Memorial Day–Labor Day, 9am-6pm rest of year) is surprisingly fun. An egg-shaped tram (very *2001*) clanks its way there. Try to pre-purchase tickets in summer.

The world's largest (no one claims the best) beer plant, the **Anheuser-Busch Brewery** (☎ 314-577-2626; 12th & Lynch Sts; ☺ 9am-4pm Mon-Sat, 11:30am-4pm Sun), gives free tours, free samples and a glimpse of those Clydesdales (one's named 'Scott').

Sleeping

The cheapest chain motels are 8 miles east on I-64 in Illinois, along city-encircling I-270, or northeast of St Louis (via I-70) in quaint St Charles.

HI Huckleberry Finn Hostel (☎ 314-241-0076; 1904–8 S 12th St; dm $18) In a couple of old Soulard townhouses, this clean hostel has five rooms (one is co-ed) and a few bathrooms. Bus No 73 heads downtown. H-Finn is planning to open a hostel in Hannibal, 116 miles north, by 2005.

Eating & Drinking

Up to the neck in tasty Cajun offerings, the Soulard district is where to eat and drink. **John D McGurk's** (☎ 314-776-8309; 1200 Russell Blvd; mains $7-19) is a landmark Irish pub. **Joanie's Pizzeria** (☎ 314-865-1994; 2101 Menard St; large pie from $10) serves thin St Louis–style pies.

In Grand South Grand, **MoKaBe's Coffeehouse** (☎ 314-865-2009; 3606 Arsenal St; sandwiches $5) is a laid-back café with patio seats and serves meat and vegetarian meals; Sunday brunch is $11. Northwest of Forest Park (several miles west), along east–west Delmar Blvd, the **Loop** buzzes with Washington University students. Here Chuck Berry plays the small basement bar monthly at **Blueberry Hill** (☎ 314-727-0880; www.blueberryhill. com; 6504 Delmar Blvd; burgers $5.25).

Getting There & Around

Lambert–St Louis International Airport (☎ 314-426-8097) is 12 miles northwest of the Arch. **Greyhound** (☎ 314-231-4485; 1450 N 13th St) and **Amtrak** (☎ 314-331-3300; 550 S 16th St) stop downtown. **Yellow Cabs** (☎ 314-361-2345) charge $1.70 per mile.

KANSAS CITY

With one peeling Dingo booted foot plopped in Kansas, the other in a stylin' leather pump with gold lace in Missouri, Kansas City (KC) keeps its choice bits – jazz lore, spicy barbecue, European-style fountains – on the Missouri side.

Orientation & Information

In downtown, I-70 meets the northeast-southwest running I-35, which crosses the

---

IF YOU'VE GOT A FEW MORE DAYS IN KANSAS

In southwestern Kansas, **Dodge City** is a popular stop, for its shoot-outs and slangified singing at **Boot Hill Museum** (☎ 620-227-8188; admission $8; ☺ daily). See worn ruts made by 19th-century wagons, 9 miles west of town. The grain elevators occasionally let you go up to the top.

Wizard of Oz-heads must pop into **Liberal** (near the southwest corner, via US83) to visit the **Land of Oz & Dorothy's Home** (☎ 620-624-7624; 567 Yellow Brick Rd; admission $5).

GREAT PLAINS

Missouri River, as well as I-29, heading north to the airport. The encircling I-435 takes in all of KC's sprawl. The **CVB** (☎ 816-221-5242, 800-767-7700; www.visitkc.com; 1100 Main St) is in City Center Sq downtown.

Sights

The glossy **American Jazz Museum** (☎ 816-474-8463; 1616 E 18th St; admission $6, combo ticket with baseball museum $8; ☼ 9am-6pm Tue-Sat, noon-6pm Sun) and the fascinating **Negro Leagues Baseball Museum** (☎ 816-221-1920; admission $6) are worthy stop-offs in KC's historic African-American district, southeast of downtown. In the former, you can play drums along with 'Sonny Rollins'; the latter highlights the little-known days when hall-of-fame players like Satchel Paige weren't allowed in the majors.

East of the Spanish-style, fountain-filled **Country Club Plaza**, about 4 miles south of downtown via Main St, the grand **Nelson-Atkins Museum of Art** (☎ 816-561-4000; 4525 Oak St; admission free; ☼ Tue-Sun), was fashioned in the Spanish style during KC's rabble-rousing 1930s, and has giant shuttlecocks outside.

Take an eerie drive through the 800-acre **SubTropolis**, just east of I-435 on Hwy 210 (northeast of downtown), a bizarre free-trade zone built inside limestone cliffs.

Sleeping

Cheap motels are way outside the city center along city-encircling I-435, *not* in the city proper. Just east of KC on I-70 is Independence, Harry Truman's old town and a good place to stop. On I-70, **American Inn** (☎ 816-373-8300; 4141 S Noland Rd; d $39-45) has wild karaoke nights catering to a fun 18-wheeler crowd.

Eating

Hickory-and-oak smoked brisket, pork or ribs in KC is a must for any meat eater. **Arthur Bryant's** (☎ 816-231-1123; 1727 Brooklyn Ave; sandwiches $8), east of 18th and Vine, and local chain **Gates & Sons Bar-B-Q** (☎ 816-753-0272; 3201 Main St) generally assume you're having a frosted mug of beer with your sauced-up slabs of pork, brisket or turkey.

Entertainment

Jazz musicians have been stumbling into the quite kept-real **Mutual Musicians Foundation** (☎ 816-471-5212; 1823 Highland Ave), next to a transient hotel, for late post-gig weekend jams since 1917 (Count Basie used to drop by).

Come by from midnight – if you're a player, join along. You can tour the site 11am to 4pm Tuesday to Sunday for free. Pick up a copy of *Pitch Weekly* for other listings.

Getting There & Around

KC International Airport (KCI; ☎ 816-243-5237) is located 17 miles north of downtown. **Greyhound** (☎ 816-221-2885; 12th & Troost Sts) has a daily bus service. **Amtrak** (☎ 816-421-3622) is behind recently restored Union Station. Call **Yellow Cab** (☎ 816-471-5000) for taxi service.

LAWRENCE

The nicest city in Kansas (36 miles west of KC on I-70), Lawrence is home to **Kansas University** (KU), and **Haskell Indian Nations University**, the country's only intertribal university. Lawrence's chain-free and lively downtown stems from Massachusetts St (with good food, beer joints and live music).

Just west of Mass St, **Halcyon House B&B** (☎ 785-841-0314; www.thehalcyonhouse.com; 1000 Ohio St; r from $49) has cozy rooms with shared bathrooms. Motels tend to be cheaper in Topeka or Abilene.

WESTERN KANSAS

Chants of 'westward ho' wane as I-70 opens up into a rolling, wide-open sea of wheat. Break up the journey at otherwise grim Topeka's **Brown vs Board of Education National Historic Site** (☎ 785-354-4273; 15th & Monroe Sts; admission free; ☼ 9am-5pm), at the Monroe Elementary School; there's a compelling video on the landmark 1954 Supreme Court case that banned segregation in US schools.

An hour west is cheerful **Abilene**, home of president Dwight Eisenhower's (with museum and library for Ike), plus a free greyhound dog museum nearby. Founded in 1877 by African-American settlers seeking a promised land, remarkable **Nicodemus**, 59 miles northwest of Hays (on I-70), is one of the oldest surviving towns of its kind. There's a small **museum** (☎ 785-839-4233).

IOWA & NEBRASKA

Other than Iowa's hilly overlooks of the Mississippi to the east (p388) and Nebraska's bluff-bursting west, much of I-80 spreads along turf flat enough to unnerve pancakes.

IOWA CITY & AROUND

The University of Iowa campus mingles with riverfront parks and downtown restaurants (around Clinton St and Iowa Ave).

In West Branch, 11 miles east on I-80, the worthwhile **Herbert Hoover Birthplace & Library** (☎ 319-643-2541; admission $4; 🕙 9am-5pm) makes a good case that the namesake of Depression-era 'Hoovervilles' was a stand-up guy. Stop in the Amana Colonies (20 miles west of Iowa City) for a 15-mile loop that takes in a German commune settled in the 1850s – excellent food abounds.

In Iowa City, the antique-packed 1908 Edwardian **Haverkamps Linn Street Homestay B&B** (☎ 319-337-4363; 619 N Linn St; r $35-50) is cheaper than most highway motels.

DES MOINES

Des Moines, meaning 'of the monks' not 'corn' as the surrounding fields might suggest, is Iowa's spread-out capital and has a few good free attractions. I-235 leads to downtown, where you'll find the **visitors center** (☎ 515-286-4960; www.seedesmoines.com; 405 6th Ave).

Sights

Downtown, the **State Historical Museum** (☎ 515-281-6412; www.iowahistory.org; 600 E Locust St; admission free; 🕙 9am-4:30pm Tue-Sat, noon-4:30pm Sun, also Mon in summer) has an inventive 'favorite things of the 20th century' exhibit, which includes pacemakers and miniskirts. See the nearby **capitol**, with the smell of fried chicken from the basement grill wafting through its hallowed halls. The **Des Moines Art Center** (☎ 515-277-4405; 4700 Grand Ave; admission free; 🕙 11am-4pm Tue-Sat, noon-4pm Sun, open till 9pm Thu), south of I-235 42nd St exit, features IM Pei's sculpture garden, and (on occasion) a talking 'butter cow.'

Sleeping & Eating

Find chain motels at I-80/I-35 exit 131 in Urbandale, such as **Best Inn** (☎ 515-270-1111;

5050 Merle Hay Rd; d incl breakfast $58; 🌊 🔀). Across from the airport, south of town, is **Motel 6** (☎ 515-287-6364; 4817 Fleur Dr; s/d $34/40).

Tasty Tacos (☎ 515-266-4242; 1418 E Grand St; tacos $2.25-2.75; 🕙 Mon-Sat) is an old-time taco seller near the capitol.

Getting There & Away

Greyhound (☎ 515-243-1773; 1107 Keosauqua Way) stops en route to Chicago and Omaha.

OMAHA

Malcolm X and Gerald Ford took their first steps in Omaha, Nebraska's biggest city. It has a quainter-than-average cobbled eating/drinking district, a few good attractions, but pricy accommodation. The **Nebraska I-80 Information Center** (☎ 402-595-3990; 1212 Bob Gibson Blvd) has city and state details.

Sights

The grand **Old Market**, situated between 10th and 13th Sts and Farnam and Jackson Sts, has century-old warehouses, plus good eating and nightlife to enjoy.

Omaha leads the US in millionaires per capita, evident in its rich art scene. Notably the art deco **Joslyn Art Museum** (☎ 402-342-3300; 2200 Dodge St; admission $6, free 10am-noon Sat; 🕙 10am-4pm Tue-Sat, noon-4pm Sun), which is open late on Thursday.

The ever-growing **Henry Doorly Zoo** (☎ 402-733-8401; www.omahazoo.com; 3701 S 10th St; admission $9.75; 🕙 9:30am-5pm), off I-80 exit 454, has a giant cat complex and the world's largest nocturnal exhibit. As zoos go, it's a doozy.

Sleeping & Eating

There plenty of motels located along I-80 and I-680 N exits. The best are far west of downtown, or in Council Bluffs or Lincoln.

Best Western Redick Tower Hotel (☎ 402-342-1500; 1504 Harney St; r from $91; 🅿 🔀) is a comfortable downtown hotel near Old Market.

IF YOU'VE GOT A FEW MORE DAYS IN IOWA & NEBRASKA

One of the Mississippi's great river towns, Victorian **Dubuque** – 84 miles north of I-80 via riverside Hwy 67 in Iowa – has a fun up-the-cliff elevator to ride. The 19th-century **Julien Inn** (☎ 563-556-4200, 800-798-7098; 200 Main St; d $49; 🔀) sports a hilarious 1960s makeover. Some 20 miles west on US 20, you can run the bases from the film *Field of Dreams*, outside Dyersville.

In north-central Nebraska, **Valentine** wins its hearts with the cowboy boot-clicking center and super canoe trips along the Niobrara River. The **CVB** (☎ 402-376-2969; 🕙 Mon-Sat) has information. Camp by the river at **Smith Falls State Park** (☎ 402-376-1306; campsites per person $3).

McFoster's Natural Kind Café (☎ 401-345-7477; 302 S 38th St; mains $5-10; ☺ 10am-10pm Mon-Sat, 10am-3pm Sun) serves fresh veggie fare. It's best for a Sunday brunch.

Getting There & Around
Greyhound (☎ 402-341-1906; 1601 Jackson St) has daily buses. Trains go to the **Amtrak station** (☎ 402-342-6699; 1003 9th St).

AROUND ASHLAND
Near Ashland, midway between Omaha and Lincoln, the fascinating **Strategic Air & Space Museum** (☎ 402-827-3100, 800-358-5029; 28210 West Park Hwy; admission $7; ☺ 9am-5pm), at I-80 exit 426, boasts two massive hangars housing more than 30 aircraft and a real flight simulator to ride. Bring Boy Scout repellent.

LINCOLN
Nebraska's capital ('Star City') is the I-70's best road stop if you're looking for a cheap bed, phallic art-deco capitol, beer-soaked student life and football – all within walking distance.

The **visitors center** (☎ 402-434-5348; 201 N 7th St) is in the historic Haymarket District, north of downtown.

Sights
Museum of Nebraska History (☎ 402-471-4754; cnr P & 15th Sts; admission free; ☺ 9am-4:30pm Tue-Sun) has a good First Nebraskans exhibit, including prehistoric bones dug up by a chicken. On most weekdays, you can visit or take a guided tour of the Cornhuskers football team's field and Heisman Room at **Memorial Stadium** (☎ 402-472-1132; admission free).

Sleeping & Eating
HI Cornerstone Hostel (☎ 402-476-0926; 640 N 16th St; dm member/nonmember $10/13) In a church between two fraternity houses (walkable from downtown to west), this hostel has a few basic dorm rooms. There's no admission from 11pm to 7am – to be considered if arriving late by train or car.

There are budget motels aplenty off I-80, including tidy **Horizon Inn** (☎ 402-474-5252; 2901 NW 12th St, exit 399; r from $45; ☺).

Lincoln's Haymarket District has a good variety of grub (Indian, steaks and café fare) and drink (beer mostly). **Maggie's Vegetarian Vittles** (☎ 402-477-3959; 311 N 8th St; mains $4-6; ☺ 8am-3pm Mon-Fri) serves vegan wraps.

> ### BACKROADS: NEBRASKA PANHANDLE
> Nebraska's western stub sports some of the region's most awe-inspiring road adventures (massive rocky cliffs jutting over plains). About 85 miles northwest of I-80, via I-26 from Ogallala, are the **Courthouse & Jail Rocks**. North 40 miles along US 385 is rural Alliance, home to **Carhenge**, a Stonehenge replica made from 34 discarded cars in a field two miles northeast.
>
> West on US 26 some 30 miles, the massive **Scotts Bluff National Monument** (☎ 308-436-4340; Hwy 92; admission per car $5; ☺ daily) pops into view. The Sioux called it *me-a-pa-te* ('hill that is hard to go around') millennia ago. Today you can drive up it in a flash. There are views to Wyoming.
>
> Up north on US 20, remote **Fort Robinson State Park** (☎ 308-665-2900; admission per vehicle $3), 4 miles west of Crawford, is where captive Crazy Horse was killed in 1877.

Getting There & Around
Greyhound (☎ 402-474-1071; 940 P St) stops here. **Amtrak** (☎ 402-476-1295; 201 N 7th St) arrives in the wee hours.

SOUTH DAKOTA

No doubt, the Great Plains' highlights – with the Black Hills and Badlands, and some tacky stuff serving as leg-stretching turf – woos cross-country drivers to the flat I-90. Off the interstate, many highways are pink (made of quartzite) and several Indian Reservations give reality checks to US history.

SIOUX FALLS TO WALL
Sioux Falls has pricier motels than nearby towns, but its namesake falls, downtown, are worth a look if you're stopping here.

Made annually from 275,000 ears of real South Dakotan corn, the Moorish-style **Corn Palace** (☎ 605-996-5031; 6th & Main Sts; admission free; ☺ daily May–Sep, Mon-Fri Oct–Apr) in **Mitchell**, 66 miles west, is the de facto civic center with graduations and basketball games.

Stop in **Chamberlain** to see the **Akta Lakota Museum & Cultural Center** (☎ 605-734-3452; 800-798-3452; admission free; ☺ daily May–Sep, Mon-Fri Oct–Apr). Many of its pieces were used in *Dances With Wolves*.

Wall Drug (☎ 605-279-2275; 510 Main St), near the hills, has cheap breakfasts, singing cowboy machines, 1970s-era toys and fudge.

BADLANDS NATIONAL PARK

These lunar-like mountains of eroded spires and canyons get their name from French-Canadian trappers who called it a 'bad land to travel through.' There are views along the wall-hugging 41-mile loop road, via Hwy 240 through the north unit, off I-90 between Cactus Flats and Wall, six short walks (under 2 miles) and a 10-mile one; watch for rattle snakes. The less developed south unit is at White River, 43 miles southwest of Wall.

Stop by the **Ben Reifel visitors center** (☎ 605-433-5361; Cedar Pass), 8 miles south of Cactus Flats. Camp or sleep at nearby **Cedar Pass Lodge** (☎ 605-433-5460; www.cedarpasslodge.com; campsites $8-10, cabins $55-60); its restaurant cooks up Indian tacos.

BLACK HILLS

Much more than the presidents of stone seen at Mt Rushmore, this 8000-sq-mile mountainous region of 7000ft 'hills' (called 'black' for their dark Ponderosa pines) is huge – far bigger than Yosemite or Yellowstone. There's outdoor fun, including 353 miles of hiking, rock-climbing, abundant wildlife and caving. Cyclists and big-time hikers can go the hills' length on the 114-mile **Mickelson Trail.**

The Black Hills National Forest covers most of the area, with Custer State Park occupying some truly enviable terrain to the southwest.

The Lakota Sioux, many of whom live in Pine Ridge Reservation to the southwest, were promised the hills (their sacred, ancestral home) for 'eternity' in the 1868 Laramie Treaty. Gold changed that. As one Lakota Sioux priest recently said, 'there's no controversy, they're ours.'

Orientation & Information

The best access points are along I-90 from Spearfish, Sturgis or Rapid City – all slightly outside the hills. The best place for information is the **Black Hills Visitors Center** (☎ 605-355-3700; 1851 Discovery Circle), east of Rapid City on I-90.

Room rates skyrocket between Memorial Day and Labor Day. Try for last-minute accommodations from **Black Hills Central Reservations** (☎ 800-529-0105; 68 Sherman St, Deadwood). The national forest has 30 basic **campgrounds** (☎ 877-444-6777; campsites $9-18) and allows backcountry camping.

Mt Rushmore National Monument

Nothing says 'USA' more than four giant stone faces, carved 60ft from neck to crown in granite cliffs. Not Medusa's leftovers, these guys – George Washington, Thomas Jefferson, Abraham Lincoln and Theodore Roosevelt – were built by Gutzon Borglum between 1927 and 1930. Close-up nostril views and the summer light show (9pm) can seriously sway a deep-rooted sceptic.

The **national monument** (☎ 605-574-2523; admission free; ☯ 8am-10pm May–Aug, 8am-5pm Sep–Apr) is 25 miles southwest of Rapid City (below) via US 16. Free parking is 400yd towards Keystone from the $8 lot.

There are several chain motels in nearby **Keystone**, and just north on US 16A. The **Holy Smoke Resort** (☎ 605-666-4616, 866-530-5696; cabins $50-135; ⚇) has log cabins with TV.

Crazy Horse Memorial

A 'Native American rebuttal' to presidential Rushmore, the in-progress **Crazy Horse Memorial** (☎ 605-673-4681; www.crazyhorse.org; person/car $9/20, walkers & cyclists $3.50; ☯ 7am-9pm summer, 8am-4:30pm winter), 4 miles north of Custer, is the world's largest monument, though it may not be finished for (literally) hundreds of years. Visitors can admire the beginnings (mostly just the face) of the famed Sioux leader astride his horse. It's privately funded; federal support was turned down.

You can stay in a tepee at the **Heritage Village** (☎ 605-673-4761; tepee/campsites $22/15), 1 mile to the south.

The town of **Custer**, a few miles south, ha many campgrounds and motels, includir

---

> **SCENIC DRIVES: BLACK HILLS**
>
> The forest's many gravel **'fire roads'** are where locals go to avoid tourists in summer. Dusk and dawn trips take in critters. A superb, more-trodden road is the 70-mile **Peter Norbeck Byway** in Custer State Park. Enter via the rock-spire Needles Hwy (Hwy 87), take the southerly Wildlife Loop Rd (past begging burros) and north on Iron Mountain Rd to see perfectly framed tunnel views of Mt Rushmore.

the cute 1930s **Shady Rest Motel** (☎ 605-673-4478, 800-567-8259; 238 Gordon St; cabins $55-205; ⌘). Its nine cottages have kitchenettes; half sleep two for under $70.

Hot Springs

Cute, with mineral springs, Hot Springs is south of the main circuit. Take a hot springs splash at **Evans Plunge** (☎ 605-745-5165; 1145 N River St; admission $9; ⊙ daily) – or in free swimming holes west of town. See 27,000-year-old mammoth remains at the left-as-found **Mammoth Site** (☎ 605-745-6017; 1800 US 18; admission $6.75; ⊙ daily). The audio of young mammoths wailing in agony at the sinkhole here is both heartbreaking and hilarious.

The hilltop **Historic Log Cabin Motel** (☎ 605-745-5166; US 385; cabins from $50), just north, has a basketball court and bikes.

Pine Ridge Indian Reservation

Visiting the country's poorest 'county', 64 miles southeast of Hot Springs, is a real eye opener. Wrecked cars lay in fields as many locals walk to-and-fro along dusty roads. Twenty miles northeast is the **Wounded Knee Massacre Site** where 300 unarmed participants of the Ghost Dance were killed in 1890.

Deadwood

Settled illegally by miners in the 1870s, **Deadwood** (www.deadwood.org) plays up its wild past. Up Boot Hill, see many gunslingers' graves at **Mt Moriah Cemetery**.

The clean **HI Penny Motel** (☎ 605-578-1842, 877-565-8140; www.pennymotel.com; 818 Upper Main St; dm members/nonmembers $13/16, d from $39) has a couple of dorm rooms, several private rooms, a TV lounge and kitchen. It rents bikes (per day $24, 50% off for guests) and offers shuttle service to Mickelson Trail.

Rapid City

This major gateway provides a good back-up for sleeping. Older motels line Hwy 79 (St Joseph St), east of downtown, including **Lamplighter Inn** (☎ 605-342-3385; www.lamplighter inn.net; 27 St Joseph St; d summer/off-season from $58/42; Ⓟ ⌘ ✕ ☎).

Jefferson Lines (☎ 605-348-3300; 333 6th St) buses stop here.

Sturgis

'Iog' lovers (Harley-Davidsons, not pigs) 'ghta stop in Sturgis for a biker shirt or brew at a biker bar. In early August, half a million bikers visit during the **Sturgis Rally & Races** (☎ 605-720-0800; www.sturgismotorcyclerally .com) when temporary campsites are set up and motels boost rates to the hundreds.

Twelve miles north on Hwy 79, away from the hills, is impressive **Bear Butte State Park** (☎ 605-347-5240; vehicle admission $5, camping $6) with camping and a lone mountain top (where Crazy Horse saw his visions).

Starlite Motel (☎ 605-347-2506, 888-214-3352; 2426 Junction Ave, exit 32; d in summer $60; Ⓟ ⌘) is of the cheaper motels.

NORTH DAKOTA

Crossed east–west by I-94, the USA's least-visited state has vast flat plains, badlands in the southeast and Native American reservations. It has considered changing its name to 'Dakota' for years, much to chagrin of its southerly neighbor.

To the east, spread-out Fargo is ho-hum, but neighboring **Moorhead**, Minnesota, has a cool Viking ship replica and rock bars.

Mid-state, the capital **Bismarck** is an excellent base for Lewis and Clarking; the duo wintered near Washburn. In New Salem, on I-94, stop to see Sue, the **World's Largest Holstein Cow** – udders are out of reach, but the view's tops.

THEODORE ROOSEVELT NATIONAL PARK

Far overlooked, the superb, wildlife-packed **Theodore Roosevelt National Park** (☎ 701-623-4466; admission per person/car $5/10), near the Montana border, has two parts. The South Unit, near I-94 at Medora, has rolling badlands and a 36-mile scenic loop, while the remote North Unit is 68 miles north on US 85. The main visitors center is in Medora.

Herds of bison sometimes surround cars. There's good walking and horseback opportunities. The best is the 96-mile **Maah Daah Hey Trail**, which connects the units in several days by foot, horse or bike. For more information, call ☎ 701-225-5151.

The park has three **campgrounds** (campsites $10). In Medora (www.medorand.com), **Custer's Cottage** (☎ 701-623-4378, 888-383-2574; www.custerscottage.com; r $40-50) has kitchenettes; call ahead.

Greyhound buses stop in Medora.

Texas

HIGHLIGHTS

- **Austin** Hundreds of bands, miles of trails and millions of bats make it the state's hippest and most memorable city (p396)
- **West Texas** Stark desert, chiseled mountains, mysterious lights and little-visited national parks (p408)
- **Hill Country** Wineries, a pink-granite monolith and a refreshing river float (p400)
- **Houston** Goofy folk art and the Gulf coast beaches of nearby Galveston (p402)
- **Off the beaten track** Cadillac Ranch's quirky car sculpture (p408)
- **Best journey** The River Rd (Hwy 170) between Presidio and Lajitas (p408)

FAST FACTS

- **Area** 261,950 sq miles (about the size of Germany and Poland combined)
- **Big cities** Houston (population 1.9 million), Dallas-Fort Worth (1.7 million), San Antonio (1.1 million), Austin (680,000)
- **Budget** $50–80 per day
- **Costs:** hotel room in Austin $60, Houston to Dallas bus ticket $30, long horn cow skull $55
- **Driving times** Houston to Austin 2½ hours, Austin to Dallas 3 hours, Austin to Big Bend National Park 8 hours
- **Famous for** cowboys, the Dallas Cowboys, barbecue, the Alamo, Willie Nelson, JR Ewing, LBJ, George W Bush
- **Languages** English, Spanish
- **Population** 21,779,893
- **Phrases** *I'll tell you what...* (Listen to this), *vee-hi-cul* (car or truck), *all hat and no cattle* (a person who is more show than substance)

- **Seasons** best weather Mar–Apr and Sep–Oct
- **Tasty treats** beef brisket, sausage-filled *kolaches* (pastries), Shiner Bock beer
- **Time** GMT minus 6 hours (daylight savings observed)
- **Top hostel** HI Austin (p398)

TRAVEL HINTS

Get a copy of the *Texas State Travel Guide* at one of the visitors centers: it gives a minihistory lesson about almost every town you'll pass through. In rural areas, streams often cross roads rather than vice versa. Never drive across water unless you're certain it's shallow and slow moving.

Yep, it's big. But to those who have never seen it, Texas can seem a big bunch of nothing much: flat land, few trees, the Alamo. That opinion dies quickly once you get there. Big size means big diversity, everything from seashores and lush bayou to high mountains and majestic desert – and, yes, the treeless plains. The people are just as varied as the geography. Their differences have produced strong rivalries (ask a local his or her opinion of another Texas city and you'll get an earful). But distinctive people make for distinct experiences, be it eating barbecue brisket at a Hill Country picnic table, attempting a two-step in an Austin honky-tonk, or sipping a beer beside the sun-seared residents of the Big Bend.

HISTORY

Texans' reputation for independent thinking began in the 1830s, when settlers (many of them Anglos from the US) butted heads with the Mexican government over religion, politics and slavery. The resulting Texan Revolution was an odd war, consisting of just two major battles. The first was at the Alamo in San Antonio, where a small group of Texans held out for 12 days before being slaughtered. The rest of the Texan army seemed intent on retreating all the way to New Orleans, but managed a surprise attack one afternoon on a bayou east of present-day Houston. A half-hour later they had routed the Mexican army and the Republic of Texas was born. For the next nine years it stood alone as an independent country, which explains the solo constellation on the state flag (as well as Texans' delight in decorating everything with big stars).

Sick and tired of being alone, the Lone Stars united with the rest of the USA in 1845 after the US-Mexican War, only to secede 16 years later with the rest of the Confederate states. The cowboys arrived after the Civil War to help round up the wild cattle that were roaming around Texas. In the early 1900s, the discovery of Texas oil helped America fall more deeply in love with fossil fuels. Oil is one of many boom-and-bust businesses that have flourished in Texas, with high tech and Enron energy trading being more recent examples.

THE CULTURE

Texas has gathered in a diverse mix of people, and the different ethnic groups have a very visible presence. Mexico, of course, remains one of the largest influences. In some southern towns it would be more accurate to say that Anglo-American traits are a subset of Hispanic culture rather than vice versa. African Americans are most prevalent in eastern Texas, the same area where slave-driven agriculture took hold in the pre–Civil War era. East Texas is also a center of Cajun (French-Canadian) culture, which derives from the French Canadians who settled in neighboring Louisiana in the 1700s. Eastern and central Europeans settled many of the towns in the middle portion of the state. Czech *kolaches* (pastries) are a popular breakfast item there, and German accents are still detectable in several Hill Country towns.

SPORTS

Football (American-style) is an obsession. The state's pro and college teams have enormous followings, but the best place to observe gridiron devotion is at a high-school game. For a truly fascinating look at the phenomenon, read HG Bissinger's *Friday Night Lights*. Rodeos are another great slice of local color, especially the small-town variety.

ARTS & ENTERTAINMENT

Texans have made their mark in all kinds of fields, but music is where they really show who they are. The mix of cultures has nurtured a who's who of legendary musicians; Blind Lemon Jefferson, Lightin' Hopkins, Buddy Holly, Bob Wills, Roy Orbison, Lydia Mendoza, Janis Joplin, Willie Nelson, ZZ Top, Flaco Jimenez, Stevie Ray Vaughan, Selena, the Butthole Surfers,

THE BIG ISSUE: THE BORDER

This border state deals directly with the complexities of illegal immigration from Mexico and Central America. Texas' politically conservative voters and politicians (there are a lot of them) often favor strict enforcement of the immigration laws, but the large Hispanic population (avidly courted by both major parties) views the illegals more sympathetically. In addition, the state's economy gets a large boost from the flow of inexpensive labor.

TEXAS

To Flagstaff (AZ)

108°W · 106°W · 104°W · 102°W · 100°W

36°N

To Denver (CO)
56 412

84

SANTA FE
25

Dalhart
Dumas

54

287 Lake Meredith
Pampa

Albuquerque
40

285 84

Amarillo
40

60

Canyon Palo Duro Canyon State Park 287

New Mexico

380

34°N

60

285

385 27 Caprock Canyons State Park
207 Turkey Quitaque Childress

70

70 84 Plainview

25

207 82 70

Roswell 380

Lubbock 82 83

82 82

Brownfield 380

385 87 84 Stamford

To Phoenix (AZ)
10

70 54 Las Cruces

Carlsbad Caverns National Park

62 180 Sweetwater 180
20 Abilene

32°N

Hueco Tanks State Park

Big Spring
20 Colorado River

Mountain Time Zone
El Paso
Central Time Zone

62 180 Guadalupe Mountains National Park 285

Odessa Midland 87 San Angelo 277 83

Ciudad Juárez Fabens

Pecos 20 385

MEXICO

10

Van Horn Kent 118 Balmorhea 10 Fort Stockton 67 Sonora 10

30°N

McDonald Observatory
17 Fort Davis 67
90 Marfa Alpine 285 Marathon 90 Lost Maples State Park 377

170 67 118 385 277

Big Bend Ranch State Park Study Butte
Presidio International Amistad Reservoir/ Presa de la Amistad Del Rio

Chihuahua

Ojinaga 16 Lajitas Terlingua Big Bend National Park

Ciudad Acuña Uvalde 83
47 277 Eagle Pass

CHIHUAHUA Piedras Negras Carrizo Springs

28°N

Cuauhtémoc

Rio Grande

Coahuila

45D 57

Durango

Monclova

Nuevo León

26°N

85

MONTERREY

SALTILLO

106°W · 104°W · 102°W · 100°W

0   150 km
0   90 miles

98°W
To Wichita (KS)
96°W
94°W
92°W
36°N

N Canadian River
Enid
75
44
Fayetteville
65
Arkansas
67
To Memphis (TN)
60
412
Tulsa
Muskogee
540
35
OKLAHOMA CITY
OKLAHOMA
40
Oklahoma
Arkansas River
Conway
LITTLE ROCK
40
S Canadian River
Eufaula Lake
270
Hot Springs National Park
530
79
49
44
Lawton
35
69
71
Pine Bluff
34°N
62
Red River
75
59
65
61
Vernon
Lake Texoma
30
Wichita Falls
82
Gainesville
Sherman
82
24
Paris
Texarkana
79
167
82
281
287
Commerce
Denton
35E
Sulphur Springs
Mount Pleasant
59
167
To Jackson (MS)
Mineral Wells
Fort Worth
30
69
271
Longview
20
180
Dallas
Shreveport
165
Weatherford
Arlington
80
Louisiana
65
32°N
283
Stephenville
67
35W
35E
Ennis
20
Tyler
Carthage
71
Red River
84
183
Corsicana
175
Jacksonville
79
96
Coleman
377
Hillsboro
287
Nacogdoches
Toledo Bend Reservoir
49
84
Mexia
Palestine
Angelina National Forest
Sabine National Forest
61
377
Brownwood
84
Waco
45
287
Lufkin
Alexandria
Brady
190
Killeen
79
Davy Crockett National Forest
Sam Rayburn Reservoir
171
To New Orleans
87
Lampasas
Temple
190
Lake Livingston
Jasper
165
49
Enchanted Rock State Park
281
35
190
Bryan
190
Livingston
190
BATON ROUGE
Johnson City
College Station
Huntsville
Sam Houston National Forest
10
Lafayette
30°N
Fredericksburg
77
San Jacinto
59
290
AUSTIN
Brenham
6
Conroe
Beaumont
Kerrville
290
90
Liberty
Orange
San Marcos
Lockhart
10
Port Arthur
90
Bandera
New Braunfels
10
Houston
45
Texas City
San Antonio
Gonzales
ALT 90
Wharton
Clear Lake
Galveston
90
Floresville
59
Edna
Pleasanton
181
183
87
Victoria
35
37
77
Port Lavaca
Beeville
Aransas National Wildlife Refuge
Gulf of Mexico
28°N
Sinton
Matagorda Island
59
Alice
Corpus Christi
Laredo
Kingsville
Padre Island National Seashore
Nuevo Laredo
Padre Island
281
77
Rio Grande City
MEX 2
83
McAllen
Harlingen
South Padre Island
26°N
Reynosa
MEX 40D
Matamoros
Brownsville
Tamaulipas
98°W
96°W
94°W
92°W

TEXAS

Beyonce Knowles, the list goes on. But what's more impressive for visitors is the way that music is so entwined in everyday life. Bands play anywhere a crowd might gather, and wherever bands are playing, people are usually dancing.

ENVIRONMENT

The coastal plain along the Gulf of Mexico is like neighboring Louisiana: humid, swampy and rainy. As you go west, the weather gets dryer and the trees get smaller. The Hill Country begins just west of Austin and San Antonio, marking the place where the coastal plain meets the limestone ridges of the Edwards Plateau. Northwest of the Hill Country, extending up into the Texas Panhandle, are flat plains that continue north into Oklahoma and Kansas. West Texas – the part of the state that tucks under New Mexico – is a dramatic place of mountains, desert, brilliant sun and few people.

TRANSPORTATION

Dallas (DFW) and Houston (IAH) are the state's major air hubs. Austin (AUS) and San Antonio (SAT) are well served but are usually a bit more expensive to fly in and out of. Southwest Airlines serves all the major cities and is a good choice for one-way tickets, which usually cost about $50 within Texas. See the Transportation section (p705) for more details.

AUSTIN

Troubadour Jerry Jeff Walker may have put it best: 'I don't live in Texas,' he said. 'I live in Austin.' The capital city's no-worries attitude and no-suits dress code stand apart from the fast pace and flashy style of Dallas and Houston, and its liberal politics divide it from the largely conservative lands that surround it. Though no Texas town lacks for music, Austin has so many bands, they've become an industry and a lifestyle. The city also has a knack for attracting filmmakers, artists, writers, and just plain offbeat characters. Many of them wandered into town, had a beer, heard some tunes – and they never went home. It can happen.

HISTORY

When Texas won its independence, the future site of Austin was a tiny river settlement known as Waterloo. Thriving it wasn't, but the centrally located village was chosen as the capital in 1839, taking its new name from Stephen F Austin, who had led settlers into Texas. After the University of Texas was established in the 1880s, Austin became a college town as well as a political center. 'UT' has grown into one of the largest colleges in the country in terms of student population (now numbering about 45,000), and it's responsible for a lot of Austin's hipness. Student club-goers are the backbone of the city's music scene, which caught fire in the early '70s thanks to Willie Nelson and like-minded 'cosmic cowboys.' Digital cowboys settled into Austin, too, laying the groundwork for the high-tech boom of the 1990s. Until the technology industry sputtered in the early 2000s, Austin was growing too fast for its own good. The pace has slowed in recent years, but there's still concern that the town will become one more nondescript big city. Traditionalists hoping to retain its offbeat character have a rallying cry: 'Keep Austin Weird.'

ORIENTATION

Downtown sits on the north bank of Town Lake (the Colorado River) and is home to the state capitol and the E Sixth St and Warehouse District entertainment areas. South Congress Ave (SoCo), lined with shops, galleries and restaurants, is a 20-minute walk from downtown. The University of Texas (UT) is just north of the capitol.

The **Austin Visitor Information Center** (☎ 866-462-8784; www.austintexas.org; 209 E 6th St; ☯ 9am-6pm Sun-Thu, 9am-7pm Fri & Sat) is downtown. Free Internet access is available at **Faulk Central Library** (☎ 512-974-7400; 800 Guadalupe St; ☯ 10am-9pm Mon-Thu, 10am-6pm Fri & Sat, noon-6pm Sun).

AUSTIN

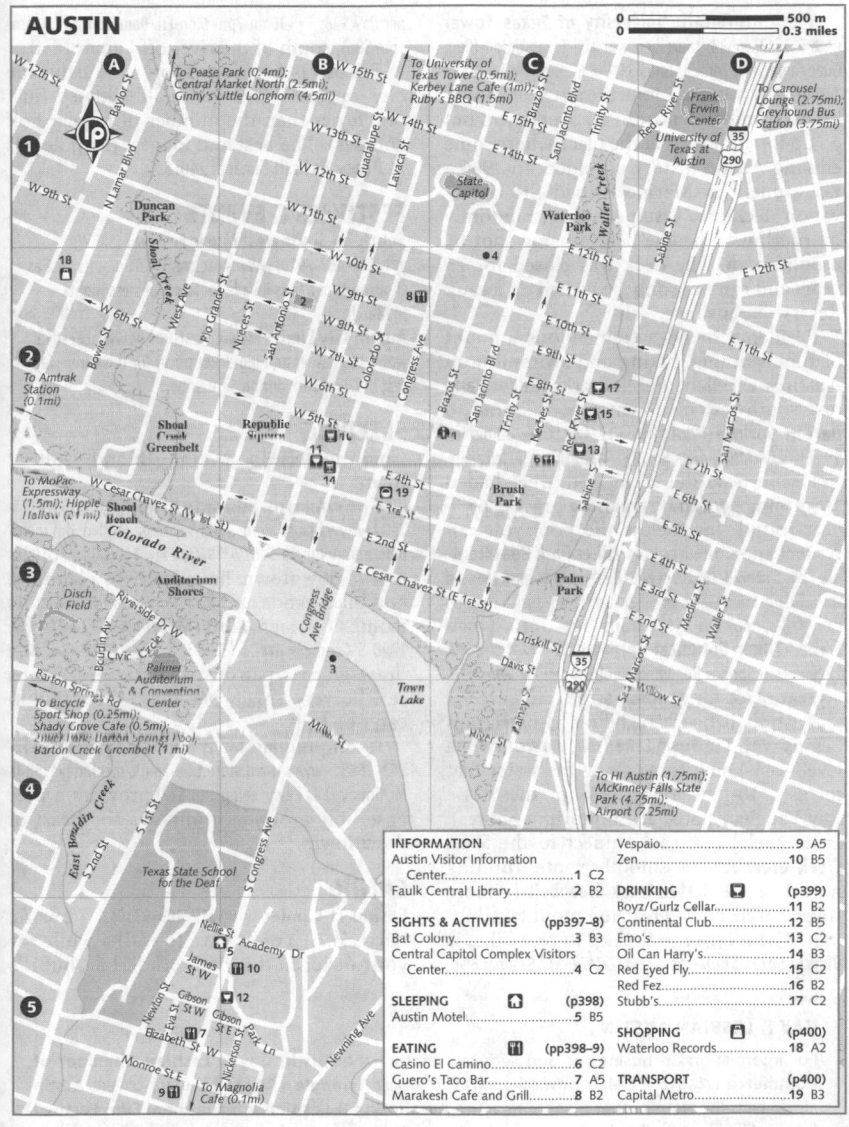

INFORMATION		Vespaio....................................9 A5
Austin Visitor Information		Zen...10 B5
Center...............................1 C2		
Faulk Central Library.............2 B2		**DRINKING** 🍸 (p399)
		Boyz/Gurlz Cellar...................11 B2
SIGHTS & ACTIVITIES (pp397–8)		Continental Club....................12 B5
Bat Colony.............................3 B3		Emo's....................................13 C2
Central Capitol Complex Visitors		Oil Can Harry's......................14 B3
Center.............................4 C2		Red Eyed Fly.........................15 C2
		Red Fez.................................16 B2
SLEEPING 🛏 (p398)		Stubb's..................................17 C2
Austin Motel...........................5 B5		
		SHOPPING 🛍 (p400)
EATING 🍴 (pp398–9)		Waterloo Records..................18 A2
Casino El Camino....................6 C2		
Guero's Taco Bar....................7 A5		**TRANSPORT** (p400)
Marakesh Cafe and Grill.........8 B2		Capital Metro........................19 B3

SIGHTS & ACTIVITIES

Austin's most unusual sight is the nightly emergence of the enormous **Bat Colony** (☎ 512-416-5700, ext 3636 for information; Congress Ave at Town Lake) from beneath the Congress Ave Bridge in downtown. Under perfect conditions, clouds of bats are silhouetted against the dusky sky. The colony, some 1.5 million strong, is in residence from March to early November, with optimal viewing during late July to mid-August.

The pink-granite **Texas State Capitol** (☎ 512-305-8400; Congress Ave at 11th St; admission free; ☀ 7am-10pm Mon-Fri, 9am-8pm Sat & Sun) can be visited on your own, or check with the visitors center about free tours.

TEXAS

The 300ft-tall **University of Texas Tower** (☎ 512-475-6633; tours begin at the Texas Union Bldg, Guadalupe St at 24th St; tours $5; 🕓 6-8pm Thu-Fri & Sat, 1-8pm late May-late Aug, shorter hr on Sat & Sun late Aug-late May) can be seen from all over town, but go up top for a look at the place where some chilling Austin history unfolded. In 1966 a UT student/ex-Marine turned the observation deck into a sniper's nest, randomly murdering 15 people before being shot by a policeman. The deck was closed for 25 years and can now only be visited on a tour. Reserve in advance.

Residents spend a tremendous amount of time running, biking and swimming in Austin's excellent public parks. **Zilker Park**, just southwest of downtown, is home to **Barton Springs Pool** (☎ 512-476-9044; admission $3; 2101 Barton Springs Rd; 🕓 5am-10pm, closed 9am-7pm Thu), a beautiful spring-fed, tree-shaded swimming spot that remains a bracing 68°F year-round. Just below the pool you can rent a canoe or kayak at **Zilker Park Boat Rentals** (☎ 512-478-3852; per hr $10; 🕓 11am-dusk Mon-Fri spring-early fall, 9am-dusk Sat & Sun; 11am-dusk Sat & Sun early fall-spring) for a paddle out onto Town Lake. **Zilker Botanical Garden** (☎ 512-477-8672; 2220 Barton Springs Rd; admission free; 🕓 7am-dusk) is a great place for a shady stroll.

Austin's network of hike-and-bike trails begins with the **Town Lake Trail**, downtown, a level, easy-going route along the water that forms a 10-mile loop (look for the Stevie Ray Vaughan statue at Auditorium Shores). From there, you can connect to the **Shoal Creek Greenbelt** (a smooth route running north) or the **Barton Creek Greenbelt** (a more rugged trail that's great for mountain biking). The most central place to rent bikes is **Bicycle Sport Shop** (☎ 512-477-3472; 517 S Lamar Blvd; per day $28; 🕓 10am-7pm Mon-Fri, 9am-6pm Sat, 11am-5pm Sun), south of the river off Lamar Blvd.

Frisbee is a serious sport in Austin: the city operates five disc golf courses (just one fewer than the number of regular golf courses). The best and longest (21 holes) is at **Pease Park** (N Lamar at 24th St).

FESTIVALS & EVENTS

South-by-Southwest Music Festival (SXSW; ☎ 512-467-7979; www.sxsw.com) Austin at its best as thousands of bands invade for four sleepless nights in March.

Austin City Limits Music Festival (www.aclfestival.com) Big names and big ticket prices for this three-day fest in Zilker Park during September.

SLEEPING

Chain motels line I-35 north and south of town.

The cheerful, lakeside **HI Austin** (☎ 512-444-2294; www.hiaustin.org; 2200 S Lakeshore Blvd; dm members/nonmembers $16.75/19.75; 🅿 🕱 🔲), southeast of downtown, has a kitchen, a laundry, and bike, canoe and kayak rentals. With its iconic neon sign, **Austin Motel** (☎ 512-441-1157; 1220 S Congress Ave; s $53-87, d $70-87; 🅿 🕱 🔊) draws repeat patrons; the cheaper rooms can be very small, but the SoCo location can't be beat.

If camping, **McKinney Falls State Park** (☎ 512-243-1643; www.tpwd.state.tx.us/park/mckinney; 5808 McKinney Falls Pkwy; campsites $17) provides a nice base only around 20 minutes southeast of downtown.

EATING

Casino El Camino (☎ 512-469-9330; 517 E 6th St; burgers $5.75) You'll have to wait a while for your order in this dark 6th St bar, but it's

---

GAY & LESBIAN AUSTIN

For information on businesses and services, contact the **Austin Gay & Lesbian Chamber of Commerce** (☎ 512-474-4422; www.aglcc.org). The **Texas Triangle** (☎ 512-476-0576) covers Austin along with the state's other major cities. The **Austin Gay & Lesbian International Film Festival** (www.agliff.org) takes place in late August and early September.

The club scene is concentrated in the downtown Warehouse District. Both **Oil Can Harry's** (☎ 512-320-8823; 211 W 4th St) and **Boyz Cellar** (☎ 512-479-8482; 213 W 4th St) have dance shows and DJs that stoke the floor until the wee hours. On Tuesday nights, Boyz Cellar is transformed into **Gurlz Cellar**, a popular lesbian gathering (the back bar at the club also caters to the gals on Sunday, Monday & Wednesday).

The misnamed **Hippie Hollow** (Commanche Trail, west of Hwy 620, on Lake Travis; per vehicle $10) is a public, clothing-optional beach that draws a large gay and lesbian contingent.

TEXAS

LATE NIGHT GRUB

Austin has two all-night standbys with menus so similar (Mexican and sandwiches, with lots of veggie options) that it's easy to confuse them. **Kerbey Lane Cafe** (☎ 512-477-5717; 2606 Guadalupe St; mains $5-10; ☽ 24hr) is in the university area. **Magnolia Cafe** (☎ 512-445-0000; 1920 S Congress Ave; mains $5-10; ☽ 24hr) is on South Congress. Both have additional locations around town.

---

worth it: these are the biggest and best burgers in town, and you can get them until 1:30am.

Guero's Taco Bar (☎ 512-447-7688; 1412 S Congress Ave; mains $6-15, tacos $1.40) The best option is to stay in the bar and order three or four tacos *al pastor* (pork and pineapple) along with one or two margaritas.

Marakesh Cafe & Grill (☎ 512-476-7735; 906 Congress Ave; mains $4-10) Middle Eastern food in big portions at cheap prices. The pita-wrapped *shuwarma* (kebab) sandwiches are an especially good deal.

SPLURGE!

Vespaio (☎ 512-441-6100; 1610 S Congress; mains $12-30) A cozy place with Italian-inspired gourmet fare, much of it incorporating produce from the restaurant's own garden.

Ruby's BBQ (☎ 512-477-2529; 512 W 29th St; mains $6-14; ☽ 11am-midnight) All-natural beef brisket is the star at this university-area favorite. Check out the autographs from many blues greats who have eaten here.

Taco Xpress (☎ 512-444-0261; 2529 S Lamar Blvd; tacos $2) As Austin as an eatery can get – ramshackle, tasty and indisputably cool. The Imperial Golden Crown Harmonizers play Sunday at 1pm and should not be missed.

Zen (☎ 512-444-8081; 1303 S Congress Ave; mains $5) Japanese-inspired stir-fry and sushi. Tasty, filling, inexpensive. Two additional locations in town.

DRINKING

Live music is the best reason to visit Austin, with bands playing in more than 100 venues around town. Downtown's E 6th St is the city's famous bar district, but 6th St proper is mostly dance clubs and shot bars. The three blocks of Red River St north of E 6th St have the biggest collection of live music clubs in town, a lot of it loud, fast

and hard. More music clubs thrive outside the city center.

Bars & Live Music

Broken Spoke (☎ 512-442-6189; 3201 S Lamar Blvd) There's simply no better place to experience a Texas dance hall. It has top-rank pickers and hoofers and a cool museum about the 'Spoke's star-studded 40-year history.

Continental Club (☎ 512-441-2444; 1315 S Congress Ave) Local and touring acts in the blues, roots rock and alternative country vein. In addition to the late-night headliners, there are shows most weekdays at 6:30pm and Saturday from 3pm to 7pm.

Emo's (☎ 512-477-3667; 603 Red River St) Has two stages with a mix of indie, punk, hip-hop and more.

Red Eyed Fly (☎ 512-474-1084; 715 Red River St) Serves up local rock and punk.

Red Fez (☎ 512-478-5120; 209 W 5th St) With an interior like a Moroccan pleasure palace and lots of wacky cocktails, this is a fun place to drink, but it transforms into a happening DJ/dance scene later in the evening.

Stubb's (☎ 512-480-8341; 801 Red River St) Big-name touring acts of all stripes play the outdoor stage; an indoor stage plays host local acts.

THE PICK OF THE PITS

You can argue barbecue for hours in Texas, but the following – all found in small Central Texas towns – get our vote as the state's best. Try to arrive between noon and 3pm; pickings get slim during the late afternoon.

- **Cooper's Old-Time Pit Bar-B-Que** (☎ 325-247-5713; 505 W Dallas St, Llano)
- **Kreuz Market** (☎ 512-398-2361; 619 N Colorado St, Lockhart)
- **Southside Market** (☎ 512-281-4650; 1212 US 290 E, Elgin)

TEXAS

TOP FIVE (ALMOST) FREE MUSIC VENUES

You'll be encouraged to toss a buck in the hat at some of these places – and you should do so – but it's still great music at bargain prices.

- **Ginny's Little Longhorn** (☎ 512-548-1813; 5434 Burnet Rd) This lovable honky-tonk has the town's best retro country acts and extremely cheap beer. Sunday afternoon's chicken shit bingo (with a live chicken and live music by Dale Watson) is an Austin must.

- **Waterloo Records CD Release Parties** (☎ 512-474-2500; 600 N Lamar St) What's better than free music? Free beer and free music. There's usually at least one of these afternoon showcases each week – check with the store.

- **Central Market North** (☎ 512-206-1000; 4001 N Lamar Blvd) The café attached to this gourmet grocery has free outdoor shows every Friday and Saturday at 6:30pm. The store's south location has a similar schedule.

- **Carousel Lounge** (☎ 512-452-6790; 1110 E 52nd St) A very wacky place with a dancing wait person named Stella and bands that range from anything from punk to rock to alternative country.

- **Shady Grove Cafe** (☎ 512-474-9991; 1624 Barton Springs Rd) Each Thursday evening from April to June one of Austin's bigger names performs on the outdoor patio. Be sure to arrive early to get in.

GETTING THERE & AROUND

Austin Bergstrom International Airport (AUS; ☎ 512-530-2242; www.ci.austin.tx.us/austinairport) is on the southeast side of town. The **bus station** (☎ 512-458-4463; 916 E Koenig Lane) is served by **Greyhound** (☎ 800-229-9424; www.greyhound .com) and the **Kerrville Bus Co** (☎ 800-474-3352; www.iridekbc.com). **Amtrak** (☎ 512-476-5684; 250 N Lamar Blvd) stops on the western edge of downtown.

Capital Metro (☎ 512-474-1200; www.capmetro.org; 323 Congress Ave) runs Austin's buses (50¢ a ride; 20-ticket book $5) and the free 'Dillo shuttles that run in the central city. Most of Austin's buses are equipped with bike racks.

AROUND AUSTIN

HILL COUNTRY

West of Austin is a land of limestone canyons, tree-covered hills, beautiful rivers and charming towns. It's a big area that's best divided into two trips.

For the westerly route, start at **Hamilton Pool Nature Preserve** (☎ 512-264-2740; FM 3238, Hamilton Pool Rd, 13 miles west of Bee Cave; $8 per vehicle; ☼ 9am-6pm), a stunning limestone grotto filled by a 60ft waterfall. It's a great place for a swim, but check on conditions before changing into your suit – bacteria levels sometimes make the water unsafe.

Further west, Hwy 290 between Johnson City and Fredericksburg is loaded with peach orchards and wineries. **Becker Vineyards** (☎ 830-644-2681; ☼ 10am-5pm Mon-Thu, 10am-6pm Fri & Sat, noon-6pm Sun), off Hwy 290 just west of Stonewall, is a good choice for wine – pretty grounds and generous with the free samples.

Fredericksburg is full of German heritage and lots of cutesy craft shops make for nice shopping. Not your bag? Head north on Hwy 16 to **Enchanted Rock State Park** (☎ 325-247-3903; 16710 Ranch Rd 965; admission $5), a 400ft-high dome of pink granite. You can hike a trail to the top, and there are also spots for technical rock climbing. **Camping** (campsites $8-10) is available. You should try to arrive early: the park is very popular and admission is limited.

The small Hill Country town of **Kerrville** becomes a low-volume Woodstock each spring when it plays host to the two-week **Kerrville Folk Festival** (☎ 830-257-3600; www.kerrville -music.com).

The southwestern Hill Country route centers on **New Braunfels**, where watery fun is the prime draw. There's a massive man-made water park, **Schlitterbahn**, but the better option is to go floating on the **Guadalupe River**, which plunges over small rapids and flows through limestone canyons on its way to town. (The nearby Comal River is a less exciting alternative.) The classic way to do the Guadalupe is in inner tubes – one for you, one for your cooler. Huge flotillas of attached tubers throng the river on summer weekends. **Rockin 'R' River Rides** (☎ 800-553-5628; www.rockinr.com; 1405 Gruene Rd; tubes $13-15, raft per person $26) is one of many companies that rents gear.

When you are finished soaking, visit the **Gruene Historic District** (pronounced *green*), an old cotton town perched above the river on the outskirts of New Braunfels. The highlight is **Gruene Hall** (☎ 830-606-1281; www .gruenehall.com; 1281 Gruene Rd; ⏰ 11-1am Fri & Sat, closes earlier Mon-Thu), which has been functioning as a dance hall since 1878 and hosts a great lineup of bands.

SAN ANTONIO

Decidedly more Hispanic than the state's other big towns, you could mistake San Antonio for a charming Mexican city – at least until you meet the throngs of conventioneers along the River Walk. If time is tight, consider seeing San Antonio on a side trip from Austin; the best attractions are close together and can be covered in a long day. The town's Fiesta blowout takes place for 10 days in late April, with parades, concerts, and sporting events throughout the city.

Sights & Activities

Begin at the shrine of Texas shrines, the **Alamo** (☎ 210-225-1391; 300 Alamo Plaza; admission free; ⏰ 9am-5:30pm Mon-Sat, 10am-5:30pm Sun), where Davy Crockett, William Travis and other independence patriots met their valiant end in 1836. It seems small and out of place amid the downtown skyscrapers. (When the battle was fought, the compound took up a lot more space.) Two historic buildings remain, both originally built in the 1700s. The displays inside give a good overview of the battle.

Next, walk across the street and enter the **River Walk** area. Almost 3 miles of stone walkways follow an inlet of the San Antonio River, with cute stone bridges arching above the water and sightseeing boats motoring past. The area was constructed as a Works Progress Administration (WPA) project in the 1930s. Now, it's mostly a bar and restaurant scene, overpriced on the whole, but fun to amble around for an hour or two. Flanking the River Walk's south side is **La Villita National Historic District**, a collection of renovated buildings from the 1800s that now house artisan shops.

When you've had enough of the River Walk proper, you can follow the riverside walkway a half-mile south to reach the **King William Historic District** (King William St at Beauregard St), a residential neighborhood made up of beautifully restored Victorian homes from the late 1800s.

Also within walking distance of the River Walk is **Market Sq** (Commerce St at Santa Rosa St). Mexican restaurants line the square, and you're likely to see a mariachi band or a spangly-attired Tejano singer. **El Mercado** (⏰ 10am-8pm summer, 10am-6pm winter), which is part of the square complex, is jam-packed with Mexican crafts and gives you a sense of the shopping available in border towns such as Nuevo Laredo.

To understand how deep the Hispanic roots run, check out the churches that make up the **San Antonio Missions National Historic Park**. They're located along a route that begins downtown and extends south for 8 miles. The Alamo (originally Mission San Antonio de Valero) is the oldest of the missions, but the other four give a better sense of the colonial communities that were established in the 1700s.

Head first to **Mission San Jose** (☎ 210-932-1001; 6701 San Jose Dr; admission free; ⏰ 9am-5pm), which is the most elaborate of the missions and houses the park's visitors center. The others are easily accessed along the Mission Trail driving route.

Sleeping

HI San Antonio Hostel (☎ 210-223-9426; 621 Pierce St; dm members/nonmembers $20/23, r $51-99; Ⓟ 🐾 ⓡ) Cheap sleeps north of downtown.

Eating

To taste the Mexican influence, you've got a lot of choices, but two of the town's best Tex-Mex eateries are **El Mirador** (☎ 210-225-9444; 722 S Saint Marys St; mains $8-20), in the King William Historic District, and **Los Barrios** (☎ 210-732-6017; 4223 Blanco; mains $5-10), north of downtown. To sample the culinary mark left by German immigrants (another prominent group), try **Schilo's Delicatessen** (☎ 210-223-6692; 424 E Commerce St; mains $5-10), just off the River Walk, which has been serving up fabulous split-pea soup and corned beef since 1917.

TEX

Getting There & Around

San Antonio International Airport (SAT; ☎ 210-207-3450; www.sanantonio.gov/airport) is north of downtown. The downtown **bus station** (500 N St Mary's St) is served by **Greyhound** (☎ 210-270-5824) and **Kerrville Bus Co** (☎ 800-474-3352; www.iridekbc.com). **VIA** (☎ 210-362-2020; www.viainfo.net; 260 E Houston St) runs the city buses (80¢). **Amtrak** (☎ 210-223-3226; 350 Hoefgen Ave) stops just north of the Alamodome.

HOUSTON & AROUND

East Texas means beaches, big highways, and surprisingly high art and quirky culture in Houston.

HOUSTON

Too large even for a Texan? That's almost the case with Houston. Its clogged freeways and sprawling developments make even the locals a little sheepish – but only a little. They know their city's size and business muscle has also brought it a grandeur that's visible in its majestic skyscrapers, lavish residential areas and top-rank museums. If you find your way to the correct off ramps, you'll discover there's also a zany and hip side to the state's biggest city.

Orientation

Main St (take Exit 769B off the I-10) runs southwest from downtown to the Museum District and Hermann Park and is the route for Houston's new light-rail service. The Menil Collection and lots of bars and restaurants are found in the Montrose District (Exit Hwy 527 from Hwy 59), which lies to the west of Main St, roughly from Elgin and Westheimer on the north to Hwy 59 on the south.

The Rice Village area is about a mile west of Main St and Hermann Park, on the far side of the Rice University campus.

The **Greater Houston Convention & Visitors Bureau** (☎ 713-437-5556, 800-446-8786; www.houston-guide.com; 901 Bagby) is downtown in the art-deco city hall. **Houston Public Library** (☎ 832-393-1313; 500 McKinney St; ☼ 9am-9pm Mon-Thu, 9am-6pm Fri & Sat, 2-6pm Sun) offers free Internet access.

Dangers & Annoyances

The section of Main St between Hwy 59 and the southern edge of downtown can be a bit dicey after nightfall. The light-rail stations are usually well populated, but avoid lengthy nighttime walks in this area.

Sights

There are several well-respected institutions in the **Museum District** (Main St at Hermann Dr, Fannin St Exit off Hwy 59), including the Museum of Fine Arts and Museum of Natural Science. But Houston's best museum is the **Menil Collection** (☎ 713-525-9400; www.menil.org; 1515 Sul Ross St, Montrose District; admission free; ☼ 11am-7pm Wed-Sun). The excellent collection (Picasso, Magritte, Matisse and lots of ancient and tribal art) is allowed to speak for itself – no tedious signs or audio guides. Be sure to see the adjacent **Rothko Chapel** (☼ 10am-6pm) and the **Byzantine Fresco**

GETTING GOOFY IN HOUSTON

Balancing Houston's elegance is a big bunch of folk-art weirdness that's fun and cheap. The **Orange Show** (☎ 713-926-6368; www.orangeshow.org; 2402 Munger St, take I-45 southwest of downtown, exit at Telephone Rd & turn right at third street; $1; ☼ noon-5pm Sat-Sun mid-Mar–mid-Dec, 9am-1pm Wed-Fri Memorial Day-Labor Day) is a house-sized agglomeration of tractor seats, ceramic tiles, and lots and lots of steel wagon wheels. The late Jeff McKissack constructed it as a monument to his favorite fruit, and the walls are adorned with oddball quotations about the majesty of the orange.

Viewable from the outside only, the **Beer Can House** (222 Malone St, Exit 764 off I-10, take Washington Ave southwest to Malone & turn right) is covered with huge curtains of aluminum fashioned from 50,000 beer cans.

If you can transform houses, why not cars? The **Art Car Museum** (☎ 713-861-5526; www.artcarmuseum.com; 140 Heights Blvd, off I-10; admission free; ☼ 11am-6pm Wed-Sun) showcases 10 or so of the zany contraptions from the annual Art Car Parade held in Houston in early May: giant rolling roaches, scorpion mobiles, vehicles constructed of spoons and the like. They're great fun, and the staff can clue you in to other offbeat happenings around town.

GAY & LESBIAN HOUSTON

The *Houston Voice* is a gay and lesbian weekly with loads of event listings. The prime nightlife district is along Pacific St (near the intersection of Westheimer and Montrose). The dance floors are jammed at **South Beach** (☎ 713-529-7623; 810 Pacific St) and **Montrose Mining Company** (☎ 713-529-7488; 808 Pacific St). Whoop it up with the cowboys at **Brazos River Bottom** (☎ 713-528-9192; 2400 Brazos St). **Mary's Lounge** (☎ 713-527-9669; 1022 Westheimer) draws a lot of lesbians on Sunday and plays host to the leather crowd on other nights.

Chapel Museum (☿ 11am-6pm Fri-Sun), two modern art meditative spaces.

The Menil (which began as one couple's private collection) gives a sense of Houston's stylish affluence. For a streetside look at luxury living, drive or walk through the **River Oaks** neighborhood, just east of Montrose. Start with River Oaks Blvd (running north from Westheimer, a few blocks east of Kirby Dr).

Festivals & Events

Houston Livestock Show & Rodeo (☎ 832-667-1000; www.hlsr.com) Runs for two and a half weeks in early March at Reliant Stadium, drawing more than a million visitors every year.

Orange Show Art Car Weekend (☎ 713-926-6368; www.orangeshow.org/artcar.html; 2402 Munger St, take I-45 southwest of downtown, exit at Telephone Rd & turn right at third street; admission $1) Takes place in mid-May, with the main parade of wacked-out autos on Saturday.

Sleeping

Houston International Hostel (☎ 713-523-1009; www.houstonhostel.com; 5302 Crawford, Southmore Exit off Hwy 288, west on Southmore, south on Crawford; dm $15; ⊠) Good central location, a few blocks from the Museum District light-rail stop.

Some decent budget motels are found in the Reliant Stadium/Astrodome area (Exits 1B and 1C off I-610). They're south of the action but convenient to the light-rail line. **Palm Court Inn** (☎ 713-668-8000; 8200 S Main St; s/d $48/58; Ⓟ ⊠ ☒) has a nice pool and grounds. The **Homestead Medical Center/Reliant Park** (☎ 713-797-0000; www.homesteadhotels.com; 7979 Fannin St; s/d $59/64; Ⓟ ⊠) offers small kitchenettes.

Eating

Brasil (☎ 713-528-1993; 2604 Dunlavy, at Westheimer; mains $6-9) Order one of the tasty sandwiches or salads at the counter, then find a seat on the plant-filled patio to watch Montrose life pass by. Good selection of beer, wine, and coffee.

Goode Co Barbecue (☎ 713-522-2530; 5109 Kirby Dr; sandwiches $5, plates $8) Houston's best choice for the national food of Texas.

Hot Bagel Shop (☎ 713-520-0340; 2009 S Shepherd Dr; mains $1-4, cash only) Quality bagels are not an easy thing to find in Texas, and this small shop has them. Good coffee, too.

Istanbul Grill & Deli (☎ 713-526-2800; 5613 Morningside Dr; mains $8-10, appetizers $3; ☿ Tue-Sun) Delicious and affordable Turkish cuisine in Rice Village. You can make a cheap meal with a couple appetizers. Try the *mantar* (stuffed mushrooms) or *coban salata* (shepherd salad with cucumber and tomato).

Drinking

BARS

Market Sq, downtown, has two one-of-a-kind bars: **La Carafe** (☎ 713-229-9399; 813 Congress Ave), a candlelit hideout in one of Houston's oldest buildings; and **Warren's Inn** (☎ 713-247-9207; 307 Travis St), a crowded cocktail spot once owned by a boyfriend of pianist Liberace.

For the Texas phenomenon of an 'ice house' (an outdoor beer joint), stop in at **West Alabama Ice House** (☎ 713-528-6874; 1919 W Alabama) in Montrose. The Rice University area has **Volcano** (☎ 713-526-5282; 2349 Bissonnet), a hip tiki bar.

LATE NIGHT GRUB

For pizza and beer in Montrose, try **Late Nite Pie** (☎ 713-529-5522; 502 Elgin; ☿ 5pm-3am; small/medium pizzas $6/10, subs $7). If 3am isn't late enough for you, head for **Ruchi's Taqueria Las Americas** (☎ 713-524-6993; 3102 S Shepherd Dr; mains $3-8, tacos $1; ☿ 24hr). Downtown, the wee-hours choice is **Frank's Pizza** (☎ 713-225-5656; 417 Travis St; large pizzas $14; ☿ to 9pm Mon-Wed, to 1am Thu, to 3am Fri & Sat).

TEX

WHAT'S UP WITH TEXAS BEACHES?

Before heading for the Gulf Coast, know this: the water isn't blue, the waves usually aren't large and many of the beaches are, well…kind of cruddy. Thanks to the Gulf currents, the sand is often littered with debris – mostly seaweed but also man-made trash such as plastic jugs and the occasional tar ball. In some resort areas, the beaches are rigorously cleaned. Still determined? Here are two of the best options:

■ **Padre Island National Seashore** Gloriously undeveloped beaches and some of the country's best windsurfing.

■ **South Padre Island** The state's best seaside resort, just miles from the Mexican border.

LIVE MUSIC

Continental Club (☎ 713-529-9899; www.continental club.com; 3700 Main St) Serves up the same musical mix as its sibling in Austin: roots rock, rockabilly and alternative country.

Engine Room (☎ 713-654-7846; 1515 Pease) This downtown club books touring acts ranging from metal to alternative to hip-hop.

Getting There & Around

There are two airports: **George Bush Intercontinental Airport** (IAH; ☎ 281-230-3100; http://iah .houstonairportsystem.org) and **William P Hobby Airport** (HOU; ☎ 713-640-3000; http://hou.houstonair portsystem.org), which is used mostly by Southwest Airlines. **Houston Bus Terminal** (☎ 713-759-6565; 2121 Main St) serves both **Greyhound** (☎ 800-229-9424; www.greyhound.com) and **Kerrville Bus Company** (☎ 800-474-3352; www.iride kbc.com). **Amtrak** stops at the **Downtown Depot** (☎ 713-224-1577; 902 Washington Ave).

Houston's Metropolitan Transit Authority or **Metro** (☎ 713-635-4000; 720 Main St; www.ride metro.org) runs the bus and MetroRail light-rail systems. The light-rail line extends for 7.5 miles along Main St, connecting downtown, the Astrodome/Reliant Stadium area and points in between. Fares for local-service buses and trains are $1. Commuter buses cost $1.50. A day pass costs $2.

DETOUR: SPACE CENTER HOUSTON

A half-hour southeast of downtown, off I-45, is **Space Center Houston** (☎ 281-244-2100; 1601 NASA Rd 1; admission $18; ☻ 10am-5pm Mon-Fri, 10am-6pm Sat & Sun, closes later Jun-Aug), the visitors center for NASA's Johnson Space Center. It's a bit overhyped, but astronaut buffs won't want to miss the lunar landers, rockets and moon rocks.

GALVESTON

Part beach town and part historic center, Galveston has just enough decay to keep it from being touristy. Its faded elegance was caused by a hurricane that leveled half the city in 1900, killing more than 6000 people – the most deadly natural disaster in US history. The best way to soak up the vintage vibe is to stroll the **Strand Historic District.** The Victorian buildings now house shops, restaurants and bars. To see inside one of the historic residences, check out **Ashton Villa** (☎ 409-762-3933; 2328 Broadway; tours $6; ☻ 10am-4pm Mon-Sat, noon-4pm Sun), which doubles as one of the town's visitor centers.

Head south from the Strand to reach the beach: the **Galveston Island Trolley** ($1) connects the two areas. The 17ft-high seawall (built after the big hurricane) forms an elevated promenade for several miles along the water. Have a seaside drink at the **Balinese Room** (☎ 409-762-9696; 2107 Seawall Blvd), an illegal casino in the 1940s and 1950s that showcased performers such as Frank Sinatra and Groucho Marx.

The original South Seas décor is way cool. There's a free beach along the seawall, or head east to **Stewart Beach Park** (Seawall Blvd at Broadway; per vehicle $7) or **East Beach** (Seawall Blvd at 6th St; per vehicle $7), which has an outdoor bar.

HI Galveston Hostel (☎ 409-765-9431; 201 E Seawall Blvd; dm members/nonmembers $18.50/21.50, r Sep-Mar $50-70, Apr-Aug $80-100; ℗ ☒ ☐) is right on the beach. Camping is available at **Galveston Island State Park** (☎ 409-737-1222; 14901 FM 3005; campsites $18-23). Rates are cheaper in all motels fall to early spring, but don't expect any discounts during **Mardi Gras** (in February or March, depending on the year), which offers several weekends of concerts and shirt lifting.

DALLAS & AROUND

North Texas backs the stereotypes, with oil money, flashy homes, rail and livestock legacies, and public art made from old Cadillacs.

DALLAS

On first glance, Dallas is a place of sleek surfaces - mirrored-glass buildings, luxury cars, carefully preened customers striding in and out of Neiman Marcus (where top cosmetic salespeople rake in six-figure incomes). But when you scrub off the surface layer, the Big D is as lively as it is manicured. Its nightlife includes both gritty music and low-key chilling. Add in the museums and cowboy cool of nearby Fort Worth and these towns have as much substance as sheen.

Catch concerts, livestock shows, rides and Big Tex the giant talking cowboy at the **Texas State Fair** (☎ 214-565-9931; www.bigtex .com), held late September to mid-October at Fair Park.

Orientation

Dallas is part of the huge 'Metroplex' that also includes Fort Worth and dozens of other towns. Downtown Dallas includes Dealey Plaza on its west side. The Deep Ellum nightlife district is about a mile northeast along Commerce and Elm. To get to the restaurants and bars of Greenville Ave, follow Ross Rd northeast out of downtown or take Hwy 75 (Central Expressway) north to Exit 2/Monticello and go east.

The **Dallas CVB Visitor Center** (☎ 214-571-1300; 100 S Houston St; ☺ 8am-5pm Mon-Fri, 9am-5pm Sat & Sun) occupies the Old Red Courthouse, downtown. The **Central Library** (☎ 214-670-1700; 1515 Young St; ☺ 9am-9pm Mon-Thu, 9am-5pm Fri & Sat, 1-5pm Sun) offers free Internet access.

Sights

Dealey Plaza (Elm St at Houston St, downtown) is where President John F Kennedy was assassinated in 1963. The **Sixth Floor Museum** (☎ 214-747-6660; www.jfk.org; 411 Elm St; admission $10; ☺ 9am-6pm) is housed in the Texas School Book Depository building, from which Lee Harvey Oswald allegedly fired on the motorcade. The spookiest sight is a mock-up of Oswald's sniper nest, but this isn't a tacky museum; it offers a thoughtful look

at the event and the era that surrounded it. You don't need the museum to get a sense of the assassination, however. An 'X' is painted on Elm St at the point where Kennedy was shot, and you can stand on the grassy knoll where, according to some theories, additional assassins were hidden. A block east and south of the plaza is the stark **Kennedy Memorial** (Main St at Market St), designed by architect Phillip Johnson.

A few blocks away, **Pioneer Plaza** (Young St at Griffin St) is filled with larger-than-life sculptures of 50 longhorns and several mounted cowboys. Climb up on a steer for a great Texas photo-op. The waterfall and stream make this a nice place to kick back in the middle of downtown.

Sleeping

Downtown Dallas lacks budget sleeping options, and the freeway motels pose transportation problems for those without a car.

The most central of the freeway motel strips is the Market Center area along I-35E (the Stemmons Freeway), northwest of downtown.

Quality Inn Market Center (☎ 214-747-9551; www .qualityinn.com; 1955 Market Center Blvd, Exit 430B off I-35E; r $66; ☐ ☒ ☒) A clean place with free shuttle service.

Candlewood Suites Dallas/Market Center (☎ 214-631-3333; www.candlewoodsuites.com; 7930 N Stemmons Fwy, Exit 433B off I-35F; s/d $62/72; ☐ ☒) Tidy rooms with kitchens and refrigerators.

Cedar Hill State Park (☎ 972-291-3900; www .tpwd.state.tx.us/park/cedarhil; 1570 FM 1382, Cedar Hill; campsites $23) Pretty lakeside campsites about a half-hour southwest of downtown

---

GAY & LESBIAN DALLAS

The **Dallas Voice** (☎ 214-754-8710; www .dallasvoice.com) is the local gay and lesbian paper. Cedar Springs Rd and nearby Maple Ave (Exit 430A off I-35E and go northeast on Oak Lawn) host the busiest club scene. Among the many choices are **Buddies II** (☎ 214-526-0887; 4025 Maple Ave), which is a lesbian hangout, with revues and an outdoor pool; **Round-up Saloon** (☎ 214-522-9611; 3912 Cedar Springs Rd), the gay-country hot spot, and **Village Station** (☎ 214-559-0650; 3911 Cedar Springs), where the boys dance and live shows take place in the Rose Room.

DALLAS

TEXAS

0	0.6 km
0	0.4 miles

INFORMATION
Central Library....................1 C3
Dallas CVB Visitor Center.......2 A3
Post Office..........................3 B3

SIGHTS & ACTIVITIES (p405)
Kennedy Memorial.................4 A3
Pioneer Plaza.......................5 B3
Sixth Floor Museum................6 A3

EATING (p407)
Crescent City Cafe.................7 D2

DRINKING (p407)
Club Clearview......................8 E2
Curtain Club/Liquid Lounge......9 E2
Deep Ellum Blues.................10 D2
Gypsy Tea Room..................11 D2

TRANSPORT (p407)
DART Office........................12 B2
Greyhound Bus Station..........13 B3

To Melba's Brós Char Bar (2.5mi);
Blarney Stone (2.5mi); Blue Goose
Cantina (3.25mi); Hurricane Grill (3.25mi);
Greenville Ave (4.5mi); Campisi's Egyptian (4.0mi)

To Quality Inn Market Center (1.5mi);
Buddies II (1.75mi); Round-up Saloon
(2.5mi); Village Station (2.5mi);
Sue Ellen's Smokehouse (2.5mi);
Candlewood Suites Dallas Market Center (5mi);
Dallas-Fort Worth International Airport (18mi)

To Dallas Market Center (2mi);
Dallas Love Field (5mi)

To Texas Stadium (8mi)

To Fort Worth (24mi)

To I-20 (9mi);
Cedar Hill State Park (20mi)

To Fair Park (0.25mi)

Dallas. Boats can be rented at the marina and there's an excellent mountain-biking trail.

Eating

Lower Greenville Ave in particular has a number of cheap tasty options.

Blue Goose Cantina (☎ 214-823-8339; 2905 Greenville Ave; mains $10-20) One of the popular stops for Greenville Ave's café society, the Goose offers Mexican food and a mix of young singles and nondangerous bikers.

Campisi's Egyptian (☎ 214-827-0355; 5610 E Mockingbird Lane; large pizza $13-15) Open since the 1940s. Supposedly Jack Ruby ate here the night before he shot Oswald. If true, he probably had great pizza, which is what you still get today.

Crescent City Café (☎ 214-745-1900; 2615 Commerce St; mains $6-12) Stop here if you need to eat in Deep Ellum. The New Orleans food is fairly priced and squarely made.

Melios Bros Char Bar (☎ 214-826-8800; 2026 Lower Greenville Ave; breakfast $3-6) This friendly diner has been serving up hearty and affordable breakfasts since 1969. Sandwiches and steaks, too, till 10pm.

Sonny Bryan's Smokehouse (☎ 214-357-7120; 2202 Inwood Rd, Exit 432A off I-35E; mains $5-9; ⏰ lunch only) It looks like a shack, but that's a plus when it comes to good barbecue. The sliced brisket sandwich is good value and good eating.

Drinking

Nightlife is concentrated in two areas. One is Deep Ellum, where they were moanin' the blues way back in the early 1900s. You can still see blues there, but modern musical moaners are more prevalent. Lots of dance clubs, too. Lower Greenville Ave is the other hot spot, drawing a clientele that's a little more upscale and a little less dependent on an all-black wardrobe. Check www.dallas observer.com for entertainment listings.

LIVE MUSIC

Curtain Club/Liquid Lounge (☎ 214-760-9785; www .curtainclub.com; 2800 Main St) Two Deep Ellum clubs under one roof – and one cover gets you into both on weekends (along with **Club Clearview**, across the street). Music varies, but loud, thrashy acts are usually in the Club, introspective strummers in the Lounge.

> **BIG D PINT NIGHTS**
>
> Draft beers go for $1 on Monday and Tuesday at **Hurricane Grill** (☎ 214-827-2112; 2831 Greenville Ave). A little further south, the **Blarney Stone** (☎ 214-821-7099; 2116 Greenville Ave) is the only Irish pub we've ever seen with a giant salt-water aquarium. Do a little swimming of your own on Wednesday when all imported pints go for $2. The Wednesday pints are even cheaper ($1) at **July Alley** (☎ 214-747-2990; 2809 Elm St) in Deep Ellum.

Deep Ellum Blues (☎ 214-760-9338; www.deep ellumblues.com; 2612 Main St) Carrying on the district's tradition with live blues Wednesday to Sunday.

Gypsy Tea Room (☎ 214-744-9779; www.gypsytea room.com; 2548 Elm St) This Deep Ellum landmark is the town's best live-music club, with local and big-name touring bands in all styles.

Getting There & Around

Dallas-Fort Worth International Airport (DFW; ☎ 972-574-8888; www.dfwairport.com) is the larger airport. Take the free airport shuttle to the Remote North station, then pick up Bus 202 to downtown ($2.25, 40 minutes). Monday to Saturday you can take the shuttle to the Remote South station and connect with the Trinity Railway Express to downtown ($2.25, 30 minutes). **Dallas Love Field** (DAL; ☎ 214-670-6073; www.dallas-lovefield.com) is used by Southwest Airlines. Take Bus 39 to downtown ($1.25, 35 minutes).

The **Greyhound Bus Station** (☎ 800-229-9424; www.greyhound.com; 205 S Lamar St) is downtown. **Amtrak** stops at downtown's **Union Station** (☎ 214-653-1101; 401 S Houston St).

Dallas Area Rapid Transit (DART; ☎ 214-979-1111; www.dart.org; office in the Akard Station, 1401 Pacific Ave) operates the bus and light-rail systems. Fares are $1.25 around downtown, $2.25 for outlying destinations. Useful lines are Rte 60, which connects downtown and Deep Ellum, and Rte 1 between downtown and Lower Greenville. **Trinity Railway Express** (TRE; ☎ 817-215-8600; www.the-T.com) connects Union Station in Dallas with ITC Station in downtown Fort Worth (one way $2.25, one hour). The Rte 1 bus (one way $1.25) runs to the Stockyards.

TEXAS

DETOUR: CADILLAC RANCH

Just off I-40 near Amarillo sits one of the great roadside oddities in the US: 10 vintage Cadillacs buried nose down with their tail fins pointing up to the Texas sky. Created by Stanley Marsh III in 1973, the car sculpture undergoes regular repaintings by graffiti artists and occasionally by Marsh himself. Take the I-40 10 minutes west of Amarillo to Exit 60/Arnot Rd. Always open, always free.

E-Z Rent-a-Car (☎ 972 574 3360; www.e-zrentacar .com) is at both airports and has some of the best rates. When checking prices, make sure taxes are included in the quote – they're a big part of the bill.

FORT WORTH

Dallas's sibling about 25 miles to the west, Fort Worth has long been shadowed by the Big D, but it has come up with two ways to set itself apart: cows and culture.

The legendary Chisholm Trail cattle drives passed through the city in the mid-1800s. That heritage is celebrated at the **Stockyards National Historic District** (☎ 817-626-7921; www.fortworthstockyards.org; Main St at Exchange Ave), which is a bit touristy but lots of fun. There are several small museums, oodles of Western-wear and souvenir shops, mock gunfights, vintage train excursions and two cattle drives a day (11:30am and 4pm, unless the weather turns mean or the long-horns turn ornery).

You can eat and drink at the Stockyards, too – Western style. The most memorable watering hole is **Billy Bob's Texas** (☎ 817-624-7117; www.billybobstexas.com; 2520 Rodeo Plaza). It can hold 6000 cowboys and cowgirls and keep them entertained with everything from big-name concert acts to professional bull riding on real bulls every Friday and Saturday

(beginners can take a shot at the mechanical toros). **White Elephant Saloon** (☎ 817-624-8273; www.whiteelephantsaloon.com; 106 E Exchange Ave) has a more authentic cowboy feel and live music on most nights.

The **Cultural District**, southeast of downtown, has several top-notch museums. The two standouts are quite good and they're free. **Kimbell Art Museum** (☎ 817-332-8451; www .kimbellart.org; 3333 Camp Bowie Blvd; ⊙ 10am-5pm Tue-Thu & Sat, noon-8pm Fri, noon-5pm Sun) has works by Picasso, Matisse, Rembrandt, Monet and more. **Amon Carter Museum** (☎ 817-738-1933; www.cartermuseum.org; 3501 Camp Bowie Blvd; ⊙ 10am-5pm Tue, Wed, Fri & Sat, 10am-8pm Thu, noon-5pm Sun) features works by cowboy artists such as Frederic Remington and Charles M Russell. The **National Cowgirl Museum & Hall of Fame** (☎ 817-336-4475; www.cowgirl.net; 1720 Gendy St; admission $6; ⊙ 10am-5pm Tue-Sat, noon-5pm Sun) isn't free but it's worth a look – a tribute to females with 'pioneer spirit,' which includes everyone from Dale Evans to Georgia O'Keeffe.

WEST TEXAS

Vast deserts, mountains and tiny, windblown towns make the west the most beautiful part of the state. **El Paso** is the transit hub where Texas and Mexico meet; the **Big Bend Region**, tucked into the sweeping bow of the Rio Grande, is on the way to nowhere, but its stark beauty makes it worth a detour. **Big Bend National Park** is the highlight, but you can easily fill another day or two at **Big Bend Ranch State Park**, almost as scenic and large as the national park. Stop into the **Barton Warnock Center** (☎ 432-424-3327; Hwy 170 just east of Lajitas; ⊙ 8am-4pm) for information on hiking, driving and mountain-biking routes in the park. There are several primitive camping areas as well as beds at **Sauceda Bunk House** (dm $20).

SCENIC DRIVE: THE RIVER RD

The hands-down winner for the best drive in Texas is Hwy 170, better known as the River Rd (Camino del Rio), which traces 67 miles of the Rio Grande's 'Big Bend,' from Presidio to Lajitas. The epic scenery includes Grand Canyon–like cliffs and panoramic river overlooks, and the terrain makes for a two-hour roller-coaster ride (the abrupt drop-offs get you squealing on every hill). Turnoffs lead to the river, and there are also picnic areas and even a frontier movie set to explore. At the western end of the road, stop at **Fort Leaton State Historic Site** (☎ 432-229-3613; admission $2; ⊙ 8am-4:30pm), a restored adobe trading post.

IF YOU'VE GOT A FEW MORE DAYS IN WEST TEXAS

Detours tempt around most every bend; these destinations are worth making time for:

- **Hueco Tanks State Park** A forest of boulders for scramblers of all levels, Hueco Tanks is part park, part climbers' convention, part rainbow gathering and simply beautiful.

- **Guadalupe Mountains National Park** Excellent hiking, including a trail to the top of the state's highest peak, 8749ft El Capitan.

- **Lubbock** Learn how extremely flat land breeds extremely good music in the West Texas town that spawned Buddy Holly and other Lone Star legends.

Between the national and state parks is **Terlingua**, Big Bend's quirky crossroads. A one-time mining community, it has a few dozen permanent residents and a handful of eating and drinking spots. Try **La Kiva** (☎ 432-371-2250; barbecue plates $8-12) or **Starlight Theatre** (☎ 432-371-2326; southwestern mains $10-15). If nothing else, stop at the general store, buy a beer and join the locals sitting on the big covered porch. Gaze off at the Chisos Mountains. Watch the dust blow around. Occasionally say 'yup' for no real reason. That's Big Bend living at its best.

BIG BEND NATIONAL PARK

This **park** (7-day pass per vehicle $15) has a mix of high mountains and majestic desert that makes humans feel small – partly because there are so few humans around. It's one of the country's least visited national parks, though the scenery and wildlife (including mountain lions and bears) are nothing short of fantastic.

Grab some info at **Panther Junction Visitor Center** (☎ 432-477-2251; ⏰ 8am-6pm). If you only have one day, plan to spend it in the **Chisos Basin**, which is tucked into the mountains, 2000ft above the surrounding desert. It's the most beautiful part of the park and has the coolest temperatures. (The rest is as hot as a blast furnace in summer.) Several excellent hiking trails begin in the basin.

Head west from Panther Junction to pick up the **Ross Maxwell Scenic Dr**, a 22-mile paved route that drops down to the Rio Grande at **Castolon**. From there, you can continue on to the mouth of **Santa Elena Canyon**, a sheer gorge that's a favorite spot for float trips on the Rio Grande. You can get a look at the canyon by hiking to an overlook.

The park's other principal paved route runs to **Rio Grande Village**, far downstream

from Castolon. Nearby is **Boquillas Canyon**, which can be seen from an overlook if you make the hour-long hike.

There are **campgrounds** (☎ 877-444-6777; www .reserveusa.com; campsites $10) at Chisos Basin, Costolon and Rio Grande Village. Only Rio Grande Village has showers. Most campsites are first come, first serve, but a limited number of reservations are accepted for stays between November 15 and April 15. Free camping at primitive backcountry sites is available by permit. Motel rooms are available at **Chisos Mountain Lodge** (☎ 432-477-2291; s/d $78/88; **P** **⏰**).

MARFA

One of the three gateway towns to the Big Bend on Hwy 90 (the others are Alpine and Marathon), Marfa's biggest attraction is the **Marfa Lights**, a spooky nighttime phenomenon best seen from a special roadside viewing center 9 miles east on Hwy 90. Lights flicker on and off to the southwest, looking somewhat like car headlights. Skeptics say that they *are* headlights, but they don't move like cars and they've been reported since the 1800s. Aliens? Spirits? Kids with flashlights? You decide.

While in Marfa, pay a visit to the **El Paisano Hotel** (☎ 432-729-3669; www.hotelpaisano.com; 207 N Highland), which serves as a mini tribute to James Dean and Elizabeth Taylor, who came to town in 1955 to film *Giant* – Dean's final film (the happy-hour margaritas on the outdoor patio shouldn't be missed). Today, Marfa is an art center: the **Chinati Foundation** (☎ 432-729-4326; www.chinati .org; 1 Cavalry Rd; adult/student $10/5, tours Wed-Sun) occupies many buildings around town. The pretension factor is high, but the metal-box sculptures by Donald Judd (Chinati's founder) are quite cool.

Southwest

HIGHLIGHTS

- **Las Vegas** Let it ride in Sin City, a full-on, 24/7, anything-goes fantasyland (p416)
- **Grand Canyon** Ponder the frailty of human existence while overlooking Arizona's world-famous, mile-deep gaping maw (p428)
- **Southern Utah's National Parks** From the wilds of Canyonlands and the graceful Arches to Bryce's weirdly wondrous hoodoos and Zion's thrilling Narrows, Canyon Country is chock-full of wow factor (p441)
- **Taos & Santa Fe** Tuck into some green chili, shred the steep slopes, and wander the adobe alleys of the USA's oldest capital (p454)
- **Off the beaten track** Explore the North Rim of Grand Canyon – same great views, one-tenth the crowd, 100% more peaceful (p429)
- **Best journey** Southern Utah National Parks Loop, especially Hwy 12 between Capitol Reef and Bryce Canyon (p441)

FAST FACTS

- **Area** 427,332 sq miles

- **Big cities** Salt Lake City (population 1.7 million), Las Vegas (1,430,000), Phoenix (1,390,000), Albuquerque (450,000), Santa Fe (62,000)

- **Budget** $25-75 per day

- **Costs** urban hostel $10-20, bowl of green chili $3.50, mountain bike rental $25-30

- **Driving times** Phoenix to Albuquerque 10 hours, Albuquerque to Salt Lake City 12 hours, Phoenix to Las Vegas 6 hours

- **Famous for** natural wonders, world-class winter sports, cactus-studded deserts

- **Languages** Spanish, Españglish, several Native American dialects

- **Population** 11.6 million

- **Phrases:** *ya'at'eeh* (Navajo greeting), *bienvenidos* (Spanish, welcome)

- **Seasons** sunny year-round with a high season from Jun-Sep; best seasons to visit Apr-May and Nov-Oct

- **States** Nevada, Arizona, Utah, New Mexico

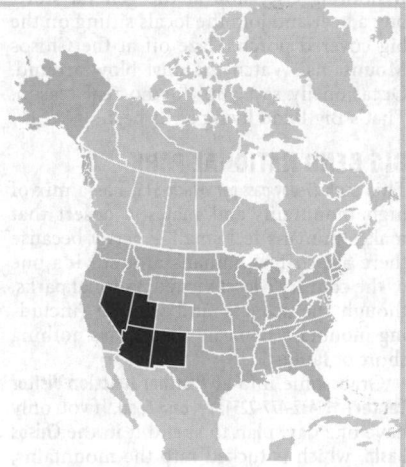

- **Tasty treats** blue corn enchiladas, *carne adobada* (marinated pork), *sopaipillas* (deep-fried pastry puffs)

- **Time** Mountain Standard Time (MST); GMT minus 7 hours (daylight savings observation varies)

- **Top hostel** Hotel Congress, Tucson (p439)

TRAVEL HINTS

Amtrak is OK for reaching the Southwest, but rail passes are poor value since routes are not integrated. Phoenix is a good spot to find long-distance auto driveaways. An annual national park pass ($50) pays for itself if you visit even a handful of the region's highlights.

Beyond the neon blinging of Las Vegas' astounding oasis of casinos, a mythic arid terrain beckons like Jim Morrison's eerie *Doors* lyrics. The immense, fabled desert is at once beautiful, awe-inspiring and ripe for exploration. What other natural landscape could spawn – and sustainably nurture – an epic creative happening on par with Burning Man?

The Southwest encompasses the Colorado River's dramatic red rock canyons, the Sonoran Desert's mighty saguaro cacti, southern Utah's maze-like canyonlands and lofty mountain ranges of the Continental Divide. It's a land of contrasts, too. The dry summer heat is often stifling, but high-elevation forests offer a cool refuge. The highest peaks are snow-mantled year-round.

Cities have mushroomed regionwide, a few now as much a part of the region's draw as the landscape. But the most rugged reaches remain virtually untouched, with endless miles of big blue sky, blazing sunshine and eroded rockscapes that beg to be climbed. Much is readily accessible by budget travelers, particularly those with cars; stellar hostels are strung throughout.

The willing inhabitants of this harsh environment have also acquired the patina of myth: the ancestral Indians and their modern descendants; the Spanish explorers and missionaries; rough-and ready miners, cowboys and outlaws; artists and eccentrics drawn to the surreal landscapes; and the US military, which appropriated vast tracts of land for nuclear dumps and weapons testing.

Only time will tell what will transpire when the reservoirs and aquifers run dry.

HISTORY

The Southwest's human history is huge, dating 12,500 years. By AD 100, three dominant cultures had emerged: the Hohokam, Mogollon, and Ancestral Puebloans (formerly known as the Anasazi).

The Hohokam abided in the Arizona deserts from 300 BC to AD 1450. Amazingly adapted to desert life, they created an incredible irrigation system, as well as earthen pyramids and a rich heritage of pottery. Their sophisticated adaptability makes their mid-15th century disappearance especially haunting. Today's Pima and Tohano O'odham Indians appear to be descendents.

From 200 BC to AD 1450, the Mogollons lived in the region's central valleys and mountains in pit dwellings on isolated mesas. Peacefully incorporated into the Ancestral Puebloans, they left historic sites such as Gila Cliff Dwellings National Monument.

The Ancestral Puebloans left behind the richest archaeological heritage, visible at Mesa Verde and Chaco Culture National Historic Park. Today, the Ancestral Puebloans' descendants are found throughout New Mexico, particularly in the Rio Grande Valley. The Hopi are descendants, too, and their village, Old Oraibi, may be North America's oldest continuously inhabited settlement.

In 1540 Francisco Vásquez de Coronado launched a Southwest expedition from México City. Instead of riches, his party found Indians, many of whom were then killed or dislocated. Half a century later, Juan de Oñate established New Mexico's first capital at San Gabriel. Much bloodshed resulted from Oñate's attempts to control Indian pueblos. He left in failure in 1608, and Santa Fe was established as a new capital in 1609.

The Southwest developed rapidly during the 19th century thanks to railroad and geological surveys. As the US pushed west, the army forcibly removed Native Americans. Gold and silver drew fortune-seekers as lawless Wild West mining towns sprang up. Soon after, the Fred Harvey Company (which built hotels and restaurants) joined forces with the Atchison, Topeka and Santa Fe Railroad to attract an ocean of tourists, who were fascinated by the West's Indian culture and rugged beauty.

THE BIG ISSUE: DROUGHT

'Where's the all the water going to come from?' This question is on the tip on everyone's tongue. Water has shaped the Southwest's history ever since the Hohokam people began irrigating centuries ago. Today, aquifers are being mined, reservoirs are drying up and the region is suffering a record drought. Projections suggest that Las Vegas, which slakes 85% of its thirst from the Colorado, may be out of H_2O by 2010. So, think twice before you flush that toilet, or, better yet, shower with a friend.

SOUTHWEST

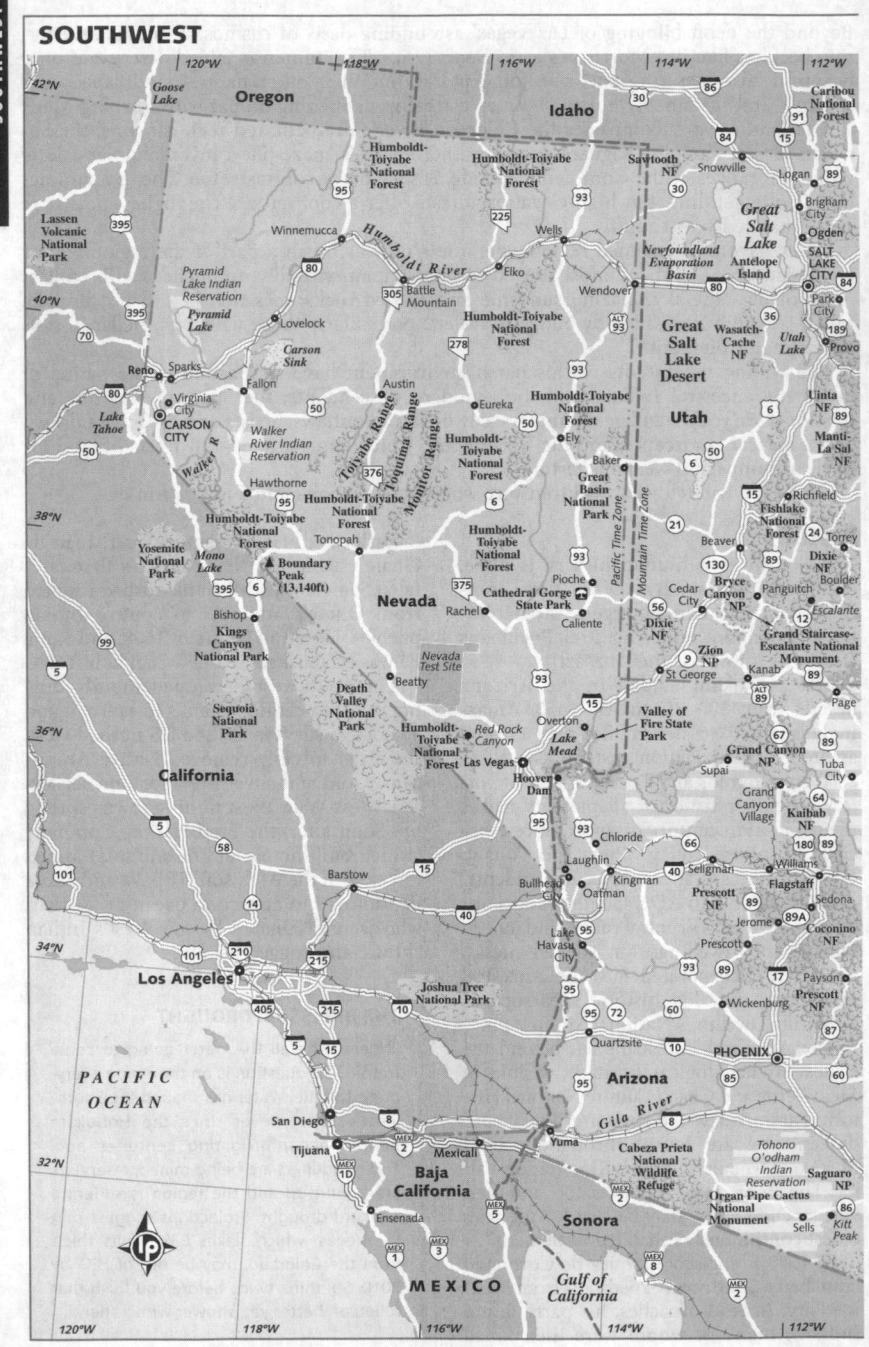

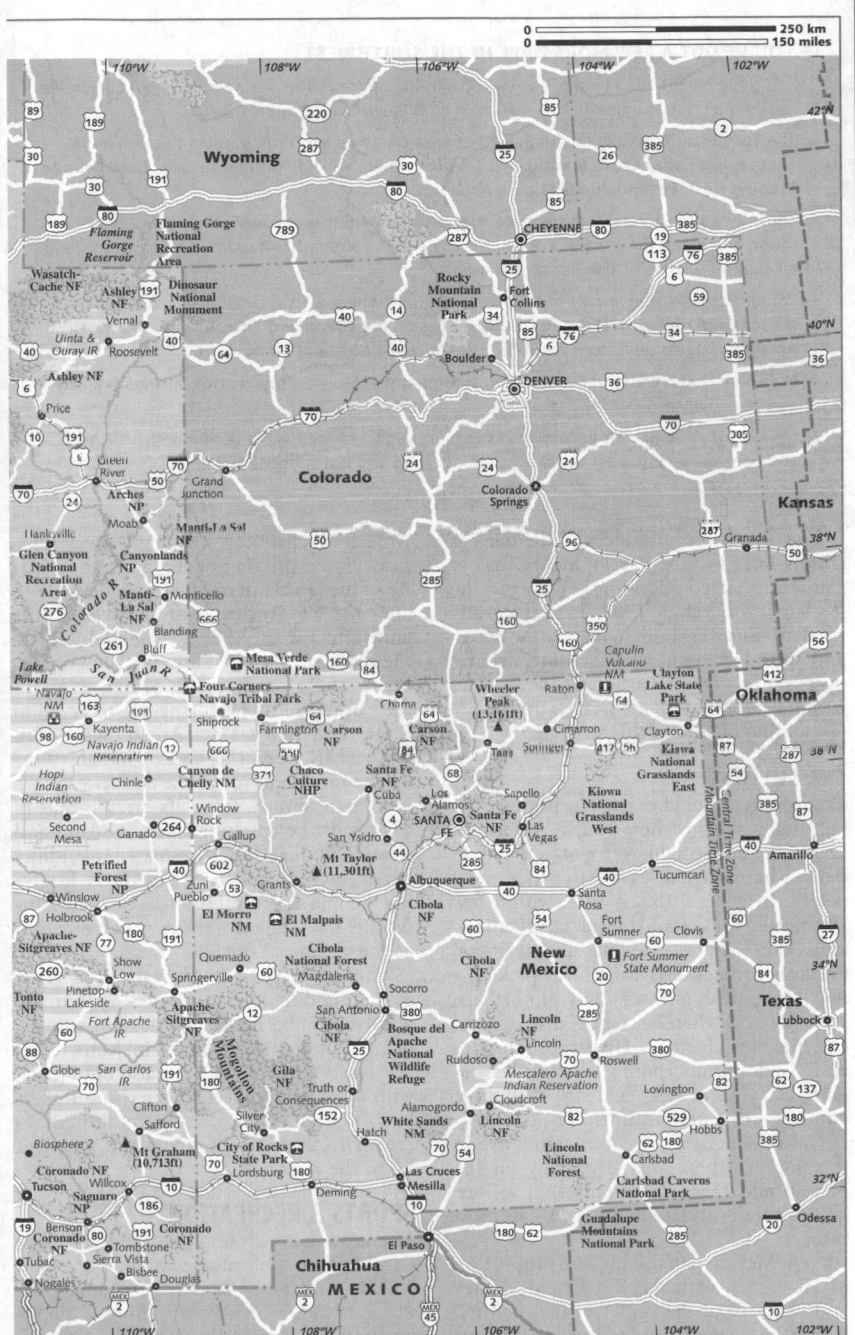

SOUTHWEST

IF YOU'VE GOT A FEW MORE DAYS IN THE SOUTHWEST

Crossing the border into **Mexico** is always an alluring option, either via walking across at **Nogales** or less-frequented **Douglas**, or driving across at **El Paso/Ciudad Juarez** (p408).

■ The **Turquoise Trail**, aka the 'High Rd' between Santa Fe and Taos, detours through quirky hamlets like **Cedar Crest**, **Madrid**, and **Cerillos**, where you'll find the whimsical **Casa Grande Trading Post, Petting Zoo & Mining Museum**.

■ The only way to access Utah's remote **High Uintas Wilderness Area** is by foot or horse – tough going, but the rewards are amazing. The high country has hundreds of stocked fishing lakes. Bunk at Defa's Dude Ranch in Hanna.

■ Wilderness adventure awaits in Northeastern Utah, where worthy detours include the scenic **Mirror Lake Highway**, **Flaming Gorge**, rafting on the **Green** and **Yampa** rivers and North America's largest prehistoric fossil beds at **Dinosaur National Monument**.

■ In Central Utah's conservative Mormon community of Monroe, **Mystic Hot Springs** is a very serene and unconservative oasis.

■ New Mexico's **Jemez Mountain Trail** winds through a ragged expanse of moody tufa grays and cool evergreens, past natural swimming holes and hot springs.

The Southwest's modern settlement is closely linked to the development of water use – and air conditioning. Following the Reclamation Act of 1902, huge federally funded dams were built to irrigate the desert and spur development. Rancorous debates over water rights continue today. Marc Resiner's book, *Cadillac Desert*, details the fascinating history of this struggle.

THE CULTURE

The Southwest pitches itself as proudly tricultural, a region where Native American, Hispanics and Anglos get along, if not in perfect harmony, at least better than most places. In general this is true, with a few simmering caveats. Interracial relationships don't merit a double-take in liberal enclaves and new arrivals quickly pick up a few key Spanish phrases. Only in northern New Mexico, where ancient Native American pueblos, historic Hispanic churches and Anglo atomic bomb laboratories coexist, can you see clear evidence of all three cultures – in a unique, intricate alliance.

Native Americans predominantly live in the Four Corners area, especially in the Navajo and Hopi Reservations. 'The Rez' is bicultural – Indian and Anglo – in most respects.

New Mexico has the highest proportion of Hispanics, with the Rio Grande Valley and Santa Fe at the center of that culture. Along the *frontera* (border), many Mexican-

Americans proudly call themselves Chicano. Some still do not recognize the legality of the US claim of Mexican land in 1848 after the US-Mexican war and refer to the land affected as Aztlan. Anglos dominate the scene in most of Mormon Utah and in many of Arizona's fast-growing cities. In the rural Southwest, many off-reservation mines and ranches are Anglo-owned, but workers are often Hispanic or Indian.

The unique flavor of the Southwest does not stem simply from its triculturalism. That must be combined with the land and climate – beautifully desolate, splendidly harsh, incredibly varied and rarely forgiving. People's survival in these extreme conditions has shaped what may be perceived as the culture of the Southwest.

The archetypal Southwestern lifestyle, as commodified by magazines, epitomizes laid-back. Folks have a taste for finer things, but go shopping for them in jeans, cowboy boots and bolo ties. It's also outdoorsy, with everyone out feeling the wind in their hair, and there's a deep commitment to creativity, attracting a young and transient lot to the region.

SPORTS & RECREATION

The mountains around Taos and Salt Lake City feature unbeatable snow play, and smaller winter resorts dot the region. During summer, white-water rafting is popular on the Colorado River and Rio Grande.

Throughout the region, in such varied terrain as Utah's Wasatch-Cache National Forest and Nevada's Red Rock Canyon, there is plenty of opportunity for hiking, backcountry camping, rock climbing, mountain biking, fishing and extreme sports like hanggliding. One of the region's most distinctive features is its variety of landscapes. Thus, while the low-lying deserts broil in summer, you can often hike or quickly ascend into cooler nearby mountains, where fly-fishing streams, alpine forests and wildflower meadows await. So what are you waiting for?

ARTS & ENTERTAINMENT

Hispanic and Native American influences have helped forge a distinctive arts scene. Much of this aesthetic is evident in the region's pottery, paintings, weavings, jewelry, sculpture, woodcarving and leatherworking. Southwestern art can be very traditional or cutting-edge contemporary.

Perhaps the region's most famous artist is Georgia O'Keeffe (1887–1986), whose Southwestern landscapes are found in major museums worldwide. Both Taos and Santa Fe have large artist communities.

The Southwest has a wide diversity of Native American art: Navajo rugs, Hopi kachina dolls, Zuni silverware, Tohono O'odham basketry and Pueblo pottery are some of the best known. Contemporary Native American art is eminently buyable, and both traditional and modern work is available in hundreds of galleries.

The Southwest's music scene, too, has its Hispanic and Native American influences. Of course, you can find anything from jazz to hip-hop in the major cities, but you can also catch *mariachis* (typically dressed in dark, ornately sequined, body-hugging cos-tumes and playing predominantly brass instruments and guitars), especially near the border. Native American dances and music are performed throughout the region.

ENVIRONMENT

The central part of the Southwest is the Colorado Plateau, a series of plateaus (5000ft and 8000ft in elevation) separated by deep canyons, among them the world-famous Grand Canyon. Four major deserts (the Great Basin, Mojave, Chihuahuan and Sonoran) comprise the vast majority of the rest of the region. Several mountain ranges run from north to south, in some areas alternating with deep desert basins (forming 'Basin and Range' country).

While mountains are blanketed with snow during the winter, most of the Southwest receives little annual rainfall. During the summer, temperatures can soar into the 90s and 100s; locals often boast 'it's a dry heat,' but it's still uncomfortable. Nights are usually cooler, and spring and fall can be downright pleasant.

Southwestern wildlife is unique and fascinating, and much of it can easily be seen. The roadrunner, New Mexico's state bird, and the coyote, the wily trickster of Navajo legend, are often seen darting across highways. Vultures wheel through the air, poisonous lizards and venomous snakes are occasionally glimpsed, tarantulas and scorpions scuttle along and jackrabbits bound with prodigious leaps. Southeastern Arizona is a mecca for birders.

National, State & Tribal Parks

The Southwest has such a wealth of parks that it's impossible to list them all. The region's most popular natural destination

---

TOP FIVE NATIVE AMERICAN SITES

Abundant archaeological sites and continuously inhabited settlements help shed light on the fascinating lives of the region's earliest inhabitants. Though in Colorado, **Mesa Verde National Park** (p488) is also often accessed from the Four Corner region.

- **Old Oraibi**, Hopi Nation (p437)
- **Taos Pueblo**, New Mexico (p458)
- **Bandelier National Monument**, New Mexico (p457)
- **Canyon de Chelly National Monument**, Arizona (p436)
- **Gila Cliff Dwellings National Monument**, New Mexico (p463)

is Arizona's Grand Canyon. Other Arizona parks include remote Organ Pipe Cactus National Monument and Canyon de Chelly National Monument.

In Utah, most national parks are located in the southern slickrock country, including Arches and Canyonlands. Cedar Breaks National Monument sees far fewer visitors than nearby Bryce and Zion, while Grand Staircase-Escalante National Monument is a mighty swath of undeveloped desert that beckons hearty adventurers.

New Mexico has impressive Carlsbad Caverns National Park and mysterious Chaco Culture National Historic Park, once a major Indian trading center. Nevada's only national park is Great Basin, a rugged mountain oasis in a remote desert area skirting the state's eastern flank.

TRANSPORTATION

Las Vegas and Phoenix are the region's busiest hubs, followed by Salt Lake City, Albuquerque and Tucson. Cheap, frequent no-frills flights on carriers such as America West and Southwest network the region.

Greyhound buses traverse the region's interstate highways several times daily, while local carriers and shuttle services link towns off major routes. Motoring is the easiest way to explore the Southwest. Phoenix and Salt Lake City are the best bets for cheap rentals. The fabled Rte 66 crossed the region; remnants of the original road parallel I-40 through Arizona and New Mexico. Amtrak train services are less extensive than buses, but they do serve several major destinations. Buses link the remaining towns.

LAS VEGAS

Sin City is all about glitz and glam for its own sake, over-the-top hustle and flash as means and end. It's crowds of big egos in polyester pantsuits, big hair and gold chains,

young hipsters on spending benders, and devotees staring at spinning lemons like deer hypnotized by headlights. Absolutely, it's an exciting place – if you like gambling and glitter, you'll adore it. And if you know where to look, you'll find lots of neon bang for your buck.

Gambling and partying dominate most visitors' agendas. Others simply want to kick back and be pampered, and Vegas brings a luxurious lifestyle within easy reach of everyone. It's typical, for instance, to spend the morning lounging by the pool, get an afternoon rubdown, shop for vintage evening wear at a funky thrift store, stuff yourself silly at a gourmet buffet, catch a 3am lounge act and then retire to your deluxe view suite – yes, the one you booked last-minute online for next-to-nothing.

HISTORY

'What history?' you ask. Looking around, you may be forgiven. Unlike the rest of Southwest, the traces of early history are few and far between in this historical town. Contrary to Hollywood legend, there was a lot more at the crossroads than some tumbleweeds and a dusty gambling parlor the day mobster Ben 'Bugsy' Siegel rolled into the one-horse town and erected a glamorous, tropical-themed casino under the searing sun. Hearty Uto-Aztecan speaking Paiute people inhabited the Las Vegas Valley for a millennium before trappers and traders blazed the Spanish Trail through the last area in the Lower 48 to be explored by Anglos. Weary travelers bestowed the name 'las vegas' (the meadows) on the shady oasis in the middle of the Mojave Desert. How long the water lasts in the drought-stricken desert, however, remains to be seen.

ORIENTATION

Downtown is home to the city's oldest hotel-casinos. The main drag is Fremont St, of which four blocks are a covered pedestrian

---

GAMBLING & PROSTITUTION

To enter a gambling area, you must be at least 18 years old. To gamble and/or drink alcohol in the casino, you must be 21 years old. Some casinos offer blackjack, roulette and craps lessons. The rub: except for poker, all gambling pits the player against the house, and the house always has a statistical edge. Prostitution is 100% illegal in Clark County (which includes Las Vegas) and Washoe County (which includes Reno) – there are legal brothels in many outlying counties.

GETTING INTO TOWN

If you're traveling light, CAT bus No 109 runs 24/7 from the airport to within a short walk of most hotels downtown. **Bell Trans** (☎ 702-739-7990; transfers $4-6) runs airport shuttles.

The **Greyhound terminal** (☎ 702-384-9561; 200 S Main St) conveniently located downtown and within easy walking distance.

mall. Heading east, Fremont St turns into the Boulder Hwy, the old main route to Hoover Dam. I-15 and I-95 bisect town.

Las Vegas Blvd is the main north–south artery. South of the city limits, this boulevard is famously known as 'the Strip,' where you'll find the titanic megaresorts.

More casinos are east of the Strip along Paradise Rd, and west of I-15 near the intersection of Flamingo Rd and Valley View Blvd. The Greyhound station is downtown.

INFORMATION
Bookstores
Gambler's Book Shop (☎ 702-382-7555, 800-522-1777; 630 S 11th St; ☘ 9am-5pm Mon-Sat) Stocks thousands of gambling-related titles.

Emergency
Police Department (☎ 702-795-3111; www.lvmpd .com; 40 Stewart Ave) Scintillating live online scanner feed.
Problem Gamblers Helpline (☎ 702-369-9740; 800 522-4700; www.nevadacouncil.org)

Internet Access
CyberStop Internet Cafe (3743 Las Vegas Blvd S; per 30min/hr $8/12; ☘ 7-2:30am) Inside Hawaiian Marketplace.

Media
Las Vegas Bugle (www.lvbugle.com) Weekly gay publication covering Southern Nevada.
Las Vegas Review-Journal (www.lvrj.com) Daily newspaper with *Neon* weekend guide on Friday.
Las Vegas Weekly (www.lasvegasweekly.com) Free weekly with good restaurant and nightlife listings.

Medical Services
Sunrise Hospital & Medical Center (☎ 702-731-8000; 3186 S Maryland Parkway)
University Medical Center (☎ 702-383-2000; 1800 W Charleston Blvd)

Money
All casinos have ATMs. Casino cashiers exchange traveler's checks and major foreign currencies, but banks give better rates.

American Express (☎ 702-739-8474; 3200 Las Vegas Blvd S; ☘ 9am-9pm Mon-Fri, 10am-8pm Sat, 11am-6pm Sun) Inside Fashion Show Mall.
Foreign Money Exchange (☎ 702-791-3301; 101 Convention Center Dr, Plaza 122) Opposite Stardust.

Post
Downtown Station (☎ 702-385-3837; 301 Stewart Ave, 89101)
Strip Station (☎ 702-735 8519; 3100 S Industrial Rd, 89109) Behind Circus Circus.

Tourist Information
Las Vegas Visitor Information Center (LVCVA; ☎ 702-892-7575, 877-847 4858; www.lvcva.com; 3150 Paradise Rd; ☘ 8am-5pm) In the parking lot across the street from the convention center; enter from Convention Center Dr.

DANGERS & ANNOYANCES
In general, The Strip is crime-free, but beware of pickpockets in crowds and on public buses. Las Vegas Blvd between downtown and the Strip gets pretty shabby, and Fremont St east of downtown is lined with fleabag motels and their habitués. If you're crashing at either of the hostels, keep your wits about you.

SIGHTS
Hotel-Casinos
Vegas is the place to flaunt it, if you've got it. And if you don't, well…get hip to an all-American tradition – freeloading! At the Strip's massive megaresorts, you can load up on free booze, cheap food and glitzy entertainment, though soothing spas and high-end shopping malls are now all the rage.

The flashiest casinos are along the Strip's southern half. The oldest 'carpet joints' are downtown and while somewhat rumpled, they retain a refreshing degree of frontier character.

What follows is a rundown of the most freeloader-friendly dens of iniquity, from north to south.

0 _____ 1 km
0 _____ 0.5 miles

DOWNTOWN

Golden Gate (☎ 702-385-1906, 800-426-1906; www
.goldengatecasino.net; 1 Fremont St) Curious what
Vegas was like a century ago? Slide into
this intimate 1906 carpet joint. The casino
retains the feel of an old West saloon, complete with ceiling fans and a honky-tonk
pianist. The West's best $1 shrimp cocktail
is obligatory – plunk down five cents for a
lemon wedge.

Binion's Horseshoe (☎ 702-382-1600, 800-622-6468;
www.binions.com; 128 E Fremont St) Another venerable downtown casino, founded in 1951
and recently re-opened by Harrah's. The
pressed-tin ceiling and red-velvet wallpaper
ooze old Vegas charm. The 'World Series
of Poker' has been held here each April for
three decades – don't miss the loose slots
and high roller Wall of Fame photos.

THE STRIP

Stratosphere (☎ 702 380 7777, 800-998-6937; www
.stratospherehotel.com; 2000 Las Vegas Blvd S) At the
Strip's north end, this casino's 1149ft tower
has a restaurant, lounge and sky-high observation deck.

The real attractions are the thrill rides:
the 32mph High Roller coaster ($4), the
teeter-totteresque X Scream ($8) and free-
falling Big Shot ($8), which exerts 4Gs of
force as it catapults up and down the tower's tip (all-day pass $25).

Circus Circus (☎ 702-734-0410, 877-224 7287; www
.circuscircus.com; 2880 Las Vegas Blvd S) The granddaddy of casino-cum-theme parks has a
variety of free circus acts in the tentlike interior. Under the Adventuredome you'll find
a double-loop roller coaster and 15 other
rides (day pass $22). For 75-cent beers,
half-pound hot dogs ($1) and cheap thrills,
grab a coupon book and head next door to
Slots-A-Fun.

Treasure Island (☎ 702-894-7111; www.treasure
island.com; 3300 Las Vegas Blvd S) It's tough to miss
the swashbuckling Sirens of TI, a seafaring
battle of the sexes, out front in the lagoon.
The free sexed-up outdoor show runs four
times nightly from 7:30pm – arrive early for
a decent view. Inside, a grown-up atmosphere has replaced the former buccaneer-
themed yo-ho-ho-ness.

Mirage (☎ 702-791-7111, 800-374-9000; www
.themirage.com; 3400 Las Vegas Blvd S) Vegas' original
ridiculously theatrical flash palace features
a Polynesian-themed casino and an iconic

TOP FIVE HOTEL-CASINOS

Now that the family-friendly days are over
and sin is in again, swaggering casinos are
back en vogue. While not great places to
learn the ropes, the swingingest places to
live it up are:

- **Bellagio** (p419)
- **Hard Rock** (p422)
- **Mandalay Bay** (p420)
- **Paris-Las Vegas** (p420)
- **Venetian** (p419)

The opening of Steve Wynn's new $2.5 bil-
lion megaresort at the former site of the
Desert Inn in mid-2005 should up the ante
considerably.

faux-volcano that erupts every 15 minutes
after dusk, with flames rising out of orange-
colored water. Alas, since Roy was mauled
by a white tiger during a live show, Siegfried
& Co are no longer performing. Don't miss
the free white tiger habitat and saltwater
aquarium in the lobby.

Venetian (☎ 702-414-1000, 877-883-6423; www
.venetian.com; 3355 Las Vegas Blvd S) This massive,
beautifully appointed $1.5 billion property
is rife with numerous nods to its namesake city. Upstairs, shops line canals that
are much cleaner than the Italian originals.
Gondola rides ($15) or the highbrow **Guggen-
heim Hermitage Museum** (admission $15; ♥ 9:30am-
8:30pm) make for good dates, but the real
action is in the swank bars and high-rollin'
casino. Watch for minstrels roaming the
Grand Canal Shoppes.

Caesars Palace (☎ 702-731-7110, 877-427-7243; www
.caesarspalace.com; 3570 Las Vegas Blvd S) A grown-up
Circus Circus, this plush hotel-casino dates
back to 1966. Wander the Forum Shops past
talking statues, and marvel at the painted
sky that changes from dawn to dusk every
three hours.

Bellagio (☎ 702-693-7111, 888-987-6667; www.bel
lagio.com; 3600 Las Vegas Blvd S) The artificial eight-
acre Lake Como in front of this glam palace
comes alive nightly every 15 minutes with
a thousand water jets dancing to Pavarotti,
Sinatra and (gulp) Lionel Richie. Inside is a
swank gaming area, numerous restaurants
and great upscale fantasy window shopping. Don't miss the glass sculptures in the

SOUTHWEST

lobby and stunning floral displays in the conservatory.

Paris-Las Vegas (☎ 702-946-7000, 877-796-2096; www.parislv.com; 3655 Las Vegas Blvd S) Play the slots under the huge legs of a half-scale mock **Eiffel Tower** (adult $9; ☉ 10-1am) or take a 460ft ride to the top, *mon ami*. The interior is like a Parisian square, with roving characters spreading the *bonhomie* (good vibes).

MGM Grand (☎ 702-891-7777, 877-880-0880; www .mgmgrand.com; 3799 Las Vegas Blvd S) Hop on the free monorail down to this massive, green-striped resort complex, one of the world's largest with more than 5000 rooms. Besides its sheer bulk, highlights include a free **Lion Habitat** (☉ 11am-10pm), one of the best race and sports books in town and major concerts at the Grand Garden Arena.

New York-New York (☎ 702-740-6969, 800-693-6763; www.nynyhotelcasino.com; 3790 Las Vegas Blvd S) The facade re-creates the Manhattan skyline, while inside are Park Ave shops, a faux Greenwich Village with restaurants and false storefronts, and a Coney Island midway. The **Manhattan Express** roller coaster (rides $12), which reaches 67mph and features a 'heartline' twist and dive maneuver, is the Strip's best nongambling adrenaline rush.

Luxor (☎ 702-262-4000, 888-777-0188; www.luxor .com; 3900 Las Vegas Blvd S) A 40-billion-candle-power beacon crowning this 30-story steel-and-glass pyramid apex illuminates the Strip's southern end. A sphinx and obelisk await out front, and inside the pyramid's hollow center is the world's largest atrium. Attractions include an **Imax Theater** (admission $8-10) with a motion simulator Ridefilm and a replica of **King Tut's Tomb** (admission $5).

The arcade is interactive, the **Oasis Spa** (day pass $25) is open 24/7 and the nightclub Ra (p424) goes off.

Mandalay Bay (☎ 702-632-7777, 877-632-7800; www.mandalaybay.com; 3950 Las Vegas Blvd S) This happening, tropically themed resort offers an 11-acre garden complete with an artificial beach (sorry, guests only) and lazy river ride. There's also quirky folk art at the House of Blues (p424) and **Shark Reef** (admission $16; ☉ 10am-11pm) with undersea sights and a 'touch tank' for the daring. If you'd rather save your coinage for the slots, check out the impressive aquariums in the lobby and Coral Reef Lounge.

Museums & Kitsch

The **Fremont Street Experience** is a covered pedestrian mall and sound-and-light extravaganza that erupts hourly each evening (dusk to midnight). It was devised to inject new life into the area and while totally weird (not to mention loud), it's great for people-watching.

At the Experience's east end, the **Neon Museum** is a free alfresco showcase of vintage signs retrieved from imploded hotels. Some are also within **Neonopolis**, an adjacent shopping and entertainment complex. All are viewable 24 hours daily.

The **Imperial Palace Auto Museum** (☎ 702-731-3311; www.autocollections.com; 3535 Las Vegas Blvd S, 5th fl; admission $7; ☉ 9:30am-9:30pm) has a phat collection of hundreds of exotic vehicles owned by the likes of Marilyn Monroe, Liberace and even Hitler. Free tickets are often handed out in front of the hotel or are available online.

VEGAS ON THE CHEAP: THE FIRST ONE IS ALWAYS FREE

Sure, you can blow your grubstake and be up to your neck in debt in no time here. *Or*, you can entertain yourself for next to nothing by taking advantage of Vegas' abundant free and low-budget options. Resist the impulse to sleep cheap away from the action. Instead, splash out for a midweek deal on a nice room at a Stripside megaresort, then soak up the freebies.

For starters, don't miss the saucy **Sirens of TI** (p419) nightly spectacle; free gambling lessons and high-flying acts at **Circus Circus** (p419) and cheap thrills at **Slots-a-Fun**, next door; the **Mirage's** (p419) tiger habitat and faux volcano (p419); **Bellagio** (p419) fountains; and **Fremont Street Experience** (p420) and **Neon Museum** (p420), both Downtown. Once you've seen your fill and are ready to participate, sidle into a casino for free drinks at sports books and gaming tables (don't skimp on the tips, cheapskate!) or play some loose penny and nickel slots Downtown.

When your stomach calls, you can either splurge on a day's worth of anti-Atkins fare at a Rabelaisian buffet at someplace classy such as the **Luxor** (p423) or **Paris-Las Vegas** (p423), or devour late-night meal deals (p423).

Tired of losing at blackjack? Try a couple of wacky air-conditioned museums. A very-Vegas favorite is the campy **Liberace Museum** (☎ 702-798-5595, shuttle 702-335-3530; www.liberace .org; 1775 E Tropicana Ave; adult/student $12/8; ☻ 10am-5pm Mon-Sat, noon-4pm Sun), complete with sequined capes, rhinestone jewelry, flashy cars and fabulous candelabra. Only suckers turn up without the ubiquitous $2-off coupon. Free shuttles run daily except Sunday from Strip resorts.

ACTIVITIES

The age-old question 'participate or spectate?' crops up daily in Vegas. Outside Circus Circus' Adventuredome at **AJ Hackett Bungy** (☎ 702-385-4321; 810 Circus Circus Dr; www.aj-hackett .com/lasvegas), first-timers can take the 52m plunge for $59. **Sky Dive Las Vegas** (☎ 702-759-3483, 800-875-9348; 1401 Airport Rd, Boulder City; www .skydivelasvegas.com) offers freefall virgins tandem skydives from $155 after a 20-minute lesson.

Most casino **spas** are reserved for registered hotel guests on weekends, but are often open to nonguests midweek. Day-use fees hover around $25; treatments fetch $100 to $150 an hour.

TOURS

Most tours appeal to seniors who prefer to leave the driving to others. It's easy enough to tour the Strip on your own via taxi, trolley, bus, foot or rental car, but Hoover Dam package deals, which include free hotel pickup and drop-off, can save a lot of ticketing headaches. Even if you're not shacking up there, check with the hostels to see what they've got on offer.

FESTIVALS & EVENTS

Dates of annual events shift from year to year. Contact the Las Vegas Visitor Information Center (p417) for a current schedule. It seems like every day there's a party (or drunken convention) here. Dates that bring the house down include **Mardi Gras** (Saturday before Ash Wednesday in February); the **St Patrick's Day Parade** (March 17) in Downtown; **Mardi Gras Too** (April) at the Rio, Orleans and Fremont Street Experience; the **World Series of Poker** (April to May) Downtown at Binion's; **Cinco de Mayo** (May 5) on Fremont Street; the **NASCAR Craftsman Truck Series** (late September) at the Las Vegas Motor Speedway; the **National Finals Rodeo** (early December) at UNLV's Thomas & Mack Center; and the days preceding **New Year's Eve,** when you should reserve a year in advance for the blockbuster celebration – or steer clear if you can't stomach sky-high room rates.

SLEEPING

If you're after a room in a Strip casino the best deals appear midweek, when doubles sometimes sink as low as $35 or $40 – surf hotel websites and online booking agents for web-only deals. Prices fluctuate wildly based on demand. The rack rates listed here are loose guidelines, not gospel, so be sure to phone ahead. The LVCVA's free **Reservation Hotline** (☎ 800-332-5333) gives current prices at local casinos and hotels – stop by to use their phone or just call and name your price to see what's available. All listed places have air-con, swimming pools and (supposedly) nonsmoking rooms.

In general, recently remodeled places on the Strip's north end are the cheapest and rates climb as you roll south down the Strip. Downtown casinos float midweek deals for as low as $25, but don't expect luxury. Many places shave $10 off for direct online bookings. There are plenty of motels, both on and off the Strip, where prices don't vary as drastically – but, if you opt for one of these ho-hum places, you're sort of missing the point, no?

Hostels, Motels & Hotels

USA Hostels Las Vegas (☎ 702-385-1150, 800-550-8958; www.usahostels.com/vegas; 1322 Fremont St; dm/s/d from $15/40/42; ▣) The facilities are clean and hospitable at this lively, party-hearty hostel in an unsavory section of downtown. Bonuses include a Jacuzzi, bar and daily tours to casinos, clubs and the Canyons. Free pickup from the Greyhound station.

Sin City Hostel (☎ 702-868-0222; www.sincity hostel.com; 1208 Las Vegas Blvd S; dm/d from $17.50/35; 🕲) Re-modeled in mid-2004, this friendly place with four-bed, single-sex dorms and semi-private rooms occupies a seedy no-mans-land, a 20-minute walk south of the Greyhound station. The new facilities are the major attraction, but only reader feedback will tell how well they stand the test of time.

Barbary Coast (☎ 702-737-7111, 888-227-2279; www .barbarycoastcasino.com; 3595 S Las Vegas Blvd; midweek/ weekend r from $40/100; 🕲) Smack dab mid-Strip, this Victorian-era casino has charming decor that carries over seamlessly to the rooms. There's free craps lessons, usually something on in the lounge and a good 24-hour coffee shop downstairs. Book ahead.

Strip Megaresorts

Circus Circus (☎ 702-734-0410, 877-224-7287; www.cir cuscircus.com; 2880 Las Vegas Blvd S; midweek/weekend r from $40/79) Popular standard rooms all have sofas and balconies or patios. Suites, like clowns, come in all shapes and sizes. Decor is tasteful and the rooms are well maintained. Millions have been invested recently to replace the kitschy carney ambience with class.

SPLURGE!

Visitors gravitate towards Vegas because they want to luxuriate, and Sin City's finest megaresorts like the **Bellagio** (p419), **Mandalay Bay** (p420) and **Venetian** (p419) oblige with spacious and finely appointed abodes. Web-only promotional deals start around $119/209 midweek/weekend for single or double occupancy (from $35 per extra person), and often include extras like casino credits, buffet and meal coupons and suite upgrades for as little as $35. For comparison, rack rates average $149 to $199 midweek and $239 to $299 on weekends. It may be hotter than Hades during the lowest summer rate periods – there's *always* a catch – but that's what the pool is for, right? So, dive on in.

Sahara (☎ 702-737-2111, 888-696-2121; www.sahara vegas.com; 2535 Las Vegas Blvd S; midweek/weekend r from $40/75) The last of the Strip's desert-themed casinos doesn't generate much excitement inside, but it does offer comfortable upgraded rooms that are often among the city's better bargains. Passable standard rooms in the older tower are slightly cheaper.

Stardust (☎ 702-732-6111, 866-642-3120; www.star dustlv.com; 3000 Las Vegas Blvd S; midweek/weekend r from $39/69) The old Rat Pack favorite retains its vintage sign and often has the lowest rates it town, which may mean a room out back.

Monte Carlo (☎ 702-730-7777, 888-529-4828; www .montecarlo.com; 3770 Las Vegas Blvd S; midweek/weekend r from $69/$109) Though less flashy than its fancy-pants neighbors, the well-located rooms all have marble tubs and are clean and comfortable. There's a stylish spa (day passes are $19 to $25, but are often 'comped' – Vegas slang for complimentary) and a wave swimming pool.

Luxor (☎ 702-262-4000, 888-777-0188; www.luxor .com; 3900 Las Vegas Blvd S; midweek/weekend r from $69/109) The rooms inside this hulking black pyramid are lined around a massive atrium (vertigo sufferers beware), but save for the angled windows, they're fairly standard and only mildly reflect the casino's Egyptian theme. Further rooms are in a tower out the back. The spa is superb, so push hard for complimentary passes.

Paris-Las Vegas (☎ 702-946-7000, 877-796-2096; www.parislv.com; 3655 Las Vegas Blvd S; midweek/ weekend r from $95/229) The elegantly appointed rooms, each at least 450 sq ft, are in a 34-story tower modeled after the famous Hotel de Ville. Room quality (and rates) rise as you climb the tower, and better views command higher prices.

Also recommended:

Bally's (☎ 702-739-4111, 888-742-9248; www.ballyslv .com; 3645 Las Vegas Blvd S; midweek/weekend r from $55/179) Perfect mid-Strip location on the monorail line. Blissfully theme-free.

Hard Rock (☎ 702-693-5000, 800-473-7525; www .hardrockhotel.com; 4455 Paradise Rd; midweek/weekend r from $69/179) Oozes stardom and seduction, with a lush tropical beach, underwater music piped into the pool and Euro-minimalist rooms as smart as the rest of the joint.

MGM Grand (☎ 702-891-7777, 877-880-0880; www.mgmgrand.com; 3799 Las Vegas Blvd S; midweek/ weekend r from $90/139) On the monorail line, in the middle of the action. Luxury suites can be worth the upgrade.

New York-New York (☎ 702-740-6969, 800-693-6763; www.nynyhotelcasino.com; 3790 Las Vegas Blvd S; midweek/weekend r from $79/159) Opposite MGM, with smaller rooms. Avoid noisy rooms facing the roller coaster.
Palms (☎ 702-942-7777, 866-942-7770; www.palms.com; 4321 W Flamingo Rd; midweek/weekend r from $89/269) MTV's *Real World* did wonders for rates at this lively off-Strip property. Score an upper floor room for a view of the Strip.

EATING
Casinos have multiple restaurants ranging from 24-hour coffeeshops to world-class gourmet restaurants fronted by celebrity iron chefs. For dinner ideas, peruse the free *Las Vegas Weekly*, which has good opinionated reviews. Keep your eyes peeled for casinos advertising dirt-cheap meal deals on billboards and marquees, especially on the North Strip and downtown. Casinos all have several options, from gourmet dining to 24 hour cafés, but they tend toward overpriced. For cheap ethnic eats, you'll have to make the trek away from the Strip. With a couple hundred 24/7 joints in town, you won't be starved for choice at 4am.

Binion's Original Coffee Shop (☎ 702-382-1600; Binion's Horseshoe, 128 E Fremont St; everything under $11; ☯ 24hr) Binion's basement diner dishes heavy-handed American, Chinese and late-night breakfast specials. the thick slabs of meat often arrive flopping off the edge of the plate.

El Sombrero (☎ 702-382-9234; 807 S Main St; mains $5-10; ☒) For high-viscosity chili, sweet agave wine margaritas and other hearty Mexican favorites, check out this diminutive, family-run eatery – ask for help with the vintage jukebox.

Meskerem Ethiopian (☎ 702-732-4250; 252 Convention Center Dr; mains under $10) In the Somerset Shopping Center just east of the Strip, this pleasant spot serves well-spiced meals in relaxed surroundings. Some dishes are vegetarian, and they even serve breakfast, which includes espresso and Ethiopian-style egg dishes.

Monte Carlo Pub & Brewery (☎ 702-730-7777; 3770 Las Vegas Blvd S; mains from $10) A spacious brewpub inside the Monte Carlo hotel-casino with decently constructed pub sandwiches and pizzas alongside a half-dozen craft-brewed ales.

DRINKING
Most boozing in Vegas happens while huddled over slot machines and gaming tables. Elsewhere, cheap pints are in short supply.

Double Down Saloon (4640 Paradise Rd) Only in Vegas: an upscale dive bar where punk rules.

BEST BUFFETS

Heed the old adage 'You get what you pay for.' The difference in quality is as apparent as filet mignon versus overcooked meatballs. **Circus Circus** (p419) boasts one of Sin City's cheapest smorgasbords, but it's heart-stopping cafeteria fare.

Most groaning 'boards feature food stations specializing in sushi, seafood, stir-fry, carved meats and so on. Among the standard entrées at the upscale resorts: fresh shrimp, lobster claws, beef tenderloin, fresh fruits, soups and heaps of salad material.

Buffet prices, like hotel rates, fluctuate. When there's a big convention in town, they're higher than usual. Expect to pay $6 to $12 for breakfast, $10 to $15 for lunch, and upwards of $15 for dinner. The best times for avoiding crushing lines are from 4pm to 5pm or after 8pm on weekdays.

Bellagio (p419), **Luxor** (p420) and **Paris-Las Vegas** (p420) compete for top honors. **Bally's** (p422) does the best Sunday champagne spread, while the **House of Blues** (p424) Sunday gospel brunch is the most unique.

The jukebox rawks garage, ska, swing, surf, lo-fi, rockabilly and broken blues. Graffiti murals decorate every square inch. Don't pass the vibrating mechanical pony by after you try the house-specialty Ass Juice. There are free live shows, never a cover. Double Down is a block south of the Hard Rock.

Houdini's Lounge (Monte Carlo, 3770 Las Vegas Blvd S) Adjacent to the baccarat area, Houdini's offers a dark, comfy respite.

Fireside Lounge (2985 S Las Vegas Blvd) The Strip's most retro romantic spot is tucked away inside the Peppermill coffeeshop. Courting couples flock here for the low lighting, sunken fire pit, '70s decor and cozy nooks built for cuddling. Skip the food and sup a Scorpion.

Ava Lounge (the Mirage, 3400 Las Vegas Blvd S) Knock a few back while you ponder life inside a terrarium.

Golden Gate (1 Fremont St) GG's old-fashioned bar is a sublime, down-to-earth spot to watch gamblers get worked up.

CLUBBING

Seemingly no expense has been spared to bring Vegas on par with New York and Los Angeles in the arena of wildly extravagant nightclubs. Peep at www.vegasafter10.com or www.coolvegas.com for listings.

Ghost Bar (☎ 702-938-2666; The Palms, 4321 W Flamingo Rd; cover $10-20; ♥ from 7pm Sun-Thu) It's a scene with a view at the Palms 55th-floor watering hole, which pulls in a hip young crowd with good DJs. There's 360° panoramas from its deck 450ft above the skyline, celeb-spotting opportunities and a smart sci-fi decor.

Ra (☎ 702-262-4949; 3900 Las Vegas Blvd S at Luxor; cover $10-20) Dress to impress at Vegas' most architecturally impressive dance club. DJs spin techno Wednesday through Saturday and house on Sunday. Line up early 'cuz it gets packed by midnight.

rumjungle (☎ 702-632-7777; 3950 Mandalay Bay, Las Vegas Blvd S; cover from $20) A tower of 150 rums looms over the dueling giant congas and open fire pit at this Brazilian eatery that morphs into a hot, Latin-inspired club after hours.

ENTERTAINMENT

Vegas boasts a constant barrage of live entertainment, from major rock concerts to flashy stage shows. Free lounge acts can be

kitschy fun or unbearable, depending on your attitude (or alcohol consumption).

Big rock venues include the **Events Center** (☎ 702-632-7580) and **House of Blues** (☎ 702-632-7600) at Mandalay Bay, **Grand Garden Arena** (☎ 702-891-7777) at MGM Grand, the **Joint** (☎ 702-693-5066; 4455 Paradise Rd) at Hard Rock and **Rain in the Desert** (☎ 702-940-7246; 4321 W Flamingo Rd) at Palms, west of the Strip.

For a classic Vegas experience, head for the Stardust's **Wayne Newton Theatre** (☎ 702-617-5577, 866-525-2077; tickets from $55), where glittery Mr Las Vegas himself headlines regularly. The hottest production shows like **Cirque du Soleil's** (www.cirquedusoleil.com; tickets $55-195) aquatic spectacular **O** (☎ 702-796-9999, 888-488-7111) at the Bellagio, **Mystère** (☎ 702-796-9999, 800-392-1999) at Treasure Island and the new adult-themed **Zumanity** (☎ 866-606-7111) at New York-New York are worth a splurge but often sell out.

SHOPPING

The Strip is the focus of shopping action. Downtown and the Westside are the places to browse trashy lingerie. Maryland Parkway, on the Eastside near UNLV, is chock-a-block with record shops and other hip stores catering to the college crowd. Malls still dominate the scene, but trendy boutiques are sprouting in low-rent districts on the Strip's fringes.

The Aladdin's impressive upscale North African–themed bazaar, **Desert Passage** (663 S Las Vegas Blvd), features wandering street performers – belly dancers, musicians and acrobats – and an emphasis on jewelry, gifts and women's apparel.

Bellagio's indoor promenade, **Via Bellagio** (3600 S Las Vegas Blvd) is home to the who's-who of fashion plate designers and makes for good window shopping.

Unique stores are scarce at the **Fashion Show Mall** (3200 S Las Vegas Blvd), but it's centrally located and the artificial cloud permanently hovering over it is worth a look-see.

GETTING THERE & AROUND

McCarran International Airport (LAS; ☎ 702-261-5743; www.mccarran.com) is a crap shoot from the Strip's southern end. It has direct flights from most US cities and some from Canada and Europe.

Downtown, the **Greyhound terminal** (☎ 702-384-9561; 200 S Main St) has regular buses to and from Los Angeles ($38, six to eight hours), San Diego ($46, eight to 11 hours) and San Francisco ($69, 15 to 20 hours). The closest **Amtrak** stations are in Needles, CA (106 miles) and Kingman, AZ (123 miles).

Air-con **Citizens Area Transport** (CAT; ☎ 702-228-7433; fares $1.25-2, day pass $5) serves all the highlights. The Nos 301 and 302 Strip Express routes shuttle 24 hours daily between the Strip and downtown.

Free monorails zip between casinos on the Strip's southern end. A private system, running from the MGM Grand north to the Sahara is scheduled to open by the end of 2004. It will operate 8am to midnight and cover the 4-mile route in under 15 minutes for $3.

AROUND NEVADA

For most visitors, Nevada (Spanish for 'snow-clad') means uninhibited nights out and a few hours of pure adrenaline at the tables. For others, however, the massive state – 86% federally owned – offers beautiful terrain to explore, from the mountains of Great Basin National Park to near-empty highways like Hwy 50. You can also sample cowboy lore in frontier waystations such as Elko, or simply pitch a tent and spend the evening under the vast, star dotted sky.

AROUND LAS VEGAS
Red Rock Canyon
The contrast between Vegas' neon lights and the natural splendor of this dramatic **National Conservation Area** (☎ 702-515-5350; admission $5, bike- & walk-ins free; ☉ 8am-dusk), a 20-mile drive west of the Strip, couldn't be greater. The canyon is actually more like a valley, with the steep, rugged Red Rock escarpment rising 3000ft on its western edge. There's a 13-mile, one-way scenic loop with access to hiking trails and shadeless **camping** (campsites $10), 2 miles east of the visitors center. Backcountry camping is possible above 5000ft with a free permit. It's a good driving day-trip or overnight bike trip, but there's no public transportation.

Lake Mead & Hoover Dam
These two sights are the most-visited places within the **Lake Mead National Recreation Area** (☎ 702-293-8907; www.nps.gov/lame; individual/car admission $3/5), which encompasses 110-mile-long Lake Mead, 67-mile-long Lake Mohave and endless miles of desert around the lakes. The excellent **Alan Bible Visitors Center** (☎ 702-293-8990; ☉ 8:30am-4:30pm), on Hwy 93 halfway between Boulder City and Hoover Dam, has details on recreation and interesting natural history exhibits. From there, North Shore Rd winds north around the lake and makes a great scenic drive to Valley of Fire State Park.

The graceful curve and art deco style of the 726ft **Hoover Dam** (www.usbr.gov/lc/hooverdam) contrasts superbly with the stark landscape. Originally called Boulder Dam, this New Deal project was completed in 1935 at a cost of $175 million. It's original intent was flood control, but it now helps supply Colorado River water (and hydroelectric power) to thirsty cities like Las Vegas. Visitors are limited to two-hour self-guided surface **tours** (adult $10), and tickets are sold at the **visitors center** (☎ 702-294-3517; ☉ 9am-5pm) – arrive as early as possible to beat the heat and crowds.

Valley of Fire State Park
Near the north end of Lake Mead NRA, 55 miles northeast of Las Vegas, Valley of Fire is a masterpiece of desert scenery, with psychedelically shaped sandstone. Hwy 169 runs past the **visitors center** (☎ 702-397-2088; http://parks.nv.gov/vf.htm; admission $5; ☉ 8:30am-4:30pm), which has hiking information and excellent desert-life exhibits. The winding side road to **White Domes** is especially scenic. The valley is at its most fiery at dawn and dusk, so consider staying overnight in one of the park's two year-round, unreservable **campgrounds** (campsites $8).

WESTERN NEVADA
The west is where the Silver State got its start. It was the site of the state's first trading post and the famous Comstock silver lode in Virginia City, which financed the Union side in the Civil War and earned Nevada its statehood. For details about the abundance of outdoor activities on the Nevada side of Lake Tahoe, see p617 in the California chapter.

Reno
'The Biggest Little City in the World' is a long way from Las Vegas. Not just in distance (445 miles) and climate, but in overall

spirit: blue-collar Reno feels more 'real.' Lately, Reno has been trying to upgrade its image with flashier casinos and an impressive new art museum.

In the 1850s, travelers on the Humboldt Trail to California needed to cross the Truckee River. Toll bridges, hotels and saloons soon sprang up, followed by a railroad depot that helped Reno cash in on the mining boom. After the mines played out, Reno made an economic virtue of quickie divorces, gambling and prostitution. Agriculture, light industry and tourism have since helped diversify the economy.

ORIENTATION & INFORMATION

Reno's downtown is north of the Truckee River and south of I-80. Most of the action is along Virginia St, between 1st and 6th Sts near the **visitors center** (☎ 775-827-7600, 888-448-7366; www.renolaketahoe.com; 300 N Center St).

SIGHTS & ACTIVITIES

Few casinos have the Vegasesque flash, although some try. The attention-grabbing **Silver Legacy** (☎ 775-325-7401, 800-687-8733; www.silver legacyreno.com; 407 N Virginia St) shows off with a 19th-century streetscape plus sound-and-light shows inside a 120ft dome. One of the city's nicest casinos is the **Siena** (1 S Lake St), featuring Tuscan styling and a more subdued atmosphere.

Veteran downtown establishments include **Fitzgeralds** (☎ 775-785-3300, 800-535-5825; 255 N Virginia St), with its 'lucky leprechaun' theme, the nearby **Eldorado** (☎ 775-786-5700, 800-648-5966; 345 N Virginia St) and the old-timey **Club Cal Neva** (☎ 775-785-3268, 877-777-7303; 140 N Virginia St), the die-hard gambler's favorite.

Reno's cutting edge **National Bowling Stadium** (☎ 775-334-2695; 300 N Center St; ☮ 6-2:30am), the 'Taj Mahal of Tenpins,' has 78 lanes and a 450ft scoreboard. Check it out from the spectator stage or get in the swing of things with a private lesson.

Nearby, the **National Automobile Museum** (☎ 775-333-9300; 10 S Lake St; admission $8; ☮ 9:30am-5:30pm Mon-Sat, 10am-4pm Sun) has a cool collection of unique vehicles, including James Dean's 1949 Mercury.

About 23 miles south of Reno off Hwy 341, **Virginia City** is a National Historic Landmark, with a main street of Victorian buildings, wooden sidewalks and some hokey but fun 'museums.' Further south on Hwy

395, Nevada's pleasant but fast-growing capital **Carson City** is a great base for exploring nearby mountains and deserts.

SLEEPING

Casinos are cheapest Sunday through Thursday, with doubles beginning around $30. Weekends, especially Saturday, can be much higher. There are many motels, and they're often much more affordable on weekends. The closest **campgrounds** are 20 miles away, at either year-round **Davis Creek Park** (☎ 775-849-0684; admission $13), south toward Carson City off Hwy 395; or summer-only **Mt Rose** (☎ 877-444-6777; admission $10; ☮ late Jun–early Sep), on Hwy 431 high in the Sierra at 9000ft.

Seasons Inn (☎ 775-322-6000, 800-322-8588; www .seasonsinn.com; 495 West St; midweek/weekend r from $42/99; ☒ ☒) This is a reliable motel with clean, fairly quiet rooms close to the casino action.

Sundowner (☎ 775-786-7050, 800-648-5490; 450 N Arlington St; www.visitreno.com/sundowner; midweek/weekend r from $35/50; ☒ ☒) The aging rooms in this tower west of Virginia St are hardly exciting but it's consistently one of Reno's cheapest options.

Siena (☎ 775-337-6260, 877-743-6233; www.siena reno.com; 1 S Lake St; midweek/weekend r from $59/99; ☒ ☒) Reno's newest resort is also one of its most luxurious, with cozy, nicely appointed rooms. Midweek rates are one of Reno's best bargains.

EATING

Most casinos have all-you-can-eat buffets, but they're less about quality and more about quantity. Keep your eyes out for dining deals in casino coffee shops. Steak dinners can run under $10, and if cheap's all 'yer after, the **Club Cal Neva** (☎ 775-785-3268, 877-777-7303; 140 N Virginia St; mains from $1) offers $1 hot dogs and $1.50 draft beers, and a 99¢ breakfast.

Brew Brothers (☎ 775-786-5700; 345 N Virginia St; mains $6-12) In the Eldorado, this hipper-than-average casino eatery serves good pizzas and several tasty microbrews. It gets packed when the nightly bands kick in.

Deux Gros Nez (☎ 775-786-9400; 249 California Ave; mains $4-8) For healthier fare, abandon the casinos for this quirky, cycling-themed café with strong coffee, excellent smoothies, sandwiches, egg dishes and vegetarian pasta dinners.

Louis' Basque Corner (☎ 775-323-7203; 301 E 4th St; mains $18) Often voted Nevada's best Basque restaurant, Louis serves an unlimited six-course family-style meal, including wine and dessert.

GETTING THERE & AROUND

Reno-Tahoe International Airport (RNO; ☎ 775-328-6870) is a few miles southeast of downtown. **Greyhound** (☎ 775-322-8801; 155 Stevenson St) has frequent buses to San Francisco and Los Angeles and one daily to Las Vegas. **Amtrak** (☎ 775-329-8638, 800-872-7245; 135 E Commercial Row) has daily services to Sacramento and Oakland.

GREAT BASIN

Much of Nevada is 'basin and range' country, its landscape almost entirely textured with range after range of mountains. Outside the major cities, the land is largely empty, save the occasional grazing cow. The highways, though, are dotted with quirky historic towns and gorgeous desert scenery. For adventurous types, cool detours lead to some deeply remote territory.

Along I-80

This old fur trappers' route along the Humboldt River was also used by the early Emigrant Trail and Central Pacific Railroad.

Heading east from Reno, the first appealing pitstop is **Winnemucca**, which has a vintage downtown and Basque restaurants as well as motels from $20. Some 50 miles north, the **Santa Rosa Mountains** offer rugged scenery and ghost towns. Southwest of Winnemucca is the folk-art sculpture garden **Thunder Mountain**, off I-80 in Imlay and open for free self-guided tours anytime.

Cowboy culture is most diligently cultivated in **Elko**, where aspiring cowpokes should check out the free **Western Folklife Center** (☎ 775-738-7508; www.westernfolklife.org; 501 Railroad St; ☼ 9am-5pm Mon-Fri), which hosts the popular **Cowboy Poetry Gathering** each January. The **Stockmen's Hotel & Casino** (☎ 800-648-2345; www.fh-inc.com; 340 Commercial St; r $40; ☒ ☒) lays on the Western hospitality heavy.

For information about the Elko backcountry, visit the **USFS Office** (☎ 775-738-5171; 2035 Last Chance Rd). North of Elko are old mining towns **Jarbridge** and **Tuscarora**. To the south, the **Ruby Mountains** are a superbly rugged range.

Along Hwy 50

'The loneliest road in America' crosses picturesque Great Basin terrain – desert mountains and wide, scenic valleys – where towns are sparse. Once part of the Lincoln Hwy, lonesome Hwy 50 follows the route of the Overland Stagecoach, the Pony Express and the first transcontinental telegraph line. It's a wonderful desert drive.

Fallon, an agricultural and military town, is the place to gas up and get groceries. The **Lariat Motel** (☎ 775-423-3181; 850 W Williams St; r $44; ☒ ☒) is a safe bet. Three miles west on Hwy 50 is **Bob's Root Beer** (4150 Reno Hwy; ☼ closed winter), a vintage drive-in.

Heading east, the next substantial town is **Austin**, rundown since its 1880s heyday but still interesting. The **USFS** (☎ 775-964-2671; 100 Midas Rd) can recommend good hiking, driving and mountain biking loops and has camping details.

During the late 19th century, $40 million worth of silver was extracted from the hills near well-preserved **Eureka**, which has a few well-kept motels. Larger **Ely** has beautiful historic murals and great old neon signs, along with some decent motels downtown.

Near the Nevada–Utah border is the awesome, uncrowded **Great Basin National Park** (☎ 775-234-7331; www.nps.gov/grba; admission free), which encompasses 13,063ft Wheeler Peak, rising abruptly from the desert. Hiking trails near the summit take in superb country with glacial lakes, ancient bristlecone pines and even a permanent ice field. The visitors center arranges guided tours of **Lehman Caves** (tours $2-8), which are richly decorated with rare limestone formations. There are four developed **campgrounds** (campsites $10), one open year-round, and free primitive sites. Nearby **Baker** has a couple of motels and restaurants.

Along Hwy 95

Hwy 95 goes roughly north–south through the western part of the state via Winnemucca, Hawthorne, Tonopah and Goldfield. The southern section is starkly scenic as it passes the Nevada Test Site (where hundreds of nuclear weapons exploded in the 1950s). Side roads head west to California and Death Valley. In Beatty, the gracious **HI-Happy Burro Hostel** (☎ 775-553-9130; happyburro@pcweb.net; dm $15-18, d $35; ☒ ☒) is a real gem, inside a refurbished antique motel with a hot tub.

Along Hwys 375 & 93

The 'Extraterrestrial Hwy' (Hwy 375) intersects Hwy 93 near top-secret **Area 51**, part of Nellis Air Force Base and a supposed hoosegow for captured UFOs. On Hwy 375 in tiny **Rachel**, **Little A'Le'Inn** (☎ 775-729-2515; www.aleinn .com; r $40) hawks extraterrestrial souvenirs and accommodates earthlings and aliens alike.

Continuing east, Hwy 93 passes through a gorgeous Joshua-tree grove before hitting **Caliente**, an ex-railroad town with a mission-style 1923 depot. Area attractions include the Rainbow Canyon scenic drive and nearby **Cathedral Gorge State Park**, with campsites amid badlands-style cliffs. Two dozen miles north is **Pioche**, an attractive hillside mining town overlooking beautiful Lake Valley.

GRAND CANYON

The Colorado River's Grand Canyon is arguably North America's most famous natural attraction. Pictures and words alone cannot grasp the scale and intensity of this massive slice through the Southwestern desert. You have to stand on the rim, peer down into it yourself and allow your eyes to soak up the multilayered rocks, cliffs and crevices; the river rushing so far below; the pale blue of the hot sky; and all that space in between.

The canyon is 277 miles long and nearly a mile deep, with most visitor services are on the busy **South Rim** and more sedate **North Rim**.

Although only 10 miles apart as the raven flies, it's 215 miles on narrow roads between visitors centers, which is why travelers usually explore the park one rim at a time. The South Rim is by far the most popular, packed every summer with camera-clad tourists, most only staying long enough to ogle from the scenic viewpoints, which are accessible by shuttle buses, short walks and roadside pullouts. To escape the crowds, the North Rim is better; or visit the South Rim during autumn and winter. Of course, hiking down into the canyon is the most breathtaking (in both senses of the word) of all Grand Canyon experiences.

INFORMATION

The park's most developed area is Grand Canyon Village, 6 miles north of the **South Entrance Station**. Here you'll find hotels, camping, restaurants, showers, rim trails, and a shuttle bus system – basically all the services of a small town – and lots and lots of people. The main visitors center is **Canyon View Information Plaza**, at the village's northeast end via a quick 0.25-mile walk or free shuttle bus. Since parking is a pain in summer, shuttle buses are the best way to get around here.

The **NPS** (☎ 928-638-7888; www.nps.gov/grca) mails out a free Trip Planner on request. Park admission costs $20 per vehicle; $10 for bicyclists and pedestrians (valid for seven days). Entering the park you'll get a free map and helpful *Visitor's Guide*. One **rim-to-rim shuttle** (☎ 928-638-2820; one way/round-trip $65/120;

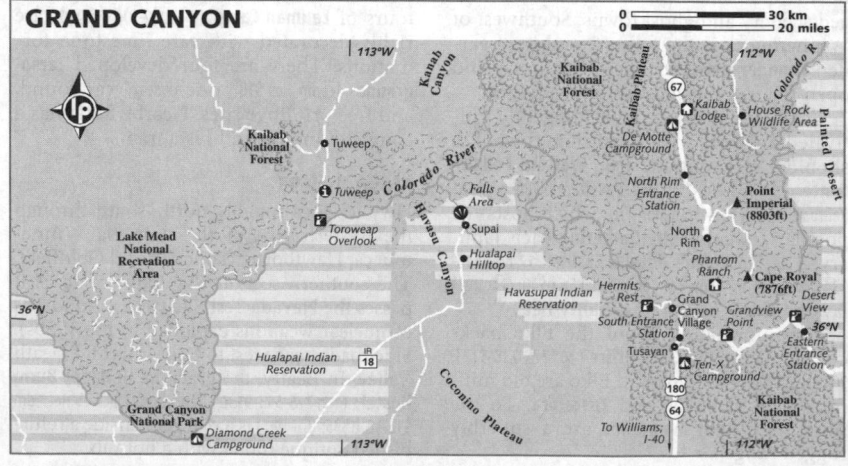

GRAND CANYON

0 ——— 30 km
0 ——— 20 miles

113°W · 112°W

Kanab Canyon · Kaibab Plateau · Colorado R.

Kaibab National Forest · Kaibab National Forest · Kaibab Lodge · House Rock Wildlife Area · Painted Desert

67 · De Motte Campground

Tuweep · Colorado River · Falls Area · North Rim Entrance Station · Point Imperial (8803ft)

Tuweep · Havasu Canyon · Supai · North Rim

Lake Mead National Recreation Area · Toroweap Overlook · Hualapai Hilltop · Phantom Ranch · Cape Royal (7876ft) · Desert View

Havasupai Indian Reservation · Hermits Rest · Grand Canyon Village · Grandview Point · Eastern Entrance Station

36°N · South Entrance Station · 36°N

Hualapai Indian Reservation · 18 · Tusayan · Ten-X Campground

Coconino Plateau · 180

Grand Canyon National Park · Diamond Creek Campground · 113°W · To Williams; I-40 · 64 · Kaibab National Forest · 112°W

May-Oct) runs each way daily; reservations required. Permits are required for all activities except day hikes.

The nonprofit **Grand Canyon Association** (☎ 928-638-2481; www.grandcanyon.org) has guidebooks and trails maps.

When to Go

June is the driest month; July and August are the wettest. January has average overnight lows of 13°F to 20°F and daytime highs of around 40°F. Summer temperatures inside the canyon regularly soar above 100°F. While the South Rim is open year-round, most visitors come between Memorial Day (late May) and Labor Day (early September), when it's very crowded. The North Rim is open from mid-May to mid-October.

Backcountry Permits

The **Backcountry Information Center** (☎ 928-638-7875, fax 928-638-2125; www.nps.gov/grca/backcountry; PO Box 129, Grand Canyon, AZ 86023; ☑ 8am-noon & 1-5pm) accepts applications for backpacking permits ($10 plus $5 per person per night) for the current month and the following four months only. Your chances are decent if you apply early and provide alternative hiking itineraries. If you arrive without a permit, don't despair. Head to the Backcountry Office, by Maswik Lodge, and get on the waiting list. You'll likely get a permit within one to six days, depending on season and itinerary.

SIGHTS & ACTIVITIES
South Rim & Scenic Viewpoints

The South Rim (7000ft) gets 90% of park visitors. To reach Grand Canyon Village take Hwy 64 north from Williams (60 miles) or west from the junction of Hwy 89 (53 miles); from Flagstaff (79 miles) follow Hwy 180

north. East of Grand Canyon Village, Hwy 64 follows Desert View Dr with numerous scenic overlooks en route to the East Entrance Station. West of the village, the Hermit's Rest Rte also passes many overlooks but is closed to private vehicles. Catch one of the frequent free shuttles, which stop at every overlook.

There are tons of great trails. The popular, recommended 12.2-mile round-trip **Bright Angel Trail** plunges 3000ft from the South Rim to Plateau Point, a strenuous all-day trek with a couple of rest houses along the way. From **Indian Gardens**, there's a campground 4.5 miles from the rim and you can continue to the Colorado River; at the bottom is **Bright Angel Campground**, 9.5 miles from the rim, and **Phantom Ranch** (p430), with water, food and a ranger station. Note: you *must* have reservations to stay at these facilities.

Carry plenty of water, and don't overdo it: the NPS recommends rim-to-river hikes be done as at least an overnight trip.

North Rim

At the North Rim (8000ft to 8800ft) summers are cooler, winters colder, the climate is wetter and the spruce-fir forest above the rim is much thicker than the forests of the South Rim. From mid-October to mid-May, all services are closed except the campground, which stays open as weather permits (no later than December 1).

The **North Rim Visitors Center** (☎ 928-638-7864), near the Grand Canyon Lodge, is 44 miles on Hwy 67 from Alt Hwy 89. The Backcountry Information Center is in the ranger station near the campground. Other services include a restaurant, gas station, bookshop, general store, coin laundry and showers. In winter, experienced skiers can

---

SPLURGE!

Every year more than 20,000 people run the canyon's white-water rapids in a variety of boats. Most are commercial trips that get fully booked many months in advance, although occasional cancellations allow folks to join a trip with just a few weeks' notice. Expect to get soaked, spend peaceful nights camping on beaches and pay at least $200 per person per day (including meals). Trips last from three to 17 days and run between April and October. Check the River section of the park's website for a list of authorized outfitters.

If you can't score a spot on a trip in the park, consider splashing out for a day-trip ($265) with **Hualapai River Runners** (☎ 888-216-0076; www.grandcanyonresort.com) on Class III Colorado rapids west of the park on the Hualapai Indian Reservation.

camp (with a backcountry permit). It takes about three days to ski in from where the road is closed. From the visitors center, 20 miles of roads lead to several scenic overlooks with picnic areas, including **Point Imperial** (8803ft).

The **North Kaibab Trail** plunges down to the Colorado River, 5750ft below and 14 miles away, connecting with trails to the South Rim. The first 4.7 miles drop well over 3000ft to **Roaring Springs**, a popular day-long hike. If you prefer a shorter dramatic day hike, walk 1 mile to the **Supai Tunnel**, 1400ft below the rim.

SLEEPING & EATING

If you can't find – or afford – lodging within the park ($64 to $285 per night), try Tusayan (at South Entrance Station), Valle (31 miles south), Cameron (53 miles east), Williams (about 60 miles south) or Flagstaff (79 miles south; p434), which all have budget motels.

Concessionaire **Xanterra** (☎ 303-297-2757, 888-297-2757, same-day inquiries 928-638-2631; www .grandcanyonlodges.com) operates all park hotels, lodges and restaurants, including the iconic **El Tovar Hotel**, where the dining room and bar are nice splurges. The **Village Marketplace**, near the visitors center, has a deli and grocery store but it's best to do your provisioning outside the park.

The best budget options are the rooms with shared bathrooms at **Bright Angel Lodge** (r $48-67). The South Rim's four other lodges have **standard motel rooms** (d $77-125).

At Grand Canyon Village is the year-round **Mather Campground** (☎ 301-722-1257, 800-365-2267; summer/winter campsites $15/10) – the South Rim's main campground; reserve up to five months in advance (not necessary December to March). Near the east entrance, the **Desert View Campground** ($10; ☽ May-Oct) has first-come, first-served sites that often fill by early morning.

At the bottom of the canyon along the Colorado River, **Phantom Ranch** (dm $26, cabins $65, dinner $18-29) is a small oasis with 11 rustic cabins, usually full with mule riders, and two single-sex, 10-bunk dorms. Plan ahead: all accommodations and meals are by advance reservation only.

The North Rim's only hotel, the stately **Grand Canyon Lodge** (☎ 303-297-2757, 888-297-2757; www.grandcanyonnorthrim.com; r $89-116) is perched on the rim and has a gorgeous **dining room**

(☎ 928-638-2611; d $15-25) with glorious canyon views (reservations required). There's also a cafeteria, coffeeshop and saloon.

The only campground between the North Rim and the river, **Cottonwood campground** (per person $5) is 7 miles and 4200ft below the rim. Phantom Ranch is 7 miles below Cottonwood. Because it's twice as far from the North Rim to the river as from the South Rim, rangers suggest three nights as a minimum to enjoy a rim-to-river and return hike.

The **North Rim Campground** (☎ 301-722-1257, 800-365-2267; www.nps.gov/grca; campsites $15) is reservable. It's located 1.5 miles north of the lodge. Free dispersed camping is allowed north of the park borders in **Kaibab National Forest** (☎ 928-643-7298).

GETTING THERE & AWAY

The only regularly scheduled bus service is **Open Road Tours** (☎ 928-226-8060, 800-766-7117), which runs twice-daily shuttles to the Grand Canyon ($20) from Flagstaff.

AROUND ARIZONA

Forget those images of saguaro cacti, rattlesnakes and Roadrunner cartoons. While the Sonoran Desert dominates the state's southern half, there's a huge variety of cultures, people and activities – even skiing – in Arizona. Tall, thickly forested mountains ring the famous Grand Canyon and the state's hottest, driest cities. You can chow down on steak 'n' beans at a cowboy saloon; learn about Indian history at Canyon de Chelly, poke around old mining towns like Jerome, and get extreme and out of doors all year-round.

PHOENIX

Though many visitors complain that the 'Valley of the Sun' lacks soul, you'll still find worthwhile places to check out. Its biggest draw is its 300 days of sunshine a year. It's baking hot in summer, but amazingly pleasant otherwise, especially during spring, when the orange blossoms lend the air a sensual aroma.

Orientation

Most of the valley sits about 1100ft above sea level, though it's ringed by mountains that range from 2500ft to more than 7000ft in elevation. Central Ave runs north–south through Phoenix, dividing west addresses from east addresses; Washington St runs west–east dividing north addresses from south addresses. Most sights described here are near the I-10/I-17 interchange.

Information
BOOKSTORES
Book Store (☎ 602-279-3910; 4230 N 7th Ave) Best selection of periodicals and magazines.
Wide World of Maps (☎ 602-279-2323; 2626 W Indian School Rd) Huge selection of maps, plus some LP guidebooks.

EMERGENCY
Phoenix Police Department (☎ 602-262-6151; 620 W Washington St)

INTERNET ACCESS
Central Phoenix Library (☎ 602-262-4636; 1221 N Central Ave; ⏲ 10am-9pm Mon-Thu, 10am-6pm Fri & Sat, noon-6pm Sun) One hour free daily.

MEDICAL SERVICES
Banner Good Samaritan Medical Center (☎ 602-239-2000; 1111 E McDowell Rd)

MONEY
Foreign exchange service is available at the airport and major bank branches around town.

POST
Downtown Post Office (☎ 602-253-9648; 522 N Central Ave)

TOURIST OFFICES
Arizona Public Lands Information Center (☎ 602-417-9300; www.publiclands.org; 222 N Central Ave)
Downtown Phoenix Visitor Information Center (☎ 602-254-6500, 877-225-5749; www.visitphoenix .com; 50 N 2nd St)

Sights
If you only visit one cultural site, make it the **Heard Museum** (☎ 602-252-8848; www.heard .org; 2301 N Central Ave; adult $7; ⏲ 9:30am-5pm), with an outstanding Southwestern Indian collection. The **Phoenix Art Museum** (☎ 602-257-1222; www.phxart.org; 1625 N Central Ave; adult $9, free Thu; ⏲ 10am-5pm Sun-Tue) has touring and permanent exhibits on Asian, European and American art.

Heritage Square (cnr 7th & Washington; tours $4) is a group of 19th-century buildings downtown that could be entirely hokey, but since Phoenix lacks historic architecture, they're a welcome respite from all the glass and steel. They house inviting bars and eateries.

In Outer Phoenix, the luxuriant 145-acre **Desert Botanical Garden** (☎ 480-941-1225; www.dbg .org; 1201 N Galvin Parkway; adult/student $9/5; ⏲ 8am-8pm Oct-Apr, 7am-8pm May-Sep) is a serene urban getaway; it's free to wander the trails outside. The surrounding **Papago Park**, an untrammeled slice of cactuscape, has hiking and biking trails.

Parts of an excavated Hohokam village remain exposed at the **Pueblo Grande Museum** (☎ 602-495-0901; 4619 E Washington St; adult $2, free Sun; ⏲ 9am-4:45pm Mon-Sat, 1-4:45pm Sun).

Sleeping
The Van Buren St strip between downtown and the airport has what once were fun older motels, but now they're popular with prostitutes. Thus, your cheapest acceptable options, sadly, are chains along the freeway exits, with the most found along I-17 north of downtown. Quoted rates are for the late winter and spring.

HI Phoenix Metcalf House (☎ 602-254-9803; www .phxhostel.com; 1026 N 9th St; dm $15-17, d $30-35; ⏲ check-in 7-10am & 5-10pm) This overgrown oasis occupies a nondescript house in a working-class residential neighborhood north of downtown (too far to walk but near the No 10 bus line). The quirky owner can be helpful.

YMCA (☎ 602-253-6181; 350 N 1st Ave; r per night/week from $20/99) The 'Y' rents rooms with shared showers. It's usually full and doesn't take reservations – show up around 11am to score a room. The guests are primarily men, but there's a women's floor, cable TV lounge, $3 dinner and everyone can use the gym for $5.

Also recommended are the **Budget Lodge Motel** (☎ 602-254-7247; 402 W Van Buren St; r $35-45), and **Motel 6 Airport** (☎ 602-244-1155, 800-466-8356; www.motel6.com; 214 S 24th St; r from $38; ⏲), 2.5 miles from the airport.

Eating
Bill Johnson's Big Apple (☎ 602-275-2107; 3757 E Van Buren St; mains $6-12) If you like cowboy kitsch (and hearty steaks or pulled pork sandwiches), git' your butt over to this western-themed classic that dates from 1956.

SOUTHWEST

PHOENIX

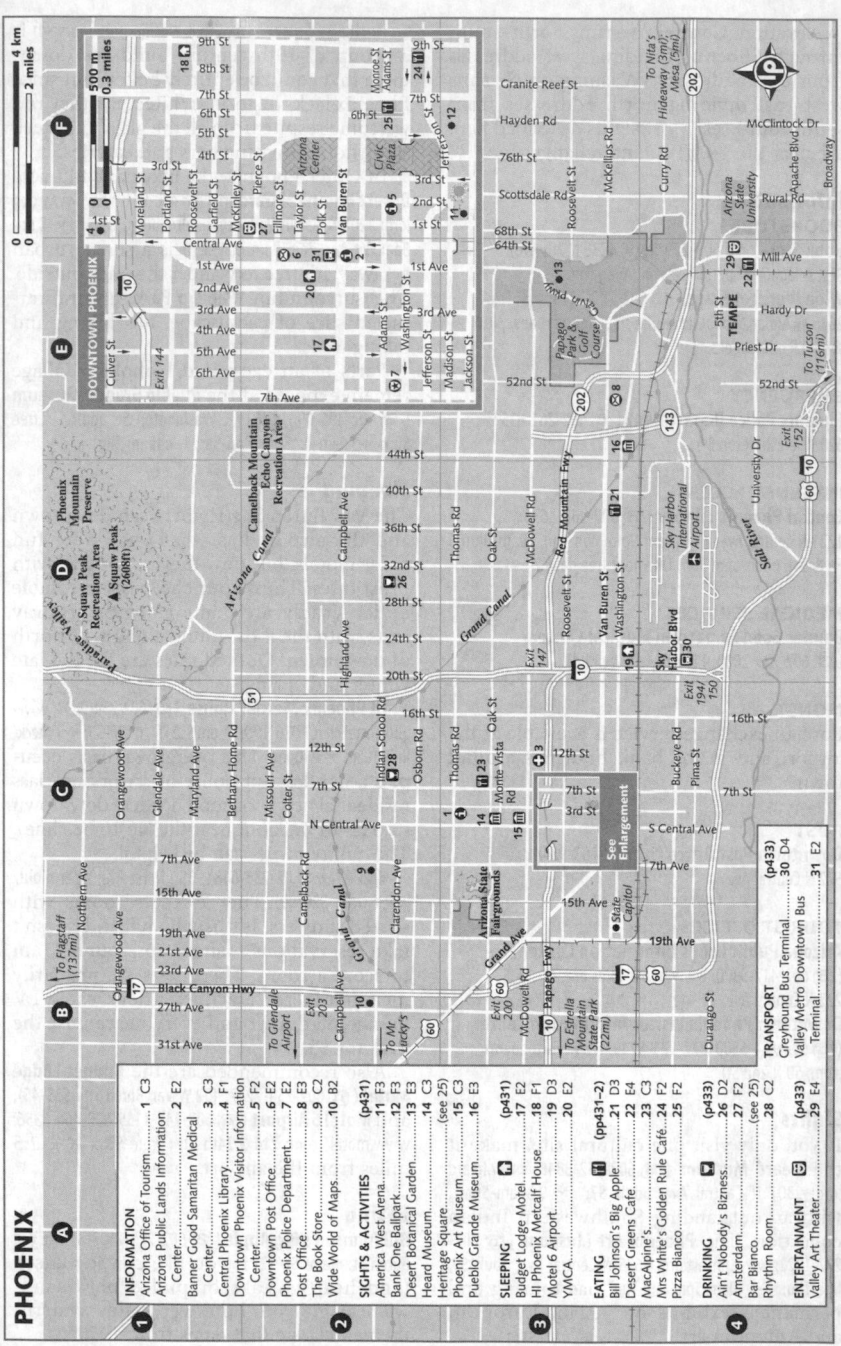

MacAlpine's (☎ 602-262-5545; 2303 N 7th St; mains $5-9, Fri buffet $15-17, dancing after 8pm $8; ☉ 11am-2pm Mon-Fri, from 6pm Fri, 11am-3pm Sat) After burgers, malts and phosphates for lunch, the doors of this classic 1928 soda fountain open every Friday evening for a lively swing dance party and dinner buffet.

Mrs White's Golden Rule Café (☎ 602-262-9256; 808 E Jefferson St; lunch $5-9; ☉ 11am-5pm Mon-Fri) Downtown within walking distance of the ballpark, this no-frills lunch spot dishes well-prepared soul food with just a dash of sass.

Pizza Bianco (☎ 602-258-8300; 623 E Adams St; mains $9-13; ☉ 5-10pm Tue-Sat, 5-9pm Sun) In a cute brick building downtown in Heritage Sq, Bianco's wood-fired pizza is divine – no surprise from a joint that grows its own herbs and makes its own mozzarella.

It's well worth the often long wait, which passes quickly if you grab a drink on the patio at the charming **Bar Bianco** located next door.

Desert Greens Cafe (☎ 480-968-4831; 234 W University Dr; mains under $10) Vegans can find solace inside Tempe's Gentle Strength Co-op, a good natural food grocery.

Drinking
To find out what's on, read the free alternative weekly *New Times* published every Thursday. On the same day, the Arizona Republic's *Rep* section also has exhaustive mainstream entertainment listings. Mill Ave between 3rd and 7th Sts in Tempe is the rowdy, frat-friendly heart of ASU nightlife.

LIVE MUSIC
Good venues for live roots, rock and blues include the friendly **Rhythm Room** (☎ 602-265-4842; 1019 E Indian School Rd; cover $4-10), where there's no cover for the Monday jam session, and **Nita's Hideaway** (☎ 480-966-7715; 3300 S Price Rd, Tempe).

GAY & LESBIAN VENUES
Ain't Nobody's Bizness (☎ 602-224-9977; 3031 E Indian School Rd) A friendly lesbian bar with a DJ spinning dance tunes.

Amsterdam (☎ 602-258-6122; 718 N Central Ave) There's never a cover at this swanky gay male dance mecca. Monday means manicures and $5 martinis and Thursday brings a diva show.

Entertainment
THEATER
Valley Art Theater (☎ 602-222-4275 ext 027; 509 S Mill Ave) Tempe's alternative film temple.

SPORTS
The men's basketball team the **Phoenix Suns** (☎ 602-379-7867) and the women's team **Phoenix Mercury** (☎ 602-252-9622) play at Phoenix's America West Arena. The **Arizona Diamondbacks** (☎ 602-514-8400) play baseball downtown at the Bank One Ballpark. Football team the **Arizona Cardinals** (☎ 602-379-0102) play at a new stadium in Glendale.

Each spring, the Cactus League Baseball Association hosts major league teams for their annual **spring training**.

For schedule and ticket details contact the Downtown Phoenix Visitor Information Center (p431).

Getting There & Around
One of the busiest airports in North America, Phoenix's **Sky Harbor International Airport** (PHX; ☎ 602-273-3300) is located 3 miles southeast of downtown. America West and Southwest are primary regional airlines. Valley Metro's Red Line buses ($1.25) serve the airport and downtown.

Greyhound (☎ 602-389-4200; 2115 E Buckeye Rd; ☉ 24hr) runs regular buses to Tucson, Flagstaff and Los Angeles, as well as many of the tiniest cities in the region Three Amtrak train routes traverse the state but don't interconnect; as with the rest of the Southwest, you're best off with a vehicle. Fortunately, rental rates here are some of the cheapest in the country.

Valley Metro (☎ 602-253-5000; www.valleymetro .org; fare $1.25) runs buses around the valley; on weekdays it also offers a free Flash service around the ASU area and a free Dash service around downtown Phoenix.

CENTRAL ARIZONA
From Phoenix you can zip 137 miles north on I-17 to Flagstaff, or you can spend quality time wandering through the region's mountains and intriguing small towns. It's a rewarding chance to visit Native American sites, cowboy and mining towns – maybe even some New Age vortexes. Hwy 89A between Prescott and Flagstaff, via Jerome and Sedona, is one of the state's most dramatic scenic drives.

Prescott & Jerome

The first territorial capital's Wild West pedigree is visible downtown in several well-preserved buildings around Courthouse Plaza. Facing the plaza is **Whiskey Row**, an infamous saloon strip that still slings plenty of booze. Residents are an intriguing mix of hippies, retirees and big-hat-no-cattle conservatives, with artists and outdoor junkies adding to the town's bohemian ambience.

The **chamber of commerce** (☎ 928-445-2000, 800-266-7534; www.prescott.org; 117 W Goodwin St) and **Prescott National Forest office** (☎ 928-443-8000; www.fs.fed.us/r3/prescott; 344 S Cortez St) provide hiking and camping tips.

It's tough to score a motel room for less than $30/40 in winter/summer. The **American Motel** (☎ 928-778-4322; 1211 E Gurley; r from $39) is the best of a bunch of similarly priced chain motels nearby.

Whiskey Row's historic watering holes are agreeable spots for a pick-me-up. A standout is the 1877 **Palace Restaurant & Saloon** (☎ 928-541-1996; 120 S Montezuma St), where the drinks are stiff. Nearby, the **Prescott Brewing Company** (☎ 928-771-2795; 130 Gurley St; mains $5-12) is the best bet for burgers and local brews. For eggs, salads, sandwiches and strong espresso, try the cozy **Prescott Coffee Roasters** (☎ 928-717-0190; 318 W Gurley St; snacks $3-5).

Greyhound (☎ 928-445-5470; 820 E Sheldon St) serves Phoenix and **Shuttle U** (☎ 928-442-1000, 800-304-6114; www.shuttleu.com; 1505 W Gurley St) runs eight vans daily to the Phoenix airport ($25).

About 34 miles northeast of Prescott on Hwy 89A, funky art galleries, antique shops and a couple of mining museums cling to the steep hillsides in the national historic district of **Jerome**.

Sedona & Red Rock Country

The stunning red-rock landscape surrounding Sedona is among the state's most awe-inspiring. The discovery of, er, energy vortexes here in the 1980s 'channeled' this once-modest settlement into a bustling New Age destination. Millions of visitors now flock here annually, keen to soak up some of the electromagnetism allegedly emanating from the region's rocks, cliffs and rivers. Mountain bikers, hikers and scenery nuts love the place, too. Caveat: if you're not a crystal worshipper, the Harmonic

Convergence birthplace might leave you feeling deflated.

The 'Y' junction of Hwys 179 and 89A marks the center. Ignore the impostors – the official **visitors center** (☎ 928-282-7722, 800-288-7336; 331 Forest Rd), just north of the junction, has heaps of handouts, including vortex maps. In Oak Creek village, the **Bike & Bean** (☎ 928-284-0210; 6020 Hwy 179; bicycle rental per day $29-40) brews strong joe.

Got wheels? If so, don't miss the gorgeous 27-mile detour north toward Flagstaff through **Oak Creek Canyon** (Hwy 89A), which traces Oak Creek through Kodachrome canyons before ascending into ponderosa forest. Don't miss **Slide Rock State Park** (☎ 928-282-3034; admission $8; ☉ 8am-7pm summer, 8am-5pm winter), 7 miles north of Sedona on Hwy 89A, where the creek sweeps swimmers through a natural rock chute.

Sedona sleeps are spendy; budget travelers are better served in Flagstaff. The best bet are the (first-come, first-served) shady, roadside **USFS campgrounds** (☎ 928-282-4119; campsites $16; ☉ May-Sep) along N Hwy 89A, six to 13 miles north of town. The **Sedona Motel** (☎ 928-282-7187; 218 Hwy 179; r $50-80; ❄) is the cheapest hostelry. Grab a sandwich or picnic fixings from **New Frontiers Natural Foods & Deli** (☎ 928-282-6311; 1420 W Hwy 89A; sandwiches $4-6; ☉ 8am-8pm).

Flagstaff & Around

Nestled among cool ponderosas on the San Francisco Peaks' southern flanks, convivial 'Flag' is northern Arizona's biggest modern-day trading post, yet it's worlds away from Phoenix's urban angst. The Grand Canyon (p428) is a 90-minute drive north, making it the perfect base for day trippers. Historic buildings line old Rte 66 (Santa Fe Ave), which roughly parallels I-40. Fifteen thousand Northern Arizona University (NAU) students add a healthy dollop of collegiate culture.

The **visitors center** (☎ 928-774-9541, 800-842-7293; www.flagstaffarizona.org; 1 E Rte 66) is downtown in the historic railway depot.

SIGHTS & ACTIVITIES

A Hopi kiva is only one of the exhibits at the **Museum of Northern Arizona** (☎ 928-774-5213; www.musnaz.org; 3101 N Fort Valley Rd; adult/student $5/3; ☉ 9am-5pm), 3 miles north of town on Hwy 180. Ask about tours of local mountains, mesas and canyons. The most famous discovery made at **Lowell Observatory** (☎ 928-774-3358; www.lowell.edu; 1400 W Mars Hill Rd; adult/student $5/4; ⊙ 9am-5pm summer, noon-5pm winter) was the planet Pluto in 1930. Call for night-time viewing hours.

The past meets the present at a trio of impressive nearby **National Monuments** (www.nps.gov/sucr/Flag_Areas/frameset.html; 3-site admission $5; ⊙ 8am-6pm summer, 9am-5pm winter). The 1000ft-tall volcano cone at the **Sunset Crater** (☎ 928-526-0502), on a loop road 12 miles north of Flagstaff along Hwy 89, was formed by volcanic eruptions in AD 1064–65. Climbing is prohibited, but trails yield great views. The **USFS Bonito campground** (☎ 928-527-1474; campsites $15; ⊙ Apr-Oct) is situated opposite the visitors center.

Follow the loop road past the crater to **Wupatki** (☎ 928-679-2365), with hundreds of Ancestral Puebloan sites, five of which are easily accessible. East of Flagstaff near I-40 exit 204, the Sinagua buildings at **Walnut Canyon** (☎ 928-526-3367) are eerily set in caves within near-vertical walls of a butte jutting splendidly from a wooded canyon.

The mountains around Flagstaff offer scores of hiking, camping and mountain-biking options around the **Coconino National Forest** (☎ 928-527-3600; www.fs.fed.us/r3/coconino; 1824 S Thompson St), as well as skiing at **Arizona Snow Bowl** (☎ 928-779-1951; www.arizonasnowbowl.com; half-day $27-34, full day $42). The best outdoor outfitters are **Peace Surplus** (☎ 928-779-4521; 14 W Rte 66), **Babbitt's Backcountry Outfitters** (☎ 928-774-4775; 12 E Aspen Ave) and **Cosmic Cycles** (☎ 928-779-1092; 901 N Beaver St).

SLEEPING

The catch to Flag's affordable motels (from $20/$50 in low/high season) is that the train lumbers through in the middle of the night. Light sleepers should head south on Milton Rd toward I-40 exit 198 for similarly priced chain motels.

Area campgrounds fill up in summer, so book ahead. **Fort Tuthill County Park** (☎ 928-774-5139; I-17 exit 337; campsites $10; ⊙ May-Sep) has 100 tent sites but no showers.

The independent **Grand Canyon International Hostel** (☎ 928-779-9421, 888-442-2696; www.grandcanyonhostel.com; 19 S San Francisco St; dm $15-17, d $30-37; 🖥) and the nearby **Dubeau International Hostel** (☎ 928-774-6731, 800-398-7112; 19 W Phoenix Ave; dm $15-17, d $32-39; 🖥) are run

separately but are jointly owned and offer free pickup. All rooms share bathrooms and the helpful owners run popular Grand Canyon day trips ($50).

Weatherford Hotel (☎ 928-779-1919; www.weatherfordhotel.com; 23 N Leroux St; midweek/weekends r from $60/65; ⊙ 1am curfew) This friendly downtown hotel's eight old-fashioned rooms (c 1898) have no TV or phone. Trains rumble close by but, hey, there are two bars on-site.

EATING

Macy's Coffeehouse (☎ 928-774-2243; 14 S Beaver St; mains $3-7) Students and outdoorsy types crowd this hip hangout for fresh-roasted coffee. Everything is veggie – many things are vegan – including house-baked pastries, waffles, sandwiches and dinner specials. There's live acoustic tunes.

Beaver Street Brewery (☎ 928-779-0079; 11 S Beaver St; mains $5-9) This modern brewpub has an antique backbar, spacious billiards room, wood-fired pizzas, outdoor patio and a good selection of craft-brewed ales.

Little Thai Kitchen (☎ 928-226-9422; 1051 S Milton Rd; mains $5-10) Never mind the strip-mall setting: this fabulous hole-in-the-wall find has fresh, inventive dishes, with lots of veggie options.

ENTERTAINMENT

The free weekly *Flagstaff Live* (www.flaglive.com) and edgy bimonthly *The Noise* review what's on. Several cinemas scattered around town screen flicks. Nightlife is lively year-round, with plenty of bars downtown. It's worth a taxi out of town to check out the **Museum Club** (☎ 928-526-9434; 3404 E Rte 66), a classic, barn-like 1931 roadhouse with something going on every night and live blues, country, rock and reggae on weekends.

GETTING THERE & AROUND

Amtrak & Greyhound both stop here.

Open Road Tours (☎ 928-226-8060, 800-776-7117; 1 E Rte 66), inside the Amtrak station, shuttles twice daily to the Grand Canyon ($20) and five times daily to the Phoenix airport ($30).

NORTHEASTERN ARIZONA

Arizona's top right quadrant is dominated by the Navajo and Hopi Indian reservations. Here Navajo *hogans* (octagonal homes made of wood and earth, with the door

---

DETOUR: CANYON DE CHELLY

The many-fingered **Canyon De Chelly National Monument** (pronounced *duh*-shay) is one of the state's most spectacular spots, a unique world unto itself that contains several Ancestral Puebloan pit dwellings (c AD 350) and some large cliff dwellings (c 1200), all within steep canyon walls that add to the monument's mystique – entering the canyon is like stepping back in time. There are two scenic rim drives, each taking about three hours, but to truly get a feel for the place you must head inside; for this you need a Navajo guide.

The **visitors center** (☎ 928-674-5500; www.nps.gov/cach) can provide details on guided hikes (per hour $15), 4WD trips (half-day $40) and horseback rides (per hour $10, plus guide $10). Nearby, the shady **Cottonwood campground** (campsites free) is open year-round.

---

facing east) and Hopi kivas nestle against some of North America's most spectacular landscapes. Equally impressive are the ancient pueblos in the Canyon de Chelly and Navajo National Monuments.

Navajo Indian Reservation

After the infamous 'Long Walk' in 1860, the surviving Diné (Navajo people) returned to their homeland in 1868 under a treaty that created a 5500-sq-mile reservation. Today, the **Navajo Nation** (population 250,000) is the USA's largest reservation – larger than 10 of the 50 US states – with 27,000 sq miles of forest and high desert covering chunks of Arizona, New Mexico and Utah.

Though some of the reservation is unmistakably poor, Navajo heritage is alive and vital. Tune in to the Voice of the Navajo Nation (KTNN AM 660) to catch music and commentary in Navajo and English. The annual **Navajo Nation Fair** (www.navajo nationfair.com) is one of the USA's biggest Native American events, held over Labor Day weekend in Window Rock, the Nation's most developed town.

Ya'aat'eeh (Welcome)! **Navajo Tourism** (☎ 928-871-6436/7371; www.discovernavajo.com) publishes a free tourist magazine, available on the reservation and in nearby towns. All backcountry activities require a permit ($5, plus $5 per person camping fee) from the **Navajo Parks & Recreation Department** (☎ 928-871-6647; www.navajonationparks.org; cnr Hwys 264 & 12).

In Window Rock, bunk in **Navajo Nation Inn** (☎ 928-871-4108, 800-662-6189; www.navajo nationinn.com; 48 W Hwy 264; s/d $62/67; 🅿 🖳), a Navajo-owned chain. Many visitors end up in Gallup, New Mexico (p463).

The **Navajo Transit System** (☎ 928-729-4002; www.navajotransitsystem.com) runs buses from Window Rock to Gallup ($2.50, one hour) and

Tuba City ($13, four hours) – with stops along Hwy 264 via the Hopi Reservation.

HUBBELL TRADING POST NATIONAL HISTORIC SITE

Thirty miles west of Window Rock in the town of Ganado, the **Hubbell Trading Post** (☎ 928-755-3475; admission free, tours $2; 🕒 8am-5pm) looks much as it would have soon after it was established in 1878. There's a small visitors center (with free coffee) alongside the trading post itself, which still sells local rugs and crafts.

MONUMENT VALLEY NAVAJO TRIBAL PARK

The magnificent buttes and mesas here are immortalized in westerns like John Ford's 1939 *Stagecoach*. The dramatic valley straddles the Arizona–Utah border, 24 miles north of Kayenta on Hwy 163. You get great views along the highway, but from the year-round **visitors center** (☎ 435-727-5870, 435-727-5874) you can get up close and personal by joining a 17-mile driving tour ($5) or, in summer, arranging 4WD and horseback tours. **Mitten View Campground** (campsites $10) has scenic sites.

NAVAJO NATIONAL MONUMENT

The Ancestral Puebloan sites of **Betatakin** and **Keet Seel** are open for public visitation and are both exceptionally well preserved, extensive and impressive. Because you need to hike 5 miles round-trip to Betatakin and 17 miles round-trip to Keet Seel, this is a good place to check out pueblo sites away from crowds. Daily hiking permits are free but limited, so call for reservations up to two months in advance. The **visitors center** (☎ 928-672-2700) is 9 miles north of Hwy 160 along paved Hwy 564. Free camping is on a first-come, first-served basis.

FOUR CORNERS NAVAJO TRIBAL PARK

You can put a foot into Arizona, another in New Mexico, a hand in Utah – do the hokey-pokey – and another in Colorado at the only place in North America where four states come together. So much fun for only $3! Honestly, there ain't much to see here. Navajo food stands and dozens of the inevitable crafts stalls ring the site, which is off Hwy 160. If you haven't had it yet, try the fry bread – with lots of honey.

Hopi Indian Reservation

The oldest, most traditional and religious tribe in the Southwest (if not the entire continent) are private people who have suffered less outside influence than most other tribes. Villages, many built between AD 1400 and AD 1700, dot the isolated mesas. **Old Oraibi**, inhabited since the early 12th century, vies with Acoma Pueblo in New Mexico for the title of North America's oldest continuously inhabited settlement.

Hwy 264 passes the three mesas (First, Second and Third Mesa) that form the heart of the reservation. There are no banks, and cash is preferred for most transactions. The Hopi are known for their kachina dolls, which can be purchased along with polychrome pottery, silver overlay jewelry and coiled baskets from artists in the villages and at roadside galleries. Photography, sketching and recording is forbidden by Hopi law – *don't even ask*.

At the end of First Mesa you'll see **Walpi** (c 1200), the most dramatic of the Hopi villages, jutting out into space from the top of a spectacularly narrow mesa. The amiable **tourist office** (☎ 928-737-2262, 928-737-3000) offers guided walking tours (admission $8) several times daily.

The **Hopi Cultural Center Restaurant & Inn** (☎ 928-734-2401; www.hopiculturalcenter.com; r winter s/d $65-70, summer $90-95, mains $5-9; 🗷), on Second Mesa, is the reservation's only hotel. The restaurant serves salads, burgers and Hopi dishes such as *noqkwivi* (lamb and hominy stew). The Cultural Center's **museum** (☎ 728-734-6650; 🕙 8am-5pm Mon-Fri) is a good first stop, with informative exhibits on Hopi history, including many historical photographs.

On I-40, **Winslow** provides the closest off-reservation accommodations to the Hopi mesas. Several vintage Rte 66 motels (in the $20s and $30s) line 2nd and 3rd Sts,

but the most memorable place to stay is the restored **La Posada** (☎ 928-289-4366; www.laposada.org; 303 E 2nd St; r from $89; 🗷), an impressive National Historic Landmark.

WESTERN ARIZONA

Along Arizona's western border, the Colorado River is alive with sun-worshippers at Lake Havasu City, while Rte 66 nuts enjoy well-preserved stretches of that classic highway near Kingman. South of I-10 toward Yuma, the wild, empty landscape is among the West's most rugged.

Founded in 1880 as a railway stop, **Kingman** is the biggest town along I-40 between California and Flagstaff. The **visitors center** (☎ 928-753-6106, 866-427-7866; www.kingmantourism.org; 120 W Andy Devine Ave) is also home to the **Route 66 Museum** (☎ 928-753-9889; admission $3).

Budget motels line Andy Devine Ave (between I-40 exits 48 and 53). The **Lido Motel** (☎ 928-753-4515; 3133 E Andy Divine Ave; r $20-29; 🗷) is a reliable choice.

The longest extant stretch of Rte 66, once called the 'Main Street of America,' winds 160 miles through empty northwestern Arizona countryside, from Seligman west to Kingman, then on through Oatman to the Arizona–California border. A former gold-mining town, **Oatman** is now a hokey but spirited tourist town, with gunfights at high noon and wild burros roaming the street. At the century-old adobe **Oatman Hotel** (☎ 928-768-4408; r $35-55) the simple rooms remain almost unchanged since Clarke Gable and Carole Lombard honeymooned here in the 1930s. All rooms share baths and have ceiling fans.

TUCSON

Rich in Latino roots and home to the University of Arizona (U of A), Arizona's second-largest city is one of the Southwest's most culturally stimulating places. For travelers seeking the region's true flavor, it's *much* more happening than Phoenix, 116 miles north. Tucson temperatures hover around 75°F during the winter, but often soar to well over 100°F in the summer.

The city is set in a Sonoran Desert valley at 2500ft, surrounded by mountains, some reaching more than 9000ft. Like Phoenix, Tucson has sprawled; luckily the areas most worth exploring are within easy walking and biking distance. The only exception is the Arizona-Sonora Desert Museum; west of town in striking Saguaro National Park.

Orientation

Downtown and the historic district are east of I-10 exit 258. The intersection of Stone Ave and Congress Sts is ground zero for Tucson addresses. The U of A campus is a mile northeast of downtown; the main drag (4th Ave) is packed with cafés, bars and hip shops.

Information

BOOKSTORES

Bookman's (☎ 520-325-5767; 1930 E Grant Rd)
Good selection of used books, music and magazines.

EMERGENCY

Tucson Police Department (☎ 520-791-4444; 270 S Stone Ave)

INTERNET ACCESS

Main library (☎ 520-791-4393; 101 N Stone Ave)
One hour free access per day.

MEDIA

89.1 FM NPR from the University of Arizona.
91.3 FM Non-commercial community station that reflects the region's cultural diversity.
Tucson Weekly (www.tucsonweekly.com)
Free alternative tabloid with best restaurant and entertainment listings.

MEDICAL SERVICES

Tucson Medical Center (☎ 520-327-5461; 5301 E Grant Rd)

POST

Downtown Station (☎ 520-903-1958; 141 S 6th Ave, 85701)

TOURIST OFFICES

Coronado National Forest Supervisor's Office
(☎ 520-670-4552; www.fs.fed.us/r3/coronado; 300 W Congress St)
Tucson Convention & Visitors Bureau
(☎ 520-624-1817, 800-638-8350; www.visittucson.org; 110 S Church Ave)

Sights

There are several worthwhile in-town stops, but most of the action is in the surrounding area. Starting downtown, wander around the 19th-century buildings and craft stores in the **Presidio Historic District**, between Court

and Main Aves and Franklin and Alameda Sts. Nearby, the **Tucson Museum of Art** (☎ 520-624-2333; 140 N Main Ave; adult/student $5/2, free Sun; ☉ 10am-4pm Mon-Sat, noon-4pm Sun) has a small collection of pre-Columbian artifacts as well as 20th-century Western art pieces.

The **University of Arizona** campus houses notable outdoor sculptures and a couple of good free museums. The top of the heap is the **Center for Creative Photography** (☎ 520-621-7968; 1030 N Olive Rd; ☉ 9am-5pm Mon-Fri, noon-5pm Sat & Sun), with an internationally renowned collection of works by American photographers and a remarkable archive (including most of Ansel Adams' and Edward Weston's work). Opposite is the free **UA Museum of Art** (☎ 520-621-7567; cnr Park Ave & Speedway Blvd; ☉ 9am-5pm Tue-Fri, noon-4pm Sat & Sun), another excellent stop.

The Buckaroos put on a spectacular non-motorized parade during the **Fiesta de los Vaqueros** (Rodeo Week; ☎ 520-741-2233, 800-964-5662; www.tucsonrodeo.com) every February.

Activities

Bicycles are the best way to get around town. Pick up a free bike map and rent a stylin' beater from the **BICAS Co-op** (☎ 520-628-7950; 44 W 6th St; bike hire per day from $5; ☉ noon-7pm Tue-Fri, 10am-5pm Sat), then freewheel across the **Diamondback Bicycle Pedestrian Bridge**, which whisks you over Broadway Blvd via a massive metal sculpture shaped like a rattlesnake. The super-friendly co-op folks put on zany events such as **bike-in film festivals** and can advise about **mountain biking** options.

The **Tucson Sidewinders** (☎ 520-434-1021; tickets $5-8; ☉ Apr-Aug) play minor league **baseball** at Tucson Electric Park.

When things heat up, locals head for the surrounding mountains for respite. **Sabino Canyon** (day pass $5), 15 miles northeast of downtown Tucson, is one of the most popular getaways; the **USFS** (☎ 520-749-8700; 5700 N Sabino Canyon Rd) has details on the numerous hikes in the Santa Catalina Mountains.

Mt Lemmon (admission $5), at 9157ft, is another popular destination. You can spend a couple of days hiking to its summit, or head east on Tanque Verde Rd to the Catalina Hwy and drive to the top in an hour. A **hiker's shuttle** ($3) facilitates several nice loop hikes, but all trails were closed at the time of writing due to a lurking mountain lion! **Mt Lemmon Ski Valley** (☎ 520-576-1400; Catalina Hwy;

half-/full-day $27/32) is the nation's southernmost ski area, and runs scenic sky rides ($9) in the summer.

Sleeping

Rack rates can vary considerably; prices are higher in winter and spring.

Hotel Congress (☎ 520-622-8848, 800-722-8848; www.hotelcongress.com; 311 E Congress St; dm with/ without HI card $20/25, r $49-99; 🖳) Downtown's very popular, beautifully restored hotel was built in 1919, and many of its fine rooms have period furnishings. What other budget digs have carpet scavenged from the Ritz Carlton? Downstairs there's a club, café and bar, so expect noise at night. If you forgot your earplugs, request a room at the far end of the hotel. Dorm rooms, with their own bathrooms and only a couple of beds, are above the nightclub. The only bummer is that there's no kitchen.

Road Runner Hostel (☎ 520-628-4709; www.road runnerhostel.com; 346 E 12th St; dm/d $18/38; 🔀 🖳) This friendly Dutch-run place is a five-minute walk from the downtown area and offers summertime deals for non-US passport holders (May through September, four nights for $36). The best private rooms are across the street. Bonuses include free Internet, a juicer in the kitchen, a big-screen TV/video room, coin laundry and air-con. They also rent cheap bicycles.

The **Lazy 8 Motel** (☎ 520-622-3336, 888-800-8805; www.lazy8motel.com; 314 E Benson Hwy; s $31-36, d $37-56; 🔀 🐾) is the best of the budget places near I-10 exit 261.

Eating

Cup Cafe (☎ 520-622-8848; 311 E Congress St; mains $5-10) Hotel Congress' casual eatery dishes gourmet breakfasts, strong coffee and decadent desserts – grab a seat outside on the patio.

Grill (☎ 520-623-7621; 100 E Congress St; mains $3-8; 🕙 24hr) A stumble away from the Congress next to Wig-O-Rama, you'll find lots of students and other boho types crowding this classic diner after shows and while contemplating the morning after – no bad hair days here.

Epic Cafe (☎ 520-624-6844; cnr 4th Ave & University; mains $4-6) In the heart of the 4th Ave shopping strip near the university, this hip and spacious café stays open until midnight and serves great lattes, sandwiches and fresh-baked pastries, some of them vegan.

Little Poca Cosa Café (20 S Scott St; mains $5-7; 🕙 7:30am-2:30pm Mon-Fri) This lively, Lilliputian offspring of the justifiably-famous Poca Cosa across the street delivers amazing Mexican breakfasts and lunches – try anything with mole – from a one-fanny kitchen. Don't be surprised if the waitress calls you 'sweetpea.' !Horale!

La Herradura (cnr St Mary's & Grande Ave; mains $3-6) If you're driving, it's worth the trek to this authentic hole-in-the-wall Sonoran-style Mexican joint just west of I-17. The fish tacos are sublime, as is the *carne asada*, and everything comes with fresh, sweet *pico de gallo*. BYOB from the drive-thru window next door.

Clubbing

The *Tucson Weekly* is the place to look for listings. Frat boys jam bars adjacent the U of A on 4th St while hipsters bar-hop downtown on 4th Ave.

Club Congress (☎ 520-622-8848; 311 E Congress St) Hotel Congress' downstairs club consistently hosts the most interesting gigs in town. From DJ dance nights to touring roots and rock bands, there's always something interesting on – not to mention the laid-back Tap Room bar where old West meets Gen Next.

Entertainment

Rialto Theatre (☎ 520-798-3333; 318 E Congress St) Opposite Club Congress, this restored theater hosts nationally touring bands, from punk to poprock.

For a free shot of nostalgia, try **Lil Abner's Steakhouse** (☎ 520-744-2800; 8500 N Silverbell Rd), where octogenarian western swing bandleader Dean Armstrong and his Arizona Dancehands have been tearing it up on Friday and Saturday nights on the outdoor stage for years. No cover.

Getting There & Around

Tucson International Airport (TUS; ☎ 520-573-8000) is 9 miles south of downtown. City Bus No 186 runs until 7pm from downtown. **Arizona Stagecoach** (☎ 520-889-1000; transfers $10-39) provides door-to-door, 24-hour airport transfers to points throughout Tucson.

Amtrak (☎ 800-872-7245; 400 E Toole Ave) has trains to Los Angeles three times weekly, and **Greyhound** (☎ 520-792-3475; 2 S 4th Ave) runs buses to Phoenix.

The **Ronstadt-Downtown Center** (cnr Congress St & 6th Ave) is the major local transit hub. From there, **Sun Tran** (☎ 520-792-9222) buses and trolleys serve metropolitan Tucson.

AROUND TUCSON

Arizona-Sonora Desert Museum

Coyotes, javelinas, bobcats, snakes, hummingbirds, scorpions and just about any other local desert animals you can think of are displayed in natural-looking outdoor settings at this excellent living **museum** (☎ 520-883-2702; 2021 N Kinney Rd; admission $12; 8:30am-5pm) off Hwy 86, 14 miles west of Tucson. A perennial local favorite, it's one of Tucson's crown jewels.

Saguaro National Park

With two separate units, east and west of Tucson, this park's purpose is to preserve large stands of the giant saguaro cactus and their associated Sonoran Desert habitat and wildlife. The **Saguaro East Visitors Center** (☎ 520-733-5153; www.nps.gov/sagu; permits $6; 9am-5pm), 15 miles east of downtown along Old Spanish Trail (take E Broadway Blvd), has information regarding day hikes, horseback riding and backcountry camping ($6 permits must be obtained by noon on the day of your hike). The park boasts 130 miles of trails, including the Tanque Verde Ridge Trail, which climbs to Mica Mountain (8666ft).

The **Saguaro West Visitors Center** (☎ 520-733-5100; admission free) is 2 miles northwest of the Arizona-Sonora Desert Museum. Night hiking (killer during a full moon) is permitted, but camping is not.

Biosphere 2

Built to be completely sealed off from Biosphere 1 (that would be earth), the $200 million experiment known as **Biosphere 2** (☎ 520-838-6200; www.bio2.edu; admission $20; 9am-5pm) is a three-acre glassed dome housing seven separate microhabitats – complete with the world's largest man-made ocean – and designed to be self-sustaining. In 1991 eight 'bionauts' entered Biosphere 2 for a two-year tour of duty, during which they were physically cut off from the outside world. They emerged thinner but in decent shape. Although this experiment could be used as a prototype for space stations, it was a privately funded endeavor and engulfed in controversy. Now it is used for various ongoing research projects. It's 30 miles north of Tucson on Hwy 77.

West of Tuscon

Hwy 86 heads west from Tucson toward some of the driest (and emptiest) parts of the Sonoran Desert.

Fifty-six miles west of Tucson, **Kitt Peak National Optical Astronomy Observatory** (☎ 520-318-8726; 9am-3:45pm) is the world's largest optical observatory. Self-guided tours are free and guided tours are available daily, as are nightly three-hour viewing sessions ($36), booked weeks in advance.

If you want solitude in stark, beautiful desert surroundings, visit **Organ Pipe Cactus National Monument** (☎ 520-387-6849; www.nps.gov/orpi; admission $5). Two unpaved loop drives and six hiking trails take you through the park, which has three types of large columnar cacti and an excellent variety of other desert flora and fauna. The **visitors center** is 22 miles south of the Hwy 86 junction at Why (Yes, Why. Don't ask.). Tent and RV **camping** (campsites $10) is available on a first-come, first-served basis.

South of Tuscon

South of Tucson, I-19 beelines for Nogales, Arizona and Viejo México. Along the way are a couple of interesting detours.

The **Titan Missile Museum** (☎ 520-625-7736; 1580 W Duval Mine Rd; admission $8; 9am-5pm daily winter, Wed-Sun summer), at exit 69, has daily tours and features an underground launch site for Cold War–era intercontinental ballistic missiles.

If history and/or shopping for crafts interest you, take exit 34 to the small village of **Tubac**, which has more than 80 galleries.

At exit 29, **Tumacácori National Historic Park** (☎ 520-398-2341; www.nps.gov/tuma; admission $3; 8am-5pm) is the well-preserved ruin of a never-completed Franciscan church started in 1800. Facilities include a visitors center, museum and gift shop.

Nogales

Arizona's most important gateway to Mexico is bustling with activity, tourists buying Mexican goods and vice versa. Keep in mind that there's a Nogales on each side of the border.

The **chamber of commerce** (☎ 520-287-3685; 123 W Kino Park Way) is in Kino Park off Grand

Ave. The **Mexican Consulate** (☎ 520-287-2521; 571 N Grand Ave) can process visa requests.

Chain motels like **Motel 6** (☎ 520-281-2951, 800-466-8356; 141 W Mariposa Rd; r from $35; ☒ ☒) are clustered at I-19 exit 4 and along Business Hwy 19.

Greyhound (☎ 520-287-5628; 35 N Terrace St) has regular services to Tucson ($8, two hours). From the bus terminal 3 miles south of the border, there are frequent bus departures further into Mexico and a train to Guadalajara and Mexico City.

Drivers heading into Mexico can obtain car insurance from friendly, helpful **Sanborn's** (☎ 520-281-1873; www.sanbornsinsurance.com; 2921 N Grand Ave). The premium is determined by the value of the car and length of your stay, but there's a $22 minimum. Insurance is available either on the spot or in advance. Sanborn's has a **second office** (☎ 520-281-1865; 850 W Shell Rd; ☑ 8am-5pm Mon-Fri, 8am-3pm Sat & Sun) in the lobby of Holiday Inn Express, conveniently located off exit 4 (Mariposa Rd). See p704 for details.

Southeastern Corner

Cochise County is a land rich with cowboys, Indians, ranchers, miners, gunslingers and all manner of Western lore. It's also an area of rugged, scenic beauty, highlighted by the Huachuca and Chiricahua Mountains.

Rural **Benson** is a quiet travelers' stop with a few motels. The best reason to come here, though, is to visit fantastic **Kartchner Caverns State Park** (☎ 520-586-4100; admission $10; ☑ 7am-6pm), a 2.5-mile-long wet limestone cave, that is touted as one of the world's best 'living' caves. It's 9 miles south of Benson on Hwy 90. Guided **tours** (reservations ☎ 520-586-2283; tours $14) are hugely popular, and advance reservations are required. However, each morning 100 same-day tour tickets are sold, and travelers often wait from before dawn to snag one in the busy winter high season. Camping with full hookups costs – ouch! – $22.

Small and remote **Chiricahua National Monument** (☎ 520-824-3560; admission $5), in the Chiricahua Mountains, offers strangely eroded volcanic geology and abundant wildlife. The **Bonita Canyon Scenic Dr** takes you 8 miles to Massai Point at 6870ft, and there are numerous hiking trails. The monument is 40 miles southeast of Wilcox off Hwy 186.

At 5500ft, in the Huachuca Mountains 10 miles south of **Sierra Vista**, the Nature Conservancy's **Ramsey Canyon Preserve** (☎ 520-378-2640; admission $5; ☑ 8am-5pm) is famous for some 170 bird species, including up to 14 types of hummingbirds.

Tombstone, formerly a rip-roaring, 19th-century silver-mining town, and the site of the famous 1881 shootout at the OK Corral. Now a National Historic Landmark that attracts crowds of tourists with its old Western buildings, stagecoach rides, and gunfight re-enactments, it's hokey, sure, but it's also a fun place to grab a beer in an old saloon. The **Visitor Information Center** (☎ 520-457 3929, 888-457-3929; www.tombstone.org; cnr 4th & Allen Sts) has a lodging list and can get you oriented.

Bisbee

Many buildings in charming Bisbee date from the heyday of the early-20th-century copper-mining boom. The town has more of a Victorian feel to it than any other in Arizona, and an intriguing mix of aging miners, gallery owners, hippies and artists.

Stop by the **chamber of commerce** (☎ 520-432-5421, 866-224-7233; www.bisbeearizona.com; 31 Subway St) for information on local attractions. A big one is the old **Queen Mine** (☎ 520-432-2071), with tours ($13) five times daily.

At funky, one-of-a-kind **Shady Dell RV & Vintage Trailer Park** (☎ 520-432-3567; 1 Douglas Rd; trailers $40-85), at the Lowell traffic circle, you can spend the night in your choice of several restored 1950s Airstreams and other vintage trailers, each decorated with period flair.

SOUTHERN UTAH

With vast expanses of undeveloped mountains, red-rock canyons, lonely deserts and wild rivers, rugged Utah is one of North America's most popular recreation wonderlands. Four-wheel-drive vehicles, loaded with mountain bikes, river rafts or skis, are a common sight almost anywhere you roam here.

Utah has two defining cultures – the ancestral Indians who left petroglyphs and remnants of early dwellings in the rocks, cliffs and canyons, and the proslytetizing Mormons, whose social and political influence reverberates throughout the region. Southern Utah harbors an incredible wealth of national parks and desert wilderness, while the state's northern half is marked by forested mountains, many boasting world-class winter resorts.

AROUND SOUTHEASTERN UTAH

Utah's bottom-right corner contains some of the world's most inhospitable and beautiful terrain in the world. Over millennia, the Colorado, Green and San Juan Rivers have carved a landscape of such sheer-walled majesty and otherworldly desolation that it can challenge one's capacity for wonder.

Every year, millions come to experience this country by foot, horseback, bicycle, car, 4WD, helicopter, raft and other means. You can camp alone in the silent desert or be catered to in exclusive lodges. However you visit, though, remember to tread lightly; millions of footsteps are taking their toll on this deceptively fragile environment.

Moab

Moab is southeastern Utah's outdoor adventure launchpad, with easy access to some of the West's most spectacular parks. The town first gained attention during the 1950s uranium boom; after the boom busted in the 1960s, however, tourists began trickling in, word having spread about the area's striking landscape. It wasn't until mountain biking took off in the mid-1980s that Moab grew to its present size.

Today it's a sprawling but trendy commercial center, home to chic restaurants, art galleries and dozens of adventure companies offering tours and rentals.

INFORMATION

Absolutely unmissable **Moab Information Center** (☎ 435-259-8825, 800-635-6622; www.discovermoab.com; cnr Center & Main Sts) is the place to head with questions about surrounding public lands, parks and forests; they post weather and road conditions and sell books and maps. Tune into community radio station KZMU 89.7/106.1FM for a slice of local insight.

The free, opinionated *Canyon Country Zephyr* newspaper is published six times annually. Look for it at **Back of Beyond** (☎ 435-259-5154, 800-700-2859; 83 N Main St), a smart bookstore. Most businesses are along Hwy 191, also called Main St.

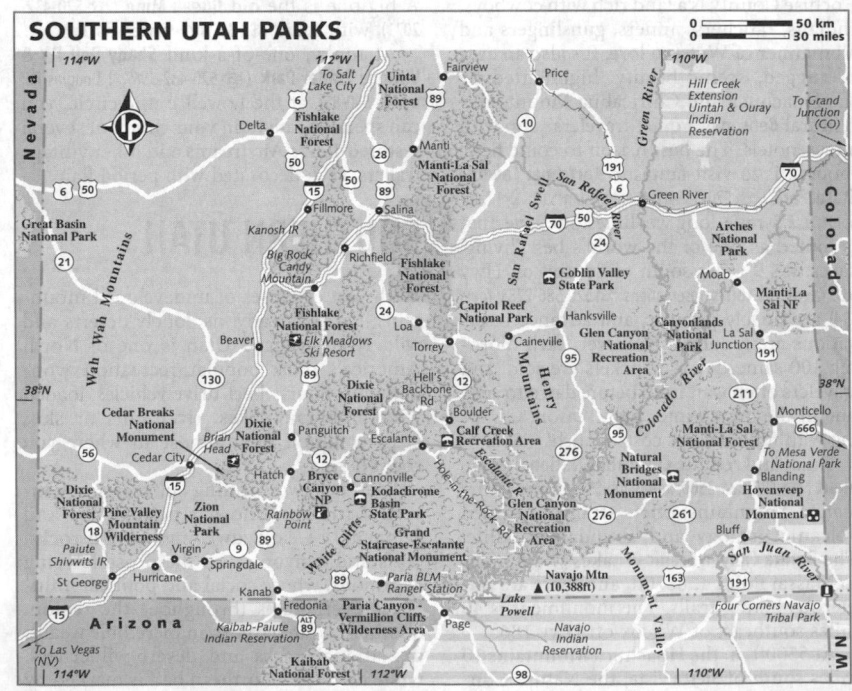

SOUTHERN UTAH PARKS

ACTIVITIES

Trip options range from day-long white-water–rafting trips (from $49) to overnight backpacking trips deep into the wilderness. The Moab Area Travel Council's (www.discovermoab.com/tour.htm) has a long list of rafting, biking, hiking and 4WD outfitters. Reader recommendations include:

Adrift Adventures (☎ 435-259-8594, 800-874-4483; www.adrift.net; 378 N Main St)

Canyon Voyages (☎ 435-259-6007, 800-733-6007; www.canyonvoyages.com; 211 N Main St)

Canyonlands Field Institute (☎ 435-259-7750, 800-860-5262; www.canyonlandsfieldinst.org; 1320 S Hwy 191)

Rim Tours (☎ 435-259-5223, 800-626-7335; www.rimtours.com; 1233 S Hwy 191)

Tex's Riverways (☎ 435-259-5101; www.texsriverways.com; 691 N 500 West)

SLEEPING

Despite a ton of hotels, B&Bs and campgrounds, the town is packed with visitors from spring to fall, and reservations are advised.

Lazy Lizard International Hostel (☎ 435-259-6057; www.lazylizardhostel.com; 1213 S Hwy 191; dm/d/cabin $9/24/29; 🖳) It doesn't get much cheaper – or laid-back – than at this easygoing place south of downtown. There's a kitchen, coin-op laundry, and nonguests can shower for $2. Look for the A-1 storage sign.

Center Street Hotel (☎ 435-259-9431, 800-653-0246; www.moab-utah.com/hotel; 96 E Center St; dm/s/d $13/35/39; ⊠ 🐾 🖳) Moab's most charming hostelry has 10 rooms that are meticulously decorated with vintage furniture, each with its own unique personality. Bathrooms are shared but clean and the ambience is about as friendly as it gets. Check in around the corner at the Kokopelli Lodge.

Apache Motel (☎ 435-259-5727, 800-228-6882; 166 S 400 East St; r $29-99; 🐾 🐕) A bit further from the main drag, this attractive two-story turquoise motel boasts that John Wayne was a regular customer (there's a suite with his name on it to prove it!).

Up The Creek Campground (☎ 435-259-2213, 435-259-6995; www.moab-utah.com/upthecreek; 210 E 300 S; campsite/shower/dog $10/5/2; 😺 Mar-Oct) Right in town, this shady spot is the backpackers' and cyclists' choice, with 20 grassy walk-in, tent-only sites and hot showers for nonguests.

Of course, there's all sorts of camping nearby, too. The visitors center (opposite)

and **BLM** (☎ 435-259-2100; www.blm.gov/utah/moab; 82 E Dogwood St) dish out advice on area campgrounds and showers.

EATING

Peace Tree Juice Cafe (☎ 435-259-8503; 20 S Main St; mains $3-8) A health-conscious bet for fresh smoothies, wraps and sandwiches, with a pleasant alfresco patio.

Breakfast at Tiffany's (☎ 435-259-2553; 90 E Center St; mains $4-7) This homey café has a funky, thrift-shop decor and delicious, creative breakfasts and lunches in the sunny patio/parking lot; service can be slow but the wait is worth it.

Red Rock Bakery & Net Cafe (☎ 435-259-5941; 74 S Main St; mains $3-6; 🖳) Another good am choice where the strong coffee is fair-trade, the pastries and sandwiches delicious. You can enjoy them while surfing the Internet ($6 per hour with purchase).

Eddie McStiff's (☎ 435-259-2337; 57 S Main; mains $6-12; 🖳) A popular microbrewery serving the best pizza in town, along with burgers, salads and a dozen tasty brews on tap. It's lively, at times rowdy, but always friendly; an upstairs 'tavern' allows you to smoke and drink without ordering food.

GETTING THERE & AROUND

Amtrak and Greyhound serve Green River, 53 miles north (p445). Both **Bighorn Express** (☎ 888-655-7433) and **Roadrunner Shuttle** (☎ 435-259-9402) run daily vans to Green River ($26 to $30) and Salt Lake City ($54). Another local bike and rafting shuttle service is **Coyote Shuttle** (☎ 435-259-8656).

Arches National Park

This gem of a **national park** (☎ 435-719-2299; www.nps.gov/arch; admission $10) boasts the greatest concentration of sandstone arches in the world. Of course, that means that Arches, 5 quick miles north of Moab on Hwy 191, is often very crowded. Even so, a visit is always worthwhile. Many of the most spectacular arches are easily reached by paved roads and relatively short hiking trails. Highlights include **Balanced Rock**, the spectacularly elongated **Landscape Arch**, the oft-photographed **Delicate Arch** and popular, twice-daily ranger-led trips into the **Fiery Furnace** (tours $8; reservations recommended). Because of the heat and scarcity of water, few visitors backpack, though it's allowed with free permits. The

---

BACKROADS: DEAD HORSE POINT STATE PARK

Whatever you do, don't miss this tiny **state park** (☎ 435-259-2614; admission $7, camping $14), which has spectacular, sweeping views of southeastern Utah's canyon country – encompassing the Colorado River, Canyonlands National Park and the distant La Sal Mountains. It's just off Hwy 313 (the road to Canyonlands), and it's absolutely worthwhile. If you only have time for one major viewpoint, this is it.

---

scenic, year-round **Devils Garden campground** (☎ 877-444-6777; campsites $10) has 30 reservable sites, plus 22 unreservable sites available after 7:30am.

Want the place to yourself? Try it under moonlight, when the rocks are spooky and the place eerily empty.

Canyonlands National Park

Utah's largest and wildest national park, **Canyonlands** (☎ 435-719-2313; www.nps.gov/cany; admission $10) encompasses 527 sq miles. Indeed, parts of it are as rugged as almost anywhere on the planet. Need proof? Just check the view from Dead Horse Point, and witness canyons tipped with white cliffs tumbling to the river 2000ft below. Arches, bridges, needles, spires, craters, mesas and buttes – Canyonlands is a crumbling, decaying beauty, a vision of ancient earth.

The difficult terrain makes it the Southwest's least developed and least visited major park. You can hike, 4WD and raft (Cataract Canyon offers some of the West's wildest white water), but be sure that you have plenty of gas, food and water before leaving Moab.

The canyons of the Colorado and Green Rivers divide the park into three districts. **Island in the Sky** is most easily reached and offers amazing views. There's also a helpful **visitors center** (☎ 435-259-4712) and some excellent short hikes (the mile-long trail to Grand View Overlook traces the canyon's edge). This section is 32 miles from Moab; head north on Hwy 191 then west on Hwy 313.

The **Needles** is on Rte 211, which heads west from US 191, 40 miles south of Moab; you'll find more great views here and a smaller **visitors center** (☎ 435-259-4711). And then there's the **Maze**, one of Southwest's wildest and most remote areas, accessible only 4WD. In **Horseshoe Canyon**, along the 32-mile-long road from Hwy 24 to the maze, is the Great Gallery, with superb life-size rock art left by prehistoric Indians.

Permits are required for all activities except day trips. **Camping** (campsites $10) is possible at several spectacular locations. Make reservations in writing or by fax (at least two weeks in advance) through the **Canyonlands National Park Reservation Office** (☎ 435-259-4351; fax 435-259-4285; 2282 S West Resource Blvd, Moab, UT 84532-3298). Or you can just show up, though reservations are wise during busy spring and fall periods.

Natural Bridges National Monument

Forty miles west of Blanding via Hwy 95, this **monument** (☎ 435-692-1234; www.nps.gov/nabr; admission $6; ⊙ 7am-sunset) became Utah's first NPS land in 1908. The highlight is a dark-stained, white sandstone canyon containing three easily accessible natural bridges. The oldest, the Owachomo Bridge, spans 180ft but is only 9ft thick. Basic developed **camping** (campsites $10) is available and there are free overflow sites four miles outside the park entrance off Bears Ears Rd.

Hovenweep National Monument

Beautiful, little-visited **Hovenweep** (☎ 970-560-4282; www.nps.gov/hove; admission $6), meaning 'deserted valley' in the Ute language, contains six sets of prehistoric ancestral Puebloan Indian sites, five of which require long hikes to reach them. There is a visitors center, ranger station and basic **campground** (campsites $10), but no facilities. The main access is east of Hwy 191 on Hwy 262 via Hatch Trading Post, 40 miles from Bluff or Blanding.

Bluff

Surrounded by red rock along the San Juan River, a couple of hours south of Moab, tiny Bluff is an ideal, sleepy basecamp for exploring the Four Corners region. **Wild Rivers Expeditions** (☎ 435-672-2200/44, 800-422-7654; www.riversandruins.com; 101 Main St) has been guiding educational river trips since 1957, and have day trips for $125. **Far Out Expeditions** (☎ /fax 435-672-2294; www.faroutexpeditions.com) organizes off-the-beaten-track trips to Monument Valley ($105) among others; ask about their cookouts and stylin' bunkhouse.

Bluff has a good selection of lodgings – from budget places to B&Bs. Besides the **BLM Sand Island campground** (campsites $10), 3 miles north of town at the river put-in, is the best budget option: the hospitable **Recapture Lodge** (☎ 435-672-2281; www.bluffutah.org/recapturelodge; Hwy 191; s $38-46, d $52-60; 🕹 🔊), a rustic property pleasantly shaded behind trees between the highway and the San Juan River.

The Four Corner's best gourmet splurge is the fun-loving **Cow Canyon Trading Post & Restaurant** (☎ 435-672-2208; cnr Hwys 163 & 191; mains $8-16; 🕑 Thu-Mon 6-9pm April Fools–Halloween), with a seasonal dinner menu featuring local ingredients, including homegrown herbs and veggie options. The year-round trading post has a great regional book selection.

Monument Valley

From the village of **Mexican Hat** – your last chance to buy beer – Hwy 163 winds southwest and enters the Navajo Indian Reservation and, after about 30 miles, Monument Valley Navajo Tribal Park (p436). Just inside the Utah border, **Goulding's Lodge** (☎ 435-727-3231; www.gouldings.com; r $68-160; 🕹 🔲 🔊) is the only hostelry near Monument Valley; each room has a balcony with a million-dollar view of the colossal red buttes. Goulding's also has a free museum, a store, gas and a year-round **campground** (campsites for 2 $16), which includes hot showers and use of the indoor heated pool (mid-March to October).

Green River

The 'world's watermelon capital' is a good base for river running on the Green and Colorado Rivers, or exploring the nearby San Rafael Swell.

The **Green River Information Center** (☎ 435-564-3526; 885 E Main St) is inside the worthwhile **John Wesley Powell Museum** (☎ 435-564-3427; admission $2), which has exhibits on the history of river running. **Moki Mac River Expeditions** (☎ 800-284-7280) and **Holiday River Expeditions** (☎ 435-564-3273) organize trips.

For basic but big rooms try the **Book Cliff Lodge** (☎ 435-564-3406, 800-493-4699; www.beattie1 .com/bookclifflodge; 365 E Main St; r from $35; 🕹 🔊). River hang at **Ray's Tavern** (☎ 435-564-3511; 25 S Broadway; mains $6-15), which serves microbrews and great hamburgers and steaks.

Greyhound stops at the West Winds Truck Stop on its way to Salt Lake City.

Amtrak carries passengers to Salt Lake City and Denver.

SOUTH-CENTRAL & SOUTHWESTERN UTAH

This section is organized roughly northeast to southwest: from Hanksville, along Hwy 24 through Capitol Reef National Park and southwest along **Hwy 12**, which passes the Grand Staircase–Escalante National Monument and Bryce Canyon and is one of USA's most scenic byways. From Hwy 12, US 89 goes south to Kanab (and continues to the North Rim of the Grand Canyon). Further west are Cedar City and St George and the gorgeous Zion National Park.

Hanksville

A couple of cheap motels and RV park/campgrounds dot this convenient pitstop at the junction of Hwys 95 and 24. The **BLM** (☎ 435-542-3461; 406 S 100 West) has information on the **Henry Mountains**, a remote, 11,000ft-high range. North along Hwy 24 is **Goblin Valley State Park** (☎ 435-564-3633; admission $5), full of delightful, alien hoodoo rock formations and a **campground** (campsites $14).

SCENIC DRIVE: MOKI DUGWAY & MULE POINT

The **Moki Dugway** (Hwy 261) heads 32 miles south from Hwy 95 to connect with Hwy 163 at Mexican Hat. Along the way is a turnoff to **Mule Point Overlook** – don't miss this cliff-edge viewpoint as it's one of the country's most sweeping and spectacular.

Back on Hwy 261, the pavement ends and the Moki Dugway suddenly descends a whopping 1100ft along a series of fist-clenching hairpin turns. At the bottom, a dirt road heads east into the **Valley of the Gods**, a 17-mile drive through monoliths of sandstone; again, it's mind-blowing scenery. Near the southern end of Hwy 261, a 4-mile paved road heads west to **Goosenecks State Park**, a small lookout with memorable views of the San Juan River, 1000ft below. Free, undeveloped camping is possible, but its windy and exposed.

About 20 miles west near Caineville, watch for **Luna Mesa Oasis** (☎ 435-456-9122; mains $5-15), a friendly spot to camp and grab a bite or a drink.

Capitol Reef National Park

Less crowded than Utah's other national parks, but equally scenic, Capitol Reef contains much of the 100-mile **Waterpocket Fold**, created 65 million years ago when the earth's surface buckled up and folded, exposing a cross-section of geological history that is almost painterly in its intensity of color. Hwy 24 through here is full of grand scenery, but a worthwhile diversion is the park's own scenic drive ($5), starting from the **visitors center** (☎ 435-425-3791; www.nps.gov/care); there's also a grassy, basic **campground** (campsites $10) and orchards for fruit picking in the summer. Backcountry camping is free with a permit, but this is a desert wilderness, so be prepared.

Torrey

This sleepy village, at the junction of Hwys 12 and 24, is a good stopover for lodging and meals. Most businesses, including the **Capital Reef Country Visitors Center** (☎ 435-425-3365, 800-858-7951; www.capitolreef.org; cnr Hwys 12 & 24) and ones listed in the following sections, close for the long winter.

Capitol Reef Inn & Café (☎ 435-425-3271; www.capitolreefinn.com; 360 W Main; s/d $44/48; mains $6-15; ▣) This inviting place has simple rooms, a hot tub and home-cooked meals, including splurge-worthy shish kebabs and vegetarian dishes.

Rim Rock Inn (☎ 435-425-3388, 888-447-4676; www.therimrock.com; r $49-79; mains $12-24; ▣) A couple miles east along Hwy 24, Rim Rock Inn has rooms with stellar views and a highly regarded restaurant serving gourmet comfort food.

Boulder

Tiny Boulder is 32 miles south of Torrey on Hwy 12. From here, the attractive **Burr Trail** heads east as a paved road across the northeastern corner of the Grand Staircase-Escalante National Monument, winding up at Bullfrog Marina on Lake Powell. If you're interested in exploring the park, definitely stop by one of the visitors centers listed here for advice and outfitter suggestions.

Next door to Boulder Mountain Lodge, **Hell's Backbone Grill** (☎ 435-335-7464; 20 N Hwy 12; breakfast $5-9) serves an amazing breakfast and elegantly prepared regional 'slow food.' Bunk down at the friendly **Hills & Hollows** (☎ 435-335-7349; 840 W Hwy 12; s/d $23/25) Conoco/C-store, which also stocks natural foods.

Escalante

Escalante Interagency Office (☎ 435-826-5499; www.ut.blm.gov/monument; 755 W Main St; ☾ Mar-Oct) is a superb resource with the scoop on all nearby public lands. Fifteen miles east on Hwy 12, **Calf Creek Recreation Area** (☎ 435-826-5499; day use/campsites $2/7) has a nice basic campground and a recommended 3-mile hike to Lower Calf Creek Falls.

Escalante Outfitters (☎ 435-826-4266; 310 W Main St; campsites/cabins $14/35; pizzas from $10; ▣) is a travelers' oasis, with maps, books, camping supplies, liquor, espresso and the state's best homemade pizza. Overnighters stay in cute, clean and cozy nonsmoking cabins with shared bath, or in the grassy campground out back.

Grand Staircase–Escalante National Monument

This 2656-sq-mile monument, established in 1996, fits in between Bryce, Capitol Reef and Glen Canyon. Infrastructure is still minimal, leaving a vast, remote desert for adventurous travelers who have the time and necessary equipment to explore.

Three unpaved roads – the Skutumpah/Johnson Canyon Rd (the least used, most westerly route), Cottonwood Canyon Rd and Smoky Mountain Rd – cross the monument roughly north–south between Hwys 12 and 89. A fourth unpaved road (the Hole-in-the-Rock Rd) begins from Hwy 12 and dead-ends at the Glen Canyon National Recreation Area. Roads get slick and impassable when wet. Wilderness camping is allowed with a permit. Before any excursions, obtain current road and travel information from the Escalante Interagency Office, or from Kanab Visitors Center (opposite), Big Water or **Cannonville** (☎ 435-679-8981; ☾ Mar-Nov).

Kodachrome Basin State Park

Dozens of red, pink and white sandstone chimneys highlight this colorful **state park** (☎ 435-679-8562; admission $5). There's a year-round **campground** (☎ 800-322-3770; campsites $14) and **cabins** (☎ 435-679-8536; www.brycecanyoninn.com; d $65) are available in summer.

Bryce Canyon National Park

The Grand Staircase, a series of steplike up-lifted rock layers stretching north from the Grand Canyon, culminates at this popular **park** (☎ 435-834-5322; www.nps.gov/brca; individual/car $10/20) in the **Pink Cliffs** formation, full of wondrous pinnacles and points, steeples, spires, and hoodoos. The 'canyon' is actually an amphitheater eroded from the cliffs.

From Hwy 12, Hwy 63 heads south for 4 miles to Rim Rd Dr (8000ft), an 18-mile dead-end road that follows the rim of the canyon, passing the visitors center, lodge, viewpoints (don't miss Inspiration Point) and trailheads, ending at Rainbow Point (9115ft). You can whisk in and out in a few hours, but for a richer experience, numerous trails wend among the spires and deeper into the heart of the landscape. In summer, there's a free (voluntary) shuttle system from Hwy 12.

Rangers lead new- and full-moon star-gazing evenings in summer. The park's a lovely sight in winter, too, and certain trails are open for snowshoeing and cross-country skiing.

The park's two **campgrounds** (campsites $10) fill by noon in summer. With a permit ($5), you can camp below the rim at 10 designated backcountry sites. There's a decent, if overpriced, restaurant at historic **Bryce Canyon Lodge** (☽ Apr-Oct), but you're best off bringing in your own rations.

One mile north of the park entrance on Hwy 63, **Ruby's Inn & Campground** (☎ 435-834-5341, 800-468-8660; www.rubysinn.com; tent/teepee/cabin $16/24/42; ☒) is a huge, 'western' complex with just about every service, including foreign currency exchange, a heated pool, hot tub, coin laundry and showers.

A couple of standard motels sit near the junction of Hwys 63 and 12, including **Bryce View Lodge** (☎ 435-834-5180; www.bryceviewlodge.com; 991 S Highway 63; r $47-66; ☒ ☒). Cheaper motels are in **Tropic**, 8 miles east along Hwy 12.

Kanab & Around

Surrounded by desert wilderness, Kanab was an isolated Mormon community until the advent of roads. In the 1930s, Hollywood 'discovered' the area and paved roads now lead to the area's famous national parks: Zion (40 miles), Bryce Canyon (80 miles), the north rim of the Grand Canyon (80 miles) and Glen Canyon National Recreation Area (74 miles). Hwy 89 has a good selection of motels and restaurants, making it a popular travelers' stopover.

The Grand Staircase-Escalante National Monument's **Kanab Visitors Center** (☎ 435-644-4680; 745 E Hwy 89) has information on the monument (p446). The county **visitors center** (☎ 435-644-5033; www.kaneutah.com; 78 S 100 East) and **BLM** (☎ 435-644-4600; 318 N 100 East) have further details.

Reservations are recommended at the **USA Hostels Grand Canyon** (☎ 435-644-5554, 877-205-7136; www.usahostels.com; 143 E 100 S; dm/d $15/32; ☒), where there's only one private room and the dorms are segregated (by sex, silly) and have their own bathrooms. They run frequent shuttles to Las Vegas in summer. Otherwise, there are several budget motels from the low $40s.

Less than an hour's drive northeast of Zion on the I 15, **Cedar City** is a natural pitstop. For area information, chat up the **Iron County Tourism Bureau** (☎ 435-586-5124; www.scenicsouthernutah.com; 585 N Main St). From June to September, the nationally renowned **Shakespearean Festival** (☎ 800-752-8499; www.bard.org) keeps the town buzzing.

For basic digs, **Cedar Rest Motel** (☎ 435-586-9471; 479 S Main St; r $45; ☒) is a clean cut above your average motor lodge.

Many folks pass through **Springdale** on their way to Zion National Park, since its on Hwy 9 just outside the park's southern entrance. It's a pleasant, relaxed community, catering mostly to park visitors; the **visitors bureau** (☎ 888-518-7070; www.zionpark.com) can answer questions and has a helpful website.

Springdale also has an abundance of good restaurants and charming lodging options. Try friendly **Terrace Brook Lodge** (☎ 435-772-3932; r $49; ☒ ☒). **Zion Pizza & Noodle** (☎ 435-772-3815; 868 Zion Park Blvd; mains $8-14), set inside a 1930s Mormon church, has a large selection of microbrews, nice beer garden and, as the name implies, plenty of carb-loaded dishes. The **Bit & Spur Restaurant & Saloon** (☎ 435-772-3498; 1212 Zion Park Blvd) has a lively bar.

Zion National Park

The white, pink and red rocks of **Zion National Park** (☎ 435-772-3256; www.nps.gov/zion; car/individual admission $20/10) are huge, overpowering and magnificent – you're guaranteed to be awed upon your first glimpse. For most visitors, the main attraction is the 6-mile drive into

Zion Canyon, a half-mile-deep slash formed by the Virgin River. Because it's so popular, the park now shuts the road to cars each summer (April to October) and runs a free shuttle bus.

This has resulted in a much quieter park, but it's still very crowded. To find some solitude, come in late spring or fall (the weather's better, too), or escape by taking a hike into the spectacular backcountry.

The most popular road into the park is the Zion–Mt Carmel Hwy (Hwy 9). From the south entrance at Springdale, the road leads to Zion Canyon, then climbs hairpin turns to meet a very narrow tunnel. East of the tunnel is dramatic, colorful slickrock country.

The **Zion Canyon Visitors Center** (8am-6pm) and **Human History Museum** (8am-5pm) are near the south entrance. Park in the lot near the visitors center for the shuttle bus, which comes every 10 minutes during summer. One bus loops north into Zion Canyon; the other heads south into Springdale (where there are further lots to leave your car, often a better bet).

It costs nothing to enter the park along Kolob Terrace Rd (closed from November to May), which leaves Hwy 9 at the village of Virgin and climbs more than 4000ft to Lava Point.

However, there are no facilities, only a ranger station and primitive campground.

At the park's northwestern corner (I-15 exit 40), you can enter via Kolob Canyons Rd (per car $10), which leads to the much smaller **Kolob Canyons Visitors Center** (435-586-9548) and wonderful views and hikes.

More than 100 miles of trails offer everything from leisurely strolls to wilderness camping.

The most well-known backpacking trip is through the **Narrows**, a 16-mile journey through dramatic canyons along the Virgin River (June to September). Overnight permits ($5) from the visitors centers are issued only on the day of or the day before your hike.

At the south gate, two shady **campgrounds** (reservations 800-365-2267; campsites $14) have 300 first-come, first-served sites, but come early.

In the canyon, the upscale **Zion Lodge** has a café and restaurant, but thrifty travelers will want to bring their own mess kit.

NORTHERN UTAH

Utah gets its name from the nomadic Ute people who, along with the Paiute and Shoshone, inhabited the Great Basin desert over 8000 years ago. Europeans arrived as early as 1776; led by Brigham Young, the Mormons fled religious persecution to Utah, establishing Salt Lake City on July 24, 1847. After the US acquired the Utah Territory from Mexico, the Mormons petitioned Congress for statehood six times. Their petitions were consistently rejected because of Mormon polygamy (the practice of having more than one spouse at the same time), which was outlawed by the US government. Tensions grew between the Mormons and the federal government until 1890, when Mormon Church President Wilford Woodruff announced that God had told him that Mormons should abide by US law. Polygamy ceased, and soon after Utah became the 45th state in 1896. Today, Mormons are in the majority in Utah and continue to exert a powerful conservative influence on the state.

SALT LAKE CITY

Much-maligned Salt Lake (aka SLC) is the headquarters of the LDS (Mormon) Church. The church's presence is certainly felt – most notably in the state's archaic drinking laws – but the bohemian backlash against all the up-tightness means there's a vibrant underground arts and culture scene. It's also a key regional transport hub and a beautiful, outdoorsy place set spectacularly at the foot of the towering Wasatch Mountains, at the gateway to endless summer recreation and world-class skiing and winter snow play. Impressive winter sports parks built for the 2002 Winter Olympics are scattered throughout the region.

Orientation

Salt Lake City's international airport, with frequent regional connections and Delta as the major carrier, is the region's third most important after Phoenix and Las Vegas. Buses network the main thoroughfares and an Amtrak route traverses the state, but, as elsewhere in the Southwest, private transport is essential for reaching many of the highpoints.

THE MORMONS

The members of the Church of Jesus Christ of Latter-Day Saints (LDS; www.lds.org) – or Mormons – prize family above all else, and Mormon families tend to be huge. Hard work and strict obedience to church leaders are very important. Smoking, alcohol, and caffeine are forbidden. Women are forbidden to take leadership roles, as were African-Americans until 1978. The faith considers missionary service important, and most young men are sent overseas on missions to push the faith. There are now more than 11 million Mormons worldwide.

Sorting out street names in Utah takes a little getting used to. Salt Lake City is laid out in a grid, with major streets aligned north–south and east–west and assigned numbers. It's a little confusing, yes, but once you get the hang of it, you'll always know, more or less, where you are. The city's zero point is Temple Square. North Temple is a busy, utilitarian road running west from downtown to the airport. State St (which takes the place of 100 East) is a busy north–south route. The main artery east from downtown to the university is 400 South. Ski resorts are east of town in the Wasatch Mountains.

Information

BOOKSTORES
Sam Weller's Zion Bookstore (☎ 801-328-2586, 800-333-7269; 254 S Main St; ◷ Mon-Sat)
Huge independent downtown shop, with new and used maps and guidebooks.

EMERGENCY
Police Department (☎ 801-799-3000; 315 E 200 South)

INTERNET ACCESS
Main library (☎ 801-524-8200; 210 E 400 South; ◷ 9am-9pm Mon-Thu, 9am-6pm Fri & Sat, 1-5pm Sun)
Free wi fi and Internet access, comfy chairs and fireplaces. Nice view from sunny rooftop gardens.

MEDIA
City Weekly (www.slweekly.com) Free alternative weekly with good restaurant and club listings; publishes the free, useful City Guide.

MEDICAL SERVICES
Salt Lake Regional Medical Center
(☎ 801-350-4111; 1050 E South Temple)

MONEY
Wells Fargo (☎ 801-246-2677; 79 S Main St; ◷ 9am-4:30pm Mon-Fri) Exchanges foreign currency, which is tough to do elsewhere in UT.

POST
Downtown Station (☎ 801 532-2906; 230 W 200 South)

TOURIST OFFICES
Gay & Lesbian Community Center of Utah
(☎ 801-539-8800, 888-874-2743; www.glccu.com; 355 N 300 West) Has bar and club listings.
Public Lands Information Center (☎ 801-466-6411; 3285 E 3300 South; ◷ 10:30am-7pm Tue-Sat)
Multi-agency information desk inside REI.
Utah Travel Council Information Center
(☎ 801-538-1030, 800-200-1160; www.utah.com; 300 N State St) Statewide information center, in Council Hall on Capitol Hill, with a large selection of guidebooks and maps.
Utah State Parks Office (☎ 801-538-7220, 800-322-3770; www.stateparks.utah.gov; 1594 W North Temple) Good free map, camping reservations.
Visitor Information Center (☎ 801-521-2822, 800-541-4955; www.visitsaltlake.com; 90 S West Temple St) In the Salt Palace Convention Center.

Sights
Enclosed by 15ft-high walls at the center of town, **Temple Square** (☎ 801-240-2534; www.lds.org; ◷ 9am-9pm) features 19th-century Mormon buildings, history exhibits and the towering **Salt Lake Temple**. LDS docents give free 30-minute tours; meet at the flagpoles in front of the **Tabernacle**. The famous **Mormon Tabernacle Choir** performs Sunday mornings (get there by 9am) and rehearses on Thursday evenings at 8pm. Adjoining Temple Sq, the **Museum of Church History and Art** (☎ 801-240-3310; 45 N West Temple St; admission free) has exhibits of pioneer history. Perhaps the most interesting thing to do here is research genealogy for free at the ▮▮▮▮rial Building (☎ 801-240-3400; ◷ 9am-9pm Mon-Fri, 9am-5pm Sat,

There are many Daughte▮ neers (DUP) museums in th▮ free **Pioneer Memorial Museum**

A▮
alta.co.
past Snow.

TOP FIVE UTAH WINTER RESORTS

It's no brag when Utah boasts that it has some of the greatest snow on earth. And up to 500 inches of powder falls on the western side of the Wasatch Front every year.

■ **Snowbird** (www.snowbird.com) Snowboarders rule at northern Utah's highest resort, with a 7760ft base elevation.

■ **Alta** (www.alta.com) The SLC local skiers' choice, with cheap lift tickets, a laid-back vibe and snowboarding ban.

■ **Park City** (www.parkcitymountain.com) The Olympic giant slalom and snowboarding site is the perfect all-round choice with short lines.

■ **Canyons** (www.thecanyons.com) Utah's largest resort has room for everyone and a killer snowboarding half-pipe park.

■ **Sundance** (www.sundanceresort.com) The wide variety of terrain makes Robert Redford's upscale getaway worth a splurge.

300 N Main St; 9am-5pm Mon-Sat), a vast treasure trove of pioneer artifacts, is the best. The walls of the impressive **Utah State Capitol** (☎ 801-538-1563; 8am-8pm), just north of Temple Sq, are covered with historical murals.

The site of the 2002 Olympic Village, the **University of Utah** (☎ 801-581-7200; www.utah.edu) has several free museums, including the **Utah Museum of Fine Arts** (☎ 801-581-7332; 410 Campus Center Dr; 10am-5pm Mon-Fri, noon-5pm Sat & Sun).

Activities

Millcreek, Big Cottonwood and Little Cottonwood canyons, all on the west side of the Wasatch Mountains and within easy reach of Salt Lake City, offer abundant opportunities for hiking, mountain biking, camping and cross-country skiing. Inside **REI** (☎ 801-486-2100; 3285 E 3300 South), the friendly **Public Lands Information Center** (p449) is a great place to get tips on exploring the area. Full-suspension mountain bike rentals run around $30 a day at **Wasatch Touring** (☎ 801-359-9361; 702 E 100 South) and **Guthrie Bicycle** (☎ 801-363-3727; 156 E 200 South).

Within 40 minutes of Salt Lake City are four world-class ski resorts in Little Cottonwood and Big Cottonwood Canyons, famous for getting some 500 powdery inches each year. There are plenty of accommodations at the resorts, but easy public transport makes it convenient and cheaper to stay in SLC. For a free *Winter Vacation Planner* contact **Ski Utah** (www.skiutah.com). Resorts nearby SLC are:

Ski Area (☎ 801-742-3333, 888-782-9258; www ; full/half-day $42/33) The skier's choice, 2 miles bird, with no snowboards.

Brighton Ski Area (☎ 801-532-4731; www.ski brighton.com; day pass $40) Snowboard half-pipe and night skiing.

Snowbird Ski Area (☎ 801-742-2222, 800-232-9542; www.snowbird.com; day pass $56) Epic snowboarding 25 miles east of town.

Solitude Ski Area (☎ 801-534-1400; www.skisolitude .com; day pass $44) Snowboard-friendly, with 1200 skiable acres, 50% intermediate.

Sleeping

The cheapest independent motels ($25 to $35) are along W North Temple St between the airport and downtown and along State St south of 1700 S, though they can be grungy. Chain hotels and motels cluster on W North Temple St near the airport; others are along S 200 West near 500 South and 600 South. Both summer and winter are high seasons; during late spring and fall prices may be a bit lower.

Ute Hostel (☎ 801-595-1645; www.infobytes.com/ utehostel; 21 E Kelsey Ave; dm/d $15/35;) South of downtown, clustered among some attractive craftsman houses, this basic but friendly hostel is homier than the Avenues.

There's no curfew or lockout and free pickups from the airport, bus and train station.

HI The Avenues (☎ 801-359-3855; 107 F St; dm/s/d $17/ 26/36;) A no-frills place in a big brick building on a pleasant, tree-lined street in a residential neighborhood. No curfew, no lockout.

USFS campgrounds (☎ 801-524-3900, 877-444-6777; campsites $14) Four basic, summer-only public campgrounds can be found in Big

Cottonwood and Little Cottonwood canyons, in the Wasatch Mountains.

Skyline Inn (☎ 801-582-5350; www.skylineinn.com; 2475 E 1700 South; s $49, d $54-69; ❂ 💻 ❂) South of the university on a hill overlooking downtown, this modest, well-maintained hotel is a great choice for those who prefer sleeping away from the city center. It also works well for skiers who don't want the expense of a slopeside hotel, as it affords easy access to Big and Little Cottonwood Canyons.

There's a year-round pool and hot tub, and some rooms have jetted tubs.

City Creek Inn (☎ 801-533-9100, 866-533-4898; www.citycreekinn.com; 230 W North Temple St; s/d $48/58; ❂) One of the best downtown budget choices, this family-owned property is simple but attractive and within walking distance of Temple Sq.

Travelodge Temple Square (☎ 801-533-8200; 144 W North Temple; r $50-75; ❂) It's nothing special but is right downtown.

Eating & Drinking

The food scene here is varied, with a huge assortment of ethnic eateries. Pick up a *City Weekly* for more reviews.

Sage's Cafe (☎ 801-322-3790; 473 E 300 South; mains $6-10; ❂ Wed-Sun) Everything is made in-house, mostly organic and entirely vegan at this comfortable restaurant, where dinner items include fajitas, pesto and wild mushroom stroganoff. Brunch is available on weekends. Beer and wine are served, as is house-made root beer and ginger ale.

Red Iguana (☎ 801-322-1489; 736 W North Temple; mains $7-12) Savvy locals head here for unpretentious Mexican grub. Try a smothered burrito, or one of the rich mole dishes, then forget about eating for the rest of the day.

Salt Lake Roasting Company (☎ 801-363-7572; 320 E 400 South; mains $3-9; ❂ Mon-Sat) The house-roasted beans are strong and flavorful here and salads, sandwiches and good pastries are served. The open, two-story space allows plenty of room to think. There's an off-shoot café in the main library.

Cafe Trang (☎ 801-539-1638; 818 S Main St; mains $6-12) A well-regarded Vietnamese place with extensive veggie options.

Squatter's Pub Brewery (☎ 801-363-2739; 147 W Broadway; pub grub $7-10) Great microbrews – try the smooth Vienna Lager or the lighter St Provo Girl.

Red Rock Brewing Company (☎ 801-521-7446; 254 S 200 West) Around the corner from Squatter's, this place is more polished and has a bigger menu.

Port O' Call (☎ 801-521-0589; 78 W 400 South; no cover Sun-Thu) If it's liquor you're after, Port O' Call is a full-service bar that spreads across four floors in a cool 1912 building. It's quiet during the day, but at night crowds pack in for burgers, DJs and bands.

Entertainment

Lift a copy of the free edgy monthly *SLUG* (www.slugmag.com) zine for insight into the diverse, rebellious SLC underground.

The Wasatch Front has an active GLBT scene; a good place to get plugged in is at the Stonewall Coffee Co at the Gay and Lesbian Community Center of Utah (p449).

LIVE MUSIC

Cup of Joe (☎ 801-363-8322; 353 W 200 South; 💻) A cool, artsy coffeehouse in an old brick warehouse that hosts acoustic music and Saturday poetry slams.

Good live-music venues include **Bricks/ Club Sound** (☎ 801-328-0255; 579 W 200 South), a

---

DRINKING IN UTAH

Can you get a drink in Utah? Absolutely, if you're over 21 and have ID. If you're hankering for a cocktail, head for one of the state's so-called 'private clubs,' and become a temporary 'member.' It costs $5 for two weeks and entitles you to bring up to five guests. You can also get 'sponsored' by another member; don't worry, it's common practice, and doormen are happy to help out.

Private clubs are full bars and they stop serving nightly at 1am. Restaurants serve wine, beer or liquor with food. 'Taverns' only sell low-alcohol (3.2%) beer. This same 'near beer' can be purchased at grocery and convenience stores, while wine and hard booze can only be purchased at state liquor stores.

Since the state has a huge range of drinking establishments – and no shortage of folks to keep the stools warm – for the most part, you won't even notice these laws.

gay-friendly place with 18-plus nights, and **Liquid Joe's** (☎ 801-467-5637; 1249 E 3300 South), with shows Wednesday through Saturday.

SPORTS

The men's professional basketball team, the **Utah Jazz**, and the women's professional basketball team, the **Utah Starzz**, play at the **Delta Center** (301 W South Temple St). The International Hockey League's **Utah Grizzlies** (☎ 801-988-7825) face off at the **E Center** (☎ 801-988-8888) in West Valley City.

Getting There & Around

Salt Lake City International Airport (SLC; ☎ 801-575-2400; www.slcairport.com) is 6 miles west of downtown. Numerous door-to-door shuttle vans and **Yellow Cab** (☎ 801-521-2100) serve downtown (fares $10 to $15). UTA runs an airport bus every 30 minutes. Call the airport's **transportation desk** (☎ 801-575-2477) for schedules.

Greyhound (☎ 801-355-9579; 160 W South Temple St) has several buses a day heading south to Las Vegas, Nevada ($53, eight to nine hours); west to San Francisco, California ($79, 16 hours); east to Denver, Colorado ($55, 13 hours); and north to Seattle, Washington ($97, 21 to 24 hours).

UTA (☎ 801-743-3882, 888-743-3882; single/day tickets $1.35/2.70) buses serve Salt Lake City and the Wasatch Front area until midnight (limited service on Sundays). During ski season they serve the four local ski areas ($2.50). The TRAX light-rail system runs east from the Delta Center to the university; the center of downtown Salt Lake is a free-fare zone.

National car rental agencies have offices at the airport and around town.

Amtrak's *California Zephyr* stops daily at the **Rio Grande Depot** (☎ 801-322-3510; 340 S 600 West) going east to Chicago ($136 to $199, 35 hours) and west to Oakland, California ($79 to $135, 18 hours).

WASATCH FRONT & NORTHERN UTAH

Salt Lake City, Ogden and Provo rump up against the Wasatch Front. The mountains are home to 11 ski resorts within 55 miles of Salt Lake City, and offer abundant hiking, camping, fly-fishing and mountain biking.

Ogden

After the completion of the first transcontinental railway in 1869, Ogden became an important railway town. Today its restored, mid-19th-century downtown is a major draw. During its heyday, historic 25th St between Union Station and Grant Ave was lined with brothels and raucous saloons; now it has the city's nicest selection of restaurants and bars. Ogden lies about 38 miles north of Salt Lake City.

The restored **Union Station** contains the **visitors center** (☎ 801-627-8288, 866-867-8824; www.ogdencvb.org; 25th St & Wall Ave); it's also home to several worthy **museums** (☎ 801-629-8535; adult $4; ⏲ 10am-5pm Mon-Sat) covering vintage trains, firearms, cars and more. Also in Union Station is the **National Forest Information Center** (☎ 385-625-5306), with maps and information on area hiking, biking and kayaking on the Ogden and Weber Rivers.

At the north end of town, the **Millstream Motel** (☎ 801-394-9425; 1450 Washington Blvd; r $30-40; ⊠) has a classic car museum and retains the flavor of its 1940s heyday.

SKIING

The steep-walled **Ogden Canyon** heads 40 miles northeast through the Wasatch Mountains to Monte Cristo Summit (9148ft), passing the following resorts:

Nordic Valley Ski Area (☎ 801-392-0900; day pass $20) Tiny 85-acre resort with the state's cheapest skiing.

Snowbasin Ski Area (☎ 801-620-1000, 888-437-5488; www.snowbasin.com; day pass $52) 3200 acres, hosted downhill and super-G Olympic events.

Powder Mountain Ski Area (☎ 801-745-3722; www.powdermountain.net; day pass $39) Appropriately named.

Park City

About 30 miles east from Salt Lake City via I-80, Park City (elevation 6900ft) is the Southwest's largest ski town and a hive of summer outdoor activity. A silver-mining community during the 19th century, its attractive Main St is remarkably well-preserved and lined with galleries, shops, hotels, restaurants and bars. And despite the sea of pre-fab housing that has spread across the valley, the town remains relatively charming.

Park City is also famous for hosting the **Sundance Film Festival** (☎ 801-328-3456; www.sundance.org) every January, which brings independent films and their makers, stars and fans to Park City for two weeks.

Get local info from the **Visitor Information Center** (☎ 435-658-4541; www.parkcityinfo.com;

750 Kearns Blvd) or the free **Park City Historic Museum** (☎ 435-649-6104; 538 Main St; ☼ 9am-7pm Mon-Sat, noon-6pm Sun).

The **public library** (1255 Park Ave) has free Internet access.

ACTIVITIES

Park City is home to three of Utah's preeminent winter resorts. A chairlift in town can take you to **Park City Mountain Resort** (☎ 435-649-8111; www.parkcitymountain.com; adult lift ticket $45), which hosted the Olympic giant slalom and snowboarding events. The **Canyons** (☎ 435-649-5400; www.thecanyons.com; adult lift ticket $62) is Utah's largest resort. All host **summer activities** as well, including mountain biking and hiking via chairlift, gondola rides at the Canyons ($12) and, at Park City Resort, the ZipRider ($15).

The **Utah Olympic Park** (☎ 435-658-4200; www .utaholympicpark.com; adult $8), on Hwy 224 outside Park City, has tours of the facilities and, if you're lucky, you can watch the pros practice (call for rates, schedules and reservations). Daring souls with deep pockets can test their nerve by **bobsledding** (☎ 435-658-4206; summer/winter $65/200), or take classes in **ski jumping** and **luge riding**.

SLEEPING

While winter rates quoted here are sky-high, prices drop in summer. Some places may also have minimum stay requirements. Park Ave runs parallel to Main St and has a rugged western feel; there are several interesting lodging choices in restored buildings here.

Park City Base Camp (☎ 435-655-7244; 888-980-7244; www.parkcitybasecamp.com; 1299 Norfolk Ave; dm $25-50, r $85-105; ☐) Modern facilities, with a big kitchen and four-bed dorms, some of which are coed. It's a very social place in-season.

Chateau Après Lodge (☎ 435-649-9372, 800-357-3556; www.chateauapres.com; 1299 Norfolk Ave; dm/r $30/85; ☒) Near the ski lifts, this longstanding lodge is popular with budget travelers as rates (including a basic breakfast) are among the area's most reasonable. Rooms are basic and sleep from one to four people.

Edelweiss Haus (☎ 435-649-9342, 800-245-6417; www.pclodge.com; 1482 Empire Ave; summer/winter r from $59/70; ☒) This modern condo complex offers standard hotel rooms as well as one- and two-bedroom apartments.

EATING

Morning Ray Café & Bakery (☎ 435-649-5686; 255 Main St; mains $3-9) Open at 7am and closing late, this place is hugely popular for its New York–style bagels, omelets and sandwiches.

Alpine Internet Coffeehouse (☎ 435-649-0051; 738 Main St; mains under $5; ☐) The coffee and pastries are good and the T1 internet access is spendy (per hour $10).

Wasatch Brew Pub (☎ 435-649-0900; 250 Main St; mains $6-10) Fine microbrewery with good pub grub and a couple dozen drafts.

Eating Establishment (☎ 435 649-8284; 317 Main St; breakfast & lunch $5-9, dinner $9-20) Famous for its filling breakfasts, served until 4pm.

ENTERTAINMENT

A half dozen crowded private clubs, most with live music, line Main St. The most popular is **Harry O's** (☎ 435-647-9494; 427 Main St) with interesting bands, including big names, and dancing most nights. The **Egyptian Theatre Company** (☎ 435-649-9371, 888-243-5779; 328 Main St) has plays in summer.

GETTING THERE & AROUND

Neither Greyhound nor Amtrak serve Park City. **Lewis Bros Stages** (Park City ☎ 435-649-2256, Salt Lake City ☎ 801-359-8677, 800-826-5844) runs daily year-round shuttles to/from Salt Lake City (one-way/round-trip $29/56); reserve a day ahead.

The frequent Park City Transit buses around town and to the ski resorts (7:30am to 10:30pm daily) are free, making it easy not to rent a car.

Logan & Around

North of Ogden, the mountains get smaller but are no less beautiful. Logan is a quintessential all-American community with strong Mormon ties. Tucked in rustic Cache Valley, it offers year-round outdoor activities, particularly hiking, camping and cross-country skiing. Founded in 1859, it's home to Utah State University. Get oriented at the **Cache Valley Tourist Council** (☎ 435-752-2161, 800-882-4433; www.tourcachevalley.com; 160 N Main St).

The **Wellsville Mountain range** is reputedly one of the highest in the world rising from such a narrow base. Get information and maps from the **Logan Ranger Station** (☎ 435-755-3620; 1500 E Hwy 89).

The 40-mile drive through **Logan Canyon** (Hwy 89 to Garden City) is beautiful any time of year, but in fall it is jaw-dropping. Enjoy hiking and biking trails, rock climbing, fishing spots and the seasonal campgrounds.

Perhaps the best of its kind, the **American West Heritage Center** (☎ 435-245-6050, 800-225-3378; self-guided tours $6; ☉ 10am-5pm Mon-Sat Memorial Day–Labor Day), on Hwy 89 south of town, offers authentic re-creations of frontier communities and lots of hands-on activities. It also hosts the popular week long **Festival of the American West** in July, a must for frontier buffs.

Besides tenting at **Riverside RV Park** (☎ 435-245-4469; 445 W 1700 S; campsites $12), the best budget options are mid-range **chain hotels** (r from $59-70) on Main St. For a down-home meal, try the classic 1920s-style **Bluebird Restaurant** (☎ 435-752-3155; 19 N Main St; mains $4-9). The slick **Caffé Ibis** (☎ 435-753-4777; 52 Federal Ave; mains under $6) is popular with the university crowd for gourmet coffees, breakfast burritos and healthy sandwiches.

NORTHERN NEW MEXICO

With its strong tricultural heritage (Native, Latin and Anglo), its luminescent desert landscape and desolate mountains, New Mexico is as much a unique culture as a beautiful place to visit. Wander through dusty villages in the northern mountains; explore ancient Indian sites such as Chaco Canyon; peruse native arts at roadside trading posts; puzzle over the alien magnet of Roswell and the atomic city of Los Alamos; savor green-chili cheeseburgers at vintage diners; hike among ponderosa pines and lava flows; extreme ski in Taos; and soak your cares away in natural hot springs along the Rio Grande.

SANTA FE

Artsy and aloof, ancient and tranquil, New Mexico's state capital has as many nicknames as personalities. Thirty years ago, most roads in this high-altitude town were unpaved and the only visitors were off-the-grid hippies and artists who came to paint the desert landscape in cruisey contemplation. Today, its one of the USA's top tourist destinations.

Initially established in 1610, Santa Fe is the oldest European community west of the Mississippi. Tourism focuses on the small downtown plaza, which at any given time may be teeming with artists, craftspeople, wealthy travelers and outdoor enthusiasts.

The city and its environs are loaded with fantastic museums, historic sites, colorful festivals and surreal landscapes. Santa Fe offers a golden opportunity to dig deep into Hispanic and Native American traditions, but it's also a fantastic place to kick back on the cheap, whether in a local café to watch fascinating people pass by, or wandering the Canyon Rd art galleries.

Orientation

The downtown plaza is within walking distance of many historic buildings and museums. Guadalupe St is the main north–south drag through downtown. The State Capitol is on Paseo de Peralta, which circles the center of town. Cerrillos Rd (I-25 exit 278) enters town from the south. St Francis Dr (I-25 exit 282) marks the western border of downtown and turns into US 285, which heads north toward Los Alamos and Taos.

Information
BOOKSTORES
Collected Works (☎ 505-988-4226; 208B W San Francisco St) Small downtown store with no periodicals.
Travel Bug (☎ 505-992-0418; 328 S Guadalupe St) Specializes in travel books.

EMERGENCY
Police (☎ 505-428-3710; 2515 Camino Entrada)

INTERNET ACCESS
Santa Fe Public Library (☎ 505-955-6780; free access; 145 Washington Ave)

MEDIA
Santa Fe Reporter (www.sfreporter.com) Free alternative weekly.

MEDICAL SERVICES
St Vincent Hospital (☎ 505-983-3361; 455 St Michael's Dr)

POST
Main Post Office (☎ 505-988-6351; 120 S Federal Place)

TOURIST OFFICES
Public Lands Information Center (☎ 505-438-7542; www.publiclands.org; 1474 Rodeo Rd) BLM and USFS share the building, at I-25 exit 282B.

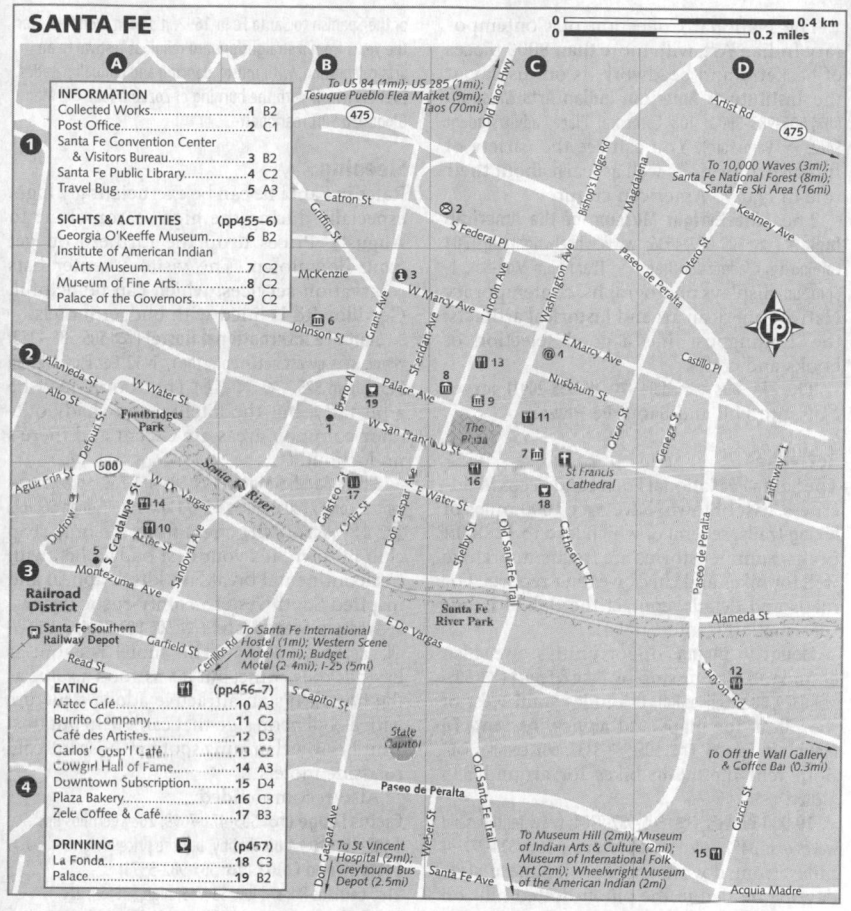

SANTA FE

0 ____ 0.4 km
0 ____ 0.2 miles

INFORMATION	
Collected Works	1 B2
Post Office	2 C1
Santa Fe Convention Center & Visitors Bureau	3 B2
Santa Fe Public Library	4 C2
Travel Bug	5 A3

SIGHTS & ACTIVITIES	(pp455–6)
Georgia O'Keeffe Museum	6 B2
Institute of American Indian Arts Museum	7 C2
Museum of Fine Arts	8 C2
Palace of the Governors	9 C2

EATING	(pp456–7)
Aztec Café	10 A3
Burrito Company	11 C2
Café des Artistes	12 D3
Carlos' Gosp'l Café	13 C2
Cowgirl Hall of Fame	14 A3
Downtown Subscription	15 D4
Plaza Bakery	16 C3
Zele Coffee & Café	17 B3

DRINKING	(p457)
La Fonda	18 C3
Palace	19 B2

To US 84 (1mi); US 285 (1mi); Tesuque Pueblo Flea Market (9mi); Taos (70mi)

To 10,000 Waves (3mi); Santa Fe National Forest (8mi); Santa Fe National Ski Area (16mi)

To Santa Fe International Hostel (1mi); Western Scene Motel (1mi); Budget Motel (2–4mi), I-25 (5mi)

To Off the Wall Gallery & Coffee Bar (0.3mi)

To St Vincent Hospital (2mi); Greyhound Bus Depot (2.5mi)

To Museum Hill (2mi); Museum of Indian Arts & Culture (2mi); Museum of International Folk Art (2mi); Wheelwright Museum of the American Indian (2mi)

Santa Fe Convention Center & Visitors Bureau

(☎ 505-955-6200, 800-777-2489; www.santafe.org; 201 W Marcy St)

Sights

Action pivots around the central **Plaza**. The **Museum of New Mexico** (☎ 505-476-5060; www.museumofnewmexico.org; ☼ Tue-Sun) administers four museums: **Palace of the Governors** (105 W Palace Ave; admission $7, free 5-8pm Fri), with regional history inside one of the country's oldest buildings; the **Museum of Fine Arts** (107 W Palace Ave; admission $7, free 5-8pm Fri); **Museum of Indian Arts & Culture** (710 Camino Lejo; admission $7); and **Museum of International Folk Art** (706 Camino Lejo; admission $7). Save and see them all with a four-day pass ($15).

The **Georgia O'Keeffe Museum** (☎ 505-946-1000; 217 Johnson St; adult/student $8/free; ☼ 10am-5pm, until 8pm Fri year-round, closed Wed Nov-Jun), housed in a former Spanish church, features the artist's paintings of flowers, bleached skulls and adobe architecture. Tours ($22) of O'Keeffe's house in Abiquiu, a tiny farming valley on Hwy 84, about 45 minutes northwest of Santa Fe, require advance reservations.

At one time **Canyon Rd**, on the southeastern edge of downtown, was a dusty artists' community. Today over 100 upscale galleries and several restaurants hug this small, adobe-lined street. It's a lovely and worthwhile stroll, even if you can't afford anything. Watch for Friday night openings offering free wine and cheese.

The National Collection of Contemporary Indian Art, with more than 8000 pieces of basketry and beadwork, is on display at the **Institute of American Indian Arts Museum** (☎ 505-983-8900; 108 Cathedral Place; adult/student $4/2; ☺ 9am-5pm). You can see the variety of Indian art forms as well as learn about their role in Native American culture.

The **Wheelwright Museum of the American Indian** (☎ 505-982-4636; www.wheelwright.org; 704 Camino Lejo; admission free; ☺ 10am-5pm Mon-Sat, 1-5pm Sun) displays photographs, contemporary Native American art and historical artifacts; the 'tradingpost' has a good selection of books and crafts.

The **'M' bus** (schedule ☎ 505-955-2001) serves Museum Hill and Santa Fe Plaza.

Activities

The Santa Fe National Forest and Pecos Wilderness, east of town, have over 1000 miles of **hiking** trails, several of which lead to 12,000ft peaks. Summer storms are frequent; prepare well for hikes and check weather reports. For maps and details, contact the Public Lands Information Center (p454).

Mountain biking opportunities are also abundant. Call or stop by **Bike & Sport** (☎ 505-820-0809; 1829 Cerillos Rd), 0.5 miles southwest of the plaza, for maps and advice, or **Santa Fe Mountain Sports** (☎ 505-988-3337; 607 Cerillos Rd). Both rent mountain bikes for around $35 a day.

10,000 Waves (☎ 505-982-9304; www.tenthousand waves.com; 3451 Hyde Park Rd; tubs per person $14-27), 4 miles from downtown, is a Japanese-style day spa nestled in the piñon-dotted hills on the road to the ski basin. It's a relaxing treat, with body treatments and outdoor hot soaking pools.

Ski Santa Fe (☎ 505-983-9155; www.skisantafe .com; beginners/half-day/full-day $23/33/45), 16 miles northeast of downtown on Hwy 475, offers 1700 vertical feet of snowboarding and downhill skiing, plus hiking in summer.

Festivals & Events

Indian Market (☎ 505-983-5220; www.swaia.org) Third weekend in August. Tens of thousands of collectors and nonaficionados alike deluge Santa Fe for the, a juried show featuring the work of artists from some 100 tribes. Book hotels way in advance.

Santa Fe Fiestas (☎ 505-988-7575; www.santafe fiesta.org) Weekend following Labor Day. Celebrated since 1712, Santa Fe Fiestas commemorates the peaceful return of the Spanish to Santa Fe in 1692. It's been modified over the years from a straightforward religious festival to an arts celebration, with music, dancing and oddball parades. Events kick off with the burning of Zozobra (aka Old Man Gloom), a 50ft marionette.

Sleeping

Rates in Santa Fe can be excruciatingly high, especially during the high season (June to August). Prices drop the further you get from downtown. The visitors center lists reservation services, which can be helpful. Cerrillos Rd is lined with budget motels.

Santa Fe International Hostel (☎ 505-988-1153; www.users.qwest.net/~epreston1; 1412 Cerrillos Rd; dm $15, r from $25; ⊠ ☒ ▣) The rooms may be a bit tatty, but the kitchen and shady outdoor common areas are decent and there's no lockout.

Silver Saddle Motel (☎ 505-471-7663; www.motel santafe.com; 2180 Cerrillos Rd; s/d low $40/45, high $60/66; ⊠ ☒) Across the street from the only strip club in town, it's your best budget bet, with free continental breakfast, kitsch appeal and inspired Southwestern comfy-rustic decor.

Western Scene Motel (☎ 505-983-7484; 1608 Cerrillos Rd; r from $39; ☒) This motel is about as basic as they come, but it's as good a value as the hostel. It's an attractive adobe structure with a cool neon sign that can't help but turn your head; a charming spot for those into old roadside motels.

Also recommended:

Cactus Lodge (☎ 505-471-7699; 2684 Cerrillos Rd; d $32-49; ☒) A bit shabby, but the price is right.

Cottonwood Court (☎ 505-982-5571; 2180 Cerrillos Rd; s/d low $36/45, high $48/64; ☒) Perfect if you consider mismatched furniture 'character.'

Luxury Inn (☎ 505-473-0567; 3752 Cerrillos Rd; d low/high $45/80, ste $55/92; ⊠ ☒ ▣) Some of the huge suites have kitchenettes and hot tubs.

El Rey Inn (☎ 505-982-1931, 800-521-1349; www.elreyinnsantafe.com; 1862 Cerrillos Rd; r $75-140; ⊠ ☒ ▣) Two miles south of the plaza. For the money, this is the nicest place to stay in Santa Fe.

Eating

Check for reviews and coupons in the *Santa Fe Reporter*, or the free monthly *Local Flavor*.

Downtown Subscription (☎ 505-983-3085; 376 Garcia St; mains $2-7) Start your day at this Santa Fe favorite with excellent coffee, unusual teas, pastries, desserts and a superb newsstand.

Café des Artistes (☎ 505-820-2535; 223b Canyon Rd; mains $4-8) Starving artists flock to the sunny patio for French-inspired dishes like brie-and-berry salads and flaky almond croissants.

Off the Wall Gallery & Coffee Bar (☎ 505-983-8337; 616 Canyon Rd; snacks $3-7) In addition to arts and crafts, this place prepares sandwiches, noodles and pastries.

Carlos' Gosp'l Café (☎ 505-983-1841; 125 Lincoln Ave; mains $4-9; Mon-Sat) Join locals on the sunny patio for creative sandwiches or vegetarian hangover stew.

Burrito Company (☎ 505-982-4453; 111 Washington Ave; mains $4 9) Plaza-side place with blue-corn enchiladas and killer chorizo breakfast burritos until 3pm.

Also recommended:

Aztec Café (☎ 505-820-0025; 317 Aztec St; sandwiches $6) Fuels the tattoos-and-climbing gear crowd. Good people-watching spot.

Plaza Bakery (☎ 505-988-3858; cnr San Francisco & Shelby Sts; mains $2-8) Breakfast anytime, soup, salads, sandwiches, ice cream – day-old baked goods are hidden in back.

Zele Coffee & Café (☎ 505-982-7835; 201 Galisteo St; mains $6-9) Breakfast, lunch and great coffee anytime.

Drinking

Browse the free *Santa Fe Reporter* (www.sfreporter.com) for thorough arts and entertainment listings.

La Fonda (☎ 505-982-5511; 100 E San Francisco St) The rooftop bar at one of the city's most historic hotels is an atmospheric place for a sunset cocktail.

Palace (☎ 505-982-9891; 142 W Palace Ave) The service can be terrible, but the old bar – with its red-all-over lighting, old West atmosphere and strange Indian princess oil painting – is wacky enough to merit a stop.

Shopping

From carved howling coyotes to fine turquoise jewelry, Santa Fe draws shoppers of all budgets. On weekends, don't miss the sprawling, high-quality **Tesuque Pueblo Flea Market** (☎ 505-995-8626; 8am-5pm Fri-Sun Mar-Dec), 9 miles north of town on US 285.

Getting There & Around

Greyhound (☎ 505-471-0008; 858 St Michael's Dr) runs daily buses to Albuquerque ($12, one hour), Taos ($15, 90 minutes) and beyond. **Sandia Shuttle** (☎ 505-474-5696, 888-775-5696) runs

> **SPLURGE!**
>
> With iron-saddle bar stools, a rustic interior and genuinely friendly service, the **Cowgirl Hall of Fame** (☎ 505-982-2565; 319 S Guadelupe St; mains $7-14; Mon-Sat;) is an easy favorite for salmon tacos, buffalo burgers and veggie options like butternut squash casserole. After the daily $2 happy hour specials, the microbrews start flowing and live music (cover $1 to $5) – rarely country – kicks in around 9pm.

13 times daily between Santa Fe hotels and the Albuquerque airport ($23, 70 minutes). **Twin Hearts** (☎ 505-751-1201, 800-654-9456) serves Taos ($25, 90 minutes).

Amtrak (☎ 505-466-4511) stops at Lamy, 18 miles south of Santa Fe; the **Lamy Shuttle** (☎ 505-982-8829) shuttles back and forth by reservation ($16).

AROUND SANTA FE

North and east of Santa Fe, the red rocks and pine forest of the Pajarito Plateau and Jemez Mountains shelter a wealth of hiking and undeveloped hot springs. Within miles of each other, Valles Caldera National Preserve, Bandelier National Monument and Los Alamos encapsulate the iconographic geological, human and atomic history of the American West.

Los Alamos

Perched among thick green forest – of which 48,000 acres burned catastrophically in 2000 – atop a series of steep-walled mesas, Los Alamos (elevation 7355ft) is a surprisingly beautiful place – ironic since it's best known as the birthplace of the atomic bomb, developed here in secret as the 'Manhattan Project' during WWII.

Behind the historic 1928 Fuller Lodge art center, the free **Los Alamos Historical Museum** (☎ 505-662-4493; 1921 Juniper St; daily) has atomic popular-culture artifacts in spades, plus exhibits probing life 'on the hill' during the project.

Bradbury Science Museum (☎ 505-667-4444; cnr Central Ave & 15th St; admission free; 9am-5pm Tue-Fri, 1-5pm Sat-Mon) gives a detailed account of US atomic history. However, it's disturbing to find only the slightest mention of the destruction of Hiroshima and Nagasaki

SOUTHWEST

DETOUR: JEMEZ SPRINGS

This small resort town is squeezed into a valley along the incredible 132-mile **Jemez Mountain Trail National Scenic Byway**, following Hwys 4, 44 and 126 past Cuba and San Ysidro. There are several B&Bs and restaurants, a few monasteries a Zen Buddhist center, and a vintage bathhouse. Ask about the free undeveloped **hot springs** and **camping** ($10) at the **Santa Fe National Forest Ranger Station** (☎ 505-829-3535), a mile north of town on Hwy 4.

(check the guest book for revealing personal reactions).

After sunset the town clears out. Visit as a day trip, or as a stopover on your way to see Bandelier, the spectacular **Valles Caldera National Preserve** (www.vallescaldera.gov), a former volcano viewable from Hwy 4, and other wild areas in the Jemez Mountains.

Bandelier National Monument

Rio Grande Puebloans lived here till the mid-16th century. Today several sites, a convenient location and a spectacular landscape make **Bandelier** (☎ 505-672-0343; www.nps .gov/band; admission $10; ☺ dawn-dusk) an intriguing visit for those interested in ancient pueblos. The **Juniper campground** (campsites $10) sometimes closes in winter.

Cuba

In an old adobe lodge set in 330 acres of the Nacimiento Mountains, seven miles out of town, the friendly and very beautiful **Circle A Ranch Hostel** (☎ 505-289-3350; www.circlea ranch.info; 510 Los Pinos Rd; dm $20, r $35-55; ☺ May-Oct) is favored by those with a car who are looking for a quiet retreat. The best in-town budget option is **Frontier Motel** (☎ 505-289-3350; 6474 Hwy 44/550; r from $27). Splurge on steak at charming **El Bruno's Restaurante y Cantina** (☎ 505-289-9429; cnr Hwys 44/550 & 126; mains $6-16), northwest New Mexico's best eatery.

TAOS

Once a laid-back outpost for hippies, artists and other back-to-the-land bohemians, Taos has grown to become one of the state's most popular destinations, with numerous hotels, restaurants and even resorts. The town's biggest attraction, however – and

justifiably so – is the Taos Pueblo, built in the 15th century and still home to many residents.

At 6967ft and set amid some spectacular landscape bordered by the Rio Grande and the Taos Plateau to the west, and the Sangre de Cristo Mountains to the north, Taos offers a seemingly endless array of year-round outdoor activities.

Orientation & Information

Entering from the south, Hwy 68 becomes Paseo del Pueblo Sur, lined with motels and shopping centers. It becomes Paseo del Pueblo Norte at Kit Carson Rd (Hwy 64), the intersection of which marks the center of town. Taos Plaza is directly east. At the traffic signal several miles north of town, Hwy 150 leads northeast to Taos Ski Valley, and Hwy 64 heads west toward the Rio Grande Gorge Bridge. Kit Carson Rd (Hwy 64) runs east to Eagle Nest and Cimarron.

The **visitors center** (☎ 505-758-3873, 800-732-8267; www.taosguide.com; cnr Paseo del Pueblo Sur & Paseo del Cañon) can help you get your bearings.

Sights

Constructed around AD 1450 and inhabited continuously ever since, **Taos Pueblo** (☎ 505-758-1028; www.taospueblo.com; adult/student $10/5; ☺ 8am-4:30pm), about 3 miles north of the plaza, is North America's largest existing multistory pueblo structure and one of the best surviving examples of traditional adobe construction. It's worth a visit. An informal tour is offered daily (no fee, but tip the guide); there's a photography fee of $5. The pueblo may be closed for sacred ceremonial dances in February, March and August. Also on site is a café serving native cuisine and the state's only 100% nonsmoking gaming facility, **Taos Mountain Casino** (☎ 505-737-0777, 888-946-8267; www.taosmountaincasino.com).

Taos Historic Museums (☎ 505-758-0505; adult 1/2/3 homes $5/7.50/10; ☺ 10am-5pm) run three houses: the **Kit Carson Home** (Kit Carson Rd), one block from the plaza; the **Blumenschein Home** (222 Ledoux St); and the **Martínez Hacienda** (Ranchitos Rd), a former colonial trader's home.

Four miles north of the plaza, **Millicent Rogers Museum** (☎ 505-758-2462; 1504 Millicent Rogers Museum Rd; adult $6; ☺ Tue-Sun Nov-Mar), filled with pottery, jewelry, baskets and textiles, is considered one of the USA's best collections of Indian and Spanish colonial art.

At 650ft above the Rio Grande, the steel **Rio Grande Gorge Bridge** is the USA's second-highest suspension bridge; it's 11 miles northwest of the plaza, and the view down is eye-popping. Just west of the bridge is a fascinating community of **Earthships** (☎ 505-751-0462; www.earthship.org; ⊙ 10am-4pm), which are solid, self-sustaining, environmentally savvy houses built with recycled materials that survive completely off the grid. Self-guided tours ($5) are worthwhile but overnight accommodations are spendy.

Activities

During the summer, **white-water rafting** is popular in the Class IV Taos Box, the steep-sided cliffs that frame the Rio Grande. Day-long trips start at around $90 per person; ask at the visitors center about local outfitters. **Hiking** is plentiful, and trailheads line the road to the ski valley. With a peak elevation of 11,819ft and a 2612ft vertical drop, **Taos Ski Valley** (☎ 800-347-7414; ticket $51) offers some of North America's most challenging **skiing**, yet remains refreshingly low-key.

Sleeping

The **USFS campgrounds** (campsites $8; ⊙ May-Oct) nearest to here are east of town nestled between Hwy 64 and a creek in the Carson National Forest. There are also five basic (no water) sites ($3-5) on the road to Ski Valley.

HI Taos Snow Mansion (☎ 505-776-8298; www .taoswebb.com/hotel/snowmansion; 476 Taos Ski Valley Rd; camping per person $6, dm $19-22, teepee $34, d $42-48; 🖵) Ten minutes north of Taos in the charming Arroyo Seco, this is a friendly place with lodging options from a simple bunk to a campsite, teepee, cabin or private room. It has an inviting communal atmosphere and is ski bum heaven.

Adobe Wall Motel (☎ 505-758-3972; 227 E Kit Carson Rd; r from $55) This cute little motel is in a lovely, tree-shaded courtyard just a short jaunt east of the plaza. Many of the homey adobe rooms have their own kiva-style fireplace.

Laughing Horse Inn (☎ 505-758-8350, 800-776-0161; www.laughinghorseinn.com; 729 Paseo del Pueblo Norte; s $54-98, d $62-118) A convivial travelers' hangout with free loaner bicycles and a lot of heart and soul. The property is over a century old and the 11 rooms are in a comfy structure that feels more like an Earthship than a crackerbox motel. Except for the penthouse, all rooms share baths.

Eating & Drinking

Taos Bakery (☎ 505-751-3734; 1223 Gusdorf Rd & Paseo del Pueblo Norte; treats $1-3) The Parisian-trained owners craft the best pastries in town, hands down.

Bean (☎ 505-758-5123; 900 Paseo del Pueblo Norte & 1033j Paseo del Pueblo Sur; mains $4-6) This local fuel stop roasts its own great coffee and rolls bomber breakfast burritos until 2pm at two locations.

El Pueblo Cafe (☎ 505-758-2053, 625 Paseo del Pueblo Norte; mains $4-10) Four wines on tap, great Frito pies and perfect hours for partying. A hard-drinking, smoky local favorite.

Orlando's New Mexican Cafe (☎ 505-751-1450; 1114 Don Juan Valdez Lane; mains $6-10) This homey, family-owned restaurant, 1.8 miles north of the plaza along Paseo del Pueblo Norte, serves affordable Southwestern meals.

Getting There & Around

From Santa Fe, take either the scenic 'High Rd' along Hwy 76 and Hwy 518, with galleries, villages and quirky museums, or trace the Rio Grande on Hwy 68.

Greyhound (☎ 505-758-1144; 1384 D Paseo del Pueblo Sur) goes daily to Santa Fe and Albuquerque. **Twin Hearts** (☎ 505-751-1201, 800-654-9456) runs shuttles to Albuquerque airport ($40) and Santa Fe ($25).

ALBUQUERQUE

Bustling and businesslike, casual and inviting, 'the duke city' is New Mexico's economic and cultural crossroads, and the largest city for hundreds of miles around. It sits at about

---

SCENIC DRIVE: ENCHANTED CIRCLE

The scenic 84-mile loop drive known as the **Enchanted Circle** snakes north and east of Taos through barren windswept high desert, alpine forests and mountain streams. Follow Hwy 522 north to Questa; head east on Hwy 38 through Red River to Eagle Nest; then return on Hwy 64. West of Questa is the spectacular **Wild Rivers Recreation Area** (☎ 505-770-1600; admission $3), at the Rio Grande and Red River confluence, where water has cut 800ft canyons into the plateau.

5300ft above sea level, with surrounding mountains topping 10,000ft. Like many western cities, its suburbs sprawl across the desert, though its core surrounds a historic plaza.

Albuquerque is a favorite of **Rte 66** junkies, who cruise the historic 'Mother Rd' as it winds through downtown. The students at the University of New Mexico (UNM) bring the city a healthy dose of youthful energy and plenty of cultural events. Though Albuquerque is not as quaint as nearby Santa Fe, it definitely has its charms. It also has inexpensive accommodations and makes a convenient base for exploring nearby mountains, deserts and pueblos.

Orientation

Albuquerque's major boundaries are Paseo del Norte Dr (north), Central Ave (south), and Tramway Blvd (east) and Rio Grande Blvd (west). Central Ave (old Rte 66) links Old Town, downtown, the university and Nob Hill. The intersection of Central Ave and the railroad tracks just east of the downtown area serves as the center point of the city's four-quadrant (NW, NE, SW and SE) system.

Information

BOOKSTORES
Page One (☎ 505-294-2026; 11018 Montgomery Blvd NE) Huge shop 5 miles east of I-25. Used-book branch Page One Too! is across the street.

EMERGENCY
Police (nonemergency ☎ 505-242-2677; 400 Roma St NW)

INTERNET ACCESS
Main Library (☎ 505-768-5140; 501 Copper Ave NW; computer fee $3)

MEDIA
Alibi (www.alibi.com) Free weekly with good entertainment listings available in cafés and bookstores.

MEDICAL SERVICES
Presbyterian Hospital (☎ 505-841-1234; 1100 Central Ave SE) Cafeteria serves good enchiladas.
University Hospital (☎ 505-272-2111; 2111 Lomas Blvd NE) On the UNM campus.

POST
Downtown Station (☎ 505-346-1674; 201 5th St SW)

TOURIST OFFICES
Albuquerque Convention & Visitors Bureau
(☎ 505-842-9918, 800-284-2282; www.itsatrip.org; cnr 2nd St & Martin Luther King Jr Ave) Downtown inside Convention Center.
New Mexico State Parks (☎ 888-667-2757; www.emnrd.state.nm.us/nmparks)
Public Lands Information Center (☎ 505-345-9498, 877-851-8946; www.publiclands.org; 6501 4th St NW) Statewide camping and recreation information.

Sights

From its foundation in 1706 until the arrival of the railroad in 1880, **Old Town Plaza** was the hub of Albuquerque; today it's the city's most popular tourist area. Many original structures are still standing, along with galleries, gift shops and museums.

Get an excellent overview of the city's history and exhibits by New Mexican artists at the **Albuquerque Museum** (☎ 505-243-7255; 2000 Mountain Rd NW; adult $3; ☺ Tue-Sun). North of Old Town, the must-see **Indian Pueblo Cultural Center** (☎ 505-843-7270, 800-766-4405; www.indianpueblo.org; 2401 12th St NW; adult/student $4/1; ☺ 9am-5pm) is the perfect starting point if you're planning to visit any of the state's pueblos. It's owned by New Mexico's 19 Pueblos. Traditional dances are demonstrated at 11am and 2pm on Saturday and Sunday. The Harvest Café serves traditional dishes and there's a drive-thru smoke shop.

The **National Hispanic Cultural Center** (☎ 505-246-2261; www.nhccnm.org; 1701 4th St SW; adult $3; ☺ Tue-Sun) is a sprawling complex including galleries celebrating Hispanic arts. It's south of downtown and well worth a trip.

Trip out on the Cold War and the potent collection of nuclear weapons at the **National Atomic Museum** (☎ 505-245-2137; www.atomicmuseum.com; 1905 Mountain Rd NW; admission $4; ☺ 9am-5pm).

The **Sandia Peak Tramway** (☎ 505-856-7325; www.sandiapeak.com; one-way/round-trip $8/15; ☺ 9am-9pm) is a 2.7-mile ride that begins in the desert and soars to 10,678ft atop Sandia Peak. Take I-25 north and turn east at Tramway Blvd (exit 234).

The University of New Mexico area has loads of popular restaurants, casual bars, offbeat shops and casual college hangouts. The main drag is Central Ave between University and Carlisle Blvds.

Near the hostel in Cedar Crest, the **Tinkertown Museum** (☎ 505-281-5233; www.tinkertown.com;

123 Sandia Crest Rd; admission $3; 9am-6pm Apr-Nov), an inspiring assortment of animated wood-carvings surrounded with antique toys and junk, is a highly recommended excursion, as is the deceased owner's intimation to eat more mangoes naked!

Northwest of downtown, on Albuquerque's West Mesa, **Petroglyph National Monument** (505-899-0205; www.nps.gov/petr; I-40 exit 154; weekday/weekend $1/2; 8am-5pm) has hiking trails and protects volcanic cones and 25,000 prehistoric rock etchings dating from AD 1300.

Activities

The omnipresent Sandia Mountains and the less crowded Manzano Mountains offer outdoor activities including hiking, skiing, mountain biking and camping. The **Sandia Ranger Station** (505-281-3304; 11776 Hwy 337), off I-40 exit 175 south, has maps and information. For equipment, try **REI** (505-247-1191; 1550 Mercantile Ave NE), just west of I-25 at the Montagno Rd exit.

Reach the top of the Sandias via the eastern slope on the lovely **Sandia Crest National Scenic Byway** (I-40 exit 175 north), which passes several trailheads; or take the Sandia Peak Tramway up the western side. An alternative is to take NM 165 from Placitas (I-25 exit 242), a dirt road through Las Huertas Canyon that passes the prehistoric dwelling of Sandia Man Cave.

The 8-mile (one way) **La Luz Trail** takes you to the top of the Sandias. To reach the trailhead, take I-25 north to Tramway Blvd, head east, then left onto USFS Rd 333.

The **Sandia Peak Ski Area** (505-242-9052; www.sandiapeak.com; half-/full-day $29/38) is at the top of the Sandia Peak Tramway. The ski/snowboard season runs mid-December to mid-March. On summer weekends and holidays (May to October), one lift stays open for mountain bikers, and combo bike rental and lift packages are available.

Festivals & Events

Gathering of the Nations Powwow (505-836-2810; www.gatheringofthenations.com) Late April.
The biggest gathering in Native America, with a week of dancing, drumming, art shows and the Miss Indian World pageant.
New Mexico State Fair (505-265-1791)
Late September. Featuring food, music, prize livestock, rodeos and creaky carnival rides. Wahoo!

Sleeping

Central Ave (old Rte 66) is lined with vintage motels. Look for more budget motels west of downtown along Central Ave near Rio Grande Blvd, or along Central Ave in the UNM district. If you've got wheels, primitive **camping** (campsites $3) is allowed in the forest off the road up the Sandia Crest.

Route 66 Hostel (505-247-1813; www.members.aol.com/route66hos/htmlRT66; 1012 Central SW; dm $15, d $20-30;) A friendly place within walking distance of Amtrak/Greyhound, Old Town and the action downtown. No curfew.

El Vado (505-243-4594; elvado@comcast.net; 2500 Central Ave SW; r $32;) Built in 1936, it claims to be the 'purest' surviving Rte 66 motel in town – meaning it hasn't been overly modernized. Cute and clean, it's definitely a roadside gem, with guests staying in duplex-type buildings, each with its own carport.

Sandia Mountain Hostel (505-281-4117; 12234 Hwy 14 N; campsites/dm/d $7/14/32) This tidy hostel 20 miles northeast of the city (I-40 exit 175 north) in Cedar Crest affords easy access to the Sandia mountains. It's more family-friendly than party-hearty. With board games and table tennis as the only entertainment options, it's a great place to meditate on the sweetness of life. Call ahead and they might even be able to pick you up from the end of the SunTran line in Albuquerque.

Eating

Albuquerque offers plenty of good, abundant meals, particularly if you like Southwestern cuisine.

Route 66 Malt Shop (505-242-7866; 1720 Central Ave SW; mains $4-6) The original vintage interior of this tiny diner is worth a look on its own, but if you're hungry, pull up a stool and tuck into their signature green-chili cheeseburger and a chocolate malt.

Winning Coffee Company (505-266-0000; 111 Harvard St NE; mains $4-6) Strong coffee is the key draw at this large, laid-back favorite with locals and students near UNM. It serves breakfast and lunch, and there's often poetry or acoustic music at night.

Frontier (505-266-0550; 2400 Central Ave SE; mains $3-8; 24hr) Inexpensive meals served round-the-clock opposite UNM.

Entertainment

Ticketmaster (505-883-7800; www.ticketmaster.com) handles many major concerts and sports events. The free weekly *Alibi* has reviews and listings.

KiMo Theatre (☎ 505-768-3544, 505-768-3522; 423 Central Ave NW) A pride and joy of downtown, this restored 1927 place was designed with a mixture of pueblo and art deco stylings. It hosts various theater, art and music events.

Several music clubs and bars line Central Ave downtown and in the UNM/Nob Hill area, including **Launchpad** (☎ 505-764-8887; 618 Central Ave SW), with a full roster of good indie-rock and roots bands, and **El Rey** (☎ 505-242-2353; 624 Central Ave SW), in an old movie theater. **Pulse** (☎ 505-255-3334; 4100 Central Ave SE) is a popular gay-friendly nightclub just east of Nob Hill.

Getting There & Around

The **Albuquerque International Sunport** (ABQ; ☎ 505-244-7733) airport is 4 miles south of downtown, just east of I-25. Most major US airlines service Albuquerque; **Southwest** (☎ 800-435-9792) has the largest presence.

SunTran Route 50 runs from the airport to town (no Sunday or evening service). Cabs between the airport and downtown fetch around $13. **Sandia Shuttle** (☎ 888-775-5696) runs from the Albuquerque airport to Santa Fe ($23, 70 minutes) multiple times daily. **Twin Hearts** (☎ 800-654-9456) has shuttles from the airport to Taos ($40, three hours).

The *Southwest Chief* stops daily at Albuquerque's **Amtrak station** (☎ 505-842-9650; 214 1st St SW).

Greyhound (☎ 505-243-4435, 800-231-2222; 300 2nd St SW) runs buses to/from Santa Fe (one hour), Taos (three hours), Roswell (3½ hours), Carlsbad (5½ hours) and beyond.

The **Alvarado Transportation Center** (cnr 1st St & Central Ave) is the hub for all local **SunTran** (☎ 505-843-9200; fares $1) buses serving metropolitan Albuquerque.

ALONG I-40
To The East

Sections of old Rte 66 parallel I-40 throughout New Mexico. In **Santa Rosa**, 114 miles east of Albuquerque, the **Route 66 Auto Museum** (☎ 505-472-1966; 2766 Old Rte 66; admission $5; ☵ 7:30am-7pm) pays homage to the mother of all roadtrips. Ask about snorkeling and scuba diving in the nearby **Blue Hole**.

The last pitstop before the Lone Star state is **Tucumcari**, 173 miles east of Albuquerque. The **Blue Swallow Motel** (☎ 505-461-9849; www .blueswallowmotel.com; 815 E Rte 66 Blvd; s/d from $30/35; ☷) is a lovingly restored vintage motor court dating from 1939, with a stucco exterior and 11 clean, cozy rooms. The five-person suite ($58) is a steal.

To The West

Although you can buzz between Albuquerque and Flagstaff in less than five hours, the national monuments and pueblos along the way are well worth a visit. For a **scenic loop**, take Hwy 53 southwest from Grants, which leads to all the following sights except Acoma. Hwy 602 takes you north to Gallup.

Lava flows, lava tubes, Anasazi ruins and ice caves define the eerie landscape of **El Malpais National Monument**, 200 sq miles of 'bad land.' An **Information Center** (☎ 505-783-4774; www.nps.gov/elma), 22 miles southwest of Grants on Hwy 53, has details on hikes and free primitive camping at the **Narrows**.

At **Zuni Pueblo**, check out the delicately inlaid silverwork, sold in stores lining Hwy 53. Walk past stone houses and beehive-shaped mud ovens to the massive **Our Lady of Guadalupe Mission**, featuring impressive murals. The **A:shiwi A:wan Museum & Heritage Center** (☎ 505-782-4403; 02E Oho Caliente Rd; admission $7; ☵ on Indian time) displays photos and other

---

DETOUR: CHACO CULTURE NATIONAL HISTORIC PARK

Featuring massive Ancestral Puebloan buildings set in an isolated high-desert environment, this intriguing **park** (☎ 505-786-7014; www.nps.gov/chcu; admission per vehicle $8; ☵ dawn-dusk) contains evidence of 5000 years of human occupation. At its prime, the community was the region's major trading and ceremonial hub. Pueblo Bonito, masterful in its design, is four stories tall and may have had 600 to 800 rooms and kivas. Sites have been stabilized but not reconstructed. Apart from taking the self-guided loop tour, you can hike various **backcountry trails**.

The visitors center is in a remote area 75 miles south of Farmington. The park is open year-round, but all routes involve driving on rough dirt roads, which are sometimes impassable in the wet. First-come, first-served **Gallo Campground** (campsites $10) is a mile east of the visitors center.

tribal artifacts from the ancestral Hawikku village.

The classic Rte 66 town of **Gallup** functions as the Navajo and Zuni peoples' major trading center, and the many trading posts, pawn shops, and galleries attract those seeking affordable jewelry, rugs, and other arts and crafts. There's loads of vintage motels. The town's true lodging jewel is **El Rancho** (☎ 505-863-9311, 800-543-6351; www.elranchohotel .com; 1000 E Rte 66; s/d from $58/68; 🔀 🖭), which dates from 1937. It has a beautiful Southwestern lobby, an eclectic assortment of rooms and a nice bar.

Farmington & Around

Northwestern New Mexico's largest town is a good basecamp for exploring the Four Corners region. For help, rouse the **visitors center** (☎ 505-326-7602, 800-448-1240; www.farmingtonnm.org; 3041 E Main St). **Shiprock Pinnacle**, a 1700ft-high volcanic plug that looms eerily to the west, was a landmark for the Anglo pioneers and is a Navajo sacred site. The low-key **Three Rivers Brewhouse** (☎ 505-324-2187; 101 E Main St; mains $5-15) brews its own in a 1912 building and has pool tables and a game room.

Some 37 miles south of Farmington off Hwy 371, the undeveloped **Bisti/De-Na-Zin Wilderness** is a surreal landscape of fossils, colorful rock formations, and petrified logs – it's like stepping onto a sci-fi film set. Desert enthusiasts shouldn't miss it. Get details about free primitive camping from the **BLM** (☎ 505-599-8900; 1235 La Plata Hwy).

The **Navajo Transit System** (☎ 520-729-4111) has a weekday service to Window Rock; for information on visiting the Navajo Nation, see p436.

Las Vegas

Travelers on the Santa Fe Trail (roughly paralleled today by I-25) traversed this region on their way from Missouri to Santa Fe. Plenty of Wild West heritage remains in towns like Las Vegas.

Dinosaurs romped here, too, adding to the stark allure of these high plains. **Las Vegas** has one of the west's most amazingly well-preserved downtown districts; over 900 buildings are listed on the National Register of Historic Places. It's no surprise, then, that Hollywood regularly uses it as a film set. It's 64 miles east of Santa Fe on I-25.

SOUTHERN NEW M

The Rio Grande Valley runs so Albuquerque to El Paso, Texas, by I-25. Much of the region is populated ranchland, dominated Chihuahuan Desert. Along New M western border, the Continental snakes through the Gila National high country near Silver City. The scape here is wild and woodsy, offering of hiking and camping opportunities; perfect place to get away from it all. the east, things take an Atomic Age tu at White Sands National Monument, an 'did-that-UFO-crash-here?' Roswell.

SILVER CITY & AROUND

The **Gila National Forest** and **Gila Wilderness** is rugged country suitable for remote cross-country skiing, camping and backpacking. On the southern edge of this mountainous region, Silver City is a small, easygoing college and old West mining town. The **chamber of commerce** (☎ 505-538-3785, 800-548-9378; www .silvercity.org; 201 N Hudson St) and **USFS** (☎ 505-388-8201; www.fs.fed.us/r3/gila; 3005 E Camino del Bosque) have details on camping and wilderness activities.

Forty-two curvy miles north of Silver City, the recommended **Gila Cliff Dwellings National Monument** (☎ 505-536-9461; www.nps .gov/gicl; admission $3; 🕑 8am-6pm summer, 9am-4pm winter) was occupied in the 13th century by Mogollon people. Free primitive **camping** is possible a few miles south of the entrance off Hwy 15.

Strangely rounded volcanic towers make up **City of Rocks State Park** (☎ 505-536-2800; day-use $4, campsites $10; 🕑 7am-9pm), southeast of Silver City on Hwy 61; secluded camp spots lie among the towers. Nearby, lovely **Faywood Hot Springs** (☎ 505-536-9663; www.faywood .com; 165 Hwy 61; day-use $10, campsites s/d $15/24, cabins $80; 🕑 10am-10pm) has public and private pools, plus camping and log cabins.

Silver City's restored **Palace Hotel** (☎ 505-388-1811; www.zianet.com/palacehotel; 106 W Broadway; r $47-57) dates from 1882. The area around the hotel is crawling with cozy cafés and art galleries on Frankie St.

TRUTH OR CONSEQUENCES

Settled on the site of natural hot springs in the 1880s, this funky little town was

---

DETOUR: VERY LARGE ARRAY

For those heading west into Arizona from Socorro, Hwy 60 is a scenic alternative to I-40. Past the town of Magdalena, and 47 miles west of Socorro, is the **Very Large Array** radio telescope facility, a complex of 27 huge antenna dishes sprouting like giant mushrooms from the high plains. Near Quemado, the **Lightning Field** (☎ 505-898-3335; www.lightningfield.org; cabins per person $135; ☙ May-Oct) is a 1977 art installation by Walter De Maria, consisting of 400 stainless-steel poles in a remote desert location. The only way to visit is to spend the night in a six-person in-situ cabin; advance reservations required.

---

renamed Truth or Consequences ('T or C') in 1950, after an eponymous radio program. Wander around the cubbyhole cafés, peruse the second-hand shops and definitely take a dip in one of the hot springs. It's tricky getting here and away without your own wheels since Greyhound stops in the middle of the night.

The **chamber of commerce** (☎ 505-894-3536; www.truthorconsequencesnm.net; 201 N Foch St) has local tourist info.

Many local motels include spas and allow day-use ($3 to $6). The backpackers' favorite is **Riverbend Hot Springs** (☎ 505-894-6183; www.nmhotsprings.com; 100 Austin Ave; camping/dm $12/18, d $36-55; ☙) a friendly hostel with dorms, private rooms (in trailers), camping and – the main attraction – communal soaks (up to 102°F) in outdoor tubs by the river. These are free to guests but only available from 7am to 10am and 7pm to 10pm. There's an occasional drum circle or guitar jam but facilities are hit-or-miss, depending on the vicissitudes of the all-volunteer staff.

Nearby, the **Charles Motel & Bath House** (☎ 505-894-7154, 800-317-4518; www.charlesspa.com; 601 Broadway; s/d $39/45; ☙) has various body treatments as well as remodeled, 1940s-style motel rooms. Grab a thick banana shake and juicy half-pound avocado burger at **TRC's Big-A-Burger** (Broadway at Austin Ave; burgers $2-5), which has video games and a decent jukebox. Hardly the place to start a diet, it's a great place to catch up on local bingo, rodeo and fishing gossip.

LAS CRUCES & AROUND

Perched at 3900ft between the Rio Grande and the strangely fluted Organ Mountains, New Mexico's second-largest city is a farming center. The village of **Hatch**, 40 miles north, is the state's fragrant chili-growing capital. New Mexico State University's 15,000 students spice up a few pockets of town, but otherwise it's painfully utilitarian. The **visitors center** (☎ 505-541-2444; www.lascrucescvb.org; 211 N Water St) has local and regional information.

Three miles southwest of downtown Las Cruces is **Mesilla**, established in 1850 by Mexican settlers who were reluctant to join the USA after the Mexican-American War. Souvenir shops and tourist-oriented restaurants dominate Mesilla's historic Plaza.

The best budget motel is **Day's End Lodge** (☎ 505-524-7753; 755 N Valley Dr; r from $29; ☙ ☙), which offers free popcorn but doesn't take reservations – 'just come by.'

The university crowd hangs out at **Spirit Winds Coffee Bar** (☎ 505-521-1222; 2260 S Locust St; mains $4-6), a chill place with sandwiches, pastries and salads. **Nellie's Café** (☎ 505-524-9982; 1226 W Hadley Ave; mains $5-7; ☙ 8am-4pm Tue-Sat) dishes up good Mexican meals. Nearby, the **High Desert Brewing Company** (☎ 505-525-6752; 1201 W Hadley Ave; mains $5-8) offers handcrafted suds, pub grub and live music.

Las Cruces Shuttle (☎ 505-525-1784, 800-288-1784) runs a dozen vans daily from Las Cruces to El Paso Airport ($30), plus less frequent services to Silver City ($43) and other regional destinations.

WHITE SANDS NATIONAL MONUMENT

Sixteen miles southwest of Alamogordo, gypsum blankets 275 sq miles to create a dazzling white landscape at the crisp, stark **White Sands National Monument** (☎ 505-679-2599; admission $3; ☙ 7am-sunset). A 16-mile loop leads into the heart of the park. Feel free to climb and romp around the dunes; there are picnic sites and hiking trails, but no car camping (backcountry only, apply at the visitors center). Ask about full-moon activities.

Phallic projectile fans shouldn't miss the **White Sands Missile Range Museum** (☎ 505-678-8824; admission free; ☙ 8am-4pm Mon-Fri, 10am-3pm Sat & Sun), 22 miles east of Las Cruces on Hwy

70. It's on the military base, a major testing range and also home to the 'Trinity Site,' where the first atomic blast took place.

The outdoor 'missile park' is an odd place that fills with wildflowers in spring. At the entrance gate, be prepared to show the national guard your driver's license and car registration.

ALAMOGORDO & AROUND

Founded as a railroad town, Alamogordo later became home to Holloman Air Force Base. It's at 4350ft in the Tularosa Basin, though it's not as picturesque as nearby Cloudcroft or Ruidoso. White Sands Blvd (WSB) is the main north–south drag.

The **New Mexico Museum of Space History** (☎ 505-437-2840, 877-333-6589; adult $2.50; ☺ 9am-5pm) is a five-story glass cube at the east end of Indian Wells Rd. Inside are exhibits about space research and flight and a huge wraparound IMAX theater (tickets $6; call for schedule).

Numerous motels (from $25) front the White Sands Blvd within spittin' distance of Greyhound. If for some reason you get stuck here, try the **Townsman Motel** (☎ 505-437-0210; 710 N WSB). **Plaza Pub** (☎ 505-437-9495; cnr N WSB & 10th St; mains $4-6) has decent pub grub, cheap daily specials and microbrews.

From Alamogordo, Hwy 82 climbs from 4700ft within 16 miles to forested **Cloudcroft**, a welcome relief from the desert heat. In town, the **USFS office** (☎ 505-682-2551) has details about free dispersed camping options and several nearby **campgrounds** (campsites $8-10). The popular **Western Bar & Café** (☎ 505-682-2445; Burro St; mains $6-14), just off Hwy 82, is straight out of a Wild West movie.

RUIDOSO

Surrounded by thick forest in the Sacramento Mountains, **Ruidoso** (elevation 7000ft) has seen its share of commercial development, but it's still an attractive place. Serious horse racing happens May through September at **Ruidoso Downs** (☎ 505-378-4431; www.ruidosodownsracing.com; 1461 Hwy 70 W; admission free). Western and cowboy enthusiasts will enjoy the more than 10,000 items in the **Hubbard Museum of the American West** (☎ 505-378-4142; admission $6; ☺ 10am-5pm), just east of Ruidoso Downs on Hwy 70. North of Ruidoso is the **Ski Apache** (☎ 505-336-4356; adult $45) downhill resort.

Numerous motels, hotels and cute little cabin complexes line the streets. The **Sitzmark Chalet** (☎ 505-257-4140, 800-658-9694; www.sitzmark-chalet.com; 627 Sudderth Dr; r from $40; ☒ ☒ ☐) has simple but nice rooms.

Besides USDA Choice sides of beef, the lively **K-Bob's Steakhouse** (☎ 505-378-4747; Hwy 70 at the Y; mains $5-15) has a full, meal-worthy chuckwagon salad bar for $6.79. **Circle J BBQ** (☎ 505-257-4105; 1825 Sudderth Dr; mains $4-10) offers five-cent coffee, cheap sandwiches and all-you-can-eat BBQ for $12.50.

ROSWELL

On the surface an unassuming ranch community, this is one odd little town that's full of surprises. Much of its quirky personality comes thanks to a single event – the crash of a mysterious 'spacecraft' in a field near here in 1947, and the alleged recovery of alien bodies. The 'Roswell Incident' claimed national headlines at the time, and debates still rage today about what *really* happened. The army officially says it was a weather balloon; we, of course, know differently.

All kinds of people now flock to this out-of-the-way town to try and figure it out for themselves. Roswellians, though, seem to be having fun with the concept, creating an entire tourist industry around the crash – eg downtown street lights are adorned with alien eyes.

The friendly folks at the town **visitors bureau** (☎ 505-624-7704, 888-767-9355; www.roswellcvb.com; 426 N Main St) have the facts.

Believers and skeptics alike will want to head immediately to the free **International UFO Museum & Research Center** (☎ 505-625-9495; www.iufomrc.com; 114 N Main St; ☺ 9am-5pm), the town's chief attraction. Displays are wordy and sometimes difficult to follow; they explore the history of UFO encounters worldwide. Informative, yet still good, wacky fun. Aficionados shouldn't miss the annual **Roswell UFO Festival** over the July 4 weekend.

Roswell has a surprising number of alien-free museums, too. Make time for the **Roswell Museum & Art Center** (☎ 505-624-6744; www.roswellmuseum.org; 100 W 11th St; admission free; ☺ 9am-5pm Mon-Sat, 1-5pm Sun), which includes a planetarium and exhibits on liquid-fuelled rockets and other sexy space-science technology.

Hotels and cheap motels line Main St north of downtown (the best place to look), and 2nd St heading west. The best choice is the **Frontier Motel** (☎ 505-622-1400; www.frontier motelroswell.com; 3010 N Main St; s/d from $28/32; ☒ ▢ ▣).

All-you-can-eat buffets are big business here. Keep your eyes peeled on Main St for gut-busting $5.50 Mexican lunch specials, MSG-free Chinese and Mongolian grill deals and meaty dinner deals under $10.

Scotty's Pit BBQ (☎ 505-622-9550; 109 E Deming; mains $5-9; ☽ 5:30am-2pm) Maybe it's the proximity to Texas, but the beef brisket is great at Scotty's, which also has an old jukebox of vintage 45s.

Nuthin' Fancy Café (☎ 505-623-4098; 2103 N Main St; mains all under $8.25; ☽ 6am-9pm) Surprise: this place features standard blue plate diner specials, espresso and 14 beers on tap.

Crash Site Cafe (☎ 505-627-7904; 1303 W 2nd St; mains $4-9; ☽ 6am-2pm) Delights such as the Galactic Gobbler and Space Burger.

If you've had enough, **Greyhound** (☎ 505-622-2510; 1100 N Virginia Ave) buses depart daily for Albuquerque and Carlsbad.

CARLSBAD CAVERNS NATIONAL PARK

The impressive **Carlsbad Caverns National Park** (☎ 505-785-2232, 800-967-2283; www.nps.gov/cave; admission $6; ☽ 8:30am-6:30pm summer, until 5pm winter) covers 73 sq miles and includes more than 100 known caves, including the 60-mile **Lechugilla Cave** and the justly famous **Big Room** (it's one of two free self-guided tours). Additional guided cave tours ($7 to $20) vary from moderate walks to difficult climbs; call for reservations.

Another major park attraction is the Mexican free-tail **bat colony** that comes to roost here (April to October). Backcountry desert backpacking trips are allowed by free permit.

Motels line Canal St, including the **Economy Inn** (☎ 505-885-4914; 1621 S Canal St; r from $35; ☒). Locals and visitors crowd **Lucy's** (☎ 505-887-7714; 701 S Canal St; mains $6-12) for cheap, tasty New Mexican meals.

Greyhound (☎ 505-887-1108; 1000 S Canyon St) leaves daily for Albuquerque and El Paso.

Rocky Mountains

HIGHLIGHTS

- **Breckenridge** Hit the slopes at the resorts around Breckenridge by day then party the night away in town (p483)
- **Boulder** Tube down Boulder Creek, people watch on the Pearl St Mall or chat up friendly locals at a rooftop bar (p477)
- **Yellowstone & Grand Teton National Parks** Soak in natural hot pots in the world's most volatile hotspot, home to the lower 48's wildest concentration of megafauna (p490)
- **Glacier National Park** Hoof it through hanging valley, around glacial horns, up stunning cirques; skinny-dip in titillating tarns; and establish a rapport with abundant wildlife (p505)
- **Off the beaten track** Sandboard slick dunes and spend a full-moon night under the stars, just you and tons upon tons of sand at the Great Sand Dunes National Monument & Preserve (p486)
- **Best journey** Drive the Million Dollar Highway to Ouray and let the mountains reach out and grab you (p489)

ROCKY MOUNTAINS

FAST FACTS

- **Area** 4,835,076 sq miles
- **Big cities** Denver (population 2,501,500), Colorado Springs (360,900), Boise (185,800), Billings (92,300), Cheyenne (53,000)
- **Budget** $30-50 per day
- **Costs** hostel bed in Denver $16, Denver to Billings bus ticket $95, happy-hour appetizers $2-5
- **Driving times** Denver to Boulder 30 minutes, Denver to Breckenridge 2½ hours, Denver to Durango 7 hours, Yellowstone to Glacier 9 hours
- **Famous for** stunning natural attractions, national parks, outdoor activities, breweries
- **Languages** English
- **Population** 7,469,500
- **Phrases** *Let's lay some fresh tracks* (being the first to ski on freshly fallen snow)
- **Seasons** high (Jun-Aug), low (Sep-Nov & Mar-May), ski resorts high (Dec-Mar)
- **States** Colorado, Wyoming, Montana, Idaho

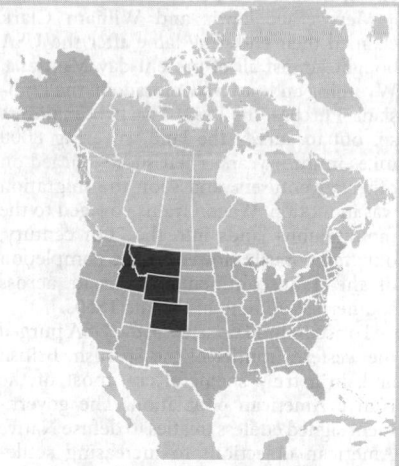

- **Tasty treats** microbrews, southwestern cuisine (especially green chili, game meat, rocky mountain oysters)
- **Time** GMT minus 7 hours
- **Top hostel** Crested Butte Mountain Resort (p487)

TRAVEL HINTS

Look for happy-hour specials at bars and restaurants – you can score seriously cheap grub if you're willing to eat between 3pm and 6pm.

ROCKY MOUNTAINS

If road trips have a soundtrack, it may be the voice of the Rockies – the babble of a brook, the call of an elk, the whoosh of air across your sun-drenched face. Here landscapes pile up, collide and constantly change. The byways of Colorado, Wyoming, Montana and Idaho ease you through alpine valleys and golden windswept prairies then up past lofty snow-capped peaks once considered impassable by humans. Home to some of the country's most spectacular vistas, it's no wonder people migrate from across the country to live here. Outdoor enthusiasts can choose from an all-you-can eat buffet of adventures – rivers fat with winter snowmelt, virgin powder ski bowls and remote trails to crystal mountain lakes.

It seems the sky is always blue, and the sun always shining in this corner of the world. Even the air smells different – sharp and fresh with a hint of pine. Whatever you crave, you'll find it here – a solitary spot amidst an endless big sky in Montana, cowboys and bulls at the old West rodeo in Cheyenne, a cold pint with friends at a Boulder microbrewery. There are cosmopolitan cities with classy clubs, big national parks with grizzlies and moose, and hole-in-the-wall bars where the air is smoky, the accents thick and the hamburgers cheap and greasy.

HISTORY

Before the late-18th century, when French trappers and Spaniards stepped in, the Rocky Mountain area was a land of many tribes, including the Nez Percé, Shoshone, Crow, Lakota and Utes.

Meriwether Lewis and William Clark claimed their enduring fame after the USA bought almost all of present-day Montana, Wyoming and eastern Colorado in the Louisiana Purchase in 1803. The two explorers set out to survey the land, covering 8000 miles in three years. Their success urged on other adventurers, and soon the migration was in motion. Wagon trains voyaged to the mountainous lands into the 20th century, only temporarily slowed by the completion of the Transcontinental Railroad across southern Wyoming in the late 1860s.

To accommodate settlers, the USA purged the western frontier of the Spanish, British and, in a truly shameful era, most of the Native American population. The government signed endless treaties to defuse Native American objections to increasing settlement, but always reneged and shunted tribes onto smaller reservations. Gold miners' incursions into Native American territory in Montana and the building of US Army forts along the Bozeman Trail ignited a series of

wars with the Lakota, Cheyenne, Arapaho tribes, among others.

Gold and silver mania preceded Colorado's entry to statehood in 1876. Statehood soon followed for Montana (1889), Wyoming (1890) and Idaho (1890). Along with miners, white farmers and ranchers were the people with power in the late 19th century.

Mining, grazing and timber played major roles in the area's economic development, sparking the growth of cities and towns to provide financial and industrial support. They also subjected the region to boom-and-bust cycles by their unsustainable use of resources, and left a legacy of environmental disruption.

After the economy boomed post–WWII, the national parks started attracting vacationers. Tourism is now a leading industry in all four states.

THE CULTURE

By reputation and ideology, the Rocky Mountain states (and all of the West) are the most individualistic region of an individualist country. It is also a socially conservative area. The conservatism is heightened by constant change and threats to the 'old way of life.' Even in the most progressive cities of the Rocky Mountain states you will

---

THE BIG ISSUE: WHERE'S THE WATER?

Water is the topic sliding off everyone's tongues these days. Where it's going, and how little of it there is. The region's been in a severe drought for years, and water rationing is no joke. Lawn watering is restricted, and some restaurants only serve a glass of aqua if you request it. In addition, many locals grumble because the water in their rivers is being diverted to quench the thirst of people as far away as Los Angeles.

encounter people whose lives depend (now or generations hence) on mining, logging and ranching. Change is coming quickly through younger generations, yet these are still the traditional cornerstones of the region's economy and need to be accepted if not necessarily agreed with.

Visitors to rural areas of the Rockies will most often find the locals extremely friendly and polite. You are, however, likely to encounter strong conservatism in such areas, especially in places that rely on agriculture, ranching or logging. Visitors should try to be aware of local political issues; don't broadcast your animal rights convictions in a bar full of hunters, or denounce clearcutting in a mill town, without first having some understanding of your audience and their experiences and upbringing.

That said there are liberal and progressive cities spread throughout the region. These tend to be places with large concentrations of university students, many of whom hail from the East or West coasts. A notable example is Boulder, Colorado, where the population leans heavily towards the left and all topics are open for debate (this is a city where residents cry bloody murder at city council meetings over the slaughter of prairie dogs).

SPORTS & RECREATION

Colorado claims fame to the region's national sports franchises, all located in Denver. For more on pro sports see p476.

The University of Colorado at Boulder is a major college football power, and the other state universities in Colorado, Wyoming, Montana and Idaho also field teams.

ARTS & ENTERTAINMENT

Underestimated because of its small population, the West has nevertheless inspired generations of artists and writers. The earliest were the Native Americans who left petroglyphs and pictographs in the canyons of the Colorado Plateau and other regions.

In recent years, resort towns like Jackson and Cody in Wyoming and Aspen, Denver and Boulder in Colorado have gained national recognition as being centers for the arts.

Thanks to the region's prevailing cowboy culture, country-and-western music is the most widespread musical style in the region. Bluegrass is also popular, particularly in Colorado where celebrated bands like Leftover Salmon and Yonder Mountain String formed. Telluride, Colorado, holds a nationally acclaimed bluegrass (as well as film) festival every year. Both draw visitors from around the world. Red Rocks Amphitheatre (outside Denver, Colorado) is highly regarded for both its views (towering red rocks) and its acoustics, and many bands record live albums here.

ENVIRONMENT

Environmental issues are constant topics of debate. The spectacular environmental bounty of the Rocky Mountain states is coveted by numerous competing interests. Timber and mining companies have drawn enormous wealth from the land, while farmers must partly thank dams on the mighty rivers for the increasingly greater harvests. Ranchers are proponents of 'open space,' but only when their cattle graze on it. Facing this coalition of 'mixed-use' supporters are those who call for no more exploitation of natural resources: leave the land to animals and to low-impact humans such as hikers.

Hot environmental issues include the role of the US Forest Service. In Colorado and Montana, the forest service has tried repeatedly to sell parcels of land to timber or energy firms, and has been caught between powerful business interests and extremely vocal angry environmental groups. Wildlife issues are also highly controversial. Debates between animal rights activists and ranchers have been sparked by the reintroduction of grizzly bear and wolf in Montana and lynx in Colorado.

The region is home to some of the USA's biggest national parks. In Colorado there is Rocky Mountain National Park, offering awesome hiking through alpine forests and tundra, and Mesa Verde National Park, in southwestern Colorado, which is primarily an archaeological preserve with elaborate cliffside dwellings.

Wyoming has Grand Teton National Park, with dramatic granitic spires; and Yellowstone National Park, the world's first national park, and a wonderland of volcanic geysers, hot springs and forested mountains. In Montana you'll find Glacier National Park, with high sedimentary peaks, small glaciers and lots of wildlife, including grizzly bear. Idaho is home to Hells Canyon National Recreation

ROCKY MOUNTAINS

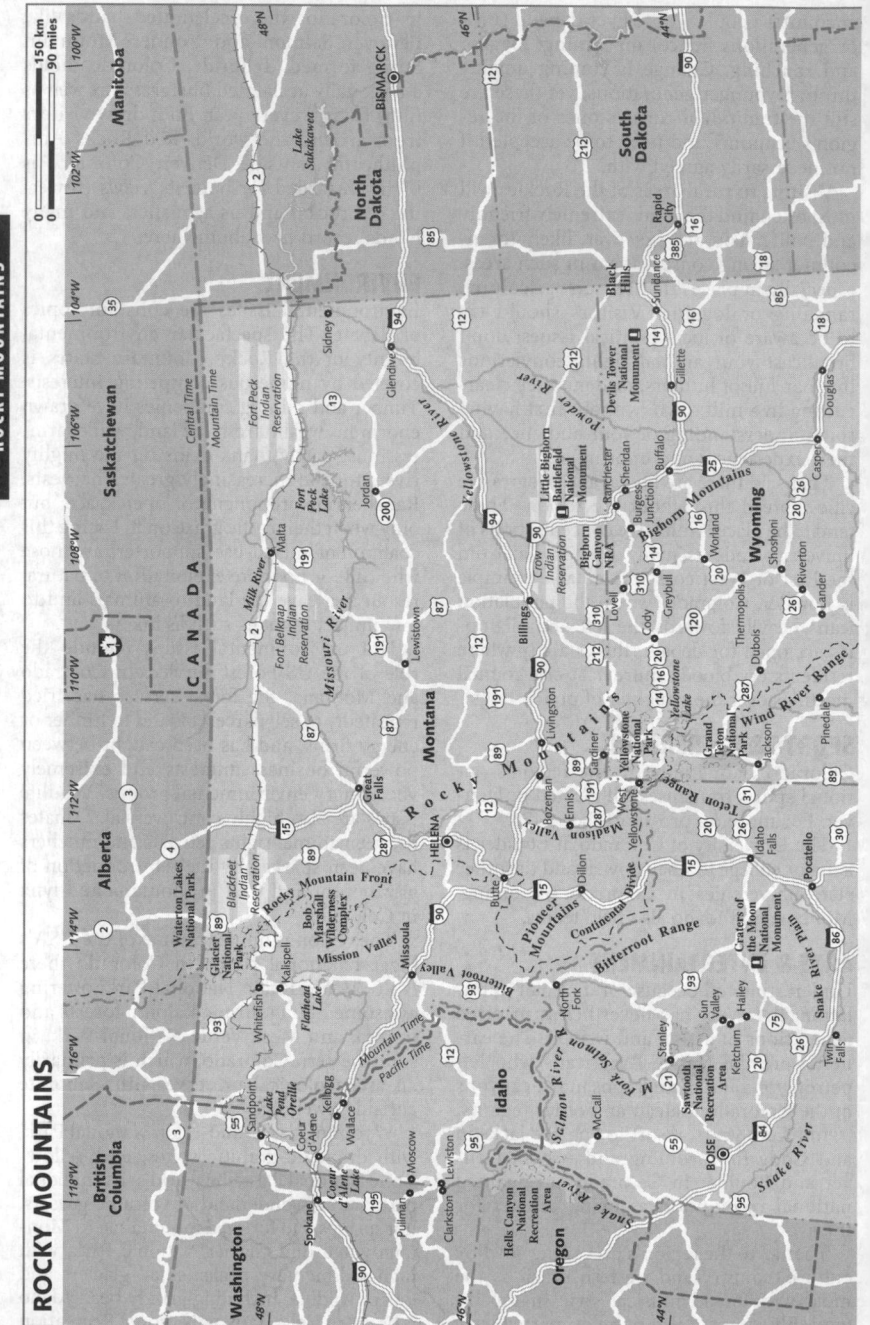

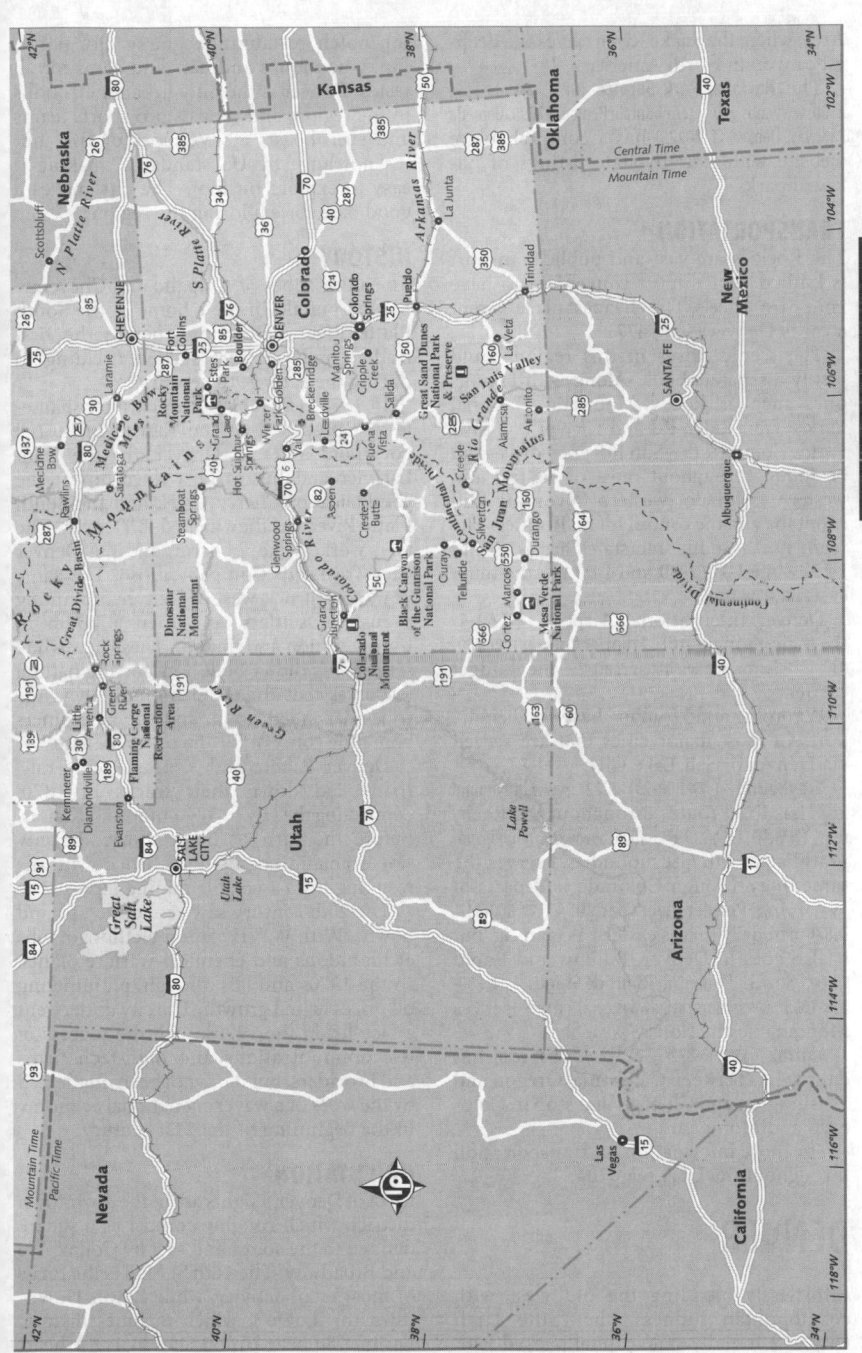

Area, where the Snake River carves the deepest canyon in North America.

The **National Park Service** (NPS; ☎ 303-969-2500; www.nps.gov; Intermountain Region, 12795 Alameda Parkway, Denver, CO 80225) has a comprehensive website with state-by-state listings of national parks.

TRANSPORTATION

The Rockies are vast and public transport is limited, so it's most convenient to have your own wheels. The cheapest place to rent a car is Denver (see p477).

The scenic drives in this region could justify a separate book. Along with famous ones such as Rocky Mountain National Park's Trail Ridge Rd and Glacier National Park's Going-to-the-Sun Rd, great drives can be found throughout most of central and western Colorado, western Wyoming and Montana and the central Idaho Rockies. The main north–south interstates are I-25 and I-15, while I-70, I-80 and I-90 are the main east–west veins.

Denver International Airport (DIA) is the region's main hub. **Frontier Airlines** (☎ 800-432-1359; www.frontierairlines.com) is the budget carrier.

Wyoming and Montana have smaller airports in most major cities that are served via Denver or Salt Lake City.

Greyhound (☎ 800-231-2222; www.greyhound.com) has fixed routes throughout the Rockies. **TNM&O** (☎ 719-635-1505; www.greyhound.com) is affiliated with Greyhound and serves the same lines through Colorado and parts of Wyoming. **Powder River Coach USA** (☎ 800-442-3682) primarily serves eastern Wyoming, but it also goes to Denver, Billings and Rapid City, South Dakota. **Rimrock Stages** (☎ 800-255-7655; www.rimrocktrailways.com) also serves Montana destinations.

Amtrak (☎ 800-872-7245; www.amtrak.com) has daily trains between California, Oregon and Washington and Chicago that stop in Colorado and Montana.

For more information on transportation throughout the USA see p704.

DENVER

Effortlessly blending the old west with cosmopolitan hipness, the 'Mile High City' is a friendly state capital packed with top-notch restaurants, grassy city parks, funky boutiques and bars and clubs for all tastes. Denver is the only urban metropolis in the region, and it hosts pro sports teams and even boasts a skyscraper or two, but it's not huge by US standards, making it easy to explore on foot. The city makes a good base for exploring the region.

HISTORY

The allied tribes of Arapaho and Cheyenne hunted buffalo in their home of the South Platte River Valley long before the first traders and trappers started trickling in during the early 19th century.

In 1858 General William Larimer shamelessley proposed to the Kansas territorial governor, James W Denver, that he grant Larimer and his party a township at the confluence of Cherry Creek and the South Platte River – if they named it 'Denver.' The plan worked like a charm, and the Denver City Township Company arose. The same year, gold struck west of Denver prompting a rush of settlers, and then a boom in transportation and finance. These new white settlements didn't bode well for the natural resources that the Arapaho and Cheyenne tribes depended upon, and the newcomers bore little concern for the tribes' welfare.

Denver Pacific and Kansas Pacific railroads laid down their tracks in 1870, connecting the city to Wyoming and Kansas. Before the turn of the century, the city saw dramatic booms and then downturns resulting from a volatile mining industry.

The 20th century saw economic ups and downs. With WWII came a plethora of jobs at munitions and chemical-warfare plants. In the 1970s and 80s, though, plummeting oil prices halted growth. The city underwent a face-lift in the 1990s, with the success of telecommunications and high-tech firms and providers, but it has not been unaffected by the woes of a wavering national economy in the beginning of the 21st century.

ORIENTATION

Most of Denver's sights are in the downtown district, which roughly comprises a square defined to the south and east by Colfax Ave and Broadway. The 16th St Mall is the focus of most retail activity, while Lower Downtown (or 'LoDo'), which includes historic Larimer Sq near Union Station, is the heart of Denver's restaurant and nightlife scene. To access LoDo and the 16th St Mall, exit I-25 at Speer Blvd.

INFORMATION

Bookstores

Book Garden (☎ 303-399-2004; 2625 E 12th Ave) Books for women, and gay and lesbian readers.

Reel Books Audio Bookstore (☎ 303-629-5528; 1580 Blake St) Books on tape and CD for sale or rental.

Tattered Cover Bookstore (☎ 303-436-1070; 1628 16th St) Denver's most loved bookstore.

Emergency

In the event of a city-wide emergency, AM radio station 850 KOA is a designated point of information.

Denver Police/Fire/Paramedics Communications Center (☎ 720-913-2000)

Police Headquarters (☎ 720-913-2000; 1331 Cherokee St)

Rape Assistance & Awareness Program (☎ 303-322-7273) Can assist victims of rape and domestic violence; 24-hour hotline.

Rocky Mountain Poison & Drug Center (☎ 303-739-1123, 800-332-3073; 1001 Yosemite St)

Internet Access

Denver Public Library (☎ 720-865-1111; 10 W 14th Ave) Free Web access.

Media

The mainstream newspapers are the *Denver Post* and the *Rocky Mountain News*. The best source for local events is the free weekly *Westword*. Monthly glossy-mag *5280* has a comprehensive dining guide.

Medical Services

Denver Health Medical Center (☎ 303-436-6000; 777 Bannock St)

Rose Medical Center (☎ 303-320-2121; 4567 E 9th Ave)

University Hospital (☎ 303-399-1211; 4200 E 9th Ave)

Money

American Express (☎ 303-383-5050, 800-291-9598; 555 S 17th St)

Thomas Cook (☎ 303-333-5713; 299 Detroit St)

Wells Fargo Bank (☎ 303-861-8811; 1740 Broadway)

Post

Post Office (☎ 303-296-4692; 951 20th St) This is the main branch.

> **GETTING INTO TOWN**
>
> If you're arriving by bus you'll be dropped off at **Denver Bus Station** (1055 19th St). From here it's an easy walk to the 16th St Mall (the heart of downtown Denver). Turn right on Curtis St and follow it to 16th St. From the airport look for the SkyRide buses that will take you downtown ($8, one hour, hourly).

Tourist Information

Denver Visitors Center (☎ 303-892-1505; www.denver.org; 918 16th St; 9am-5pm Mon-Fri) Invaluable resource for both city and state information.

SIGHTS & ACTIVITIES

Denver makes a great base for exploring the region, although the city itself holds less interest for shoestringers than the surrounding areas. The best way to experience Denver is on foot. The **16th St Mall**, a pedestrian-only strip of downtown, is lined with shops, restaurants and bars and is a great place to stretch your legs or people watch from an outdoor café. Another not-to-be missed area is funky **LoDo**, centered around Larimer Square. This is the place to have a drink or browse the boutiques.

Fifteen miles southwest of Denver on Hwy 93 is **Red Rocks Park & Amphitheatre** (☎ 303-640-2637; www.redrocksonline.com; 16352 County Rd 93; park admission free, concerts from $30; 5am-11pm). This 9000-seat outdoor amphitheatre is set between 400ft-high red sandstone rocks and provides acoustics so good that many artists record live albums here. The theater offers stunning views and draws big-name bands all summer long. Even if you can't afford a show, visit the park to hike through the bizarrely placed rocks. Also hanging out in the parking lot during a popular gig (like when the Dead play) can be great fun – arrive around 3pm with a couple of six-packs of beer and drink with the locals. Who knows, you may even score discount tickets.

If museums are your thing, the excellent **Black American West Museum & Heritage Center** (☎ 303-292-2566; 3091 California St; admission $5; 10am-2pm Mon-Fri, 10am-5pm Sat & Sun, closed Mon-Tue winter) chronicles the explorations of African-Americans in the West during the 19th century. You'll be introduced to many intriguing characters – from black cowboys

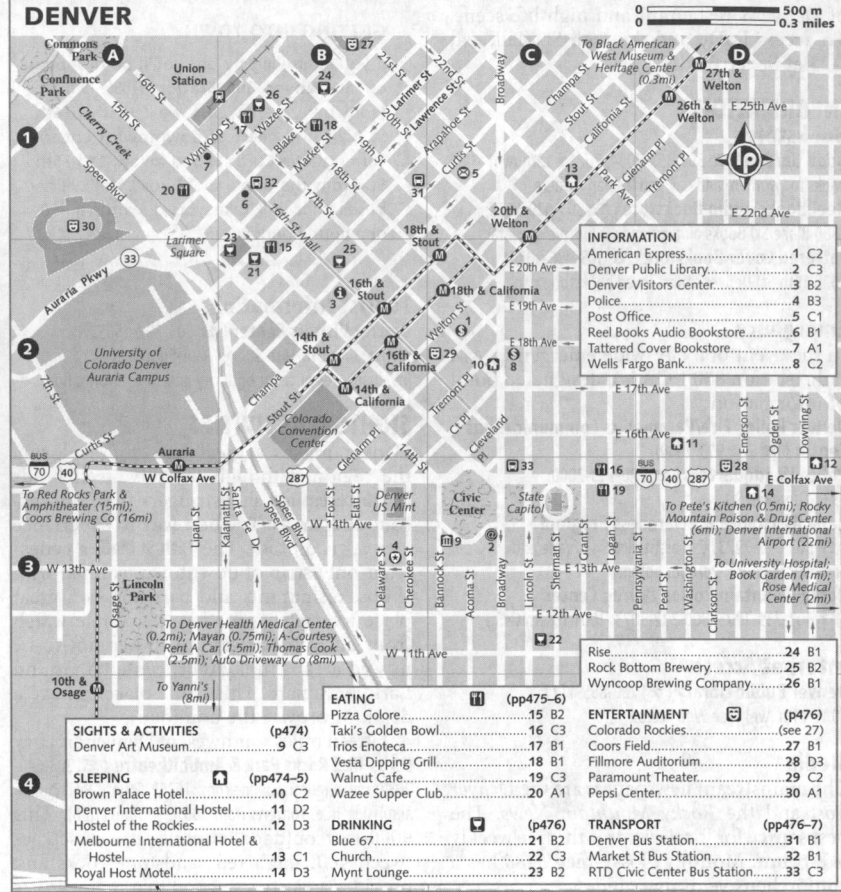

DENVER

to rodeo riders. The museum offers a glimpse at often overlooked contributions of African-Americans during this era.

Also try the **Denver Art Museum** (720-865-5000; www.denverartmuseum.org; 100 W 14th Ave; adult/student $8/6; 10am-5pm Tue-Sat, 10am-9pm Wed, noon-5pm Sun), which houses fine Asian, European and Western American departments as well as one of the largest Native American art collections in the USA.

FESTIVALS & EVENTS

Following are just a few highlights of Denver's festival-laden year. Ask the visitors center for a complete schedule.

Cinco de Mayo (303-534-8342; www.newsed.org) Salsa music and margaritas at one of the country's biggest Cinco de Mayo celebrations. held on the first weekend in May.

Great American Beer Festival (303-447-0816; www.beertown.org) A whole gamut of brew in early September.

Taste of Colorado (303-295-6330; www.ataste ofcolorado.com) More than 50 restaurants cook up their specialties at various food stalls on Labor Day. In addition, there's booze, live music and lots of arts and crafts vendors.

SLEEPING

Besides the places mentioned here there are various chain and independent motels scattered throughout the city with rooms starting at $50. The closest campground is 15 miles north of the city in Broomfield.

Denver International Hostel (☎ 303-832-9996; fax 303-861-1376; 630 E 16th Ave; dm $9) With the cheapest beds in town, this hostel is very fine value. The same-sex rooms are a little cramped but cheerful, and there are rarely more than five people in a dorm.

Hostel of the Rockies (☎ 303-861-7777; 1530 Downing St; dm from $16, r $40) It's the busiest hostel in town, offering same-sex dorms that are slightly spacious, with just four beds to a room. A free, basic breakfast is available daily.

Melbourne International Hotel & Hostel (☎ 303-292-6386; www.denverhostel.com; 607 22nd St; dm from $13, s/d with shared bathroom $23/32; 🖵) This clean hostel's greatest asset is its cheap private rooms, which are basic but not impersonal. The hostel operates an on-site coffee house, perfect for lounging with a good book.

Royal Host Motel (☎ 303-831-7200; 930 E Colfax Ave; r $50; ✹) It's a little run-down and slightly sleazy, but it's quite secure and located near a popular music venue and bar strip. Rooms are basic, and roomy enough for wheelchair users. Some rooms don't have a phone, so request one if needed.

SPLURGE!

Brown Palace Hotel (☎ 303-297-3111; www .brownpalace.com; 321 17th St; r from $235; ✹) This distinguished historic landmark is the place to stay in Denver. Within walking distance of restaurants and nightlife, the Brown Palace is elegantly decorated and provides old world atmosphere and excellent service. It has hosted everyone over the years – from the Beatles to Winston Churchill. Don't let the published rates deter you; there are often specials if booked online through brokers like www.hotels.com. It makes for a great end of the trip splash out.

EATING

Denver has restaurants for all tastes and budgets. Cheap street meals can be found on the 16th St Mall.

Yanni's (☎ 303-692-0404; 2225 S Monaco Parkway; mains $11-20) The flavors explode in your mouth, and you won't be able to put your fork down at this atmospheric Greek restaurant with its generous portions. As if that's not enough, the owner comes by frequently

---

LATE NIGHT GRUB

Pete's Kitchen (☎ 303-321-3139; 1962 E Colfax Ave; mains from $3; ☯ 24hr) This Denver institution is where everyone heads for breakfast after the clubs close. Lines start forming at 1:30am, so arrive early or prepare to wait! All the American diner basics are here – steak and eggs, waffles, greasy burgers, weak coffee – waiting to sop up the alcohol flowing through your system. Pete's is great for people watching.

---

with complimentary ouzo shots. It's well worth the effort it takes to reach this pleasant family-run south Denver restaurant. Try one of the daily specials.

Pizza Colore (☎ 303-534-6884; 1512 Larimer St; mains from $6) Big portions of inexpensive pasta and wood-oven pizzas are served at this casual Italian restaurant. The food is delicious (especially considering the price). There's ample outdoor seating if the weather cooperates.

Taki's Golden Bowl (☎ 303-832-8440; 341 E Colfax Ave; mains $4-8) In this casual space, you can slurp down healthy Japanese noodles, scarf down big bowls of rice and drink down miso-ginger soup (aka 'flu killer soup'). It's a good-value option with plenty for the vegetarian diner.

Trios Enoteca (☎ 303-293-2887; 1730 Wynkoop St; happy hr pizza $5) Art-glass lampshades, bare brick walls and exposed timber create the atmosphere at this sleek LoDo joint, and might make you question if the posh place is out of your price range. But arrive between 4pm and 7pm Tuesday through Thursday, and you're in for a pleasant surprise – gourmet pizzas are half-price, as is the wine (and there are more than 50 varieties to choose from).

Wazee Supper Club (☎ 303-623-9518; 1600 15th St; mains $7-9, pizzas $10-18) Once you step into Wazee, there's little chance you'll turn around – it smells that delicious. Known for some of the best pizza in the city, this longtime local favorite is a friendly, buzzing place.

Walnut Cafe (☎ 303-832-5108; 338 E Colfax Ave; mains $5-7; ☯ 7am-2pm) This is *the* breakfast spot in the 'hood, with a diverse range of offerings, from American standards like waffles and egg variations to breakfast burritos; healthy lunches are also served. Get there early, or be patient.

SPLURGE!

Vesta Dipping Grill (☎ 303-296-1970; 1822 Blake St; mains $15-25; ☾ dinner only) Pick a type of meat and then choose from 30 different sauces to dip it into. It's a simple concept that works exceedingly well. The melt-in-your mouth quality of the creative dishes – many Asian inspired – makes Vesta one of Denver's top restaurants, and the lines form early. The atmosphere is relaxed yet funky and there's a full bar.

DRINKING

Most bars and nightspots are in LoDo, though you'll also find action on the grittier E Colfax Ave, east of the State Capitol. The biweekly gay newspaper *Out Front*, found in coffee shops and bars, has entertainment listings.

Mynt Lounge (☎ 303-825-6968; 1424 Market St) This is one of the best happy hours in town – from 3pm to 9pm the martinis are just $3, and there is a massive list to choose from. Mynt is an ultra-swank white-themed minimalist lounge with a very sexy vibe.

Wyncoop Brewing Company (☎ 303-297-2700; 1634 18th St) The big Wyncoop is arguably the city's most rocking brewery. It offers an interesting selection of beers and there are over 20 pool tables upstairs.

Rock Bottom Brewery (☎ 303-534-7616; 1001 16th St) This place has people-packed booths, a bustling bar, sports-screening TVs and an outdoor patio prime for sunny afternoons with a pitcher.

Blue 67 (☎ 303-260-7505; 1475 Lawrence St) The true-blue draw at this suave bar and restaurant is the drink – it offers over 60 styles of martini. Flavors include chocolate strawberry, Japanese pear and a token 'cowboy martini.' Live jazz plays nightly from about 9:30pm.

CLUBBING

Rise (☎ 303-383-1909; 1909 Blake St; admission $10) One of Denver's hottest clubs, the music changes nightly. Downstairs the atmosphere is trippy light show and go-go dancers, scantily clad waitresses and Chinese pole dancers. Upstairs it's more sedate with a tranquil lounge and outdoor palm-lined patio. Locals say Rise is one of Denver's best spots for singles. On Friday and Saturday

from 9pm to 10pm drinks are free. Girls, arrive before 11pm on Wednesday and score free drinks, food and no cover.

Church (☎ 303-832-3538; 1160 Lincoln St; admission $10) There's nothing like ordering a stiff drink inside an old cathedral. Yes, this club, which draws a large and diverse crowd, is in a former house of the Lord. There are three dance floors, a couple of lounges and even a sushi bar! Arrive before 10pm Friday through Sunday to avoid the cover charge. On Thursday the club opens its doors to the 18-plus crowd.

ENTERTAINMENT
Theater

To find out everything that is happening with music, theater and other performing arts, pick up a free copy of *Westword*. In town, the main venues for national acts are **Paramount Theater** (☎ 303-534-8336; 1621 Glenarm Pl) and **Fillmore Auditorium** (☎ 303-837-0360; 1510 Clarkson St).

Sports

Denver is a city known for manic sports fans and boasts five pro teams. The **Colorado Rockies** (☎ 303-762-5437, 800-388-7625) play baseball at the highly rated Coors Field. The **Pepsi Center** (☎ 303-405-1111) hosts the Denver Nuggets basketball team and the Colorado Avalanche hockey team. The much-lauded **Denver Broncos** (☎ 720-258-3333) football team and the **Colorado Rapids** (☎ 303-299-1599, 800-844-7777) soccer team play at **Mile High Stadium** (☎ 720-258-3000).

GETTING THERE & AWAY

Denver International Airport (DIA; www.flydenver .com; 8500 Peña Blvd) is served by around 20 airlines and offers flights to nearly every major US city. Located 24 miles from downtown, DIA is connected with I-70 exit 238 by the 12-mile-long Peña Blvd.

Greyhound buses stop at the **Denver Bus Station** (☎ 303-293-6555; 1055 19th St), which runs services to Cheyenne ($19, three hours, daily) and Billings ($95, 14 hours, daily). **Powder River Coach USA** (☎ 800-442-3682) and **TNM&O** (☎ 806-763-5389) also stop here.

Amtrak's (☎ 800-872-7245) *California Zephyr* runs daily between Chicago and San Francisco via Denver. Trains arrive and depart from **Union Station** (☎ 303-825-2583; 17th & Wynkoop Sts).

GETTING AROUND

Street parking can be a pain, but there are slews of pay garages in downtown and LoDo. Nearly all the major car rental firms have counters at DIA.

For those lacking a credit card, **A-Courtesy Rent A Car** (☎ 303-733-2218, 800-441-1816; 270 S Broadway; ☿ 7:30am-5pm Mon-Fri) accepts cash deposits, but its vehicles cannot be driven outside the state.

For drive-aways (rented from vehicle transport companies that need drivers to move cars from one place to another), try **Auto Driveaway Co** (☎ 303-757-1211; autodriveaway@ quest.net; 5777 E Evans Ave; ☿ 9am-5pm Mon-Fri).

Public Regional Transit District (RTD; ☎ 303-299-6000; www.rtd-denver.com) provides public transportation throughout the Denver and Boulder area. Buses cost $1.25. Useful free shuttle buses run along the 16th St Mall.

RTD also operates a light-rail line serving 16 stations on a 12-mile route through downtown. Fares are the same as for local buses.

For a taxi try **Yellow Cab** (☎ 303 777-7777).

COLORADO'S FRONT RANGE

The Front Range of the Rockies stretches from Colorado Springs north to Fort Collins along I-25 and includes a stretch of cities and towns, many little more than satellite communities of Denver. A few places west of the I-25 (eg Rocky Mountain National Park and Cripple Creek) make easy day trips from the Front Range.

BOULDER

Tree-hugging hippies, wealthy trust funders, well-heeled young professionals and hard-drinking college kids (the 30,000-student-strong University of Colorado is here – with a reputation of party, party, party) all give the city its unique independent vibe. Boulder has an ongoing love affair with the outdoors – the first thing you'll notice is the slew of mountain bikers peddling up and down the main roads. The city is a long ways from the conservative mind-set found in much of Colorado, in fact some residents take pride in saying they live in the 'People's Republic of Boulder.' Hang out on the pedestrian-only Pearl St Mall – packed with boutiques, restaurants and bars, bars, bars – and catch a street performance. Down a pint or two at one of the microbreweries or pick up a six-pack and tube down the Boulder Creek on a hot summer day; whatever your whim Boulder will indulge.

Orientation & Information

Boulder's two areas to see and be seen are the downtown Pearl St Mall and the University Hill district (next to campus), both off Broadway. Overlooking the city from the west are the Flatirons, an eye-catching rock formation. Boulder is north of Denver. From I-25 exit at Hwy 36 (it's a left-hand exit) and follow this road for about 20 miles into town.

Boulder Bookstore (☎ 303-447-2074; 1107 Pearl St) Large selection of travel guides and recent fiction.

Boulder Visitors Center (☎ 303-442-2911; www .bouldercoloradousa.com; 2440 Pearl St; ☿ 8:30am-5pm Mon-Thu, 8:30am-4pm Fri) Offers information and Internet access.

SCENIC DRIVE: PEAK TO PEAK HIGHWAY

Stretching some 40 miles between Nederland and Estes Park, this route takes you past a series of breathtaking mountains, including the 14,255ft Longs Peak, lush valleys and grassy meadows. You can break up the ride by stopping at one of the little towns along the way. Our favorite is Ward. Just opposite the turnoff for Ward is a road leading up to Brainard Lake. The lake itself is tiny but in a gorgeous setting and there are some great hiking trails leading from it. Afterwards stop in at the Millsite Inn, just north of the turnoff. On sunny fall days it's packed with colorful characters and features greasy hamburgers and dripping cold microbrews in an old crumbling wooden structure with a creaky porch.

End your day at the Stanley Hotel in Estes Park (gateway to Rocky Mountain National Park – see p480). Best known for inspiring Stephen King's horror novel the *Shining*, it's an atmospheric old hotel. The bar and outdoor patio are pleasant spots for a late afternoon drink.

To reach the Peak to Peak Highway from Boulder, drive west on Hwy 119 until you reach Nederland, then take Hwy 72. Allow between three and five hours.

ROCKY MOUNTAINS

Sights & Activities

Shop, hike, bike and drink until you drop. The main feature of downtown Boulder is the **Pearl St Mall**, a lovely, vibrant pedestrian zone filled with shops, bars, galleries and restaurants.

Head west on Arapahoe Ave until it dead-ends into Eben G Fine Park. Here you'll find Boulder Creek. In the summer locals buy tubes at the **Conoco Gas Station** (☎ 303-442-6293; 1201 Arapahoe Ave; tubes $14) then float down the creek. The rapids are mild to slightly wild – there's a few small waterfalls sure to flip your tube, and there are good swimming holes. Cross over the bridge in the park and follow one of the numerous hiking trails for high-above-the city views and red rock scrambles.

From the popular Chautauqua Park, at the west end of Baseline Rd, **hiking** trails head in many directions, including up to the Flatirons. Other nice hikes head up Gregory Canyon and Flagstaff Mountain. The easy Mesa Trail runs north 7 miles from Chautauqua to Eldorado Canyon and offers access to more difficult routes, such as Shadow Canyon, Fern Canyon and Bear Canyon, which leads up to Bear Peak (elevation 8461ft).

The 16-mile Boulder Creek Trail is the main **cycling** route in town and leads west to an unpaved streamside path to Four Mile Canyon. Challenge-seekers can also ride 4 miles

---

COLORADO'S TOP FIVE MICROBREWERIES *Aaron Anderson*

There's a microbrewery around every corner in Colorado, so how do you pick the best? We offer a sampling.

- **Avery Brewing Co** (☎ 303-440-4324; 5763 Arapahoe Ave, Boulder) If it's big, bold, hoppy beers you're craving, Avery will become an instant favorite. Not a brewpub (there's no food), it is a pure microbrewery and you can find the beers at most liquor stores. Try the holy trinity of ales: the Reverend, a 10% alcohol quadruple containing Belgian dark candy sugar, will make you a believer in Avery's philosophy of 'small brewery, big beers,' while the Salvation, another Belgian-style ale, goes down so smoothly you won't believe it is 9% alcohol. Finally an outright testament to the glory of the hop is Hog Heaven. At 9.2% alcohol and 100 IBUs (that's a lot of hops), this barley wine is perhaps the best around.

- **Mountain Sun Pub & Brewery** (☎ 303-546-0886; 1535 Pearl St; Boulder) Winning gold recently at the Great American Beer Festival for its Pearl Street Porter, Mountain Sun offers the best of Boulder with a variety of hoppy, full-bodied unfiltered ales. Try the Pearl Street Porter, a dark, robust, dryly hopped porter or the XXX beer, a high alcohol, very hoppy, super-pale ale. If that's not enough, try the Java Porter and get your coffee/beer buzz simultaneously. See also p479.

- **New Belgium Brewing Co** (NBB; ☎ 800-622-4044; 500 Linde St, Fort Collins; guided tours 2pm & 4pm Mon-Fri, 11am-4pm Sat) Choose your own destiny with a self-guided tour and complimentary tasting of the flagship and specialty brews. Recognized as one of the world's most environmentally conscious breweries, NBB was the first totally wind-powered operation thanks to a 100,000kW turbine. Best known for its Fat Tire Ambler Ale, we recommend leaving the herd and trying the Loft, Trippell or Sunshine Wheat. Fort Collins is an hour north of Boulder on I-25.

- **Ska Brewing Co** (☎ 970-247-5792; 545 Turner Dr, Durango) Another gold winner at the Great American Beer Festival, Ska makes beers that are huge on character, like the Pinstripe Red Ale or the Buster Nut Brown Ale. Go even lighter with the True Blond Ale and Mexican Logger. Also not a sit-down brewpub, Ska is available at most liquor stores. If you're in Durango give the brewery a call to set up a tour.

- **Smugglers Brewpub & Grille** (☎ 970-728-0919; 225 South Pine St, Telluride) Smugglers is a casual place to hang out in the mountains any season. With at least seven beers on tap, this brewpub is big on variety. And with the pint of the day only $2 between 3pm and 5pm, you can afford to sample the best they have. Our picks are the chocolately Two Plank Porter, the Smuggler's Scottish Strong Ale, and you'll always strike gold with an Ingrams IPA.

up Flagstaff Rd to the top of Flagstaff Mountain. Bike rentals, maps and information are available from **University Bicycles** (☎ 303-444-4196; 839 Pearl St) and **Full Cycle** (☎ 303-440-7771; 1211 13th St).

Eldorado Canyon State Park (☎ 303-494-3943; visitors center ⊙ 9am-5pm) is one of the country's most favored **rock-climbing** areas, offering Class 5.5 to 5.12 climbs. The park entrance is on Eldorado Springs Dr, west of Hwy 93. Information is available from **Boulder Rock Club** (☎ 303-447-2804; 2829 Mapleton Ave).

In the winter city buses leave from the corner of 14th and Walnut Sts (round-trip $7) and take you to **Eldora Mountain Resort** (☎ 303-440-8700; www.eldora.com; Hwy 130; lift ticket $50), where you can spend the day skiing and snowboarding on quite decent terrain – it's not as big as some of Colorado's resorts, but it's cheaper.

Sleeping

Like much else in Boulder, sleeping doesn't come cheap.

Boulder International Youth Hostel (☎ 303-442-0522; www.boulderhostel.com; 1107 12th St; dm $17, s/d with shared bathroom $39/45; 🖳) Near all the action on University Hill, this tidy place has the town's cheapest accommodation and boasts kitchen and laundry facilities. There's a three-day limit on the dorms, and room rates are reduced after the first night.

Boulder Mountain Lodge (☎ 303-444 0882; www .bouldermountainlodge.com; 91 Four Mile Canyon Rd; campsites $14, r winter/summer from $60/70; 🐾) Set in a shady canyon, 4 miles west of Boulder on Hwy 119, this lodge is gorgeously placed amid pines and cottonwood trees. It offers shady camping, as well as clean, uncrowded motel-style rooms.

Boulder Outlook Hotel & Suites (☎ 303-443-3322; www.boulderoutlook.com; 800 28th St; r $90; 🖳) This very unique hotel with a funky paint job has a fitting motto: 'cure for the common hotel.' There's a large indoor pool with rocks for scrambling and a Jacuzzi. Rooms are big, there's free Internet access and it's close to the center of town. It's good value for money. For a cheaper deal, try booking on a website like www.hotels.com.

Foot of the Mountain Motel (☎ 303-442-5688; www.footofthemountainmotel.com; 200 Arapahoe Ave; r winter/summer from $60/70; Ⓟ) For both remoteness and convenience to the city, this attractive motel may be ideal. Near the entrance to

Boulder Mountain Park, it has cozy wood-paneled rooms.

University Inn (☎ 303-442-3830, 800-258-7917; www.u-inn.com; 1632 Broadway; r winter/summer from $70/85; 🐾 🖳) The basic rooms here are comfortable, and it's hard to beat the location if you're looking to drink the night away on University Hill and the Pearl St Mall – it's a short walk to both.

Eating & Drinking

The best way to eat in Boulder is during happy hour. Many restaurants feature this between 3pm and 6pm when everything – from appetizers to burgers – is on bargain basement sale. Boulder has a number of microbreweries; for more on these see p478.

Boulder Cafe (☎ 303-444-4884; 1247 Pearl St; mains from $10, happy-hr appetizers from $3) Eat during happy hour, and you're in for a seriously cheap meal at a fancy (and delicious) restaurant. Appetizers and many drinks are half-price during these hours, including the seafood raw bar. And believe us, order a few appetizers and you can consider it dinner. Even better, the outdoor patio is prime real estate for people watching.

Sherpa's Adventurers Restaurant & Bar (☎ 303-440-7151; 825 Walnut St; mains $3-13, lunch special adult/student $7/5.50) Part restaurant, part travel adventure center, this place is run by a Nepalese sherpa and has a large menu consisting of bits of Tibet, portions of Nepal and a few pinches of India. Plates are enormous – the *saag* appetizer ($5) alone can make a meal. For something different try the yak noodles ($13).

Lucille's Creole Cafe (☎ 303-442-4743; 2142 14th St; mains $4-8) Boulder's favorite breakfast spot. Lines form early, but the wait is oh-so-worth-it. There's a Creole lunch menu, but everyone orders breakfast. Try the eggs Sardou ($7) or the daily special.

Boulder Dushanbe Teahouse (☎ 303-442-4993; 1770 13th St; mains $8-14) Incredible Tajik craftsmanship envelops the phenomenal interior of this teahouse presented by Boulder's Russian sister city, Dushanbe. The international fare ranges from Amazonian to Mediterranean to, of course, Tajik.

Mountain Sun Pub & Brewery (☎ 303-546-0886; 1535 Pearl St; burgers $6) A rainbow of brews is available in this tapestry-lined pub, includig fruity beers, and they won't break the bank either at $4 a pint. The place manages to feel relaxed even when busy with its usual eclectic mix of students and locals. The burgers are large and delicious.

West End Tavern (☎ 303-444-3535; 926 Pearl St; mains from $7) Another happy-hour cheapie: Monday through Friday from 4pm to 6pm a dozen wings go for $1 and the meal deal (burger, side and a beer) is just $7. Don't miss the great rooftop deck – Boulder's best.

Reef Piano Bar & Grill (☎ 303-209-3740; 1801 13th St) This super-trendy piano bar is the spot to be on Sunday, when any drink in the house – and we mean anything – is just $3! Otherwise it's a place to watch the beautiful people dance the night away to live music.

Catacombs Bar (☎ 303-443-0486; 2115 13th St) One of the few places in Boulder where you can have a cigarette with your drink (the town has a no smoking ordinance in bars and restaurants), it's full of young college kids looking to get rowdy and hook-up, and there are daily, very cheap, happy hours.

Getting There & Around

RTD (☎ 303-299-6000, 800-366-7433; www.rtd-denver .com) buses provide frequent service in and around Boulder ($1.25); maps are available at **Boulder Station** (14th & Walnut Sts). RTD buses (route B) operate between Boulder Station and Denver's Market St Station ($3.50, one hour). RTD's SkyRide bus (route AB) heads to DIA ($10, 1½ hours, hourly). **SuperShuttle** (☎ 303-444-0808) provides hotel ($19) and door-to-door ($25) shuttle service from the airport.

ROCKY MOUNTAIN NATIONAL PARK

Towering peaks, fields of grazing elk and high-alpine tundra are only a few of the perks that make this stunningly beautiful national park one of America's favorites. It's so alluring, in fact, that over three million visitors mosey in annually. The most popular driving route is **Trail Ridge Rd** (US 34; ✪ Jun–mid-Oct), which winds through spectacular alpine tundra environment. Those who prefer communing with nonhuman nature should venture on foot away from the road corridor; the reward is quiet, superlative scenery.

The most direct route to the park from Boulder follows US 36 through Lyons to the east entrances – it's an easy day trip. Another approach from the south, mountainous Hwy 7, provides access to campsites

and trailheads (including Longs Peak) on the east side of the Continental Divide. Winter closure of US 34 through the park makes access to the west side dependent on US 40 at Granby. Unfortunately, buses from Denver and Boulder will take you only as far as Lyons; from here you'll need to hitch a ride or have your own wheels.

For park information visit the **Fall River Visitors Center** (☎ 970-586-1415; Trail Ridge Rd; ✪ 9am-5pm daily summer, Sat & Sun only winter). Entry to the park (per vehicle/hiker $15/5) is valid for seven days. Backcountry permits ($15) are required for overnight trips.

Rocky Mountain National Park offers lots of hiking opportunities. The bustling **Bear Lake Trailhead** is perfect for easy hikes to several lakes. Another busy area is **Glacier Gorge Junction Trailhead**.

Forested **Fern Lake**, 4 miles from the Moraine Park Trailhead, is dominated by craggy Notchtop Peak. You can complete a loop to the Bear Lake shuttle stop in 8.5 miles for a rewarding day hike, or head into the upper Fern Creek drainage to explore the backcountry. The strenuous **Flattop Mountain Trail** is the only cross-park trail, linking Bear Creek on the east side with either Tonahutu Creek Trail or the North Inlet Trail on the west side.

If you want to summit a 14,255ft mountain, try the strenuous hike to the top of **Longs Peak**, which usually doesn't open until July.

Trail Ridge Rd crosses the Continental Divide at **Milner Pass** (10,759ft), where trails head 4 miles (and up 2000ft!) southeast to Mt Ida, which offers fantastic views.

Before July, many of the trails are snowbound, and high-water runoff makes passage difficult.

The only overnight accommodations in the park are at campgrounds. The park has five formal campgrounds, all with seven-day limits during summer. Fees are $18 ($10 in winter, when the water supply is off). The Moraine Park, Longs Peak and Timber Creek campgrounds are open year-round.

Aspenglen (54 sites) 5 miles west of Estes Park on US 34.

Glacier Basin (150 sites) 7 miles west of BeaverMeadows Visitors Center.

Longs Peak (26 sites) 12 miles south of Estes Park on Hwy 7; provides Longs Peak hikers with an early trail start.

Moraine Park (247 sites) 2.5 miles from BeaverMeadows Visitors Center.

Timber Creek (100 sites) 7 miles north of Grand Lake.

A free shuttle bus provides frequent summer service from the Glacier Basin parking area to Bear Lake. Another shuttle operates between Moraine Park campground and the Glacier Basin parking area. Shuttles run daily from mid-June to early September, and thereafter on weekends only until mid-October.

COLORADO SPRINGS

A bizarre amalgamation of evangelical conservatives, tourists and military installations, this city is home to a large military base, the US Air Force Academy and the North American Radar Air Defense (the command center monitoring US and Canadian airspace is located in a hollowed out mountain and is where the president would weather a nuclear missile strike). Colorado's second-largest city is in a picture-perfect location below famous Pikes Peak and offers a host of activities.

Orientation & Information

I-25 bisects the sprawling metropolitan area; to the east is the central business district, centered around Tejon St between Kiowa St and Colorado Ave. Here you will find restaurants, bars, clubs and shops. To the west of the interstate are Old Colorado City, Garden of the Gods and Manitou Springs. To reach downtown take exit 142. **Colorado Springs Visitors Center** (☎ 719-635-7506; www.coloradosprings-travel.com; 515 S Cascade Ave; ☺ 8:30am-5pm summer, closed Sat & Sun winter) has all the usual tourist info.

Sights & Activities

The bewitching red sandstone formations at the **Garden of the Gods** (the rocks are smack in the middle of town and seem so out of place you won't quite believe your eyes) draw around two million visitors each year to see highlights like Balanced Rock, High Point and Central Garden. Soak up the beauty on one of the park hiking trails.

Since 1891 travelers have been making the trip on **Pikes Peak Cog Railway** up to the summit of Pikes Peak (14,110ft). Katherine Lee Bates was inspired to write *America the Beautiful* after her 1893 journey up the mountain. Now Swiss-built trains smoothly make the round-trip in 3¼ hours, which includes 40 minutes at the top. Trains leave the **Manitou Springs depot** (☎ 719-685-5401; www.cograilway.com; 515 Ruxton Ave, Manitou Springs; admission $26; ☺ Apr-Jan). The depot is 6 miles

from downtown Colorado Springs. Take US 24 west to Manitou Ave; head westward on Manitou Ave, from where you'll make a left onto Ruxton Ave.

Hike the tough 12.5-mile **Barr Trail** to reach the summit for free. From the trailhead, just above the Manitou Springs depot, the path climbs 7300ft. Fit hikers should reach the top in about eight hours. Leave in the early morning, as afternoon thunderstorms can prove deadly. Make sure your body is acclimatized to the altitude before setting out. It's easy to hitch a ride down the mountain once you reach the top.

From the town of Divide, west of Manitou Springs on US 24, you can drive the **Pikes Peak Toll Rd** (per person/car $10/35; ☺ 9am-3pm winter, 7am-7pm summer) to the summit. Due to weather, it's sometimes closed in winter.

Sleeping

Cheap 1950s-style independent motels (quite unique looking, really) line Nevada Ave about 1 mile north and 1 mile south of the CBD. Many of these places are run-down, and some are victims of frequent prostitute stings, but rooms can start as low as $30 a night, and the motels are generally safe. If you're interested in staying longer, ask about weekly and monthly rates.

J's Motor Hotel (☎ 719-635-8539; 820 N Nevada; r from $45; 🅿 🈳) Within walking distance of the downtown nightlife, this place is clean and plain and will do for a night if you just want to sleep.

Garden of the Gods Motel (☎ 719-636-5271; 2922 W Colorado Ave; r from $45; 🅿 🈳) With spacious rooms, an indoor swimming pool and a sauna, this motel is good value. It's conveniently situated within walking distance of Old Colorado shops and restaurants.

El Colorado Lodge (☎ 719-685-5485, 800-782-2246; www.pikes-peak.com/elcolorado; 23 Manitou Ave; d/q from $60/95; 🅿) These comfortable abodes have a fireplace, and the larger ones (for up to six people) are split-level. It's a good deal if you're traveling with four people.

Garden of the Gods Campground (☎ 719-475-9450, 800-248-9451; www.coloradocampground.com; 3704 W Colorado Ave; campsites $28, cabins $40; 🈳) For camping close to town you could do worse than this place. There are only a few trees, and most of the area is paved, but the pool is refreshing and the basic cabins not bad value for money.

Eating & Drinking

The Tejon strip downtown is the place to eat and drink in Colorado Springs.

Western Omelette (☎ 719-636-2286; 16 S Walnut St; breakfast from $4) If you're hungover, do as the locals do and head to the Western Omelette for a green chili cure. The Mexican breakfast dishes like huevos rancheros (with green chili, of course) are superb greasy-spoon fare. The Omelette's a big place completely lacking in character, which oddly gives it its charm.

Tony's (☎ 719-228-6566; 311 N Tejon St; mains $4-7) For greasy sandwiches or mac and cheese, you don't get much cheaper than Tony's (and the quality is not bad either). Pretty much an institution since it opened, Wisconsin-themed Tony's is a neighborhood bar that serves the cheapest pitchers in town. There's often live music at night.

32 Bleu (☎ 719-955-5664; 32 S Tejon St; lunch $7-9, dinner $13-24) Downstairs, this snazzy place makes 32 different glasses of wine available to accompany its internationally influenced nosh. Upstairs, the nightclub books national acts and its recent arrival completely changed Colorado Springs' live music scene (there wasn't really much of one before). Live bands perform nightly (admission is $3 to $20).

Hotel Bar (☎ 719-577-5733; 1 Lake Ave, Broadmoor Hotel) On a warm summer afternoon there's no better spot for a drink with a view than this bar overlooking a private lake. The hotel, one of the finest in the USA, enjoys a magnificent location up against the mountains. Order a chilled glass of wine and a cigar and sit back and watch the ducks pass by. When the weather turns cool they light the outdoor stone fireplaces.

Phantom Canyon Brewing Co (☎ 719-635-2800; 2 E Pikes Peak Ave; mains from $6) In an old exposed warehouse building, this local brewery serves a variety of pints and American cuisine in a casual atmosphere. The appetizers can be large enough for a meal. Locals flock to the upstairs bar for pool and socializing at night.

Rum Bay (☎ 719-634-3522; 20 N Tejon St; admission $5) There are seven clubs in one at this very popular and absolutely giant place. Dance to pulsating techno, sing karaoke, hear live jazz in a romantic lounge or two-step the night away to country music. The cover charge allows you entrance to the equally popular **Tequila's** (☎ 719-630-0500; 25 N Tejon St) across the street.

Getting There & Around

The **Colorado Springs Municipal Airport** (☎ 719-550-1900; 7770 Drennan Rd) offers a viable alternative to DIA. The **Yellow Cab** (☎ 719-634-5000) fare from the airport to the city center is between $20 and $25.

TNM&O buses between Cheyenne, Wyoming and Pueblo stop daily at the **depot** (☎ 719-635-1505; 120 Weber St; ☽ 5am-10pm). The **transportation center** (☎ 719-385-7433; 127 E Kiowa St; ☽ 8am-5pm Mon-Fri) offers information and route maps for all 31 city bus lines.

CRIPPLE CREEK

Just an hour from Colorado Springs, yet worlds away, a visit to Cripple Creek is like stepping back into the Wild West of lore. The booze still flows and gambling still thrives but yesteryear's saloons and brothels have been converted into tasteful casinos. Despite the flashing neon signs, Cripple Creek manages to retain a lot of its old charm, and most casinos are tucked away inside the original century-old buildings still lining the main street.

At the turn of the 20th century the city was one of the most important in the state – producing $340 million worth of gold between 1891 and 1916, and a staggering $413 million worth by 1952.

If nothing else Cripple Creek is a wonderful day trip from Colorado Springs. The road climbs quickly as you head west into the mountains and the last 18 miles, especially in the fall when the trees turn golden, are quite breathtaking.

As far as casinos go, try **Womack's Hotel & Casino** (☎ 719-689-0333; 210 E Bennett Ave) for classy, **JP McGills** (☎ 719-689-2446; 232 E Bennett) for something reminiscent of Las Vegas, and the **Brass Ass** (☎ 719-689-2104; 264 E Bennett), with a giant brass donkey in the doorway, for an old west gambling experience.

If you want to stay the night, the **Cripple Creek Gold Campground** (☎ 719-689-0131; 12654 Hwy 67; campsites $15; ☽ May-Oct), 2 miles northeast of the city, offers leafy and secluded campsites.

Most of the casinos feature on-site restaurants with palatable food at good prices. **Goldie's** (☎ 719-689-2142; Johnny Nolan's Saloon, 301 E Bennett; mains $5-13), upstairs from the saloon, has tables overlooking the casino and daily specials for $5.

Nightlife in Cripple Creek is centered around gambling and the casinos serve free drinks as long as you're playing the slots (get a roll of nickels and feed them into the machine very slowly – you may score some cash, you'll definitely score a lot of free booze). For dancing, darts and pool try the **Horseshoe Saloon** (☎ 719-689-7463; 123 E Bennett). The place retains the charm of a turn-of-the century booze hall with a wine-red carpet and old photographs stretched mural-like across the walls.

Cripple Creek is 50 miles southwest of Colorado Springs on Hwy 67. Catch the **Ramblin' Express** (☎ 719-590-8687; www.ramblin express.com) from Colorado Springs for $22. The bus departs hourly between 7am and 10pm from the 8th St depot and leaves from JP McGills Casino hourly between 8:30am and 2:10am.

NORTHERN COLORADO

Famed for their ski resorts, Colorado's northern mountains also offer numerous opportunities for hiking and white-water rafting in summer.

BRECKENRIDGE & AROUND

When in Breckinridge do as the locals do – ride hard all day, play hard all night. This resort town with a 19th-century mining feel is full of young people looking to party (many migrate to Breck after university to spend a few years 'ski bumming'). With four of Colorado's best resorts less than an hour's drive away, Breckenridge makes an ideal base. The town is about 80 miles west of Denver off I-70. Take exit 203.

Information

The **Visitors Center** (☎ 970-453-6018, 800-221-1091; www.gobreck.com; 309 N Main St; ⊙ 9am-5pm) has information on accommodations.

Activities

In the winter, it's all about the snow. **Breckenridge** (☎ 800-789-7669; www.snow.com; lift tickets $63), spanning 600 acres over four mountains, features some of the best beginner and intermediate terrain around (the green runs are flatter than most in Colorado), as well as killer steeps and chutes for experts, and a renowned snowboard park (it has the USA's largest half-pipe and plenty of jumps).

Arapahoe Basin Ski Area (☎ 970-468-0718, 888-272-7246; www.arapahoebsin.com; lift tickets $50), North America's highest resort, is smaller and less commercial and you can ride A-Basin until mid-June. Full of steeps, walls and back-country terrain, it's a local favorite because it doesn't draw herds of package tourists. The outdoor bar is a great place to kick back with a cold microbrew, and people are always grilling burgers and socializing at impromptu tailgate parties in the parking lot (known as the beach). **Keystone Ski Resort** (☎ 970-496-2316, 877-625-1556; www.keystoneresort.com; lift tickets $61) is another option and has night skiing.

Then there's **Vail Mountain** (☎ 970-476-9090; www.snow.com; lift tickets $70), with world-class skiing at world-class prices. This is where the movie stars ski, and it's not odd to see Texans in 10-gallon hats and ladies in mink coats zipping down the slopes. That said, for terrain, Vail is our favorite resort in Colorado. Wide open and immense, the back bowls (which cater to intermediate and expert skiers) are nothing short of spectacular, especially on a powder day.

In the summer these towns offer loads of hiking and mountain biking. Ride up and bike down the lifts at Breckenridge (single ride/day pass $12/28). The resort rents bikes (half-/full day $20/28).

Sleeping

Breckenridge is a friendly town, so who knows, a local just might take pity on you at the bar and offer a couch or floor to sleep on – especially if you have a cute accent.

Fireside Inn B&B and Hostel (☎ 970-453-6456; www.firesideinn.com; 114 N French St; dm $30, r summer/winter from $65/100; 🖵) This welcoming hostel offers a very comfortable stay, as well as ski and bike storage and a hot tub. Breakfast is free for private-room guests, and $3 for dorm dwellers.

Abbett Placer B&B (☎ 970-453-6489, 888-794-7750; www.abbettplacerbnb.com; 205 S French St; r $85-130) In a restored Victorian home, this is also a personable choice. It is well run, has a hot tub and most of the rooms have a fireplace.

Eating & Drinking

Most of the eating and drinking in Breckenridge takes place along a few blocks of Main St.

ROCKY MOUNTAINS

Downstairs at Eric's (☎ 970-453-1401; 111 S Main St; lunch special $5, dinner from $6) Say you're a local to score the lunch special – a soft drink with small pizza, burger or sandwich and a side. A basement joint, it's a colorful and lively place with filling pub grub that keeps locals returning. There are more than 120 beers to choose from.

Fatty's (☎ 970-453-9802; 106 S Ridge Rd; pizzas from $13) The pizzas are large and yummy and feed at least two. Locals frequent the bar, so it can get rowdy at night. In the summer sit outside on the patio and people watch.

Hearthstone (☎ 970-453-1148; 130 S Ridge St; happy-hr appetizers $5) Try to hit happy hour between 4pm and 6pm at this very cozy Victorian restaurant. It's the perfect place to watch the snow fall over a quiet cocktail. The deal is the breaded jumbo shrimp stuffed with jalapeno. It's 75¢ per shrimp, but after four or five you'll be full. Drinks are $1 off during this time.

Cecilia's (☎ 970-453-2243; 520 S Main St) Breckenridge's most popular late night hang-out, Cecilia's packs in crowds all week long. There's a large dance floor with mostly DJ music, a few pool tables and a corner couch or two.

Sherpa & Yettis (☎ 970-547-9299; 320 S Main St) Another popular nightclub, this one in a basement, Sherpa's is a trendy place with mod art on the walls. Saturdays are hip-hop nights with lots of drink specials; other nights feature live bands, including some big names.

Getting There & Around

Breckenridge is off I-70, 104 miles west of Denver. The **Resort Express** (☎ 970-468-7600, 800-334-7433) offers services between Breck and DIA ($53, two hours, multiple trips daily). To get between the resorts, hop on the free **Summit Stages** (☎ 970-668-0999) buses, which connect Breckenridge with the rest of Summit County and with Vail. It's also easy to hitchhike during the ski season. While this is never entirely safe, most people don't have a problem in this region.

GLENWOOD SPRINGS

Located just outside a spectacular canyon, Glenwood Springs, 150 miles west of Denver on I-70, is a pleasurable place to kick up your heels. Aside from its world-famous hot springs, it offers outdoor adventures ranging from the adventurous to soothing.

For area information, hit the **visitors center** (☎ 970-945-6589; www.glenwoodchamber.com; 1102 Grand Ave; ◷ 9am-5pm Mon-Fri, 10am-5pm Sat & Sun).

The **Hot Springs Lodge & Pool** (☎ 970-947-2955; www.hotspringspool.com; 401 N River St; admission $10; ◷ 7:30am-10pm summer, 9am-10pm winter) is one of Colorado's favorite family vacation spots. It's not a secluded retreat, but there is much to keep you happy – ample shallow areas, deeper areas with diving boards, water-slides and mini-golf.

There's its tip-top road and mountain **biking** as well as tons of **hiking** around Glenwood Springs; pick up a free trails guide at the visitors center. Rent bikes at **BSR Sports** (☎ 970-945-7317; 210 7th St).

Glenwood Canyon offers Class III and IV **white-water rafting** below the Shoshone Dam, 7.5 miles east of town. For guided tours, try **Rock Gardens Rafting** (☎ 970-945-6737, 800-958-6737; tours $20-64). About 20 motels and hotels are in the Glenwood area, and those closest to the city center fill up quickly in summer.

Glenwood Springs Hostel (☎ 970-945-8545, 800-946-7835; 1021 Grand Ave; dm from $12, r from $19; ▯) is a welcoming and relaxed place with kitchens, common lounges and over 3000 records for your listening pleasure. Discounts for hostel guests are available at some area restaurants and sites.

Hotel Denver (☎ 970-945-6565, 800-826-8820; www.thehoteldenver.com; 402 7th St; r from $75; ▨) is a modern hotel with spacious rooms; it has two wheelchair-friendly rooms, one with roll-in shower. It's an easy stroll to the hot springs and the town center.

Before hitting the trails, fuel up at the **Glenwood Cafe** (☎ 970-945-2639; 311 8th St; mains $4-8). Breakfast is of the eggs, hash browns and hotcakes variety, but not greasy enough to leave you comatose after your meal.

Glenwood Canyon Brewing Company (☎ 970-945-1276; Hotel Denver, 402 7th St; sandwiches from $7, mains from $9) has a large menu and a variety of beers named for local attractions or interstate exits. It's a lively rustic place with a fun atmosphere.

Colorado Mountain Express (☎ 970-926-9800, 800-525-6363; www.cmex.com) offers shuttle service to and from DIA ($75, four hours, daily). Amtrak's *California Zephyr* stops daily at the **train depot** (☎ 970-945-9563; 413 7th St). Buses stop at the Greyhound **bus station** (☎ 970-945-8501; 118 W 6th St).

Roaring Fork Transit Authority (☎ 970-920-1905; www.rfta.com) has buses that leave from the Greyhound station and connect Glenwood with Aspen.

ASPEN

Home to great skiing and beautiful alpine scenery, Aspen, Colorado's glitziest high-octane resort, plays host to some of the wealthiest skiers in the word – where else in Colorado can you shop at Prada or Gucci? The scenery, especially in the fall when the Aspen trees put on a spectacular display, is just extra sugary eye-candy. The historic town is charming, and the rock stars that vacation here must like to party, because the bars are happening. Aspen is 150 miles southwest of Denver on Hwy 82.

Information

Aspen Visitors Center (☎ 970-925-1940, 888-290-1324; www.aspenchamber.org; 425 Rio Grande Pl; ☼ 8am-5pm Mon-Fri) Has all the usual info.

Activities

SKIING & SNOWBOARDING

Aspen Skiing Company (☎ 970-925-1220, 800-308-6935; www.aspensnowmass.com; lift tickets $70) operates the area's four ski resorts. **Aspen** (or Ajax) is an athlete's mountain, offering more than 3000ft of steep vertical drop. **Aspen Highlands** has outstanding extreme skiing and breathtaking views. **Buttermilk Mountain** provides gentle slopes for beginners and intermediate skiers, while **Snowmass** offers a mix of intermediate and extreme expert terrain, and boasts the longest vertical drop in the USA (4400ft).

HIKING & BIKING

The three wilderness areas surrounding Aspen offer bountiful **hiking** trails. The Hunter Valley Trail leads through wildflower meadows and into the Hunter–Fryingpan Wilderness Area. Hot springs are the reward after 8.5 miles of moderate climbing on the Conundrum Creek Trail. Another awesome area to hike is the stunningly beautiful Maroon Bells–Snowmass Wilderness Area.

Plenty of quite heavily used **mountain-biking** routes ply Aspen Mountain and Smuggler Mountain. Hunter Valley and the Sunnyside trails provide a challenging single-track loop north of town. The Montezuma Basin and Pearl Pass rides offer extreme cycling experiences, well above the timberline, south of

town from Castle Creek Rd. The **Hub** (☎ 970-925-7970; 315 E Hyman Ave) rents mountain bikes.

Sleeping

Surprisingly, Aspen has a few budget places to stay.

St Moritz Lodge (☎ 970-925-3220; www.moritzlodge.com; 334 W Hyman Ave; dm summer/winter $30/39; r summer/ winter from $60/95; 🖳 🖾) Neat and congenial, this European-style lodge offers a variety of options, from nice dorms to two-bedroom condos. Continental breakfast is served, and there is a pool and steam room.

Mountain Chalet (☎ 970-925-7797, 800-321-7813; 333 E Durant Ave; r from $85; 🖾) Stay here for convenience to both the lifts and town center. Some rooms have a mountain view, and the lounge is well suited for lounging. Amenities include a hot tub and sauna.

The **USFS White River National Forest's Aspen Ranger District** (☎ 970-925-3445; 806 W Hallam; ☼ 8am-4:30pm Mon-Fri winter, also 8am-4:30pm Sat summer) operates nine **campgrounds** (campsites $14) around the area. Watch out for bears, they are plentiful in the area.

Eating & Drinking

Main St Bakery (☎ 970-925-6446; 201 E Main St; mains $6-10) It's a hit, especially at breakfast time, for its gamut of sweet and savory goods (granola and pancakes to chicken pot pie) in its convivial room and outdoor patio.

Woody Creek Tavern (☎ 970-923-4285; 2 Woody Creek Plaza) If you can make it down the valley about 8 miles, do so. This local hang-out is the popular watering hole of gonzo journalist Hunter S Thompson, and quite a few other celebrities. There's cheap beer on tap, walls jam-packed with stuff, and a flavor that's just like the bar back home.

Red Onion (☎ 970-925-9043; 420 E Cooper Ave; mains $8-12) Aspen's oldest saloon, first opened in 1892, is a long-standing favorite of the local ski patrol. There's the usual pub grub to eat.

Cooper St Bar (☎ 970-925-7758; 508 E Cooper Ave; mains $7-12) A good place to start your night with a pint and a burger and to maybe shoot a little pool. The place gets rowdy early.

Double Diamond (☎ 970-920-6905; 450 S Galena St; admission from $5) When live music acts – from rock and blues to salsa and reggae – come into town, they play at this spacious club. It's seen George Clinton, G-Love and many others. Shows generally get rocking at 10pm.

ROCKY MOUNTAINS

IF YOU'VE GOT A COUPLE MORE DAYS IN COLORADO

Pretty much any destination west of I-25 is worthy of exploration, so if you have a little extra time just hit the road and see where it takes you. Here are three destinations worth a red circle on your map.

- **Steamboat Springs** Another classic Colorado ski town, Steamboat, in northwestern Colorado, is full of character and charm. In the winter there's consistently satisfying powder skiing. In the summer you can camp, hike, mountain bike, raft or soak in natural hot springs.

- **Leadville** The air is thin in 10,200ft Leadville, aka 'Cloud City.' A wonderfully scenic town with a dramatic mining legacy, it's well suited for ambling. Hikers come here to scale Colorado's highest peak 14,433ft Mt Elbert and the slightly smaller 14,421ft Mt Massive. Leadville is 100 miles southwest of Denver on Hwy 24.

- **Black Canyon of the Gunnison National Park** Awe and vertigo are natural reactions to this dark, 2000ft-deep chasm over the Gunnison River. The 7-mile S Rim Rd winds along the canyon edge and past overlooks. It's in southwestern Colorado off Hwy 50.

Getting There & Around

Colorado Mountain Express (☎ 970-947-0506, 800-525-6363; www.cmex.com) offers frequent services to DIA ($100, four hours).

BUENA VISTA

Buena Vista won't stick in your mind after you leave, but shooting the rapids of the Arkansas River or soaking in a hot spring under the stars sure will. A bit of a jumping-off point, the area around Buena Vista is certainly worth at least a day of your time. Buena Vista is 90 miles west of Colorado Springs on Hwy 24.

For rafting, stop by **Wilderness Aware Rafting** (☎ 719-395-2112; www.wildernessaware.com; tours from $40). You'll want to run Brown's Canyon (class III-IV), the Narrows (III-IV) or the Numbers (IV-V), and the earlier in the season the better (try for late April or early May when the river is bloated with snow run-off and the rapids are much more intense). The company is located at the junction of Hwys 285 and 24 at Johnson Village, 2 miles south of Buena Vista.

After a day on the river, forget the bruises incurred after the boat flipped with a soak in the five pools at **Cottonwood Hot Springs Inn & Spa** (☎ 719-395-6434; 18999 County Rd 306; admission $15, r from $90). The pools are rustic with fantastic views (the stars can be amazing). Clothing is optional after dark between October and May, and the resort discourages children. The hot springs are about 6 miles south of Buena Vista.

West of town the USFS operates two campgrounds. **Cottonwood Lake** (USFS Rd 344; campsites $10) is on the South Cottonwood Creek about 5 miles down from the County Rd 306 turnoff (near the hot springs). Mountain goats are often spotted on the way to the camp. The large **Collegiate Peaks** (County Rd 306; campsites $10) is on Middle Cottonwood Creek, 11 miles west of Buena Vista. Both are scenic spots.

In Buena Vista itself you'll find a string of motels and lodges with rooms starting at about $80 in the summer, less in winter. There is no public transport to Buena Vista.

SOUTHWESTERN COLORADO

The southern reaches of Colorado's Rockies offer plenty of stunning alpine scenery, some world-class ski resorts and the sprawling San Luis Valley. A broad swath of agricultural land, it is home to the scenic wonders of the Great Sand Dunes and the Sangre de Cristo Mountains and retains a strong sense of its Hispanic heritage.

GREAT SAND DUNES NATIONAL PARK

Landscapes collide in a shifting sea of sand at the **Great Sand Dunes National Park** (☎ 719-378-2312; 11999 Hwy 150; admission $3; Visitors Center ☺ 9am-5pm), making you wonder whether a spaceship has whisked you to another continent. The USA's newest national park, Great Sand Dunes is in the vast San Luis Valley. Squeezed between the jagged 14,000ft peaks of the Sangre de Cristo and

San Juan Mountains and flat, arid scrub brush are 30 sq miles of dunes, the tallest of which rise 700ft from the valley floor.

Plan your visit around a full moon. Stock up on supplies, stop by the visitors center for your free back-country camping permit then hike into the surreal landscape and set up camp in the middle of nowhere. You won't be disappointed.

There are numerous hiking trails, or the more adventuresome can try sandboarding (where you ride a snowboard down the dunes). You'll need your own equipment, but Colorado is jam-packed with snowboard rental shops. Spring is the best time for boarding, when the dunes are most moist. For the slickest boarding arrive a few hours after it rains – when the dunes are wet underneath, but dry on top.

Try riding down Star Dune, roughly 750ft high. It's a strenuous 3-mile hike from the Dunes parking lot. The High Dune, about 650ft tall, is another option. Be sure to bring lots of water. Walking in loose sand is difficult, and summer temperatures on the dunes can exceed 130°F.

There is a campground ($12 per tent) in the preserve. Otherwise, just south of the entrance you'll find the **Great Sand Dunes Oasis** (☎ 719-378-2222; 5400 Hwy 150; campsites $14, d cabins $35; 🏵 May-Oct). Cabins are rustic one-room affairs with shared facilities. The place has a restaurant and grocery store.

The sand dunes are about 35 miles northeast of Alamosa, and 250 miles south of Denver. From Denver, take I-25 south to Hwy 160 west and turn onto Hwy 150 north. There is no public transport.

CRESTED BUTTE

Remote and beautiful Crested Butte feels real. Despite being one of Colorado's best ski resorts (some say *the* best) it doesn't put on airs. There's nothing haughty, or even glossy, about the town – just fresh mountain air, a laid-back attitude and friendly folk.

Crested Butte is 230 miles southwest of Denver. Almost everything in town is on Elk Ave, including the **visitors center** (☎ 970-349-6438, 800-545-4505; www.crestedbuttechamber.com; 601 Elk Ave; 🏵 9am-5pm).

Crested Butte Mountain Resort (☎ 970-349-2333, 800-544-8448; www.skicb.com; lift tickets $60) sits 2 miles north of the town at the base of the impressive mountain of the same name. Surrounded by forests, rugged mountain peaks and the West Elk, Raggeds and Maroon Bells–Snowmass Wilderness Areas, the scenery is wet-your-pants beautiful. It caters mostly to intermediate and expert riders.

Crested Butte is also a **mountain-biking** mecca, full of excellent high-altitude single-track trails. For maps, information and mountain-bike rentals visit the **Alpineer** (☎ 970-349-5210; 419 6th St).

The attractive **Crested Butte International Hostel** (☎ 970-349-0588, 888-389-0588; www.crestedbuttehostel.com; 615 Teocalli Ave; dm $20-27, r with shared bathroom from $60) is one of Colorado's nicest. Bunks come with reading lamps and lockable drawers, and the communal area is mountain rustic with a stone fireplace and comfortable couches.

For more privacy try the handsome cedar-flavored **Inn at Crested Butte** (☎ 970-349-1225, 800-949-4828; www.innatcrestedbutte.com; 510 Whiterock Ave; r incl breakfast from $70). It has comfy doubles

---

DETOUR: ALIEN ENCOUNTERS

The sand dunes may have you thinking you've left the planet, but to really watch for outer space visitors you have to stop by the **UFO Watchtower & Campground** (☎ 719-378-2271; www.ufowatchtower.com; admission by donation; campsites $10; 🏵 11am-10pm), 2.5 miles north of Hooper on Hwy 17, en route to the sand dunes.

Judy Messoline built the watchtower and opened her property up to UFO fanatics in 2000 after her cattle-ranching endeavors failed. The San Luis Valley is known for its high levels of UFO activity. Those who believe in the paranormal say the area is a giant antenna that attracts alien life forms, while Indian legend says it's a window to other worlds. There have been hundreds of unexplained sightings – everything from mile-long crafts to fireballs filling the night sky.

Today people from all over the country make the pilgrimage to her humble dome with its 2nd-story viewing deck. In August hundreds gather for an annual night of close encounters with the third kind. A visit is definitely a unique, and if you're lucky, otherworldly, experience. If nothing else, the sunsets are phenomenal.

and triples, an outdoor hot tub and a free shuttle to the ski resort. There's a wheelchair-accessible room on the ground floor.

The closest large campground to Crested Butte is the reservable USFS **Lake Irwin** (campsites $12), west of town before Kebler Pass.

Certainly not a secret, the **Secret Stash** (☎ 970-349-6245; 21 Elk Ave; pizzas $13-17; ☺ from 5pm) is an enticing pizza place with a joyful interior. Sit on the floor upstairs, or park yourself in a velvety chair.

For pastries, coffee and a chance to surf the web try **Buckaroo Beanery** (☎ 970-349-5252; 601 6th St; mains $2-5; ☐). Cheap breakfasts and lunches are served at the pleasant **Paradise Cafe** (☎ 970-349-6233; cnr 4th St & Elk Ave; mains $4-7). If you have a hankering for Thai or Vietnamese head to **Ginger Cafe** (☎ 970-349-7291; 313 3rd St; mains $8-12). Crested Butte has an interesting music scene year-round and the lively **Eldo** (☎ 970-349-6125; 215 Elk Ave) is where most out-of-town bands play. From the great outdoor deck you can peep at street life below. The **Princess Wine Bar** (☎ 970-349-0210; 218 Elk St) is an intimate bar perfect for sitting and chatting. First-rate live music of the local singer/songwriter flavor is on show nightly.

The free **Mountain Express** (☎ 970-349-7318) connects Crested Butte with Mt Crested Butte every 15 minutes in winter, less often in other seasons; check departure times at bus stops.

DURANGO

A picturesque mountain town on the banks of the Animas River, Durango attracts travelers for a ride on the steam-driven train, and mountain biking, rafting and skiing.

The **visitors center** (☎ 800-525-8855; www.du rango.org; 111 S Camino del Rio; ☺ 8am-6pm daily summer, 8am-5pm Mon-Fri winter) is south of town at the Santa Rita exit from US 550.

Climb aboard the steam-driven **Durango & Silverton Narrow Gauge Railroad** (☎ 970-247-2733, 888-872-4607; round-trip admission from $55), which makes a scenic 45-mile trip north to Silverton, a National Historic Landmark. The journey is best in fall, when the trees put on a magnificent show.

The town's other main draw is **Durango Mountain Resort** (☎ 970-247-9000, 800-693-0175; www.durangomountainresort.com; lift ticket $52), 25 miles north on US 550, which offers skiing during winter and mountain biking, rafting and more in summer.

The family-owned **Siesta Motel** (☎ 970-247-0741; fax 970-247-0971; 3475 N Main Ave; s/d from $45/55; ☒) is one of the town's cheapest options. It's a welcoming place offering spacious and comfortable rooms. There's a little courtyard on-site with a barbecue grill.

The nicest camping option near town is the riverside **United Campground** (☎ 970-247-3853; 1322 Animas View Dr; campsites $20; ☒). The city trolley, part of Durango's public transport system, makes a stop here.

The relaxed **Carver Brewing Co** (☎ 970-259-2545; 1022 Main Ave; lunch $5-7, dinner $10-15) churns out 1000 barrels of brew annually; enjoy a pint with burgers and sandwiches in the outdoor beer garden. If you want to know more about microbrews, see p478.

Greyhound/TNM&O buses run daily from **Durango Bus Center** (☎ 970-259-2755; 275 E 8th Ave) north to Grand Junction and south to Albuquerque, New Mexico.

MESA VERDE NATIONAL PARK

Shrouded in mystery, **Mesa Verde** (7-day pass hiker/car $5/10) is a fascinating, if slightly eerie, park to explore. It is here that a civilization of Ancestral Pueblo Indians appears to have disappeared into thin air in 1300.

Ancestral Puebloan dwellings here first evolved from simple natural structures in AD 450 to great cliff cities that were inhabited around 1200 and were then mysteriously abandoned in 1300. Their disappearance after only a century still defies explanation. The cliff dwellings remained undisturbed until 1849, when a US Army lieutenant stumbled upon them. Today magnificent sites dot the canyons and mesa tops. Hiking and biking opportunities are slim, but immersion into the past is readily on offer.

From the entrance, it's 15 miles to the **Far View Visitors Center** (☎ 970-529-5034; ☺ 8am-5pm), where visitors must stop for compulsory tickets ($2.50) for tours of the magnificent Cliff Palace or Balcony House.

The largest concentration of Ancestral Puebloan sites in the area is at **Chapin Mesa**, including the densely clustered Far View Site and the large Spruce Tree House. At **Wetherill Mesa**, the second-largest concentration, visitors may enter stabilized surface sites and two cliff dwellings, including the Long House, open late May through August. South from park headquarters, the

---

SCENIC DRIVE: MILLION DOLLAR HIGHWAY

Between Silverton and Ouray, US 550 is known as the Million Dollar Highway because the road-bed fill contains valuable ore. One of the state's most memorable drives, it's a breathtaking stretch of pavement that passes old mine head-frames and larger than life Alpine scenery – at some points the spectacular peaks are so close they seem ready to grab you. The road is scary when raining or snowing, so take extra care.

In the heart of the lush San Juan Mountains, little Ouray is known for the **Ouray Hot Springs** (970-325-4638; pool admission $8) and **Ouray Ice Park** (☎ 970-325-4061; www.ourayicepark.com), the world's first dedicated ice-climbing area. Even without these the town would still be an eye-catching place. The imposing peaks leave barely 0.25 miles of valley floor in town. Allow between two and four hours.

6-mile-long **Mesa Top Rd** connects excavated mesa-top sites, accessible cliff dwellings and vantages of inaccessible cliff dwellings from the mesa rim.

You can camp at **Morefield Campground** (☎ 970-533-1944, 800-449-2288; campsites $19; ☼ Apr-Oct). There are also motels aplenty in Cortez and a few places in the town of Mancos, including the charming and gay-friendly **Old Mancos Inn** (☎ 970-533-9019; fax 970 533 7138; 200 W Grand Ave; s/d with shared bathroom $30/35).

TELLURIDE

It's been a hunting ground for the Utes, a saloon-swinging mining mecca and a ghost town. But nowadays, folks flock to this archetypal mountain town for outdoor adventures galore, fantastic festivals and an all around laid-back feel. Easy on the eyes, Telluride, located 360 miles southwest of Denver, boasts not only a well-preserved Victorian downtown, but picture-perfect Colorado mountain views.

The **visitors center** (☎ 970-728-3041, 800-525-3455; 398 W Colorado Ave; ☼ 10am-7pm daily summer, 9am-5pm Mon-Fri winter) will be happy to assist.

Telluride has two giant festivals each year. The **Telluride Bluegrass Festival** (☎ 800-624-2422; www.planetbluegrass.com; admission $55; ☼ late Jun) sells out months in advance and attracts thousands. It is an awesome party. National and international films are premiered at the **Telluride Film Festival** (☎ 603-433-9202; www.telluridefilmfestival.com; ☼ early Sep). The event attracts big-name stars.

Covering three distinct areas, **Telluride Ski Resort** (☎ 970-728-6900, 866-287-5015; www.telluride skiresort.com; lift tickets $70) is served by 16 lifts. Much of the terrain is for advanced and intermediate skiers, but there's still ample choice for beginners.

Surrounding mountains offer great **mountain biking** and **hiking. San Juan Hut Systems** (☎ 970-626-3033; www.sanjuanhuts.com) is a series of huts accessible to mountain bikers along a 206-mile route from Telluride to Moab, Utah. **Easy Rider** (☎ 970-728-4734; 101 W Colorado Ave) rents out bikes.

Telluride does not boast much budget lodging; your best bet is to camp. Its exterior doesn't look very Victorian, but the **Victorian Inn** (☎ 970-728-6601, 800-611-9893; www.tellurideinn.com; r from $80) has comfortable rooms (some with kitchenettes) with a hint of the era. There's a hot tub and sauna outside.

In town, **Telluride Town Park Campground** (☎ 970-728-2173; 500 W Colorado Ave; campsites $10; ☼ mid-May–mid-Sep) has 20 sites with shower access ($1.50 for a hot shower).

For a fill-up on pizza, sandwiches, salads and calzones, head to the counter at **Baked in Telluride** (☎ 970-728-4775; 127 S Fir St; mains $6-10). It's a very casual place with a front deck that's all the rage.

Other recommended places for your dining pleasure include low-key **Fat Alley** (☎ 970-728-3985; 128 S Oak St; mains $6-9) for barbecue, and atmospheric **Tellurice** (☎ 970-728-8787; 142 E Colorado Ave; mains $9-16) for Asian cuisine. Popular with locals for a drink is the **Last Dollar Saloon** (☎ 970-728-4800; 100 E Colorado Ave). You can sip whiskey by the fireplace on a snowy night. For live music, the best place in town is the **Fly Me to the Moon Saloon** (☎ 970-728-6666; 132 E Colorado Ave). If you're interested in a local microbrew check out the boxed text on p478.

GRAND JUNCTION

Western Colorado's main urban hub, Grand Junction has a pleasant downtown district. Most travelers just stop for a night on their

---

DETOUR: COLORADO NATIONAL MONUMENT

The 32-sq-mile scenic wonder called **Colorado National Monument** (hiker/car $3/5) is one of the most rewarding sidetrips possible off an interstate highway. With about half a dozen accessible colorful sandstone canyons precipitously descending to the flatlands, this beauty is exceptional for hiking and camping, as well as biking on Rim Rock Rd, which links the eastern and western entrances.

The monument is 4 miles west of Grand Junction. The **visitors center** (☎ 970-858-3617; ☾ 9am-5pm winter, 8am-6pm summer) is 7 miles south of Fruita, on the plateau at the north end of the park. **Saddlehorn Campground** (campsites $10), near the visitors center, has the only formal sites within the park. Backcountry camping is free (permits required – pick one up at the visitors center).

---

way to Utah's national parks – it's on I-70, just east of the Utah border.

If you linger, you'll learn a local secret – some of Colorado's very finest **mountain biking** can be found around here, particularly near Fruita, 13 miles west. **Ruby Canyon Cycles** (☎ 970-241-0141; 301 Main St; from $20) rents bikes.

The historic **Hotel Melrose** (☎ 970-242-9636; www.hotelmelrose.com; 337 Colorado Ave; dm $20, r $33-45) is full of character and close to downtown.

Two Rivers Inn (☎ 970-245-8585; 141 N 1st St; s/d $50/55; ☒ ☒), along a traffic-heavy street, is a basic motel with comfortable enough rooms. It has a hot tub and pool.

The innocently attractive **Crystal Cafe & Bake Shop** (☎ 970-242-8843; 314 Main St; mains $4-8), with low Muzak playing and wine glasses on the table, is where locals come for their sweets injection; it also serves excellent breakfasts and lunches.

Visit **Rockslide Brewery** (☎ 970-245-2111; 401 Main St; mains $9-15) for food and beer.

Buses leave the **Greyhound depot** (☎ 970-242-6012; 230 S 5th St) for Denver, Durango, Salida and more. Amtrak's daily *California Zephyr* stops at the **train depot** (☎ 970-241-2733; 339 S 1st St).

YELLOWSTONE & AROUND

Saddle up, hoss. The rough-and-tumble Cowboy State's unbroken northwestern corner epitomizes both the myth and reality of the Wild West. Sure, the high-noon shootouts are now staged, but plenty of charismatic wildlife still roams the Lower 48's most remote regions. Outdoor enthusiasts are spoiled for choice outside the gateway towns of Jackson, Cody and Lander, ideal launchpads for epic hiking, camping, fishing, climbing and skiing adventures.

YELLOWSTONE NATIONAL PARK

The world's first national park is home to half the world's geysers and the Lower 48's motliest concentration of free-roaming wildlife. Its copious alpine lakes, rivers and waterfalls are world-renowned. This natural cornucopia attracts up to 30,000 visitors daily in summer and three million gate-crashers annually. To escape the crowds, take a hike.

When John Colter became the first white man to visit the area in 1807, the only inhabitants were Tukudikas, a Shoshone-Bannock people who hunted bighorn sheep. Colter's reports of the soaring geysers and boiling mud holes (at first dismissed as tall tales) brought in expeditions and tourism interest. The park was established in 1872 to preserve Yellowstone's spectacular geography: the geothermal phenomena, the fossil forests and Yellowstone Lake.

Orientation

The 3472-sq-mile park is divide into five distinct regions (clockwise from the north): Mammoth, Roosevelt, Canyon, Lake and Geyser Country.

Of the park's five entrance stations, only the North Entrance, near Gardiner, MT, is open year-round. The others, typically open May to October, are the Northeast (Cooke City, MT), the East (Cody), the South (north of Grand Teton National Park) and the West (West Yellowstone, MT). Most sights are accessed from the scenic 142-mile Grand Loop Rd drive, the park's main road.

Information

The park is open year-round, but most roads close during winter. Park entrance permits

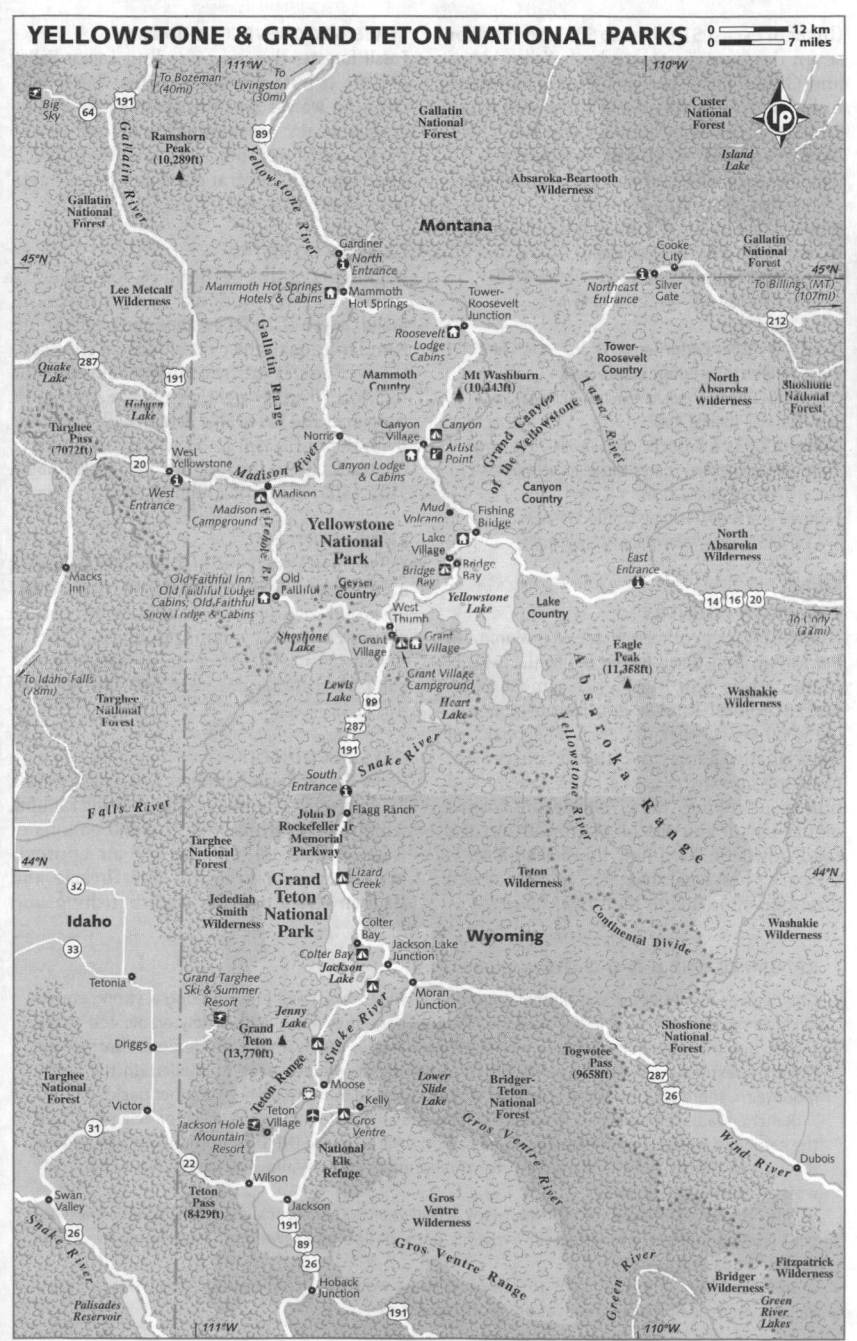

YELLOWSTONE & GRAND TETON NATIONAL PARKS

(hiker or cyclist $10, vehicle $20) are valid for seven days for entry into both Yellowstone and Grand Teton National Parks. Summer-only visitors centers are evenly spaced every 20 to 30 miles along Grand Loop Rd.

Albright Visitors Center & Park Headquarters (☎ 307-344-2263/7381; www.nps.gov/yell; Mammoth; ☺ 8am-7pm summer, 9am-5pm winter)

NPS Backcountry Office (☎ 307-344-2160; Box 168, Yellowstone NP, WY 82190, Mammoth)

Old Faithful Visitors Center (☎ 307-545-2750; ☺ 9am-5pm mid-Apr–May 29, 8am-8pm May 30–mid-Apr)

Road & Weather Conditions (☎ 307-344-2114/2117)

West Yellowstone Public Lands Desk (☎ 406-646-4403; ☺ 8am-4pm mid-Apr–May 29, 8am-8pm May 30–mid-Apr)

Xanterra Parks & Resorts (☎ 307-344-7311; www .travelyellowstone.com) Concessionaire for activities, camping and accommodations.

Yellowstone Association (☎ 307-344-2294, 877-967-0090; www.yellowstoneassociation.org)

Sights
MAMMOTH COUNTRY
Known for its geothermal areas at **Mammoth Hot Springs** and **Norris Geyser Basin**, the Mammoth area is North America's most volatile and oldest-known continuously active (115,000 years) thermal area. The peaks of the Gallatin Range rise to the northwest, towering above the area's lakes, creeks and numerous hiking trails. Astride the Continental Divide outside of Mammoth on the road down to Gardiner, the **Boiling River** is the park's best legal soak; it's typically closed until mid-June due to high river levels.

TOWER-ROOSEVELT COUNTRY
Fossil forests, the commanding **Lamar Valley** and its tributary trout streams, **Tower Falls**, denning **wolves** and the **Absaroka Mountains'** craggy peaks are highlights of one of the park's most remote, scenic and undeveloped regions. Several good day hikes begin near **Tower-Roosevelt**.

CANYON COUNTRY
Highlights of this beautiful region include a series of scenic overlooks and a network of **Grand Canyon of the Yellowstone** rim trails. South Rim Dr leads to the canyon's most spectacular overlook at **Artist Point**. **Mud Volcano** is the region's primary geothermal area. Notable trails include **Seven Mile Hole**, which descends from the north rim into the canyon, and scenic tracks up to the lookout atop **Mt Washburn** (10,243ft), the park's highest peak.

LAKE COUNTRY
Yellowstone Lake, one of the world's largest alpine lakes, is the centerpiece of this less-crowded region and is also home to the country's largest inland population of cutthroat trout. The often-snowcapped Absaroka Mountains rise east and southeast of the lake.

GEYSER COUNTRY
Upper Geyser Basin contains 180 of the park's 250 geysers. The most famous is **Old Faithful**, which spews from 3700 to 8400 gallons of water 100ft to 180ft into the air approximately every 1½ hours. The **Firehole** and **Madison Rivers** provide superb fishing and

---

RETURN OF THE H-O-O-O-OWL

Gray wolves *(Canis lupus)*, the ultimate symbol of wilderness, have been making a strong comeback. Originally protected in Yellowstone National Park, they were deliberately eradicated in the 1920s, but then Canadian wolves were reintroduced in 1995 amid considerable controversy. Since the extremely successful reintroduction efforts the wolves have multiplied. In the Rocky Mountains, there are now more than 650 wolves roaming in more than 40 distinct packs.

Ranchers adjacent the park were predictably suspicious of the reintroduction, claiming that the carnivore would prey on livestock. The National Park Service (NPS) compromised: they revised the wolves' status from 'endangered' to 'threatened,' thereby allowing ranchers to shoot any wolves attacking their stock.

The nonprofit **Defender of Wildlife** (www.defenders.org), a self-proclaimed 'champion of wolves,' continues to reimburse ranchers for livestock depredation and rewards those who allow wolves to raise pups on their land.

In Yellowstone, the best spot to see (and hear) wolves is from road pullouts in the Lamar Valley, where aficionados often set up spotting scopes.

wildlife viewing. The lukewarm **Firehole Canyon** swimming area, one of the park's few legal frontcountry swimming holes, is off the scenic, one-way **Firehole Canyon Dr**.

Activities

Over 85 trailheads give access to 1200 miles of **hiking** trails. A free backcountry use permit is required for overnight trips. Backcountry camping is allowed in 300 designated sites, two-thirds of which can be reserved in advance by mail for a $20 fee.

Bicycling is best April to October, when the roads are usually snow-free. Cyclists can ride on all paved roads, but not on backcountry trails.

Most park trails are not groomed in winter, but unplowed routes are open for **snowshoeing** and **cross-country skiing**. The rapids of Yankee Jim Canyon on the Yellowstone River lure white-water **rafting** day-trippers. **Yellowstone Raft Company** (☎ 800-858-7781; www.yellowstoneraft .com) offers a range of guided adventures out of Gardiner starting in late May.

Sleeping

Reservations are essential in summer. The best budget options are the seven NPS-run campgrounds ($12 to $14), in Mammoth (open year-round), Roosevelt and Geyser Countries, which are first-come, first-served. Xanterra's runs five reservable campgrounds ($18 per night for up to six people), all with cold-water bathrooms, flush toilets and drinking water. Hot showers ($3) are available at Canyon, Fishing Bridge, Grant Village, Mammoth and Old Faithful.

Bridge Bay Campground (Lake Country) Near the west shore of Yellowstone Lake. There are 43 sites.

Canyon Campground (Canyon Country) Centrally located with pay showers and coin laundry nearby. There are 272 sites.

Fishing Bridge RV Park (Lake Country) There are 346 full hook-ups for hard-shell RVs only ($32; no tents). Pay showers and coin laundry.

Grant Village Campground (Lake Country) On Yellowstone Lake's southwest shore. Pay showers and coin laundry nearby. There are 425 sites.

Madison Campground (Geyser Country) Generator-free, tent-only area. There are 280 sites.

Xanterra-run **cabins** ($44-119), **hotels** (from $73) and **lodges** (from $140) are and are spread around the park and are all open May or June to October – except for Mammoth Hot

Springs Hotel and Old Faithful Snow Lodge, which are also open mid-December through March. The best budget options, which fill first and have shared bathrooms, are the cozy cabins at Old Faithful and Roosevelt Lodge. All places are nonsmoking and none have air-con or TV.

Slightly cheaper lodging can be found in the gateway communities of **Cody** (see p497), **Gardiner** (☎ 406-848-7971; www.gardiner chamber.com; 222 Park St) and **West Yellowstone** (☎ 406-646-7701; www.westyellowstonechamber.com; cnr Yellowstone Ave & Canyon St), where motels start around $45 in the off-season and $65 in summer.

Three miles north of West Yellowstone on US 191, the tent-friendly USFS **Bakers Hole Campground** (campsites $13) has water and flush toilets.

In West Yellowstone, the historic **Madison Motel** (☎ 406-646-7745, 800-838-7745; 139 Yellowstone Ave; dm $22, r $35-80; ☺ May-Oct; ✂ 🖳) has rooms with or without bathroom; hostel rooms are on its 2nd floor, but there's only a microwave.

In Gardiner, the best thrifty option is **Rocky Mountain Campground** (☎ 406-848-7251; 14 Jardine Rd; campsites $18, cabins $20-25; ☺ Apr-Oct), with super views but little shade. About 2 miles up the same winding dirt road is the woodsy USFS **Eagle Creek Campground** (campsites $7).

Eating

Snack bars, delis, burger counters and grocery stores are scattered around the park. Breakfast buffets, salad bars and lunches at the hotel restaurants and cafeterias are decent value, but dinners at the fancier lodge dining rooms are overpriced. It's best to stock up on provisions outside the park.

Getting There & Around

The closest year-round airports are: Cody (53 miles); Jackson Hole (55 miles); Gallatin Field (Bozeman, 79 miles); and Idaho Falls (107 miles). The airport in West Yellowstone, Montana, is usually open June to September. It's often cheaper to fly into Salt Lake City, Utah (390 miles), or Denver, Colorado (563 miles) and rent a car.

No public transport exists to or within Yellowstone. During the summer, commercial buses operate from Jackson and Cody. Buses serve West Yellowstone and Gardiner from Bozeman year-round.

ROCKY MOUNTAINS

ROCKY MOUNTAINS

GRAND TETON NATIONAL PARK

To escape the RV circuit, head south of Yellowstone. Twelve jagged, glacier-carved granite spires rise above 12,000ft, crowned by the singular Grand Teton (13,770ft), the focal point of this intimate, less-crowded park. This 40-mile-long Teton Range towers over Jackson Hole, where lakes and streams, including the nascent Snake River, mirror the soaring peaks.

Orientation & Information

The national park has two entrance stations: Moose (south), on Teton Park Rd west of Moose Junction; and Moran (east), on US 89/191/287 north of Moran Junction. The park is open year-round, although most roads and entrances close from November to May 1, including part of Moose–Wilson Rd. Entrance permits (hiker or cyclist $10, vehicle $20) are valid for seven days and include Yellowstone National Park.

Park Headquarters (☎ 307-739-3300; www.nps.gov/grte; Box 170, Moose, WY 83012; 🕑 8am-5pm winter, 8am-7pm summer) shares a building and hours with **Moose Visitors Center** (☎ 307-739-3309, backcountry permits 307-739-3399), 0.5 miles west of Moose Junction. Summer-only visitors centers are at Colter Bay and Jenny Lake.

Three concessionaires run accommodations, restaurants and activities:

Dornan's (☎ 307-733-2415; www.dornans.com)

Grand Teton Lodge Company (☎ 307-543-3100, 800-628-9988; www.gtlc.com)

Signal Mountain Lodge (☎ 307-543-2831, 800-672-6012; www.signalmtnlodge.com)

Sights & Activities

The 5-mile, summer-only **Signal Mountain Summit Rd**, east of Teton Park Rd, goes to Signal Mountain's summit. Another nice route is the **Jenny Lake Scenic Loop Rd**, which abuts Grand Teton.

There are interesting **historic buildings** at Menor's Ferry, half a mile north of Moose Village, and along **Mormon Row**, east of Blacktail Butte, where bison are a common sight.

The park has 200 miles of **hiking trails**; visitors centers have free maps. A free backcountry use permit is required for overnight trips. Reservations can also be made by mail from January to May by writing park headquarters. The **Teton Crest Trail**, which runs just west of the main summits, can be accessed from trailheads that wind up steep canyons. Easier scenic trails include the Jenny Lake, Moose Ponds and String Lake loops.

The Tetons offer world-class **rock climbing**. Challenging short routes abound, as well as classic longer summits like Mt Moran, Mt Owen and the Grand Teton. The summer-only **Jenny Lake Ranger Station** (☎ 307-739-3343; 🕑 8am-7pm) is ground zero for alpinists. For instruction and guided climbs, contact **Exum Mountain Guides** (☎ 307-733-2297; www.exumguides.com) or **Jackson Hole Mountain Guides** (☎ 307-733-4979, 800-239-7642; www.jhmg.com; 165 N Glenwood St).

Adventure Sports (☎ 307-733-3307; Moose Village) has maps, rents bikes ($25 to $30 per day) and can suggest road- and mountain-biking routes. Next door, **Moosely Seconds** (☎ 307-733-7176) rents alpine outfits and sells top-quality gear at deep discounts.

Fishing is also a draw – several species of trout thrive in park rivers and lakes. Land a license at the Moose store, Signal Mountain Lodge or Colter Bay Marina. **Cross-country skiing** and **snowshoeing** are the best ways to explore the park in winter.

Sleeping

Most campgrounds and accommodations (all nonsmoking and without phones or TVs) are open May to October, weather depending. Demand is highest early July to Labor Day. Most campgrounds fill by noon (Jenny Lake fills much earlier; Gros Ventre rarely fills). The best in-park deals are the unreservable bunks at the **American Alpine Club Climbers' Ranch** (☎ 307-733-7271; www.americanalpineclub.org; dm $10; 🕑 mid-Jun–mid-Sep), 4 miles north of the Moose Visitors Center.

The **NPS** (recorded info ☎ 307-739-3603) operates the park's five **campgrounds** (campsites $12, hikers & cyclists pay $5 only), all first-come, first-served:

Colter Bay Campground (3 miles north of Jackson Lake Junction) 350 large, wooded sites on Jackson Lake's east shore, with pay showers, tent-only sites and a separate RV park.

Gros Ventre Campground (Near Gros Ventre Junction) 100 tent-only sites out of 372 total, shaded by cottonwoods.

Jenny Lake Campground (8 miles north of Moose Junction) 51 tent-only and hiker/cyclist sites convenient to many trailheads. Maximum stay is seven days.

Lizard Creek Campground (8 miles north of Colter Bay Junction; 🕑 Jun-Aug) 60 sites, several walk-in, on a peninsula on Jackson Lake's north shore.

Signal Mountain Campground (5 miles south of Jackson Lake Junction) 86 sites among lodgepole pines on Jackson Lake's southeast shore.

The **Grand Teton Lodge Company** (☎ 307-543-3100, 800-628-9988; www.gtlc.com) runs **Colter Bay Village** (tents $36, cabins $35-110), **Jackson Lake Lodge** (from $160) and the exclusive **Jenny Lake Lodge** (from $450).

Signal Mountain Lodge (cabins $95-140, r $120) fronts Jackson Lake, and Dornan's **Spur Ranch Log Cabins** (cabins $140-170, $40 less in winter) is in Moose.

Eating

There are several restaurants near Colter Bay, Jackson Lake and Moose Village. The **John Colter Chuckwagon** (Colter Village) has reasonably priced breakfasts, lunch and dinner buffets in a relaxed atmosphere. **Dornan's** (Moose Village) is an open-air eatery with pancake-and egg breakfasts, salad and sandwiches and unlimited prime rib dinners. There's also a good deli and general store for groceries at the gas station.

GATEWAY TOWNS

Yellowstone and the Grand Tetons can be accessed through several gateway towns, each with distinct personalities. To the south, tony **Jackson** offers some surprisingly affordable lodgings. Raucous **Cody** to the east trades on its Wild West image and dramatic approach to the park; further afield, **Lander** has loads of outdoors enthusiasts. In Montana, **West Yellowstone** is known for its outfitters operations, while **Gardiner** to the north is Yellowstone's oldest gateway. Tiny **Cooke City**, at Yellowstone's northeastern corner, sports three bars for its 100 denizens, and connects the parks with the dramatic **Beartooth Hwy** (p502).

Jackson & Jackson Hole

In cinema speak, if Jackson is Wyoming's establishing shot, then the Tetons are its scenic climax. Ungulates cruise the valley floor, set against the titillating backdrop of the *trois* Tetons, while recreation fuels the buzz of the state's most jet-set destination. Though world-class downhill skiing dominates, summer visitors can hike, bike, raft and explore outdoors up the wazoo.

ORIENTATION

The 'Hole' is a valley bounded by the Gros Ventre and Teton Ranges to the east and west, respectively. Most of the area's amenities are concentrated in the ritzy town of Jackson. Teton Village is 12 miles northwest of town.

INFORMATION

Public Library (☎ 307-733-2164; 125 Virginian Lane; ☺ 10am-9pm Mon-Thu, 10am-5:30pm Fri, 10am-5pm Sat, 1-5pm Sun) Behind the Virginian Lodge, provides free express Internet access.

Soap Opera Laundromat (☎ 307-733-5584; 835 W Broadway; ☺ 24hr)

USFS Bridger-Teton National Forest Headquarters (☎ 307-739-5500; 340 N Cache Dr) Dishes sage advice about outdoor possibilities.

Valley Bookstore (☎ 307-733-4533; 125 N Cache St) Stocks a superb selection of maps and local guidebooks.

Visitors Center (☎ 307-733-3316; www.jacksonhole chamber.com; 532 N Cache Dr) Info outside 24/7/365.

SIGHTS

Downtown Jackson has a handful of **historic buildings** and, in summer, a free **town square shoot-out** (☺ 6:15pm Mon-Sat). The free **Jackson Hole Historical Society Museum** (☎ 307-733-9605; 105 Mercill Ave; ☺ 8am-5pm Mon-Fri) explores the region's native and pioneer history. About 2 miles northeast of town, the **National Elk Refuge** (☎ 307-733-9212) protects thousands of wapiti from November to May and runs winter sleigh rides. It's also free to tour the **National Fish Hatchery** (☎ 307-733-2510; ☺ 8am-4pm), 2 miles north of town.

ACTIVITIES

Smack bang in town, the year-round 400-acre **Snow King Resort** (☎ 307-733-5200, 800-522-5464; www.snowking.com; full-/half-day lift tickets $35/23) offers night skiing, ice skating ($4t to $5) and snow tubing ($10). After the snow melts, you can mountain bike or ride the alpine slide or scenic chairlift.

From the 6311ft base at Teton Village to the summit of Rendezvous Mountain (10,450ft), **Jackson Hole Mountain Resort** (☎ 307-733-2292, 888-333-7766; www.jacksonhole.com; full-/half-day lift tickets $64/47) boasts the USA's greatest continuous vertical rise and is one of the country's top ski destinations, with advanced terrain. In summer, there's an aerial tram ($16) to topnotch mountain-biking and hiking trails.

Teton Cyclery (☎ 307-733-4386; 175 N Glenwood St) is an excellent shop with friendly, knowledgeable service and rentals. **Hoback Sports** (☎ 307-733-5335; 40 S Millward St) has a good map of the area's bike trails.

Rendezvous River Sports (☎ 307-733-2471, 800-733-2471; www.jhkayakschool.com; 945 W Broadway) offers kayak instruction. For rig rentals, try **Leisure Sports** (☎ 307-733-3040; 1075 S US 89).

ROCKY MOUNTAINS

ROCKY MOUNTAINS

Singles seeking a climbing partner swear by the bulletin board at **Teton Mountaineering** (☎ 307-733-3595; 170 N Cache Dr).

SLEEPING

Reservations are essential in summer and winter. Cheaper rates are available October 1 until the first big snowfall, and from early April until Memorial Day weekend. The closest USFS campground is the scenic first-come, first-served **Curtis Canyon** (campsites $12), 8 miles east of the Elk Refuge off USFS Rd 30440.

Teton County Recreation Center (☎ 307-739-9025; 155 E Gill St; ⏰ 1-9pm Mon-Sat, 1-7pm Sun summer, 3:30-8pm Mon-Fri, 1-9pm Sat, 1-7pm Sun winter; day pass $6.50) For campers, this place has showers, a pool, hot tub, sauna, gym and steam room.

Bunkhouse (☎ 307-733-3668, 800-234-4507; www .anvilmotel.com; 215 N Cache Dr; dm $25, r from $49, shower for nonguests $5 from 8am-8pm; ✗) The Anvil Motel's 25-bed hostel is the only in-town budget option. The basement-level space has clean dorm beds, laundry, ski lockers, a TV lounge and a basic kitchen. It's quiet most of the year but becomes party central when the powder is fresh. Hostellers can use the motel's hot tub.

Wagon Wheel Village (☎ 307-733-4588; www .wagonwheelvillage.com; 435 N Cache Dr; campsites winter/summer $20/24) Popular with climbers, these cramped creekside campsites encourage socializing with your neighbors.

Teton Gables Motel (☎ 307-733-3723; 1140 W Hwy 22; s/d winter $35/45, summer $55/65; ✗) Basic cinderblock construction hides recently refurbished rooms at the local workingman's favorite.

Hostel X (☎ 307-733-3415; www.hostelx.com; d/q $52/65) Teton Village's only budget option is a relaxed place with basic rooms with private bathroom (and maid service) plus a full-on entertainment room. There's a five-night minimum in winter, when the fireplace is blazing and reservations are advised.

EATING

Jackson excels at the B and C food groups – bagels, baked goods, burgers, burritos, cafés and coffee – and is home to Wyoming's most sophisticated grub. For groceries, hit Food Town (cheapest) or Albertson's (fanciest), both within walking distance of the square, west of town off Broadway.

Harvest Bakery & Cafe (☎ 307-733-5418; 130 W Broadway; mains $4-8) This natural foods store is loaded with organic produce, fresh breads and baked goods and serves up wholesome soups, sandwiches, smoothies and a great salad bar in its cozy café.

Bunnery (☎ 307-733-5474; 130 N Cache; mains $4-8) Wide veggie selection and superb baked goods.

Bubba's BBQ (☎ 307-733-2288; 515 W Broadway; mains $5-15) Get the biggest, fluffiest breakfast biscuits for miles at this friendly BYOB eatery. Later on, it's got a decent salad bar and serves a range of ribs and racks.

Snake River Brewing Co (☎ 307-739-2337; 265 S Millward St; mains $5-11; ✗) Happy-hour pints ($2.50) and $6 lunch specials attract locals here, where pub grub like wood-fired pizza stands up well to the smooth microbrews.

Jedediah's (☎ 307-733-5671; 135 E Broadway; breakfast $4-8, mains $7-15) It tends toward greasy, but Jedediah's is popular thanks to its huge portions and patio seating.

Other worthy quick bites include:

Pearl Street Bagels (☎ 307-739-1218; 145 W Pearl Ave; snacks $2-5) Good coffee and sandwiches.

Sanchez Mexican Food (☎ 307-732-2326; 65 S Glenwood St; ⏰ Mon-Sat) Giant *tortas* (type of Mexican sandwich) and boffo burritos.

Wild Flour Bakery (☎ 307-734-2455; 345 N Glenwood St; sweet treats $1-3) Fresh and bargain day-old goodies.

DRINKING & ENTERTAINMENT

Like all resort towns with restless bunches of seasonal workers and play-hard visitors, Jackson has an animated nightlife.

Rancher (☎ 307-733-3886; 20 E Broadway) Overlooking the square, this pool hall is the hard-drinkin' local happy-hour hang-out.

Mangy Moose Saloon (☎ 307-733-9779; www .mangymoose.net; admission free-$35) In Teton Village, this lively place hosts a wide variety of live shows, from free local bands to big-name national touring acts.

Stagecoach Bar & Grill (☎ 307-733-4407; 5755 W Hwy 22) Worth the 5-mile drive from Jackson, particularly on Tuesday for free pool, Wednesday for DJed reggae or Thursday for disco hits. Herb tokers and cowpokers mingle here like no other place in the Wild West.

Million Dollar Cowboy Bar (☎ 307-733-2207; 25 N Cache Dr) Everyone should saddle up (at least briefly) to this entertaining landmark, which has a chop shop that dishes decent Philly cheesesteaks.

Silver Dollar Bar (☎ 307-732-3939; cnr Glenwood St & Broadway) A bit fancier than the Cowboy Bar, this place has a happy hour from 10pm to midnight and live bluegrass most nights in summer.

GETTING THERE & AROUND

Jackson Hole Airport (JAC; ☎ 307-733-7682) is 7 miles north of Jackson off US 26/89/191. Daily flights serve Dallas, Denver, Houston and Salt Lake City, while weekend flights connect with Chicago.

Alltrans' Jackson Hole Express (☎ 307-733-1719, 800-652-9510; www.jacksonholebus.com) buses depart at 6:30am daily from Jackson's **Exxon Station** (cnr Hwy 89 S & S Park Loop Rd) for Salt Lake City ($56, 5½ hours).

Free **Southern Teton Area Rapid Transit** (Start; ☎ 307-733-4521; www.startbus.com) buses connect Jackson and Teton Village.

Cody

Boisterous Cody to the east ropes in Yellowstone-bound visitors with rodeo and a streak of yeehaw. The **visitors center** (☎ 307-587-2777; www.codychamber.org, 836 Sheridan Ave, ☽ 9am-5pm) and the **USFS** (☎ 307-527-6921; 203a Yellowstone Ave) are logical starting points.

Cody's major tourist attraction is the **Buffalo Bill Historical Center** (☎ 307-587-4771; www.bbhc.org; 720 Sheridan Ave; admission $15; ☽ 7am-8pm summer, 10am-3pm Tue-Sun winter). Several museums are dedicated to Buffalo Bill, Western art, Plains Indians, the Yellowstone region's ecosystem and American firearms.

Also popular is the **Cody Nite Rodeo** (☎ 307-587-5155, 800-207-0744; Stampede Park, 421 W Yellowstone Ave; admission from $12), which giddyups nightly June to August.

Accessed 20 miles west of Cody, the North Fork Shoshone River is a favorite among **white-water rafting** fans. A variety of wildlife, including elk and moose, are often seen from the river.

Gateway Campground (☎ 307-587-2561; 203 Yellowstone Ave; campsites $12, r & cabins $55-65; ☐ ☒) has a nice range of accommodations: shady sites for camping, cozy cabins and motel rooms.

Pawnee Hotel (☎ 307-587-2239; 1032 12th St; www.cjswalkerswyoming.com/PawneeHotel; s $22-36, d $28-48; ☒) is smoky but real hospitable, and has a 'beauty shop' and hilarious musical website. Rooms with shared bathroom are dirt cheap.

Whole Foods Trading Company (☎ 307-587-3213; 1239 Rumsey Ave; ☽ Mon-Sat) stocks bulk and organic provisions.

Maxwell's Fine Food & Spirits (☎ 307-527-7749; 937 Sheridan Ave; mains $5-17; ☽ Mon-Sat) has a comfortable interior devoid of trophy animal heads and a good selection of sandwiches, pasta, pizza and more; vegetarians will do just fine here.

A mile east of town, **Yellowstone Regional Airport** (COD; ☎ 307-587-5096; www.flyyra.com) has daily flights to Denver and Salt Lake City. **Powder River** (☎ 800-442-3682) buses pause at **Palmer's Outpost** (1521 Rumsey Ave) en route to Billings, MT.

LANDER & AROUND

A stone's throw from the Wind River Indian Reservation, laid-back Lander is a mixed cultural bag, from longtime ranchers to outdoors enthusiasts. The National Outdoor Leadership School (NOLS) campus lends an interesting flavor and a college-town feel.

Explore your options at the **Lander Visitors Center** (☎ 307-332-3892, 800-433-0662; www.landerchamber.org; 160 N First St) or the **USFS** (☎ 307-332-5460; 333 E Main St), which has useful information on the **Popo Agie** (pah-*poh*-za) **Wilderness Area** and other awesome backcountry.

Lander's location at the foot of the glaciated Wind River Range (including Wyoming's highest mountains) makes it a perfect base for **rock climbing** and **mountaineering**. The rugged areas around Lander are also reputed for **mountain biking**, **hiking** and **fishing**.

Wild Iris Mountain Sports (☎ 307-332-4541; 333 Main St) is the climbers' mecca, while cyclists and powder hounds make tracks for **Freewheel Ski & Cycle** (☎ 307-332-6616; 378 W Main St).

Sinks Canyon State Park (☎ 307-332-3077), 6 miles south of Lander on Sinks Canyon Rd (Hwy 131), is a beautiful spot with perplexing natural features. The Middle Fork of the Popo Agie River flows through the narrow canyon, disappears into the soluble Madison limestone called the Sinks, and pops up faster and warmer 0.25 miles downstream in a pool called the Rise – what the water does underground is up for debate. There's a summer-only visitors center near the two scenic **campgrounds** (campsites $8).

The cheapest motel is the **Western Lodge** (☎ 307-332-2300, 877-622-2300; 151 9th St; s/d $28/30). Camping is free (three-night maximum) at **Lander City Park** (405 Fremont St), but you get a hot

RESERVATION RADIO

In central Wyoming, home of the Wind River Indian Reservation, tune into KWRR 89.5 FM for music and talk-radio from the Native American perspective. You might hear some Arapahoe tunes, the syndicated Native America Calling current affairs program or Shoshone language lessons. KWRR also broadcasts quirky local news and National Public Radio (NPR) and Public Radio International (PRI) programming.

shower, free continental breakfast and use of the hot tub if you tent it at the riverfront spots at **Holiday Lodge** (☎ 307-332-2511, 800-624-1974; 210 McFarlane Dr; campsites per person $8).

For espresso, smoothies and truffles, chomp your sweet tooth into **Chocolates for Breakfast** (☎ 307-332-9273; 329 Main St). Pizza, sandwiches and salads go down well on the outdoor deck at **Gannett Grill** (☎ 307-332-8228; 126 Main St; mains $5-8), especially it's sunny.

Wind River Transportation Authority (☎ 307-856-7118, 800-439-7118; www.wrtabuslines.com) has weekday service to Riverton Regional Airport ($15).

EASTERN WYOMING

CHEYENNE

An obvious pitstop at the junction of I-25 and I-80, Wyoming's state capital and largest settlement retains much of its former cattle-town heyday giddyup. Visitors don't tend to linger long here, but the city (if you can call it that) has a couple of enjoyable sites and events.

Information

The **Cheyenne Visitors Center** (☎ 307-778-3133, 800-426-5009; www.cheyenne.org; 1 Depot Sq) is a great resource. **City News** (☎ 307-638-8671; 1722 Carey Ave) coffeehouse stocks a fair range of regional titles.

Sights & Activities

A sign warns those offended by taxidermy to steer clear of the **Nelson Museum of the West** (☎ 307-635-7670; 1714 Carey Ave; admission $3; 🕒 8am-5pm Mon-Sat summer, closed Sat winter), which boasts a unique private Old West collection, from train gangs to movie posters.

Frontier Days Old West Museum (☎ 307-778-7290, 800-266-2696; cnr 8th & N Carey Aves; admission $5; 🕒 9am-5pm Mon-Fri, 10am-5pm Sat & Sun), at I-25 exit 12, shines a lively spotlight on early Cheyenne.

It's difficult not to play dress-up at the **Wrangler** (☎ 307-634-3048; 1518 Capital Ave), a huge Western-wear outfitter with hundreds of boots, hats for every noggin' and huge silver belt buckles.

In late July, **Cheyenne Frontier Days** (☎ 307-778-7222, 800-227-6336; www.cfdrodeo.com; 4501 N Carey Ave) features 10 days of high-octane rodeos (admission $10 to $23) at Frontier Park, plus concerts, chili cook-offs and a free pancake breakfast.

Sleeping

Reservations are a must during Frontier Days, when rates double and everything within 50 miles is booked.

Lincoln Court (☎ 307-638-3302; 1720 W Lincolnway; s/d from $45/50; ✱ ▣) The best-value motel in summer, when it shares facilities with the pricier Best Western next door. A string of other motels lines noisy Lincolnway (I-25 exit 9).

Curt Gowdy St Park (☎ 307-632-7946; 1351 Hynds Lodge Rd; campsites $12) The closest public camping is this scenic park, 25 miles west.

AB Camping (☎ 307-634-7035; abcamping@juno.com; 1503 W College Dr; campsites $13; 🕒 Mar-Oct) Campers will like this tidy option on I-25 exit 7.

Eating

Whalen's Deli (☎ 307-637-7400; 318 W 17th St; mains $3-6; 🕒 6am-8pm Mon-Sat) Quality coffee, healthy sandwiches, soup, bagels and waffles.

Sanford's Grub & Pub (☎ 307-634-3381; 115 E 17th St; mains $7-15) Walls aflutter with sports bric-a-brac and road signs, the fun Sanford's has a novella-length menu of tasty eats, including burgers, chicken, ice-cold brews and a range of 'porker' plates.

Getting There & Around

Cheyenne Airport (CYS; ☎ 307-634-7071; www.cheyenneairport.com; 200 E 8th Ave) has daily flights to Denver. The **bus depot** (☎ 307-634-7744; 222 E Deming Dr) sends Powder River and Greyhound services daily to Denver ($19, 3½ hours), Chicago and San Francisco.

LARAMIE

Wyoming's only four-year university injects a welcome vibrancy and political diversity

---

DETOUR: DEVILS TOWER NATIONAL MONUMENT

Known as Bears Lodge by Native Americans who consider it sacred, **Devils Tower National Monument** (☎ 307-467-5283; www.nps.gpv/deto; hiker & cyclist/car $5/10) rises dramatically above the Belle Fourche Valley. It's a must-see detour for those cruising I-90 between the Black Hills and western Wyoming. In 1977 it was the point of alien contact in Spielberg's *Close Encounters of the Third Kind*. Covering only 2 sq miles, the park offers good hiking, camping and rock climbing. The **Belle Fourche Campground** (campsites $12; ☼ Apr–Oct) fills early. You can also camp in the Bearlodge Mountains, Black Hills and in the sleepy burg of Sundance.

---

into the state's cultural capital. The quaint historic downtown has plenty of eats, drinks and nightlife.

Information

Laramie Visitors Center (☎ 307-745-7339, 866-876-1012, event hotline 307 721-7345; www.laramie.org; 800 S 3rd St)

USFS Medicine Bow-Routt National Forest (☎ 307 745-2300; www.fs.fed.us/r2/mbr; 2468 Jackson St)

Sights

Spend an afternoon wandering Laramie's interesting 1860s-era **historic district**. The **University of Wyoming** (UW) ☎ 307 766 1121; www.wyoming.edu) has several free museums, including the **University of Wyoming Art Museum** (☎ 307-766-6622; 2111 Willett Dr; ☼ 10am–5pm), with an interesting rotating range of modern paintings and sculptures. **Wyoming Territorial Prison & Old West Park** (☎ 307-745-6161, 800-845-2287; www.wyoprisonpark.org; 975 Snowy Range Rd; adult $11; ☼ mid-May–Sep) is a curious restoration of an early prison and frontier town.

Sleeping

Lodging reservations are recommended (and rates are much higher) for UW graduation (mid-May), Fourth of July, Cheyenne Frontier Days (see p498) and fall UW football weekends. Numerous budget options await off I-80 exit 313.

Sunset Inn (☎ 307-742-3741, 800-308-3744; 1104 S 3rd St; s/d $50/65; ☒ ☒) Comfortable, spacious rooms, pool and hot tub, plus a few cheaper bare-bones rooms.

The best camping options are **USFS sites** (campsites $10) in the Pole Mountain area, 10 miles east of town. If you're headed east, **Curt Gowdy St Park** (see p498) on the backroad to Cheyenne is a better option. **Riverside Campground** (☎ 307-721-7405; Curtis St; campsites $10), east of I-80 exit 310 has bleak, exposed campsites.

Eating & Drinking

Sweet Melissa's Vegetarian Cafe (☎ 307-742-9607; 213 S 1st St; mains $4-6) Popular with students, this mellow place serves veggie foods for protein intake, plus coffee, chai and yummy desserts.

Old Buckhorn Bar (☎ 307-742-3554; 114 Ivinson St) For live country-and-western music and a drink or three.

3rd St Bar & Grill (☎ 307-742-5522; 220 Grand Ave) Smoky, but quieter.

Getting There & Away

Laramie Regional Airport (LAR; ☎ 307-742-4164), 4 miles west of town off I-80 exit 311, has daily flights to Denver. **Greyhound** (☎ 307-742-5188) and **Powder River** (☎ 800-442-3682) buses stop at the **Tumbleweed Express** (4700 Bluebird Lane) gas station at the east end of town (I-80 exit 316).

MEDICINE BOW MOUNTAINS & SNOWY RANGE

The Snowy Range's lofty summits cap the rugged Medicine Bow Mountains west of Laramie. Southwest are the Sierra Madre and the Continental Divide – the Medicine Bow National Forest spans both.

The 29-mile **Snowy Range Scenic Byway** (Hwy 130) traverses Snowy Range Pass (10,830ft; open Memorial Day to mid-October) between Centennial and Saratoga. Wildflowers and wildlife are abundant, as are overlooks, trails, rafting and campgrounds. Grab a map at the **Centennial Visitors Center** (☎ 307-742-6023), 1 mile west of Centennial on Hwy 130.

MONTANA

Whoa, pardner! The 'live and let live' state's countryside remains sparsely populated – the livestock to human ratio is 12:1 – but its gorgeous wildlands lure a steady stream of migrant artists, students, Hollywood starlets and real-estate developers. With its feet firmly planted in mountains and plains, and its head floating in the big sky, Montana – from *montaña* (Spanish for 'mountain') – is the type of place that, once you've visited, lives on in memory. Visitors will find that even the biggest draws, Flathead Lake and Glacier National Park, offer quiet beauty and opportunities for remote exploration.

Once you've seen more forest than you can shake a lodgepole pine at, a healthy dose of rollicking entertainment awaits in the state's population centers. And only the ahistorical are bored by the goldmine of colorful lore in boom-gone-bust mining hotspots like Butte.

History

If these lands could talk: Montana saw many conflicts between white settlers and Native Americans. Gold fever struck in 1863, with a discovery near Bannack. Soon after, Marcus Daly found the world's largest copper vein in Butte. In 1889, Montana became the USA's 41st state. Though tourism began to sweep through the Rockies in the late 19th century, the boom didn't really reach Montana until the 1980s, hence the easy-going, insular feel.

BOZEMAN

'Bozeangeles' may have agricultural roots, but today it's a vibrant, fast growing hub, where ranchers rub shoulders with hipster college students in boutique shops lining Main St. Rumped up against the Bridger Mountains, Bozeman is also a natural beauty.

Information

Visitors center (☎ 406-586-5421, 800-228-4224; www.bozemanchamber.com; 1003 N 7th Ave) Has all the info.

Sights & Activities

The free **Gallatin County Pioneer Museum** (☎ 406-582-3195; 317 W Main St; ☺ Mon-Sat) is worth a look for its collection of photos documenting 1920s cowgirls. The nonprofit **Emerson Cultural Center** (☺ 406-587-9797; 111 S Grand Ave) is Bozeman's artistic hub, with retail galleries, studios and changing exhibits.

Montana State University's **Museum of the Rockies** (☎ 406-994-2251; www.museumofthe rockies.org; 600 W Kagy Blvd; museum admission $7, with planetarium $9; ☺ 8am-8pm daily summer, 9am-5pm Mon-Sat, 12:30-5pm Sun winter) is Montana's most

entertaining museum, with early Native American art, dinosaur exhibits and planetarium laser-light shows.

With every passing digital year the calculating 'dinosaurs' (slide rules, room-sized electronic computers, key punch machines) at the **American Computer Museum** (☎ 406-582-1288; www.compustory.com; 2304 N 7th Ave; admission $4; ☺ 10am-4pm Tue, Wed, Fri & Sat, 4pm-8pm Thu) seem more comical. Don't miss the prototypes of first-run video games.

Eleven miles south of town, **Hyalite Canyon** is great for climbing, mountain biking and trail running. Sixteen miles north of town, the Bridger Mountains offer superb hiking and snow play at **Bridger Bowl Ski Area** (☎ 406-587-2111, 800-223-9609; www.bridgerbowl.com; day pass $35) and **Bohart Ranch Cross-Country Ski Center** (☎ 406-586-9070). For maps, trail guides and gear rentals, drop by **Barrel Mountaineering** (☎ 406-582-1335; 240 E Main St).

Soak away your aches and pains in the pools, sauna and steam room at **Bozeman Hot Springs** (☎ 406-586-6492; admission $5; ☺ 8am-10pm Sun-Thu, 8am-midnight Fri & Sat), 8 miles west of Bozeman off US 191.

Sleeping

There are three campgrounds at **Hyalite Canyon Recreation Area** (campsites $12), 11 to 18 miles south of town on Hyalite Canyon Rd. There are a few passable budget motels (from $30) east of downtown on Main St, plus a host of pricier chain motels north of downtown on 7th Ave, near I-90.

Window Rock Cabin (☎ 406-522-2520; cabin $30) A mile south of the reservoir, this USFS 1940s field station sleeps four and is equipped with wood stoves.

Bear Canyon Campground (☎ 406-587-1575; 800-438-1575; www.bearcanyoncampground.com; campsites $15; ☺ May-Oct; ☒) This private RV park is 3 miles east of Bozeman at I-90 exit 313.

Bozeman Backpacker's Hostel (☎ 406-586-4659; bozeman4hostel@yahoo.com; 405 W Olive St; dm/r $16/35; ☺ year-round) This Aussie-run independent hostel's casual approach means a relaxed ambience, mixed dorms and no lockout – but also erratic cleanliness and uncomfortable beds. Whatever. It's *the* place to rendezvous with active globestompers.

Eating

Community Food Co-Op (☎ 406-587-4039; 908 W Main St; mains $3-9) The co-op has a salad bar, full-service deli and organic picnic fixings. Head upstairs to the café for decadent desserts, fair-trade coffee, mountain views and occasional live acoustic music.

Cateye Café (☎ 406-587-8844; 23 N Tracy Ave; mains $5-9; ☯ Wed-Mon) Heaping plates of eggs, mimosas and more are served up here in the morning, though vegans can chew happily at lunch, too.

Burrito Shop (406-586-1422; 203 N 7th Ave; 1lb burrito $6; ☯ Mon-Sat) You can stuff yourself on the cheap at this student hang-out where happy hour runs from 2:30pm to 4pm.

La Parillia (☎ 406-582-9511; 1533 W Babcock; mains $4-8; ☯ 11am-9pm) Feeling adventurous? Tuck into a cross-cultural Thai or Cajun wrap, but don't let them talk you into adding gorgonzola cheese *and* wasabi to the same wrap.

Drinking

No joke: bar-hopping is one of the most popular majors at MSU.

Haufbrau (22 S 8th Ave) Enroll in freshman 101 with $2 pints and $7 pitchers at the Haufbrau.

Molly Brown (S 8th Ave) Stumble across the parking lot from Haufbrau for some graduate-level study at this noisy dive which has eight pool tables and 20 beers on tap.

Pick up a free copy of *BoZone* for Boozeman's latest event listings.

Getting There & Away

The **Gallatin Airport** (BZN; ☎ 406-388-6632), 8 miles northwest of downtown, has flights to Denver, Minneapolis, Salt Lake City and Seattle. Greyhound and Rimrock Trailways serve Montana towns along I-90 from the **bus depot** (☎ 406-587-3110; 1205 E Main St), 0.5 miles east of downtown. **Karst Stage** (☎ 406-388-2293, 800-287-4759; www.karststage.com) runs daily buses to Big Sky ($27, one hour) and West Yellowstone ($37, two hours) from December to April; summer service is by reservation only.

GALLATIN & PARADISE VALLEYS

Outdoorsy types can explore the expansive beauty around the Gallatin River for days. **Big Sky Resort** (☎ 800-548-4486; www.bigskyresort.com; full-/half-day lift tickets $60/47), with three mountains, 400 inches of annual powder and Montana's longest vertical drop (4350ft), is the valley's foremost winter destination. In summer it offers hiking and mountain

biking. For backpacking and backcountry skiing, head for the **Lee Metcalf Wilderness Complex**, which covers 389 sq miles of Gallatin and Beaverhead National Forest west of US 191. Scenic USFS campgrounds flank the Gallatin Range on the east side of US 191.

Fisherfolk will prefer to tie their flies in the Paradise Valley, which is full of blue-ribbon **fishing** access sites. Rafts, kayaks and canoes take over the river June to August.

Twenty miles south of Livingston off US 89 en route to Yellowstone, unpretentious **Chico Hot Springs** (☎ 406-333-4933, 800-468-9232; www.chicohotsprings.com; r from $39, soaks for nonguests $6.50) has a couple of suave year-round soaking pools and its lively bar hosts swinging country-and-western dance bands on weekends.

BILLINGS

Montana's largest town is a friendly ranching and oil center with big-city conveniences but little stress. Hardly a must-see, it's a decent place to break the monotonous journey along I-90/I-94. Worthwhile cultural sites include the free **Western Heritage Center** (☎ 406-256-6809; 2822 Montana Ave; ☯ 10am-5pm), which celebrates the harshness of homesteading.

Ask the **visitors center** (☎ 406-245-4111, 800-735-2635; www.billingschamber.com; 815 S 27th St) about **hiking trails** in the area.

The best central budget bet is the humble **Big 5 Motel** (☎ 406-245-6646, 888-544-9358; s/d $35/40; ❄), which boasts that it's rooms are 'comfortable and decent.'

The only nearby camping option is the USA's original 'kampground,' **Billings KOA** (☎ 406-252-3104, 800-562-8546; www.koa.com; 547 Garden Ave; campsite $18-28, cabin $32-60), in a beautiful riverfront spot, 0.5 miles south of I-90 off exit 450.

Perk up at the chipper **McCormick Cafe** (☎ 406-255-9555; 2419 Montana Ave; mains $4-7; ☯ Mon-Sat) with hot and cold breakfasts, or soups, salads and pizza at lunchtime. There's Internet access too.

Cheers, mate! There's Guinness on tap at **Pug Mahon's** (☎ 406-259-4190; 3011 1st Ave N; mains $6-15), an affable Irish pub. The Sunday champagne brunch pulls in hard-working crowds from acres around.

For a slice of authentic Americana, catch a minor league **Billings Mustangs** (☎ 406-252-1241; Cobb Field, 901 N 27th St; tickets $5; ☯ Jun-Sep) baseball game.

ROCKY MOUNTAINS

Logan International Airport (BIL; ☎ 406-238-3420), 2 miles north of downtown, has direct flights to Denver, Minneapolis, Phoenix, Salt Lake City and Seattle. The 24-hour **bus depot** (☎ 406-245-5116; 2502 1st Ave) has services to Bozeman ($30, three hours), Butte ($41, five hours), Missoula ($59, eight hours), Denver, Portland and Seattle.

ABSAROKA BEARTOOTH WILDERNESS

This vista-packed, 943,377-acre wilderness area saddles up next to Paradise Valley in the west and Yellowstone National Park in the south. The thickly forested Absaroka Range dominates the area's western half and is most easily accessed from Paradise Valley or the Boulder River Corridor.

The Beartooth Range's jagged peaks are best reached from Hwy 78 and US 212 near Red Lodge. Because of its proximity to Yellowstone, the Beartooth portion gets two-thirds of the area's traffic. A plethora of uncrowded alpine tundra awaits in the rugged interior.

A picturesque old mining town with fun bars and a good range of accommodations, **Red Lodge** (visitors center ☎ 406-446-1718, 888-281-0625; www.redlodge.com; 601 N Broadway Ave) is loaded with hiking and backpacking options and, in winter, skiing near town. A mile south of town, the **Beartooth Ranger Station** (☎ 406-446-2103; 6811 Hwy 212 S) has maps and recreation suggestions.

The awesome **Beartooth Hwy** (US 212; usually open June to mid-October) links Red Lodge to Cooke City (p495) and Yellowstone's northeast entrance via an incredible 68-mile journey (allow at least three hours) that passes soaring peaks and wildflower-sprinkled tundra. There are five reservable USFS campgrounds along the highway within 12 miles of Red Lodge.

BUTTE

With a skyline of massive mining headframes and vacant ornate buildings, Butte feels lost in time. Though more staid nowadays than during its late-19th-century boom times, the town – and its fascinating bars – still carry an air of political intrigue. Grab a free *Uptown Butte* walking tour map of one of the USA's largest **historic districts** from the **visitors center** (☎ 406-723-3177, 800-735-6814; www.butteinfo.org; 1000 George St; ☾ 8am-8pm summer, 8am-5pm winter), north of I-15/I-90, or stroll along Granite, Broadway and Park Sts and read the National Register of Historic Places plaques.

If it's open, visit the **Dumas Brothel Museum** (☎ 406-723-6128; 45 E Mercury St; tour $4; ☾ 9am-5pm summer), at the center of what used to be a huge red-light district, where the cribs remain 'as is' since it closed in 1986.

Montana Tech's free **Mineral Museum** (☎ 406-496-4414; 1300 W Park St; ☾ 9am-6pm summer, 9am-4pm winter) is more than just a bunch of rocks. It has impressive displays of minerals, including 'Big Daddy,' Montana's largest quartz crystal. Rockhounds should also assay the **World Museum of Mining** (☎ 406-723-7211; 155 Museum Way; admission $7; ☾ 9am-5:30pm Apr-Oct), with an old mining town that's worth an hour or two.

If you can't swing a big, well-maintained room with a view at the historic **Finlen Hotel** (☎ 406-723-5461, 800-729-5461; www.finlen.com; 100 E Broadway; s $44-48, d $54-58), try the basic **Capri Motel** (☎ 406-723-4391, 800-342-2774; 220 N Wyoming St; r from $40) nearby.

The only camping option near town is the **Butte KOA** (☎ 406-782-8080; campsite/cabin $22/35), near I-90 exit 126.

Gamer's (☎ 406-723-5453; 15 W Park St; mains $4-8) is a local favorite for big American breakfasts and pasties (pass-tees), compact yet hearty pies native to Cornwall, England, filled with meat, onions and potatoes or turnips. At **Pekin** (☎ 406-782-2217; 117 S Main St; s & d $5-10), the garish pink walls and dining cabins are more interesting than the MSG-laced food.

Butte's watering holes retain a gritty, authentic feel and deserve museum status. Highlights include the **M&M Bar** (9 N Main St), the **New Deal Bar** (333 S Arizona St) and the **Irish Times** (cnr Main & Galena Sts), which has draft Guinness and live music most weekends.

Rimrock and Greyhound buses stop at Butte's **depot** (☎ 406-723-3287; 103 E Front St) en route to Bozeman and Missoula.

MISSOULA

Locals joke that 'Missou' has 10 months of winter and two months of relatives, but its climate is actually milder than much of the rest of Montana.

The enjoyable town is within spittin' distance of an endless outdoor romper room: the Rattlesnake Recreation Area and the Bitterroot Range span its western edge and the floatable Clark Fork River courses right through it. The dreadlocks, global import shops and veggie restaurants near the University of Montana add an unexpected dash of cultural flavor.

Information

Tune in to University of Montana stations KUFM (89.1 FM) and KUKL (89.9 FM) for National Public Radio (NPR), quirky local news and groovy free-form alternative music mixes.

Adventure Cycling Association (☎ 406-721-1776, 800-755-2453; www.adventurecycling.org; 150 E Pine St) Maps and touring information.

Trail Head (☎ 406-543-6966; www.trailheadmontana .net; 110 E Pine St) Maps, abundant advice, camping and kayaking rental gear.

USFS Northern Region Headquarters (☎ 406-329-3511; www.fs.fed.us/r1; 200 E Broadway)

Visitors center (☎ 406-532-3250, 800-526-3465; www.missoulacvb.org; 1121 E Broadway)

Sights & Activities

Downtown, the contemporary installations at the **Art Museum of Missoula** (☎ 406-728-0447; 335 N Pattee St; admission $2, free Tue; ☯ 10am-6pm Tue-Sat) are worth a look.

Seven miles west of downtown on W Broadway is the **Smokejumper Visitors Center** (☎ 406-329-4900; free tours 10am-4pm in summer), the active base for the heroic men and women who parachute into forests to combat raging wildfires. Take bus No 10 to get there.

Nearby, the free **Rocky Mountain Elk Foundation's Wildlife Visitors Center** (RMEF; ☎ 800-225-5355; 2291 W Broadway; ☯ 8am-6pm) has a huge collection of stuffed North American big-game animals and related art. Bus No 2 or 10 will get you there.

One of the area's most accessible **hikes** is along the south side of Clark Fork from McCormick Park (west of the Orange St bridge) into Hellgate Canyon. At sunset, join the steep pilgrimage from the football stadium to the 'M' on Mt Sentinel for spectacular views.

Advanced skiers love **Snowbowl Ski Area** (☎ 406-549-9777; www.montanasnowbowl.com; lift tickets $32), 17 miles north of Missoula, for its 2600ft vertical drop. **10,000 Waves** (☎ 406-549-6670, 800-537-8315; www.10000-waves.com) runs a range of rafting and kayaking trips ($35 to $80) on the Class III and IV rapids.

Sleeping

Most lodging is on Broadway between Van Buren and Orange Sts within walking distance of downtown and the campus. Contact the **USFS** (☎ 406-329-3511) about nearby out-of-town camping options.

Downtown Motel (☎ 406-549-5191, 800-303-5191; 502 E Broadway; s/d $40/45) Super-clean with floppy beds and paper-thin walls.

City Center Motel (☎ 406-543-3193; 338 E Broadway; s/d $45/50; ▨) Comfortable rooms with subtle western touches.

Creekside Inn (☎ 406-549-2387, 800-551-2387; 630 E Broadway; s/d $50/65; ▨ ▨) Also recommended is the nicer Creekside with free continental breakfast.

Missoula/El-Mar KOA (☎ 406-549-0881, 800-562-5366; www.koa.com; 3450 Tina Ave; campsites $21-26) The only in-town campground is 3 miles west of downtown off W Broadway.

Eating

Bernice's Bakery (☎ 406-728-1358; 190 S 3rd St; everything under $4; ☯ 6am-10pm) Start your day right with coffee and toothsome sweets.

Food for Thought (☎ 406-721-6033; 540 Daly Ave; mains $4-8; ☯ 7am-9pm) Across from the university with heaping portions of health-conscious food.

Tipu's (☎ 406-542-0622; 115 1/2 S 4th St; buffet $7, mains $5-10; ☯ 11:30am-9pm) Missoula's only all-vegetarian eatery brews flavorful chai and East Indian chow. It's tasty and filling – don't pass over the fresh chutneys.

Drinking & Entertainment

In Missoula, bar-hopping ranks right up there with hiking, rodeo, disco dancing and cowtipping. For live music listings, browse the *Independent* (www.missoulanews.com) or the Entertainment section of Friday's *Missoulian*.

Carmike 10 (☎ 406-541-7467; 3640 Mullan Rd; admission $7.25, before 6pm $5) Check the schedule for first-run releases.

Wilma Theatre (☎ 406-728-2521; 131 S Higgins; admission $7) Screens foreign and independent flicks.

For bar-hopping, you can't go wrong with the Ryman St trio of the **Ritz** (No 208), **Reds** (No 217) and the **Rhino** (cnr Ryman & Front Sts), all with bottomless kegs and nightly drink specials.

Raven Café (☎ 406-829-8188; 130 E Broadway) Nonsmoking, with several pool tables, beers, comfy chairs and loaded bookshelves. Also offers Internet access.

Iron Horse Brewpub (☎ 406-728-8866; 501 N Higgins Ave) An upbeat student favorite with plenty of places to sit and sip, including an outdoor patio.

Top Hat (☎ 406-728-9865; 134 W Front St) Bluegrass, blues and rock bands, plus pool and table tennis, get this big, open space moving at night.

Old Post (☎ 406-721-7399; 103 W Spruce St) This cozy wood-walled number draws crowds with its happy-hour specials and upscale pub grub. Jazz and blues bands saunter in on weekends.

Other Side (☎ 406-543-3405; 1100 Strand Ave) It's worth the trek west of town for poker, cheap booze and live shows, some all-ages.

Sean Kelly's (☎ 406-542-1471; 130 W Pine St) Often packed for sports on the TV.

Getting There & Around
Missoula County International Airport (MSO; ☎ 406-728-4381; Hwy 12 W), 5 miles west of town, has flights to Boise, Denver, Minneapolis, Portland, Salt Lake City and Seattle.

Greyhound buses serve Montana's four corners from the **depot** (☎ 406-549-2339; 1660 W Broadway), a mile west of town.

WHITEFISH & KALISPELL
A fine gateway to Glacier National Park, Whitefish sports a new West getup of hip bars, shops and restaurants. It sits in the shadow of **Big Mountain Resort** (☎ 406-862-2900; www.bigmtn .com; lift tickets $49), one of Montana's premier year-round resorts, with downhill skiing plus gondola-served hiking and mountain biking in summer. **Glacier Cyclery** (☎ 406-862-6446; 326 2nd St) has maps and rents bikes.

Though not as charming as Whitefish, Kalispell, 13 miles south, is Flathead Valley's cheapest place to resupply.

Kalispell Area Visitors Center (☎ 406-758-2800; www.kalispellchamber.com; 15 Depot Park) and **Whitefish Visitors Center** (☎ 406-862-3501, 877-862-3548; www.whitefishmt.com; 520 E 2nd St) offers the usual tourist information. **Tally Lake Ranger Station** (☎ 406-862-2508; 1335 Hwy 93 N) has camping info and maps.

In Whitefish, the **Downtowner** (☎ 406-862-2535; 224 Spokane Ave; dm $20; 🖳) bunks include use of the adjacent gym and sauna. There are several basic budget motels south of Whitefish on US 93. For satisfying shady campsites, try **Whitefish RV Park** (☎ 406-862-7275; www.whitefishrvpark.com; 6404 Hwy 93 S; campsites $16), a mile south of town.

Glacier Park International Airport (FCA; ☎ 406-257-5994; 4170 Hwy 2), halfway between Whitefish and Kalispell on US 2, has flights to Minneapolis, Salt Lake City and Seattle. The **Airport Shuttle Service** (☎ 406-752-2842, 406-752-4022) serves Kalispell ($7.50) and Whitefish ($18).

Amtrak stops in Whitefish en route to West Glacier ($8 to $10) and East Glacier ($19 to $24). Intermountain Transport connects Kalispell's **bus station** (☎ 406-755-4011; 1301 S Main St) to Whitefish's railroad depot; buses also run to Bozeman and Missoula.

The free Shuttle Network of Whitefish (SNOW) runs between Whitefish and Big Mountain during ski season.

BOB MARSHALL WILDERNESS COMPLEX
The essence of Montana's wildlands can be well sampled in the vast Bob Marshall Wilderness Complex, which runs roughly from the southern boundary of Glacier National Park in the north to Rogers Pass (on Hwy 200) in the south. Within the complex, three designated wilderness areas (Bob Marshall, Great Bear and Scapegoat) hum with a medley of geology, plants and wildlife. National Forest lands begirding the complex offer campgrounds, road access to trailheads and quieter country when 'the Bob' hosts hunters in autumn. The core lands are 40 miles from the nearest road. The easiest (and busiest) access routes are from the Benchmark and Gibson Reservoir trailheads in the Rocky Mountain Front.

Trails generally start steep, reaching the wilderness boundary after around 7 miles. It takes another 10 miles or so to really get into the Bob's heart. Good day hikes run from all sides. Two USFS districts tend to the Bob:

> ## BACKROADS: FLATHEAD LAKE
>
> Thanks to picture-pretty bays and 128 miles of wooded shoreline, fish-filled Flathead is one of Montana's most favored attractions. The **Flathead Lake Marine Trail** makes paddling from one access point to another a fun way to venture; two marine **campsites** (reservations ☎ 406-751-4577; campsites $8) are available. If you have a car, you can circumnavigate the lake in four hours, but stopping at the fruit stands is a must.
>
> On the Indian Reservation at the lake's south end, fast-growing **Polson** (visitors center ☎ 406-883-5969; www.polsonchamber.com; 4 2nd Ave E) is the region's biggest service center, with several gas stations, fast food and motels.
>
> At the lake's opposite end, **Bigfork** (visitors center ☎ 406-837-5888; www.bigfork.org; 8155 Hwy 35) is an artsy village with good grub. West of Bigfork, the **Swan Lake Ranger District Station** (☎ 406-837-5081; 200 Ranger Station Rd) has camping details.
>
> Between Polson and Bigfork are lakefront campgrounds, summer camp–style resorts, and, on the lake's east side, orchards festooned with plump cherries. In either town you can join a boat tour to visit **Wild Horse Island**, where wild mares, thought to be descendants of Pend d'Oreille and Flathead steeds, roam. Watch for Flathead Nessie, a distant cousin to the Loch Ness Monster (or was that a sunk log bobbing to the surface?). **Flathead Raft Co** (☎ 406-883-5838, 800-654-4359; www.flatheadraftco.com; from $40) runs kayaking and river-rafting trips.

Flathead National Forest Headquarters
(☎ 406-758-5204; www.fs.fed.us/r1/flathead/; 1935 3rd Ave E, Kalispell)
Lewis & Clark National Forest Supervisors
(☎ 406-791-7700; www.fs.fed.us/r1/lewisclark; 1101 15th St N, Great Falls)

GLACIER NATIONAL PARK

This stunner of a park is a veritable body of natural wonders and Montana's most revered attraction. Most of July and August's visitors stick to developed areas and short hiking trails. Explore the extensive backcountry for some one-on-one time with nature.

Those who don't have the time to investigate the remote reaches can still get a dose of divine scenery by traveling the Going-to-the-Sun Rd, which displays tremendous examples of glacial activity and often mountain goats and bighorn sheep. In winter, when Going-to-the-Sun Rd is closed but surrounding access roads lead to snowshoe and cross-country ski trails, the park is left to wildlife and adventurous souls.

The less crowded **Waterton Lakes National Park** (p667) extends north into Canada. In 1995 the parks were declared a World Heritage Site for their vast cross section of plant and animal species.

In 2003, 15% of the park's acreage was scorched by wildfires.

Orientation

Glacier's 1562 sq miles are divided into five districts, each centered on a ranger station: Polebridge (northwest); Lake McDonald, including the West Entrance and Apgar village (southwest); St Mary (east); Two Medicine (southeast); and Many Glacier (northeast). The 50-mile Going-to-the-Sun Rd is the only paved road that traverses the park.

Information

Visitors centers and ranger stations sell field guides and hand out hiking maps. Those at Apgar and St Mary are open daily May to October; the Logan Pass center is open when Going-to-the-Sun Rd is open. The Many Glacier, Two Medicine and Polebridge Ranger Stations close at the end of September. **Park headquarters** (☎ 406-888-7800; www.nps.gov/glac; ☒ 8am-4:30pm Mon-Fri), in West Glacier between US 2 and Apgar, is open year-round.

Entry to the park (vehicles/individuals $20/5) is valid for seven days. Day hikers don't need permits, but overnight backpackers do. Half of the permits ($4 per person per day) are available on a first-come, first-served basis from the Apgar Backcountry Permit Center, St Mary's Visitors Center and the Many Glacier, Two Medicine and Polebridge Ranger Stations. The other half can be reserved at the Apgar Backcountry Permit Center, visitors centers and ranger stations. Advance reservations ($20) can be made at

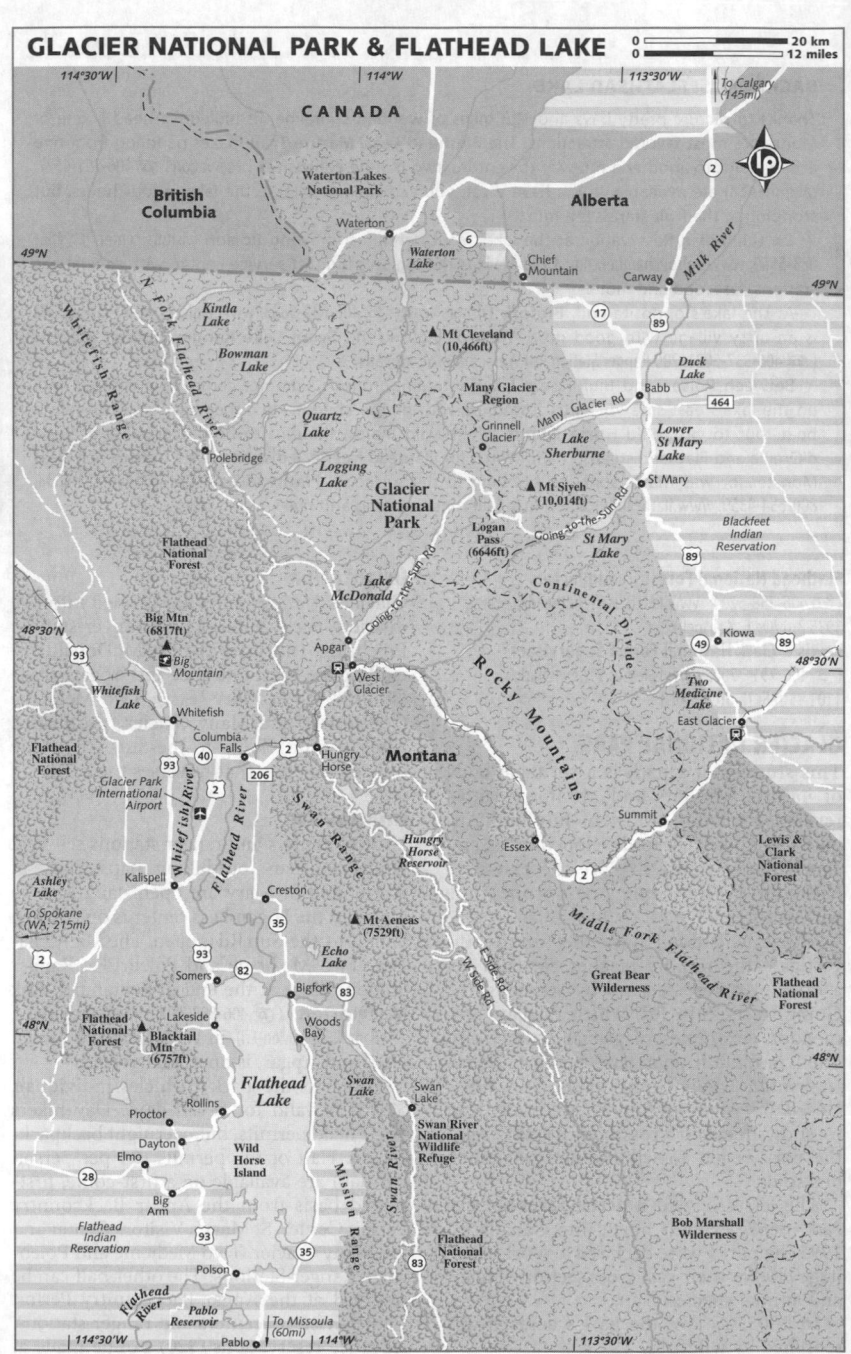

ROCKY MOUNTAINS

the permit centers or after April 1 by writing to: Backcountry Reservations, Glacier National Park, West Glacier, MT 59936.

Sights & Activities

Starting at Apgar, the phenomenal **Going-to-the-Sun Rd** skirts shimmering Lake McDonald before angling sharply to the Garden Wall – the main dividing line between the west and east sides of the park. At Logan Pass you can stroll 1.5 miles to **Hidden Lake Overlook**; heartier hikers can try the 7.5-mile **Highline Trail**. About halfway between the pass and St Mary Lake, the **Continental Divide Trail** crosses the road at Siyeh Bend, a good starting point for multiday hikes.

Busier routes include the 5-mile **Grinnell Glacier Trail**, which climbs 1600ft to the base of the park's most visible glacier, and the 6-mile **Cracker Lake Trail**, a 1400ft climb to some of the park's most dramatic scenery. For more solitude, try trails in the North Fork or Two Medicine areas.

Mountain bikes are prohibited on park trails. Road bikes can ply the park's pavement but are banned from parts of Going-to-the-Sun Rd from 11am to 4pm in summer.

Glacier Park Boat Co (☎ 406-257-2426; www.glacier parkboats.com) rents kayaks and canoes and runs popular guided tours ($10 to $12) from five locations in Glacier National Park. For **rafting** trips and guided day hikes and backpacking trips, contact **Glacier Wilderness Guides** (☎ 406-387-5555, 800-521-7238; www.glacierguides.com) in West Glacier.

ICEBERG LAKE HIKE

The five-to six-hour 9-mile day hike to Iceberg Lake is justifiably a favorite. Enclosed by stunning 3000ft vertical headwalls on three sides, it's one of the most impressive glacial lakes in North America. The 1200ft ascent is gentle and the approach is mostly at or above treeline, affording awesome views. Wildflower fiends will delight in the meadows around the lake.

Iceberg Lake was named in 1905 by George Grinnell, who saw icebergs calving from the glacier at the foot of the headwalls. The glacier is no longer active, but surface ice and avalanche debris still provide sizeable flotillas of bergs as the lake melts out in early summer. The trail was built in 1914 and the Great Northern Railway tried to attract visitors to the lake with fabricated stories of the 'furred' trout that could be caught in the frigid waters.

Scientists predict that, if global climate warming trends continue, all of the park's 50-some moving ice masses will be completely melted by 2030, so there's no better time than now to see some of the ancient ice for yourself.

The hike begins and ends at Iceberg Lake trailhead near the Many Glacier Ranger Station.

Sleeping

Within the park, campgrounds and lodges are mainly open mid-May to the end of September. East Glacier and West Glacier offer overflow accommodations year-round.

Dating from the early 19th century, Glacier's seven historic lodges are now operated by **Glacier Park, Inc** (☎ 406-892-2525; www.glacierparkinc.com; r $95-399). All are completely nonsmoking, and rooms do not have TV or air-con. The best budget deal is the **Swiftcurrent Motor Inn** (☎ 406-732-5531; www.swiftcurrent motorinn.com; Many Glacier Valley; cabin $43-53, with bathroom $73, r $94-105; 🖰 mid-Jun–early Sep), where no-frills cabins are a pebble's toss from fantastic trailheads – book ahead.

In East Glacier, friendly **AYH Brownie's** (☎ 406-226-4426; Hwy 49; dm/s/d $16/21/29; 🖰 May-Sep; 💻), above Brownie's Grocery & Deli, is always in demand but gets mixed reviews. It offers dorm rooms, private rooms, coin laundry and a kitchen.

Also in East Glacier, the **Backpacker's Inn** (☎ 406-226-9392; Dawson Ave; dm $10, s/d cabins $20/30), behind Serrano's, is a quieter alternative with single-sex dorms and a couple of cozy cabins. Check-out is 10am – sharp, bub – and there's no kitchen or indoor common area, neither.

In Polebridge, the ultra-rustic (no electricity), year-round **Northfork Hostel & Square-peg Ranch** (☎ 406-888-5241; www.nfhostel.com; tent & tepee/dm $10/15, cabins $30-65) has bunks, cabins and a kitchen and the veggie-friendly Northern Lights Cafe next door. Guests can use the hostel's bikes, cross-country skis, snowshoes and kayaks for free; nonguests can rent equipment. Pickup from West Glacier Amtrak station is $30/35 summer/winter.

Of the 13 **NPS campgrounds** (☎ 800-365-2267; reservations.nps.gov; campsites $12-17), only campsites at **Fish Creek** and **St Mary** can be reserved up to five months in advance. All other sites are first-come, first-served. Sites fill up by mid-morning, particularly July and August. Even during the busiest days, there's usually at least one vacant space somewhere in the park. Only Apgar Picnic Area and St Mary campground offer winter camping ($7.50).

A mile west of West Glacier off Hwy 2, **Glacier Campground** (☎ 406-387-5689; campsites $18, cabins $30-40) has campsites spanning 40 acres of lovely wooded grounds, as well as a cute cluster of basic wooden cabins.

Eating

In summer there are grocery stores with limited camping supplies in Apgar, Lake McDonald Lodge, Rising Sun and at the Swift-current Motor Inn. In general, it's cheaper to stock up in gateway towns.

In East Glacier, **Serrano's Mexican Restaurant** (☎ 406-226-9392; 29 Dawson Ave; mains $7-12) serves up good Mexican dinners in casual environs year-round. **Brownie's Grocery & Deli** (Hwy 49) has a well-rounded grocery supply and makes its own breads. Dining options in West Glacier are unexciting; if you can, head to Whitefish.

Getting There & Around

Amtrak's *Empire Builder* stops at East Glacier (Glacier Park Station) and West Glacier (Belton Station). **Glacier Park, Inc** (☎ 406-892-2525) runs shuttles over Going-to-the-Sun Rd, including the unreservable Hiker's Shuttle ($8 to $24) from West Glacier or Many Glacier.

IDAHO

Sandwiched between the Pacific Northwest and the Rockies, mountainous and lake-speckled Idaho is a paradise for hikers, bikers, rafters, fisherfolk, skiers, sledders and horseback riders. It's second only to Alaska for most national forests and wilderness areas, contains the deepest gorge on the continent (Hells Canyon, shared with Oregon) and is perhaps the USA's river-rafting capital, with tons of options along wild waterways including the Salmon and Snake rivers. I-84, I-90 and US 95 are major throughways, taking in diverse geography from arid plains to bursting-green forests.

For more information on Idaho, call ☎ 800-635-7820, or check www.idahorec .org or www.visited.org.

BOISE

Idaho's capital and largest city is a surprisingly hip place with an outdoors slant and a hassle-free feel. Much of its late–19th-century architecture remains, cafés and restaurants stay open late, and crowds from nightspots spill onto the streets on hot summer nights. Locals consider Boise a gay-friendly city, and the city has an active gay and lesbian community.

Orientation & Information

Delve into the main business district, bounded by State, Grove, 4th and 9th Sts. Restaurants and nightspots are found downtown in the brick-lined pedestrian plaza of the Grove, the gentrified former warehouse district at 8th St Marketplace and Old Boise, just east of downtown. Along Grove St between 6th St and Capitol Blvd, the Basque Block has sites commemorating Idaho's Basque pioneers.

Stop by the **visitors center** (☎ 208-344-5338, 800-635-5240; www.boise.org; 850 Front St; ☻ 10am-5pm Mon-Fri, 10am-2pm Sat summer, 9am-4pm Mon-Fri winter).

Sights & Activities

Of interest are the architecturally impressive **state capitol** (built in 1905, it's the only statehouse in the USA to be heated by geothermal water); riverfront Julia Davis Park, containing the **Idaho Historical Museum** (☎ 208-334-2120; 610 N Julia Davis Dr; admission $2; ☻ 9am-5pm Mon-Sat, 1-5pm Sun) and **Boise Art Museum** (☎ 208-345-8330; 670 Julia Davis Dr; admission $8; ☻ 10am-5pm Tue-Sat, 10am-8pm Thu, noon-5pm Sun); and the fascinating but chilling **Old Idaho Penitentiary** (☎ 208-368-6080; 2445 Old Penitentiary Rd; admission $4; ☻ noon-5pm winter, 10am-5pm summer).

Northeast of Boise, **hiking** trails span the mountains of the Boise Front.

White-water rafting opportunities nearest to Boise lie on the Payette River, an hour's drive from the city. Local outfitters such as **Headwaters River Company** (☎ 800-800-7238; www .idahorivertours.com) offer day and multiday trips on the rapids; **kayaking** ventures can also be arranged.

Sleeping

You'll find other budget accommodations along Capitol Blvd near the university.

Hostel Boise (☎ 208-467-6858; 17322 Can-Ada Rd, Nampa; www.hostelboise.com; dm/s/d $14/31/35; ☐) Just outside of town, this country-style hostel's rooms have a max of four beds each. There's a barbecue on the back patio and lots of yard space for laying around and digesting after grilling up those tasty Boca Burgers. Staff offer lifts to and from the airport ($10) and Nampa's Greyhound stop.

Cabana Inn (☎ 208-343-6000; cabanainn@interplus .net; 1600 Main St; s/d $40/45; Ⓟ ⊠) A few hops west of downtown, the Cabana is run by helpful folk and offers well-kept motel rooms.

Eating

River City Bagel & Bakery (☎ 208-338-1299; 908 Main St; bagels $2-6) A good place for morning fuel. It has sidewalk seating and a bookstore.

Gernika (☎ 208-344-2175; 202 S Capitol Blvd; mains $6-8) For good bar food and 'Beef tongue Saturday' (commences at 11:30am), head to this friendly bar on the Basque Block.

Also recommended are:

Tablerock Brewpub & Grill (☎ 208-342-0944; 705 Fulton St; mains $7-16) Cranks out hefty pub food and tasty hand-crafted beer; try the White Bird Wheat.

Boise Co-op (☎ 208-472-4500; 888 W Fort St) Serves natural foods.

Drinking

Emerald City (☎ 208-342-5446; 415 S 9th St) Proud to be 'straight friendly,' this gay bar and nightclub has DJs spinning every night except Saturday, when a show gets the spotlight.

Getting There & Around

Boise Municipal Airport (☎ 208-383-3110; I-84 exit 53) has daily flights to Seattle, Spokane and elsewhere. Greyhound and Northwestern Trailway services depart from the **bus station** (☎ 208-343-3681; 1212 W Bannock St) and travel along three main routes: I-84, US 95 and I-15/I-20/I-287/I-91.

Boise Urban Stages (BUS; ☎ 208-336-1010) operates local buses, including an airport route (No 13).

KETCHUM & SUN VALLEY

Largely due to the highly rated Sun Valley ski resort, Ketchum and Sun Valley are Idaho's premier destinations and the most happening cluster of towns in Idaho. The area has long buzzed with high flyers: the truly wealthy live in their 'trophy homes,' and it's not uncommon to see a shining Hollywood face cruising down a slope. But this is no LA: the year-round destinations of Ketchum and Sun Valley, nestled among resplendent natural beauty, are places to get away from it all.

Ketchum is the main commercial hub, with many restaurants, hotels and boutiques. Nobel-prize-winning author (and avid sportsman) Ernest Hemingway (1899–1961) was a frequent visitor to the area, and spent his last years in Ketchum, where he's buried. Twelve miles south on Hwy 75, Hailey (lived in and half-owned by Bruce Willis) is where most seasonal workers and ski bums live.

Information

Sun Valley/Ketchum Visitors Center (☎ 208-726-3423, 800-634-3347; www.visitsunvalley.com; 411 Main St; ☺ 9am-6pm) and **USFS Sawtooth National Forest Ketchum Ranger Station** (☎ 208-622-5371; 206 Sun Valley Rd, ☺ 8am-5pm Mon-Fri) offer area advice.

Activities

Sun Valley Resort (☎ 800-786-8259; www.sunvalley.com; lift tickets winter/summer $46/20) is famous for its prime powder and excellent slopes. West of Ketchum, world-class **Bald Mountain** (☎ 208-622-6136; lift tickets winter/summer $66/20) has mostly advanced terrain, while older **Dollar Mountain** (☎ 208-622-2242; lift tickets winter/summer $49/35) offers easier runs. In summer, both offer **hiking** and **mountain biking**, which are also popular along the very well-maintained Wood River Trail System (WRTS), winding 20 miles through Ketchum and Sun Valley. The 10-mile Sun Valley Trail connects to the WRTS, and there are several other excellent trails near Ketchum.

> ### DETOUR: WALLACE
>
> A wee dot on the Idaho panhandle, Wallace is an old silver-mining town that preserves the Western flavor of its historic town center. Of curious note is the **Oasis Bordello Museum** (☎ 208-753-0801; 605 Cedar St; admission $5; ☺ 9:30am-6:30pm Mon-Sat, 10am-5pm Sun), a brothel until 1988. Twenty-minute tours unveil the mystery of the ladies' hasty departure and offer sneak peeks at lingering items like the Madam's dressing table, just as she left it.
>
> Wallace's environs offer outdoorsy treats such as **white-water rafting** the Class III run of the St Joe National Wild & Scenic River and **jet-skiing** on the 60-plus lakes around Coeur d'Alene.

RAFTING THE WEST'S WILDEST WHITE-WATER *Andrew Dean Nystrom*

The Wild West, especially the US **Rocky Mountains**, California's **Sierra Nevada** (p613) and the **Southwest** (p441) desert, is synonymous with wilderness, and there's no better way to access and experience many of these regions' untamed lands than via the wild rivers that run through them, in a white-water kayak, paddle raft, 'cataraft' or even inflatable 'rubber duckie' kayak.

Whatever craft/vessel you choose, options range from hour-long guided scenic flat-water floats and noncommercial tubing trips to the marathon seven- to 30-day voyage down the Colorado River through the **Grand Canyon** (p428) in northern Arizona. Without joining a private or commercial trip it's impossible to get on the river, since the 15- to 20-year waiting list has been closed indefinitely by the National Parks Service (NPS) while they try to come up with a new permit system!

While there are innumerable western white-water outfitters who will rent you all the gear necessary for a self-guided trip, there's really no substitute for experienced guides, especially when it comes to picking campsites, securing permits and safely navigating Class V rapids. It's well worth a splurge for a guided commercial trip to secure a launch date on the most popular rivers, such as Idaho's Wild and Scenic **Middle Fork of the Salmon River**, part of the Lower 48's longest undammed river system. Once on the water, few folks complain about being served coffee in their sleeping bag and having guides whip up eggs Benedict and Dutch oven desserts while they float, fish, soak and dream their cares away.

The rugged, remote Middle Fork is often rated as one of the world's top 10 white-water and fly-fishing trips, and for good reason. The three- to eight-day journey begins its 3000ft vertical drop (an average descent of 28ft per mile) surrounded by conifer forest at 6000ft at the

Sleeping

Budget accommodations are difficult to come by; you could consider camping relatively close to town.

Lift Tower Lodge (☎ 208-726-5163, 800-462-8646; ltowerl@micron.net; 703 S Main St; r $65-90) This friendly small motel in downtown Ketchum offers free continental breakfasts and a hot tub. It sits next to a landmark exhibition chairlift (c 1939).

Meadows RV Park (☎ 208-726-5445; 13 Broadway Run, Hwy 75; campsites/RV sites $15/27) About 2 miles south of Ketchum.

Boundary Campground (campsites $11) You can't reserve at this campground, off Trail Creek Rd, 3 miles east of the Ketchum ranger station.

Eating

Bigwood Bread (☎ 208-726-2034; 270 Northwood Way; mains $4-8) With a cheery and upbeat atmosphere, art-lined Bigwood Bread has hearty sandwiches, salads and healthy-start offerings like organic muesli ($2.50).

Desperado's (☎ 208-726-3068; 211 4th St; mains $7-9) A bright and busy eatery specializing in reasonably priced Mexican food and $17 pitchers of margaritas.

Grumpy's (860 Warm Springs Rd; mains $4-8) For big burgers and bigger personality, follow

locals to the sunny deck at Grumpy's, decorated with old beer cans.

Getting There & Around

The region's airport is Hailey's **Friedman Memorial Airport** (☎ 208-788-4956), 12 miles south of Ketchum. **Ketchum Area Rapid Transit** (KART; ☎ 208-726-7576; ☉ 8am-6pm Mon-Fri) operates a free daily bus service between Ketchum and Sun Valley.

AROUND KETCHUM

Craters of the Moon National Monument (☎ 208-527-3257; vehicle/hiker or biker $4/2), an hour's drive southeast of Ketchum, is an 83-sq-mile volcanic showcase.

Lava flows, cinder cones, lava tubes and trailheads lie along the 7-mile **Crater Loop Rd** (☉ Apr-Nov), traversed by skiers and snowshoers in winter. A surreal **campground** (campsites $10) near the entrance station has running water only in summer.

Drive 30 miles north of Ketchum on Hwy 75, which winds past timbered slopes and along the Salmon River, and you will ascend Galena Summit (8701ft), with truly breathtaking views.

The 1180-sq-mile **Sawtooth National Recreation Area** spans the Sawtooth, Smoky, Boulder and Salmon River mountains and has

Boundary Creek put-in outside Stanley. There are over 100 rapids (Class II to IV+) and no roads reach the river's banks for 100 miles, until the confluence with the Main Fork of the Salmon.

Unique highlights along the way include visits to early 20th-century homesteader cabins, several soakable hot springs, wildlife-watching opportunities (eagles, river otters, big horn sheep), day hikes to well-preserved native Tukudeka pictograph (rock art) sites and blue-ribbon, catch-and-release angling in gin-clear riffles for native cut-throat and rainbow trout.

Early season (late May to mid-June) features peak flow and thrilling, chilly white-water, while mid-season (mid-June to August) means warmer water and better fishing. Late season (mid-August to September) options during lower water include specialized fishing and hiking trips. Other thematic options include spiritual women-only and co-ed yoga retreats and family-focus trips.

For details about Middle Fork trips, contact Idaho's premier river outfitter, Coeur d'Alene–based **River Odysseys West** (ROW; ☎ 208-765-0841, 800-451-6034; www.rowinc.com).

All-inclusive rates (excluding pre- and post-trip transportation to and from the put-in and take-out) for most trips start around $40 for half-day floats, $75 for full-day trips and run $200 to $300 per day for overnight trips, depending on the season, demand and remoteness of the river.

Trips in Colorado tend to be a bit more expensive. The majority of trips run between May and September, with a few options available year-round. Check outfitters' websites and sign up for email newsletters for last-minute deals, two-for-one offers and shoulder season specials – then gear up for an adrenaline-filled experience of a lifetime.

ROCKY MOUNTAINS

40 peaks over 10,000ft, over 300 high-alpine lakes, 100 miles of streams and 750 miles of trails.

The adjacent 340-sq-mile Sawtooth Wilderness Area centers on the rugged Sawtooth Range. Though most tourists come in summer and winter, boundless recreation is possible year-round.

The **area headquarters** (☎ 208-727-5000, 800-847-4843; Hwy 75; ☯ 8am-4:30pm winter, 8am-5pm summer), 8.5 miles north of Ketchum, refers visitors to guides for climbing, fishing and backcountry skiing, and has information on yurt rentals and camping.

It also sells Trailhead Parking Passes (three-day/year passes $5/15).

Pacific Northwest

HIGHLIGHTS

- **Olympic National Park** Admire the view from Hurricane Ridge or step into what could be a *Lord of the Rings* set in the Hoh Rain Forest (p529)
- **Crater Lake** Gaze longingly into its deep, deep blue eye (p553)
- **Oregon Coast** Count starfish in tidal pools or wander aimlessly on pristine beaches (p549)
- **Bumbershoot** Rock out at Seattle's hippest music festival (p522)
- **Off the beaten track** Delve into the wild depths of Hells Canyon, North America's deepest chasm (p545)
- **Best journey** Cruise Hwy 30 through the unbelievably scenic Columbia River Gorge (p543)

FAST FACTS

- **Area** 169,689 sq miles (about the same as Iraq)
- **Big cities** Seattle (population 3.5 million), Portland (530,000)
- **Budget** $40-60 per day
- **Costs** yurt in an Oregon coast state park $29, Seattle–Portland train ticket $24, pint of ambrosial microbrew $2.40
- **Driving times** Vancouver, BC to Seattle 3 hours, Seattle to Portland 3 hours, Portland to San Francisco 11 hours
- **Famous for** coffee, microbrews, political activism, outdoor adventure
- **Languages** English, several Native American languages in the Algonquian-Wakashan and Penutian families
- **Population:** 15 million
- **Phrases** *Partly sunny* (mostly cloudy), *Why bother?* (decaf, nonfat latte), *Ory-gun* (proper state-name pronunciation – not or-ee-gone)
- **Seasons** high (May to Labor Day)

- **States** Washington, Oregon
- **Tasty treats** Columbia River salmon, local apples, morel mushrooms, micro-brewed beer
- **Time** PST; GMT minus 8 hours (daylight-saving observed)
- **Top hostel** McMenamins Edgefield (p545)

TRAVEL HINTS

Call ahead for road conditions and room reservations, self-cater from local organic markets instead of constantly eating out and always carry an umbrella.

Oregon and Washington possess some of the USA's most wild and diverse landscapes. Few other regions offer misty, moss-laden rain forests, soaring snow-capped mountains, churning rivers, arid plateaus and rugged coastline – all within two state borders. From the awe-inspiring glaciers of Mt Rainier to the gaping crater of Mt St Helens, the winding chasm of the Columbia River Gorge to the expansive Oregon coast, the Pacific Northwest offers unlimited opportunities for exploration and adventure for nature lovers and armchair (well, car seat) travelers alike.

All this natural wonder is anchored by two vibrant, cosmopolitan cities. Seattle's coffeehouses and music venues provide innumerable retreats from inclement weather, as do Portland's bookstores and brewpubs. But in the Pacific Northwest, you're expected to get outdoors – even if it's raining. So make like the locals and get your latte to go.

HISTORY

If humans did arrive via a land bridge from Russia to Alaska, the coasts, islands and river valleys of the Pacific Northwest must have been among the continent's first populated areas. When Europeans arrived in the 18th century, Native American societies already had well-established, prosperous communities. Inland, cultures such as the Nez Percé and Spokane thrived.

Three hundred years after Columbus landed in the New World, Spanish and British explorers were probing the northern Pacific coast, still seeking the fabled Northwest Passage. In 1792 Captain George Vancouver claimed British sovereignty over the entire Puget Sound region. From then to the 1820s, exploration was all the rage, and explorers Lewis and Clark helped extend US claim on the territory and usher in waves of settlers. This had a devastating impact on the indigenous cultures, assailed as they were by the double threat of European diseases and alcohol.

The USA formally acquired the territory from the British by treaty in 1846. By 1855 some 53,000 settlers came to the Northwest via the 2000-mile-long Oregon Trail, and most of the major cities in the Pacific Northwest had been established by 1860. Meanwhile the indigenous people had been moved to reservations, where illness, starvation and dislocation almost led to their extinction.

With the appearance of the Northern Pacific Railroad (1873) and the Great Northern Railroad (1893), the region's future was set. Agriculture and lumber became the pillars of the regional economy until 1914, when the new Panama Canal and WWI brought increased trade to Pacific ports. Shipyards opened along Puget Sound, and aircraft Goliath Boeing set up shop near Seattle.

WWII offered another boost for aircraft manufacturing and shipbuilding, and agriculture continued to thrive. In the post-war period Washington's population, especially around Puget Sound, grew to twice that of Oregon. But hydroelectricity production and the massive irrigation projects along the Columbia have nearly destroyed the river's ecosystem beyond repair. Logging has also left its scars, especially in Oregon. The environment remains a contentious issue in the Northwest; flash points are the logging of old-growth forests and the destruction of salmon runs in streams and rivers (see p513).

In the 1980s and '90s, the economic emphasis shifted again as the high-tech industry – embodied by Microsoft in Seattle and Intel in Portland – took hold in the region. More recently the tech industry has suffered from the troubled national economy, and unemployment in the Northwest has soared; in 2003 Oregon and Washington had the first- and third-highest jobless rates in the USA, respectively.

THE CULTURE

Pacific Northwesterners are passionate about many things – outdoor adventure, beer and recycling among them. West of the Cascades,

---

THE BIG ISSUE: DAM IT

For 65 years, hydroelectric dams along the Snake and Columbia Rivers have been driving the Pacific Northwest's economy – and blocking salmon from reaching their traditional spawning grounds. In the late 1990s a politically explosive controversy erupted over breaching these dams in an effort to save dwindling populations of wild salmon. Environmentalists and Native Americans support breaching, which would force the hydroelectric plants to shut down, yet the shipping and irrigation interests that depend on the dams stiffly oppose it. In 2000 federal agencies began an effort to restore salmon habitats and improve fish survival through the dams – five- and eight-year assessments of which will determine whether breaching is really necessary.

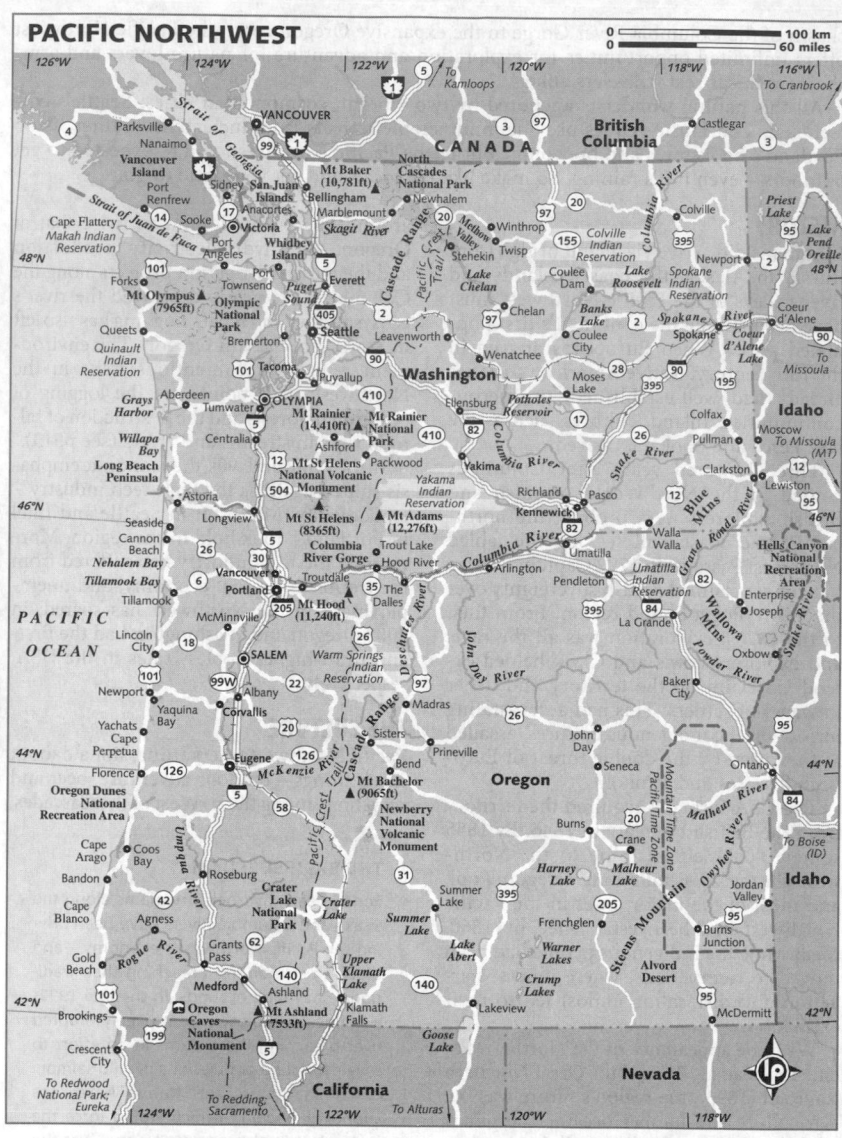

folks are progressive and politically active; east of the mountains, things tend to be more conservative. Yet certain issues, such as unemployment, span the peaks.

Despite the region's addiction to coffee, residents remain phenomenally laid back. True, they're still suffering from growing pains after the grunge and high-tech explosions that drew flocks of East Coasters to the area. But they're easing out of the national spotlight and into their newfound sleek sophistication (goodbye flannel, hello Fendi). As a result, lifestyles are melding. Many finer establishments, anxious not to lose business, are offering scaled-down, more-affordable menus. The result: a blended atmosphere of neo-hippie emanating from sushi bars, and yuppies who are comfortable sipping microbrews and cavorting with outdoorsy types.

SPORTS & RECREATION

Pacific Northwesterners are some of the most adventure-loving Americans you'll meet. The outdoor-recreation industry is colossal here, with hiking, backpacking, mountaineering, cycling, kayaking, white-water rafting, snowboarding/skiing/snowshoeing, windsurfing and whale-watching outfitters in nearly every nook. More esoteric, hardcore pursuits, such as skysurfing and mountain boarding, have crannies as well. For excellent information on everything outdoors, visit or call the **Outdoor Recreation Information Center** (☎ 206-470-4060; 222 Yale Ave N), in the REI flagship store in Seattle.

Spectator sports are gigantic too, with college teams vying with professional franchises for the allegiance of Northwest fans.

ARTS & ENTERTAINMENT

With everything from Portland's **Imago Theater** (p542) to the **Seattle Symphony** (p526) to Ashland's world class **Shakespeare Festival** (p551), there are plenty of cultural offerings in the Pacific Northwest. And if that's not enough, there's always baseball's Mariners.

Seattle is the cultural center of the region. With more bookstores per capita than any other US city, it has bred a stable of internationally recognized writers. The rest of the area shares the love, and not just for literature; it's become a hotbed of cutting-edge music and visual arts. Portland's live-music venues are packed nightly, and the region's art museums host international traveling exhibits.

Books, films and TV shows (such as *Frasier*) have been set in the Pacific Northwest and many films produced here have been set somewhere else (such as the Cascades posing as the Rockies in *The Shining*).

ENVIRONMENT

Environmental issues dominate politics and civic life in the Pacific Northwest. Trees are both holy altars and cash cows, and the logging industry's presence is a powerful point of contention. Endangered fish runs, especially for sea-going salmon, are another concern. Yet many residents exhibit a profound

---

TOP FIVE MICROBREWERIES

There are more microbreweries per capita in Oregon than anywhere in the world, and Washington nearly birthed the industry. Before you go blindly brewpub-hopping, start with these surefire goodies:

- **Rogue Ales Brewery**, Newport, OR (p550)
- **Lucky Labrador Brewing Company**, Portland, OR (p541)
- **Full Sail Brewery**, Hood River, OR (p544)
- **Jolly Roger Taproom**, Seattle, WA (p525)
- **Fishbowl Brewpub**, Olympia, WA (p529)

---

appreciation of their surroundings, both in accessing nature and preserving it – try to find a house in Eugene without a compost bin.

The Cascades effectively divide the Northwest into two ecosystems. West of the mountains are mossy, heavily forested valleys, and arid uplands and high deserts stretch east of the range. They also divide microclimates: the Pacific's marine air doesn't penetrate the mountains, so coastal winters are moderate and moist while a continental weather pattern prevails in the east. Flora and fauna are similarly varied. Dense coastal forests are full of old-growth Douglas firs and madrones; dry eastern upland forests contain ponderosa and lodgepole pines. Wildlife abounds in both, with populations of myriad species of bird, salmon, elk and antelope.

Oregon has one national park – Crater Lake (p553) – and Washington has three – Mt Rainier (p533), Olympic (p529) and North Cascades (p533). National forests are numerous, but 16% of these are open to logging. State and county parks and wildlife refuges offer local retreats, as do day-use parks (some of which charge a $3 parking fee).

TRANSPORTATION

For general transportation information, see p702. Also see p702 for details on crossing the USA–Canada border.

Seattle and Portland receive most of the region's airborne visitors. **Sea-Tac International**

(☎ 206-433-5388; www.portseattle.org) is the main airport in the Northwest, with international and regional service; second-most frequented is **Portland International Airport** (PDX; ☎ 877-739-4636; www.flypdx.com). See p702 for a listing of major airlines; Southwest, Alaska and Horizon are top budget options.

Both passenger-only and car ferries, operated by Washington State Ferries (p527), ply Puget Sound and across to British Columbia; details are in serviced-town sections.

Local and national buses connect to ferries. **Greyhound** (☎ 800-229-9424; www.greyhound .com) provides service along the I-5 corridor and the main east–west routes, with links to some smaller communities. For a more eccentric travel experience, explore the **Green Tortoise bus** (www.greentortoise.com), which has a hostel in Seattle (p523).

Driving your own vehicle is the most convenient way to tour the area. I-5 is the Pacific Northwest's main thoroughfare, stretching through Washington and Oregon en route to California. Snaking Hwy 101 hugs the coast and offers stunning coastal panoramas. Major car-rental agencies can be found throughout the region; see p707 for details.

More pleasant and scenic than the bus, and comparably priced, **Amtrak** (☎ 800-872-7245; www.amtrak.com) runs trains to, from, around and beyond the Northwest. Routes include the Cascades (Portland and Eugene to Seattle and Vancouver, BC), Coast Starlight (Seattle to Los Angeles) and Empire Builder (Seattle or Portland to Chicago).

SEATTLE

The birthplace of überinfluential trends like grunge music and gourmet coffee, Washington's largest city (population 571,900) epitomizes the region's transformation from hick to hip. Pre-1980s provincialism and conservatism gave way to '90s Nirvana and Starbucks, and TV and film crews often base themselves here to capture Seattle's chic cultural and social idiosyncrasies. Today the city's rapid growth spurt is slowing, and residents find themselves re-settling into face-lifted neighborhoods where rents are higher and the folks next door are Californians. Yet Seattlites tend to be happy; maybe it's the glorious surrounding Cascade and Olympic mountains, Puget Sound's watery fingers and alluring islands, and the bountiful lattes.

HISTORY
Named 'Seattle' for the chief of the Duwamish tribe who originally inhabited the Lake Washington area, Washington's largest city was settled by David Denny in 1851. The Great Fire of 1889 devastated the wooden frontier village, yet the seeming catastrophe was somewhat of a blessing – the city was rebuilt with handsome structures of brick, stone and steel. The railroad linked Seattle to the rest of the country in 1893, and the city's first boom came shortly after. In 1897 it became the provisioning point for prospectors headed to the Yukon gold territory, and the banking center for the fortunes made there.

The boom continued through WWI, when Northwest lumber was in great demand and the Puget Sound area prospered as a shipbuilding center. In 1916 William Boeing founded the aircraft manufacturing business that would become one of the largest employers in Seattle, attracting tens of thousands of newcomers to the region during WWII. In more recent years, the growth of Microsoft and other software developers has made it increasingly difficult to find someone who isn't a contractor, caterer or car dealer for the Microsoft crowd.

In November 1999 Seattle made international headlines when protesters and police clashed violently outside a World Trade Organization summit. Then, in 2001 a 6.8-magnitude earthquake near the state capital caused billions of dollars' worth of damages (though, miraculously, little loss of life). Later that year came the ultimate kick in the teeth: Boeing relocated its headquarters to Chicago.

ORIENTATION
Seattle sits on a slim isthmus between Puget Sound (to the west) and Lake Washington (to the east), while Mt Rainier looms to the south and the ocean laps the shore 125 miles away. Traffic creeps on the north–south I-5, which bisects the city, and the I-90, which joins I-5 south of downtown and heads east to New York.

The city is very neighborhood-oriented; locals give directions in terms of district, so try to learn the lingo. Basically, heading north from the compact downtown core, Capitol

Hill and the U District are east of I-5, while Seattle Center (spottable landmark: Space Needle), Fremont and Ballard (burgeoning artist/hipster neighborhood) lie to the west. Aurora Ave (Hwy 99) is a major north–south artery. Eastlake Ave goes from downtown to the U District.

Good maps are invaluable and abundant; Lonely Planet's *Seattle* map is handy.

INFORMATION
Bookstores
Bailey/Coy Books (☎ 206-323-8842; 414 Broadway E; ☿ 10am-10pm Sun-Thu, 10am-11pm Fri & Sat) Friendly local bookshop

Beyond the Closet Books (☎ 206-322-4609; 518 E Pike St; ☿ 10am-6pm) Gay-focused bookstore since 1988.

Bulldog News & Espresso (☎ 206-632-6397; 4208 University Way NE, U District; ☿ 8am-9pm Sun-Thu, 8am-10pm Fri & Sat, espresso bar opens 6:30am daily) Mag-browsers and espresso-sippers.

Elliott Bay Book Company (☎ 206-624-6600; www .elliottbaybook.com; 101 S Main St; ☿ 9:30am-10pm Mon-Sat, 11am-7pm Sun) Labyrinthine store in historic Pioneer Square; readings almost every day. Downstairs Elliott Bay Café has light fare and the beloved Top Pot handcrafted doughnuts.

Left Bank Books (☎ 206-622-0195; 92 Pike Pl; ☿ 10am-7pm Mon-Sat, 11am-6pm Sun) Socialist intellectual heaven.

Metsker Maps (☎ 206-623-8747; 1511 1st Ave; ☿ 9am-6pm Mon-Fri, 10am-5pm Sat & Sun) Maps and guidebooks galore.

University Bookstore (☎ 206-634-3400; 4326 University Way NE, U District; ☿ 9am-9pm Mon-Fri, 9am-6pm Sat, noon-5pm Sun) Readings, events and books, books, books.

Emergency
Community Info Line (☎ 206-461-3200) Information on emergency services, housing, legal advice etc.
Seattle Police (☎ 206-625-5011)
Seattle Rape Relief (☎ 206-632-7273)
Washington State Patrol (☎ 425-649-4370)

Internet Access
For free Internet access, stop by any of Seattle's public libraries. There are a gazillion WiFi spots around, and Internet cafés (most of whom offer 30 minutes free if you buy a coffee or snack) include the following:
Aurafice (☎ 206-860-9977; 616 E Pine St; per hr $6; ☿ 8am-midnight Wed-Mon, 8-2am Tue) DJ on Tuesday night.
CapitolHill.net (☎ 206-860-6858; www.capitolhill.net; 216 Broadway E; per hr $6; ☿ 8am-midnight) Sunlight-

GETTING INTO TOWN

Most visitors arrive at Sea-Tac International Airport. **Airport Express shuttles** (☎ 206-626-6088, 800-426-7532; one way/roundtrip $8.50/14; ☿ 5am-11pm) run every 30 minutes. Or catch Metro Transit bus No 174 or 194 ($1.75, 30 minutes).

A taxi is about $35. City buses and taxis abound at the Amtrak and Greyhound stations.

starved place on the main drag serving food ($3 to $6) from 11am to 11pm.

Online Coffee Co Capitol Hill (☎ 206-328-3731; 1720 E Olive Way; ☿ 8am-midnight Mon-Sat, 9am-midnight Sun); Downtown (☎ 206-381-1991; 1111 1st Ave; per hr $8; ☿ 7am-10pm Mon-Fri, 9am-10pm Sat, 9am-8pm Sun) Ample terminals at mellow, couch-filled cafés.

Libraries
Central Library (☎ 206-386-4636; www.spl.org; 1000 4th Ave; ☿ 10am-8pm Mon-Wed, 10am-6pm Thu-Sat, 1-5pm Sun) Everything about Seattle's brand new, $165 million public library is amazing if not overwhelming, from its massive book collection to its 300 computers to its shrine-to-glass-and-steel architecture to the all-red 4th floor.

Media
KEXP 90.3 FM Alt-rock university station.
KPLU 88.5 FM National Public Radio.
KUOW 94.9 FM The University of Washington's NPR affiliate.
Seattle Post-Intelligencer (www.seattlepi.com) The morning daily.
Seattle Times (www.seattletimes.com) The state's largest daily paper.
Seattle Weekly (www.seattleweekly.com) Free weekly with news and entertainment listings.
Stranger (www.thestranger.com) Free weekly with the best alternative news and entertainment listings; home of racy 'Savage Love.'

Medical Services
45th St Community Clinic (☎ 206-633-3350; 1629 N 45th St, Wallingford) Medical and dental services; call for hours.
Harborview Medical Center (☎ 206-731-3000; 325 9th Ave) Full medical care with 24-hour emergency room.
US Healthworks Denny Way (☎ 206-682-7418; 1151 Denny Way; ☿ 7am-6pm Mon-Fri); Aurora Ave (☎ 206-784-0737; 8313 Aurora N; ☿ 8am-7pm, 9am-5pm Sat) Nonemergency walk-in clinics.

Money
American Express (☎ 206-441-8622; 600 Stewart St; ◷ 8:30am-5:30pm Mon-Fri)
Travelex Foreign Exchange Airport (☎ 206-248-0401; ◷ 6am-8pm); Westlake Center (☎ 206-682-4525; 400 Pine St, Level 3; ◷ 9:30am-6pm Mon-Sat, 11am-5pm Sun) The booth at the main airport terminal is behind the Northwest Airlines counter.

Post
Broadway station (☎ 206-324-5474; 101 Broadway E; ◷ 8:30am-6pm Mon-Fri, 8:30am-3pm Sat)
Main post office (☎ 206-748-5417; 301 Union St; ◷ 7:30am-5:30pm Mon-Fri)
University station (☎ 206-675-8114; 4244 University Way NE; ◷ 7:30am-6pm Mon-Fri, 8:30am-3pm Sat)

Telephone
Within Seattle, even for local calls, you must dial the full 10-digit number (without a 1).

Tourist Information
Citywide Concierge Center (☎ 206-461-5888; www.seeseattle.org; cnr 7th Ave & Pike St; ◷ 9am-5pm Mon-Fri with some summer weekends) Seattle's helpful, brilliantly colorful tourist office (and TicketMaster outlet) is on the main floor of the Washington State Convention & Trade Center.

SIGHTS
You just *have* to visit Seattle Center (Space Needle and Experience Music Project) and downtown (Pike Place Market and Waterfront). But Seattle is filled with other sights, neighborhoods and parks worth roaming around and getting lost in. And when your feet tire, there's always a corner coffeeshop to keep you humming.

If you're hitting the big attractions, consider a Seattle CityPass ($39.50), which covers admission to six sights including the Space Needle and the aquarium. Art buffs will enjoy First Thursdays, when 35-plus venues – including Seattle Art Museum and the Burke Museum, and many Pioneer Square galleries – offer free entry.

Downtown & Belltown
The tourist-thronged heart of downtown Seattle is **Pike Place Market**. It's good theater, though usually claustrophobically crowded. The Main and North Arcades are the most popular areas, with bellowing, halibut-tossing fishmongers, rows of gem-like produce and myriad arts-and-crafts vendors.

Tiny shops and eateries of all descriptions fill the market's labyrinthine lower levels. Go on a weekday morning to avoid the throngs. From here, steps and streets lead to the scenic **Waterfront**. And yes, the **Starbucks** (1912 Pike Pl) here is the original.

A 48ft-high mechanized *Hammering Man* towers over the **Seattle Art Museum** (SAM; ☎ 206-654-3100; www.seattleartmuseum.org; 100 University St; adult/student $7/5; ◷ 10am-5pm Tue-Sun, 10am-9pm Thu). The museum's permanent collection includes European and Asian paintings and sculpture, and an excellent display of pieces from Northwest coastal tribes. Some question whether the admission price is worth it, and prices rise for special local and international exhibits (which can be phenomenal). SAM's expansion is slated to open in spring 2007.

On Pier 59 is the **Seattle Aquarium** (☎ 206-386-4320; www.seattleaquarium.org; 1483 Alaskan Way; admission $13; ◷ 10am-5pm). Full of open-air and hands-on exhibits for ogling octopi and massaging skates, it features local habitats and marine life. Surrounded by touching pools, a salmon ladder and a jellyfish arch, the aquarium's centerpiece is the Dome, a spherical underwater room where you can see deep-water denizens from all angles; don't miss the daily feeding frenzy at 1:30pm. Note that the building may be closed for a month or two in fall 2005 due to construction; call ahead.

Just north of downtown is the hip neighborhood of **Belltown**, a former warehouse district sprinkled with bars, boutiques, and yoga studios. Stroll the streets, sip a double-tall nonfat flat mocha and feel beautiful.

Seattle Center & Queen Anne
The archetypal Seattle attraction is the *Jetsons*-esque **Space Needle** (☎ 206-905-2100; www.spaceneedle.com; admission $13; ◷ 9am-11pm Sun-Thu, 9am-midnight Fri & Sat), a 605ft-high observation station built for the 1962 World's Fair with a sweeping 360° view. Other futuristic-yet-retro-looking vestiges of the fair are on view at the **Seattle Center** (☎ 206-684-8582; www.seattlecenter.com; 400 Broad St).

On the eastern side of the Center, that giant blob of undulating, colorful metal is nothing other than the **Experience Music Project** (EMP; ☎ 206-367-5483; www.emplive.com; 325 5th Ave N; admission $20; ◷ 9am-6pm Sun-Thu, 9am-9pm Fri & Sat). The lovechild of Microsoft cofounder Paul Allen's fat wallet and rock-and-roll heart, this interactive music museum is worth a look for the architecture alone; but it'll cost ya. The shimmering, abstract Frank Gehry–designed building houses 80,000 music artifacts, including handwritten lyrics by Nirvana's Kurt Cobain and a fabulous Hendrix Gallery (Jimi's buried in nearby Renton). To serious music fans, the exhibits may seem a little basic, although the video archive is excellent. The Sky Church theater, **Liquid Lounge** (p526) and Turntable restaurant are accessible free of charge. The EMP opens at 10am in winter.

Aptly placed under the flying-saucer-like Space Needle is the new **Science Fiction Museum** (☎ 206-724-3428; www.sfhomeworld.org; 325 5th Ave N; admission $13, ☑ 10am-3pm Tue-Thu, 10am-9pm Fri & Sat, 10am-6pm Sun). Another Allen investment ($20 million), this brand-new shrine to kitschy and classic science-fiction artefacts features Captain Kirk's command chair, robots and androids, and the interactive orbital Spacedock. A $27 combo ticket gets you into the neighboring EMP, too.

To get even closer to outerspace, trek up Highland Dr in posh **Queen Anne** for a little exercise and killer views of the skyline and Mt Rainier. Explore the narrow staircases crisscrossing Queen Anne hill.

Pioneer Square

The birthplace of Seattle, the enclave of red-brick buildings known as Pioneer Square languished for years until cheap rents and Historic Register status brought in art galleries, antique shops and cafés. Today the Waterfront Streetcar drops you amid tourists and locals frequenting the establishments around Yesler Way, the area's original 'skid road.' In Seattle's early days timber would skid down the road from a lofty logging camp to Henry Yesler's pierside mill. With the decline of the area, the street became a haven for homeless people. The nickname Skid Rd (or 'Skid Row') came to mean the opposite of 'Easy St' in cities across the USA.

Just south of Pioneer Square, on Occidental Ave S, concrete **Occidental Park** has totem poles carved by Chinookan artist Duane Pasco. Between S Main and Jackson Sts, the park turns into a tree-lined pedestrian mall.

At the **Klondike Gold Rush National Historic Park** (☎ 206-553-7220; 117 S Main St; admission free; ☑ 9am-5pm), one of the few *indoor* national parks in the country, learn what kind of provisions you would've needed were you to stake a claim in the Yukon Territory.

Capitol Hill

This long-time countercultural oasis has an unmatched vitality. Cruise Broadway north of E John St (which becomes E Olive Way west of Broadway), pulsing with trendy and commercial life (though there are more eateries than shops), and where tattooed locals cram restaurants' sidewalk tables on rare sunny afternoons.

For a break from urbania, head up to stately **Volunteer Park** (E Prospect St), originally Seattle's cemetery. Here the **Seattle Asian Art Museum** (☎ 206-654-3100; 1400 E Prospect St; suggested donation $3; ☑ 10am-5pm Tue-Sun, 10am-9pm Thu; ℗) houses an extensive collection including Japanese, Korean and Himalayan art. Flash your ticket stub for $3 off SAM (opposite) admission within seven days. Also in the park is the glass-paned Victorian **conservatory** (☎ 206-684-4743; admission free; ☑ 10am-4pm), filled with botanical enchantments.

If you're driving, there's a paid parking lot ($1.75/15 half-hour/day) on E Harrison St behind the Broadway Market.

The U District

The lush University of Washington (aka U dub) campus sits on Lake Union about 3 miles northeast of downtown. The neighborhood's main drags, **'the Ave'** (University Way) and NE 45th Ave, teem with affordable food stops, thrift shops and cafés. U-dub's core is **Central Plaza**; get information and a campus map at the **visitors center** (☎ 206-543-9198; 4014 University Way; ☑ 8am-5pm Mon-Fri).

On the campus border, the **Burke Museum** (☎ 206-543-5590; www.washington.edu/burkemuseum; cnr 17th Ave NE & NE 45th St; adult/student $8/5; ☑ 10am-5pm) beautifully represents Northwest-coast Indian cultures. The sophisticated **Henry Art Gallery** (☎ 206-543-2280; www.henryart.org; adult/student $8/free; ☑ 11am-5pm Tue-Sun, 11am-8pm Thu) holds contemporary art, photography and visual arts in a modern Charles Gwathmey–designed edifice.

International District

Just east of Pioneer Square, this neighborhood is bustling with Asian groceries and restaurants (come for late-night dim sum). The thought-provoking **Wing Luke Asian Museum** (☎ 206-623-5124; www.wingluke.org; 407 7th Ave S; adult/student $4/3; ☑ 11am-4:30pm Tue-Fri, noon-4pm Sat & Sun) explores the culture, art and history of Asian Pacific Americans. It documents the

Volunteer Park

To Seattle Asian Art Museum & Volunteer Park Conservatory (0.25mi)

16th Ave E
E Ward St
E Valley St
E Aloha St
E Mercer St
16th Ave E
15th Ave E
14th Ave
16th Ave
Malden Ave E
14th Ave E
13th Ave E
12th Ave E
11th Ave E
Federal Ave E
E Roy St
10th Ave E

Capitol Hill

E John St
E Denny Way
E Howell St
E Olive St
E Pine St
E Union St
E Spring St
E Marion St
13th Ave
11th Ave

Lincoln Reservoir

Bobby Morris Playfield

Nagle Pl
Broadway
Broadway E
10th Ave
Broadway Ct

Seattle University

E Prospect St

Harvard Ave E
Harvard Ave
Boylston Ave E
Belmont Pl E
Belmont Ave E
Belmont Ave E
E Mercer St
E Republican St
E Harrison St
Summit Ave E
Boylston Ave E
E Thomas St
Bellevue Ave E
E Loretta Pl
E John Pl

Seattle Central Community College

E Pine St
E Olive St
Belmont Ave
Summit Ave
Crawford Pl
Bellevue Ave
Union St
Boylston Ave

Melrose Ave E
Melrose Ave
Eastlake Ave E

To U District (1.5mi); Gas Works Park (1.5mi); Wallingford (1.5mi); US Healthworks (2.5mi)

Yale Ave N
Pontius Ave N
Minor Ave N
Thomas St
John St
Howell St
Yale St
Minor Ave
Boren Ave
Olive Way

Cascade Playground

Fairview Ave N
Boren Ave N
Terry Ave N
Terry Ave
9th Ave
8th Ave

Washington State Convention & Trade Center

Hubbell Pl
5th Avenue Theatre

Downtown

Eastlake

Thomas St
John St
9th Ave N
8th Ave N
Republican St
Harrison St
Dexter Ave N
Denny Way
Westlake Ave
Lenora St
Virginia St
7th Ave
6th Ave
Pine St
Stewart St

Denny Park

Westlake Center
Bon Marché
Century Plaza
Coliseum Theater

To Fremont (2mi); Ballard (3mi)

Aurora Ave N
6th Ave N
Taylor Ave N
Mercer St
Ward St
Aloha St

Memorial Stadium

Bagley Wright Theatre

Children's Theatre

Seattle Center

Belltown

Regrade Park

Bell St
Blanchard St
Battery St
Bell St
Vine St
Cedar St
Wall St
5th Ave
4th Ave
3rd Ave
2nd Ave
Western Ave
Elliott Ave
Alaskan Way

Pike Place Market

Victor Steinbrueck Park

The Waterfront

To Queen Anne (0.5mi)

3rd Ave N
2nd Ave N
Warren Ave N
1st Ave N
Ward St
Prospect St
3rd Valley St
Roy St
Thomas St
Denny Way
Broad St
Clay St
Eagle St
Pier 66 (Bell St Pier)
Pier 69
Pier 67
Pier 70
Broad St

0 — 500 m
0 — 0.3 miles

INFORMATION

American Express	1 C3
Auralice	2 E3
Bailey/Coy Books	3 E2
Beyond the Closet Books	4 E3
CapitolHill.net	5 E2
Central Library	6 D5
Citywide Concierge Center (Visitor Center)	7 D4
Elliott Bay Book Company	8 D6
Harborview Medical Center	9 E5
Left Bank Books	10 C4
Main Post Office	11 C4
Metsker Maps	12 C4
Online Coffee Co	13 C5
Online Coffee Co	14 E2
Outdoor Recreation Information Center	15 D2
Post Office	(see 38)
REI	(see 15)
Seattle University Bookstore	16 E4
US Healthworks	17 D3

SIGHTS & ACTIVITIES (pp518–22)

Experience Music Project	18 B2
Frye Museum	19 E5
Klondike Gold Rush National Historic Park	20 D6
Original Starbucks	21 B4
Pike Place Market	22 C4
Science Fiction Museum	(see 18)
Seattle Aquarium	23 B5
Seattle Art Museum	24 C5
Space Needle	25 A2
Wing Luke Asian Museum	26 E6

SLEEPING (p523)

Ace Hotel	27 B3
Commodore Hotel	28 B4
Gaslight B&B	29 F3
Green Tortoise Guest House	30 C4
HI Seattle	31 C5
Moore Hotel	32 C4

EATING (pp523–5)

13 Coins	33 C3
Bakeman's	34 D6
Bimbo's Bitchin' Burrito Kitchen	35 E2
Café Hue	36 D6
Café Septieme	37 E2
Dick's Drive-In	38 E2
Elliott Bay Café	39 D6
Five Point Cafe	40 B3
Hing Loon	41 E7
Jai Thai	42 B4
Joe Bar Libation Front	43 E1
Macrina	44 B3
Mama's Mexican Kitchen	45 B3
No Boundaries Cafe	(see 22)
Noodle Ranch	46 B3
Shanghai Garden	47 E7
Siam on Broadway	48 E2
Than Brothers	49 E2
Two Bells Tavern	50 B3
Wasabi Bistro	51 C4
Wild Ginger	52 C5

DRINKING (pp525–6)

B&O Espresso	53 E2
Bookstore Bar	54 C5
Central Saloon	55 D6
Cha-Cha Lounge	(see 35)
Chop Suey	56 E3
Comet	57 E2
Crocodile Cafe	58 B4
Elysian	59 E3
Lava Lounge	60 B3
Liquid Lounge	61 B2
New Orleans Creole Restaurant	62 D6
Nitelite	(see 32)
Pike Pub & Brewery	63 C5
Shorty's	64 B4
Showbox	65 C4
Zeitgeist	66 D6

ENTERTAINMENT (pp526–7)

A Contemporary Theatre (ACT)	67 D4
Benaroya Concert Hall	68 C5
Egyptian	69 E3
Elite	70 E1
Graceland	71 D3
Harvard Exit	72 E1
Key Arena	73 A2
McCaw Hall	74 A2
Neighbours	75 E2
R Place	76 E3
Re-bar	77 D3
Safeco Field	78 D8
Seahawks Stadium	79 D7

SHOPPING (p527)

Uwajimaya	82 D7
Wall of Sound	83 D6

TRANSPORT (pp527–8)

Greyhound Bus Depot	84 C3
King County Metro Transit	85 D6
Victoria Clipper (Ferry to San Juan Island & Victoria BC)	86 A4
Washington State Ferries (to Bainbridge Island & Bremerton)	87 C6
Washington State Ferries (to Vashon Island & Bremerton)	88 C6

OTHER

Bill Speidel's Underground Tour	89 D5
Gray Line of Seattle	90 D4

Ticket/Ticket booth | (see 22) |
Ticket/Ticket booth | 80 E2 |
Wildrose | 81 F3 |

often difficult and violent meeting of Asian and Western cultures in Seattle with artwork, special exhibits, historic photographs, a replica of a WWII Japanese–American internment camp and some recorded interviews with internees.

The district's **Jackson St**, particularly around 12th Ave, was once home to an African American contingent and a thriving jazz scene. As teens in the late '40s and early '50s, Quincy Jones and Ray Charles used to hustle their way into jazz clubs here and play into the wee hours of the morning with the likes of Duke Ellington.

Other Neighborhoods

If you have energy for more neighborhood-prowling, wander around fun-loving **Fremont**, about 2 miles north of Seattle Center, known for its unorthodox public sculpture – namely *Waiting for the Interurban* (N 34th St at Fremont) and the scary-eyed VW-devouring *Fremont Troll* (beneath the Aurora Bridge at 36th St) – summer outdoor film festival and general high spirits. **Fremont Ave N** is the lively main strip.

On sunny days, see and be seen walking the 2.8 miles around delightful **Green Lake**. Or loll about in Wallingford's **Gas Works Park**, the epitome of urban reclamation and a fabulous July 4 fireworks viewpoint.

In First Hill near Seattle University, the **Frye Museum** (☎ 206-622-9250; www.fryeart.org; 704 Terry Ave; admission free; ♥ 10am-5pm Tue-Sat, noon-5pm Sun, 10am-8pm Thu) is a marvelous gathering of visual art, mainly from the 19th century to today.

Head 30 miles north to Everett to watch the world's largest commercial planes being built in the world's biggest building – the **Boeing Everett factory** (☎ 206-544-1264, 800-464-1476; admission $5; tours ♥ 9am, 10am, 11am, 1pm, 2pm & 3pm Mon-Fri). Even though the company's headquarters are in Chicago, you can still take the grand tour in Seattle.

TOURS

Bill Speidel's Underground Tour (☎ 206-682-4646; 610 1st Ave; adult/student $10/8) Explores a network of dank subterranean sidewalks that predate the 1889 fire and subsequent rebuilding of the Pioneer Square district above the tide flats. Entertaining guides share snippets of Seattle's not-so-glorious past. Tours are popular, so arrive 15 to 30 minutes early.

Gray Line of Seattle (☎ 206-626-5208, 800-426-7505; www.graylineofseattle.com; 800 Convention Place; $29) City Sights Tour runs year-round.

FESTIVALS & EVENTS

Bumbershoot (☎ 206-281-8111; www.bumbershoot .com; Labor Day weekend, Sep) This four-day musical extravaganza draws huge names and huge crowds to Seattle Center. Almost as much of a draw as the bands are the numerous food and crafts hawkers.

Chinese New Year (☎ 206-382-1197; www.internationaldistrict.org; Jan or Feb) Colorful parades, fireworks and food liven up the International District.

Northwest Folklife Festival (☎ 206-684-7300; www.nwfolklife.org; Memorial Day weekend, May; suggested donation $5) Seattle Center fills with international music, dance, arts and crafts vendors, and food, food, food.

Seattle International Film Festival (SIFF; www .seattlefilm.com; ☎ 206-324-9996; late May–mid-Jun) Hundreds of screenings run during this annual three-week celebration of indie filmmakers and brilliant never-heard-of actors.

GAY & LESBIAN SEATTLE

It's no surprise that super-hip-and-liberal Seattle is all-around gay-and-lesbian-friendly (although much of the Northwest is more conservative) with a club scene that's less segregated than in many American cities. Capitol Hill is the principal gay and lesbian neighborhood, home to numerous entertainment venues. For a mostly gay male disco scene, check out **Neighbours** (☎ 206-324-5358; 1509 Broadway Ave E), **Elite** (☎ 206-324-4470; 622 Broadway Ave E) or three-storied **R Place** (☎ 206-322-8828; 619 E Pine St). Nirvana held album releases at **Re-bar** (☎ 206-233-9873; 1114 Howell St), which welcomes gay, straight, bi or undecided revelers to its dance floor nightly. Nearby, comfortable **Wildrose** (☎ 206-324-9210; 1021 E Pike St) is Seattle's only primarily lesbian bar.

The **Seattle Gay News** (www.sgn.org) covers the GLBT scene; other publications include the *Lesbian & Gay Pink Pages*. For a listing of gay-friendly businesses, contact the **Greater Seattle Business Association** (☎ 206-363-9188; www.thegsba.org). Bailey/Coy and Beyond the Closet (p517) have queer-oriented books and excellent community information.

SPLURGE!

Ace Hotel (☎ 206-448-4721; www.acehotel.com; 2423 1st Ave, Belltown; r with shared bathroom $65-95, with private bathroom $130-175; Ⓟ ☒) Seattle's hippest hotel, hands down. This scenester spot helped usher in boutique hotels nationwide. It sports minimal, ultramodern décor (everything from the sofas to the TVs is white, unless it's stainless steel or wood), hardwood floors, platform beds, antique French army blankets, condoms instead of pillow mints, and copies of the *Kama Sutra* instead of the Bible. All is perfectly immaculate, including the shared bathrooms; the private bathrooms are stashed in back of revolving mirrored doors or clear-glass partitions behind the beds. Too hip. Reserve up to a month in advance, especially in summer.

If it's a B&B experience you're after, **Gaslight B&B** (☎ 206-325-3654; www.gaslight-inn.com; 1727 E 15th Ave; r with shared bathroom $78-98, r with private bathroom $118-178; Ⓟ ☒ ▣ ▣) is a restored 20th-century house with a warm, dark-wood atmosphere, 15 rooms, a pool and a hot tub. The owners have amassed an impressive art collection over the years, and they make a mean brekkie. Gaslight is a good value given the amenities and location – and hey, it's a B&B.

SLEEPING

As amazing as Seattle is, it's no lie that budget beds are hard to find. There are two great hostels in the city (from the airport, take bus No 174 or 194); another is perched on Vashon Island (p528). Some inexpensive places exist in Belltown, the U District and near Seattle Center, and chain motels ring the city. You can always try the **Seattle Hotel Hotline** (☎ 800-361-1029) or, better yet, check out **www.seattlesupersaver.com** (☎ 206-461-5882, 800-535-7071), the city's one-stop-hotel-shop. Overall, rates grow in summer and on weekends, and they shrink in winter. Wherever you want to stay, strive to reserve a month or more in advance, especially in summer.

Downtown

Green Tortoise Guest House (☎ 206-340-1222, 888-424-6783; www.greentortoise.com; 1525 2nd Ave; dm/s $20/50; ☒ ▣) The Tortoise is right in the middle of the action – and it feels like it. Inside can be as frenetic and happening as outside, as backpackers settle into this worn-in hostel for their often-long stands in Seattle. There are six- and eight-bed dorms, comfy beds, free breakfast, a great kitchen and other free meals during the week.

HI Seattle (☎ 206-622-5443, 888-622-5443; www.hiseattle.org; 84 Union St; dm $19-26, r $39-69; ☒ ▣) Central to the Waterfront and Pike Place Market, this 145-bed hostel is more sterile than nearby Green Tortoise. It's clean, friendly and open 24 hours. The dining room has a great view, there's a free pool table and the staff can load you up with information on everything Seattle. Bonus: the Pike Pub & Brewery (p526) is right up the stairs.

Belltown

Moore Hotel (☎ 206-448-4851; www.moorehotel.com; 1926 2nd Ave; r with shared bathroom $39, s/d with private bathroom $59/67) Rooms at this once-grand hotel are nothing fancy, but they're clean and elegant, and you can hardly beat the price. Don't miss the adjoining Nitelite, an unpretentious retro lounge featuring small plastic animals.

Commodore Hotel (☎ 206-448-8868, 800-714-8868; www.commodorehotel.com; 2013 2nd Ave; r with shared/private bathroom from $55/67) Rates at this no-frills, friendly hotel include a continental breakfast. Aim for a room with a view of the sound, and be careful on the stairs – the carpets are dizzying.

The U District

College Inn (☎ 206-633-4441; 4000 University Way NE; r from $50; Ⓟ ☒ ▣) The closest thing this neighborhood has to a hostel, the friendly, no-frills College Inn is a perfect spot to bed down while visiting UW. The elevatorless 1909 building has 25 European-style guestrooms (with sinks, but bathrooms are shared). South-facing rooms get the most light. Rates include a continental breakfast served in the communal lounge.

EATING

Ah, eating in Seattle. You can't do enough of it, but you can do it on the cheap. Neighborhood main drags – as in Fremont, Capitol Hill, and the U District – are lined with eateries, and many bars applaud early birds with celebrated happy-hour specials. **Farmers markets** (www.seattlefarmersmarkets.org) often have delicious organic meals and self-catering provisions.

PACIFIC NORTHWEST

Downtown & Belltown

Downtown's affordable food is in Pike Place Market – forage for fresh produce and baked goods and along Pike St and Post Alley, where sandwiches, salads and chowder abound.

No Boundaries Cafe (☎ 206-223-0998; 93 Pike St) Head here for grilled focaccia sandwiches ($5.50).

Macrina (☎ 206-448-4032; 2408 1st Ave; lunch $5-11) This Belltown bakery has homemade artisan bread, panini sandwiches, light lunches (weekdays only) and pastries.

Mama's Mexican Kitchen (☎ 206-728-6262; 2234 2nd Ave; mains $4.50-10) Rock-and-roll-themed Mama's is always enjoyably packed, thanks to huge portions, cheap burritos and great happy-hour margaritas ($4).

Two Bells Tavern (☎ 206-441-3050; 2313 4th Ave; burgers $7-8; kitchen ☯ 11am-10pm; ✗) This venerable pub is a welcoming place to enjoy one of Seattle's best burgers or all-you-can-eat-spaghetti Mondays ($6).

Noodle Ranch (☎ 206-728-0463; 2228 2nd Ave; mains $5-11) Latish-night (until 11pm) crowds swarm here for Pan-Asian cuisine.

Pioneer Square & International District

Shanghai Garden (☎ 206-625-1688; 524 6th Ave S; mains $5.50-15) This is known as the best place in town for inventive Chinese cuisine. Portions are heaping.

Hing Loon (☎ 206-682-2828; 628 S Weller St; mains $5-9.25) Around the corner from Shanghai Garden, this much-liked seafood-focused restaurant is open late.

Bakeman's (☎ 206-622-3375; 122 Cherry St; sandwiches $3-3.50; ☯ 10am-3pm Mon-Fri) Grab a meatloaf or turkey sandwich (they roast their own meat!) with the nine-to-fivers at this cafeteria-style treasure.

Cafe Hue (☎ 206-625-9833; 312 2nd Ave S; mains $3-9) This café serves meat-heavy Vietnamese food with colonial French influences.

Capitol Hill

Bimbo's Bitchin' Burrito Kitchen (☎ 206-329-9978; 506 E Pine St; mains $4.25-7.95) It looks like a hipster exploded in here, with over-the-top Mexikitsch décor covering every inch of the tiny space. The food is cheap, fresh, massive and served until 2am on weekends. Don't miss happy hour, when drinks are $2.50 between 4pm and 7pm at the adjoining Cha-Cha Lounge, a cool, comfortable tiki bar.

Café Septieme (☎ 206-860-8858; 214 Broadway E; mains $6-21) This trendy, modern French-inspired space serves fancy drinks, gourmet salads and light meals. Dinner's not a deal, but breakfast ($6 to $8) is reasonably priced given the neighborhood.

Siam on Broadway (☎ 206-324-0892; 616 Broadway E; mains $9-12) Thai-food favorite Siam has good lunch specials ($7 to $8, Monday to Friday only).

Joe Bar Libation Front (☎ 206-324-0407; 810 E Roy; mains $2.25-6.75) Local artists' works adorn the walls of this super hip coffee/crepe/panini shop/pub.

The U District

Than Brothers (☎ 206-633-1735; 4027 University Way NE; soup $3.85-6) Students and professors alike fill up on generous bowls of steaming *pho* (Vietnamese noodle soup). Other locations are **Capitol Hill** (☎ 206-568-7218; 516 Broadway E) and **Green Lake** (☎ 206-527-5973; 7714 Aurora Ave N).

Aladdin Falafel (☎ 206-548-9539; 4541 University Ave NE; sandwiches $3.20-5.50) This family-run 'gyro-cery' and falafel shop serves delicious Middle Eastern sandwiches on homemade pita bread.

Schultzy's Sausages (☎ 206-548-9461; 4142 University Way NE; mains $5-7.50) A good budget option along University Way, busy Schultzy's grills up sausages, burgers and 'sausage burgers.' Despite all the meat, it even does a decent a veggie burger.

LATE-NIGHT GRUB

It's 1:42am, and you're hungry. Fortunately, unlike some US cities, Seattle has numerous midnight-snack options. Twenty-four-hour **Beth's** (p525) and **Five Point Cafe** (p525) offer similar gargantuan meals (which are hard to see for the cigarette smoke). In Capitol Hill **Bimbo's Bitchin' Burrito Kitchen** (p524) rolls burritos until 2am, and **Dick's Drive-In** (☎ 206-323-1300; 115 Broadway E; burgers $1.10-2; Ⓟ) will satisfy your greasy-burger fix until 1:59am. Within staggering distance of downtown and Seattle Center bars is all-night **13 Coins** (☎ 206-682-2513; 125 Boren Ave N; mains $10-47; ☯ 24hr; Ⓟ), perfect for when you're too buzzed to care if you're eating overpriced (though tasty) diner food.

SPLURGE!

Exquisite eateries infiltrate nearly every Seattle neighborhood, so how to decide where to spend your coveted big bills? Go no further than trendy Belltown.

For tops sushi, it doesn't get fresher than **Wasabi Bistro** (☎ 206-441-6044; 2311 2nd Ave; appetizers $8-14, rolls $6-15; ☉ until 1am). Chic hipsters and camera-bedecked tourists sip cucumber martinis ($7.50) before munching elaborate rolls washed down with cold unfiltered sake. Complimentary *edamame* (boiled soybeans) break your wallet's fall – barely.

Or gussy up (sort of – after all, it's laid-back Seattle) for **Wild Ginger** (☎ 206-623-4450; 1401 3rd Ave; satays $3-10, mains $8-30; ☉ until 2am), Seattle's definitive Pan-Asian fusion restaurant. Sit at the revered Satay Bar or watch the show from the 2nd-story cocktail lounge. Staff are as phenomenal as the food: rich coconut-milk soups, exotic seafood-heavy dishes and incredible daily specials.

Other Neighborhoods

Jai Thai (☎ 206-770-7884; 2132 1st Ave, Belltown; mains $6-8) Delicious Thai food that delights the steady stream of locals. There's another in **Fremont** (☎ 206-632-7060; 3423 Fremont Ave N).

Five Point Cafe (☎ 206-448-9993; 415 Cedar St; mains $4-9; ☉ 24hr) Cheeky servers sling all-you-can-eat hash browns (weekdays only) in this all-hours landmark dive near Seattle Center. It touts with pride: 'Alcoholics serving alcoholics since 1929.' Home of the famous periscope urinal – see the Space Needle from the men's room!

Beth's (☎ 206-782-5588; 7311 Aurora Ave N; mains $5-9; ☉ 24hr) This Green Lake icon serves infamous 12-egg omelettes on pizza pans to oft-hungover patrons slumped in Naugahyde booths. Nonsmokers beware – it's thick with the stuff.

Hattie's Hat (☎ 206-784-0175; 5231 Ballard Ave NW; mains $6-12) Weekend brunch ($4.25 to $8) is in high demand at this Ballard hot spot.

Madame K's (☎ 206-783-9710; 5327 Ballard Ave NW; pizzas from $14) An elegant, red-and-black pizza parlor with an old bordello feel (the building was once a brothel), this small, chic place is packed at dinner. It's also popular for drinks, and the aptly named desserts – like the Chocolate Chip Orgasm ($6.50) – are sinful.

DRINKING

Drinking in Seattle falls into three general categories: coffeehouses, brewpubs and everything else. For late-night action, head to Capitol Hill's Pike-Pine Corridor (Broadway to 12th Ave), home to a plethora of arty live-music clubs and taverns. For a less vigorous, but still very busy, bar scene, check out the pubs along Ballard Ave. And for a terrific overview of the Pioneer Square club scene, spring for the joint cover (before/

after 10pm Friday and Saturday $10/12, cheaper other nights) that's good for 10 clubs, including **Central Saloon** (☎ 206-622-0209; 207 1st Ave S) – Seattle's oldest restaurant – with live music every night of the year, and jazz-and-blues **New Orleans Creole Restaurant** (☎ 206-622-2563; 114 1st Ave S).

Coffeehouses

Begin or end your day at one of Seattle's independent coffeeshops, which tend to close by 11pm.

B&O Espresso (☎ 206-322-5028; 204 Belmont Ave E) Pleasant for some postcard-scribbling or emailing on Capitol Hill.

Café Allegro (☎ 206-633-3030; 4214 University Way NE) Supposedly the city's first espresso bar; on an alley behind the university in the U District.

Still Life in Fremont (☎ 206-547-9850; 709 N 35th St) A hippie/boho hangout in Fremont with vegan food and organic coffee.

Zeltgeist (☎ 206-583-0497; 171 S Jackson St) Seattle's best caffeine source: a high-ceilinged, brick-walled café with great coffee and lip-smacking whipped cream, plus WiFi for the 'working artist' crowd.

Brewpubs

Aside from often-amazing microbrews, many brewpubs also have decent (but not inexpensive) food. Most close by midnight.

Jolly Roger Taproom (☎ 206-782-6181; 1514 NW Leary Way) A secret treasure tucked away in Ballard, Maritime Pacific Brewing's tiny, pirate-themed brewpub pours its delicious hand-crafted beer into real, 20oz pints ($3.75).

Elysian (☎ 206-860-1920; 1221 E Pike St) This vast Capitol Hill brewpub's windows are really great for people-watching. Try a seasonal beer if there's one on tap.

Hale's Ales Brewery & Pub (☎ 206-706-1544; www .halesales.com; 4301 Leary Way NW) Between Fremont and Ballard, the Hale's Brewery offers a mini self-guided tour, friendly service and, of course, great beer – try the ambrosial Cream Ale.

Old Town Ale House (☎ 206-782-8323; 5233 Ballard Ave NW, Ballard; ☽ until 4am Sat & Sun) This cavernous, warmly lit, red-brick pub serves giant sandwich 'wedges' ($9) and luscious microbrewed beer.

Pike Pub & Brewery (☎ 206-622-6044; 1415 1st Ave) Steps from Pike Place Market, this split-level brewpub has pool tables, a cigar room, and squishy leather chairs littered about the checkerboard floor.

Bars

Whether chic or casual, bars in Seattle are usually open 5pm to 2am.

Shorty's (☎ 206-441-5449; 2222 2nd Ave) A totally unpretentious oasis in a block of trés-chic lounges, Shorty's has cheap beer, hot dogs and a pinball-wizard's heaven out back. The tabletops alone are worth a look.

Liquid Lounge (☎ 206-770-2777; 325 5th Ave N) Located upstairs at the EMP, this bar's sleek, high-tech atmosphere is supported by DJs or live music most nights, and happy-hour bargains on food and drink.

Peso's (☎ 206-283-9353; 605 Queen Anne Ave N, Queen Anne) This beautiful-people lair is worth the trip to Queen Anne for fabulous happy-hour food (mains $3 to $4 from 3pm to 6pm) and an impressive Day-of-the-Dead barback.

Also recommended:

Bookstore Bar (☎ 206-382-1506; 1007 1st Ave) Cool book-nook bar adjoining the rather pretentious Library Bistro in the Alexis Hotel (note the colossal Chihuly hanging in the lobby).

Comet (☎ 206-323-9853; 922 E Pike St) A no-frills institution with cheap beer, loyal locals and occasional bands.

Lava Lounge (☎ 206-441-5660; 2226 2nd Ave) Fiery den with massive hipster cachet – and shuffleboard!

Linda's Tavern (☎ 206-325-1220; 707 E Pine St) Amazingly popular cool-kids hangout with a tiki-themed patio and $1.50 bottles of Black Label.

Live Music

Once Seattle's bread and butter, a thriving music community still exists in Seattle despite grunge's fade. Most covers are around $5. Some of the best dancing is at gay clubs; see p522 for listings.

Crocodile Cafe (☎ 206-441-5611; www.thecrocodile .com; 2200 2nd Ave) This beloved Belltown institution helped launch the whole grunge movement. It still hosts local and touring bands.

Töst (☎ 206-547-0240; 513 N 36th St; ☒) Scenesters fill this Fremont lounge, pumping DJ-spun tunes or live music most nights.

Chop Suey (☎ 206-324-8000; 1325 E Madison St) A dark, high-ceilinged space with ramshackle faux-Chinese motif, this venue currently has some of the best live rock shows in town.

Also recommended:

Graceland (☎ 206-381-3094; 109 Eastlake Ave) A gritty gem for lovers of sweat, booze and rock and roll; formerly the Off Ramp; all-ages all the time.

Showbox (☎ 206-628-3151; 1426 1st Ave) Big rock venue for touring bands.

Tractor Tavern (☎ 206-789-3599; 5213 Ballard Ave NW, Ballard) An atmospheric place for folk/acoustic acts.

ENTERTAINMENT

Consult the *Stranger*, *Seattle Weekly* or daily papers for listings. Big-event tickets are available at **TicketMaster** (☎ 206-628-0888). To pick up half-price day-of-performance tickets, stop by a cash-only **Ticket/Ticket booth** (☎ 206-324-2744; ☽ Tue-Sun), with outlets at **Capitol Hill** (Broadway Market, 401 Broadway E, 2nd fl) and **Pike Place Market** (Market Information Booth, cnr 1st Ave & Pike St).

Performing Arts

Seattle boasts one of the most vibrant theater scenes on the West Coast.

A Contemporary Theatre (ACT; ☎ 206-292-7676; 700 Union St) Located at Kreielsheimer Pl, this theater produces excellent performances year-round featuring Seattle's best thespians and big-time actors.

Seattle Symphony (☎ 206-215-4747; Benaroya Concert Hall, 200 University St) Under maestro Gerard Schwartz, the symphony has risen to prominence as a major regional ensemble.

Seattle Opera (☎ 206-389-7676; McCaw Hall, Seattle Center) The Seattle Opera isn't afraid to tackle weighty or nontraditional works.

Pacific Northwest Ballet (☎ 206-441-9411; McCaw Hall, Seattle Center) This troupe is the foremost dance company in the Northwest.

Cinemas

At opposite ends of Capitol Hill are two of the city's best art cinemas, the **Egyptian** (☎ 206-323-4978; 805 E Pine St) and the **Harvard Exit** (☎ 206-323-8986; 807 E Roy St), featuring foreign films, classics and documentaries. Both are key venues during SIFF (see p522) and the **Seattle Gay & Lesbian Film Festival** (☎ 206-323-4274; ☺ Oct).

Sports

With new stadiums and fun-loving fans, Seattle is a passionate sport-watching town.

Seattle Mariners (☎ 206-628-3555; www.mariners .org) Locally loved baseball team, which plays in Safeco Field.

Seattle Seahawks (☎ 206-827-9777; www.seahawks .com) Pro football in the avant-garde new Seahawks Stadium.

Supersonics (☎ 206-283-3865; www.nba.com/sonics) NBA franchise and huge crowds at Seattle Center's Key Arena.

Huskies (☎ 206-543-2200; www.gohuskies.com) Enormously popular University of Washington football and basketball teams.

SHOPPING

Seattle has the best of both shopping worlds: big-name highbrow stores flood downtown's Westlake Center, and quirky ultra-independent shops are sprinkled all over the city.

Of course, shopping is religion in Pike Place Market and its environs, around which you can wander for eternity. Capitol Hill and the U District, catering to pop and youth culture, host great lose-track-of-time bookstores, worth-picking-through vintage-clothing stores and legendary record shops, including **Wall of Sound** (☎ 206-441-9880; 915 E Pine St). Fremont's main drag features a mixed bag of chic boutiques and tchotchke shops.

The International District's cornerstone is **Uwijamaya** (☎ 206-624-6248; 600 5th Ave S), a gargantuan Asian supermarket. And in Ballard, **Archie McPhee** (☎ 206-297-0240; 2428 NW Market St) is kitsch and ephemera heaven. Go on, buy something you *totally* don't need.

GETTING THERE & AWAY
Air

Seattle's airport, **Seattle-Tacoma International Airport** (Sea-Tac, SEA; ☎ 206-433-5388; www.portseattle .org) is 12 miles south of Seattle on I-5. Southwest and Alaska Airlines offer frequent inexpensive flights to and from Portland (from $39 one way), Vancouver, BC (from $89 one way), and other destinations in the west and beyond. Small commuter airlines link Seattle to the San Juan Islands and smaller Northwest towns like Bellingham and Spokane.

Boat

Washington State Ferries (☎ 206-464-6400, in Washington 888-808-7977; www.wsdot.wa.gov/ferries) runs frequent passenger-only and passenger-and-auto ferries daily throughout and outside Puget Sound. Boats to Bainbridge Island (vehicle and driver/passenger $12.50/5.70 one way) and Bremerton (vehicle and driver/passenger $12.50/5.70) sail from Pier 52. The Vashon Island passenger-only ferry ($7.70 one way) departs Pier 50; the passenger-and-auto ferry (vehicle and driver/passenger $16.25/3.70 one way) leaves from Fauntleroy (West Seattle). **Clipper Navigation** (☎ 206-448-5000, outside Seattle & Victoria 800-888-2535; www.victoria clipper.com) runs the passenger only *Victoria Clipper* (from $64/106 one way/roundtrip), which departs Pier 69 for Victoria, BC (one daily via San Juan Island).

Bus

Greyhound (☎ 206-628-5526; cnr 8th Ave & Stewart St), on the north edge of downtown, has daily connections to Portland (from $20.50 one way) and points east.

Quick Shuttle (☎ 800-665-2122; www.quickcoach .com) runs daily express buses between Vancouver, BC, and Sea-Tac ($41) or downtown ($33; stops at Travelodge, 2213 8th Ave).

Train

Amtrak (☎ 800-872-7245; King St Station, 303 S Jackson St) connects Seattle daily with countless US and Canadian cities, including Portland (from $24 one way) and Vancouver, BC (from $24 one way).

GETTING AROUND
Car & Motorcycle

Seattle traffic is among the worst in the country. Add to that the scarce and expensive parking, and you might consider relying on public transit. If you do drive, take a friend; some Seattle freeways have High-Occupancy Vehicle (HOV) lanes for vehicles carrying two or more people.

National rental agencies have offices at the airport and around town. Taxes on rental cars are a steep 18.3%.

Public Transportation

Seattle's public transit system is good and getting better. **Metro Transit** (☎ 206-553-3000, in Washington ☎ 800-542-7876) serves the greater Seattle metropolitan area with buses and a

Waterfront streetcar (both $1.50/1.25 peak/off-peak). Bus rides are free from 6am to 7pm in much of downtown (neither Seattle Center nor the streetcar is within the ride-free zone). Buy tickets or day passes ($5) in advance and get a system map at the **King County Metro Transit office** (☎ 206-553-3000; http ://transit.metrokc.gov; 201 S Jackson St), at the Westlake Center bus tunnel station, or at the Citywide Concierge Center (p518).

The Waterfront's Vintage green Australian streetcars run every 20 to 30 minutes from Broad St (Pier 70, a 10-minute walk from Seattle Center) through Pioneer Square to the International District; service stops around 7pm. Note that red streetcars also run along the Waterfront; these are operated by **Gray Line** (☎ 206-626-5208, 800-426-7505) and are for jump-on, jump-off sightseeing ($17).

A 1.5-mile mass-transit experiment built for the 1962 World's Fair, the monorail ($3) runs every 10 minutes (7:30am to 11pm Monday to Friday, 9am to 11pm Saturday and Sunday) from Westlake Center to Seattle Center, passing through a crumple in the smashed-guitar hull of the EMP (p518).

Taxi

Farwest Taxi (☎ 206-622-1717)
Yellow Cabs (☎ 206-622-6500)

AROUND SEATTLE

PUGET SOUND

It's almost criminal to be in Seattle and not get out on Puget Sound's islands, which make a fantastic and popular escape from the city.

Getting to **Bainbridge Island** is half the fun: the views of Seattle and the Sound from the ferry are stunning. Once you're there, stroll around lazily or cycle around the countryside – all the while being sure to *relax* – until heading back.

More rural and countercultural than Bainbridge, **Vashon Island** is covered with farms, gardens and artist enclaves. It offers unencumbered views of the Cascades and scenic cycling or driving between 'you-pick' berry and fruit farms. Another highlight is the unique family-run **Vashon AYH Ranch** (☎ 206-463-2592; www.vashonhostel.com; 12119 SW Cove Rd; campsites/dm/r $9/13/45), a rustic summer HI hostel with fold-up mattress pads

laid in teepees and covered wagons on 10 acres butted up against a nature preserve. Bike use, pancakes and shuttles into town are free.

Washington State Ferries (p527) dock at both islands.

TACOMA

Tacoma is home to renowned glassblowing artist Dale Chihuly, member of the Studio Glass movement – moving from solitary, studio-confined artistry to collaborative teams sharing the creative process. The city also boasts the **Museum of Glass** (☎ 253-284-4750, 866-468-7386; www.museumofglass.org; 1801 E Dock St; adult/student $10/8; ☽ 10am-5pm Wed-Sat, noon-5pm Sun) a contemporary art museum that concentrates on this fragile medium. It features three galleries of changing exhibits (not always glass), a theater and a hands-on art studio staffed by visiting artists. The highlight of the museum is the Hot Shop (closed 1pm to 2pm), a 90ft steel cone housing a working glass studio where visitors can watch glassblowers at work.

Walk across Chihuly's impressive **Bridge of Glass**, connecting the museum with downtown's copper-domed neobaroque **Union Station** (1911), designed by the folks who built New York's Grand Central Terminal (the ironwork on the windows is nearly identical). Renovated in the early 1990s, the station now houses the federal courts (and more Chihuly pieces). Next door is the **Washington State History Museum** (☎ 888-238-4373; 1911 Pacific Ave; admission $7; ☽ 10am-5pm Tue-Sat, noon-5pm Sun), with good exhibits on Northwest Coast tribes.

From Seattle or Olympia, take I-5 exit 133 and follow the signs to the museum. You can also take the Sound Transit Seattle Express bus (route 594; $2.50) or train ($4).

OLYMPIA

Olympia, the state capital, lives up to its surprising reputation as an indie-rock/hipster hub (it birthed 'riot grrrl' and lady-rockers Sleater-Kinney). Its diminutive yet quaint downtown marries politicians, businessfolk and countercultural grads (and dropouts) of innovative liberal-arts Evergreen State College, where *The Simpsons* creator, Matt Groening, studied.

The **State Capitol Visitors Center** (☎ 360-586-3460; www.ga.wa.gov/visitor/index.html; 14th Ave & Capitol

Way; ☺ 8am-5pm Mon-Fri, plus 10am-4pm Sat & Sun in summer) provides information on the Capitol campus and the Olympia area.

Amtrak links Olympia daily to Seattle and Portland; bus No 64 shuttles between the station and downtown Olympia.

Sights & Activities

At the **Washington State Capitol** you can tour the vast, domed 1927 **Legislative Building** (☎ 360-586-8687; admission free; ☺ tours every hr 10am-3pm) or, on a self-guided campus tour, explore the Temple of Justice and Capitol Conservatory, housing a large collection of tropical plants. The **State Capital Museum** (☎ 360-753-2580; www.wshs.org/wscm; 211 W 21st Ave; admission $2; ☺ 10am-4pm Tue-Fri, noon-4pm Sat) has exhibits on the Nisqually Indians. Browse the fun **Olympia Farmers Market** (☎ 360-352-9096; ☺ 10am-3pm Thu-Sun Apr-Oct, Sat & Sun only Nov-Dec), at the north end of Capitol Way, then zen out in the **Yashiro Japanese Garden** (☎ 360-753-8380; 1010 Plum St SE; admission free; ☺ daily until dusk).

Sleeping

Olympia Inn (☎ 360-352-8533, 800-407-7734; 909 Capitol Way; r from $49) This carefully maintained downtown motel is frequented by legislators.

Carriage Inn Motel (☎ 360-943-4710; 1211 Quince St SE; s/d $50/60) Off I-5 exit 105, the rooms here are older in style, but have microwaves and include free local calls.

Eating & Drinking

Urban Onion (☎ 360-943-9242; 116 Legion Way E; mains $4.50-8) Classy vegetarian haunt in an old hotel. It serves cheap breakfast and affordable lunch (salads and quiche), but prices rise for dinner.

Spar Bar (☎ 360-357-6444; 114 E 4th Ave; mains $4-8) A stylish old café/tobacco store with a cool façade and a cozy back-room bar, the Highclimber (with live music Saturday from 6pm to midnight).

Oldschool Pizzeria (☎ 360-786-9640; 108 Franklin St; pizzas $8.50-19) For a quick cheesy fix, hit this local-fave.

Fishbowl Brewpub (☎ 360-943-3650; 515 Jefferson St SE) This place is acked with locals sipping home-brewed English-style Fish Tale ales.

4th Ave Alehouse (☎ 360-786-1444; 210 4th Ave E) Catch live local bands at this busy pub.

OLYMPIC PENINSULA

OLYMPIC NATIONAL PARK

Olympic is one of the USA's most popular national parks, and deservedly so. Its wilderness hiking, dramatic scenery and widely varying ecosystems offer a visit as serene or as adventurous as desired. The heavily glaciated Olympic Mountains reign supreme, with Mt Olympus (7965ft) at the helm.

Few roads penetrate more than a few miles into the park proper, but visitors willing to hike a bit will find magnificent waterfalls, wide-open alpine meadows, moss-bearded rain forests and remote lakes. Most lower valley trails are passable year-round, but expect rain, or at least clouds, at any time.

Information

Park entry is $5/10 per person/vehicle, valid for one week, payable at park entrances. Many park visitor centers double as United States Forest Service (USFS) ranger stations, where you get permits for wilderness camping ($5 per group plus $2 per person per night, valid up to 14 days).

Forks Visitor Information Center (☎ 360-374-2531, 800-443-6757; 1411 S Forks Ave; ☺ 10am-4pm) Suggested itineraries and seasonal information.

Olympic National Park Visitor Center (☎ 360-565-3130; 3002 Mt Angeles Rd, Port Angeles; ☺ 9am-5pm) Very helpful center at the Hurricane Ridge gateway. Just behind is the Wilderness Information Center, where you'll find maps, permits and trail information.

Northern Entrances

The dizzying vistas at must-see **Hurricane Ridge** are well worth the winding 18-mile drive up. Just shy of the top, there's an interpretive center in a flower-strewn meadow from which you can see Mt Olympus and dozens of other peaks (on a clear day). At the end is the lovely 1.6-mile **Hurricane Hill Trail**, offering more fabulous views. Hurricane Ridge Rd begins at the visitors center in Port Angeles; 5 miles along is **Heart O' the Hills campground** (☎ 360-956-2300; campsites $10).

East Beach at idyllic **Lake Crescent** offers swimming. From **Storm King Information Station** (☎ 360-928-3380; ☺ summer only) on the lake's south shore, a 0.25-mile hike climbs through old-growth forest to Marymere Falls. Along the Sol Duc River, the **Sol Duc Hot Springs Resort** (☎ 360-327-3583; www.northolympic.com/solduc;

campsites/RV/cabin $12/20/112; ♥ Oct-Mar) has sooth-ing **hot-spring pools** (admission $10.25) and great day hikes. Nearby is the 1.6-mile-roundtrip trail to romantic **Sol Duc Falls**.

Eastern Entrances

Off Hwy 101, the graveled Dosewallips River Rd leads to **Dosewallips Ranger Station**, where two long-distance trails begin (even short jaunts on these paths are worth a visit to the valley); call ☎ 360-565-3130 for road conditions. Another eastern entry for hikers is the **Staircase Ranger Station** (☎ 360-877-5569; ♥ summer only), 15 miles from Hoodsport on Hwy 101.

There are two camper-heavy state parks along the park's eastern edge: **Dosewallips** and **Lake Cushman** (☎ 888-226-7688; campsites/RV $15/21).

Western Entrances

Isolated by distance and inclement weather, and facing the Olympic Coast National Marine Sanctuary, the Pacific side of the Olympics remains its wildest. Only Hwy 101 offers access to its noted temperate rain forests and rugged coastline.

The green **Hoh Rain Forest** can get 12ft to 14ft of precipitation annually. Trails from the **visitors center & campground** (☎ 360-374-6925; ♥ 9am-4:30pm Sep-Jun, 9am-6pm Jul & Aug), at the end of 19-mile Hoh River Rd, plunge into thick clusters of old-growth trees wearing furry green sweaters of moss. Was *The Lord of the Rings* filmed here?

The **Queets River Valley** is the most remote – and, hence, pristine – part of the park. A gentle, 3-mile day hike starts at primitive **Queets Campground & Ranger Station** (☎ 360-962-2283; campsites $8).

Further south on Hwy 101 is **Lake Quinault**, a picturesque glacial lake popular for fishing and swimming. A number of short trails begin just below Lake Quinault Lodge, on South Shore Rd, near lakeside **Falls Creek Campground** (☎ 360-288-2525; campsites $15). At the end of South Shore Rd, 19 miles off Hwy 101, the 13-mile **Enchanted Valley Trail** begins at the **Graves Creek Ranger Station & Campground** (☎ 360-565-3000; campsites $12). The trail climbs up to a large meadow (a former glacial lakebed) that's resplendent with wildflowers and copses of alder trees.

Olympic Coast

The coastal strip of the park protects more than 60 miles of wild shoreline. Access is limited to a few roads, but easy-to-reach Rialto Beach and Ruby Beach are excellent samples of the coast's beauty. Near Rialto, stay at **Mora campground** (☎ 360-374-5460; campsites $10), 13 miles off Hwy 101 on Rte 110.

PORT TOWNSEND

One of the best-preserved Victorian-era seaports in the USA, Port Townsend resembles an old sepia-toned photograph. The city's 1890 architectural splendor is largely intact, especially along Water St, making for pleasant pre- or post-ferry meandering. For information try the **visitors center** (☎ 360-385-2722; www.ptchamber.org; 2437 E Sims Way; ♥ 9am-5pm Mon-Fri, 10am-4pm Sat, 11am-4pm Sun).

Historic **Fort Worden** (☎ 360-385-4730), 2 miles north of the ferry landing (take Cherry St from uptown), was featured in the film *An Officer and a Gentleman*. Up the hill behind the park office, former barracks house the **HI Olympic Hostel** (☎ 360-385-0655; olyhost@olympus .net; 272 Battery Way; dm $14-17) has impeccable if spartan quarters and a piano in the common room. A cab from town is about $5. The grand, central **Waterstreet Hotel** (☎ 360-385-5467, 800-735-9810; www.waterstreethotelporttown send.com; 635 Water St; r from $59) offers old-world charm at reasonable rates.

For no-nonsense breakfast, join the local marina folk at sunny **Landfall Restaurant** (☎ 360-385-5814; 412 Water St; mains $5-8). Grab a slice at **Waterfront Pizza** (☎ 360-385-6629; 951 Water St; slice $2) or a taco at **El Sarape** (☎ 360-379-9343; 628 Water St; mains $4.50-10). **Sirens** (☎ 360-379-1100; 832 Water St) is a cozy upstairs bar with a balcony overlooking the port.

From Seattle, take the ferry to Bainbridge Island; buses go the remainder. Washington State Ferries (p527) sail daily to and from Whidbey Island.

PORT ANGELES

Port Angeles is an excellent launchpad for exploring the Olympic Peninsula. Ignore the stripmalls and head for the **visitors center** (☎ 360-452-2363; 121 E Railroad Ave; ♥ 9:45am-6pm Mon-Sat, 1-5pm Sun), adjacent to the ferry terminal. Go to Olympic Mountaineering for outdoor-gear rentals and climbing tours (see opposite).

A block off the **Waterfront Trail** – really perfect for watching the sunset behind Vancouver Island – is the homey, relaxed **Thor Town Hostel** (☎ 360-452-0931; www.thortown.com;

316 N Race St; dm/r $12/28; (P X □). Camp at shady **Salt Creek County Park** (☎ 360-928-3441; www.clallam.net; campsites $14), 16 miles west on Hwy 112, with stunning views across the Strait of Juan de Fuca.

Olympic Bagel Company (☎ 360-452-9100; 802 E 1st St; bagels 85¢-$5.75) has an impressive, if not overwhelming, menu of breakfast and lunch bagels. **India Oven** (☎ 360-452-5170; 222 N Lincoln; mains $8-11) has a $4 lunch buffet. One local dubbed **Crazy Fish** (☎ 360-457-1944; 229 W 1st St; mains $4-8) 'the town's saving grace,' with live music and good Mexican food ($2 tacos and tequila on Tuesdays!).

The **Coho Vehicle Ferry** (☎ 360-457-4491) and the passenger-only **Victoria Express** (☎ 360 452-8088; www.victoriaexpress.com; ☾ Jun-Sep) cross the border to Victoria, BC. **Olympic Bus Lines** (☎ 360-417-0700) run to Seattle, and **Clallam Transit buses** (☎ 360 452-4511) go to Forks and Sequim.

SPLURGE!

Don't just gawk at Mt Olympus – climb it! **Olympic Mountaineering** (☎ 360 452 0240; www.olymtn.com; 140 W Front St) leads summit tours ($295); climbing and mountaineering experience isn't necessary, as guides help at the summit, but as you trek 19 miles to base camp yourself, solid backpacking experience *is* necessary. Reserve in advance.

NORTHWEST PENINSULA

The Indian reservations that cling to this corner of the continent welcome respectful visitors. On the east end of Neah Bay, the **Makah Cultural & Research Center** (☎ 360-645-2711; www.makah.com/mcrchome.htm; Hwy 112; admission $4; ☾ closed Mon & Tue in winter) is the sole repository of artefacts from nearby Ozette, home of the ancient Makah. Seven miles beyond, a short boardwalk trail leads to **Cape Flattery**, the most northwesterly point in the lower 48 states.

Convenient to the Hoh Rain Forest and the Olympic coastline, stay at the Waltons-esque **Hoh Humm Ranch** (☎ 360-374-5337; 171763 Hwy 101; r from $35), a B&B in a working farm-house where balconies gaze over riverside herds of sheep, cattle and llamas. Or crash at the remote **Rain Forest Hostel** (☎ 360-374-2270; www.rainforesthostel.com; 169312 Hwy 101; dm/d $12/25), 8 miles south of Hoh River Rd, where bikers and busers can camp for $6.

NORTHWEST WASHINGTON

BELLINGHAM

Bellingham, 18 miles south of the USA–Canadian border, is more than just a port city. Western Washington University fills the city with young bar-goers, and the good culinary scene is equally populated. Bellingham's action is divided between the downtown, grouped around Commercial and Holly Sts, and Fairhaven, a cluster of red-brick buildings 3 miles to the south.

Information

ReSport (☎ 360-733-3133; 1411 Railroad Ave; ☾ 10am-6pm Sat-Mon, 10am-7pm Tue-Fri; per hr $3) Across from the bus terminal, you can access the Internet here.

Visitors center (☎ 360-671-3990, 800-487-2032; www.bellingham.org; 904 Potter St; ☾ 8:30am-5:30pm) Off I-5 exit 253, the office is loaded with the requisite tourist materials.

Sleeping

Most of the inexpensive motels are on Samish Way, off I-5 exit 252.

Shangri-La Downtown Motel (☎ 360-733-7050; 611 E Holly St; s/d from $35/40) Just avoid the 'fishing rooms' at this otherwise fine downtown motel.

Bellingham Inn (☎ 360-734-1900; 202 E Holly St; s/d from $45/50) Also worth a try for its central location.

Birch Bay Hostel (☎ 360-371-2180; www.biz.birch bay.net/hostel; 7467 Gemini St; dm/r $17/36; ☾ May-Sep) North of town, this place has clean dorm beds that fill with travelers en route to or from Canada.

Eating & Drinking

Community Food Co-op (☎ 360-734-0542; 1220 N Forest St) Grab lunch at the mouth-watering Swan Cafe & Deli, inside this mainly organic market.

Old Town Cafe (☎ 360-671-4431; 316 W Holly St; mains $3-7) The food is just plain good here. Budget breakfasts and organic, all-natural ingredients draw happy crowds of smiling locals.

Casa Qué Paso (☎ 360-738-8226; 1415 Railroad Ave; tacos $2-3, burritos $3-6) For tasty tacos and burritos the size of your face.

Bagelry (☎ 360-676-5288; 1319 Railroad Ave; bagel sandwiches $1-5) Located near Casa Qué Paso, the Bagelry satisfies every carb craving.

Three Bs Tavern (☎ 360-734-1881; 1226 N State St) Raucous student hang out with pool tables and live music on weekends ($5 cover).

Boundary Bay Brewery (☎ 360-647-5593; 1107 Railroad Ave) Pours soulful homebrews, ladles out creamy smoked salmon chowder ($4.25), and often features bands on weekends.

Archer Ale House (☎ 360-647-7002; 1212 10th St; snacks $4-8) In Fairhaven, this smoke-free pub offers tempting pub fare and a good draft-beer selection.

Getting There & Away

San Juan Islands Shuttle Express (☎ 360-671-1137, 888-373-8522) offers daily summer service to the San Juan Islands. **Alaska Marine Highway Ferries** (☎ 360-676-0212, 800-642-0066; www.state .ak.us/ferry) goes to Skagway and other south-east Alaskan ports. The **Bellair Airporter Shuttle** (☎ 800-423-4219; www.airporter.com) runs to Sea-Tac airport with en-route connections to Anacortes and Whidbey Island.

WHIDBEY ISLAND

Green, low-lying Whidbey Island snakes 41 miles along the Washington mainland from the northern suburbs of Seattle to Deception Pass – so named because Captain George Vancouver realized he had been 'deceived' in thinking Whidbey was attached to the mainland. **Deception Pass State Park**, with for-est trails, lakes and more than 17 miles of shoreline, encompasses the narrow channel traversed by a dramatic bridge that links the two islands.

Camp in the park or stay in historic **Coupe-ville**, 10 miles south of Whidbey's main town, Oak Harbor. Coupeville has an attractive seafront filled with antique stores and old inns. Sample local oysters and mussels at the **Captain's Galley** (☎ 360-678-0241; 10 Front St).

Washington State Ferries (p527) takes you to the island, and Island Transit buses whisk you around.

SAN JUAN ISLANDS

The San Juan archipelago contains 457 is-lands sprawled across 750 sq miles of Pa-cific waters. Despite a developed economic dependency on tourism, the islands retain their bucolic charm that is imposed by the farming and fishing residents. Visitors seek R&R and outdoor activities – cycling, kay-aking, sailing, whale-watching – and most come in summer, the best time to go.

For information, contact the San Juan Is-lands **visitors bureau** (☎ 888-468-3701; www.guide tosanjuans.com). During July and August, ac-commodations reservations are essential.

Sea kayaks, a popular means of exploring the shores of the San Juans, are available for rent on Lopez, Orcas and San Juan Islands. Expect a guided half-day trip to cost $30 to $45. Note that most beach access is barred by private property, except at state or county parks.

Washington State Ferries (p527) leave Anacortes (Fidalgo Island) for Lopez and San Juan Islands; some continue to Sidney, BC, near Victoria. To visit all the islands, it's cheapest to go to San Juan first and work your way back through the other islands. On the islands, public transportation is pretty much nonexistent, but most motels will pick up guests at the ferry landing with advance notice. Bike rentals are available.

Lopez Island

The most agricultural of the San Juan Islands, Lopez is also the closest to the mainland. For pastoral charm, it's a hard place to beat. South of the ferry landing (1.3 miles) is **Odlin County Park** (☎ 360-468-2496; campsites $11-19).

San Juan Island

San Juan offers the most hospitable blend of sophisticated amenities and rural land-scapes. The main settlement is Friday Harbor. **San Juan Island National Historical Park** (☎ 360-378-2240; ☷ 8:30am-4pm) commemorates a mid-19th-century British–US territorial conflict; the American Camp, on the island's southeast end, features a splendid hike up Mt Finlayson, from which three mountain ranges can be glimpsed on a clear day. On the western shore, **Lime Kiln Point State Park** (☷ 8am-5pm Oct-Mar, 6:30am-10pm Apr 1–Oct 15) is de-voted to whale-watching and sunsets.

Camp on San Juan or stay at **Wayfarer's Rest** (☎ 360-378-6428; www.rockisland.com/~wayfarersrest; 35 Malcolm St; dm/cabins $22/55), Friday Harbor's backpackers' hostel and a welcome addition to an isle of pricey inns.

Orcas Island

Ruggedly beautiful Orcas Island is the larg-est of the San Juans. The ferry terminal is

---

DETOUR: NORTH CASCADES NATIONAL PARK

This park contains some of Washington's most dramatic and diverse landscapes. Remote and thus nearly untouched, North Cascades is a (free!) paradise for hikers, cross-country skiers, mountaineers and kayakers seeking a bit of solitude. From Whidbey Island (p532), scenic North Cascades Hwy (Hwy 20) heads up the Skagit River Valley into glaciated heaven.

Hundreds of great **backcountry hikes**, including the Pacific Crest Trail, crisscross the park; **Cascade Pass Trail** is a popular day hike. **Campgrounds** abound, too, with 19 facilities accessible from Hwy 20, but bring food and supplies. **Newhalem**, a dam-workers' town, is the jumping-off point for recreation, and pictorial **Diablo Lake and dam** are nearby. The park's **visitors center** (☎ 206-386-4495; 502 Newhalem St; ◷ 9am-6pm), off Hwy 20 near Newhalem, has information on trails, camping and rafting on the Skagit River; also check out www.nps.gov/noca.

13.5 miles south of the main population center, Eastsound. On the island's eastern lobe is **Moran State Park** (☎ 360-376-2326, camping reservations 888-226-7688; campsites from $10), dominated by Mt Constitution (2409ft), with 40 miles of trails; get a map at headquarters.

For help with accommodations, call the **Orcas lodging hotline** (☎ 360-376-8888; www.orcas -island.com/lodging.html). The backwoods hippie hangout **Doe Bay Resort & Retreat** (☎ 360-376-2291; www.doebay.com; dm/campsites $25/35, r $55-185), on the island's easternmost shore, has myriad accommodations options, plus hot tubs, yoga classes, guided tours and other fringe benefits.

SOUTH CASCADES

Rocky, glaciated and wild, the Cascade Mountains are the backbone of the Northwest. They are a source of unremitting adventure, much of which can be experienced as day trips from urban centers. The term 'North Cascades' refers to the chiseled alpine peaks in northern Washington (see p533), and the 'South Cascades' are the majestic, wildflower-covered slopes whose mighty crests captivate the southern part of the state.

MT RAINIER NATIONAL PARK

At 14,410ft Mt Rainier, 95 miles southeast of Seattle, is the highest peak in the Cascades – and an active volcano. The park has four entrances; the main one, Nisqually (on Hwy 706 via Ashford, near the park's southwest corner), is the only entrance open in winter for the cross-country skiers and snowshoers. Call ☎ 800-695-7623 for road conditions.

For detailed park information, contact the **superintendent's office** (☎ 360-569-2211, ext 3314; www.nps.gov/mora); download maps and trail descriptions from the website. Park entry is $10/5 per car/pedestrian. Get trail information and backcountry permits (free) at the **Longmire Hiker Information Center** (☎ 360-569-2211, ext 3317; ◷ summer only), the **Jackson Visitor Center** (☎ 360-569-2211, ext 2328; Paradise), or ranger stations.

The most popular route up to the summit of Mt Rainier starts in Paradise, near the Nisqually entrance, known for its alpine wildflower meadows laced with hiking trails. Some of the best views of Rainier are from Sunrise, which is often crowded with hikers. The remote Carbon River entrance gives access to the park's inland rain forest. The **ranger station** (☎ 360-829-9639; ◷ summer only) is just inside the entrance.

Reservations are strongly advised during summer at the park's six **campgrounds** (reservations ☎ 800-365-2267; www.mount.rainier.national -park.com/camping.htm; campsites from $9) and can be made up to two months in advance.

Packwood (on US 12) is the closest town to the White River and Ohanapecosh entrances, both of which have campsites ($15). The **Packwood Ranger Station** (☎ 360-494-0600) is near the east end of town. **Hotel Packwood** (☎ 360-494-5431; 104 Main St; s/d $29/39) has clean, charming rooms and a mountain-view veranda.

The **Rainier Shuttle** (☎ 360-569-2331) runs between Sea-Tac airport and Ashford or Paradise. Gray Line (p522) runs tours from Seattle ($54).

MT ST HELENS NATIONAL VOLCANIC MONUMENT

On May 18, 1980, Mt St Helens (8365ft) disappeared from the Space Needle's view. It erupted with a force of a 24-megaton blast, leveling hundreds of square miles of forest

WILL HISTORY REPEAT ITSELF?

In late September 2004, the USGS started monitoring 'volcanic unrest' within Mt St Helens, and ash and steam plumes were seen rising from her once again. At the time we went to press, growth of the new lava dome inside the crater (in layman's terms, eruption) continued. Reports stated that changes in eruptive activity could occur (and increase) over days, weeks and even months, but full-scale eruption comparable to that of 25 years ago was unlikely.

and blowing 1300ft off its peak. Slowly regenerating from the effects of nature's fury, the mountain-with-her-peak-lopped-off and the surrounding 171 sq miles of volcano-wracked wilderness can be visited as a day trip from Portland or Seattle.

The **Mt St Helens Visitor Center** (☎ 360-274-2100; 9am-5pm), just off I-5 exit 49 near Castle Rock, presents an overview of the site's history and geology. At the end of Hwy 504, in the heart of the blast zone, the **Johnston Ridge Visitors Center** (☎ 360-274-2131; 10am-6pm May-Oct) provides views directly into the mouth of Mt St Helens' north-facing crater. A more remote vista point, with good views of the lava dome inside the crater, is on the northeastern side of the mountain along **Windy Ridge**, the terminus of USFS Rd 99 (closed in winter). Single/multiple-site passes cost $3/6.

To climb Mt St Helens, get a permit ($15) in advance from **monument headquarters** (☎ 360-449-7861; www.fs.fed.us/gpnf/mshnvm). The climb takes six to 12 hours in total; check weather conditions before ascending.

MT ADAMS

Mt Adams (12,276ft) is one of the most beautiful of the Cascade peaks, with enchanting hikes, an easy summit ascent and the unique activity of huckleberry picking (permits required). For information on hiking or climbing, inquire at the **Trout Lake ranger station** (☎ 509-395-3400; 2455 Hwy 141). There are numerous campgrounds around Mt Adams and B&Bs on Trout Lake. Maps cost $4.25 at the ranger station.

The eastern slope is part of the Yakama Indian Reservation and mostly closed to non-tribal members. A notable exception is the 3-mile **Bird Creek Meadow Trail**, one of the best-loved hikes in the Northwest, which gently climbs to an alpine meadow showered by waterfalls and ablaze with wildflowers. It begins in a small, western portion of the reservation that is open to non-Yakamas ($10 vehicle fee). Near Bird Creek Meadows are three lakeside **campgrounds** (☎ 509-865-2405).

The easiest access to Mt Adams is from the Columbia River Gorge, from either I-84 or Hwy 14. Take Hwy 141 to Trout Lake, which is the focal point of recreation in the area.

IF YOU'VE GOT A FEW MORE DAYS IN THE NORTHWEST

Washington and Oregon are riddled with off-the-I-5 treasures. While it's fabulous to stay sleepless in Seattle and partying in Portland, consider veering off the freeway toward these more remote gems:

- **Oregon Caves National Monument, OR** Forty-eight miles southeast of Grants Pass, explore 3 miles of formation-filled underground chambers with the fast-moving River Styx running the length of the marble cave (despite the name, there's only one cave). Entry is by **guided tour** (☎ 541-592-2100; www.nps.org/orca; adult/National Parks passholder $7.50/free; Apr-Nov) only. Dress for cold and wet conditions.

- **Spokane, WA** The prosperous trade center of the Inland Northwest, Spokane has a touch of spunk and culture worth checking out en route to Minneapolis. Its wineries make some mean merlots, and the city hosts the famed 7.2-mile Bloomsday Run (1st Sunday in May), the world's largest timed road race.

- **Mt Baker, WA** Snowboarders love this 10,781ft mountain, which boasts the greatest annual snowfall of any ski area in North America; see www.skiwashington.com for links to resort websites. Hiking and climbing are big, too, even though Baker is the second-most-active Cascades volcano after Mt St Helens.

PORTLAND

Second to Seattle only in size, Portland is an urban garden blooming with culture, friendliness and microbreweries. The city is beautiful, especially in springtime when those infamous rains turn its many parks a supernatural green and vivid rhododendrons grace every street. Dotted with busy coffeehouses, hipster bars, and sales-tax-free boutiques, it's obvious why Portland regularly finds itself on the 'most livable cities of the USA' list. Its residents are generally a left-leaning bunch who tend to read and recycle with equal devotion. With easy access to the coast, as well as the Columbia River Gorge and Cascades range, Portland offers far more than just great city life.

HISTORY

The Portland region was initially settled by retired trappers from the fur-trading post at nearby Fort Vancouver; the first building was erected in 1829. The city was named by the flip of a coin (the other choice was Boston), and due to it prime location on the Columbia, it quickly became the shipping center for much of the Northwest. During the 20th century it enjoyed steady growth, with a shipbuilding boom from WWII.

The port and shipping operations have since moved north of downtown, and much of the city's rough-and-tumble waterfront feel went with it. The Old Town has been substantially revitalized, and the once-industrial Pearl District now brims with expensive lofts.

These days high-tech firms such as Intel and outdoor-gear companies such as Columbia Sportswear fuel economic growth, and they do so primarily from the suburbs (both Intel and Nike headquarters are west of the city).

ORIENTATION

The Willamette River bisects the city into east and west, and Burnside St divides north from south, giving rise to the city's four quadrants. At the confluence of the Columbia and Willamette Rivers, nine bridges link Portland's diverse neighborhoods. Downtown is in Southwest Portland; the historic Old Town, Chinatown and trendy shopping areas are in Northwest. Northeast contains

> **GETTING INTO TOWN**
>
> Tri-Met's MAX light-rail train runs between the Portland International Airport (p543) and downtown ($1.55); in the reverse direction, catch it northbound along SW Yamhill St. Taxis cost about $30.

the commercial Lloyd District – home to the USA's first full-blown shopping mall – and quickly gentrifying Alberta, abuzz with hipsters and arts-and-crafts galleries. In Southeast, the gay-friendly Hawthorne District, between 30th and 45th Aves, is a neo-hippie hangout, while Belmont St and Clinton St both house clusters of cool.

The Portland Streetcar connects Northwest and the Pearl with downtown, while Tri-Met's MAX light-rail system links the city center with Southeast Portland and the airport.

INFORMATION
Bookstores

CounterMedia (☎ 503-226-8141; 927 SW Oak St; ☼ 11am-7pm Mon-Sat, noon-6pm Sun) Next to Reading Frenzy, beautiful, glossy, expensive books of erotica and fringe culture.

Excalibur (☎ 503-231-7351; 2444 SE Hawthorne Blvd, Hawthorne District; ☼ 11am-8pm Mon-Thu, 10am-8pm Fri & Sat, 11am-7pm Sun) Comic books and graphic novels galore.

In Other Words (☎ 503-232-6003; www.inotherwords .org; 3734 SE Hawthorne Blvd, Hawthorne District; ☼ 10-9pm Mon-Sat, 11am-6pm Sun) Feminist bookstore and resource center.

Independent Publishing Resource Center (IPRC; ☎ 503-827-0249) Upstairs from Radio Frenzy, it has a zine library and self-publishing resources available to the public.

Powell's City of Books (☎ 503-228-4651; www .powells.com; 1005 W Burnside St; ☼ 9am-11pm) Portland landmark better than the Pyramids to a bibliophile – and nearly as big, covering a city block and stocking more than one million titles.

Reading Frenzy (☎ 503-274-1449; 921 SW Oak St; ☼ 11am-7pm Mon-Sat, noon-6pm Sun) Kitty-corner from Powell's; indie-rock-zine and small-press-book emporium.

Emergency
Oregon State Police (☎ 503-731-3030)
Poison Control (☎ 800-222-1222)
Portland Police/Fire (☎ 503-823-3333)
Portland Women's Crisis Line (☎ 503-235-5333)
Rape Crisis Center (☎ 503-640-5311)

PACIFIC NORTHWEST

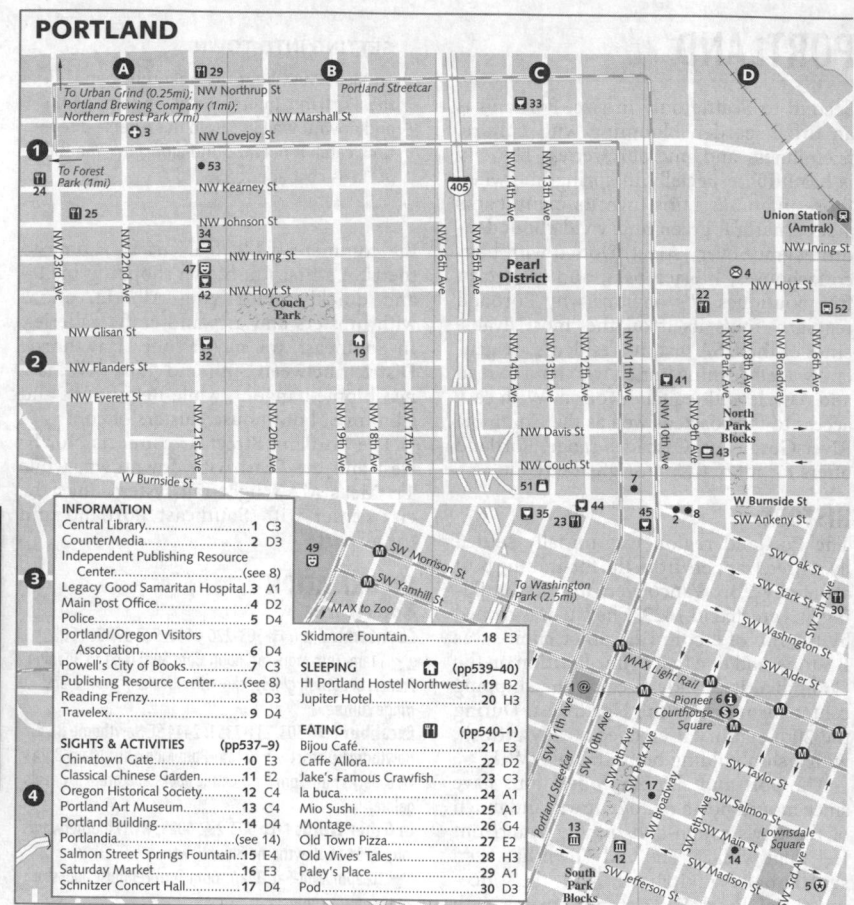

PORTLAND

Internet Access

Free wireless Internet access is available at many neighborhood cafés – such as **Urban Grind** (☎ 503-546-0649; 2214 NE Oregon; ☻ 7am-4pm Mon-Fri, 8am-4pm Sat), which also has one community computer (free for customers) – and at the Hawthorne hostel (p540). The Northwest hostel (p540) has a lone terminal.

There's free one-hour access – if you can wrangle a spot – at the **Central Library** (☎ 503-988-5123; www.multcolib.org; 801 SW 10th Ave; ☻ 9am-9pm Mon-Thu, 9am-6pm Fri & Sat, 1-5pm Sun), the oldest library on the West Coast.

Media

A&E Friday entertainment section in the state's largest daily, the *Oregonian*.

Barfly (www.barflymag.com) Pint-sized glossy distributed monthly in bars, with sassy, spot-on reviews of drinking establishments.

KBOO 90.7 FM Progressive local station run mostly by volunteers and offering alternative news and views.

KOPB 91.5 FM The National Public Radio (NPR) station.

Portland Mercury (www.portlandmercury.com) Local sibling of Seattle's *Stranger*; free on Thursdays; plugged into the indie-rock scene.

Willamette Week (www.wweek.com) Free on Wednesdays; local news and entertainment coverage.

Medical Services

Legacy Good Samaritan Hospital (☎ 503-413-7711; www.legacyhealth.org; 1015 NW 22nd Ave; ☻ 24hr)

Walgreens (☎ 503-238-6053; 940 SE 39th Ave, Hawthorne District; pharmacy ☻ 24hr)

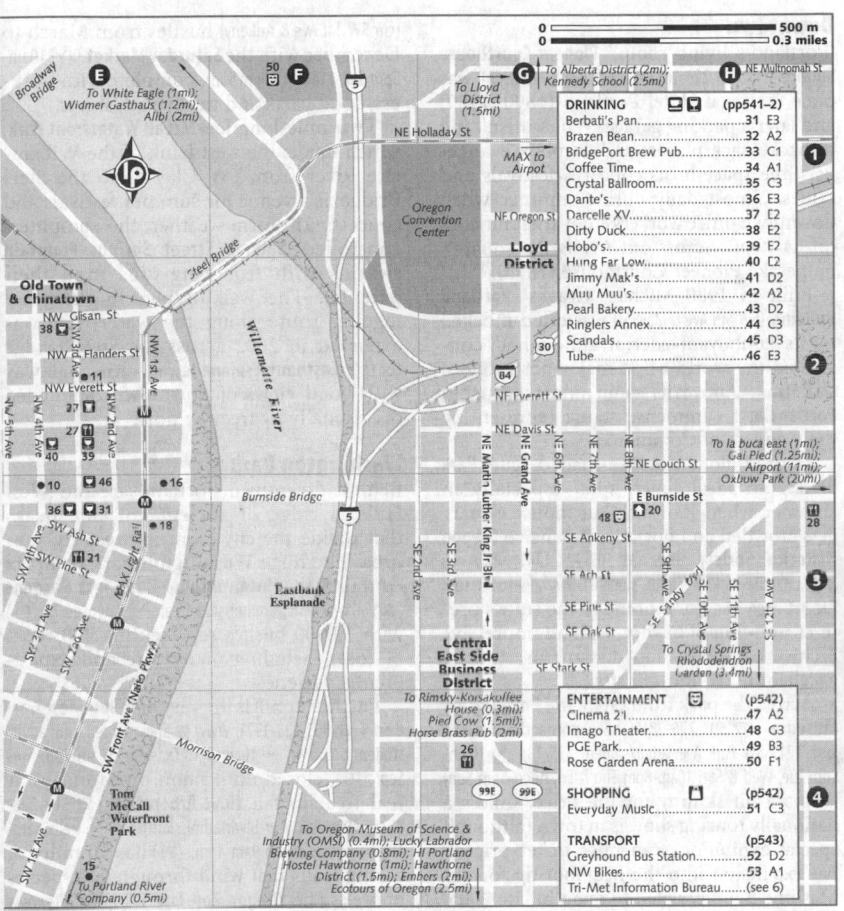

DRINKING (pp541–2)
Berbati's Pan	**31** E3
Brazen Bean	**32** A2
BridgePort Brew Pub	**33** C1
Coffee Time	**34** A1
Crystal Ballroom	**35** C3
Dante's	**36** E3
Darcelle XV	**37** E2
Dirty Duck	**38** E2
Hobo's	**39** E2
Hung Far Low	**40** E2
Jimmy Mak's	**41** D2
Muu Muu's	**42** A2
Pearl Bakery	**43** D2
Ringlers Annex	**44** C3
Scandals	**45** D3
Tube	**46** E3

ENTERTAINMENT (p542)
Cinema 21	**47** A2
Imago Theater	**48** G3
PGE Park	**49** B3
Rose Garden Arena	**50** F1

SHOPPING (p542)
Everyday Music	**51** C3

TRANSPORT (p543)
Greyhound Bus Station	**52** D2
NW Bikes	**53** A1
Tri-Met Information Bureau	(see 6)

PACIFIC NORTHWEST

Money

Foreign-currency exchange office (Portland International Airport; 5:30am-4:30pm)
Travelex (☎ 503-222-2665; 7601 SW 6th Ave; 9am-5:30pm Mon-Fri, 11am-2pm Sat)

Post

Main post office (☎ 503-525-5398; 715 NW Hoyt; 7am-6:30pm Mon-Fri, 8:30am-5pm)

Telephone

If you find yourself within the Portland area, even for local telephone calls, you must dial the full 10-digit number (without including the 1).

Area codes are ☎ 503 and, seen less frequently, ☎ 971.

Tourist Information

Portland/Oregon Visitors Association (☎ 503-275-8355, 877-678-5263; www.travelportland.com; 701 SW 6th Ave; 8:30am-5:30pm Mon-Fri, 10am-4pm Sat) This office in Pioneer Courthouse Square restrains the usual avalanche of tourist materials and has a small theater where you can watch a free, 12-minute film about the city.

SIGHTS

Portland has many highlights and they lie squarely within its vibrant neighborhoods: exclusive residential areas with impressive architecture, upscale shopping districts, übertrendy main drags, magnificent parks, and historical and cultural attractions.

Downtown

'Portland's living room,' **Pioneer Courthouse Square** (☎ 503-223-1613; SW 6th Ave & Morrison) was once the regal Hotel Portland (1890–1950) and later a parking garage. When it isn't full of hackeysack players and soapbox evangelists, the space hosts concerts, festivals and rallies, almost daily during summer when downtown office workers enjoy their lunches on its steps. Across 6th Ave is the square's namesake Pioneer Courthouse (1875).

Built in 1980 Michael Graves' **Portland Building** (SW 5th Ave & Main St) was often mocked for its flamboyant exterior, although it's considered the world's first major postmodern structure. Above its main doors crouches **Portlandia**, an immense statue representing the Goddess of Commerce.

Housed along the tree-shaded **South Park Blocks** (an ideal lunch spot, especially in summer when Pioneer Courthouse Square gets crowded and hot), the expansive **Oregon Historical Society** (OHS; ☎ 503-222-1741; www.ohs.org; 1200 SW Park Ave; adult/student $8/7; ☼ 10am-5pm Tue-Sat, noon-5pm Sun) is home to the state's premier museum of history, with an impressive archive of photos and documents, and an excellent book-and-gift store.

Across the park from OHS, the **Portland Art Museum** (☎ 503-226-2811; www.portlandartmuseum.org; 1219 SW Park Ave; adult/student $15/13; ☼ 10am-5pm Tue, Wed & Sat, 10am-8pm Thu & Fri, noon-5pm Sun) seems a bit skimpy for the price, unless a nationally touring show is in town (although special exhibitions can raise ticket prices). An expansion into the neighboring former Masonic temple, slated to open in late 2005, will house modern and contemporary art.

Old Town & Chinatown

The core of 1890s Portland, **Old Town** once felt dodgy but, thanks to a number of new clubs, it's now among the liveliest sections of town after dark.

The ornate **Chinatown gate** (cnr Burnside & SW 4th Ave) welcomes visitors to lively Chinatown. The authentic Suzhou-style **Classical Chinese Garden** (☎ 503-228-8131; cnr NW 3rd Ave & Everett; adult/student $7/5.50; ☼ 9am-6pm summer, 10am-5pm winter) is a one-block haven of calming tranquility with a teahouse in the 'Tower of Cosmic Reflections.' Tours (free with admission) leave at noon and 1pm daily.

A preserve of Victorian-era architecture, the district that surrounds **Skidmore Fountain** (cnr SW 1st Ave & Ankeny) bustles from March to December with the **Saturday Market** (☼ 10am-5pm Sat, 11am-4:30pm Sun), complete with buskers, food carts and tie-dyed T-shirts.

Two-mile-long **Tom McCall Waterfront Park**, which flanks the west bank of the Willamette River from SW Clay St to the Steel Bridge, is a venue for summer festivals and concerts. In warm weather, the computer-controlled **Salmon Street Springs Fountain** swarms with frolicking kids (and their parents). The walking/bicycling/skating/jogging route along the waterfront was extended in 2002 across the Steel Bridge to the **Eastbank Esplanade**, a 1-mile walkway with good views of downtown dampened occasionally by freeway noise.

Washington Park

Behind downtown Portland are the West Hills, a ridge of ancient volcanic peaks that divide the city from its westerly suburbs. The huge Washington Park complex contains the **International Rose Test Gardens** (☎ 503-823-3636; admission free; ☼ dawn-dusk; ℗) with 10,000 bushes representing 400 types of rose, including many rare and experimental varieties.

Further uphill is the very lush **Japanese Garden** (☎ 503-223-1321; www.japanesegarden.com; adult/student $6.50/4; ☼ 10am-4pm Oct-Mar, 10am-7pm Apr-Sep; ℗), closed until noon on Mondays. A real treat in fall, **Hoyt Arboretum** (☎ 503-228-8733; 4000 Fairview Blvd; admission free; ☼ trails 5am-10pm, visitors center 9am-4pm; ℗) has 10 miles of hiking trails that wind through 900 species of tree. The **Oregon Zoo** (☎ 503-226-1561; www.oregonzoo.org; 4001 SW Canyon Rd; admission $9; ☼ 9am-6pm mid-Apr–mid-Sep, 9am-4pm mid-Sep–mid-Apr; ℗) specializes in Asian elephants and maintains one of the world's most successful elephant-breeding programmes.

You can feel like old-money Portland without even paying admission at **Pittock Mansion** (☎ 503-823-3624; www.pittockmansion.com; 3229 NW Pittock Dr; admission $5.25; ☼ 11am-4pm Jun-Aug, noon-4pm Sep-May, closed Jan; ℗). Stroll the grounds and pretend you're lord of all you survey.

Southeast

The **Oregon Museum of Science & Industry** (OMSI; ☎ 503-797-6674; www.omsi.edu; 1945 SE Water St; admission from $5; ☼ 9:30am-5:30pm Tue-Sun Sep-May, 9:30am-7pm Jun-Aug) is a hands-on museum and Omnimax theater that enthralls kids and adults alike. If you do only one thing here, make it the submarine tour.

The **Hawthorne District** is an activity in and of itself; get your goddess gear and fair-trade sneakers in shops on Hawthorne Blvd, then fuel yourself with wheatgrass shots or organic falafel. End the day in serene **Crystal Springs Rhododendron Garden** (SE 28th Ave & Woodstock).

ACTIVITIES

Hikers will find more than 50 miles of **hiking** trails in **Forest Park**, the nation's largest natural urban park. Pick up a park map at the Hoyt Arboretum Visitor Center. The Wildwood Trail starts near the zoo and winds through 30 miles of forest. Another easily accessible entry point is in Macleay Park at NW Thurman and 26th Ave.

For good **mountain biking**, head uphill to the western end of NW Thurman and continue past the gate onto Leif Erikson Dr, an old dirt logging road leading 11 miles into Forest Park (don't bike on the hiking trails!).

Kayakers can check out **Portland River Company** (☎ 503-229-0551, 888-238-2059; www.portlandrivercompany.com; 315 SW Montgomery St; tours $43-60, classes $50-150, rentals $20-60), offering year-round kayak tours of the Willamette River, as well as kayaking classes and unguided rentals.

TOURS

Ecotours of Oregon (☎ 503-245-1428, 888-868-7733; www.ecotours-of-oregon.com; 3127 SE 23rd Ave; tours $40-100) Naturalist tours of northwest Oregon include microbrewery, Mt St Helens and whale-watching trips; scheduled on demand.

Portland Walking Tours (☎ 503-774-4522; www.portlandwalkingtours.com; tours $15) One of several guided strolls, the 'A Walk Through Time' tour, highlighting Old Town and Chinatown, leaves from Pioneer Courthouse Square Fridays at 3pm. The 'Best of Portland' walk is popular, too.

Shanghai Tunnels (☎ 503-622-4798; shanghaitunnels@onemain.com; tours $11) Running beneath Old Town are a series of underground corridors through which nefarious ship captains used to shanghai drunken sailors, dragging them aboard as indentured workers.

FESTIVALS & EVENTS

Locals and suburbanites stake out prime parade-viewing territory days in advance for the springtime **Portland Rose Festival** (☎ 503-227-2681; www.rosefestival.org). Other highlights of the city's biggest celebration include a seedy riverfront carnival in Tom McCall Waterfront Park, roaming packs of wild-eyed sailors, beauty queens and blooming roses.

Other festivals include the following:

Waterfront Blues Festival (☎ 503-282-0555; www.waterfrontbluesfest.com; Jul 4 weekend) Blues music fills Tom McCall Waterfront Park; proceeds go to the Oregon Food Bank.

Waterfront Park Oregon Brewers Festival (☎ 503-778-5917; www.oregonbrewfest.com; Jul) Sample spring and summer microbrews from Oregon and beyond at this ultimate beerfest.

SLEEPING

Portland's pricey hotels are easily avoidable thanks to lower-cost motels, boutique hotels and hostels. Freeway exits around the outskirts of town (like I-205 exit 24) are good places for budget options.

GAY & LESBIAN PORTLAND

Leftist Portland's primary gay-friendly neighborhood is the Hawthorne District. **Just Out** (www.justout.com) is a publication serving the Portland area's gay community; pick it up at **Gai-Pied** (☎ 503-331-1125; 2544 NE Broadway; ☾ noon-8pm Mon-Thu, 11am-9pm Fri & Sat, noon-6pm Sun). A good resource for GLBT visitors is www.travelportland.com/glbt/glbt.html.

Gay venues are in no short supply in Portland. Many are downtown on SW Stark near 11th Ave and on NW 3rd Ave; Hawthorne Blvd is another hot spot, especially for women. Energetic **Scandals** (☎ 503-227-5887; 1038 SW Stark) is a linchpin of Portland's gay nightlife. Lesbians of all stripes gather at **Embers** (☎ 503-236-8689; 3701 SE Division) for dancing, pool and karaoke. Other recommendations include:

- **Darcelle XV** (☎ 503-222-5338; 208 NW 3rd Ave) Portland's landmark drag club.
- **Dirty Duck** (☎ 503-224-8446; 439 NW 3rd Ave) Working-class bear den, with pool tables.
- **Hobo's** (☎ 503-224-3285; 120 NW 3rd Ave) Stylish piano bar with no cover.

HI Portland Hostel Hawthorne (☎ 503-236-3380, 866-447-3031; www.portlandhostel.org; 3031 SE Hawthorne Blvd; dm $18-21, r $38-48; ☐) This popular hostel is in a great location, and has good facilities in a lovely old house. Check out the ecofriendly 'living roof.' Guests traveling by bicycle get a $3 discount. Take bus No 14 from downtown.

HI Portland Hostel Northwest (☎ 503-241-2783, 800-909-4776, code 178; www.2oregonhostels.com; 1818 NW Glisan St; dm/s/d $18/49/59; ☐) Quieter and perhaps more adult-friendly than the Hawthorne location, this very homey hostel in a tree-lined residential area is another well-positioned base, right between the cosmopolitan Pearl District and trendy Northwest Portland. Take bus No 17 from downtown.

White Eagle (☎ 503-335-8900, 866-271-3377; 836/838 N Russell St; dm $30, r $40-50) Opened in 1905, this musicians' hangout in an oft-ignored industrial corner of town is supposedly haunted (thanks to a nasty occurrence in room No 2). The 11 super-clean, European-style rooms with shared bathrooms are upstairs from a tavern where live acoustic music is played nightly, so it's best for night owls (room Nos 7 and 8 are noisiest). But it's a great bargain, a fabulously unique sleeping experience and a piece of Portland music history.

Oxbow Park (☎ 503-663-4708; 3010 SE Oxbow Pkwy, Gresham; campsites/extra vehicle $9/2) The best place to camp nearest Portland is 20 miles east of town in the Sandy River Gorge. Sites are first-come first-served, but there are 45 of them.

EATING

From upscale, gourmet places (where you can still wear jeans) to super-cheap dives, many kitchens throughout Portland (and Oregon) take pride in using local and organic ingredients. Self-catering is easy, with multiple options for organic grocery shopping (most such places have good delis). Downtown, food trucks referred to as the **'Pod'** (SW 5th Ave at Stark) offer cheap lunches.

Downtown & Northwest

The best eats this side of the Willamette are sprinkled throughout the single-digit avenues, and along and around the NW 21st Ave strip.

Caffe Allora (☎ 503-445-4612; 504 NW 9th Ave; mains $6-10) You can savor a wonderful Italian meal in this cozy neighborhood bistro for as little as $6, but beware: Edmondo may charm you into spending more. Stop by in the morning for pastries and coffee; the perfect bread is from nearby Pearl Bakery.

Jake's Famous Crawfish (☎ 503-226-1419; 401 SW 12th Ave; mains $8-25) The best reason to visit this old-school seafood-and-steak establishment is the cheap happy-hour menu (mains from $2 to $4 between 3pm and 6pm Monday to Friday); arrive early for a table.

Old Town Pizza (☎ 503-222-9999; 226 NW Davis St; pizzas from $6) Antique lamps, brick walls, low lights and velvet couches give away this rambling pizza parlor's past life as a bordello.

Mio Sushi (☎ 503-221-1496; 2271 NW Johnson St; mains $4-14) Mio is worthy of its multiple 'Best Sushi in Portland' awards and accolades.

Other recommendations:

Bijou Café (☎ 503-222-3187; 132 SW 3rd Ave; omelettes $6-8) Slightly pretentious but the best place for breakfast downtown.

la buca West (☎ 503-279-8040, 2309 NW Kearney; mains $6-9); East (☎ 503-238-1058, 40 NE 28th Ave) Inexpensive Italian eatery with good daily specials.

SPLURGE!

McMenamins Kennedy School (☎ 503-249-3983; www.mcmenamins.com; 5736 NE 33rd Ave; r incl breakfast $99-109; Ⓟ) Finally, your chance to drink and smoke in detention! McMenamins is a personality-infused hotel housed in a former elementary school. The former-classroom rooms are spacious, the beds are comfortable and the nightstands have fill-it-yourself, resealable beer jars for imbibing on the go. Decorated in classic McMenamins style, there's artwork all over the place, a Japanese-style soaking pool (at a balmy 100°F), a movie theater, a restaurant and a pub down every hall. Make reservations in advance for this unique Portland sleeping – and eating and drinking – experience.

Jupiter Hotel (☎ 503-230-9200, 877-800-0004; www.jupiterhotel.com; 800 E Burnside; s/d from $79/89; Ⓟ ⊠) The 82 immaculate and comfortable rooms at this newly remodeled boutique hotel have chalkboard doors and mod Ikea-style décor. On the premises are a bar, club and diner-style restaurant.

SPLURGE!

Paley's Place (☎ 503-243-2403; 1204 NW 21st Ave; mains $18-28) Set aside an entire evening for nothing but sheer gastronomic ecstasy and make a reservation at this fine place. Opened in 1995, Paley's immediately took Portland's culinary world by storm, winning awards left and right for its spectacular use of fresh, local products and ambitious pairings of alluring flavors. Kimberly Paley and her staff offer unprecedented service and hospitality while her husband, Vitaly, rules the creative kitchen with flawless precision, wooing Alaskan halibut with sauce gribiche ($28) into poached perfection.

Northeast & Southeast

Restaurants are concentrated along the Hawthorne and Alberta main drags.

Old Wives' Tales (☎ 503-238-0470; 1300 E Burnside St; mains $5-12) This cornerstone of progressive Portland serves upscale organic comfort food, such as tofu scrambles and parchment-baked halibut with wild rice. Super family- (and gay- and low-sodium-diet) friendly, there's a children's playroom off to the side.

Montage (☎ 503-234-1324; 301 SE Morrison; mains $4-14) The beloved cash-only Creole nightspot under the Morrison Bridge has long, white-clothed community tables, an aggressively oddball wait staff, oyster shooters, and legendary macaroni and cheese.

Cup & Saucer Cafe (☎ 503-236-6001; 3566 SE Hawthorne Blvd, Hawthorne District; mains $4-7) Breakfast is served all day at this vegan-friendly joint, where customers and staff sip coffee and compare tattoos.

Bread & Ink Café (☎ 503-239-4756; 3610 SE Hawthorne Blvd, Hawthorne District; mains $6-12) A Portland standby; for brunch, try blintzes ($7.50) or the salmon sandwich ($9.25).

Tin Shed (☎ 503-288-6966; 1438 NE Alberta St, Alberta District; breakfast $5-8; ⏱ 7am-3pm) Great breakfast-menu items with clever names; try the Fetch, Roll Over, or Good Dog potato-cake stacks ($6.25 each).

Other recommendations:

Hawthorne Street Cafe (☎ 503-232-4982; 3354 SE Hawthorne Blvd, Hawthorne District; ⏱ 7:30am-3pm daily plus 5-9pm Thu-Sat; mains $4.50-7) All-day breakfasts and outdoor seating.

Vita Cafe (☎ 503-335-8233; 3024 NE Alberta St, Alberta District; mains $5-8) A vegan joint that serves burgers! Glorious patio, too.

DRINKING

When in doubt about how to spend an evening out in Portland, make like the locals and drink. In addition to spots listed here, you're bound to be within staggering distance of a **McMenamins** (www.mcmenamins.com; or check phone book), always a surefire brewpub.

Coffeehouses

Coffee Time (☎ 503-497-1090; 712 NW 21st Ave; ⏱ 6:30-2:30am) Quasi-intellectual bohemian hangout where some die-hards stay until closing, then wait outside for the café to reopen.

Pearl Bakery (☎ 503-827-0910; 102 NW 9th Ave) Delicious breads and pastries, and lunch for under $5.

Pied Cow (☎ 503-230-4866; 3244 SE Belmont; ⏱ 4pm-midnight Tue-Thu, 4pm-1am Fri, noon-1am Sat, noon-midnight Sun) Elegant historic mansion with loads of atmosphere, gourmet munchies and an excellent patio.

Rimsky-Korsakoffee House (☎ 503-232-2640; 707 SE 12th Ave; ⏱ 7pm-midnight Sun-Thu, 7pm-1am Fri & Sat) Eccentric place with an unmarked façade that looks like a private home and blasts classical music. Rotating tabletops!

Brewpubs

Lucky Labrador Brewing Company (☎ 503-236-3555; 915 SE Hawthorne St) Quintessentially Portland, this cavernous brewhall in industrial Southeast has a cool back patio that invites people to bring their dogs. Post a pic of your pooch on the wall.

BridgePort Brew Pub (☎ 503-241-7179; www .bridgeportbrew.com; 1313 NW Marshall St) Portland's oldest microbrewery, BridgePort is a vast gathering place with top-notch beer (try the great Black Strap Stout or the flagship Blue Heron).

Widmer Gasthaus (☎ 503-281-3333; 929 N Russell St) Quaff Hefeweizen and nibble schnitzel under the Fremont Bridge. Brewery tours are at 3pm Friday, and 1pm and 2pm Saturday and Sunday.

Portland Brewing Company (☎ 503-228-5269; 2730 NW 31st Ave) The taproom here, in the outer industrial section of Northwest, has a patio and food that is worth going the extra half-mile.

PACIFIC NORTHWEST

Bars

Horse Brass Pub (☎ 503-232-2202; 4534 SE Belmont St) This authentic English pub comes complete with weekend football matches and smokers galore.

Brazen Bean (☎ 503-294-0636; 2075 NW Glisan; ☽ Mon-Sat) Crowds wait outside this dark, posh house-turned-cigar-bar until 5pm – opening time and start of happy hour (5pm to 8pm). Famous for more than 25 specialty martinis ($3 each).

Muu Muu's (☎ 503-223-8169; 612 NW 21st Ave) The eclectic international food is as good as the innovative cocktails in this industrial-tiki lounge full of 30-somethings worthy of much people-watching.

Alibi (☎ 503-287-5335; 4024 N Interstate Ave) Vehemently tiki-themed, this karaoke favorite has peppy servers and absurdly complicated tropical drinks. Show up before 9pm or hide in a black-lit corner to avoid the karaoke.

Hung Far Low (☎ 503-223-8686; 112 NW 4th Ave) Beyond the cruelly fluorescent-lit Chinese restaurant is a dark and cozy hideout, blessed by Buddha and a bartender who knows that quantity trumps quality.

Also recommended:

Ringlers Annex (☎ 503-525-0520; 1223 SW Stark St) A multitiered bar in a triangle building, with a candlelit crypt in the basement.

Space Room (☎ 503-235-8303; 4800 SE Hawthorne St) Flying saucers hang over the bar at this black hole in the Hawthorne District's 'Stumbling Zone;' killer Bloody Marys.

Tube (☎ 503-241-8823; 18 NW 3rd Ave) Are you sleek enough to be seen in a faux–*Space Odyssey* mint-green cylindrical bar?

Live Music

Dante's (☎ 503-226-6630; 1 SW 3rd Ave) National acts and vaudeville shows heat up this red, velvety bar, with an intimate stage, toasty fire pit and frosty barmaids.

Berbati's Pan (☎ 503-248-4579; 10 SW 3rd Ave) Big and buzzing with the sound of chatter, this place features pricey drinks and eclectic billing.

Crystal Ballroom (☎ 503-778-5625; 1332 W Burnside St) Major touring bands play at this (usually all-ages) historic ballroom; the 'floating' dance floor bounces at the slightest provocation.

Jimmy Mak's (☎ 503-295-6542; 300 NW 10th Ave) This venue features lively jazz and serves Greek food.

ENTERTAINMENT

Check the *Mercury* or *Willamette Week* for event information.

Performing Arts

Chamber Music Northwest (☎ 503-223-3202; www .cmnw.org) Has chamber music concerts in summer.

Imago Theater (☎ 503-231-9581; 17 SE 8th Ave; admission $24) Well regarded for its innovative puppet theater, including the long-running *Frogz*.

Oregon Ballet Theatre (☎ 503-222-5538; www .obt.org) Portland's resident dance troupe; classical and contemporary programmes.

Cinema

Bagdad Theater (☎ 503-232-6676; 3702 SE Hawthorne Blvd, Hawthorne District; admission $2-3) Visit this gorgeous old faux-Moorish theater for second-run films, beer and pizza.

Cinema 21 (☎ 503-223-4515; 616 NW 21st Ave; admission $4-6) This longstanding arthouse cinema shows indie films and classics.

Sports

Portland Trail Blazers (☎ 503-231-8000) This pro basketball team plays at the Rose Garden Arena. Tickets are expensive and often sold out well in advance.

Portland Timbers (☎ 503-553-5400; admission $8) This minor-league soccer team plays in PGE Park; head for Section 107, where beer and testosterone flow freely, and local boys practice their British hooligan accents.

Portland Winter Hawks (☎ 503-238-6366; admisison $14.25) Check out this pro-junior hockey team at the Rose Garden Arena.

SHOPPING

Portland's mecca for high-end shopping is Northwest; NW 23rd between Everett and Lovejoy is lined with clothing stores, expensive gift shops, home décor boutiques and other trendy businesses. Parking is available on side streets, and buses and streetcars run regularly from downtown. The Pearl District is crammed with chic interior-design shops and is home to the city's best CD store, **Everyday Music** (☎ 503-274-0961; 1313 W Burnside St; ☽ 9am-midnight). Hawthorne is the place to find quirky gifts, while quickly developing NE Alberta St is lined with shops from 14th to 31st Aves.

GETTING THERE & AWAY

At **Portland International Airport** (PDX; ☎ 877-739-4636; www.flypdx.com), 11 miles from downtown, Horizon, Southwest, Alaska and United Airlines offer frequent flights to and from Seattle, San Francisco and afar.

Greyhound (☎ 503-243-2310; 550 NW 6th Ave) connects Portland with cities along I-5 and I-84. Regular service includes Seattle, Bend, Ashland, San Francisco, and Vancouver, BC.

Trains run regularly to and from **Amtrak's Union Station** (☎ 503-241-4290; NW 6th Ave & Irving). Destinations include Seattle, Los Angeles and Chicago. Amtrak's fun *Coast Starlight* train leaves Portland daily for Seattle and Vancouver at 4:05pm, and for San Francisco and LA at 2:25pm.

GETTING AROUND

Portland is phenomenally friendly toward bicycles. Rent a two-wheeler at **NW Bikes** (☎ 503-248-9142; 916 NW 21st Ave; day/overnight/additional day $15/25/10; ☯ 10am-6pm Mon-Sat). A map of metro-area bike routes is available from bike shops. Portland's streets are easily navigated, and metered parking in the city is generally available, surprisingly. Or park free on an inner-Southeast street and walk across a bridge to the city center.

Oregon law prevents you from pumping your own gas, so don't even try it.

Tri-Met operates local buses and the MAX light-rail system; visit its **information bureau** (☎ 503-238-7433; www.trimet.org; 701 SW 6th Ave; ☯ 8:30am-5:30pm Mon-Fri) at Pioneer Courthouse Square. A streetcar runs from Portland State University, south of downtown, through the Pearl District to NW 23rd Ave. Within the downtown core, public transportation is free; outside downtown, fares are $1.30 to $1.60. Bus services stop running at around 1:30am.

Call, don't hail, taxis in Portland. Try **Broadway Cab** (☎ 503-227-1234) or **Radio Cab** (☎ 503-227-1212).

COLUMBIA RIVER GORGE & AROUND

The enormous Columbia River divides Washington and Oregon, and her canyon is one of the Pacific Northwest's (and the USA's) most dramatic destinations.

Hard winds and fast water have warranted the region's nickname 'the adrenaline capital of the Northwest.' On the Oregon side, river-level I-84 provides the quickest access to the most popular sites. If time permits, opt for the slower but far more scenic Historic Columbia River Hwy (Hwy 30; see p544). Washington's Hwy 14, also slower going than I-84, offers spectacular vistas from the other side of the river. Campers will find state parks on both sides, although campsites are scarce on summer weekends and traffic noise can be bothersome.

HOOD RIVER & AROUND

The cool town of Hood River, 63 miles east of Portland on I-84, is a slender wedge of outdoorsy shops and outfitters, cafés and a few hotels. The Columbia River here is a famous windsurfing hot spot, and there's great mountain biking south of town off Hwy 35 and USFS Rd 44.

Information

Downtown information office (☎ 541-386-3058; 104 Oak St, ☯ 9am-5pm) Smaller than the visitors center, but equally informative.

Hood River Wine & Internet Bar (☎ 541-386-3239; www.thewinebar.com; 106 3rd St; per hr $5; ☯ 4-11pm Mon-Thu, 2-11pm Fri & Sat, 2-8pm Sun, closed Sun & Mon in winter) Sip a local pinot while surfing the Web.

Visitors center (☎ 541-386-2000, 800-366-3530; www.hoodriver.org; 405 Portway Ave; ☯ 9am-5pm Mon-Fri, plus 10am-5pm Sat & Sun Apr-Oct) Adjacent to the Expo Center, across I-84 from the city center.

Sleeping

Bingen School Inn (☎ 509-493-3363; www.bsi-cgoc.com; cnr Cedar & Humbolt Sts; dm/d $16/40; ⓟ ⊠) Across the Columbia in Bingen, Washington, this former schoolhouse has bunk beds and private rooms in wooden classrooms. It's popular with windsurfers and other adventurers, and with local school groups. Shoot some hoops in the old gym and enjoy an organic salad ($1) from the garden.

Lone Pine Motel (☎ 541-387-8882; 2429 Cascade Ave; r $25-60) Area hotels can be pricey, but this motel is good value.

Campgrounds are the cheapest accommodations around, and all the following choices are good.

Tucker Park (☎ 541-386-4477; Tucker Rd/Hwy 281; campsites/RV $13/14) Newly renovated and 5 miles south of town.

SCENIC DRIVE: HISTORIC COLUMBIA RIVER HWY (HWY 30)

The first paved road in the Northwest (opened 1915) and America's first scenic highway, this lushly forested, winding route between Troutdale and The Dalles wows all who drive it. Between breathtaking vistas of the Columbia River are parking lots for the gorge's most visited state parks, waterfalls and hiking trails. If you just gawk and don't stop much, the drive can be as brief as an hour. But don't cheat yourself – take the time to marvel.

Famous as the western entry to the gorge, the **Vista House at Crown Point** (☎ 503-695-2230; admission free; ☽ 9am-6pm) is an interpretive center perched atop a craggy cliff of basalt offering dramatic views.

Heading east, some of the gorge's most popular trails begin at cascading **Wahkeena Falls**. Next, ogle the 642ft, two-tiered **Multnomah Falls** (the second-highest non-seasonal falls in the USA) and hike the steep 1-mile switchback trail to the top. The **Forest Service visitors center** (☎ 503-695-2372; ☽ 9am-5pm) here is a good place to get information – including the invaluable *Hiking the Columbia River Gorge* – on other gorge hikes.

Continue east to **Horsetail Falls**, whose easy 2.6-mile roundtrip trail leads behind smaller Ponytail Falls and through quiet Oneonta Gorge. Then drive on to Yeon State Park, home to stunning **Elowah Falls** (despite freeway and train noise); access is via a 0.8-mile trail with some steep switchbacks. Past **Bonneville Dam** (☎ 541-374-8820; ☽ 7am-5pm), with its informative visitor center and fish ladders, is **Wahclella Falls**, maybe not the most famous but maybe the most spectacular waterfall in the gorge. The easy 2-mile loop trail leads past delicate East Fork

---

Viento State Park (☎ 541-374-8811, reservations 800-452-5687; I-84 exit 56; campsites/RV $14/16) Popular with windsurfers, this is 8 miles west of town.

Toll Bridge County Park (☎ 541-352-5522; Hwy 35; campsites/RV $13/15) Woodsy, quiet with private sites and hot showers; 17 miles west of town.

Eating & Drinking

Hood River dining is culinary joy and not particularly inexpensive – a dream!

Holstein's Coffee Co (☎ 541-386-4115; 12 Oak Ave; sandwiches $3-6) Great coffee and sandwiches.

Bette's (☎ 541-386-1880; 416 Oak St; mains $5-8) The best meal deals are here, where windsurfers and old-timers hunker down over breakfast.

SPLURGE!

6th St Bistro & Loft (☎ 541-386-5737; 509 Cascade Ave; mains $12-18) Treat yourself to a meal at Hood River's best restaurant, which strives to use only local ingredients (and organic ones whenever possible). The result is amazing, super-fresh creations – try the always-incredible specials – served by excellent, jovial staff. The small bar is the perfect place to wait for an outside table, which you'll undoubtedly have to do.

Andrew's Pizza (☎ 541-386-1448; 107 Oak St; pizzas $12.50-22) Grab a salad-and-slice lunch for $5.25.

Hood River City Market (☎ 541-386-9876; 406 Oak St; half/whole sandwiches $3.50/6) For gourmet self-catering provisions and sandwiches.

Full Sail Brewery (☎ 541-386-2247; 506 Columbia St; burgers $5-6) This stellar brewery has a tasting room with a small pub menu – skip the snacks and just drink. Award-winning and lesser-known brews are on tap, and they're all tasty. Free 20-minute brewery tours leave on the hour from 1pm to 4pm daily.

Getting There & Around

Greyhound runs between Hood River and Portland four times daily. Amtrak's on the Washington side, in Bingen (two trains daily).

If you're driving from Washington, cross the river via the 75¢ Hood River Toll Bridge, in White Salmon. From Portland, follow I-84 or the Columbia River Hwy (see above); from the south, picturesque Hwy 35 is dotted with sno-parks (cross-country ski areas) and fruit farms. Parking is ample in town but standoffs for spots happen in summer.

MT HOOD

The state's highest peak at 11,240ft, majestic Mt Hood is visible on a sunny day from much of northern Oregon. It is accessible

Falls, and offers a true sense of the gorge and her waterfalls. Beyond Hood River is **Rowena Crest**, offering spectacular bidirectional views and vast meadows now preserved as a wildflower sanctuary; come in springtime for full-bloom glory. Across the river, go **mushroom- and huckleberry-picking** in White Salmon.

After cruising the sights, ditch the car and bike, walk or jog along two stretches of the old highway that have been renovated for nonautomotive use. The western section of the trail runs between Tanner Creek (at the I-84 Bonneville Dam exit) and Eagle Creek; another, longer stretch runs 4.5 miles from Hood River to Mosier.

Accommodations along and around the highway include the following (also see p543):

■ **McMenamins Edgefield** (☎ 503-669-8610, 800-669-8610; www.mcmenamins.com; 2126 SW Halsey St, Troutdale; dm $20) The old county poor farm now houses some of the best dormitory lodging in the Pacific Northwest. You can eat, drink and sleep at this sprawling complex, which includes the hotel, two restaurants, a vineyard, a brewery, and a movie theatre, all decorated in classic McMenamins style.

■ **Ainsworth State Park** (☎ 503-695-2301, 800-551-6949; campsites/RV $14/16) Three miles east of Multnomah Falls, this roadside campground is noisy. The park offers easy access to Horsetail and Elowah Falls trails.

To reach the Columbia River Hwy from Portland, take exit 17 or 35 off I-84. From Mt Hood, Rte 35 runs right into it. Access is also via three bridges along Washington's Rte 14.

year-round via US 26 from Portland and via scenic Hwy 35 from Hood River; call ☎ 800 977 6368 to check road conditions. Together with the Historic Columbia River Hwy (see left), these routes constitute the **Mt Hood Loop**, one of the supreme scenic-road excursions in the USA.

Barely there **Government Camp**, 56 miles from Portland and 44 miles from Hood River at the pass, has some food and lodging. The **Mt Hood Information Center** (☎ 503-622-4822, 888-622-4822; 65000 E Hwy 26, Welches; ◷ 8am-5pm Mon-Sat, 8am-4pm Sun) is next to Mt Hood Village.

The hype here is about skiing, which is available year-round at majestic Timberline Lodge (see p546). Seasonal **Mt Hood Meadows** (☎ 503-337-2222; www.skihood.com; lift ticket $44), 76 miles from Portland, is the largest ski area on Mt Hood and often has the best conditions. **SkiBowl** (☎ 503-272-3206; www.skibowl.com; lift ticket $32), off US 26 just west of Government Camp, has night skiing and summer mountain biking.

Hiking buffs should get the free USFS pamphlet *Day Hikes Around Mt Hood*, which details 30 hikes, from the visitors center. After Japan's Mt Fuji, Mt Hood is the world's most-climbed peak over 10,000ft, with a typical route from Timberline taking 10 to 12 hours roundtrip (for experienced climbers). Climbing is best from May to mid-July.

Huckleberry Inn (☎ 503-272-3325; 88611 E Government Camp Loop; r from $65) has standard rooms and an adjoining folksy café. There's feverish competition for campsites around Mt Hood; try 27-site **Still Creek** (☎ 503-668-1700, reservations 877-444-6777; campsites $14), 1 mile east of Government Camp on Hwy 26, or the larger postcard-perfect **Trillium Lake** (☎ 503-668-1700, reservations 877-444-6777; campsites $14), 1 mile east of Government Camp off Hwy 26, both of which are at 3600ft and are closed in winter. **Mt Hood Village** (☎ 503-622-4011, 800-255-3069; www.mthoodvillage.com; 65000 E Hwy 26; campsites $34-39) is a huge year-round resort complex near Brightwood, 14 miles from Government Camp.

HELLS CANYON & AROUND

East of the Wallowa Mountains (among Oregon's most beautiful and isolated areas), the earth suddenly gives way to the yawning chasm of **Hells Canyon**, North America's deepest. Wild adventures and an even more dramatic landscape are found here, where the Snake River has been carving out an 8000ft-deep trench for about 13 million years.

Fishing, boating and hiking reign throughout this national recreation area (NRA), and white-water action starts just below Hells Canyon Dam, 28 miles north (downriver) from the small campground community of Copperfield, a nexus of activity on the

SPLURGE!

A mammoth-timber and native-stone masterpiece of the Works Progress Administration (WPA) era, the 1937 **Timberline Lodge** (☎ 503-231-5400, 800-547-1406; www.timberlinelodge.com; P ☒ ☒ ☐ ☒) was built and decorated in grand rustic style as a hotel, ski resort and restaurant. Over 500 workers were employed to build the edifice, and for many of them Timberline was more than a job – it was an expression of cultural ideal, fostering pride in their work and capturing the 'mystic strength that lives in the hills.'

Now also a National Historic Landmark, Timberline offers luxurious accommodations at 6000ft, halfway to the summit of Mt Hood. Rooms start at $125, and dormitory accommodations are available for $85 for two people, then $25 per additional person in the room. Dorm rooms sleep two to 10, totaling 46 dorm beds. Reservations are encouraged.

Even if you don't stay, admire the 92ft central fireplace, sip a hot chocolate on the mezzanine and revel in this magnificent old building's history. Or spend a blustery winter day or warm summer night at Timberline's **ski area** (☎ 503-622-0717; lift ticket $39), which is renowned for being open year-round. Ski teams and snowboarders flock here for summer training.

Shining fans, don't expect a hedge maze: only the front exterior of the lodge was used in Stephen King's classic horror film. However, it's still chilling to walk by 'redrum' room No 217, named in the book – which Timberline owners successfully entreated director Stanley Kubrick to change to nonexistent room No 237 for the film.

Timberline looms 7.5 miles north of Government Camp, off US 26, at the end of Timberline Rd.

river. Contact **Hells Canyon Adventures** (☎ 541-785-3352, 800-422-3568; www.hellscanyonadventures.com; 4200 Hells Canyon Dam Rd, Oxbow) for popular and noisy jet-boat tours (from $32) or pricier rafting trips ($160). For perspective, drive up to the spectacular lookout at **Hat Point** (USFS Rd 4240), 23 miles from Imnaha, with dramatic views of the gorge and surrounding mountains. The road is open from late May until snowfall; allow two hours and call ☎ 541-426-5546 first for conditions.

The Hells Canyon NRA spans the Idaho–Oregon state line, but the Oregon section is not readily accessible from Idaho. US 95 parallels its eastern boundary; a few unpaved roads lead from US 95 between the tiny towns of Riggins (a big rafting center) and White Bird into the NRA. Only one road leads from US 95 to the Snake River itself, at Pittsburg Landing.

Travelers with time (and high-clearance vehicles) can drive to the canyon rim on unpaved roads for dramatic views: Idaho's USFS Rd 517 (open July to October), 0.25 miles south of the Hells Canyon Riggins office, climbs 17 miles to the rim and ends 2 miles later at the breathtaking **Heaven's Gate Lookout**.

Serving both areas, the **Wallowa Mountains Visitor Center** (☎ 541-426-5546; 88401 Hwy 82, Enterprise; ☼ 8am-5pm Mon-Sat, noon-5pm Sun in summer) has good trail maps, camping information, and

backcountry hiking tips. In Idaho, the **Hells Canyon NRA Riggins** (☎ 208-628-3916; US 95; ☼ 8am-5pm Mon-Fri) has similar services. **Copperfield Park Campground** (☎ 541-785-3323; www.idahopower.com/riversreccopperfield.htm; Hwy 86; campsites/RV $6/10), just below Oxbow Dam at the beginning of Hells Canyon, has 62 riverside campsites. Or stay in Joseph at the often-full **Indian Lodge Motel** (☎ 541-432-2651, 888-286-5484; 201 S Main; s/d $40/53).

CENTRAL OREGON

EUGENE

Eugene's vibrancy and mellowness lie in the shade of every tree, of which there are a delicious number. Both a studious college town and a hotbed of countercultural activity, Eugene has birthed establishments as disparate as alternative hippie communes and Nike. Former radicals own many of the city's businesses, and environmental activism is *de rigueur* among the students here.

Information

Convention & Visitors Association of Lane County (☎ 541-484-5307, 800-547-5445; www.cvalco.org; 115 W 8th Ave, Ste 190; ☼ 8am-5pm Mon-Fri) For brochures and maps galore.

Eugene Public Library (☎ 541-682-5450; 100 W 10th Ave; www.ci.Eugene.or.us/library; ☼ 10am-8pm

Mon-Thu, 10am-6pm Fri-Sun) Internet access is free for 15 minutes (or an hour if you stop at reception first and smile).

Sip & Surf Cybercafé (☎ 541-343-9607; 99 W 10th Ave; per hr $6; ⊙ 7:30am-6pm Mon-Fri, noon-5pm Sat) Across the street from the library, drop $1 for a cuppa and 15 minutes of computer time.

Sights & Activities

Meandering through Eugene's dynamic neighborhoods, such as the anarchistic/artistic/punk-rock **Whiteaker district** or the **University of Oregon** area (namely student-infested 13th Ave), can be wildly entertaining. For concentrated commerciality, **Fifth St Public Market** (E 5th Ave btwn Pearl & High Sts) is the heart of a small but lively shopping and café area. The famous waffle iron used to make the first Nike soles is displayed at the **Nike Factory Store** (☎ 541-342-5155; 296 E 5th Ave). Hippies and yuppies converge at the colorful **Saturday Market** (⊙ 9am-4pm Apr-Oct) to procure everything from organic produce to homemade crafts.

Housed in a replica of a Native American longhouse, the university's newly expanded **Museum of Natural & Cultural History** (☎ 541-346-3024; http://natural-history.uoregon.edu/Pages/home.html; 1680 E 15th Ave; admission $2; ⊙ noon-5pm Wed-Sun) highlights Oregon's geological, natural and cultural history – and the country's oldest pair of shoes.

In spring, lose yourself in the blooming beauty of the aromatic **Owen Rose Garden** (☎ 541-687-5347) and the paradisaical **Hendricks Park Rhododendron Garden** (☎ 541-682-5324), both free. Year-round, extensive paths along the Willamette and in Alton Baker Park are great for **biking**. At sunset, climb or drive atop **Skinner Butte** for nice views.

The **Oregon Country Fair** (☎ 541-343-4298; Jul) is a riotous three-day celebration of Eugene's folksy, hippie past and present. It's held on a farm 13 miles west of Eugene, near Veneta.

About 55 miles east of Eugene is tranquil **Cougar Hot Springs** (Terwilliger Hot Springs; Rte 126). Take Rte 162 toward Bend, turn right at Rd 19, drive 8 miles and park in the lot on the left. The 0.25-mile trailhead is across the street along the guardrail. Alternatively, take bus No 91 ($2.50 roundtrip).

Sleeping

Eugene International Hostel (☎ 541-349-0589; eugenehostel@hotmail.com; 2352 Willamette St; dm/s/d $19/30/40; ⊙ closed 11am-5pm) Super-friendly and nearly as tidy, this extremely casual hostel has dorms and one private room inside, and plenty of yard space for lolling around. The kitchen is vegetarian-only, and there's a wonderful health food market right down the street. Be sure to give Celie, the hostel dog, lots of love. Reservations are recommended in summer, especially for the private room. There is talk of moving to a new location, so call ahead.

Downtown Motel (☎ 541-345-8739, 800-648-4366; 361 W 7th Ave; s/d $35/40) A great bargain, the Downtown is much nicer than you might think at first glance, with spacious rooms, helpful staff, and a good location.

Options, other than the hostel, are a bit out of town:

Eugene Kamping World (☎ 541-343-4832, 800-343-3008; 90932 S Stuart Way; campsites/RV $15/23) Six miles north of Eugene in Coburg, off I-5's exit 199.

Richardson Park Campground (☎ 541-935-2005; Richardson Park Rd; campsites $20) On the Fern Ridge Reservoir, 16 miles west of Eugene.

Eating & Drinking

The cheapest eats can be found along 13th Ave by the university (between Kincaid and Alder), including popular **Glenwood Campus Cafe** (☎ 541-687-0355; 1340 Alder; mains $4.45-8.50). But generally, better meals are elsewhere.

Sundance (☎ 541-343-9142; 748 E 24th Ave; ⊙ until 11pm) Of Eugene's several natural foods markets, Sundance is the preferred destination – after all, it has a bulk foods map!

Red Barn (☎ 541-342-7503; 357 Van Buren; ⊙ until 10pm) Red Barn is comparable to Sundance but in the slightly grittier Whiteaker neighborhood (and no bulk foods map).

Morning Glory Cafe (☎ 541-687-0709; 450 Willamette St; mains $4.25-9) Local and culinary flavors abound at this revered vegan-friendly place.

Keystone Cafe (☎ 541-342-2075; 395 W 5th Ave; mains $3.75-7.25) The owners of Morning Glory recently bought this greasier Eugene-staple that also features some vegan options.

Studio One (☎ 541-342-8596; 1473 E 19th Ave) Giant plates of French toast ($7) are king here; try to get a table outside.

Toshi's Ramen (☎ 541-683-7833; 1520 Pearl St; ⊙ closed 3rd Sat of the month; soups $4-8) Noodle buffs flock here for generous bowls of homemade noodles, veggies, and marinated pork (optional) in choose-your-favorite broth.

Café Yumm (☎ 541-484-7302; 296 E 5th Ave; mains $3.50-6.25) Serves satisfying rice bowls and wraps in the 5th St Public Market, home to other eateries and an enticing bakery. There are other branches at the **Meridian** (☎ 541-431-0204; 1801 Willamette St) and the **Oakway Center** (☎ 541-225-0120; Oakway & Cuburg Rds).

Sam Bond's Garage (☎ 541-431-6603; 407 Blair Blvd; mains $6-8) In the Whiteaker district, this hip place serves great vegetarian fare.

Cafe Paradiso (☎ 541-484-9933; 115 W Broadway; mains $3.75-6) Home to Eugene's longest-running open-mic night (8pm Tuesday). Paradiso has good coffee, sandwiches and pasta.

Max's Tavern (☎ 541-349-8986; 550 E 13th Ave) College-dive-bar pouring cheap beer (in 32oz mugs!); *Simpsons* fans may recognize Max's as the inspiration for Moe's.

Getting There & Around

Getting in and out of Eugene is a cinch thanks to **Amtrak** (☎ 541-687-1383; cnr E 4th Ave & Willamette St), which runs trains and Thruway buses to regional destinations, and **Greyhound** (☎ 541-344-6265; 987 Pearl St).

Lane Transit District (☎ 541-687-5555; www.ltd.org) bus routes are extensive; No 91 bus hauls all the way out to McKenzie Bridge, the gateway to the spectacular Willamette National Forest and popular Cougar Hot Springs (p547). In town, stroll or rent bikes from **Paul's Bicycle Way of Life** (☎ 541-344-4105; www.bicycleway.com; 152 W 5th Ave; day/overnight $18/25; ☺ 9am-7pm Mon-Fri, 10am-5pm Sat & Sun).

BEND & MT BACHELOR

Bend, growing seemingly larger every day, teems with triathletes and nature lovers thanks to its backyard of sheer outdoor adventure. Don't let stripmall-heavy Hwy 97 fool you: quaint if not ritzy downtown is lined with pleasant cafés, shops and bars, and lovely **Drake Park** is perfect for people-watching. The large **visitors center** (☎ 541-382-8048; www.visitbend.com; 63085 N US 97; ☺ 9am-5pm Mon-Sat) has a fabulous map of Oregon campgrounds. It's for reference only (not for sale), but it's invaluable for planning the rest of your impromptu camping trip.

Perhaps the state's best museum, Bend's **High Desert Museum** (☎ 541-382-4754; www.high desert.org; 59800 S Hwy 97; 2-day ticket $12; ☺ 9am-5pm) has impeccable exhibits on early cultural life and the fascinating natural history of the High Desert. Get an up-close glimpse of the famous spotted owl at the raptor center.

Lava Lands Visitor Center (☎ 541-593-2421; admission free; ☺ 9am-5pm May-Sep), on US 97 about 11 miles south of Bend, has exhibits revealing the geology, wildlife and archeology of the **Newberry National Volcanic Monument**. Nearby Lava Butte rises 500ft above the surrounding lava flows.

Twenty-two miles southwest of Bend, 9065ft **Mt Bachelor** (☎ 541-382-2442, 800-829-2442; www.mtbachelor.com; lift ticket $44; ☺ 9am-4pm Mon-Fri, 8am-4pm Sat & Sun) has Oregon's best skiing, with 3100ft of vertical and more than 300 inches of snow per year; it's known for fine dry powder. The season begins in November and can last until June.

Sleeping

Central Oregon Reservation Center (☎ 541-382-8334; ☺ 8am-5pm Mon-Fri) can help with accommodations. There's a motel strip along US 97 (here called 3rd St).

Chalet Motel (☎ 541-382-6124; 510 SE 3rd St; s/d from $30/35; P ✗ ✗) For some of the best rates in town, you get clean rooms and friendly staff, although it's nothing at all fancy.

Rainbow Motel (☎ 541-382-1821; 154 NE Franklin; s/d from $35/40; P ✗ ✗) For a few dollars more that the Chalet, you still don't get fancy, but you get a microwave in your room and the warm hospitality of the family who runs the place.

Eating & Drinking

Soba (☎ 541-318-1535; 945 NW Bond St; noodle & rice bowls $4.50-7) Wander along downtown's Wall and Bond Sts for this inexpensive eatery.

Deschutes Brewery & Public House (☎ 541-382-9242; 1044 NW Bond St; mains $4-9) Squeeze into this crowded pub and grab a pint of the signature Mirror Pond Pale Ale or incomparable Black Butte Porter at the bar while you wait for a table.

Getting There & Around

Bend is about 140 miles east of Eugene. Follow Rte 126 to 20 or 242 (closed in winter), or take Amtrak or Greyhound.

The winter-only **Mt Bachelor Shuttle** (☎ 541-382-2442) provides service from Bend for $1 one way.

OREGON COAST

Thanks to a farsighted state government in the 1910s, Oregon's 362-mile Pacific coast was set aside as public land. Today all Oregon beaches are open to the public, even in developed areas. The northern stretch is more resorty, while the south (below Florence) approaches pristine wilderness.

Best budget accommodations are coastal campgrounds, which are abundant. State parks offer some of the most private and scenic sites; see p549; private and USFS campgrounds are listed in appropriate sections.

ASTORIA & AROUND

Astoria, with its seafaring history and scruffy charm, sits at the mouth of the Columbia River, where the 4.1-mile **Astoria Bridge** crosses to Washington. After the Lewis and Clark expedition reached the Pacific and bedded down here for winter, John Jacob Astor and his Pacific Fur Trading Company established a small fort here in 1811, making this the first US settlement west of the Mississippi. Find regional information at the **visitors center** (☎ 503-325-6311; 111 W Marine Dr; ☼ 8am-6pm summer, 9am-5pm winter).

For a loftier history lesson, climb 164-step **Astoria Column** (☎ 503-325-2963; admission free; ☼ dawn-dusk), atop Coxcomb Hill for a 360° view of the lush coastal geography; the monument's painted exterior chronicles the region's past. Learn more about the mighty Columbia at the **Columbia River Maritime Museum** (☎ 503-325-2323; www.crmm.org; 1792 Marine Dr; admission $8; ☼ 9:30am-5pm). Astoria's main drag hosts the surprisingly large **Sunday market** (12th St; ☼ May-Oct), where local vendors sell everything from rainboot planters to deep-fried Twinkies ($3).

For diehard Lewis and Clark fans: reconstructed **Fort Clatsop** (☎ 503-861-2471; admission $3; ☼ 8am-5pm), 8 miles south of Astoria off US 101, is worth a stop. The Lewis and Clark party spent a miserable winter here in 1805–06. Diehard cult-film fans should check out the **Goonies house** (368 38th St), from Spielberg's 1984 pirate-kids movie.

On perpendicular Commercial St, find healthful fare and Internet access at vegetarian **Wombat Moon Café** (☎ 503-338-4490; 1008 Commercial St; per hr $3.60; wraps $5). Nearby **Rusty Cup** (☎ 503-325-8265; 1213 Commercial St; sandwiches $4-6) is good for sandwiches and strong coffee.

Walk around town or ride the **Riverfront Trolley** (☎ 503-325-6311; $1; ☼ daily May-Oct, Sat & Sun

---

CAMPING IN OREGON STATE PARKS

Over 70 coastal state parks along Hwy 101 offer some of the most scenic and private campgrounds in Oregon. Several of these are listed here in north–south order. Low-season rates are campsites/RV/yurt $18/22/29 unless otherwise noted; many parks reward hikers and bikers with $4 sites.

For park information and reservations (some campgrounds are first come first-served), contact **Oregon State Parks** (☎ 503-731-3411, 800-452-5687; www.oregonstateparks.org).

- **Fort Stevens** (☎ 503-861-1671) Ten miles west of Astoria. On Clatsop Spit, close to Hammond beaches; check out photogenic wreck of English sailing ship, *Peter Iredale*.
- **Oswald West** (☎ 503-368-5154; campsites $14) Ten miles south of Cannon Beach. Wheelbarrows are provided for hauling gear to 30 wooded, walk-in campsites. Trails offer beach access.
- **South Beach** (☎ 541-867-4715; site/yurt $22/29) Two miles south of Newport. Beachfront campground features primitive sites 0.25 miles from the ocean ($9).
- **Beverly Beach** (☎ 541-265-9278) Seven miles north of Newport. This is the giant mother of Oregon's state-park campgrounds.
- **Beachside** (☎ 541-563-3220; ☼ Mar-Oct) Five miles south of Yachats. Beach bums love Beachside.
- **Jessie M Honeyman** (☎ 541-997-3641) Three miles south of Florence. Has lake swimming and is convenient for recreation in ODNRA (p551).
- **Umpqua Lighthouse** (☎ 503-271-4118) Six miles south of Reedsport. Has deluxe yurts with TV and fridges ($45).

Nov-Apr). To or from Portland, hop an Amtrak Thruway bus or the new Lewis and Clark Train, which runs along the Columbia during summer only for $29.

Across the river, the **Long Beach Peninsula** claims to have the world's longest beach (28 miles). Fact or fiction, this sandy state highway (yes, really) is beautiful, but watch for pickup trucks. Campgrounds and eateries dot the peninsula.

CANNON BEACH & AROUND

Fronting upscale Cannon Beach are miles of stunning beaches, broken by immense basalt promontories and rocky tide pools. Get a town map at the **visitors center** (☎ 503-436-2623; 2nd St; ☽ 10am-5pm Mon-Sat, 11am-4pm Sun). The souvenir shops along the town's touristy main drag (Hemlock St) are numerous but are hard-pressed to coax visitors off the alluring beach.

Park free at Tolovana Beach (off Warren Way; take the third Cannon Beach exit off Hwy 101) for access to the deservedly much-photographed **Haystack Rock**. On June's renowned Sandcastle Day, teams compete for sand-sculpture originality and execution. North of town, trails in **Ecola State Park** lead through moss-dripping trees to secluded beaches. Dramatic views at photogenic Ecola Point continue along the **Oregon Coast Trail** to Indian Beach (good surfing and primitive hike-in camping), looming Tillamook Head and Seaside.

Stay comfortably at riverfront **Seaside International Hostel** (☎ 503-738-7911; www.2oregonhostels .com; 930 N Holladay Dr; dm/r $16/39; P ⊠ ⛄ ▣), 9 miles north of Cannon Beach. Each meticulous six- or eight-bed dorm has a bathroom, and you can rent kayaks for $9 per two hours. Greyhound stops in front.

Cannon Beach restaurants tend to be upscale. Get sandwiches at **Bill's Tavern** (☎ 503-436-2202; 188 N Hemlock; mains $4-14) or huge slices at **Pizza a Fetta** (☎ 503-436-0333; 231 N Hemlock; slice $2.75-3.25).

NEWPORT

This fabulously scruffy little port town has lively, old-fashioned seafood markets facing Yaquina Bay, some excellent marine-life museums and the picturesque and historic Nye Beach. Get details at the **visitors center** (☎ 541-265-8801, 800-262-7844; 555 SW Coast Hwy; ☽ 8:30am-5pm Mon-Fri, plus 10am-4pm Sat May).

The **Oregon Coast Aquarium** (☎ 541-867-3474; www.aquarium.org; 2820 SE Ferry Slip Rd; admission $10.75; ☽ 10am-5pm Sep-May, 9am-6pm Jun-Aug) has arresting marine exhibits, including an enormous Plexiglas tunnel through a shark tank. Less glamorous, but cheaper and also interesting, is the **Hatfield Marine Science Center** (☎ 541-867-0100; 2030 SE Marine Science Dr; suggested donation $2; ☽ 10am-5pm May-Sep, 10am-4pm Thu-Mon Oct-Apr), with a touch pool.

The **Sylvia Beach Hotel** (☎ 541-265-5428; www .sylviabeachhotel.com; 267 NW Cliff St; dm $27, d incl breakfast $88-173; P ⊠ ⛄) has 12 dorm beds and some private rooms brilliantly decorated after famous writers; the Edgar Allan Poe is inspired, with a raven in the corner and a pendulum swinging over the bed. Drastically plainer **City Center Motel** (☎ 541-265-7381, 800-687-9099; 538 SW Coast Hwy; s/d from $29/39; P ⊠ ⛄) is on stripmalled Hwy 101.

Start your day at the **Coffee House** (☎ 541-265-6263; 156 SW Bay Blvd; mains $2-10; ☽ 8am-4pm), with brewed-to-order coffee and a waterfront deck. Later, slurp clam chowder at **Mo's Annex** (☎ 541-265-7512; www.moschowder.com; 657 SW Bay Blvd; mains $3-11). The **Rogue Ales Brewery** (☎ 541-867-3660; 2320 SW OSU Dr) makes some of the best beers on the planet; try the decadent Chocolate Stout (available only in winter).

YACHATS & AROUND

Volcanic intrusions south of Yachats form some of Oregon's most beautiful shoreline. Surf explodes against the shore to create dramatic effects at **Cape Perpetua**, where visitors can prowl among intertidal rock pools and sandy inlets, or hike or drive 2 miles up to a fantastic viewpoint. Ten miles south of Yachats, the 1894 **Heceta Head Lighthouse** perches above the churning ocean; a trail leads there from enchanting Devil's Elbow State Park. The **Sea Lion Caves** (☎ 541-547-3111; www.sealioncaves.com; 91560 Hwy 101; admission $7.50), filled with glossy Steller sea lions, are a highlight of the central Oregon coast.

Camp at creekside **Cape Perpetua Campground** (☎ 541-547-3289, reservations 877-444-6777; campsites $17), 3 miles south of Yachats, or secluded and woodsy **Rock Creek Campground** (☎ 877-444-6777; Hwy 101; campsites $17), 7 miles further.

Breakfasts rule homey **Joes' Town Center Cafe** (☎ 541-547-4244; W 4th & Hwy 101; mains $2-8.50; ☽ 8am-3pm Thu-Tue). There's also good food at friendly **Drift Inn** (☎ 541-547-4477; 124 Hwy 101; mains $4.50-10), the local watering hole.

OREGON DUNES NATIONAL RECREATION AREA & FLORENCE

Fifty miles of shifting sand between Florence and Coos Bay form the **Oregon Dunes National Recreation Area** (ODNRA), the largest expanse of coastal dunes in the USA. There are established hiking (primarily in the northern section), boating and swimming areas, and the region teems with birds and other wildlife. Unfortunately, dune buggies and dirt bikes scream up and down the dunes, especially the stretch south of Reedsport; be careful out there. Area **headquarters** (☎ 541-271-3611; 855 Highway Ave; ☺ 8am-4:30pm Mon-Fri) is in logged out Reedsport (host to chainsaw-carving championships in June).

USFS campgrounds like **Eel Creek** (☎ 541-759-4462, 800-452-5687; campsites $13), 10 miles south of Reedsport, offer the best dune access.

In Florence, fuel up with brewed-by-the-cup coffee at **Siuslaw River Coffee Roasters** (☎ 541-997-3443; 1240 Bay St). **Beachcomber Tavern** (☎ 541-997-6357; 1355 Bay St; mains $4-12) is the best bet for inexpensive dining.

BANDON

Old Town Bandon is a small nucleus of cafés, gift shops, taverns and a **visitors center** (☎ 541-347-9616; www.bandon.com; 300 2nd St; ☺ 9am-5pm). Beach Loop Dr leads south of town to Bandon's best beaches, with towering seastacks (coastal rock pillars that have resisted the surrounding erosion) and monoliths that host large numbers of seabirds. **Coquille Point**, at the end of 11th St, is a popular place to spot migrating whales in winter and spring.

The central **HI Sea Star Hostel** (☎ 541-347-9632; 375 2nd St; dm $16, r $35-75; P ✕) has an adjoining café, **Stan's Place** (☺ 7am-noon Wed-Sat,

9am-1pm Sun), with heavenly coffee and the greatest breakfast in town. **Table Rock Motel** (☎ 541-347-2700, 800-457-9141; www.tablerockmotel.com; 840 Beach Loop Rd; r from $40), on a shrubby bluff, has rooms and apartment-style quarters with kitchenettes (from $80).

Bandon Channel House (☎ 541-347-9057; 480 1st St SW; lunch $7-13, dinner $15-25) has bay-view dining, but is closed for lunch on Sundays.

GOLD BEACH & BROOKINGS

There's not much to these towns, hovering 33 and 6 miles (respectively) north of the California border, but they offer access to pristine coastline, redwood forest, and the Wild Rogue Wilderness (p552).

From Gold Beach – whose visitors center is at the **Gold Beach Ranger Station** (☎ 541-247-7526, 800-525-2334; www.goldbeach.org; 29279 S Ellensburg Ave; ☺ 9am-5pm Mon-Fri) – zip up the Rogue River with **Jerry's Rogue Jets** (☎ 541-247-4571, 800-451-3645; www.roguejets.com), offering scenic jet-boat trips (from $34). For about the same price you can ride to Agness on a **mail boat hydrojet** (☎ 541-247-7033, 800-458-3511; www.mailboat.com). There are great riverside campgrounds up USFS Rd 33.

The USA's largest Easter lily–bulb producer, charmless Brookings is just minutes from rugged coastline and redwood forest. Consider the **visitors center** (☎ 541-469-3181, 800-535-9469; www.brookingsor.com; 16330 Lower Harbor Rd; ☺ 9am-5pm Mon-Fri), then head inland along the Chetco River to the western edge of remote **Kalmiopsis Wilderness Area**, the state's largest. Oregon's only redwood forests, as well as old growth myrtle, are found here, notably in **Alfred A Loeb State Park** (☎ 541-469-2021, reservations 800-551-6949; N Bank Chetco River Rd; campsite/cabin $12/35), 10 miles east of Brookings. North of town is **Samuel H Boardman State Park**, with over 11 miles of Oregon's most beautiful coastline.

SPLURGE!

Highly respected and wildly popular, the **Oregon Shakespeare Festival** (OSF; www.osfashland.org) has defined Ashland as Oregon's cultural center since 1935. Though the core of OSF's repertoire is Shakespearean and Elizabethan drama, it also features revivals and contemporary theater from around the world. Productions run February through October in three theaters (the outdoor Elizabethan Theatre, the Angus Bowmer Theatre and the intimate New Theatre) and often sell out months in advance. To get last-minute seats – often your only chance – wait at the **box office** (☎ 541-482-4331; 15 S Pioneer St) for unclaimed tickets ($22 to $55), released at 9:30am and 6pm daily (noon for matinees).

SOUTHERN OREGON

ASHLAND

This artsy, granola town, 285 miles south of Portland on I-5, is famed for its Shakespeare fest, yet is attractive nonetheless. Nestled among crafts shops and fancy restaurants are affordable cafés, a lively youth hostel and some bohemian and friendly locals. Get information at the **visitors center** (☎ 541-482-3486; www.ashlandchamber.com; 110 E Main St; ☺ 9am-5pm).

Consider splurging for a Shakespeare Festival ticket while lollygagging in verdant **Lithia Park**, created by San Francisco's Golden Gate Park designer and filled with swans, picnic baskets, concert-goers (in summer) and ice-skaters (in winter). Nearby Mt Ashland (7533ft) offers hiking and mountain biking as well as skiing at **Mt Ashland Ski Resort** (☎ 541-482-2897; www.mtashland.com; lift ticket $34). Rent outdoor gear at **Ashland Mountain Supply** (☎ 541-488-2749; 31 N Main St).

Greyhound passes through at 4pm daily.

Sleeping

Ashland is loaded with quaint Victorian B&Bs, though they're rather expensive and booked solid in summer.

Ashland Hostel (☎ 541-482-9217; www.ashlandhostel.com; 150 N Main St; dm/s $21/50; ☺ 5-10pm; P X 🖳) Convivial Victorian home with a broad front porch, a fireplace in the common room, a spacious kitchen and clean dorms. The location is ace, a few hundred yards from the central Plaza.

Jackson WellSprings (☎ 541-482-3776, in Oregon 800-482-3776; www.wellspringsnet.com; 2253 Hwy 99 N; campsites/RV $14/20) Relaxed camping where you can stagger from your tent into onsite hot springs. A bike path here leads into town and to nearby Medford.

Glenyan Campground (☎ 541-488-1785, 877-453-6926; www.glenyancampground.com; 5310 Hwy 66; campsites/RV $18.50/25) Six miles out of town near Emigrant Lake is pet-friendly Glenyan, which has some shady sites. Reservations are advised.

Eating & Drinking

Ashland has countless eateries, perhaps because it's the only place in Oregon with a restaurant tax (5%).

Evo's (☎ 541-482-2261; 376 E Main St; ☺ 7am-4pm Mon-Fri, 7am-3pm Sat & Sun; 🖳) Killer coffee, organic granola with yogurt and berries ($3), and free Internet access.

Breadboard (☎ 541-488-0295; 744 N Main St; mains $4-8; ☺ 7am-2:30pm) Get something eggier at this local-fave, on the north end of town.

Pilaf (☎ 541-488-7898; 18 Calle Guanajuato; mains $4-8) A lovely vegetarian oasis with a creekside seating.

Black Sheep (☎ 541-482-6414; 51 N Main St; mains $5-15; ☺ 11-1am; X 🖳) For dinner and drinks by the fire, Brit-flavored Black Sheep has surprisingly good pub grub, including untraditional grilled Szechwan tofu ($12).

Ashland Creek Bar & Grill (☎ 541-482-4131; 92½ N Main St; mains $3-7) It's all about the expansive deck, on which you can imbibe to your heart's delight with the locals.

Q's (☎ 541-488-4880; 140 Lithia Way) The college bar scene thrives here with live music on Wednesday.

ROGUE RIVER

Just northwest of Medford, the Wild Rogue Wilderness lives up to its name, with the turbulent Rogue River cutting through 40 miles of untamed, roadless canyon. The area is known for hardcore white-water rafting (classes III-IV+) and long-distance hikes.

Rafting the Rogue here is not for the faint of heart; rapids are serious, and trips can run several days and several hundred dollars. Outfitters in **Grants Pass**, the gateway to Rogue adventure, include **Rogue River Raft Trips** (☎ 541-476-3825, 800-826-1963; www.rogueriverraft.com) and **Rogue Wilderness Inc** (☎ 541-479-9554, 800-336-1647; www.wildrogue.com). These outfitters also offer shorter trips ($50 to $75) to the 'recreational' (read: calmer) section of the Rogue, as does **Noah's River Adventures** (☎ 541-488-2811, 800-858-2811; www.noahsrafting.com; 53 N Main St), in Ashland, who also rafts the rowdy Upper Klamath ($109 to $135).

The 40-mile **Rogue River Trail** was once a supply route from Gold Beach. The full hike takes about five days; day hikers might aim for Whiskey Creek Cabin, a 7-mile round-trip from the Grave Creek trailhead. There are primitive campgrounds along the way.

Greyhound and Amtrak Thruway buses run daily to Portland and elsewhere from the **Grants Pass station** (☎ 541-476-4513; 460 NE Agness Ave).

CRATER LAKE NATIONAL PARK

Eerily symmetrical and uncannily blue, **Crater Lake** is the deepest lake in the USA and Oregon's only national park.

On offer are unbelievable vistas, hiking and cross-country skiing trails, and scenic drives around the 33-mile crater lip. The park's popular south entrance, 90 miles from Ashland, is open year-round, although it can be rough going in winter; chains are advised.

In summer, there's a $10 park-entry fee. For information, contact **park headquarters** (☎ 541-594-3000). Facilities in the park are closed in winter, but cross-country skiers still visit.

Travelers tend to daytrip from Medford, Ashland or Klamath Falls. There are two campgrounds in the park. **Mazama Village** (☎ 541-830-8700; campsites/RV $18/20) has 200 first-come, first-served sites near the park's south entrance. **Lost Creek** (☎ 541-594-3000), southeast of Rim Village, has 16 dusty sites for tents only. For overnight backcountry stays, get a free permit from a visitor center. If park lodging is booked up, try lodges and USFS campgrounds around Union Creek and Prospect, west on Hwy 62.

California

HIGHLIGHTS

- **San Francisco** The planet's most livable city has it all: hip hostels, boho bars and outdoors galore (p593)
- **North Coast** Admire the towering ancient, moody mammoths in Redwood National Park (p628)
- **SoCal beaches** Strap on your skates and surf the electric scene at Venice Beach (p564)
- **Sierra Nevada** Shred, schuss and hike the slopes around sapphire-jewel Lake Tahoe (p617)
- **Off the beaten track** Wander Joshua Tree National Park's surreal Dr Seuss desert of twisted trees, rugged rocks and capricious cacti (p583)
- **Best journey** Serpentine and mythic, epic Hwy 1 winds past many of the Golden State's highlights while tracing the coast (p584)

FAST FACTS

- **Area** 155,959 sq miles (third-largest US state, bigger than Italy or Great Britain)

- **Big cities** Los Angeles (population 3.9 million), San Diego (1.3 million), San Francisco (770,000), Sacramento (440,000)

- **Budget** $25-75 per day

- **Costs:** urban hostel $15-25, theme park admission $45, beaches free

- **Driving times** LA to San Francisco 7 hours on I-5, all day on Hwy 1, San Francisco to Yosemite 3 to 4 hours, LA to Las Vegas 5 to 6 hours

- **Famous for** endless coastline, sunshine, Hollywood, Silicon Valley, gold rush, redwoods, earthquakes, liberal politics, epic national parks, amusement parks

- **Languages** English, Spanish, Españglish, many Asian dialects

- **Population** 35.6 million (2002 estimate), 50 million (projected 2025)

- **Phrases** *killer, bitchin', stylin'* (really good), *bunk, nappy* (really bad), *gnarly* (extreme), *hella* (very)

- **Seasons** high season is Jun-Sep, shoulder is Apr-May and Oct-Nov; weather is sunny year-round

- **Tasty treats** organic farm-stand fruit, microbrew and wine tasting, fresh seafood, artisan breads and cheeses, boffo burritos, fish tacos, creative vegan cuisine

- **Time** Pacific Standard Time (PST); GMT minus 8 hours (daylight-saving time observed)

- **Top hostels** Pigeon Point Lighthouse (p592), Pescadero and HI Redwood National Park Hostel (p629), North Coast

---

TRAVEL HINTS

Scan hostel notice boards for lifts along the coast, or consider renting or buying a bomb. Camp for free in national forests, then splurge in cities. Don't forget your bathing suit.

California defines cutting edge. Most people have a preconception of the fantasyland that's given the world snowboards, mountain biking, frozen health-food pizzas, psychedelic rock, hand-held computers, cryogenics, kite surfing and Governor Arnold Schwarzenegger. California is all that, and more.

American dreamers have long found the Left Coast to be a fertile, free-thinking enough place to embrace techies, hippies, religious cults, surf goddesses, diehard environmentalists, world-class winemakers, defense industry bigwigs and biotech wizards.

The USA's most populous state is also its most diverse: over a quarter of residents are foreign-born, accounting for nearly a third of the nation's immigrants. California's economy would rank sixth in the world if it were a nation. It's the home of Hollywood – the arbiter of American pop culture – and a bottomless well of invention, spawning everything from Mickey Mouse to the Macintosh computer.

For the shoestring traveler, all this might mean little if California weren't a land of unparalleled natural beauty. The Pacific Coast, the nonnegotiable edge of westward migration, is by turns dramatically rugged and soporifically mild. The state has ancient forests to dwarf your imagination, as well as granite mountains and brutal, awesome deserts.

By all means, go west. You just might end up staying for good.

HISTORY

The Spanish, who conquered Mexico in the early 1500s, explored California through the 1540s in search of a fabled 'city of gold,' but left empty-handed. It wasn't until the Mission period (1769–1810) that Spain launched a serious settlement attempt by establishing 21 Catholic missions and several military forts (presidios) to defend against Russian and British interests.

Mexican rule over California ended with defeat in the 1841–45 Mexican–American War. The US took possession of California and the Southwest with the signing of the 1848 Treaty of Guadalupe Hidalgo; tough for Mexico, gold was discovered in northern California almost simultaneously. With the gold rush drawing people from around the globe, California's population exploded from 14,000 to 90,000 by the end of 1849. Wealth and lawlessness combined most famously in San Francisco, a hotbed of gambling and prostitution. In 1850, California was admitted to the USA as a non-slave state.

In the mid-19th century, the building of the transcontinental railroad (the eastern terminus of which was Sacramento) led to the arrival of 15,000 Chinese laborers, who suffered under a wave of anti-Chinese legislation once the railroad was completed in 1869.

Despite the devastating 1906 San Francisco earthquake, the 20th century resulted in exponential growth for California. Mexican immigrants arrived during the 1910–21 Mexican Revolution; families from Oklahoma fleeing the Dust Bowl came in the 1930s. During WWII, African Americans came to fill jobs for the war effort, while resurfaced anti-Asian sentiments lead to internment of Japanese Americans.

Since the 1930s Hollywood has mesmerized the world with its dreams and fashions, while San Francisco reacts against the banal complacency of suburbia. The 1950s Beat literary movement mushroomed there, as did 1960s hippie counterculture, and then the Gay Pride movement of the 1970s and 1980s. The Internet revolution, driven by Silicon Valley high-tech giants, rewired the country and culminated in a 1990s gold rush in overspeculated stocks.

While that bubble popped in the early 21st century, unprecedented state deficits rolled back jobs and income. In 2003

THE BIG ISSUE – THE GOVERNATOR

In a bizarre and historic 2003 recall election, Californians voted in Arnold Schwarzenegger as governor. A former body builder and silver-screen action hero from Graz, Austria, Schwarzenegger won the contest that terminated former governor Gray Davis. In addition to politicians and lawyers, the star-studded recall ballot included child actor Gary Coleman (from the TV series *Different Strokes*), porn publisher Larry Flint, and voluptuous billboard model Angelyne. Arnold, a moderate Republican, is well-liked in the state, and obviously takes the job seriously: he commutes from his LA home to the state capital, Sacramento, every week.

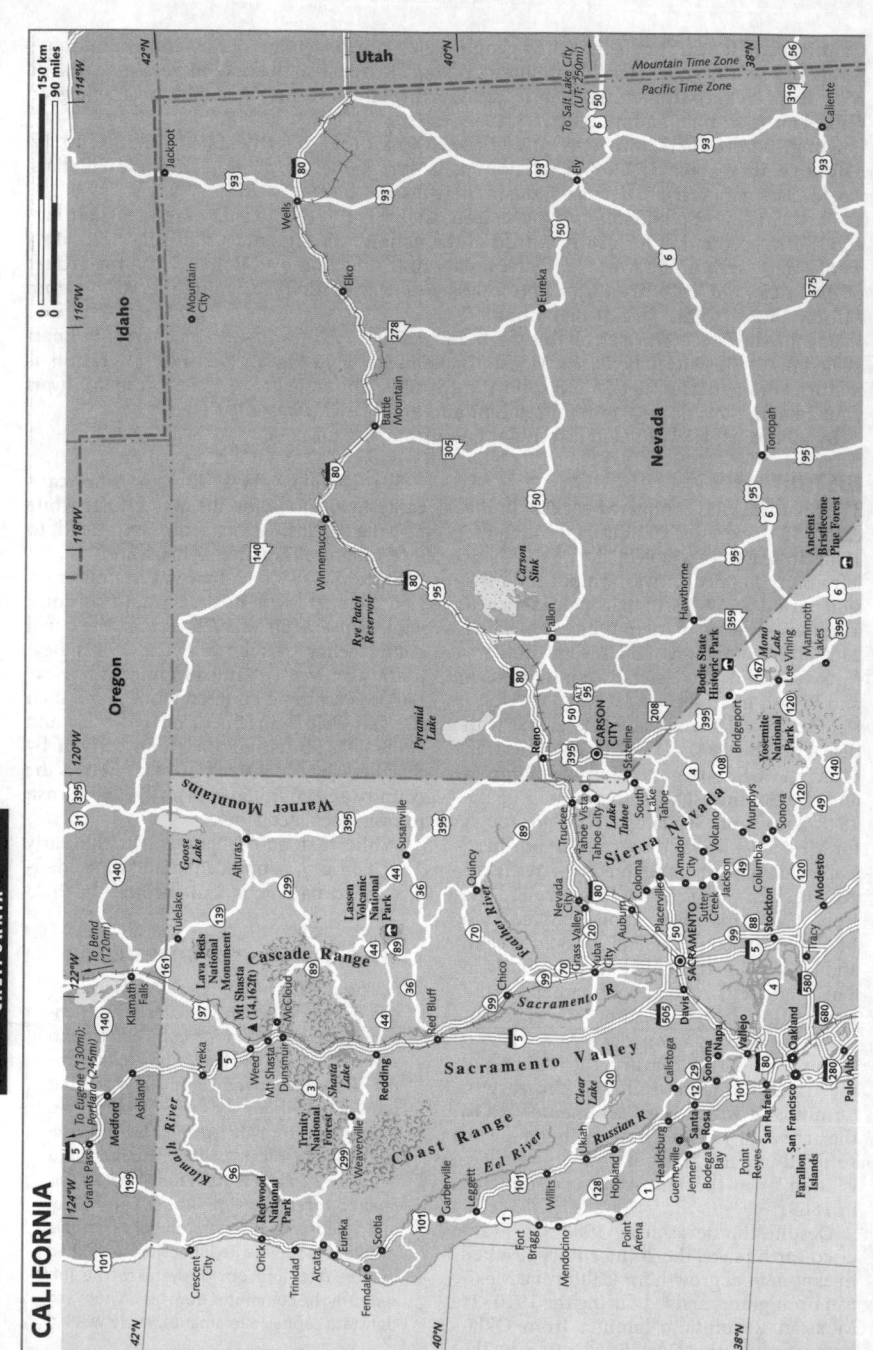

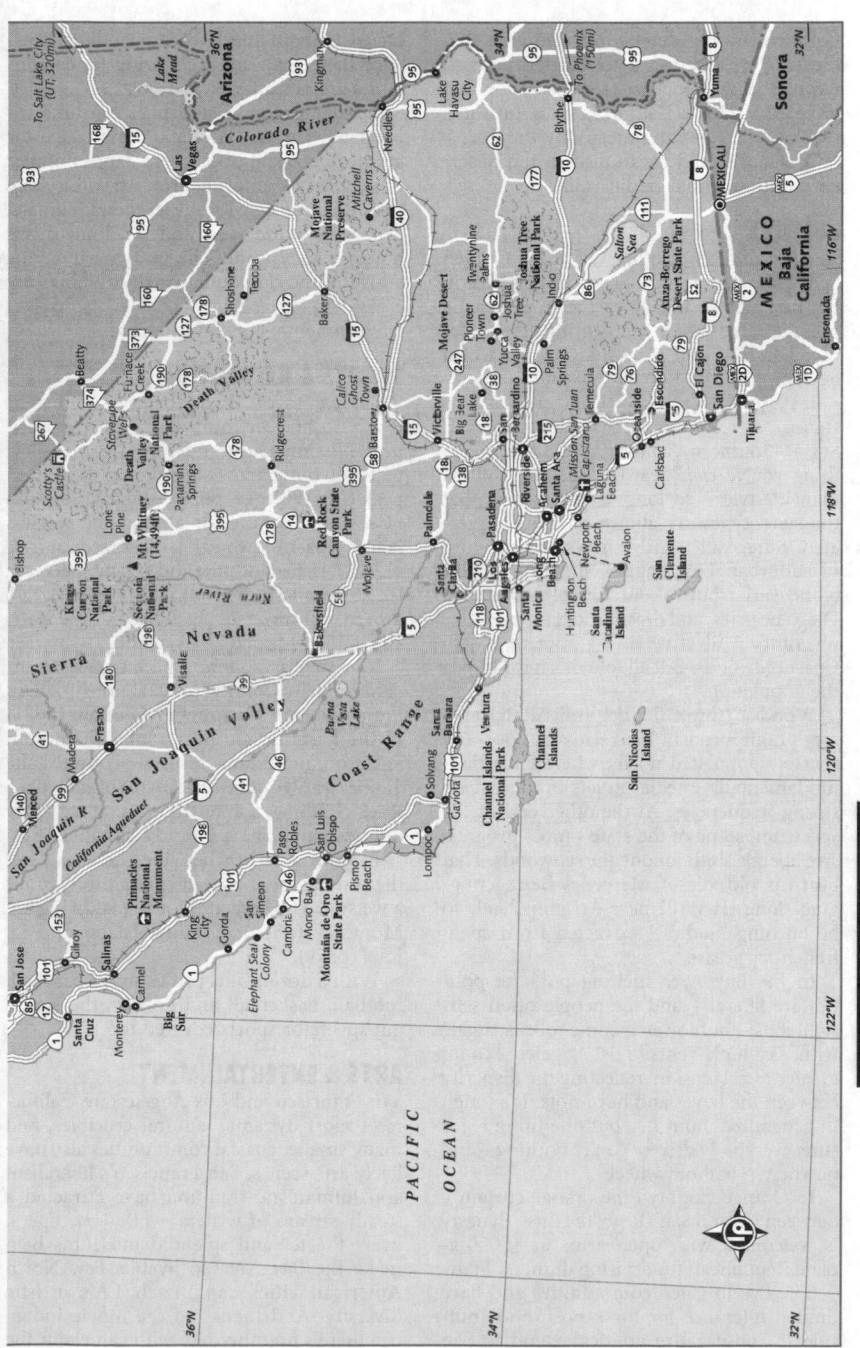

Californians registered their growing displeasure by electing actor-turned-politico Arnold Schwarzenegger (see the boxed text on p555). That's California in a nutshell: revolutionary one minute, loony the next – only a fool would try to discern the difference until the final credits roll.

CULTURE

The rest of the world marvels at the Golden State, never quite sure how to categorize it. It's best not to try, since the hyperkinetic populace is forever reinventing itself. Remember: this is the place that gave the world both hippies *and* Ronald Reagan.

It's useful to think of California as two states: NorCal (Northern California) and SoCal (Southern California). Believe everything you've ever heard about the Californian lifestyle – so long as you realize that the stereotypes are almost always exaggerated. Sure, valley girls snap chewing gum in suburban Los Angeles shopping malls, blond surfer boys shout 'Dude!' across San Diego beaches, and dreadlocked hippies toke on joints while tree-sitting ancient North Coast redwoods. But all told, it's hard to peg the population.

Woodsy (think flannel and mesh caps) types homestead in the relatively poor and sparsely populated north, where Christian-fundamentalist media outlets broadcast on strong frequencies. At the other end of the spectrum, some of the state's most progressive liberals abide among the redwoods. That beat-up old diesel Mercedes-Benz chugging along Hwy 101 near Arcata is likely to be burning biodiesel extracted from spent french-fry grease.

In the Bay Area melting pot, the politics are liberal – and the people often self-righteous – but lower-income folks struggle with sky-high rents. Los Angeles exudes greater racial tension, reflecting the disparity between the haves and have-nots. It's tough to generalize about LA, but one thing is for sure: everybody drives. You're nothing – and nowhere – without wheels.

In Orange County ('the orange curtain'), between LA and San Diego, the Bush dynasty is welcomed with open arms at $5000-a-plate Republican fundraising dinners. Many people live in gated communities and have limited tolerance for (or exposure to) outsiders. Conservative politics extend to San Diego, perhaps due to the large military presence there. Extreme right-wing fundamentalists are not unknown.

Residents along California's coastline appreciate what they have and don't take it for granted; probably because a large number of people in California grew up somewhere else and came here for the temperate climate, expansive world view and freedom to live however they want. The unifying theme is a love of the outdoors, which explains why a majority of residents consider themselves environmental conservationists.

SPORTS & RECREATION

What can't you do in balmy California? Ready to hike or camp out? You can do it in the nation's hottest desert (Death Valley; p584); in the shadow of the Lower 48's tallest peak (Mt Whitney; p621); along 1100 miles of scenic coastline; or among the world's tallest (coast redwood), largest (sequoia) or oldest (bristlecone pine) trees. The spectacular 2638-mile **Pacific Crest Trail** (☎ 916-349-2109; www.pcta.org) traverses the length of the state, en route to Mexico and Canada.

The state's mountain-biking meccas include Marin County (p608), north of San Francisco, and Mammoth Mountain (p621) in the Eastern Sierra. In winter Mammoth and the mountain resorts around Lake Tahoe (p617) offer endless acres of snowplay. Rock climbing, fishing and rafting are other quintessential Sierra Nevada activities.

Famous surf beaches line the coast, but the water is usually cold enough to warrant a wetsuit. The best sites for scuba diving are Monterey (p589), Catalina Island and La Jolla (p579).

With a dozen-plus pro teams in baseball, football, basketball and hockey, the state's got spectator sports covered too.

ARTS & ENTERTAINMENT

San Francisco and Los Angeles are California's most dynamic cultural crucibles, and many smaller coastal communities also have lively arts scenes. San Francisco's liberalism and humanistic tradition have attracted a steady stream of writers, while jazz, opera, lively theater and splendid museums help make the Bay Area so livable. Few North American cities can match LA's artistic diversity. And thanks to the movie industry, there's no other city who can claim the cultural influence – both high and low – that Hollywood exports worldwide.

Rock or rap, rhythm and blues or Mexican ranchero, odds are good that those brand-spankin'-new recording artists on *MTV* kick it in California. In the realms of architecture and visual arts, the state excels again. From Frank Lloyd Wright to Frank Gehry, roller coasters to radical dwellings, the coast is full of constructions and contraptions that epitomize the state's reputation as a mecca for artists and dreamers.

ENVIRONMENT

California's development has often come at the expense of the environment, but the news isn't all bad. Californians are acutely environmentally aware: come prepared to recycle *everything*, and to answer 'Paper or plastic?' at the store as if your life depended on it.

Along the coast, air pollution isn't stifling, thanks to the prevailing westerly ocean breezes. But travel inland, particularly in the LA Basin, and the air takes on a thick haze, obscuring vistas and creating health hazards. Fortunately, California leads the nation in emissions controls.

Of equal concern is water. There never seems to be enough to quench the thirst of every lawn, orchard and fountain. Most precipitation comes from the Sierra Nevada. If it rains little in the Sierra – or doesn't snow at all – there's nothing to melt into the reservoirs that feed inland farms and coastal cities. Fortunately, folks have learned to conserve. And you will too: don't bitch about that low-flow showerhead.

Every season has its charms in the north and eastern mountain regions, although winter snows can close certain roads through May. The deserts are best in early spring, when wildflowers are blooming. Along the coast, summer temperatures never get really hot, especially in foggy northern California, and winters are mild but wet. This changes dramatically inland, where the valleys become frying pans from June to August. For Southern California beaches, come in May to October. The best time to visit northern California is September to October, when summer fog gives way to the warmest days.

Coastal wildlife aplenty means elephant and harbor seals, sea lions and sea otters, migrating gray whales, dolphins and

---

TOP 10 CALIFORNIA STATE PARKS

The following would merit national park status in most other states. See www.parks.ca.gov for a map, park guide and reservation information.

- **Prairie Creek Redwoods**, North Coast (p628) An uncrowded alternative to Redwood National Park, with miles of wild, untouched coastline, spectacular hiking, great camping and resident elk herds.
- **Hearst Castle**, Central Coast (p588) An extraordinary monument to wealth and ambition, overlooking the Pacific Ocean.
- **Año Nuevo**, Central Coast (p592) Book well ahead to experience the mid-winter breeding season at this entertaining elephant seal colony.
- **Julia Pfeiffer Burns**, Big Sur (p589) Enjoy an easy hike to the Golden State's only coastal waterfall, then let the sound of the waves lull you to sleep in your tent.
- **Calaveras Big Trees State Park**, Sierra Nevada (p615) Giant sequoias and abundant conifer forests.
- **Emerald Bay**, Lake Tahoe (p617) Hiking, camping and emerald waters.
- **Santa Cruz State Beaches**, Central Coast (p591) Sand, sun, surf. These scenic stretches of coastline have it all – except warm water.
- **Mono Lake**, Sierra Nevada (p620) An Ice Age remnant formed more than 700,000 years ago.
- **Anza-Borrego Desert State Park**, Southern California (p583) Vast swathe of desert that's a more accessible alternative to Death Valley and an ideal winter camping getaway.
- **Mt Tamalpais**, San Francisco Bay Area (p609) 6300 acres of redwood groves and oak woodlands with a spectacular view from the 2571ft peak.

CALIFORNIA

porpoises. In the sky, look for gigantic California condors, migrating monarch butterflies and millions of seabirds. In the mountains, you'll walk in beauty among mule deer, bighorn sheep and black bears. Elusive desert wildlife includes roadrunners, sloth-like tortoises, foxes, wily coyotes and bobcats.

National & State Parks

A huge chunk of California is protected in seven national parks, plus 16 other areas managed by the National Park Service, and 266 state parks. For details, contact the following agencies:

California State Parks (☎ 916-653-6995, 800-777-0369; www.parks.ca.gov)

California State Park Camping Reservations (☎ 916-638-5883, 800-444-7275; www.reserve america.com)

National Park Camping Reservations (☎ 800-365-2267; http://reservations.nps.gov) Yosemite (p613) has a different reservation number.

TRANSPORTATION

Los Angeles and San Francisco have major international airports. No-frills airlines run frequent cheap regional flights.

Greyhound (☎ 800-231-2222; www.greyhound.com) reaches most major towns in California and **Green Tortoise** (☎ 800-867-8647; www.greentortoise .com) budget bus adventures for independent travelers depart from LA and from San Francisco.

National and local agencies in Los Angeles, San Diego and San Francisco are the best places to rent wheels. Rideboards are prevalent but hitchhiking is hit-or-miss. An independent form of locomotion is handy for touring iconic highlights such as Hwys 1 and 395, which are infrequently served by public transit.

Four Amtrak train routes link California with the rest of the USA. For Mexico border crossing tips, see (p704).

LOS ANGELES

One of the world's most complex, intriguing cities, Los Angeles both equals and transcends its clichés. For sure, cruising Sunset Strip with the top down, sidewalk-stargazing on Hollywood Blvd and shredding the perfect wave are all part of the LA experience. But once you've starred in the movie of your imagination, move on and check out the 'other' LA, with its superb art museums, killer parks, cool architecture and cutting-edge shopping. Pick from a UN of culinary experiences – Afghani to Zambian – then go and take in some live hip-hop or a hip nightclub.

What makes LA so very fascinating is its wealth of human experience – its near-utopian mosaic of cultures living side by side in relative, well-tanned peace. Not even earthquakes, freeway gridlock or smog can stop LA from thriving. Reality here is never far from the myth, and vice versa, which is part of what makes LA so intriguing – that, and its storybook seaside setting.

HISTORY

Southern California has always been a region of migrants, dating back to as early as 6000 BC, when Chumash and Gabrielino peoples hunted and gathered around what is now LA. The arrival of the Spanish missionaries and settlers from Mexico in the late 18th century ended the Native Americans' idyllic existence.

El Pueblo de la Reina de Los Angeles (the Village of the Queen of the Angels), as the first civilian settlement was known, became a thriving farming community but remained a far-flung outpost for decades.

In the Mexican-American War (1846–48), American soldiers encountered resistance from General Andrés Pico, but eventually LA and the rest of Alta California came under US rule. The city was incorporated on April 4, 1850. A series of seminal events caused LA's population to swell to two million by 1930: the collapse of the Northern California gold rush in the 1850s, the arrival of the transcontinental railroad in the 1870s, establishment of the citrus industry, discovery of oil near Downtown in 1892, construction of a harbor in San Pedro and the opening of the LA aqueduct in 1913.

During WWI, the Lockheed brothers and Donald Douglas established aircraft manufacturing plants in LA. Two decades later, the aerospace industry – helped by billions of federal dollars for military contracts – was among the industries that contributed to a real estate boom and sparked suburban sprawl. Another, of course, was the film industry, which took root in this city as early as 1908.

GETTING INTO TOWN

Bus No 58 goes from the Greyhound depot downtown to the transit plaza at Union Station, with onward service around town, including Metro Rail's Red Line to Hollywood. Door-to-door shuttles ($12 to $20) operate from the lower terminal level of all terminals. Most hostels and airport-area hotels offer free or discounted deals with shuttle companies. Free shuttles go to the Metro Rail Green Line Station and MTA Bus Center. Santa Monica's Big Blue Bus Line 3 (Montana Ave and Lincoln Blvd) serves the airport frequently from 6am to midnight. Otherwise, dispatchers can summon a taxi. Average fares range from $23 to $28 to Santa Monica, $28 to $38 to Hollywood.

ORIENTATION

Los Angeles may be vast and amorphous, but the areas of visitor interest are well-defined. Northwest of downtown, sprawling Hollywood encompasses the trendy 'hoods of Silver Lake and Los Feliz, while most TV and movie studios are actually in the suburban San Fernando Valley. West Hollywood is LA's gay and lesbian epicenter.

South of Hollywood is Mid-City, home to Museum Row, and to the west is ritzy Beverly Hills. Other Westside communities are linked by Sunset Blvd. Of the beach towns, sophisticated-yet-relaxed Santa Monica and funky Venice Beach are the most visitor-friendly.

Due to LA's size, a car is the ideal way to get around, though if you limit explorations to specific neighborhoods, public transit is adequate. Lonely Planet publishes a handy laminated *Los Angeles* city map.

INFORMATION

Bookstores

Book Soup (☎ 310-659-3110; 8818 Sunset Blvd, West Hollywood) Celebrity-heavy general-interest bookstore.

California Map & Travel Center (Map p565; ☎ 310-396-6277; 3312 Pico Blvd, Santa Monica) Guidebooks galore.

Midnight Special Bookstore (Map p565; ☎ 310-393-2923; 1450 2nd St, Santa Monica) Politically oriented indie shop.

Internet Access

Cyber Java (Map p566; 7080 Hollywood Blvd, Hollywood; per hr $6) Free wi-fi, and good coffee.

Interactive Café (Map p565; 215 Broadway, Santa Monica; per 5 min $1) Good newsstand.

Global Gossip (Map p565; 80 Windward Ave, Venice; per hr $8) Full-service digital communications center.

Media

LA Weekly (www.laweekly.com) Free alternative weekly with good eating and nightlife listings.

Los Angeles Times (www.latimes.com)

KCRW 89.9 fm (www.kcrw.org) BBC, NPR and eclectic new music mix.

KPFK 90.7 fm (www.kpfk.org) Indie Pacific radio network; news, tunes and talk.

Medical Services

Cedars-Sinai Medical Center (☎ 310-855-5000; 8700 Beverly Blvd, West Hollywood)

Los Angeles Free Clinic (appointments ☎ 323-653-1990; www.lafreeclinic.org) Beverly (8405 Beverly Blvd); Hollywood (Map p566; 6043 Hollywood Blvd) Wilshire (5205 Melrose Ave)

Rite-Aid 24-hour Pharmacies (☎ 800-748-3243; www.riteaid.com) Call to locate one of 86 pharmacies

UCLA Medical Center (Map pp562-3; ☎ 310-825-9111; 10833 LeConte Ave, Westwood)

Money

American Express (☎ 310-659-1682; 8493 W 3rd St, West Hollywood; ☺ 9am-6pm Mon-Fri, 10am-3pm Sat)

Thomas Cook/Travelex (all branches ☎ 800-287-7362; www.travelex.com) West Hollywood (806 Hilldale Ave; ☺ 10am-5pm Mon-Fri); Beverly Hills (421 N Rodeo Dr; ☺ 10am-5pm Mon-Fri)

Post

Hollywood (Map p566; 1615 Wilcox Ave, Los Angeles, CA 90028)

Santa Monica (Map p565; 248 5th St, Santa Monica, CA 90401)

Telephone

Pay phones are widespread, but often in rough shape and many won't accept incoming calls. Local calls cost a minimum of $0.35; it's cheaper to make long-distance calls with calling cards. If you must use a public phone, look inside malls or nicer hotel lobbies.

Toilets

Public 'restrooms' are few and far between – and usually filthy. The exception are at

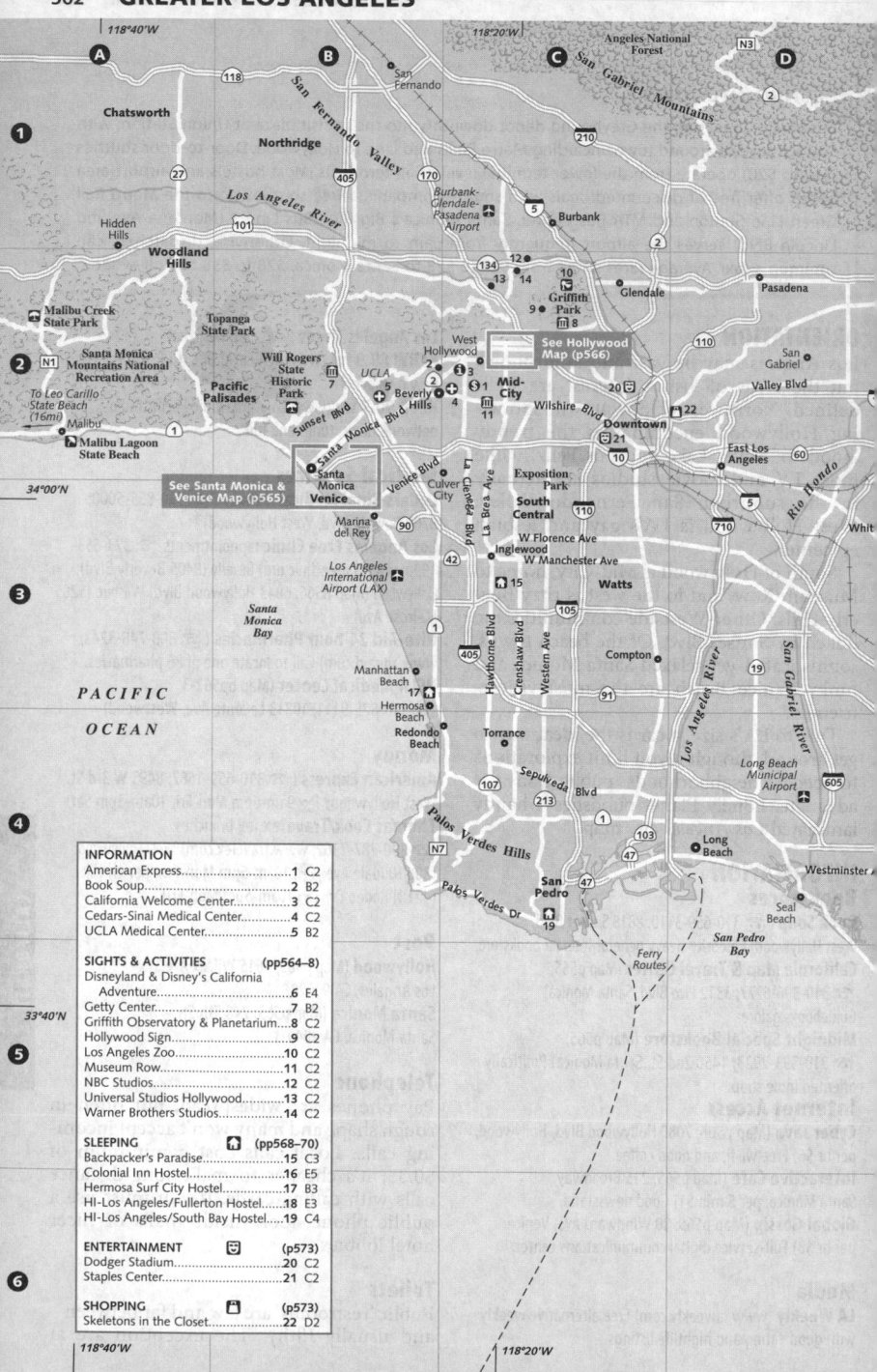

beach communities, which have well-kept public facilities near the ocean. Otherwise, try shopping malls, department stores, libraries or hotel lobbies.

Tourist Information

California Welcome Center (☎ 310-854-7616; www.visitcalifornia.com; 8500 Beverly Blvd, West Hollywood; ☽ 10am-6pm Mon-Sat, 11am-6pm Sun) Inside Beverly Center.

Downtown Visitors Center (☎ 213-689-8822; www.lacvb.com; 685 S Figueroa St; ☽ 8am-5pm Mon-Sat)

Hollywood Visitors Center (Map p566; ☎ 323-467-6412; cnr Hollywood Blvd & Highland Ave; ☽ 10am-10pm Mon-Sat, 10am-7pm Sun)

Santa Monica Visitors Center (Map p565; ☎ 310-393-7593, 800-544-5319; www.santamonica.com; Santa Monica Place Mall; ☽ 10am-6pm)

DANGERS & ANNOYANCES

Wandering around LA in the daytime is generally no problem, although extra caution should be exercised in MacArthur Park, East and South Central LA, which are plagued by gang activity and drugs. Hollywood also yields dangers, especially in poorly lit side streets; ditto for Venice. If you're unlucky enough to experience an earthquake, duck for cover, stay clear of potential crashing glass and give downed power lines wide berth.

SIGHTS

All of LA's neighborhoods have their unique charms. Where you focus your sightseeing depends on your personal interests. Beach bums gravitate toward Santa Monica and Venice for wandering and soaking up the SoCal vibe, while museums and distinctive architecture cluster in Hollywood and downtown.

Santa Monica, Venice & Getty Center

Santa Monica, LA's most agreeable seaside city, features wide beaches, a pedestrian-friendly downtown and excellent dining. The **Third Street Promenade** (Map p565) pedestrian mall extends for three blocks from Wilshire Blvd south to Broadway. Ocean Ave parallels **Palisades Park** (Map p565), perched on a bluff overlooking the Pacific. The main draw at **Santa Monica Pier** (Map p565) is **Pacific Park** (Map p565; rides $2-4; ☽ 11am-11pm Sun-Thu, to midnight Fri & Sat), an amusement

---

QUIRKY, WACKY, WILD: VENICE

If aliens landed on Venice's famous **Ocean Front Walk** (known locally as Venice Boardwalk), they'd probably blend right into the human zoo of bikini-clad bicyclists, chainsaw-juggling entertainers, Muscle Beach body builders and zealous 'meat is murder' activists. This is the place to get your hair braided, your skin tattooed or your aura adjusted. It's a freak show that must be seen to be believed, preferably on hot summer weekends when its at its most surreal.

This quintessential bohemian playground was the brainchild of eccentric and dreamer *extraordinaire*, cigarette heir Abbot Kinney (1850–1920). Kinney's vision was to create a cultural theme park he dubbed 'Venice of America' on marshy land just south of Santa Monica, complete with canals and imported gondoliers to pole people around his beachfront paradise. The park declined soon after Kinney's death, but 3 miles of the original canals were recently restored and are now flanked by flower-festooned villas. The **Venice Canal Walk** threads through this idyllic neighborhood, best accessed from either Venice or Washington Blvds near Dell Ave.

Such counterculture royalty as beatniks Lawrence Lipton and Stuart Perkoff, and Lizard King Jim Morrison all made their homes here. These days it's still a cauldron of creativity peopled by karmically correct New Agers, eternal hippies, cool-conscious musicians, and artists and architects of all stripes. Galleries, studios and public art abound, hardly surprisingly much of it with a surreal bent. Case in point: Jonathan Borofsky's tutu-clad *Ballerina Clown* at Rose Ave and Main St. Nearby at 340 Main St stands star architect Frank Gehry's **Chiat/Day Building**, another famous Venice landmark, fronted by a pair of four-story binoculars by Claes Oldenburg.

Abbot Kinney would probably be delighted that one of LA's most individualistic streets bears his name. Sort of 'seaside Melrose Ave' with a 'Venetian' flavor, the 1-mile stretch of **Abbot Kinney Blvd** between Venice Blvd and Main St is chock-a-block with unique boutiques, galleries, vintage clothing stores and interesting restaurants. When you require 'quirk,' Venice definitely provides your quota.

INFORMATION
California Map & Travel Center..1 D1
Global Gossip.....................................2 C3
Interactive Café.................................3 A1
Midnight Special Bookstore.......4 A1
Post Office...5 B1
Santa Monica Visitors Center....6 A1

SIGHTS & ACTIVITIES (pp564–5)
Pacific Park.......................................7 A2

SLEEPING (p569)
Cadillac Hotel...................................8 B3
HI Los Angeles–Santa Monica....9 A1
Hostel California...........................10 C3
Sea Shore Motel............................11 B2
Venice Beach Cotel.......................12 B3
Venice Beach Hostel..............(see 12)

EATING (pp570–1)
Eatz...13 A1
Jody Maroni's Sausage
Kingdom......................................14 C3
Newsroom Café..............................15 A1
Omelette Parlor..............................16 B2
Real Food Daily..............................17 A1
Rose Café..18 B3
Sidewalk Café.................................19 B3
Wolfgang Puck Express.................20 A1
Ye Olde King's Head.....................21 A1

DRINKING (p572)
Circle Bar...22 B2
Temple Bar......................................23 A1
Toppers...24 A1

park with a small roller coaster and solar powered Ferris wheel. A mile inland, the **Santa Monica Museum of Art** (2525 Michigan Ave; adult/student $5/3; 11am-6pm Tue-Sat, noon-5pm Sun) is the irreverent home of changing contemporary exhibits. It's located within **Bergamot Station**, an old trolley stop that's now LA's artistic nexus.

To the north, idyllic **Malibu Beach** stretches for 12 miles of coastline, harboring surf breaks and beachfront homes of the cool and famous.

North of Santa Monica, looming above the 405 Fwy, is the $1 billion hilltop **Getty Center** (Map pp562-3; ☎ 310-440-7300; 1200 Getty Center Dr; admission free, parking $5; 10am-6pm Tue-Sun, to 9pm Fri & Sat). It presents triple delights: a respectable art collection (Renaissance to David Hockney), the fabulous architecture of Richard Meier and beautiful gardens. On clear days, you'll also get breathtaking views of city and ocean. There's a good café and bus No 233 stops outside.

Hollywood & Griffith Park

Aging movie stars know that a facelift can do wonders for a sagging career, and the same holds true for Hollywood neighborhoods. Millions have been injected recently to rejuvenate the legendary entertainment district. It's still far from glamorous, but at least it's ready for its 'close-up.' East of Hwy 101 (the Hollywood Fwy), **Los Feliz** and **Silver Lake** have evolved into hip enclaves with off-beat shopping and hopping nightlife.

Whether it's Hollywood history or just silly fun you're after, you'll find it along **Hollywood Blvd** (Map p566). The most interesting stretch is the mile between Vine St and La Brea Blvd, the beginning of the **Walk of Fame** (Map p566). Nearby is a focal point of Hollywood revitalization in the form of the humongous **Hollywood & Highland** (Map p566)

INSTEAD OF...

...aimlessly wandering around Hollywood Blvd, head for Griffith Park for scenic picnicking and hiking to the edge of the Hollywood sign. Or, walk up the hill to the Getty Center around 9am, grab a latte and tour the rooftop gardens before the first tram arrives.

shopping and entertainment complex, which dwarfs the famous **Mann's Chinese Theater** (Map p566; 6925 Hollywood Blvd). Across the street is the beautifully restored **El Capitan Theater** (Map p566; 6838 Hollywood Blvd).

If you're titillated by stars' undies, don't miss the free **Frederick's of Hollywood Lingerie Museum** (Map p566; 10am-9pm Mon-Sat, 11am-6:30pm Sun) in the rear of the saucy store, then continue to the fabled corner of Hollywood and Vine, which in reality is pretty drab. Exceptions are the art deco **Pantages Theater** (Map p566), which hosts Broadway blockbusters, and the **Capitol Records Tower** (1956; Map p566), the world's first circular office building.

Sprawling **Griffith Park** (Map p566) is a great escape from LA's hectic velocity. Five times the size of New York's Central Park, it embraces the **Los Angeles Zoo** (Map pp562-3; ☎ 323-644-6400; admission $10; 10am-5pm), the landmark 1935 **observatory** (Map pp562-3; ☎ 323-664-1181) – where James Dean fought it out in *Rebel Without a Cause* – hiking trails and the city's most recognizable landmark,

the **Hollywood Sign** (Map pp562-3). Access is easiest via the Griffith Park Dr or Zoo Dr exits off the I-5 (Golden State Fwy). Bus No 96 stops in front of the zoo.

West Hollywood

West Hollywood (WeHo) is one of LA's liveliest 'hoods, teeming with clubs and shopping. Most of the action concentrates along the famous **W Sunset Strip** (see Drinking, p571, for listings). It's also the heart of LA's queer scene, with most hang-outs fronting Santa Monica Blvd between Robertson and La Cienega Blvds (see the boxed text, p568). **Hustler Hollywood** (8920 Sunset Blvd) is a one-stop adult super shop.

Further south, close to the western end of trendy **Melrose Ave**, is the architecturally striking **Pacific Design Center** (PDC; 8687 Melrose Ave), which incorporates a small branch of the **Museum of Contemporary Art** (admission $3, free Thu; 11am-5pm Tue-Sun, to 8pm Thu). The surrounding **Avenues of Art & Design** are excellent for strolling, people-watching, and vintage-clothing shopping.

HOLLYWOOD

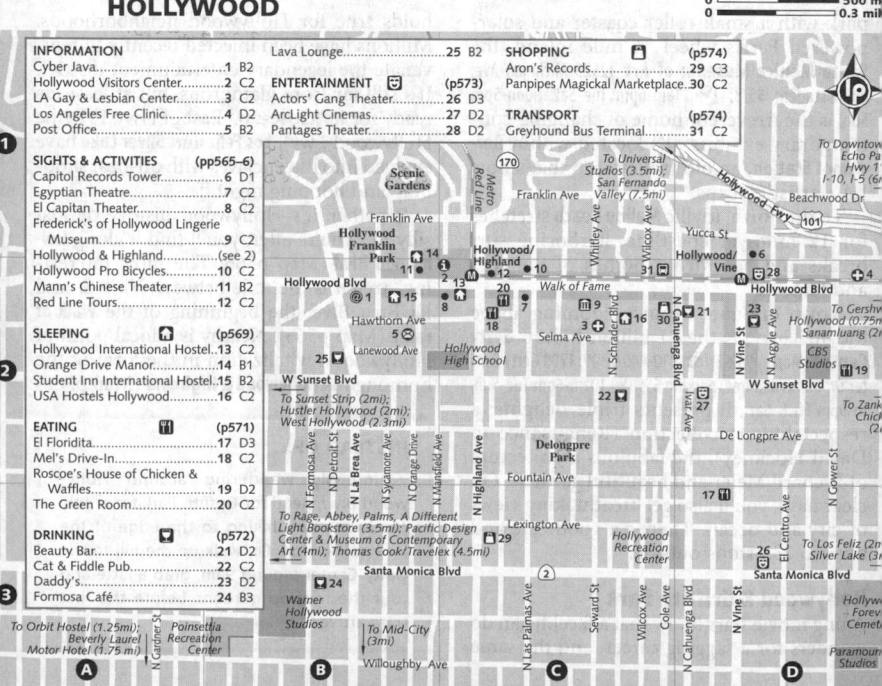

0 —————— 500 m
0 —————— 0.3 mi

INFORMATION	
Cyber Java	1 B2
Hollywood Visitors Center	2 C2
LA Gay & Lesbian Center	3 C2
Los Angeles Free Clinic	4 C2
Post Office	5 B2

SIGHTS & ACTIVITIES	(pp565–6)
Capitol Records Tower	6 D1
Egyptian Theatre	7 C2
El Capitan Theater	8 C2
Frederick's of Hollywood Lingerie Museum	9 C2
Hollywood & Highland	(see 2)
Hollywood Pro Bicycles	10 B2
Mann's Chinese Theater	11 B2
Red Line Tours	12 C2

SLEEPING	(p569)
Hollywood International Hostel	13 C2
Orange Drive Manor	14 B1
Student Inn International Hostel	15 B2
USA Hostels Hollywood	16 C2

EATING	(p571)
El Floridita	17 D3
Mel's Drive-In	18 C2
Roscoe's House of Chicken & Waffles	19 D2
The Green Room	20 C2

DRINKING	(p572)
Beauty Bar	21 D2
Cat & Fiddle Pub	22 C2
Daddy's	23 D2
Formosa Café	24 B3

Lava Lounge	25 B2

ENTERTAINMENT	(p573)
Actors' Gang Theater	26 D3
ArcLight Cinemas	27 C2
Pantages Theater	28 D2

SHOPPING	(p574)
Aron's Records	29 C3
Panpipes Magickal Marketplace	30 D3

TRANSPORT	(p574)
Greyhound Bus Terminal	31 C2

Beverly Hills

Mere mention of this ritzy enclave conjures images of 'the lifestyles of the rich and famous,' the reality is not far from the *90210* myth. Stylish and sophisticated, the well-heeled still frolic here. However, there's no telling how current the maps of stars' homes hawked by street-corner vendors might be.

Beverly Hills' commercial heart beats within the so-called **Golden Triangle** (bordered by Wilshire Blvd, Santa Monica Blvd and Rexford Dr), where **Rodeo Dr** is lined with high-fashion boutiques. The **Museum of Television & Radio** (☎ 310-786-1000; 465 N Beverly Dr; adult/student $10/8; ☼ noon-5pm Wed-Sun) is a giant archive of the 20th century's breakthrough media, all available for viewing in a computerized library.

Miracle Mile & Fairfax Districts

South of Melrose Ave is a cluster of three must-see museums along Wilshire Blvd known as **Museum Row**. The **Los Angeles County Museum of Art** (LACMA; ☎ 323-857-6000; 5905 Wilshire Blvd; adult/student $7/5; ☼ noon-8pm Mon, Tue & Thu, noon-9pm Fri, 11am-8pm Sat & Sun) displays a vast collection of fine art, sculpture and decorative arts from Europe, Asia and America, as well as ancient and Islamic art. The **Page Museum** (☎ 323-936-2230; 5801 Wilshire Blvd; adult/student $6/3.50; ☼ 9:30am-5pm Mon-Fri, 10am-5pm Sat & Sun) displays fossilized skeletons of long-extinct mammals that died in the adjacent **La Brea Tar Pits**. LA's love affair with the automobile is celebrated at the **Petersen Automotive Museum** (☎ 323-930-2277; 6060 Wilshire Blvd; admission $10; ☼ 10am-6pm Tue-Sun).

North of Museum Row, the highlights of the **Fairfax District** are the **Original Farmers Market** (6333 W 3rd St) and the adjacent **Grove**, an open-air shopping mall.

Downtown

Few LA neighborhoods have as much to offer as the city's Historic Core, worth a wander for a look at vintage architecture around Pershing Sq and glimpses of futuristic high-rises nearby in the modern business district. Serious shoppers should trawl the **Fashion District**, a 56-square-block area south of 7th St that's more Arabic bazaar than American mall. Bargains abound, and haggling is accepted in most places.

The cluster of landmark government buildings are collectively known as the **Civic Center**. In 2003 City Hall's top-dog status got competition from the stunning **Walt Disney Hall** (111 S Grand Ave), a Frank Gehry–designed architectural symphony of curving and billowing stainless steel, home to LA's Philharmonic Orchestra. Just east of here is the **Music Center of LA County** (☎ 213-972-7483; 135 N Grand Ave; free tours 10am-1:30pm Tue-Sun).

Also on Grand Avenue's 'cultural corridor' is the world-renowned **Museum of Contemporary Art** (MOCA; ☎ 213-626-6222; 250 S Grand Ave; adult/student $8/5, admission free Thu; ☼ 11am-5pm Mon, 11am-8pm Thu, 11am-5pm Fri, 11am-6pm Sat & Sun). Tickets are valid for same-day admission to the nearby **MOCA Geffen Contemporary** (☎ 213-626-6222; 152 N Central Ave) and the Pacific Design Center (see opposite) branch.

The 44-acre **El Pueblo de Los Angeles** state historic park preserves many early buildings, including the 1818 **Avila Adobe**, a 1930s open-air Mexican marketplace, on Olvera St. Get a self-guided tour brochure at the **visitors center** (☎ 213-625-3800; Olvera St s/n; ☼ 10am-3pm) in the 1877 Sepulveda House.

Across the street, **Union Station** is a classic 1939 Spanish Mission–style beauty that was the last of the USA's grand railroad stations. To make room for its construction, LA's original Chinatown was razed and relocated to an area just north of El Pueblo. The new **Chinatown** is a vibrant cultural and social hub and is a good bet for authentic Cantonese or Szechuan delicacies, shopping for tea and silk clothing, or having a herbalist whip you up a magical potion. Just south, **Little Tokyo** has a mix of sushi bars, traditional gardens, outdoor shopping malls and Buddhist temples.

ACTIVITIES

Relentless sunshine and unlimited activity potential draw devoted flocks to the shorefront year-round. Surfing, sailing, swimming, volleyball, beachcombing – or simply strolling the sand and sunbathing – are all popular. Grab your suntan lotion and hit the beach.

Swimming & Surfing

Santa Monica, Venice, Hermosa, Manhattan and Malibu are the most popular beaches. Water temperatures are tolerable by late spring and are highest (about 70°F or 21°C) in August and September. Water quality is mostly good, although the ocean is often

SPLURGE!

If you can't land some free TV studio audience tickets – contact **Audiences Unlimited** (☎ 818-753-3470, ext 812; www.tvtickets.com). Then splash out on a behind-the-scenes 1½-hour guided tour at the **NBC Studios** (Map pp562-3; ☎ 818-840-3537; 3000 W Alameda Ave, Burbank; tours $7.50; ☼ 9am-3pm Mon-Fri), **Warner Brothers Studios** (Map pp562-3; ☎ 818-972-8687; 4000 Warner Blvd, Burbank; tours $32; ☼ 9am-3pm Mon-Fri) or **Universal Studios Hollywood** (Map pp562-3; ☎ 818-508-9600; 100 Universal City Plaza; tickets $47; ☼ call for seasonal hr), the world's largest movie studio.

off-limits after storms. Nonprofit **Heal the Bay** (☎ 310-453-0395, in California 800-432-5229; www .healthebay.org) monitors water quality. Surfing is good at Malibu Lagoon State Beach (Map pp562-3; aka Surfrider Beach) and near the Manhattan Beach pier.

Cycling & In-line Skating

Los Angeles has 200 miles of designated bike and multi-use trails. The most popular cruising stretch is along the paved 22-mile beachfront trail from Temescal Canyon Rd north of Santa Monica to Torrance Beach. Bike and in-line skate rental outfits are plentiful in beach towns. Mountain bikers can hit the Santa Monica Mountains. For inspiration, see www.labikepaths.com. For rentals and self-guiding tour maps, contact **Hollywood Pro Bicycles** (Map p566; ☎ 323-466-5890, 888-775-2453; 6731 Hollywood Blvd; per day $25-30).

Hiking   Map pp562-3

There's excellent hiking in the **Santa Monica Mountains**, the outer fringes of which reach all the way to the Pacific Coast Hwy. **Will Rogers State Historic Park**, **Topanga State Park** and **Malibu Creek State Park** are among the gateways to a variety of hikes – one-hour to all-day, easy to strenuous – through beautiful terrain. Maps are available at park entrances.

TOURS

Most hostels offer some sort of Hollywood tour, plus many longer all-day excursions.

Los Angeles Conservancy (☎ 213-623-2489; www.laconservancy.org; tours $8-10) Thematic walking tours of downtown, with an architectural focus.

Red Line Tours (Map p566; ☎ 323-402-1074; www.redlinetours.com; 6773 Hollywood Blvd; adult/student $20/18) Fun-filled 90-minute guided audio walking tours of Hollywood and downtown.

FESTIVALS & EVENTS

Rose Parade (☎ 626-449-4100; www.tournament ofroses.com) A huge cavalcade of flower-festooned floats in Pasadena on New Year's Day.

Cinco de Mayo (☎ 213-625-5045) Celebrated with bands and parades in downtown's El Pueblo in early May.

West Hollywood's Halloween Party (☎ 310-289-2525) A rambunctious street fair with eccentric costumes on Santa Monica Blvd on October 31.

Hollywood Christmas Parade (☎ 323-469-2337; www.hollywoodchristmas.com) Late November; features film and TV celebrities on flashy floats.

SLEEPING

When deciding where to sleep in LA, consider what type of experience you desire. For

GAY & LESBIAN LOS ANGELES

Though the focus is primarily gay, a few of West Hollywood's queer hang-outs cater to lesbian and mixed audiences. Beauty reigns supreme in 'Boyz Town' and the intimidation factor can be high unless you're buff, bronzed and styled-out. A more low-key vibe pervades Silver Lake, where bars are more mixed. The beach towns, historically havens of queerness, now have relaxed, neighborly scenes, especially in Venice.

Santa Monica Blvd boasts action 24-7 at party palaces like **Rage** (☎ 310-652-7055; 8911 Santa Monica Blvd), one of West Hollywood's top dance clubs. Nearby, the **Abbey** (☎ 310-289-8410; 692 N Robertson Blvd) attracts a laid-back breakfast and lunch crowd but turns up the heat at night in the back bar with its semiprivate alcoves. The **Palms** (☎ 310-652-6188; 8572 Santa Monica Blvd) is WeHo's oldest lesbian bar.

A Different Light Bookstore (☎ 310-854-6601; 8853 Santa Monica Blvd, West Hollywood) is the city's number-one gay bookstore. The **LA Gay & Lesbian Center** (Map p566; ☎ 323-993-7400; www .laglc.org; 1625 N Schrader Blvd, Hollywood) is a one-stop health agency.

CALIFORNIA

the beach, stay in Santa Monica or Venice. Urban explorers should crash near West Hollywood and its bars and nightlife. Hollywood is the hostel ghetto. A tax of 12% to 14% is added to all room rates.

Santa Monica & Venice   Map p565

Cadillac Hotel (☎ 310-399-8876; www.thecadillacho tel.com; 8 Dudley Ave, Venice; dm $22, r $89-160; 🖳) Dorm rooms are sparse at this beachfront art deco landmark, but all have airy ocean views and the sun deck is very social. Save a bit by booking online.

Venice Beach Cotel (☎ 310-399-7649; www.venice beachcotel.com; 25 Windward Ave, Venice; dm $16-20, r $36-53; 🖳) A hostel-plus, including extras like ready-made beds, maid service and private bathroom in some of the six-bed dorms. Private rooms are small but have TVs – No 319, with an ocean view, is a super choice. The downside? It's above a noisy nightclub.

HI Los Angeles-Santa Monica (☎ 310-393-9913, 800-909-4776; www.hilosangeles.org; 1436 2nd St; dm $22-25, r $60-75; 🖳) Despite complaints (sterile, soulless, poor beds), this well-situated place packs 'em into spick-and-span rooms. Hey, it's only two blocks from the beach and there's a helpful travel center. It's often recommended as a comfortable place for solo women.

Venice Beach Hostel (☎ 310-452-3052; www.cap rica.com/venice-beach-hostel; 1515 Pacific Ave, Venice; dm/r $20/55; 🖳) This eccentric, well-worn rabbit warren of a place is a favorite crash pad of artists and street buskers. There's a large kitchen, a convivial atmosphere and women-only dorms. Americans must show ID.

Hostel California (☎ 310-305-0250; www.hostel california.net; 2221 Lincoln Blvd, Venice; dm $13-18, r $36-40; 🖳) Looks like a tornado-hit trailer park in the chaotic 30-room dorm! Try for one of the smaller dorms or private rooms. Long-term guests take full advantage of the pool table and big-screen TV. Bummer – it's a 20-minute walk to the beach.

Hollywood, West Hollywood & Mid-City

USA Hostels Hollywood (Map p566; ☎ 323-462-3777, 800-524-6783; www.usahostels.com; 1624 Schrader Blvd; dm $17-25, r $45-65; 🖳) A well-run, central hostel. Private rooms have satellite TV and private bathrooms. Twice-weekly comedy nights, free pancake breakfast and a stellar kitchen encourage guests to mingle. Call for pickup from Greyhound and LAX (Los Angeles International Airport).

> **SPLURGE!**
>
> **Sea Shore Motel** (Map p565; ☎ 310-392-2787; www.seashoremotel.com; 2637 Main St, Santa Monica; r $75-135) Fronting the boutique- and restaurant-filled Main St, two blocks from the beach, this recently slicked-up motor court's assets include multiple creature comforts, with a laundromat, Internet access and a good café next door.

Orbit Hostel (☎ 323-655-1510; 7950 Melrose Ave, Mid-City; www.orbithotel.com; dm $18-21, r $49-89; 🖾 🖳) Retro and well-run, with clean six-bed dorms and a groovy movie lounge, all in a former retirement home near the epicenter of LA hipness. Dorms have private bathrooms and some private rooms have balconies.

Gershwin Hollywood (☎ 323-464-1131; 5533 Hollywood Blvd; www.gershwinhollywood.com; dm from $20, r $39-50) A converted apartment building sporting colorful Ikea-inspired design. Half the rooms have kitchenettes and the Red Line is out front.

Orange Drive Manor (Map p566; ☎ 323-850-0350; www.orangedrivehostel.com; 1764 N Orange Dr; dm $20-24, r $40-56; 🖳 🖾) Unsigned, in a rambling 1920s mansion complete with high ceilings and creaky hardwood floors, just off Hollywood Blvd. The roomy two- to four-bed dorms are single-sex and the vibe is low-key, with movies as the preferred after-dark diversion. Parking $5 a day, no curfew.

Student Inn International Hostel (Map p566; ☎ 323-462-6781; www.studentinn.com; 7038½ Hollywood Blvd; dm $14-18, d $48; 🖳) All rooms have private bathrooms at the newest hostel near the Walk of Fame. Couples can share a large dorm bed, and penny pinchers can sometimes work the front desk in exchange for room and board.

Hollywood International Hostel (Map p566; ☎ 323-463-0797, 800-750-6561; www.hollywoodhostels .com; 6820 Hollywood Blvd; dm/d from $17/40; 🖳) This lowbrow option attracts a rambunctious, sociable globe-trotting crowd in its 40-plus single-sex dorms, which sleep three to four. The kitchen, however, is nonexistent. Don't expect cleanliness, security or to cook, and you'll have a blast.

Beverly Laurel Motor Hotel (☎ 323-651-2441, 800-962-3824; 8018 Beverly Blvd, Mid-City; r $79-89; 🖾 🖳) Want to ride the retro wave? Check into one of the arty rooms at this venerable

1950s motel, one of the city's best-value hotels. The attached Swingers diner crawls with hipsters until the wee hours.

Also recommended:

Backpacker's Paradise (Map pp562-3; ☎ 310-672-3090, 800-852-0011/12, in Canada ☎ 800-648-6363; www.backpackersparadise.com; 4200 W Century Blvd, Inglewood; dm $12, r $55-85; ☒) All about the poolside party and free airport pickup. Venice hostels, however, are only 5 miles from LAX, and don't suffer from as much overflight noise.

HI-Los Angeles/South Bay Hostel (Map pp562-3; ☎ 310-831-8109, 800-909-4776; www.hilosangeles. org; 3601 S Gaffey St, San Pedro; dm $17-21, d $38-41; ☺ May-Sep) Overlooking the Pacific in Angels Gate Park, a peaceful getaway.

Hermosa Surf City Hostel (Map pp562-3; ☎ 310-798-2323, 800-305-2901; www.lasurfcityhostel .com; 25 Pier Ave, Hermosa Beach; dm/d $17/45) Killer beach location. Weekly dorm deals from $100.

Colonial Inn Hostel (Map pp562-3; ☎ 714-536-3315; www.huntingtonbeachhostel.com; 421 8th St, Huntington Beach; dm/d $21/50) Wicked! Three blocks from Orange County's best surfing beach, a bus ride from Disneyland. Weekly rate $130.

Outer Los Angeles

LA County has many campgrounds, but none are very central and many only allow RVs. Some folks end up sleeping in their cars, but it's hardly recommendable. Your best bet is shady **Leo Carrillo State Beach Campground** (☎ 805-488-5225, 800-444-7275; 9000 Pacific Coast Hwy; campsites $13-20), 28 miles northwest of Santa Monica, a popular spot with 138 campsites. Extras include flush toilets, coin-op hot showers and a sandy beach with cool tide pools. Reserve ahead in summer.

EATING

As a cosmopolitan crossroads, one of the Southland's great pleasures is its motley mélange of cheap, authentic ethnic eats. There's plenty of requisite healthy California cuisine bandied about in trendy culinary temples, but it's the mom-and-pop Mexican, Thai, Korean, Ethiopian and Middle Eastern places that pack the savory bang for the buck. For unadventurous palates, there are plenty of reliable fast-food chains and healthy, veggie-friendly options, too.

Santa Monica & Venice   Map p565

Venice's stretch of Ocean Front Walk has cheap fast-food stands like **Jody Maroni's Sausage Kingdom** (☎ 310-822-5639; north of Venice Blvd, Venice boardwalk; sandwiches $3-5), where even finicky folks will be pleased by the free samples and plump all-natural 'haut dogs.' Otherwise, your best bet is to head inland.

Omelette Parlor (☎ 310-399-7892; 2732 Main St, Santa Monica; mains under $8) Delightfully old-fashioned, this joint has been preparing stuffed omelettes, fruit-topped pancakes and beefy sandwiches (like the $4 weekday half-pound-burger lunch special) since 1967. Expect long lines on weekends, especially for sunny seats at the spick-and-span counter.

Real Food Daily (☎ 310-451-7544; 514 Santa Monica Blvd, Santa Monica; mains $6-13) Superb organic and vegan lunch and dinner daily. Casual setting and sizable celebrity following.

Eatz (ground fl, Santa Monica Place, Santa Monica; mains $2-9) Hands down, this is LA's best shopping mall food court, with choices spanning the world's four corners. Highlights include heaping plates at the Mongolian BBQ and the crazy get-ups at Hot Dog on a Stick.

Rose Café (☎ 310-399-0711; 220 Rose Ave, Venice; stand-up café under $5, sit-down restaurant $9-16) The self-service café/deli at this popular standby serves yummy baked goods in its tree-fringed patio. In the restaurant, the accent is on fresh salads, light pastas and seafood.

Sidewalk Café (☎ 310-399-5547; 1401 Ocean Front Walk, Venice; breakfast $5-9, lunch $9-13) Tourists flock here for old-fashioned American fare, all-day breakfast and front-row views of the

---

LATE-NIGHT GRUB

Bars closed and you're still hungry? It's never too late to cross town for a late-night bite. Chow on garlicky chili dogs at **Pink's** (709 N La Brea Ave, Melrose/La Brea; dogs $3-6; ☺ to 2am Sun-Thu, 3am Fri & Sat); on NY-style pies at **Damiano Mr Pizza** (412 N Fairfax Ave, Fairfax District; slices $1.75, full pies $10; ☺ to 6am Sun-Thu, 7am Fri-Sat); at **Roscoe's House of Chicken & Waffles** (Map p566; 1514 N Gower St; mains $7-12; ☺ to midnight Sun-Thu, 4am Fri & Sat), a no-frills soul shack; on a triple-decker pastrami at **Greenblatt's Deli** (8017 W Sunset Blvd, West Hollywood; mains $6-12; ☺ to 2am); or on anti-Atkins, all-American fare at the **Original Pantry Cafe** (877 S Figueroa St, Downtown; mains $8-14; ☺ 24hr).

stream of bizarre humanity parading along the beachfront.

Also recommended in Santa Monica:

Newsroom Café (☎ 310-319-9100; 530 Wilshire Blvd; mains $5-13) Great choice for star spotting and gourmet health food.

Wolfgang Puck Express (☎ 310-576-4770; 1315 Third Street Promenade; mains $7-10) Get pizza or Chinese chicken salad.

Ye Olde King's Head (☎ 310-451-1402; 116 Santa Monica Blvd; mains $6-13) Cheap lunch specials and super fish and chips.

Hollywood, West Hollywood & Mid-City

Original Farmers Market (cnr Fairfax Ave & W 3rd St) Pull together a picnic or enjoy a sit down meal right amid the market bustle. Good options include the New Orleans–style **Gumbo Pot** (☎ 323-933-0358; mains $5-9) and **Pampas Grill** (☎ 323-931-1928; salad bar per lb $6.25) for the delicious Brazilian-style buffet of meats and veggies.

Green Room (Map p566; ☎ 323 860-0775; 6752 Hollywood Blvd; mains $4-9) This little café provides an excellent vantage point for watching the endless parade of freaks milling down the Hollywood strip. Breakfast is served until 4pm daily and there are decent salads, sandwiches and live jam sessions.

Sanamluang (☎ 323-660-8006; 5176 Hollywood Blvd; mains $4-8) One of LA's best Thai restaurants is tucked away in a nondescript mini-mall. The menu is as complex as an algebra equation, so we'll make it simple: order a noodle dish like the delectable *pad kee mow*.

Zankou Chicken (☎ 323-665-7842; 5065 Sunset Blvd; mains $3-9) Even virgins of Armenian cuisine will become instantaneous fans when trying out the lip-smacking rotisserie chicken, especially after slathering on all that garlic sauce.

Fred 62 (☎ 323-667-0062; 1850 Vermont Ave; mains $3.60-13.60; ☉ 24hr) This updated '50s-style diner in the heart of Los Feliz Village feeds hipsters huge plates of polyethnic sandwiches, salads and noodles.

Mel's Drive-in (Map p566; ☎ 323-465-2111; 1660 N Highland Ave; mains $7-10) Catch the *American Graffiti* vibe at this fun '50s diner where the big menu features all the classics.

El Siete Mares (The Seven Seas; 3131 W Sunset Blvd, Silver Lake; mains under $5) Casual taco stands abound in LA, but this place is famous for its consistently excellent – and huge – fish tacos, burritos and seviche tostadas.

SPLURGE!

El Floridita (Map p566; ☎ 323-871-0936; 1253 N Vine St; mains $9-15, cover without dinner $10) Cubans aren't the only ones who give this supper club with floor-to-ceiling mirrors the thumbs up for its authentic food, energetic atmosphere, live Latin music and free dance lessons. Perennial favorites include the Cuban roast pork sandwiches and the *ropa vieja* ('old clothing'), which consists of shredded beef simmered in Creole sauce. Dinner reservations advised.

Griddle Café (☎ 323-874-0377; 7916 W Sunset Blvd, West Hollywood; mains $5-12) Feast on comfort food with out-of-work actors.

Palermo (☎ 323-663-1178; 1858 Vermont Ave, Los Feliz; mains $8-13; ☉ Wed-Mon) Delicious pizza.

Yuca's (☎ 323-662-1214; 2056 Hillhurst Ave, Los Feliz; mains $3-6) Takeout-only Yucatan-style burritos, tacos and *tortas* (sandwiches).

Downtown

Downtown is a great place for cash-strapped people, at least for breakfast and lunch. At multiethnic **Grand Central Market** (317 Broadway) **Maria's Pescado Frito** (central aisle; tacos $1-2) and **China Café** (upper level; mains $2-5) are recommended, as is French bistro **Angélique Cafe** (☎ 213-623-8698; 840 S Spring St; mains $6-11).

Clifton's Brookdale Cafeteria (☎ 213-627-1673; 648 S Broadway; mains $2-6) The ultra-campy setting – an enchanted forest with fake trees, squirrels etc – is what sets this ex-Salvation Army cafeteria apart. For spiritual sustenance, duck into the diminutive chapel.

Philippe the Original (☎ 213-628-3781; 1001 N Alameda St; mains $2-5; cash only) Off-duty gourmet chefs regularly join the throngs at the long service counter for juicy roast beef sandwiches. Get a side of coleslaw and a decent glass of red wine. Coffee is still 9¢. It's handy to the train station.

DRINKING

To plug into the buzz, pick up the free *LA Weekly* at cafés, boutiques and pubs or surf its website (www.laweekly.com). Its 'Scoring the Clubs' section gives a blow-by-blow rundown of the week's best gigs. LA.com also has extensive nightlife listings.

You can't fling a screenplay without plonking somewhere to drown your sorrows:

CALIFORNIA

Hollywood, West Hollywood (including Los Feliz and Silver Lake) and Santa Monica are bar- and club-hopping hot spots where live music and mixed drinks go hand in hand. Note: Smoking is banned inside California bars, but many circumvent the law by providing outdoor patios.

Bars

Good Luck Bar (☎ 323-666-3524; 1514 Hillhurst Ave, Los Feliz; ☒ Mon-Sat) The clientele is cool and single, the jukebox loud and the drinks seductively strong at this cultish watering hole decked out in Chinese opium den–inspired carmine red.

Tiki Ti (☎ 323-669-9381; 4427 W Sunset Blvd, Silver Lake; ☒ from 6pm Wed-Sun) The trick is finding out when this legendary Tiki shrine actually opens, since the owner reportedly goes surfing a lot. The ambience is hole-in-the-wall tropical tavern, with a wicked collection of kitsch and surreal junk. No credit cards, smoking allowed.

Cat & Fiddle Pub (Map p566; ☎ 323-468-3800; 6530 Sunset Blvd, Hollywood) Order up a $3 happy hour pint (4pm to 7pm), grab an outdoor table, chuck some darts and enjoy live Sunday night jazz at this ever-popular Brit expat favorite.

Formosa Café (Map p566; ☎ 323-850-9050; 7156 Santa Monica Blvd, Hollywood) The one-time watering hole of Bogart, Monroe and Gable is a cool place to sop up some Hollywood nostalgia along with your pre-dinner or after-hours cocktail. Mao-tais and martinis are beverages of choice.

Beauty Bar (Map p566; ☎ 323-464-7676; 1638 N Cahuenga Blvd, Hollywood) At this pint-sized cocktail bar, decorated with hair-salon paraphernalia from the Kennedy era, you can sip a martini, get your nails done or peruse the crowd while seated beneath plastic hairdryers.

Toppers (Map p565; ☎ 310-393-8080; 1111 2nd St, Santa Monica) Get a buzz from the margaritas, fill yourself up at one of LA's best happy hours (4:30pm to 7:30pm daily) and watch the sun drop into the ocean at this buzzing bar atop the Radisson Huntley Hotel.

Conga Room (☎ 323-549-9765; 5364 Wilshire Blvd, Mid-City) Gorgeous Latin dance club with the heady feel of pre-revolution Havana. Come dressed up.

Also recommended:

Dresden Room (☎ 323-665-4294; 1760 N Vermont Ave, Los Feliz; ☒ Mon-Sat) Swank lounge featuring the campy lyrical stylings of inimitable crooners Marty and Elayne.

Daddy's (Map p566; ☎ 323-463-7777; 1610 N Vine St, Hollywood) Pick-up joint with sensuously curved booths.

Lava Lounge (Map p565; ☎ 323-876-6612; 1533 N La Brea Ave, Hollywood) Tiki-themed bar, often with live music.

Circle Bar (Map p565; ☎ 310-450-0508; 2926 Main St, Santa Monica) Strong drinks and DJ dancing.

Largo (☎ 323-852-1073; 432 N Fairfax Ave, Mid-City) Supper club with an eclectic musical menu.

Troubadour (☎ 310-276-6168; 9081 Santa Monica Blvd, West Hollywood) Old-time good timer.

Viper Room (☎ 310-358-1880; 8852 Sunset Blvd, West Hollywood) Celeb-heavy crowd.

Live Music

Spaceland (☎ 213-833-2843; 1717 Silver Lake Blvd, Silver Lake; cover $7-12, Mon usually free) At the epicenter of Silver Lake's indie rock scene, local alt-rock, skate-punk and surf bands take the stage, all hoping to make it big. Turn up early, boss.

House of Blues (☎ 323-848-5100; www.hob.com; 8430 Sunset Blvd, West Hollywood) Top talent of all stripes plays at this faux–Mississippi Delta shack. The Sunday Gospel Brunch (seatings at 10am and 1pm; $27 to $33) is a finger-lickin' institution.

Roxy (☎ 310-276-2222; 9009 Sunset Blvd, West Hollywood) This Sunset fixture is still a launchpad for bands on the verge of stardom. Big names have been known to pop in for impromptu concerts.

Temple Bar (Map p565; ☎ 310-393-6611; 1026 Wilshire Blvd, Santa Monica) One of the more happening hang-outs west of Hollywood. The bands are hit-or-miss, but the drinks are strong, the crowd's heavy on the eye candy and the ambience is fairly relaxed.

CALIFORNIA

PINT NIGHTS

In swanky LA, you won't find many $1 pint nights. In fact, you're lucky to get a free manicure with your $10 martini. Though you won't meet many locals, there's no better place in Santa Monica to watch the sunset (margarita-in-hand) than at happy hour at rooftop **Toppers** (right). In Hollywood, happy hour pints of British ales at the **Cat & Fiddle** (above) fuel a lively pick-up scene. Drinks are half-price from 8:30pm to 10pm at the **Lava Lounge** (right), which helps lubricate the crowd for Kinky Karaoke.

Derby (☎ 323-663-8979; 4500 Los Feliz Blvd, Los Feliz) The best swing dancers in town jump and jive around the pint-sized dance floor, while stylish retro bands play on. Call about free dance lessons.

ENTERTAINMENT

Los Angeles has got it all, from sporting thrills and spills to world-class performing arts. The best source for mainstream entertainment reviews is the daily Calendar section of the *Los Angeles Times* and its Sunday magazine supplement. Events tickets are available either from each venue's box office or via **Ticketmaster** (☎ 213-480-3232; www .ticketmaster.com) or **TicketWeb** (☎ 866 777 8932; www .ticketweb.com).

Theater

Score half-price tickets for shows taking place that week by reserving online via **Theatre LA** (www.theatrela.org).

Actors' Gang Theatre (Map p566; ☎ 323-465-0566; 6209 Santa Monica Blvd, Hollywood) Co-founded by Tim Robbins, this socially mindful troupe presents daring and offbeat interpretations of classics and new works pulled from ensemble workshops.

Geffen Playhouse (☎ 310-208-5454; 10886 Le Conte Ave, Westwood) Cutting-edge productions by leading American playwrights, often featuring a star-studded cast.

Mark Taper Forum (☎ 213-628-2772; 135 N Grand Ave, Downtown) Part of the Music Center complex and known for its high-caliber premieres, often with celebrity casts. Rush tickets ($12) go on sale 10 minutes before curtain.

Groundlings Theater (☎ 323-934-9700; 7307 Melrose Ave, Mid-City) This first-rate improv school and comedy ensemble is also recommended.

Cinemas   Map p565

ArcLight Cinemas (☎ 323-464-4226; 6360 W Sunset Blvd, Hollywood; tickets $11) At the historic Cinerama Dome, this multiplex is a romp through 1960s-style fashion. New releases, special director's cuts and classic revivals are also shown in the main hall of the dome.

Egyptian Theatre (☎ 323-466-3456; 6712 Hollywood Blvd, Hollywood; tickets $8) In the same year that King Tut's tomb was discovered, this faux-Egyptian temple screened its first all-star Hollywood premiere. Now run by the non-profit American Cinematheque, it screens independent, avant-garde and foreign films.

Sports

Dodger Stadium (Map pp562-3; ☎ 323-224-1448; www.dodgers.com; 1000 Elysian Park Ave; tickets from $6) LA's Major League Baseball team plays ball April to September in this legendary stadium.

Staples Center (Map pp562-3; ☎ 213-742-7340; www .staplescenter.com; 1111 S Figueroa St, Downtown; tickets from $20) This state-of-the-art venue is home to all three of LA's professional basketball teams: the LA Lakers, the female LA Sparks and the LA Clippers. The LA Kings professional hockey team also face off here.

Classical Music & Opera

LA Philharmonic Orchestra (☎ 323-850-2000; tickets from $15) The world-class LA Phil fills Walt Disney Hall in the fall with works by obscure composers to obscure works by famous composers.

LA Opera (☎ 213-972-8001; tickets from $30) Now under the stewardship of Plácido Domingo, the LA Opera has fine tuned its mostly high-caliber repertory. Performances with English subtitles take place in the Music Center's **Dorothy Chandler Pavilion** (135 N Grand Ave, Downtown).

Hollywood Bowl (☎ 323-850-2000; 2301 N Highland Ave, Hollywood; tickets from $1) From late June through September the sounds of Mozart, Gershwin, The Who and other music greats ring out at this lovely outdoor venue. BYOB and a picnic to enjoy before the show.

SHOPPING

Countless unique offbeat shops will reward those with a knack for browsing and a flair for the unusual. For cutting-edge designs, Melrose Ave between La Brea and Fairfax Aves has a great concentration of quirky and hip boutiques. Silver Lake and Los Feliz have lots of thrift, secondhand and vintage clothing shops. Many folks want to cruise up upscale Rodeo Dr, even if their credit card limit won't even buy a foot inside the guarded door. Some great bargains (and faux brands) turn up downtown in the Fashion District, while the boardwalk at Venice Beach is the place for cheap, kitschy souvenirs.

Aron's Records (Map p566; ☎ 323-469-4700; 1150 N Highland Ave, Hollywood; ☽ Mon-Sat) LA's best indie record shop has been supplying alpha-male customers for four decades with racks of used vinyl and CDs from the lands of punk, hard-core, obscure electronica and beyond.

CALIFORNIA

SHOP TILL YOU DROP?

Shopping in LA can be uplifting, or a near-death experience. **Necromance** (☎ 323-934-8684; 7220 Melrose Ave, Hollywood) sells animal and human bones, pickled frogs and vampire repellent. Up the street, **Panpipes Magickal Marketplace** (Map p566; ☎ 323-462-7078; 1641 Cahuenga Blvd, Hollywood) mixes metaphysical blends to solve whatever problem's ailing you. Where else but LA would you find a coroner's office giftshop called **Skeletons in the Closet** (Map pp562-3; ☎ 323-343-0760; 1104 N Mission Rd, Downtown) selling personalized toe tags?

It's a Wrap! (☎ 818-567-7366; 315 W Magnolia Blvd, Burbank) For surprisingly little money, this shop resells studio clothes worn by actual TV stars. Of course, you may only be told the name of the show or network. Still, designer labels are in tip-top condition.

Wacko (☎ 323-663-0122; 4633 Hollywood Blvd, Silver Lake) A huge gallery of kitsch and pop culture, sold out of pure love. A punching rabbi? Encyclopedia of bizarre SoCal architecture? Jumping plastic goldfish? Yep, they are all here. Next door, Ozzie Dots hawks vintage Hollywood costumery.

GETTING THERE & AWAY
Air
The most popular routes, with dozens of daily departures, are (for one-way advance purchase fares): Los Angeles–Las Vegas ($59 to $129), Los Angeles–San Francisco ($89 to $219) and San Francisco–San Diego ($149 to $299).

Los Angeles International Airport (LAX; Map pp562-3; ☎ 310-646-5252; www.lawa.org) is the biggie, but several regional airports are often used by no-frills carriers:

Burbank-Glendale-Pasadena (BUR; Map pp562-3; ☎ 818-840-8847; www.burbankairport.com)
John Wayne Airport (SNA; Map pp562-3; ☎ 949-252-5200; www.ocair.com)
Long Beach (LGB; Map pp562-3; ☎ 562-570-2600; www.lgb.org)

For a list of other US carriers see p705.

Bus
The **Greyhound** (☎ 213-629-8401; 1716 E 7th St) terminal is in a fairly forlorn part of downtown, so try not to arrive after dark. Some Greyhound buses arrive at the **Hollywood bus terminal** (Map p566; ☎ 323-466-6381; 1715 N Cahuenga Blvd, Hollywood). Common routes include: San Francisco–Los Angeles (up to 16 daily), Los Angeles–San Diego (hourly), Los Angeles–Las Vegas (hourly).

Other long-distance options include:
California Shuttle Bus (☎ 800-387-3319; www.cashuttlebus.com) Daily shuttles between LA and San Francisco ($40) area hotels.
Missing Link Tours (☎ 800-209-8586; www.tmltours.com) Shuttles between LA and Vegas ($39) and LA and San Francisco ($49 or $69) several times a week.

Car
Renting a car is a viable alternative to public transportation, especially if you land an unlimited mileage deal and share gas costs with as many people as you can squeeze in. Try **Super Cheap Car Rental** (☎ 310-645-3993; www.supercheapcar.com; 10212 La Cienega Blvd), which offers free pickup from the LAX transit center and rents older subcompacts (one week minimum, including full insurance and unlimited mileage) to folks aged 20 and older, starting at $169 per week for local use or $199 within California and to Las Vegas. Other rental outfits may impose a surcharge on drivers under 25 years of age.

Train
Daily intrastate **Amtrak** (☎ 800-872-7245; 800 N Alameda St) trains stopping downtown at historic Union Station are the *Coast Starlight* to Oakland (for San Francisco, $66) and the *Pacific Surfliner* to San Diego ($29), Santa Barbara ($20) and San Luis Obispo ($30).

GETTING AROUND
Contrary to popular belief, LA does have a comprehensive public transit system (day/week pass $3/14). Still, cars remain the favored weapon of mass destruction. All the major international car-rental agencies have counters at LAX airport and throughout Los Angeles (see p710 for toll-free reservation numbers).

Public Transportation
The **Metropolitan Transportation Authority** (MTA; ☎ 800-266-6883; www.mta.net; fare $1.35) operates

CALIFORNIA

an extensive bus and rail system. To plan trips, call or use the online tool, or pick up a free network map from a customer center **downtown** (Arco Plaza, 515 S Flower St; ☺ 7:30am-3:30pm) or near Museum Row in **Mid-City** (5301 Wilshire Blvd; ☺ 9am-5pm).

The fastest way across town is aboard Metro Rapid bus No 720, which travels along Wilshire Blvd from Santa Monica to downtown and into East LA via Westwood, Beverly Hills, Fairfax and Mid-City. Downtown, Hollywood and Mid-City are also served by **DASH minibuses** (☎ 213-808-2273; www.ladottransit.com; ticket 25¢; ☺ 7am-7pm Mon-Sat). Santa Monica–based **Big Blue Bus** (☎ 310-451-5444; www.bigbluebus.com) serves much of western LA, including Santa Monica, Venice, Westwood and LAX (75¢). Express bus No 10 runs from Santa Monica to downtown ($1.75).

The MTA-operated Metro Rail is a network of four routes: the Blue Line (downtown to Long Beach), the Red Line (downtown's Union Station to North Hollywood, via central Hollywood and Universal Studios), the Green Line (Norwalk to Redondo Beach) and the new Gold Line from downtown to Pasadena.

Except for taxi ranks at airports, train stations, bus stations and major hotels, cabbies will only respond to phone calls. Fares are metered: $2 at flag fall plus $2 per mile. Companies include **Checker** (☎ 800-300-5007), **Independent** (☎ 800-521-8294) and **Yellow Cab** (☎ 800-200-1085).

SOUTH COAST

Not to be confused with OC, Ocean City (p242), *the* OC – Orange County – is wedged between Los Angeles to the north and San Diego to the south. It's home to SoCal's most popular attraction – Disneyland (see below) in Anaheim – but is also justly famous for its 42 miles of wonderful coastline.

Surfers, artists and retirees give Orange County's beach towns such as relaxed **Huntington Beach** (aka Surf City, USA), artsy **Laguna Beach** and sophisticated **Newport Beach** their distinct vibe.

DISNEYLAND

Ever since Walt Disney opened the original **Disneyland** (Map pp562-3; ☎ 714-781-4400; www.disneyland.com; 1313 Harbor Blvd, Anaheim; admission $50)

in 1955, the mother of all theme parks has captured the heart, minds and pocketbooks of millions of folks. It's divided into seven thematic 'lands,' that include the space-age Tomorrowland, jungle-themed Adventureland, and Fantasyland, where classic Disney characters reside. The most popular thrill rides are Indiana Jones Adventure, Space Mountain and Pirates of the Caribbean.

In 2001 a second, smaller park called **Disney's California Adventure** opened adjacent to the original, with caricatures of the natural and cultural glories of the Golden State. If you can't experience the real thing, not-to-be missed attractions include Soarin' over California, a virtual hang gliding ride, and California Screamin', a roller coaster built around a Mickey Mouse silhouette.

Also part of Disneyland Resort are three hotels and **Downtown Disney**, a pedestrian mall stuffed with dining, shopping and entertainment venues.

You can see either park in a day, but it requires at least two days to go on all the rides (three for both parks), especially in summer when lines are gargantuan – visit midweek and arrive when the gates open. When getting to the parks, familiarize yourself with the FastPass system, which gives you pre-assigned time slots for faster boarding.

A variety of multi-day passes good at both parks are available. Check the website to buy tickets and verify park hours. These vary daily, although in peak season the parks are usually open from 8am to midnight.

The area around Disneyland – especially along Harbor Blvd and Katella Ave – has plenty of lodging options, mostly of the chain hotel/motel variety. The only budget option is the **HI-Los Angeles/Fullerton Hostel** (Map pp562-3; ☎ 714-738-3721, 800-909-4776; www.hostelweb.com/losangeles/fullerton.htm; 1700 N Harbor Blvd; dm $17-20; ☺ Jun-Sep; 🖳), quite a decent option five miles from Disneyland with no curfew.

SAN DIEGO

It's easy to fall in love with San Diego. When much of the USA shivers under blankets of rain and snow, San Diegans picnic outdoors or slice through waves on surfboards. So, what's not to like? Detractors – mostly from success-driven, angst-ridden LA – point to a degree of solar-induced complacency that all this perfection has inspired. San Diegans, however, are fiercely proud of their city, which they shamelessly, yet endearingly, promote as 'America's Finest City.' After a few days of sunny exploration, you might agree.

Orientation

The heart of San Diego is its compact downtown, especially the historic, gentrified Gaslamp Quarter. Southwest of here, upscale Coronado is reached either via ferry or a stunning bridge, while Balboa Park and the San Diego Zoo are to the north. The park segues into Hillcrest, the nerve center of the city's gay community. Communities west of here include tourist-oriented Old Town and Mission Bay, a water playground. Coastside, Ocean Beach, Mission Beach and Pacific Beach all epitomize the laid-back SoCal lifestyle, while further north, La Jolla sits pretty as an enclave of sophistication. The I-5 Fwy cuts through the city north–south, while I-8 is the main east–west artery.

Information

BOOKSTORES

5th Avenue Books (☎ 619-291-4660; 3838 5th Ave, Hillcrest) Used books.

Le Travel Store & STA Travel (☎ 619-544-0005; 745 4th Ave, Gaslamp) New maps and guidebooks.

INTERNET ACCESS

Central Library (820 E St, Downtown; Internet access free; ☼ 10am-9pm Mon-Thu, 9:30am-5:30pm Fri & Sat, 1-5pm Sun)

Cyber Zone (193 Horton Plaza, cnr 1st Ave & F St, Downtown; per hr from $4; ☼ 10am-11pm)

MEDIA

San Diego Union-Tribune (www.signonsandiego.com) Major daily.

San Diego Reader (www.sdreader.com) Independent weekly.

Update (www.sandiegogaynews.com) Serves the GLBT community.

MEDICAL SERVICES

Mission Bay Memorial Hospital (☎ 619-274-7721; 3030 Bunker Hill St, Mission Bay)

Scripps Mercy Hospital (☎ 619-294-8111; 4077 5th Ave, Hillcrest)

MONEY

Travelex (☎ 800-287-7362; ground level, Horton Plaza, Downtown) Foreign-currency exchange.

POST

Downtown Post Office (815 E St, San Diego, 92101) Downtown, for General Delivery mail.

TOURIST INFORMATION

Downtown Visitors Center (☎ 619-236-1212; www .sandiego.org; 1040 W Broadway; ☼ 9am-5pm Mon-Sat)

Sights

DOWNTOWN & LITTLE ITALY

Downtown's main drag, 5th Ave, was once a notorious strip of saloons, bordellos and gambling joints. These days, the restored **Gaslamp Quarter** is downtown's heart and soul, a bustling playground of restaurants, bars, clubs, shops and galleries. For the full historical picture, take a guided tour with the **Gaslamp Quarter Historical Foundation** (☎ 619-233-4692; 410 Island Ave; tours $3; 11am Sat), headquartered in the 1850 **William Heath Davis House**, one of San Diego's oldest buildings; it also contains a small museum.

Adjacent to the Gaslamp Quarter, downtown's newest building is the 42,000-seat **Petco Park** Major League Baseball stadium, home of the **San Diego Padres** (tickets ☎ 877-374-2784; tickets $12-40; Apr-Oct).

The initial spark for downtown's redevelopment in the 1980s was a giant shopping mall, the postmodern **Horton Plaza** (Broadway). West of here, the free **Museum of Contemporary Art** (☎ 619-234-1001; 1001 Kettner Blvd; ☼ 11am-5pm Thu-Tue) has changing exhibitions of post-1960s painting and sculpture.

North of the Gaslamp Quarter, **Little Italy** is an increasingly hip neighborhood, with antique stores and good restaurants along India St.

Further west you'll find the **Embarcadero**, San Diego's well-manicured waterfront area geared towards pedestrian pleasure seekers. A harborside stroll might start at the **Maritime Museum** (☎ 619-234-9153; 1492 N Harbor Dr; admission $8; ☼ 9am-9pm) with its historic sailing vessels. Stroll south past the cruise ship piers to **Seaport Village** (☎ 619-235-4014; ☼ 10am-9pm), a collection of novelty shops, restaurants and snack outlets.

BALBOA PARK

With its museums, gardens and its famous zoo, immaculately landscaped Balboa Park tops San Diego's must-see list. Many of the ornate beaux-arts and Spanish Colonial buildings are replicas of those constructed

DOWNTOWN SAN DIEGO & BALBOA PARK

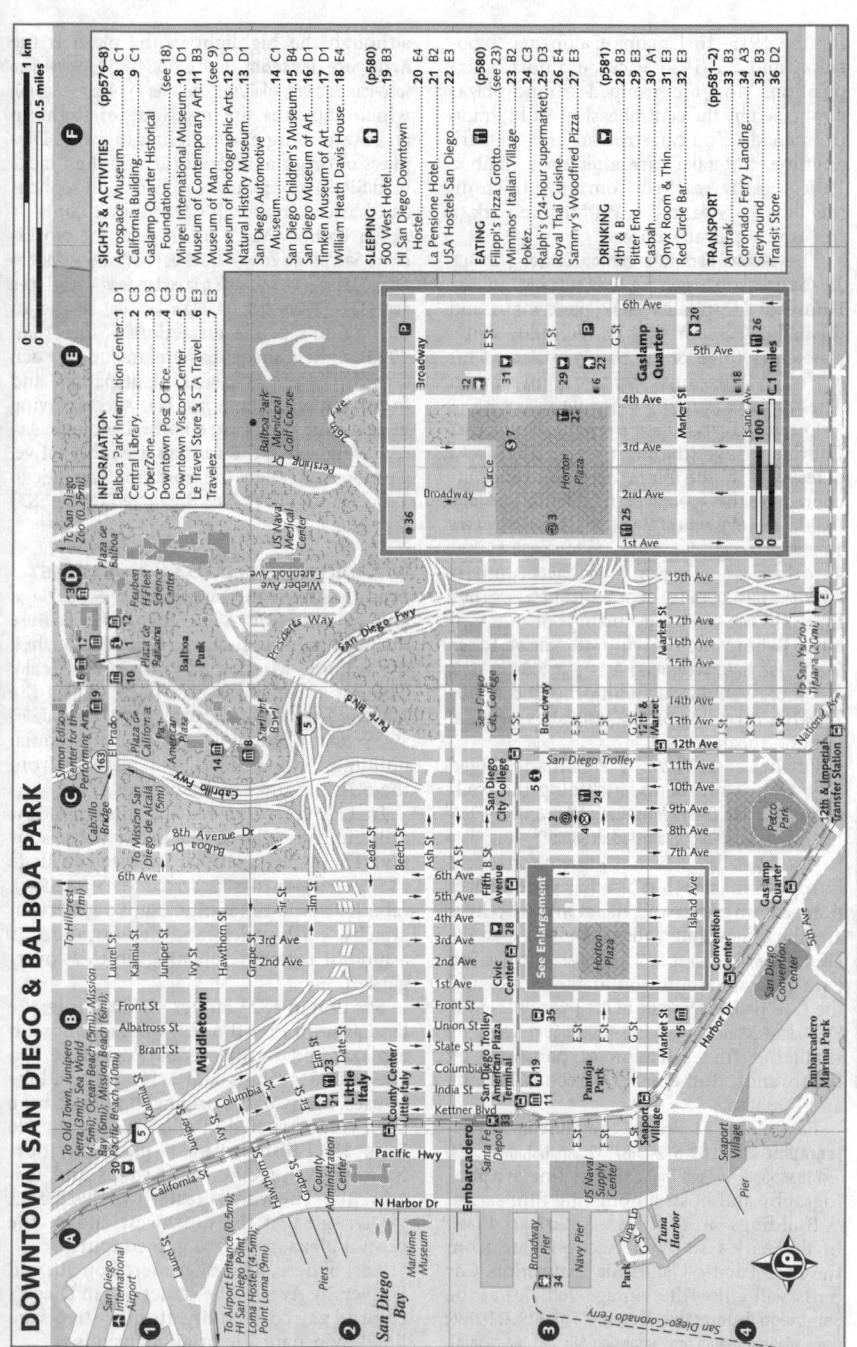

INFORMATION
Balboa Park Information Center..1 D1
Central Library...............2 C3
CyberZone....................3 D3
Downtown Post Office.........4 C3
Downtown Visitors Center.....5 C3
Le Travel Store & S*A Travel..6 E3
Travelex.....................7 E3

SIGHTS & ACTIVITIES (pp576–8)
Aerospace Museum..............8 C1
California Building............9 C1
Gaslamp Quarter Historical
 Foundation..............(see 18)
Mingei International Museum...10 D1
Museum of Contemporary Art..11 B3
Museum of Man.............(see 9)
Museum of Photographic Arts..12 D1
Natural History Museum.......13 D1
San Diego Automotive
 Museum....................14 C1
San Diego Children's Museum..15 B4
San Diego Museum of Art......16 D1
Timken Museum of Art.........17 D1
William Heath Davis House....18 E4

SLEEPING (p580)
500 West Hotel...............19 B3
HI San Diego Downtown
 Hostel.....................20 E4
La Pensione Hotel............21 B2
USA Hostels San Diego........22 E3

EATING (p580)
Filippi's Pizza Grotto.......23 B2
Mimmos' Italian Village......24 C3
Poké......................(see 23)
Ralph's (24-hour supermarket).25 D3
Royal Thai Cuisine...........26 E4
Sammy's Woodfired Pizza......27 E3

DRINKING (p581)
4th & B......................28 B3
Bitter End...................29 B3
Casbah.......................30 A1
Onyx Room & Thin............31 E3
Red Circle Bar...............32 E3

TRANSPORT (pp581–2)
Amtrak.......................33 B3
Coronado Ferry Landing.......34 A3
Greyhound....................35 B3
Transit Store................36 D2

CALIFORNIA

for the 1915–16 Panama-California Exposition and the 1935 Pacific-California Exposition. Most are grouped around plazas connected by the central east–west El Prado promenade. You can stroll around the park anytime, but take care after dark. Balboa Park is easily reached from downtown on bus Nos 7, 7A and 7B. Within the park, a free tram links attractions.

The **Balboa Park Information Center** (☎ 619-239-0512; www.balboapark.org; 1549 El Prado), in the House of Hospitality, sells park maps and the Balboa Passport ($30), which allows one-time entry to 13 of the park's museums for one week. Museums offer free admission on Tuesday on a rotating schedule.

Entering Balboa Park from the west across Cabrillo Bridge (the most scenic approach) takes you to the Plaza de California, anchored by the spectacular **California Building**. Inside, the **Museum of Man** (☎ 619-239-2001; www.museumofman.org; admission $6; ☽ 10am-4:30pm) has a world-class collection of artifacts (pottery, jewelry, baskets etc) representing a journey through the cultural history of humankind. Behind the museum, the **Simon Edison Centre for the Performing Arts** (☎ 619-239-2255) has three venues, including the Old Globe Theatre, a replica of Shakespeare's original London theater.

Further east, Plaza de Panama is ringed by a trio of museums, including the well-respected **San Diego Museum of Art** (☎ 619-232-7931; www.sdmart.org; adult/student $8/6; ☽ 10am-6pm Tue-Sun, to 9pm Thu), which is known for its old European masters but also has good collections of American and Asian art. Also here are the **Mingei International Museum** (☎ 619-239-0003; adult/student $6/3; ☽ 10am-4pm Tue-Sun) with folk art from around the globe, and the free **Timken Museum of Art** (☎ 619-239-5548; ☽ 10am-4:30pm Tue-Sat, 1:30-4:30pm Sun) with its small but fine selection of paintings by Rembrandt, Rubens, El Greco, Cézanne and Pissarro.

East along El Prado, the **Museum of Photographic Arts** (☎ 619-238-7559; adult/student $7/4; ☽ 10am-5pm, to 9pm Thu) exhibits fine art photography and hosts an ongoing film series.

Buildings around Pan-American Plaza in the park's southern section date from the 1935 Pacific-California Exposition. Car buffs will enjoy the vintage vehicles at the **San Diego Automotive Museum** (☎ 619-231-2886; www.sdautomuseum.org; admission $8; ☽ 10am-5pm),

although the highlight in the plaza is the **Aerospace Museum** (☎ 619-234-8291; www.aerospacemuseum.org; adult/student $8/6; ☽ 10am-4:30pm), which captures the mystique of flight in an entertaining and enlightening way. Displays of original aircraft include the Blackbird SR-71 spy plane as well as such replicas as Charles Lindbergh's *Spirit of St Louis*.

On Balboa Park's north side, the world-class **San Diego Zoo** (☎ 619-231-1515; www.sandiegozoo.org; admission $21, with guided bus tour & aerial tram ride $32; ☽ 9am-4pm, to 10pm Jun-Sep) is one of the region's prime attractions. More than 4000 animals shack up here, including such crowd pleasers as koalas, giant pandas and forest buffalo. There are 800 species living in beautifully re-created natural habitats. Arrive early, when the animals are most active. Combo tickets to the zoo and San Diego Wild Animal Park (see the boxed text, p583) cost $56.

PRESIDIO HILL, OLD TOWN & HILLCREST

Presidio Hill is the birthplace of San Diego and, by extension, of California. It was here during 1769 that Junípero Serra established the original Mission San Diego de Alcalá. The attractive site is now occupied by the **Junípero Serra Museum** (☎ 619-297-3258; admission $5; ☽ 10am-4:30pm Fri-Sun), a Spanish colonial building with artifacts and pictures from the mission and rancho periods.

In 1773 Serra moved the mission a few miles upriver, closer to a better water supply. These days, **Mission San Diego de Alcalá** (☎ 619-281-8449; Friars Rd; admission $3; ☽ 9am-5pm), rebuilt several times after Native American attacks, earthquakes and deterioration, is a modest rectangle opening up to a lovely garden.

Starting in 1821, under Mexican rule, the land around Presidio Hill was laid out with a plaza, and by the 1830s Pueblo de San Diego had 40 huts and a few large adobe houses. Many of the original buildings have been reconstructed in what is now the **Old Town State Historic Park**, a pleasant, tourist-oriented precinct with shops and restaurants. The **visitors center** (☎ 619-220-5422; ☽ 10am-5pm), at the northwest end of the central plaza, runs free guided tours.

East of here, **Hillcrest**, centered on 5th and University Aves, is the center of San Diego's colorful gay community. Its hilly streets are lined by ornate Victorian mansions.

POINT LOMA

This peninsula protectively wraps around the entrance to San Diego Bay like an arm around a shoulder. At its southern tip, the **Cabrillo National Monument** (☎ 619-557-5450; $5 per car, $3 by bike or bus; ☷ 9am-5:15pm) commemorates the man who led the first Spanish exploration of the West Coast and offers stunning bay panoramas. The exhibits at the visitors center are worth a look. Also here is the 1854 **Old Point Loma Lighthouse**, in operation until 1891 and now a museum. Access to the point is along Catalina Blvd (Hwy 209) or bus No 6A from downtown.

SEA WORLD, MISSION BAY & THE BEACHES

After WWII, coastal engineering turned the swampy San Diego River mouth into a 7-sq-mile playground of parks, beaches and bays. Facilities run from free outdoor activities to luxurious resorts. Kite flying is popular, along with water sports and cycling the miles of paved bike paths.

San Diego's best-known attraction, **Sea-World** (☎ 619-226-3901; www.seaworld.com; 500 Sea-World Dr; admission $50; ☷ 9am-11pm Jul-Aug, shorter hr at other times) combines live shows starring trained animals with zoo-like animal exhibits. Must-do's include shows starring Shamu the killer whale, and the sea lions Clyde and Seamore, as well as the Wild Arctic motion-simulator ride. Lines can get long in summer. Look for discount coupons in hotels and tourist offices.

Three main beaches is where the action's at. South of Mission Bay is the boho of **Ocean Beach** (OB), with a fishing pier, good surf and sunset barbecues. Newport Ave is chock-a-block with bars, eateries, bikini shops and outlaw grommet skateboarders pulling 'ollies' on the sidewalks. West of Mission Bay, **Mission Beach** (MB) and its northern neighbor, **Pacific Beach** (PB), are connected by a paved **Ocean Front Walk**, which attracts skaters, joggers and cyclists. In summer it's a *Baywatch* scene, with end-to-end bodies, cafés, bars and impossible parking. **Belmont Park** in MB is an old-fashioned amusement park with a wooden roller coaster. The activity in PB spreads inland along Garnet Ave, with lively bars and restaurants.

LA JOLLA

On one of Southern California's most scenic stretches of coast is a ritzy suburb, with a compact, upscale downtown packed with galleries, boutiques and restaurants. Noteworthy sights include the **Children's Pool**, **La Jolla Cove** and, marked by buoys, the offshore **San Diego-La Jolla Underwater Park**, a great spot for scuba diving (below). The slick **Museum of Contemporary Art** (☎ 858-454-3541; 700 Prospect St; admission $6; ☷ 11am-5pm Thu-Tue, to 7pm Thu) has good collections of 1960s and '70s minimalist and pop art, as well as conceptual works and cross-border pieces from Tijuana.

La Jolla is also home to the **University of California at San Diego** (UCSD). The **Stephen Birch Aquarium-Museum** (☎ 858-534-3474; 2300 Exhibition Way; adult/student $9/6; ☷ 9am-5pm) has brilliant displays of marine life (recommended). Further north, the **Salk Institute** (☎ 858-453-4100, 10010 N Torrey Pines Rd), designed in 1965 by Louis Kahn, is a masterpiece of modern architecture; call to arrange a free weekday tour. There's superb coastline at **Torrey Pines State Reserve** (per car $4; ☷ 8am-sunset) with gorgeous ocean-view trails.

Activities

San Diego has good **surfing** and **windsurfing** (surf report ☎ 619-221-8824), but the water can get crowded. First-timers might try **Pacific Surf School** (☎ 619-742-2267; www.pacificsurf.org; lessons $45-65) in Mission Beach. The best scuba diving is at the **San Diego-La Jolla Underwater Park**, with giant kelp forests and the 100ft-deep La Jolla Canyon; local outfitters include **OE Express** (☎ 858-454-6195; www.oeexpress .com; 2158 Av de la Playa, La Jolla).

Festivals & Events

Mardi Gras (February) Fat Tuesday street party in the Gaslamp.

Ocean Beach Kite Festival (early March) Contests and intense competition at the OB Rec Center.

Cinco de Mayo (early May) Mexican national day celebrated with *mucho tequila* in Old Town and beyond.

American Indian Cultural Days (mid-May) Dancing, music and art displays in Balboa Park.

US Open Sandcastle Competition (early July) Amazing constructions at Imperial Beach.

World Bodysurfing Championships (August) Look dude, no board! In Oceanside.

San Diego Street Scene (early September) Street music festival in the Gaslamp.

Dia de los Muertos (late October) Traditional Mexican Day of the Dead processions and altars in Bazaar del Mundo.

Sleeping

Where you'll want to stay depends on what sort of experience you envisage. If you want to be within walking distance of plentiful dining and entertainment options, opt for a hostel downtown. Sun worshippers should hang their hat in one of the beach towns. In summer (late May to early September) hotels book up early and rates skyrocket, especially in the beach towns. There's plenty to choose from, so poke around. Our listed rates don't include the 10.5% room tax.

USA Hostels San Diego (☎ 619-232-3100, 800-438-8622; www.usahostels.com; 726 5th Ave; dm $19-21, r $53-54; ☒ ☐) The original link in this chain is a friendly Victorian-era hotel refitted with six-bed dorms, a nice lounge and good kitchen. There's always something on tap, like keg parties, TJ booze tours and pub crawls, and guests can hang out until 10pm after checking out.

> **SPLURGE!**
>
> **La Pensione Hotel** (☎ 619-236-8000, 800-232-4683; www.lapensionehotel.com; 606 W Date St; r $75) One of San Diego's top bargains, this Little Italy gem brings European flair to the Left Coast, complete with black marble lobby, free wi-fi Internet and well-equipped rooms.

Ocean Beach International Hostel (☎ 619-223-7873, 800-339-7263; www.californiahostel.com; 4961 Newport Ave; dm/r from $16/40) It's all about hangin' out and hookin' up at this fun, laid-back place. It's within stumbling distance of way too many bars and only a couple of blocks from some of the best surf in town. US travelers must show proof of foreign travel, so it's mostly an international crowd.

HI San Diego Downtown Hostel (☎ 619-525-1531, 800-909-4776; www.sandiegohostels.org; 521 Market St; dm $19-26, r $47-58; ☒ ☐) This popular, party-friendly Gaslamp Quarter hostel has a big kitchen and is handy to nightlife and public transit – but it's a ways from the beach. It's a wee bit institutional but skylights throughout create a pleasant vibe.

Also recommended:

Banana Bungalow (☎ 858-273-3060, 800-546-7835; www.bananabungalow.com; dm/r from $20/49; ☐) Fronting Mission Beach boardwalk, with a nonstop beach-party atmosphere. Don't plan on getting any sleep, dude.

HI San Diego Point Loma Hostel (☎ 619-223-4778, 800-909-4775; www.sandiegohostels.org; 3790 Udall St; dm $15-21, r $38-48; ☒ ☐) In quiet Loma Portal, a 20-minute walk from the heart of Ocean Beach. No lockout. Bus Nos 23 (from downtown, weekdays only) and 35 (daily from Old Town) run along nearby Voltaire St.

500 West Hotel (☎ 619-269-9172; www.500westhotel.com; 500 W Broadway; r from $69; ☐) The old YMCA morphed into a hyper-modern boutique hotel lavished with high-tech amenities like flat-screen TVs and in-room DSL.

Eating

You can enjoy Mexican *huevos rancheros* (fried eggs on tortillas, covered in salsa) for breakfast, an Indian curry for lunch and wrap up the day with a killer lobster taco. The best cheap options tend to be near the beach, rather than in town.

Pokéz (☎ 619-702-7160; 947 E St; mains less than $6) Healthy, vegetarian Mexican in a funky, artsy space.

Kono's (☎ 858-483-1669; 704 Garnet Ave, Pacific Beach; mains under $6) This quintessential surf shack draws long lines for its tasty breakfasts, burgers and sandwiches served until the early afternoon.

Hodad's (☎ 619-224-4623; 5010 Newport Ave, Ocean Beach; burgers $3-9) Grab a stool at the communal longboard with other 'wannabe surfers' and scope the street scene at the ultimate burger shack

Royal Thai Cuisine (☎ 619-230-8424; 467 5th Ave; mains $9-13) Enjoy San Diego's best Thai food in an airy dining room sprinkled with classic statues. Lunch specials ($8) are popular.

Old Town Mexican Café (☎ 619-297-4330; 2489 San Diego Ave; mains $4-12) No-frills favorite with locals for sit-down dining.

Sammy's Woodfired Pizza (☎ 619-230-8888; 770 4th Ave; mains $8-15) Creative pizzas are the star of the show at this cafeteria-style eatery, although the appetizers and big salads have their fans as well.

Supermarkets are ubiquitous. **Ralphs** (☎ 595-1581; 101 G St; ☾ 24hr) is just south of Horton Plaza and upscale **Whole Foods** (☎ 294-2800; 711 University Ave, Hillcrest) stocks organic produce.

Also recommended:

Mimmos' Italian Village (☎ 619-239-3710; 1743 India St, Little Italy; sandwiches from $5) Hot and cold hoagies from a classic deli case.

Filippi's Pizza Grotto Little Italy (☎ 619-232-5094; 2061 India St); Pacific Beach (☎ 858-483-6222; 962 Garnet Ave; pizzas from $10) The classics: pizza, Chianti and Sinatra.

Drinking

Watch out for happy-hour tours run by hostels, and all-you-can-handle booze day trips to Tijuana – and compromising pictures of you on the Internet afterwards. Don't say we didn't warn you.

BARS

Onyx Room & Thin (☎ 619-235-6699; 852 5th Ave) Come for cocktails and conversations at the ultra-cool, industrial look Thin, or the plusher, candle-lit Onyx in the basement. The latter also has a dance floor.

Red Circle Bar (☎ 619-234-9211; 420 E St) Order a martini (choose from over 100 vodkas), raise your pinkie and peruse the Soviet-era memorabilia and lissome crowd bathed in sexy red lighting at this trendy Russian-themed *boîte* (small restaurant or nightclub).

Bitter End (☎ 619-338-9300; 770 5th Ave) On busy nights all three levels of this fabulous bar bustle with bodies of all shapes and sizes. There's dancing in the basement, beer at street level and martinis in the upstairs.

Coaster Saloon (☎ 858-488-4438; 744 Ventura Pl, Mission Beach) An old-fashioned, unpretentious neighborhood bar with good margaritas and front-row views of the Belmont Park roller coaster.

LIVE MUSIC & CLUBBING

The *San Diego Reader* hits the free stands every Thursday and contains comprehensive listings.

Casbah (☎ 619-232-4355; 2501 Kettner Blvd, Little Italy) Nirvana and the Smashing Pumpkins cut their teeth at this alternative venue, where couches, pinball machines and dimly lit alcoves offer respite from the dance floor.

4th & B (☎ 619-231-4343; 345 B St) It's mostly local bands at this popular venue with a huge dance floor, energetic crowd and eclectic music schedule – soul to Latin to alternative rock.

Barefoot Bar & Grill (☎ 858-274-4630; 1404 W Vacation Rd, Mission Bay) The time to be at Barefoot, in the Paradise Point Resort, is on summer Sundays for the wild all-day weekend wrap-up parties. Things cool down on other days.

Still standing? Other fun party places:

Canes (☎ 858-488-1780; 3105 Ocean Front Walk, Mission Beach) Tropical.

Winston's (☎ 619-222-6822; 1921 Bacon St, Ocean Beach) Reggae-infused.

Blind Melons (☎ 858-483-7844; 710 Garnet Ave, Pacific Beach) Edgy, popular with military.

Getting There & Around

San Diego International Airport (SAN; ☎ 619-400-2400; www.san.org) is 3 miles west of downtown. Catch the *Flyer*, bus No 992 ($2.25) downtown along Broadway. Airport shuttles and taxis cost from $8 to $13.

Greyhound (☎ 619-239-8082; 120 W Broadway) has frequent departures in every direction.

Amtrak's (☎ 619-239-9021; Santa Fe Depot) *Pacific Surfliner* service runs up the coast several times daily.

GOING TO TIJUANA & BAJA CALIFORNIA

You've come all this way, so why not cross the line? The US–Mexican border at San Ysidro, 20 miles south of downtown San Diego, is the world's busiest frontier, with an average of more than 200,000 people crossing each day. Downtown Tijuana and its infamous R&R party spots fronting Avenida Revolución (La Revo) are a 15-minute walk past the international border. Take care if straying even a block off the main drag, even in broad daylight and especially north of La Revo bordering the Zona Norte red-light district. Nearly all businesses (and *maldito* cops – resist attempts to extract bribes) accept US dollars.

Pick up a free map showing cafés, restaurants, hotels and museums from the friendly, bilingual **visitors center** (☎ 664-683-1405; www.tijuanaonline.org) on the pedestrian walkway.

The cheapest, easiest and most efficient way to reach the border is via the **San Diego Trolley Blue Line** ($3 one way). Frequent trains make the 45-minute journey from early in the morning to late at night and around the clock on Saturday. The other alternative to driving is **Greyhound**, with hourly departures ($5 one way) – oddly, it's cheaper to stay on board the bus and go direct to Tijuana than to get off in San Ysidro ($8 to $9.50) and walk across the border.

Unless you're planning on exploring the Baja Peninsula south of Tijuana, driving is more hassle than it's worth. Due to heightened post-9/11 security, expect delays when returning to the USA. See Visas (p698) and Customs (p687) for border requirements.

CALIFORNIA

Most hostels post current auto driveaway opportunities (see p707). Major car rental companies (see p710) have desks at the airport.

Local buses and the San Diego Trolley are operated by **Metropolitan Transit Service** (MTS; ☎ 800-266-6883; www.sdcommute.com). The **Transit Store** (☎ 619-234-1060; Broadway & 1st Ave) has maps, tickets and one-/two-/three-/four-day passes ($5/9/12/15).

Buses blanket the metro area, while the Trolley's main route travels south to the Mexican border from Old Town. *Coaster* commuter trains serve communities in northern San Diego county.

THE DESERTS

Forget about green. After a while the starkness of the desert landscape, the clarity of the light and the spaciousness are beautiful in their own way. Be warned that the deserts present real dangers from extreme weather: hot days (120°F or 49°C and up), freezing, windy nights and flash flood potential. Resist the temptation to explore abandoned mine shafts. And bring lots and *lots* of water.

Music fans gather in Indio each May for the Coachella Valley Music and Arts Festival (see the boxed text, opposite).

PALM SPRINGS

Hemmed in by the austere Colorado Desert and lorded over by the rugged San Jacinto Mountains, the ritziest of Coachella Valley's desert resorts is a pretty pastiche of swaying palms, abundant flowers and emerald golf courses. Its pedigree as a posh playground dates back to the roaring 1920s when Hollywood starlets retreated here for indiscretions.

There's plenty to do here besides sip maotais poolside, but few backpackers detour here en route to Las Vegas. A big gay and lesbian scene flourishes along Arenas Rd. Most visitors come in the cooler months (October to April), but some rock-bottom rates help things stay busy even in summer, when temperatures rarely drop below 100°F (38°C).

The **Main Visitors Center** (☎ 760-778-8415, 800-927-7256; www.palm-springs.org; ☿ 9am-6pm) is north of town, at the tramway turnoff.

Sights & Activities

Escape the summer heat by riding the **Aerial Tramway** (☎ 760-325-1391; www.pstramway.com; $21; ☿ 10am-10pm Mon-Fri, 8am-10pm Sat & Sun) up Mt San Jacinto to an elevation of 8516ft, an eight-minute journey through five vegetation zones equivalent to a trip from Mexico to Alaska. As well as awesome desert views, 54 miles of hiking trails beckon in **Mt Jacinto State Park**, including a 5.5-mile trek to the 10,804ft summit. In winter, explore the forest on snowshoes or cross-country skis, for hire at the mountain station.

Another cool place is **Knott's Soak City** (☎ 760-327-0499; 1500 S Gene Autry Trail; www.soakcityusa .com; admission $24, after 3pm $14; ☿ 10am-6pm daily mid-Mar–Aug, Sat & Sun only Oct) with slides, tube rides, wave pools and rock climbing center next door. Day use of the mineral pools at **Desert Hot Springs** (☎ 800-808-7727; 10805 Palm Dr; admission $3-8) includes a dry sauna and showers.

In the cooler months, especially during the spring wildflower season, a hike through the lovely, scenic **Indian Canyons** (☎ 760-325-3400, 800-790-3398; www.indian-canyons.com; admission $6; ☿ 8am-5pm), 2 miles south of downtown and on the Agua Caliente Indian Reservation, is a delight. Tribal members also lead tours of sacred **Tahquitz Canyon** (☎ 760-416-7044; www .tahquitzcanyon.com; 500 W Mesquite Dr; $12.50; ☿ 8am-3pm, closed Jun-Sep), famous for its 60ft waterfall and ancient rock art.

Sleeping

The thriftiest motels are along East Palm Canyon/South Palm Canyon Dr. Four miles south of La Quinta at the western end of 58th Ave, RV-mobbed **Lake Cahuilla County Park** (☎ 760-564-4712; campsites $10-15) is the closest campground, but Mt Jacinto State Park (see above) and Joshua Tree National Park (see opposite), an hour's drive east, are nicer options.

Iron Tree Inn (☎ 760-325-8237, 877-696-9668; 1600 Calle Palo Fierro; r from $55; ☿ Sep–mid-Jun; ✿) looks a bit dumpy from the outside, but you won't notice this inside the Southwestern-themed rooms. It's quiet and central, with kitchenettes. Nearby is the leafy **Alpine Gardens Hotel** (☎ 760-323-2231, 888-299-7455; www.alpinegardens.com; 1586 E Palm Canyon Dr; r $50-85; ✖ ✖ ✿).

Eating

Grab any meal at **Rock Garden Café** (☎ 760-327-8840; 777 S Palm Canyon Dr; mains $8-17), a casual eatery with a large patio and extensive menu offering everything from roast-beef sandwiches to vegetarian quiche. **Bit of Country** (☎ 760-325-5154; 418 S Indian Canyon Dr; breakfast $4-9) serves big, hearty breakfasts, while **Native Foods** (☎ 760-416-0070; 1775 E Palm Canyon Dr; mains $9-13) offers vegan fare.

Getting There & Around

Palm Springs International Airport (PSP; ☎ 760-318 3800; www.palmsprinqsairport.com) has direct flights to and from major US cities. **Greyhound** (☎ 760-325-2053; 311 N Indian Canyon Dr) goes to LA, while local service is via **SunBus** ($1, day pass $3).

JOSHUA TREE NATIONAL PARK

Made famous by the band U2, **Joshua Tree National Park** welcomes backpackers, rock climbers and rock-and-roll pilgrims. It's especially popular in spring when the whimsical gnarled trees dramatically send up a huge single white flower. Highlights include dramatic rock formations in **Hidden Valley**; **Keys View**, with vistas as far as Mexico (best at sunset); and the **Cholla Cactus Garden**.

Near the park's northern entrance is the Twentynine Palms **visitors center** (☎ 760 367-5500; www.nps.gov/jotr; admission $10), with the Cottonwood Springs **visitors center** (☉ 8am-4pm) just inside the south entrance.

Bunk where Bono and co stayed while recording the album *Joshua Tree* in 1987 at the **Harmony Motel** (☎ 760-367-3351; www.harmonymotel .com; 71161 29 Palms Hwy 2000 Twentynine Palms; r $60-100; 🔊), complete with pool, private units and sweeping desert views.

A couple of the park's nine **campgrounds** (☎ 800-365-2267; http://reservations.nps.gov; campsites $5-10) are reservable and free backcountry camping is permitted. Note that aside from

> ### COACHELLA ROCKS!
>
> Music fans brave the desert each May for the **Coachella Valley Music and Arts Festival** (www.coachella.com), an open-air weekend festival with the likes of Radiohead, Beck, Air, the Flaming Lips, Stereolab and the Beastie Boys on recent bills. Bring a hat and sunscreen!

restrooms the park has no facilities, so bring food and plenty of water.

If you can't get enough of the desert, you should check out the sand dunes, volcanic outcrops and fabulous rock formations in the vast, undeveloped **Mojave National Preserve** (☎ 760-733-4040; www.nps.gov/moja), sandwiched between the I-10 and I-40, with access via Baker and Needles.

MOJAVE DESERT

The I-15 Fwy bisects the Mojave (mo-*ha*-vee) Desert. Midway between LA and Vegas, it enters **Barstow**, a pit-stop oasis. The Barstow Rd exit leads to the **California Desert Information Center** (☎ 760-255-8760; 831 Barstow Rd). A few miles east is **Calico Ghost Town** (☎ 760-254-2122; www.calicotown.com; admission $6, campsite/cabin $18/28; ☉ 8am-dusk), rebuilt but only marginally more authentic than Disney's Frontierland. It's still a fun place to stop and take a break.

About 25 miles north of Mojave, via Hwy 14, **Red Rock Canyon State Park** (☎ 661-942-0662; day-use fee $3) straddles Hwy 14. Its dramatically eroded sandstone cliffs are especially spectacular at sunrise and sunset and featured in the opening scenes of the film *Jurassic Park*. For front-row stargazing, pitch a tent at **Ricardo Campground** (campsites $9; first-come, first-served).

IF YOU'VE GOT A FEW MORE DAYS IN SOUTHERN CALIFORNIA

- Explore **Anza-Borrego Desert State Park** (www.anzaborrego.statepark.org), east of San Diego, perfect for adventurers seeking a quintessential desert experience: solitude, remote camping, stargazing, meditating, whatever.
- Go on safari at the 1800-acre **San Diego Wild Animal Park** (☎ 760-747-8702; www.sandiegozoo .org; 15500 San Pasqual Valley Rd, Escondido; admission $27; ☉ 9am-10pm Jun-Sep, closes 5pm other times) that lets its denizens roam freely on the open valley floor. You'll encounter herds of giraffes, zebras, rhinos and other animals while riding the Wgasa Bush Line Railway or touring the Heart of Africa and other habitats.
- Ferry to **Catalina Island**, 88% protected backcountry.

CALIFORNIA

DEATH VALLEY NATIONAL PARK

The name itself evokes all that is harsh and hellish – a lifeless place hotter than Satan's hoof. True, but only half-baked. Death Valley is a mesmerizing medley of rugged canyons, sand dunes, ghost towns, oases and colorful mountains. It holds the US records for hottest temperature (134°F, or 56°C, measured in 1913), lowest point (Badwater, 282ft below sea level) and largest national park outside Alaska (4687 sq miles). Bring plenty of water for you and your car. There's no public transportation to or within the park.

Orientation & Information

Centrally located **Furnace Creek** has the most facilities, including a general store, restaurants, public showers and a **visitors center** (☎ 760-786-3200; www.nps.gov/deva; admission $10; ✹ 8am-5pm) that doubles as a museum. **Stovepipe Wells**, 24 miles northwest, has a store, gas station, motel with restaurant, and a ranger station. Gas and sustenance are also available at **Scotty's Castle**, in the north, and **Panamint Springs**, on the park's western edge.

Sleeping

During the peak months of March–April (wildflower season) campgrounds fill up by mid-morning. Crowds thin considerably from June to September.

Basic motel rooms can be found in various sizes at **Stove Pipe Wells Village** (☎ 760-786-2331; r $55-99; ✹ ▯ ✺) while the pet-friendly **Panamint Springs Resort** (☎ 775-482-7680; www.deathvalley.com; campsites $12, r $65-139; ✹) is on the park's western edge. Both have restaurants and campgrounds.

The summer heat makes camping at the lower levels intolerable, while winter nights can be surprisingly cold. Death Valley has nine other campgrounds (several seasonal and free), but none are that attractive. Only **Furnace Creek** (☎ 800-365-2267; www.reservations.nps.gov; campsites $10-16), the most pleasant and shady campground, accepts reservations. Nearby – at 190ft below sea level! – is the 1000-site, RV-oriented **Sunset** (campsites $10) and the much nicer, hillside **Texas Spring** (campsites $12). Both are open mid-October to mid-April. For free backcountry camping, pick up a permit from the visitors center or ranger station.

OUTSIDE THE PARK

More lodging options are available within a one- to two-hour drive from Furnace Creek. The pit stops of Ridgecrest and Beatty, Nevada, are the best bet for budget motels. Any hard-core shoestringers should steer for the **HI Desertaire Hostel** (☎ 760-852-4580, 877-907-1265; www.desertairehostel.com; 2000 Old Spanish Trail Hwy; dm/r $15/50; ✺), near free public hot springs – sort of redundant in this weather, no? – in Tecopa, 60 miles southeast near Shoshone.

CENTRAL COAST

California's Central Coast, stretching from Ventura north to Monterey Bay, covers nearly 300 miles of prime shoreline. Hwy 101 is the region's main conduit, though for outstanding coastal views take Pacific Coast Hwy (Hwy 1) between San Luis Obispo and Monterey. Greyhound and Amtrak have frequent service up and down the coast.

SCENIC DRIVE: DEATH VALLEY

This tour can be done in a single day (even starting from outside the valley), if you start early. Begin by catching the sunrise at either **Zabriskie Point** or **Dante's View**. From the latter, it's possible to see both Mt Whitney (14,494ft) and Badwater, the highest and lowest points respectively in the contiguous USA. Head down to Furnace Creek, then cruise to Stovepipe Wells to enjoy the interplay of light and shadow while clambering around the **sand dunes**.

Another 36 miles north is **Scotty's Castle** (☎ 760-786-2392; admission $9; ✹ 7am-6pm), at 3000ft above sea level and noticeably cooler, a richly furnished ex-home of an insurance magnate. Eight miles west, **Ubehebe Crater** is the result of a massive volcanic eruption. The round-trip hike to the bottom takes about 30 minutes. Backtrack south for 60 miles past Furnace Creek to **Badwater**, where you can walk onto the constantly evaporating bed of salty, mineralized water. A few miles back north, the valley floor is filled with lumps of crystallized salt in what is called the **Devil's Golf Course**. Conclude your day on **Artists Drive** by watching the mountains erupt in a riot of color in the late-afternoon sun.

SPLURGE!

Ventura Harbor, southwest of Hwy 101 via Harbor Blvd, is where boats depart for the Channel Islands, whose unique flora and fauna has garnered them the nickname 'California's Galápagos'. Five of the eight islands in this chain stretching from Newport Beach to Santa Barbara comprise **Channel Islands National Park**. The National Park Service operates a **visitors center** (☎ 805-658-5730; www.nps.gov/chis; 1901 Spinnaker Dr; ⏱ 8:30am-5pm) in Ventura Harbor. Anacapa is closest to the mainland and thus gets the most visitors. Santa Cruz is the largest and the best suited for explorations on your own. San Miguel, the most remote island, offers solitude and wilderness but is often shrouded in fog. Santa Barbara supports a sizable elephant seal colony, and Santa Rosa, with its many bird species and sandy beaches, is the best island for longer trips. Swimming, snorkeling, diving, bird-watching and kayaking are all popular activities on the islands, all of which have primitive **campgrounds** (reservations ☎ 800-365-2267; campsites $10); bring food and water. One air and two boat operators offer camper transportation, and a variety of day trips and packages. Expect to pay about $37/34/20 adult/senior/child for an eight-hour boat trip to Anacapa Island.

- **Islands Packers** (☎ 805-642-7688; www.islandpackers.com; 1867 Spinnaker Dr) Next to the NPS Visitors Center.
- **Truth Aquatics** (☎ 805-962-1127; wwwtruthaquatics; 301 W Cabrillo Blvd) In Santa Barbara.
- **Channel Islands Aviation** (☎ 805-987-1301; 305 Durley Ave, Camarillo; flights $106) Flights to Santa Rosa Island from airports in Camarillo and Santa Barbara.

SANTA BARBARA

Sitting prettily between the Pacific Ocean and the Santa Ynez Mountains, its red-tile roofs and white stucco visible from afar, Santa Barbara is a Central Coast highlight. The historic downtown retains an architectural integrity, a real masterpiece of a courthouse and museums that are balanced well by five colleges, including the University of California at Santa Barbara (UCSB), which lend the town youthful verve and balance its affluent yachting and retirement communities. State St is downtown's main drag. Lower State St (south of Ortega St) is bar central, while upper State St harbors boutiques and museums.

Information

Chaucer's (☎ 805-682-6787; 3321 State St)
Best bookstore in town, with a good travel section.
Hot Spots (36 State St; Internet access per hr $8; ⏱ 24hr) Erratic coin-op Internet kiosks, biased visitor info and handy all-night café.
Visitors Center (☎ 805-965-3021; www.santa barbaraca.com; 1 Garden St; ⏱ 9am-5pm Mon-Sat, 10am-5pm Sun) Helpful; sells Lonely Planet books.

Sights & Activities

Though pricy, Santa Barbara is a great walking town. Ask at the visitors centers for the free Red Tile Tour pamphlet for self-guided tours of downtown.

Start your explorations at the exquisite **Santa Barbara County Courthouse** (☎ 805-962-6464; 1100 Anacapa St; ⏱ 8:30am-5pm Mon-Fri, 10am-4:30pm Sat & Sun). Built in Spanish–Moorish Revival style, it features hand-painted ceilings, tiles from Tunisia and Spain and wrought-iron chandeliers. Look around on your own or take one of the free docent-led tours (Monday, Tuesday and Friday at 10:30am and 2pm). Don't miss the panoramic view from the clock tower and the 2nd-floor Mural Room.

The nearby **Santa Barbara Museum of Art** (☎ 805-963-4364; 1130 State St; adult/student $7/4, admission free Sun; ⏱ 11am-5pm Tue-Sat, noon-5pm Sun) presents American and European hotshots – Hopper, O'Keefe, Monet and Matisse – plus Asian art, photography and classical sculpture. There's a nice café and, out front, an engaging free mural, *Portrait of México Today, 1932*, by David Alfaro Siqueiros.

Serra stopped in Santa Barbara in 1786 long enough to found **Mission Santa Barbara** (☎ 805-682-4713; 2201 Laguna St; admission $4; ⏱ 9am-5pm), nicknamed 'Queen of the Missions.' Chumash decorations adorn the church, which abuts a large cemetery.

Back on the waterfront, stroll the rough wooden **Stearns Wharf** and sample the town's briny history at the **Santa Barbara Maritime Museum** (☎ 805-962-8404; 113 Harbor Way; adult/

CALIFORNIA

student $5/3; 🕑 11am-5pm Thu-Tue), which often hands out two-for-one coupons.

Near the beach end of State St, several outfits rent bikes and in-line skates ($7 an hour). On the waterfront, **Truth Aquatics** (301 W Cabrillo Blvd) rents sea kayaks.

Sleeping

Stylish Santa Barbara is not known for its budget digs. From mid-May through mid-September, even budget places jack up their rates two or even three times low-season prices. Chain motels cluster along upper State St, near Las Positas Rd, several miles north of downtown (bus No 6 or 11). In a pinch, try **Travelers Motel** (☎ 805-687-6009; 3222 State St; r $39-65; 🖳).

Santa Barbara Tourist Hostel (☎ 805-963-0154; www.sbhostel.com; 134 Chapala St; dm $19-21, r $45-55; 🖳) Brand new and noisy, within a somersault of the train station. It's friendly, lively and there's always something going on.

Hotel State Street (☎ 805-966-6586; ewtrade@ix .netcom.com; 121 State St; r $45-80; 🗶) This freshly painted place with spacious rooms and cable TV is adjacent to Amtrak (bring earplugs), a couple of blocks from the beach. All rooms but one have shared bathroom.

Haley Cottage Studios (☎ 805-455-1485; www .haleycottages.com; 227 E Haley St; r $47-85; 🖳) Cozy two-person kitchenette flats grouped around common patios in an old apartment complex. There's a coin-op laundry and a pool table.

Nearby state parks have nice beachfront campgrounds (☎ 805-968-1033). **Refugio State Beach** (campsites $15) and **El Capitan State Beach** (campsites $13-16) are 17 miles west of town off Hwy 101.

Eating

Authentic *taquerías* (taco joints) line Milpas St, an easy nine-block walk northwest of State St.

La Super Rica (☎ 805-963-4940; 622 N Milpas St; mains under $6) The best Mexican food in town comes out of this unassuming little self-service shack. The handmade tortillas and daily specials are standouts.

Pierre Lafond Bistro (☎ 805-962-1455; 516 State St; mains $4-8) This stylish self-serve café brings the best of casual French and California cuisine (espresso, pastries, salads, sandwiches) within reach of the masses at its sidewalk tables. Free wi-fi Internet.

Esau's Coffee Shop (403 State St; mains $4-8) No-attitude institution with orange booths, wacky décor, veggie options and a satisfying menu of classic American breakfasts and lunches.

Go Fish & Chips (☎ 805-962-7090; 50 S State St; buffet $9) All-you-can-eat fish and chips all day, every day for $8.95. We dare you to beat the iron-stomached champ who finished off 20 pieces!

Drinking

Lower State St is asses-to-elbows with bars, pubs and cafés – dress to impress to get past the bouncers at the thumping meat markets.

Wild Cat (☎ 805-962-7970; 15 W Ortega St) This funky revival lounge resembles something like a cross between a warehouse and a love shack.

Press Room (☎ 805-963-8121; 15 E Ortega St) An exception to the look-alike places lining State St, with punk posters, a jukebox and no-nonsense bar staff pulling smooth pints.

James Joyce (☎ 805-962-2688; 513 State St) An old-world place with plenty of character (read: peanut shells on the floor) that comes alive with live Dixieland jazz on Saturday nights.

Santa Barbara Brewing Co (☎ 805-730-1040; 501 State St; mains $5-10) A dozen homemade brews on tap, plus hearty lunch and dinner.

Getting There & Around

Greyhound (☎ 805-965-7551; 34 W Carrillo St) has daily buses to Los Angeles and San Francisco, while **Amtrak** (☎ 805-963-1015; 209 State St) has a direct train and more expensive coach service to Los Angeles and San Luis Obispo.

The **Downtown-Waterfront Shuttle Bus** (25¢; 🕑 10am-6pm) runs two routes: along State St to Stearns Wharf, and along Cabrillo Blvd from the yacht harbor to the zoo.

SAN LUIS OBISPO

North of Santa Barbara, Hwy 101 snakes along the coast and veers inland at Gaviota. Hwys 101 and 1 reunite 75 miles later at Pismo Beach, a dog-eared tourist town known for clams and sand dunes. Back at Gaviota, Hwy 1 swings northwest past Vandenberg Air Force Base.

San Luis Obispo is lively yet low-key, with a high quality of life and community spirit. Like most other Californian towns, it grew up around a mission, founded in 1772 by Junípero Serra. California Polytechnic State University's 17,000 students inject a healthy hubbub into the streets, pubs and cafés. The helpful **visitors center** (☎ 805-781-2777; www .visitslo.com; 1039 Chorro St) has maps and a phone for free hotel bookings. The best time to visit is Thursday from 6pm to 9pm year-round, when Higuera St turns into a giant street party during the famous **farmers market**.

Sights & Activities

San Luis Obispo's attractions cluster around **Mission Plaza**, a shady oasis with restored adobes. The plaza is lorded over by the **Mission San Luis Obispo De Toloso** (☎ 805-781-8220; church admission free, museum $2), with an endearingly old-fashioned museum about the Chumash and mission periods. For an in-depth look at local history, visit the free **San Luis Obispo County Historical Museum** (☎ 805-543-0430; 696 Monterey St; ❤ 10am-4pm Wed-Sun), adjacent to the mission. On the plaza's south end, the free **San Luis Obispo Art Center** (☎ 805-543-8562; 1010 Broad St; ❤ 11am-5pm Wed-Mon) showcases local artists. San Luis Obispo's quirkiest attraction is **Bubblegum Alley**, a narrow passageway, accessed between 733 and 737 Higuera St, covered with wads of discarded chicle.

Ask at the visitors center about **hiking** the **Nine Sisters** volcanic peaks and area **mountain biking** options.

Sleeping

Many major chains (rooms from $60) are represented on San Luis Obispo's motel row along Monterey St, north of downtown. Even if you can't splurge on the kitschy **Madonna Inn** (☎ 805-543-3000, 800-543-9666; www.madonnainn .com; r from $129), don't miss the urinal in the men's room – sorry ladies, no peeking.

The well-kept **HI Hostel Obispo** (☎ 805-544-4678; www.hostelobispo.com; 1617 Santa Rosa St; dm $18-20, r $45-60; ❤ closed 10am-4:30pm; ✕ ▣), in a homey Victorian building, has a bit of a B&B feel and is close to downtown and the Amtrak station. The dorms are cramped, but the bomber pancake breakfast makes up for it.

Eating

Linnaea's Café (☎ 805-541-5888; 1110 Garden St; mains $3-6) is a cool, relaxed locals hang-out with good coffee and live acoustic tunes at night. Upscale pub grub and fun décor get a thumbs up for **Mother's Tavern** (☎ 805-541-8733;

725 Higuera St; mains $4-7); at night, a sophomoric college crowd invades, not least for the live entertainment.

MORRO BAY TO BIG SUR

North of San Luis Obispo is one of the most dramatic stretches of Hwy 1. The first town you reach is **Morro Bay**, home to a large commercial fishing fleet and its namesake **Morro Rock**, a 578ft volcanic peak. Leading south from the rock is the Embarcadero, a waterfront walkway cluttered with tourist shops.

For a nicer experience, head south to **Morro Bay State Park**, which has a natural history museum and a heron reserve. Even further south is the largely undeveloped **Montaña de Oro State Park**, featuring coastal bluffs, sand dunes and a 4-mile-long sand spit.

There's camping at the **Morro Strand State Beach** (☎ 805-772-8812; campsites $13), **Morro Bay State Park** (☎ 805-772-7434; campsites $12) and at **Montaña de Oro State Park** (☎ 805-528-0513; campsites $7). For in-town eats, try **Frenchie Creperie Sophie** (☎ 805-772-4727; 355 Morro Bay Blvd; mains $5-9), which also serves beer.

Twenty miles north of Morro Bay, the artists village of **Cambria** features a fab roadside folk art attraction: **Nit Wit Ridge** (tour reservations ☎ 805-927-2690; 881 Hillcrest Dr; 'donation' $5), a homemade dwelling cobbled together entirely from recycled materials – from abalone shells to beer cans to toilet seats.

In **Harmony** (population 18), some 15 miles north of Morro Bay, don't miss the old-fashioned post office, Lilliputian chapel and killer glass-blowing studio-gallery – and the barbecue cart during summer. Visit the rustic **Harmony Cellars** (☎ 800-432-9239; 3255 Harmony Valley Rd) for free wine tastings.

The region's best budget lodging option is the charming **Bridge Street Inn** (☎ 805-927-7653; www.bridgestreetinncambria.com; 4314 Bridge St; dm $20, r $40-70), a B&B/hostel with considerable comfort. **Linn's** (☎ 805-927-0371; 2277 Main St; mains $6-12) is a casual eatery known for its pot pies, Sunday brunch and outlandish desserts. Linger on the patio at the **Redwood Cafe** (☎ 805-927-4830; 2094 Main St; mains $4-8) over hearty breakfasts and burgers until 2pm.

The coastline north of Hearst Castle (see p588) is home to California's largest **elephant seal colony**. There's a viewpoint 5 miles north of the castle. The seals are here year-round but are at their most plentiful between December and February.

> **SPLURGE!**
>
> California's most famous monument to wealth and ambition (and that's saying a lot in these parts), **Hearst Castle** (☎ 916-414-8400, 800-444-4445; www.hearstcastle.com; ◷ 8:20am-6pm summer, shorter hr off-season; tour 1 $18, tours 2, 3 & 4 $12, evening tour $24), a state Historic Monument, sprawls over 127 acres overlooking the Pacific. Newspaper magnate William Randolph Hearst created this estate of luxuriant gardens, accentuated by shimmering pools and ancient Greek statuary. The visit is worthwhile, if only to see something so ostentatious. Four estate tours are offered; tour 1 is best for first-time visitors. All tours last 90 minutes and reservations are recommended.

As you continue north, Hwy 1 leaves civilization far behind, hugging the rugged Pacific shore and traversing vast stretches of coast where services – let alone towns – are few and far between. After 30 miles you hit tiny **Gorda**, with an expensive gas station, deli and café. Next stop is the Central Coast's blockbuster – **Big Sur**.

CCAT/RTA buses (☎ 805-541-2228; $1-2.50) shuttle between San Luis Obispo, Morro Bay and San Simeon/Hearst Castle.

BIG SUR

The 'Big South' is an awe-inspiring symphony of nature. At times, Hwy 1 clutches at the cliffs as if in desperation, providing vista-point junkies with a steady fix. This sparsely populated region consists mainly of three state parks (Julia Pfeiffer Burns State Park, Pfeiffer Big Sur State Park and Andrew Molera State Park) and a slew of restaurants, inns and posh resorts tucked away off the highway. The **USFS Big Sur Ranger Station** (☎ 831-667-2315; ◷ 8am-4:30pm, to 6pm summer), a half-mile south of Pfeiffer Big Sur State Park, has information on all the parks and issues backcountry permits. Each park's $5 entrance fee is also valid on the same day at the other two parks.

Appropriately, the physical and spiritual beginning to Big Sur (if coming from the south) is the **Esalen Institute** (☎ 831-667-3000; www.esalen.org), a renowned retreat offering workshops and classes that explore 'human potential.' To experience Esalen without

enrolling, see if the sign on the road says 'vacancy' ($90 to $180 for sleeping bag spots to rustic private rooms), or make a same-day reservation for either a massage ($125), which includes time in the sumptuous hot springs, or '**night bathing**' ($20; ◷ 1-3am) in the famous tubs perched over the ocean.

Seven miles north, the **Henry Miller Memorial Library** (☎ 831-667-2574; www.henrymiller.org; ◷ 11am-6pm Wed-Mon, variable hr off-season) is, in essence, a sophisticated bookstore emphasizing Miller's works, but, more importantly, it strives to keep the author's iconoclastic spirit alive amid a gale of 21st-century conservatism. Stop by for inspiration, a squizz at the outdoor sculpture garden and by-donation coffee. Internet use is free.

Big Sur Center, 2 miles north, contains the first clutch of traveler services: a post office, general store, deli, restaurant and gas station. There's also a heart-warming bakery.

Ventana Wilderness is popular with backpackers; get $4 overnight parking permits, free backcountry permits and trail details from the rangers. **Point Sur** is that compelling hump of volcanic rock jutting into the ocean. The only way to visit is to join the three-hour tour of the 1899 **Point Sur Light Station** (☎ 831-625-4419; $5; ◷ Sat & Sun year-round, additional days in summer).

Sleeping

Accommodations are pricey, and fill up on weekends. If you turn up without camping reservations in summer, every site is likely to be taken. Also, pack a full cooler – groceries are expensive too.

Deetjen's Big Sur Inn (☎ 831-667-2377; www.deetjens.com; r $75-195, mains $5-25) This cozy homestead, just south of the Henry Miller Memorial Library, occupies a historic ranch with bona fide rustic credentials. If you can't swing a room, try to stop at the atmospheric restaurant for breakfast or dinner.

Eating

Half a mile north of Deetjen's, Nepenthe's casual **Café Kivah** (☎ 831-667-2345; mains $7-15) has amazing ocean views and blue jays who aren't shy about stealing the mouthwatering cinnamon rolls at breakfast. There's also a fancier restaurant for romantic tête-à-têtes.

A couple of miles north of Big Sur Center, **Ripplewood Resort** has a general store and **cafe** (mains $6-9) serving breakfast and lunch.

BIG SUR CAMPING

The best way to see Big Sur is also the cheapest – by camping. Three of California's top state parks line Hwy 1 along the Pacific. None are secret though, and campers reserve sites up to seven months in advance. You should, too.

Julia Pfeiffer Burns State Park (☎ 831-667-2315), several miles north of Esalen, has two highlights. The first is the easy 0.25-mile hike to 50ft McWay Falls, which drops into the sea. The second is Julia Pfeiffer's two environmental campsites, secluded high above the surging waves.

A further mile north, **Pfeiffer Big Sur State Park** has plenty of coastal hiking trails; the 1.4-mile round trip to Pfeiffer Falls is a fine experience of redwoods. Ask at the ranger station for directions to the rugged **Pfeiffer Beach** (parking $5); it's so nice that locals keep taking the sign down.

Andrew Molera State Park, 4.5 miles north of Pfeiffer Big Sur, features a gentle mile-long trail that leads to a beautiful beach.

Camping at **Julia Pfeiffer Burns** (campsites $13-17) and the 218-site **Pfeiffer Big Sur State Park** ($13-17) can be reserved through **ParkNet** (☎ 800-444-7275; www.reserveamerica.com). **Andrew Molera State Park** (per person $4) has 24 first-come, first-served campsites.

The best private campground is **Big Sur Campground & Cabins** (☎ 831-667-2322; campsites $30, tent cabins $60, deluxe cabins from $100), near Big Sur River Inn.

MONTEREY PENINSULA
Carmel & Around

When the 1906 San Francisco earthquake forced artists to find abodes, **Carmel-by-the-Sea** became a bohemian retreat. Today, it's an example of a self-ordered California community driven by the dreams of a sophisticated upper class. Local bylaws ensure that it remains modestly picturesque – there are no streetlights or sidewalks – even as refinement and wealth drips from every awning. Ocean Ave, the main drag, slopes down past tony galleries and eateries to a pristine beach.

Carmel and Monterey are linked by Hwy 1 and by the spectacularly scenic **17-Mile Drive**. Though this road is justifiably famous, you can get the same views for free – minus the signature Lone Cypress, the exclusive mansions and golf courses – by touring the coast around Pacific Grove. There are five entry gates to **Pebble Beach** (☎ 831-647-7500; per car/bicycle & pedestrian $8.25/free). On weekends, hikers and bicycles must use the Pacific Grove gate.

Point Lobos State Reserve (☎ 831-624-4909; www .ptlobos.org; per car $8; ☼ 9am-5pm, to 7pm summer), 3.5 miles south of Carmel, is a scenic jewel. Its rocky coastline encompasses 554 aboveground acres and 750 submarine acres that are ideal for scuba diving. Gorgeous, easy hikes crisscross the point, from where you can spot whales, sea lions and otters.

Monterey & Around

Monterey enjoys an envious position at the edge of the uniquely diverse Monterey Bay, protected as the nation's largest marine sanctuary. The city's rich Latino heritage is well preserved in numerous museums and restored 18th-century adobes from California's Spanish and Mexican periods. Most of these are concentrated in downtown 'Old Monterey,' while the world-famous aquarium and Cannery Row are just northwest in 'New Monterey.'

The friendly **visitors center** (☎ 831-649-1770, 888-221-1010; www.montereyinfo.org; cnr Camino El Estero & Franklin St; ☼ 9am-6pm Mon-Sat, 9am-5pm Sun) provides peninsula-wide information and lodging availability.

SIGHTS

If the peninsula contained nothing else, it would still be worth visiting for the mighty **Monterey Bay Aquarium** (☎ 831-648-4888, tickets ☎ 800-756-3737; www.montereybayaquarium.org; 886 Cannery Row; adult/student $20/16; ☼ 10am-6pm), the must-see temple to Monterey's underwater universe. Highlights include the two-story Kelp Forest tank, the million-gallon Outer Bay tank where sea turtles and ponderous sunfish glide by, feeding time with the sea otters and the new shark exhibit (yikes!). The aquarium receives nearly two million visitors a year. To avoid queues, reserve tickets ($3 booking fee) at least a day ahead.

Located downtown at the Custom House Plaza, **Monterey State Historic Park** is a collection of Monterey's finest historical buildings. The free **Pacific House Museum** (☎ 831-649-7118; ☼ 10am-3pm Fri-Sun & Wed), near the wharf,

CALIFORNIA

contains the park's headquarters and exhibits. All cargo once brought to Mexico's Alta California had to be unloaded at **Monterey Custom House** (🕑 Thu-Mon), which now displays a collection of these antique goods. The **Larkin House** is a prime example of 'Monterey colonial' architecture, an adobe/New England hybrid, and the **Stevenson House**, now housing a superb memorabilia collection, is where Robert Louis Stevenson reputedly wrote *Treasure Island* in the 1880s. Hours vary for park buildings, so call ahead.

Also at Custom House Plaza, the **Maritime Museum** (☎ 831-372-2608; admission $5; 🕑 10am-5pm Mon & Wed-Sun) features a great ship-in-a-bottle collection plus displays on the rise and rapid fall of the local sardine industry. A short jaunt from the state historic park, **Fisherman's Wharf** is a low-key tourist trap with plenty of restaurants, seafood stands and gift shops.

In its heyday, **Cannery Row** was a hectic and very smelly place, and John Steinbeck's eponymous novel made it famous. Sardine canning operations began here in 1926, expanding until the peak in 1945, when the annual sardine catch reached 250,000 tons. By 1950, overfishing and climate changes caused the industry to crash in a hurry. Nowadays Cannery Row nets only tourists in its seven blocks of restaurants and souvenir shops.

In Pacific Grove, follow signs from Lighthouse Ave to find the **Monarch Grove Sanctuary** (☎ 831-648-5716; admission free), an October-to-March wintering site for monarch butterflies on their amazing north–south migration. They cluster in the pine trees like dead leaves, only opening as the sun warms them. Volunteer docents are often on hand.

ACTIVITIES

From Cannery Row, you can walk or bike a path that follows the ragged, scenic coastline. Knowledgeable and friendly **Adventures by the Sea** (☎ 831-372-1807; 201 Alvarado St & 299 Cannery Row) rents bikes ($18 for four hours) and kayaks ($30 per day). **Monterey Bay Kayaks** (☎ 831-373-5357, 800-649-5357; 693 Del Monte Ave; kayaks per day $30) can also get you afloat.

For surfing gear and board rentals, head to **On the Beach** (☎ 831-646-9283; 711 Cannery Row; surf gear per day $20).

Guided single-tank scuba dives cost $65, plus $60 for equipment, at the **Aquarius Dive Shop** (☎ 831-375-1933; 2040 Del Monte Ave & 32 Cannery Row); it also rents snorkel gear with wetsuits.

Several outfits run whale-watching trips from the wharf year-round, but only the recommended **Monterey Bay Whale Watch** (☎ 831-375-4658; www.gowhales.com; 3-6hr trips $27-41) has marine biologists for guides; reservations required.

SLEEPING

High-season rates listed here can drop by a third or more in winter, while special-event weekends might be half again as much. Call ahead! Some places here impose a two-night minimum during summer weekends. For a relatively economical motel, try downtown's Munras Ave or N Fremont St, 2.5 miles from downtown and east of Hwy 1 (Casa Verde exit).

Four blocks from Cannery Row, **HI Monterey Hostel** (☎ 831-649-0375; www.montereyhostel.org; 778 Hawthorne St; dm $22-25, r from $60) has plain and simple dorm rooms, and is a model of water conservation. Reservations are required June through September and the 11pm curfew is strict. Take bus No 1 from the Transit Plaza.

The centrally located **Veterans Memorial Park Campground** (☎ 831-646-3865; campsites per vehicle $18, walk-ins $5; 3-day maximum) has 40 unreservable campsites. From Hwy 1, take Hwy 68 to Skyline Forest Dr to Skyline Dr north. From downtown Monterey, follow Jefferson St west into the park.

DETOUR: NATIONAL STEINBECK CENTER

The **National Steinbeck Center** (☎ 831-796-3833; www.steinbeck.org; 1 Main St, Salinas; admission $11; 🕑 10am-5pm) is well worth the 20-mile inland detour to Salinas, through the flat, fertile valley that was Steinbeck's home and passion. The interactive exhibits, displays and short movie bring together all the strands of the author's life, whose Pulitzer- and Nobel prize–winning work captured the troubled spirit of rural and working-class America. The attached Valley of the World center explores the region's agricultural heritage.

EATING

Lighthouse Ave above Cannery Row is the place to go for an affordable meal, while the *only* place to go for breakfast is downtown's **Old Monterey Cafe** (☎ 831-646-1021; 489 Alvarado St; ❤ 7am-2:30pm; mains $5-10): lumberjack portions, and pancakes as big as hubcaps. There's a good bakery and deli next door.

GETTING THERE & AROUND

Greyhound buses traveling between Los Angeles ($40) and San Francisco ($18) stop at the **gas station** (1024 Del Monte Ave), just east of El Estero Lake. The closest Amtrak station is 17 miles east in Salinas, with shuttles ($8) linking the towns all day. **Monterey-Salinas Transit** (MST; ☎ 831-899-2555; www.mst.org) operates buses around the peninsula to Carmel and Pacific Grove, and south to Big Sur. The Monterey Transit Plaza, at the south end of Alvarado St, is the main MST terminal.

SANTA CRUZ

Santa Cruz is where SoCal beach culture meets NorCal counterculture. As the home of the University of California, Santa Cruz (UCSC; www.ucsc.edu) and its 15,000 left-of-center students, it is far more youthful, hip and political than touristy Monterey, and with over one-sixth of the county composed of state parks, it offers ample opportunities to wander among the redwoods.

Orientation & Information

Restaurants and shops line parallel Pacific Ave and Front St, the main drags. For the beach and Boardwalk, head south on Front St and turn left on Beach St. The helpful **visitors center** (☎ 831-425-1234, 800-833-3494; www.santacruz.org; 1211 Ocean St; ❤ 9am-5pm Mon-Fri, 10am-4pm Sat, 10am-3pm Sun) has accommodations availability (from $40); you can book online via the website.

Bookshop Santa Cruz (☎ 831-423-0900; 1520 Pacific Ave) is as busy on a Friday night as any bar. **Logos** (☎ 831-427-5100; 1117 Pacific Ave) is a usedbook and music-lover's paradise. **Cruzio** (903 Pacific Ave; per 15 min $2) and the **public library** (224 Church St; Internet access free; ❤ Mon-Thu 10am-8pm, Fri & Sat 10am-5pm, Sun 1-5pm) have Internet access.

Sights & Activities

The classic 1906 **Beach Boardwalk** (☎ 831-423-7433; www.beachboardwalk.com; 400 Beach St; rides $2-4, all-day ticket $26; ❤ daily from 11am mid-Apr–mid-Nov, from noon Sat & Sun mid-Nov–mid-Apr) is the West Coast's oldest beachfront amusement park, with a 1923 Giant Dipper coaster and a 1911 Looff carousel – both National Historic Landmarks; call for hours, which vary weekly.

The free **Surfing Museum** (☎ 831-420-6289; ❤ noon-4pm Wed-Mon, closed Wed winter) is a small tribute to the history and art of wave riding. It's at Lighthouse Point on W Cliff Dr and overlooks Steamer's Lane, the most popular surf break in Santa Cruz.

Just north of town, **Natural Bridges State Beach** (☎ 831-423-4609; 2531 W Cliff Dr; admission $5; ❤ 8am-sunset) has a good beach, tide pools and trees where monarch butterflies hibernate October through March.

Established in 1902, **Big Basin Redwoods State Park** (☎ 831-338-8860; www.bigbasin.org; per car $5, campsites $13-16; ❤ sunrise-sunset), 23 miles north of Santa Cruz via Hwys 9 and 236, is the birthplace of California's conservation movement. It contains 18,000 acres of redwood forest and 80 miles of trails, one of which drops to the Pacific Ocean.

The **Mystery Spot** (☎ 831-423-8897; www.mysteryspot.com; admission $5; ❤ 9am-7pm summer, to 4:30pm winter), 3 miles north of Santa Cruz on Branciforte Dr, is a classic bit of odd-ball Americana: objects defy gravity by rolling uphill, and buildings lean at unexplained angles. It really is mysterious. Don't forget your bumper sticker.

It wouldn't be Santa Cruz without meditative, holistic and therapeutic spas. **Well Within** (☎ 831-458-9355; 417 Cedar St) and **Kiva House** (☎ 831-429-1142; 702 Water St) are local

---

LET'S GO SURFING NOW

Everybody's surfing now at Santa Cruz, or so it seems sometimes. If you've never, here's a great place to try your feet. Recommended beginner breaks are **Cowell's** and **38th Ave**. If all you need is a board, try **Go Skate** (☎ 831-425-8578; 601 Beach St; skateboards per day from $10). Wahines should make waves for the women-owned **Paradise Surf Shop** (☎ 831-462-3880; www.paradisesurf.com; 3961 Portola Dr), which has board sales, plus rentals and knowledgeable staff.

For lessons, try the venerable **Richard Schmidt Surf School** (☎ 831-423-0928; www.richardschmidt.com; 849 Almar Ave; 2hr group lesson $80).

institutions; hourly tub rates range from $9 to $33 and massages merit a splurge.

Hiking or **biking** on the beautiful W Cliff Dr is satisfying anytime, but particularly at sunset. Check Beach St for bike-rental shops. **Kayak Connection** (☎ 831-479-1121; 413 Lake Ave; kayaks per 4hr $30-50) has kayak rentals.

Sleeping

In a pinch, try the chain motels along Riverside Ave and Ocean St.

HI Carmelita Cottages Hostel (☎ 831-423-8304; www.hi-santacruz.org; 321 Main St; dm $18-21, d $46-80; ⊗) One of the Left Coast's busiest hostels, which explains why attitudes and the 40 bunks in four cottages can get a little frayed. No alcohol, 10am to 5pm lockout, strict 11pm curfew. Reservations advised.

Public campgrounds (☎ 800-444-7275; $13-20) You can tent it among the redwoods in the nearby Henry Cowell and Big Basin State Parks, north of town off Hwy 9, and at New Brighton State Beach, 4 miles south of Santa Cruz near Capitola. Reservations are advised.

Eating & Drinking

Downtown Santa Cruz, especially on Pacific Ave and Front St, is full of eateries of all stripes.

Saturn Cafe (☎ 831-429-8505; 145 Laurel St; mains $5-9; ☯ 11:30-3am Sun-Thu, 11:30-4am Fri & Sat; ▣) A Santa Cruz classic, this late-night vegetarian place is a pop culture–fever dream: flame-painted walls, thatched tiki awnings and whacked-out dioramas beneath every booth table. Don't pass on the 'chocolate madness.' Everything on the Cheap Eats menu, which is available until 5pm weekdays, is under $6.

Seabright Brewery (☎ 831-426-2739; 519 Seabright Ave; mains $8-14; ☯ 11:30am-11:30pm) The only true brewpub in Santa Cruz serves passable pub grub and great microbrews to a loud, lively crowd. There's a crowded patio and occasional live bands.

Mobo Sushi (☎ 831-425-1700; 105 S River St; hand rolls $3-5.50; ☯ lunch Mon-Fri, dinner nightly) This atmospheric place is known for inventive, especially veggie, hand rolls: try the Mad Dog, Crop Burning or the UCSC favorite, Banana Slug.

If you're in town Wednesday afternoon, don't miss the **farmers market** (cnr Lincoln & Center Sts; ☯ 2:30-6:30pm).

Entertainment

Check the free weekly *Metro Santa Cruz* (www.metroactive.com/cruz) for schedules of big-name touring musicians, who appear regularly at the classy **Kuumbwa Jazz Center** (☎ 831-427-2227; www.kuumbwajazz.org; 320-2 Cedar St) and the 800-seat **Catalyst** (☎ 831-423-1338; 1011 Pacific Ave), which includes a pool room upstairs. **Club Dakota** (☎ 831-454-9030; 1209 Pacific Ave) is a popular queer-friendly dance club with an award-winning bar and a hoppin' 4pm to 7pm weekday happy hour.

Getting There & Away

Santa Cruz Metropolitan Transit (☎ 831-425-8600; www.scmtd.com) operates from the **Santa Cruz Metro Transit Center** (920 Pacific Ave; fare $1.50, day pass $4.50) and serves the greater Santa Cruz region. From the Transit Center, **Greyhound** (☎ 831-423-1800; 425 Front St) runs daily buses to San Francisco ($11) and Los Angeles ($44). There are also regular bus connections to/from the CalTrain/Amtrak station in San Jose ($6).

SAN MATEO COAST

The most scenic approach from Santa Cruz to San Francisco is via narrow, coastal Hwy 1. **Año Nuevo State Reserve** (Map p594; ☎ 650-879-0227; ☯ 8am-sunset, closed Dec 1-14), 5 miles south of Pigeon Point off Hwy 1, is highly recommended for its resident elephant seal colony. During the mating and birthing season (December 15 to March), visitors are allowed only on heavily booked guided tours ($4 parking, $4 each additional person); for reservations call ☎ 800-444-4445. Otherwise, reservations are not required.

HI Pigeon Point Lighthouse Hostel (Map p594; ☎ 650-879-0633; dm $17/20) is one of the busiest hostels in the US. No wonder: it occupies a quiet, windswept coastal perch next to the historic lighthouse.

Five miles north, **Pescadero** is a good stop for sandwiches and supplies; it's home to the locally renowned **Duarte's Tavern** (☎ 650-879-0464) and its famous artichoke soup.

Tiny **San Gregorio**, 10 miles north at the Hwy 84 junction, is worth a stop for one reason: its general store/café, which maintains a distinctive Northern California ambience.

South of quiet **Half Moon Bay**, public beaches are strung like pearls. The welcoming **nurseries** along Hwy 92 reveal Californian flora in all its divergent glories.

Close by, the **HI Point Montara Lighthouse Hostel** (Map p594; ☎ 650-728-7177; dm $16-19), on Hwy 1 at 16th St, is a clean and very popular hostel with a hot tub and private beach. Just south, **Moss Beach Distillery** (☎ 650-728-5595; cnr Beach Way & Ocean Blvd) is a former prohibition-era speakeasy with an ocean-view deck.

Just north of Montara, the **Gray Whale Cove State Beach** is a popular, unsigned clothing-optional strand.

SAN FRANCISCO

Tony Bennett and Steve Perry pretty much got it right. A love affair with the 'city by the bay' often begins with those heart-stopping views of majestic bridges, of dainty Victorian houses, of little cable cars ascending impossibly steep hills with apparent ease as the light goes down on the 'sit-tay.' The infatuation deepens as you walk the streets of San Francisco to discover the city's vibrant neighborhoods, its sexiness, its unhesitant embrace of all things eccentric, its abiding appreciation of creativity, and its astounding array of restaurants, bars and nightclubs. No other American city gets under your skin quite like San Francisco.

HISTORY

Ohlone Indians were inhabiting the Bay Area when the first Europeans arrived. By 1776 Gaspar de Portolá and Father Junípero Serra had established a mission and presidio here, and within a few decades the Ohlone were nearly wiped out by introduced diseases.

However, 1848 marks the true birth of the city: it received its current name then (after Mexico ceded California to the USA), and its first rush of citizens, crazed by the prospect of gold.

The nefarious entertainments of miners turned San Francisco into a notorious place, full of casinos, saloons, brothels and opium dens. The 'Barbary Coast' (now Chinatown and Jackson Sq) was a place of reckless criminality, where sailors were routinely knocked out, robbed and 'Shanghai'd' – awaking to find themselves indentured to a ship that was already out to sea.

The 1906 earthquake and fire leveled most of the city, and frantic years of construction followed. This continued through the 1930s, when the San Francisco–Oakland Bay (1936) and the Golden Gate (1937) Bridges were built.

The years after WWII were distinguished by colorful countercultures: the Beats spearheaded the '50s poetry movement, and hippies brought flower power and free love in the '60s. During this same period, San Francisco's nascent gay community coalesced and, by the 1970s, firmly established itself.

While the economic boom of the 1980s sparked a culinary renaissance among the city's restaurants, this was overshadowed by the dot-com revolution of the late 1990s, which, driven by the same greedy delirium of the gold rush, sent rents and real estate skyrocketing and refashioned the social landscape, driving out artists and the middle class and marginalizing the poor even further. The inevitable bust was felt nationally, but the hangover is sharpest here. However, just as some people take strange pleasure in their hangovers, San Francisco is enjoying catching its breath as rents have dropped and the manic consumerism has subsided.

ORIENTATION

San Francisco occupies the tip of a 30-mile-long peninsula, with the ocean to the west and the bay to the east. The city can be divided into three sections. The downtown district

---

GETTING INTO TOWN

From both San Francisco International Airport (SFO) and Oakland International Airport, the best way to get into the heart of the city is to take **BART** (Bay Area Rapid Transit; ☎ 510-465-2278; www.bart.gov), which connects directly to downtown San Francisco ($4.70). SFO's AirTrain, an automated people mover, connects the terminals and the BART station. From Oakland International Airport, a shuttle leaves the main terminal ($2) every 10 to 15 minutes, connecting with BART at Coliseum Station. By comparison, a taxi from SFO costs at least $35, from Oakland airport to downtown San Francisco costs at least $45. Traveling by bus is possible, but requires multiple transfers and is not much cheaper than BART.

0 ___ 20 km
0 ___ 12 miles

38°30'N 123°00'W 122°30'W 122°00'W 38°30'N

A **B** **C** **D**

To Calistoga (5mi)

To Sacramento (22mi)

Jenner

1

Bodega Bay

Santa Rosa

Oakville

Silverado Trail

(116)

(12)

Wine Country

(29)

(121)

Fairfield

(12)

Tomales

Petaluma

(101)

(116)

Petaluma River

(121)

(12) (121)

Sonoma

Napa

(29)

(80)

(680)

Grizzly Bay

2

Point Reyes National Seashore

Inverness

Point Reyes Station

Novato

(37)

Vallejo

(780)

Benicia

Suisun Bay

Pittsburg

Nicasio

(101)

San Pablo Bay

Crockett

(4)

Martinez

Concord

(242)

38°00'N

Drakes Bay

Olema

Fairfax

San Rafael

San Pablo

Richmond

Wildcat Canyon Regional Park

Pleasant Hill

Walnut Creek

(680)

Mount Diablo State Park

Point Reyes

10

Golden Gate National Recreation Area

Larkspur

Stinson Beach

Mill Valley

(580)

Albany

Tilden Regional Park

Berkeley

(24)

3

Farallon National Wildlife Refuge

Bolinas

Mount Tamalpais State Park

5

Tiburon

Angel Island State Park

Alcatraz Island

(123)

Redwood Regional Park

Danville

San Ramon

Sausalito

Golden Gate National Recreation Area

7

Fort Baker

11

Berkeley

(13)

To I-5; Tracy (25mi)

Golden Gate Bridge

1

4

12

Oakland

Alameda

(185)

Anthony Chabot Regional Park

Castro Valley

(580)

See Downtown San Francisco Map (pp596–7)

2

Oakland International Airport

San Leandro

(880)

Hayward

4

PACIFIC OCEAN

(35)

Daly City

South San Francisco

San Francisco Bay

San Lorenzo

(238)

Union City

Pleasanton

37°30'N

(280)

San Bruno

Gray Whale Cove State Beach

Pacifica

San Francisco International Airport

(92)

(880)

Fremont

Newark

Sunol Regional Wilderness

(84)

Sunol

9

Montara

San Mateo

Foster City

(101)

(84)

37°30'N

Moss Beach

Half Moon Bay

Half Moon Bay

(92)

Redwood City

(280)

(84)

Palo Alto

East Palo Alto

(237)

San Jose International Airport

Milpitas

5

(1)

(35)

Woodside

San Gregorio

San Jose

(82)

(87)

La Honda

(84)

(35)

Saratoga

Campbell

(85)

Los Gatos

Pescadero

(236)

Big Basin Redwoods State Park

Pigeon Point

8

Año Nuevo State Reserve

Boulder Creek

Scotts Valley

(9)

(17)

Davenport

Santa Cruz

Capitola

To Monterey (40mi)

37°00'N

6

SIGHTS & ACTIVITIES	(pp595–601)
California Palace of the Legion of Honor	1 B3
Candlestick Park	2 C3
Fort Point	3 C3
Golden Gate Park	4 B3
Jack London Square	(see 12)
Muir Woods National Monument	5 B3
University of California at Berkeley	6 C3

SLEEPING	🏠	(pp602–3)
HI Marin Headlands Hostel	7 B3	
HI Pigeon Point Lighthouse Hostel	8 C5	
HI Point Montara Lighthouse Hostel	9 B4	
HI Point Reyes Hostel	10 A2	

TRANSPORT	(pp607–8)
Amtrak Terminal Emeryville	11 C3
Amtrak Terminal	12 C3

122°30'W 122°00'W

LP

is in the northeast between Van Ness Ave, Market St and the bay, and includes the Embarcadero, Union Sq, the Financial District, Civic Center, the Tenderloin, Chinatown, North Beach, Nob Hill, Russian Hill and Fisherman's Wharf.

The South of Market District, or SoMa, is a trendy warehouse zone that fades into the Mission, the city's Latino quarter, and then the Castro, the city's gay quarter.

The residential western part of the city stretches from Van Ness Ave all the way to the Pacific Ocean, encompassing upscale The Marina and Pacific Heights, Japantown, the Haight, the Richmond and Sunset Districts, and Golden Gate Park.

INFORMATION
Bookstores
A Different Light Bookstore (☎ 415-431-0891; 489 Castro St) The USA's largest gay and lesbian bookseller.
City Lights Bookstore (☎ 415-362-8193; 261 Columbus Ave, North Beach) A North Beach institution; Beat poetry and progressive literature.
Get Lost (☎ 415-437-0529; 1825 Market St) Specializes in travel.

Internet Access
Free terminals (15 minute limit) include:
CompUSA (☎ 415-391-9778; 750 Market St, Union Sq)
Main Library (☎ 415-557-4400; www.sfpl.org; cnr Larkin & Grove Sts, Civic Center)

Media
San Francisco Chronicle (www.sfgate.com) The main daily newspaper; its website is a great resource.
San Francisco Bay Guardian (www.sfbg.com) Free weekly; alternative news and entertainment.
SF Weekly (www.sfweekly.com) Free weekly; alternative news and entertainment.

Medical Services
Haight Ashbury Free Clinic (☎ 415-487-5632; 558 Clayton St) Appointments required, but free treatment.
San Francisco General Hospital (☎ 415-206-8000; 1001 Potrero Ave)

Money
ATMs are all over town at banks and in corner markets and even some bars.

Post
Civic Center post office (☎ 415-563-7284, 800-725-2161; www.usps.com; 101 Hyde St, San Francisco, CA 94142) The city's most central post office.

Telephone
Public phones are becoming rare in the age of cell phones but can generally be found in the same places: near elevators in department stores and large hotels and at the rear of bars and restaurants.

Toilets
The city has put green, self-cleaning sidewalk commodes in areas where pedestrian traffic is particularly heavy. Public libraries have toilets, as do department stores, large hotels, bars and restaurants.

Tourist Information
San Francisco Visitor Information Center
(☎ 415-391-2000; www.sfvisitor.org; cnr Market & Powell Sts; 🕙 9am-5pm Mon-Fri, 9am-3pm Sat & Sun) On the lower level of Hallidie Plaza, offers comprehensive information and access to an online reservation service.

DANGERS & ANNOYANCES
Beyond the usual city smarts, be wary in the rough Tenderloin at any time, and after dark in SoMa and the areas around the 16th St and 24th St BART (Bay Area Rapid Transit) stations in the Mission.

SIGHTS
Union Sq, Chinatown, North Beach, Civic Center, SoMa, Nob Hill and the Embarcadero are all jammed up against one another, and despite the hills most visitors find the central part of the city very walkable. Easy public transit can get you to attractions in the Mission, Castro, Marina, Haight-Ashbury and Golden Gate Park.

Alcatraz
The infamous **Alcatraz prison** was long ago transformed into San Francisco's most inviting tourist trap. Alcatraz's extraordinary history is related in an engrossing audio tour, bringing the old walls and bars back to life. From 1933 to 1963 the 12-acre rocky island located in the middle of the bay was the nation's most famous penitentiary, supposedly escape-proof and home to such notorious convicts as Al Capone, 'Machine Gun' Kelly and Robert Stroud (the 'birdman of Alcatraz'). A few inmates did manage to escape from Alcatraz, but it's never been established whether any aged very quietly in the woods somewhere or if all were food for sharks. **Blue & Gold Ferries** (☎ 415-705-5555;

A

INFORMATION
A Different Light Bookstore........ 1 D6
City Lights Bookstore................... 2 F2
Civic Center Post Office.............. 3 F4
CompUSA................................... 4 G3
Get Lost...................................... 5 E5
Haight-Ashbury Free Clinic........ 6 C5
Main Library............................... 7 F4
San Francisco Visitor Information
   Center.................................... 8 F4

SIGHTS & ACTIVITIES   (pp595-601)
Bank of America Building........... 9 G3
Blazing Saddles........................ 10 F1
Cable Car Barn & Museum....... 11 F2
Cartoon Art Museum................. 12 G3
Chinatown Gate........................ 13 F3
City Hall................................... 14 E4
Coit Tower............................... 15 F2
Ghirardelli Square.................... 16 E1
Mission Dolores....................... 17 E6
Palace of Fine Arts.................. 18 C2
Portsmouth Square................... 19 F2
Saints Peter & Paul Church...... 20 F2
San Francisco Museum of
   Modern Art (SFMOMA)....... 21 G3
Skates on Haight...................... 22 B5
Spinnaker Sailing..................... 23 H4
Transamerica Pyramid.............. 24 G2
Yerba Buena Gardens.............. 25 G4

SLEEPING   (pp602-3)
24 Henry.................................. 26 D6
Adelaide Hostel & Hotel.......... 27 F3
Central YMCA Hotel................. 28 F4
Globe Hostel............................ 29 F5
Grant Hotel.............................. 30 F3
Green Tortoise Hostel............... 31 F3
HI San Francisco City Center.... 32 E4
HI San Francisco Downtown..... 33 F3
HI San Francisco Fisherman's
   Wharf.................................. 34 D1
Hotel des Arts.....................(see 44)
Hotel Triton............................. 35 G3
Metro Hotel............................. 36 D5
Mosser.................................... 37 G4
Obrero Hotel........................... 38 F2
Pacific Tradewinds Backpacker
   Hostel.................................. 39 G3
Phoenix Motel.......................... 40 E4
Red Victorian B&B................... 41 D5
Willows Inn.............................. 42 D5

EATING   (pp603-6)
Cafe Flore............................... 43 D6
Café de la Presse.................... 44 G3
Chow....................................... 45 D5
Dol Ho.................................... 46 F2
Dotty's True Blue Café............. 47 F3
Ferry Building Marketplace...(see 101)
Gold Mountain......................... 48 F2
Golden Boy Pizza.................... 49 F2
House of Nanking.................... 50 F2
L'Osteria del Forno................. 51 F2
Lefty O'Doul's......................... 52 F3

B

Liguria.................................... 53 F2
Lucky Creation........................ 54 F2
Magnolia Pub & Brewery........ 55 C5
Mario's Bohemian Cigar Store..56 F2
Mo's Burgers........................... 57 F2
Molinari's Delicatessen............ 58 F2
Pancho Villa Taqueria.............. 59 E6
Pho Hoa................................. 60 F3
Pork Store Cafe...................... 61 C5
Puerto Alegre......................... 62 E6
Red's Java House.................... 63 H3
Taquería Can-Cun................... 64 E6
Thep Phanom......................... 65 D5
Truly Mediterranean............... 66 E6
WeBe Sushi.....................(see 62)
Yank Sing............................... 67 H3

DRINKING   (pp606-7)
Boom Boom Room.................. 68 D4
Bottom of the Hill................... 69 G6
Cafe du Nord......................... 70 D6
Café....................................... 71 D6
Club Deluxe............................ 72 C5
Edinburgh Castle.................... 73 E3
Elbo Room............................. 74 E6
EndUp..................................... 75 G4
Great American Music Hall...... 76 E4
Harry Denton's Starlight
   Room................................... 77 F3
Lexington Club........................ 78 E6
Mad Dog in the Fog............... 79 D5
Murio's Trophy Room.............. 80 B5
Paradise Lounge..................... 81 F5
Slim's..................................... 82 F5
Stud.. 83 F5
Tonga Room............................ 84 F3
Tosca Café.............................. 85 F2
Up & Down Club..................... 86 F5
Vesuvio................................... 87 F2
Zam Zam................................ 88 C5
Zeitgeist.................................. 89 E5

ENTERTAINMENT   (p607)
Castro Theatre........................ 90 D6
Club Fugazi............................. 91 F2
Davies Symphony Hall............. 92 E4
Fillmore Auditorium................ 93 D4
Geary Theater......................... 94 F3
Lumiere.................................. 95 E3
Magic Theatre......................... 96 D1
Roxie Cinema......................... 97 E6
War Memorial Opera House.... 98 E4
Warfield.................................. 99 F4

TRANSPORT   (pp607-8)
Blue & Gold Ferries.............. 100 H2
Ferry Building........................ 101 H2
Transbay Terminal................. 102 G3

www.blueandgoldfleet.com; tours $16) runs to the island from Pier 41; tickets include the ferry trip and audio tour, and must be booked in advance.

Golden Gate Bridge

Talk about eye-pleasing engineering feats. Designed by Joseph Strauss and constructed between 1933 and 1937, the elegant **Golden Gate Bridge** (☎ 415-921-5858), 2 miles in length with a main span of 4200ft, links San Francisco with Marin County at the edge of the Western world. At the time of completion it was the longest suspension bridge in the world. Painting the bridge is a never-ending job – a team of 25 painters adds another 1000 orange gallons every week. A prime spot for snap photography is **Fort Point Lookout**, on Marine Dr at the bridge's San Francisco end. But you really must cross the bridge, preferably on foot, skates or bicycle (no toll). The bridge can be reached on foot from the Fort Mason area, and there are parking lots on either end of the bridge if you want to drive to it and walk across. Cars pay a $5 toll for southbound (Marin to San Francisco) travel; northbound traffic crosses toll-free.

Chinatown

Every city seems to have one, but San Francisco's bustling, chaotic, vibrant **Chinatown** has an allure all its own. Neon and ersatz Sino-Disney architecture built just after the 1906 quake have attained their own authenticity over the years. Culturally, the neighborhood is thriving, thanks to a steady influx of Chinese immigrants. Cantonese remains the first language for many. **Grant Ave**, between Bush and Jackson Sts, is the main thoroughfare catering to tourists, but Chinatown is best experienced by wandering its side streets and alleys – many of which, in the late 1800s, were notorious for brothels, opium dens and gambling. Cheap eats, herbal cures and whimsical curios are the neighborhood's commercial calling cards.

North Beach

The city's atmospheric Italian-American quarter is great for wandering, bar hopping, café lounging and sampling the many delicacies on offer. The adopted home of writers Jack Kerouac and Allen Ginsberg, **North Beach** was the birthplace of the '50s Beat movement, and it remains a center for peculiar poetry and progressive politics. Along Broadway, touts and neon signs keep alive another North Beach tradition from the early 1960s, that of the golden age of nude dancing.

Washington Sq, North Beach's playground, is a spot of greenery that's perfect for tai chi, kicking a ball around or just lounging. Nearby, atop Telegraph Hill, is the 210ft **Coit Tower** (☎ 415-362-0808; admission free; ☉ 10am-5pm), one of San Francisco's most prominent landmarks. The tower's lobby is adorned with superb WPA murals illustrating San Francisco industry, commerce and life. **Elevator rides** ($3) to the top are worth it for the views.

Haight

This is still a groovy part of town. In 1967 a heavy concentration of trippin', free-lovin' hippies made the Haight the epicenter of the 'Summer of Love,' and it was here also that the psychedelic 'San Francisco sound' emerged, epitomized by rock bands like the Grateful Dead and Jefferson Airplane. Bluesy Janis Joplin also lived in the neighborhood. Today, Haight St is more about quirky fashion and nightlife than returning to Eden, but it maintains a unique aura.

The **Upper Haight**, also known as Haight-Ashbury, stretches from Golden Gate Park to Buena Vista Park and is lined with used clothing shops, boutiques, cafés and cheap restaurants. Deadheads will want to snap a photo at **710 Ashbury St**, the onetime communal home of the Grateful Dead (now a private residence). Around the corner of Haight and Fillmore Sts, the **Lower Haight** is a scruffy few blocks of top-notch dive bars.

Mission

The city's Latino district is also its hippest neighborhood. Here you'll find some of the best cheap meals (you have to try a San Francisco burrito) and the city's most interesting range of bars and clubs. By disembarking at the 24th St BART station you'll find yourself in the heart of the Hispanic Mission, with block after block of colorful shops selling tortillas, votive candles and mariachi CDs. Areas with the strongest hipster pull are around 16th St between Mission and Guerrero and along Valencia St between 20th and 24th Sts.

The 1782 adobe **Mission Dolores** (☎ 415-621-8203; cnr Dolores & 16th Sts; admission $3; ☉ 9am-4pm) was the sixth California mission founded by Father Junípero Serra, and is the oldest building in the city. The adjoining 1913 basilica is a must-visit for its stained glass and tile work, and the historic cemetery is also interesting.

Narrow **Balmy Alley**, off 24th St near Folsom, is resplendent with intensely vibrant murals depicting everything from San Francisco's labor history to Central American independence. Get a map with mural information at **Precita Eyes Mural Arts Center** (☎ 415-285-2287; www.precitaeyes.org; 2981 24th St; 🕑 10am-5pm Mon-Fri, noon-4pm Sat & Sun).

Castro

The compact Castro, the gay center of San Francisco, is great for strolling, people-watching, shopping and dining. The magnificent **Castro Theatre** (☎ 415-621-6120; 429 Castro St), where the city's most important film festivals are held, is the primary landmark on busy Castro St. See Entertainment (p607) for a sampling of the neighborhood's never-dull nightlife.

Russian Hill

West of North Beach, the steep streets of Russian Hill offer scenic stairway gardens and the oft-photographed 1000 block of **Lombard Street**, between Hyde and Leavenworth Sts, which is famously billed as 'the world's crookedest street.'

The cable car was invented by Andrew Hallidie for the most part to make it easier for the city's ruthless 19th-century 'Silver Kings' – Mark Hopkins, Collis P Huntington, James Grantham Fair and Leland Stanford – to reach their stately homes on the summit of Nob Hill. This effort is recounted in the **Cable Car Barn & Museum** (☎ 415-474-1887; www.cablecarmuseum.com; 1201 Mason St; admission free; 🕑 10am-5pm, until 6pm summer), which also showcases the noisy churning of the cables themselves as they power the vehicles over the hills.

Union Sq

The corner of Powell and Market Sts is quite a scene at weekends – a crush of shoppers, buskers, hustlers, sidewalk chess matches and tourists lined up at the **cable car turnaround**. The blocks north and east of here are lined with high-end shops and extravagant hotels that are fun to snoop through.

INSTEAD OF

Instead of going to the overcrowded, overhyped Fisherman's Wharf, head further east along the San Francisco waterfront while exploring the revitalized **Embarcadero**. Once cut off from the city by a highly loathed highway, the Embarcadero now is a pedestrian-friendly esplanade with historic streetcars, palm trees, fishing piers, bars and restaurants, kayak rentals and utterly fabulous bay views. Chow down at the foot of Market Street and the **Ferry Building Marketplace** (p603), or cheer on the Giants at the fantastic **SBC Park** (p607).

SoMa

South of Market, or SoMa, refers to a vast area that includes long corridors of loft apartments and former warehouses long-since converted into hot clubs and nightspots. This is also where many of the city's celebrated museums are.

Chief on the list is **San Francisco Museum of Modern Art** (SFMOMA; ☎ 415-357-4000; www.sfmoma.org; 151 3rd St; adult/student $10/6; 🕑 10am-6pm Fri-Tue, 10am-9pm Thu). This eye-catching redbrick landmark, designed by Swiss architect Mario Botta, is one of the nation's premier modern art showcases. The museum's strength is American abstract expressionism, but all great American and European modern artists are represented, and it has a distinguished collection of American photography.

Across the street, **Yerba Buena Gardens** (Mission St), between 3rd and 4th Sts, is a relaxing urban green space and sculpture garden bordered by cultural institutions and highrise buildings. It's especially inviting during free outdoor concerts, usually around lunch time from May to October.

The nearby **Cartoon Art Museum** (☎ 415-227-8666; www.cartoonart.org; 655 Mission St; adult/student $6/4; 🕑 11am-5pm Tue-Sun) takes the funnies seriously, with original works from such diverse artists as Charles Schultz and R Crumb.

Financial District

Visiting the Financial District, densely concentrated in the blocks from Union Sq to the bay, is essentially a neck-straining architectural experience. When it was completed in 1969, the 761ft **Bank of America building** (555 California St) ushered in a new era for San

CALIFORNIA

ROLL WITH THE MASSES

On the last Friday of every month, hundreds of festive cyclists take over the evening rush hour like merry pranksters crashing a corporate meeting. The event is called **Critical Mass** (🕑 5pm last Fri monthly), and anyone on wheels can join in. Riders usually gather at the foot of Market St around 5pm before following a different course through the city. There's no organization, and no stated political point, though clearly the monthly ride is a show of pedal power.

Remember the Bay City Rollers? Rent skates and become one. On Friday nights the **Midnight Rollers** (☎ 415-752-1967; www.cora.org; 🕑 9pm Fri) meet at Justin Herman Plaza, near the Embarcadero and Market St, and skate through the night. The number of skaters typically tops 20, stops sometimes include a bar, and anyone is welcome to join them.

Francisco's previously low-rise skyline, and its top-floor **Carnelian Room** (☎ 415-433-7500) restaurant/bar provides amazing views. San Francisco's tallest building, the 853ft **Transamerica Pyramid** (600 Montgomery St), was completed in 1972.

Marina & Presidio

The northwestern edge of the peninsula, rimmed with parks, beaches, museums and one singular bridge, makes for dreamy biking and strolling.

The Marina was born in time for the 1915 Panama-Pacific International Exposition, when waterfront marshland was filled in with rubble from the 1906 quake to create the exhibition grounds. One of the few surviving Expo structures is Bernard Maybeck's stately **Palace of Fine Arts**, off Baker St bordering the Presidio.

The scenic **Presidio** (☎ 415-561-4323) is a former Spanish and US military fort now part of the Golden Gate National Recreation Area. Windsurfers launch from the **Crissy Field** beaches, which lead to **Fort Point** and the view of the Golden Gate Bridge Alfred Hitchcock made famous in *Vertigo*.

Golden Gate Park & Around

San Francisco's biggest park was designed in 1871 by 24-year-old William Hammond Hall, who transformed 1017 acres of windswept sand dunes into the largest developed city park in the world.

The park's oldest building is the graceful **Conservatory of Flowers** (☎ 415-666-7001; adult/student $5/3; 🕑 9am-5pm Tue-Sun), an 1879 Victorian glasshouse with gorgeous tropical plant exhibits. The **Japanese Tea Garden** (☎ 415-752-1171; admission $3.50, free after 4pm; 🕑 8:30am-5pm) is an immaculate garden with a stylized pagoda and a horseshoe-shaped footbridge.

The park is packed with sporting facilities, including 7.5 miles of bicycle trails, 12 miles of bridle trails, a challenging nine-hole golf course and 21 tennis courts. Rowboats and pedal boats can be rented on **Stow Lake** (☎ 415-752-0347; boats per hr $11-15), along with surreys ($15 per hour), bikes ($8 per hour) and in-line skates ($7 per hour).

The **California Palace of the Legion of Honor** (☎ 415-863-3330; www.thinker.org; admission $8, free Tue; 🕑 9:30am-5pm Tue-Sun), in Lincoln Park north of Golden Gate Park, is one of San Francisco's premier art museums, with a world-class collection of European art from medieval times to the 20th century.

ACTIVITIES

For bicycle rentals, try **Blazing Saddles** (☎ 415-202-8888; 1096 Columbus Ave; bicycles per hr/day $7/28), with a North Beach location that's a convenient starting point for a ride over the Golden Gate Bridge (Blazing Saddles also

---

SPLURGE!

The sight of sailboats on San Francisco Bay on a sunny day is very inviting, so imagine how gorgeous the bay and the city must look from the sailor's perspective. Luckily, getting out on the water doesn't necessarily require connections, just a willingness to splurge. **Spinnaker Sailing** (☎ 415-543-7333; www.mspinnaker-sailing.com; Pier 40; charters from $265) provides three-hour chartered sailboats with skipper. If the costs are split among a small group, it's really quite reasonable. **Hawaiian Chieftain** (☎ 415-331-3214; www.hawaiianchieftain.com; Marina Plaza Dock, Sausalito; cruises $40-50) is a replica of a 19th-century European merchant sailing ship that operates cruises around the bay.

---

has a pick-up stall by Fisherman's Wharf). In-line skates can be rented at **Skates on Haight** (☎ 415-752-8375; 1818 Haight St; skates per hr/day $6/24), near Golden Gate Park.

GoCar Rentals (☎ 800-914-6227; www.gocarsf.com; 1st hr $40, per day $110) offers a fun and unique way to zip around the city – in a three-wheel, two-seat racing car that goes 35mph. The little yellow cars are equipped with GPS-triggered commentary on sights as you pass them. You must be 18 years or older and have a valid driver's license.

WALKING TOUR

San Francisco is great for sidewalk treks in search of interesting neighborhoods and stunning hilltop vantage points. This tour takes in two of the city's most colorful enclaves – Chinatown and North Beach – and ends with one of the best up-and-downs the city offers. Done leisurely, this makes a good day.

Start at the corner of Grant Ave and Bush St, where the stone dragons and jade-green awnings of the **Chinatown Gate (1)** announce the entrance to Chinatown. Walk north on bustling Grant Ave, with its neon chop suey signs and faux 'ornamental-oriental' façades that reflect an early 20th-century romanticism. Grant St's theme park image fails to mask the fact that the surrounding blocks comprise one of the USA's most vital immigrant quarters.

At Sacramento St, turn left and then right onto Waverly Pl, an atmospheric alley lined with medicinal ginseng displays and filigreed open balconies. At Clay St, turn west uphill. The **Chinese Historical Society of America Museum (2;** ☎ 415-391-1188; www.chsa.org; 965 Clay St; adult/student $3/2; ☺ noon-5pm Tue-Fri, noon-4pm Sat & Sun), with the largest collection of Chinese American artifacts in the US, is just half a block up.

Return east on Clay St and continue north along Waverly Pl. At Washington St, jog left and enter Ross Alley, a hidden pedestrian walkway. That enticing scent will be coming from the **Golden Gate Fortune Cookies (3;** 56 Ross Alley), a dimly lit warehouse where you can watch women operate two old-fashioned machines churning out fortune cookies, a San Francisco invention. Try a hot sample and buy a bag!

Return to Washington St and walk east to **Portsmouth Sq (4)**, where crowds of old men

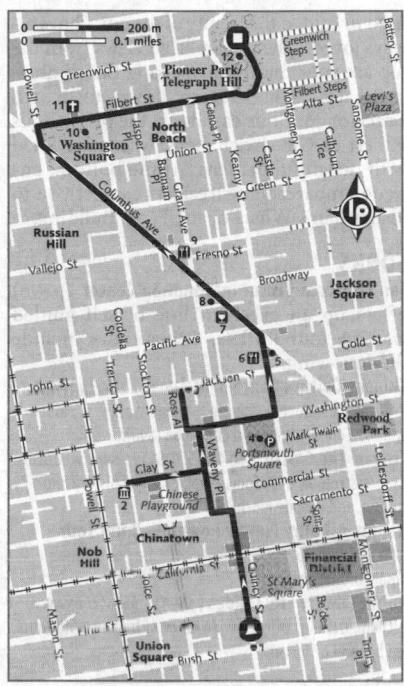

gamble on park benches while just a few feet away children romp on a playground. Turn north on Kearny St to Columbus Ave. Here, Chinatown and North Beach meet. The striking 1905 **Sentinel Building (5)**, on the corner, is owned by filmmaker Francis Ford Coppola. If it's lunch time, stop at the **House of Nanking (6;** p604).

Columbus Ave leads into the heart of North Beach. Flanking Jack Kerouac Alley, **Vesuvio (7;** p606), an eccentric old bar, faces **City Lights Bookstore (8;** p595) still owned by poet Lawrence Ferlinghetti, who opened the store in 1953. A publisher as well as a bookseller, City Lights remains a vital and passionate San Francisco countercultural institution.

Rest your dogs over a cappuccino within the Italo-beatnik digs of **Caffe Trieste (9)** or on the lawn at **Washington Sq (10)**, where you can admire the ornate 1924 **Saints Peter & Paul Church (11;** 666 Filbert St). Then ascend steep Filbert St until you reach the top of Telegraph Hill and **Coit Tower (12;** p598). The tower was financed by the eccentric Lillie Hitchcock Coit, who asked that a third of her estate be used to 'add to the beauty of the city I have always loved.' The unparalleled views from the top are your reward for making the climb.

Finally, either return down to North Beach or continue east down the precipitous Filbert or Greenwich steps, which are lined with delightful gardens. At the bottom, antique Embarcadero streetcars can get you to Fisherman's Wharf or the Ferry Building.

TOURS

San Francisco Visitor Information Center (p595) offers up an excellent line of self-guided walking-tour leaflets. Other tours include the following:

Chinese Culture Center (☎ 415-986-1822; www .c-c-c.org) Conducts a Chinese Heritage Walk ($17) and a Chinese Culinary Walk and Luncheon ($40).

Cruisin' the Castro (☎ 415-550-8110; www.webcastro .com/castrotour; $45) Tours emphasize gay history and culture, and include lunch.

Haight-Ashbury Flower Power Walking Tour (☎ 415-863-1621; $15; Tue & Sat) A traipse through hippie ground zero.

Public Library City Guides (☎ 415-557-4266; www .sfcityguides.org) Offers a wide range of free walking tours led by local historians.

FESTIVALS & EVENTS

Chinese New Year Parade (☎ 415-982-3000; www .chineseparade.com) One of the nation's largest, this winds through Chinatown in January or early February. The famous 200ft Golden Dragon ends the parade to the explosions of 600,000 firecrackers.

Noise Pop (www.noisepop.com) San Francisco's independent music fest is highly touted for bringing the best of the nation's up-and-coming bands to play in clubs around town. Also includes rock-related film screenings.

SF International Film Festival (☎ 415-561-5000; www.sffs.org) The nation's oldest film festival occurs in late April.

SF Gay Pride Month June begins with the Gay & Lesbian Film Festival, and the last Sunday of the month sees the **Lesbian, Gay, Bisexual & Transgender Pride Parade** (☎ 415-864-3733; www.sfpride.org), which makes a spectacle of itself along Market St in front of a million people. The Saturday before is the **Dyke March** (☎ 415-241-8882; www.dykemarch.org).

Open Studios (www.sfopenstudios.com) Artists citywide welcome the public to their workspaces throughout October.

SLEEPING

Hotels can be very expensive in San Francisco, but luckily the city has an abundance of central hostels, including three HI facilities, and there are a surprising number of older hotels with reasonable rates. The city's hotel tax is 14%.

HI San Francisco Downtown (☎ 415-788-5604; www.norcalhostels.org; 312 Mason St; dm $24-29, r $55-69; 🖳) The city's main HI property is just a block from Union Sq, amid five-star hotels at a tiny fraction of the price. Each dorm has three or four beds and private rooms can accommodate two people.

HI San Francisco City Center (☎ 415-474-5721; www.norcalhostels.org; 685 Ellis St; dm $23-29, r $67-70; 🅿 $11; 🖳) This comfy gem in the rough Tenderloin occupies a vintage 1920 hotel, and the small four-bed dorms all have private bathrooms.

HI San Francisco Fisherman's Wharf (☎ 415-771-7277; www.norcalhostels.org; Fort Mason Bldg 240; dm $22-29, r $69-78; 🅿 🖳) This top-notch hostel is set within the expansive lawns of Fort Mason, mere paces from the bay, and has great public rooms, tons of activities and a café. Most of the dorms have eight to 12 beds. From Transbay Terminal take a No 42 bus to the corner of Van Ness Ave and Bay St.

Pacific Tradewinds Backpacker Hostel (☎ 415-433-7970; 680 Sacramento St; dm $18-24) San Francisco's most intimate and friendly hostel (only 32 beds) has a travel-savvy and multilingual staff. It's on the edge of Chinatown, very convenient to public transportation.

Adelaide Hostel & Hotel (☎ 415-359-1915, 877-359-1915; www.adelaidehostel.com; 5 Isadora Duncan Lane; dm $20, r $55-65; 🖳) A cheery hostel at the end of a safe alley, the Adelaide is a good option near Union Sq. The private rooms have shared bathroom.

Elements New Mission Hostel (☎ 866-327-8407; www.elementssf.com; 2516 Mission St; dm $19-22) Opened in 2004, this brand-new facility introduces affordable lodging to the vibrant Mission District. The roof deck is a great social space and all rooms have private bathroom. Perfect if you're planning on indulging in the Mission's hip scene. BART is nearby.

Central YMCA Hostel (☎ 415-885-0460; 220 Golden Gate Ave; dm $24, r $44-55; 🅿 🖳) The 'Y' takes up most of a city block in the hardscrabble Tenderloin, and offers clean unisex rooms for men and women. Fitness facilities are available to guests. Dorms have shared bathroom, while the more expensive private rooms have their own bathroom.

Globe Hostel (☎ 415-431-0540; 10 Hallam Pl; dm $16-18, d $46; ☒) In the thick of SoMa nightlife, this large, worn hostel attracts a partying international crowd. No real kitchen, but bathrooms are private to each dorm room. US citizens need to show a passport to stay.

Green Tortoise Hostel (☎ 415-834-1000; www.greentortoise.com; 494 Broadway; dm $19-22, r $48-58) This mid-sized hostel, located on North Beach's seedy strip-joint strip, is run by the funky long-distance bus people, so expect similarly relaxed, slightly offbeat accommodations here. The location, while sinful, poses no real threat, and offers instant access to many San Francisco fun spots. Private rooms at the high-end price accommodate up to four people.

Hotel des Arts (☎ 415-956-3232; www.sfhoteldesarts.com; 447 Bush St; r $59-119) Small rooms are clean and comfortable and the lobby is an art gallery in this unassuming hotel near Chinatown and Union Sq. Cheapest quarters have shared bathroom.

Grant Hotel (☎ 415 421 7540, 800 522 0979; www.granthotel.citysearch.com; 753 Bush St; r $40-85) Basic, clean rooms all have private bathroom in this old hotel. The downtown location is unbeatable.

Obrero Hotel (☎ 415-989-3960; 1200 Stockton St; s/d $45/55) On one of Chinatown's busiest corners, this small family-run hotel has 12 tidy rooms with shared bathroom. The street gets quiet in the evening but can be very noisy in the morning.

Metro Hotel (☎ 415-861-5364; 319 Divisadero St; d $66-77; ☒) Plain but clean, this hotel near the Haight is close to lots of public transit, and its pretty courtyard is relaxing. Avoid street-side rooms.

Mosser (☎ 415-986-4400, 800-227-3804; www.themosser.com; 54 4th St; r with bathroom $129-180, without bathroom $69-90; ☒ $25; ☒) The small rooms with shared bathroom are the best deal: public facilities are sparkling, and the crisp modern décor is the same throughout. Double-paned windows keep out the street noise.

EATING

San Francisco, as everyone knows, is a gourmand's paradise. The really good news, though, is that the city's high standards are not only found in white-tablecloth establishments. Some of the city's best meals are served in authentic taquerías, dim sum parlors, Italian delis, all-American diners and takeout pizza joints, as well as places to get a good burger, a bowl of noodles or a satisfying veg meal.

Downtown

Union Sq, the Financial District, Civic Center and the Tenderloin all have their friendly nosheries.

The refurbished **Ferry Building**, where the Embarcadero meets Market St, hosts an outstanding **farmers market** (☒ 8am-2pm Sat & Sun, 10am-2pm Tue, 3-7pm Thu). Inside the building, the stylish **Ferry Building Marketplace** is a food mall, with cafés, restaurants and stalls selling high-quality goods in a historic setting.

Yank Sing (☎ 415-957-9300; 101 Spear St; mains $10-15, dim sum $2-10; ☒ lunch) In the Rincon Center,

---

SPLURGE!

As in any city, in Frisco you can blow more dough on one night in a hotel suite than you spend on a month's rent back home, but that's not really the point in this town. Much more appropriate for San Francisco is the supply of intriguing digs catering to your imaginative, creative side (at relatively down-to-earth prices).

Phoenix Motel (☎ 415-776-1380, 800-248-9466; www.thephoenixhotel.com; 601 Eddy St; r from $130; ☒ ☒) This renovated motor court is a Civic Center oasis that takes its rock-and-roll pretensions seriously, with tropical hues, leopard prints, an arty mosaic-lined pool, complimentary Pop Tarts for breakfast and on-call stylists.

Red Victorian B&B (☎ 415-864-1978; www.redvic.com; 1665 Haight St; r with bathroom $120-126, without bathroom $96-110) Big wow factor here. Each comfortable room in this earnestly trippy B&B remains faithful to every '60s cliché. Décor varies from door to door, but each is wigged-out, wild and unforgettable.

Hotel Triton (☎ 415-394-0500, 800-433-6611; www.hotel-tritonsf.com; 342 Grant Ave; r $239-269; ☒ $30; ☒ ☒) This shagadelic designer hotel in Union Sq rewards guests with its cheeky humor. Expect crushed velvet spreads, Mad-Hatter striped wallpaper and blown-glass chandeliers.

Yank Sing serves the city's best dim sum, although the dining room lacks the colorful, chaotic atmosphere of the Chinatown restaurants.

Lefty O'Doul's (☎ 415-982-8900; 333 Geary St; mains $5.50-12; ☉ 11-2am) This old-school sports bar, with baseball bat legs on the stools, has a steaming hofbrau, along with freshly-carved open-faced turkey sandwiches smothered in gravy – an effective hangover cure.

Dotty's True Blue Café (☎ 415-885-2767; 522 Jones St; mains $6-9) Hefty hotcakes, eye-popping omelets and strong coffee are the calling cards of this cordial and very popular Tenderloin diner.

Red's Java House (The Embarcadero; mains $1-3; ☉ 6am-4pm Mon-Fri) A beloved relic of the old port, this barren little tinderbox slings absurdly cheap (and somewhat greasy) double-cheeseburgers and ice-cold Bud in a bottle. Coffee and doughnuts anchor the breakfast menu. It's along the waterfront, towards the ballpark.

For a lunch-time escape from the Union Sq madness, try the French **Café de la Presse** (☎ 415-398-2680; 352 Grant Ave; mains $10-15). Cheap Vietnamese noodles can be had at **Pho Hoa** (☎ 415-673-3163; 431 Jones St; mains $4-8) in the Tenderloin.

Chinatown & North Beach

Small restaurants and huge dim sum halls jammed with tables and carts are what make these neighborhoods so well-loved. Also, North Beach's Italian cafés can be counted on for pastries and, in some cases, light meals prepared to order.

House of Nanking (☎ 415-421-1429; 919 Kearny St; mains $4-8) It's cramped, crowded, rushed and sometimes rude – in other words, vintage Chinatown. Hoards of diners keep returning for the delicious food.

Lucky Creation (☎ 415-989-0818; 854 Washington St; mains $5-7) This unpretentious, simple Buddhist vegetarian restaurant is a star in the heart of Chinatown.

Gold Mountain (☎ 415-296-7733; 644 Broadway; mains $7-16, dim sum $2-5) A formidable armada of dim sum carts makes the rounds in this huge, raucous hall, bearing fresh and finely prepared plates and steamer pots.

Dol Ho (☎ 415-392-2828; 808 Pacific Ave; dim sum $2-3) The place is small, crowded and lacks atmosphere, but excellent and inexpensive dim sum is churned out of its steaming kitchen.

Mario's Bohemian Cigar Store (☎ 415-362-0536; 566 Columbus Ave; mains $7-13) Small pizzas and focaccia sandwiches – not cigars – are what the patrons chomp on at this comfortable little corner tavern on Washington Sq. A good place to knock back a few beers and a light meal with friends.

Liguria (☎ 415-421-3786; 1700 Stockton St; half-sheet focaccia $3.25) From Washington Sq follow your nose to this no-frills bakery for freshly baked focaccia (with tomato sauce, onions or plain). Along with a soda from a Grant St grocery, you've got a simple picnic.

Molinari's Delicatessen (☎ 415-421-2337; 373 Columbus Ave; sandwiches $5-8) North Beach denizens have been flocking to this aromatic deli for a century. Cold cuts are of high quality, and the vegetarian Joe's Special (fresh mozzarella, dried tomatoes, sweet peppers, basil and garlic) is excellent.

L'Osteria del Forno (☎ 415-982-1124; 519 Columbus Ave; mains $11-17, lunch $5-10; ☉ Wed-Mon) Superb handmade raviolis and pizzas are dished up in this intimate North Beach spot. Drop by for a quiet lunch.

Golden Boy Pizza (☎ 415-982-9738; 542 Green St; slices $2-3) It look's like a grunge band's practice space, but Golden Boy's pizza is terrific. A good pit stop between bars.

Mo's Burgers (☎ 415-788-3779; 1322 Grant Ave; mains $6.25-10) Some of the city's best hand-patted burgers are charbroiled at this fun North Beach spot. Cows and stooges adorn the walls.

Mission

Since the Mission is one of the city's better nightlife zones, it's awfully convenient that so many of the area's eateries offer cheap and filling fare.

Puerto Alegre (☎ 415-255-8201; 546 Valencia St; mains $5-14) The ordinary Mexican fare at this fun spot tastes good after your party has downed a couple of cheap margarita pitchers. The place gets truly jolly during happy hour (3pm to 6pm Monday to Friday).

La Palma Mexica-tessen (☎ 415-647-1500; 2884 24th St; mains $2-4; ☉ Mon-Sat) In the back of this Mexican grocery there's a takeout counter that's famous for its handmade tamales. You can also order tacos and burritos here.

Chow (☎ 415-552-2469; 215 Church; mains $6-11) In a Castro/Mission overlap zone (just off Market St), this lively restaurant attracts all types. The menu proffers a range of pizzas, grilled sandwiches and pan-Asian noodle dishes at a fraction of what you'd expect to pay for food this good.

WeBe Sushi (☎ 415-565-0749; 538 Valencia St; sushi $2-4) Even WeBe's biggest fans don't consider it a place for fine sushi, but all appreciate the lite price for such tasty, healthful morsels amid Mission District bars.

Truly Mediterranean (☎ 415-252-7482; 3109 16th St; mains $5-7) The tasty kebabs, shwarmas and meatless falafels make this little dive a good pit stop between bars.

Haight

The Haight is good for a quick bite while shopping or bar hopping, with plenty of international cuisines to choose from.

Thep Phanom (☎ 415-431-2526; 400 Waller St; mains $9-12; ☻ dinner) This dependable, atmospheric Lower Haight favorite serves some of San Francisco's best Thai food – focus on the specials.

Pork Store Cafe (☎ 415-864-6981; 1451 Haight St; mains $3-8) Wondering what San Francis-

co's hippies ate? No doubt many of 'em ate the truck stop slop at this place, which has been slinging cheap short-order fare since 1919. A bustling counter and rickety

---

> ### MISSION: FIND PERFECT BURRITO
>
> Tracking down the perfect Mission District burrito is a matter of some urgency for anyone hoping to gain some cred in San Francisco; start your quest at one of the following:
>
> - **La Taquería** (☎ 415-285-7117; 2889 Mission St; burritos $5-9) Riceless burritos leave more room for perfectly cooked meats; a block from 24th St BART.
> - **Taquería Can-Cun** (☎ 415-252-9560; 2288 Mission St; burritos $4-8) The city's best veg burrito.
> - **Pancho Villa Taquería** (☎ 415-864-8840; 3071 16th St; burritos $4-6) Tasty, filling burritos near 16th St bars and BART.

> ### GAY FRISCO
>
> San Francisco requires no introduction as the USA's gay cultural capital. The Castro District is the hub for gay activities, but the Mission, Bernal Heights and the Tenderloin have their scenes as well.
>
> The local events calendar is marked by several gay-centric occasions, such as the following:
>
> - **Sisters of Perpetual Indulgence Easter Celebration** (☎ 415-552-0220; www.thesisters.com) Easter Sunday.
> - **AIDS Candlelight March & Vigil** (☎ 415-552-0220; www.thesisters.com) Third Sunday in May.
> - **San Francisco Gay & Lesbian Film Festival** (☎ 415-703-8650; www.frameline.com) Late June.
> - **Dyke March** (☎ 415-241-8882; www.dykemarch.org) Last Saturday in June.
> - **Lesbian, Gay, Bisexual & Transgender Pride Parade** (☎ 415-864-3744; www.sfpride.org) Last Sunday in June.
> - **Folsom St Fair** (☎ 415-861-3247; www.folsomstreetfair.com) Last Sunday in September.
> - **Castro St Fair** (☎ 415-841-1824; www.castrostreetfair.org) First Sunday in October.
>
> The city has a bunch of gay-friendly hotels, including **24 Henry** (☎ 415-864-5686, 800-900-5686; www.24henry.com; 24 Henry St; r with bathroom $110, without $65-85; ☐), in an old Victorian house in the Castro, and the pricey but comfortable **Willows Inn** (☎ 415-431-4770; www.willowssf.com; 710 14th St; r $110-130) – check for web specials.
>
> Grab a bite at **Cafe Flore** (☎ 415-621-8579; 2298 Market St at Noe; mains $10-13), aka 'Cafe Hairdo.' It's the classic Castro meeting place, where the food is second to the moving scenery.
>
> The Castro is chock-a-block with gay bars. **Harvey's** (☎ 415-431-4278; 500 Castro St), a peachy, tourist-friendly spot, is a good starting point. In the Mission, **Lexington Club** (☎ 415-863-2052; 3464 19th St) is *the* lesbian hang-out. The **Stud** (☎ 415-252-7883; 399 9th St) is a legendary gay dance club that hosts numerous theme nights for all persuasions. Check the Clubbing listings (p606) for more interesting nightlife.

tables and sleepy-headed wait staff add to the authenticity.

Magnolia Pub & Brewery (☎ 415-864-7468; 1398 Haight St; mains $6-12) Great food and excellent beer brewed in the basement make this friendly spot one of the Haight's top draws.

DRINKING
Bars

The Mission, the Haight and North Beach are famous for their bars and pubs.

Tonga Room (☎ 415-772-5278; cnr California & Mason Sts) In the swank Fairmont Hotel, atop Nob Hill, this is the swizzle stick for any evening: a fake jungle, tropical drinks, cover bands on a raft and a twice hourly 'monsoon.'

Vesuvio (☎ 415-362-3370; 255 Columbus Ave) This North Beach prototypical Beat hang-out draws the scenesters of yesterday and today.

Tosca Cafe (☎ 415-986-9651; 242 Columbus Ave) Politicos and local celebrities gather at this forever-cool North Beach institution.

Elbo Room (☎ 415-552-7788; 647 Valencia St) This always-packed Mission spot defies its own name, whether around the bar, pool tables or upstairs dance floor.

Make-Out Room (☎ 415-647-2888; 3225 22nd St) A lesson in Mission hip, this casually cool place features alternative music most nights. Up the street, drop by the tranquil **Latin American Club** (☎ 415-647-2732; 3286 22nd St).

Zam Zam (☎ 415-861-2545; 1633 Haight St) The exotic décor and swinging jukebox at this swanky den of dissolution conjure a mood

---

BILL GRAHAM PRESENTED

It wouldn't have been the 1960s in San Francisco had it not been for Bill Graham, the groundbreaking rock and roll concert promoter/impresario who helped launch the careers of Janis Joplin, Santana, the Jefferson Airplane, the Grateful Dead and countless others. Though Graham died in a 1990 helicopter crash (he went down while scouting a concert site), his legacy endures at the two San Francisco nightclubs he put on the map: the **Fillmore Auditorium** (☎ 415-346-6000; www.thefillmore.com; 1805 Geary Blvd) and the **Warfield** (☎ 415-775-7722; 982 Market St), both of which continue to draw top touring acts from all genres.

---

for mixed beverages. If such pre-hippy trappings don't suit your Haight yearnings, slouch into the more neighborly **Murio's Trophy Room** (☎ 415-752-2971; 1811 Haight St), where you're more likely to overhear conversations that reveal the strangeness of the district.

Edinburgh Castle (☎ 415-885-4074; 950 Geary St) All types converge on this old Tenderloin hall for British beers, Scotch whiskies, the occasional live bagpiper and an upstairs performance space.

Zeitgeist (☎ 415-255-7505; 199 Valencia St) On the central edge of the Mission, Zeitgeist's festive beer garden is the in spot for city bikers and punk hipsters.

Mad Dog in the Fog (☎ 415-626-7279; 530 Haight St) Lower Haight denizens gather at this friendly Anglophile pub for darts, draft Guinness, *futbol* on the telly and hearty grill fare.

Live Music

Cafe du Nord (☎ 415-861-5016; 2170 Market St) This former speakeasy in the Castro-Mission cross-over zone books jazz and salsa, and patrons dance like they know how.

Bottom of the Hill (☎ 415-621-4455; 1233 17th St) Always something interesting going on in this club, with music ranging from jazzy-funk to folky-punk.

Great American Music Hall (☎ 415-885-0750; 859 O'Farrell St) This former bordello retains some lurid plushness, but is now one of San Francisco's classiest performance spaces. An excellent venue in which to see acts ranging from rock, alt, country, jazz and blues.

Slim's (☎ 415-621-3330; 333 11th St) A full slate of rock and R&B artists keeps this large club hopping.

Paradise Lounge (☎ 415-861-6906; cnr 11th & Folsom Sts) This place has three stages and two floors, so something's always on, from punk to poetry. Pool tables, too.

Boom Boom Room (☎ 415-673-8000; 1601 Fillmore St) Live blues and funk occur nightly at this refurbished, historic Fillmore haunt.

Club Deluxe (☎ 415-552-6949; 1511 Haight St) The crowd dresses the part at this retro Haight spot, which spins the appropriate swing and big-band tunes.

CLUBBING

The Mission and the Castro have tons of action, but don't forget the swanky, Union Sq hotel lounges and their great views.

Harry Denton's Starlight Room (☎ 415-395-8595; 450 Powell St) On the top floor of the Sir Francis Drake Hotel, Harry Denton's has the views and nightly dancing.

El Rio (☎ 415-282-3325; 3158 Mission St at Cesar Chavez) World beat and salsa get their due at this diverse Mission club with an outdoor patio.

Café (☎ 415-861-3846; 2367 Market St) A lively, multifaceted Castro club that draws a mixed gay and lesbian crowd onto its dance floor and has a large street-view deck.

Up & Down Club (☎ 415-626-2388; 1151 Folsom St) Go up for DJ-spun hip hop and down for live jazz.

EndUp (☎ 415-357-0827; 401 6th St) One of the city's most popular dance clubs. 'Fag Fridays' start the weekend, which finishes with Sunday's day-long tea dance.

ENTERTAINMENT

Extensive entertainment listings can be found in the city's free weeklies – the *San Francisco Bay Guardian* and *SF Weekly* – and at www.sfarts.com, which also lists free events. For tickets to the theater, big music acts and other shows, call **BASS** (☎ 415-776-1999; www.tickets.com). **TIX Bay Area** (☎ 415-433-7827; www.theatrebayarea.org; ☯ Tue-Sun), at Union Sq, also sells half-price tickets to opera, dance and theater events.

Performing Arts

Davies Symphony Hall (☎ 415-864-6000; 201 Van Ness Ave) The renowned San Francisco Symphony performs here from September to May.

War Memorial Opera House (☎ 415-864-3330; 301 Van Ness Ave) Both the acclaimed San Francisco Opera and the **San Francisco Ballet** (☎ 415-865-2000) perform here.

Theater

San Francisco has numerous small theater companies and one major company, the American Conservatory Theater (ACT).

Geary Theater (☎ 415-749-2228; 415 Geary St) ACT performs primarily here.

Magic Theatre (☎ 415-441-8822; Bldg D, Fort Mason) Made famous by Sam Shepard, this is an important breeding ground for new playwrights.

Club Fugazi (☎ 415-421-4222; 678 Green St) The ribald *Beach Blanket Babylon* plays here – San Francisco's longest-running theater-comedy extravaganza.

Cinemas

Castro Theatre (☎ 415-621-6120; 429 Castro St) This grand old-style cinema has the city's best calendar of art, independent and foreign films.

Other independent and just plain weird films can be seen at:

Red Vic Movie House (☎ 415-668-3994; 1727 Haight St)

Roxie Cinema (☎ 415-863-1087; 3117 16th St)

Lumiere (☎ 415-885-3200; 1572 California St)

Sports

Tickets for the local pro teams are difficult but not impossible to come by.

San Francisco Giants (☎ 415-467-8000; http://san francisco.giants.mlb.com) The Major League baseball club plays at the stunning SBC Park, along the Embarcadero near downtown.

San Francisco 49ers (☎ 415-468-2249; www.sf49ers .com) The city's NFL football team plays at windy Candlestick Park, off Hwy 101 in the southern part of the city.

SHOPPING

Besides eating, there's nothing a San Francisco visitor likes more than shopping, and the city does not disappoint.

For major department stores and international designers, head for Union Sq. Other places for hip clothing boutiques include Union and Chestnut Sts in the Marina and Fillmore St north of Geary Blvd. Youth culture and vintage vultures are served in the Haight and the Mission. Polk St north of Broadway is a fun, eclectic shopping destination. And only New York has a better range of bookstores and vinyl record shops; they're everywhere in San Francisco.

GETTING THERE & AWAY

Air

San Francisco International Airport (SFO; ☎ 650-821-8211; www.flysfo.com) is situated 14 miles south of downtown off Hwy 101. SFO is a United Airlines hub, and most other domestic and international carriers fly in and out of here.

Bus

The **Transbay Terminal** (425 Mission St), at 1st St in SoMa, is the city's major bus station. If you're heading out to neighboring communities, you can take **AC Transit** (☎ 510-817-1717; www.actransit.org) buses to the East Bay, **Golden Gate Transit** (☎ 415-923-2000; www.goldengate.org)

CALIFORNIA

buses north into Marin and Sonoma Counties, and **SamTrans** (☎ 800-660-4287; www.samtrans.com) buses south to Palo Alto and along the Pacific Coast.

Greyhound (☎ 415-495-1569, 800-229-9424; www.greyhound.com), also serving the Transbay Terminal, has several buses daily to Los Angeles, Lake Tahoe and other destinations.

Train
CalTrain (☎ 800-660-4287; www.caltrain.com) operates down the Peninsula. From the depot at 4th and Townsend Sts in San Francisco, it links to Palo Alto and San Jose. **Amtrak** (☎ 800-872-7245; www.amtrakcalifornia.com) runs free shuttle buses to San Francisco's Ferry Building and CalTrain station from its terminals in Emeryville and Oakland's Jack London Sq. Trains arriving from the north connect with the bus at Emeryville; those from the south connect with the bus at Oakland.

GETTING AROUND
Operated by the Metropolitan Transportation Commission, www.transitinfo.org is an excellent resource, covering transit options for the entire nine-county Bay Area. You can also call ☎ 511, an automated Bay Area transit information service.

Boat
Blue & Gold Ferries (☎ 415-773-1188; www.blueandgoldfleet.com) runs the Alameda–Oakland ferry from Pier 41 and the Ferry Building. It also serves Alcatraz Island. **Golden Gate Ferry** (☎ 415-923-2000; www.goldengate.org) has regular service from the Ferry Building to Larkspur and Sausalito in Marin County.

Car & Motorcycle
Avoid driving a car in San Francisco: street parking is notoriously competitive, tickets expensive and the hills daunting.

However, convenient downtown parking lots are at the Embarcadero Center, at 5th and Mission Sts and at Sutter and Stockton Sts.

National car rental agencies have 24-hour offices at the airport and regular offices downtown. See p710 for toll-free contact information.

Public Transportation
San Francisco's **Municipal Transit Agency** (Muni; ☎ 415-673-6864; www.sfmuni.com) operates comprehensive bus and streetcar lines and three cable car lines; two cable car lines leave from Powell and Market Sts, and one leaves from California and Market Sts. The general fare for buses or streetcars is $1.25; cable car fare is $3. A Muni Passport, available in one-day ($9), three-day ($15) or seven-day ($20) versions, allows unlimited travel on all Muni transportation, including cable cars; it's sold at **San Francisco Visitor Information Center** (p595) and at the TIX Bay Area kiosk at Union Sq.

The **Bay Area Rapid Transit system** (BART; ☎ 415-989-2278; www.bart.gov) is the commuter train system linking San Francisco with the East Bay. In the city, BART runs beneath Market St, down Mission St and south to SFO and Millbrae, where it connects with CalTrain. Fares are $1.25 to $7. Most ticket machines won't make change, so it's best to have change in hand.

Taxi
Fares run about $2.25 per mile. Some of the major cab companies are:
DeSoto Cab (☎ 415-970-1300)
Veteran's Taxicab (☎ 415-552-1300)
Yellow Cab (☎ 415-626-2345)

SAN FRANCISCO BAY AREA

MARIN COUNTY
Just across the Golden Gate Bridge, wealthy 'Marin' is as warm and green as San Francisco is foggy and urban. **Sausalito** is a pleasant bayside community that makes a good destination for bike trips over the bridge (take the ferry back).

Marin Headlands
These hilly, windswept promontories are interlaced with prime hiking trails and offer spectacular views of San Francisco and the Pacific Ocean. To reach the **visitors center** (☎ 415-331-1540) by bike, take the Alexander Ave exit from the Golden Gate Bridge, go past Fort Baker and head west on Conzelman Rd.

The only public transit is the hourly No 76 Muni bus from San Francisco on Sunday and holidays. Attractions include the Point Bonita lighthouse and a mammal center, plus there's free walk-in camping. Near the visitors center, private rooms in the commanding officer's house at the historic **HI Marin Headlands Hostel** (☎ 415-331-2777, 800-909-4776; www.norcalhostels.org; dm/r $18/54; 💻) feel like hostelling in name only.

Mt Tamalpais State Park & Around

Majestic 'Mt Tam' (2517ft) has breathtaking views of the ocean, bay and surrounding rolling hills. **Mt Tamalpais State Park** (☎ 415-388-2070; per car $4) encompasses 6300 acres of wilderness, plus over 200 miles of hiking and biking trails. Panoramic Hwy climbs from the quiet town of Mill Valley through the park to Stinson Beach.

Golden Gate Transit only runs buses on weekends. **Park headquarters** is at **Pantoll Station** (801 Panoramic Hwy), where there are trailheads and a first-come, first-served **campground** ($12). Steep Ravine Trail follows a wooded creek to the coast (2 miles each way), where there are six magnificent **campsites** (reservations ☎ 800-444-7275).

Nearby, the foggy surf mecca of **Stinson Beach** and '60s outpost **Bolinas** make for interesting day trips, if you have a car.

Muir Woods National Monument

The slopes of Mt Tam were once carpeted with mighty redwoods. The only surviving remnant is 550-acre **Muir Woods** (☎ 415-388-2595; per car $3), which was named after Sierra Club founder John Muir in 1908. The easy 1-mile Main Trail Loop leads past the splendor of the 1000-year-old trees at Cathedral Grove and returns via Bohemian Grove. Muir Woods is 12 miles north of the Golden Gate Bridge via Hwy 101, with no direct public transit. Arrive early or stay late to avoid the crowds. There's a ranger station, but no camping or picnicking.

Point Reyes National Seashore

The triangle-shaped peninsula of **Point Reyes National Seashore** comprises 110 sq miles of windswept beaches, lagoons and forested cliffs. The westernmost point of the peninsula, Point Reyes Headlands, is crowned by the **Point Reyes Lighthouse**, the best spot in the Bay Area for onshore whale-watching, while the peninsula's northern tip is home to a tule elk herd. The **Bear Valley Visitors Center** (☎ 415-464-5100) has trail maps and park displays. Point Reyes has four hike-in **campsites** (reservations 9am-2pm Mon-Fri ☎ 415-663-8054; campsites $12), two near the beach.

If you can't score a campsite, head for the simple **HI Point Reyes Hostel** (☎ 415-663-8811, 800-909-4776; dm/r $16/54), off Limantour Rd, 8 miles from the Bear Valley Visitors Center. It offers a solid roof over 16-bed dorms in an idyllic location. Nearby, **Point Reyes Station** is a pleasant small town for a meal or picnic supplies.

WINE COUNTRY

The USA's best wine is produced in the warm, picturesque Sonoma and Napa Valleys, an hour or two north of San Francisco. It's an easy day trip from the city, but an overnight stay is recommended, especially if you're driving. Sophisticated country living is what the Wine Country is all about, so indulging in the region's pleasures may require digging a little deeper into your pockets. However, many prefer the inexpensive joys of merely driving the valleys' rustic scenic highways, or touring by bicycle, and gathering picnic fixings from any of the Wine Country's gourmet delis.

Reasonably priced tours, with a knowledgeable guide, can be arranged through the HI hostels in San Francisco. The days when tastings were free are just about over; most tastings include a 'flight' of several varieties and cost from $3 to $10. Many wineries scale down their tours and tastings in winter; call ahead.

> **SPLURGE!**
>
> A deluxe way to explore the Wine Country is by rail on the **Napa Valley Wine Train** (☎ 707-253-2111, 800-427-4124; www.winetrain.com; lunch $65-95, dinner $85-110), which offers three-hour lunch and dinner trips daily.

Sonoma Valley

Seventeen-mile-long Sonoma Valley is less heavily trafficked than Napa and most of its wineries are on or just off Hwy 12.

The state of California first passed into US control in 1846, when a band of Americans seized the Mexican governor in the town of **Sonoma**, at the valley's southern end. They declared the state a republic, and raised the 'bear flag' over the plaza. The **visitors center** (☎ 707-996-1090, 800-576-6662;

www.sonomavalley.com; 453 1st St E; 9am-5pm) is on the plaza, which is surrounded by nice restaurants and shops. The **Sonoma State Historical Park** (707-938-1519; per person $2; 10am-5pm) includes the nearby 1823 Sonoma Mission, the Sonoma Barracks, the Governor Vallejo home a half-mile away and the Petaluma Adobe, 15 miles west near suburban Petaluma, itself a pleasant slice of small-town California.

Sonoma's historic **Buena Vista** (707-938-1266, 800-926-1266; 18000 Old Winery Rd) is where the California wine industry was launched, when it was purchased by pioneering Hungarian vintner Count Agoston Haraszthy in 1857.

In Glen Ellen, the small, relaxed **Valley of the Moon** (707-996-6941; 777 Madrone Rd) is far enough off busy Hwy 12 to escape the crowds. Sample the super wines that are produced here before tucking into your picnic lunch.

On the road to Jack London State Historic Park, **Benziger** (707-935-3000, 888-490-2739) is a highly educational winery with do-it-yourself vineyard walks and tractor-driven tours of the whole winery.

You won't be charmed by sprawling **Santa Rosa**, at the valley's northern end, but it's very convenient and affordable. However, charming is just the word for the **Charles M Schulz Museum** (707-579-4452; www.schulz museum.org; 2301 Hardies Ln; admission $8; noon-5pm Mon & Wed-Fri, 10am-5pm Sat & Sun), dedicated to Santa Rosa's native son and his enduring creation, Charlie Brown and the Peanuts gang. Warm-hearted exhibits remind you why 'Sparky' was without peer among cartoonists, and the original ice-skating rink is next door.

SLEEPING

Sandman Hotel (707-544-8570; 3421 Cleveland Ave; r from $75; P) Santa Rosa's Cleveland Ave has several decent chain motels, among them the dependably neat and clean Sandman hotel.

Motel 6 (707-765-03331368; N McDowell Blvd; r $45) Just north of Petaluma, it offers the usual cheap accommodations.

EATING

Artisan Bakers (707-939-1765; 750 W Napa St; sandwiches $5-8) In Sonoma, it's worth tracking down the Artisan Bakers, which sells pastries, sandwiches and award-winning breads.

Sonoma Cheese Factory (707-996-1931; 2 W Spain St; sandwiches $5-8) The 'home of Sonoma Jack' is right on Sonoma Plaza, where you can enjoy a picnic lunch among ducks in the shade.

Napa Valley

There are over 200 wineries crowding the 30-mile-long Napa Valley along two main arteries: busy St Helena Hwy (Hwy 29) and the more scenic Silverado Trail, a mile or two east. Napa is known for cabernet sauvignon; search out the boutique wineries for the best.

Most wineries are open for tours and tastings 10am to 4pm or 5pm daily.

Get information in Napa, at the valley's southern end, which is itself decidedly plain. Follow signs for the **Napa Valley Visitors Bureau** (707-226-7459; www.napavalley.com; 1310 Napa Town Center; 9am-5pm), which has oodles of brochures, lodging updates and the informative free tabloid *Inside Napa Valley*, which contains a comprehensive winery map and guide.

In Yountville, **Domaine Chandon** (707-944-2280), west off Hwy 29, makes excellent 'sparkling wines' (it ain't champagne unless it's grown in Champagne, France) and has an exquisite restaurant.

On the St Helena Hwy in Oakville, **Robert Mondavi** (707-226-1335, 888-766-6328; tours $10) is a big commercial winery with a good tour about the wine-making process.

In Rutherford the modern **St Supéry** (707-963-4507, 800-942-0809; 8440 St Helena Hwy) has very informative and free exhibits illustrating the wine-making process.

Across the highway, the **Niebaum-Coppola Winery** (707-968-1100; tours $20) is owned by filmmaker Francis Ford Coppola. The tour focuses on the dramatic and imposing 1887 Inglenook chateau, while a free movie 'museum' includes such memorabilia as a Tucker car and the Oscar Coppola won for *Godfather*.

St Helena is a charming historic town. Just north of it is **Beringer** (707-963-7115; 2000 Main St), with an atmospheric manse and an interesting tour.

Calistoga is the best town for lingering, particularly if you want to treat yourself at one of its famous **thermal spas**. **Indian Springs**

(☎ 707-942-4913; 1712 Lincoln Ave) and Golden Haven (opposite Indian Springs) are both well regarded; spa packages last about an hour and start at around $50, not including extras like massages and facials. For the completely Northern Californian, clothing-optional experience, head to the **Harbin Hot Springs** (☎ 707-987-2477; www.harbin.org; day use mid-week/weekend $20/25), 4 miles north of Middletown, which is 12 miles north of Calistoga. There's a vegetarian restaurant and dorms ($35/50 midweek/weekends; bring your own linen).

SLEEPING

Golden Haven (☎ 707-942-6793; 1713 Lake St; www .goldenhaven.com; r $75-99) In Calistoga, this spa offers a full range of massage and mud-bath options. You can just stay here, too, in one of the standard rooms that are very reasonably priced. Jacuzzi suites run from $115 to $189.

Calistoga Inn (☎ 707-942-4101; www.calistoga inn.com; 1250 Lincoln Ave; r $75-125) The local institution. All rooms share a bathroom, and none have TVs or phones, but just amble downstairs to the friendly restaurant and bar, a popular watering hole.

Napa has a selection of mid-range chain hotels, such as Discovery Inn, Budget Inn and Travelodge.

Bothe Napa Valley State Park (☎ 707-942-4575; campsites $13-20) Off Hwy 29 between St Helena and Calistoga, this woodsy state park offers camping as well as good hiking options. It's a very convenient base for exploring the valley.

Sugarloaf Ridge State Park (☎ 707-833-5712; reservations 800-444-7275; campsites $15) Another camping place north of Kenwood on Adobe Canyon Rd.

EATING

Taylor's Automatic Refresher (☎ 707-963-3486; 933 Main St; mains $3-12) In St Helena, this perfectly preserved 1950s drive-in prepares burgers and shakes of the highest quality, and its impressive menu features gourmet tacos and seafood items. Top-notch dining on a lawn strewn with picnic tables – best done on lazy summer evenings.

Gordon's Cafe & Wine Bar (☎ 707-944-8246; 6770 Washington St; sandwiches & salads $5-10; ♡ until 3pm) In Yountville, Gordon's makes a nice, unpretentious mid-valley lunch stop.

Oakville Grocery (☎ 707-944-8802) On Hwy 29 in minuscule Oakville, the lovely Oakville Grocery sells gourmet picnic fixings and deli sandwiches.

Getting There & Around

Public transportation can get you to the valleys but is not ideal for vineyard hopping. **Greyhound buses** (☎ 800-231-2222) run daily from San Francisco up Napa Valley to Calistoga. **Golden Gate Transit** (☎ 415-923-2000, 707-541-2000) has buses from San Francisco to Sonoma, Petaluma and Santa Rosa. **Sonoma County Transit** (☎ 707-576-7433; www.sctransit.com) serves Sonoma Valley.

Rent bicycles in Napa at **Napa Valley Bike Tours** (☎ 800-707-2453; www.napavalleybiketours.com; 1988 Wise Dr; bikes per hr/day $6/25) and in Sonoma at **Sonoma Valley Cyclery** (☎ 707-935-3377; www .bikeroute.com; 20093 Broadway; bikes per hr/day $6/20).

EAST BAY

Across from San Francisco, the East Bay boasts fantastic sunsets, lively towns, and a good number of hipsters who've fled the big city's huge rents.

Berkeley

The Bay Area is a liberal enclave, but its radical core is **Berkeley**. Although it has mellowed since the 1960s heyday of the student-led free speech movement and anti-Vietnam War protests, it remains an iconoclastic fiefdom.

Founded in 1868, the **University of California at Berkeley** – 'Cal' to students and locals – is one of the country's top universities and home to 33,000 ethnically diverse, and politically conscious students. The university's **Visitor Services center** (☎ 510-642-5215; www .berkeley.edu; 101 University Hall, 2200 University Ave at Oxford St; ♡ 8:30am-4:30pm Mon-Fri) has information and leads free **tours** (♡ 10am Mon-Sat, 1pm Sun) of the pretty campus. Cal's landmark is the 1914 Campanile, which was modeled on St Mark's Campanile in Venice; anyone can ride the **elevator** ($2) to the top. The **Bancroft Library** displays the surprisingly small gold nugget that started the California gold rush in 1848.

Telegraph Avenue, immediately south of the campus, is a prime student hang-out that retains some of the free-spirited 1960s energy. It's packed with cafés, cheap eateries, record stores and bookstores – including the used-music emporium **Amoeba** (☎ 510-549-1125; 2455 Telegraph Ave) and acclaimed **Cody's Books** (☎ 510-845-7852; 2454 Telegraph Ave).

One prime student pick is **Café Intermezzo** (2442 Telegraph Ave; mains $4-6), with huge fresh salads.

Meanwhile, the **Gourmet Ghetto**, on Shattuck Ave north of University Ave, is home to many highly regarded restaurants, such as **Gregoire** (☎ 510-883-1893; 2109 Cedar St; mains $5-15), a takeaway with a pair of sidewalk tables just off Shattuck, where seasonal freshness and careful preparation rule the Francophile menu.

Nearby is the birthplace of California cuisine, Alice Waters' **Chez Panisse** (☎ 510-548-5525; www.chezpanisse.com; 1517 Shattuck Ave; café mains $15-18; ♥ Mon-Sat). Head straight upstairs, where the relaxed café serves relatively inexpensive lunch and dinner (downstairs it's three times as expensive).

From San Francisco, it's a short trip on BART to the downtown Berkeley station ($2.75), which is four blocks from the main UCB campus gate.

Oakland

Oakland is a city of remarkable racial and economic diversity that in recent years has been refurbishing and polishing its downtown area. Parts of the nation's fifth-busiest port still suffer from urban decay, but the city and its rich history make for pleasant exploring.

Oakland's **Chinatown**, a less touristy version of the one in San Francisco, is east of Broadway between Franklin and Webster Sts. The 1931 **Paramount Theatre** (☎ 510-465-6400; 2025 Broadway at 21st St) is a gorgeous art deco movie theater that screens a variety of films and hosts concerts.

Quality, inexpensive Asian restaurants abound. Try the *pho* soup at the Vietnamese **Pho Hoa Lao II** (☎ 510-763-8296; 333 10th St; mains $5). **Battambang** (☎ 510-839-8815; 850 Broadway; mains $5-9) is a less-hectic choice for fine Cambodian. Also downtown, **Pacific Coast Brewing Co** (☎ 510-836-2739; 906 Washington; mains $8-10) is a fun place for American pub grub or pizza and a microbrew.

From **Oakland International Airport** (☎ 510-563-2984), shuttle buses ($2) to the Coliseum BART station run about every 15 minutes until midnight daily. From San Francisco, take BART to the 12th St station in downtown Oakland ($2.35). Far more pleasant is the **Alameda–Oakland ferry** (☎ 510-522-3300), which operates from two locations in San Francisco (Pier 39 and the Ferry Building) to Jack London Sq up to 12 times daily ($5 one way).

SIERRA NEVADA

Just a couple of hundred miles from the sea, this jagged cordillera reaches for the stratosphere as it runs along the California-Nevada border. It's a glacier-scarred granite world interwoven with ancient forests, azure lakes and alpine meadows. Its highest peaks, including 14,494ft Mt Whitney, are along the Sierra Nevada Crest in the east, while Yosemite, Sequoia and Kings Canyon National Parks are mostly accessible from the west. Lake Tahoe can be easily reached from either direction.

YOSEMITE NATIONAL PARK

Yosemite can be described in four words: *bee you tea full.* (Say 'em fast.) Or, as the 19th-century naturalist John Muir put it, 'No temple made with hands can compare with Yosemite.' But that's stating the obvious (although the religious imagery is interesting). Yosemite is simply incomparable.

As anyone who has laid eyes on the 'crown jewel' of the USA's National Parks System will tell you, few places on earth pack as much ravishing natural beauty, tranquil serenity and cliff-hanging drama as Yosemite. While the downside is that the park attracts an astounding 3.5 million visitors a year, it's impossible to arrive and not be awed by the grandeur of Half Dome (8842ft) and El Capitan (7569ft), or be lured into the untamed wilderness of the park's vast hinterlands.

Spending just a day in Yosemite Valley, as most visitors do, is truly memorable; however, a week's explorations could be the highlight of a lifetime.

Come in spring to see the valley's spectacular waterfalls at their fullest, and to avoid summer's crushing crowds and campfire smog. Fall is also tranquil, and after a fresh winter snow the park looks as quiet and dainty as a bride.

Balancing tourists' needs with those of the environment is an ongoing battle in

YOSEMITE NATIONAL PARK

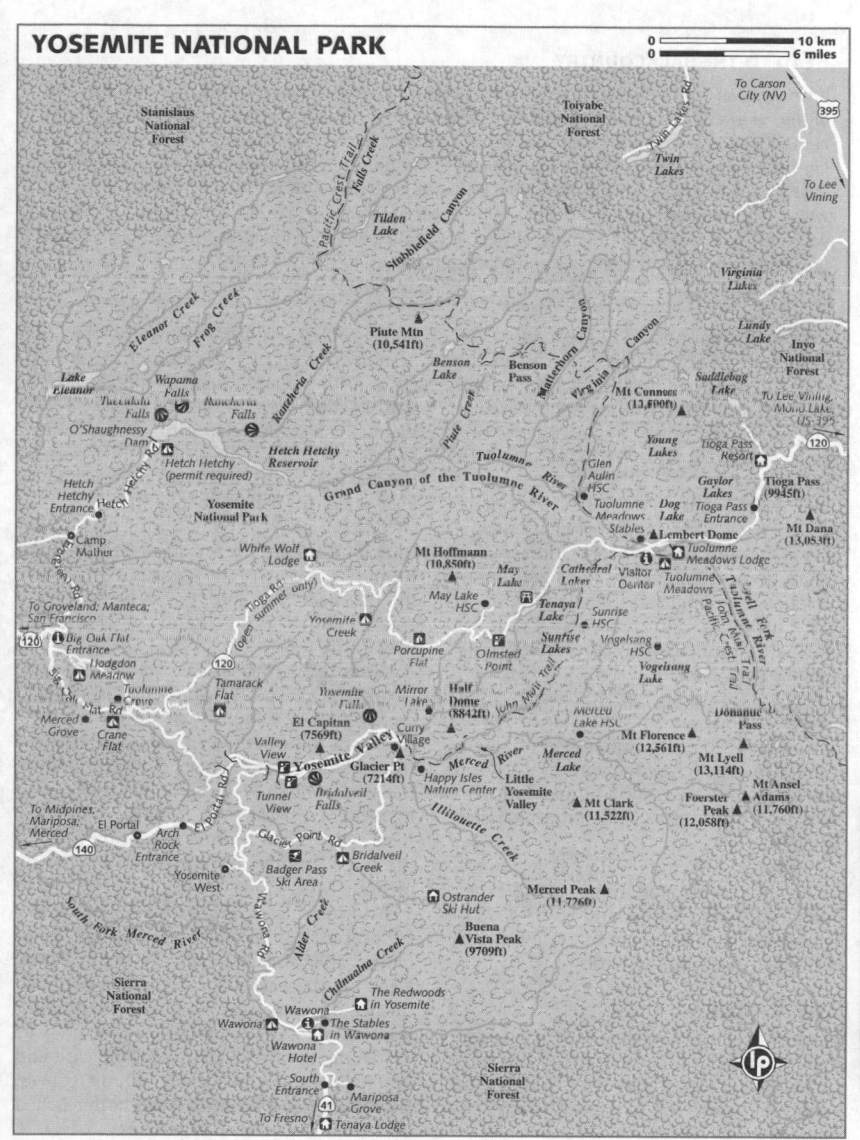

Yosemite, though the ultimate 'radical' solution – banning or limiting cars – is unlikely to be adopted soon.

Orientation & Information

Yosemite's entrance fee ($20 per vehicle, $10 for those on bicycle or foot) is valid for seven days. There are four primary en-

trances to **Yosemite National Park**: South Entrance (Hwy 41), Arch Rock (Hwy 140), Big Oak Flat (Hwy 120 west) and Tioga Pass (Hwy 120 east). Hwy 120 traverses the park as Tioga Rd (which is closed in winter), connecting the valley with Mono Lake via 9945ft Tioga Pass. Yosemite Valley, located on the southwest side of the park, is the

HEAD TO THE BACKCOUNTRY

If smoky, overcrowded campsites don't float your boat, you can, with a little planning, hike out of the valley and pitch your tent in the wilds of Yosemite's backcountry. Free wilderness permits are required year-round for overnight trips. A quota system limits the number of people leaving from each trailhead. About 60% of permits can be reserved between six months and two days in advance through the **Yosemite Wilderness Center** (☎ 209-372-0740; reservation fee $5), which is a wonderful resource for planning excursions once you're here. To reserve a permit, you must first provide the number of people in your party, entry and exit dates, starting and finishing trailheads and then your principal destination.

foremost destination and home to most visitor facilities. Tuolumne Meadows, on the east end of Tioga Rd, is a hub for backpackers as well as climbers. Wawona, located at the southern entrance, has a hotel, store, pioneer museum and Mariposa Grove of giant sequoias.

The **visitor center** (☎ 209-372-0299; www.nps.gov/yose; 9am-5pm, longer hr summer) in **Yosemite Valley** is the park's main information source, though there are ranger stations with maps and posted campground availability at all park entrances. For recorded Yosemite information and road/weather conditions, call ☎ 209-372-0200.

There is no gas in Yosemite Valley itself, but gas stations are in Wawona, El Portal, Crane Flat (Tioga Rd junction) and Tuolumne Meadows (closed in winter). In Yosemite Village, there is a 24-hour ATM near the Village Store and a 24-hour **medical clinic** (☎ 209-372-4637).

In winter, Yosemite Valley is a magical place, and accommodations are cheaper. Valley roads are plowed, and Hwys 41, 120 and 140 are kept open, but buy snow chains before approaching the park.

Yosemite Valley

Seven-mile-long Yosemite Valley is the thrilling center of the national park, with all facilities, campgrounds, lodges and trailheads connected by a mostly one-way loop road.

The hub is **Yosemite Village**, with the main visitors center, a post office, the Wilderness Center, an Indian museum, gift shops, a grocery store and basic eateries. West of the village, world-famous **Yosemite Falls** is actually a three-tiered affair cascading 2425ft – considered the tallest waterfall in North America. An easy hike leads to the base. While in spring the falls – and the entire valley – gush beautifully, they can actually dry up by late summer. At the valley's southeast end, the well-done **Happy Isles Nature Centure** (admission free; 9am-noon & 1-4pm May-Sep) is a popular spot for Merced River swims, picnics and leisurely strolls, and it's the starting point for the strenuous hike to ever-watchful **Half Dome** (8842ft).

Valley View Turnout is a good place to admire El Capitan, the world's largest granite monolith from base to summit. Peer closely up its sheer face and you'll probably see ropes, haul bags and climbers working their way to the top.

Mirror Lake, at the valley's northeast end, is an unforgettable, wheelchair-accessible destination, particularly in spring.

Words fail when one is met with the view from **Glacier Point**, a sheer cliff overlooking the entire valley. Glacier Point Rd (closed in winter), off Hwy 41, leads right to it, or reach it by cross-country skis or on foot via the steep, highly recommended Panorama or Four Mile Trails.

Another 'classic' Yosemite Valley view – encompassing majestic El Capitan, Half Dome and **Bridalveil Falls** – is from **Tunnel View**, on the east side of the Wawona Rd tunnel. The steep, aptly named Inspiration Point Trail starts from here.

Just north of the valley, near the west end of Tioga Rd, are two giant sequoia groves: **Merced Grove** and **Tuolumne Grove**, both reached by 2- to 3-mile round-trip hikes.

Tuolumne Meadows

About 55 miles from Yosemite Valley, Tuolumne (*twol*-uh-mee) Meadows, at 8600ft, is the largest subalpine meadow in the Sierra. It provides a dazzling contrast to the valley, with lush open fields, clear blue lakes, ragged granite peaks and domes, and cooler temperatures. Hikers and climbers will find a paradise of options, and campgrounds are somewhat less crowded.

Tioga Rd (Hwy 120) provides access to Tuolumne and is the only road to traverse the park from east to west. The road and all facilities are open only in summer. At the meadow's west end, **Tuolumne Meadows Visitor Center** (☎ 209-372-0263; 🕙 9am-5pm) has a large selection of maps and guidebooks. About a mile east, the **Tuolumne Meadows Store** (☎ 209-372-8428) sells groceries and camping supplies. A ranger kiosk, off the road near Tuolumne Meadows Lodge, issues wilderness permits.

Activities

With over 800 miles of **hiking** trails, Yosemite is a delight for trekkers of all abilities. In addition to the trails mentioned above, the **Mist** and **John Muir Trails** can be overcrowded during peak season, as one would expect from fairly easy hikes that lead to some spectacular scenery. They leave from Happy Isles Nature Center and lead around Vernal and Nevada Falls and up into idyllic Little Yosemite Valley.

The Muir trail continues on into Yosemite's back country and beyond, for hundreds of miles.

The main stop for **rock climbing** and camping supplies is the **Curry Village Mountain Shop** (☎ 209-372-8396), in Yosemite Valley; the **Tuolumne Meadows Mountain Shop** (☎ 209-372-8435) is smaller and is closed in winter. Novice and intermediate climbers might want to take an all day class (gear included, shoe rental extra) or guided climb with the excellent **Yosemite Mountaineering School** (☎ 209-372-8344; www.yosemitemountaineering.com; full-day class from $117), in Curry Village. It also has skiing, backpacking and hiking programs.

SCENIC DRIVE: GOLD COUNTRY

California gold was first discovered on January 24, 1848, when James Marshall was inspecting the lumber mill he was building for John Sutter, near present-day Coloma. From the mill's tailrace water Marshall pulled out a gold nugget 'roughly half the size of a pea' – an inauspicious beginning to a legendary era. By 1849 the gold rush was in full swing, with thousands of miners known as the '49ers migrating to California in search of the 'Mother Lode.'

Hugging the foothills of the western Sierra Nevada, California's Gold Country winds 300 miles north to south along Hwy 49; the most interesting stretch is from Nevada City to Sonora, which boasts a wealth of restored mining towns and historic hotels soaked in Old West atmosphere. Some of the towns are a bit precious, catering to antique hunters and arts and crafts collectors, but it's well worth working this scenic route into a drive up to Lake Tahoe or Yosemite. From the I-80, catch Hwy 49 at Auburn. Driving this section of the highway can be done in a day.

Nevada City is a busy tourist town full of fancy cafés, nice accommodations, well-preserved Victorian buildings and small museums tracing the area's mining and immigrant history.

In summer, stop for a **swim** at the confluence of the North and South Forks of the American River, 3 miles south of Auburn on Hwy 49. Ask around for the best swimming holes.

Sutter Creek is a less-polished, more endearing version of Nevada City, with its high-balconied buildings free of modern additions. It gets quite busy on weekends.

Scruffy **Jackson** contains the dusty **Amador County Museum** (☎ 209-223-6386; 225 Church St; admission free; 🕙 10am-4pm Wed-Sun), which in addition to history displays has unique 'model mine' **tours** ($1) on weekends. These are worth seeing before visiting the nearby **Kennedy Gold Mine** (☎ 209-223-9542; www.kennedygoldmine.com; admission $9; 🕙 10am-3pm Sat & Sun Mar-Oct), on Hwy 49.

Fifteen miles north of Murphys on Hwy 4, **Calaveras Big Trees State Park** (☎ 209-795-2334; per car $2, campsites $14-19) has giant sequoia groves and nice campsites. Hwy 4 itself is a scenic alternate route into the mountains and to Tahoe.

Columbia is now a state **historic park** (☎ 209-536-1672; www.columbiacalifornia.com), with four full blocks of authentic 1850s buildings and concessionaires in period costumes. It provides a real flavor of the Old West, without the smelly miners. The park itself doesn't close, but most businesses are open from 10am to 5pm.

In winter, downhill **skiing** and **snowshoeing** are available at **Badger Pass** (☎ 209-372-1000; www.badgerpass.com; half-/full-day lift tickets $22/31), and cross-country skiing at Badger Pass and Crane Flat. Two backcountry ski huts – with beds, cooking facilities and water – are available for overnight stays (reservations required). Contact the **Yosemite Association** (☎ 209-372-0740) and **Yosemite Cross-country Ski School** (☎ 209-372-8444). Badger Pass also offers **tubing** in summer.

Bike rentals are available at Yosemite Lodge and Curry Village, which also has a winter-only **ice-skating** rink.

Sleeping

Yosemite Bug Lodge & HI Hostel (☎ 209-966-6666; www.yosemitebug.com; dm $16, r with bathroom $40-70, without bathroom $55-115, tent cabins $30-50, campsites $17; 🖳) About 20 miles from the park on Hwy 140, in Midpines, this friendly place is the region's best budget option. Hostel rooms are extremely clean, the nice cabins have rustic charm and the café is a relaxing place to hang out. The Yarts (Yosemite Area Region Transportation; see opposite) bus stops here.

Within the park your choice is inexpensive campsites, mid-range tent-cabins (priced high for what they are but a bargain in Yosemite) and exorbitant cabins and lodges. All cabin and hotel room reservations are made through **Yosemite Concession Services** (YCS; ☎ 559-252-4848; www.yosemitepark.com; 5410 E Home Ave, Fresno, CA 93727). Wherever you stay, make reservations as early as possible, even a year in advance. Most rates decrease in the off-season. Unless otherwise noted, all lodging listed here is in the valley.

Character-lacking **Yosemite Lodge** (hotel/lodge r $110/161, mains $18-25) gets large tour groups and has 'standard' hotel rooms and modern, slightly larger 'lodge' rooms. There's an all-day food court, a buffet restaurant and a pricier, dinner-only restaurant with a popular bar.

Near the park's south entrance, the 1879, New England-style **Wawona Hotel** (r with private/shared bathroom $170/115) has relaxing lawns and pleasing Victorian rooms. The restaurant is a top choice.

Yosemite campgrounds (☎ 310-722-1257, 800-436-7275; http://reservations.nps.gov; campsites $18) tend to fill up fast, and not just in summer.

For many, reservations are required; you can and should make them up to five months in advance. Don't expect a wilderness experience: the folks in the RV one site over might be as big as bears, and the bears might be as intrusive as nosy neighbors. Campsites on the reservation system, including all those in Yosemite Valley, have flush toilets, picnic tables, fire rings and food-storage boxes.

First-come, first-served campgrounds include those with water and flush toilets, such as **Bridalveil Creek** (campsites $12) and **White Wolf** (campsites $12), and those without, including **Tamarack Flat** (campsites $8) and **Yosemite Creek** (campsites $8), which are more secluded. The only first-come, first-served camping in the valley is the ever-popular, 35-site **Camp 4** (campsites per person $5). The 304-site (half first-come, first-served) **Tuolumne Meadows Campground** (campsites $18; 🌣 summer only) is more pleasant than its size may suggest it is.

Curry Village (tent cabins $64, cabins with private/shared bathroom $88/80, r $110), with its long lines of tightly spaced cabins and tent cabins, could double as a labor camp (a step up from a prison camp, for sure). There are rough-and-simple tent cabins, nicer wooden cabins with and without bathroom, and standard motel rooms. The Curry Village **Dining Pavilion** (mains $6-12) has an all-day self-service cafeteria, a pizza window and, in the evening, a convivial, backpackers après-hike atmosphere.

Housekeeping Camp (bunkers $67) is a compound with a grocery store, laundry, pay showers, outdoor grills and three-sided concrete structures with plastic roofs that are like permanent tents. This should be your last resort in the price range, as it really has a refugee camp feel.

In the High Sierra, **Tuolumne Meadows Lodge** (tent cabins $71) has spartan tent cabins with four beds, a woodstove and candles (no electricity). A mile north of Tioga Rd, **White Wolf Lodge** (tent/wooden cabins $67/84) has similar tent cabins and a few wooden ones. Both have dining halls.

Eating

Hands-down the park's best grocery is the Village Store in Yosemite Village, while nearby, Degnan's Deli is just that, and Degnan's Loft serves pizza.

Getting There & Around

Amtrak (☎ 209-722-6862, 800-872-7245) operates a train/bus system from San Francisco and Los Angeles into Yosemite Valley via its Merced depot.

The **Yosemite Area Region Transportation** (Yarts; ☎ 877-989-2787; www.yarts.com) runs daily buses to the valley from Merced and other towns along Hwy 140. Another **Yarts bus** (☎ 800-626-6684) runs in summer only from Mammoth, east of the park, stopping in Tuolumne Meadows.

A free **shuttle bus** (☎ 209-372-1240) is available year-round for getting to points within Yosemite Valley itself.

LAKE TAHOE

The sparkly sapphire known as Lake Tahoe sits in a stadium-like bowl of evergreenery and rugged snow-capped peaks. In summer, vacationers flock to its shores and abundant parks, and in winter, skiers attack its famous slopes, which are mainly on the north side. Because it straddles the California-Nevada state border, Lake Tahoe also offers gaudy casinos, particularly along the south shore (via Hwy 50). It is often mused that many a mobster weighted with cement boots sleeps with the fishes within Tahoe's bottomless depths.

In winter, Hwy 89 (Emerald Bay Rd) is usually closed, and tire chains are often required for driving on the I-80 and Hwy 50; for winter road information, call ☎ 800-427-7623.

North & East Shores

Tahoe's northeastern shore is dominated by **Lake Tahoe-Nevada State Park** (☎ 775-831-0494; per car $6), which has cross-country skiing in winter and a nice, often-crowded beach at Sand Harbor. **Crystal Bay** is an aging casino town, while affluent Incline Village is home to touristy **Ponderosa Ranch** (☎ 775-831-0691; www.ponderosaranch.com; admission $12.50; ☺ 9:30am-6pm mid-Apr–Oct), where the TV Western *Bonanza* was filmed.

On the I-80 northwest of Tahoe, **Truckee** (www.truckee.com) is a onetime mining and railroad town with restaurants, shops and hotels. **Tahoe City** is the north shore's largest town.

Heading northeast on Hwy 28, Tahoe Vista and Kings Beach have attractive lodgings convenient to the slopes and sandy beaches. Hiking, biking and cross-country skiing can be enjoyed at North Tahoe Regional Park, north of Hwy 28 at the end of National St.

West & South Shores

DL Bliss State Park (☎ 530-525-7277; per car $5, campsites $12) is an ideal summer destination: clear turquoise water, white-sand beaches, lots of camping and access to unspoiled hiking trails.

The 6-mile Rubicon Trail rims narrow Emerald Bay – containing the lake's only island and waters that truly justify its name – and leads all the way to **Vikingsholm Castle** (admission $3; ☺ 10am-4pm Jun-Sep), a 1928 Scandinavian mansion at the lake's edge. The castle and **Emerald Bay State Park** (☎ 530-541-6498; per car $5) are also accessible via Hwy 89.

About 3 miles southeast on Emerald Bay Rd, the **Tallac Historic Site** (☎ 530-541-5227; admission free; ☺ 10am-4pm Jun-Sep) encompasses three historic estates and a museum.

South Lake Tahoe is a parade of cheap motels and a **visitors center** (☎ 530-541-5255; ☺ 9am-5pm Mon-Sat). Immediately across the Nevada border is **Stateline**, where you can engage in the Old West tradition of gambling all your money away at Caesar's Tahoe, Harrah's and Harvey's.

Activities

Lift passes for a full day of skiing are not cheap in the Tahoe area, and fluctuate throughout the ski season. They can peak at about $60 and tend to drop to about $30 in the spring.

A FEW FRIENDS FOR DINNER

Not far from Lake Tahoe, gorgeous **Donner Lake** is surrounded by small, woodsy resorts and is a low-key alternative to the Tahoe action. It wasn't so pleasant in the winter of 1846, though. That's when a combination of winter storms and poor planning wiped out half of the 87-person Donner party, and famished survivors notoriously resorted to consuming human flesh to stave off their hunger. At the east end of Donner Lake, the **Emigrant Trail Museum** (☎ 530-582-7892; admission $2; ☺ 10am-4pm, to 5pm summer) does a tasteful (ahem) job chronicling the Donner party's fateful journey.

SPLURGE!

An unforgettable part of any visit to California is a rafting trip on the American, Tuolumne, Kings and Stanislaus Rivers. **Whitewater Connection** (☎ 800-336-7238; www.whitewaterconnection .com; half-day trips $109-129) and **Zephyr Whitewater Expeditions** (☎ 800-431-3636, 209-532-6249; www .zrafting.com; half-day trips from $85) offer half-day trips and longer excursions.

It makes sense to call around before strapping on the skis.

Alpine Meadows (☎ 530-583-0963, 800-441-4423; www.skialpine.com) Large, popular, family-friendly resort; off Hwy 89 near Tahoe City.

Heavenly (☎ 775-586-7000, 800-243-2826; www .skiheavenly.com) Best all-around resort, massive new upgrade; near Stateline in South Lake Tahoe.

Kirkwood (☎ 209-258-6000, 877-547-5966; www .kirkwood.com) Locals' choice and popular with snowboarders; 35 miles south of Lake Tahoe on Hwy 88.

Squaw Valley USA (☎ 530-583-6985, 800-403-0206; www.squaw.com) World-class resort, host of 1960 Winter Olympics; off Hwy 89, 10 miles north of Tahoe City.

Near Donner Pass on the I-80, the Sierra Club's **Clair Tappaan Lodge** (☎ 530-426-3632) has 7.5 miles of cross-country ski trails and rentals, and **Alpine Skills International** (☎ 530-426-9108; www.alpineskills.com) has rentals and runs backcountry programs.

On Hwy 89 a few miles north of South Lake Tahoe, **Camp Richardson** (☎ 530-542-6584) has marked cross-country trails, and it can point you to more, but it really excels in summer with a full-service **marina** (☎ 530-542-6570) and bike rentals.

Summer or winter, the **cable car ride** (round-trip fare $19) to **High Camp** at Squaw Valley is a true Tahoe experience: you'll find an ice-skating rink, heated swimming pool, Olympic museum and restaurants and bars, all at 8200ft.

In summer, shops at **Ski Run Marina** (☎ 530-544-0200; www.tahoesports.com), in South Lake Tahoe, will set you up for all sorts of water sports – kayaking, powerboating, parasailing, jet skiing. The **Tahoe Queen** (☎ 800-238-2463; www.laketahoecruises.com; 2½hr cruise $26) runs Emerald Bay Cruises aboard a lovely old-fashioned paddle-wheeler.

Hikers have oodles of choices. A favorite trek is the strenuous 5-mile climb up Mt Tallac in the **Desolation Wilderness**. Pick up maps and permits at the **USFS Visitor Center** (☎ 530-573-2674; ☼ summer only) near to the Tallac Historic Site. Another highlight is the 150-mile **Tahoe Rim Trail**, which can be divided into good one-day sections and is open to hikers and bikers.

For further details, contact the **Tahoe Rim Trail Association** (☎ 775-588-0686; www.tahoerim trail.org).

Sleeping

Note that high-season (which may mean summer, winter or both) rates are quoted here; off-season rates can be 30% less.

If you're bargain-hunting, check out South Lake Tahoe's cheap hotels and mid-range chains along Hwy 50 west of Hwy 89; midweek deals can often go below $30. The casinos only offer good deals when business is slow.

Doug's Mellow Mountain Retreat (☎ 530-544-8065; 3787 Forest Ave; dm $15) Independent travelers will find more of their own kind at this independent hostel located in a tract-style house.

Camp Richardson (☎ 530-541-1801, 800-544-1801; www.camprichardson.com; campsites $18-28, r $85-175) On the west shore, this spiffy complex has two campgrounds and a very comfortable hotel where pine-log bed frames set the rustic tone. Cabins are rented nightly in winter (from $75), weekly in summer (from $620).

El Dorado Motel (☎ 530-544-5757, 800-935-3672; 4139 Lake Tahoe Blvd; r $49-109) In South Lake Tahoe, this small motor lodge is a good cheapie in the 1950s mold.

North Lake Lodge (☎ 530-546-2731, 888-923-5253; www.northlakelodge.com; 8716 N Lake Blvd; cabins $85-105) In Kings Beach, this family-run place has traditional Alpine efficiencies – very woodsy, with tacky furniture – and is pet-friendly.

There is lots of camping at the state parks and at **USFS sites** (reservations ☎ 877-444-6777; campsites $12). Open year-round is **Sugar Pine Point State Park** (reservations ☎ 530-525-7982, 800-444-7275; campsites $12), located on the western shore.

Eating

Dining choices are abundant, and the resorts have good options. In Tahoe City, the **Bridgetender** (☎ 530-583-3342; 65 West Lake Blvd; mains $5-8) is a classic Tahoe brew-and-burger joint that attracts the younger après-ski crowd.

Getting There & Around

Greyhound buses (☎ 800-231-2222) run daily between Truckee and Sacramento and San Francisco. Amtrak also stops in Truckee.

Tahoe Area Rapid Transit (TART; ☎ 530-550-1212; www.laketahoetransit.com; $1.25) buses connect Tahoe City, Truckee, Tahoe Vista and other towns. In summer service is extended down the west shore to Meeks Bay Resort, where you can transfer to the **South Lake Tahoe Stage** (☎ 530-542-6077) network. In winter, some ski resorts have free shuttles, as do larger casinos.

SEQUOIA & KINGS CANYON NATIONAL PARKS

If Yosemite's crowds are making you crazy, come here, where you don't have to hike very far into the backcountry to leave behind the cares of humanity. These adjacent parks receive only a quarter to a third the number of Yosemite's visitors, even though they encompass some of California's finest alpine scenery and awe-inspiring groves of giant sequoia trees.

The highlights, of course, are the giant sequoias. These are rare and awkward beauties (cousins to the coast redwoods), found only in sparse pockets above the snow line of the Sierras' western slope. Their trunks are massive, growing 300ft high and 40ft in diameter, with what look like smaller trees growing out of their tops. No living thing on earth can match them in overall volume.

Orientation & Information

Sequoia was designated a national park in 1890 (the second in the USA), Kings Canyon in 1940. The two parks, though distinct, are operated as one unit with a single admission of $10 per car and $5 per person on a bicycle or by foot. Admission is valid for seven days.

Enter the parks via Grant Grove (Hwy 180) or Ash Mountain (Hwy 198), the latter a series of narrow switchbacks. The parks are connected by the 48-mile, north–south Generals Hwy.

Grant Grove Village (☎ 559-565-4307), in Kings Canyon, and **Lodgepole** (☎ 559-565-3782), in Sequoia, are the two hubs. Each has a year-round **visitors center** (⊙ 9am-4:30pm, longer hr in summer), a market, showers, a post office and ATMs. Also open all year is **Foothills Visitors Center** (☎ 559-565-3135; ⊙ 8am-5pm), at the southern Ash Mountain entrance. There's also **Cedar Grove Visitors Center** (☎ 559-565-3793; ⊙ summer only) and the rangers station at remote **Mineral King** (☎ 559-565-3768; ⊙ summer only). For 24-hour recorded information, call ☎ 559-565-3341.

Kings Canyon Lodge and Hume Lake, both north of Grant Grove, have gas stations.

Sequoia National Park

The prime destination for first-time visitors is the **Giant Forest**. Park in the lot for the General Sherman Tree, the world's largest; it's hardly 20 paces from the road. Continue from here along the popular Congress Trail, a 2-mile pathway among awesome sequoias; other trails lead further into the forest.

Two miles south, the **Giant Forest Museum** (☎ 559-565-4480; admission free; ⊙ 9am-4:30pm) has exhibits about sequoia ecology and history, and accesses more trails, one of which is wheelchair accessible. For mind-boggling views of the Great Western Divide, climb the steep quarter-mile staircase up **Moro Rock**.

Discovered in 1918, 3-mile-long **Crystal Cave** has formations estimated to be 10,000 years old. **Cave tours** ($9, 45 minutes, summer only) cover a half-mile of chambers; tickets are available at the Lodgepole and Foothills visitors centers, not at the cave.

Kings Canyon National Park

Just north of Grant Grove Village, **General Grant Grove** contains numerous majestic giants. North of here, Hwy 180 descends into **Kings Canyon**, a spectacular, winding 36-mile drive (closed in winter) that includes sweeping mountain vistas, a surging river, waterfalls and dramatic granite cliffs. The canyon itself, plunging 8200ft, is the deepest in the contiguous 48 states. Far into the canyon is **Cedar Grove**, with seasonal campgrounds, lodging and a visitors center. It's worth the hour it takes to get

CALIFORNIA

to **Roads End**, if only for a short hike and picnic at beautiful Zumwalt Meadow. A ranger kiosk here issues wilderness permits for overnight backpackers.

Activities

With trail mileage 10 times greater than its road mileage, the parks are a **backpacking** heaven. Kings Canyon, Lodgepole and Mineral King, in Sequoia, provide backcountry access; the Jennie Lakes Wilderness Area, in the adjacent Sequoia National Forest, has pristine meadows and lakes at lower elevations. Trails are usually open by mid-May. Wilderness permits ($15) are required for all overnight trips; since quotas have recently been instituted, reservations, particularly for midsummer, are advised. You can make a **reservation** (☎ 559-565-3766; fax 559-565-4239; Wilderness Permit Reservations, HCR 89, Box 60, Three Rivers, CA 93271) by fax or post no earlier than March 1.

In winter, Grant Grove Village and Wuksachi Lodge near Lodgepole rent equipment for **cross-country skiing**; both parks have marked trails.

Sleeping

At Lodgepole, the busy **Lodgepole** and **Dorst campgrounds** (☎ 800-365-2267; http://reservations.nps .gov; campsites with/without flush toilet $20/12) can be reserved ahead. All others are on a first-come, first-served basis; those at Grant Grove are particularly nice. Most have water and flush toilets, while a few have vault or pit toilets. **Lodgepole, Azalea, Potwisha** and **South Fork** campgrounds are open year-round; the rest, including the four inside Kings Canyon, are usually open May to October. Call ☎ 559-565-3341 for updates.

Park-operated lodging uses the same **reservation service** (☎ 559-335-5500, 866-522-6966; www .sequoia-kingscanyon.com). In Grant Grove Village (which has a grocery store and restaurant), **John Muir Lodge** (tent cabins $45, cabins with bathroom $110-117, r $110-150; ☯ year-round), has nice hotel rooms, and some cabins come with a private bathroom.

In the canyon itself are two mediocre, seasonal options. **Cedar Grove Lodge** (r $105-115) has motel-style rooms. About halfway down, the privately run **Kings Canyon Lodge** (☎ 559-335-2405; r/cabins $90/180) has plain accommodations, though its café and gas pumps have nostalgic appeal.

Three Rivers, 6 miles south of Sequoia, is the best place outside the parks to stock up on food and supplies; it also has about a dozen mid-range **independent** and **chain motels** along Hwy 198.

EASTERN SIERRA

The jagged and majestic eastern side of the Sierra Nevada mountains is a sublime region where granite peaks abruptly plunge into the Great Basin desert. Hwy 395 runs at the feet of the entire range, with turnoffs offering side trips to lakes and mountains, where hikers, bikers, fishers and skiers can have a ball. The main towns here are Bridgeport, Lee Vining, Mammoth Lakes and Bishop.

A bona fide highlight in these parts is **Bodie State Historic Park**, one of the West's most picturesque ghost towns. Bodie was founded in 1859, and still has a large number of sturdy gold rush–era buildings that are slowly and gracefully decaying.

The **visitors center** (☎ 760-647-6445; admission $2; ☯ 10am-4pm late May-Sep) is excellent. To get there, exit Hwy 395 at the Hwy 270 turnoff, about 7 miles south of Bridgeport. From Hwy 395 the drive is 13 miles, the last three are unpaved and these are often closed in winter.

Mono Lake is an Ice Age remnant formed more than 700,000 years ago. Appearing like drip sand castles rising more than a dozen feet above the water, Mono's peculiar tufa towers form as calcium-bearing freshwater bubbles up through the alkaline lake. The most photogenic concentration is at the **South Tufa Reserve** (admission $3), on the lake's southern rim. Nearby, Lee Vining is a gateway town with two helpful information centers.

Immediately north of town, the USFS runs the **Mono Basin Scenic Area Visitors Center** (☎ 760-647-3044; ☯ 9am-4:30pm), which also has camping information. In town, the **Mono Lake Committee Information Center** (☎ 760-647-6595; www.monolake.org; Hwy 395 & 3rd St; ☯ 9am-5pm) is a good source of information on regional travel .

For a relaxing diversion, drive the 16-mile **June Lake Loop**. The scenic road, signposted midway between Mono Lake and Mammoth, follows Hwy 158 west into the mountains, passing Grant, Silver, Gull and June Lakes. The town of June Lake is a small resort community with grocery stores and motels.

Mammoth Lakes is a laid-back resort town amid stellar mountain surroundings, which offer great hiking. Though mainly an unattractive conglomeration of shopping centers and condominiums, the town now also boasts the brand-new, pedestrian-friendly Mammoth Village, with upscale shopping, eating, lodges and a 1-mile gondola ride directly to the area's main attraction, **Mammoth Mountain** (☎ 760-934-0745, 800-626-6684; www .mammothmountain.com). This four-season resort has world-class skiing and a very popular summertime **mountain-bike park** (lift tickets $31, bike rental packages $35-64).

The **Mammoth Lakes Ranger Station** (☎ 760-924-5500) and **Mammoth Lakes Visitor Bureau** (☎ 760-934-2712, 888-466-2666; www.visitmammoth .com; ☽ 8am-5pm) share a building on the north side of Rte 203, just before Old Mammoth Rd. This one-stop information center issues wilderness permits, has campground listings and offers a 24-hour courtesy phone to local hotels.

Bishop, the largest town south of Mammoth Lakes, is an important stop for hikers, since it provides access to the John Muir Wilderness.

The central district has some character, with covered sidewalks, 1950s neon signs and hunting and fishing stores, and there is an interesting railroad museum and a Paiute Shoshone cultural center. Restaurants, motels and gas stations line the highway at either end of town.

Some of California's most stunningly surreal topography is in the **Ancient Bristlecone Pine Forest** (☎ 760-873-2500); camp overnight, and drag yourself out of your tent before sunrise. Above 10,000ft in the White Mountains, the gnarly, spooky-looking bristlecone pines are Earth's oldest living things, with some dating back around 4000 years. They positively thrive on parched-looking slopes, where the sandy earth turns varying shades of red and orange as the sun emerges over the desert to the east.

The road (closed in winter) is paved to the top, where there are hikes of varying length, primitive camping and a visitors center. Wear sunscreen and a hat. From Bishop drive 15 miles south to Big Pine, then head east on Hwy 168 another 13 miles to the marked turnoff.

At 14,494ft high, **Mt Whitney** is the tallest point in the Lower 48, and the climb to its peak is among the most popular in the country.

To get there, drive 13 miles east of Lone Pine to Whitney Portal, where there is a store, café, campgrounds and access to the main trail, which leads 10.7 miles to the mountaintop.

The **Lone Pine Ranger Station** (☎ 760-876-6200; ☽ 7am-4:30pm May-Oct), located on Main St, has trail information and issues wilderness permits. However, trail quotas apply from May 1 to November 1, and **reservations** (per person $15) are awarded by lottery. To enter, overnight and day hikers should fax or mail applications to the **Wilderness Permit Office Inyo National Forest** (fax 760-873-2485; 873 N Main St, Bishop, CA 93514). Applications can be submitted only in February; check **USFS** (www.fs.fed.us/r5/inyo) for printable applications and tons of really good hiking advice.

Sleeping

Campgrounds abound in the Eastern Sierra. On public land outside developed campgrounds, however, you'll need a free fire permit, even for a camp stove. They're obtainable at any ranger station.

Silver Maple (☎ 760-932-7383; 310 Main St; r from $60) In Bridgeport, this is a clean and friendly motel.

Davison St Guest House Hostel (reservations ☎ 760-924-2188, 619-544-9093; www.mammoth-guest. com; 19 Davison St; dm summer/winter $22/30) In Mammoth Lakes, this excellent hostel has five tidy rooms and 22 beds – book ahead.

Bishop has a number of dependable chain motels – such as Comfort Inn, Motel 6 and Best Western.

Elms Motel (☎ 760-873-8118, 800-848-9226; www.395.com/elms; 233 E Elm St; r $30-50) Plain but cozy, it's a good budget choice.

Lee Vining Motel (☎ 647-6440; I-395; r from $50) In Lee Vining, this is a photogenic 1940s traveler's stop.

Eating

Whoa Nellie Deli (☎ 760-647-1088; mains $6-18) Also in Lee Vining, this is an unexpected delight, inside the Mobil gas station minimart on Hwy 120 near the Hwy 395 junction; it serves great sandwiches and steak dinners.

Getting There & Around
Greyhound (☎ 775-882-3375; Carson City) buses travel Hwy 395 between Los Angeles and Carson City, Nevada, stopping in most towns. Free Mammoth Mountain shuttle buses make loops through Mammoth during ski season.

NORTHERN MOUNTAINS

North of the I-80, along the I-5 and east to the Nevada line, are some of California's most beautiful – and least visited – features, including majestic Mt Shasta, Lassen Volcanic National Park and Lava Beds National Monument.

LASSEN VOLCANIC NATIONAL PARK
Vastly underappreciated, even by Californians, **Lassen Volcanic National Park** (www .nps.gov/lavo; per car $25, campsites $10-16) is an astounding natural attraction. In addition to spectacular Lassen Peak (10,457ft), the world's largest plug-dome volcano, the park contains all the steaming geothermal sulfur pools and cauldrons of Yellowstone, only without the geyser; good hikes include a 17-mile portion of the Pacific Crest Trail.

The park has two entrances, both with visitor centers: the smaller is on Hwy 44 at Manzanita Lake, and the main one is in the south off Hwy 89, via a turnoff 5 miles east of Mineral, where the **park headquarters** (☎ 530-595-4444) is located.

Hwy 89 through the park is only open June through October. All camping is first-come, first-served, and various lodges and cabins line Hwy 89 leading to the southern entrance.

MT SHASTA & AROUND
If Shasta, California's sixth-highest mountain (14,162ft), appears especially magnificent, it's because the dormant volcano rises alone on the landscape.

Everitt Memorial Hwy goes up the mountain to 7900ft; to access it, simply head east from Mt Shasta town on Lake St and keep going. Rangers can suggest a number of good hiking trails, depending on what the weather conditions are. To climb higher than 10,000ft, obtain a $15 permit from the **Mt Shasta Ranger Station** (☎ 530-926-4511; 204 W Alma St; ☺ 8am-4:30pm Mon-Sat, 9am-3pm Sun). On the south slope, off Hwy 89, **Mt Shasta Ski Park** (☎ 530-926-8610, 800-754-7427; www.skipark .com) offers skiing in winter, and mountain biking and chairlift rides in summer. Note that camping on Mt Shasta can be cold and mosquito-plagued.

An excellent base for area explorations, the little town of **Mt Shasta** is dwarfed by its neighboring namesake mountain. The **Mt Shasta Visitor Center** (☎ 530-926-4865, 800-926-4865; www.mtshastachamber.com; 300 Pine St; ☺ 9am-5:30pm Mon-Sat, 9am-4pm Sun) provides regional information. The **Sisson Museum** (☎ 530-926-5508; 1 North Old Stage Rd; admission free; ☺ 1-4pm Apr-Sep, from 10am Jun-Sep, closed Jan-Mar) is a well-done small-town museum right next to a fish hatchery.

Shasta Lake (☎ 530-275-4463; www.shastalake .com; ☺ 8:30am-4:30pm) is the state's largest reservoir; it has numerous hiking trails, campgrounds and boat rentals along its shores. Tours of stunning **Lake Shasta Caverns** (☎ 530-238-2341; admission $18) include a catamaran ride across Shasta Lake.

At the north end of the Sacramento Valley, **Redding** is an unremarkable but highly convenient stopover.

Maps as well as backcountry permits for northern California's national forests are available at the **Shasta-Trinity National Forest Headquarters** (☎ 530-244-2978; 2400 Washington Ave;

SCENIC DRIVE: HWY 299

A highly recommended detour from the Shasta area is Hwy 299, the **Trinity Scenic Byway**, which courses through the **Trinity Alps**, where fog catches the trees like tufts of cotton; there's loads of camping, backpacking and river-running.

The drive is three hours between Redding and Arcata, on the North Coast. **Weaverville**, a pleasant mountain town, has an interesting Chinese temple museum and several decent budget motels and restaurants. **Weaverville Ranger Station** (☎ 530-623-2121; 210 N Main St; ☺ 8am-4:30pm Mon-Fri) has outdoor information and can issue backcountry permits. Visitor information for Trinity can be gathered at the **Shasta-Trinity National Forest Headquarters** (☎ 530-244-2978; 2400 Washington Ave; ☺ 7:30am-4:30pm Mon-Fri, to 5pm summer).

7:30am-4:30pm Mon-Fri, to 5pm summer). Comprehensive public lands and tourist information is also available 10 miles south of Redding at the **California Welcome Center** (530-365-1180, 800-474-2782; www.shastacascade .org; 9am-5pm Mon-Fri, 10am-3pm Sat & Sun), off Hwy 5 in Anderson at the south end of the Prime Outlets Mall.

Yreka (y-*ree*-kuh), which is inland California's northernmost city, is a pleasant spot to stay and eat. The **Yreka Western Railroad** (530-842-4146, 800-973-5277; www.yrekawesternrr.com; fare $10), a 1915 Baldwin steam engine, chugs to the tiny town of Montague in summer.

McCloud is an atmospheric, historic mill town 10 miles east of the I-5 on Hwy 89 at the foot of Shasta's southern slope. Hiking is good in the area, especially the Squaw Valley Creek Trail, an easy 5-mile loop south of town.

Sleeping

Redding has several older budget motels downtown on Pine St, such as the acceptably average **Stardust Motel** (530-241-6121, info@StarDustRedding.com; 1200 Pine St; d $40-75;). Several modest restaurants are around the Downtown Mall, also off Pine St.

In the quiet railroad town of Dunsmuir, **Bavaria Lodge** (530-235-4707; www.bavarialodge .net; 4601 Dunsmuir Ave; cabins $40-60) might make homesick Germans feel better, and is a neat and comfortable complex of 1940s cabins, most with kitchens.

The area's most unusual place to stay is in one of the 23 vintage railroad cabooses at the **Railroad Park Resort** (530-235-4440; www.rrpark.com; 100 Railroad Park Rd; r $90-110, campsites $20;), off the I-5 slightly south of Dunsmuir.

Several comfortable motels line Yreka's Main St, including the **Klamath Motor Lodge** (530-842-2751, 800-551-7255; www.klamathmotorlodge.com; 1111 S Main St; r from $54;).

Eating

In Dunsmuir, the **Hitching Post** (530-235-4336; 4917 Dunsmuir Ave; mains $5-12) has a friendly small-town atmosphere and specializes in all-American vittles.

McCloud Soda Shoppe (530-964-2747; 245 Main St; mains $4-12), in McCloud, is an old-fashioned soda fountain where solid short-order fare is flipped off the griddle.

Getting There & Around

Amtrak services Redding and Dunsmuir; Greyhound serves those towns plus Yreka. By car, San Francisco to Redding is 215 miles (four hours). **Stage buses** (530-842-8295) run from Dunsmuir to Yreka ($3.50, 1½ hours). For road conditions call **Siskiyou County** (530-842-4438).

NORTH COAST

Coastal California's top half is markedly different to its bottom half. As you wend your way north from San Francisco, Alta California's Pacific edge continues its dramatic aria of lush forests, rocky beaches and fog-shrouded cliffs.

The Pacific Coast Hwy (Hwy 1) courses leisurely along the coast, while the Redwood Hwy (Hwy 101) zips less scenically through fertile inland valleys.

The two highways join again at Leggett, north of which old-growth redwoods predominate.

RUSSIAN RIVER

North of San Francisco, about two hours by car via Hwys 101 and 116, the lower Russian River snakes through redwoods, vineyards and a few tiny towns; canoeing the river is popular in summer, when the area gets crazy-busy.

Guerneville is the region's hub, with plenty of hotels and restaurants. It's also a popular gay-and-lesbian playground. The local **visitors center** (707-869-3533, 877-644-9001; www .russianriver.com; 16209 1st St) has maps and lodging ideas.

Korbel Cellars (707-824-7000; www.korbel.com; 3250 River Rd), a picturesque 1886 winery noted for its sparkling wines, gives free daily cellar tours.

Armstrong Redwoods State Reserve (707-869-2015; per car $4, campsites $12), 2 miles north of Guerneville, has a magnificent stand of old-growth redwood trees. Camping is at nearby Austin Creek.

Nine miles west from Guerneville, tiny, *über*-quaint **Duncans Mills** has kayak rentals and the friendly **Blue Heron** (707-865-9135; mains $6-20) restaurant, which often hosts interesting live music.

The **Bohemian Hwy**, south of Guerneville, is an easy-going and scenic drive leading to quiet discoveries in charming **Occidental** and **Freestone**.

Burke's Canoe Trips (☎ 707-887-1222; www.burkes canoetrips.com; 8600 River Rd), a mile due north of Forestville, offers camping and is *the* place to rent complete DIY canoeing outfits ($50) for lazy Russian River paddles; rates include shuttle service.

BODEGA BAY TO FORT BRAGG (HWY 1)

Like a panther, this famous stretch of coastline is irresistible to look at, but unpredictable – weather is mildest in spring and fall, but cool fog and cold rain can hit anytime. Frigid ocean water and rip tides make swimming a cautious enterprise; surfing is only for the hardy. From November to April, California gray whales migrate down the coast, and whale-watching trips become popular. Overall, this stretch of Hwy 1 takes at least five hours without picnic stops.

Bodega Bay is an idyllic fishing town; from here, a series of great state beaches extends north to Jenner. Along with its inland sister city, endearing little **Bodega**, it was a location for Hitchcock's 1963 thriller *The Birds*. **Bodega Bay Sportfishing** (☎ 707-875-3344; $25) offers whale-watching trips. **Bodega Bay Surf Shack** (☎ 707-875-3944; www.bodegabaysurf.com; surfboards per day $13, bicycles per half-day $18, kayaks per 4hr $45) rents much of outdoor gear you may need for your activities.

Jenner is perched on picturesque coastal hills at the mouth of the Russian River, where there is a resident harbor seal colony; look for them from Hwy 1 turnouts north of town.

The centerpiece of the **Fort Ross State Park** (☎ 707-847-3286; per car $4, campsites $10) is a reconstructed 1812 Russian trading post and interesting historical exhibits. It also has first-come, first-served camping.

Salt Point State Park (☎ 707-847-3221; per car $4, campsites $12) has hiking trails, tide pools, two campgrounds and the Gerstle Cove Marine Reserve and the Kruse Rhododendron State Reserve, where pink blooms spot the green, wet woods in springtime.

Gualala (wah-*la*-la), founded in 1858 as a lumber mill, has a breathtaking coastal location. A mile south of town, **Gualala Point Regional Park** (☎ 707-785-2377; campsites $16, parking $3) has an attractive campground, hiking trails and a windswept beach.

Charming **Point Arena** has interesting old buildings and a fishing pier. A few miles north, the 1908 **Point Arena Lighthouse & Museum** (☎ 707-882-2777; admission $5; ☺ 10am-4:30pm May-Oct, 10am-3pm Oct-Apr) offers knockout coastal views and worthwhile tours.

Eight miles north of Elk, **Van Damme State Park** (☎ 707-937-5804; per car $4, campsites $16) has good camping and the popular Fern Canyon Trail, that passes through an unusual pygmy forest.

Upscale, photogenic **Mendocino** puts the 'Q' in quaint. Perched on a scenic headland perfect for strolling, it's noted for its Cape Cod–style architecture and a plethora of art galleries, fine restaurants and tourist shops. The **visitors center** (☎ 707-937-5397, 866-466-3636; www.gomendo.com; 735 Main St; ☺ 11am-4pm) is in the Ford House. The **Mendocino Art Center** (☎ 707-937-5818; 45200 Little Lake St; ☺ 10am-5pm) is a hub of artistic efforts.

Fort Bragg is more of a blue-collar town; it has a nice, unpretentious old town section, and food and lodging are cheaper. You can join fishing and whale-watching trips at Noyo Harbor, at the south end of town.

Sleeping & Eating

If you've been waiting to splash out on something romantic, this is the place to do it. Otherwise, pack your tent to take advantage of several nice coastal campsites.

Independent travelers will want to beeline for the big-hearted **Jug Handle Farm & Nature Center** (☎ 707-964-4630; r/cabins per person $27/35), in Caspar opposite Jug Handle State Reserve. Hostel-like private rooms and cabins share a bathroom (linen provided, but bring a blanket); the nice farmhouse has a full kitchen. Hiking trails connect to the reserve, and a one-hour stewardship on the farm nets you a $5 discount.

The **Bodega Harbor Inn** (☎ 707-875-3594; www.bodegaharborinn.com; r $65-95), on Hwy 1 in Bodega Bay, has plain but comfortable cottage-style rooms.

The historic **Gualala Hotel** (☎ 707-884-3441, 800-482-5252; www.thegualalahotel.com; r with shared bathroom $58-68, with private bathroom $85-105), located on Hwy 1 in Gualala, was recently spruced up by new owners. Also in Gualala, **St Orres** (☎ 707-884-3303; www.saintorres.com; r $90-105) has a gorgeous, Russian-style main hotel (where rooms have shared bathroom) and secluded

CALIFORNIA

cottages. Its gourmet restaurant is highly recommended.

Mendocino is a costly, if stylish, place to stay. The visitors center website (www.gomendo.com) is a good resource. **Sweetwater Spa & Inn** (☎ 800-300-4140; www.sweetwaterspa.com; 44840 Main St; group tub & sauna $10, r $80-175) runs over a baker's dozen of attractive lodgings, and rates include use of the spa, which can also be enjoyed on its own.

Fort Bragg has a number of nondescript motels and eateries. Just south of Hwy 20, the **Coast Motel** (☎ 707-964-2852; 18661 Hwy 1; r from $45) is one of the best cheapies. Fort Bragg also boasts the **North Coast Brewing Co** (☎ 707-964-2739; 455 N Main St), which serves its award-winning brews in its pub and attached restaurant, and the **Headlands Coffeehouse** (☎ 707-964-1987; 120 Laurel St), where local musicians jam.

Getting There & Away

The **Mendocino Transit Authority** (MTA; ☎ 800-696-4682; www.4mta.org) runs bus No 65 every morning from Fort Bragg south to Santa Rosa via Willits and Ukiah ($16, three hours); at Santa Rosa the San Francisco–bound bus No 70/80 ($6.30) is operated by **Golden Gate Transit** (☎ 415-923-2000; www.goldengate.org). Note: Amtrak and Greyhound do not serve towns along Hwy 1.

HEALDSBURG TO SCOTIA (HWY 101)

Affable **Healdsburg** is centered on a green Spanish-style plaza. The Russian River – plus 60 wineries within a 30-mile radius – attracts a million visitors each year annually. Get a Wine Country map from the **Healdsburg Visitors Center** (☎ 707-433-6935, 800-648-9922; www.healdsburg.org; 217 Healdsburg Ave) and sample local vintages at the attractive **Hop Kiln Winery** (☎ 707-433-6491; www.hopkilnwinery.com; 6050 Westside Rd; ☺ 10am-5pm).

A detour to **Anderson Valley**, which is studded with vineyards and apple orchards, is far prettier than the equivalent stretch of Hwy 101; take Hwy 128 west to tiny Boonville, then Hwy 253 northeast to Ukiah. In many ways, **Hopland**, 15 miles south of Ukiah on Hwy 101, is the ideal small town, with historic buildings and a sophisticated country feel. For instance, on the edge of town is the **Real Goods Solar Living Institute** (☎ 707-744-2017; www.solarliving.org; 13771 S Hwy 101; admission free; ☺ 10am-6pm), where the attractive, inviting

grounds are actually a rather compelling 12-acre demonstration site for permaculture, environmentally friendly building methods and alternative energy sources. The **Fetzer winery** (☎ 707-744-7600, 800-846-8637; www.fetzer.com; 13601 East Side Rd) has a deli, nice gardens, free tasting and tours.

Ukiah is the largest town for miles. It's a good pit stop, but has few tourist attractions. The **visitors center** (☎ 707-462-7417, 866-466-3636; www.gomendo.com; 525 S Main St) has county-wide info. **Orr Hot Springs** (☎ 707-462-6277; springs day use $22, dm $40-45, r & cottages $115-185; ☺ 10am-10pm), 15 miles west of Ukiah (Hwy 101 to N State St exit), is a rustic, clothing-optional hot springs (for which reservations are required).

After the highways rejoin at tiny **Leggett**, keep heading north on Hwy 101 to **Richardson Grove State Park** (☎ 707-247-3318; per car $4, campsites $15) for a full immersion in a giant redwood forest. Rangers are here year-round, and the summer-only **visitors center** (☺ 9am-5pm) has good exhibits. The campground is spread beneath towering redwoods next to the South Fork of the Eel River.

Garberville and environs became famous in the 1970s for the sinsemilla marijuana grown in the surrounding hills. Today it's a quiet town with basic services, cheap motels and a few places to eat.

Lost Coast became 'lost' when the state's highway system bypassed the rugged mountains of the King Range, which rises to around 4000ft only a few miles from the ocean. Today the region is mostly untouched and undeveloped and affords stunning scenery. From Garberville it's 23 miles on a rough road to **Shelter Cove**, a seaside resort with a deli and hotels. Other roads crossing the mountains are equally slow.

On Hwy 101, the 80-sq-mile **Humboldt Redwoods State Park** (campsites $12) protects some of the world's oldest redwood trees. The park's awe-inspiring **Avenue of the Giants**, a 32-mile stretch of two-lane road winding through wonderful old-growth forests, runs parallel to Hwy 101 and the Eel River. Near the informative **visitors center** (☎ 707-946-2409; ☺ 9am-5pm), campsites are magnificent, so book ahead.

Ferndale, at the northern tip of the Lost Coast, has restored Victorian buildings and a funky rural sensibility, epitomized by the

HEADING TO HAWAII?

Those who haven't experienced the magic of Hawaii cannot fully comprehend the islands' allure. Sure, tourist brochures paint a glossy portrait of the picturesque beaches and colorful *luaus* (Hawaiian feasts), but they fail to capture Hawaii's impossibly beautiful landscapes, its vibrant cultural diversity and the aloha spirit of hospitality that ties it all together. Critics point to the state's mass tourism, high-rise hotels and crowded beaches – and indeed, overdevelopment and cultural erosion are legitimate threats to the Hawaiian way of life. But anyone who truly dislikes Hawaii probably hasn't been there. Those who come expecting to get *leied* by hula dancers and serenaded by steel guitars won't be disappointed, but they will soon realize that this is only a thin slice of the true Hawaiian experience. Naturally, the great outdoors is a huge draw. The islands are amazingly varied – with spectacular gorges and lush valleys, stunning beaches ranging from alabaster white to jet black, and the world's most active volcano. The weather is brilliant year-round, and the state boasts some of the planet's top water-sports hotspots.

For all these reasons, the USA's 50th state remains first in the hearts of its lucky inhabitants and those travelers fortunate enough to visit. Aloha, indeed.

Orientation & Information

The Hawaiian Island chain stretches 1523 miles from the Kure Atoll in the northwest to the Big Island in the southeast. Ka Lae, on the Big Island, is the southernmost point in the USA. The equator is 1470 miles south of Honolulu and all the main islands are south of the Tropic of Cancer. Hawaii is on the same latitude as Hong Kong, Bombay and Mexico's Yucatán Peninsula. The **Hawaii Visitors & Convention Bureau** (☎ 808-923-1811, 800-464-2924; www.gohawaii.com) sends out a free annual *Islands of Aloha* travel planner and serves all the islands. For brochures and to make camping reservations, contact the **Division of State Parks** (☎ 808-587-0330; www.state.hi.us/dlnr/dsp).

Useful websites for independent travelers include **Planet Hawaii** (www.planet-hawaii.com) and **Alternative Hawaii** (www.alternative-hawaii.com).

When to Go

Hawaii enjoys warm weather year-round, with average temperatures differing only 7°F from winter to summer, thanks to the moderating effect of the trade winds. Near the coast the daily high averages 83°F (28°C), with a low average of 68°F (20°C). Summer and fall are the driest seasons, winter the wettest. December to March is also the busiest tourist season, when affordable rooms are in short supply. Fall and spring are slow seasons, with the best discounts between April and November. Whenever you turn up, you really can't go wrong.

Getting There & Around

Honolulu is a major Pacific hub and an intermediate stop on many flights between the US mainland and Asia, Australia, New Zealand and the South Pacific. Passengers on any of these routes can often arrange a free stopover. From Europe, ask about an add-on fare from the US West Coast or perhaps a RTW ticket. From mainland USA, the cheapest round-trip fares generally start at around $650 to $900 (depending on the season) from the East Coast (11 hours), $350 to $650 from the West Coast (5½ hours). If you're coming from beyond the West Coast, it can work out cheaper to first buy a no-frills ticket to California, then catch a separate flight to the islands from LA or San Francisco. If you're flexible with your dates (and final destination) and want to fly in and out of the same mainland airport, **AirTech** (☎ 212-219-7000; www.airtech.com) can get you to the islands from the West Coast for as little as $129 one-way, on a space-available basis.

Most flights arrive in Honolulu; travelers to other islands must then make the short hop to their final destination. Frequent interisland flights with **Aloha** (☎ 808-484-1111; www.alohaair.com) and **Hawaiian** (☎ 808-838-1555; www.hawaiianair.com) between the main islands cost $55 to $105 one way. Ask about discount coupons and air passes.

Once you hit the ground, you can easily get around Oahu on public buses, but service is more limited on Kauai and the Big Island. If you really want to get off the beaten track, rental car rates are around $150 to $200 a week when reserved in advance. Moped rentals are another option.

CALIFORNIA

Highlights

- Experiencing the Big Island getting bigger via fiery lava at **Hawaii Volcanoes National Park**
- Sea-cliff hiking on Kauai's spectacular **Na Pali Coast**
- Feeling dwarfed by majestic humpback whales off **Maui**'s magic coast
- Getting away from it all in the slow lane on rural **Molokai**
- Surfing in winter and snorkeling in summer off **Oahu**'s North Shore

Sights

While there are a few must-sees, Hawaii really isn't about running around sightseeing, per se. Many folks are content to chill on the beach for a week watching amazing endless sunsets and don't make it to any of the following attractions. Hawaii's **national parks** are both volcano-intensive. On the Big Island, **Hawaii Volcanoes NP** (www.nps.gov/havo) is a jaw-dropping mélange of wilderness environments ranging from tropical beaches to sub-arctic mountaintops, centered on two active volcanoes. **Chain of Craters Drive** is an awesome route that ends at an amazing lava flow (best at night). On Maui, **Haleakala NP** (www.nps.gov/hale) focuses on the dormant Haleakala Crater (best at sunrise), which could envelop a large city. The islands' state parks range from well-developed, with plenty of campsites and facilities, to completely wild.

If you're hanging in Honolulu, relax at local favorite **Ala Moana Beach Park** instead of touristy **Waikiki**, or hike to the summit of **Diamond Head** for a good morning workout. The **Circle Island** bus route can shuttle you all the way around much of Oahu in a day, but doesn't leave much time for sightseeing at hotspots like the **North Shore**. Top activities include snorkeling at **Hanauma Bay** and windsurfing in the turquoise waters off **Kailua Beach**. On the Big Island, escape Kailua in favor of **Kealakekua Bay** for super snorkeling, or the perfect beaches at undeveloped **Kona Coast State Park** up north in rural Kohala. Over on Maui, eschew Lahaina for whale-watching near beaches like gold-sand **Wailea** and secluded **Makena**. If you rent a car, head 'upcountry' and don't miss the beautiful **road to Hana**. On Kauai, the least developed of Hawaii's four major islands, the 100% natural beauty is best experienced outside Lihue while hiking the stunning **Na Pali Coast** (North Shore) or lush **Waimea Canyon** (West Shore).

If you're itching to get off the trodden track, you can't do much better than the sparsely populated **Molokai**, the most traditional of the islands – except for tiny Niihau, which is off-limits to outsiders.

Activities

Hawaii's diverse geography means there's an endless variety of outdoor activities. The islands' leeward (southwestern) coasts are sunny, dry and desert-like, with white sands and turquoise waters. The mountainous windward (northeastern) sides have tropical jungles, cascading waterfalls and pounding surf. The uplands are cool and green, with small farms and ranches.

You could easily spend the better part of a year exploring the lovely assortment of **beaches**, while **swimming, surfing, bodysurfing, boogie boarding, windsurfing, snorkeling, kayaking, fishing, sailing, whale-watching** and **scuba diving** to your heart's content. Off the water, inland options range from **hiking, backpacking, mountain biking** and **horseback riding** to extreme thrills like **skydiving** and **hanggliding**.

Sleeping & Eating

If you come prepared to camp out, cook for yourself and are willing to make your way around without a vehicle, you can explore the islands for weeks for less than the price of your airplane ticket. All the islands have inexpensive state and county park campgrounds, and wilderness camping is free in the national parks. The main islands each have a couple of hostel-style places for under $20 and either simple B&Bs or spartan hotels for around $50. By picnicking on locally grown produce from farmers markets, you can avoid extra costs tacked on by shipping that account for grocery prices averaging about 25% higher than the mainland. Chowing down on 'plate lunch' specials with locals at mom-and-pop eateries can lead to some of the best entertainment around.

CALIFORNIA

Kinetic Sculpture Race on Memorial Day weekend. If you can't make the race, visit the free **Kinetic Sculpture Museum** (☎ 707-786-9259; 580 Main St; ☺ 10am-5pm Mon-Sat, noon-4pm Sun).

Scotia is a rarity in the modern world: a 'company town' entirely owned and operated by Pacific Lumber Company (Palco). It's a wholesome little place with free self-guided mill **tours** (☺ 8am-2pm Mon-Fri); check in at the **Scotia Museum & Visitors Center** (☎ 707-764-2222; www.palco.com; ☺ 8am-4:30pm Mon-Fri summer only), on Main St. In winter, follow signs straight to the mill.

Sleeping

Once again, camping is your best bet in this upscale region. The best options are in the state parks mentioned earlier. In Ukiah, chain motels line S State St. In Ferndale, you can pitch your tent at the **Humboldt County Fairgrounds** (☎ 707-786-9511; 1250 5th St; campsites $5), where grazing sheep will keep you company.

Eating & Drinking

In Hopland, the **Mendocino Brewing Company Tavern** (☎ 707-744-1015; S Hwy 101), the nation's oldest brewpub, serves some of the nation's best beer. A couple of doors down, the Phoenix Bread Co has hand-crafted loaves, wood-fired pizzas and succulent barbecue.

Getting There & Around

Greyhound (☎ 800-229-9424) makes frequent stops along Hwy 101 from San Francisco, including Ukiah ($24, 3½ hours). **Redwood Transit System** (☎ 707-443-0826; www.hta.org) runs buses daily except Sunday between Scotia and Trinidad ($2, 2½ hours).

EUREKA TO CRESCENT CITY

From Hwy 101, **Eureka**, the largest town before you get to Oregon, seems like nothing but a thunder of traffic, motels and strip malls. However, venture to Eureka's old town, and you'll find a relaxing mix of historic Victorian buildings, interesting shops and good eateries. The **Eureka visitors center** (☎ 707-442-3738, 800-356-6381; www.eurekachamber .com; 2112 Broadway) has maps and information. In the old town, **Going Places** (☎ 707-443-4145; 328 2nd St) is a great travel bookstore.

The free **Clarke Memorial Museum** (☎ 707-443-1947; 240 E St; ☺ 11am-4pm Tue-Sat) has an impressive American Indian collection. The unique **Blue Ox Millworks** (☎ 707-444-3437, 800-248-4259; 1 X St; www.blueoxmill.com; admission $7.50; ☺ 9am-4pm Mon-Sat) hand-mills Victorian detailing using traditional carpentry and authentic 19th-century equipment. Fascinating, self-guided tours let you watch the craftspeople work.

Nine miles north of Eureka, **Arcata** is a laid-back university town that has the same alternative bent as San Francisco's Haight St. Downtown's Arcata Plaza is the center of the action. On the northeast side of town, **Humboldt State University** (☎ 707-826-3011; www.hum boldt.edu) has an attractive campus and a good art gallery. The blissful **Finnish Country Sauna & Tubs** (☎ 707-822-2228; 5th & J Sts; per hr $15) has a good café and a secluded, outdoor complex.

At the junction of Hwys 299 and 101 is a **California Welcome Center** (☎ 707-822-3619, 800-346-3482; ☺ 9am-5pm), with tons of regional information.

Trinidad, 12 miles north of Arcata, is a working fishing town on an idyllic bay. Follow Edward St to the harbor, where there is a wonderful beach and short hikes on dramatic Trinidad Head. Nearby Luffenholtz Beach is a popular surf spot, and north of town, **Patrick's Point Rd** is dotted with lodging and campgrounds tucked into the forest.

On Hwy 101, a mile south of petite Orick, is the visitors center for the **Redwood National & State Parks** (☎ 707-464-6101; www.nps.gov/redw; ☺ 9am-5pm). Together, Redwood National Park and Prairie Creek, Del Norte and Jedediah Smith State Parks are a designated World Heritage Site, as they protect half of California's remaining old-growth redwood forests.

The national park is free, and the state parks have a reciprocal $5 day-use fee; only the state parks have developed **campsites** ($12-15), which are recommended. The visitor center has trail maps and info about all the parks and issues free permits for backcountry camping and to visit Tall Trees Grove.

The highlights at Redwood National Park are the **Lady Bird Johnson Grove** and the sublime **Tall Trees Grove**, home to several of the world's tallest trees, as well as free-roaming Roosevelt elk herds.

The **Prairie Creek Redwoods State Park** is famous for Fern Canyon, a sheer 60ft fissure overgrown with ferns. It's free to drive the 8-mile Newton B Drury Scenic Parkway through redwood forests and parallels Hwy 101.

IF YOU'VE GOT A FEW MORE DAYS IN NORTHERN CALIFORNIA

■ Find yourself during a wild 24-mile north-to-south hike along the rugged **Lost Coast Trail** up north in Humboldt County.

■ Hike or kayak the **Smith River National Recreation Area**, the state's last remaining undammed waterway.

■ Create your own itineraries in untouristed **Sacramento** and **San Jose**.

■ Wander the freaky high desert craters, lava flows and lava tubes of **Lava Beds National Monument**, near the Oregon state line.

There's not much in **Klamath** except a giant redwood carving of Paul Bunyan and Babe the Blue Ox at the entrance to the silly **Trees of Mystery** (☎ 800-638-3389; admission $12; ☺ 9am-5pm, later in summer), though its free **End of the Trail Museum** has a good collection of American Indian artifacts. A few miles northof here, **Del Norte Coast Redwoods State Park** contains beautiful redwood groves and 8 miles of absolute pristine coastline.

On a crescent-shaped bay, **Crescent City** is the only sizable coastal town north of Arcata. It has few old buildings, since half the town was destroyed by a 1964 tidal wave. The 1865 **Battery Point Lighthouse** (☎ 707-464-3089; admission $2; ☺ Apr-Sep), at the south end of A St, is accessible whenever the tide is out.

Jedediah Smith Redwoods State Park, 5 miles northeast of Crescent City, is less crowded than the other national parks but no less beautiful and lush. Its summer-only **Hiouchi Information Center** is on Hwy 199 in Hiouchi, 5 miles east of Hwy 101.

Sleeping

The highly recommended **HI Redwood National Park Hostel** (☎ 707-482-8265, 800-909-4776; www.norcalhostels.org; 14480 Hwy 101; dm $16-19, r $45; ☺ closed Dec-Feb; ✕), about 7 miles north of Klamath, enjoys an enviable perch on the coast and makes a perfect base camp for exploring the nearby national parks. Dozens of plain-Jane motels line Hwy 101 in Arcata and Eureka. In Eureka, try the **Downtowner Motel** (☎ 707-443-5061, 800-862-4906; 424 8th St; r from $59; ✆), which has spacious rooms, a hot tub and sauna, and includes continental breakfast.

Eating

Outside Eureka on the Samoa Peninsula, the popular **Samoa Cookhouse** (☎ 707-442-1659; all-you-can-eat $9-14) is the dining hall of an 1893 lumber camp. It's a fun place where plentiful, if not memorable, grub with all the fixings is served at long communal tables.

Getting There & Around

Greyhound (☎ 800-231-2222) hits most major towns along Hwy 101 from San Francisco to Crescent City ($60, nine hours). **Redwood Transit System buses** (☎ 707-443-0826) stop in Arcata on their weekday Trinidad–Scotia and Eureka–Blue Lake routes.

Western Canada

HIGHLIGHTS

- **Vancouver** Stand on Burrard St bridge during sunset then say it doesn't deserve top-10 standing (p638)
- **Lake Louise** Not even a million camera-clickers can dumb-down her beauty (p665)
- **Biggest surprise** Moose Jaw has more stories to tell than anyone would expect from a 'buttf*ck town' (p670)
- **Off the beaten track** Waterton Lakes National Park gets less attention than it deserves, but doesn't seem to care (p667)
- **Best journey** Start in Calgary and head west through the Rockies, stopping in Banff, Jasper and Kelowna on the way to Vancouver. Pop over to Victoria if you've got time

FAST FACTS

- **Area** 6,246,254 sq km
- **Big cities** Vancouver (population 2.1 million), Calgary (943,000), Winnipeg (620,000), Victoria (325,000)
- **Budget** $40-80 per day
- **Costs** campsite $15-30, hostel $18-30, pint/six-pack BC-brewed beer $5/9
- **Driving times** Vancouver to Kelowna 3½ hours, Vancouver to Calgary 10 hours, Calgary to Winnipeg 16 hours
- **Famous for** stunning mountain scenery, Hollywood North, Calgary Stampede
- **Language** English; various ethnic enclaves
- **Population:** 9,073,840
- **Phrases** End question with 'or…?' 'So, are you in Canada for long or…?'; 'Do you wanna get something to eat or…?'
- **Seasons** summer is hot and dry, mild on the coast; winter on the coast is wet, on the Prairies cold and long
- **Provinces** British Columbia, Alberta, Saskatchewan, Manitoba Territories: Yukon, Northwest Territories, Nunavut

- **Tasty treats** Vancouver sushi, Okanagan fruit and wine, Alberta beef
- **Time** Central, Mountain and Pacific Time Zones; no daylight saving in Northeastern BC and Saskatchewan
- **Top hostel** Whalers on the Point, Tofino (p652)

TRAVEL HINTS

Hitchhiking Vancouver Island's west coast can produce new friends and backyard-tent-pitching possibilities. Jasper may add another day, but is less crowded than Banff. 'Buffalo' are 'bison.' Pot ain't legal, but you'll rarely be far from a toke or bong hit (peace-pipe-style passing is the norm). You'll want to stay here longer than you expected, so budget a few more days. DON'T FEED THE ANIMALS.

WESTERN CANADA

Making a case for 'The West is the Best,' Canada's 'left' half runs from Western Ontario across the underrated Prairies before the majestic and young Rockies spike from the wheatfields, then disappear into the Pacific. In this part of the country you'll see things that won't remind you of anything you've seen before – massive skies, caribou herds, scraggly and jagged mountains, surfing Canadians, arid valleys only hours away from rain forests…the list goes on.

There aren't really any secrets; it's all in your face once you get here. Do make detours from the Trans Canada Hwy – it was designed as a way of crossing the country, not as a highlight route.

HISTORY

BC's first people arrived via land-bridge during the last ice age 15,000 to 20,000 years ago, and followed caribou herds and migrating whales until relatively recently.

Western Canada's history follows the Canadian Pacific Railway. Before that, the only way to the coast was by boat, bird, mountain trekking or catapult.

Far-northern Churchill, settled in the 17th century, became Canada's closest port to Europe, and agricultural communities emerged in the south along trade lines for the north. As more Europeans – mostly English, Scottish and Ukrainian – arrived, settlement spread westwards across the Prairies, following the railway (there it is again). When gold was discovered in the Fraser River in 1858, the single largest US-to-Canada emigration occurred. Fearing a repeat, Canada has kept discoveries quiet ever since.

Getting the railway through the peaks, valleys, avalanches and rockslides of the mountains produced much head scratching, but was achieved mostly on the backs of Chinese immigrants, who were forced into hard labor and suffered untold losses of life. When the first train pulled into Vancouver in 1885, cross-country harmony rang.

Alberta experienced a huge boom in the 1970s when cowboy hats became chic and an influx of money arrived from around the continent to exploit huge natural gas and oil deposits.

With all this going on, Cree, Salish, Blackfoot and dozens of other aboriginal groups have watched the land get settled and exploited, and dream of caribou herds and migrating whales.

THE CULTURE

Technically, the geographic longitudinal center of Canada is east of Winnipeg (there's a sign that says so). So Western Canada is like a collection of cultural pockets including cooler-than-California BC, better-than-Texas Alberta, the-'Midwest'-is-such-a-ridiculous-name Prairies and no-place-like-here North.

The Continental Divide, running down the spine of the Rockies, also politically divides Liberal-with-Conservative-tendencies BC and strictly Conservative Alberta. Vancouver and Calgary have frequent spats over who's younger, hipper, fresher and funner, while Saskatoon quietly builds its own reputation. Winnipeg stopped caring long ago and just says, 'Whatever, we're Winnipeg.'

At the end of the day, they're all Canadian. As with any sibling rivalry, they'll back each other up if need be.

SPORTS & RECREATION

It'll be a long time before Vancouver Canuck fans and players forget tying Game 7 with 5.7 seconds remaining in the first round of the 2004 Stanley Cup playoffs…only to lose

---

THE BIG ISSUE: 2010 OR BUST

In July 2003, Vancouver and Whistler were formally announced as hosts for the 2010 Olympic (and Paralympic) Winter Games. After the euphoria wore off, officials got straight to work preparing for dozens of sporting events, hundreds of competitions, thousands of athletes, tens-of-thousands of volunteers and millions of visitors. The main focus is on building or renovating venues and improving the Sea to Sky highway, which would be a traffic nightmare without additional room for the increase in traffic. Road construction has been ongoing for years, but the successful Olympic bid has given the budget a much-needed shot in the arm. A straighter road with additional lanes is currently being built.

WESTERN CANADA

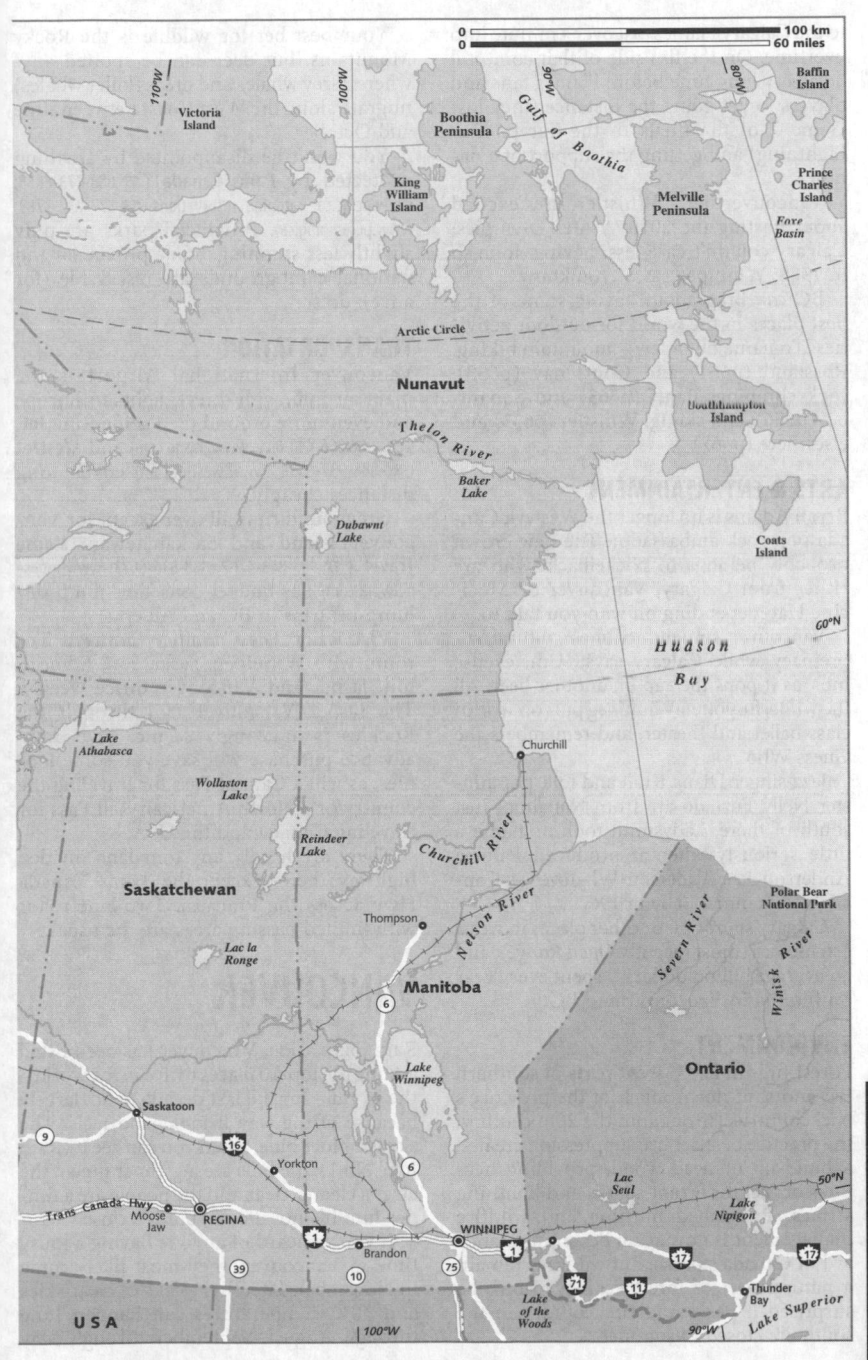

to the Calgary Flames just over a minute into overtime. On the flip side of that coin, it'll be a very long time before Flames fans and players forget going the distance (they lost Game 7 of the finals to the Tampa Bay Lightning) and getting the support of a nation.

Vancouver and Whistler are excited about hosting the 2010 Winter Olympics; Calgary couldn't care less, having done so in 1988; Winnipeg says…you know.

BC *can* brag about having some of the best places in the world for outdoor activities. To name but a few – mountain biking: Rossland (p661) and Courtenay (p653); rock climbing: Banff (p663) and Squamish (p656); and skiing: Whistler (p655) and elsewhere (p662).

ARTS & ENTERTAINMENT

Bryan Adams is no longer the Western Canada pop rock ambassador. The new crown probably belongs to Nickelback, who are either from Calgary, Vancouver or Medicine Hat, depending on who you talk to.

Vancouver smugly assumes cultural supremacy while Calgary says, 'Um, excuse me?' as it pops the cap on another beer. All the while, forgotten Winnipeg puts on world-class ballet and theater, and remembers the Guess Who.

Jazz singer Diana Krall and folk-pop hipster Nelly Furtado are from Nanaimo. Just south of there, Ladysmith took its name a little seriously when it produced Pamela Anderson-Lee-Anderson-Whatever as Canada's Centennial Baby in 1967.

Calgary stands in for other places in western movies (most recently *Open Range*), and an average billion dollars is spent every year on filming in Vancouver and BC.

ENVIRONMENT

Forest fires in 2003 swept parts of southern BC and shut down much of the province's backcountry. Throughout the 20th century, the practice of strict fire suppression created a build-up of dead wood, providing hectares of fuel for errant sparks and lightning strikes. Prescribed burning and wildfire management is now again becoming standard in Canada's parks, but wildfires remain a natural part of forest ecology. Don't be surprised if parks and backcountry in the south are closed in summer.

Your best bet for wildlife is the Rocky Mountains, but deer can be spotted anywhere. Grey whales and orcas (killer whales) migrate along the West Coast between June and October.

You won't be disappointed by anything protected by **Parks Canada** (☎ 888-773-8888; www.pc.gc.ca; camping reservations ☎ 877-737-3783; www.pccamping.ca). Provincial parks are only slightly less stunning. Some provincial and national campgrounds are reservable (for a fee): do so.

TRANSPORTATION

Vancouver International Airport is the main air hub, with direct flights to Europe and even more around the Pacific Rim. **Jetsgo** (☎ 866-440-044; www.jetsgo.com) and **WestJet** (☎ 888-937-8538; www.westjet.com) cover long distances cheaply.

Greyhound runs all over except for Vancouver Island and Saskatchewan. **Moose Travel** (☎ 905-853-4762, 888-816-6673; www.moose network.com) has budget-conscious jump-on/jump-off trips in BC and Alberta.

VIA Rail's *The Canadian* connects Toronto with Winnipeg, Saskatoon, Edmonton, Jasper and Vancouver thrice weekly. The Jasper–Vancouver trip through the Rockies is amazingly scenic. Five days' advance purchase will save you some loonies, as will a Canrail Pass for traveling the country or a North American Rail Pass for traveling Canada and the USA.

There are hardly any four-lane divided highways here (except the Trans Canada Hwy across the Prairies). Two-lane roads with limited passing areas are the usual.

VANCOUVER

Rain jokes aside, Vancouver has been listed among the top-10 places to live in the world – the *world* – for the last decade or so, largely because of the way it looks and feels. The sky is a bluer blue, when you can see it (Rain Joke No 1), the hills are a greener green, the air is a clearer clear and the people are a funner fun. It's not utopia, but it's close.

If you've heard of anyone having a lousy time in Vancouver, they most likely came in November. Literally, weeks of clear skies and 30°C temperatures can happen June through August. September through May sees about 134 minutes of sunlight total (Rain Joke No 2). Your first (or even hundredth) sight of the city is an endorphin-producing view of: sky-reaching buildings dwarfed by the Coast Mountains behind; sailboats drifting in the foreground of False Creek and, stage left, English Bay; and people lying on the beaches or moving along the shoreline paths.

About those people? Well, they are some of the most laid back around adopting westcoast *and* Canadian thinking while somewhat humbled by the precipitation (Rain Joke No 3).

Warning: some people come here for a visit but stay for a lifetime. Could be you, yes you. To better your chances, tell fewer rain jokes but get used to hearing them.

HISTORY

Captain George Vancouver arrived in 1792 (about 17,792 to 12,792 years after the Coast Salish arrived via land-bridge from Asia) only to discover Spain had already claimed the formidable location between mountain and ocean. Undismayed and bull-headed, Vancouver met captains Valdez and Galiano on what is now Spanish Banks and struck a deal where the area became British property.

During the mid-1800s: Simon Fraser (fray-zhur, not Frasier like the TV show)

arrived via the river that now bears his name, despite the fact he thought he was traveling the Columbia (the river that separates Washington and Oregon); 'Gassy' Jack Deighton arrived on the north shores of downtown with a bottle of whiskey, a yellow dog, $12 and opened a saloon for foresters and the city's first official name was Gastown, despite Gassy being a bit of a jackass and storyteller; the railway arrived near the end of the century; CPR vice president William Van Horne felt Vancouver was a more deserving city name and declared, 'This is destined to become a great city, perhaps the greatest city in Canada,' despite the fact it had burnt to the ground a year earlier.

During the 20th century Vancouver grew as a place of commerce and recreation. It had a real chance to showcase itself during the World Exposition in 1986 (Expo '86) and hasn't looked back since. Thousands of new residents flocked during the late 1990s and cranes and under-construction condominiums will continue to occupy the Vancouver skyline.

ORIENTATION

Downtown is a peninsula with Stanley Park at its northwestern tip. Robson and Georgia Sts are the main downtown southeast–northwest thoroughfares, while Granville St

---

GETTING INTO TOWN

Vancouver International Airport is in Richmond, 13km from downtown. It's not impossible to walk (three to four hours). Follow Grant McConachie Way over the Arthur Laing Bridge and then Granville St all the way from there. Bus information is available at the arrivals-level visitors centers. Catch bus No 424 ($2 to $3) from the domestic terminal's Level 1 for the five-minute ride to Airport Station, and transfer to bus No 98 for downtown.

Mint-green **Vancouver Airporter** (☎ 604-946-8866, 800-668-3141; www.yvrairporter.com; one way/round-trip $12/18; ⏱ 5:30am-11:45pm) buses take around 90 minutes to hit Pacific Central Station and the major hotels.

A taxi costs $25. If you're in a group (maximum six), consider a $42 limo.

Main St/Science World SkyTrain stop is opposite the bus and train Pacific Central Station. Some hostels have shuttles, or you can walk through Thorton Park, cross Main St to Quebec St and go right, around False Creek towards BC Place. At GM Place turn right on Abbott St for Gastown, or follow Pacific Blvd to Terry Fox Way around BC Place for downtown-bound Smithe St.

Take bus No 640 ($2 to $4) from Tsawwassen ferry terminal to Ladner Exchange, then bus No 601 downtown. Bus No 250 or 257 ($2 to $3) go downtown from Horseshoe Bay terminal. A cab ride from either terminal is around $35.

At the US–Canada border (listen to 1130AM for traffic updates as the Pacific Hwy crossing – Exit 275, or Route 543 – will probably be less busy), the I-5 turns into Hwy 99, which goes over Oak St Bridge. A detour to Cambie or Granville Sts (follow the 'City Centre' signs) leads downtown. Coming from the east on the Trans Canada Hwy (Hwy 1), take the Hastings St exit.

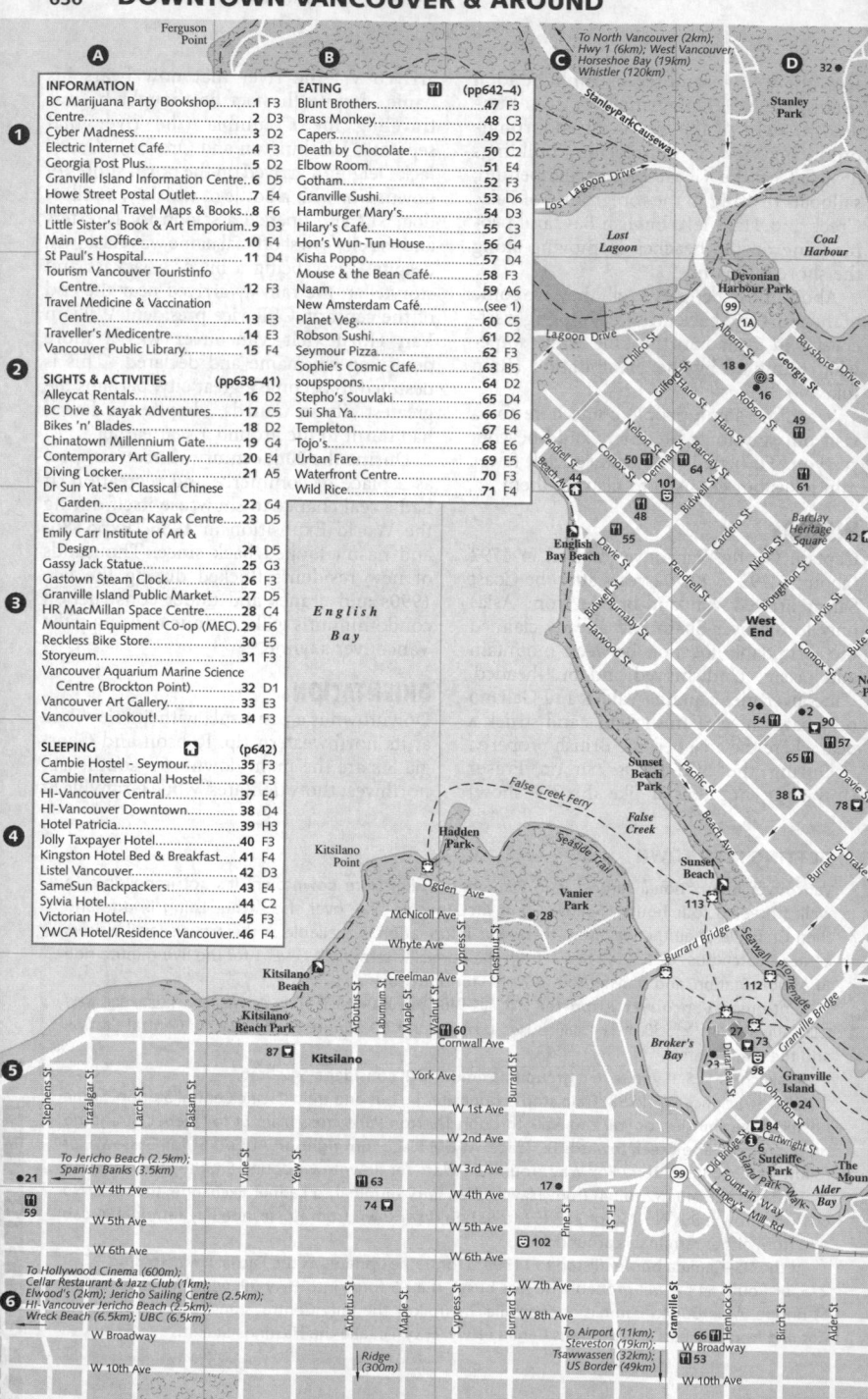

INFORMATION

BC Marijuana Party Bookshop...........1 F3
Centre...2 D3
Cyber Madness...................................3 D2
Electric Internet Café.........................4 F3
Georgia Post Plus...............................5 D2
Granville Island Information Centre...6 D5
Howe Street Postal Outlet.................7 D4
International Travel Maps & Books....8 F6
Little Sister's Book & Art Emporium..9 D3
Main Post Office..............................10 F4
St Paul's Hospital.............................11 D4
Tourism Vancouver Touristinfo
Centre..12 F3
Travel Medicine & Vaccination
Centre..13 E3
Traveller's Medicentre......................14 E3
Vancouver Public Library.................15 F4

SIGHTS & ACTIVITIES (pp638–41)

Alleycat Rentals...............................16 D2
BC Dive & Kayak Adventures..........17 C5
Bikes 'n' Blades...............................18 D2
Chinatown Millennium Gate...........19 G4
Contemporary Art Gallery...............20 E4
Diving Locker..................................21 A5
Dr Sun Yat-Sen Classical Chinese
Garden..22 G4
Ecomarine Ocean Kayak Centre.....23 D5
Emily Carr Institute of Art &
Design...24 D5
Gassy Jack Statue.............................25 G3
Gastown Steam Clock......................26 F3
Granville Island Public Market.........27 D5
HR MacMillan Space Centre............28 C4
Mountain Equipment Co-op (MEC).29 F6
Reckless Bike Store..........................30 E5
Storyeum...31 F3
Vancouver Aquarium Marine Science
Centre (Brockton Point)................32 D1
Vancouver Art Gallery......................33 E3
Vancouver Lookout!........................34 F3

SLEEPING (p642)

Cambie Hostel - Seymour................35 F3
Cambie International Hostel............36 F3
HI-Vancouver Central......................37 E4
HI-Vancouver Downtown................38 D4
Hotel Patricia..................................39 H3
Jolly Taxpayer Hotel.........................40 F3
Kingston Hotel Bed & Breakfast......41 F3
Listel Vancouver..............................42 D3
SameSun Backpackers.......................43 E4
Sylvia Hotel.....................................44 C2
Victorian Hotel................................45 F3
YWCA Hotel/Residence Vancouver..46 F4

EATING (pp642–4)

Blunt Brothers.................................47 F3
Brass Monkey...................................48 C3
Capers...49 D2
Death by Chocolate.........................50 C2
Elbow Room....................................51 E4
Gotham...52 F3
Granville Sushi.................................53 D6
Hamburger Mary's...........................54 D3
Hilary's Café....................................55 C3
Hon's Wun-Tun House.....................56 G4
Kisha Poppo.....................................57 C5
Mouse & the Bean Café...................58 F3
Naam...59 A6
New Amsterdam Café.................(see 1)
Planet Veg.......................................60 C5
Robson Sushi...................................61 D2
Seymour F3......................................62 F3
Sophie's Cosmic Café.......................63 B5
soupspoons......................................64 D2
Stepho's Souvlaki.............................65 C5
Sui Sha Ya.......................................66 D6
Templeton..67 E4
Tojo's...68 E6
Urban Fare.......................................69 E5
Waterfront Centre............................70 F3
Wild Rice...71 F4

DRINKING 🍺🍷 (pp644–5)

Alibi Room	72 G3
Backstage Lounge	73 D5
Bimini's Tap House	74 B6
Blarney Stone	75 G3
Caffe Artigiano	76 E3
Caprice	77 E4
Celebrities	78 D4
Commodore Ballroom	79 E4
Dix	80 F4
Doolin's Irish Pub	81 F4
DVB	82 E3
Glowball/Afterglow	83 D5
Granville Island Brewery	84 D5
Irish Heather	85 G3
Lick	86 F4
Malones	87 B5
Mo'Butta	88 G3
Odyssey	89 E4
Pumpjack Pub	90 D4
Railway Club	91 F3
Richard's on Richards	92 E4
Roxy	93 F3
Shine	94 F3
Steamworks Brewing Co.	95 F3
Yale	96 E4
Yaletown Brewing Co.	97 E4

ENTERTAINMENT 🎭 (pp645–6)

Arts Club Theatre Company	98 D5
BC Lions	(see 99)
BC Place Stadium	99 F4
Centre for Performing Arts	100 F4
Denman Place Discount Cinema	101 C3
Fifth Avenue Cinemas	102 C6
GM Place	103 F4
Orpheum Theatre	104 E4
Queen Elizabeth Theatre	105 F4
Shark Club Bar & Grill	106 F4
TheatreSports League	(see 98)
Vancouver Canucks	(see 103)

SHOPPING 🛍 (p646)

Coastal Peoples Fine	107 F4
Arts Gallery	107 F4
Hill's Native Art	108 F3
Kawabata-ya	109 F3
True Value Vintage	110 E4
Vancouver Flea Market	111 H5

TRANSPORT (p646)

Aquabus	112 D5
False Creek Ferries	113 D4
Pacific Central Station	114 G5
Seabus	115 F3

is the main northeast-southwest artery. If you get lost, red-suited Downtown Ambassadors walk the streets to assist visitors.

The 'sails' in north downtown mark **Canada Place** (☎ 604-647-7390; 999 Canada Place Way) a promenade with panoramic views of Stanley Park, mountains and yellow sulfur piles. The marshmallow dome of **BC Place** (777 Pacific Blvd) draws architectural attention from downtown's southeast shore.

The West End is the long-standing residential part of downtown. Newcomer Yaletown occupies the southeastern chunk, Gastown and Chinatown mark the eastern entrance and the true 'City Centre' is in the middle of it all. Lighthearted Kitsilano looks across False Creek to downtown from the south, whereas West and North Vancouver (aka the North Shore) sit north across Burrard Inlet.

INFORMATION
Bookstores
International Travel Maps & Books (☎ 604-879-3621; 530 W Broadway) Best map shop in Western Canada.

Emergency
Crisis Centre (☎ 604-872-3311) Emotional crisis counseling.
Rape Crisis Centre (☎ 604-255-6344)

Internet Access
Cyber Madness (☎ 604-633-9389; 779 Denman St; per hr $3.50)
Electric Internet Café (☎ 604-681-0667; 605 W Pender St; per hr $3)
Vancouver Public Library (☎ 604-331-3600; 350 W Georgia St; per 30min free) Has 27 green-tagged express terminals.

Media
Georgia Straight Best free entertainment newspaper; check two-for-one coupons.
Province Daily tabloid.
Vancouver Sun Main daily.
Westender Quirky downtown community newspaper.
Xtra! West Gay and lesbian newspaper.

Medical Services
Traveller's Medicentre (☎ 604-683-8138; Bentall Centre Mall, 1055 Dunsmuir St; 8am-4:30pm Mon-Fri) Walk-in clinic for visitors.
St Paul's Hospital (☎ 604-682-2344; 1081 Burrard St) Offers 24-hour accident and emergency services.

Travel Medicine & Vaccination Centre (☎ 604-681-5656; 314-1030 W Georgia St) Shots and medical advice for onward travel.

Money
Banks and ATMs are located throughout the city. Also, check for 24-hour QuickEx currency-exchange machines.

Post
Georgia Post Plus (☎ 604-632-4226; 1358 W Georgia St; 9:30am-6pm Mon-Fri, 10am-4pm Sat)
Howe Street Postal Outlet (☎ 604-688-2068; 732 Davie St; 8am-8pm Mon-Fri, 9am-5pm Sat)
Main Post Office (☎ 604-662-5723; 349 W Georgia St; 8am-5:30pm Mon-Fri)

Tourist Information
Granville Island Information Centre (☎ 604-666-5784; 1398 Cartwright St; 9am-6pm)
Information Desks (Vancouver International Airport) Domestic terminal (baggage carousel); International terminal (after customs)
Tourism Vancouver Tourist Info Centre (☎ 604-683-2000; www.tourismvancouver.com; 200 Burrard St; 8:30am-6pm daily mid-May–Sep, 8:30am-5pm Mon-Fri, 9am-5pm Sat Oct–mid-May)

DANGERS & ANNOYANCES
Overall, Vancouver is a safe city for visitors. But cyclists should use a good bike lock on their seat and both wheels. Never leave valuables visible in your vehicle.

Downtown Eastside is just dirty and depressing, but not dangerous per se, though women won't feel comfortable on their own. Street begging across the city has almost become street theater where the 'usual suspects' target gullible tourists with made-up sob stories.

Stanley Park is a casual nighttime pick-up spot for gay men. Violent assaults by homophobes are not uncommon.

SIGHTS
Downtown is geared towards wandering and watching, and a walk across Granville or Burrard St Bridges to Kitsilano offers postcard photo ops. Other sights around town can be reached via public transit.

Downtown
Seen from the outside, downtown is a compact, upwards-growing, glass-tower-meets-nature sci-fi backdrop. **Robson St** is the main

pedestrian artery full of coffeehouses, restaurants, tourist shops and fashion stores. **Denman St** is another good walking street with zero pretense and a collection of locally owned, anti-chain restaurants. Slum with Vancouverites on **Granville St** and get a tattoo or piercing of some kind. During breezy summer days, it's rarely better (especially sunsets) than the beaches of **English Bay**, literally seconds from downtown action.

Relax by the series of waterfalls outside the Arthur Erickson-designed **Provincial Law Courts** (☎ 660-2910; 219 Smithe St; ☺ 8:30am-4:30pm) before heading into it's sloped-glass-roof tranquility and walk (shhhhhhh, these are real courts) all the way to the 7th floor. Outside the courts, people-watching **Robson Square** leads across Robson St to **Vancouver Art Gallery** (☎ 604-662-4719; 750 Hornby St; adult/student $15/10, donation after 5pm Thu; ☺ 10am-5:30pm, to 9pm Thu). BC legend Emily Carr's mountain, forest and aboriginal scenes live on the 4th floor, Group of Seven pieces are part of the permanent gallery, and temporary exhibits are provocative if nothing else.

Get your bearings and revel in Vancouver's glory 169m above the ground at **Vancouver Lookout!** (☎ 604-689-0421; www.vancouverlookout .com; 555 W Hastings St; adult/student $10/7, coupon online; ☺ 8:30am-10:30pm). Come back during the impressive twilight (tickets good all day).

Stanley Park

More than just a park, this 404-hectare greenery is an urban oasis enclosed by the seawall. Make it to eastern **Brockton Point** for views of downtown, a collection of **totem poles** and the chance to scare the crap out of your traveling buddies at the **Nine O'clock Gun** (show up at, oh, say 8:57pm and wait).

In the center of Brockton Point, **Vancouver Aquarium Marine Science Centre** (☎ 604-659-3474; adult/student $16.50/12.50; ☺ 9.30am-7pm late-Jun–early Sep, 10am-5:30pm early Sep–late-Jun) impressively displays 9000 sea creatures, including sharks, belugas and octopi in indoor and outdoor tanks.

Gastown & Chinatown

Walk Gastown's restored cobblestone streets where yuckster 'Gassy' Jack Deighton opened his saloon in 1867 in Vancouver's first settled area. The 1970s restorations kept the heritage buildings, added the photogenic **steam clock** (cnr Cambie & Water Sts) – show

up on the hour to make it worthwhile – and paid homage to good ol' **Gassy** (cnr Cordova & Water Sts) bronze style.

The story is told and acted out at **Storyeum** (☎ 604-687-8142, 800-687-8142; 142 Water St; admission $22; ☺ 8:30am-7pm) in worth-it, 70-minute underground performances.

Chinatown Millennium Gate (W Pender & Taylor Sts) leads to Chinatown and all its associated Asian remedies, fish heads, clamor and smells. This is the place for noodles and chaos. Amidst it all are the purposeful pathways and manicured trees of **Dr Sun Yat-Sen Classical Chinese Garden** (☎ 604-662-3207; 578 Carrall St; admission $8.25; ☺ 9:30am-7pm).

Granville Island

Across False Creek from downtown, underneath the Granville St Bridge, Vancouver's one-time industrial hub is a current cultural focal point. Spend at least an afternoon here shopping for crafts, eating on a patio, taking in some theater or getting picnic things at **Granville Island Public Market** (☎ 604-666-6477; Johnson St; ☺ 9am-6pm). Hit the public galleries of **Emily Carr Institute of Art & Design** (☎ 604-844-3800; 1399 Johnson St; admission free; ☺ noon-5pm Mon-Fri, 10am-5pm Sat & Sun).

Other Neighborhoods

Abandoned for years after Expo '86, **Yaletown** has recently cultivated crops of glass condos, and former brick warehouses now house cafés, lounges and houseware shops. Very pedestrian friendly with a gorgeous waterfront, the late-20s crowd comes to life here. Step into the **Contemporary Art Gallery** (☎ 604-681-2700; 555 Nelson St; admission free; ☺ 11am-5pm Wed-Sat, noon-5pm Sun) to see local artists.

West of Granville Island, '60s hipsters settled **Kitsilano** ('Kits') and while students and young folk have moved in and the hipsters have settled into professions, it's kept a granola vibe. On hot summer days **Jericho Beach** and **Kitsilano Beach** get packed (for a little more privacy try **Spanish Banks** further west). A grassy contrast, **Vanier Park** affords great city views and **HR MacMillan Space Centre** (☎ 604-738-7827; 1100 Chestnut St) has **planetarium** (admission $10; ☺ Thu-Sat evening) shows like Laser Zeppelin or Laser Pink Floyd.

Trying to San Francisco-ize itself as 'SoMa,' the bohemian energy of **South Main** is captured in restaurants, shops and cargo

---

WHAT ARE YOU LOOKING AT?

Wreck Beach (www.wreckbeach.org), Vancouver's let-it-all-hang-out beach, has been a naturists' haven for years. Locals and in-the-know visitors share the sand with independent vendors and an appreciation of being themselves, not gawking at others. Until you add 1900 horny students with binoculars.

UBC has a green light to build four 20-story student residences on the cliffs looking down on the beach. Needless to say, this poses a bit of a privacy issue for beach users and constructions plans are being highly protested.

To get to Wreck (hopefully still unwatched), follow steep-stepped No 4, 5 or 6 trails from Marine Dr.

---

pants. Vancouver's most multicultural strip, easily accessed by SkyTrain, is **Commercial Drive** in East Vancouver ('East Van'), where cheap restaurants, soccer enthusiasts and communal energy come together.

Before the **University of British Columbia** (UBC) campus, you'll pass through the huge, forested Endowment Lands with ample opportunities for hiking and biking. On the campus, the **Museum of Anthropology** (☎ 604-822-3825; www.moa.ubc.ca; 6393 NW Marine Dr; adult/student $9/7, free Tue 5-9pm; ☺ 10am-5pm, to 9pm Tue, closed Mon Sep–mid-May) offers the best collection of Pacific Northwest aboriginal art.

Around Vancouver

Those with wheels or the will might want to visit Vancouver's supporting cast.

A SeaBus trip goes to **North Vancouver** and the fresh foodiness of **Lonsdale Quay Market**. Up in the hills via Lynn Canyon Rd, touristy **Capilano Suspension Bridge & Park** (☎ 604-985-7474; 3735 Capilano Rd; adult/student $22/16.50; ☺ 9am-dusk) swings 70m above the Capilano River. A bit further north, **Lynn Canyon Park** has a smaller (and scarier) bridge for free.

Look past the tackiness and see the real, working fishing village of **Steveston** in Richmond's southwest corner. Sights, smells and activity radiate from the docks, where fisherfolk sell fresh catches right off the boat. Walk through **Britannia Heritage Shipyard National Historic Site** (☎ 604-718-8050; 5180 Westwater Dr; donation; ☺ dawn-dusk) for a fascinating look at cannery and shipyard buildings.

ACTIVITIES

Vancouver is outside. Look around. Try and keep up with locals who sail in the morning, hike in the afternoon, ski (or bike) at night, and then brag about it over drinks. You'll be tired, but evening libations will taste better and, really, where else could you do such a thing? Canada's favorite outdoor toy store, **Mountain Equipment Co-op** (MEC; ☎ 604-872-7858; 130 W Broadway; camping $9-21, climbing $22, snow sports $12-35; lifetime membership $5) rents equipment and has weekend specials (you use equipment Thursday evening to Monday morning but only pay for Saturday and Sunday).

Cycling & Rollerblading

Stanley Park's seawall is the obvious popular route, but the area around Yaletown has been getting some much-needed attention. For thrashin', head to UBC Endowment Lands. Most shops rent roller-blades for the same price.

Alleycat Rentals (☎ 604-684-5117; 1779 Robson St; per day $10) Down the alley is your best, no-nonsense bet.

Bikes N' Blades (☎ 604-602-9899; 718 Denman St; per day $12)

Reckless Bike Store (www.reckless.ca; per day $25) Kitsilano (☎ 604-731-2420; 1810 Fir St); Yaletown (☎ 604-648-2600; 110 Davie St)

Hiking

Vancouverites will try and sell you the right-of-passage **Grouse Grind**, a 3km outdoor stairmaster with no views straight up the North Shore mountain. If you want a bit more peace and a lot more nature, try Baden-Powell or Howe Sound Crest trails in **Cypress Provincial Park**, 12km west of Vancouver.

Lighthouse Park, especially rocky Point Atkinson, 10km west of Lion's Gate Bridge in West Vancouver, is an awesome picnic spot with 13km of rain-forest hiking trails.

And there's always a forested trail through **Stanley Park**.

Kayaking & Canoeing

False Creek and Burrard Inlet make for calm paddles. Rent from **Ecomarine Ocean Kayak Centre** (www.ecomarine.com; single/double kayak per day $59/85, lessons from $50) Jericho Beach (☎ 604-222-3565; 1300 Discovery St; lessons from $65; rentals per day $52-74; ☺ closed Oct-Apr); Granville Island (☎ 604-689-7575; 1668 Duranleau) or **Mountain Equipment Co-op** (MEC; ☎ 604-872-7858; 130 W Broadway; kayak/canoe full day $30/45).

Scuba Diving

Hardy divers brave cold temperatures of North Shore waters with wolf eels and giant octopi. For equipment, training and trips try **BC Dive and Kayak Adventures** (☎ 604-732-1344; www.bcdive.com; 1695 W 4th St; wetsuit/drysuit package $50/80) or **Diving Locker** (☎ 604-736-2681; www.kochersdiving.com; 2745 W 4th Ave; package $50).

Swimming

People do swim at English Bay beach, but the water's much cleaner at Kitsilano and Jericho Beaches or the shores off UBC, like Vancouver's nudie, Wreck Beach.

Windsurfing & Sailing

Huge winds whipping through English Bay make it fun and frustrating to zip around on a laser or catch some windsurf air off the whitecaps. **Jericho Sailing Centre** (1300 Discovery St) houses the outfitters:

Windsure Windsurfing School (☎ 604-224-0615; 2hr lesson/full-day rental $39/100)

Mac Sailing (☎ 604-224 7245; www.macsailing.com; drop-in/courses $20/225, rental per hr $25-45; ♥ closed Oct–mid-Apr)

Winter Sports

Vancouver has always had decent local skiing, and the 2010 Winter Olympics will enhance that. **Cypress Mountain** (☎ 604-926-5612; Cypress Bowl Rd; admission $45) is the most popular and has the best vertical drop. **Grouse Mountain** (☎ 604-984-0661; 6400 Nancy Greene Way; adult/student $42/30) has awesome views of the city; **Mount Seymour**

(☎ 604-986-2261; 1700 Mt Seymour Rd; day pass adult/student $34/24) is smaller and much less busy. Check newspapers and radio for discounts.

TOURS

The best way to explore Vancouver is to put one foot in front of the other and wander aimlessly. But if you'd rather follow someone else's lead:

Watershed Tours (☎ 604-432-6430; www.gvrd.bc.ca/watershed; free; Thu-Sun, mid-Jun–mid-Sep) Popular city-run ecosystem tours; book ahead.

Erik's City & Canyon Tour (HI-Vancouver Downtown; admission $10; 9am Tue & Fri) Freewheeling day-long tour covers city highlights and Lynn Canyon Park.

FESTIVALS & EVENTS

Bard on the Beach (☎ 604-739-0559; www.bardonthebeach.org; Jun-Sep) Open tents at Vanier Park stage entertaining Shakespeare.

Celebration of Light (☎ 604-641-1193; www.celebration-of-light.com; late-Jul–early-Aug) Countries compete for biggest-bang bragging rights during choreographed fireworks competition at English Bay.

Vancouver Early Music Festival (☎ 604-732-1610; www.earlymusic.bc.ca; Jul) Stretching over three weeks, the lutes and harpsichords players combine complex and accessible performances.

Vancouver Fringe Festival (☎ 604-257-0350; www.vancouverfringe.com; mid-Sep) Lively, wacky and weird $10 shows.

Vancouver International Writers & Readers Festival (☎ 604-681-6330; www.writersfest.bc.ca) Local and international scribblers host seminars and public forums.

GAY & LESBIAN VANCOUVER

Fully integrated into Vancouver's culture, gay men and lesbians live and party mainly along Davie St in the West End. Free weekly *Xtra! West* gives an overview of the scene.

The **Centre** (☎ 604-684-5307; www.lgtbcentrevancouver.com; 1170 Bute St) provides discussion groups, library, health clinic and legal advice, including BC's recent recognition of same-sex marriages (www.vs.gov.bc.ca/marriage/howto.html). They also staff **Prideline** (☎ 604-684-6869; ♥ 7-10pm) a phone-in peer support and information service.

Little Sisters Book & Art Emporium (☎ 604-669-1753; 1238 Davie St) One of North America's widest selections of specialist literature, an active bulletin board and a hyper-knowledgeable staff.

Pumpjack (☎ 604-685-3417; 1167 Davie St) This popular pub is loud and proud and the patio and open-window seats are 'the' place for happy hour.

Celebrities (☎ 604-681-6180; 1022 Davie St) After an extended absence, complete renovations with new sound, lights & theme-nights have this former top gay club ready to regain its crown.

Odyssey (☎ 604-689-5256; 1251 Howe St) Young crowd and reputation as the wildest club.

Lick (☎ 604-685-7777; 455 Abbott St) A club for women in the Lotus Hotel has topless bartenders and Trouble Fridays.

SPLURGE!

Victorian Hotel (☎ 604-681-6369, 877-681-6369; www.victorian-hotel.com; 514 Homer St; s/d $109/119) This renovated European-style Victorian with European-style hospitality – muffins and tea in the morning – is right downtown yet quiet and comfortable.

Funky furniture and colors at **Listel Vancouver** (☎ 604-684-8461; www.listel-vancouver.com; 1300 Robson St; s/d from $125/150) mingle with art (the 4th and 5th floors are 'Gallery Floors'), indiscreet lighting, wood and granite. Well-loved and ivy-covered **Sylvia Hotel** (☎ 604-681-9321; www.sylvia hotel.com; 1154 Gilford St; from s/d/tr $65/65/110) is on the shores of English Bay.

Why stay near the airport when you can stay *at* the airport behind soundproofed floor-to-ceiling windows? At **Fairmont Vancouver Airport** (☎ 604-207-5200; www.fairmont.com/vancouverairport; s/d/ste from $150/175/250) enjoy your first (or last) views of the coast mountains and sleep until literally minutes before your flight.

SLEEPING

Most hostels in town are excellent, but some are unsafe dumps. Trust your gut and do your research. Prices are given for non-members.

HI-Vancouver Central (☎ 604-685-5335, 888-203-833; vancouver.central@hihostels.ca; 1025 Granville St; dm/r $28/66) A busy hostel with above-hostel amenities (thick mattresses; private bathrooms, some with claw-foot tubs) in the middle of downtown's action. The attached bar is always a gas and the hostel owns several Canucks' season-tickets.

SameSun Backpackers (☎ 604-682-8226; www .samesun.com; 1018 Granville St; dm/d $23.50/45) Loud and colorful, this hostel of funk is also in the thick of it. Enough grunge to be cool, but not too much to be dirty.

Cambie International Hostel (☎ 604-684-6466, 877-395-5335; www.cambiehostels.com; 300 Cambie St; dm $15.50-20, s/d $45/50) An always-party-time hostel, it shares a location just outside Gastown with the best blue-collar pub in town. No cooking facilities but the café is cheap and your first breakfast is free. The spin-off **Cambie Hostel – Seymour** (☎ 604-684-7757; www.cambie hostels.com; 515 Seymour St; dm/r $20/50) is quieter with narrow hallways and comfy beds.

HI-Vancouver Downtown (☎ 604-684-4565, 888-203-4302; vancouver.downtown@hihostels.ca; 1114 Burnaby St; dm/r $28/66) Low-key and clean, this hostel is close to Davie St's action and the beach.

YWCA Hotel/Residence Vancouver (☎ 604-895-5830; www.ywcahotel.com; 733 Beatty St; from s/d/tr $51/56/73) Modernly redone, this ain't your typical Y. It's a Yaletown tower of fun and comfort, packed with amenities. Ask for student and weekly discounts.

HI-Vancouver Jericho Beach (☎ 604-224-3208; vancouver.jericho@hihostels.ca; 1515 Discovery St; dm/r $22.50/67.50; ☯ May-Sep) This old military something in Kits with an industrial-sized kitchen and café is seconds from the beach.

If poor planning has you without a bunk, the 5th-floor rooms at **Hotel Patricia** (☎ 604-255-4301; www.budgetpathotel.bc.ca; 403 E Hastings St; s/d with bathroom $89/99) have great views. **Jolly Taxpayer Hotel** (☎ 604-681-3550; www.jollytaxpayerhotel .com; 828 W Hastings St; s/d $69/79) or **Kingston Hotel Bed & Breakfast** (☎ 604-684-9024; www.kingstonhotel vancouver.com; 757 Richards St; d with shared bathroom $68) are better than most budget hotels.

EATING
Downtown & Around

Street dogs in Vancouver rival anywhere else then raise the intensity a notch. Go big: get a sausage and cram it full of relishes, peppers and onions from the southeast corner of **Robson and Burrard Sts** (dogs $3-6), one of the best, or **Hot Dog Johnny's** (☎ 604-913-3647; 1061 Denman St; dogs $3-6) in Stanley Park. For the cheapest eats (sandwiches, soups, sushi, pizza) Seymour St and Pender St are full of take-out and $1 slices of pizza joints; **Seymour Pizza** (☎ 604-685-7468; 547 Seymour St; slices $1) has considerably less grease than the others.

Residential West End and Yaletown have plenty of local grocers and mega-marts for self-catering and picnics. Industrially decorated **Urban Fare** (☎ 604-975-7550; 177 Davie St) and the neighborly, friendly **Capers** (☎ 604-687-5299; 1675 Robson St; deli $4-8) are organically exhaustive and, though not cheap grocery stores, have delicious deli-deals. Shopping-center food courts like **Waterfront Centre** (☎ 604-630-5306; 200 Burrard St) are excellent value. Don't forget **Granville Island Public Market** (☎ 604-666-6477; Johnson St; ☯ 9am-6pm).

Mouse & the Bean Café (☎ 604-633-1781; 207 W Hastings St; mains $4-7) Relocated and revamped from a hole-in-the-wall to very colorful, but the inexpensive Mexican menu's the same.

Hilary's Café (☎ 604-608-6808; 1184 Denman St; items $3-6) The best cinnamon buns in town and a gem for English Bay mornings.

Hon's Wun-Tun House (☎ 604-685-0871; 268 Keefer St; soups $5-8, noodles $6-11) The flagship of several locations has predictable sights, smells and huge bowls of delicious soup and noodles in the heart of Chinatown.

Stepho's Souvlaki (☎ 604-683-2555; 1124 Davie St; mains $7-13) Get in line and wait for stucco walls, dim lighting and tangy Greek food.

Hamburger Mary's (☎ 604-687-1293; 1202 Davie St; mains $7-10) Burgers are her specialty and $10 pitchers make them more special.

Templeton (☎ 604-685-4612; 1087 Granville St; meal $6-10) Traditional chrome-and-vinyl diner serves untraditional organic burgers and vegetarian sausages.

Elbow Room (☎ 604-685-3628; 560 Davie St, burgers $6-8) Have fun with the churlish servers. The 'You've Got to be F-ing kidding' is the kind of two-beef-patties-and-bacon burger that tastes better in a hole-in-the-wall café. All day breakfasts.

soupspoons (☎ 604-328-7687; 990 Denman St; soups $5-7) A dozen delicious soups and 20% off happy hour (3pm to 5pm).

Death by Chocolate (☎ 604-899-2462; 1001 Denman St; desserts $5-15) Screw the diet and get a chocolate burger.

Hip and moderately priced **Brass Monkey** (☎ 604-685-7626; 1072 Denman St; mains $8-18) has spare-parts furniture. East meets West meets lounge meets martini at **Wild Rice** (☎ 604-642-2882; 117 W Pender St; appetizers $6-10, meals $8-18).

Kitsilano

Sophie's Cosmic Café (☎ 604-732-6810; 2095 West 4th Ave; mains $6-12) Need eggs? Love good food? Got a hangover? Go to Kits' favorite, fun and casual Sophie's.

Planet Veg (☎ 604-734-1001; 1941 Cornwall Ave; mains $4-7) Great value Indian fusion vegetarian spot where meat-eaters will be more than satisfied.

Naam (☎ 604-738-7151; 2724 W 4th Ave; meal $8-16; ☯ 24hr) This pocket of Kitsilano tradition is an always-busy, vegetarian eatery even attracting non-veggies for sesame fries with miso gravy.

Commercial Drive

Belgian Fries (☎ 604-253-4220; 1885 Commercial Dr; poutine $4-6, sandwiches $5-8) For a little slice of Québecois, come for smoked meat sandwiches, poutine or Québec beer. For a little slice of artery-clogging insanity, go for deep-fried Mars bars.

La Casa Gelato (☎ 604-251-3211; 1033 Venables St; cones $2-5) Make a few-blocks detour for

---

ALL THE RAW FISH YOU CAN EAT

You're into getting the most for your dollar and when you order an aquarium, you want the ocean. Not only is the sushi in Vancouver knock-you-on-your-ass good, several places around town have all-you-can-eat.

Kisha Poppo (☎ 604-681-0488; 1143 Davie St; lunch/dinner $11/19) Almost melt-in-your-mouth sushi and authentic bamboo, lightwood and frenzied service lead to instant gratification. Other eat-until-you-drop options:

- **Granville Sushi** (☎ 604-738-0388; 2526 Granville St; lunch/dinner $10/19)
- **Robson Sushi** (☎ 604-688-4789; 1542 Robson St; lunch/dinner/after 9:30pm $10/14/11)
- **Sui Sha Ya** (☎ 604-733-8886; 101-1401 W Broadway; lunch/dinner $10/19)

Vancouver's favorite ice-cream/gelato parlor. After vanilla and chocolate, the 200 flavors get ridiculous: salmon and fudge, blackbean and white chocolate, wasabi...

Havana (☎ 604-253-9119; 1212 Commercial Dr; mains $8-18) Funky live theater and gallery with an Afro-Cuban-Southern fusion menu.

DRINKING
Cafés
Caffe Artigiano (☎ 604-696-9222; 763 Hornby St) Painted cups and artistic steamed milk heads and the award winning coffee is the best in town.

Calabria Coffee Bar (☎ 604-253-7017; 1745 Commercial Dr) Whether the marble floor is Italian or not, the music, kitsch and we're-not-baristas behind the counter are.

Bars
If you know what's good for you, you'll at least *try* the locally-crafted drafts at one of the wood-and-brick brewpubs before going back to bad beer.

Granville Island Brewery (☎ 604-687-2739; 1441 Cartwright St) Vancouver's most popular brewery has a small, basic pub, but the **tour and samples** ($8; ☽ 10am-4pm) will teach you some appreciation.

Steamworks Brewing Co (☎ 604-689-2739; 375 Water St) In Gastown, this brickhouse has outstanding views of the North Shore.

Yaletown Brewing Co (☎ 604-681-2739; 1111 Mainland St) Yaletown's entry is rustically trendy with Sunday specials.

Dix (☎ 604-682-2739; 871 Beatty St) Its own pitchers are $12 and the applewood grill is always fired up.

Irish Heather (☎ 604-688-9779; 217 Carrall St) An old-country labyrinth of brick-lined nooks great for slamming down pints. Or find the back-room Shebeen Whisky House, with its 'Excuse me, how many?' selection of 140.

Doolin's Irish Pub (☎ 604-605-4343; 654 Nelson St) The central bar gets busy, and honest pints get drunk.

Bimini's Tap House (☎ 604-732-9232; 2010 W 4th Ave) 'Couch by the fireplace' relaxing mid-week or 'get loose' nightclubbing weekends in Kits.

Elwood's (☎ 604-736-4301; 3145 W Broadway) Tall pints on the patio at 'the Wood' brings you close to Kitsilanoty.

VANSTERDAM

You've heard the stories and you're so very, very excited and you've been punching your buddies in the shoulder on the plane/bus/train ride here and saying, 'Dude, legal pot' and you can't wait to walk down streets lined with all-night cafés of every little thing's gonna be alright. Chill.

Some of the stories you've heard are untrue; it's not legal in Canada, you can get arrested and 'Vansterdam' is just one block on the north side of W Hastings St. Sorry to harsh your mellow. Step into **BC Marijuana Party Bookshop** (☎ 604-682-1172; 307 W Hastings St) to share your outrage with the legitimate provincial governmental **party** (☎ 604-684-7076; www.bcmarijuanaparty.ca).

Some of the stories you've heard are very true. BC Bud is some of the best naturally grown stuff in the world and this mini-strip of stoner-friendly cafés, hemp shops and hydroponics stores has been raved by *High Times* as the best tourist spot for pot enthusiasts. An unfortunate mishap on the way to enlightenment occurred when a couple of the buildings were destroyed in an April, 2004 fire. Looking on the bright side of life, **Blunt Brothers** (www.bluntbros.com) – 'a respectable joint' – bought a bigger and better building (at 300 W Hastings St) planned for a February, 2005 opening. The new pot-friendly place will have you munching on 'The Cheech' (sandwich with THC: turkey, ham and cheddar) while playing Donkey Kong or sharing a fatty with Mike the lawyer or Cheryl the bike messenger. Also check out **New Amsterdam Café** (☎ 604-682-5868; 301 W Hastings St; munchies $5-7) across the street for chillin' or the **BC Marijuana Party Bookshop** (see above) where every style of glass pipe you've hallucinated is for sale.

US and Canadian marijuana laws are basically the same, but have been 'interpreted' differently in Canada. However, there's been a recent push for tougher enforcement. US customs has *really* tightened the strings. Smuggling into the States is now incredibly difficult(er), so dealers and suppliers have been forced to drop prices (good for you), but anyone caught at the border with anything related to marijuana will be questioned and possibly detained (bad for you). If you're going to take that pipe home, don't use it until you get there. Talk to the Marijuana Party; the lyrics to *Rainy Day Women 12 & 35* won't get you far with authorities.

Malones (☎ 604-737-7777; 2210 Cornwall Ave) Patio fun and cold beer across the street from Kits Beach where 'sports watching' is popular.

Blarney Stone (☎ 604-687-4322; 216 Carrall St) Honest Gastown fun.

Live Music

Commodore Ballroom (☎ 604-739-4550; www.hob .com/venues/concerts/commodore; 868 Granville St) Legendary venue for mid-sized shows has great sound, classic architecture and bouncy dance floor.

WISE Hall (☎ 604-254-5858; www.wisehall.ca; 1882 Adananc St) Comfortably ragged former church brings locals for (what? live? really?) folk, ska and disco.

Railway Club (☎ 604-681-1625; www.therailway club.com; 579 Dunsmuir St; cover $4-10) Upstairs and intimate, 'the Rail' has been a well-kept secret for no-names (future big-names) since the 1930s. Daily pint specials $4.35.

Mo'Butta (☎ 604-688-6439; 52 Powell St) Gastown speakeasy, brick-walled jazz and blues club has no covers.

Cellar Restaurant & Jazz Club (☎ 604 738 1959; www.cellarjazz.com; 3611 W Broadway; cover free-$10 Mon-Fri) A serious, small, underground jazz club with cheap weekday shows and pints.

Yale (☎ 604-681-9253; www.theyale.ca; 1300 Granville St) Loud rhythm-and-blues joint with a large stage and weekend jams for hard-drinking music lovers.

Richard's on Richards (☎ 604-687-6794; 1036 Richards St) Two-leveled 'Dick's on Dicks' has been a top live-music club for years

Backstage Lounge (☎ 604-687-1354; 1585 Johnston St) A grungy Granville Island hangout with occasional local bands and constant great view. Tuesday $2.50 beer specials.

CLUBBING

Granville St between Robson St and Davie St is nightclub central and Gastown's Water St boasts the same.

Check the lines for dress codes and age limits.

Roxy (☎ 604-684-7699; 932 Granville St) Has withstood tests of time and fickle tastes with reliable, loud, good times.

DV8 (☎ 604-682-4388; 515 Davie St) Open all day, not loungy until late-night, when noisy Granville escape is necessary.

Glowball/Afterglow (☎ 604-602-0835; 1082 Hamilton St) The girls, naturally followed by boys, come for the sexy pink interior and a flirty cocktail list specializing in 'ini' drinks.

Alibi Room (☎ 604-623-3383; 157 Alexander St) Famous among famous people; they pitch and bitch in dark corners upstairs or hunker in the low-ceilinged basement.

Shine (☎ 604-408-4321; 364 Water St) An intimate house-funk cozy cave with 40ft chill-out sofa. 'Saturday's Big Sexy Funk' is…read the name again.

Caprice (☎ 604-681-2114; 967 Granville St) This former cinema flips between bad and popular.

ENTERTAINMENT

Georgia Straight should be your first entertainment paper; *Westender and Terminal City* are also good. The *Province* and the *Vancouver Sun* publish entertainment sections on Thursday.

Get tickets through venues or **Ticketmaster** (performing arts ☎ 604-280-3311; concerts 604-280-4444; sports 280-4400; www.ticketmaster.ca). **Tickets tonight** (☎ 604-684-2787; www.ticketstonight.ca) In the tourist info center sells half-price tickets for day of events, and sells some advance tickets online.

Cinemas

Major first-run downtown theaters face each other on Granville.

Fifth Avenue Cinemas (☎ 604-734-7469; 2110 Burrard St) is a popular indie- and foreign-movie screener. **Hollywood Cinema** (☎ 604-515-5864; 3123 W Broadway; admission $5) and the **Ridge** (☎ 604-738-6311; 3131 Arbutus St; admission $5) show between-theater-and DVD movies.

Denman Place Discount Cinema (☎ 604-663-2201; 1779 Comox St) shows $6 double features, and three films for $4 Tuesdays.

Sports

Except for Canucks, tickets will usually be available game day, so ignore scalpers until after the game's started – they'll be desperate.

GM Place (800 Griffiths Way) To tap into Vancouver's cultural heartbeat, a **Vancouver Canucks** (☎ 604-899-4625; www.canucks.com; ticket from $30) National Hockey League (NHL) game is a good start. Games are consistently sold out (try scalpers on Georgia St, not at the arena) but the **Shark Club Bar & Grill** (☎ 604-687-4275; 180 West Georgia St) is TV-watching headquarters.

Pacific Coliseum (100 North Renfrew St) Catch an eastbound bus down Hastings St to catch the **Vancouver Giants** (☎ 604-444-2687; www.vancouvergiants.com; ticket $10-25), a cheaper Canucks alternative with enough skill, hitting and fighting to entertain.

BC Place (p638) In a dome on fake turf, the **BC Lions** (☎ 604-589-7627; www.bclions.com; ticket $20-60) still play exciting Canadian Football League (CFL) football.

Nat Bailey Stadium (4601 Ontario St) 'The prettiest little ballpark in the world' hosts inexpensive **Vancouver Canadians** (☎ 604-872-5332; www.canadiansbaseball.com; ticket $7.50-20) games, perfect for sunny afternoons and cold beer.

Swangard Stadium (cnr Boundary Rd & Kingsway) The **Vancouver Whitecaps** (☎ 604-669-9283; www.whitecapsfc.com; ticket $12-22) men's and women's teams play competitive soccer in Burnaby. Take the SkyTrain to Patterson Station.

Theater

Arts Club Theatre Company (☎ 604-687-1644; www.artsclub.com; admission $25-45; Granville Island Stage 1585 Johnston St; Stanley Theatre 2750 Granville St) Vancouver's leading theater company mixes works by regional playwrights with popular classics.

TheatreSports League (☎ 604-738-7013; www.vtsl.com; New Revue Stage, 1601 Johnston St; admission $10-16.50) Hilarious improv high jinks is a Granville Island don't-miss. Two-for-one coupons in *Georgia Straight*.

Vancouver's multi-functional venues:

Centre for Performing Arts (☎ 604-602-0616; 777 Homer St)

Queen Elizabeth Theatre (☎ 604-665-3050; 600 Hamilton St)

Orpheum Theatre (☎ 604-665-3050; 884 Granville St) Home to **Vancouver Symphony Orchestra** (☎ 604-876-3343; www.vancouversymphony.ca; admission $25-45).

SHOPPING

Fashionably trendy Robson St is Vancouver's attempt at Rodeo Drive but also battles Gastown's Water St for '*I ♥ Canada*' T-shirts and shot glasses. Independent stores in Yaletown and South Main St, Commercial Dr and Kitsilano's W 4th Ave galleries and clothing stores showcase local artists and designers. Broadway east of Cambie St is an outdoor gear haven started by Mountain Equipment Co-op (p640).

Honestly, the smoked salmon you've heard about will probably be cheapest at grocery stores (get the vacuum-sealed packages if you're taking it home), but check prices at Granville Island's or Steveston's docks while you're there. Pacific Northwest art won't come cheap, but can be found at **Hill's Native Art** (☎ 604-685-4249; 165 Water St; ☯ 9am-9pm) or **Coastal Peoples Fine Arts Gallery** (☎ 604-685-9298; 1024 Mainland St).

Near the bus station, **Vancouver Flea Market** (☎ 604-685-0666; 703 Terminal Ave) is a giant indoor garage sale hawking lampshades, LPs, plaid shirts and everything else. Hunting vintage clothing at **Kawabata-ya** (☎ 604-806-0020; 437 Hastings St) and **True Value Vintage** (☎ 604-685-5403; 710 Robson St) may uncover that *Dukes of Hazzard* baseball shirt.

GETTING THERE & AWAY

Vancouver International Airport (code: YVR; ☎ 604-207-7077; www.yvr.ca) serves all major airlines. BC Ferries' Tsawwassen terminal (south) serves Victoria, Nanaimo and the Gulf Islands; the Horseshoe Bay terminal (north) is used for Nanaimo and the Sunshine Coast.

Major bus lines use **Pacific Central Station** (1150 Station St) near Chinatown. **Quick Coach Lines** (☎ 604-940-4428; www.quickcoach.com; downtown/SeaTac $33/41) makes limited stops to/from Seattle–Tacoma airport and Vancouver locations. Pacific Central Station is also the western terminus for trains, including VIA Rail's *Canadian* and Amtrak's *Cascades* (shuttle buses are sometimes used to Seattle).

GETTING AROUND

Aquabus Ferries (☎ 604-689-5858; www.aquabus.bc.ca; one way/daypass $2/10) and **False Creek Ferries** (☎ 604-684-7781; www.granvilleislandferries.bc.ca; one way/daypass $2/12) operate mini pedestrian-only vessels on different routes around and across False Creek.

TransLink (☎ 604-953-3333; www.translink.bc.ca; single/daypass/10-tickets $2/8/18) operates Vancouver's extensive bus, SkyTrain and SeaBus network. Progressively costlier zones are in effect mid-week, but they're only for those branching into the suburbs or heading to the ferries or airport.

Robson, Georgia and Granville Sts or major hotels are the easiest spots to flag a taxi. Main operators include **Yellow Cab** (☎ 604-681-1111), **Black Top** (☎ 604-681-3201) and **Vancouver Taxi** (☎ 604-871-1111).

VANCOUVER ISLAND

Seemingly adrift from BC's southwest coast, Vancouver Island isn't on the way to anywhere but is on almost everyone's itinerary. The forested hump rising from the Georgia Strait puts all the things that make the province what it is (forests, coastlines, wildlife, low-key affability) in a nice little package.

Victoria's European prettiness and up-island's wild ruggedness play off each other and offer an extended invitation.

TRANSPORTATION

Some surprisingly good deals can be found on WestJet flights between Victoria or Comox and Canadian cities. Pacific Coastal flies around the island and to mainland coastal towns.

BC Ferries (☎ 250-386-3431, 888-223-3779; www .bcferries.com) employs a seemingly complicated and always changing schedule from several terminals to connect Vancouver Island, the Gulf Islands and the mainland. Prices vary depending on season and destination. Schedules are available online or from info centers everywhere. Vancouver Island–mainland reservations are recommended if you're taking a vehicle on the weekend. The *Queen of the North* sails up the spectacular **Inside Passage** (adult $103, car $242, bike $6.50) between Port Hardy and Prince Rupert – one of the great ferry journeys of the world – on 15-hour, daylight sailings every second day between May and October.

Other operators connect Victoria with points in Washington State.

COME SAIL AWAY

BC Ferries offers a great value and hassle-free way to explore this gorgeous corner of the world with its multi-day **Sail Pass** (www.becferries.com/sailpass; 4-/7-day pass $139/179) good for two adults and a vehicle on four or seven consecutive days travel on any of the 20 southern routes. A favorite week-long itinerary is: Tsawwassen–Gulf Islands–Victoria–Denman & Hornby Islands–Comox–Powell River–Sunshine Coast–Vancouver.

GETTING INTO TOWN

AKAL Airport Shuttle Bus (☎ 250-386-2525; $14) shuttles between the airport and Victoria accommodations. Bus No 70 goes to the ferry terminal all day and the airport sometimes (within 1km at other times). A taxi from the airport or ferry terminal costs $45 to $55.

VICTORIA

British Columbia's provincial capital has gone from a grandma-visiting, traditionally British town to a properly mannered city infused with young energy.

Orientation

The Inner Harbour is the heart of Victoria, watched over by the Empress Hotel and stone-and-copper Parliament Buildings. Douglas St (Hwy 1 aka Trans Canada Hwy) is downtown's main north–south thoroughfare and usual entrance to the city. Blanshard St is the other northern entrance/exit to/from the city, leading to Hwy 17, the airport and BC Ferries terminal.

Information

Major banks have branches on Douglas St and ATMs are everywhere.

Downtown Medical Centre (☎ 250-380-2210; 622 Courtney St)

Main Post Office (☎ 250-953-1352; 706 Yates St)

Munro's Books (☎ 250-382-2464; 1108 Government St) Victoria institution.

Royal Jubilee Hospital (☎ 250-370-8000; 1952 Bay St; 🕑 24hr)

Stain Internet Café (☎ 250-382-3352; www.stain cafe.com; 609 Yates St; per hr $3)

Visitor Info Centre (☎ 250-953-2033; www.tourism victoria.com; 812 Wharf St; 🕑 8:30am-6pm) At the Inner Harbour.

Sights

The 3rd-floor aboriginal exhibit at highly-acclaimed **Royal British Columbia Museum** (☎ 250-356-7226, 888-447-7977; www.rbcm.gov.bc.ca; 675 Belleville St; adult/student $22.50/16.25; 🕑 9am-6:30pm) contains a re-created, 19th-century Haida village and Nawalagwatsi, 'the cave of supernatural power.' Second-floor 'Living Land, Living Sea' has a mean-looking woolly mammoth. For those who like to pretend to be giants, there's **Miniature World**

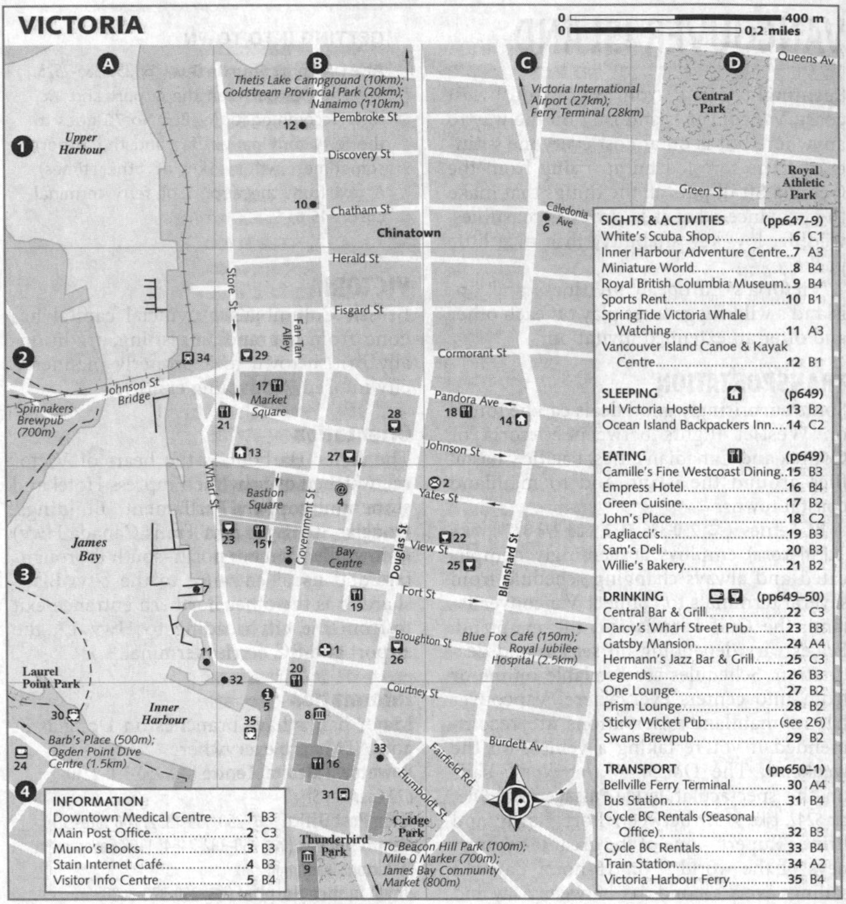

(☎ 250-385-9731; www.miniatureworld.com; 649 Humboldt St; admission $8; 🕑 9am-5pm Sep-May, 8:30am-9pm Jun-Aug).

In the northwest part of downtown, the formerly rough-and-tumble Fort Victoria – with courthouse, jail, gallows and brothel – has been converted into hip **Bastion Square**. Small and authentic, Victoria's **Chinatown** is Canada's oldest; narrow **Fan Tan Alley** (btwn Fisgard St & Pandora Ave) was the place for opium in the 1800s.

Next to the museum, **Thunderbird Park** is full of totem poles and possibly carvers at work. South of there, 61-hectare **Beacon Hill Park** offers gardens, ponds, the world's second-tallest totem pole and a 100-year-old cricket pitch. The end of Douglas St marks the Trans Canada Hwy's **Mile 0**; roughly 8000km east in Newfoundland is its counterpart.

Activities

Inner Harbour Adventure Centre (☎ 250-995-2211; www.marine-adventures.com; 950 Wharf St; 🕑 9am-6pm) houses several outfitters and charters. **Sports Rent** (☎ 250-385-7368; www.sportsrentbc.com; 1950 Government St) is cheap for all equipment rentals.

If you're heading up-island, you'll find cheaper and better **whale-watching** places. If you're just hitting Victoria, research prices and success rates of the dozen outfitters, like **SpringTide Victoria Whale Watching** (☎ 250-386-6016, 800-470-3474; www.springtidecharters.com; 950 Wharf St; $90), which set out to see the 90 orcas at the island's southern tip April to October.

Victoria's nutrient-rich waters are amazingly clear, supporting diverse underwater ecosystems. Good shore dives include **10 Mile Point**, **Ogden Point Breakwater**, **Race Rocks** and **Saanich Inlet**. For details and rentals contact **Frank White's Scuba Shop** (☎ 250-385-4713; 1855 Blanshard St) or **Ogden Point Dive Centre** (☎ 250-380-9119; www.divevictoria.com; 199 Dallas Rd).

For **kayaking**, the waters around Victoria are amazingly peaceful. **Sports Rent** (kayak/canoe rental $45/35) is the best deal just for gear. **Vancouver Island Canoe & Kayak Centre** (☎ 250-361-9365, 877-921-9365; www.canoeandkayakcentre.com; 575 Pembroke St; kayak/canoe $50/30) offers lessons and trips.

Tours
A retired, uniformed London Bobby (police officer), and history buff leads **Victoria Bobby Walking Tours** (☎ 250 995-0233; $15; 11am May–mid-Sep).

Festivals & Events
First People's Festival (www.vnfc.ca/culturecomm relation.html; early Aug) Three days of cultural celebrations.
Great Canadian Beer Festival (www.gcbf.com; early Sep) Long weekend of nothing but beer.

Sleeping
Ocean Island Backpackers Inn (☎ 250-385-1785, 888-888-4180; www.oceanisland.com; 791 Pandora Ave; dm $17-23, s/d/r $30/40/60) For good ol' fun, this super-colorful, four-floor veteran near downtown does the trick. Some rooms are windowless; all have fridges.

HI-Victoria Hostel (☎ 250-385-4511, 888-883-0099; www.hihostels.ca/victoria; 516 Yates St; dm $17-24) This old converted warehouse near the Inner Harbour offers bunks in barracks-style dorms.

The best camping is at **Goldstream Provincial Park** (☎ 250-391-2300; Island Hwy; campsite $18.50), 20km from town. Closer is **Thetis Lake Campground** (☎ 250-478-3845; thetislake@shaw.ca; 1938 W Park Lane; campsite $6).

Eating
Street-food isn't the best, but carts at **Market Square** (cnr Johnson & Wharf Sts) are decent, **Green Cuisine** (☎ 250-385-1809; 560 Johnson St; buffet $2/100g) is a pay-by-weight vegetarian buffet with vegans in mind and **James Bay Community Market** (☎ 250-381-5323; 547 Michigan St; 9am-3pm Sat) is a great farmers' market.

Sam's Deli (☎ 250-382-8424; 805 Government St; sandwiches $7-8), for sandwiches, and **Willie's Bakery** (☎ 250-381-8414; 537 Johnson St; mains $6-10), for grab-and-go breakfasts, are popular cafeteria-style places.

Barb's Place (☎ 250-384-6515; 310 St Lawrence St; fish & chips $7-9) Fish and chips at Fisherman's Wharf can't be beat.

John's Place (☎ 250-389-0799; 723 Pandora Ave; mains $7-11) Greasy spoon without the greasy.

Pagliacci's (☎ 250-386-1662, 1011 Broad St; mains $8-12) Popular, cramped, boisterous and delicious, this Italian place rewards loyalty with inventive dishes and low prices.

Blue Fox Café (☎ 250-380-1683; 101-919 Fort St; mains $6-9) Granola hole-in the-wall.

Drinking
Mmmmm, beer. The golden ales and dark stouts of the micro-brewed beers in Victoria are some of BC's finest. Check out *Monday Magazine*'s calendar to see what's happening.

Spinnakers Brewpub & Restaurant (☎ 250-386-2739; 308 Catherine St) A harbor ferry and short walk to Spinnakers gives great patio views of the city; over a dozen taps line the bar.

SPLURGE!
Camille's Fine Westcoast Dining (☎ 250-381-3433; 45 Bastion Sq; mains $18-20) If you really want to treat yourself to tasty and elegant local cuisine, head underground to one of Victoria's favorites. The seasonally changing menu combines island produce and game with international preparation.

High Tea
Traditional British high tea is an irresistible and artery-hardening assortment of scones, sandwiches, pastries, cream and berries – and tea of course – and Victoria does it right.

Empress Hotel (☎ 250-348-8111, 800-441-1414; 721 Government St; $50; noon-5pm) She's the Queen of Victoria's high tea and priced to match; book two weeks ahead in summer.

For a little less decadence at a lot less price, **Gatsby Mansion** (☎ 250-663-7557; 309 Belleville St; $22) is in an old Victorian building on the harbor.

Swans Brewpub (☎ 250-361-3310; 506 Pandora St) In town, enjoy some of the purest pints in the courtyard here.

Sticky Wicket Pub (☎ 250-383-7137; 919 Douglas St) The rooftop patio (with volleyball pits) at this pub is always packed.

Bands rolling through town usually rock at **Legends** (☎ 250-383-7137; 919 Douglas St) or **Central Bar & Grill** (☎ 361-1700; 708 View St).

Darcy's Wharf Street Pub (☎ 250-380-1322; 1127 Wharf St) Crowds line up on weekends for cover bands at this mid-week hangout.

Hermann's Jazz Bar & Grill (☎ 250-388-9166; 753 View St; cover $5) Excellent acoustics and cool tunes go well with single malts. First set (5:30pm) usually free.

Formerly BJ's, **Prism Lounge** (☎ 250-388-0505; 642 Johnson St) is still the main gay and lesbian club. Fun early-20-somethings crowd the **One Lounge** (☎ 250-384-3557; 1318 Broad St).

Getting There & Away

Victoria International Airport (code: YYJ; ☎ 250-953-7500; www.cyyj.ca), 18km north, is used mainly for flights to Vancouver or Seattle, but does serve other Canadian destinations.

Vancouver Island Coach Lines stops at the **bus station** (700 Douglas St); Greyhound has an office for Mainland travel. VIA Rail runs the *Malahat* up-island and the **train station**

(☎ 250-842-7245; 450 Pandora Ave) is only open during arrivals and departures.

BC Ferries operates service to Tsawwassen and the Southern Gulf Islands from Swartz Bay, 27km north via Hwy 17.

US FERRIES

Seasonal ferries to Washington State depart from **Belleville Ferry Terminal** (254 Belleville St): **Black Ball Transport** (☎ 250-386-2202; www.cohoferry.com; adult US$9, car US$36) To Port Angeles.

Passenger Only

Passenger-only services:

Clipper Navigation (☎ 250-382-8100; 800-555-2535; www.victoriaclipper.com; one way/round-trip US$70/116) Year-round, three-hour catamarans trips to Seattle.

Victoria Express (☎ 250-361-9144; www.victoriaexpress.com; US$10, bicycle US$5) To Port Angeles.

Victoria-San Juan Cruises (☎ 250-443-4552; www.whales.com; one way/round-trip US$50/90) To Bellingham.

Getting Around

Cycle BC Rentals (☎ 250-380-2453, 866-380-2453; www.cyclebc.ca; bicycle/scooter/motorcycle per day from $20/50/90 Main Office 747 Douglas St; Summer Kiosk 950 Wharf St) and **Sports Rent** (☎ 250-385-7368; road/mountain bike per day from $25/20) are both central.

BACKROADS VANCOUVER ISLAND

Carmanah Walbran Provincial Park

Accessed over 45km of private logging roads from Lake Cowichan, the Island's last remaining old-growth forest (1000-year-old cedars) is serene and eerily compelling.

Yellow Point

North of Ladysmith, follow the turn off for Yellow Point Rd, a beautiful bucolic route to Nanaimo. Stop at **Crow & Gate** (☎ 250-722-3731; 2313 Yellow Point Rd; mains $8-11) for a properly poured Guinness and shepherd's pie.

Denman & Hornby Islands

Reached by mid-island (Buckley Bay) ferries, Denman and Hornby have artistic tendencies and backpacking-hippie appeal. You may plan on an afternoon, but after a hike to Denman's lighthouse in **Boyle Point Provincial Park**, a swim in Hornby's **Tribune Bay** and new friends at **Denman Island Bakery & Pizza** (☎ 250-335-1310; Northwest Rd; mains $7-11; ☒ Mon-Sat), you'll be playing and singing acoustic-guitar-campfire tunes until the sun comes up.

Alert Bay

Take the ferry from Port McNeill to see world's tallest totem pole and traditional totem carvers at work. Learn true aboriginal culture at Kwakwaka'wakw **U'Mista Cultural Centre** (☎ 250-974-5403; www.umista.org; admission $5) and dances at the **Big House** (☎ 250-974-5403; admission $15; ☒ 1pm Thu-Sun).

BC Transit (☎ 250-382-6161; www.bctransit.com; one/two zone $1.75/2.50, daypass $5.50) buses run frequently.

Victoria Harbour Ferry (☎ 250-708-0201; www .harbourferry.com; from $3.50) provides scheduled services within the Inner Harbour.

NANAIMO

Nanaimo, 110km north of Victoria, is a transportation hub for Vancouver Island, and most use it for just that. It lacks the polished appeal of Victoria, but the redone harbor, shoreline parks and marine activities reward those who spend a day.

Hudson's Bay Company built the **Bastion** (cnr Front & Bastion Sts) in 1853 for protection. Never used save for the odd disturbance quelling, it still fires daily at noon.

Vehicle free **Newcastle Island Provincial Marine Park** (☎ 250-753-5141) offers unpolluted picnicking, cycling, hiking, and beaches. The **campground** (☎ 250-753-3481; campsites summer/winter $14/9) has only 18 walk in campsites, no reservations and no services, but hey, you're on an island. It's reached via 10-minute **ferry** ($7; ☼ 10am-7pm May–mid-Oct).

Small dorms, large bunks and lots of chaos make **Cambie International Hostel** (☎ 250-754-5323, 877-754-5323; www.cambiehostels .com/nanaimo; 63 Victoria Cres; dm/r $22.50/45) popular. No cooking facilities, but breakfast is included at the **bakery/café** (mains $3-5). Gotta have a Nanaimo bar, and the pub has cheap beer and live music. It's a walk up the hill to friendly and family-run **Nicol St Hostel** (☎ 250-753-1188; www.nanaimohostel.com; 65 Nicol St; campsite/dm/r $10/17/45) but the backyard views are worth it.

Armani's Grill (☎ 250-754-5551; 22 Victoria Cres; burgers $6-11) uses ground sirloin in individually prepared not-*just*-a-burger creations. It doesn't get better than fresh-from-the-ocean **Trollers Fish & Chips** (☎ 250-741-7994; 104 Front St; fish & chips $7-10) on the docks.

BC Ferries sails from Departure Bay (north of town) to Horseshoe Bay and from Duke Point (south) to Tsawwassen. Bus No 2 City Centre goes to Departure Bay. **Nanaimo Seaporter** (☎ 250-753-2118; Departure Bay/Duke Point $6/14) goes to both terminals. **Harbour-Lynx** (☎ 604-688-5465; www.harbourlynx.com; one way/return $25/45) runs a high-speed service between Vancouver and Nanaimo downtowns. Vancouver Island Coach Lines and VIA Rail stop here.

PACIFIC RIM NATIONAL PARK RESERVE

Wild storms, crashing waves, sandy beaches, amazing sunsets, abundant wildlife, rain forests; welcome to Canada's real West Coast. The 'left' side of Vancouver Island is untamed and wisely protected by the federal government in three 'units': Long Beach, Broken Group Islands and West Coast Trail.

Easily accessed by Hwy 4, **Long Beach Unit** (parking $10, annual parking pass $45) is the most visited and features wildly beautiful beaches and short walks showcasing the park's biodiversity. The **Park Information Centre** (☎ 250-726-4212; Hwy 4; ☼ 10am-5pm mid-Mar–mid-Oct) is just inside the southern boundary. Also, check out interpretive exhibits at **Wickaninnish Centre** (Wick Rd; ☼ 9am-6pm mid-Mar–mid-Oct).

Interpretive signs direct **Nuu-chah-nulth Trail** (5km round-trip) through shoreline, forest and aboriginal culture from Wickaninnish Beach to Florencia Bay.

A Pacific Rim park excursion will give lifelong memories. Whether it's good or bad will depend on preparation, so **Research** (☎ 250-726-7721; www.pc.gc.ca) before you go.

After five-to-nine days, $120 (fees and ferries) and an ass kicking, you'll have completed one of North America's best-known and toughest hiking routes – the **West Coast Trail** – and you'll want to do it again.

Comprising 100 rugged, forested islands, the **Broken Group Islands** provide protection for sea otters, sea lions, orcas, gray whales and kayakers. Unless you're really experienced, sign up with a guided trip.

The 94 drive-in campsites at **Green Point Campground** (☎ 250-689-9025; drive-in/walk-in campsites $20/14) can be reserved three months ahead; it's first-come, first-served for 20 walk-in campsites. Privately run **Long Beach Golf Course Campground** (☎ 250-725-3314; www .longbeachgolfcourse.com; campsite $25) has wooded camping.

Vancouver Island Coach Lines stops here and **Tofino Bus** (☎ 250-725-2871, 866-986-3466) shuttles up and down the coast, stopping within the park.

TOFINO

At the north end of Hwy 4, Tofino is no dead-end town. Set on Clayoquot (klayqwot) Sound (a Unesco World Biosphere Reserve) the serene and spectacular scenery is mirrored by the ecologically minded hippies who live here.

WESTERN CANADA

IF YOU'VE GOT A FEW MORE DAYS ON THE ISLANDS

The 'Other' Gulf Islands

Mayne's historic importance is evident at Georgina Point Heritage Park. Ecologically sensitive, dirt-cheap houses at **Cobworks** (☎ 250-539-5253; 640 Horton Bay Rd; campsite/cobhouse $15/80, tour/course $5/200-2600; tour 2pm last Sun May-Aug) can be built or slept in. **Pender** is appealingly unpretentious, offering the simple pleasures of sun, sky, forest and beach. **Saturna** is the most remote and beautiful with free whale-watching from East Point Regional Park.

The **Visitor Info Centre** (☎ 250-725-3414; www .island.net/~tofino; 1426 Pacific Rim Hwy; ☉ 10am-6pm May-Sep) is 6km south of town.

Sights & Activities

Most sights are north in Clayoquot Sound. **Hot Springs Cove**, the central attraction for **Maquinna Provincial Marine Park** (☎ 250-248-9460), is one of the most rewarding where natural hot pools rejuvenate the body. **Meares Island** has thick old-growth forest, and was the site of anti-logging protests that kicked-off the Clayoquot Sound environmental movement (see the boxed text opposite). On Flores Island, **Ahousat** is home to a Nuu-chah-nulth community, a plethora of wildlife-viewing opportunities and a spectacular-but-difficult 11km **Wild Side Heritage Trail** (☎ 250-670-9586; fee $20). **Walk the Wild Side** (☎ 250-670-9586, 888-670-9586; without/with First Nations guide $75/120) leads guided hikes.

The island system means kayaking around Tofino is superb, **Tla-ook** (☎ 250-725-2656, 877-942-2663; www.tlaook.com; 2/4/6hr $45/60/140) uses authentic, aboriginal dugout canoes. **Tofino Sea Kayaking Co** (☎ 250-725-4222; www .tofino-kayaking.com; 320 Main St; half-/full-day $35/50, tours $55-100) paddles to Meares Island and rents to soloists.

With nothing between Japan and Vancouver Island's west coast, surf-ready waves pound the beaches. Among the many surf shops, **Longbeach Surf Shop** (☎ 250-725-3800; 630 Pacific Rim Hwy; 24hr board/wetsuit $20/20) gets you in, out and on the water and **Live to Surf** (☎ 250-725-4464; www.livetosurf.com; 1180 Pacific Rim Hwy; board/ wetsuit $25/20) has been doing it the longest.

Sleeping & Eating

Whalers on the Point Guesthouse (☎ 250-725-3443; www.tofinohostel.com; 81 West St; dm/d/tr/q $26/75/85/115) A secluded waterfront location and huge windows makes Whalers the spacious and comfortable Rolls Royce of hostels.

Hummingbird Hostel (☎ 250-670-9679; www .hummingbird-hostel.com; dm/r $20/70) This restored 1904 house on Ahousat's waterfront pays the Wild Side Heritage Trail fee for guests.

There's camping in Pacific Rim National Park Reserve, and it's been known for residents to let backpackers pitch a tent in their yard (ask the people wearing flip-flops, not turtle-necks).

Bella Pacifica Resort & Campground (☎ 250-725-3400; www.bellapacifica.com; 400 Mackenzie Beach Rd; campsite $29-41) Right on the ocean's edge are superb beachfront campsites worth booking in advance.

So Bo (☎ 250-725-2341; 1180 Pacific Rim Hwy; lunches $4-5; ☉ Wed-Sun) Not just any roach-coach, So Bo serves inexpensive gourmet salads, soups and tacos from the lunch-wagon behind Beaches Grocery.

Beaches Grocery (☎ 250-725-2270; 1184 Pacific Rim Hwy) has organic products. The huge deck outside the **Coffee Pod** (☎ 250-725-4246; 151 Fourth St; mains $4-7) is always full of locals. **Common Loaf Bake Shop** (☎ 725-3915, 180 First St; items $2-5) is a tree-house local gathering spot.

Getting There & Around

Vancouver Island Coach Lines stops here, and **Tofino Bus** (☎ 250-725-2871, 866-986-3466; www .tofinobus.com; 564 Campbell St) makes daily runs (with extra service during summer) to/from Victoria ($50, five hours) and Nanaimo ($32, three hours) hostels as well as Vancouver connections ($43 to $55). It also runs the three-times-a-day Beach Bus ($3.50 to $9) up and down the coast with stops along the way.

A regular **seabus** ($14; ☉ 10:30am-4pm) goes to Ahousat; **Tom's Water Taxi** (☎ 250-725-3747; $20) goes to Meares.

COMOX VALLEY

The Comox Valley is known for biking and **Mount Washington Alpine Resort** (☎ 250-338-1386; www.mtwashington.bc.ca; $44) is *the* place to ski on

Vancouver Island and has plenty of summertime hiking. **Mt Washington Guest House** (☎ 250-898-8141; www.mtwashingtonguesthouse.com; 1203 Fosters Pl; dm/r $22/60) is a chalet-turned-hostel with nature right outside the door.

Designed for activity seekers, **Riding Fool** (☎ 800-313-3665; 2705 Dunsmuir; dm/r $18/45) is a red-walled, hardwood-floored funky hostel in Cumberland. Six km west of Courtenay, you can literally hike into Strathcona from **Comox Lake Hostel** (☎ 250-338-1914; comoxlakehostel@telus .net; 4787 Lake Trail Rd; campsite/dm $10/17).

Centered around 2200m Mt Golden Hinde, 250,000-hectare **Strathcona Provincial Park** (☎ 250-337-2400, frontcountry/backcountry campsite $14/5) is BC's oldest protected area and is definitely a hikers' park with large tracts of wilderness and pristine alpine.

Vancouver Island Coach Lines, VIA Rail, West Jet and Pacific Coastal stop here. BC Ferries makes four daily trips near Comox to Powell River.

NORTHERN VANCOUVER ISLAND

Whale-watching is the best on the Island from Telegraph Cove and **Stubbs Island Whale Watching** (☎ 250-928-3185/17, 800 665-3066; www .stubbs-island.com; Beaver Cove Rd) goes to Johnstone Strait on three-hour tours to see them; reservations required. The 9:30am and 1pm tours cost $70 and the 5:30pm tours cost $60.

Port Hardy is a hub for Cape Scott hikes and Inside Passage ferries and draws international attention among spelunkers for reappearing rivers, sinkholes and land bridges. Contact **Vancouver Island Nature Exploration** (☎ 250-902-2662; www.nature-exploration .com; half/full day from $65/90).

North Shore Inn (☎ 250-949-8500; north_shore _inn@hotmail.com; 7370 Market St; s/d/tw from $70/80/ 100) has been much used, but there's plenty of room and balconies overlook the bay. Camp at the **Quatse River Campground** (☎ 250-949-2395; 5050 Hardy Bay Rd; campsite $14). There's pizza, Chinese or fish and chips in the town center, beer at **IV's Quarterdeck Pub** (☎ 250-949-6922; 6555 Hardy Bay Rd).

Pristine and challenging, **Cape Scott Provincial Park** (backcountry $5) is 70km west of Port Hardy over an active logging gravel road. Easily-accessible San Josef Bay, is 2.5km along a well-maintained trail. Beyond there, accessibility becomes more difficult and dares you to go further. The 24km mud-fest to Cape Scott, an old Danish settlement, is a hiking rite-of-passage. Mentally prepare for stuck feet and unpredictable storms and you'll be rewarded with waking up on fine, white sand and endless west-coast views.

Nearby **Raft Cove Provincial Park** has similar reward with less effort. A 2km rough, but passable, hike brings you to crescent beaches and beautiful lagoons perfect for free camping.

Along the road to the parks: a **crushed car, boot-tree** and **Ronning's Garden**.

Pacific Coastal Airlines flies to Port Hardy; Vancouver Island Coach Lines stops along Hwy 19.

BC Ferries' Port Hardy terminal is just south of town. **North Island Transportation** (☎ 250-949-6300; nit@island.net; $5.25) runs some shuttles.

TREE HUGGIN'

Environmentally conscious folks'll appreciate environmentally active organizations in Tofino – stop in and chat.

Friends of Clayoquot Sound (☎ 250-725-4218; www.focs.ca; 331 Neill St) is a grassroots organization defending rain forests and marine ecosystems. Working smartly rather than acting irrationally, indiscriminate logging in the area has dropped significantly since massive protests in 1993. The group also concerns itself with salmon farming and the impact of sewage and antibiotics use.

The **Rainforest Interpretive Centre** (☎ 250-725-2560; www.tofinores.com; 451 Main St) is a project of the Raincoast Education Society, part of a growing international network to explore sustainable forest management.

Built with a minimal-environmental-impact focus using – among other techniques and materials – 100% reclaimed timber, 9000-sq-ft **Cedar Corner** (cnr Fourth & Campbell Sts; www.cedarcorner.com) greets you as you enter Tofino as an example of ecologic friendliness. Constructed from wood originally milled in 1881, it was vacant at press-time but will hopefully soon become the new home of **Tofino Brewhouse** (www.tofinobrewpub.com).

SOUTHERN GULF ISLANDS

Sandwiched between the mainland and Vancouver Island, the Southern Gulf (not really a 'gulf,' you know) Islands enjoy tranquil waters and mild climate contrasting the storm-tossed ruggedness of Vancouver Island's west coast.

SALT SPRING ISLAND

The most popular Gulf Island, Salt Spring is well known for the Market, amazing views and artsy residents.

Ganges is the heart of the island, and Fulford-Ganges Rd, Long Harbour Rd and Vesuvius Bay Rd are its aortas leading to BC Ferries' three terminals: Fulford Harbour (via Swartz Bay) on the south; Long Harbour (via Tsawwassen or Gulf Island) on the east; or Vesuvius Bay (via Crofton) on the west.

The Ganges **Visitor Info Centre** (☎ 250-537-5252; 121 Lower Ganges Rd; ☉ 10am-4pm) has helpful staff and good maps.

Internationally famous **Market in the Park** (☎ 250-537-4448; www.saltspringmarket.com; Centennial Park; ☉ 8:30am-3:30pm Sat Apr–mid-Oct) is *the* Saturday event where everything is locally grown, baked or made.

Mt Maxwell Provincial Park (☎ 250-248-9460) has mind-blowing views peering out from thick stands of old-growth Douglas fir. **Salt Spring Guided Rides** (☎ 250-537-5761; per hr $35) leads horseback riding on Mt Maxwell.

Walk-in, beachside campsites at **Ruckle Provincial Park** (☎ 250-539-2115; parking $3, campsite $14), also BC's oldest farm (1872), let you wake up to unbelievably colored sunrises.

On four hectares of woodlands with ducks, tree houses, caravans and tipis, **Salt Spring Island Hostel** (☎ 250-537-4149; www.beacom .com/ssihostel; 640 Cusheon Lake Rd; dm/tipi/d/treehouse/ caravan $21/50/70/80/80; ☉ mid-Mar–mid-Oct) also has regular dorms.

Hobbit-like **Treehouse Café** (☎ 250-537-5379; 106 Purvis Lane, Ganges; mains $5-11) makes wholesome breakfasts, good sandwiches and excellent coffee.

Ganges Faerie (☎ 250-537-6758; www.ganges faerie.com) shuttles between ferry terminals, the hostel, Ganges and Ruckle.

GALIANO ISLAND

Long and narrow Galiano Island doesn't feel crowded despite being closest to the mainland and having the best activities.

Galiano Chamber of Commerce (☎ 250-539-2233; www.galianoisland.com) has an information shack on your right as you leave the ferry.

Enjoy sunrises *and* sunsets from the sheltered peninsula of **Montague Harbour Provincial Marine Park** (☎ 250-539-2115; parking $3, campsite $17), which has an incredible ecologically diverse trail and 25 drive-in and 15 walk-in (snag one of Nos 34 to 38 if you can) campsites. **Bluffs Park** boasts great views of Active Pass, **Bodega Ridge Provincial Park** has wildlife and Lovers' Leap viewpoint.

For excellent diving among friendly wolf eels, caves, anemone walls, and the sunken *Point Grey* tugboat, contact **Galiano Island Diving** (☎ 250-539-3109; 1005 Devina Dr; rental $49).

Appreciate Galiano's sandstone cliffs offshore with rentals and tours from **Gulf Island Kayaking** (☎ 250-539-2442; www.seakayak.ca; Montague Marina; 3hr/full-day rental from $28/50, tours from $40).

Cycling the island's narrow, hilly roads is thrilling and dangerously close to danger; **Galiano Bicycle Rental & Repair** (☎ 250-539-9906; 36 Burrill Rd; 4hr/full-day $23/28), near Sturdies Bay, has rentals.

Run by young, wandering travelers like yourself, **Bodega Resort** (☎ 250-539-2677; 120 Cook Rd; r/cabin $80/100) is set on fruit-tree and sheep-lived pastoral farmland with incredible views.

Grab some grub from **Max & Moritz Spicy Island Food House** (☎ 250-539-5888; items $3.50-8), Indonesian-German fusion from the lunch wagon at the ferry. Beer-drinkers gravitate to **Hummingbird Pub** (☎ 250-539-5472; 47 Sturdies Bay Rd; mains $8-12); don't be tempted by the pie.

Go Galiano Island Shuttle (☎ 250-539-0202; $4; ☉ daily summer, Fri-Sun May, Jun & Sep) meets the ferries for island transport and also makes Hummingbird Pub evening runs.

MAINLAND BC

As if you didn't know: BC is beautiful. Maybe you really didn't know: BC is diverse. The cool, damp, almost always foggy northwest coast could be a world away from the hot and dry, almost always on fire, Okanagan and Kootenays. Vancouver is undoubtedly beautiful, but it enjoys relative climatologic

---

IF YOU'VE GOT A FEW EXTRA DAYS IN BC

Bowron Lakes Provincial Park – A 116km, 10-lake, eight-portage, six-to-10-day, world-famous canoe circle provides stunning scenery and plenty of wildlife. Numbers are limited; reserve with BC Parks (☎ 250-387-1642, 800-435-5622; person $60, reservation $18).

Queen Charlotte Islands (Haida Gwaii) – Off the west coast, Canada's 'Galapagos' is a wild, rainy home to flora and fauna entirely different from the mainland and steeped in aboriginal tradition. Don't be in a rush and do make it to Gwaii Haanas National Park Reserve.

Okanagan Valley Wineries – With over 50 vineyards, the Okanagan is a wine-lovers dream. Most offer, often free, tours and tastings to plug their product (try the icewines). Hostels work with tour operators and **BC Wine Information Centre** (☎ 250-493-4055, 800-663-5052; 888 Westminster Ave W, Penticton; ☉ 8am-8pm summer) and **Wine Museum** (☎ 250-868-0441; 1304 Ellis St, Kelowna; ☉ 10am-5pm Mon-Sat, noon-5pm Sun) are good resources.

---

protection from Vancouver Island and the Coast Mountains. Travel east or north and it's just you and nature, buddy.

WHISTLER

Long touted as an international ski destination, Whistler, along with Vancouver, has bolstered its image with the successful bid for the 2010 Winter Olympic Games. An engaging village, vibrant nightlife and activities from golf to climbing have added a legitimate 'year-round' title to the region where grubby backpackers share the same goal as crusty millionaires: play. Most of the action is at **Whistler Village** (Village Gate Blvd off Hwy 99).

Along with kiosks at Village North and Upper Village, the **Activity & Information Centre** (☎ 604-938-2769, 877-991-9988; www.tourism whistler.com; 4010 Whistler Way; ☉ 8am-6pm) is busy but well-staffed.

Summer Activities

Whistler gondola cheatingly takes **hikers** ($24; ☉ 8am-5pm late Jun-Aug) to the top for easy alpine hiking on 48km of forever-view trails. The bottom half **Bike Park** (admission $40, rental $60; ☉ 10am-5pm Jun-Sep) makes for awesome gravity-fed trail rides.

No powder, but slap on the planks in August and ride **Horstman Glacier** ($45; ☉ noon-3pm Jun-Aug) on top of Blackcomb (1609m).

Winter Activities

The area centerpiece, as well as the reason people come, **Whistler-Blackcomb** (☎ 604-932-3434, 800-766-0449; www.whistlerblackcomb.com; admission $70) has over 7000 acres of terrain and 200 longer-than-average trails, not including the backcountry. The season *can* run until June on Whistler.

Mountain Adventure Centres (www.whistlerblack comb.com/rentals; admission from $32; Whistler ☎ 604-905-2252; Blackcomb ☎ 604-938-7737) rents from the base of both mountains and 14 other locations around Whistler. There are more pick-up locations if you reserve online.

Whistler Municipality (☎ 604-935-8300; www .whistler.ca; Lot 4a off Lorimer Rd; day/night $10/4; ☉ 8am-9pm Nov-Mar) grooms more than 30km of cross-country ski trails through Lost Lake Park and the valley. **Lost Lake Cross-Country Connection** (☎ 604-905-0071; www.crosscountryconnection.bc.ca; rentals from $24) rents from beside the ticket booth.

Sleeping

Anytime of year, book a bunk ahead or risk shelling out $150 for a room.

Southside Lodge (☎ 604-932 3644; www.snow boardwhistler.com; 2102 Lake Placid Rd; night/week $30/200) The most convenient bunkhouse to the lifts has been spruced up since its decrepit days. Each of the 24 bunkrooms has a bathroom and shower.

Shoestring Lodge (☎ 604-932-3338; shoe@direct .ca; 7124 Nancy Greene Dr; summer dm/r $21/80, winter dm/r $31/125) A 15-minute walk from the village, this is the place to party until 3am before getting up at 8am to tackle the day. The Boot Pub attracts the rowdies for strippers and live bands.

HI-Whistler (☎ 604-932-5492; www.hihostels.ca /whistler; 5678 Alta Lake Rd; dm $25) This rustic lodge

---

BUDGET TIP

Before wasting the morning shopping around, prices run pretty much the same at village rental shops; if possible, rent in Vancouver.

WORKING AT WHISTLER-BLACKCOMB

Those who can't get enough of the white stuff consider being a liftie a pretty sweet gig. **Whistler-Blackcomb** (☎ 604-938-7366; www.whistlerblackcomb.com; Whistler-Blackcomb, 4896 Glacier Dr, Whistler BC, V0N 1B4, Canada) hires several thousand each year for seasonal jobs ranging from lift operators to food servers. Most jobs go to Canadians or people with Canadian work authorization, but you can still chase the dream. October-November and February-March are peak recruiting times. Hourly wages range from $7.50 to $12, plus benefits: a season-pass, 50% food discounts and free lessons.

The resort makes bunks available through its Glacier Residence program; rental rates range from $8.25 to $15 per night. Call ☎ 604-938-7500 for information.

---

is remote (4km from Whistler Village; local bus passes close), but the beautiful setting on Alta Lake's west side has awesome views of Blackcomb.

In Nordic Estates off Hwy 99 between Creekside and Whistler Village, **Fireside Lodge** (☎ 604-932-4660; 2113 Nordic Dr; $25) and the **UBC Lodge** (☎ 604-932-6604; 2124 Nordic Dr; summer/winter $30/21.25) offer dormitory accommodations. **Riverside RV Resort & Campground** (☎ 604-905-5533, 877-905-5533; www.whistlercamping .com; 8018 Mons Rd; campsite/RV $30/45) has camping and mini-golf.

Eating

Ingrid's Village Cafe (☎ 604-932-7000; 4305 Skiers Approach; mains $4-9) For the best value, standard breakfasts ($4 to $8) stand out here, and there's plenty for hungry vegetarians.

Other options for a quick bite include **Auntie Em's Kitchen** (☎ 604-932-1163; 4340 Lorimer Rd; light meals $5-8) and **Mogul's Coffee** (☎ 604-932-4845; 203-4204 Village Sq; snacks $2-6).

Hearty and huge bowls of noodles are had at **Whistler Noodle House** (☎ 604-932-2228; 9-4330 Northlands Rd; mains $8-12).

Locals shop at **Nesters Market** (☎ 604-932-3545; 7019 Nesters Rd), tourists use **Marketplace IGA** (☎ 604-938-2850; 4330 Northlands Blvd).

Drinking

Pick up a copy of *Pique Newsmagazine* for entertainment listings.

Brewhouse Restaurant & Pub (☎ 604-905-2739; 4355 Blackcomb Way) Try brew-masterpieces like Twin Peaks Pale Ale or Lifty Lager.

Front row seats to crash-n-burn victims, **Black's Pub & Restaurant** (☎ 604-932-6408; 4270 Mountain Sq), at the bottom of Whistler, has 100 kinds of beer, and **Merlin's Bar & Grill** (☎ 604-938-7700; Upper Village, base of Blackcomb) has a patio.

The usual stop for real bands, **Garfinkel's** (☎ 604-932-2323; 1-4308 Main St) plays hip-hop and dance with rock thrown in other nights.

Getting There & Around

Greyhound stops here and **WAVE** (☎ 604-932-4020; www.whistler.net/transit; adult/student $1.50/1.25) is the Whistler area's public transit. The shuttle between Whistler Village, Village North and Upper Village is free.

SQUAMISH

Halfway between Vancouver and Whistler, Squamish is a mecca for those who want the rush without Whistler crowds. The imposing Stawamus Chief monolith overlooks the town and its spectacular natural setting at the meeting of ocean, river and alpine forest.

The well-stocked **Visitor Info Centre** (☎ 604-892-9244; www.squamishchamber.bc.ca; 37950 Cleveland Ave; 🕑 9am-6pm Jun-Sep) is near the far end of Cleveland Ave.

An American defection? Thousands of **bald eagles** gather near Brackendale, just north of Squamish, each winter to feed on migrating salmon. **Brackendale Art Gallery** (☎ 604-898-3333; www.brackendaleartgallery.com/eagles; cnr Government & Depot Rds) has info about them.

Five access roads leave Hwy 99 between Squamish and Whistler for rugged and immense **Garibaldi Provincial Park** (backcountry $5). The 195-sq-km mountain wilderness playground is known for excellent hiking; the trek to **Garibaldi Lake** (9km; 3-4hr) is a crashcourse in Beautiful BC.

Stawamus Chief ('the Chief') has over 200 **climbing** routes from simple to Spiderman level; contact **Squamish Rock Guides** (☎ 604-815-1750; www.squamishrockguides.com). Named 'Mother of the Winds' by Coast Salish for the 60km/h winds up Howe Sound into Squamish Harbour, there's powerful **windsurfing** in these parts; contact **Squamish Windsurfing Society** (☎ 604-892-2235; www.squamishwindsurfing.org). **Mountain-biking** enthusiasts love the rugged parks and 100 trails in the area. Rentals and information are at **Tantalus Bike Shop** (☎ 604-898-2588; www.tantalusbikeshop. com; 40446 Government Rd; half-/full-day rental $15/35).

Popular with climbers, **Stawamus Chief Provincial Park** (campsite $9) has camping, and **Squamish International Hostel** (☎ 604-892-9240, 800-449-8614; www.squamishhostel.com; 38220 Hwy 99; dm/r $20/40), across the highway from town, is bright and colorful with free bikes, climbing wall and rooftop deck.

Rustically inviting with a small patio looking up at the Chief, **Howe Sound Inn & Brewing Company** (☎ 604-892-2603, 800-919-2537; www.howe sound.com; 37801 Cleveland Ave) brews tasty beers (a good diversion when Whistler-Vancouver traffic sucks).

SUNSHINE COAST

The formidable Coast Mountains and waters of Howe Sound separate Southern BC's ruggedly gorgeous zone from the Lower Mainland. BC Ferries runs ferries between Vancouver (Horseshoe Bay) and Gibsons on the southern Sunshine Coast; Earl's Cove and Saltery Bay mid-way; and Powell River and Vancouver Island. **Malaspina Coach Lines** (☎ 604-485-5030, 877-227-8287) runs buses from Vancouver up the coast.

Sechelt has the best cold-water diving in the province with a dozen sites to explore, including the wreck of the HMCS *Chaudiere* and Tuwanek Point Marine Park. **Suncoast Diving & Watersports** (☎ 604-740-8006; www .suncoastdiving.com; 5643 Wharf St; rentals $75, dives from $135) takes you deep.

Tides plus narrow inlet equals gravity-defying rapids in **Skookumchuck Narrows Provincial Park** (☎ 604-885-3714) near Egmont.

Powell River

This plain little town was built around the mill, but knows how to take advantage of its surroundings. The **Visitor Info Centre** (☎ 604-485-4701; 4690 Marine Ave; ☻ 9am-5:30pm) has good information on activities.

The 180km **Sunshine Coast Trail** (www.sunshine coast-trail.com) wanders through forests and marine environments from Saltery Bay to Sarah Point. The 57km **Powell Forest Canoe Route** is a relatively secret, fantastic 12-lake trip. Beautiful Desolation Sound can be explored for a couple of hours or several days with **Powell River Sea Kayak** (☎ 604-485-2144; www.bcseakayak.com; 6812E Alberni Pl; tours from $110).

The old courthouse and jail has been re-invented as **Old Courthouse Inn & Hostel** (☎ 604-483-4000, 877-483-4777; oldcourthouseinn@armourtech .com; 6243 Walnut St; r $20-75) where bunks are in the judge's chambers or jail. Stay here for info on area adventures.

Willingdon Beach Campsite (☎ 604-485-2242; 4845 Marine Ave; campsite/RV $15/20) is on the water with a large plastic Popeye.

Captain Billy's Old Fashioned Fish & Chips (☎ 604-485-2252; mains $6-8; ☻ Apr-Nov) has been at the ferry terminal for over 25 years. **Shinglemill Pub** (☎ 604-483-2001; 6233 Powell Pl; mains $7-12) is on Powell Lake north of the town.

Malaspina Coach Lines stops here. BC Ferries goes from here to Comox on Vancouver Island four times daily.

SOUTHWESTERN BC

On your way from Vancouver to the interior of the province, gas-up and get snacks in **Hope**, 150km east. Also hit the **Visitor Info**

SPLURGE!

The mighty Fraser and Thompson Rivers are some of the wildest waters in the country, making for awesome white-water rafting trips. One-day excursions including lunch run $100 to $120 per adult – worth it – and most places offer discounts on Sundays. Lytton-based **Kumsheen Raft Adventures** (☎ 800-663-6667, 250-455-2296; www.kumsheen.com; day-trips from $100, site/cabin $19/79), 6km east of town, offers both power (motor) and paddle (your muscles) trips; either way, you'll get soaked. After-rafters can after-party at the campsites or furnished four-person cabin tents. Other outfitters rendezvous at various spots along area rivers.

- **Fraser River Raft Expeditions** (☎ 800-363-7238; www.fraserraft.com; from $120)

- **REO Rafting Adventure Resort** (☎ 800-736-7238; www.reorafting.com; from $110) Like Fraser River Raft Expeditions, this outfit also runs lesser-known but very fast Nahatlatch River.

- **Hyak River Rafting** (☎ 800-663-7238; www.hyak.com; from $100) Runs out of Chilliwack, close to Vancouver.

Centre (☎ 604-869-2021; 919 Water Ave; ☺ 9am-5pm) for information on area parks.

The Trans Canada Hwy (Hwy 1) passes through gold-rush towns like Yale and Spuzzum northwards on a geomorphology fieldtrip through steep-faced Fraser Canyon to Kamloops.

The Crowsnest Hwy (Hwy 3) winds west through forested mountains, passing through the **Hope Slide** and Vancouver's favorite daytrip, **Manning Provincial Park** (☎ 604-795-6169). Stop for swimming or fishing at Lightning Lakes or hike from dry interior to alpine climate on **Dry Ridge Trail** (3km round-trip, 45 minutes). The Crowsnest continues to Osoyoos and southern Okanagan Valley.

Your third option is multi-laned Coquihalla Hwy (Hwy 5; toll $10), which speeds (unless it's a long weekend) its way over the mountains north to Kamloops, or branches off, via Hwy 97C, to Kelowna.

The judge's chambers can be slept in at **HI Kamloops** (☎ 250-828-7991, 866-782-9526; www.hihostels.ca; 7 W Seymour St; dm/d $20/50) on the western edge of downtown 'Loops.'

Greyhound stops everywhere, VIA Rail stops at Kamloops.

GOLD RUSH TRAIL

North from Cache Creek (70km west of Kamloops on Hwy 1), Cariboo Hwy (Hwy 97) follows prospector's routes through Williams Lake, Prince George, Dawson Creek, Fort St John and Fort Nelson as you cross the Rockies into the purple-skied Peace River Valley, the grasslands of the Interior Plains

---

TAKE OFF TO THE GREAT WHITE NORTH

Not just a Rush song, getting to the rugged charm north of the 60th parallel is worth the trip. Towns built on permafrost, herds of caribou and bison, flocks of migratory birds all live under the green-and-yellow dance of the Northern Lights.

Hwys 97 and 37 lead through northern BC to **Whitehorse**, where a Sourdough Ale fresh from **Yukon Brewing Company** (☎ 867-668-4183; 102 Copper Rd) tastes so much better. Rest at **Beez Kneez Bakpakers** (☎ 867-456-2333; www.bzkneez.com; 408 Hoge St; dm/r $20/40) or **Hide on Jeckell Guesthouse** (☎ 867-633-4933; www.hide-on-jeckell.com; 410 Jeckell St; dm $20).

The **Gold Rush Trail** (Hwy 2; Klondike Hwy) follows the 1898 northbound route of 40,000 gold seekers. **Dawson City** launches you back a century to unpaved streets, boarded sidewalks and a gritty, edge-of-the-world feel. **Diamond Tooth Gertie's Gambling Hall** (☎ 867-993-5575; cnr Queen St & 4th Ave; $8) has small-time gambling, honky-tonk piano and dancing girls. See the midnight sun barely set before rising again from **Midnight Dome**. Party during **Dawson City Music Festival** (☎ 867-993-5384; www.dcmf.com) and **Discovery Day** (☺ mid-Aug). **Dawson City River Hostel** (☎ 867-993-6823 summer; www.yukonhostels.com; dm/r $19/39) is no-electricity rustic and having-too-much-fun-in-the-Yukon funky.

North enough? Drive the scenic 106km **Top of the World Hwy** (Hwy 9; ☺ Jun-Aug) along ridgetops to Alaska, or brave the Arctic Circle and Northern Tree Line. **Dempster Hwy** (Hwy 5; ☎ 800-661-0750) makes full north–south North American road travel possible as the 747km gravel road from Dawson City passes through mountains, valleys, rivers and vast open tundra to **Inuvik**, Northwest Territories (NWT).

Rte 77 (often closed), near Fort Nelson, and the more-traveled Hwy 35, through northern Alberta, also lead into the Northwest Territories. **Wood Buffalo National Park** is confusingly wood-buffalo-less, though they do (as 'bison' remember) flourish along Hwys 1, 7 and particularly Hwy 3, which passes through **Mackenzie Bison Sanctuary** and the world's largest free-ranging herd.

Slave River has monster rapids along the Canadian Shield; splurge with **Slave Kayak Lodge** (☎ 250-318-3278, 866-588-3278; www.slavekayaklodge.com).

At the end of Hwy 3, **Yellowknife** is the best place in Canada to buy northern art and the only place in Canada to see igloo-shaped **Legislature Buildings**. The gritty action of the dim **Gold Range Hotel** (☎ 867-873-4441; 5010 50th St; ☺ 10-2am) is good for a drink or seven after a **dogsled tour**. Not just a Tom Cochrane song, **Ragged Ass Rd** is lined with sagging gold-rush-era cabins and antique trucks.

Nunavut, as magical and remote as any place in the north, is accessed by air or boat only; wire home for money (lots of it) if you really want to go.

SCENIC DRIVE: STEWART–CASSIAR HWY

While the usual route to the Yukon is the Alaska Hwy (Hwy 97), Hwy 37 makes a sometimes slow, but always spectacular loop through the northwest corner of the province. There's never less than 150km between service stations; have good spares and don't trust that quarter-tank for long. Salmon spawn and bears feed at **Fish Creek** (☼ Jul-Sep) near Hyder. Undeveloped and full of wildlife, **Spatsizi Plateau Provincial Wilderness Park** (☎ 250-771-4591) is 28km from Tatogga; prepare well for hikes. Relax and sleep at **Red Goat Lodge** (☎ 250-234-3261, 888-733-4628; www .karo-ent.com/redgoat.htm; campsite/dm $13/20, r 55-95) on Eddontenajon Lake. **Mt Edziza Provincial Park** (☎ 250 771-4591) protects a volcanic landscape accessed by hiking trails.

---

and back into the Rocky Mountain foothills on the 1850km trek to the Yukon. This is where you realize just how big and unique this province is. Cheap motels and cheaper beer can be found along the way, as can excellent camping in parks and reserves. **Dawson Creek** (no relation to the similarly named TV show) marks the starting point (Mile 0) of the Alaska Hwy (2237km to Fairbanks, AK).

Greyhound takes this route and VIA Rail stops overnight in Prince George on its way between Jasper and Prince Rupert.

PRINCE RUPERT

True wilderness is evident everywhere in northwest BC. Acting as a gateway, Rupert, on the mouth of the Skeena River flanked by mountains and rugged coastlines, can leave you awestruck.

A shouldn't-miss, the **Museum of Northern British Columbia** (☎ 250-624-3207; www.museumof northernbc.com; 100 1st Ave W; admission $5; ☼ 9am-8pm Mon-Sat, until 5pm Sun summer, 9am-5pm winter) has an excellent collection inside a replicated longhouse.

Food and beer is in town. The awesome, warped-walled and colorfully decorated historic **Pioneer Hostel** (☎ 250-624-2334, 888-794-9998; www.citytel.net/pioneer; 167 3rd Ave E; dm $16-21, s/d 35/43) has a barbecue out back.

VIA Rail ends it trip here from Jasper; Greyhound also stops here.

BC Ferries sails to Port Hardy on Vancouver Island and the Queen Charlotte Islands from the harbor southwest of town. **Alaska Maritime Highway** (☎ 250-627-1744, 800-642-0066; www.alaska.gov/ferry; to Skagway adult $175, car from $200, bicycle $28, cabin from $130) has a terminal behind fences at the same place for boats to Skagway, with stops along the way four times a week in summer and twice in winter. Book for all ferries.

OKANAGAN VALLEY

Yeah it's hot, but it's a semi-dry heat. The highly popular and gorgeous fertile valley, centered by long and skinny Okanagan Lake, is best explored by the 'big three': Kelowna, Penticton and Vernon.

Ravaged by fires in 2003, some of the parks may still be closed during your visit – all of them will if it's been a hot, dry summer. Fruit-stands lining the roads still sell Canada's best and cheapest produce. Stock up.

At the valley's southern end, small **Osoyoos** 'enjoys' a hot (up to 45°C in summer) and dry (less than 200mm per year precipitation) climate, producing an uncharacteristic Canadian desert: rattlesnakes, turtles, (Wile E) coyotes and cacti. Twenty-seven hectares can be interpreted (guided tours mandatory) along boardwalks at **Desert Centre** (☎ 250-495-2470; www.desert.org; Hwy 97; $6; ☼ 9am-7pm May-Sep) north of town. Break from the dry heat in blissful, sandy-beached, dark-blue and incredibly warm **Osoyoos Lake**.

Vernon (most northerly of the big three) is surrounded by parks like **Ellison Provincial Park** (☎ 800-689-9025; Okanagan Landing Rd; campsite $17) with a fun beach and easy trails. **HI Lodged Inn** (☎ 250-549-3742, 888-737-9427; www.hihostels.ca /vernon; 3201 Pleasant Valley Rd; dm $20) will help you find swimming, fishing and camping, paragliding, skydiving, climbing and hiking.

Penticton, a perfect beach town at the southern end of Okanagan Lake, is world famous for rock-climbing at **Skaha Bluffs**. For courses ranging from rookie to technical, **Skaha Rock Adventures** (☎ 250-493-1765; www.skaharockclimbing .com; courses from $125) harnesses you up. **Peach Festival** (☎ 800-663-5052; www.peachfest.com; ☼ early Aug) is the city's national-popular, weeklong party. A bit on the scruffy side with a homey vibe and huge activity board, **HI Penticton Hostel** (☎ 250-492-3992; 464 Ellis St; dm/r $24/40) is a downtown 1901 home.

BACKROADS BC

Barkerville

Like most BC gold-rush towns at one point, Barkerville was the largest city west of Chicago and north of San Francisco after Billy Barker made $1000 in two days of prospecting in 1862. Now a **historic site** (☎ 250-994-3332; www.heritage.gov.bc.ca; admission $12.50; ☾ 8am-8pm), 89km east of Quesnel along Hwy 26, the town makes the most of its history with 125 restored buildings.

Hwy 5 to Jasper

North from Kamloops, Hwy 5 passes through **Wells Gray Provincial Park** (☎ 250-674-2194), a waterfall-filled jewel where 137m **Helmcken Falls** is the misty-abyss centerpiece. Just outside the south gate, **Wells Gray Guest Ranch** (☎ 250-674-2792, 866-467-4346; www.wellsgrayranch.com; campsite $14, teepee $30, d $85-120) offers horseback-riding, hiking, mountain biking, fishing, dog-sledding and snow-shoeing.

North of Nelson

From Nelson, Hwy 3A goes north to lakeside **Kaslo** where the SS *Moyie* stern-wheeler sits. Slow and rugged Hwy 31A heads east to **New Denver** where **Nikkei Internment Memorial Centre** (☎ 250-358-7288; www.newdenver.ca/nikkei; 306 Josephine St; admission $4; ☾ 9am-5pm Jun-Sep) is an eye-opening museum, formerly a WWII Japanese internment camp. Stop at the gorgeous and rugged **Valhalla Provincial Park**, for hiking, swimming or camping. It's then another 48km north on Hwy 6 to **Nakusp**. Brand-new **Nakusp International Hostel** (☎ 250-265-3069; 1950 Hwy 23 N; www .nakusphostel.com; dm/r $20/45) has hammocks on the lake.

Greyhound stops at Vernon, Osoyoos and Penticton.

Kelowna

Placed on the eastern mid-section shore of Okanagan Lake and backdropped by scrubby grassland hills, followed by the high, jagged peaks of the Monashee Mountains, Kelowna makes a good base; it's also Okanagan's party town.

Pick up the brochure at the **Visitor Info Centre** (☎ 250-861-1515, 800-663-4345; www.tourism kelowna.org; 544 Harvey Ave; ☾ 8am-7pm summer, 8am-5pm Mon-Fri, 10am-3pm Sat & Sun winter) for a self-guiding tour of the **Cultural District**.

BC Orchard Industry Museum (☎ 250-763-0433; www.kelownamuseum.ca; 1304 Ellis St; admission by donation; ☾ 10am-5pm Tue-Sat) has a cool collection of old, packing-crate labels among other displays chronicling the Okanagan Valley's transformation from ranchland to orchards.

SPLURGE!

Kelowna Parasail Adventures (☎ 250-868-4838; www.parasailcanada.com; 1310 Water St; from $50) Parasailing is offered daily in summer in front of the Grand Okanagan Hotel.

Modern and sterile looking, **Kelowna SameSun International Hostel** (☎ 250-763-9814, 877-562-2783; www.samesun.com; 245 Harvey Ave; dm/d $22/40), on the edge of downtown, loads up with fun and international travelers. For more time and space to relax, **Kelowna International Hostel** (☎ 250-763-6024; www.kelowna -hostel.bc.ca; 2343 Pandosy St; dm from $13) is an old house a short walk from the beach.

Hipsters, students and businesspeople hang at the stylish café-bistro **Verve** (☎ 250-860-8086; 345 Lawrence Ave; meals $10) for fine coffee and an ever-changing menu. With *Uncle Tom's Band* on repeat (not really), **Grateful Fed Psyche Deli** (☎ 250-862-8621; 509 Bernard Ave; sandwiches $5) makes *c'est bon* Montréal smoked-meat sammies.

Spill and swill on the patios of **Rose's Waterfront Pub** (☎ 250-860-1141; 1352 Water St) or Guinness-loving **Kelly O'Bryan's** (☎ 250-861-1338; 262 Bernard Ave). Leon St is the place for clubbing. **Gotcha** (☎ 250-860-0800; 238 Leon Ave; cover varies; ☾ 7pm-late Tue-Sat) is the two-story place of choice.

Enthusiastic fans watch **Kelowna Rockets** (☎ 250-860-7825; www.kelownarockets.com) hockey games live at **SkyReach Place** (☎ 250-979-0888; www.skyreachplace.com; Water St & Cawston Ave; ticket from $10) or talk, drink, breathe the team at **Sturgeon Hall** (☎ 250-860-4664; 1481 Water St), self-proclaimed hockey headquarters full of memorabilia.

Westjet (sometimes cheaper than Greyhound) and Air Canada fly to **Kelowna Airport** (code: YLW; ☎ 250-765-5125; www.kelownaairport.com), 20km north on Hwy 97. Greyhound stops in Kelowna.

THE KOOTENAYS

The quicker, northern Trans Canada Hwy (Hwy 1) or the picturesque, southern Crowsnest (Hwy 3) both wind through the Selkirks, Monashee, Purcell and Rocky Mountains from the Okanagan to Alberta. The pumping-heart of avalanche country, contact the **Canadian Avalanche Association** (☎ 250-837-2435, 24hr information 800-667-1105; www.avalanche.ca) in Revelstoke if you're backcountry hiking/camping.

Revelstoke

Almost eerily perfect in a David Lynch way, picturesque Revelstoke is marred by frequent train whistles.

The **Visitor Info Centre** (☎ 250-837-5345, 800-487-1493; www.seerevelstoke.com; 206 Campbell Ave; 8:30am-4:30pm Mon-Fri) also has a **summer office** (111 Mackenzie St; 8:30am-6pm). **Parks Canada** (☎ 250-837-7500; 301 3rd St; 8am-4:30pm Mon-Fri) has an office here, too.

Enjoy free live music at **Grizzly Plaza** (btwn Mackenzie & Orton Aves). **Revelstoke Railway Museum** (☎ 250-837-6060, 877-837-6060; www.railwaymuseum.com; 719 Track St W; admission $6; 9am-8pm summer) documents the CPR's essential east–west linking of Canada.

Once you find your bunk in the labyrinth, **SameSun Budget Lodge** (☎ 250-837-4050, 877-562-2783; www.samesun.ca; 400 2nd St W; dm/d $22/45) will hook you up with activities and offer a deck for evening relaxing.

East on Hwy 1

The Trans Canada Hwy is the most-traveled Kootenays route to Banff and Jasper.

Mt Revelstoke National Park (admission $5) has incredible views from the jagged 2220m summit of Mt Revelstoke. You can hike if you want, or take the **Meadows in the Sky Parkway** (Jul-Sep) through forests and meadows to Balsam Lake, 2km from the peak, and the **shuttle** (10am-4:20pm) the rest of the way.

Creatively named **Glacier National Park** (admission $7) has more than 430 glaciers with stunning hiking and climbing, but you gotta

register at **Rogers Pass Centre** (☎ 250-814-5233; 8am-7pm summer, varies seasonally; backcountry $8).

A good base for Rocky Mountain adventures, **Golden** has only recently started to take advantage of its location close to everything: rafting, mountain biking, hiking, skiing, hang-gliding. The **Visitor Info Centre** (☎ 250-344-7125, 800-622-4653; www.goldenchamber.bc.ca; 500 10th Ave N; 9am-5pm, Mon-Fri Sep-Jun) helps arrange activities. **Glacier Raft Company** (☎ 250-344-6521; www.glacierraft.com; from $55) and **Wet 'n' Wild** (☎ 250-344-6546, 800-668-9119; www.wetnwild.bc.ca; from $55) brave local Class III and IV rapids. Basic **Mary's Motel** (☎ 250-344-7111, 866-734-6279; www.marysmotel.com; 603 8th Ave N; r $60-90;) is on the river.

Rossland

Small Rossland on Hwy 22 near the US border has BC's best mountain biking, with a well-developed trail system radiating from downtown. **Powderhound** (☎ 250-362-5311; 2044 Columbia Ave; from $35) offers rentals.

Nelson

A Hwy 3A or Hwy 6 detour from the Crowsnest leads to this backpacker's, adrenaline seeker's and stoner's paradise town surrounded by the Selkirk Mountains. With a pretty little downtown and sweet aroma of BC Bud, it draws the creative types who are sick of the city.

The **Visitor Info Centre** (☎ 250-352-3433, 877-663-5706; www.discovernelson.com; 225 Hall St; 8:30am-8pm summer; 8:30am-5pm weekdays winter) is on an outlandishly steep hill. **Nelson Brewing Company** (☎ 250-352-3582; 512 Latimer St) has frequent tours and tastings.

From town, the two-hour climb to **Pulpit Rock** gives great views. **Kokanee Creek Provincial Park** (☎ 250-825-4212; campsite $22) and **Kokanee Glacier Provincial Park** (☎ 250-825-3500; backcountry campsite $5) have camping, glacier-accessible hiking trails and awesome biking.

WATCH THIS

Confusingly, the eastern part of the Kootenays is in the mountain time zone (like Alberta and Idaho) and the western Kootenays are in the Pacific Time Zone. Simply, as you're traveling east (towards Alberta), set your watch ahead an hour at Glacier National Park (Hwy 1) or Creston (Hwy 3).

THE WHITE STUFF

If your first winter-activity stop from Vancouver is Whistler, you've made a good call but also a terrible mistake. For a few more hours driving, you could save loonies, avoid rookies and carve with real downhillers on the icing-sugar-fine and haystack-deep powder of BC's interior.

Hostels usually have discounted lift-tickets or ski-and-stay packages and some hills offer a 'good excuse' to stay with on-mountain hostels. Most are open in summer (around $10) for hikers and bikers.

In very particular order (although they're all good) the best are:

- **Big White** (☎ 250-765-8888, 800-663-2772; www.bigwhite.com; 55km east of Kelowna; admission $60) You may get socked in with fog for five days straight, but with 777m of vert, and the best powder and aprés-ski scene, you won't care. Ski-in, ski-out at well-kept **SameSun-Big White** (☎ 250-765-7920; www.samesun.com; 7470 Porcupine Rd; dm/r $25/60).

- **Fernie** (☎ 250-423-4655, 877-333-2339; www.skifernie.com; Fernie; admission $60) Astounding 8.75m of snowfall per year only a five-minute drive from downtown. Despite 107 runs and five bowls, still considered their little secret and hidden gem.

- **Apex Mountain** (☎ 877-777-2739; www.apexresort.com; 37km west of Penticton; admission $48) Still a small ski resort despite having the most double-black-diamonds in the area. Brand-spanking new **Apex Double Diamond Hostel** (☎ 250-292-8256, 866-273-9737; www.apexaccommodation.com; dm/r $20/60) is log-built everything.

- **Kicking Horse** (☎ 250-439-5400, 866-754-5425; www.kickinghorseresort.com; Golden; admission $55) A jaw-and-stomach dropping 1260m vertical is accessed by only three lifts. Little wind means lots of snow and 60% of 96 runs are Advanced or Expert.

- **Sun Peaks** (☎ 250-578-5474, 800-807-3257; www.sunpeaksresort.com; 53km northeast of Kamloops; admission $55) Has some of the longest runs, limiting wait-in-line time. Stay at almost-an-A-frame **Sun Peaks International Hostel** (☎ 250-578-0057; www.sunpeakshostel.com; 1140 Sun Peaks Rd; dm $20).

- **Silver Star** (☎ 250-542-0224, 800-663-4431; www.silverstarmtn.com; 22km northeast of Vernon; admission $56) Though it has 760m of vertical, most of the runs are flat and good for beginners; hard-cores hit the steeper summit. Stay at **SameSun Budget Lodge** (☎ 250-545-8933, 877-562-2783; www.samesun.com; 9898 Pinnacles Rd; dm/d $25/60).

- **Red Mountain** (☎ 250-362-7384, 800-663-0105; www.ski-red.com; Rossland; admission $50) Some of the best technical trails on 880m of vertical.

- **Powder Springs** (☎ 250-837-5151, 877-991-4455; www.catpowder.com/indexsprings.html; Revelstoke; admission $28) No high-speed lifts; yes heavy snowfall (up to 1200cm), loads of backcountry, almost no crowds and cheap as hell.

- **Whitewater** (☎ 250-354-4944, 800-666-9420; www.skiwhitewater.com; 12km south of Nelson; admission $42) Only two chairs and a tow-rope, but tons of powder.

Named after active animals, HI-affiliated **Dancing Bear Inn** (☎ 250-352-7573, 877-352-7573; www.dancingbearinn.com; 171 Baker St; dm/d $20/40) is an immaculately restored home with dark woodwork, but without dancing bears. Nearby, **Flying Squirrel International Hostel** (☎ 250-352-7285; www.flyingsquirrelhostel.com; 198 Baker St; dm/r $20/39) is brick walled and pleasantly used, with a fun bar. Nope, no squirrels.

Get fluffy omelettes from **Stanley's on Baker** (☎ 250-354-4458; 402 Baker St; mains $5-10); **Outer Clove** (☎ 250-354-1667; 536 Stanley St; mains

$8-15) has spicy (some vegetarian) dishes. Go to **Mike's Place** (☎ 250-352-5331; 422 Vernon St) for drinkin'.

East on Hwy 3

As you drive through southern BC mountains, you'll approach a clearing and think you've reached the summit...until you switchback to discover another hill to climb; repeat.

Cranbrook is an unfortunately unattractive working town, but the fine collection of Canadian trains at the **Canadian Museum of Rail Travel** (☎ 250-489-3918; www.traindeluxe.com; admission $8; ☺ 10am-6pm summer, 10am-5pm Tue-Sat winter) elicits 'woo-wooooos.' Detour north on Hwy 95A for mountain activities at Bavarian look-alike **Kimberly** with modern **SameSun Budget Lodge** (☎ 250-427-7191, 877-562-2783; www.samesun.com; 275 Spokane St; dm/d $22/59).

Attractively Victorian with young and artistic residents, **Fernie** is humble almost to a fault. The skiing is superb and summer rafting is hard to pass up. Check with the **Visitor Info Centre** (☎ 250-423-6868; www.fernie chamber.com; 102 Commerce Rd; ☺ 9am-7pm summer, 9am-5pm Mon-Fri winter). Basic-but-fun **HI Raging Elk Hostel** (☎ 250-423-6811; www.hihostels.ca/fernie; 892 6th Ave; dm $22) also helps with activities.

CANADIAN ROCKIES

You've seen the postcards, coffee-table books and magazine spreads; been told of dizzying views and adrenaline rushes felt months later; and heard the stories of countless wildlife. But nothing can truly prepare you for your first glimpse of a sky-kissing, serrated peak cradling a tongue-shaped, city-sized glacier feeding an emerald lake flanked by a dozen bighorn sheep. Welcome to [insert Deity here]'s country.

GETTING AROUND

Brewster Transportation (☎ 780-852-3332; www .brewster.ca) runs between Calgary (including the airport) and Jasper, with stops, and more frequent runs between, Banff and Lake Louise.

True North Tours (☎ 403-912-0407; www.backpacker -tour.com/truenorthtours/home.asp; mid-May–mid-Oct), works with HI-Calgary for Rocky Mountain trips, including a six-day one to Calgary, Banff, Lake Louise, Jasper and Calgary ($360 including hostels). **SunDog Tour Co** (☎ 780-852-4056; www.sundogtours.com) runs a cheaper-than-Greyhound shuttle between Banff and Jasper in addition to guided tours.

Rocky Mountain Discount Travel (☎ 888-287-7638; www.rmdtravel.ca; $75) runs between Vancouver and Calgary hostels, with extended Rocky Mountain stays allowed.

BANFF NATIONAL PARK

Everyone's Rockies-first-to-do, **Banff** (☎ 403-762-1550; adult/group $7/14) exemplifies the majesty of the area. Full of cold lakes, colder glaciers, dangerous peaks, dangerouser wildlife, tough hikes and tougher climbs, the park earns its place as centerpiece of the Rockies.

Spend months in Banff and you still wouldn't explore all the park's trails. **Bow River** near town is a quiet stroll, **Tunnel Mountain** is a bit of a leg-burner to views from St Julien Rd. **Warner Guiding & Outfitting** (☎ 800-661-8352; www.horseback.com; 132 Banff Ave) offer a variety of horseback-riding trips from covered-wagon cookouts ($63) to an hour-long ride along Spray River ($30).

Canoe rentals are from **Bow River Canoe Rentals** (☎ 403-762-3632; Bow Ave & Wolf St; per hr/day $16/40) for water-level wildlife-viewing at **Vermilion Lakes**.

Banff's rocky crags boast the best climbing in the Rockies and **Banff Adventure Centre** (☎ 403-762 8536; www.mountainguide.com; 724 Bear St; courses $69-240) is a good place to start.

The snowy peaks just beg to be conquered in the winter. A **three-day pass** ($175) is good for all three resorts. **Sunshine Village** (☎ 403-762-6500, 877-542-2633; www.skibanff.com; $60) straddles the continental divide with a ton of expert territory (you'll need avalanche beacon, shovel, probe and partner to hit the backcountry). **Lake Louise** (☎ 403-522-3555, 800-258-7669; www.skilouise.com; $59) is one of Canada's most popular (ie busy) and largest ski areas, with 17 sq km of skiable terrain spread over four mountain faces. **Ski Banff @Norquay** (☎ 403-762-4421, 866-464-7669; www.banffnorquay.com; Mt Norquay Rd; $46) is the original hill 6km north of downtown Banff. Local buses **shuttle** (one way/round-trip from $6/10) riders to all three resorts every half hour during the season.

Banff Townsite

Wood-and-stone architecture, tourists and hipsters everywhere and mountains all around make the town of Banff an attraction in itself

Parks Canada Information Centre (☎ 403-762-1550; 224 Banff Ave; ☺ 8am-8pm summer) and **Banff/ Lake Louise Tourism Bureau** (☎ 403-762-8421; www .banfflakelouise.com) are in the same building. Pick up *Day Hikes in Banff National Park* and *Backcountry Visitors' Guide*.

See the historic photographs at **Whyte Museum** (☎ 403-762-2291; www.whyte.org; 111 Bear St; admission $6; ☺ 10am-5pm). Four kilometers south (shuttle $5), **Banff Gondola** (☎ 403-762-2523; Mountain Ave; admission $22; ☺ 7:30am-9pm

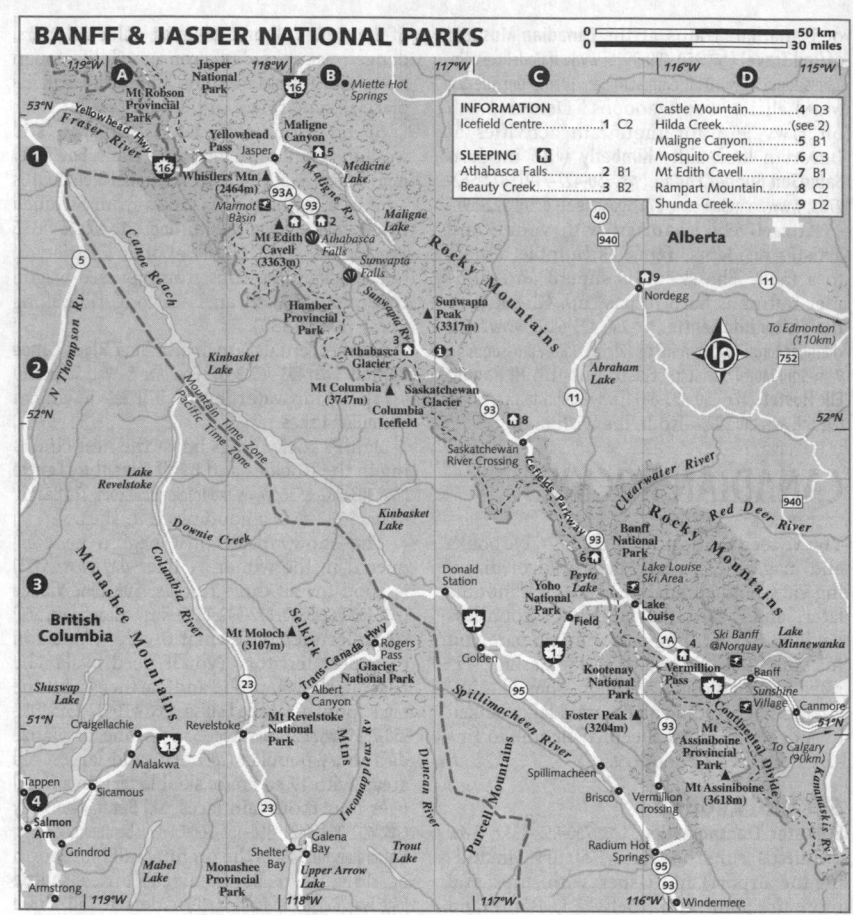

BANFF & JASPER NATIONAL PARKS

INFORMATION
Icefield Centre..............1 C2

SLEEPING
Athabasca Falls.............2 B1
Beauty Creek...............3 B2

Castle Mountain.............4 D3
Hilda Creek.............(see 2)
Maligne Canyon............5 B1
Mosquito Creek.............6 C3
Mt Edith Cavell...........7 B1
Rampart Mountain..........8 C2
Shunda Creek.............9 D2

---

summer) rides 2285m to the summit of Sulphur Mountain for panoramic views.

The **park** (frontcountry/backcountry campsites $13-22/6) has 13 first-come, first-served campgrounds and many backcountry sites. **Johnston Canyon Campground** (Bow Valley Pkwy; ☻ early Jun–mid-Sep) is one of Banff's finest and **Two Jack Main Campground** (Minnewanka Loop Dr; ☻ mid-May–mid-Sep) has more campsites. **Tunnel Mountain Village** (Tunnel Mountain Rd) is open year-round.

INSTEAD OF BANFF GONDOLA

Hike (two hours) up the mountain's steep east side from Upper Hot Springs parking lot and take the gondola down (free).

With a central courtyard (including waterfall), hot tub and frequent barbecues, **Samesun-Banff** (☎ 403-762-5521, 888-844-7875; www .samesun.com; 449 Banff Ave; dm/r $26/67) is always ready to party.

Cavernous and a bit loud but with cozy fireplaces and huge decks, **HI-Banff Alpine Centre** (☎ 403-762-4122, 866-762-4122; www.hihostels .ca/banff; 801 Coyote Dr; dm/d $28/80) makes the most of its location with chalet architecture. Up Tunnel Mountain, take a free shuttle from the bus station.

Evelyn's Coffee Bar (☎ 403-762-0352; 201 Banff Ave; lunches $6-8) has the best local coffee and homemade sandwiches, wraps and soups. There's a great vegetarian menu at **Sunfood Café** (☎ 403-760-3933; 215 Banff Ave; mains $5-8).

WESTERN CANADA

Legendary Bill Peyto made Banff famous with climbing adventures and bobcat fights. **Wild Bill's Legendary Saloon** (☎ 403-762-0333; 201 Banff Ave) is a true cowboy hangout only slightly less tame.

Greyhound stops here. **Rocky Mountain Sky Shuttle** (☎ 403-762-5200, 888-762-8754), **Brewster Transportation** (☎ 403-762-6767, 800-661-1152) and **Banff Airporter** (☎ 403-762-3330, 888-449-2901) run buses to Calgary and the airport for around $40/75 one way/round-trip.

Lake Louise

Fifty-seven kilometers north of Banff, Lake Louise is the park's classic reflecting emerald-green lake surrounded by granite slopes. Fortress-like Chateau Lake Louise poses at the north end. Lesser-known and more ruggedly, naturally impressive, **Moraine Lake** is an impossibly-deep teal. For a more rigorous venture, take the switchbacks up to **Mirror Lake**.

The village of Lake Louise, 5km south of the lake, has the **Lake Louise Visitor Centre** (☎ 403-522-3833; beside Samson Mall, Lake Louise Village; ☉ 9am-7pm summer, varies seasonally). Here you should check weather reports before heading out on extended hikes (it can snow in July) like the 20km **Valley of the Ten Peaks** between Moraine Lake and Lake Louise. **Lake Louise Trail** makes an afternoon trip following the lake's northern banks westward to the **Plain of Six Glaciers**.

HI-Lake Louise (☎ 403-522-2200; www.hihostels.ca/lakelouise; Village Rd; dm/d $28/82) is friendly and borderline luxurious (mints on the pillows). The bunks are solid, the lofts are cool, the lounge is huge and some furniture is twig. They put a lot of thought into ski-packages and outdoor programs. In the hostel, **Bill Peyto's Café** (☎ 403-670-7580; mains $7-10) is lively and popular with guests and locals.

The closest campground to Lake Louise, **Lake Louise Tent & Trailer** (☎ 403-522-3833; off Lake Louise Dr; campsite from $22; ☉ late-Jun–late-Sep) has an electric fence to keep you in (or maybe the bears out).

Greyhound and Brewster stop here. In summer, Parks Canada runs the Vista shuttle bus from the village to both Moraine Lake and Lake Louise. It's 45 minutes from the village to Lake Louise on the footpath.

ICEFIELDS PARKWAY

Hwy 93 curves around jagged mountains, turquoise lakes and retreating glaciers along

> **SCENIC DRIVE: HWY 93A**
>
> At Athabasca Falls, Hwy 93A sneaks quietly off to the left. Take it. Literally the road less traveled, this old route into Jasper offers a blissfully traffic-free experience as it slips serenely through deep dark woods past small placid lakes and meadows.

the spine of the Rockies between Banff and Jasper. Always keep your eyes peeled and camera ready for grizzly, moose and big-horn sheep. Numerous roadside stops offer fantastic viewpoints and trails for getting lost. The 230km road can be done in a few hours, but take your time.

One of the world's most beautiful road-side glacial scenes, robin-egg-blue **Peyto Lake** should be visited in early morning before the tour buses arrive.

About halfway between Lake Louise and Jasper, **Athabasca Glacier** is one of 30 glaciers of 350m thick Columbia Icefield. You can walk or drive to the toe of the glacier; to hike onto it you'll need a guide. Much-hyped and touristy 'snocoach' ice tours by **Brewster** (☎ 877-423-7433; www.brewster.ca; admission $30) drive out onto the ice past what can be seen from the road. **Icefield Centre** (☎ 780-852-6288; ☉ 9am-6pm May–mid-Oct) is across the highway with well-designed displays on glaciers and a Parks Canada information desk.

Sunwapta Falls and the 'please-ignore-the-utility-road-bridge' **Athabasca Falls** are close to Jasper.

JASPER NATIONAL PARK

Jasper's (☎ 780-852-6176; adult/group $7/14) greatest asset is its relative solitude. It offers the same cougars, mountains, bears, lakes, moose, glaciers, camping and activities as Banff, but lacks its southern neighbor's crowds. The forests seem a little denser, the lakes a little bluer, the glaciers a little bigger, the wildlife a little more plentiful and the people a little friendlier.

Maligne Canyon, 11km east of the townsite, is a narrow and deep limestone gorge with waterfalls, crystalline pools and interesting rock formations. Skip the crowds and walk the lower canyon; turn off the main road at Fifth Bridge. About 21km further up the road, **Medicine Lake**'s water level rises, falls and disappears completely with the seasonal

WILD(ER(NESS)) NIGHTS

HI runs a string of wilderness hostels along Icefields Parkway designed for natural adventures without the bother of tents, gear etc. They all have solar showers, outhouses, no electricity, outdoor firepits and equipped kitchens. Most will have seasonal closures and 'office hours' (pick a bunk when you arrive and pay later). All are unique (wood-burning saunas at some) and capture the spirit of the true backpacker.

Heading north from Banff to Jasper:

- **Castle Mountain** (www.hihostels.ca/castlemountain; dm $24) Hard to call 'rustic' with wrap-around windows and access to Banff and Lake Louise.

- **Mosquito Creek** (www.hihostels.ca/mosquitocreek; dm $24) Grounds are a little wild but buildings are well maintained in a forest setting.

- **Rampart Mountain** (www.hihostels.ca/rampartcreek; dm $25) At the base of huge cliff (ice-climbing in winter) sit a couple of quaint, 12-bunk bungalows popular with climbers.

- **Shunda Creek** (www.hihostels.ca/nordegg; dm $22) Off the parkway, east on Hwy 11, this two-story lodge is revered by hikers, bikers and climbers as a hidden gem.

- **Hilda Creek** (www.hihostels.ca/hildacreek; dm $24) Closest to Columbia Icefield. May still be closed due to 2002 fire.

- **Beauty Creek** (www.hihostels.ca/beautycreek; dm $17) Three bunkhouses built into the hillside looking over creekside locations; area hiking is spectacular.

- **Mt Edith Cavell** (www.hihostels.ca/mountedithcavel; dm $18; ☉ mid-Jun–mid-Oct) Totally worth 13km drive/walk/ski west of Hwy 93A. Nestled in incredibly remote mountains with access to glaciers and turquoise lakes. Ski in by appointment in winter.

- **Athabasca Falls** (www.hihostels.ca/athabascafalls; dm $18) Very cool common room, including ping-pong table, and the three 14-bunk cabins are impeccably kept.

- **Maligne Canyon** (www.hihostels.ca/malignecanyon; dm $18) East of Jasper, close to Skyline Trail and above scenic canyon.

flow of one of the western hemisphere's largest underground river systems.

INSTEAD OF BANFF OR JASPER

East of 'those other parks,' BC's Rockies offer similar stunning scenery without the crowds.

- **Yoho National Park** (☎ 250-343-6783; adult $7, campsite $14-22) Emerald Lake, 10km north of the Trans-Canada, has a flat hike around the real-life postcard. A short walk from waterfalls, **HI Whiskey Jack Hostel** (☎ 403-762-4122, 866-762-4122; www.hihostels.ca; dm $23; ☉ Jun-Sep) offers 27 bunks.

- **Kootenay National Park** (☎ 250-347-9615; adult $7, campsite $17-30) Rockies' most moderate climate and the only Canadian national park to contain both glaciers and cacti. Take the scary wooden bridges to **Marble Canyon**.

Jasper National Park visitor guide details backcountry trails (the 45km-above-the-treeline **Skyline Trail** is popular). For shorter trips, **Mt Edith Cavell** and **Miette Hot Springs** areas have good day hikes.

A good cycling route close to the townsite is along **Maligne Lake Rd**. If you're bikeless, rent from **Vicious Cycle** (☎ 780-852-1111; 630 Connaught Dr; day $20) or the **hostel** (hr/day $7/25).

Calm to turbulent **white-water rafting** is exhilarating on Jasper's rivers. **Maligne Rafting Adventures** (☎ 780-852-3370; www.mra.ab.ca; 627 Patricia St; from $44) and **Rocky Mountain River Guides** (☎ 780-852-3777; www.rmriverguides.com; 626 Connaught Dr; from $45) lead trips for all levels.

Jasper National Park's only ski area is **Marmot Basin** (☎ 780-852-3816; www.skimarmot .com; Marmot Basin Rd; admission $54), 19km southwest of the townsite.

Jasper Townsite

Jasper townsite is almost in the middle of the park, where the Icefields Parkway meets

Hwy 16. Parks Canada's **Jasper Information Centre** (☎ 780-852-6176; 500 Connaught Dr; ☼ 9am-7pm summer, 9am-4pm winter) has the *Day-hikers' Guide to Jasper National Park* and *Mountain Biking Guide, Jasper National Park*.

Seven kilometers south of town (shuttle $3), **Jasper Tramway** (☎ 780-852-3093; Whistlers Mountain Rd; admission $21; ☼ 8:30am-10:30pm summer) takes you up 973m for glaciers, mountains and grouchy goats to see and a summit to conquer.

The **park** (frontcountry/backcountry campsites $13-22/6) has 10 campgrounds. You can get backcountry permits at the information centre.

Big, multi-bed dorms and multi-couch common rooms are found in **HI-Jasper** (☎ 780-852-3215, 877-852-0781; www.hihostels.ca /jasper; Whistlers Mountain Rd; dm from $18), 7km (last 2km uphill) southwest of the townsite; take the tramway shuttle ($3). Jasper's 10 park campgrounds are generally open from mid-May until first snowfall.

The townsite is full of little cafés. Amond the best are **Bear's Paw Bakery** (☎ 780-852-3233; 4 Cedar Ave; items $3), for sweet treats, and **Coco's Café** (☎ 780-852-4550; 608 Patricia St; mains $4-7), for healthy breakfasts and vegetarian lunches.

Pool, darts and cheap beer are at **Whistle Stop Pub** (☎ 780-852-3361; cnr Connaught Dr & Miette Ave) and **De'd Dog Bar & Grill** (☎ 780-852-3351; Astoria Hotel, 404 Connaught Dr). **Pete's on Patricia** (☎ 780-852-6262; 614 Patricia St) is the after-10pm hotspot.

Greyhound, Brewster, SunDog and VIA Rail stop here.

CANMORE

Those who appreciate the natural splendor of the area, but not the forced tourism embrace Canmore, 26km west of Banff. Particularly popular with mountain bikers and climbers, the fast-growing village is a good base camp.

Mountaineers stay 5km southeast of town at the Alpine Club of Canada's **Canmore Clubhouse** (☎ 403-678-3200; www.alpineclubofcanada.ca; Indian Flats Rd; dm $19) just footsteps away from trailheads. Classes are offered, as is access to backcountry huts.

WATERTON LAKES NATIONAL PARK

When mountains and prairie collide in a lake basin at the southeasternmost edge of the Canadian Rockies, visitors to **Waterton Lakes National Park** (☎ 403-859-2224; adult/group $5/12.50) win. Despite being magnificently scenic,

stocked with wildlife and, combined with **Glacier National Park** (☎ 406-888-7800; www.nps.gov /glac) to make Waterton-Glacier International Peace Park (see p661), an international handshake between bitter rivals, Waterton is far less visited than Banff and Jasper.

The park is open year-round though most services in Waterton townsite, where bighorn sheep 'share' the roads, are only open during summer. **Waterton Visitor Centre** (☎ 403-859-5133; ☼ 8am-7pm mid May–mid-Sep) is across the road from the can't-miss Prince of Wales Hotel.

The park was designed for backpackers, and most trailheads are accessible from the townsite. Join rangers on the not-to-be-missed **International Peace Park Hike** (☼ 10am Sat Jun-Aug), an eight-hour guided hike (including lunch stop) from Waterton Village to Goat Haunt, MT. Solo hiking is possible, but it crosses the border so check about immigration requirements; non-North Americans may be denied. The 8.7km **Crypt Lake Trail** is a popular, challenging and exhilarating hike over a ladder, along a ledge and through a tunnel. The only way to the trailhead is with **Waterton Shoreline Cruises** (☎ 403-859-2362; round-trip $13; ☼ May-Aug)

The park has three vehicle-accessible, un-reservable **campgrounds** (campsite/RV/backcountry $17/30/8). Backcountry campsites are limited and must be reserved through the visitor center. If you need a bed before you tackle the wilderness, book one of the 21 solid bunks ASAP at spotless **HI-Waterton** (☎ 403-859-2151, 888-985-6343; www.hihostels.ca/Alberta; Cameron Falls Dr at Windflower Ave; dm/r $35/105; ☼ mid-May–Nov). Beer-slamming and dirty-dancing happen at **Thirsty Bear Saloon** (☎ 403-859-2111; Main St).

Hwy 6 crosses into Port of Chief Mountain, MT east of the park.

THE PRAIRIES

In the land of big skies and wild storms, resist the urge to say 'Are we there yet?' Instead, as you travel the Trans Canada or Yellowhead Hwys, appreciate the small agricultural towns and enjoy the larger metropolises. Watch for wagon-wheel ruts, plains dropping into badlands and signs of aboriginal culture and consider what takes hours today, took days (or weeks) only a century ago.

Saskatchewan Bus Company (STC; ☎ 800-663-7181; www.stcbus.com) takes over Greyhound's routes within Saskatchewan.

CALGARY

The Wild West meets the young and wild in this pimple on the prairie long written-off as 'Cow Town.' These days, university graduates are lured to the land of 10-gallon hats by high-tech jobs and the low cost of living. Things really come alive during the colossal Calgary Stampede.

Tourism Calgary (☎ 403-263-8510, 800-661-1678; www.visitor.calgary.ab.ca; 220 8th Ave SW; ☽ 8am-5pm) operates information centers on Stephen Ave Walk and the airport.

Sights & Activities

Eau Claire Market, north of downtown on Bow River, is people-watching, free-music and festival central.

The 1988 Winter Olympics grounds, **Canada Olympic Park** (☎ 403-247-5452; www.coda.ab.ca; 88 Canada Olympic Rd SW; admission $15; ☽ 8am-9pm Mon-Fri, 9am-5pm weekends), are east of town. The **bobsled** ($45) track, made famous by Jamaicans (see *Cool Runnings*), can be ridden. In summer the park becomes a lift-serviced **mountain biking** (daypass $14) park.

Calgary is known for its **zoo** (☎ 403-232-9300, 800-588-9993; www.calgaryzoo.ab.ca; 1300 Zoo Rd NE; admission $15; ☽ 9am-5pm), with more than 900 animals in simulated natural habitats.

Sleeping & Eating

HI-Calgary (☎ 403-269-8239; www.hihostels.ca/calgary; 520 7th Ave SE; dm $30) At the shady-looking but safe east side of downtown this huge, impeccable and modern place has a barbecue in the big backyard and Ms Pac-Man in the front lounge.

CALGARY GONE WILD (WEST)

Though the 10-day **Calgary Stampede** (☎ 403-261-0101, 800-661-1260; http//:calgarystampede.com; tickets from $24; ☽ mid-Jul) mostly takes place at Stampede Park in organized events like calf-roping, branding and bucking-bronco-riding, the entire city blows up in a gigantic party. The actual rodeo is a hoot and North America's biggest and roughest, but even if you can't get a ticket, you'll have a blast.

Alberta beef should be eaten in steak ($15 to $25) or beef dip ($5 to $7) form. The latter is thinly sliced roast beef served in a bun manually 'dipped' (by you) in its own juices. Wood and leather **Buzzard's Cookshack & Watering Hole** (☎ 403-264-6959; 140 10th Ave SW; mains $8-26) has 80 taps of beer and 'yeehaw' good meat. **Good Earth Coffeehouse & Bakery** (☎ 403-265-2636; 119 8th Ave SW; mains $6-10) spells I ♥ Alberta (roast) beef (sandwiches). A breakfast dynasty in Calgary, **Nellie's Break the Fast Café** (☎ 403-265-5071; 516 9th Ave SW; mains $6.50-9) or **Nellie's Kitchen** (☎ 403-244-4616; 738B 17th Ave SW; mains $5-9) have tasty pancakes. The silhouettes don't lie. **Burger Inn** (☎ 403-244-9293; 1711 4th St SW; burgers $2.50-6) does make burgers from ostrich, wild boar and other creatures.

Drinking

The entertainment rag is *ffwd*. Seventeenth Ave NW was dubbed 'The Red Mile' during the Flames Stanley Cup run as bars were full of red-T-shirt-wearing fans.

Melrose Cafe & Bar (☎ 403-228-3566; 730 17th Ave SW) Trendy spot with terraced patio.

Ship & Anchor (☎ 403-245-3333; 534 17th Ave SW) The patio, with trees, is full of beer-drinking, semi-grubby types.

Entertainment

Saddledome (Stampede Park) Technically the opposite of a 'dome,' and realistically a 'saddle,' it sold-out regularly before the **Calgary Flames** (☎ 403-777-0000; www.calgaryflames.com; ticket from $12) got hot in 2004.

McMahon Stadium (1817 Crowchild Trail NW) hosts CFL **Calgary Stampeders** (☎ 403-289-0258; www.calgarystampeders.com; ticket from $25).

Shopping

Alberta Boot Co (☎ 403-263-4605; www.albertaboot.com; 614 10th Ave SW) The real Western boot factory can be visited, and real Western boots (kangaroo, ostrich, python, rattlesnake, lizard, alligator or just cowhide) bought ($235 to $1700).

Getting There & Away

Calgary International Airport (code: YYC; ☎ 403-735-1372; www.calgaryairport.com) is 15km northeast of the center off Barlow Trail. Bus No 57 goes to the C-Train Whitehorn stop.

Greyhound Bus Station (☎ 403-265-9111; 850 16th St SW) has a free city shuttle to the C-Train 10th St SW stop.

BACKROADS ALBERTA

Bison & Dinosaurs

For a long and eventful day, roam the ranges for Alberta's unique sights.

Hwy 2 south from Calgary leads to signs for **Head-Smashed-In Buffalo Jump** (☎ 403-553-2731; www.head-smashed-in.com; Spring Point Rd/Secondary Hwy 785; interpretive center $6.50; 9am-6pm). Used by Blackfoot for millennia to stampede bison over the cliff for meat and supplies, the name comes from the legend of a young brave crushed while sneaking a closer look.

Hwy 3 east to Rte 36 north over Trans Canada to the 76½-million-year-old dinosaur graveyard, **Dinosaur Provincial Park** (☎ 403-378 4342; www3.gov.ab.ca/env/parks/prov_parks/dinosaur; off Hwy 544). More than 300 complete skeletons have been uncovered. **Royal Tyrrell Museum Field Station** (☎ 403-378-4342; $2.50; 8:30am-9pm daily, 9am-4pm Mon-Fri only early Sep–late May) has four behind glass and archaeologists on hand. Guided **tours** (☎ 403-378-4344; admission $8, reservations required; May-Oct) lead past interpretive trails into fossil-country. There is **camping** (☎ 403-378-3700; reservation $6, campsite $15).

Backtrack and go west on the Trans Canada Hwy then head north on Rte 56 through badlands to kitschy-but honest **Drumheller**, where (not real) dinosaurs sit on street corners. The **information center** (☎ 403-823-1331; 60 1st Ave W; 10am-6pm) has a huge **T-Rex** and maps (ask about **Hoodoo Drive** and **Dinosaur Trail**).

The outstanding **Royal Tyrrell Museum of Palaeontology** (☎ 403-823-7707, 888-440-4240; www.tyrrellmuseum.com; admission $8.50; 9am-9pm Tue-Sun, 10am-5pm Tue-Sun Sep–mid-May) has earth-explaining science and three-dozen dinosaur skeletons. Play pretend-paleontologist on **digs** ($85) and dig-site **hikes** ($12). Impressive **Horseshoe Canyon** is west on Hwy 9.

Rooms are tidy and standard at **Badlands Motel** (☎ 403-823-5155; fax 403-823-7653; 801 N Dinosaur Trail; winter/summer r $44/80). Attached **Whif's Flapjack House** (☎ 403-823-7595; breakfast $4-7) maybe has whifs, definitely has flapjacks. Side-trip to Wayne for beer at old-fashioned **Last Chance Saloon** (☎ 405-823-9189).

Hammerhead Tours (☎ 403 260-0940; www.hammerheadtours.com; $60; May-Nov) runs full-day tours from HI-Calgary to Drumheller or Head-Smashed-In.

EDMONTON

Edmonton became 'Oil Capital of Canada' in the 1970s, when the entire province boomed and shrugged off its cowboy image.

The North Saskatchewan River drifts through town, separating downtown (north) from Old Strathcona (south) with beautiful riverbanks in between (take the long staircases down to park trails). **Edmonton Tourism** (☎ 780-426-4715, 800-463-4667; www.edmonton.com; 9990 Jasper Ave; 8am-5pm) opened a new office in 2004.

Historic **Old Strathcona**, along 82nd (Whyte) Ave, has funky shops, bars, theaters and nightclubs and a young, edgy vibe.

The *Wild Alberta* display at the **Provincial Museum of Alberta** (☎ 780-453-9100; www.pma.edmonton.ab.ca; 12845 102nd Ave; admission $10, half-price to 11am weekends; 9am-5pm) is excellent and hands on.

West Edmonton Mall (☎ 780-444-5330, 800-661-8890; www.westedmontonmall.com; 170th St), clinging to 'World's Largest' title, is used more for amusement rides, fake beach and indoor attractions like **Fanstyland Hotel** (☎ 780-444-3000; www.fantasylandhotel.com; r from $120, free daily tours 2pm) – with themed-rooms from African to pickup trucks – than for actual shopping.

In memory of lies, deceit and false tales of a gold rush trail from Edmonton to Dawson City, **Klondike Days** (☎ 780-423-2822; www.klondikedays.com; late Jul) is Edmonton's biggest fest.

Institutional yet comfortable with lots of chesterfields and common space, **HI-Edmonton** (☎ 780-988-6836, 877-467-8336; www.hihostels.ca/edmonton; 10647 81st Ave; dm/d $23/45) is in Old Strathcona.

Silk Hat (☎ 780-425-1920; 10251 Jasper Ave; mains $6-10) is a charismatic diner since 1912 (has latest-edition *Star Wars* posters).

Iron Horse (☎ 780-438-3710; 8101 103rd St) was a cavernous 1907 train station, now cheap bar, in Old Strathcona.

Globe (☎ 780-426-7111; 10045 109th St) has half-priced (everything) Thursdays and more kinds of wings (32) than beer.

At the **Skyreach Centre** (7424 118th Ave NW), decades after Gretzky played here and the **Edmonton Oilers** (☎ 780-414-4625, 866-414-4625; www.edmontonoilers.com; ticket from $24) were winning Stanley Cups, the team is still fast and fun to watch.

Among the ranks of possibly-un-PC teams, the **Edmonton Eskimos** (☎ 780-448-3757, 800-667-3757; www.esks.com; ticket from $23) have CFL-fan support around the country and play at **Commonwealth Stadium** (11000 Stadium Rd).

Edmonton International Airport (code: YEG; ☎ 780-890-8382) is 30km south of downtown. **Sky Shuttle Airport Service** (☎ 780-465-8515, 888-438-2342; $11) runs shuttles.

Greyhound stops downtown. **VIA Rail station** (☎ 780-448-2575; 12360 121 St) is north, 4km down Kingsway to 109th St for downtown.

MOOSE JAW

Really, it has nothing to do with the Jaw of a Moose. English translation of the Cree word 'moosegaw' ('warm breezes') put this nondescript, but surprising, town on the map, acting as a whiskey-smuggling hangout for Al Capone during US prohibition made it famous.

Take the exit off Hwy 1 and follow Main St south past the chain restaurants and hotels into downtown boomtown. Used as 'Little Chicago' during the 1920s and 30s, Al Capone really (no, really) did live here part-time and walked the streets of the town – for all intents and purposes – he owned. Under those same streets, **Tunnels of Moose Jaw** (☎ 306-693-5261; 108 Main St; 1/both tours $12/19; ☺ 10am-7pm Mon-Thu & 10am-9pm Fri-Sun summer, varies seasonally) gives hour-long reinacted tours of hidden history. With a backdrop of hookers and booze, 'Chicago Connection' puts you in bootleggers' shoes and leads through old time saloons and hideouts for Capone and his tommy-gun toting goons. Also a part of Moose Jaw's history is that of Chinese immigrants who literally lived underground in order to stay in Canada; 'Passage to Fortune' tells their heart-wrenching tales. If you're hungry, swing by (try and avoid lunch hour) **Burger Palace** (☎ 306-693-5353; 80 1st Ave; burgers & fries $4-8) for better-than-average grub.

Greyhound and STC stop here.

REGINA

Saskatchewan's commercial and political capital, Regina (yes it rhymes with vagina,

but the original name was 'Pile of Bones') has pretty **Wascana Park**, and the **Royal Saskatchewan Museum** (☎ 306-787-2815; www.royalsaskmuseum.ca; 2445 Albert St; donation $2; ☺ 9am-5:30pm), with its mind-altering look at Saskatchewan's geologic past.

The white Victorian **Turgeon Hostel** (☎ 306-791-8165; hihostels.sask@sk.sympatico.ca; 2310 McIntyre St; dm/d $24/52) has balconies everywhere, and spacious rooms.

The fun Old Warehouse District, north of downtown, includes **New Yorx** (☎ 306-356-7771; 2300 Dewdney Ave) for lunch, dancing or the 3-D model of Manhattan behind the bar.

Regina International Airport (code YQR; ☎ 306-761-7555; 5200 Regina Ave) is located 5km from downtown.

Greyhound and STC stop here.

SASKATOON

The prettiest city on the Prairies is a jolly good enough reason to take the northern route (Yellowhead or Hwy 9) through Saskatchewan.

The **Meewasin Valley Trail** lines both sides of the South Saskatchewan River; south bank's **Rotary Park** is the best for city views. On the downtown side, **Mendel Art Gallery & Conservatory** (☎ 306-975-7610; 950 Spadina Cres E; free; ☺ 9am-9pm) has local art.

From the southern end of Broadway Bridge (known as **Five Corners**) the town's oldest district runs south to Main St. **Broadway Café** (☎ 306-652-8244; 818 Broadway Ave; breakfast $5-7) is 'the' diner, always packed for breakfast. Fire Hall No 5, *sans* fire engine, is now **Hose Brew Pub** (☎ 306-477-3473; 612 11th St E).

The cheapest sleeps are on the outskirts along Circle Dr. Downtown. **Hotel Senator** (☎ 306-244-6141; www.hotelsenator.ca; 243 21st St E; s/d/ste $65/80/100) has Winston's pub and **Patricia Hotel** (☎ 306-242-8861; 345 2nd Ave N; r $40) has bed-sized rooms and 'The Pat' nightclub.

Mr Hockey's **Gordon Howe Campground** (☎ 306-975-3328, Ave P south of 11th St; campsites $16; ☺ mid-May–Oct) is west of downtown.

Diefenbaker International Airport (code YXE; ☎ 306-975-8900; 2625 Airport Dr) is 8km northeast of the city.

Greyhound and STC stop here. So does VIA Rail, but trains arrive between 1am and 3am, 8km from downtown. Make accommodation arrangements before you arrive and friends on the train to share an $18 **Blueline Taxi** (☎ 306-653-3333).

IF YOU REALLY WANT TO BLOW THE BUDGET

Churchill – The chance to be inches from a polar bear (September to November) or shoreline spectator to beluga whales (June to August) won't come cheap (budget $1000 to $2000), but it will be the trip of a lifetime. The train (the only way there besides a plane) leaves from Winnipeg, but try to get to Thompson if you can (to save money and time). HI in Winnipeg offers packages.

WINNIPEG

Of Manitoba's funny-named places, Winnipeg is a crop of prairie cosmopolitan compared to Chicago's Midwest culture, but is very much its own mid-Canadian scene.

The **Forks** is the 6000-year-old meeting place, with markets, history and parks. Across the river is the very French neighborhood of **St Boniface**, birthplace and resting place of Canada's last publicly tried and executed traitor, Louis Riel. **Downtown** is good for walking (Randy Bachman and Neil Young wrote a song about *Portage & Main*, nationally famous for frigid winds and temperatures). The **Exchange District** to the north is good for commercial history, and partying.

Two blocks from each other west of downtown, **Guest House International Hostel** (☎ 204-772-1772, 800-743-4423; www.backpackers winnipeg.com; 168 Maryland St; s/d $22/42; ✆ Jun-Oct) is lived in and cluttered but is well kept, and **HI-Ivey House Hostel** (☎ 204-772-3022, 866-762-4122; 210 Maryland St; s/d $24/42) is a super friendly, creaky, old turreted house.

Close to the hostels, **Bistro Dansk** (☎ 204-775-5662; 63 Sherbrooke St; soups $4-6; ✆ Tue-Sat) is a delicious locally-owned Danish café. Downtown, **Wagon Wheel** (☎ 204-942-6695; 305 Hargrove St; mains $5-9) is a hole-in-the-wall famous for clubhouse sandwiches.

Dance at **Coyote Cafe** (☎ 204-957-7665; 171 McDermont St) and lounge at **Phat Daddy's** (☎ 204-284-7428; 165 McDermont St).

Honestly, all kidding aside, Winnipeg has an international reputation for **Royal Winnipeg Ballet** (☎ 204-956-2792, 800-667-4792; www.rwb.org; cnr Graham Ave & Edmonton St; admission $12-35) performances, which are cheap and unfussy.

The **MTS Centre** (cnr Portage Ave & Donald St) is where the **Manitoba Moose** (☎ 204-780-7328; www.moosehockey.com; ticket $15-30), a minor-league team for the NHL's Vancouver Canucks, are a hot (cool) ticket.

At **CanadInns Stadium** (1430 Maroons Rd) the **Winnipeg Blue Bombers** (☎ 204-784-2583; www .bluebombers.com; ticket $12-45) play CFL games.

The basement of the **Bay** (☎ 204-783-2112; cnr Portage Ave & Memorial Blvd) has fur-trade-era style and blankets.

WestJet and JetsGo flights from **Winnipeg International Airport** (code YWG; 2000 Wellington Ave) can be extremely cheap to/from Toronto. Take bus No 15 from downtown to the airport ($1.80).

Greyhound and VIA Rail stop here.

ALASKA

Alaska

HIGHLIGHTS

- **Kenai Fjords National Park** Ogle awesome glaciers, watch whales and wilderness kayak (p678)
- **Homer** Bohemian enclave with beach-side camping in stunning Kachemak Bay (p678)
- **Denali National Park** Admire 37 species of mammals and one big-ass mountain in this immense subarctic wilderness (p679)
- **Off the beaten track** Alaska Marine Highway from Kodiak to Dutch Harbor in the Aleutian Islands
- **Best journey** Cruising the Inside Passage fjords past islands, glaciers and isolated outposts (p680)

FAST FACTS

- **Area** 586,412 sq mi (20% of the entire USA)
- **Big cities** Anchorage (population 261,000), Fairbanks (85,000), Juneau (31,000)
- **Budget** $35-100 per day
- **Costs** campsites free-$25, salmon bake $15-20, subcompact rental car $30-45 per day
- **Famous for** Northern lights, biting insects, Eskimos, grizzly bears
- **Languages** English, Inupiaq, 19 other native languages
- **Population** 635,000
- **Phrases** *breakup* (winter's end), *the Bush* (anyplace not accessible by road or ferry), *cheechako* (greenhorn or tenderfoot, Alaska newcomer), *Outside* (anywhere but Alaska), *sourdough* (anyone who's survived a winter)
- **Seasons** thawed (Jun–Aug), shoulder (May & Sep), frozen (Oct–Apr), rainy (year-round)

- **Tasty treats** Eskimo ice cream, barbecue seafood, wild berries, stinkhead (fermented salmon)
- **Time** Alaska Time; GMT minus 9 hours; 24 hours of daylight mid-summer
- **Top hostel** Denali Mountain Morning, Denali National Park (p679)

TRAVEL HINTS

Prices increase as you head north. Allow at least three weeks if visiting the Southeast, a month if heading farther north, two months if driving from the Lower 48. Save on expenses and make long-term travel pals on the Green Tortoise (p698).

It isn't just the fantastic wildlands that draw travelers to Alaska, but the magic in the land. No region in North America possesses a more mystical pull. The lure inherent in its moniker as the Final Frontier is as strong today as it was a century ago, when get-rich-quick adventure sparked the first invasion of miners. Today they have been replaced by wayfaring backpackers, but the spirit of exploration remains.

Drawn to the North Country by its colorful reputation, cheechakos (newcomers) are stunned by the state's grandeur. Sure, there are mountains, glaciers and rivers elsewhere in North America, but few match the scale as those here. Spying a brown bear rambling up a mountainside or watching a glacier calve from a kayak are experiences that can permanently alter your reality.

Alaska is a major – and expensive – detour but the juice is worth the squeeze. If you're going to make the trek, allow at least three weeks. Hop on a ferry from Bellingham and cruise the Inside Passage, take in the Kenai Peninsula, then head north to Denali and Mt McKinley. Once here, many find it difficult to leave.

HISTORY

Indigenous Alaskans' ancestors migrated across the Bering Strait 35,000 years ago. In the 18th century Europeans, whalers and fur traders descended upon the area, introducing guns, alcohol and diseases. In 1867, the USA purchased the territory from Russia for less than 2¢ an acre. After Japan attacked Alaskan islands in WWII, the military built the Alcan (Alaska–Canada) Hwy, which proceeded statehood in 1959.

A 1964 earthquake left Alaska in shambles, but recovery was sparked by the discovery of oil at Prudhoe Bay and the subsequent construction of the 789-mile Trans-Alaska Pipeline to Valdez. The party ended in 1986 when oil prices plummeted, then the hangover came in 1989 when the *Exxon Valdez* fuel tanker spilled 11 million gallons of crude into Prince William Sound.

Alaska is now considering implementing state sales and income taxes, and recent years have seen fees at parks rise sharply. One proposal for economic revival is the opening of the Arctic National Wildlife Refuge (ANWR) to oil production. Environmentalists fought to protect the 1.5 million-acre Coastal Plain – 8% of ANWR – and got a scare in 2003 when the Senate rejected a pro-drilling proposal by George Bush II by a single vote. Although Republicans have promised to revisit the issue, the Plain remains in limbo.

THE CULTURE

Alaska is the USA's largest and most sparsely populated state in the union. This situation, coupled with a large influx of seasonal workers, dovetails to create a unique cultural landscape. The male-dominated singles' scene is summed up by eligible females as 'the odds are good, but the goods are odd.'

An estimated 30% of the state's residents are native-born. Of the rest, 25% have moved here within the past five years. The typical resident is young, say 27, mobile and often from the US West Coast. Inupiaqs and other indigenous groups make up around 15% of the population.

Despite modernization, indigenous peoples retain some of their culture, languages and traditional ceremonies like the potlatch.

The peak tourist season is early July to mid-August, when the best-known parks are packed and it's essential to make reservations for ferries and accommodations. May and September have mild weather, less crowds and lower prices.

THE BIG ISSUE: ANWR – TO DRILL OR NOT?

Oil companies and Alaskan politicians are pushing hard to open the 1.5-million-acre Arctic National Wildlife Refuge (ANWR), one of the USA's last great wilderness areas, to oil and gas drilling. Former President Bill Clinton stifled efforts to open ANWR to pipelines, but many Alaskans believe it's only a matter of time before the inevitable happens in a state where 80% of the revenue comes from resource extraction. Environmentalists say that what ultimately happens depends on who ends up in the White House in 2005. The issue is only the tip of a much larger iceberg surrounding the consequences of increased US dependence on foreign oil sources.

ALASKA

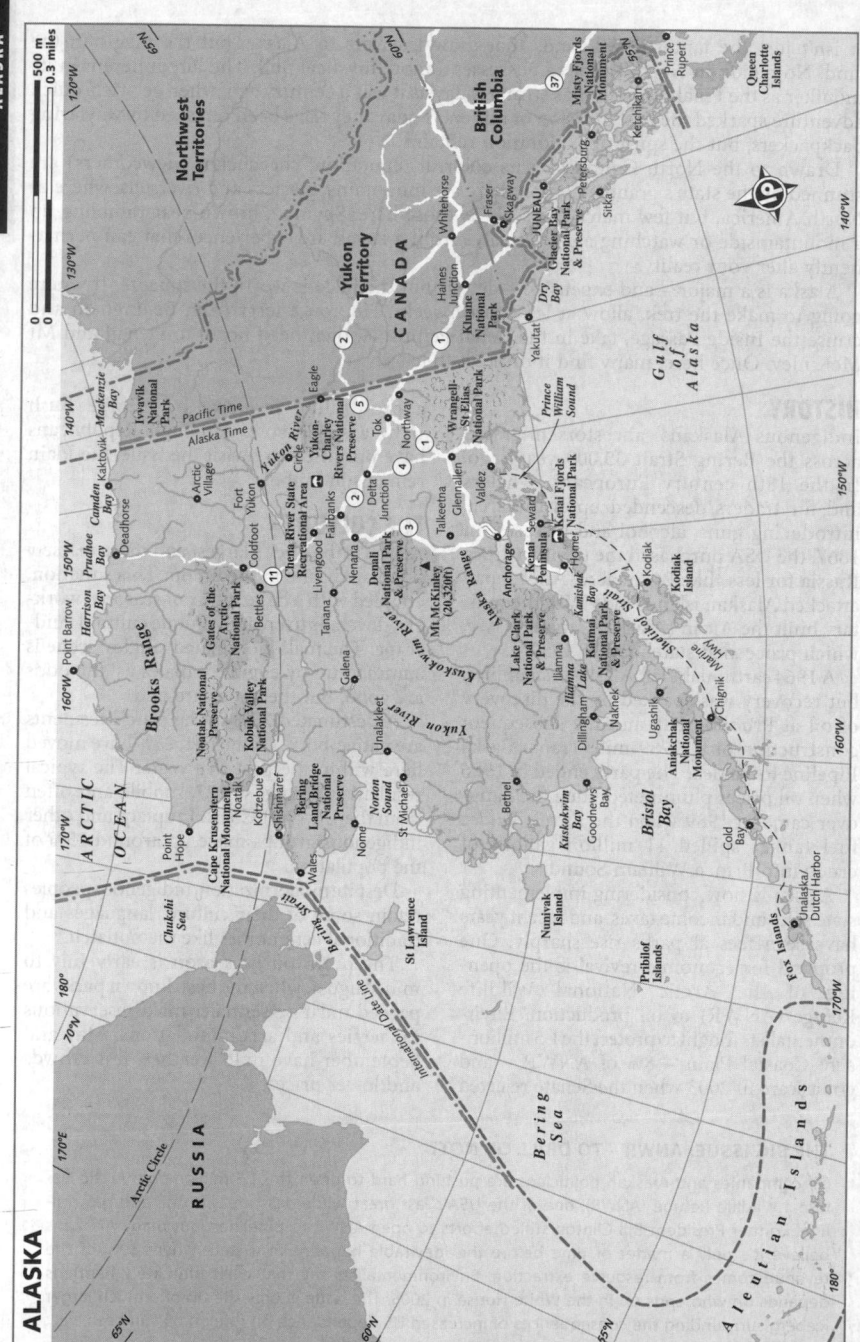

ENVIRONMENT

At latitudes spanning the Arctic Circle, Alaska's main body is about 800 sq miles, with the Aleutian Island chain stretching some 1600 miles south and west, and a 'panhandle' stretching 600 miles southeast down the North American coast.

Alaska's flora is diverse. The coastal regions have lush coniferous forests, while the Interior is dominated by boreal forest. Further north is a taiga zone – a moist subarctic forest characterized by muskeg, willow thickets and stunted spruce – then the treeless Arctic tundra.

Alaska has an extremely variable climate and famously unpredictable weather. The Interior can top 90°F during the summer. For the most part, a good summer week will include three sunny days (with average temperatures of 55°F to 70°F), two overcast ones and two when you need to pull your rain gear out or duck for cover. In winter expect long nights, minus 50°F temperatures and the fantastic northern lights.

Alaska is notorious for its biting insects. In town you'll have few problems, but expect a variety of flying pests in the backcountry. The most effective protection is an insect repellant containing a high percentage of Deet (diethyltoluamide). Unfortunately, repellants are more effective against mosquitoes than black flies and more annoying 'no-see-ums.' Foil them by wearing light colors, tucking in your pant legs and wearing a snug hat.

A great variety of wildlife can easily be seen, notably moose, deer and bears. Harder to spot are the large herds of caribou that inhabit the Interior; mountain goats and Dall sheep; and reclusive wolves. Marine life includes seals, porpoises, whales, sea otters and walruses. During summer, millions of spawning salmon imbue rivers and streams.

Encountering a bear is often a highlight of a trip to Alaska, but heed commonsense rules so you don't attract unwanted ursine attention: sing or clap when traveling through thick bush; hang your food at least 10ft off the ground; and, whatever you do, don't take any food (or toothpaste, lotions or anything odoriferous) into your tent. That said, don't let paranoia keep you out of the wilds – bears rarely attack unless they feel trapped, are enticed by food, or if their cubs are threatened.

National & State Parks

Alaska's main draw card is its 54 million acres of national parks, preserves and monuments. State parks account for another three million acres. Chugach State Park near Anchorage and Chena River State Recreational Area both possess the wow factor of the more well-known national parks, with a fraction of the crowds. The best one-stop shops for outdoor recreation information are all in Anchorage (see p677).

TRANSPORTATION

The **Alaskan Center** (www.alaskan.com) has tourist information as well as bus, ferry, air and train schedules. Other useful sites include **Alaska One** (www.alaskaone.com) and **Alaska Guidebook** (www.alaskaguidebook.com).

ALASKA

The **Alaska Travel Industry Association** (www .travelalaska.com) distributes a free *Vacation Planner*, maps, ferry and railroad schedules. The **Alaska Department of Transportation** (☎ 511 within AK, 866-282-7577 in USA; www.511.alaska.gov) delivers real-time road updates.

If you're planning on covering lots of ground in a short spell, consider an **AlaskaPass** (☎ 800-248-7598, 206-463-6550; www.alaskapass.com; passes $649-1049), which allows for unlimited travel on the Alaska Marine Highway, Holland America Motorcoach tours and the Alaska Railroad and limited White Pass & Yukon Railroad services.

Alaska Airlines (☎ 800-252-7522; www.alaskaair .com) is the major carrier. Regional airlines serve small towns, and chartered bush planes serve remote areas.

The **Alaska Marine Highway System** (☎ 800-642-0066; www.ferryalaska.com) links major ports. See the Cruising the Inside Passage boxed text (p680) for details. The **Inter-Island Ferry Service** (☎ 907-826-4848, 866-308-4848; www .interislandferry.com) covers Southeastern routes. To experience untouristed Alaska, you can try disembarking at any of the secondary ports.

Regular bus services link Alaska's main towns, with connections to Canada and the Lower 48. Busing it isn't cheaper than flying, but you do get to experience the epic Alaska Hwy. From Seattle, **Greyhound** (☎ 206-628-5526, 800-229-9424; www.greyhound.com; 811 Stewart St, Seattle) trundles the 1768 miles to Whitehorse, Canada (via Vancouver; from $169) in three and a half l-o-o-o-ng days. From Whitehorse, **Alaska Direct** (☎ 403-668-4833, 800-770-6652; www.tokalaska.com/dirctbus.shtml) heads to Anchorage ($165, 15½ hours). Green Tortoise (see p698) runs good-value trips from San Francisco via Seattle over two-weeks ($790 plus return airfare) or one-month ($1990 including airfare).

If driving, allow at least a week to motor from the Pacific Northwest through Canada to Fairbanks on the paved Alcan Hwy (Hwy 2). It's not worth the long haul unless you spend a few weeks in Alaska. Rental cars – from $35 a day with 100 miles free or $50 with unlimited miles – are the best way to explore the countryside; book ahead in summer.

The **Alaska Railroad** (☎ 907-265-2494, 800-544-0552; www.akrr.com) has one scenic passenger route, from Seward on the Gulf of Alaska to Anchorage, and north from there via Denali to Fairbanks. Reserve ahead and check online for web-only deals.

ANCHORAGE & AROUND

ANCHORAGE

Within 30 minutes' drive of the Alaskan wilderness, Anchorage has the comforts of a major US city. Founded in 1914 as an Alaska Railroad work camp, the city was devastated by a 1964 earthquake. Boomtime oil money has paid for the glut of modern amenities.

Information

BOOKSTORES

Cook Inlet Book Company (☎ 907-258-4544; 415 W 5th Ave) Downtown indie shop with one of state's best selections of Alaska-related titles.

REI (☎ 907-272-4565; 1200 W Northern Lights Blvd) Guidebooks and a huge selection of backpacking and kayaking gear.

Title Wave Books (☎ 907-277-5127; 1360 W Northern Lights Blvd) Huge and well-organized, both new and used titles.

EMERGENCY

Anchorage Police (☎ 907-786-8500; 4501 S Bragaw St)

INTERNET ACCESS

ZJ Loussac Public Library (3600 Denali St; free; ✆ 10am-8pm Mon-Thu, 10am-6pm Fri & Sat)

MEDICAL SERVICES

Alaska Regional Hospital (☎ 907-276-1131; 2801 DeBarr Rd) Emergency care.

MONEY

Wells Fargo (301 W Northern Lights Blvd; ✆ 7am-6pm Mon-Fri, closes 4pm Sat) Exchanges many foreign currencies.

POST
Post office (344 W 3rd Ave) Downtown in Ship Creek Center.

TOURIST OFFICES
Alaska Public Lands Information Center (☎ 907-271-2737; www.nps.gov/aplic; 605 W 4th Ave; ☼ 9am-6pm summer, 10am-5:30pm Mon-Fri winter) Park, trail and cabin details.

Division of Parks & Outdoor Recreation (☎ 907-269-8400; www.dnr.state.ak.us/parks; 550 W 7th Ave) Useful visitors center.

Log Cabin Visitors Center (☎ 907-274-3531, recorded info ☎ 907-276-3200; www.anchorage.net; cnr 4th Ave & F St; ☼ 7:30am-7pm)

NPS Alaska Regional Office (☎ 907-644-3501; www.nps.gov/akso; 240 W 5th Ave)

Sights & Activities
The impressive **Anchorage Museum of History & Art** (☎ 907-343-4326; 121 W 7th Ave; admission $7) celebrates Alaskan history and indigenous culture, while the free **Heritage Library Museum** (☎ 907-265-2834; 301 W Northern Lights Blvd, admission free) displays Native Alaskan costumes, weapons and artwork. The **Saturday Market** (☎ 907-272-5634; W 3rd Ave & E St; ☼ 10am-6pm Sat) is a fantastic place for cheap eats and souvenir shopping.

The best of the beautiful city parks include Earthquake Park, Russian Jack Springs Park (the Municipal Greenhouse) and the 4000-acre Far North Bi-Centennial Park, where the Hilltop Ski Area morphs into a summertime mountain biking oasis.

Sleeping
Spenard Hostel (☎ 907-248-5036; www.alaskahostel .org; 2845 W 42nd Pl; tent & dm $18-19, r $72-76; ☐) A friendly, well-equipped, community-oriented hangout with weekly potluck dinners.

Anchorage Guest House (☎ 907-274-0408; www .akhouse.com; 2001 Hillcrest Dr; dm $25-28, r $68-78; ☐) More like a B&B than a hostel. You can rent a bike or chill in the immaculate common areas.

HI-AYH Anchorage International Hostel (☎ 907-276-3635; www.anchorageinternationalhostel.org; 700 H St; dm $20) A convenient downtown option with a festive atmosphere, but the quarters tend toward less-than-salubrious.

Brown Bear Motel (☎ 907-653-7000; Mile 103 Seward Hwy; r from $49) Well south of town, the rooms are clean, but get noisy when the adjacent Brown Bear Saloon is hopping.

The city-run **Centennial Park Campground** (campsites $15) is 4.5 miles from downtown on Glenn Hwy via bus Nos 3, 4 and 75. **Lion's Camper Park** (campsites $15) is in Russian Jack Springs Park.

Eating
Snow City Café (☎ 907-272-2489; 1034 W 4th Ave; mains $4-9) The crowd is often tattooed and the grub slightly trendy. Hangout over late breakfast and mondo mugs of joe.

Cyrano's Books & Café (☎ 907-274-2591; 413 D St; mains $4-8) Lose yourself in a paperback over tempting French and Mediterranean sweets, soups, salads and wraps. Come back in the evening for eclectic entertainment.

Sweet Basil Café (☎ 907-274-0070; 335 E St; mains $3-10) Most everything is healthy, except the coffee and desserts, at this centrally-located oasis.

Twin Dragon (☎ 907-276-7535; 612 E 15th Ave; buffet lunch/dinner $8/12) The unlimited Mongolian BBQ is a bargain, and the a la carte Chinese food ain't bad, either.

Fred Meyer Supermarket (1000 E Northern Lights Blvd) Widest selection, best prices.

Drinking
Raven (☎ 907-276-9672; 708 E 4th Ave) Jumpstart your evening with some pool at this well-lit, smoky, queer-friendly haunt.

Cheechako Bar (☎ 907-274-6132; 317 W Fireweed Lane) A queer-friendly, Irish-themed pub with pool tables and the occasional jam session.

Mad Myrna's (☎ 907-276-9762; 530 E 5th Ave; weekend cover $3) Cruisy non-smoking bar with dancing, drag shows and danceable music.

Humpy's (☎ 907-276-2337; 610 W 6th Ave) Live music nightly – from acoustic folk to ska to disco – plus 40 draft beers.

Getting There & Around
Anchorage International Airport (ANC; ☎ 907-266-2526) has frequent inter- and intrastate flights. **Alaska Airlines** flies to all major Alaskan towns. **Era Aviation** (☎ 800-866-8394; www.flyera .com) serves nearby towns. **Pen Air** (☎ 800-448-4226) circles around the Southwest.

Downtown Connection (☎ 907-344-6667) shuttles to the train station ($3) and the airport ($6).

Parks Hwy Express (☎ 888-600-6001) goes to Fairbanks via Denali, Tok, Valdez and Dawson City, Canada. **Seward Bus Lines**

(☎ 907-563-0800; www.sewardbuslines.com) goes to Seward. **Homer Stage Lines** (☎ 907-868-3914; 3335 Fairbanks St) serves Homer.

KENAI PENINSULA

When red salmon run in the summer, Kenai gets incredibly crowded. Escape the wading throngs by exploring the seemingly endless backcountry.

Seward & Kenai Fjords National Park

This scenic town is flanked by rugged mountains and overlooks salmon-filled Resurrection Bay. The downtown **visitors center** (www.seward.net/chamber; Jefferson St & 3rd Ave) is in a Pullman railroad car. There's also a **USFS office** (☎ 907-224-3374; 4th Ave & Jefferson St). The **Kenai Fjords National Park Visitors Center** (☎ 907-224-3175; 1212 4th Ave) has tips on hiking and paddling.

SIGHTS & ACTIVITIES

Alaska SeaLife Center (☎ 907-224-3080, 800-224-2525; 301 Railway Ave; adult $13; ⌚ 8am-8pm) is the western hemisphere's only cold-water marine-science facility. Plan to spend the better part of one of your best afternoons here watching puffins, otters and 1000-pound Stellar sea lions glide past viewing windows.

The **Mt Marathon Trail** is a killer 3-mile round- Ztrip to spectacular views overlooking Seward. Rent boats at **Kayak Adventures** (☎ 907-224-3960, 800-288-3134; 328 3rd Ave).

South of town, the main features of **Kenai Fjords National Park** are the 917-sq-mile **Harding Icefield** and the calving tidewater glaciers like **Exit Glacier**. A 0.25-mile trail goes to a glacier overlook and hikers can gumshoe a worthwhile 5 miles to the edge of the ice field for breathtaking views.

The state's best marine-wildlife cruises are the splurge-worthy, ranger-narrated viewing tours that sail into the fjords. **Major Marine Tours** (☎ 907-274-7300, 800-764-7300; www.alaskaone.com/mmt) offers half-day and full-day options (from $69).

SLEEPING

Moby Dick Hostel (☎ 907-224-7072; www.mobydickhostel.com; 432 3rd Ave; dm $17, r $45-60) It's friendly, well located and clean (enough) for budget-savvy travelers.

Snow River Hostel (☎ 907-440-1907; Mile 16 Seward Hwy; dm/d $15/40) This hostel is out of town but recommended for its sauna and wood-fired stove.

Waterfront Campground (Ballaine Blvd; campsites $8) Between downtown and the boat harbor.

EATING & DRINKING

Terry's Fish & Chips (☎ 907-224-8807; 1210 4th Ave; mains $3-9; ⌚ 24hr) Get your snack on at the harbor's best cheapie fish stand.

Sue's Teriyaki (☎ 907-224-4593; 303 S Harbor St; mains $6-13) Might not look like much, but the kim chee is phat and the sushi's even better.

Tony's (135 4th Ave) and the **Yukon Bar** (☎ 4th Ave & Washington St) have live music.

GETTING THERE & AWAY

Ferries (☎ 907-224-5485) sail every few days. **Seward Bus Lines** (☎ 907-224-3608) goes daily to Anchorage, and the Alaska Railroad choo-choos daily to Anchorage via a spectacular route.

Homer

At the end of Sterling Hwy, colorful Homer sits on beautiful Kachemak Bay amid awe-inspiring mountains. Alternative types got hip to the place in the Flower Power days and artists have followed. The **visitors center** (☎ 907-235-7740; www.homeralaska.org; 135 Sterling Hwy) has courtesy phones to book rooms and the **library** (141 W Pioneer Ave) has Internet access.

SIGHTS & ACTIVITIES

The slick **Pratt Museum** (☎ 907-235-8635; 3779 Bartlett St; admission $6) has a good display on the *Exxon Valdez* oil spill.

Homer Spit has **clamming** and beach **camping**. The best **hiking** is found along the beaches and across the bay at **Kachemak Bay State Park**.

SLEEPING

Seaside Farms (☎ 907-235-7850; seaside@xyz.net; 40904 Seaside Farms Rd; dm $15, r $40-50, cabins $55) Five miles east of E End Rd, this hostel is more Burning Man than regulation HI. Work in exchange for a place to stay, crash on hay bales in the barn, whatever, it's all negotiable.

Driftwood Inn (☎ 907-235-8019, 800-478-8019; 435 W Bunnell Ave; campsites $15, s $55-100, d $65-130) Fall asleep to the sound of the waves in the quiet campground or inside the tiny 'ship quarters.'

There's (often rowdy) beach camping at **Homer Spit Public Campground** (Homer Spit Rd;

campsites $6). **Karen Hornaday Memorial Campground** (Bartlett St; campsites $6) is a better bet for light sleepers.

EATING & DRINKING

Two Sisters Bakery (☎ 907-235-2280; 106 W Bunnell Ave; mains $4-9) The best of Homer's many excellent coffee houses.

Smoky Bay Natural Foods (☎ 907-235-7252; 248 W Pioneer Ave) Co-op with organic veggies, groceries, herbs, a big bulk-foods selection and a deli.

Glacier Drive-In (☎ 907-235-7148; Homer Spit Rd; mains $2-9) is one of the better cheap eateries, while nearby is the iconic **Salty Dawg Saloon** (Homer Spit Rd).

GETTING THERE & AWAY

Era Aviation swoops in frequently from Anchorage. The **MV Tustumena** (☎ 907-235-8449) sails twice weekly to Seldovia and Kodiak. **Kachemak Bay Transit** (☎ 877-235-9101) and **Homer Stage Lines** (☎ 907-235-2252) both bus it to Anchorage.

DENALI & AROUND

DENALI NATIONAL PARK

A single road lined with campsites, trailheads, wildlife and stunning panoramas curves 91 miles through the heart of this breathtaking wilderness area. This road can be used only by official shuttle buses, which have limited seating. Numbers in the campsites and wilderness zones are also strictly limited. This means great mecca-like crowds at the entrance, but relative solitude once you're inside.

Spotting wildlife is as easy as falling off a chair. Caribou, wolves and brown bears are crowd favorites. The main attraction, however, is the magnificent Mt McKinley (20,320ft), North America's highest peak, which clouds will obscure more often than not; you'll need to be prepared to wait for the amazing view.

Information

The park entrance is at Mile 237.3 George 'Parks' Hwy. Park entry (per person/family $5/10) is good for a week. The highway north and south of the park entrance is a touristy strip of private campgrounds, lodges and restaurants.

Denali National Park Reservation Service (☎ 907-272-7275, 800-622-7275; www.reservedenali .com) If possible, plan the exact days you will be in the park, and reserve bus seats and campsites through this organization.

Mountaineering Ranger Station (☎ 907-733-2231; cnr 1st & B Sts; ☒ 9am-6pm) Handles expeditions to Mt McKinley and has details about scenic view flights (from $125).

Talkeetna-Denali Visitors Center (☎ 907-733-2688, 800-660-2688; Parks Hwy & Talkeetna Spur Rd; ☒ 7am-8pm) In town, this place is super-helpful.

Visitor Access Center (VAC; ☎ 907-683-2294; www .nps.gov/dena; ☒ 7am-8pm) The place to organize your trip.

Sights & Activities

For permit-free day hiking, get off the shuttle bus at any valley, riverbed or ridge that takes your fancy. For a guided walk, book ahead at the VAC. For backcountry camping, get a permit from the VAC one day in advance. The park is divided into 43 zones, each with a regulated number of visitors. Watch the Backcountry Simulator Program video and check the quota board for an area you can access. Then go to the counter to book a camper shuttle bus and buy maps.

Cycling is permitted only on roads. Most cyclists book campsites then carry their bikes on the camper shuttle. Rent mountain bikes from **Denali Outdoor Center** (☎ 907-638-1925, 888-303-1925; www.denalioutdoorcenter.com; Mile 238.5 Parks Hwy) for $35 to $40 per day.

Several whitewater rafting companies offer daily floats on the Nenana River. **Denali Raft Adventures** (☎ 907-683-2234, 888 683-2234; www.denaliraft.com; Mile 238 Parks Hwy) offers a two-hour canyon run ($68) and a four-hour Class IV paddle raft trip ($95).

Sleeping

Denali Mountain Morning Hostel (☎ 907-683-7503; www.hostelalaska.com; Mile 224.5 Parks Hwy; dm/r $25/65, cabins $75-130; ☐) This recommended, rustic place has free park shuttles and is a good spot to stash your gear (or rent some). Book ahead!

Carlo Creek Lodge (☎ 907-683-2576; www.alaska one.com/carlocreek; Mile 224 Parks Hwy; tent/cabins from $16/77) Twelve miles south of the park entrance, with hot showers and a variety of creek-side accommodations.

Talkeetna Hostel International (☎ 907-733-4678; www.talkeetnahostel.com; I St; dm/s/d $25/50/60; ☐) Is a wonderful hostel only a 10-minute stroll from Main St.

Most campsites ($9 to $18) are spaced along the park road and can be reserved for a $4 fee. It can be tough to score a campground, so take anything available and change campgrounds later. The nicest in-park option is **Wonder Lake** (Mile 85 Park Rd; campsites $16), with 26 spots looking onto Mt McKinley. Tent-only **Sanctuary River** (Mile 23 Park Rd; campsites $9) is a great day-hike area. At the park entrance, year-round **Riley Creek** (campsites $12) gets overrun by RVs, but tenters rarely feel overwhelmed.

Denali Grizzly Bear Campground (☎ 907-683-2696, 866-583-2696; www.alaskaone.com/dengrzly; Mile 231 Parks Hwy; campsites $19, tent cabins $26-30, cabins $49-79) has a hot shower and laundry services.

Eating

The only food inside the park entrance area is at **McKinley Mercantile**, which sells fresh, dried and canned food. As ever, it's best to stock up on supplies when you are well outside the park.

Getting There & Around

Parks Hwy Express (☎ 888-600-6001) dashes to Anchorage and Fairbanks. The Alaska Railroad makes a scenic daily run between Fairbanks and Anchorage. **Talkeetna Shuttle Service** (☎ 907-733-1725, 888-288-6008) hustles between Anchorage and Talkeetna.

Within the park, shuttle buses provide access for day hiking and sightseeing, and can be reserved from late February for that summer. In the backcountry you can get on or off buses at any point along their routes. Buses leave the VAC regularly for Eielson Visitors Center and Wonder Lake. Camper shuttles, with room for backpacks and bikes, charge $23 to anywhere along the road.

SOUTHEASTERN ALASKA

KETCHIKAN

This character-filled town is the ferry's first northbound Alaskan stop. The **visitors center** (☎ 907-225-6166, 800-770-3300; www.visit-ketchikan.com; 131 Front St) has a walking-tour map. For details of trails, cabins, outdoor activities and trip planning assistance, visit the **Southeast Alaska Discovery Center** (☎ 907-228-6220; www.fs.fed.us/r10/tongass; 50 Main St).

HI-AYH Ketchikan Hostel (☎ 907-225-3319; ktnyh@eagle.ptialaska.net; 400 Main St; dm $12-15) Two miles south of the ferry terminal, it's basic but bustling, with a kitchen, daytime lockout and lights out at 10:30pm, sharp.

Eagle View Hostel (☎ 907-225-5461; www.eagleviewhostel.com; 2303 Fifth Ave; dm $25) Perched like an aerie above the Plaza Mall, with great Tongass Narrows views, separate-sex dorms and a couples room. Owner Dale is an inveterate traveler.

The closest camping is 10 miles north of town in the **Ward Lake Recreation Area** (campsites $10).

Carr's (2417 Tongass Ave; ☽ 24hr) supermarket is next to Plaza Mall. **Chico's** (435 Dock St; mains $5-12) dishes up pizza, gyros and heaping plates of Mexican fare. Hip **New York Café** (211 Stedman St; breakfast $5-9, lunch $12-19) flips the best pancakes in town. The fishing crowd frequents **Potlatch Bar** (126 Thomas St), but **Eagles Club** (Creek St) pours cheaper pitchers.

WRANGELL

Since the cruise-ship biz is in its infancy here, Wrangell is the least gentrified of the major ferry ports. The **visitors center** (☎ 907-874-3901, 800-367-9745; www.wrangell.com) and **USFS** (☎ 907-874-2323; 525 Bennett St) have information.

CRUISING THE INSIDE PASSAGE

Alaska's Panhandle is linked to 'the Outside' by the Alaska Marine Hwy. You can also fly in, but your best bet is cruising the Inside Passage. Unlimited hiking, kayaking, whale-watching and sightseeing await at the 14 ports. In the following section is a south-to-north listing of primary ports along the way.

Ferries call at main ports almost daily in summer. Smaller boats make less frequent stops at minor settlements. The complete trip ($306, without meals or berth), from Bellingham, Washington (see p532), to Skagway takes a minimum of a week; stops at ports along the way can only be arranged in advance. You can take a car onboard, but it costs a bundle and space must be reserved months ahead. If you can't hop a ferry in Bellingham, head for Prince Rupert, British Columbia (p659).

The austere **Wrangell Hostel** (☎ 907-874-3534; 206-220 Church St; r $15) is two blocks from the ferry terminal in the Presbyterian church. If you drink or smoke, pitch your tent for free (24-hour limit) in the waterfront **City Park Campground** (Zimovia Hwy), a mile south of the ferry terminus.

Diamond C Café (223 Front St; mains $6-10; 🕙 6am-3pm) is the best spot to grab a bite, while **J&W's** (120 Front St; mains $5-8) is the place for fast food. Locals still call **Bob's Supermarket** (223 Brueger St) by its old name, Benjamin's.

Mingle with the natives at **Totem Bar** (116 Front St) or the **Marine Bar** (Shakes St), or boogie with them at **Stikine Inn Lounge** (107 Stikine Ave).

PETERSBURG

At the north end of spectacular Wrangell Narrows, this very picturesque Norwegian-founded community is home to Alaska's largest concentration of humpback whales, nearby calving tidewater glaciers and the state's biggest halibut fleet

The **visitors center** (☎ 907-772-3646; www.petersburg.org; Fram & 1st Sts) and **USFS** (☎ 907-772-3871; 12 N Nordic Dr) have recreation tips.

Petersburg Bunk & Breakfast Hostel (☎ 907-772-3632, mobile 907-723-5340; www.bunkandbreakfast .com; 805 Gjoa St; dm $23; 🖳) is 1.5 miles from the ferry terminal. It offers separate-sex dorms, free breakfast and BBQ grills. Call for reservations and directions – especially if you are arriving by ferry in the middle of the night.

Camping options include the central **LeConte RV Park** (☎ 907-772-4680; partners@alaska .net; 4th St & Haugen Dr; campsites $7) and the sociable, city-run **Tent City** (☎ 907-772-4224; Haugen Dr; campsites night/week $5/30), 2 miles from town between the airport and Sandy Cove, a favorite with cannery workers since it has raised wooden platforms.

The hippest eatery is **Alaskafe** (306 N Nordic Dr; mains $6-15; 🖳), mainly a coffee house but also dishing up creative breakfasts and grilled sandwiches. Wednesday through Friday it cooks gourmet dinners, usually with a veggie option. **Helse Health Foods & Deli** (17 Sing Lee Alley) is cheap and wholesome.

Locals shoot pool at **Harbor Bar** (310 Nordic Dr), while wild **Kito's Kave** (11 Sing Lee Alley) has live music and dancing.

SITKA

The southeast's cultural center is a well-set gem. Buses ply the 5 miles from the ferry terminal into town. The **visitors center** (☎ 907-747-5940; www.sitka.org; 330 Harbor Dr) and **USFS** (☎ 907-747-6671; 204 Siginaka Way) have hiking and kayaking particulars.

The **HI-AYH Sitka Youth Hostel** (☎ 907-747-8661; 303 Kimsham St; dm member/nonmember $13/16; 🕙 Jun-Aug), in a basic church basement bunkhouse, is 8 miles from the ferry. You can rent a sleeping bag, but it's best to bring your own. There's a lockout with a strict 11pm curfew. Reservations essential.

USFS campgrounds are: **Starrigavan** (Halibut Point Rd; campsites $8), a mile north of the ferry; and **Sawmill Creek** (Blue Lake Rd; campsites free), 6 miles east of town.

Back Door Café (104 Barracks St; mains under $5) is a calm eye in the cruise-ship storm, with *simpatico* staff slinging supremo coffeehouse fare. Institutional slop never tasted so good as at **Sheldon Jackson College Cafeteria** (Sweetland Hall; breakfast/lunch/dinner $5/7/10) – and there's nobody to tip! Near the hostel, **Lakeside Grocery** (705 Halibut Point Rd) has sandwiches, soups and a salad bar.

JUNEAU

Juneau boasts a bustling waterfront and snow-mantled peaks. Downtown clings to a mountainside; the rest of town spreads north into Mendenhall Valley. The ferry terminal is 14 miles northwest of downtown in Auke Bay, with shuttles to/from the city center. The main visitors center is **Davis Log Cabin** (☎ 907-586-1737, 800-587-2201; www.traveljuneau.com; 101 Egan Dr). The **USFS** (☎ 907-586-8800; Centennial Hall) has details on surrounding wildlands.

Historic **South Franklin St** is lined with bustling bars, shops and restaurants. The area's numerous glaciers include famous 'drive-in' **Mendenhall**; the informative **visitors center** (☎ 907-789-0097; admission $3; 🕙 8am-6:30pm) is 13 miles northwest of town.

The area is wonderful for kayaking. **Alaska Boat & Kayak** (☎ 907-789-6886; www.juneaukayak .com; 6105 Thane Rd, Auke Bay) rents boats.

Juneau International Hostel (☎ 907-586-9559; www.juneauhostel.org; 614 Harris St; dm $10; 🖳) is alcohol-free and has single-sex dorms. Take the MGT shuttle ($5 to $6) from the ferry. The **USFS Auke Village Campground** (☎ 907-586-8800; Glacier Hwy; campsites $8) has 12 unreservable, scenic sites 1.5 miles west of the ferry. Basic **Thane Public Campground** (☎ 907-463-4463; Thane Rd; campsites $5) is 1 mile south of downtown.

IF YOU'VE GOT A FEW MORE DAYS IN ALASKA

■ Scope bears aplenty in their natural habitat on mountain-bike friendly **Kodiak Island**, then explore the **Aleutian Islands** via the Alaska Marine Highway.

■ Gape at the calving **Childs Glacier** and abundant sealife on **Prince William Sound**.

■ Pan for gold alongside real miners way up north in far-out **Nome**.

■ Discover **Arctic Alaska** via the Dalton Hwy and experience life in the bush on a wildlife tour in **Point Barrow**, North America's northernmost tip of firmament.

Carr's (Vintage Blvd & Egan Hwy; ⊙ 24hr) supermarket has some prepared foods. **Rainbow Foods** (224 4th St) is a groovy natural-foods grocery, deli and happening lunch spot. **Silverbow Inn Bakery** (120 2nd St; sandwiches $3-7) has sandwiches and fresh bagels. Downtown, **Bullwinkle's Pizza Parlor** (318 Willoughby Ave; pizzas from $12) tosses cheap pies and is open late on Friday and Saturday.

HAINES

This gateway to Interior Alaska and Canada's Yukon Territory is surrounded by mountains. Get oriented at the **visitors center** (☎ 907-766-2234, 800-458-3579; www.haines.ak.us; 2nd Ave & Willard St), which has details about numerous hiking and rafting possibilities.

Bear Creek Cabins & Hostel (☎ 907-766-2259; www.bearcreekcabinsalaska.com; Small Tract Rd; campsites/dm/cabins $14/16/42) is 2.5 miles south of town. Call ahead to arrange pickup ($3) from the ferry. **Port Chilkoot Camper Park** (☎ 907-766-2000, 800-542-6363; www.hotelhalsingland.com; campsites $10) is adjacent Fort Seward.

Bamboo Room (☎ 907-766-2800; 11 2nd Ave; mains $6-8) has big stacks of blueberry pancakes. **Grizzly Greg's Pizzeria** (☎ 907-766-3622; 2nd & Main; pizzas from $12) has the best pizza in town, but no booze. The **Fogcutter Bar** (Main St) and **Pioneer Bar** (13 2nd Ave) get lively while the **Hotel Hälsingland Pub** (13 Fort Seward Dr) is more sober.

Wings of Alaska is the cheapest of several local air-charter companies. **Alaska Direct Bus Line** (☎ 800-770-6652; www.tokalaska.com/dirctbus.shtml) plies the Fairbanks–Haines route.

SKAGWAY

The Marine Highway's northern terminus was once a lawless gold-rush town. The driftwood-clad **visitors center** (☎ 907-983-2854; www.skagway.org; Broadway & 2nd St) is in the Arctic Brotherhood Hall.

Near the ferry terminal is **Pullen Creek RV Park** (☎ 907-983-2768, 800-936-3731; www.pullencreekrv.com; campsites $14), while **Skagway Mountain View RV Park** (☎ 907-983-3333, 888-778-7700; 1450 Broadway St; campsites $14) has laundry facilities. The waterless **Dyea Camping Area** (☎ 907-983-2921; campsites free) is 9 miles north of town.

For breakfast, try **Sweet Tooth Café** (Broadway St & 3rd Ave; mains $4-8). Skagway Inn's bistro **Olivia's** (mains $4-11) serves tasty snacks and lunches, plus heavenly desserts.

There are regular flights between Skagway and Juneau, Haines and Glacier Bay; Skagway Air is generally cheapest. Northbound, **Gray Line buses** (☎ 907-983-2241, 800-544-2206) depart daily at 8:45am for Whitehorse. White Pass & Yukon Railroad (see p676) goes to Fraser, BC, where buses connect to Whitehorse.

Directory

CONTENTS

This alphabetized directory covers general information for the USA and Canada. Also see region-specific Fast Facts boxes starting each chapter.

ACCOMMODATIONS

This book focuses on where to stay on the cheap. The dodgiest of the dodgy, such as motels doubling as drug or prostitute centers, are not included. Some 'splurge' boxes feature stays that are worth the extra dollar. Prices vary – some camping is free

while a hostel bunk may cost you US$30, the same as a Motel 6 in mid-America. Also see Dream Sleeps (p29).

Camping

Tent camping options, for roadtrip stop-offs or in mountains, are everywhere. National and state parks are usually nicer (nature-wise) and cheaper than private ones – though generally require park entrance fees. Sites fill quickest in July and August. Many public campgrounds run on the honor system – so have plenty of small bills ready.

The US **National Park Service** (NPS; ☎ 800-365-2267, 301-722-1257; http://reservations.nps.gov) has campsites ranging from free to US$25, often not including park entrance fees. Primitive 'backcountry' sites have no facilities, 'basic' sites have pit toilets and drinking water, 'developed' sites have hot showers and RV folk. An annual fee to visit all parks is US$50. Call to book a site up to five months in advance.

Parks Canada's reservation program (☎ 877-737-3783; 905-426 4648; www.pccamping.ca) covers eight national parks, but plans to expand its program in 2005. Other sites go on a first-come, first-served basis. Sites run about C$8 to C$30 per night, backcountry sites are C$5 to C$9. An annual pass for Canadian parks costs C$45.

For state or provincial park information, contact state tourist centers (p696).

Other useful websites:

Recreation.gov (www.recreation.gov) Links to US playgrounds (national and state parks, national forests, BLM) via state links.

ReserveAmerica (www.reserveamerica.com) Reservation service for 13 states (including California, Utah and New York) and Manitoba of all things.

ReserveUSA (☎ 877-444-6777; www.reserveusa.com) Has listings and reservations for all US national forests, national parks and BLM lands. It costs US$10 per reservation.

Private campgrounds tend to cater to an older crowd pulling RVs and families, but usually have tent sites (plus stuff like swimming pools and ping-pong tables). **KOA** (www .koa.com) is a giant network of functional in-and-out tent, cabin and RV sites throughout

DIRECTORY

TOP 10 WAYS TO SAVE ON SLEEPING

Brave New Rooms

Several online booking engines offer rooms for remarkably less than hotel rack rates. If you're wanting to stay central and stylin' for a few days, definitely try www.priceline.com, www.hotels.com, www.travelocity.com, www.orbitz.com and www.hotwire.com – even for same-day finds.

Here's some savings on swank sleeps our authors snared via www.priceline.com while researching this book:

City	Quoted Price	Listed Price
Atlanta	US$40	US$139
Chicago	US$45	US$154
Edmonton	C$35	C$129

Nine More Tips

- Get discount coupons from gas stations and information centers.
- On road trips, stay off the interstate in small towns.
- Motel rates vary by town – even in the middle of nowhere; if one town seems a little high, it could be US$20 cheaper 15 miles away.
- Ask for a discount – many motels will budge on a one-night stay.
- AAA (p707) and CAA (p707) car clubs offer discounts.
- Look for off hours – many business-oriented hotels drop rates on weekends.
- See what rate Motel 6 posts on its sign (they always do); it's the cheapest chain (US$25 to US$60 per night) and a good gauge of what you can expect elsewhere; most of the indie-run motels are about the same price or a little less.
- Many B&Bs cater to high-paying travelers, though not all. State or province visitors guides include B&Bs, and some list prices. In less-visited areas, you'll find country-style B&Bs offering motel-type rates (from US$30 to US$60), and discounts during the week.
- Some university dorms open for travelers in summer; ask in a uni town.

---

the USA and Canada. Many locations are just off the interstate. The KOA 'Value Kard' (US$12) offers 10% discounts.

Car Sleeping

Sleeping in your car is obviously a free option, provided you find a well-lit place in a secure area. It's generally fine to sleep in your vehicle at highway rest stops, but not on the highway shoulder. If you pull into a hotel or mall parking lot, local security may ask you to leave, or late-night burglars may come thinking it's a vacant abandoned car. Some truck stops boom all hours with action (and dozed-off drivers in their cabs). No matter where you are, lock up. Sleeping in a car is not always safe, so use common sense when doing it. Always keep in mind that crime is not strictly an inner-city problem in the USA.

For stats on overnight driving, see p710.

Hostels

Both the USA and Canada have Hostelling International (HI) – called HI-USA or HI-AYH (American Youth Hostels) south of the border – and private hostels with varying conditions. HI hostels are generally gender-segregated and prohibit alcohol and smoking. In the USA, hostels are not widespread, mainly clustered in the northeast, the Rockies and along the west coast. Big-city hostels tend to be open 24 hours, while those in the sticks have closed hours (and might ask you to help clean a little). Many have private rooms, though not necessarily for cheaper rates than motels.

Dorms of three to 10 bunks generally run US$20 to US$35. See Fast Facts in regional chapters for a top hostel pick of the area.

Some indie hostel owners have resisted joining HI, but many of them are excellent. Check out reviews at www.hostels.com or www.backpackers.com. Or pick up the **Hostel Handbook** (www.hostelhandbook.com; US$5); the site has loads of budget links.

Reservations are a good idea, particularly in summer. In the USA, you can book at most HI-USA hostels through a **booking service** (☎ 800-909-4776, 202-783-6161; www.hiusa .org); you'll need the hostel's access code, available online. The organization also publishes a handbook with listings.

See p14 for five of the best hostels.

Motels

Scores of chain motels will greet you aside highways and interstates. Only especially good deals, or areas with clustered offerings far outside a bigger city's center, are listed in this book. Motel 6 tends to be the cheapest chain motel, with clean but barebone rooms (no alarm clocks, but there's a TV).

The following chains are generally found in both countries. More budget-oriented chains:

Budget Host (☎ 800-283-4678; www.budgethost.com)
Days Inn (☎ 800 329 7466; www.daysinn.com)
Econo Lodge (☎ 877-424-6423; www.econolodge.com)
Motel 6 (☎ 800-466-8356; www.motel6.com)
Super 8 Motel (☎ 800-800-8000; www.super8.com)

These chains price rooms a bit higher:
Best Western (☎ 800-780-7234; www.bestwestern.com)
Clarion Hotel (☎ 877-424-6423; www.clarionhotel.com)
Comfort Inn (☎ 877-424-6423; www.comfortinn.com)
Fairfield Inn (☎ 800-228-2800; www.fairfieldinn.com)
Hampton Inn (☎ 800-426-7866; www.hamptoninn.com)
Holiday Inn (☎ 800-465-4329; www.holiday-inn.com)
Howard Johnson (☎ 800-446-4656; www.hojo.com)
La Quinta (☎ 800-531-5900; www.lq.com)
Quality Inn (☎ 877-424-6423; www.qualityinn.com)
Red Roof Inn (☎ 800-733-7663; www.redroof.com)
Rodeway Inn (☎ 877-424-6423; www.rodewayinn.com)
Sleep Inn (☎ 877-424-6423; www.sleepinn.com)
Travelodge (☎ 800-578-7878; www.travelodge.com)

ACTIVITIES

Whether you think museums are for wussies or just like sweating, there's plenty to do. Regional chapters contain activities listings – some are splurges (eg skydiving in New York, p108, isn't the price of a popsicle), but hiking trails and climbing walls are free, and renting a canoe can be cheap as well. State, provincial and national parks and forests brim with options, particularly in the countries' western halves where sun and nature beg locals to grow up outdoors.

Also see p13 for the best canoeing, rafting, rock climbing, skiing and skydiving options in the region.

Canoeing, Kayaking & Rafting

White-water canoeing and rafting is best in West Virginia (seriously; p246), the Rocky Mountains (p510), Sierra Nevada (p613), and both in and around the Grand Canyon (p428). 'Tubing' in summer is the definition of 'laid back,' with beer-gurglers floating peacefully down streams in inflated tubes. Boulder (p477) has a very good DIY option.

Cycling

More cities are painting up bike lanes and commonly rent bikes for US$15 to US$30 per day. Bikes are usually banned from wilderness areas and national park trails, but bikes are permitted on many trails in US national forests (www.fs.fed.us) and lands watched over by the **Bureau of Land Management** (www.blm.gov)

Many cyclists spend the better part of summer crossing the country (about 4200 miles). **Adventure Cycling** (www.adventurecycling .org) sells downloadable bike routes crisscrossing the USA (and some of western Canada). Plenty of cross-country pedalers post bike-a-logues online that show routes; one interesting one is at www.rideacross .com. **Cycle America** (www.cycleamerica.com) offers bike tours – the two-month coast-to-coast crossing runs US$5195.

For routes and bike tips in Canada, check out **Cycle Canada** (www.cycle-canada.com) and the **Canadian Cycling Association** (☎ 613-248-1353; www. canadian-cycling.com).

Biking highlights abound. In the USA, good choices include a 206-mile hut-to-hut trail between Telluride, Colorado and Moab, Utah (p489); the Tahoe Rim Trail along Lake Tahoe, California (p617); through thick forests of Grand Island on Michigan's Upper Peninsula (p367); the 100-plus mile Mickelson Trail through South Dakota's Black Hills (p390) and in Marin County outside San Francisco (p608).

Up in Canada, Alberta's Icefields Parkway near Banff (p663) and British Columbia's coastal Fraser River Delta are highlight bikeways.

Many ski slopes in summer operate lifts for mountain bikers, including Colorado's Crested Butte (p487), slopes in Grand Teton National Park (p494) and Mammoth Lakes, California (p621).

Super bike-friendly cities include Montréal (p195); Portland, Oregon (p535); Tucson (p437); Austin (p396); Boulder, Colorado (p477) and many college towns.

Diving

Scuba diving and snorkeling is done all over – including off New York City and in the Great Lakes. The best diving locations, no doubt, are around Florida's Key West (p330), near California's Monterey (p589), and Hawaii (p626).

Florida is super for BYOS (bring your own snorkel) dips.

Dives in the cold and clear lakes off Ontario's spectacular Bruce Peninsula (p194) take in shipwrecks.

Hiking & Rock Climbing

All national parks and most state or provincial parks have short and long trails – the farther you go, the fewer people you'll see. National parks give out handy maps, good for day hikes. Overnighters should pick up topographical maps (p694). Check to see if permits are needed before heading out.

Pick up Bradford Angier's classic *How to Stay Alive in the Woods* for tips, and check with **Leave No Trace Center** (☎ 303-442-8222, 800-332-4100; www.lnt.org) for low-impact camping information. The **Rails-to-Trails Conservancy** (www.railtrails.org/content.html) has information on some 1200 hiking trails made from abandoned railroad corridors.

Three famed long trails include the **Appalachian Trail** (☎ 304-535-6331, 888-287-8673; www.appalachiantrail.org) connecting Maine with Georgia; the expanding **Continental Divide Trail**, which is a mountain-hopping link between Canada and the USA (see p699 for volunteering options) and the **Pacific Crest Trail** (☎ 916-349-2109, 888-728-7245; www.pcta.org), which zigzags between Canada and Mexico along the USA's west coast.

Rock-climbing pursuits reach their peak in the West, particularly in the Sierra Nevada and Yosemite National Park (p613), the Rockies (p467) and Utah's southeast deserts (p442).

Skiing & Snowboarding

Ski resorts are found along with most mountains in the USA and Canada. Colorado is a prime-time resort destination: famous resorts include Aspen (p485), Breckenridge (p483), Crested Butte (p487) and Steamboat Springs (p486).

Idaho's Sun Valley (p509) draws the Hollywood set. Mt Whistler in British Columbia (p655) and Banff (p663) are two of the top slopes in Canada. To the east, slopes can be icier and shorter. Vermont generally has the best, though New York's Lake Placid (p111) hosted the 1980 winter Olympics and Québec's Mont Tremblant (p204) sees a lot of skiing.

Snowboarding (Vermont honed the sport during its early days) is everywhere.

Surfing

Hawaii and Southern California reign over the area's surf scene. Oahu's North Shore is legendary, while great California spots to catch a wave are Rincon, south of Santa Barbara (p585) and at Malibu near Los Angeles (p567). Other options include Santa Cruz (p591), for first-timers San Diego's Mission Beach (p579) and even at North Carolina's Cape Hatteras (p298), best in fall.

For information, check **Surfer** (www.surfer mag.com/travel).

BOOKS

If you're looking to linger in one place for longer, check out Lonely Planet's comprehensive city and regional guides to the USA and Canada. Key US titles include *New England, Southwest, Pacific Northwest, Hawaii* and *Alaska;* there are titles for *Québec, British Columbia* and the *Maritime Provinces.* If you're continuing your trip to the south, pick up *Mexico* or *Central America on a Shoestring.*

See p32 for a list of inspiring roadtrip reads.

BUSINESS HOURS

This book's Information sections assume bank, tourist offices, Internet cafés and the like are open roughly 9am to 5pm Monday to Friday. Any deviations (if open Saturday or Sunday) are listed.

Restaurant and bar hours aren't listed unless deviating from expectation (open daily, roughly 8am or 9am to 8pm or 9pm for restaurants, or 2pm or 3pm to midnight or 1am for bars).

Most shops in the USA and Canada are open later hours (until 8pm or 9pm), and often on weekends. Supermarkets, delis and small grocery shops are generally open daily, sometimes 24 hours.

CLIMATE

For general advice on climate and the best times to travel in the USA and Canada, see Seasons in the Fast Facts box at the start of each regional chapter. The climate charts on p688 provide a snapshot of the weather patterns in the USA and Canada.

CUSTOMS

For the USA, unless you're planning on bringing in more than 1L of liquor, hundreds of cigarettes or cigars, over US$100 of gifts (they tend to let US$200 slide actually), US$10,000 in cash or traveler's checks, or a pet, you should be OK with customs. There's no duty on computers, accessories or 'tools of the trade' (including camping gear). Contact the quite helpful **US Customs & Border Protection** (in Los Angeles ☎ 310-215-2414; www.customs.gov) if you have questions, and check for duty restrictions on the 'Know Before You Go' list on the travel page of the website. You're eligible for the full exemptions every 30 days.

In Canada, restrictions are different (eg, only C$60 for gifts, 1.5L of liquor) and the allowances can be made again if you spend at least 48 hours outside of Canada. Again, personal stuff – like camping gear and laptops – won't be a problem. Declare if you're bringing in over C$10,000. For more details, check with the **Canadian Border Services Agency** (CBSA; ☎ 506-636-5064, 800-461-9999; www.cbsa-asfc.gc.ca).

DANGERS & ANNOYANCES
Driving

The biggest danger is car wrecks. In 2002, crash-related deaths exceeded murder victims by 4.4 times, car injuries exceeded violent crime victims by two times. Heed wildlife crossing warnings; if you should face a moose on the road, get down: deaths occur after a giant animal crashes through the windshield.

Don't leave any valuables within view in parked cars, particularly in cities.

Always buckle up: it's the law. Keep blankets if driving in the winter, extra water in the summer.

Scams

In big cities, three-card 'you pick it' games are always rigged. (The game, involving three bent cards shuffled very quickly on a cardboard box, is like a shell game in which the dealer's slight of hand stacks the odds against unsuspecting suckers.) Most scams in the USA are variations of online fraud. Some call ATM charges and airline date-change penalties scams. See recent scams (mostly business oriented) under 'Consumer Protection' at http://firstgov.gov.

Street Crime

Though even idle chat on BBC's *The Office* warns travelers of the crime and danger in the USA, it's exaggerated. Crime since the late 1990s has dipped gradually (in 2002 Britain recorded three times the number, per capita, of crime victims than the USA!) Still travelers should always be wary for 'grab and run' incidents or car break-ins. Use ATMs in well-trafficked areas, preferably one inside a bank or mall.

Canada has the reputation of being quieter and safer, though on paper crime rates are actually not far off those of the USA.

Guns are much more available in the USA and Canada than most places abroad, but guns rarely affect the traveler. If you're in the wild during hunting season, wear bright colors. In Alaska, some hikers carry guns for safety purposes (eg grizzlies).

Wildlife

In the woods, biting mosquitoes, ticks and blackflies can deflate a trip. Building a fire keeps mosquitoes away. Minimize skin exposure and wear insect repellent.

Most animals are timid. OK, so the USA leads the world in shark attacks, but it's still very very rare. If you're still too scared to swim, consider that in 1996, 11,000 Americans were injured by buckets whereas 18 were by sharks (no joke). *Stay away from buckets.* Also you're 125 times more likely to be hit by lightning than face a shark attack.

Never keep food stored in your tent; wildlife – including a lot of bears and cougars (particularly in the West), plus pesky raccoons – will snoop around for it.

CHICAGO, IL 182m (595ft)

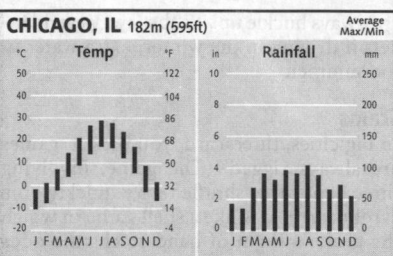

LAS VEGAS, NV 658m (2162ft)

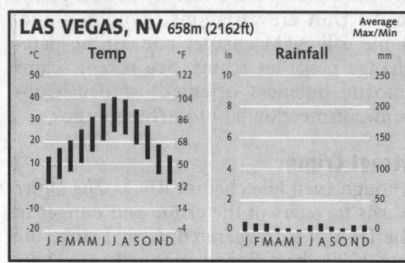

LOS ANGELES, CA 78m (256ft)

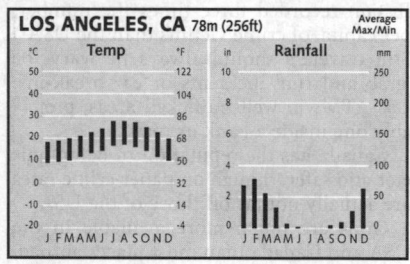

MIAMI, FL 3m (12ft)

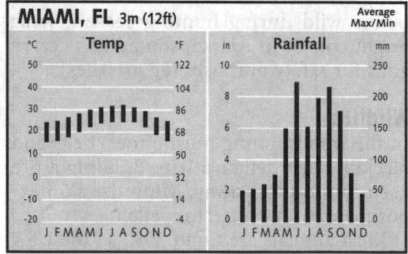

MONTRÉAL, QC 35m (118ft)

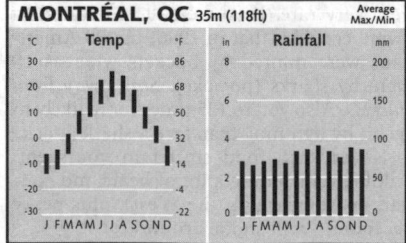

NEW ORLEANS, LA 5m (16ft)

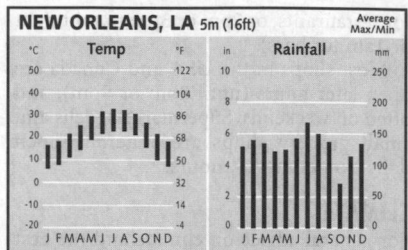

NEW YORK, NY 39m (131ft)

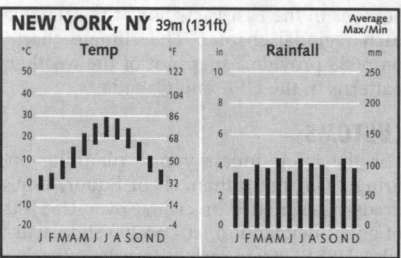

TORONTO, ON 116m (379ft)

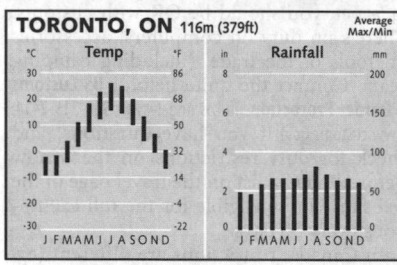

VANCOUVER, BC 3m (9ft)

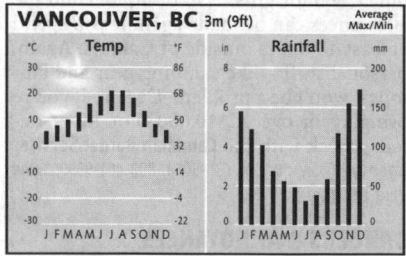

WASHINGTON, DC 9m (30ft)

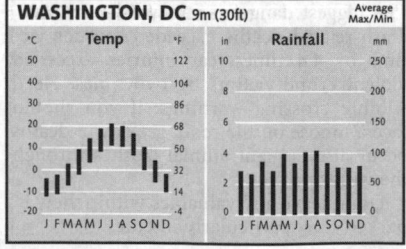

You could see rattle snakes out west; be wary of your footsteps in tall grass.

DISABLED TRAVELERS

The USA is a world leader in providing facilities for the disabled. Technically all public buildings, including hotels, restaurants, museums, bathrooms and public transit, should be wheelchair accessible. It's not always the case. Greyhound buses and Amtrak trains assist disabled travelers.

Canada is moving toward providing more disabled facilities, and many public buildings do have ramps and wheelchair-accessible WCs.

Some helpful organizations:

Access-Able Travel Source (www.access-able.com) Excellent links and state-by-state service listings.

Access to Travel (www.accesstotravel.gc.ca) Canadian information source on accessible transportation throughout the country.

Disabled Sports USA (www.dsusa.org) Scheduled events around the USA.

Travelin' Talk Network (www.travelintalk.net) Global network with information on disabled services providers.

DISCOUNT CARDS

If you're a student, bring along an **International Student Identity Card** (ISIC; www.isiccard.com) for discount on bus passes, travel insurance, air tickets, museums, theater and other sights in the USA and Canada. If you're under 26 but not a student, get an **International Youth Travel Card** (IYTC) or the **Euro26 Card** (www.euro26 .org), which offer much the same savings and benefits.

A car-club membership with the AAA (p707) offers discounts on accommodation and other services.

Discount coupons, available at welcome centers and gas stations, offer good discounts to chain motels.

See p31 for budget tips.

DISCRIMINATION

The smaller the town, the more looks you'll get just for being an outsider. This is almost always just plain curiosity, though it doesn't always feel that way – things can get friendly quick with just a smile or a 'howdy.'

Discrimination, however, against Middle Eastern people, including Sikhs and Turks, has grown recently, particularly following September 11. Reported 'racial profiling'

incidents include airlines refusing to board a 'too talkative' Pakistani businessman from San Francisco or a Sikh who refused to remove his turban. The more liberal cities, and neighborhoods, are more accepting. Be wary in some bars. See how Borat (the convincing character from Kazakhstan) on the *Ali G Show* interacts with small-town America.

There's been much press over police abuse of African Americans in the USA. Some have reported that black drivers get pulled over purely because of their race.

In some pockets of the country, French travelers may get an earful over the conflicting administrations' policies in the events before the US invasion of Iraq (when french fries were briefly renamed 'freedom fries'), but it's unlikely to pop up until way after a conversation has started.

Cities, in general, are far more tolerant to the different.

DRIVER'S LICENSE

Turn to p707 for information on driver's licenses.

EMBASSIES & CONSULATES
Embassies & Consulates in the USA

Most countries have an embassy in Washington, DC. Call ☎ 202-555-1212 or check www.embassy.org for details.

Australia Washington, DC (☎ 202-797-3000; 1601 Massachusetts Ave NW); Chicago (☎ 312-419-1480; Suite 1330, 123 N Wacker Dr); Los Angeles (☎ 310-229-4800; 19th fl, Century Plaza Towers); New York (☎ 212-351-6500; 34th fl, 150 E 42nd St); San Francisco (☎ 415-536-1970; Suite 200, 625 Market St)

Canada (see Canadian Embassies & Consulates Abroad, p690)

France Washington, DC (☎ 202-944-6000; 4101 Reservoir Rd NW); Los Angeles (☎ 310-235-3200; Suite 300, 10990 Wilshire Blvd); Miami (☎ 305-372-9799; Suite 1710, 2 S Biscayne Blvd,); New Orleans (☎ 523-5772; 1340 Poydras St); New York (☎ 212-606-3688; 934 Fifth Ave); San Francisco (☎ 415-397-4330; 540 Bush St)

Germany Washington, DC (☎ 202-298-4000; 4645 Reservoir Rd NW); Chicago (☎ 312-580-1199; Suite 3200, 676 N Michigan Ave); Los Angeles (☎ 323-930-2703; Suite 500, 6222 Wilshire Blvd); Miami (☎ 305-358-0290; 22nd fl, 100 N Biscayne Blvd); New York (☎ 212-610-9700; 871 UN Plaza); San Francisco (☎ 415-775-1061; 1960 Jackson St)

Ireland Washington, DC (☎ 202-462-3939; 2234 Massachusetts Ave NW); New York (☎ 212-319-2562; 17th fl, 345 Park Ave); San Francisco (☎ 415-392-4214; 33rd fl, 100 Pine St)

Japan Washington, DC (☎ 202-238-6700; 2520 Massachusetts Ave); Chicago (☎ 312-280-0400; Suite 1100, 737 N Michigan Ave); Miami (☎ 305-530-9090; Suite 3200, 80 SW 8 St); New Orleans (☎ 529-2101; 639 Loyola Ave); New York (☎ 212-371-8222; 299 Park Ave)

Mexico Washington, DC (☎ 202-728-1600; 1911 Pennsylvania Ave NW); Austin (☎ 512-478-2866; Suite 330, 800 Brazos St); Los Angeles (☎ 213-351-6800; 2401 W 6th St); Miami (☎ 786-268-4900; Suite 301, 5975 SW 72nd St); New York (☎ 212-217-6400; 27 E 39th St)

New Zealand Washington, DC (☎ 202-328-4800; 37 Observatory Circle); Chicago (☎ 773-714-9461; 8600 W Bryn Mawr); Los Angeles (☎ 310-207-1605; Suite 1150, 12400 Wilshire Blvd); New York (☎ 212-832-4038; 780 Third Ave)

UK Washington, DC (☎ 202-588-6500; 3100 Massachusetts Ave NW); Chicago (☎ 312-970-3800; 400 N Michigan Ave); Los Angeles (☎ 310-481-0031; Suite 1200, 11766 Wilshire Blvd); Miami (☎ 305-374-1522; Suite 2800, 1001 Brickell Bay Dr); New Orleans (☎ 524-4180; 321 St Charles Ave); New York (☎ 212-745-0200; 845 Third Ave); San Francisco (☎ 415-617-1300; Suite 850, 1 Sansome St); Seattle (☎ 206-622-9255; Suite 3001, 900 4th Ave)

Embassies & Consulates in Canada

The principal diplomatic representations to Canada are in the capital Ottawa, listed here. Other offices can be found in major cities throughout Canada.

Australia (☎ 613-236-0841; 50 O'Connor St, Ottawa)
France (☎ 613-789-1795; 42 Sussex Dr, Ottawa)
Germany (☎ 613-232-1101; 1 Waverley St, Ottawa)
Ireland (☎ 613-233-6281; 130 Albert St, Ottawa)
Japan (☎ 613-241-8541; 255 Sussex Dr, Ottawa)
New Zealand (☎ 613-238-5991; 727-99 Bank St, Ottawa)
UK (☎ 613-237-1530; 80 Elgin St, Ottawa)
USA (See US Embassies & Consulates Abroad, below)

US Embassies & Consulates Abroad

The **US Department of State Bureau of Consular Affairs** (http://travel.state.gov/index.html) has links for all US embassies abroad on its website.

Australia Canberra (☎ 2-6214-5600; Moonah Pl, Yarralumla ACT 2600); Melbourne (☎ 3-9526-5900; 553 St Kilda Rd, Melbourne, VIC 3004); Sydney (☎ 2-9373-9200; Level 59 MLC Cenrte, 19–29 Martin Pl, Sydney NSW 2000)

Canada Ottawa (☎ 613-238-5335; 490 Sussex Dr, Ottawa, Ontario, K1N 1G8); Calgary (☎ 900-451-2778; Rm 1000, 615 Macleod Trail SE, Calgary, AL, T2G 4TB); Montréal (☎ 514-398-9695; 1155 Rue St-Alexandre, Montréal, Québec, H3B 1Z1); Toronto (☎ 416-595-1700; 360 University Ave, Toronto, ON, M5G 1S4); Vancouver

(☎ 900-451-2778; 1095 W Pender St, Vancouver, BC, V6E 2M6)

France (☎ 1-43 12 22 22; 2 Av Gabriel, 75008 Paris)
Germany (☎ 30-8305-0; Neustädtische Kirchstrasse 4-5, 10117 Berlin)
Ireland (☎ 1-668-8777; 42 Elgin Rd, Dublin 4)
Japan (☎ 3-3224-5000; 1-10-5 Akasaka, Minato-ku, Tokyo 107-8420)

Mexico Mexico City (☎ 55-5080-2000; Paseo de la Reforma 305, Cuauhtémoc, 06500 Mexico City); Ciudad Juárez (☎ 656-611-3000; Av Lopez Mateos 924 Nte, Ciudad Juárez); Tijuana (☎ 664-622-7400; Av Lapachula 96, Colonia Hipodromo, 22420 Tijuana)

New Zealand Wellington (☎ 4-462-6000; 29 Fitzherbert Terrace, Thorndon, Wellington); Auckland (☎ 9-303-2724; 3rd fl, 23 Customs St, Auckland)

UK London (☎ 20-7499-9000; 24 Grosvenor Sq, London W1A 1AE); Belfast (☎ 28-9038-6100; Danesfort House 223 Stranmills Rd, Belfast, Northern Ireland BT9 5GR); Edinburgh (☎ 131-556-8315; 3 Regent Terrace, Edinburgh, Scotland EH7 5BW)

Canadian Embassies & Consulates Abroad

Check out the full list of embassies ande consulates at www.dfait-maeci.gc.ca/world/embassies/menu-en.asp.

Australia Canberra (☎ 02-6270-4000; Commonwealth Ave); Melbourne (☎ 03-9653-9674; Level 50, 101 Collins St); Sydney (☎ 02-9364-3000; Level 5, 111 Harrington St)

France (☎ 01-44 43 29 00; 35 Ave Montaigne, Paris)
Germany (☎ 30-20312-0; Friedrichstrasse 95, Berlin)
Ireland (☎ 01-417-4100; 65 St Stephen's Green, Dublin 2) Note: offers no immigration services.
Japan (☎ 03-5412-6200; 3-38 Akasaka 7-chome, Minato-ku, Tokyo)
Mexico (☎ 55-5724-7900; Schiller 529, Polanco, Mexico City)
New Zealand (☎ 04-473-9577; 61 Molesworth St, Thorndon, Wellington) Note: visa and immigration inquiries are handled by the Consulate General of Canada in Sydney, Australia.
UK London (☎ 020-7258-6600; 1 Grosvenor Sq); Belfast (☎ 02891-272-060; 8 Cromac Ave)
USA Washington DC (☎ 202-682-1740; 501 Pennsylvania Ave, NW); Buffalo (☎ 716-858-9500; 3000 HSBC Center); Chicago (☎ 312-616-1860; 180 N Stetson Ave, Suite 2400); Detroit (☎ 313-567-2340; Suite 1100, 600 Renaissance Center); Los Angeles (☎ 213-346-2700; 9th fl, 550 S Hope St); Miami (☎ 305-579-1600; Suite 1600, 200 S Biscayne Blvd); New York City (☎ 212-596-1628; 1251 Sixth Ave); San Francisco (☎ 415-834-3180; www.cdntrade.com; Suite 1288, 555 Montgomery St); Seattle (☎ 206-443-1777; 412 Plaza 600)

FESTIVALS & EVENTS
Here's a list of some of the two countries' greatest let-loose events. Some require pre-planning to find rooms. See destination chapters for more details and contact local tourist offices for more info.

These days, most North American cities have dedicated film and fringe festivals, and gay pride celebrations in June. Check city visitor centers for details.

January & February
Rose Parade (January 1) Los Angeles (p568)
Mummers Parade (January 1) Philadelphia (p96)
St Paul Winter Carnival (January) Minnesota (p377)
Chinese New Year Parade (January or February)
San Francisco (p602)
Mardi Gras (January or February) New Orleans (p263)
Winterlude (February) Going on ice in Ottawa (p191)
Winter Carnival (February) More ice in
Québec City (p206)
Noise Pop (late February) Music festival in
San Francisco (p602)

March & April
St Patrick's Day (March 17) Boston (p133)
Calle Ocho Festival (March) Cuban fest in Miami (p325)
South by Southwest (March) Music frenzy in Austin,
Texas (p398)
National Cherry Blossom Festival (late March to early
April) Washington, DC (p224)
Patriot's Day & Boston Marathon (third Monday in
April) Boston (p128)

May
New Orleans Jazz & Heritage Festival (late April &
early May) New Orleans (p263)
Cinco de Mayo (May 5) Los Angeles (p568)
Memorial Festival (Memorial Day) Electronica music in
Detroit (p366)

June & July
Chicago Blues Festival (June) Chicago (p347)
Elvis Presley Festival (June) Tupelo, Mississippi (p276)
Gospel Festival (June) Chicago (p347)
Red Earth Native American Cultural Festival (June)
Oklahoma City (p385)
Spoleto Festival USA (early June) Charleston,
South Carolina (p301)
Volksmarch (June) Walk up the Crazy Horse monument,
South Dakota (p390)
International Jazz Festival (June & July) Montréal (p200)
Canada Day (July 1) Ottawa (p191)
Independence Day (July 4) Washington, DC (p224) or
New York City (p73)

Just for Laughs Comedy Festival (July)
Montréal (p200)
Celebration of Light (late July) Vancouver (p641)

August
World Bodysurfing Championships (August)
San Diego (p579)
Elvis Week (mid-August) Memphis (p281)

September & October
Great American Beer Festival (early September)
Denver (p474)
Bumbershoot (Labor Day weekend) Music in Seattle (p522)
Texas State Fair (late September to early October)
Dallas (p405)

November
Thanksgiving Day Parade (November)
New York City (p73)

GAY & LESBIAN TRAVELERS
Generally the USA and Canada are tolerant when it comes to gays and lesbians, with regional variation. Note that outward displays of affection (including hand-holding) can threaten the sensibilities of folks who haven't faced it before (outside major cities, particularly in mid-America). Though some would argue that the buff Roman statue at Vulcan Park in Birmingham, Alabama (p315) states a different case. Same-sex marriage, with some debate, was legalized in 2003 and 2004 in Vermont, Massachusetts, Ontario, British Columbia and Québec.

See the index (p721) for boxed coverage of the gay and lesbian scenes throughout this book.

Resources
Damron (☎ 415-255-0404, 800-462-6654; www.damron.com) Publishes three travel guides and offers juicy tours of the US.
Gay Canada (www.gaycanada.com) Online community.
Gay & Lesbian National Hotline (☎ 888-843-4564;
www.glnh.org) Hotline for help and information.
Gay & Lesbian Yellow Pages (☎ 212-674-0120, 800-
697-2812; www.glyp.com) Listings for 28 locations.
National Gay/Lesbian Task Force (☎ 202-393-5177;
www.ngltf.org) National advocacy group.
Our World (www.ourworldmagazine.com) Online magazine with back-issues talking up international gay & lesbian scenes.
Out & About (www.outandabout.com) Online source with state-by-state links (including much of Canada).
Queer Canada (www.queercanada.ca) Dozens of links.

DIRECTORY

Scenes

US cities often have gay and lesbian neighborhoods. The most famed scenes include Greenwich Village and Chelsea in New York City (p59); the Castro and the parades in San Francisco (p593); South Beach in Miami (p324); West Hollywood in Los Angeles (p566); around Dupont Circle in DC (p223); the Lower Quarter of New Orleans (p254); Seattle's Capitol Hill (p519); the Hawthorne in Portland, Oregon (p535); San Diego's Hillcrest (p575); and 'Hotlanta' (aka Atlanta, p303), home to Elton John.

In Canadian cities, things get, if anything, crazier, in Montréal's Village (p195), and in Toronto (p175) and Vancouver (p634).

Beach resorts often cater to the gay and lesbian community, notably Key West (p330) in Florida; Fire Island (p72) outside New York City; Provincetown, Massachusetts (p140) and – get this – Rehoboth, Delaware (p245). College towns are, generally, far more open-minded. Even Lincoln, Nebraska, has a gay bar. Austin, Texas (p396) has a notable scene, with a nude beach on a nearby lake.

HOLIDAYS

Much is closed on some holidays. The following days are observed in the USA and Canada:

New Year's Day (January 1)
Labor Day (first Monday of September)
Veterans Day or **Remembrance Day** (November 11)
Christmas Day (December 25)

Key US holidays:
Martin Luther King Jr Day (third Monday in January)
Presidents' Day (third Monday in February)
Memorial Day (last Monday in May)
Independence Day (July 4)
Columbus Day (second Monday in October)
Thanksgiving Day (fourth Thursday in November)

And in Canada:
Victoria Day (Monday before May 25)
Civic Holiday (first Monday of August; all except Québec and Yukon)
Canada Day (July 1, called Memorial Day in Newfoundland)
Thanksgiving (second Monday of October)
Boxing Day (December 26)

INSURANCE

Often overlooked, adequate travel insurance is important no matter how long or short your trip may be. A good policy – covering luggage theft or loss, and trip cancellation insurance – should cost about 5% to 7% of your total trip budget. One sample was US$75 for one-month coverage with US$100 deductible.

Start by talking with a travel agency about options. Agencies offering good policies:
Access America (☎ 800-284-8300; www.access america.com)
Insure.com (☎ 800-556-9393; www.insure.com)
Quoteline Direct (☎ 0870-444 0870; www.quoteline direct.co.uk)
Travelex (☎ 800-228-9792; www.travelex.com)
Travel Guard (☎ 888-859-4181; www.travelguard.com)

See p713 for information on medical treatment in the USA and Canada.

INTERNET ACCESS

Almost all public libraries in the USA and Canada offer free Internet access, though often there are time limits, waits and slower connections. Most hostels offer Internet access for free or a small charge. Internet cafés, plentiful in more touristed places, usually cost US$3 to US$5 (C$4 to C$8) per hour.

Nicer hotels offer modem lines in rooms. Accommodations with Internet access are indicated in text by ▣ .

INTERNET RESOURCES

For information on air tickets and transport, see the Transportation chapter (p702). The best resource – said in complete sincerity – is Lonely Planet's Thorn Tree bulletin board (www.lonelyplanet.com), where you can post and answer trip-related questions, or post show-off minutiae once your trip is done.

Other good websites:
An American's Guide to Canada (www.icomm.ca /emily/) A sassy look at the critical differences between the USA and its northern neighbor.
Canada's Cultural Gateway (www.culture.ca) All the facts about Canada, including what Royal Mounties actually do.
Canadian Tourism Commission (www.travelcanada .ca) Official tourist information site, packed with details on all aspects of travel to and within Canada.
CIA World Factbook (www.cia.gov/cia/publications /factbook) Rather serious, but packed with useful and frequently updated tidbits – geopolitics and whatnot – for *todo del mundo* (including the USA and Canada).
Firstgov.gov (http://firstgov.gov) US government's official website with loads of links.

Government of Canada (http://canada.gc.ca) All things Canada from immigration to the lyrics to *O Canada*.

Recreation.gov (www.recreation.gov) Full run-down on US public lands.

Roadside America (www.roadsideamerica.com) One-stop look at Wackemerica.

StudentTraveler (www.studenttraveler.com) US-oriented student magazine with back issues online.

Travel Cuts (www.travelcuts.com) Loads of information on passes and tours.

LANGUAGE

American mocking a Canadian: 'Hey, how's aboot a game a hockey, eh?' Canadian mocking an American: 'Nah, but y'all have a nice day, now, y'hear?' Though the USA doesn't have an 'official language,' English is spoken practically everywhere. French reigns in Louisiana's Cajun Country (p269) and in parts of Canada like Québec, where the province's French roots are tributed on all vehicle license plates ('je me souviens' or 'I remember'). Canada has two official languages, English and French. See Ethnic Enclaves (p26) for areas where a 'good morning' might prompt a shoulder shrug.

Of course, lovely dialect differences in English run state and provincial lines, if not country lines, across this broad bulk of land. As in the movie *Fargo*, you can count 'you betchas' and 'alrighty thens' in Minnesota (and North Dakota), part of the local brand of Scandinavian-ified English.

In the South and Texas, generous use of 'y'all' corrects a flaw in the English language (lack of plural 'you'). When people in these parts are about to do something, they're 'fixin' to do it. You say 'howdy' not 'hello sir, how are you doing?' Less endearing southern accents tend to hover in Texas and Oklahoma, where 'oh shit' usually comes out in syllables as a long 'aww sheeeeyit' just like a cud-chewing cow would cuss. Things are more honey-dewed in Georgia and the Carolinas.

In comparison, much of New England and New York talk in brutal, quirk burps. New York's well-known 'Brooklynese' – an ongoing amalgam from the Dutch, Germans, Irish, Southern blacks, Jews and Latinos – made parents 'muddas and faddas,' and 'I'm certain that that girl thinks she's the most perfect thing in the world' into 'I'm soitun dat goil tinks sheez da most poifect ting in da woild.'

Bill Bryson's *Made in America* (1994) tackles the ins and outs of American lingo.

LEGAL MATTERS

Under the USA's controversial Patriot Act, passed following September 11, foreign visitors and immigrants can be detained for extended amounts of time without submitting charges or bringing them to trial. Only a handful of the thousands detained (mainly Arabs and Muslims) have been arrested.

Otherwise most other US laws remain unchanged. If arrested (in either country), you can keep silent and are permitted one phone call (police will give you an embassy number).

US drug laws can be very strict – marijuana possession charges in the US are sometimes taken more seriously than violent crime. In Canada, it's said half of those caught with pot get off with a warning; also use of marijuana for medical purposes was legalized in 2001 (still debated in the USA).

You must be 16 and have a driver's license to drive in both countries. Do not risk heavy penalties for driving drunk (max blood-alcohol level is 0.08%).

TOP FIVE WAYS TO HAVE FUN IN PRISON

You don't have to get arrested to see things from inside a jail cell. Try these instead:

- **Alcatraz**, San Francisco (p595) For US$16, visit the USA's most famous prison where inmates had Golden Gate views.
- **HI Ottawa** (p191) Sleep in a (haunted?) 18th-century cell in the Canadian capital's hostel.
- **Castillo de Marcos**, St Augustine, Florida (p328) Crumbling fort with past prisoners' scrawlings eerily lining cell walls.
- **Eastern State Penitentiary**, Philadelphia (p94) For US$9, see Al Capone's former cell in this 1829 prison.
- **Jailer's Inn**, Bardstown, Kentucky (p291) Splurge for a cell bunk in a Bourbon Country B&B.

DIRECTORY

MAPS

State, province and city information centers give out free maps. If you're driving, spring for a road atlas (at any bookstore), essential for backroad rambles. A perk for members of car-clubs AAA or CAA (p707) are high-quality free road maps. Download free maps online from **MapQuest** (www.mapquest.com) – the directions can get dodgy along tricky one-way big-city streets, but they're dandy otherwise.

For hiking, good topographical maps are made by the **US Geological Survey** (USGS; ☎ 888-275-8747; www.usgs.gov) and in Canada by the **Centre for Topographic Information** (http://maps.nrcan.gc.ca).

Lonely Planet publishes several durable compact city maps, including ones for Chicago, New Orleans, New York City, San Francisco, Toronto, Vancouver and Washington, DC.

MEDIA

See city Information sections for newspaper and radio recommendations. Most cities have freebie weekly papers with entertainment listings.

The biggie newspapers are the *New York Times* (www.nytimes.com), *Los Angeles Times* (www.latimes.com) and the *Washington Post* (www.washingtonpost.com), as well as *USA Today* (www.usatoday.com) and the *Wall Street Journal* (www.wsj.com).

Some excellent alternative reads include the *Onion* (www.onion.com), *Mother Jones* (www.motherjones.com) and the *Nation* (www.thenation .com).

In the USA, National Public Radio (NPR) is usually on the lower end of the FM dial.

The big TV broadcasters in the USA are ABC, CBS, NBC, Fox and PBS (public broadcasting). Major cable channels include CNN (news), ESPN (sports, the king of), HBO (movies, *The Sopranos)* and the Weather Channel.

MONEY

Prices in this book are in US dollars ($) for US chapters, and Canadian dollars (also $) for Canadian chapters. In chapters with both figures included (like this one), Canadian dollars are represented as 'C$' and US dollars as 'US$.'

The very stable US dollar – or 'buck' – is divided into 100 cents (¢). Coins of both nations come in pennies (1¢), nickels (5¢), dimes (10¢), quarters (25¢) and the rare half-dollar (50¢) and US$1 coins. In Canada, the loon-decorated C$1 coin is called a 'loonie,' and a C$2 coin is a 'toonie.' A lot of joking about that south of the border.

Paper currency, or bills, come in US$1, US$2, US$5, US$10, US$20, US$50 and US$100 – the same in Canada excepting the US$1. Canadian currency is less stable.

For an overview of how much things cost, see p30.

ATMs

ATMs (automated teller machines) are available 24 hours a day at most banks, shopping centers, airports, grocery stores and casinos. Most are linked with international networks such as Cirrus, Plus, Star and Maestro. Exchange rates are usually as good as you can get. Some ATMs have a US$1.50 or so charge lopped on top. Many spit out cash for a credit card, but the fees are often high.

Credit Cards

Major credit cards are accepted nearly everywhere, and you'll most likely need one to rent a car or book tickets by phone or Internet. Good to have in case of emergencies, even if you don't plan on using it. Note that some airlines, curiously, mandate that your credit card billing address be in the USA (or Canada), making picking up domestic flights a bit of a hassle once here. Keep copies of your credit card numbers separately in case they are lost or stolen.

Toll-free phone numbers for credit-card companies:

American Express (in the USA ☎ 800-528-4800, in Canada 866-296-5198; www.americanexpress.com)
Diners Club (in the USA ☎ 800-234-6377, in Canada 800-363-3333; www.dinersclub.com)

Discover (in the USA ☎ 800-347-2683, in Canada 801-902-3100; www.discovercard.com)
MasterCard (in the USA ☎ 800-826-2181, in Canada 800-307-7309; www.mastercard.com)
Visa (in the USA ☎ 800-336-8472, in Canada 800-847-2911; www.visa.com)

Exchanging Money

This table shows currency rates at the time this book went to press. For the latest exchange rates check out www.oanda.com/convert/classic.

country	currency		exchange rate
Australia	A$1	=	US$0.77, C$0.93
Canada	C$1	=	US$0.83
Euro zone	€1	=	US$1.34, C$1.61
Japan	¥100	=	US$0.96, C$1.16
Mexico	10 pesos	=	US$0.89, C$1.08
New Zealand	NZ$1	=	US$0.72, C$0.86
UK	£1	=	US$1.93, C$2.33
USA	US$1	=	C$1.20

Taxes & Refunds

It's important to note that prices quoted in this book are before sales tax is added, generally 5% to 8%. In the USA sales taxes are left to the state (Oregon has 0% and Louisiana actually offers tax back for foreign visitors' purchases).

In addition to provincial sales taxes, Canada adds a hefty 7% GST (goods and services tax) to just about everything you buy – so it's 12% to 14% in all! If you leave Canada within 60 days of purchase, you can get the GST back on any single receipt breaking C$50 before taxes (so don't haggle down a room from C$52 to C$48).

Present receipts at immigration to get stamped by a customs agent, then mail with a rebate application.

For more details, contact the **Visitor Rebate Program** (☎ 902-432-5608, 800-668-4748; www.ccra-adrc.gc.ca/visitors).

Tipping

In city restaurants, the 15% of the pretax bill is considered low; 20% is in vogue. Bar tenders expect US$1 per drink. Taxi drivers and hairdressers expect 10% to 15%.

If you're hotel-splurging, give the bellhop US$1 or US$2 per bag. 'Tip jars' – in cafés and at least one San Francisco newsstand – have been all the rage in recent years; up to you.

Traveler's Checks

The flood of ATMs means traveler's checks aren't a necessity for getting around. American Express is the most widely accepted traveler's check (in Canada too).

PASSPORT

All foreign citizens must show a passport to enter the USA or Canada, with the exception of Canadians entering the USA (from Canada) and Americans entering Canada (from the USA), both of whom can show proof of citizenship (certified birth certificate or naturalization card plus a photo ID). It's easier just to bring a passport, and some hostels require a passport for check-in, even for US and Canadian guests. See also Visas (p698).

PHOTOGRAPHY

Color print film is everywhere; stock up on black-and-white or slide film in a bigger city. Ask before taking photos of people close-up, and military bases. Some Native American communities frown on photos. At airports, you can try asking inspectors to visually check high-speed film. Or just upgrade to a digital camera.

If you're sick of taking crap photos, pick up Lonely Planet's *Travel Photography: A Guide to Taking Better Pictures*.

POST

US Postal Service (☎ 800-275-8777; www.usps.com) rates for letters up to 1oz within the USA are 37¢ (23¢ for each additional ounce) and 23¢ for post cards. International rates are 60¢ for a letter 50¢ for a post card to Mexico and Canada, 80¢ and 70¢ elsewhere. Post offices keep different hours, some open daily; check online for nearby locations.

General delivery mail (ie poste restante) can be sent to you c/o General Delivery at any post office with its own zip code (postal code). Mail is usually held 10 days. Or try an American Express or Thomas Cook office.

More expensive services are available via **Federal Express** (☎ 800-463-3339; www.fedex.com) or **United Parcel Service** (UPS; ☎ 800-782-7892; www.ups.com).

With **Canada Post** (☎ 800-267-1177; www.canadapost.ca), letters up to 30g (about 1oz) and postcards cost 50¢ within Canada, 85¢ to the US and US$1.45 to all other countries.

STUDYING

Scores of US and Canadian universities and colleges accept international students. Students come via various programs (check with a student-based agent like STA Travel) or contact schools on their own. Also check out www.studyabroadlinks.com for international listings.

In the USA

Foreign students need one of a few different study visas, all arranged before arrival. The F-1 visa is most common and is for colleges, the J-1 or Q-1 visa is for exchange programs and the M-1 visa is to study at non-academic institutions. Get application forms from a US embassy or consulate. The federal-run **Education USA** (www.educationusa .state.gov) has international locations offering advice and a long *If You Want to Study in the USA* download online.

Study in the USA (www.studyusa.com) lists by state schools with programs and outlines the application (and visa) process.

In Canada

You can take a short-term course in Canada (under six months) without acquiring a Study Permit, which must be arranged in advance. **Citizenship & Immigration Canada** (www.cic.gc.ca) outlines the steps. Note that Québec requires an additional application for students. Hit 'English' at www.immig ration-quebec.gouv.qc.ca, then 'Immigration' to read about temporary student visit forms.

TELEPHONE

The US phone system – composed of numerous regional companies (many are Bell subsidiaries) – is geared toward local users. Don't make long calls from hotel rooms or on pay phones (with or without phone cards). It's always cheaper to use a regular landline.

Mobile Phones

Cell phones in the USA and Canada use GSM 1900 or DCMA 800, a different frequency than other countries. The only foreign phones that work are tri-band models operating on GSM 1900 and also some other frequencies; check with your service provider before traipsing your unit (ha, they said 'unit') to the USA.

You may be able to take the SIM card from your home phone and install it in a rented mobile phone that's compatible with the US systems, and use the same number and billing. Ask your company. Renting a phone is around US$45 a week.

T-Mobile (www.t-mobile.com) rents GSM 1900 compatible phones which have set prepaid call time; it's not cheap though.

Huge rural pockets of the USA and Canada won't pick up a signal. If you go mobile, check various regional plans, which vary in coverage and cost plenty.

Pay Phones

Local calls cost 25¢ to 50¢ at US pay phones (25¢ in Canada), and they don't give change. Long-distance calls from pay phones are prohibitively expensive and take higher rates for phonecards. Use a private line whenever possible.

Phone Codes

Area codes in the USA and Canada are three digits. Usually you don't have to use an area code if it's a local call. Some toll-free numbers (not all) work in both countries. Toll-free numbers begin with 800, 888, 877 or 866. Numbers beginning with 550, 554, 900, 920, 940 and 976 attract a premium rate.

Phonecards

Cheap rates on prepaid phonecards are available at newsstands at bigger cities. Or check online for 'phonecards in the USA'. Some offer rock-bottom prices (a cent a minute to the UK) with no connection fees. The ones sold in airports tend to be the worst deals.

TOURIST INFORMATION

Always stop at state and province welcome centers (and town info centers) for free maps, motel coupons and free coffee. **STA Travel** (☎ 800-781-4040; www.sta-travel.com) run 88 offices throughout the USA and seven in Canada. Contact the following tourist boards for information or get info online.
Alabama (☎ 334-242-4169, 800-252-2262; www.touralabama.org)
Alaska (☎ 907-465-2010; www.travelalaska.com)
Arizona (☎ 602-230-7733, 800-842-8257; www.arizonaguide.com)
Arkansas (☎ 501-682-7777, 800-628-8725; www.arkansastravel.com)

California (☎ 916-322-2881, 800-462-2543; www.visitcalifornia.com)
Colorado (☎ 800-265-6723; www.colorado.com)
Connecticut (☎ 860-270-8081, 800-282-6863; www.ctbound.org)
Delaware (☎ 302-739-4271, 866-284-7489; www.visitdelaware.org)
Florida (☎ 850-488-5607, 888-735-2872; www.flausa.com)
Georgia (☎ 404-656-3590, 800-847-4842; www.georgia.org)
Hawaii (☎ 808-923-1811; www.gohawaii.com)
Idaho (☎ 208-334-2470, 800-635-7820; www.visitid.org)
Illinois (☎ 800-226-6632, www.enjoyillinois.com)
Indiana (☎ 800-289-6646; www.enjoyindiana.com)
Iowa (☎ 515-242-4705, 800-345-4692; www.traveliowa.com)
Kansas (☎ 785-296-2009, 800-252-6727; www.kansascommerce.com)
Kentucky (☎ 502-564-4930, 800-225-8747; www.kentuckytourism.com)
Louisiana (☎ 225-342-8119, 800-633-6970; www.lousianatravel.com)
Maine (☎ 888-624-6345; www.visitmaine.com)
Maryland (☎ 410-767-3400, 800-543-1036; www.mdwelcome.org)
Massachusetts (☎ 617-973-8500, 800-227-6277; www.massvacation.com)
Michigan (☎ 800-543-2937; www.michigan.org)
Minnesota (☎ 800-657-3700; www.explore minnesota.com)
Mississippi (☎ 601-875-0705, 800-927-6378; www.visitmississippi.org)
Missouri (☎ 573-751-4133, 800-877-1234; www.missouritourism.org)
Montana (☎ 406-444-2654, 800-847-4868; www.visitmt.com)
Nebraska (☎ 800-228-4307; www.visit nebraska.org)
Nevada (☎ 800-638-2328; www.travelnevada.com)
New Hampshire (☎ 603-271-2665, 800-386-4664; www.visitnh.gov)
New Jersey (☎ 609-292-2470, 800-537-7397; www.state.nj.us/travel)
New Mexico (☎ 505-827-7400, 800-733-6396; www.newmexico.org)
New York (☎ 518-474-4116, 800-225-5697; www.iloveny.com)
North Carolina (☎ 919-733-4147, 800-847-4862; www.visitnc.com)
North Dakota (☎ 701-328-2525, 800-435-5663; www.ndtourism.com)
Ohio (☎ 800-282-5393; www.ohiotourism.com)

Oklahoma (☎ 405-521-2409, 800-652-6552; www.travelok.com)
Oregon (☎ 503-986-0000, 800-547-7842; www.traveloregon.com)
Pennsylvania (☎ 717-232-8880, 800-847-4872; www.visitpa.com)
Rhode Island (☎ 401-222-2601; www.visitrhode island.com)
South Carolina (☎ 803-734-1700; www.discover southcarolina.com)
South Dakota (☎ 800-732-5682; www.state.sd.us /tourism)
Tennessee (☎ 615-741-2159, 800-462-8366; www.tnvacation.com)
Texas (☎ 800-452-9292; www.traveltex.com)
Utah (☎ 001-530-1030, 800-200-1160; www .utah.com)
Vermont (☎ 802-828-3676, 800-837-6668; www.travel-vermont.com)
Virginia (☎ 800-321-3244; www.virginia.org)
Washington (☎ 360-725-5052; www.tourism .wa.gov)
West Virginia (☎ 304-558-2200, 800-225-5982; www.callwva.com)
Wisconsin (☎ 800-432-8747; www.travel wisconsin.com)
Wyoming (☎ 307-777-7777, 800-225-5996; www.wyomingtourism.org)

In Canada:
Alberta (☎ 780-427-4321, 800-661-8888; www.travelalberta.com)
British Columbia (☎ 250-356-6363, 800-435-5622; www.hellobc.com)
Manitoba (☎ 204-945-3777, 800-665-0040; www.travelmanitoba.com)
New Brunswick (☎ 506-753-3876, 800-561-0123; www.tourismnbcanada.com)
Newfoundland & Labrador (☎ 800-563-6353; www.gov.nf.ca/tourism)
Northwest Territories (☎ 867-873-7200; 800-661-0788; www.nwttravel.nt.ca)
Nova Scotia (☎ 902-425-5781, 800-565-0000; www.explorens.com)
Nunavut (☎ 867-979-4636, 866-686-2888; www.nunatour.nt.ca)
Ontario (☎ 800-668-2746; www.ontariotravel.net)
Prince Edward Island (☎ 902-368-4444, 888-734-7529; www.peiplay.com)
Québec (☎ 514-873-2015, 877-266-5687; www.bonjourquebec.com)
Saskatchewan (☎ 306-787-9600, 877-237-2273; www.sasktourism.com)
Yukon (☎ 867-667-5036, 800-789-8566; www.touryukon.com)

TOURS

Lauded by many a trip-taker, **Green Tortoise** (☎ 800-867-8647, 415-956-7500; www.greentortoise .com) run free-spirited budget trips of diverse (primarily 20-something) travelers on sleeper coaches. The two-week traipse around Alaska is US$700 (plus US$195 for food), the popular six-day Northern California loop is US$300 (US$55 for food), the nine-day Southwest canyon trip is US$380 (US$125 for food) and a two-week cross-country jaunt is US$449 to US$549 ($151 for food). It's a very good way to meet people and get to remote places if you're without transport.

Also try **Trek America** (☎ 800-221-0596, 973-983-1144; www.trekamerica.com) or **Contiki** (☎ 866-266-8454; www.contiki.com).

For shoestring-oriented trips in Canada, contact the **Moose Travel Network** (Eastern Canada tours ☎ 416-504-7514, 888-816-6673; Western Canada tours ☎ 604-777-9905, 888-244-6673; www .moosenetwork.com), which offers jump on-and-off tours of British Columbia and Alberta, Québec and Ontario. Its West Pass (C$450) is a 10-day loop that starts in Vancouver and reaches Whistler, Jasper and Banff. Accommodation will cost extra, but Moose pre-books dormitory beds for all its tour-goers.

Salty Bear Adventure Tours (☎ 902-446-3866; 866-458-2327; www.saltybear.ca) offers trips in the Maritime Provinces. Its two-day circuit of Novia Scotia is C$110/100 without/with ISIC card.

VISAS
To the USA

Entry requirements continue to change post-9/11, so double-check requirements before arriving. The new Department of Homeland Security absorbed the old Immi-

---

REGISTRATION

Starting in 2005, all of the 35 million annual visitors to the USA will purportedly undergo a 20-minute 'registration' (aka National Security Entry Exit Registration System; NSEERS), which will consist of a short interview in a separate room, and having a photo and electronic fingerprints taken. Time will tell how much extra time this will mean to immigration lines.

---

gration and Naturalization Service (INS), and the **Bureau of Citizenship & Immigration Services** (BCIS; www.bcis.gov) now handles visa and immigration processing. For visa details check out www.unitedstates.gov or www .travel.state.gov/visas.

DO YOU NEED A VISA?

Canadians do not need a visa to enter the US, but will need to show proof of citizenship (a birth certificate or naturalization card) and photo ID if entering from Canada. A passport is easier.

Under the Visa Waiver Program citizens of 27 other countries – including all of Western Europe (which includes the UK, Ireland, France, Germany), Scandinavia, Iceland, Slovenia, Australia, New Zealand and Japan – can enter the USA, with a passport, for a visit of up to 90 days without extensions. It's no longer automatically 90 – sometimes a few weeks. You'll need to show a round-trip or onward ticket.

The 'grounds for exclusion' apply to visa waivers too (opposite). All other nationalities require a visa.

If you go to Canada for a couple of days on a single-entry tourist visa (not multi-entry), you start from scratch when crossing back to the USA.

IF YOU NEED A VISA

Apply for a visa at a US consulate or embassy, or from an agent or by mail, at least a month before your flight. It's easier to apply from your home country due to restrictions than from another country on the road. Check www.travel.state.gov/visa_services.html or the BCIS website for more details.

All passports must be valid for six months or longer than your extended stay in the USA. There's a US$100 processing fee, and you'll need to provide a recent photo. In addition to the main nonimmigrant visa form (DS-156), all men aged 16 to 45 must complete a DS-157 form that outlines travel plans.

In almost all cases, applicants must show documents of financial stability, a round-trip or onward ticket and 'binding obligations' that ensure a return home, such as a job, home or family ties.

The most common visa is a nonimmigrant visitor visa, type B1 for business, B2 for tourism or visiting people. A visitor's visa allows multiple entries over one to five years and prohibits paid employment in the USA.

If you're going to the US to work or study, you'll need a different visa, and the company or school should make the arrangements. The F1 visa is for students; H1, H2 or H3 visas are for temporary employment; the J1 visa for approved exchange programs; the K1 visa for a fiancée or fiancée of a US citizen; and the L1 visa is for intracompany transfers. Allow six months to process the visas.

Green Cards are for permanent residence. The easiest way to get one is through an employment or family connection in the USA. Each year, the Green Card Lottery randomly selects an additional 50,000 candidates to receive Green Cards.

GROUNDS FOR EXCLUSION & DEPORTATION

The visa application asks many questions, including whether you're a drug trafficker or plan to engage in terrorist activities. Also if you admit to being a prostitute, junkie, ex-Nazi or smuggler, you may well be denied entry. If you have a 'communicable disease of public health significance' (including HIV, SARS, tuberculosis and the Ebola virus); a criminal record, or made a previous false statement in a US visa application, you may have to request an exemption – many do and are granted. Don't attempt to enter on a Visa Waiver Program if you have a criminal record – apply for a visa from home.

US immigration is far more lenient to those who admit to an old criminal charge or a communicable disease than someone who wilfully tries to mislead immigration on a visa application. Tell the truth.

ENTERING THE USA

Those with a non-US passport should fill in Form I-94 (an arrival/departure record) before reaching immigration. Give the address of a motel or hostel you plan to stay at the first night for 'Address While in the United States.' Immigration officers will ask questions. It's a good idea to have an itinerary (even a rough one) handy, plus a credit card and your onward ticket.

VISA EXTENSIONS

Go to a local BCIS office (call ☎ 800-375-5283 for information) well before the stamped date.

SHORT-TERM DEPARTURES & REENTRY

The days when visitors popped over to Canada to get a new visa of 90 days are largely gone. While it's kinda easy to make day trips to Canada (see below) or Mexico (its border area, including Baja California, is a visa-free zone), you will be subjected to the full immigration procedure. If your visa has expired, it helps to turn it in when you leave the USA and have all the necessary visa documentation (described left). If you return after a couple days and expect to get a new visa, you may be questioned thoroughly.

To Canada

Citizens of dozens of countries – including the US, most western European and Commonwealth countries, Japan, South Korea and Israel – don't need visas to enter Canada for stays up to 180 days. US permanent residents are also exempt from obtaining visas regardless of their nationality.

Nationals of around 150 other countries, including South Africa, Hong Kong and Poland, need to apply for a 'temporary resident visa' (TRV) with the Canadian visa office in their home country. The website maintained by **Citizenship and Immigration Canada** (CIC; www .cic.gc.ca) has full details. A separate visa is required if you plan on studying or working in Canada. Single-entry TRVs (C$75) are valid up to six months, while multiple-entry TRVs (C$150) are valid for two or three years.

Visa extensions (C$75) need to be filed with the CIC Visitor Case Processing Centre in Alberta at least one month before your visa expires.

A passport and/or visa do not guarantee entry. The admission and duration of a permitted stay is based on various factors, including good health, being law abiding, having sufficient money and, possibly, having a return ticket out of the country.

VOLUNTEERING

Short-term programs can break up a long-haul journey and are often the most memorable part of a trip. There are countless opportunities: working on mountain trails, volunteering off-season at a national park visitor center, reading to kids, building housing for the poor. No prices here include airfare.

VFP (Volunteers for Peace; ☎ 802-259-2759; www.vfp .org; 1034 Tiffany Rd, Belmont, VT 05730) offers dozens of short-term (two or three weeks mostly) volunteer programs – such as working on the Appalachian Trail etc – around the US and Canada. Prices range from US$200 to US$400, including room and board. It's a good deal. A popular choice in summer is working with kids on Native American reservations, such as the Standing Rock Sioux Tribe in North Dakota, which attracts college students. From abroad, you may need to book with one of VFP's partners.

Global Volunteers (☎ 651-407-6100; www.global volunteers.org; 375 E Little Canada Rd, St Paul, MN 55117) hosts programs in the US – working with struggling communities in the Mississippi Delta, the Blackfeet Nation in Montana etc – for US$750 per week (room and board).

The **Continental Divide Trail Alliance** (☎ 888-909-2382; www.cdtrail.org) recruits volunteers for one-day to two-week programs helping expand the trail between Montana and New Mexico, and has some last-minute opportunities too.

Other organizations include:

Charity Guide (charityguide.org/charity/vacation.htm) Links to volunteer programs in USA and Canada.

Earthwatch Institute (www.earthwatch.org) Programs start around US$1500.

Global Volunteer Network (www.volunteer.org.nz) Month-long Alaska programs for US$1500.

Responsible Travel (www.responsibletravel.com) Links to US and Canadian programs, such as six weeks working on Nevada trails, including cabin (not flight) for US$650.

Volunteer Abroad (www.volunteerabroad.com) Links to many programs.

Volunteer America (www.volunteeramerica.net)

WOMEN TRAVELERS

Women traveling alone or in groups should encounter no particular problems in the USA or Canada. Avoid being alone on empty streets and be wary of 'help' from men that lead you away from crowded areas. Saying 'no thank you' politely is usually enough to end an unwanted conversation in a bar.

Physical attacks are very unlikely. Many larger cities have rape crisis centers (below).

Mace or cayenne-pepper spray is a popular deterrent, but is illegal in Canada and some US states. Also note sprays cannot be taken aboard planes.

Resources

Call ☎ 911 in an emergency. In the USA, **Rape, Abuse & Incest National Network** (RAINN;

☎ 800-656-4673; www.rainn.org) has a 24-hour hotline and the website lists help centers by state. In Canada, contact the **Canadian Association of Sexual Assault Centers** (☎ 604-876-2622; www.casac.ca) for hotlines and centers.

For general information, check out the community website www.journeywoman. com, which has many links. Other good organizations include **National Organization for Women** (NOW; ☎ 202-628-8669; www.now.org) and **Planned Parenthood** (☎ 212-541-7800; www.planned parenthood.org), which offers medical advice.

WORKING

Lonely Planet's *Gap Year Book* outlines how to work on the road. Another great book is *Work Abroad: The Complete Guide to Finding a Job Overseas*, by Clayton A Hubbs, et all; also see www.transitionsbroad.com.

In the USA

To work legally, foreigners need to apply for a US work visa before leaving home. A J-1 visa, for exchange visitors, is issued to young people for study, student vacation employment, work in summer camps, and short-term traineeships.

Hostels sometimes offer exchange programs, rather informally.

PROGRAMS

Students aged 24 and under have an easier go getting short-term work and travel gigs. For a fee, the following organizations help locate jobs, arrange J-1s (four-months work, one-month travel) for all nationalities. The stress is time and experience over money. Many jobs are targeted to tourism and peak seasons (winter for ski resorts, summer for summer resorts). It takes some nationalities longer to get visas – a British citizen should plan at least a couple of months in advance.

Alliance Abroad Group (☎ 512-457-8062; www.alliancesabroad.com) Helps locate seasonal jobs (on ski slopes and summer camps).

American Institute for Foreign Study (AIFS; ☎ 800-727-2437; www.aifs.com) Works with several organizations (including Camp America) to get short-term resort, camp, education and nanny gigs.

Back Door Jobs (www.backdoorjobs.com) Lists scores of jobs (national parks, resorts, youth programs) in the USA and Canada.

Bunac (☎ 020-7251-3472; www.bunac.org; 16 Bowling Green Lane, London) Recently opened its Work Canada program to non-students under 35.

Camp America (☎ 020-7581-7377; www.campamerica .co.uk; 37A Queens Gate, London) Organized camp work for free room and board and usually a flight.

Council on International Educational Exchange (CIEE; ☎ 1800-407-8839, in Boston 617-247-0350; in London 020-7478-2020; www.ciee.org)

InterExchange (☎ 212-924-0446; www.interexchange .org) Camp programs and au pair programs for those 18 to 26 (as live-in nanny).

International Exchange Programs (IEP; ☎ 1300-300-012; www.iep-australia.com; ☎ 09-366-6255; www.iepnz.co.nz) For Australians and New Zealanders.

Work & Travel USA (www.workandtravelusa.net) Run with CIEE, helps full-time students (aged 18 to 30) get four-month gigs in certain time frames (from June 1 for Europeans, from November 15 for Australians).

In Canada

Other than for a few employers hiring temp workers (at hotels, bars, resorts, construction and forestry projects and farms), you'll need a valid work permit to work in Canada. If you get caught working without

one, get your bags out. See www.cic.gc.ca /english/work for details.

Students aged 18 to 25 from a dozen-plus countries (including the UK, Australia, New Zealand and Ireland) can apply for the **Student Work Abroad Program** (SWAP; www.swap .ca), which allows a one-year, nonextendable visa to work in any job you can get (usually in bars, hotels or on farms).

Nonstudents can apply to spend up to a year on a **Working Holiday Program** (WHP). You must be between 18 and 30 years old and a citizen of Australia, France, Germany, Ireland, Japan, Netherlands, New Zealand, South Korea, Sweden or the UK. National quotas are filled on first-come, first-served basis. An application takes about three months. Check out www.dfait -maeci.gc.ca/123go/workholiday-en.asp for further details.

Bunac's Work Canada program (see programs p700) is now open to nonstudents.

See p656 for more specific information on working in Whistler, BC.

Transportation

CONTENTS

Key transportation hubs and routes within United States and Canadian regions are listed in Transportation sections near the front of each chapter. refer to the individual city Getting There & Away sections for the locations of airports, train stations and bus stations.

GETTING THERE & AWAY

Most people reach the USA and Canada by air. Cruises and passenger ship lines are prohibitively expensive, but do occur.

AIR

Many international flights require transfers in another city.

Airports & Airlines

AIRLINES

Following is a list of the main international carriers:

Aer Lingus (☎ 800-474-7424; www.aerlingus.com)
Aerolíneas Argentinas (☎ 800-333-0276; www.aeroargentinas.com)
Air Canada (☎ 888-247-2262; www.aircanada.ca)
Air France (☎ 800-237-2747; www.airfrance.com)
Air New Zealand (☎ 800-262-1234; www.airnewzealand.com)
Alitalia (☎ 800-223-5730; www.alitalia.com)
American Airlines (☎ 800-433-7300; www.aa.com)
British Airways (☎ 800-247-9297; www.britishairways.com)

Cathay Pacific (☎ 800-233-2742; www.cathaypacific.com)
Continental Airlines (☎ 800-231-0856; www.continental.com)
Delta Air Lines (☎ 800-241-4141; www.delta.com)
El Al (☎ 800-223-6700; www.elal.co.il)
Garuda Indonesia (☎ 800-342-7832; www.garuda-indonesia.com)
Iberia (☎ 800-772-4642; www.iberia.com)
Icelandair (☎ 800-223-5500; www.icelandair.com)
Japan Airlines (JAL; ☎ 800-525-3663; www.jal.com)
KLM (☎ 800-374-7747; www.klm.com)
Korean Air (☎ 800-438-5000; www.koreanair.com)
Kuwait Airways (☎ 800-458-9248; www.kuwait-airways.com)
Lufthansa (☎ 800-645-3880; www.lufthansa.com)
Northwest Airlines (☎ 800-447-4747; www.nwa.com)
Polynesian Airlines (☎ 800-264-0823; www.polynesianairlines.com)
Qantas (☎ 800-227-4500; www.qantas.com)
Scandinavian Airlines (SAS; ☎ 800-221-2350; www.scandinavian.net)
Singapore Airlines (☎ 800-742-3333; www.singaporeair.com)
Song (☎ 800-359-7664; www.flysong.com)
South African Airways (☎ 800-722-9675; www.flysaa.com)
Thai Airways International (THAI; ☎ 800-426-5204; www.thaiair.com)
United Airlines (☎ 800-538-2929; www.ual.com)
US Airways (☎ 800-622-1015; www.usairways.com)
Virgin Atlantic (☎ 800-862-8621; www.virgin-atlantic.com)

AIRPORTS – USA

Atlanta Hartsfield International (code ATL; ☎ 404-209-1700; www.atlanta-airport.com)
Boston Logan International (code BOS; ☎ 800-235-6426; www.massport.com/logan)
Chicago O'Hare International (code ORD; ☎ 800-832-6352; www.ohare.com/ohare/home.asp)
Dallas-Fort Worth (code DFW; ☎ 972-574-8888; www.dfwairport.com)
Honolulu (code HNL; ☎ 808-836-6413; www.honoluluairport.com)
Houston George Bush Intercontinental (code IAH; ☎ 281-230-3000; www.houston-iah.com)
Los Angeles (code LAX; ☎ 310-646-5252; www.lawa.org/lax/laxframe.html)
Miami (code MIA; ☎ 305-876-7000; www.miami-airport.com)

New York John F Kennedy (code JFK; ☎ 718-244-4444; www.panynj.gov/aviation/jfkframe.HTM)
Newark (code EWR; ☎ 973-961-6000; www.panynj.gov /aviation/ewrframe.HTM)
San Francisco (code SFO; ☎ 650-821-8211; www .flysfo.com)
Seattle Seattle-Tacoma International (code SEA; ☎ 206-433-5388; www.portseattle.org/seatac/default.htm)
Washington, DC Dulles International (code IAD; ☎ 703-572-2700; www.metwashairports.com/dulles/)

AIRPORTS – CANADA
Montréal Dorval (code YUL; ☎ 514-394-7377; www .admtl.com)
Toronto Pearson International (code YYZ; ☎ 416-776-3000; www.toronto-yyz.com)
Vancouver (code YVR; ☎ 604-207-7077; www.yvr.ca)

Tickets
Plan ahead, and get quotes before buying your tickets. Online ticket bookers offer the cheapest tickets, but often run out months in advance. High-season fares generally run mid-June to mid-September, plus Thanksgiving and Christmas/New Year's Day. Save by traveling during curb seasons (particularly February, March, October and November). Consider this:

- A good value open-jaw ticket (into Los Angeles and out of New York) may save you money and time from backtracking cross-country; a couple of sample fares from London–LA, NYC–London cost US$803/514 summer/fall, a third more than a return London–LA ticket was US$519/343.
- Buy a roundtrip ticket with a free stopover (eg, London to San Francisco with a free stop in New York), then bus around each hub.
- A round-the-world (RTW) ticket only pays off if you're planning multiple stops outside the region.
- Flexible return dates will save you US$150 or higher penalties to change your ticket once issued.

COURIER FLIGHTS
Sadly, the heyday of cheap courier flights was all but grounded after September 11.

Check out www.courier.org or www .courier travel.org for info on routes from London to New York, Newark or Miami (some have max stays on a couple weeks, however).

From Africa
Most flights come via a European hub, most commonly London. Useful agents include:
Flight Centre (in South Africa ☎ 0860-400-747; www.flightcentre.co.za)
STA Travel (in South Africa ☎ 021-418-6570; www.sta travel.co.za)
Let's Go Travel (in Kenya ☎ 4447-151; www.letsgo safari.com)

From Asia
Bangkok, Singapore, Kuala Lumpur, Hong Kong, Seoul, Taipei and Tokyo have good connections to the US and Canada. A few flights allow a stopover in Honolulu.
Four Seas Tours (in Hong Kong ☎ 2200 7760; www .fourseastravel.com/english)
No 1 Travel (In Japan ☎ 03-3200-8871; www.no1 -travel.com)
STA Travel Bangkok (☎ 662-236-0262; www.statravel .co.th); Hong Kong (☎ 852-2736-1618; www.statravel .com.hk); Japan (☎ 03-5391-2922; www.statravel.co.jp); Singapore (☎ 65-6737-7188; www.statravel.com.sg)

From Australia
Flights go from Melbourne or Sydney to the USA and Canada via Los Angeles and San Francisco. Qantas, Air New Zealand and United are the main airlines on the route.
Flight Centre (☎ 1300-133-133; www.flightcentre .com.au)
STA Travel (☎ 1300-733-035; www.statravel.com.au)
Trailfinders (☎ 03-9600-3022; www.trailfinders.com.au)
Travel.com (☎ 1300-130-482; www.travel.com.au)

From Central & South America
Most flights connect the region with Dallas/ Ft Worth, Houston, Los Angeles and Miami. Other common gateways are Atlanta, Chicago, Newark, New York, San Francisco, Toronto and Washington, DC.
Asatej (in Argentina ☎ 54-011-4114-7595; www.asatej .com)
IVI Tours Venezuela (in Venezuela ☎ 0212-993-6082; www.ividiomas.com)
Mundo Joven (in Mexico ☎ 5518-1755; www.mundo joven.com)
STA Travel Guatemala (in Guatemala ☎ 502-219-9217; www.statravel.com, www.isyta.com; Antigua)
Student Travel Bureau (in Brazil ☎ 3038-1555; www .stb.com.br)

From Continental Europe
Nonstop flights connect Europe with many US and Canadian cities, though discounted

TRANSPORTATION

fares often involve indirect routes and transfers. The main airlines on the routes are Air Canada, Air France, Alitalia, American Airlines, British Airways, Continental, Delta, KLM, Lufthansa, Scandinavian Airlines, TWA and United. Zoom Airlines (below) also flies to Canada from Paris.

France

Lastminute (☎ 08-92-70-50-00; www.fr.lastminute.com)
Nouvelles Frontieres (☎ 0825-00-07-47; www.nouvelles-frontieres.fr)
OTU Voyages (☎ 08-25-00-40-27; www.otu.fr)
Specializes in student travel.
Usit Connections (☎ 08-92-88-88-88) Specializes in student travel.

Germany

Just Travel (☎ 089-747-3330; www.justtravel.de)
Last Minute (☎ 01805-284-639; www.lastminute.de)
Reiseboerse.com (☎ 030-2800-2800; www.reiseboerse.com)
STA Travel (☎ 01805-456-422; www.statravel.de)

From New Zealand

Air New Zealand has regular flights from Auckland direct to Los Angeles.

Flight Centre (☎ 0800-24-35-44; www.flightcentre.co.nz)
STA Travel (☎ 0508-782-872; www.statravel.co.nz)
Travel.com (☎ 0800-468-332; www.travel.co.nz)

From the UK & Ireland

One of the busiest and most competitive air sectors in the world is from the UK to the USA, with hundreds of scheduled flights by British Airways, American Airlines, United, Delta, Northwest, Continental, Kuwait, Air India, TWA and discount specialist Virgin Atlantic. **Zoom Airlines** (www.flyzoom.com) offers discounted one-way fares to Canada from London, Glasgow and Paris.

Bucket shops that sell discounted fares abound in London and the UK. Look in *Time Out,* the free *TNT* magazine or the *Evening Standard*. Check to see if the agent is bonded by organizations (such as ATOL, ABTA or AITO) that give some protection to buyers if the company goes broke.

Bridge the World (☎ 0870-444-7474; www.b-t-w.co.uk)
Cheap Flights (www.cheapflights.co.uk)
Ebookers.com (☎ 0870-010-7000; www.ebookers.com)
Flight Centre (☎ 0870-890-8099; www.flightcentre.co.uk)
Lastminute.com (http://engb.lastminute.com) Discounts on everything, including travel.

North-South Travel (☎ 01245-608-291; www.northsouthtravel.co.uk) Part of its profit funds developing-world projects.
Quest Travel (☎ 0870-442-3542; www.questtravel.com)
STA Travel (☎ 0870-160-0599; www.statravel.co.uk) Discount and student travel specialist.
Trailfinders (www.trailfinders.co.uk)
Dublin (☎ 01-677-7888); Glasgow (☎ 0141-353-2224); London (☎ 020-7937-5400)
Travel Bag (☎ 0870-890-1456; www.travelbag.co.uk)
Travelocity (www.travelocity.co.uk)

LAND

Greyhound and Amtrak have direct connections across the long US/Canadian border. Many car rental agencies allow border hops, but keep your registration papers in order. For visa and border-crossing info between the USA and Canada, see p699.

Since September 11, customs are sticking to the book more carefully at all ports of entry, including the US/Canada border. Some borders are open 24 hours, but not all – one Vermont/Québec crossing is a 'one-man operation.' Random checks prompt long waits. Always have your papers in order.

From Mexico, **Greyhound Mexico** (www.greyhound.com.mx) send direct buses over the border, though you can expect a wait if crossing into the USA. **Autobus Americanos** (☎ 800-784-8333) sends buses to/from Houston and San Antonio to various points in Mexico. Check www.ticketbus.com.mx for Mexican domestic bus info. Generally it's best to walk across and catch another bus. Some 'direct' services will require transfers anyway.

The main US/Mexico crossings include San Diego/Tijuana (California), Nogales/Nogales (Arizona), El Paso/Ciudad Juárez (Texas) and Brownsville/Matamoros (Texas).

US car insurance is not valid in Mexico, but short-term agencies cluster at many border crossings. Generally you can walk into Mexico and back for the day; if you're not American, ensure your visa allows re-entry.

GETTING AROUND

Train, bus, plane, car, bike or boots? If you have a car, or can rent one, and you're planning to cover a lot of ground, you'll get more out of the trip – it is car country. Discount airlines exist, without the Ryan Air prices familiar to Europeans; but good deals do pop up. Amtrak trains are fun but pricey and tend to run behind schedule, with sparse service outside the northeast and west coast. Tough on the legs for the long haul, cheaper Greyhound buses (and other smaller services) cover more miles but can get a little mangy after several hours. Bus and train passes can be good, perhaps in tandem with a one-way flight.

See the Without Wheels trip on p25 for key destinations where you don't have to have a car when you get there.

AIR

US routes coast-to-coast are usually cheaper than ones north of the border. And you may save more by flying from Boston to Seattle then catching a bus north to Vancouver than by flying directly to Canada. Domestic flights are often a bit cheaper to buy within the US than abroad, though most US-based search engines online won't sell tickets to those outside the country.

Airlines

Following are the main domestic carriers in the USA:

AirTran (☎ 800-247-8726; www.airtran.com)
Alaska Airlines (☎ 800-252-7522; www.alaska air.com)
America West (☎ 800-235-9292; www.america west.com)
American Airlines (☎ 800-433-7300; www.aa.com)
American Trans Air (☎ 800-435-9282; www.ata.com)
Continental Airlines (☎ 800-523-3273; www.contin ental.com)
Delta Air Lines (☎ 800-221-1212; www.delta.com)
Frontier Airlines (☎ 800-432-1359; www.frontier airlines.com)
Hawaiian Airlines (☎ 800-367-5320; www.hawaiian air.com)
JetBlue (☎ 800-538-2583; www.jetblue.com)
Midwest Express (☎ 800-452-2022; www.midwest express.com)
Northwest Airlines (☎ 800-225-2525; www.nwa.com)
Southwest Airlines (☎ 800-435-9792; www.ifly swa.com)
Spirit Airlines (☎ 800-772-7117; www.spiritair.com)
United Airlines (☎ 800-864-8331; www.ual.com)
US Airways (☎ 800-428-4322; www.usairways.com)

Significant Canadian carriers include:
Air Canada (☎ 888-247-2262; www.aircanada.com)
Tango (☎ 800-315-1390; www.flytango.com)
WestJet (☎ 800-538-5696; www.westjet.com)

Tickets

Air ticket prices are confusing, and prices change frequently with patterns impossible to understand. Check a few websites (such as www.orbitz.com, www.travelocity.com, www.sta.com, www.hotwire.com) and find which airlines are posting the cheapest deal, then check that airline's website. At research

---

TAKE OFF YOUR SHOES PLEASE

Since September 11, US airports have upped the security-measure ante. Before getting on your flight, you're likely to de-belt, de-shoe, go through a couple metal detectors, get a quick frisk-down, and show your ID (you must have it) at check-in to airport security to get to the gate and when boarding. If you can, avoid wearing hidden body piercings or underwire bras. The checks take time, so don't be late.

All checked luggage is screened for explosives (after check in). It's recommended not to lock luggage, as it will be broken if it's necessary to open a bag. Put personal items in clear plastic bags if you don't want them handled. Avoid stacking books or papers in bags, and don't pack food and drinks. Keep undeveloped film with your carry-ons.

Be sure to check the following, which will be confiscated if you try to board with it:

■ Pocket knives, even keychain size

■ Scissors (blunt-tipped ones are OK)

■ Corkscrews

■ Carpentry tools

■ Straight razors

For up-to-date information, contact the **Transport Security Administration** (TSA; ☎ 866-289-9673; www.tsa.gov/public). For advice, check www.airsafe.com.

time, return flights between New York and Los Angeles ran US$222 to US$301 on these sites (with American Airlines the cheapest in this case), while American Airlines' site undercut them all (a bit) at US$217.

JetBlue sells useful one-way tickets between the northeast and the West Coast and Florida – usually the best deals if you're not looking for roundtrip tickets. (Also date-change fees with JB are just US$25.)

Stick with hub cities for the cheapest fares. Sample fares from New York to Seattle runs around US$300, while a flight from nearby Hartford to Olympia is US$580. Though sometimes a hub's secondary airport (eg Newark vs JFK, Oakland vs SFO) offers the best deals.

For last minute deals, check www.priceline.com (you'll be at their mercy time-wise) or www.travelzoo.com (with great package deals too).

If booking from abroad, usually you'll have to use a home-based search engine (eg www.expedia.co.uk or www.opodo.co.uk in Britain); www.hotfares.com quotes prices abroad.

Sample fares

Sample airfares for a two-week roundtrip flights in July: Note that prices sway and shift daily.

From	To	Price
New York	Los Angeles	US$222
New York	Miami	US$226
New York	Chicago	US$181
Los Angeles	Vancouver	US$236
New Orleans	San Francisco	US$278
San Francisco	Seattle	US$200
Toronto	Vancouver	C$547

BOAT

Ferries send passengers and cars to nearby islands along the seashore in many places. Short boat tours go through the bayou in Louisiana and the swamps in Florida. Longhaul cruises, such as going down the Mississippi, are prohibitively expensive.

BUS

With frequent service and (generally) clean reclining seats, US and Canadian buses are not only a bit cheaper than the train, but usually quicker. Some bus stations can be in dodgy areas, so if you're arriving in the wee hours, spend the money on a taxi. Many stations have left luggage facilities.

Bus Companies

Greyhound (☎ 800-229-9424, 214-849-8966; www.greyhound.com) is the USA's chief long-distance bus company, connecting most of the US (as well as routes to Montréal, Toronto and Vancouver). A student discount card ($20) offers savings of up to 15% on regular walk-up fares. Check online for discounted eSaver tickets, companion fares of advance-ticket deals. Trips starting Monday to Thursday are cheapest. At the time of writing, Greyhound was planning to cut 260 smaller towns from its routes, which would trim back long-haul trip times considerably.

Greyhound's biggest US competitor, **Trailways** (☎ 703-691-3052; www.trailways.com) generally has lower fares (but is less convenient for long-haul trips). A few regional Trailways carriers include:

Atlantic Coast Trailways (☎ 800-548-8584; www.atlanticcoasttrailways.com)

Pacific Trailways of Southern California (☎ 714-892-5000; www.pacificcoachways.com)

Peter Pan Trailways (☎ 800-237-8747; www.peterpanbus.com) In the northeast.

New **Chinatown buses** connect New York City (p85) with Boston (p135), Philadelphia (p99) and Washington, DC (p230), for half the price of the big boys.

Handling domestic journeys north of the border, **Greyhound Lines of Canada** (☎ 800-661-8747; www.greyhound.ca) has pricing schemes that fluster the most measured of minds. Call. Regular fares allow unlimited stop-overs (so a C$340 one-way ticket for the 72-hour trip from Toronto to Vancouver lets you spend up to 60 days stopping off as you like), while non-stopover tickets bought a day or a week in advance save 50% or more. Students get a 10% discount. **Coach Canada** (☎ 800-461-7661; www.coachcanada.com) sometimes sells tickets (around Ontario and into New York) for cheaper than Greyhound.

Bus Passes

Greyhound offers such an array of passes allowing unlimited travel in the lower 48 states and parts of Canada that much of its staff will fumble at information.

If coming from abroad, talk to a travel agent beforehand.

TRANSPORTATION

Available for US and Canadian travelers, the Discovery Pass comes in various day intervals (seven, 10, 15, 21, 30, 45 and 60); the seven-day pass costs adult/student US$239/215 in peak season (mid-May through September), the 21-day is US$419/377, and the 60-day costs US$662/602. The International Ameripass, for foreign travelers, ranges from the 15 day pass ($419/377) to the 60-day pass ($679/611). These include cities in Canada such as Toronto and Vancouver.

A good deal (available to all) are **regional passes** including West Coast (from Colorado west actually, including Vancouver), Northeast (including Montréal) and Southeast (from Florida to New Orleans and up to Kentucky). These come as 10-day passes ($299/269) or 21-day passes ($399/359). Greyhound also offers CanAm passes for western and eastern Canada.

If you have trouble getting information, the **Greyhound International Office** (☎ 212-971-0492; Port Authority Bus Terminal, New York City; ☷ 8am-4pm Mon-Thu, 8am 6pm Fri, 9am-3pm Sat) can help international travelers and sells regional passes to anyone. Or try ☎ 888-454-7277 for pass information.

Sample Fares

The following one-way fares are for Greyhound buses in summer mid-week. Duration times are likely to drop a bit following small-town cuts.

Origin	Destination	Duration	One Way	Round-Trip
New York	Montréal	8hr	US$73	US$114
New York	Chicago	17-20hr	US$87	US$162
New York	New Orleans	28-34hr	US$112	US$191
Washington, DC	Orlando	19hr	US$104	US$178
Chicago	Seattle	53hr	US$131	US$233
Chicago	Los Angeles	44hr	US$131	US$233
San Francisco	Vancouver	25hr	US$86	US$149

CAR & MOTORCYCLE

Driving is the way to go (outside main cities). Try www.craigslist.org or hostel boards for ride shares.

Car Clubs

In the US, the **American Automobile Association** (AAA; ☎ 800-874-7532; www.aaa.com) is the main auto club, offering hotel discounts, 24-hour

---

TOP TRANSPORT SAVINGS

- **Greyhound in Canada** (p706) – allows unlimited stop-offs on cheap purchase-in-advance long-haul trips meaning you see Canada with one one-way ticket.
- **Rent-a-Wreck** (p711) – get slightly used rental cars from secondary towns for less.
- **JetBlue one-way airfare** (p703) – this discount airline usually posts the cheapest cross-country get-there tickets (not roundtrip); also try WestJet in Canada (p702).
- **Drive away Cars** (p707) – drive others' wheels for gas money, for new-age Kerouacs over 21.
- **Get a car full** – the best way is with your own wheels and as many gas-providing bodies as you can legally fit in.
- **Chinatown buses** – new cheap bus services from Chinatowns connect Boston, New York, Philadelphia and DC.
- **Hidden track** – Greyhound's 'West Coast' bus pass (p706) includes Vancouver, all of the Southwest and Colorado.

---

roadside assistance, and free maps. Another is the more environmentally friendly **Better World Club** (☎ 866-238-1137; www.betterworld.com).

In Canada, the **Canadian Automobile Association** (CAA; ☎ 800-268-3750; www.caa.ca) provides similar services.

Driver's License

You can drive up to 12 months with your home driver's license in the USA, but only for three months in Canada. If yours doesn't have a photograph; or you are planning to get a drive-away car; or planning longer drive periods up north, bring an International Driving Permit (IDP).

Drive-Away Cars

The lure of snagging a drive-away car – a car requiring a driver to get from X to Y, for fuel costs only, with insurance thrown in – is real, but whether it'll work depends on timing and availability.

If you are 21 or over, have a valid driver's license (non-US citizens need an International Driving Permit; IDP), you can

TRANSPORTATION

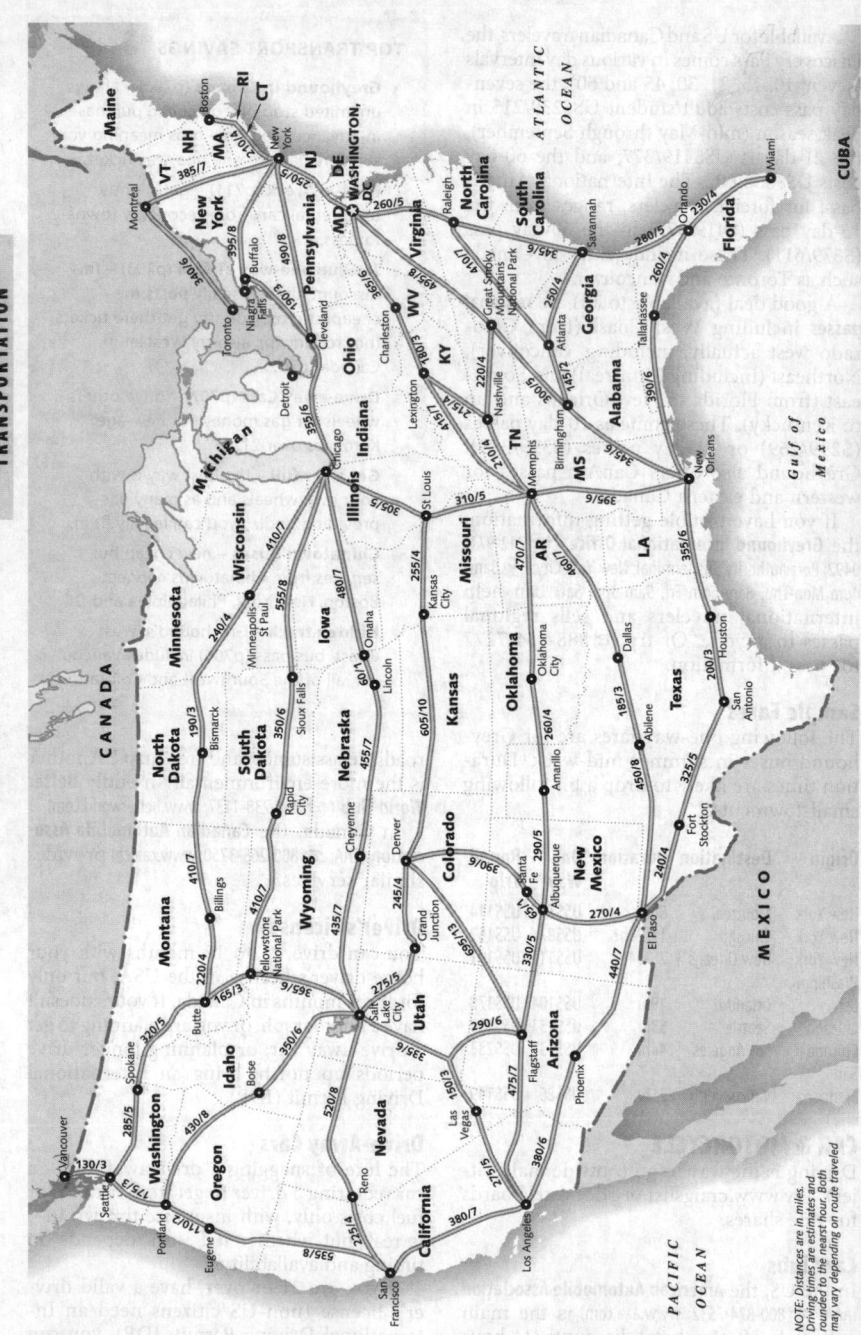

NOTE: Distances are in miles.
Driving times are estimates and
could be longer or shorter
depending on route traveled

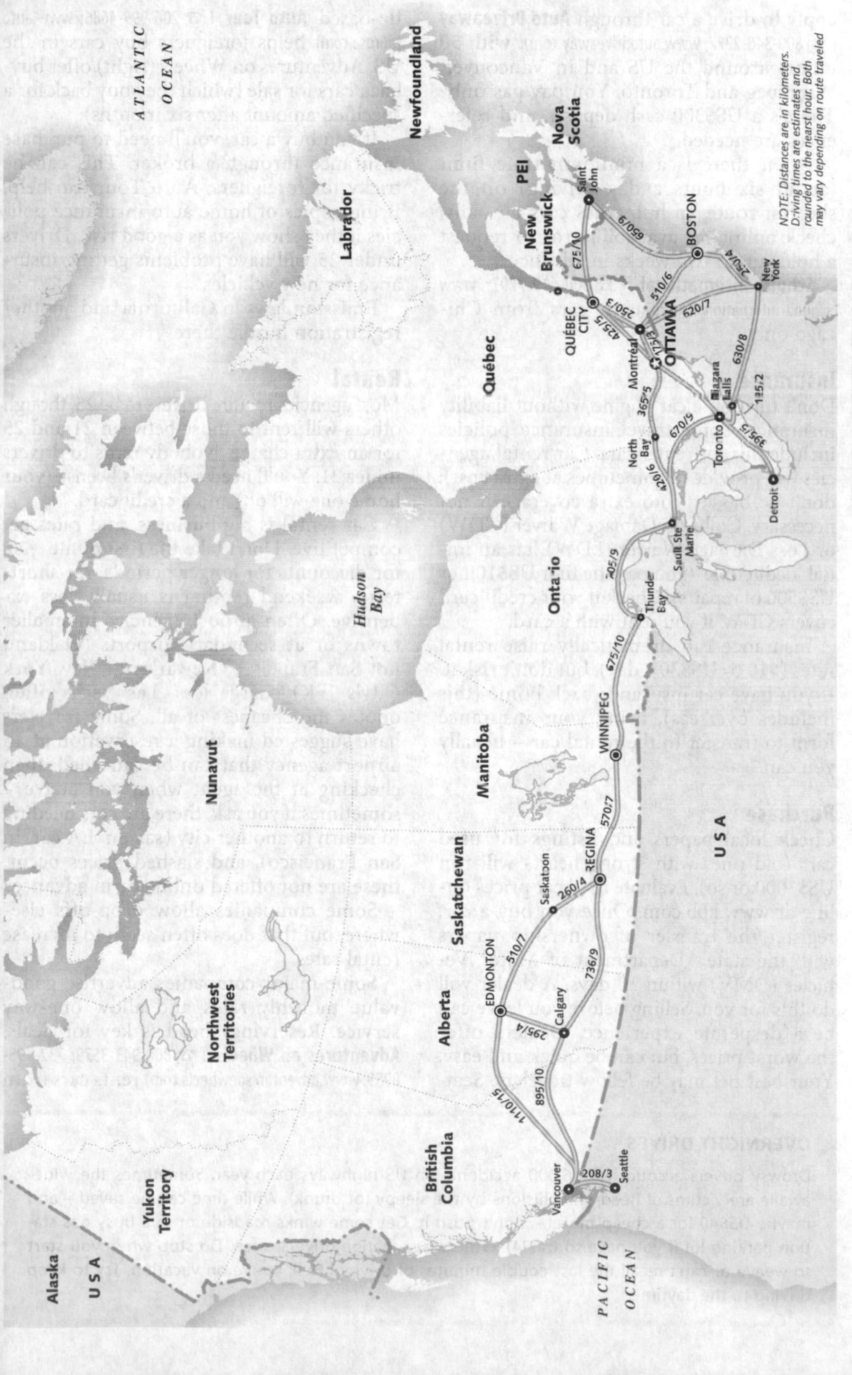

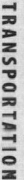

NOTE: Distances are in kilometres. Driving times are estimates and rounded to the nearest hour. Both may vary depending on route traveled.

apply to drive a car through **Auto Driveaway** (☎ 800-346-2277; www.autodriveaway.com), with 50 offices around the US and in Vancouver, Winnipeg and Toronto. You pay gas only. There's a US$300 cash deposit, and references are needed.

Often there is a minimum time limit (about six hours a day driving) on the shortest route. In hub cities cars go daily; check online for availability (or to request a hold) up to two weeks in advance.

Schultz-International (☎ 800-619-7707; www.schultz-international.com) sends cars from Chicago only.

Insurance

Don't turn on a car engine without liability insurance. Some travel insurance policies include this for rental cars. Car rental agencies will provide it (sometimes at extra cost); don't be hassled into extra coverage if not necessary. Collision Damage Waiver (CDW) or Loss Damage Waiver (LDW) has an initial 'deductible' (you pay the first US$100 or US$500 of repairs). Check if your credit card covers CDW if you rent with a card.

Insurance can dramatically raise rental rates ($10 to US$30 a day), but don't risk it. If you have car insurance back home (this includes overseas), bring your insurance form to transfer to the rental car – usually you can.

Purchase

Check local papers and listings for used cars (old ones with strong hearts will run US$3000 or so). Evaluate used car prices online at www.kbb.com. Once you buy a car, register the transfer of ownership papers with the state's Department of Motor Vehicles (DMV) within 10 days. A dealer will do this for you. Selling before you leave can be a desperate experience. Dealers offer the worst prices, but can be quick and easy. Your best bet may be fellow travelers. Seat-

tle-based **Auto Tour** (☎ 206-999-4686; www.autotourusa.com) helps foreigners buy cars in the US. Adventures on Wheels (right) offer buyback cars for sale (which they buy back for a specified amount after six months).

If you buy a car, you'll need to purchase insurance through a broker. This can be tricky for foreigners; Auto Tour can help. Bring copies of home auto insurance policies if they show you as a good risk. Drivers under 25 will have problems getting insurance for new vehicles.

Emission laws in California add another registration hurdle there.

Rental

Most agencies require drivers to be 25, though others will rent to those between 21 and 25 for an extra charge. Nobody rents to drivers under 21. You'll need a driver's license (your home one will do) and a credit card.

Car rental is big business, and rates get competitive. Don't take the first quote. Ask for discounts for longer periods; for short-term, weekend renting is usually less expensive. Often airport agencies in smaller towns or at secondary airports (Oakland not San Francisco, Newark not New York City's JFK) charge less. Las Vegas often quotes the cheapest of all. Some travelers have suggested making a reservation at an airport agency that can be cancelled, then checking at the agent when you arrive – sometimes if you ask, there are cars needing to return to another city (say an 'LA car' in San Francisco), and slashed prices occur; these are not offered online or in advance.

Some companies allow drop-offs elsewhere, but that does often seem to increase rental rates.

Some major companies advertise good-value monthly rates and allow one-way service. Reserving ahead is key for deals. **Adventures on Wheels** (☎ 800-943-3579; 732-495-0959; www.adventuresonwheels.com) rents cars from

---

OVERNIGHT DRIVES

Drowsy drivers account for 56,000 accidents on US highways each year. Sometimes the wide-awake are victims of head-on collisions by the sleepy (or drunk). While time can be saved – and maybe US$40 for a cheap motel – don't push it. Get some winks roadside or in a busy gas station parking lot if you have to (p684). Otherwise, change drivers often. Do stop when you start to weave or can't recall the last couple minutes of driving. Hell, you're on vacation. Try to keep driving to the daytime.

US$25 per day. **Autoteam USA** (p85), outside New York City, has US$30 daily rates.

Here's a list of major companies:

Alamo (☎ 800-462-5266; www.alamo.com)
Avis (☎ 800-230-4898; www.avis.com)
Budget (☎ 800-527-0700; www.drivebudget.com)
Dollar (☎ 800-800-4000; www.dollar.com)
Enterprise (☎ 800-736-8222; www.enterprise.com)
Hertz (☎ 800-654-3131; www.hertz.com)
National (☎ 800-227-7368; www.nationalcar.com)
Thrifty (☎ 800-847-4389; www.thrifty.com)

Best for short-haul loops, **Rent-a-Wreck** (☎ 800-944-7501; www.rent-a-wreck.com) is a US network of nice, slightly used, cars for rent; each location sets their own prices, age restriction (usually 25) and mileage limit (often a teensy 100 miles per day).

There are no drop offs. Call secondary offices. Brooklyn charges US$280 per week, some Jersey locations US$180; a quick bus ride up to Rhode Island can save you another US$30 per week. The west coast is even cheaper (around US$140 outside San Francisco).

For motorcycle rental, contact **EagleRider** (☎ 888-900-9901; www.eaglerider.com). In most places, helmets are mandatory.

Road Rules

Traffic in the USA and Canada is on the right side of the road. Use of seat belts is required everywhere. In many states, open container laws prohibit open alcohol bottles in the vehicle, even if empty. Keep them in the trunk. Observe strict 'DUI' laws (driving under the influence); the max legal blood alcohol concentration is 0.08%. Get caught littering and you'll pay up to US$1000.

Four-lane interstates have the highest speed limits (65mph, 70mph or 75mph). In Canada, it goes metric. Outside the cities, speed limits are 90km/h to 100km/h.

HITCHING

It's done, but it's not a good idea. It's potentially dangerous, and most drivers are equally afraid of those sticking their thumbs out. Hitching on many freeways is prohibited, though you'll see more thumbing (and stopping) in rural Canada and Alaska.

A good alternative is ride-share services offered by **Autotaxi** (www.autotaxi.com), a free web-based bulletin board for both coun-

tries. Some macho types jump on freight trains to get around, hobo-style. It's unwise.

LOCAL TRANSPORTATION

Most big cities have (at least iffy) bus systems (free to US$2 per ride) to ply around spread-out metropolis grids. Outside the big cities, you'll need to call for a taxi. Taxi drivers expect a 10% to 15% tip (at least a buck). See the Without Wheels trip (p25) for places easily visited without a car.

TRAIN

Amtrak (☎ 800-872-7245; www.amtrak.com) runs its rails through the USA, with Amtrak Thruway buses providing convenient connections to notable hubs and parks. Fun though they may be, trains aren't cheap. Generally you'll spend far longer and more money than by airplane and sometimes bus. Most routes go daily, others go every three to five days.

Some discounts are available. For example, while Amtrak's scenic New York–Montréal leg is US$130 roundtrip, the AAA (p707) discount saves US$13 or the student discount saves US$19. Fares are less from early January to mid June, and from late August to mid December. First class or sleeping compartments, obviously, will hike up prices considerably.

Sample undiscounted Amtrak fares for July trips follow:

Origin	Destination	Duration	One Way	Round-Trip
New York	Montréal	10¼hr	US$62	US$130
New York	Chicago	8½hr	US$106	US$191
New York	New Orleans	28½hr	US$129	US$326
Washington, DC	Orlando	19hr	US$132	US$233
Chicago	New Orleans	19½hr	US$114	US$205
Chicago	Seattle	46hr	US$259	US$400
Chicago	Flagstaff, AZ	31hr	US$221	US$362

Up Canada way, **VIA Rail** (☎ 888-842-7245; www.viarail.ca) connects Québec City, Montréal, Toronto, Ottawa, Winnipeg, Jasper (not Calgary) and Vancouver among other places. One sample ticket found a summer one-way ticket from Montréal to Vancouver (which allows pre-planned stop-offs along the way) was only about C$30 more than the Canrailpass (see p712).

TRANSPORTATION

Train Passes

Amtrak's good-value USA Rail Pass is available to international travellers (not US or Canadian citizens). Prices depend on region, days (15 or 30) and season. The 30-day West Rail Pass, for example, will set you back US$405/270 in high/low season and covers tracks from Chicago to New Orleans and west. VIA Rail offers passes to anyone. Its unlimited 30-day North American Rail Pass covers Amtrak routes too (meaning Americans could stick with Amtrak exclusively on a VIA Rail pass); it's mid-October–May/rest of the year C$711/1004 with no tax. The Canrailpass allows 12 days of use in a 30-day period for C$461/741 (before tax). The Corridorpass gives you 10 days between Québec City, Montréal, Toronto, Ottawa and Niagara Falls for C$218 all year.

Health Dr David Goldberg

CONTENTS

The North American continent encompasses an extraordinary range of climates and terrains, from the freezing heights of the Canadian Rockies to tropical areas in southern Florida. Because of the high level of hygiene here, infectious diseases will not be a significant concern for most travelers, who will probably experience nothing worse than a little diarrhea or a mild respiratory infection.

BEFORE YOU GO

INSURANCE

The United States and Canada offer some of the finest health care in the world. The problem is that, unless you have citizenship or good insurance, it can be prohibitively expensive. It's essential to purchase travel health insurance if your regular policy doesn't cover you when you're abroad.

Bring any medications you may need clearly labeled in their original containers.

A signed, dated letter from your physician that describes all your medical conditions and medications, including generic names, is also a good idea.

If your health insurance does not cover medical expenses abroad, consider supplemental insurance. Check the Subwwway section of the **Lonely Planet website** (www.lonelyplanet.com /subwwway) for more information. Find out in advance if your insurance plan will make payments directly to providers or reimburse you later for overseas health expenditures.

RECOMMENDED VACCINATIONS

No special vaccines are required or recommended for travel to North America. All travelers should be up-to-date on routine immunizations, see box below.

ONLINE RESOURCES

There is a wealth of travel health advice on the Internet. The World Health Organization publishes a superb book, *International Travel and Health*, which is revised annually and is available free online at www.who.int /ith/. Another website of interest is **MD Travel Health** (www.mdtravelhealth.com), which provides complete travel health recommendations for every country, updated daily at no cost.

It's usually a good idea to consult your government's travel health website before departure, if one is available:
Australia (www.dfat.gov.au/travel/)
Canada (www.hc-sc.gc.ca/english/index.html)
United Kingdom (www.doh.gov.uk/traveladvice /index.htm)
United States (www.cdc.gov/travel/)

HEALTH

ROUTINE IMMUNIZATIONS

Vaccine	Recommended for	Dosage	Side Effects
tetanus-diphtheria	all travelers who haven't had booster within 10 years	one dose lasts 10 years	soreness at injection site
measles	travelers born after 1956 who've had only one measles vaccination	one dose	fever, rash, joint pains, allergic reactions
chicken pox	travelers who've never had chicken pox	two doses a month apart	fever, mild case of chicken pox
influenza	all travelers during flu season (November through March)	one dose	soreness at the injection site, fever

MEDICAL CHECKLIST

- acetaminophen (Tylenol) or aspirin
- anti-inflammatory drugs (eg ibuprofen)
- antihistamines (for hay fever and allergic reactions)
- antibacterial ointment (eg Bactroban) for cuts and abrasions
- steroid cream or cortisone (for poison ivy and other allergic rashes)
- bandages, gauze, gauze rolls
- adhesive or paper tape
- scissors, safety pins, tweezers
- thermometer
- pocket knife
- DEET-containing insect repellent for the skin
- permethrin-containing insect spray for clothing, tents and bed nets
- sun block

IN THE USA & CANADA

AVAILABILITY & COST OF HEALTH CARE

In general, if you have a medical emergency, the best bet is to find the nearest hospital and go to its emergency room. If the problem isn't urgent, you can call a nearby hospital and ask for a referral to a local physician, which is usually cheaper than a trip to the emergency room.

Pharmacies are abundantly supplied, but you may find that some medications that are available over-the-counter in your home country require a prescription in the United States or Canada and, as always, if you don't have insurance to cover the cost of prescriptions, they can be shockingly expensive.

INFECTIOUS DISEASES

In addition to more common ailments, there are several infectious diseases that are unknown or uncommon outside North America. Most are acquired by mosquito or tick bites.

West Nile Virus

Cases of West Nile virus were unknown in North America until a few years ago, but have now been reported in most of the continent. The virus is transmitted by culex mosquitoes, which are active in late summer and early fall and generally bite after dusk. Most infections are mild or asymptomatic, but the virus may infect the central nervous system, leading to fever, headache, confusion, lethargy, coma and sometimes death. There is no treatment for West Nile virus. For the latest update on the areas affected by West Nile, go to the **US Geological Survey website** (http://westnilemaps.usgs.gov/) or the **Health Canada website** (www.hc-sc.gc.ca/english/westnile/index.html).

Lyme Disease

Most documented cases occur in the northeastern part of the United States and southern Canada. Lyme disease is transmitted by deer ticks, which are only 1mm to 2mm long. Most cases occur in the late spring and summer. The US-based Centers for Disease Control and Prevention (CDC) has an informative, if slightly scary, **Lyme disease website** (www.cdc.gov/ncidod/dvbid/lyme/).

The first symptom is usually an expanding red rash that is often pale in the center, known as a bull's eye rash. However, in many cases, no rash is observed. Flu-like symptoms are common, including fever, headache, joint pain, body aches and malaise. When the infection is treated promptly with an appropriate antibiotic, usually doxycycline or amoxicillin, the cure rate is high. Luckily, since the tick must be attached for 36 hours or more to transmit Lyme disease, most cases can be prevented by performing a thorough tick check after you've been outdoors (see p716).

Rabies

Rabies is a viral infection of the brain and spinal cord that is almost always fatal. The rabies virus is carried in the saliva of infected animals and is typically transmitted through an animal bite, though contamination of any break in the skin with infected saliva may result in rabies. In the USA and Canada, most cases of human rabies are related to exposure to bats. Rabies may also be contracted from raccoons, skunks, foxes and unvaccinated cats and dogs.

If there is any possibility, however small, that you have been exposed to rabies, you should seek preventative treatment, which consists of rabies immune globulin and rabies vaccine and is quite safe. In particular, any contact with a bat should be discussed with health authorities, because bats have small teeth and may not leave obvious bite marks.

Giardiasis

This parasitic infection of the small intestine occurs throughout North America and the world. Symptoms may include nausea, bloating, cramps and diarrhea, and may last for weeks. To protect yourself from giardia, you should avoid drinking directly from lakes, ponds, streams and rivers, which may be contaminated by animal or human feces. The infection can also be transmitted from person to person if proper hand washing is not performed. Giardiasis is easily diagnosed by a stool test and readily treated with antibiotics.

HIV/AIDS

As with most parts of the world, HIV infection occurs throughout the United States and Canada. You should never assume, on the basis of someone's background or appearance, that they're free of this or any other sexually transmitted disease. Be sure to use a condom for all sexual encounters.

ENVIRONMENTAL HAZARDS
Heat

Dehydration is the main contributor to heat exhaustion. Symptoms include weakness, headache, irritability, nausea or vomiting, sweaty skin, a fast, weak pulse and a normal or slightly elevated temperature. Treatment involves getting out of the heat and/or sun, fanning the victim and applying cool wet cloths to the skin, laying the victim flat with their legs raised and rehydrating with water containing a quarter of a teaspoon of salt per liter. Recovery is usually rapid and it is common to feel weak for days afterwards.

Heatstroke is a serious medical emergency. Symptoms come on suddenly and include weakness, nausea, a hot dry body with a body temperature of over 41°C, dizziness, confusion, loss of coordination, fits and eventually collapse and loss of consciousness. Seek medical help and commence cooling by getting the person out of the heat, removing their clothes, fanning them and applying cool wet cloths or ice to their body, especially to the groin and armpits.

Cold

Cold exposure may be a problem, especially in the northern regions of the countries. To prevent hypothermia, keep all body surfaces covered, including the head and neck. Synthetic materials such as Gore-Tex and Thinsulate provide excellent insulation. Because the body loses heat faster when it is wet, stay dry. Change inner garments promptly when they become moist. Keep active, but get enough rest. Consume plenty of food and water. Be sure not to have any alcohol. Caffeine and tobacco should also be avoided.

Watch out for the 'Umbles' – stumbles, mumbles, fumbles and grumbles – signs of impending hypothermia. If someone appears to be developing hypothermia, you should insulate them from the ground, protect them from the wind, remove wet clothing or cover them with a vapor barrier such as a plastic bag, and get them immediately to a warm environment and a medical facility. Warm fluids (but not coffee or tea – noncaffeinated herbal teas are OK) may be given if the person is alert enough to swallow.

Altitude Sickness

Acute Mountain Sickness (AMS), aka 'Altitude Sickness,' may develop in those who ascend rapidly to altitudes more than 2500m. Being physically fit offers no protection. Those who have experienced AMS in the past are prone to future episodes. The risk increases with faster ascents, higher altitudes and greater exertion. Symptoms are headaches, nausea, vomiting, dizziness, malaise, insomnia and loss of appetite. Severe cases may be complicated by fluid in the lungs (high-altitude pulmonary edema) or swelling of the brain (high-altitude cerebral edema).

The best treatment for AMS is descent. If you are exhibiting symptoms, do not ascend. If symptoms are severe or persistent, descend immediately. When traveling to high altitudes, avoid overexertion, eat light meals and abstain from alcohol. If your symptoms are more than mild or don't resolve promptly, see a doctor. Altitude sickness should be taken seriously; it can be life-threatening when severe.

Bites & Stings

Common sense approaches to these concerns are the most effective: wear boots when hiking to protect from snakes, wear long

HEALTH

sleeves and pants to protect from ticks and mosquitoes. If you're bitten, don't overreact. Stay calm and follow the recommended treatment.

MOSQUITO BITES

When traveling in areas where West Nile virus or other mosquito-borne illnesses have been reported, keep yourself covered (wear long sleeves, long pants, hats, and shoes rather than sandals) and apply a good insect repellent, preferably one containing DEET, to exposed skin and clothing. In general, adults and children over 12 should use preparations containing 25% to 35% DEET, which usually lasts about six hours. Children between two and 12 years of age should use preparations containing no more than 10% DEET, applied sparingly, which will usually last about three hours. Neurologic toxicity has been reported from DEET, especially in children, but appears to be extremely uncommon and generally related to overuse. DEET-containing compounds should not be used on children under age two.

Insect repellents containing certain botanical products, including oil of eucalyptus and soybean oil, are effective but last only 1½ to two hours. Products based on citronella are not effective.

TICK BITES

Ticks are parasitic arachnids that may be present in brush, forest and grasslands, where hikers often get them on their legs or in their boots. Adult ticks suck blood from hosts by burrowing into the skin and can carry infections such as Lyme disease.

Always check your body for ticks after walking through high grass or thickly forested area. If ticks are found unattached, they can simply be brushed off. If a tick is found attached, press down around the tick's head with tweezers, grab the head and gently pull upwards – do not twist it. (If no tweezers are available, use your fingers, but protect them from contamination with a piece of tissue or paper.) Do not rub oil, alcohol or petroleum jelly on it. If you get sick in the following couple of weeks, consult a doctor.

MAMMAL BITES

Do not attempt to pet, handle or feed any animal, with the exception of domestic animals known to be free of any infectious disease. Most animal injuries are directly related to a person's attempt to touch or feed the animal.

Any bite or scratch by a mammal, including bats, should be promptly and thoroughly cleansed with large amounts of soap and water, followed by the application of an antiseptic such as iodine or alcohol. The local health authorities should be contacted immediately for possible post-exposure rabies treatment, whether or not you've been immunized against rabies. It may also be advisable to start an antibiotic, since wounds caused by animal bites and scratches frequently become infected.

SNAKE BITES

There are several varieties of venomous snakes in North America, but unlike those in other countries they do not cause instantaneous death, and antivenins are available. First aid is to place a light constricting bandage over the bite, keep the wounded part below the level of the heart and move it as little as possible. Stay calm and get to a medical facility as soon as possible. Bring the dead snake for identification if you can, but don't risk being bitten again. Do not use the mythic 'cut an X and suck out the venom' trick; this causes more damage to snakebite victims than the bites themselves.

SPIDER & SCORPION BITES

Although there are many species of spiders in the USA and Canada, the only ones that cause significant human illness are the black widow, brown recluse and hobo spiders. The black widow is black or brown in color, measuring about 15mm in body length, with a shiny top, fat body, and distinctive red or orange hourglass figure on its underside. It's found throughout North America, usually in barns, woodpiles, sheds, harvested crops and bowls of outdoor toilets. The brown recluse spider is brown in color, usually 10mm in body length, with a dark violin-shaped mark on the top of the upper section of the body. It's usually found in the south and southern Midwest, but has spread to other parts of the USA in recent years. The brown recluse is active mostly at night, lives in dark sheltered areas such as under porches and in woodpiles, and typically bites when trapped. Hobo spiders are found chiefly in the northwestern United States and western Canada.

If bitten by a black widow, you should apply ice or cold packs and go immediately to the nearest emergency room. Complications of a black widow bite may include muscle spasms, breathing difficulties and high blood pressure. The bite of a brown recluse or hobo spider typically causes a large, inflamed wound, sometimes associated with fever and chills. If bitten, apply ice and see a physician. The symptoms of a hobo spider bite are similar to those of a brown recluse, but milder.

The only dangerous species of scorpion in the United States is the bark scorpion, which is found in the southwestern part of the country, chiefly Arizona. If stung, you should immediately apply ice or cold packs, immobilize the affected body part and go to the nearest emergency room. To prevent scorpion stings, be sure to inspect and shake out clothing, shoes and sleeping bags before use, and wear gloves and protective clothing when working around piles of wood or leaves.

HEALTH

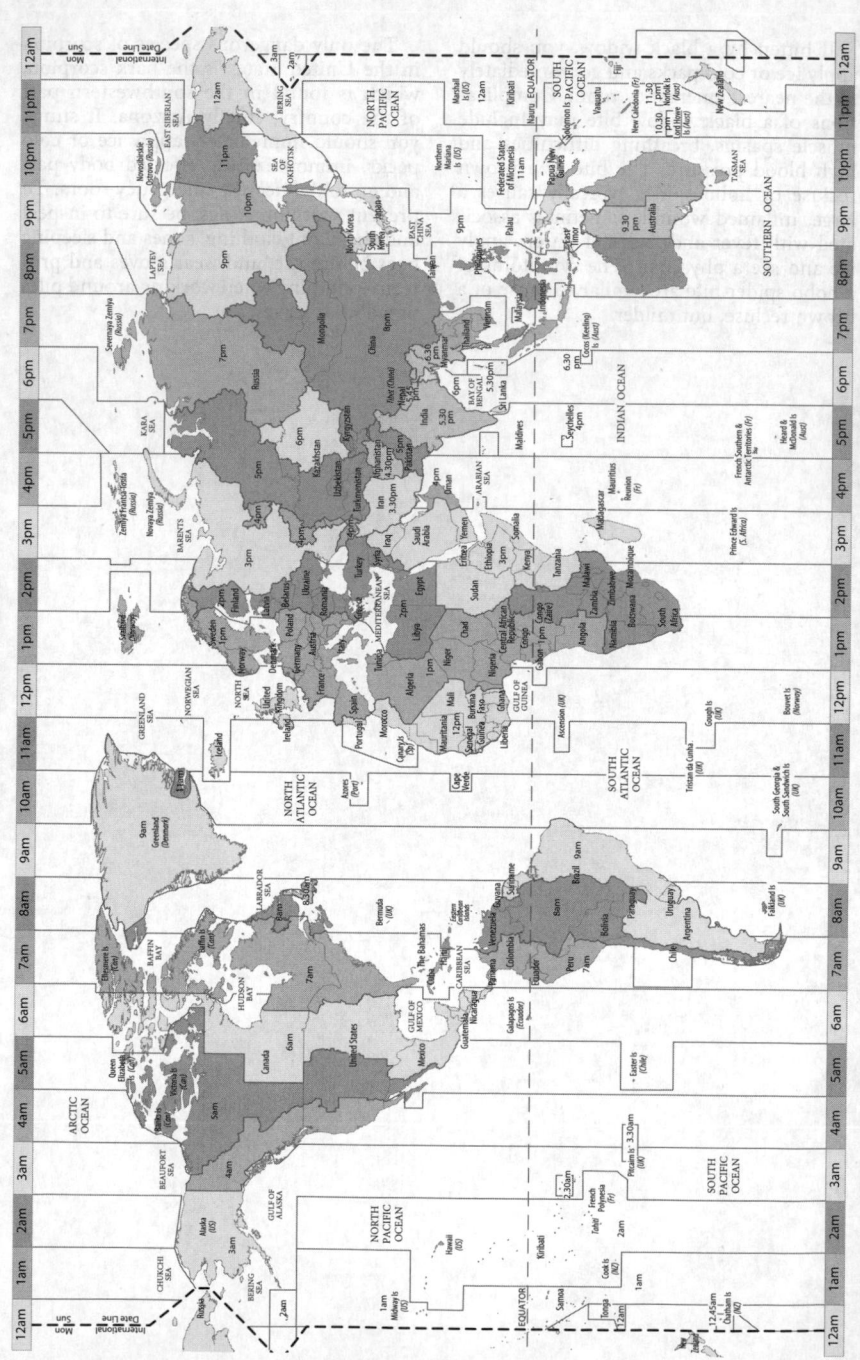

Behind the Scenes

THIS BOOK

This 1st edition of *USA & Canada on a Shoestring* was researched and written by an intrepid team of authors, led by the supremely diligent and inspiring Robert Reid. Robert wrote the chapters on New York City and the Great Plains, as well as the book's front and rear sections. Contributing authors Becca Blond (Rocky Mountains and Washington, DC & the Capital Region), Loretta Chilcoat (Florida), Jeremy Chipman (New England), Tom Downs (California, Great Lakes and the South), Michael Grosberg (Mid-Atlantic), Jeff Hill (Texas), Graham Neale (Eastern and Western Canada), Andrew Dean Nystrom (Alaska, California, Rocky Mountains and the Southwest), Michael Read (the South) and Emily Wolman (Pacific Northwest) canvassed the continent and lent their expertise throughout. Dr David Goldberg wrote the Health chapter. Jeff Greenwald contributed the USA & Canada Outdoors chapter.

THANKS from the Authors

Robert Reid Big thanks to Jay Cooke for signing me up and eagerly collaborating on this lovely and fun 1st edition. More thanks to all the authors for dealing with my questions and thoughts, Mr Justin Flynn in Melbourne for overseeing production and Wampus Reynolds for the *Louis Riehl* book that helped Manitobize my intellect a bit. Thanks also to Beth Greenfield, whom I had the pleasure to work with on the latest *New York City* guide. And thanks to Mai for putting up with my whining.

Becca Blond In DC, thanks to Jesi Kettler and Patricia and Harper Caron for opening up their homes to me. Also thanks to all my friends in both regions who offered invaluable tips on what was in and what was out and where to go for a drink. Thanks always to my family, David, Patricia, Jessica, Jennie and Vera for their support. To Jay Cooke and the rest of the shoestring team, it was a pleasure to work with you all. Finally, to Aaron (and the pocket moose), thanks for always being there. I couldn't do this without you.

Loretta Chilcoat Many thanks to Jay Cooke for a monumental undertaking with this 1st edition, and to Justin Flynn for his stellar edits and making me laugh. Thanks to Michelle Revuelta, Keith Salwoski, Carol Shaughnassy and Andrea Hender-

son. To my incredible family for watching my three-month-old daughter while I ran around Florida. And a special thanks to Travis Plowman and his roommates for letting me crash with them in Orlando (and for those amazing peanut butter cookies!).

Jeremy Chipman Thanks to Jay Cooke and Robert Reid for their support. The visitor bureaus throughout New England were extremely helpful. I'm grateful to the Zelmans (Eric, Alyssa, Henry and Oliver) for their friendship, hospitality and laptop computer. Ted Collins, Kristen Crean, Carol Deanow, Jodi Fisher, Marc Gidal, Jen Hazlett, Julie Kitchell, Michael Lee, Mod Ono, Ralph Pratt, Ed Schwartzreich and Emily Sunderman all provided valuable suggestions. Last but not least, thanks to my family.

Michael Grosberg Thanks go out especially to Kathy Vidal and Farhan Khawaja for taking me under their wing and showing me the hotspots in Philadelphia. To Darren and Leslie Roberts for their hospitality and free access to their refrigerator and advice on Philadelphia and surroundings. To Isabel Cuadrado for her enthusiasm and curiosity and helping me see the area from a foreigner's perspective. To Peter Guryan and Olaitan Senbanjo for hints on Ithaca, Rich Burkitt and Bennet Zamoff for their Pittsburgh expertise, Lucas Rubin and Asad Raza for advice and insight into unfairly maligned Buffalo, and finally to my brother Joel Grosberg for joining me on a trip to Cooperstown, and points north, and my parents Sheldon and Judy Grosberg for the memories of childhood trips which I only partly block out.

Jeff Hill First and foremost, thanks to my wife, Lori Hill, for her advice, patience, and insatiable desire to read every piece of written material that she comes across on the road, be it the *Twisted Parrot* newspaper or the 'Our Story' section of the restaurant menu. Thanks to Jay Cooke and Robert Reid at Lonely Planet for answering my tiresome questions and making the process easier. I'm much obliged to Steve Hall for his wisdom about the Gulf Coast and to Shirley Allaway for her expertise on various parts of the state. Finally, a shout-out to the motor vehicles: to the (mostly) trusty Ford Focus, which died halfway up a West Texas mountain but miraculously came back to life; and to the aging pickup truck whose well-worn clutch survived several stop-and-go days in Dallas.

Graham Neale Canada's big. I thank all of it (except Celine Dion and the Leafs), especially my sister. Sarah and Chloé started this endeavor on the best foot (remember bowling?). I love Jane (saved my soul), Laurel (opened my heart) and Allison (kept me safe) for helping me finish. I also like pie.

Andrew Dean Nystrom Many thanks to Susan, Johnny, Tanya, Bryan and Ethan in LA; the Muhlenbecks; Jenny Wow and the Sacred Passage *sangha*; Laurel in Santa Fe; Charlie and the Wild Rivers crew; Michele and Bob in Moab; Jacob in Jackson; and Bryan and Becca in CO. Much love to Dolores, Joe, John and Barbra for making it all possible. No thanks to the *maldito* TJ cops – except the one who recognized me on the LP *San Diego* cover!

Michael Read Special thanks to hitchhiker Tony Jones, who opened my eyes to the way things *really* work in Birmingham, and to my beloved iPod, whose constant companionship kept me from focusing on my truck's lack of an air-conditioner. A nod goes to the helpful hostel managers in Nags Head, Knoxville and Atlanta for sharing their observations on the peculiar traveling habits of Danish backpackers. Most of all, thanks to traveling companions Gerard Granucci

and Irene Rietschel for sharing my delight in the quirky charms of the American South.

Emily K Wolman Heartfelt gratitude to everyone who lent a hand, car, or sofa, including Joe Pasquariello, Aaron Snyderman, Rhiannon Wood, Steve Ingrao, Sandra Bao, Ben Greensfelder, and those missionaries with the can opener at Mora campground. Immeasurable love to Bernice Hunt, my grandmother and idol; and to John, for his ever-enduring optimism and support. *Namaste.*

CREDITS

USA & Canada on a Shoestring was commissioned in Lonely Planet's Oakland office by Jay Cooke with input from Maria Donohoe, Erin Corrigan, Errol Hunt and Vivek Wagle and regional publishing manager David Zingarelli.

This new edition was coordinated in Lonely Planet's Melbourne office by Justin Flynn (editing), Herman So (cartography) and Pablo Gastar (layout). Justin was assisted with editing by Katrina Webb, Bruce Evans, Kate McLeod, Nina Rousseau, Tom Smallman, Kim Hutchins, Meg Worby, Emily Coles, Alan Murphy, Nancy Ianni, Sasha Baskett, Susannah Farfor, Lucy Monie, Julia Taylor, Suzannah Shwer and Laura Gibb. Herman was given superb assistance by Celia Wood, Tim Lohnes, Laurie Mikkelsen and Daniel Fennessy, with managing cartographer Alison Lyall supervising. The project was, at first, managed inhouse by Celia Wood before Eoin Dunlevy took over. Lachlan Ross and Mark Germanchis provided technical assistance when the heat was on in the home straight.

Index

000 Map pages
000 Photograph pages

INDEX

INDEX

THE LONELY PLANET STORY

The story begins with a classic travel adventure: Tony and Maureen Wheeler's 1972 journey across Europe and Asia to Australia. There was no useful information about the overland trail then, so Tony and Maureen published the first Lonely Planet guidebook to meet a growing need.

From a kitchen table, Lonely Planet has grown to become the largest independent travel publisher in the world, with offices in Melbourne (Australia), Oakland (USA) and London (UK). Today Lonely Planet guidebooks cover the globe. There is an ever-growing list of books and information in a variety of media. Some things haven't changed. The main aim is still to make it possible for adventurous travelers to get out there – to explore and better understand the world.

At Lonely Planet we believe travelers can make a positive contribution to the countries they visit – if they respect their host communities and spend their money wisely. Every year 5% of company profit is donated to charities around the world.

SEND US YOUR FEEDBACK

We love to hear from travelers – your comments keep us on our toes and help make our books better. Our well-traveled team reads every word on what you loved or loathed about this book. Although we cannot reply individually to postal submissions, we always guarantee that your feedback goes straight to the appropriate authors, in time for the next edition. Each person who sends us information is thanked in the next edition – and the most useful submissions are rewarded with a free book. See the Behind the Scenes section.

To send us your updates – and find out about Lonely Planet events, newsletters and travel news – visit our award-winning website: **www.lonelyplanet.com/feedback**

Note: We may edit, reproduce and incorporate your comments in Lonely Planet products such as guidebooks, websites and digital products, so let us know if you don't want your comments reproduced or your name acknowledged. For a copy of our privacy policy, go to www.lonelyplanet.com/privacy

Published by Lonely Planet Publications Pty Ltd
ABN 36 005 607 983

© Lonely Planet 2005

© photographers as indicated 2005

Cover montage by Wendy Wright & Gerylin Atterbery. Cover artwork by Wendy Wright. Photographs by Lonely Planet Images: John Hay, Ross Barnett, Ray Laskowitz, Lee Foster, Richard Cummins, Christine Osborne, Kim Grant & Cheyenne Rouse-Braumberger. Many of the images in this guide are available for licensing from Lonely Planet Images: www.lonelyplanetimages.com

Printed through SNP SPrint Singapore Pte Ltd at KHL Printing Co Sdn Bhd, Malaysia

LONELY PLANET OFFICES

Australia
Head Office
Locked Bag 1, Footscray, Victoria 3011
☎ 03 8379 8000, fax 03 8379 8111
talk2us@lonelyplanet.com.au

USA
150 Linden St, Oakland, CA 94607
☎ 510 893 8555, toll free 800 275 8555
fax 510 893 8572, info@lonelyplanet.com

UK
72–82 Rosebery Ave,
Clerkenwell, London EC1R 4RW
☎ 020 7841 9000, fax 020 7841 9001
go@lonelyplanet.co.uk